A CHILD'S WORLD

INFANCY THROUGH ADOLESCENCE

A CHILD'S WORLD
INFANCY THROUGH ADOLESCENCE

Diane E. Papalia and Sally Wendkos Olds are also the coauthors of *Human Development*, Sixth Edition, and *Psychology*, Second Edition

Diane E. Papalia is coauthor, with Cameron Camp and Ruth Duskin Feldman, of *Adult Development and Aging*.

A CHILD'S WORLD

INFANCY THROUGH ADOLESCENCE

SEVENTH EDITION

DIANE E. PAPALIA
SALLY WENDKOS OLDS

McGRAW-HILL, INC.

New York St. Louis San Francisco Auckland Bogotá Caracas
Lisbon London Madrid Mexico City Milan Montreal
New Delhi San Juan Singapore Sydney Tokyo Toronto

A CHILD'S WORLD

INFANCY THROUGH ADOLESCENCE

Acknowledgments appear on pages A-1 to A-5, and on this page by reference.

This book is printed on acid-free paper.

2 3 4 5 6 7 8 9 0   VNH   VNH   9 0 9 8 7 6

ISBN 0-07-048765-0

This book was set in Palatino by York Graphic Services, Inc.
The editors were Michael R. Elia, Jane Vaicunas, and David A. Damstra;
the designer was Joan E. O'Connor;
the production supervisor was Paula Keller.
The photo editor was Inge King.
New drawings were done by Fine Line Illustrations, Inc.
Von Hoffmann Press, Inc., was printer and binder.

Cover photo: Peter Pagan, FPG International

Library of Congress Cataloging-in-Publication Data
Papalia, Diane E.
    A child's world: infancy through adolescence / Diane E. Papalia,
Sally W. Olds.—7th ed.
        p.   cm.
    Includes bibliographical references and indexes.
    ISBN 0-07-048765-0
    1. Child development.   2. Child psychology.   3. Adolescence.
I. Olds, Sally Wendkos.   II. Title.
HQ767.9.P36   1996
305.23′ 1—dc20   95-10671

ABOUT THE AUTHORS

As a professor, *Diane E. Papalia* has taught thousands of undergraduates at the University of Wisconsin. She received her bachelor's degree, majoring in psychology, from Vassar College and both her master's degree in child development and family relations and her Ph.D. in life-span developmental psychology from West Virginia University. She has published numerous articles in such professional journals as *Human Development, International Journal of Aging and Human Development, Sex Roles, Journal of Experimental Child Psychology,* and *Journal of Gerontology.* Most of these papers have dealt with her major research focus, cognitive development from childhood through old age. She is especially interested in cognitive development and factors that contribute to the maintenance of cognitive functioning. She is a Fellow in the Gerontological Society of America.

Sally Wendkos Olds is an award-winning professional writer who has written more than 200 articles in leading magazines and is the author or coauthor of six books addressed to general readers in addition to the three textbooks she has coauthored with Dr. Papalia. Her books *The Complete Book of Breastfeeding* and *The Working Parents' Survival Guide* have both been issued in completely updated and expanded editions. She is also the author of *The Eternal Garden: Seasons of Our Sexuality* and the coauthor of *Raising a Hyperactive Child* (winner of the Family Service Association of America National Media Award) and *Helping Your Child Find Values to Live By.* She received her bachelor's degree from the University of Pennsylvania, where she majored in English literature and minored in psychology. She was elected to Phi Beta Kappa and was graduated summa cum laude.

To our parents,
Madeline and Edward Papalia
and Leah and Samuel Wendkos,
for their unfailing love, nurturance, and
confidence in us, and for their abiding conviction
that childhood is a wondrous time of life.

And to our children,
Anna Victoria
and Nancy, Jennifer, and Dorri,
who have helped us revisit childhood
and see its wonders and challenges
with new eyes.

CONTENTS IN BRIEF

CONTENTS

BEGINNINGS

INFANCY AND TODDLERHOOD

MIDDLE CHILDHOOD

◆ CHAPTER 11 PHYSICAL DEVELOPMENT AND HEALTH IN MIDDLE CHILDHOOD

LIST OF BOXES

PREFACE

With the publication of this seventh edition, *A Child's World* celebrates its twenty-first birthday. Like a person achieving majority at the same age, this book at 21 is quite different from its original nature. It is even different from its earlier editions in key ways. This seventh edition, in fact, represents the most thorough of all revisions of this text. Yet while *A Child's World* has developed, changed and matured, it, like a 21-year-old person, still retains some of the qualities that have contributed to its continued popularity over these years.

Some of the changes that you will see in this edition stem from shifts in society as we address issues that have achieved new importance over these past two decades. Some changes respond to differences in our readership, as the population of college students continues to widen to include many more than the traditional undergraduate. Some changes reflect an even sharper sensitivity to the impact of culture and ethnicity on children's development. And some changes are due to the maturing perspectives of the two coauthors of this book, whose own life experiences have helped us to look differently at many of the issues discussed in these pages.

When the two of us began working together in 1973, Diane Papalia was a single, childless assistant professor at the University of Wisconsin in Madison. Sally Olds, a professional writer, was a married mother of three children—one in elementary school, one in junior high, and one in high school.

Since then, as both of us have moved from young adulthood into midlife, both our lives have changed in many ways. Diane took on more responsibilities as she moved up the ranks of academia, becoming an associate professor, then a dean, then a full professor, while continuing to publish her research papers in eminent psychology journals. What may be more significant for the evolution of *A Child's World* is that she married and, with her husband, adopted a baby girl, who is now nine years old. Meanwhile, Sally Olds's daughters grew up, went to college, chose careers, and established homes of their own. Two married—one in her early twenties, one in her mid-thirties—and had their own children.

Revisiting childhood personally, through these children, has helped both authors evaluate the importance of many of the issues we report on in this book and has given us new bases for interpreting the implications of both traditional and cutting-edge research.

Meanwhile, along with our family experiences in what Urie Bronfenbrenner in his ecological approach (which we discuss throughout the book as we put child development into context) calls our microsystem, we have seen the macrosystem of the wider world change around us. Societal phenomena, like the gender revolution, the sexual revolution, and the computer revolution have stamped their impressions on children growing up today. These children—whether they experience them directly or not—are also influenced by such darker visitations as the AIDS epidemic, racial unrest, and homelessness.

As worldwide communication has expanded, we have access to information about children's lives in many societies around the world, and this knowledge helps us learn about the lives of children close to home. It also supports our conviction that development in western cultures, and theories derived from studies of children in these cultures, should not be considered the "norm" for all children.

Vicky and Jason—fictional characters based on real children—reflect all these changes. You will still see these two children growing up in the pages of this book. You will still hear the words they say and see how they handle various aspects of their development. They are referred to primarily to introduce topics throughout the book, generally by being the focus of a relevant anecdote drawn from real life. But in the realization that there is no "average" or "typical" child, but that each child is an individual with a unique personality and a unique set of life circumstances, we show more of the individual differences among children as we describe the experiences of Vicky and Jason, and of other children in their world—some of whom they will never meet. Vicky and Jason are products of their culture, as are the other children whose stories we'll tell.

We have been especially gratified by the feedback we have received over the years from former students who first encountered *A Child's World* as a text and who have kept the book on their home library shelves and referred to it as they have worked with children in classrooms or hospitals or have brought up their own children. While the book is not a child-rearing manual, we consistently seek to draw conclusions from the study of child development that can be applied to the everyday lives of real children.

In the prefaces to the previous editions of *A Child's World,* we described the way this book continues to develop—just as do Vicky and Jason, the prototypical children you will come to know well through these pages. In some ways, the seventh edition of this book is much like the earlier editions—just as children of any age continue to display many of the same characteristics they were born with. Yet there are some very important differences.

Each chapter has been extensively updated to include the most recent research findings. In response to the growing interest among professors in presenting child development as a rigorous scientific enterprise, we present clear, understandable discussions of this research. For many of the studies cited, we provide enough detail for students to grasp the methods used, the conclusions drawn, and the implications of the findings. In addition to keeping up with the newest research in a rapidly expanding discipline, we have sharpened our focus in several areas.

OUR AIMS FOR THIS EDITION

Our goal for this edition remains the same: to make the study of child development come alive to those of you with a professional interest in children, to those of you who have an intellectual curiosity about how we all develop from conception through adolescence, and, of course, to those of you who will be rearing children or have already raised your families.

One of the ways we work toward this goal is by telling stories about "Vicky" and "Jason." These stories describe incidents from the lives of real children (either children whom the authors know or children who have taken part in research projects), which illustrate important principles in child development. We see, for example, how Vicky feels about the birth of her little brother and how Jason feels about his parents' divorce.

We continue to offer many specific examples instead of talking in vague or abstract generalities. We also continue to treat the most important theories and research findings in the field, always with a special emphasis on how they can actually be used in real life. We know that you want to know how this information can help you as you teach, examine, interview, test, heal, counsel, parent, or otherwise deal with children.

To meet our goal, we are still asking the same basic questions: What factors influence the way children develop? What can adults do to help children realize their potential? How much control do children exert over their own lives? What aspects of development are typical for most children? In what ways is each child unique? What is normal? What is cause for concern?

We are also asking some new questions and coming up with some new answers. Virtually every topic in this book has been updated with new information or new interpretation. We continue to be sensitive to issues of cultural diversity, gender roles, social context, and other issues that are especially relevant in the 1990s. Furthermore, we have expanded our efforts to synthesize research findings and to help students interpret them and think critically about controversial issues. One way in which we encourage critical thinking is through thought-provoking questions posed throughout the text.

Our work on two other college textbooks, *Human Development* (for courses in development throughout the life span) and *Psychology* (for introductory courses), has helped us refine and sharpen our thinking about child development. The changes in this revision, then, represent growth and development in our own ideas.

THE SEVENTH EDITION

ORGANIZATION

There are two major approaches to writing about and teaching child development. The *chronological* approach looks at the functioning of all aspects of development at different stages of life, such as infancy or adolescence. The other, the *topical* approach, traces one aspect of development at a time, such as perception, memory, moral reasoning, the self-concept, or attachment to other people. Each of these approaches has advantages and drawbacks.

We have chosen the chronological approach, since we believe that this is the most effective way to understand the intertwining and interdependence of all aspects of development. Following growth from conception through adolescence provides a sense of the multifaceted sweep of child development, as we get to know first the infant and toddler, then the young child, the schoolchild, and finally the adolescent on the brink of adulthood. By choosing this path, we sometimes have to interrupt the description of one domain of development in one stage and to pick it up a few chapters later. We employ a number of techniques to make these discussions more cohesive, such as charts providing an overview of a certain aspect of development, cross-references between chapters, and brief reminders in the text that look ahead or back at related discussions.

In line with the chronological approach we have divided this book into five parts. After the Introduction (Part I), we discuss the physical, the cognitive, and the personality and social development for each of the four age-based stages outlined above.

Readers who prefer a topical approach may read the book in a different order. For an introduction to child development, first read Chapters 1, 2, 3, and 4, which present theories and basic issues, the influences of heredity and environment, prenatal development, and birth and the neonate. To read about physical development, read Chapters 5, 8, 11, and 14. To follow children's cognitive development, read Chapters 6, 9, 12, and 15. And to trace personality and social development from infancy through adolescence, read Chapters 7, 10, 13, and 16.

CONTENT

We still emphasize the importance of those crucial first nine months of development, the prenatal period. We are more keenly aware than ever that children grow up in many different worlds in many different kinds of families, and we talk about the influences of many kinds of family situations and of different cultures and subcultures. We still include such topics of contemporary social significance as the ethics of research; the effects of divorce, single parenthood, and parents' employment; emotional disturbances in childhood and ways of treating them; the development of moral judgment; and changing sexual attitudes and behavior among adolescents, with special attention to the problems of teenage pregnancy, delinquency, and drug abuse.

There is also much that is new. While we have retained the scope, emphasis, and level of previous editions, we have made many important changes in this seventh edition. In addition to a greater emphasis on the interrelationships among the different stages of development and among various influences on children, we have updated material whenever new findings or interpretations have been available, reorganized material to make it more effective, and added completely new sections. This edition, even more so than the previous one, provides a wealth of information about cross-cultural and ethnic diversity. We are not content with describing development in western majority cultures. Instead, we point out how different cultural practices affect child development and how normal development occurs in many different settings. We have also made major changes in Chapter 1, in the interests of a clearer presentation of the basic theories about development.

Among the important changes in this edition you will find:

- *New sections* on ethological and Vygotsky's contextual perspectives, Jean Baker Miller's relational theory, sex chromosome abnormalities and genetic disorders, sleep patterns, early literacy and literacy development, environmental deprivation, homelessness, cognitive advances and limitations, self-understanding and self-esteem, Alice Miller's concept of "poisonous pedagogy," rough-and-tumble play, mathematics development, the social implications of cognitive growth, the cultural context of the family, adolescent depression, Sternberg's triarchic theory, and ethnic factors in identity formation.
- *Important revisions* of discussions on Bronfenbrenner's ecological perspective, heredity and environment (including reaction range and canalization), brain development, the role of the environment in motor development, information processing, autism, day care, attachment, gender differences, child maltreatment, memory development, language delay, schooling, self-concept, AIDS, and eating disorders.

Boxed Material in This Edition

- *Around the World.* Almost all chapters contain one of these boxes, which present windows on child development in various cultures and subcultures, showing that children grow up in many different kinds of societies, under many different influences. These discussions treat such issues as differences in eastern and western learning styles, childbirth and school in Himalayan villages, preschools in Asia and the United States, peekaboo games across cultures, day care in Sweden, cultural attitudes toward health care, the implications of the one-child family in China, and an Asian perspective on moral development.
- *The Everyday World.* Every developmental chapter presents one or more boxes that show a practical way to apply research findings on some aspect of child development. These boxes cover such topics as prenatal diagnosis of birth defects, how to comfort a crying baby, helping children sleep well, improving children's safety, raising boys and girls without gender-role stereotypes, and preventing sexually transmitted diseases and adolescent pregnancy.
- *Food for Thought.* These boxes, which appear in almost every chapter, present current material of a research or controversial nature, with an eye to encouraging students to think critically. In this category are such contemporary concerns as what we can learn from longitudinal studies, the pros and cons of genetic testing, how homelessness affects children, theory of mind, "good-enough" parenting, self-esteem and disability, living with chronic violence, moral leadership, and gender differences in personality.

Learning Aids

We also provide a number of basic teaching aids, including:
- Part overviews
- Chapter-opening outlines
- Introductory one-paragraph chapter overviews

- A "running glossary"—definitions of key terms in the margins of the text
- End-of-chapter lists of key terms in the order in which they are discussed
- Case examples
- End-of-chapter summaries of major points
- Recommended readings for each chapter (either classic or lively contemporary books)
- Bibliography
- Indexes for names and for subjects
- A full-color illustration program of photographs and art that underscores and expands upon the textual discussions, captioned to emphasize important points

Supplementary Materials

An extensive package of supplementary materials adds to the value of this book as a teaching and learning tool:

- *Study Guide with Readings* by Ruth Duskin Feldman.
- *Instructor's Manual* by Peggy Skinner.
- *Test Bank* by Thomas Moye. Computerized test banks for use with IBM and Macintosh computers are also available.
- The *McGraw-Hill Overhead Transparency Program in Child Development.*
- *Films and videotapes.* A wide variety of films and videotapes are available. A complete listing can be found in the instructor's manual.
- *Newsletter.* The text will be supplemented regularly by a newsletter highlighting recent research and current issues, including the theme of *cultural diversity* within the United States and around the world.

ACKNOWLEDGMENTS

We would like to express our gratitude to the many friends and colleagues who, through their work and their interest, helped us clarify our thinking about child development. We are especially grateful for the valuable help given by those who reviewed the published sixth edition of *A Child's World* and the manuscript drafts of this seventh edition, whose evaluations and suggestions helped greatly in the preparation of this new edition: Marc Alcorn, University of Northern Colorado; Bettye Anne Batiste, Armstrong State College; Patricia J. Bence, Tompkins-Courtland Community College; Barbara Biales, College of St. Catherine; Julie Braungart-Rieker, University of Notre Dame; Diana Divecha, Sonoma State University; Trisha Folds-Bennett, College of Charleston; Elizabeth Gilleland, Meredith College; Bert Hayslip, Jr., University of North Texas; Patricia Jarvis, Illinois State University; William L. Johnson, Ambassador College; Eugene W. Krebs, California State University, Fresno; Richard Lanthier, Indiana University, Bloomington; Barbara Matthews, Palm Beach Community College; Richard L. Metzger, University of Tennessee, Chattanooga; Jennifer Myers, University of North Carolina at Chapel Hill; Dawn M. Niedner, Purdue University, Calumet; Christine Readdick, Florida State University; Alvin Roberts, Washtenaw Community College; Pennelope Skoglund, Northeastern Junior College; Lupita Montoya Tannatt, Santa Monica College; Pearl M. Vincent, Jackson State University; and Don Wells, Louisiana Technical University.

We appreciate the strong support we have had from our publisher and would like to express our special thanks to Jane Vaicunas, our sponsoring editor for this edition, and to Beth Kaufman and Katy Redmond, both of whom helped in innumerable ways. Mike Elia's suggestions for streamlining the draft manuscript paid off in a much tighter final version. Our Editing Supervisor, David Damstra, shepherded the book well through all its stages of production. Ursula Smith copy edited the manuscript thoroughly and unobtrusively. Inge King, photo editor of all six previous editions of *A Child's World*, again used her sensitivity to children and her good eye to find outstanding photographs. Joan O'Connor and the artists working with her produced a cover and book design noteworthy for their aesthetics as well as for their rendering of concepts. Kim Gelé devoted much care and many hours to researching the literature, assembling the suggested readings, and organizing the bibliography.

Finally, we'd like to give special thanks to all the children in our lives who were the real-life inspirations for incidents from the lives of "Vicky" and "Jason." Someday they'll all know how much they helped us.

Diane E. Papalia
Sally Wendkos Olds

INTRODUCTION
ABOUT A CHILD'S WORLD

*I'm like a child
trying to do everything
say everything
see everything
and be everything
all at once*

John Hartford, 1971

If you were to meet the child whom we call "Vicky," the first thing you would notice about her might be her physical agility. Wiry, flexible, and strong, she is usually in motion—and a joy to watch. The feature you might notice first about "Jason," a child of about the same age, is his bashfulness. Instead of answering you when you speak to him, or even look at him, he is likely, at first, to duck his head and seem to pretend that he isn't even there.

Each of these children is a unique person, unlike anyone else in this world. So far even our advanced scientific technology has not learned how to clone a human being! Both these children, of course, have many characteristics that make up their individual personalities. Some of their traits—Vicky's physical agility and Jason's shyness, for instance—are like those of the people closest to them— her mother, his father. Other traits seem to spring from nowhere.

The blend of each child's physical and psychological characteristics is distinctive to that child. How did this mix come about? How did these children become the particular individuals they are? Which events in their lives have had the greatest influence? Which of their characteristics will persist into adulthood? Which will change? The answers to questions like these are what we seek when we study child development.

We want to answer such questions for a host of reasons. First is basic curiosity: For most of us, nothing is more interesting than understanding ourselves. Then come the people we care about. By examining how children develop—from conception through adolescence—we will come to know more about ourselves and our fellow human beings. Second, the answers have practical benefits. When we understand how development occurs, we can step in—when appropriate— to help people live happier, more fulfilled lives. Finally, since no society can approach its potential unless its members fulfill their own, we help ourselves when we help others. Let's see, then, what this book is all about.

HOW THIS BOOK PRESENTS THE STUDY OF CHILD DEVELOPMENT

Each human being is like other people in some ways but unique in others. This book, too, is like other books about child development in some ways but different in others. It shows its own "personality" in the topics it discusses, the way it treats them, and how it illustrates and organizes them. Its uniqueness rests on its reflection of its authors' points of view. To help readers assess what we, the authors, say, we want to outline the perspectives from which we wrote this book. We'll start from our more philosophical stances and go on to our practical ones.

WE CELEBRATE THE HUMAN BEING

In a book about child development, it is not surprising that our emphasis is on what research and theory have to tell us about human beings and about the implications that their early development carries for their later years. We seek information that gives us insights into specifically human qualities—how children develop, how they respond to their biological legacy and their environment, and how they affect the world they live in.

Children adapt and take part in their cultures in complex ways that reflect the richness of humanity. To explore the diversity of children's lives, we examine them in a variety of settings, including those that are characteristic of a particular ethnic or cultural milieu. For example, in Chapter 7, we report research about variations among Canadian, Haitian, and Vietnamese parents' beliefs regarding child rearing and how these beliefs are reflected in parenting practices. In Chapter 10, we talk about how some Native American groups, like the Hopi and the Papago, bring up their children in ways that encourage them to share with and care about other people, whereas the parenting styles of other groups, like the Ik of east Africa, seem to encourage distrust and hostility toward others.

To explore this complexity of child development in many contexts, we discuss issues like these throughout the book, both in the main body of the text and in "Around the World" boxes.* Differences in behaviors and development among people in various cultural groups pose a warning to us as scientists: When it comes to understanding humanity, we must look to its richness before we can find any unifying simplicity.

Whenever possible, we cite research that has been performed on children rather than animals. Sometimes we *need* to refer to animal studies—for example, where ethical standards prevent us from using children in research, such as exploring the harm to a fetus when a pregnant woman takes drugs. When we do give conclusions based on animal research, we apply them with caution, since we cannot assume that they apply equally to humans.

WE BELIEVE IN THE RESILIENCE OF CHILDREN

We believe that people often have the ability to bounce back from difficult early circumstances or stressful experiences to make a good adaptation to life. This has been dramatically illustrated by the efforts made to help low-birthweight infants catch up with their peers and develop normally, which we discuss in Chapter 4. It has also shown up in longitudinal research that has followed people from childhood into at least their sixties and has found that a single experience, even one so painful as the death of a parent in childhood, is not likely to cause irreversible damage (Vaillant & Vaillant, 1990). Later events can often transform the results of early experiences.

A nurturing environment can often help a child overcome the effects of early deprivation. Studies of children on the Hawaiian island of Kauai, for example, have reinforced our belief in children's resilience. This research, which we also discuss in Chapter 4, indicates that even when children have been seriously injured at birth, the best predictor of development is the child's overall experience of growing up. In other words, the postnatal environment exerts a strong influence on the degree to which a child will be affected by birth trauma.

*See the list of boxes on page xxiii.

Children help to shape their own world, and then they respond to the world they helped to make. It is hard to tell from this picture who laughed first—mother or baby—but once the fun began, each one affected the other. The same spiral can occur with other moods, too.

WE RECOGNIZE THAT CHILDREN HELP SHAPE THEIR OWN DEVELOPMENT

Children are not passive sponges soaking up influences. They actively shape their own environment, and then they respond to the environment that they have helped to create. In other words, the influence is *bidirectional,* flowing from the outside world to the child—and from the child out to the child's world. Right from birth, a baby's inborn temperament influences the ways parents and other people react to that baby. People treat a cheerful baby differently from a cranky one, an active baby differently from an apathetic one, and a healthy baby differently from a sick one. Research that we report on in Chapter 7 found that the "fit" between parents and child—the degree to which the parents feel comfortable with the child—affects parents' feelings. Energetic, active parents may become impatient with a slow-moving, docile child, although more easygoing parents might welcome a child with such a personality.

Language is a striking area in which babies affect their world. As we report in Chapter 6, when babies babble and coo, adults are more likely to talk to them, which then makes the baby "talk" more. This cycle of conversation helps children acquire the ability to use language—and to gain better control over their own lives.

WE BELIEVE THAT KNOWLEDGE IS USEFUL

As two people who live in the real world, we examine research findings carefully to see how we or others can use them to solve practical problems. *Basic research,* the kind undertaken in the spirit of intellectual curiosity with no immediate practical goal in mind, and *applied research,* which addresses an immediate problem, complement each other and often go together. In this book we focus on three main aspects of application: for parents and caregivers, for educators, and for private and governmental setters of social policy.

Basic research, for example, can reveal how a child of a particular age learns and thinks. Applied research can use that basic knowledge to develop age-appropriate education or to help the child deal with life issues. In Chapter 9 we discuss preschool children's cognitive levels—what they understand and when they achieve certain concepts. By knowing that the understanding of death is still incomplete, parents are better able to help a child deal with grief and bereavement. Other research that we examine in Chapter 9 concerns memory development in childhood and is important in determining such social policy issues as the legal validity of children's eyewitness testimony.

This book also includes boxes titled "Food for Thought." These boxes report on new developments in either basic or applied research, reflect controversies in the field, and discuss how research can be applied in the real world. Also, each chapter from Chapter 2 on includes one or more boxes titled "The Everyday World." These boxes show how research can be applied to solve practical problems. Of course, actual research studies and applications of research are found throughout the text narrative as well.

WE BELIEVE THAT ALL DOMAINS OF DEVELOPMENT ARE INTERRELATED

The examples given above also show another relationship, that between the cognitive aspects of development and the emotional aspects. Although this book divides development into three separate domains—physical, cognitive, and personality and social—to follow children's development through adolescence, we know that each one of these aspects of development is entwined with the other two. In Chapter 5, we show how a baby's increasing physical mobility affects the sense of competence and self-esteem. And in Chapter 6, we point out how the growth of memory allows an infant the emotional security of knowing that even when his or her mother is out of sight, she has not ceased to exist. Similarly, in Chapter 14, we note the implications of the timing of puberty for adolescents' emotional and cognitive development.

WE RESPECT ALL STAGES OF THE LIFE SPAN

Although this book is about the development of children, we are fully aware that development and growth do not end, as this book does, with adolescence. We refer to the lifetime implications of many childhood experiences, and we examine some of the ways in which children's development affects their parents. We are convinced that people continue to change, often in positive ways, as long as they live. Many of these changes cannot be predicted from childhood or even adolescence, since they occur as the results of experiences or relationships later in life.

Some research, though, does permit us to look down the road to adulthood from the vantage point of childhood or adolescence. For example, a study described in Chapter 1 found that some adolescents are stronger than others in an attribute called *planful competence*, a mix of qualities that includes self-confidence, dependability, and the pursuit of intellectual achievement. Longitudinal research based on this study followed youths into middle age; it found that people who as teenagers were strong in this trait were less likely to go through a midlife crisis.

As you read this book, you will see these various attitudes reflected again and again in our discussions. To bring some of these issues to life, we have created two fictional characters, Vicky and Jason.

MEET VICKY AND JASON

Real children are not abstractions. They are living, laughing, crawling, crying, shouting, shrieking, jumping, whining, skipping, reaching, thumb-sucking, nose-picking, diaper-wetting, tantrum-throwing, question-asking human beings. To help you see children more as they really are and to personalize our statements about how children develop, we introduce two leading characters who will grow up through the pages of this text.

We follow these children, whom we have named Vicky and Jason, from the moment of their conception until we leave them (or they leave us) in adolescence. We also come to know some of the people in their world—Vicky's parents, Ellen and Charles; Jason's parents, Julia and Jess (whose divorce is one of the traumas in Jason's life); Vicky's little brother, Bobby (whose birth affects her life in many ways); and some of the people who interact with Vicky and Jason and influence them. As we trace these children's adventures, we are reminded that whenever we talk about children, we talk not about abstract concepts in imaginary space, but about real children in a real world.

These people are all composites of real people who exist in real life. Every anecdote in which they appear, every fact that relates to them is rooted in truth. *Nothing* about Vicky and Jason, their parents, their siblings, or their friends is made up. The stories about them are drawn from two sources. One wellspring is the actual lives of real children, either our own (four between the two authors) or other children whom we have observed. There is also another source: Vicky and Jason often personalize the findings of actual research.

THE SOCIAL CONTEXT OF DEVELOPMENT

No child grows up in a vacuum. All development for all of us occurs within a definite environment. Since what happens around children affects them in many ways, we look at development in the context in which it occurs. One framework for this exploration is the ecological approach formulated by Urie Bronfenbrenner. In Chapter 1 we explain Bronfenbrenner's identification of five different levels of environmental influence—going from the intimate surroundings of the home, out to institutions like the school system, and finally encompassing the cultural and sociohistorical patterns and conditions that affect home, school, and virtually everything in a child's life.

This approach helps us recognize the different strands that affect children in a variety of cultures, both in our own society and around the world. Today, one-third of the United States population consists of African Americans, Asian Americans, Hispanic Americans, and Native Americans. By the year 2000 a majority of the nation's young people will probably be from these groups (Spencer, 1990).

A major challenge facing world leaders is to diminish the gap in the quality of life between the "haves" and the "have-nots," while preserving the unique strengths in every culture's values system. Today in the United States, children from some minority groups are more likely to live in poverty; to suffer from discrimination; and to have less access to good medical care, adequate housing, and sound education. We will look at the implications of the social context of a child's world as we look at children of many different backgrounds. We will see how children's life circumstances affect their development. We do not confine our discussions to either the ideal or the typical.

These Native American children celebrating at a festival—like all children—are influenced by many aspects of the social context in which they grow up.

NORMAL DEVELOPMENT AND INDIVIDUAL DIFFERENCE

Normal development involves proceeding through recognized developmental stages at a typical rate. Wide variations in normal development, however, allow for a great deal of *individual difference.* In this book, we talk about *average* ages at which certain behaviors occur: the first smile, the first word, the first step. In all cases, these ages are only averages, because no child is exactly average in every aspect of development. Normal development includes a wide range of individual differences with respect to height and weight, walking and talking, understanding ideas, forming relationships, and so forth. Therefore all the average ages we give should be regarded as flexible. Only when children deviate drastically from the norm is there cause for considering them exceptionally advanced or delayed. The important point to remember is that normal children generally go through the same *sequence* of events, even though the *timing* varies greatly.

To understand individual differences in normal development, we try to untangle some of the many threads in children's lives and to see how they weave the fabric of an individual person's journey. These include the kind of family a child grows up in—nuclear, intergenerational, or nontraditional; the presence or absence of some physical, mental, or emotional disability; and the influences of a child's gender, social class, race, and ethnicity.

Many researchers are delving into the issue of individual differences and what we can learn from them. For example, in Chapter 6 we discuss the range among babies in the efficiency with which they process information. By testing children in infancy and then following them into the school years, researchers have found that some measures of early information processing can help to predict intelligence test scores later in childhood.

A REMINDER: THE REAL WORLD AND REAL CHILDREN

One item this book cannot provide is a living child. For that, you need to keep an eye cocked on the real world and the children in it. Jason and Vicky and the children around them can only begin to tug at you, to pull you from the laboratory into the real world. With their help and with the new knowledge of children that you will gain as you proceed through this course, you will look at every child you see with new eyes.

Observe the children about you—your sisters and brothers, nieces and nephews, daughters and sons. Observe children in supermarkets and fast-food restaurants, on buses and airplanes, in playgrounds and yards. Listen to them. Look at them. See how they get along with each other and with adults. Pause to pay attention to children as they confront and experience the wonder of life.

Look too at the child you once were yourself. Recall some of your own earlier experiences; they may help to illustrate the various concepts discussed in this book. Call up your own memories of your childhood and analyze some of the factors that made you the person you are today. Look at the world through the eyes of a child, and the wonder you see will become your own.

INTRODUCTION
ABOUT A CHILD'S WORLD

CHAPTER 1
A CHILD'S WORLD: THEORIES, ISSUES, AND METHODS FOR STUDYING IT

Children have neither a past nor a future.
Thus they enjoy the present—
which seldom happens to us.

Jean de la Bruyère, *Caractères*, 1688

This first chapter is like an atlas for the world of children. It presents routes for studying child development; traces journeys that theorists and researchers have followed in the quest for information about what makes children grow up the way they do; tells the directions researchers follow today; and poses questions about the best way to reach the destination: knowledge. After you have studied this chapter, you should be able to answer questions like the following:

PREVIEW QUESTIONS

♦ Why should we study child development?
♦ What are the main aspects and stages of children's development, and what influences it?
♦ What perspectives for looking at development should we know about?
♦ Who are the most important theorists in the field, and what are the chief points of their theories?
♦ How do researchers study children, and what are the advantages and disadvantages of each method?
♦ What ethical issues do researchers have to consider?

Vicky began to coo—to make happy squeals, gurgles, and vowel sounds—at about 2 months, a typical age for this early vocalizing. Like parents around the world, Ellen and Charles began to coo back and to talk to their baby in dozens of daily "conversations." At about 6 months Vicky added consonants to her "speech" and began to babble. At 11 months, she toddled over to a next-door neighbor and said her first word—"Hi." Excited by the response she received, Vicky immediately repeated her first word six more times. Over the next month she added three more words to her vocabulary and a few more soon after her first birthday. Vicky seemed to be right on schedule in becoming a speaker.

But then Vicky's progress slowed, and by the time she was 2½, Ellen and Charles were worried. Vicky seemed to understand what was said to her, but she spoke only a few words and was not putting them together in two-word sentences—though the average child does this at about 18 months of age. When they expressed their anxieties to their pediatrician, she suggested a language assessment at a speech clinic. There the speech pathologist told the worried parents that their daughter understood what a child her age was expected to, but that at 30 months, she had the expressive language of a 15-month-old.

The speech pathologist assured both parents that they did not seem to be to

Besides being an enjoyable shared activity, reading with a child—as Anna's mother is doing with her—is an important way to help language skills develop.

blame. Speech, she said, may be late in developing for reasons unrelated to the child's intelligence or the environment provided by the parents. She recommended a program to bring Vicky's speech up to normal for her age.

One part of the program, which began just before Vicky's third birthday, was language stimulation. A speech therapist "played" with Vicky, using toys to teach such concepts as *up-down, soft-hard,* and *big-little.* The therapist helped Vicky to say her words more clearly and communicate more effectively—to use speech the way most people use it (or try to use it) much of the time—to get what she wanted.

The other part of Vicky's language therapy rested with her parents. They had enjoyed talking and reading to Vicky, and they had generally spoken to her in the simplified speech that most adults use with babies. Now they were encouraged to simplify their speech even further. Instead of asking Vicky, "Want to get up on Mommy's lap?" they were to ask, "Want up?" Both parents carried out this suggestion, gradually moving to more advanced levels of language as Vicky's own speech improved. They also expanded on whatever Vicky said and talked about whatever she showed interest in; and they used some new reading routines (described in Chapter 6).

After 4 months of language therapy, Ellen and Charles got good news: At the age of 3 years, 4 months, Vicky had the usual vocabulary for her age. By 3 years, 9 months her vocabulary was at an *advanced* level—4 years, 4 months. She was now speaking sentences that averaged 5 to 7 words and included some of 10 words. By age 4, Vicky was chattering away, making requests, giving orders, asking questions, issuing comments. By the end of first grade she had learned about time and money, was adding and subtracting in her head, and was using a computer. She loves to read and to be read to and is an imaginative storyteller. As her first-grade class project she wrote and illustrated a 16-page book, "Kara and the Magic Fish."

Language is a good illustration of the study of human development: It involves both the changes and the consistency that are typical of development, and it lends itself to study by all the basic methods of developmentalists.

A CHILD'S WORLD: CONCEPTS AND ISSUES

WHAT IS DEVELOPMENT, AND WHY SHOULD WE STUDY IT?

development   *Change and continuity over time.*

child development
Scientific study of change and continuity throughout childhood.

quantitative change
Change in amount, such as in height, weight, or size of vocabulary.

qualitative change
Change in kind, as in the nature of intelligence.

Development comprises both change and continuity over time. *Child development* is the scientific study of the ways in which children change, as well as how they stay the same, from conception through adolescence.

There are two kinds of developmental change. *Quantitative change* is a change in *amount,* as in height, weight, and vocabulary size. *Qualitative change* involves changes in kind, like the changing nature of intelligence. Like the emergence of a butterfly from a cocoon, qualitative change is marked by the appearance of new phenomena that could not have been predicted from earlier functioning. The development of memory changes in both these ways. Jason will remember more from an array of objects shown to him at age 7 than he could remember at age 3, illustrating quantitative change. At 7 he can use memory strategies to help him remember (like grouping objects into logical categories), a skill he did not have at 3; this shows qualitative change (P. Miller, 1993).

The field of child development became a scientific discipline as its goals evolved to include *description, explanation, prediction,* and *modification* of behavior.

- *Description* leads to establishing norms (averages) for behavior at various ages.
- *Explanation* involves uncovering causes for behavior.
- *Prediction* entails forecasting later development.
- *Modification* involves intervening to promote optimal development.

We can see how these four activities work together by looking at language. To describe when most normal children reach certain levels of language development—say, when they say their first words—we study large groups of children. We then want to explain how children acquire language and get better at using it. We try to predict what language ability at a given age can tell about later behavior. (Is Vicky's delayed speech at age 2 likely to be followed by reading problems in second grade?) Finally, we may want to modify behavior (as in offering language therapy to Vicky).

What are the practical implications in the study of child development? By learning about the usual course of development, we can look at various factors in a child's life and attempt to *predict* future behavior. If our predictions suggest future problems, we can try to *modify* development through training or treatment.

Students of child development draw on a wide range of disciplines, including psychology, sociology, anthropology, family science, biology, education, and medicine. This book includes findings from research in all these fields.

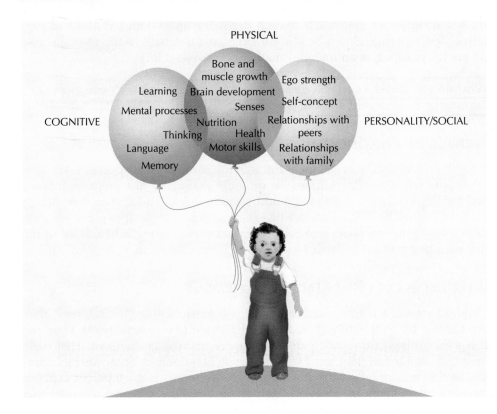

FIGURE 1-1
The aspects of development that we have divided into the physical, the cognitive, and the personality and social are often arbitrary and rarely neat. They overlap and interact with each other throughout life, since development in one sphere affects development in the others.

THE WHOLE CHILD: ASPECTS OF DEVELOPMENT

As we follow changes in Vicky and Jason, we will see that these changes affect every facet of development. To simplify discussion, we talk separately about physical development, cognitive development, and personality and social development. But we need to remember that these divisions are often arbitrary and rarely neat. They overlap and interact throughout life, since development in one sphere affects development in the others. (See Figure 1-1.)

Changes in height, weight, sensory capacity, and motor abilities; development of the brain; and health-related issues are all part of *physical development*. These changes influence personality and intellect. For example, an infant learns about the world largely through his senses and his motor activity. In infancy, physical and mental development complement each other closely. Later, the physical and hormonal changes of puberty will dramatically affect the developing concept of the self.

Mental abilities—like learning, language, memory, reasoning, and thinking—constitute *cognitive development*. Changes in these are closely related to both motor and emotional aspects of being. Thus a baby's growing memory is the root of separation anxiety, the fear that her mother will not return once she has gone away. If the baby could not remember the past and anticipate the future, she would not be anxious about her mother's absence.

For each of us, our unique way of dealing with the world, our sense of self, the way we get along with other people, and our emotions, constitute *personal-*

physical development
Changes over time in body, brain, sensory capacity, and motor skills.

cognitive development
Changes over time in mental abilities, activities, and organization.

personality and social developement *Changes in a person's unique style of behaving, feeling, and reacting.*

ity and social development. Changes in this realm affect both physical and cognitive aspects of functioning. So if a student is anxious about taking a test, he may do poorly, resulting in an underestimation of his true ability.

What do you think? *Can you think of ways in your life in which one aspect of development affects one or more other aspects?*

PERIODS OF CHILDHOOD

We will explore child development through the chronological approach. We look at various aspects of development at different periods of life: prenatal, infancy and toddlerhood, early childhood, middle childhood, and adolescence. Although each period has its own characteristic events and issues, the ages given for each time span are approximate and somewhat arbitrary. Major characteristics of the five periods are listed in Table 1-1.

INFLUENCES ON CHILDREN'S DEVELOPMENT

Children are subjected to countless influences. As we will see in Chapter 2, they are affected by both nature (heredity) and nurture (the environment). First, the genes they inherit from their parents influence many characteristics. That basic predisposition is then tempered by other kinds of influences. Some are biological and environmental influences that occur in the same way in most people at about the same age. Others are biological and environmental influences common to a

These Rwandan children are, like other children growing up at the same time and in the same place, living through the dangers of war, the sickness and death of family members, the stress of relocation, and other horrors that do not affect other cohorts of children growing up in other places at other historic times.

TABLE 1-1

MAJOR DEVELOPMENTS IN CHILDHOOD AND ADOLESCENCE	
AGE PERIOD	**MAJOR DEVELOPMENTS**
Prenatal stage (Conception to birth)	Basic body structure and organs form. Physical growth is most rapid in life span. Vulnerability to environmental influences is great.
Infancy and toddlerhood (Birth to age 3)	Newborn is dependent but competent. All senses operate at birth. Physical growth and development of motor skills are rapid. Ability to learn and remember is present, even in early weeks of life. Attachments to parents and others form toward end of first year. Self-awareness develops in second year. Comprehension and speech develop rapidly. Interest in other children increases.
Early childhood (3 to 6 years)	Family is still focus of life, although other children become more important. Fine and gross motor skills and strength improve. Independence, self-control, and self-care increase. Play, creativity, and imagination become more elaborate. Cognitive immaturity leads to many "illogical" ideas about the world. Behavior is largely egocentric, but understanding of other people's perspective grows.
Middle childhood (6 to 12 years)	Peers assume central importance. Children begin to think logically, although largely concretely. Egocentrism diminishes. Memory and language skills increase. Cognitive gains improve ability to benefit from formal schooling. Self-concept develops, affecting self-esteem. Physical growth slows. Strength and athletic skills improve.
Adolescence (12 to about 20 years)	Physical changes are rapid and profound. Reproductive maturity arrives. Search for identity becomes central. Peer groups help to develop and test self-concept. Ability to think abstractly and use scientific reasoning develops. Adolescent egocentrism persists in some behaviors. Relationships with parents are generally good.

particular generation, or *cohort,* people born at the same time and in the same place and thus subject to similar influences from historical and cultural events and conditions, like war and famine. Finally, there are unusual, unexpected events that do not happen to most people—but when they do occur, they have a major impact on a person's life (Baltes, Reese, & Lipsitt, 1980).

We explore how these influences can affect children. Vicky and Jason will be influenced similarly in some ways. Both will start elementary school at about age 6, as do most American children. Both will be affected by puberty, an experience both will share with other girls and boys. Then, since both children are growing up in the same cohort in the United States in the 1990s, both will be influenced

cohort *People growing up at the same time and in the same place.*

by television, computers, and other technologies. They will also be affected by such influences on their parents' lives as the changing roles of women and a decline in the nation's economy. Finally, they are also affected by unexpected events, like the divorce of Jason's parents and Vicky's attendance at a summer program for gifted adolescents.

We often help create influential events, showing our ability to actively shape our lives. If Vicky had not applied, she would not have won the scholarship that could open up a new world for her. Tragically, her classmate, Sean, drove his father's car after drinking several cans of beer and caused an accident that left him severely disabled.

The way we respond to external forces can change the world around us, even as it changes us. It is not only his parents' divorce that affects Jason; it is also his reaction to it that will influence him further.

What do you think? *Can you describe some of the influences on your own life that brought you to where you are today?*

CONTEXTS OF DEVELOPMENT

An Ecological Approach

ecological approach
Bronfenbrenner's system of understanding development, which identifies five levels of environmental influence, from intimate to global.

Influences occur at particular levels of the environment. In his ***ecological approach*** to understanding development, Urie Bronfenbrenner (1979, 1986, 1994) identifies five different levels of environmental influence, extending from the most intimate environment to the most global. (See Figure 1-2.) He describes them as "a set of nested structures, each inside the other like a set of Russian dolls" (1994, p. 1645). To understand individual development, we must understand each person within the context of all of these levels.

- The *microsystem* is the most intimate, everyday environment of home and school or work. It includes relationships with parents, siblings, caregivers, classmates, and teachers. These relationships are *bidirectional,* with each one affecting others. The personalities and values of Vicky's parents influenced their children's development, and the births of Vicky and then her little brother, Bobby, affected her parents. Ellen left her full-time job as an advertising copywriter, and Charles felt an increased sense of responsibility for supporting his family. Then Bobby's birth affected Vicky's life: She no longer had her parents' exclusive attention. On the other hand, she was now in the position of being older and wiser than a person close to her. The attitudes of the children's teachers affected each child's performance in school—positively when the teacher was encouraging and supportive, negatively when she or he was sarcastic or impersonal.
- The *mesosystem* is the interlocking of two or more settings containing the developing person—in other words, a system of microsystems. These include linkages between home and school, home and work, or work and community. If Jason is unhappy at home, his distress is likely to spill over to school, affecting his academic achievement and his social relationships.
- The *exosystem* involves the linkages between two or more settings, at least one of which does not contain the developing person. Three that are especially

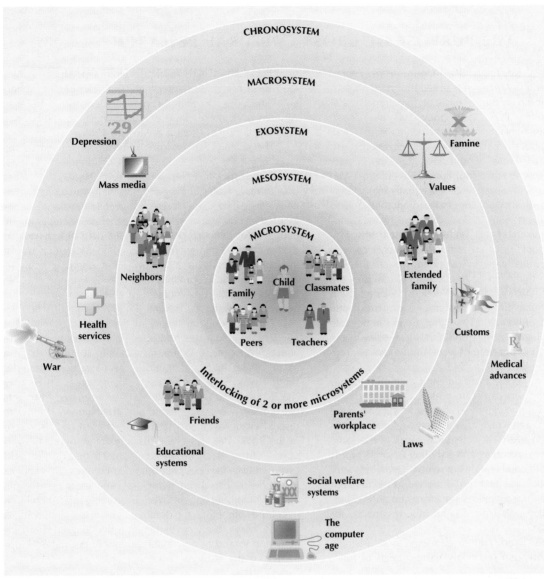

Figure content labels:

CHRONOSYSTEM

MACROSYSTEM

EXOSYSTEM

MESOSYSTEM

MICROSYSTEM

'29
Depression

Mass media

Neighbors

Health services

War

Friends

Educational systems

Social welfare systems

The computer age

Interlocking of 2 or more microsystems

Family

Child

Classmates

Peers

Teachers

Parents' workplace

Laws

Extended family

Famine

Values

Customs

Medical advances

FIGURE 1-2
Bronfenbrenner's ecological model. To understand individual development, we must understand each child within the context of five levels of environmental influence. Going from the most intimate environment to the most global, they include the *microsystem,* the *mesosystem,* the *exosystem,* the *macrosystem,* and the *chronosystem.*

likely to affect children's development are the parents' workplace, the family's social networks, and links between neighborhood and community. Thus if Jason's father is unhappy at work, his discontent is likely to spill over at home, affecting both his marriage and his relationship with his son.

■ The *macrosystem* involves the overarching patterns of culture, government, religion, education, and the economy. Vicky is affected by her country's economy, values, and policies: Because of the financial climate, both her parents need to work outside the home, and she grows up with a patchwork of child-care services, constantly having to get used to new people and new places.

■ The *chronosystem* encompasses change or constancy over time in the person and also in the environment in which she or he lives. This can include changes in family structure, place of residence, or employment. Evidence of this has

BOX 1-1 ■ AROUND THE WORLD

THE PURPOSE OF CROSS-CULTURAL RESEARCH

When Kpelle adults (people from central Liberia in Africa) were asked to sort 20 objects, they consistently did so on the basis of "functional" categories (that is, knife with orange or potato with hoe). Western psychologists associate functional sorting with a low level of thought; but since the subjects kept saying that this was the way a "wise man" would do it, the experimenter finally asked, "How would a fool do it?" He then received the "higher-order" categories he had originally expected—four neat piles with food in one, tools in another, and so on (J. Glick, 1975, p. 636).

This story illustrates one important reason why psychologists conduct research among different cultural groups—to recognize biases in traditional western theories and perspectives that often go unquestioned until they are shown to be a product of cultural influences. "Working with people from a quite different background can make one aware of aspects of human activity that are not noticeable until they are missing or differently arranged, as with the fish who reputedly is unaware of water until removed from it" (Rogoff & Morelli, 1989, p. 343).

By looking at people from different cultural and ethnic groups, researchers can learn which aspects of development are universal (and thus seem an intrinsic part of the human condition) and which are culturally determined. For example, children everywhere learn to speak in the same sequence, going from cooing and babbling to single words and then to simple combinations of words. The words vary from culture to culture, but around the world toddlers put them together to form sentences similar in structure. (Findings like this suggest that there is an inborn capacity for learning language.)

On the other hand, culture can exert a surprisingly large influence on such seemingly basic aspects of func-

tioning as babies' early motor development. African babies tend to sit and walk earlier than American babies, apparently because of cultural practices, possibly because Africans often prop infants in a sitting position and bounce them on their feet (Rogoff & Morelli, 1989).

The society that children grow up in influences the tasks they learn. In the United States, children learn to read, write, and operate computers; in rural Nepal, they learn how to drive water buffalo and find their way along mountain paths. Since so much research in child development has focused on children in western industrialized societies, many people have defined the norm, or standard of behavior, as the typical development of these children. Measuring against this "norm" leads to a narrow—and often, a wrong—notion about development. Pushed to its extreme, this belief can view the development of children in other ethnic and cultural groups as deviant (Rogoff & Morelli, 1989).

The sociocultural theory of the Russian psychologist Lev Vygotsky analyzes how specific practices in a culture affect development. When, for example, a Hindu girl in a small village in Nepal touched the plow that her older brother was using, she was severely rebuked. In this way she learned that as a female she was restricted from acts her brothers were expected to perform (Skinner, 1989). We discuss Vygotsky's theory later in this chapter and elsewhere in the book. We also cite other influential theories developed from research on western subjects that do not hold up when tested on people from other cultures. This applies to gender roles, abstract thinking, and moral reasoning, along with other concepts. We consistently look at children in cultures other than the dominant one in the United States to show how closely development is tied to culture and society and to add to our understanding of normal development in many settings.

---

surfaced in studies of people who were more or less affected by the Great Depression of the 1930s: Teenagers from economically deprived families mobilized their resources and attained greater satisfaction in life than nondeprived youngsters (Elder, 1974).

By looking at systems that affect individuals in and beyond the family, this ecological approach helps us to see the variety of influences upon human development. The relative importance of each system may vary from one society to another, or from one cultural group to another within the same society. This is why it is valuable to do cross-cultural research. (See Box 1-1.)

What do you think?   *Think of a culture other than the one you grew up in. How might you be different if you had grown up in that other culture?*

A CHILD'S WORLD: PERSPECTIVES ON CHILD DEVELOPMENT

EARLY APPROACHES

People have always had different ideas about what children are like and how they should be raised to become decent, socially useful adults. According to the French historian Philippe Ariès (1962), not until the seventeenth century were children seen as qualitatively different from adults. Before that, children were considered simply smaller, weaker, and less intelligent. Ariès based his opinion on historical sources. Old paintings showed children dressed like their elders. Documents described children working long hours, leaving their parents at early ages for apprenticeships, and suffering brutality at the hands of adults. High infant mortality rates led Ariès to conclude that parents, fearing their children would die young, were afraid to love them wholeheartedly.

Ariès's view had been widely accepted, but more recent analyses paint a different picture. David Elkind (1988) finds recognition of children's special nature in the Bible and in the works of the ancient Greeks and Romans. Also, Linda A. Pollock (1983) reexamined sources going back to the sixteenth century, analyzing autobiographies, diaries, and literature from that time to the present. She argues that children have always been seen as different from adults, and that they have, in fact, been given special treatment throughout history.

Pollock found that diaries of adults and children show parents who loved their children and saw them as playful beings who needed guidance, care, and protection. Parent-child relationships were *not* formal and distant, and there is lit-

This seventeenth-century painting by Georges de La Tour captures a tender moment between mother and baby, suggesting that—contrary to one widely held view—the recognition and appreciation of children's special nature is not a recent phenomenon.

New York State Department of Labor investigators found this 11-year-old girl trimming threads in a belt factory in New York City. More than 50 years after federal child labor laws were passed to ban children under 16 from working in factories, many children still work long hours. They often fall asleep in school—or do not attend school at all.

tle evidence of harsh discipline or widespread child abuse. Most parents wanted their children and enjoyed their company, were concerned about issues like weaning and teething, and suffered when children fell ill or died. Parents regarded child rearing as one of the most important challenges in life.

One reason for these differing interpretations of childhood lies in the sources used. Autobiographers recalled stricter discipline than diarists (Pollock, 1983), showing the need to use all available sources on a topic, to avoid the distorted view that would come from using only a few. A difference like this also confirms the need to examine data carefully before drawing conclusions from *any* research.

The first evidence of professional involvement in children's lives came in the sixteenth century. Books of child-rearing advice began to appear, relying on the pet theories and biases of their authors, generally physicians. Their lack of scientific basis shows up in advice to mothers: not to nurse their babies after feeling angry, lest the milk prove fatal; to begin toilet training when a baby was 3 weeks old; and to bind babies' arms for several months after birth to prevent thumb-sucking (Ryerson, 1961).

In the eighteenth and nineteenth centuries, several trends merged to create a fertile soil for the growth of the new scientific study of child development. Scientists had unraveled the mysteries of conception and were arguing over the roles of heredity and environment. They had discovered germs, and then immunization, which made it possible for many more children to survive infancy. Adults came to feel more responsible for the way children turned out, instead of just accepting misfortune or misbehavior. Because of an abundance of cheap labor, children were needed less as workers. The new laws that protected them from long workdays let them spend more time in school. This meant that teachers needed to know more about their pupils. The spirit of democracy filtered into home and classroom, making parents and teachers more eager to identify and meet children's needs. Also, the new science of psychology taught that people could understand themselves by learning what had influenced them as children.

By the end of the nineteenth century, all these trends had come together, and scientists were devising ways to study children. But this new discipline still had far to go. Adolescence, for example, was not considered as a stage in human development until the twentieth century when G. Stanley Hall, a pioneer in child study, formulated a theory of adolescence. His popular (if unscientific) book, *Adolescence*, published in 1904, served mainly as a platform for his ideas, which did stimulate thinking about this period of life.

TODAY'S APPROACHES

The way we explain development depends on how we view the nature of human beings. Different thinkers have come up with different explanations, or theories, about why children behave as they do.

A *theory* is a set of interrelated statements designed to explain development. Theories organize and explain *data,* the information obtained through research. Theories also predict what data might be obtained under certain conditions. Theories, then, help scientists achieve the goals of the field of child development noted earlier—to *describe, explain, predict,* and *modify* behavior.

A good theory is a rich source of **hypotheses,** or predictions that can be tested using research. Sometimes research confirms a hypothesis, providing added support for a theory. At other times, scientists must modify their theories to account for unexpected facts that emerge. Theories are dynamic; they change to incorporate new findings and they serve as a continuing source of research hypotheses.

No one theory of child development is universally accepted today, and no one theory explains all facets of development. Different theorists look from different perspectives at how children develop. These perspectives influence the questions they ask, the research methods they use, and the ways they interpret data. Therefore, to evaluate and interpret research, it is important to know the researcher's point of view. Throughout this book we will discuss studies that stem from the perspectives we introduce in this chapter. Some of the research data support the premises of a particular approach, while other findings fail to do so.

Some theories give more weight to the role of innate factors (heredity), others to experience (the environment); most contemporary theories acknowledge the interaction of the two. Theories tend to differ on the issue of continuity versus discontinuity of development. "Stage theorists" see development as a series of leaps from one level of development to another, like walking up separate flights of stairs and resting on the landings; other theorists see development as a more gradual, continuous process, like walking up a ramp. (See Figure 1-3.)

theory *Set of related statements about data, designed to integrate the data, explain behavior, and predict behavior.*

data *Information obtained through research.*

hypothesis *Possible explanation for an observation; used to predict the outcome of an experiment.*

What do you think? *Which seems a more valid theory of the development of children: the notion of stages or the idea of continuity?*

We'll now look at five perspectives on child development: (1) *psychoanalytic* (which focuses on emotions), (2) *learning* (which emphasizes observable behavior), (3) *cognitive* (which stresses thought processes), (4) *ethological* (which considers evolutionary underpinnings of behavior), and (5) *contextual* (which emphasizes the impact of cultural context on development). In this chapter we highlight the key aspects of each perspective (summarized in Table 1-2); later we discuss more fully some of the theories and the thinkers associated with them.

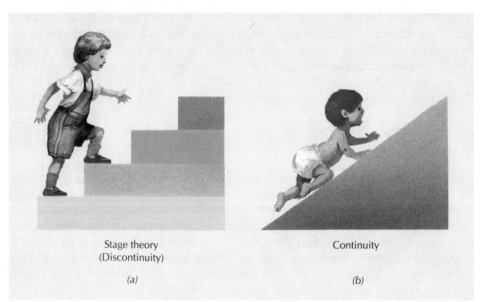

FIGURE 1-3
A major difference among developmental theories is (*a*) whether development occurs in distinct stages as Piaget, Freud, and Erikson have maintained or (*b*) whether it proceeds continuously as Miller, the learning theorists, and the information-processing theorists propose.

Stage theory
(Discontinuity)

(a)

Continuity

(b)

Psychoanalytic Perspective

psychoanalytic perspective
View of humanity that is concerned with the unconscious forces motivating behavior.

The *psychoanalytic perspective* is concerned with the unconscious forces motivating human behavior. This view originated at the beginning of the twentieth century, when Sigmund Freud, a Viennese physician, developed psychoanalysis, a therapeutic approach based on giving people insights into the unconscious conflicts that stemmed from their childhoods and affected their behavior and emotions.

The psychoanalytic perspective delves below the surface of our feelings to explore unconscious forces, which people are unaware of but which motivate behavior. Originated by Freud, this perspective has been expanded and modified by others. Even though contemporary psychologists subscribe to few Freudian concepts—partly because so few have held up to efforts to test them scientifically—Freud's theory has historic importance and has generated considerable debate.

psychosexual development
In Freudian theory, the different stages of development in which gratification shifts from one body zone to another.

The Viennese physician Sigmund Freud developed an original, influential, and controversial theory of emotional developement in childhood, based on his adult patients' recollections.

Sigmund Freud: Psychosexual Theory. Sigmund Freud (1856–1939) wanted to devote himself to medical research, but limited funds and barriers in Austria to academic advancement for Jews forced him into the private practice of medicine. One of his interests was neurology, the study of the brain and treatment of disorders of the nervous system, a branch of medicine then in its infancy. To relieve symptoms with no apparent physical cause, Freud asked questions designed to summon up long-buried memories. He then concluded that the source of emotional disturbances lay in repressed traumatic experiences of early childhood.

Freud believed that personality is formed in the first few years of life, as children deal with conflicts between their inborn biological, sexually related urges and the requirements of society. As Table 1-3 shows, he proposed that these conflicts occur in an unvarying sequence of stages of *psychosexual development,* in which pleasure shifts from one bodily zone to another—from the mouth to the anus and then to the genitals. At each stage, the behavior that is the chief source of gratification changes—from feeding to elimination and eventually to sexual activity.

TABLE 1-2

PERSPECTIVE	IMPORTANT THEORIES	BASIC BELIEF	TECHNIQUE USED	STAGE-ORIENTED	EMPHASIS
Psychoanalytic	Freud's psychosexual theory	Behavior is controlled by powerful unconscious urges	Clinical observation	Yes	Innate factors
	Erikson's psychosocial theory	Personality is influenced by society and develops through a series of crises.	Clinical observation	Yes	Interaction of innate and experiential factors
	Miller's relational theory	Personality develops in the context of emotional relationships, not separately from them.	Clinical observation	No	Interaction of innate and experiential factors
Learning	Behaviorism, or traditional learning theory (Pavlov, Skinner, Watson)	People are responders; the environment controls behavior	Rigorous and scientific (experimental) procedures	No	Experience
	Social-learning (social-cognitive) theory (Bandura)	Children learn in a social context, by observing and imitating models; person is an active contributor to learning.	Rigorous and scientific (experimental) procedures	No	Experience
Cognitive	Piaget's cognitive-stage theory	There are qualitative changes in the way children think that develop in a series of four stages between infancy and adolescence. Person is an active initiator of development.	Flexible interviews; meticulous observation	Yes	Interaction of innate and experiential factors
	Information-processing theory	Human beings are processors of symbols	Laboratory research; technological monitoring of physiologic responses	No	Interaction of innate and experiential factors
Ethological	Bowlby's attachment theory	Human beings have the adaptive mechanisms to survive; critical or sensitive periods are stressed; the evolutionary basis for behavior is important; biology is stressed; learning (environment) is also important.	Naturalistic observation	No	Innate factors
Contextual	Vygotsky's sociocultural theory	Child's sociocultural context has an important impact on development.	Cross-cultural research; observation of child interacting with more competent person	No	Experience

Stages of Psychosexual Development. Of the five stages of personality development Freud described (see Table 1-3), he considered crucial the first three—those of the first few years of life. He believed that children are at risk of *fixation*—an arrest in development—if they receive too little or too much gratification in any of the stages. A child may become emotionally "stuck" and may need help to move beyond that stage. He believed that evidence of childhood fixation shows up in adult personality.

1. *Oral Stage (Birth to 12–18 Months).** During infancy, the oral region (the mouth) is the primary erogenous zone, and feeding is the main source of sensual pleasure. Babies whose oral needs are not met may grow up to become nail-biters or develop "bitingly" critical personalities. Babies who received so *much* oral pleasure that they do not want to abandon this stage may grow up to become compulsive eaters or smokers.

2. *Anal Stage (12–18 Months to 3 Years).* During toddlerhood, the chief source of pleasure is moving the bowels. Too-strict toilet training may lead a child to hold back feces or release them at inappropriate times. An adult fixated at the anal stage may have a "constipated" personality, becoming obsessively clean and neat or rigidly tied to schedules and routines. Or the person may become defiantly messy.

3. *Phallic Stage (3 to 6 Years).* During early childhood, the site of pleasure shifts from the anus to the genitals. In this stage, boys are influenced by sexual attachments to their mothers and girls to their fathers, and by rivalry with the same-sex parent. The boy learns that little girls do not have penises, assumes they were cut off, and worries that his father will castrate him too. The girl experiences what Freud called *penis envy* and blames her mother for not having given her a penis. Children eventually resolve the anxiety from both situations by identifying with the same-sex parent.

   Boys and girls deal with guilt and fear by identifying with the same-sex parent and developing a superego. The early superego is rigid. The daughter of parents who value cleanliness may want to change her clothes six times a day; a little boy may be tormented by guilt because he wrestled harmlessly with a friend. With maturity, the superego becomes more realistic and flexible, as it is better controlled by the ego.

4. *Latency (6 to 12 Years).* Freud considered middle childhood relatively calm sexually. Youngsters have identified with the same-sex parent, adopted gender roles, and developed superegos. Because of this sexual calm, they can become socialized, develop skills, and learn about themselves and society.

5. *Genital Stage (Adolescence and Adulthood).* The physical changes of puberty reawaken the libido, the basic energy that fuels the sex drive. The sexual urges of the phallic stage, repressed during latency, now resurface to flow in socially approved channels—heterosexual relations with people outside the family. The genital stage, the final psychosexual stage, lasts through adulthood.

Id, Ego, and Superego. Freud proposed three hypothetical parts of the personality, the id, the ego, and the superego. At first, he said, newborns are governed by the *id*, a source of motives and desires that is present at birth. The id seeks immediate satisfaction under the *pleasure principle.* Initially, infants do not see themselves as separate from the outside world; all they care about is what they want. But when gratification is delayed (as when they have to wait for food),

* All ages are approximate

TABLE 1-3

DEVELOPMENTAL STAGES ACCORDING TO VARIOUS THEORIES

PSYCHOSEXUAL STAGES (FREUD)	PSYCHOSOCIAL STAGES (ERIKSON)	COGNITIVE STAGES (PIAGET)
Oral (birth to 12-18 months). Baby's chief source of pleasure is mouth-oriented activities like sucking and eating	*Basic trust versus mistrust (birth to 12-18 months).* Baby develops sense of whether world can be trusted. Virtue: hope.	*Sensorimotor (birth to 2 years).* Infant changes from a being who responds primarily through reflexes to one who can organize activities in relation to the environment. Learns through sensory and motor activity.
Anal (12-18 months to 3 years). Child derives sensual gratification from withholding and expelling feces. Zone of gratification is anal region.	*Autonomy versus shame and doubt (12-18 months to 3 years).* Child develops a balance of independence over doubt and shame. Virtue: will.	*Preoperational (2 to 7 years).* Child develops a representational system and uses symbols such as words to represent people, places, and events.
Phallic (3 to 6 years). Child becomes attached to other-sex parent and later identifies with same-sex parent. Zone of gratification shifts to genital region.	*Initiative versus guilt (3 to 6 years).* Child develops initiative when trying out new things and is not overwhelmed by failure. Virtue: purpose.	
Latency (6 years to puberty). Time of relative calm between more turbulent stages.	*Industry versus inferiority (6 years to puberty).* Child must learn skills of the culture or face feelings of inferiority. Virtue: skill.	*Concrete operations (7 to 12 years).* Child can solve problems logically if they are focused on the here and now.
Genital (puberty through adulthood). Time of mature adult sexuality.	*Identity versus identity confusion (puberty to young adulthood).* Adolescent must determine own sense of self. Virtue: fidelity.	*Formal operations (12 years through adulthood).* Person can think in abstract terms, deal with hypothetical situations, and think about possibilities.
	Intimacy versus isolation (young adulthood). Person seeks to make commitments to others; if unsuccessful, may suffer from sense of isolation and self-absorption. Virtue: love.	
	Generativity versus stagnation (middle adulthood). Mature adult is concerned with establishing and guiding the next generation or else feels personal impoverishment. Virtue: care.	
	Integrity versus despair (old age). Elderly person achieves a sense of acceptance of own life, allowing the acceptance of death, or else falls into despair. Virtue: wisdom.	

Note: All ages are approximate.

TABLE 1-4

FREUDIAN DEFENSE MECHANISMS	
MECHANISM	**DESCRIPTION AND EXAMPLES**
Regression	During stressful times, return to behavior of an earlier age to try to recapture remembered security. A girl who has just entered school may go back to sucking her thumb or wetting the bed, or a high school student may react to his parents' recent separation by asking them to make decisions for him as they did when he was a child. When the crisis becomes less acute or the person is able to deal with it, the inappropriate behavior usually disappears.
Repression	Blocking from consciousness those feelings and experiences that arouse anxiety. Freud believed that people's inability to remember much about their early years is due to their having repressed disturbing sexual feelings toward their parents.
Sublimation	Channeling of disturbing sexual or aggressive impulses into such "acceptable" activities as study, work, sports, and hobbies.
Projection	Attribution of unacceptable thoughts and motives to another person. For example, a little girl talks about how jealous of the new baby her brother is, when she herself is actually jealous of the new baby.
Reaction formation	Saying the opposite of what one really feels. Buddy says, "I don't want to play with Tony because I don't like him," when the truth is that Buddy likes Tony a lot but is afraid that Tony does not want to play with him.

they begin to see themselves as separate from their surroundings. Sometime during the first year of life they begin to develop an ego. The *ego,* which represents reason, or common sense, operates according to the *reality principle.* The ego's aim is to find realistic ways to gratify the id. Finally, at about age 5 or 6, the *superego* develops. This includes the conscience. The superego is the result of the child's identification with the parent of the same sex. It incorporates socially approved "shoulds" and "should nots" into the child's own values.

Defense Mechanisms. Freud described defense mechanisms, ways in which people unconsciously distort reality to protect their egos against anxiety. (See Table 1-4.) Everyone uses defense mechanisms at times. Only when they are so overused that they interfere with normal emotional development are they unhealthy.

Erik Erikson: Psychosocial Theory. Erik Erikson (1902–1994), a German-born psychoanalyst, received psychoanalytic training in Vienna from Freud's daughter, Anna Freud, also a psychoanalyst. Erikson fled from the threat of Nazism and came to the United States in 1933.

Greatly influenced by Freud, Erikson held many similar views, but he felt that Freud undervalued the influence of society on the developing personality. He modified and extended Freudian theory.

Erikson's Approach. Erikson believed that the major theme throughout life is the quest for identity, which he defined as a basic confidence in one's inner continuity amid change. He himself had felt confusion over his own identity, growing up in Germany as the son of a Danish mother and a Jewish adoptive father. He never knew his biological father; he floundered before settling on a vocation; and when he came to America, he needed to redefine his identity as an immigrant. All these issues found echoes in the "identity crises" he observed among such groups as disturbed adolescents, soldiers in combat, and members of minority groups (Erikson, 1968, 1973; R. I. Evans, 1967).

While Freud saw civilization as a source of discontent, an impediment to biological drives, Erikson stressed how society can shape the development of the ego, or self. Thus, a girl growing up on a Sioux Indian reservation, where females are trained to serve their hunter husbands, will develop different personality patterns and different skills from a girl who grew up in a wealthy family in turn-of-the-century Vienna, as most of Freud's patients did. Then, whereas Freud maintained that early childhood experiences shaped personality for life, Erikson contended that ego development occurs throughout life.

The psychoanalyst Erik H. Erikson departed from Freudian thought in emphasizing societal, rather than chiefly biological, influences on personality. Erikson sees development as proceeding through eight significant turning points at different times throughout life.

Erikson's Eight Crises of Personality Development. Erikson's (1950) theory of ***psychosocial development*** traces personality development across the life span. It emphasizes societal and cultural influences on the ego at each of eight age periods. Each stage involves a "crisis" in personality caused by a different major conflict. (See Table 1-3.) Each crisis is a turning point for dealing with an issue that is particularly important at that time and will remain an issue to some degree throughout life. The crises emerge according to a timetable based on a person's level of maturation. If the person adjusts to the demands of each crisis, the ego will develop toward the next crisis. If any crisis is not adequately resolved, the person's continued struggle with it will interfere with healthy ego development.

Successful resolution of each of the eight crises (discussed in Chapters 7, 10, 13, and 16) requires balancing a positive trait and a corresponding negative one. Although the positive quality should predominate, some degree of the negative is needed too. The crisis of infancy, for example, is *trust versus mistrust*. People need to trust the world and the people in it—but they also need to learn some mistrust so that they can protect themselves from danger. The successful outcome of each crisis is the development of a particular "virtue," or strength—in this first crisis, the virtue of hope.

psychosocial development
Erikson's theory of personality development through the life span, stressing societal and cultural influences on the ego at eight stages.

Jean Baker Miller: Relational Theory.

Jean Baker Miller (b. 1927), a psychiatrist who founded The Stone Center for Developmental Services and Studies at Wellesley College, originally reacted against the male orientation in prevalent theories of personality development on the grounds that these theories did not explain women's development. She came to believe that such theories do not describe well what occurs in men either.

According to Miller's "relational theory" (J. B. Miller, 1991), personality growth occurs *within* emotional connections, not separate from them, beginning in infancy. The beginnings of the concept of self are not of a static and lone person being ministered to by another, but of a person inseparable from a dynamic interaction with another.

The infant identifies with the first caregiver—not because of who that person is but because of what the person does. The baby responds to other people's emotions, becomes comfortable when others are also comfortable, and acts to move relationships forward toward closer connections. During childhood, instead of striving only for autonomy and separation, children still consider the

Jean Baker Miller developed a relational theory that maintains that personality growth occurs *within* emotional connections, not separate from them, beginning in infancy.

most important things in life their emotional connections with important people.

A split between male and female development occurs during the school years, when girls are encouraged to continue showing a deep interest in relationships, family, and emotional issues, but boys are discouraged from expressing such interests. Instead, they are steered toward personal achievements and competition. By separating these aspects of development, says Miller, both sexes are short-changed. This dichotomy widens during adolescence and adulthood, to the ultimate detriment of both men and women. Women's growth within relationships is devalued by society, and men's deficiencies in participating in growth-fostering relationships are not addressed early enough.

Evaluation of Psychoanalytic Perspective.   Freud's original thinking contributed to our understanding of children and has had a major impact on child rearing. He made us aware of unconscious thoughts and emotions, the ambivalence of early parent-child relationships, and the presence from birth of sexual urges. He also originated psychoanalysis, which influenced modern-day psychotherapy.

Freud's theory grew out of his place in history and in society. Much of it seems to demean women, no doubt because of its roots in the social system of a Victorian-era European culture convinced of male superiority. Also, Freud based his theories about *normal* development not on a population of average children, but on a clientele of upper-middle-class neurotic adults in therapy. His concentration on body-centered conflicts seems too narrow, and his emphasis on the importance of early experience does not take into account such other influences on personality as genes and later experiences. His theories are hard to test, yet research has questioned or invalidated many of his concepts. For example, research does not support Freud's contention that the superego and gender identity are outcomes of children's conflicts during the phallic stage (Emde, 1992).

Erikson's theory has held up better, especially in its emphasis on social and cultural influences on development, which takes it beyond Freud's narrow focus on biological and maturational factors. Also, Erikson covers the entire life span, whereas Freud stops at adolescence. This life-span approach sees the possibility for growth, change, and development throughout life. For Erikson, development does not stop at adolescence. But Erikson has also been criticized for an antifemale bias, since he uses the male as the norm for healthy development. His description of development in childhood as leading toward increased autonomy and independence seems inappropriate in describing female development and may be limited for healthy male development as well. Furthermore, some of his concepts are also hard to assess objectively or to use as the basis for research.

Miller's relational theory highlights relationships rather than separation for healthy development. It does not consider female development as a deviation from the norm. This theory, largely based on clinical observation, is quite new and many aspects of it need to be tested by research.

The differences among these three theories arise from a current controversy about healthy development: whether it rests on individuation (development of the self) or on connectedness (relationships with other people). A new model seeks to redress what critics see as an egocentric, individualistic bias in the theories of Freud, Erikson, and others (Guisinger & Blatt, 1994). Guisinger and Blatt (1994) believe that healthy male and female development does not rest on a narrow and incomplete focus on autonomy, separation, and the self. Instead, it comes about through the mutual interaction of mature relationships *with* mature self-identity, and it continues to develop as these two processes evolve together from birth through old age.

What do you think? *Does healthy development rest more on individuation or on connectedness? How can these two developmental aspects be joined?*

Learning Perspective: Behaviorism and Social-Learning (Social-Cognitive) Theory

Unlike psychoanalytic theorists, learning theorists are concerned with behavior that can be observed rather than with unconscious forces. They study behavior objectively and scientifically.

Learning theorists see development as quantitative (changes in amount rather than kind) and continuous (rather than occurring in stages). They predict later behaviors from earlier ones. Research spurred by this view focuses on how experiences affect behavior. Learning theorists develop laws of behavior that apply to people of all ages. Two important learning theories are behaviorism and social-learning (or social-cognitive) theory.

Behaviorism. *Behaviorism* focuses on behaviors that can be seen, measured, and recorded. Behaviorists look for immediate, observable factors that determine whether a particular behavior will continue. They recognize that biology sets limits, but they view the environment as much more influential in directing behavior. Behaviorists believe that *learning* is what changes behavior and advances development. They hold that human beings learn about the world the same way other animals do: by reacting to aspects of their environments that they find pleasing, painful, or threatening.

Behaviorists focus on two kinds of learning: classical conditioning and operant conditioning.

Classical Conditioning. Eager to capture Vicky's memorable moments on film, Charles took pictures of her smiling, crawling, "dancing," and showing off her other achievements. Whenever the flash went off, Vicky blinked. One evening when Vicky was 11 months old, she saw Charles hold the camera up to his eye—and she blinked *before* the flash. She had learned to associate the camera with the bright light, and her blinking reflex operated without the flash.

Vicky's blinking is an example of classical conditioning. While doing research on the salivating reflex of dogs, the Russian physiologist Ivan Pavlov (1849–1936) accidentally discovered that his dogs had learned to associate sound with food. The dogs would salivate when they heard the food being brought to them. Pavlov then devised experiments in which dogs learned to salivate at the sound of a bell, which had been paired with food. These experiments demonstrated *classical conditioning,* a kind of learning in which an animal or person learns a response to a stimulus that did not originally bring it, after the stimulus is repeatedly associated with a stimulus that *does* bring the response. Figure 1-4 shows the steps in classical conditioning; note the sequence:

1. *Before conditioning:* Vicky blinks when the flash goes off. The light is an un-

behaviorism *School of psychology that emphasizes the study of observable behaviors and events and the role of the environment in causing behavior.*

classical conditioning *Learning in which a previously neutral stimulus (conditioned stimulus) acquires the power to elicit a response (conditioned response) by association with an unconditioned stimulus that ordinarily elicits a particular response (unconditioned response).*

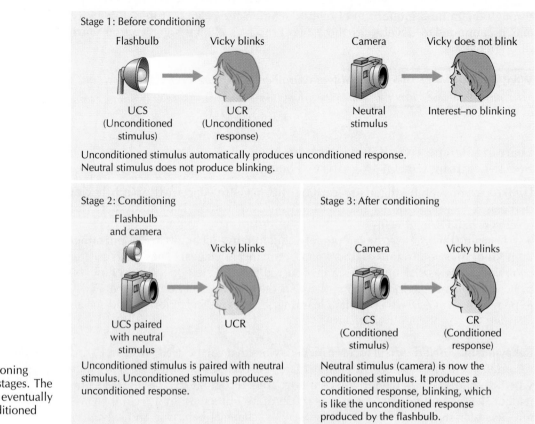

FIGURE 1-4
Classical conditioning occurs in three stages. The neutral stimulus eventually produces a conditioned response.

Stage 1: Before conditioning

Flashbulb → Vicky blinks
UCS (Unconditioned stimulus) → UCR (Unconditioned response)

Camera → Vicky does not blink
Neutral stimulus → Interest–no blinking

Unconditioned stimulus automatically produces unconditioned response. Neutral stimulus does not produce blinking.

Stage 2: Conditioning

Flashbulb and camera → Vicky blinks
UCS paired with neutral stimulus → UCR

Unconditioned stimulus is paired with neutral stimulus. Unconditioned stimulus produces unconditioned response.

Stage 3: After conditioning

Camera → Vicky blinks
CS (Conditioned stimulus) → CR (Conditioned response)

Neutral stimulus (camera) is now the conditioned stimulus. It produces a conditioned response, blinking, which is like the unconditioned response produced by the flashbulb.

conditioned stimulus; it automatically elicits an unlearned, or unconditioned, response. Blinking is an automatic, unlearned response to bright light. The camera is a neutral stimulus; it does not ordinarily cause blinking.

2. *During conditioning:* When Charles takes two series of photos indoors, he repeatedly pairs the camera with the light. Every time he holds up the camera, the light flashes. Vicky reflexively blinks at the light.

3. *After conditioning:* Vicky blinks at the sight of the camera alone. She has learned to associate the camera with the light and to respond the same way to both. The camera is now a conditioned stimulus; it was originally neutral, but after repeatedly being paired with the light, it now evokes blinking. The blinking has become a conditioned response; it is now brought by the camera.

John B. Watson (1878–1958) was an American behaviorist who applied stimulus-response theories of learning to the study of child development. He said,

> Give me a dozen healthy infants, well formed, and my own special world to bring them up in, and I'll guarantee to take any one at random and train him to become any type of specialist I might select—doctor, lawyer, artist, merchant chief, and yes, even beggar and thief, regardless of his talents, penchants, tendencies, abilities, vocations and race of his ancestors. (1958, p. 104)

Watson never got his dozen infants, but he did teach one baby, known as

"Little Albert," to fear furry white objects, using classical conditioning techniques. This famous study, which demonstrated that emotions can be learned, is discussed in Chapter 6.

What do you think? *Watson's approach is like the one in the story of Pygmalion, the basis for the show* My Fair Lady, *in which a professor turns a cockney flower seller into an aristocrat. Do you think this philosophy would work in real life? Why or why not?*

Operant Conditioning. Jason smiles peacefully in his crib. His mother sees him smile, goes over to the crib, picks him up, and plays with him. Another time his father does the same thing. If this sequence continues to be repeated, Jason will learn that something he does (smiles) can produce something that he likes (loving attention from a parent).

This kind of learning is called *operant conditioning* because the person (or animal) becomes conditioned as a result of his or her "operating" on the environment. Jason learns that if he smiles at his parents, they will play with him. Thus smiling, which began as an "accidental response," has become conditioned as the result of reinforcement.

The American psychologist B. F. Skinner (1904–1990) formulated the basic principles of operant conditioning. He believed that an organism will tend to repeat a response that has been reinforced and will suppress a response that has been punished. Skinner (1938) worked primarily with rats and pigeons but maintained that the same principles applied to human beings.

Figure 1-5 shows the sequence in operant conditioning: Jason happens to smile. This random, or accidental, response is reinforced by his parents' playing with him. He keeps smiling to attract their attention. The originally accidental response becomes a deliberate response.

Reinforcement and Punishment. In operant conditioning, the consequences of a behavior determine its fate. A consequence that follows a behavior and *increases* the likelihood that the behavior will be repeated is called a *reinforcement.* Reinforcement can be either positive or negative. *Positive reinforcement* consists of *giving* a reward like food, gold stars, money, or praise. *Negative reinforcement* con-

The American psychologist B. F. Skinner first formulated the basic principles of operant conditioning. He maintained that the same principles that governed the behavior of rats and pigeons also applied to human beings.

operant conditioning *Learning in which a response continues to be made because it has been reinforced; also called instrumental conditioning.*

reinforcement *Stimulus that follows a response and increases the likelihood that the response will be repeated.*

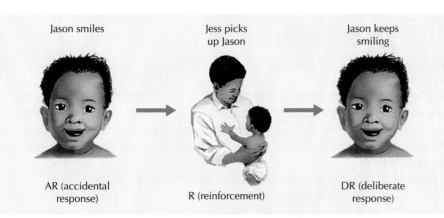

Jason smiles | Jess picks up Jason | Jason keeps smiling

AR (accidental response) | R (reinforcement) | DR (deliberate response)

FIGURE 1-5
Operant conditioning occurs in three stages. An accidental response that is reinforced will be repeated.

sists of *taking away* something that the individual does not like (known as an *aversive* event), like a bright light or a loud noise.

Negative reinforcement is sometimes confused with punishment. However, they are different. *Punishment* is a consequence that follows a behavior and *decreases* the likelihood that a behavior will be repeated. Punishment suppresses a behavior by *bringing on* an aversive event (like spanking a child or giving an electric shock to an animal) or by *withdrawing* a positive event (like watching television). Negative reinforcement encourages repetition of a behavior by *taking away* an aversive event. Whether or not something is reinforcing or punishing depends on the person involved. What is reinforcing for one child may be punishing for another.

Reinforcement is most effective when it immediately follows a behavior. If a response is no longer reinforced, it will eventually return to its original (baseline) level in a process called *extinction*. If no one picks up Jason when he smiles, he may not stop smiling; but he will smile far less than if his smiles bring reinforcement. Thus behaviors are strengthened when they are reinforced and weakened when they are punished.

Intermittent reinforcement—reinforcing a response at some times and not at others—produces more durable behaviors than reinforcing it every time. Because it takes longer to realize that reinforcement has ended, the behavior tends to persist. This is why parents who only occasionally give in to a child's temper tantrum strengthen that kind of behavior even more than if they had given in every time—and then stopped. If they had been reinforcing every tantrum, once they stopped doing so the child would realize quickly that the tantrum was not producing the desired result.

Shaping New Responses. What can be done if a child does not show any of the desired behavior? *Shaping* is a way to bring about a new response by reinforcing responses that are progressively like the desired one. For example, 3-year-old Joey stopped talking when his father left home. Joey's mother first gave him a little toy after he made any sound at all. Then she would give the toy only after Joey said a word, and then only after he spoke a sentence.

Shaping is often part of *behavioral modification*, a form of operant conditioning used to eliminate undesirable behavior. This type of learning is used to teach a variety of behaviors, including toilet training and obeying classroom rules. It is used most often for children with special needs, like mentally handicapped or emotionally disturbed youngsters, but its techniques are also effective in the day-to-day management of normal children.

Social-Learning (Social-Cognitive) Theory. An outgrowth of behaviorism, *social-learning theory* maintains that children learn social behaviors by observing and imitating models, usually their parents. Albert Bandura (b. 1925), a professor at Stanford University, developed many of the principles of modern social-learning theory, also known as social-cognitive theory, which today is more influential than behaviorism. As social-learning theory has evolved, its orientation has become more cognitive.

Social-learning theory differs from behaviorism in several ways. First, it regards the learner as an active contributor to his or her learning, rather than as primarily reactive. Second, although social-learning theorists also emphasize rigorous laboratory experimentation, they believe that theories based on animal

punishment *Stimulus that follows a behavior and decreases the likelihood that the behavior will be repeated.*

social-learning theory *Theory proposed by Bandura that behaviors are learned by observing and imitating models. Also called social-cognitive theory.*

Social-learning theory helps explain the process by which this child is learning how to examine the health of an apparently willing "patient." Children observe models, learn chunks of behavior, and mentally put the chunks together into complex new behavior patterns.

research cannot explain human behavior. People learn in a social context, and human learning is more complex than simple conditioning. Third, it acknowledges cognitive influence on behavior. It maintains that observational learning, rather than direct reinforcement or punishment, is central in development.

Of particular importance in social-learning theory is the imitation and observation of models. Children acquire new abilities through *observational learning*— by watching others. They demonstrate their new learning when they imitate the model, which they may do even when the model is no longer present. However, learning can occur even if the child does not perform the behavior observed. In any case, reinforcement is not necessary for learning to occur.

observational learning
Learning by watching others.

According to social-learning theory, children's imitation of models like parents is the most important element in how they learn a language, deal with aggression, develop a moral sense, and learn the behaviors their society holds as appropriate for their gender.

Children actively advance their own social learning. For one thing, they choose the models they imitate. The choice is influenced by characteristics of the model, the child, and the environment. A child may choose one parent over the other and choose another adult (like a teacher, a television personality, a sports figure, or a drug dealer) in addition to—or instead of—either parent. Children tend to imitate people of high status and people who reflect their own personalities. So Benji, who already has aggressive tendencies, imitates Rambo rather than Mr. Rogers.

Behaviorists see the environment as molding the child, but social-learning theorists believe that the child also acts upon the environment—in fact, *creates* the environment to some extent. For example, Vicky's classmate, Erica, by her behavior creates an environment in which people react negatively to her, whereas Vicky's cheerful, helpful behavior helps to create a positive environment in which she is well liked.

The specific behavior that children imitate depends on the behavior that is present and valued in their culture. If all the teachers in Jason's school are women, he will not model their behavior, thinking that he would not then be "manly." But if he meets a male teacher he likes, he may change his mind. He learns by observation and modifies his behavior.

Cognitive processes are at work as children observe models, learn "chunks" of behavior, and mentally put the chunks together into complex new behavior patterns. Vicky, for example, imitates the toes-out walk of her dance teacher but models her dance steps after those of Carmen, a slightly advanced student. Even so, she develops her own style of dancing in the way she puts her observations together in a *new* pattern. Cognitive factors, like the ability to pay attention and to mentally organize sensory information, affect the way a person will incorporate observed behavior. Children's developing ability to use mental symbols to stand for a model's behavior enables them to form standards for judging their own behavior.

Evaluation of Learning Perspective.   Both behaviorism and social-learning theory have helped to make the study of psychology more scientific for two reasons: They make it possible to define terms precisely, and their theories can be tested by rigorous laboratory experiments. By stressing environmental influences, learning theories explain cultural differences in behavior very well (Horowitz, 1992). But they underplay the importance of heredity and biology. Since they apply the same basic laws of learning to explain behavior from infancy through adulthood, they are not truly developmental. They are not concerned with differences in various stages of development.

Behaviorism has been useful in designing programs and therapies designed to effect rapid changes in behavior (like giving up smoking) or to teach new behaviors (like using the toilet). But because behaviorists are not interested in the causes of symptoms, they may eliminate one undesirable behavior (like stealing) by punishing it, only to see the substitution of another negative behavior (like bed-wetting), leaving the basic problem unresolved. Also, some people object to behaviorism on ethical grounds; they say behaviorists "play God" by controlling other people's behavior.

Social-learning theory serves as a bridge between behaviorism and the cognitive perspective; it acknowledges the active role people play in their own learning and the cognitive influences on behavior. It has also been used clinically, as in one program helping preschoolers to overcome fears of animals by having them observe a fearless model (C. M. Murphy & Bootzin, 1973).

Cognitive Perspective

cognitive perspective
View of humanity that sees people as active, not reactive, and emphasizes qualitative, rather than quantitative, change.

This theoretical perspective views people as living, growing beings with their own internal impulses and patterns for development. The *cognitive perspective* is concerned with the development of thought processes. It views people as active, not reactive, and it emphasizes qualitative change—changes in the way people of different ages think—rather than quantitative change.

Cognitive theorists do not try to determine how reinforcements shape a person's responses. Nor do they focus on underlying unconscious motivational forces. They are concerned with how changes in behavior reflect changes in thinking. From infancy, they say, every normal person is a doer who actively constructs his or her world.

The Swiss psychologist Jean Piaget studied children's cognitive development by observing and talking with his own youngsters and others.

The Cognitive-Stage Theory of Jean Piaget.   Much of what we know about how children think is due to the creative inquiry of the Swiss theoretician Jean Piaget (1896–1980), who applied his knowledge of biology, philosophy, and psychology to meticulous observations of children. He built theories about *cognitive development:* changes in children's thought processes that result in a growing ability to acquire and use knowledge about their world.

Jean Piaget was a serious little boy who was interested in mechanics, birds, fossils, and seashells. He published his first scientific paper at the age of 10, on an albino sparrow he had seen in a park. At about this time, he began to assist the director of a museum of natural history and thus learned about mollusks, a kind of shellfish. He wrote about them—and had to turn down the offer of a curatorship of mollusks at another museum because he was still in school!

Piaget continued his scientific studies and also took up the study of psychoanalysis, psychology, and philosophy. While studying in Paris, he set out to standardize the tests that were developed to assess the intelligence of French schoolchildren. Piaget became intrigued by the children's wrong answers, finding in them clues to their thought processes. Continuing his interest in how children's minds develop, Piaget became director of a Swiss institute for studying children and training teachers. The institute student whom he married eventually helped him study the day-by-day cognitive development of their own three children. From his observations of his own and other children, Piaget built a comprehensive theory of cognitive development.

Up to his death at age 84, Piaget studied and wrote. He wrote more than 40 books and more than 100 articles. Much of his work was done with his longtime collaborator, Bärbel Inhelder, a psychologist who did her own research on how children and adolescents come to understand the laws of natural science.

Piaget described cognitive development as occurring in a series of stages. At

Bärbel Inhelder, a child psychologist, collaborated with Piaget over many years. She also conducted her own research on how children and adolescents come to understand the laws of natural science.

scheme *In Piaget's terminology, the basic cognitive unit, an organized pattern of behavior generally named after the behavior involved.*

organization *In Piaget's terminology, the tendency to create systems that bring together all of a person's knowledge of the environment.*

adaptation *In Piaget's terminology, the complementary processes of assimilation and accommodation.*

assimilation *In Piaget's terminology, the incorporation of a new object, experience, or concept into existing cognitive structures.*

accommodation *In Piaget's terminology, changes in existing cognitive structures to include new experiences.*

each stage a new way of thinking about and responding to the world develops. Each stage constitutes a qualitative change from one type of thought or behavior to another. Each stage builds on the stage before it and constructs the foundation for the one that comes next. Each stage has many facets. All people go through the same stages in the same order, even though the timing varies from one person to another, making any age cutoff only approximate. (Piaget's stages are listed in Table 1-3 and discussed in Chapters 6, 9, 12, and 15.) Let's look at some of the principal features of Piaget's theory that apply at all ages.

Cognitive Structures. Piaget believed that the core of intelligent behavior is a person's inborn ability to adapt to the environment. Children build on their sensory, motor, and reflex capacities to learn about and act upon their world—from feeling a pebble, say, or exploring the boundaries of a living room. As they learn from their experiences, they develop more complex cognitive structures.

At each stage of development, a person has his or her individual representation of the world. Within this representation lie a number of basic cognitive structures known as *schemes*. A *scheme* is an organized pattern of behavior that a person uses to think about and act in a situation. In infancy, schemes are known by the behavior they involve—sucking, biting, shaking, grasping, and so forth. From the first days of life, infants have a variety of schemes. As babies vary the schemes, they differentiate them. For example, babies develop different ways to suck at the breast, a bottle, or a thumb.

The earliest schemes are motor actions. As children develop cognitively, their schemes become patterns of thought related to particular behaviors. They also become progressively more complex—going from concrete thinking about things they can see, hear, smell, taste, or feel to abstract thought.

Principles of Cognitive Development. Cognitive growth occurs, according to Piaget, in a two-step process: (1) taking in new information about the world (assimilation) and (2) changing one's ideas to include the new knowledge (accommodation). This involves three interrelated principles—organization, adaptation, and equilibration. All three of these principles are interrelated: They are inherited, they operate at all stages of development, and they affect all interactions with the environment.

Cognitive *organization* is a tendency to create systems that bring together all of a person's knowledge of the environment. From infancy on, people try to make sense of their world by organizing their knowledge. Development progresses from simple organizational structures to more complex ones. At first, an infant's schemes of looking and grasping operate independently. Later she integrates, or organizes, these separate schemes into a single, more complex scheme that allows her to look at an object while holding it—to coordinate eye and hand—and thus to better understand that particular part of her environment. More complex organization comes about as she acquires more information.

Adaptation is Piaget's term for how a person deals with new information. It includes the two-step complementary processes of *assimilation* and *accommodation*. When Jason begins to suck on a rubber nipple, he is showing assimilation; that is, he is adding new information to an existing scheme because the information fits the scheme. He sucks on the rubber nipple because it is similar to his mother's breast. However, when he discovers that getting milk from a bottle requires different tongue and mouth movements from those used to suck on a breast, he changes his sucking motions slightly. This change reflects accommodation because he has changed his sucking scheme to allow for the differences in sucking on different kinds of nipples. Thus assimilation and accommodation work together to produce cognitive growth.

Equilibration is a constant striving for balance between a child and the outside world and among the child's own cognitive structures. The need for equilibrium leads a child to shift from assimilation to accommodation. That is, when Jason can no longer use the "old" sucking movements, he has to accommodate by changing them. This allows a state of balance, or equilibrium.

equilibration *In Piaget's terminology, striving for cognitive balance.*

Evaluation of Piaget's Theory. Piaget was the forerunner of today's "cognitive revolution," with its emphasis on internal cognitive processes as opposed to learning theory's emphasis on outside influences and overt behaviors. Piaget has inspired more research on children's cognitive development than any other theorist. Among the offshoots of Piaget's theory are Lawrence Kohlberg's cognitive-developmental approaches to gender identity and moral reasoning (discussed in Chapters 10, 12, and 15) and information-processing theory, which is concerned with how people manipulate incoming sensory information.

Piaget's observations have yielded surprising insights. Who, for example, would have thought that not until age 6 or 7 do even very bright children realize that a ball of clay that has been rolled into a "worm" before their eyes still contains the same amount of clay? Or that an infant might think that a person no longer in sight may no longer exist? Piaget has shown that children's minds are not miniatures of adults' minds, but that children think differently. Understanding how children think makes it easier for parents to teach them about money, about illness, about family crises. And it helps teachers know how and when to introduce topics into the curriculum.

Yet Piaget spoke primarily of the "average" child and took little notice of individual differences or of the ways in which culture, education, and individual motivation affect cognitive development. He said little about emotional and personality development. Many of his ideas emerged not from scientific research, but from his personal observations of his own children and from his use of the clinical method, an idiosyncratic way of interviewing other children. Nevertheless, he seems to have underestimated the abilities of young children.

On a more basic level, Piaget's idea of clearly demarcated stages of cognitive growth is questioned by contemporary psychologists who view growth as gradual and continuous rather than as changing abruptly from one stage to the next. It also seems that many people do not reach Piaget's highest level of thought, formal logic, even in adulthood. In fact, formal logic (abstract thinking) may not even be the best model of mature thought, since it fails to acknowledge such critical aspects of adult cognitive functioning as practical problem-solving ability and the development of wisdom. The developmental psychologists known as neo-Piagetians have extended and altered Piaget's theory by integrating it with the information-processing viewpoint, described next (Case, 1985, 1992). According to Case, as children develop, their memory capacity increases in efficiency. Skills like counting, adding, and subtracting become more automatic and efficient. Thus, speed of information processing increases, expanding memory capacity.

information-processing approach *Method based on analyzing the mental processes underlying intelligent behavior.*

Information-Processing Approach. The *information-processing approach* to understanding cognitive development analyzes the mental processes underlying in-

Newly hatched chicks will follow and become attached to the first moving object they see. The ethologist Konrad Lorenz, who got newborn ducklings to "love him like a mother," called this behavior *imprinting*.

telligent behavior. To learn how people manipulate incoming sensory information, it examines processes like perception, attention, memory, and problem solving. Scientists who pursue this approach see people as active manipulators of symbols and look at the processes by which they use these symbols and transform information.

To find out, for example, how infants process information, researchers use sensitive equipment to monitor such physiological responses as eye movements, heart rate, and brain activity. They gauge the efficiency of infants' information processing by measuring variations in attention: how quickly different babies stop paying attention to familiar stimuli, how fast their attention recovers when they are exposed to new stimuli, and how much time they spend looking at the new versus the old. Through such studies we now know that even very young infants can remember and recognize something they have seen.

Robbie Case (1985, 1992), an important theorist and researcher in information processing, emphasizes a child's maximum capacity for independent schemes. He maintains that children develop cognitively by becoming more efficient rather than through equilibration. One way to do this is through practice. Thus a child who practices a skill, like counting or reading, becomes able to do it almost automatically, faster, and more proficiently. At the same time, maturation of the child's neurological processes enables cognitive development to advance.

The information-processing approach, like Piaget's, sees people as active. Unlike Piaget's theory, it does not propose stages of development. It ignores such important aspects of development as creativity, motivation, and social relations. Still, information-processing techniques provide a way to assess intelligence and to gather information about the development of memory. We discuss this important new area in the field of psychology in Chapters 6, 9, 12, and 15.

Ethological Perspective

In his studies of animal behavior, the ethologist Konrad Lorenz (1957) waddled, honked, and flapped his arms—and got newborn ducklings to follow him as they would the mother duck and to "love him like a mother."

ethological perspective
Scientific view that focuses on the biological and evolutionary basis of behavior.

The *ethological perspective* involves the study of the behavior of a species in its natural surroundings or in the laboratory. It focuses on the biological and evolutionary bases of behavior. According to the ethological approach, each species has a variety of innate, species-specific behaviors that have evolved to increase the odds of survival of that species. Ethology relies on naturalistic observation, focused mostly on animals and birds. It emphasizes critical, or sensitive, periods for the development of behavior, but also stresses the importance of predispositions for certain types of learning. As a discipline, ethology began in the 1930s in concepts developed by two European zoologists, Konrad Lorenz and Niko Tinbergen. In the 1950s, the British psychologist John Bowlby extended their perspectives to human development.

How do findings on animals apply to human beings? As Lorenz showed, newly hatched chicks will follow the first moving object they see, whether or not it is a member of their own species, and they become increasingly attached to it. Usually, this first attachment is to the mother; but if the natural course of events is disturbed, other attachments (like the one to Lorenz) can occur. This behavior, termed *imprinting*, is an example of a predisposition toward learning, in which an organism's nervous system seems ready to acquire certain information during a brief critical period in the animal's early life.

Imprinting is said to take place automatically and irreversibly. If Lorenz's chicks had no object to follow during the critical period, imprinting would not occur. Similarly, among goats and cows, certain rituals occur right after birth. If these rituals are prevented or interrupted, mother and offspring will not recognize each other. The results for the baby animal are devastating—physical withering and death or abnormal development. Does the same kind of imprinting occur between human newborns and their mothers?

John Bowlby (1951) was an important ethological researcher who was convinced of the importance of the mother-baby bond. His conviction arose partly from examining ethological studies of bonding in animals and partly from seeing disturbed children in a psychoanalytic clinic in London. He recognized the baby's role in fostering attachment and warned against separating mother and baby without providing good substitute caregiving. Mary Ainsworth, originally a junior colleague of John Bowlby, expanded his research, studying attachment at first in African babies and then in American ones and coming up with the now famous "Strange Situation" for studying attachment (Ainsworth & Bowlby, 1991).

Coming from an ethological perspective, research on attachment is based on the belief that the infant and its caregiver are both biologically predisposed to become attached and that such attachment is important for the baby's survival. (We discuss some of the ramifications of this work in Chapter 4.)

Evaluation of Ethological Perspective.   Ethology helps us look at behaviors to see which ones are important for survival and why children adopt them. It has been applied in a number of developmental areas, including attachment between infant and caregiver and interaction between peers. However, some of its methods pose problems in studying people and seem unsuited for some aspects of human development, like language and abstract thought (P. Miller, 1993).

What do you think?   *Why might it be inadvisable to apply findings from animal studies to human beings?*

Contextual Perspective: Vygotsky's Sociocultural Theory

The *contextual perspective*, first enunciated by the Russian psychologist Lev Semenovich Vygotsky (1896–1934), sees the human being as developing in a social context. This emphasis on the need to understand the context of a person's life echoes Bronfenbrenner's ecological approach and contrasts with the emphasis on the solitary individual described by Piaget and the information-processing theorists. With the translation of his work into English in the 1980s and the interest in sociocultural contexts of development, Vygotsky's theories have become increasingly influential.

Vygotsky, born into an intellectual Russian Jewish family, received a degree in law, read widely, and maintained a special interest in language and literature. His interest in cognitive development came from his efforts to help children with birth defects fulfill their potential. Because of the social upheaval following the Russian revolution, radical new theories like Vygotsky's belief in the cultural-historical view of developmental psychology were given a welcome reception.

The basis of Vygotsky's *sociocultural theory*, which is concerned mainly with

contextual perspective
View of humanity that sees the person as developing in a social context.

sociocultural theory
Vygotsky's theory, which analyzes how specific cultural practices affect development.

higher mental activities, is the active nature of the child, who is not only affected by the social-historical-cultural context in which she or he lives, but who also affects this context. Because of this emphasis, cross-cultural research is particularly relevant. (Refer back to Box 1-1.) The theory's emphasis on the child's potential for learning has had important implications for education and cognitive testing.

Vygotsky's best-known concept is the *zone of proximal development (ZPD)*. ("Proximal" means "near.") Since children learn from social interaction with adults, says Vygotsky, the adults must first direct and organize a child's learning. Then the child will master and internalize this learning. Children in this "zone" for a particular task can almost—but not completely—perform the task on their own. With the right kind of teaching, they can accomplish it successfully. A good teacher seeks out a child's ZPD and helps the child learn within it. Then the adult gradually gives less support until the child can perform the task unaided.

Researchers have applied the metaphor of scaffolds, the temporary platforms where building workers stand, to this way of teaching (D. Wood, 1980; D. Wood, Bruner, & Ross, 1976). *Scaffolding* is the temporary support that parents give a child to do a task. There is an inverse relationship between the child's current ability and the amount of support needed. In other words, the more trouble a child has doing a task, the more direction the parent should give. As the child becomes able to do more, the parent helps less. Once the job is done, the parent takes away the temporary support—or scaffold, which is no longer needed.

Vygotsky (1956) gives an example of two children, both with a mental age of 7 years (based on their ability to do various cognitive tasks). With the help of leading questions, examples, and demonstrations, Natasha can easily solve test items taken from 2 years above her level of actual development. But Ivan, with the same kind of help from an adult, can solve test items only half a year above his level of actual development. If you measure these children by what they can do on their own, their mental development is about the same. But if you measure them by their immediate potential development, they are quite different. In other words, Natasha and Ivan have different ZPDs.

To take stock, then, not only of completed stages of development, but also of those in the process of developing, testers using the ZPD approach give children test items up to 2 years above their level of actual development. They help them to answer the items by asking leading questions and giving examples. The testers can then find the child's current ZPD, or level of potential development. This tells more about a child's potential than does a traditional test score.

Evaluation of Contextual Perspective. Vygotsky's sociocultural theory's emphasis on context stresses the fact that the development of children from one culture or subculture (such as white, middle-class Americans) may not be an appropriate norm for children from other societies. Tests that focus on a child's potential, then, present a welcome change from standard "intelligence" tests that assess only what the child has already learned.

However, concepts like ZPD are vague and hard to measure. Further, there is little attention paid to developmental issues. Finally, since it is time-consuming and expensive to compare social and cultural contexts and to interpret results of such studies, there is little significant research confirming Vygotsky's theories (P. Miller, 1993).

---

zone of proximal development (ZPD) *Vygotsky's term for the level at which children can* almost *perform a task on their own and, with appropriate teaching, can perform it.*

scaffolding *Temporary support given to a child who is mastering a task.*

What do you think? *The five theoretical perspectives on child development each address different aspects of development and differ in their world views. Which approach makes the most sense to you? Can you suggest ways to combine two or more approaches to come up with a more general theory?*

A CHILD'S WORLD: HOW WE DISCOVER IT

Each of these five perspectives suggests its own questions and answers. One way to evaluate each approach is whether it can be tested scientifically. *Scientific method* is a systematic and controlled study of development. It incorporates these principles:

1. Identification of the problem to be studied
2. Formulation and testing of various hypotheses (predictions that can be tested)
3. Collection of data
4. Statistical analysis of data and formulation of conclusions about whether the data support the hypothesis
5. Public dissemination of findings to allow other observers to learn from, analyze, repeat, and build on the work
6. Revision of theories as needed

Only by doing systematic and controlled research can we reliably explain and predict human behavior. The more closely we stick to these principles, the sounder our information will be.

scientific method *System of established principles of scientific inquiry involving the systematic and controlled study of development.*

METHODS FOR STUDYING CHILD DEVELOPMENT

How do we know what children are like at various stages of development? Researchers use a variety of methods to observe children, either in daily life or in planned situations. We will look at nonexperimental research methods, at experimental techniques, and at ways of collecting data. In almost all these methods, some attempt is made to find a *correlation,* or a statistical relationship, between two or more elements in children's lives. (See Box 1-2.)

correlation *Statistical relationship between variables.*

Nonexperimental Methods

Nonexperimental methods include case studies, observations, and interviews and questionaires. Table 1-5 lists the characteristics of these methods, as well as their advantages and disadvantages.

Case Studies. *Case studies* are studies of a single case, or individual life. The first case studies were baby biographies, journals kept to record the progress of a single child. Then Freud and other psychoanalysts relied heavily on detailed notes about individual patients.

A recent case study is the poignant story of "Genie" (Rymer, 1993; Curtiss, 1977; Fromkin, Krashen, Curtiss, Rigler, & Rigler, 1974). From the age of 20 months until she was discovered at age $13\frac{1}{2}$, Genie (not her real name) had been confined in a small room where no one spoke to her. When found, she weighed only 59

case studies *Studies of a single case, or individual life.*

pounds, could not straighten her arms or legs, and did not speak. She recognized only her own name and the word *sorry*. Over the next 9 years, Genie received intensive therapy that helped her learn many words and string them together in primitive sentences. Yet at least report, when Genie was in her early thirties and in a home for retarded adults, her language was still not normal (Rymer, 1993).

Case studies offer useful, in-depth information, giving a rich description of a person. But they have shortcomings. From studying Genie, we learn much about the development of a single child. However, a case study does not yield cause-and-effect information, nor does it provide an explanation of development. Even

TABLE 1-5

CHARACTERISTICS OF MAJOR RESEARCH METHODS

TYPE	MAIN CHARACTERISTICS	ADVANTAGES	DISADVANTAGES
Nonexperimental methods			
Case study	Study of single individual in depth.	Provides detailed picture of one person's behavior and development; provides good description of behavior.	May not generalize to others; may reflect observer bias.
Naturalistic observation	Observation of people in their normal setting, with no attempt to manipulate behavior.	Provides good description of behavior; does not subject people to unnatural settings (like the laboratory) that may distort behavior; is a source of research hypotheses.	Lack of control; inability to explain cause-and-effect relationships; observer bias possible.
Laboratory observation	Observation of people in the laboratory, with no attempt to manipulate behavior.	Provides good descriptions; greater control than naturalistic observation; is a source of research hypotheses.	Inability to explain cause-and-effect relationships; observer bias; controlled situation can be artificial.
Interview and questionnaire	Participants asked about some aspect of their lives; ranges from highly structured to more flexible questioning.	Goes beyond observation in getting information about a person's life, attitudes, or opinions.	Subject may not remember information accurately or may distort responses in a socially desirable way; how question is asked may affect answer.
Clinical method	Combination of observation and individualized questioning developed by Piaget to study children.	Flexibility allows researcher to follow up on interesting responses.	Quality of insights about development depends on skill of the researcher; difficult to replicate because of individualized approach.
Experimental method			
Experiment	Controlled procedure in which an experimenter manipulates the independent variable to determine its effect on the dependent variable; may be conducted in the laboratory or field or make use of naturally occurring events.	Establishes cause-and-effect relationships; highly controlled procedure that can be repeated by another investigator. Degree of control is greatest in the laboratory experiment and least in the natural experiment.	Findings, especially when derived from laboratory experiments, may not generalize to situations outside the laboratory.

BOX 1-2 ■ FOOD FOR THOUGHT

CORRELATIONAL STUDIES

Suppose you want to measure the relationship between two separate factors, like the amount of violence children see on television and the amount of aggressive behavior they show during play. Each of these factors (the amount of violence on television and the amount of aggressive behavior) is called a *variable,* because it varies among members of a group or can be varied for purposes of an experiment.

The relationships between variables are expressed in terms of a *correlation.* Correlations show the *direction* and *magnitude* of a relationship between variables. Two variables may be related *positively:* They increase or decrease together. A *positive correlation* between televised violence and aggressiveness would exist if we found that the more violent television children watch, the more they hit, bite, or kick; and conversely, the less violent television children watch, the less aggressive their behavior is. Or two variables may have a *negative* correlation: As one increases, the other decreases. A *negative correlation* would exist if we found that the more violent television children watch, the *less* they fight.

Correlations are expressed as numbers ranging from −1.0 (a perfect negative, or inverse, relationship) to +1.0 (a perfect positive, or direct, relationship). The higher the

number (whether + or −), the stronger the relationship (either positive or negative). A correlation of zero indicates that there is no relationship between two variables. Correlations almost never reach either −1.0 or +1.0, but are somewhere between 0 and +1 or 0 and −1.

Correlations allow us to *predict* one variable on the basis of another. If, say, there is a positive correlation between watching televised violence and fighting, we would predict that children who watch "shoot-'em-ups" are more likely to get into fights. Obviously, the greater the correlation between two variables, the greater the ability to predict one from the other.

Although correlations suggest *possible* causes for outcomes, they do *not* allow us to draw conclusions about cause and effect. We cannot conclude that watching violent shows *causes* aggressive play or makes it less likely; we can conclude *only* that the two variables are related. It is possible that being aggressive makes children want to watch violence. It is also possible that a third factor—perhaps an inborn predisposition toward aggressiveness—causes a child both to watch violent programs and to act aggressively. A correlation does not let us conclude that one factor causes the other. To do this, we need to design a controlled experiment.

---

though it seems reasonable that Genie's severely deprived environment caused her language deficiency, we cannot make this connection with certainty. Also, case studies may suffer from "observer bias"; that is, the recorder may emphasize some aspects of development and minimize others. While case studies may tell a great deal about an individual child, it is questionable how much the information applies to children in general.

Observation.   Observation can take two forms: naturalistic observation and laboratory observation. Both provide good descriptions of behavior.

Naturalistic Observation. In *naturalistic observation,* researchers look at children in real-life settings like home, school, or playground. They do not try to alter behavior or the environment.

In one naturalistic observation, researchers videotaped 72 first-time mothers and their 5-month-old babies in their homes in the United States, France, and Japan. They then scored such behaviors as talking to, playing with, and caring for the baby and drawing the baby's attention to a person or a thing (Bornstein, Tal, & Tamis-LeMonda, 1991). The mothers in the different cultures were very similar in how they nurtured their babies, how they imitated the babies' babbling, and how they played with them in active ways, leading to the researchers' conclusion that some parenting activities occur automatically across cultures. But

naturalistic observation
Research method in which behavior is studied in natural settings, with no attempt to manipulate behavior.

Naturalistic studies, like this one in which psychologist David Elkind observes kindergartners, allow children to be themselves. Researchers observe but do not participate and do not establish experimental conditions or controls.

laboratory observation
Research method in which people are observed in a controlled setting, with no attempt to manipulate behavior.

since the mothers differed considerably in the degrees to which they talked to and stimulated their infants, the researchers concluded that other parenting activities may stem from cultural beliefs about childrearing.

Laboratory Observation. In *laboratory observation,* researchers observe and record behavior in a controlled situation, such as a laboratory. This method places all subjects in the same situation, to yield information on the subjects' behaviors in this structured environment. This kind of study standardizes the conditions of observation for all participants.

One research team looked at how mothers and fathers spoke to their babies of two different ages, either $2\frac{1}{2}$–$3\frac{1}{2}$ months of age or $8\frac{1}{2}$–$9\frac{1}{2}$ months, by observing them in the laboratory (Kruper & Uzgiris, 1987). The 40 mother-baby pairs and 32 father-baby pairs were equally divided between older and younger infants. Each parent-child pair was videotaped for about 10 minutes as the parent sat on a stool facing the baby. The parent had been asked to stay seated unless the baby needed attention and to play with the baby without toys as they would at home. By and large, fathers and mothers spoke similarly to the babies. They treated their children as "communicating partners" from a very early age as they asked questions, interpreted the babies' actions as answers, sometimes responded for the babies, and commented on the babies' thoughts and feelings.

Both types of observational studies are an important source of research hypotheses. But they too have limitations. For one, they do not explain behavior or determine cause and effect. For example, this second study does not tell us *why* parents talk to babies the way they do. Then too, an observer's presence can alter behavior. Observers sometimes stay behind one-way mirrors (they can see the children, but the children cannot see them) or try to blend into the background. Still, children may know that they are being watched and may act differently. Finally, the controlled situations set up by an observer can be artificial and potentially misleading.

Interviews and Questionnaires. In a face-to-face or telephone *interview,* researchers ask questions about people's attitudes or opinions or some other aspect of their lives. To reach more people, researchers sometimes distribute a *questionnaire,* which subjects fill out and return.

Interviews with nearly a hundred 7- to 18-year-olds who attended a private girls' school in Ohio formed the basis of a study on how girls negotiate the transition to womanhood (L. M. Brown & Gilligan, 1992). One 10-year-old, showing the pressures she feels from her friends, said, "Sometimes I sort of go along with them, but *sometimes I say, 'I don't know,' . . . 'cause I don't know what to say . . . I don't know . . . I just don't know what to say*" (p. 112, italics in original). Statements like this provide evidence that even in this privileged group, these girls were struggling to take their own experiences seriously, to develop self-confidence, and to form authentic relationships.

An annual self-report questionnaire given to a nationally representative sample of secondary school students has for several years provided information about trends in drug use and attitudes (National Institute on Drug Abuse [NIDA], 1994).

By interviewing or questioning a large number of people, investigators get a broad picture—at least of what the respondents *say* that they believe or do or did. Interview and questionnaire studies focus on topics such as parent-child relationships, sexual activities, occupational goals, and life in general. But respondents may not remember accurately. Some people forget when and how events actually took place, and others distort their replies to make them more acceptable to the researchers—or to themselves. Also, how a question is asked can influence the answer.

Clinical Method. The *clinical method* combines observation with careful, individualized questioning. It tailors the testing situation to the person being questioned, so that no two people are questioned in exactly the same way. This method is quite different from the standardized testing technique, which aims to make the testing situation as alike as possible for all subjects.

Piaget developed this flexible, open-ended method to find out how children think, since he believed that their wrong answers held clues to the ways they reason. He would follow up their answers to his questions by asking more questions. In an exploration of children's understanding that the number of items remains the same after being rearranged, he had Gui, aged 4 years, 4 months, exchange six pennies for six flowers and then had the following conversation with the child (Piaget, 1952):

PIAGET: What have we done?
GUI: We exchanged them.
PIAGET: Then is there the same number of flowers and pennies?
GUI: No.
PIAGET: Are there more on one side?
GUI: Yes.
PIAGET: Where?
GUI: There. (Points to row of pennies.)

Using the clinical method, Piaget discovered that a typical 4-year-old believed that pennies or flowers were more numerous when arranged in a line than when heaped or piled up. He individualized each exchange, probing further into in-

interview *Research technique in which people are asked, either face to face or on the telephone, to state their attitudes, opinions, or histories.*

questionnaire *Research technique in which people complete a form that explores their attitudes, opinions, or behaviors.*

clinical method *Type of nonexperimental research method developed by Piaget that combines observation with careful, individualized questioning.*

teresting responses, using language he thought the child would understand, and even changing to the language the child was using.

This procedure lets a researcher follow up especially interesting responses and often elicits answers that could not be discovered otherwise. But the method has drawbacks. The investigator has to be imaginative and perceptive, and it is hard for other researchers to duplicate the results exactly. Its findings can be accepted only after several researchers support one another's observations.

Experimental Methods

experiment *Highly controlled, replicable (repeatable) procedure in which a researcher assesses the effect of manipulating variables; provides information about cause and effect.*

An *experiment* is a strictly controlled procedure in which an investigator (the experimenter) manipulates variables to determine how one affects another. Scientific experiments must be conducted and reported in a way that allows another investigator to replicate (repeat) them to verify results and conclusions. A true experiment requires three features: *random assignment*, a *control group*, and *manipulation of the independent variable*. All these terms are defined in the following paragraphs. For a diagram of an experiment, see Figure 1-6.

To examine the influence of watching television on the development of both aggressive and prosocial behavior (helping behavior like sharing), researchers conducted a field experiment in a preschool. They compared two groups of children: 3- to 5-year-olds who saw a prosocial program (*Mr. Rogers' Neighborhood*), a similar group of preschoolers who saw aggressive cartoons (*Batman* and *Superman*), and a third group who saw neutral films. They assessed the groups on measures of aggressive and prosocial behavior (like hitting or cooperating) and concluded that the kinds of programs influenced how the children acted. Since the groups were similar before the program began, the differences between them afterward were attributed to the programs they had watched (Friedrich & Stein, 1973).

Variables and Groups. In such an experiment, we call the viewing of the televi-

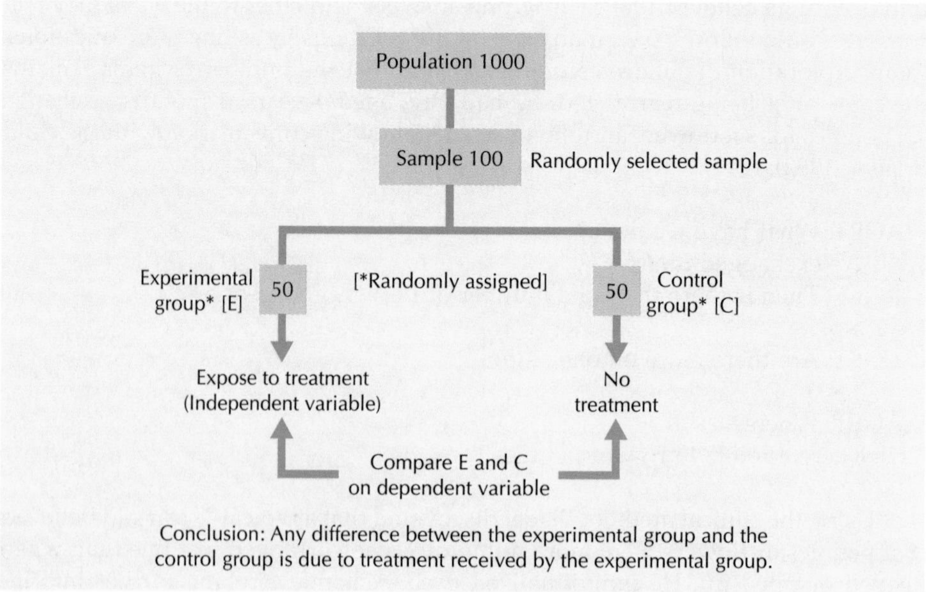

FIGURE 1-6
Design for an experiment. This experiment takes a random sample from the larger population being studied, randomly assigns subjects to either the experimental (E) or the control (C) group, and exposes the experimental group to a treatment that is not offered to the control group. By comparing the two groups after the experimental group has received the treatment, the researcher can conclude that any difference between them is due to the experimental treatment.

Population 1000

Sample 100 — Randomly selected sample

Experimental group* [E] 50 — [*Randomly assigned] — 50 Control group* [C]

Expose to treatment (Independent variable) — No treatment

Compare E and C on dependent variable

Conclusion: Any difference between the experimental group and the control group is due to treatment received by the experimental group.

sion program the *independent variable* and the child's behavior the **dependent variable.** The *independent variable* is something over which the experimenter has control. A *dependent variable* is something that may or may not change as a result of changes in the independent variable; it *depends* on the independent variable. In an experiment, we manipulate the independent variable to see how changes in it will affect the dependent variable.

To design an experiment, we need experimental groups and control groups. An *experimental group* consists of people who will be exposed to the experimental manipulation or treatment (like being shown prosocial programs). After exposure, the effect of the treatment on the dependent variable is measured one or more times. A *control group* consists of people who are similar to the experimental group but who have not received the treatment whose effects we want to measure. (In the experiment just described, the children viewing the neutral films were the control group.)

Sampling and Assignment.   Suppose we want to study the value of an enrichment program for children in day care. We find that a group of children who were in the program show higher scores afterwards on cognitive tests. How can we be sure that the relationship between being in the program and having higher test scores will hold for children in general? And how can we rule out the impact of some unknown third factor that might account for the results (like the possibility that the children in the program were brighter initially than those who were not offered the program)? The answers hinge on how subjects are selected and assigned to experimental and control groups.

Selecting the Sample.   First, the *sample* (the subjects in an experiment) must be *representative*, or typical, of the larger group that we want to study, as, say, all high school graduates of 1995 or all urban children in day care in 1994. Since it is generally too costly and time-consuming to study the entire group, experimenters choose a subgroup, or sample, of this population. Only if the sample is typical of the larger group are we able to *generalize* the experimental results, that is, apply them to the population as a whole.

The best way to ensure that a sample is typical is to choose a *random sample,* one in which each member of the population has an equal chance of being selected. Using this method, we might get our sample by putting the names of all the children in a preschool class into a hat and drawing out the number we want.

Assigning Subjects. Next, we need to assign subjects either to the experimental group or to the control group. We can assign people randomly, so that each subject has an equal chance of being in either group. In a large enough sample, the two groups will be alike in almost every respect—age, sex, race, socioeconomic status, school attendance, IQ, and so forth. With two very similar groups, only one of which will receive the independent variable (the enrichment program), we will be able to draw conclusions about the effect of that variable.

We can also divide the sample through matching. This involves identifying any characteristic that might affect the results—like age, sex, race, and socioeconomic status—and then making sure that the experimental group and the control group are alike on these characteristics. However, in matching the two groups on some factors, we may miss others, which may turn out to be just as important.

independent variable   *In an experiment, the variable that is directly controlled and manipulated by the experimenter.*

dependent variable   *In an experiment, the variable that may or may not change as a result of changes in the independent variable.*

experimental group   *In an experiment, people who receive the treatment under study; changes in these people are compared with changes in a control group.*

control group   *In an experiment, people who are similar to people in the experimental group but who do not receive the treatment whose effects are to be measured; the results obtained with this group are compared with the results obtained with the experimental group to assess cause and effect.*

sample   *In an experiment, a group of people chosen to represent the total population.*

random sample   *Sampling technique in which each member of the population has an equal chance of being selected for study.*

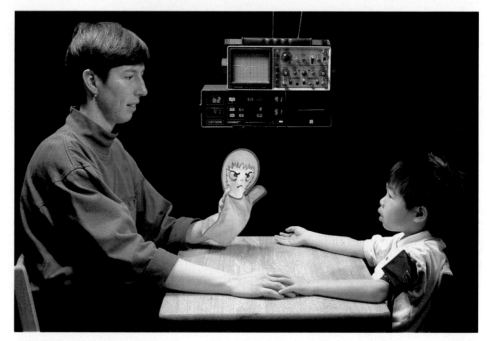

Experiments use strictly controlled procedures that manipulate variables to determine how one affects another. To study emotional resiliency, this research project at the University of California at San Francisco monitors the heart rate and blood pressure of young children as they explain their feelings in response to a hand puppet's happy or angry face.

Types of Experiments. There are three types of experiments: those conducted in the laboratory; those conducted in the field, a setting that is part of the subject's everyday life; and those that make use of naturally occurring experiences.

In a *laboratory experiment*, the subject is brought to a specific place, where she or he experiences certain controlled conditions, and his or her reaction to these conditions is recorded. It may be contrasted with the same person's behavior under other conditions or with the behavior of people who are subjected to a different set of conditions.

Field experiments take place in "the field," a familiar setting, like the school or the home. The experiment in which preschoolers watched two different kinds of TV programs (Friedrich & Stein, 1973) was a field experiment.

Natural experiments compare people whom life circumstances have accidentally divided into separate groups. These are not true experiments, since they do not try to modify behavior; but they provide a way of studying events that cannot be created artificially. For example, it would be unethical, even if it were possible, to separate twins at birth just to do interesting experiments. But finding and studying identical twins who had been separated at birth and raised in different circumstances offers the chance to compare different environmental effects on identical genes, as we will see in Chapter 2.

How the Types of Experiments Differ. The three types of experiments—laboratory, field, and natural—differ in two respects. One is the *degree of control* exerted by the experimenter. Laboratory experiments are the most rigidly controlled; field experiments are under considerable control; but control in natural experiments exists only in the way researchers collect and use the data. Because of this control, laboratory experiments are the easiest to replicate by other investigators.

The other difference between kinds of experiments is the degree to which the findings from a study can be *generalized*, or applied to a broad range of people.

The degree of generalizability is inverse to the degree of control. Laboratory experiments, which are the most highly controlled, typically are the least generalizable. Because they are carried out in an artificial setting, we cannot be sure their findings will apply outside the laboratory.

Comparing Experimental and Nonexperimental Methods

Experiments have several advantages over nonexperimental methods. Only experiments can establish cause-and-effect relationships. Furthermore, experiments are so highly regulated and carefully described that they can be replicated. By repeating studies with different subjects, researchers can assess the reliability of data.

Experiments also have drawbacks. Many look at only one or two facets of development at a time; by zeroing in so narrowly, they sometimes miss larger, more general variables in people's lives. Then too, we cannot generalize from the laboratory to other situations. Experimental manipulation shows what *can* happen if certain conditions are present—for example, that children who watch violent television shows in the laboratory *can* become more aggressive in that setting. It does not tell us what actually *does* happen in daily life: *Do* children who watch a lot of violent shows hit their little brothers or sisters more often than children who watch fewer such shows?

Greater understanding of child development results from using both nonexperimental and experimental methods. Researchers can first observe children as they go about their everyday lives, determine whether correlations exist between various factors, and then design experiments of these apparent relationships.

Developmental Data-Collection Techniques

Information about how children develop is commonly collected by conducting *longitudinal* and *cross-sectional* studies. (See Figure 1-7.) Since each of these methods has drawbacks, researchers have also developed *sequential* strategies.

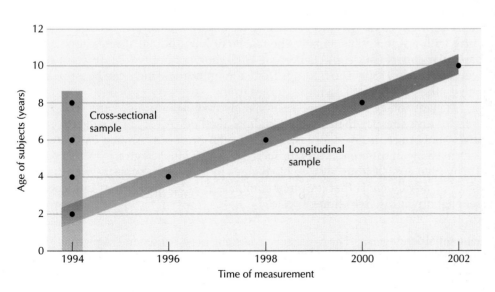

FIGURE 1-7
Two ways to obtain data about development. In a *cross-sectional* study, people of different ages are measured at one time. Here, groups of 2-, 4-, 6-, and 8-years-olds were tested in 1994, to obtain data about age differences in performance. In a *longitudinal* study, the same people are measured more than once. Here, a sample of children were first measured in 1994 when they were 2 years old. Follow-up testing of the same children was scheduled for 1996, 1998, 2000, and 2002, when the children would be 4, 6, 8, and 10, respectively. This technique shows age changes in performance.

longitudinal study
Research that follows the same person or people over a period of time.

cross-sectional study
Research that assesses different people of different ages at the same time.

Longitudinal Studies.   In a *longitudinal study,* researchers measure the same people more than once to see how they change with age. We may measure a single characteristic like vocabulary size, IQ, height, or aggressiveness. Or we may look at several aspects of development to find relationships among factors. This approach shows the *process* of development, rather than its status at any given time. (See Box 1-3 for a discussion of the Berkeley Longitudinal Studies.)

Cross-Sectional Studies.   In a *cross-sectional study,* people of different ages are assessed at one time. Cross-sectional studies provide information about differences in development among people of different ages, rather than about changes with age in the same person. One series of cross-sectional studies, described in Chapter 9, seeks to find out when children develop knowledge about the process of thinking. In one of these studies, researchers asked 3-, 4-, 6-, and 7-year-olds questions about what a pensive-looking woman was doing, or about the state of someone's mind. They have found age differences showing a striking increase with age in children's awareness of mental activity (J. H. Flavell, Green, & Flavell, 1995, 1992).

Comparing Longitudinal and Cross-Sectional Studies.   Longitudinal studies assess *changes* undergone by one or more persons over time; cross-sectional studies look at *differences* between groups of people. Each approach has strengths and weaknesses.

Longitudinal studies are more sensitive to individual patterns of change: By repeatedly studying the same people, researchers can track data about individuals. Also, *within* a study, they avoid the effects of cohort membership (the year in which subjects were born and their different life circumstances due to when they lived).

But longitudinal studies are time-consuming and expensive. It is hard to keep track of a large group of subjects over the years, to keep records, and to keep the study unified despite personnel turnover. Then there is a probable bias in the sample: Volunteers tend to be of higher-than-average socioeconomic status and intelligence, and those who stay with the study over time tend to be more competent than those who drop out. Also, the results can be affected by repeated testing or interviewing. People may do better in later tests, for example, because of familiarity with test materials. Finally, the results of longitudinal studies done on one particular cohort (say, subjects born in 1930) may not apply to a different cohort (people born in 1980). The findings from a longitudinal study can be generalized only to the cohort that its sample comes from.

The advantages of the cross-sectional method include speed and economy: It is faster and cheaper than the longitudinal method. Also, since subjects are assessed only once, it does not lose subjects who drop out. Among its drawbacks is its masking of differences among subjects since it looks at group averages. Thus it may give a misleading picture of changes in individual subjects over time. Its major disadvantage is that it cannot eliminate the effects of cohort influences on people born at different times.

Sequential Strategies.   The *cross-sequential study* is one of several sequential strategies designed to overcome drawbacks of the longitudinal and cross-sectional

BOX 1-3 ▪ FOOD FOR THOUGHT

WHAT LONGITUDINAL STUDIES CAN TELL US

Stuart Campbell, orphaned at age 6 by his mother's death and abandonment by his alcoholic father, was raised in near-poverty by his stern but loving grandmother. At age 11 he entered a longitudinal study. In junior high school and high school, he was judged to be unusually mature, intelligent, and mentally healthy, with a good sense of humor. By age 17 he knew he wanted to be a doctor. He became a pediatrician, married and divorced early, married again happily, had five children with his second wife, and established a home and a reputation in an upper-middle-class community.

Stuart was one of more than 500 children recruited for three studies known collectively as the Berkeley Longitudinal Studies. For the Berkeley Guidance Study and the Berkeley Growth Study, which were both launched in 1928, infants were enrolled right after birth. The Guidance Study gave parents help in coping with their children's problems, and the Growth Study examined mental development and physical growth. The Adolescent (Oakland) Growth Study was designed to assess how early or late puberty affected social and emotional development. This study enrolled children aged 10 to 12; Stuart was 11 when he joined it. More than 300 of the subjects in the three studies were followed into old age.

MEASURES

All subjects were given medical exams and periodic intelligence and psychological tests, including personality measures. Family histories and descriptions of current family situations were recorded. Case studies were developed for 60 subjects on the basis of recorded data and interviews.

FINDINGS

These studies showed how people help to shape their own development. Sociologist John A. Clausen (1993) concluded that "adolescent planful competence'—a combination of self-confidence, dependability, and cognitive involvement—helps a person to mobilize resources and cope with difficulties. Other aspects of personality, appearance, and social background also had long-term consequences. Planful competence did not *guarantee* success in life, nor did its absence ensure failure. But adolescent planful competence was the most powerful influence on the course of a person's life. Competent teenagers like Stuart Campbell

made good choices early in life, which often led to promising opportunities (like scholarships, competent spouses, and good jobs). Less competent adolescents made poorer early decisions and then tended to lead crisis-ridden lives.

A key goal of developmental research is the prediction of development and behavior. In these studies the personalities of people who as adolescents had shown planful competence changed less, and were less turmoil-ridden, than the personalities of less competent teenagers. For example, at age 61, Stuart Campbell was self-confident, intellectually involved, dependable, warm and agreeable, outgoing, and modestly assertive—all qualities that he had had in early adolescence.

How do people develop planful competence? In these studies, parenting that combined high standards, loving support, and firm control emerged as a major influence.

METHODOLOGY ISSUES

Planful competence in senior high school was a dependent variable and factors like parenting practices, intelligence test scores, and social class were independent variables. Then planful competence became an independent variable, with life success (as defined by the researchers) becoming the dependent variable.

Although the report of these studies is titled *American Lives,* it is actually a report of only *some* American lives. The lives studied are those of a cohort of people born in the 1920s and in one part of the country (the San Francisco Bay Area). The sample reflected the people living there at that time. It was almost entirely white, mostly native-born, Christian, and middle-class, with a few working-class subjects. Therefore its findings might well not apply to people who, say, have to deal with poverty or racial or religious discrimination.

Of the approximately 200 subjects who dropped out, a disproportionate number were from families with problems involving money, conflict, and divorce. So the skewing of the sample toward those with fewer family problems may have affected the findings. Still, with these warnings, the conclusions from these studies can be very helpful to developmentalists, parents, teachers—and individuals looking for a better life.

SOURCE: Based on Clausen, 1993.

methods. This method combines the other two: People in a cross-sectional sample are assessed more than once, and the results are analyzed to determine the differences that show up over time for the different groups of subjects.

The cross-sequential approach is not the perfect solution either, since it is complicated and expensive. Furthermore, researchers need to be sensitive to issues in which cohort membership is likely to have an effect. When this does not seem significant, the simpler longitudinal strategy may serve better than the more complex sequential one.

What do you think? *Researchers use different methods to study child development. Choose a topic of interest to you and suggest two different ways to study it. What different kinds of information would the different methods yield?*

ETHICS OF RESEARCH

The cognitive, emotional, and physical integrity of children deserves respect. At the same time, we need to probe children's cognitive, emotional, and physical natures to understand them and guide their development. Sometimes respect for the subject's integrity and the quest for knowledge conflict. To find answers to thorny ethical issues, researchers ask such questions as: Are the potential benefits of a study great enough to justify posing some risk to the subjects? Are the possible benefits more likely than the possible risks? Let's see what some of these ethical issues are.

Rights of Participants

Right to Privacy. A doctor once recommended giving psychological tests to young underprivileged children, with the aim of predicting which ones would someday become delinquent. He proposed watching these children and giving them extra social help to try to forestall their criminal tendencies. But critics pointed out that the test results might produce a self-fulfilling prophecy: Children who were labeled potential delinquents and therefore treated differently might actually *become* delinquent as a result.

This is one potentially harmful way that research results can be used. Other material, like scores on psychological tests, also has the potential for being used against a person. One-way mirrors and hidden cameras and tape recorders let psychologists observe and record behavior without a subject's knowledge. Furthermore, much private information surfaces during personal interviews—information about income, education, child-rearing techniques, and parent-child relationships. What is the researcher's obligation in collecting and storing such information? The basic rule is that confidentiality should be respected, and no information collected from research subjects should ever be used to their disadvantage.

Right to Informed Consent. Children are not always asked to give their consent to be part of experiments; even when they are, they may not be able to make mature judgments. When parents or school personnel consent to a child's participation, can we assume that they are acting in the child's best interests? How much do parents have to know about an experiment before the consent they give is "informed," or knowledgeable? Can laypeople *ever* give truly informed consent? When the true purpose of an experiment is withheld from a subject, can consent

Babies, like this one participating in a research project with the psychologist Tiffany Field, cannot give their consent to be research subjects. Thus experimenters, parents, and other concerned adults must weigh the possible consequences of such projects before allowing children to take part.

be considered informed? There are no easy answers to these questions, and responsible researchers continue to look for the best ways to resolve these issues.

Some experiments depend on deceiving subjects. Suppose children are told they are trying out a new game, when they are actually being tested on their reactions to success or failure? Experiments like these, which cannot be carried out without deception, have added significantly to our knowledge—but at the cost of the subjects' ability to give informed consent.

The National Commission for the Protection of Human Subjects of Biomedical and Behavioral Research (1978) recommends that parents and investigators ask children aged 7 and over to give their consent to take part in research and that children's objections should be overruled only if the research promises a direct benefit to them, as in the use of a new, experimental drug.

Right to Self-Esteem.   Subjects may be affected by their own behavior in an experiment. For instance, studies on the limits of children's capabilities have a built-in "failure factor": The investigator keeps presenting problems until the child is unable to answer. How will failure and the feelings connected with it affect a child? Even if an experimenter takes special pains to see that the child experiences success by the end of an experimental session, does this make up for artificially induced failure? What are the long-term effects of such failures? Is the quest for scientific truth worth the possibility of damaging the self-concept of a single child?

Social Decisions

All these issues force fundamental decisions on researchers. Researchers want to learn and to contribute to society. They need to ask how they can work in an ethical way to balance scientific independence with the rights of a democratic society. This balance is achieved first by the individual researcher, then by professional peers, and ultimately by concerned laypeople. How does this process work?

First, researchers need to think about the projects they design to see whether there is any risk to subjects or others. Second, because no researcher can anticipate all possible ethical dilemmas, safeguards must be provided. Proposed research projects should be approved by juries of professional peers. Citizens must be alert to moral concerns. In a democracy, ethical questions are too important to be reserved for the "experts." Laypeople have interests in both promoting increased knowledge about children and protecting the rights of children.

Decisions about ethics in research emerge from a complex circle of individual researchers, professional peers, citizens, and groups of citizens. The optimal result would be a society in which research into child development does no harm and offers a genuine and lasting service for us all.

A WORD TO STUDENTS

Our final word in this chapter is that this entire book is far from the final word. Researchers are still learning about children. Some research findings have put old ideas to rest forever. Others are still ambiguous and need to be pursued vigorously. Some theories seem to make sense but are hard to test. As you read this book, you will no doubt consider many issues that will raise questions of values in your mind. If you can pursue your questions through research and thought, you yourself, now just embarking on the study of child development, may in future years advance this study to the benefit of all.

SUMMARY

1 The study of child development is the scientific study of the qualitative and quantitative ways children change over time and how they stay the same. Quantitative change refers to change in amount, such as that in height, weight, or vocabulary. Qualitative change refers to change in kind, such as the nature of intelligence or memory. The goals of the field include description, explanation, prediction, and modification of behavior.

2 Although we can look separately at various aspects of development (that is, physical, cognitive, and personality/social development), we must remember that these do not occur in isolation. Each affects the other.

3 We discuss five periods: the prenatal period (conception to birth), infancy and toddlerhood (birth to age 3), early childhood (3 to 6), middle childhood (6 to 12), and adolescence (12 to about 20). Although we can describe normative behavior for each period, individual differences must be taken into account.

4 Influences on development include both hereditary and environmental factors. Influences can occur in a relatively similar way for most people of a given age or generation (cohort). Events that are unusual in their occurrence or timing can also have a major impact.

5 Bronfenbrenner's ecological approach identifies five levels of environmental influence on development. There are the microsystem, mesosystem, exosystem, macrosystem, and chronosystem.

6 The question whether children have been seen throughout history as qualitatively different from adults is controversial. Ariès (1962) held that not until the seventeenth century were children seen as qualitatively different from adults. More recent analyses suggest that children have always been regarded as qualitatively different from adults.

7   The first evidence of professional interest in child development came with books of child-rearing advice in the sixteenth century.

8   A theory is a set of interrelated statements about a phenomenon and an attempt to organize data to explain why the phenomenon occurs. In this book, we consider five theoretical perspectives about development: psychoanalytic, learning, cognitive, ethological, and contextual.

9   Theories from the psychoanalytic perspective focus on the underlying forces that motivate behavior. Although they differ markedly in some of the specifics of their theories, Sigmund Freud, Erik Erikson, and Jean Baker Miller take this perspective. Freud described a series of psychosexual stages in which gratification shifts from one body zone to another (from mouth, to anus, to genitals); the child's maturational level determines when the shift will occur. Erikson described eight stages of psychosocial development that occur between infancy and old age. Each stage involves the resolution of a particular crisis, achieving a balance between extremes; the crises emerge according to a maturationally based timetable. Miller's relational theory holds that personality growth occurs within emotional connections, not separate from them.

10   Learning theories focus on observable behaviors. Behaviorists are interested in how behavior is shaped through conditioning. Social-learning (social-cognitive) theorists maintain that children learn by observing and imitating models. Social-learning theory incorporates some cognitive aspects; the child is considered to be an active contributor to learning.

11   Cognitive theories see people as active contributors to their own development. Jean Piaget described children's cognitive development as occurring through a series of four qualitatively different stages: sensorimotor (birth to 2 years), preoperational (2 to 7 years), concrete operations (7 to 12 years), and formal operations (12 years through adulthood). The information-processing approach analyzes the processes underlying intelligent behavior. It focuses on perception, attention, memory, and problem solving.

12   The ethological perspective, represented by Lorenz, Bowlby, and Ainsworth, focuses on the biological and evolutionary basis of behavior. According to this approach, each species has innate, species-specific behaviors that have evolved to increase the odds of species survival.

13   The contextual perspective, described by Russian psychologist Lev Vygotsky, regards human beings as developing in a social context.

14   Scientific method incorporates careful observation and recording of data, development and testing of hypotheses, and public dissemination of findings. It involves the systematic and controlled study of development. There are five major nonexperimental methods for studying children. Case studies involve studying a single individual. Observations, which can be either naturalistic or laboratory, involve describing behavior rather than changing behavior. Interviews and questionnaires involve asking questions about aspects of one's life. Clinical method assesses relationships between variables. Each approach has its strengths and weaknesses. No nonexperimental method can determine cause-and-effect relationships.

16   Experiments are the only method of assessing cause-and-effect relationships. The three principal types of experiments are laboratory experiments, field experiments, and natural experiments.

17   Developmentalists use three chief methods of data collection: longitudinal, cross-sectional, and sequential. In a longitudinal study, changes with age are determined by measuring the same people more than once. In a cross-sectional study, differences between age groups are revealed by measuring people of different ages. The cross-sequential strategy combines aspects of the cross-sectional and longitudinal approaches. Each of these methods has strengths and shortcomings.

18   The study of children must reflect certain ethical considerations. In a carefully designed study, the researcher considers effects on the participants as well as potential benefits to the field of child development.

KEY TERMS

development (14)

child development (14)

quantitative change (14)

qualitative change (14)

physical development (15)

cognitive development (15)

personality and social development (16)

cohort (17)

ecological approach (18)

theory (23)

data (23)

hypothesis (23)

psychoanalytic perspective (24)

psychosexual development (24)

psychosocial development (29)

behaviorism (31)

classical conditioning (31)

operant conditioning (33)

reinforcement (33)

punishment (34)

social-learning theory (34)

observational learning (35)

cognitive perspective (36)

scheme (38)

organization (38)

adaptation (38)

assimilation (38)

accommodation (38)

equilibration (39)

information-processing approach (39)

ethological perspective (40)

contextual perspective (41)

sociocultural theory (41)

zone of proximal development (ZPD) (42)

scaffolding (42)

scientific method (43)

correlation (43)

case studies (43)

naturalistic observation (45)

laboratory observation (46)

interview (47)

questionnaire (47)

clinical method (47)

experiment (48)

independent variable (49)

dependent variable (49)

experimental group (49)

control group (49)

sample (49)

random sample (49)

longitudinal study (52)

cross-sectional study (52)

SUGGESTED READINGS

American Psychological Association. (1982). *Ethical principles in the conduct of research with human participants.* Washington, DC: Author. Ethical guidelines for psychological experimentation.

Edelman, M. W. (1992). *The measure of our success: A letter to my children and yours.* Boston: Beacon. The founder and president of the Children's Defense Fund dedicates this book to her own three sons, born of an interracial, interfaith marriage, but it has moral implications for any reader. The book's "lessons for life" emphasize service to society and a recognition of the bonds across race, class, and gender.

Erikson, E. H. (1963). *Childhood and society.* New York: Norton. A collection of Erikson's writings that includes the classic "Eight Ages of Man," in which he outlines his theory of psychosocial development from infancy through old age.

Kagan, J. (1984). *The nature of the child.* New York: Basic Books. A beautifully written and convincing argument against the idea of the irreversibility of early experience. Kagan believes that people have the ability to change throughout life and that later events transform early childhood experiences.

Marks, J. (1993). *The hidden children: The secret survivors of the Holocaust.* New York: Fawcett Columbine. Many children survived the Holocaust by remaining in hiding for months or years. In this powerful work, twenty-three of these children, now adults, share their experiences and the profound impact that these experiences have had on their lives.

Shapiro, J. P. (1993). *No pity: People with disabilities forging a new civil rights movement.* New York: Times Books. A fascinating account of the birth and development of the disability rights movement, which led to the enactment of the Americans with Disabilities Act. The book deals with many of the issues involved in this struggle and includes many personal stories of people with physical, mental, or emotional disabilities who were instrumental in changing the way such people are looked at and treated.

BEGINNINGS

By the time babies are born, they already have an impressive history, a history that began long before conception. Part of this early history is a hereditary endowment, determined when fertilization occurs. Another part is environmental, for the organism in the womb is affected by many events that occur during gestation. As Vicky and Jason grow from single cells into newborn babies, genes and experience affect their development. At birth, they are already individuals, distinguishable not just by sex, but by size, temperament, appearance, and history.

In Chapters 2, 3, and 4, we trace the earliest development of a child. Chapter 2 presents the two great contributors to individual development—genes and the environment. In Chapter 3, we see the interaction of these two elements as the organism develops in the womb. Chapter 4 describes the birth of a child, ways of evaluating a newborn's immediate condition, and the normal abilities of a newborn. In science, we never speak of miracles, but more precise words seem insufficient when we are faced with the marvel of a newborn—eyes bright, little fingers grasping a parent's thumb, and the whisper of a smile on tiny lips.

CHAPTER 2
HEREDITY AND ENVIRONMENT

Of the cell, the wondrous seed
Becoming plant and animal and mind
Unerringly forever after its kind
In its omnipotence, in flower and weed
And breast and bird and fish, and many a breed
Of man and woman from all years behind
Building its future.

William Ellery Leonard, 1923

This chapter focuses on how a human being is conceived, and explains the basic genetic and environmental influences that determine what a person will be like. After you have read about how all of us are influenced by the complex interaction between heredity and environment, you should be able to answer questions like the following:

PREVIEW QUESTIONS

♦ How does human reproduction occur?
♦ Through what genetic mechanisms do people inherit various characteristics?
♦ How are birth defects transmitted?
♦ How can genetic counseling and prenatal diagnosis help parents who are worried about bearing a child with a disability?
♦ How do heredity and environment interact?
♦ How can the effects of heredity and environment be studied?

When Ellen and Charles first thought about having a child, they tried to imagine what their baby might be like. Would it be a girl with dimples like Ellen's? Or a boy who would laugh like Charles? And what sort of world could they provide for their child? What impact would their money worries and other stresses have on the child's life? Of course, all these questions were impossible to answer. At that time, they had only a faint suspicion of the way one small child would forever alter their lives. Parents' lives change dramatically after the birth of a first child. But every child brings new satisfactions (like insights, achievements, and a reawakening of purpose) and new stresses (like responsibilities and demands on both time and money).

Throughout this book, we will talk about many of the questions that parents wonder about. The science of child development is concerned with all the factors that influence human growth from conception to adulthood. What *are* these factors? And how important is each one? These are hard questions. In this chapter, we will consider one of the greatest puzzles of them all—the importance of both hereditary and environmental influences on the developing person.

We begin by exploring what people think about when they consider having a child. The issues are deeply personal and emotional: "What do I have to offer a child?" "What can a child offer me?" Then we discuss the beginning of pregnancy: when *heredity*—the inherited factors that affect development—is most powerful in influencing development. Yet even at this initial stage of life, the *environment*—a combination of outside influences like family, community, and personal experience—plays a role. So we examine in detail the ***nature-versus-nurture controversy***. We look at how heredity (nature) and the environment (nurture) interact and how their relative effects on development are studied. This theme of interaction recurs throughout this book and is woven through almost all the accounts of Vicky's and Jason's development.

We go on to examine the mechanisms and patterns of heredity. Then we show how new genetic knowledge helps prospective parents to understand the adventure ahead. With genetic counseling and new therapeutic techniques, couples can think more clearly and confidently about becoming parents.

heredity *Inborn influences on development carried on the genes, that is, inherited from the parent.*

environment *Combination of outside influences, such as family, community, and personal experience, that affect development.*

nature-versus-nurture controversy *Debate over the relative importance of hereditary and environmental factors in influencing human development.*

CHOOSING PARENTHOOD

The choice and the timing of parenthood can have vast consequences for a child. Whether that child's birth was planned or accidental, whether the pregnancy was welcomed or unwanted, and how old the parents were when the child was conceived are all factors in the microsystem described in Bronfenbrenner's (1979) ecological approach. Whether the culture encourages large families, whether it values one sex over the other, and how much it supports families with children are macrosystem issues likely to influence that child's development.

People may have mixed feelings about the joys and burdens of parenthood, but until recently, what they thought hardly mattered. Parenthood was the nearly

One reason why parents, like this couple in Nepal, have children is the complex, challenging, and gratifying intimacy that parenthood provides.

inevitable consequence of sexual intercourse. Today, with reliable birth control, parenthood is a more freely chosen option. Still, most people in their thirties have children, and most find parenting a major source of satisfaction (Veroff, Douvan, & Kulka, 1981).

WHY PEOPLE HAVE CHILDREN

At one time, the blessing offered newlyweds in the Asian country of Nepal was "May you have enough sons to cover the hillsides!" Having children has traditionally been regarded as not only the primary reason for marriage, but its ultimate fulfillment. In preindustrial societies, large families were a necessity: Children helped with the family's work and eventually cared for their aging parents. Because the death rate in childhood was high, fewer children reached maturity. Because economic and social reasons for having children were so powerful, parenthood—especially motherhood—was revered.

Today Nepali couples are wished, "May you have a very bright son." Although sons are still preferred over daughters there, even sons are not wished for in large numbers any more. Because of technological progress, fewer workers are needed; because of modern medical care, most children survive; and because of government programs, some care of the aged is being provided. Overpopulation is a major problem in many parts of the world, and children are an expense rather than an economic asset. Furthermore, children can have negative, as well as positive, effects on a marriage.

Still, the desire for children is almost universal. Why? One research team studied 600 couples in the first 6 years of marriage. These couples tended to see children as necessary for "a real family life" and as sources of love and affection that serve as buffers against loneliness and impersonality. They also saw disadvantages in parenthood—mainly lifestyle changes, financial costs, and career problems for women (Neal, Grout, & Wicks, 1989).

Today's young adults are more ambivalent toward having children than their parents were. They know they have a choice and sometimes have trouble weighing the values of children versus a fulfilling career, time alone with a spouse, extra money, and a neat and orderly household. Parenthood *usually* outweighs the other choices, but almost half of these couples rate other values equal to or more valuable than having children.

WHEN PEOPLE HAVE CHILDREN

Today most couples who can have children do so. But they tend to have fewer children and to have them later. Often this is because people spend their early years getting an education and establishing a career. More women today—16 percent in 1987 versus 4 percent in 1970—have a first child after age 30. However, although the birth rate for those 35 and older rose between 1990 and 1991, the year 1991 saw a decrease in the birth rate for women 30 to 34 years of age and only a small increase for women over 35 (Wegman, 1993; National Center for Health Statistics, 1993). National surveys show that today's women believe in a later ideal age for first birth. The most recently married women, women with more years of education, and the most strongly feminist choose the latest "ideal ages" (Pebley, 1981). Better-educated women actually do have their children later (Rindfuss, Morgan, & Swicegood, 1988; Rindfuss & St. John, 1983).

THE BEGINNING OF PREGNANCY

Our interest in development begins long before the biologic event of conception. Psychologists seek to uncover the factors that affect a pregnancy and its outcome, including influences that might go back for generations. We will talk more about such factors later; for now, we will see how conception occurs.

HOW DOES FERTILIZATION TAKE PLACE?

Fertilization, or conception, the process by which sperm and ovum fuse to form a single new cell, is most likely to occur between 9 and 16 days after the beginning of a woman's menstrual period. The new single cell formed by the two gametes, or sex cells—the ovum and the sperm—is called a *zygote.*

A newborn girl is born with all the ova (plural of *ovum*) she will ever have—about 400,000. At birth these immature ova are in her two ovaries, each one in its own small sac, called a follicle. The ovum—only about one-fourth the size of the period that ends this sentence—is the largest cell in the human body. Ovulation—when one mature follicle in either ovary ruptures and expels an ovum—occurs about once every 28 days in a mature female. This ovum is swept along through the fallopian tube by tiny hair cells called *cilia* toward the uterus, or womb. Fertilization normally occurs during the brief time the ovum is passing through the fallopian tube.

The tadpolelike sperm—only 1/600 inch from head to tail—is one of the smallest cells in the body. Sperm are much more active than ova, and there are many more of them. Sperm are produced in the testicles (testes) of a mature male at a rate of several hundred million a day and are ejaculated in his semen at sexual climax. An ejaculation carries about 500 million sperm; for fertilization to occur, at least 20 million sperm must enter a woman's body at one time. They enter the vagina and try to swim through the cervix (the opening to the uterus) and into the fallopian tubes, but only a tiny fraction make it this far. The discovery that sperm cells have odor receptors, like those in the nose, suggests that they may locate a fertile egg by its scent (Parmentier et al., 1992). More than one sperm may penetrate the ovum, but only one can fertilize it.

If fertilization does not occur, the ovum and any sperm cells in the woman's body die. The sperm are absorbed by the woman's white blood cells, and the ovum passes through the uterus and exits through the vagina. If sperm and ovum do meet, however, they conceive a new life and endow it with a rich genetic legacy.

WHAT CAUSES MULTIPLE BIRTHS?

Unlike most animals, the human baby usually comes into the world alone. Exceptions—multiple births—occur in two different ways. One mechanism pro-

fertilization *Process by which sperm and ovum fuse to form a single new cell; also called conception.*

zygote *Single cell formed through fertilization.*

TABLE 2-1

INCIDENCE OF FRATERNAL TWIN BIRTHS IN VARIOUS ETHNIC GROUPS*	
Belgians	1 in 56 births
African Americans	1 in 70 births
Italians	1 in 86 births
White Americans	1 in 86 births
Greeks	1 in 130 births
Japanese	1 in 150 births
Chinese	1 in 300 births

*These figures do not reflect the effects of fertility drugs.
SOURCE: Behrman, 1992.

fraternal, or dizygotic, twins *Two people who are conceived and born at approximately the same time as a result of the fertilization of two ova.*

duces *fraternal, or dizygotic, twins,* the most common type of multiple births. In this case, the woman's body releases two ova within a short time of each other, and both are fertilized. Created by different ova and different sperm, dizygotic twins are no more alike in genetic makeup than any other siblings. They may be of the same sex or different sexes.

The other twinning mechanism is the splitting in two of the single ovum after it has been fertilized by a single sperm. The babies that result from this cell division are called *identical, or monozygotic, twins.* They are always of the same sex. They have the same genetic heritage, and any differences that they show must be due to the influences of the environment (including the prenatal environment). For example, the twins' locations in the uterus can result in one's receiving more oxygen than the other.

identical, or monozygotic, twins *Two people with identical genes, arising from the formation of one zygote that divided.*

Other multiple births—triplets, quadruplets, quintuplets, and so forth—result from either one of these processes or a combination of both.

Identical twins seem to be born through an accident of prenatal life; their incidence is about the same in all ethnic groups. Fraternal twins, however, are more common under certain circumstances. In recent years, more have been born because of the increased use of fertility drugs, which spur ovulation and often cause the release of more than one egg. Also, fraternal twins are more likely to be born in third and later pregnancies, to older women, and in families with a history of fraternal twins (Behrman, 1992). They are also more common in certain ethnic groups—African Americans, east Indians, and white northern Europeans; they are least common among Asians. (See Table 2-1.) The different rates may be due to inherited hormonal differences among women of different ethnic groups, which may make some more likely to release two ova at the same time.

INFLUENCES OF HEREDITY AND ENVIRONMENT

Both heredity and environment play a critical role in making us the people we are and will become. Let's see how.

THE MECHANISMS OF HEREDITY: GENES AND CHROMOSOMES

chromosome *Rod-shaped particle found in every living cell; carries the genes.*

Normally every cell in the body *except* the sex cells, or *gametes* (the sperm and the ovum), has 23 pairs of rod-shaped structures (46 in all) called *chromosomes.* The chromosomes contain all the hereditary material passed from parents to children.

But the sperm and the ovum, instead of having all 46 chromosomes like all other body cells, have only 23 each, or one member of each pair. Through a complex process of cell division called *meiosis,* in which each original cell splits into two halves, the gametes receive one of each pair. Then, when gametes fuse at conception, they endow the zygote with 46 chromosomes. (See Figure 2-1.) Thus the zygote receives half its 46 chromosomes from each parent; half of its hereditary material is from the father, half from the mother. Because the meiotic division process is complex, the hereditary material that each parent provides will differ for each child.

After the zygote is formed, it develops into an embryo through *mitosis,* the process by which the cells divide in half over and over again. Each division creates a duplicate of the original cell, with the same basic hereditary information, and continues to maintain 46 chromosomes. When development is normal, each cell in the developing embryo (except the gametes) has 46 chromosomes. Later in this chapter, we discuss disorders that can occur when there are too many or too few chromosomes.

Eventually, the new being will have trillions of cells specializing in hundreds of functions. Every cell (except the sex cells) has the same hereditary information. Each chromosome contains thousands of segments strung out on it lengthwise like beads. These segments are the *genes,* the most basic units of our inherited characteristics. Each cell in the body contains an estimated 100,000 genes, which are made of the chemical **DNA, *deoxyribonucleic acid.*** DNA carries the biochemical instructions that tell all the cells how to make the proteins that enable them to carry out all body functions. Various genes seem to be located according to their functions in definite positions on particular chromosomes.

gene *Functional unit of heredity; determines the traits that are passed from one generation to the next.*

DNA (deoxyribonucleic acid) *Chemical carrying the instructions that tell all the cells in the body how to make the proteins that enable them to carry out their various functions.*

WHAT DETERMINES SEX?

In many villages in Nepal, it is not uncommon for a man whose wife has borne no male babies to take on a second wife, with the acceptance—if not necessarily

FIGURE 2-1
Genetic transmission: how the zygote receives genes. Genes—the basic units of inheritance—are carried on the chromosomes contributed by both male and female gametes (sex cells). (*a*) Body cells of women and men each contain 23 pairs of chromosomes; each chromosome consists of thousands of genes. (*b*) Each gamete (ovum and sperm) has only 23 chromosomes, because of a special kind of cell division (meiosis) in which the total number of chromosomes is halved. (*c*) At fertilization, the 23 chromosomes from the sperm join the 23 from the ovum. The total number of chromosomes is 46, arranged in 23 pairs.

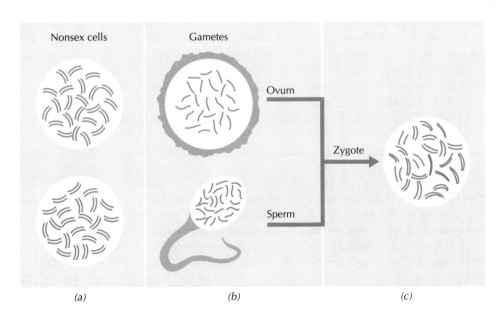

Nonsex cells | Gametes | Ovum | Zygote | Sperm

(a)　　　(b)　　　(c)

the blessing—of the first wife. In other societies, a woman's failure to produce sons is a valid basis for divorce. The irony in these customs is that it is almost always the father's sperm cell that determines the child's sex.

At the moment of conception, the 23 chromosomes from the father's sperm cell and the 23 from the mother's ovum align themselves in 23 pairs. Twenty-two pairs are autosomes, chromosomes that are not related to sexual expression; the twenty-third pair are sex chromosomes, which determine the child's sex.

The sex chromosome of every ovum from the mother is an X chromosome, whereas the sperm from the father may carry either an X or a Y chromosome. When an ovum (X) is fertilized by an X-carrying sperm, the zygote formed is XX, a female. When an ovum (X) is fertilized by a Y-carrying sperm, the resulting zygote is XY, a male.

If nothing further happens prenatally, the embryo will develop female sexual characteristics. But for the embryo to develop male characteristics, certain events must occur at about 6 to 8 weeks of gestation. At this time the sex organs of human male embryos start producing the male hormone testosterone. It is the male embryo's exposure to steady, high levels of testosterone that result in the male body plan, with its male primary sexual characteristics. Even if an embryo has the masculine genetic endowment (XY), it will retain the female body plan if it is not exposed prenatally to ongoing levels of self-produced male hormones.

Currently, however, research is exploring a gene on the X chromosome (DDS gene) that seems able to override the gene on the Y chromosome (SRY gene) that determines maleness (Camerino et al., 1994). Four patients who had a working SRY gene but who still showed external genitals that either looked female or were ambiguous were all found to have a double dose of the DDS gene on the X chromosome. It seems, then, that two copies of DDS can feminize a fetus that is chromosomally male. In chromosomally female fetuses, it seems that only one good copy of DDS is needed for normal female development.

Sex Selection

Ellen and Charles, like most expectant parents in the United States, were hoping to have first a boy, then a girl (Frenkiel, 1993). They listened politely to tips from an elderly relative about when they should have intercourse, what position they should use, and what Ellen should eat. But they sensibly ignored all this advice as invalid folklore. Furthermore, they didn't feel strongly enough about the sex of their unborn baby to pursue either of two new techniques that have had some success in conceiving one sex or the other. Without a valid reason for sex preference (like the possibility that a child of one sex would be at high risk of a sex-related birth defect), they probably would not have gained access to them.

Sperm sorting involves sorting semen samples rich in either X or Y sperm and inserting the desired sample into the woman by artificial insemination (described later in this chapter). *Preimplantation genetic diagnosis* involves analyzing the DNA from three-day-old zygotes and implanting the embryo of the desired sex into the woman's uterus. As of 1993, the techniques, which are expensive and complex, had been used in only a few cases ("Jack or Jill?", 1993).

A much more widespread—and highly controversial—means of sex selection involves learning the sex of the fetus through amniocentesis (a prenatal test described in Box 2-2 which can reveal the sex of the fetus) and terminating the pregnancy if the sex is "wrong." Here we can see the impact of the macrosystem in fostering a preference for one sex or the other. In some countries, a preference for male children is rooted in economics and religion. In others, it is encouraged by advertising that depicts the "ideal American family" as made up of two parents, an older son, and a younger daughter. (The intersection of culture and technology is discussed in Box 2-1.) Genetic counselors and other health care professionals generally consider this option ethical only when a fetus is at considerable risk of inheriting a sex-linked disorder (Burke, 1992; M. I. Evans et al., 1991).

Sex Differences

Differences between the sexes begin to appear at conception. About 120 to 170 males are conceived for every 100 females, but since males are more likely to be spontaneously aborted (miscarried) or stillborn, only 106 males are born for every 100 females (U.S. Department of Health and Human Services, USDHHS, 1982). Boys' births average 1 hour longer than girls' births; this is one reason why more boys have birth defects (Jacklin, 1989). More males die early in life, and at every age, males are more susceptible to many disorders, so that there are only 95 males for every 100 females in the United States (USDHHS, 1982).

Why are males more vulnerable throughout life? Part of the explanation most likely rests on the fact that the zygotes start out with the female body plan. The fact that males require more alterations during early development than females do, as described above, probably accounts at least in part for their poorer survivability and greater vulnerability.

BOX 2-1 ■ AROUND THE WORLD

ANCIENT CULTURES AND NEW TECHNOLOGY

What happens when state-of-the-art technology is applied in the service of ancient cultural mores? Both amniocentesis and ultrasound procedures were developed to detect birth defects; coincidentally, they disclose the sex of the fetus. When American women who undergo these procedures are asked whether they want to know their unborn babies' sex, often the answer is "no."

However, over the past few years in China and India, thousands of women have undergone amniocentesis or ultrasound solely to determine the sex of their unborn children. Females fare poorly in many Asian societies: Girls often receive less food, less schooling, and poorer medical care—and now, with the help of technology, fewer females are being born.

In China, where the government has decreed that families have no more than one child, an estimated 12 percent of female fetuses are aborted (Kristof, 1993). In India, a woman pregnant with a fifth daughter burst into tears, crying that her husband would throw her out of the house if she did not produce a son (Weisman, 1988). In Asia, sons typically support aging parents and perform religious rituals. Daughters, however, usually live with their in-laws after marriage, and in India brides are expected to have a dowry of as much as $10,000—a family's yearly income.

In one county in China, ultrasound was used in 2316 cases, resulting in 1006 abortions of female fetuses (Kristof, 1993).

As the result of protests in India by feminist groups and health officials, a law was passed by the Indian Parliament imposing prison sentences and fines on doctors and patients giving or taking prenatal tests solely to determine the sex of a fetus (Burns, 1994). However, with the availability of compact ultrasound machines, entrepreneurs operating mobile clinics are beyond the reach of the law, and the pressure to bear sons has continued to increase. In both the Indian and Chinese populations, males now predominate (Kristof, 1993).

Although the United Nations is investigating the situation and many doctors and women's groups decry it, an Indian obstetrician said to protesting foreign observers, "You cannot pass judgment on what is happening in our country—taking your norms and applying them to us. Others may regard it as a barbaric practice . . . but nobody can have a 100 percent purist view in this world. The law has been changed, but what have we done to change social attitudes?" (Weisman, 1988, p. A9). If attitudes do not change, the net effects of laws may be to drive families back to the ancient practice of killing baby girls soon after birth or neglecting them so badly that they will die young.

Other explanations include the possibility that the X chromosome may contain genes that protect females, the Y chromosome may contain harmful genes, or there may be different mechanisms in the sexes for providing immunity to various infections and diseases. One controversial hypothesis suggests that the mother's body produces damaging antibodies against a male fetus (Gualtieri & Hicks, 1985).

PATTERNS OF GENETIC TRANSMISSION

Can you curl your tongue the long way? You may never have thought about or tried it, but read on to see how this somewhat dubious ability is related to your genetic makeup. When you look in the mirror, besides seeing your tongue, you will see some of the most obvious characteristics that are influenced by your genes, like the color of your eyes and the shape of your nose. Heredity also influences a wide range of other characteristics, including your health, your intellect, and your personality.

During the 1860s, Gregor Mendel, an Austrian monk who experimented with plants, laid the foundation for our understanding of inheritance in all living things. He crossbred pea plants that produced only yellow seeds with pea plants that produced only green seeds. All the resulting plants—hybrids—produced yellow seeds, meaning, he said, that yellow was dominant over green. Yet when he bred the hybrids, only 75 percent of their offspring had yellow seeds, while the other 25 percent had green seeds.

Mendel also tried breeding for two traits at once. Mating pea plants that produced round yellow seeds with plants that produced wrinkled green ones, he found that color and shape were transmitted independently of each other. Mendel thus showed that hereditary traits are transmitted separately.

Mendel's findings were groundbreaking in his time. But today we know that the genetic picture in humans is far more complex than Mendel imagined. It is hard to find a single normal trait that people inherit through simple dominant transmission—other than the ability to curl the tongue lengthwise! Let us look at the various ways we inherit our many characteristics.

Dominant and Recessive Inheritance

If you are a "tongue curler," you inherited this ability through dominant inheritance. If you are a redhead even though both your parents have dark hair, recessive inheritance operated. How do these two types of inheritance work?

Genes that govern alternative expressions of a characteristic (like tongue-curling ability or inability) are called *alleles.* Every person receives a pair of alleles for a given characteristic, one from each parent. When both alleles are the same, the person is *homozygous* for the characteristic; when they are different, the person is *heterozygous.* In a heterozygous situation, the dominant allele is expressed. This is known as *dominant inheritance,* that is, the principle that when an offspring receives genes for contradictory traits, only the dominant trait will be expressed. *Recessive inheritance* occurs only when a homozygous person has received the same recessive allele from each parent; then the recessive trait is expressed.

If you inherited one allele for tongue-curling ability from each parent, you are homozygous for tongue curling and you express the trait. But if, say, your mother passed on an allele with the ability and your father passed an allele lack-

allele *One of a pair of genes affecting a trait; the genes may be identical or different.*

homozygous *Possessing identical alleles for a trait.*

heterozygous *Possessing different alleles for a trait.*

dominant inheritance *Principle that when an offspring receives genes for contradictory traits, only one of the traits—the dominant trait—will be expressed.*

recessive inheritance *Expression of a recessive trait, which occurs only if a person (or an animal or a plant) is homozygous for the trait (has two alleles carrying it).*

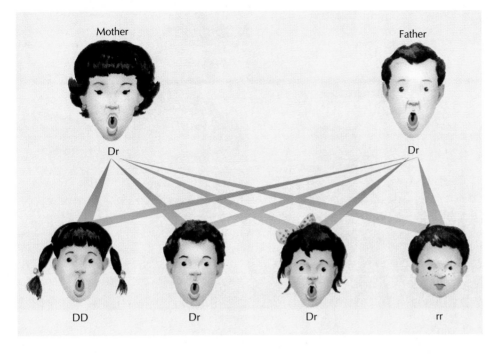

FIGURE 2-2
Phenotypes and genotypes. Because of dominant inheritance, the same observable phenotype (in this case, the ability to curl the tongue) can result from two different genotypes (DD—homozygous, and Dr—heterozygous). Each parent in this family is heterozygous for this trait, with one dominant gene (D) for the ability and one recessive gene (r) lacking the ability. Their children show the statistical 3:1 average for expressing the trait. The three children with identical phenotypes (they can curl their tongues) show two different genotypes (DD and Dr). A phenotype expressing a recessive characteristic (like the inability to curl the tongue) can have only one genotype (rr—homozygous).

ing it, you are heterozygous. Since the ability is dominant and its lack is recessive, you can curl your tongue. However, if you are heterozygous and you have four children with someone who is also heterozygous for tongue curling, the statistical probability is that one child will be homozygous for the ability, one will be homozygous lacking it, and the other two will be heterozygous. Thus three of your children will have the same phenotypes for tongue curling (they will be able to curl their tongues), but this ability will arise from two different genotypes—DD and Dr. (See Figure 2-2.)

Genotypes and Phenotypes

A *genotype* is our genetic makeup, the underlying pattern that we have inherited in the DNA. Except for identical twins, no two people have the same genotype. A *phenotype* is the observable, measurable way that a genotype is expressed. So your ability to curl your tongue, which you can feel and see, is your phenotype. As Figure 2-2 shows, this phenotype may arise from either of two different underlying genotypes: either a homozygous combination of two dominant alleles for tongue curling (DD) or a heterozygous combination of one dominant allele and one recessive allele (Dr).

While tongue curling has a strong genetic base, most characteristics that psychologists study are not inherited in such a simple way. For most traits, a person's experiences modify the way the genotype is expressed in a phenotype. We can see how this happens with regard to musical ability, a characteristic whose inheritance is more complex than simple dominant inheritance.

Let us say that Jason has inherited a genotype for musical ability. If he takes music lessons and practices, he may delight his family with his performances. If his family encourages classical music, he may play Bach preludes; if the children

genotype *Pattern of alleles carried by a person.*

phenotype *Observable characteristics of a person.*

Musical ability is one of many characteristics that are passed on in the genes from parents to children. Researchers are discovering that a large number of physical, intellectual, and personality attributes are part of a child's genetic legacy.

on his block encourage him in popular music, he may form a rock group. But if from early childhood he is not encouraged, not motivated, and has no access to lessons or a musical instrument, his musical abilities may not be expressed.

Throughout this book we will talk about how aspects of the environment interact with genetic endowment to bring about the expression of characteristics in the physical, cognitive, and personality and social domains. Throughout life, our genes interact with our environment to influence our development.

Other Forms of Genetic Transmission

Sex-Linked Inheritance. If you have trouble seeing red and green, you are probably male and you probably inherited your color blindness from your mother. In *sex-linked inheritance*, certain recessive traits are inherited differently by male and female children. Sex-linked traits are carried by genes on the X chromosome.

Most sex-linked genes are recessive. Therefore, if a girl received a dominant gene (say, for normal color vision) on the X chromosome from one parent and a recessive gene (say, for color blindness) on her other X chromosome, the dominant gene will override the recessive one, and she will not express the trait. She can still pass it on, however, since she is a *carrier* for the trait. Since genes on the X chromosome have no known alleles on the Y chromosome, any allele on a male's X chromosome will be expressed, whether or not it is recessive in the mother. Thus, when a carrier mother passes on color blindness to her son, he will express the trait and be color-blind. The most common mode of transmission, then, for sex-linked traits is from mother to son. Red-green color blindness is one of a number of conditions commonly passed on this way.

Incomplete Dominance. Sometimes a trait combines the attributes of both alleles. That is, the interaction between alleles does not always produce completely

sex-linked inheritance
Process by which certain recessive genes are transmitted differently to male and female children.

carrier *In genetics, a person with an allele which is not expressed but which can be passed on to future generations.*

dominant effects. Some genes, like blood groupings, exist in three or more allelic states and are known as *multiple alleles.* Thus someone who has alleles for two types of blood, A and B, can end up having blood type AB.

Polygenic Inheritance.   Many traits result from the interaction of several different genes, in what is known as *polygenic inheritance.* Human skin color is inherited through the interaction of three or more separate sets of genes on three different chromosomes. These genes work together to produce different amounts of brown pigment in the skin, resulting in hundreds of shades. Other physical traits, like height and weight, and behavioral traits, too, are influenced by a number of genes rather than just one.

polygenic inheritance
Interaction of a number of different genes to produce certain traits.

Multifactorial Transmission.   Some physical characteristics (like height and weight) and most psychological characteristics (like intelligence, personality traits, and certain disorders) are the result of *multifactorial transmission.* This is the interaction of genetic and environmental factors. For example, if Jason should be ill for a long time or be malnourished, he would be shorter than his genes would otherwise have allowed. That is, his phenotype would differ from his genotype as the result of environmental influences. However, he might still be taller than another boy who suffered the same kind of deprivation but inherited a tendency to shortness.

multifactorial transmission
Interaction of both genetic and environmental factors to produce certain traits.

GENETIC AND CHROMOSOMAL ABNORMALITIES

Vicky and Jason, like about 94 percent of all babies born in the United States—about 4.04 million in 1993—are healthy and normal. Each year, however, more than 250,000 infants are born with physical or mental disabilities of varying degrees of severity (March of Dimes Birth Defects Foundation, 1983). These babies constitute about 6 percent of total births and about 21 percent of deaths in the first year of life (Wegman, 1994). Nearly half of the serious malformations involve the central nervous system. (See Table 2-2 for information on the effects, the ethnic groups at greatest risk, and the treatment for various birth defects.)

While the overall picture is promising and birth disorders are rare, some disorders are devastating. Moreover, the distribution of disorders is uneven. Some people are more likely than others to be in the unfortunate 6 percent. Of course, even among children in this category, we can see dramatic evidence of human resiliency. Many people born with defects that would once have kept them institutionalized for life can now, with physical or psychological therapy, emerge into the wider world and live rich, fulfilled lives.

All of us carry genes with potentially harmful effects. Usually no harm results, since many genes are recessive and are expressed only when two people both pass the same recessive gene to the zygote. Let us see how some birth defects are transmitted genetically.

Defects Transmitted by Dominant Inheritance

Most of the time, normal genes are dominant over those carrying abnormal traits. But sometimes this situation is reversed and an abnormal trait is carried by a dominant gene. When one parent, say, the father, has one normal gene (r = recessive) and one abnormal gene (D = dominant) and the other parent has two normal

TABLE 2-2

PROBLEM	CHARACTERISTICS OF THE CONDITION	WHO IS AT RISK	WHAT CAN BE DONE
Alpha₁ antitrypsin deficiency	Enzyme deficiency that can lead to cirrhosis of the liver in early infancy and pulmonary emphysema and degenerative lung disease in middle age.	1 in 1000 Caucasians	No treatment.
Alpha thalassemia	Severe anemia that reduces ability of the blood to carry oxygen; nearly all affected infants are stillborn or die soon after birth.	Primarily families of Malaysian, African, and southeast Asian descent	Frequent blood transfusions.
Beta thalassemia (Cooley's anemia)	Severe anemia resulting in weakness, fatigue, and frequent illness; usually fatal in adolescence or young adulthood.	Primarily families of Mediterranean descent	Frequent blood transfusions.
Cystic fibrosis	Body makes too much mucus, which collects in the lungs and digestive tract; children do not grow normally and usually do not live beyond age 30, although some live longer; the most common inherited *lethal* defect among white people.	1 in 2000 Caucasians	Daily physical therapy to loosen mucus; antibiotics for lung infections; enzymes to improve digestion; gene therapy (in experimental stage); lung transplants (in experimental stage).
Down syndrome	Minor-to-severe mental retardation caused by an extra 21st chromosome; the most common chromosomal defect.	1 in 350 babies born to women over age 35; 1 in 800 born to all women	No treatment, although programs of intellectual stimulation are effective.
Duchenne's muscular dystrophy	Fatal disease found only in males, marked by muscle weakness; minor mental retardation is common; respiratory failure and death usually occur in young adulthood.	1 in 7000 male births	No treatment.
Phenylketonuria (PKU)	Metabolic disorder resulting in mental retardation.	1 in 14,000 births	Special diet begun in first few weeks of life can offset mental retardation.

TABLE 2-2

BIRTH DEFECTS (CONTINUED)

PROBLEM	CHARACTERISTICS OF THE CONDITION	WHO IS AT RISK	WHAT CAN BE DONE
Hemophilia	Excessive bleeding, usually affecting males rather than females; in its most severe form, can lead to crippling arthritis in adulthood.	1 in 10,000 families with a history of hemophilia	Frequent transfusions of blood with clotting factors.
Neural-tube defects. Two types of neural-tube defects together constitute the most common serious type of birth defect in the United States:			
Anencephaly	Absence of brain tissue; infants are stillborn or die soon after birth.	1 in 1000	No treatment.
Spina bifida	Incompletely closed spinal canal, resulting in muscle weakness or paralysis and loss of bladder and bowel control; often accompanied by hydrocephalus, an accumulation of spinal fluid in the brain, which can lead to mental retardation.	1 in 1000	Surgery to close spinal canal prevents further injury; shunt placed in brain drains excess fluid and prevents mental retardation.
Polycystic kidney disease	*Infantile form:* enlarged kidneys, leading to respiratory problems and congestive heart failure. *Adult form:* kidney pain, kidney stones, and hypertension resulting in chronic kidney failure; symptoms usually begin around age 30.	1 in 1000	Kidney transplants.
Sickle-cell anemia	Deformed, fragile red blood cells that can clog the blood vessels, depriving the body of oxygen; symptoms include severe pain, stunted growth, frequent infections, leg ulcers, gallstones, susceptibility to pneumonia, and stroke.	1 in 500 African Americans	Painkillers, transfusions for anemia, antibiotics for infections.
Tay-Sachs disease	Degenerative disease of the brain and nerve cells, resulting in death before age 5.	1 in 3000 eastern European Jews; rarer in other groups 1 in 1000 Caucasians	No treatment.

SOURCE: Adapted from Tilsdale, 1988, pp. 68–69.

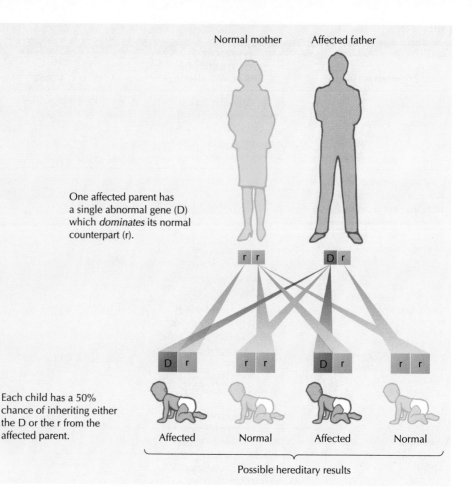

One affected parent has a single abnormal gene (D) which *dominates* its normal counterpart (r).

Normal mother   Affected father

r r   D r

D r   r r   D r   r r

Each child has a 50% chance of inheriting either the D or the r from the affected parent.

Affected   Normal   Affected   Normal

Possible hereditary results

FIGURE 2-3
Dominant inheritance of a birth defect.

genes (rr), each of their children will have a 50-50 chance of inheriting the abnormal gene from the father and of having the same defect he has. (See Figure 2-3.) Because the abnormal gene is dominant, every person who has this abnormal gene has the defect. The defect cannot be of a kind that results in the death of a person before the age of reproduction: If it did, the defect could not be passed on to the next generation. Among the more than 1800 disorders now known to be passed on this way are achondroplasia (a type of dwarfism) and Huntington's disease.

Defects Transmitted by Recessive Inheritance

Many more defects are transmitted by recessive genes, passed along by parents who are healthy themselves. Such disorders are often killers early in life. One of these is sickle-cell anemia, a blood disorder seen most often among African Americans. As we have seen, recessive traits are expressed only if a child received the same recessive gene from each parent. If only one parent—say, the father—has the abnormal recessive gene, he is a carrier for the defect: He does not suffer from it and none of his children will either. However, each child has a 50-50 chance of being a carrier and of passing on the recessive gene to his or her children. If *both*

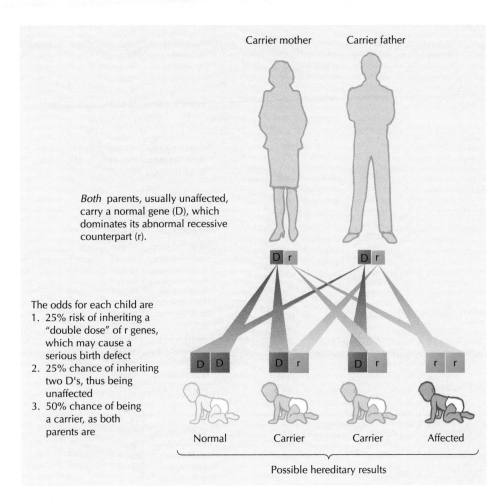

Carrier mother　　Carrier father

Both parents, usually unaffected, carry a normal gene (D), which dominates its abnormal recessive counterpart (r).

The odds for each child are
1. 25% risk of inheriting a "double dose" of r genes, which may cause a serious birth defect
2. 25% chance of inheriting two D's, thus being unaffected
3. 50% chance of being a carrier, as both parents are

| D r | D r |

| D D | D r | D r | r r |

Normal　　Carrier　　Carrier　　Affected

Possible hereditary results

FIGURE 2-4
Recessive inheritance of a birth defect.

parents carry the abnormal recessive gene, although *they* are unaffected, each of their children has a 50-50 chance of inheriting one dominant gene (D) and one recessive gene (r) and of being carriers themselves. Each child has 1 chance in 4 of inheriting the abnormal gene from both parents—and suffering the disorder. (See Figure 2-4.) Some disorders are more common among certain ethnic groups, which, through intermarriage, have passed down specific recessive genes. (See Table 2-3.)

Defects Transmitted by Sex-Linked Inheritance

Hemophilia, a disorder in which blood does not clot when it should, used to be known as the "royal" disease because it affected so many members of the highly inbred ruling family of England. Hemophilia is a sex-linked condition carried by a recessive gene on the X chromosome.

Each son of a man with two normal genes for a trait and of a woman with one abnormal gene will have a 50 percent chance of inheriting the mother's harmful gene and the disorder and a 50 percent chance of inheriting the mother's normal X chromosome and being unaffected. Daughters will have a 50 percent chance of being carriers. (See Figure 2-5.) An affected father can never pass on such a

TABLE 2-3

	THE CHANCE	
IF YOU ARE	**IS ABOUT**	**THAT**
African American	1 in 12	You are a carrier of sickle-cell anemia.
	7 in 10	You will have milk intolerance as an adult.
African American and male	1 in 10	You have a hereditary predisposition to develop hemolytic anemia after taking sulfa or other drugs.
African American and female	1 in 50	
White	1 in 25	You are a carrier of cystic fibrosis.
	1 in 80	You are a carrier of phenylketonuria.
Jewish (Ashkenazic)	1 in 30	You are a carrier of Tay-Sachs disease.
	1 in 100	You are a carrier of familial dysautonomia.
Italian American or Greek American	1 in 10	You are a carrier of beta thalassemia.
Armenian or Jewish (Sephardic)	1 in 45	You are a carrier of familial Mediterranean fever.
Afrikaner (white South African)	1 in 330	You have porphyria.
Asian	almost 100%	You will have milk intolerance as an adult.

SOURCE: Adapted from Milunsky, 1992, p. 122.

gene to his sons, since he contributes a Y chromosome to them; but he can pass the gene on to his daughters, who then become carriers.

In rare instances, a female can inherit one of these sex-linked conditions. The daughter of a hemophiliac man and a woman who is a carrier for the disorder has a 50 percent chance of inheriting the abnormal X chromosome from each parent. Should she inherit it, she will suffer from the disease. Females typically do not inherit this way, because the normal X chromosome will override the X chromosome that has the defective gene.

Chromosomal Abnormalities

Chromosomal activity almost always proceeds normally. But when something does go wrong, serious abnormalities may develop. About 1 in 156 children in western countries is estimated to have some type of chromosomal abnormality (Milunsky, 1992). Some abnormalities are inherited; others result from accidents occurring during the development of an individual organism. Accidental abnormalities are not likely to recur in the same family.

Some chromosomal disorders are caused by either a missing or an extra sex chromosome. Relatively rare conditions—for example, Klinefelter's syndrome (XXY syndrome), caused by an extra X chromosome in males—have a variety of

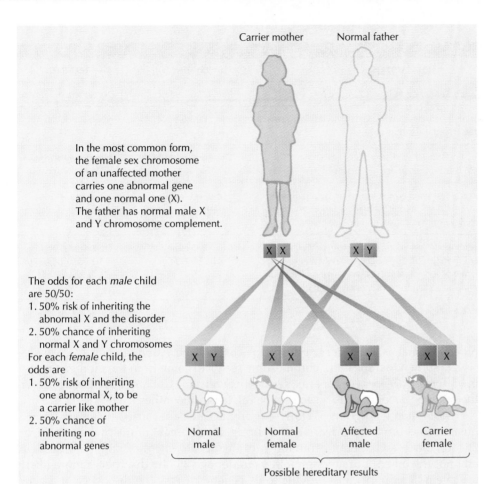

Carrier mother   Normal father

In the most common form, the female sex chromosome of an unaffected mother carries one abnormal gene and one normal one (X). The father has normal male X and Y chromosome complement.

X X   X Y

The odds for each *male* child are 50/50:
1. 50% risk of inheriting the abnormal X and the disorder
2. 50% chance of inheriting normal X and Y chromosomes

For each *female* child, the odds are
1. 50% risk of inheriting one abnormal X, to be a carrier like mother
2. 50% chance of inheriting no abnormal genes

X Y   X X   X Y   X X

Normal   Normal   Affected   Carrier
male   female   male   female

Possible hereditary results

FIGURE 2-5
Sex-linked inheritance of a birth defect.

effects. The most obvious are sexually related characteristics—underdevelopment, sterility, or secondary sex characteristics of the other sex. The long-term outlook for children with these conditions includes learning disorders (see Table 2-4).

Down syndrome is the most common chromosomal disorder. It is responsible for about one-third of all cases of moderate-to-severe mental retardation. Its most obvious characteristic is a downward-sloping skin fold at the inner corners of the eyes. Other signs are a small head; a flat nose; a protruding tongue; motor retardation; and defective heart, gastrointestinal tract, eyes, and ears. The condition is caused by *trisomy-21*, an extra twenty-first chromosome or the translocation of part of the twenty-first chromosome onto another chromosome. Today more than 70 percent of people with Down syndrome live into their sixties, although they are at risk for developing the dementia known as Alzheimer's disease (A. Hayes & Batshaw, 1993).

About 1 in every 700 babies born alive worldwide has Down syndrome (A. Hayes & Batshaw, 1993). The risk is greatest with older parents: The chances rise from 1 such birth in 2000 among 25-year-old mothers to 1 in 40 for women over 45. The risk also rises with the father's age, especially among men over 50 (Abroms & Bennett, 1981). For years, the father's influence was ignored as researchers concentrated on the mother's age, failing to consider the fact that the

Down syndrome *Disorder caused by an extra twenty-first chromosome; characterized by mental retardation and various physical abnormalities.*

TABLE 2-4

SEX CHROMOSOME ABNORMALITIES

PATTERN/NAME	CHARACTERISTIC*	INCIDENCE	TREATMENT
XYY	Male; tall stature; tendency to low IQ, especially verbal.	1 in 1000 male births	No special treatment
XXX (triple X)	Female, normal appearance, menstrual irregularities, learning disorders, mental retardation.	1 in 1000 female births	Special education
XXY (Kleinfelter's)	Male, sterility, underdeveloped secondary sex characteristics, small testes, learning disorders.	1 in 1000 male births	Hormone therapy, special education
XO (Turner's)	Female, short stature, webbed neck, impaired spatial abilities, no menstruation, sterility, underdeveloped sex organs, incomplete development of secondary sex characteristics.	1 in 3500 female births	Hormone therapy, special education
Fragile X	Minor-to-severe mental retardation; symptoms, which are more severe in males, include delayed speech and motor development, speech impairments, and hyperactivity; the most common *inherited* form of mental retardation.	1 in 1200 male births; 1 in 2000 female births	Educational and behavioral therapies when needed

*Not every affected person has every characteristic.

older a woman is, the older her husband is likely to be. Although new DNA analysis has shown that the extra chromosome seems to come from the mother's ovum in 95 percent of cases (Antonarakis & Down Syndrome Collaborative Group, 1991), the other 5 percent of cases seem to be related to the father's age.

More than 90 percent of Down syndrome cases are caused by an accident, a mistake in chromosome distribution during development of the ovum, sperm, or zygote. (Such an accident can happen in the development of one identical twin and not the other.) But among mothers under age 35, the disorder is more likely to have a hereditary cause. A clue to its genetic basis is the discovery of a gene on chromosome 21. This gene expresses a brain protein that seems to lead to Down syndrome (Allore et al., 1988).

The resilience of human beings is illustrated by the generally positive way in which Down syndrome children and their families adjust. A study that compared 34 such families with 41 families without disabled children found that the two groups were similar on all measures of individual, marital, and family functioning (Van Riper, Ryff, & Pridham, 1992). Many parents learn about the condition and deal with it with the help of support groups.

The future for children with Down syndrome is brighter than was once thought. Many live at home until adulthood and then enter a small group home. A number of them can support themselves, and they tend to do well in structured job situations. At a 1993 international conference, adult speakers with Down syndrome represented occupations that included clerks, cooks, actors, salespeople, and authors (National Down Syndrome Society, 1993). Two young men with Down syndrome recently wrote a book about their feelings of growing up with this developmental disability (Kingsley & Levitz, 1994).

genetic counseling
Clinical service that advises couples of the probable risk of having a child with a particular hereditary disorder.

GENETIC COUNSELING

Because Ellen was over 35 years old when she became pregnant for the first time, her age put her into one of the target groups for *genetic counseling*, a service that helps couples determine their chances of producing healthy children.

Besides older prospective parents, genetic counseling is advised for couples who have had problems conceiving, women who have previously miscarried, people who have already had a child with a genetic defect, prospective parents who are first cousins, and people from specific ethnic backgrounds. African Americans, for example, are at a higher-than-average risk of passing on genes for sickle-cell anemia, and couples of eastern European Jewish ancestry are at risk of having children with the nervous system disorder Tay-Sachs disease.

How Genetic Counseling Works

A genetic counselor may be a pediatrician, an obstetrician, a family doctor, or a genetic specialist. She or he takes a family history, which includes information relating to diseases and causes of death of siblings, parents, and other close blood relatives; any marriages between relatives; and previous abortions or stillbirths. Each parent and any children receive physical examinations, since physical conditions often give clues to genetic abnormalities.

Laboratory investigations of blood, skin, urine, or fingerprints may also be performed. Chromosomes from body tissues may be analyzed and photographed, with the photographs cut out and arranged according to size and structure on a chart called a *karyotype.* This chart can show chromosomal abnormalities and can indicate whether a person who appears normal could possibly transmit genetic defects to his or her children. (See Figure 2-6.)

On the basis of these tests, the counselor calculates the mathematical odds that a couple will have an afflicted child. If the couple feel the risks are too high, one partner may choose to be sterilized, or the couple may consider adoption or another type of conception. (See "Alternative Ways to Conceive" in Chapter 3.)

This lively little boy, age 2½, has Down syndrome. Although the intellectual potential of such children is limited, loving care and patient teaching helps many achieve much more than was once thought possible.

karyotype *Photograph made through a microscope showing the chromosomes when they are separated and aligned for cell division; the chromosomes are displayed according to a standard array.*

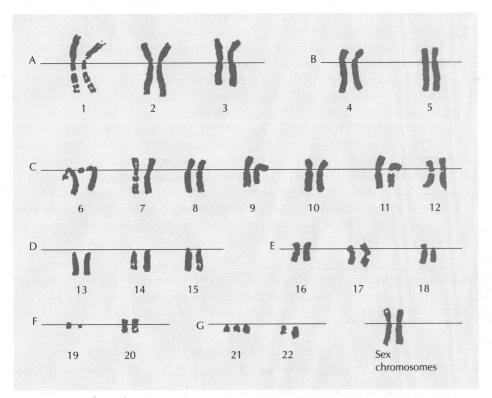

FIGURE 2-6
A karyotype is a photograph that shows the chromosomes when they are separated and aligned for cell division. We know that this is a karyotype of a person with Down syndrome, because there are three chromosomes instead of the usual two on number 21. Since pair 23 consists of two Xs, we know that this child is a girl. (SOURCE: Vanderbilt University and March of Dimes, 1987.)

A genetic counselor does not give advice on whether to take risks. Rather, the counselor tries only to find out and help a couple understand the mathematical risk of a particular condition, explain its implications, and inform the prospective parents of alternative courses of action.

Because defects occur in only 6 percent of all births, the chances of having a healthy baby are very good. To make these chances even better, prospective parents can take tests developed to identify carriers of genetic defects. If a husband and wife know they both carry a recessive gene for a disorder, they may decide to conceive a baby and then order prenatal tests to find out whether the fetus has the condition. For example, simple blood tests can identify carriers of Tay-Sachs disease, of sickle-cell anemia, and of thalassemia (another blood disorder, which affects persons of Mediterranean origin). Box 2-2 describes several techniques of prenatal diagnosis—*amniocentesis, chorionic villus sampling (CVS), ultrasound,* maternal blood tests, umbilical cord blood sampling, preimplantation genetic diagnosis, and embryoscopy.

amniocentesis *Prenatal diagnostic procedure for examining the chromosomes of a fetus; sample cells are withdrawn from the amniotic fluid in which the fetus floats and are examined for signs of birth defects.*

chorionic villus sampling (CVS) *Prenatal diagnostic procedure for obtaining sample villi from the membrane surrounding the embryo and then examining the embryo's chromosomes for birth defects.*

ultrasound *Medical procedure using high-frequency sound waves to detect the outlines of a fetus and determine whether the pregnancy is progressing normally.*

What do you think? *Suppose you are pregnant and would like amniocentesis or CVS (chorionic villus sampling) for reassurance that the fetus is developing normally, but you don't fit any high-risk category. Should you be able to have the test paid for by your medical insurance carrier, or is this a waste of health care dollars needed elsewhere?*

Suppose a genetic counselor determines that a husband and wife are both carriers of a harmful recessive allele. This means that there is a 25 percent chance that they will have a child with the disorder. Some people think that a 1 out of 4 risk means that if the first child born has the genetic defect, the next three children will not have it. But the saying "Chance has no memory" applies here: The odds are 1 out of 4 that any child born of that union will inherit the disease.

In many cases, a couple may learn that the risk they feared is slight or even nonexistent. In other cases, couples acknowledge that they run a higher risk, and they take a chance. If a disorder is not particularly disabling or can be treated, they can carry the baby to term; but if prenatal testing shows the presence of a severe disability, they can opt to terminate the pregnancy.

Geneticists have already made a great contribution to prospective parents. For example, since so many Jewish couples have been tested for Tay-Sachs genes, far fewer babies have been born with the disease (Kaback et al., 1993). (Those who are born are more often born now to non-Jewish parents.) Scientific progress in locating defective genes on chromosomes promises more help for the future.

A national registry tracking specific birth defects could help to identify people who may be at risk, provide preventive services, and help agencies meet the needs of affected people and their families.

What do you think? *To prevent the transmission of hereditary disorders, should genetic counseling be made compulsory for all people wanting to get married? Or just for people in certain categories? Give reasons for your answer.*

Geneticists are making progress in locating defective genes on chromosomes. By identifying and locating specific genes, they have been able to "map" (locate)

BOX 2-2 ■ THE EVERYDAY WORLD

PRENATAL ASSESSMENT

Not long ago, almost the only decision parents had to make about their babies before birth was the decision to conceive; most of what happened in the intervening 9 months was beyond their control. But we now have an array of new tools to assess fetal development and well-being.

AMNIOCENTESIS

In *amniocentesis,* a sample of the fluid in the amniotic sac is withdrawn and analyzed to detect the presence of about 200 (out of 4000) genetic defects, all recognizable chromosomal disorders, and other problems, including neural-tube defects (Milunsky, 1992). This fluid, in which the fetus floats in the uterus, contains fetal cells. The procedure is usually done between the fourteenth to sixteenth weeks of pregnancy; it takes about 2 weeks to get the results. Amniocentesis can also reveal the sex of the fetus, which may be crucial in the case of a sex-linked disorder like hemophilia. (See Figure 2-7.)

Amniocentesis is recommended for pregnant women if they are at least 35 years old; if they and their partners are both known carriers of diseases such as Tay-Sachs or sickle-cell anemia; or if they or their partners have a family history of such conditions as Down syndrome, spina bifida, Rh disease, or muscular dystrophy. One analysis of 3000 women who had amniocentesis indicated that it was "safe, highly reliable and extremely accurate" (Golbus et al., 1979, p. 157). But another study of 4600 women found a slightly higher risk of miscarriage in women who had the procedure (Tabor et al., 1986).

According to a Canadian study of 100 babies whose mothers had undergone amniocentesis and 56 untested infants, tested babies are no more likely to suffer problems relating to intelligence, language, or behavior. They seem to be at slightly greater risk of ear infections and middle-ear abnormalities, although their hearing is not affected (Finegan et al., 1990). Attempts are now being made to do amniocentesis before 15 weeks of pregnancy, although its safety remains unknown (D'Alton & DeCherney, 1993).

CHORIONIC VILLUS SAMPLING

Chorionic villus sampling (CVS) consists of taking tissue from the end of one or more villi—hairlike projections of the membrane around the embryo, which are made up of fetal cells. These cells are then tested for the presence of various birth defects and disorders. This procedure can be performed between 8 and 13 weeks of pregnancy (earlier than amniocentesis), and it yields results sooner (within about a week). However, there are problems with CVS,

compared with amniocentesis. Some women who used CVS experienced almost 5 percent more deaths of their fetuses or newborns than did those who chose amniocentesis. Also, CVS diagnoses can be ambiguous, so women may have to undergo amniocentesis anyway (D'Alton & DeCherney, 1993).

MATERNAL BLOOD TESTS

A blood sample taken from the mother between the sixteenth and eighteenth weeks of pregnancy can be tested for the amount of alpha fetoprotein (AFP) it contains. This *maternal blood test* is appropriate for women at risk of bearing children with defects in the formation of the brain or spinal cord (like anencephaly or spina bifida), which may be detected by high AFP levels. To confirm or refute suspected conditions, ultrasound or amniocentesis, or both, may be performed.

One study found that blood tests from samples taken from the fifteenth to twentieth weeks of gestation—for AFP and two hormones (unconjugated estriol and chorionic gonadotropin)—predicted about 60 percent of cases of Down syndrome. These could then be confirmed by amniocentesis. This blood test is important for women *under* 35 (who bear 80 percent of all Down syndrome babies), because they are not usually targeted to receive amniocentesis (Haddow et al., 1992).

FIGURE 2-7

Amniocentesis. Through amniocentesis, a sample of amniotic fluid can be withdrawn and analyzed for the presence of a variety of birth defects. A needle is inserted through the mother's abdominal wall to remove the fluid. Analysis of the sampled fluid generally takes 2 to 4 weeks. (SOURCE: F. Fuchs, 1980.)

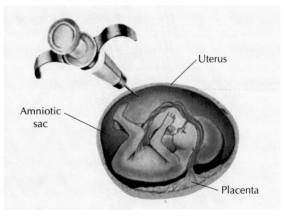

BOX 2-2 ■ THE EVERYDAY WORLD

It should be possible to detect even more disorders, with the recent discovery that fetal cells can be isolated from the mother's blood and then analyzed (Simpson & Elias, 1993). Blood tests can also identify carriers of sickle-cell anemia, Tay-Sachs disease, and thalassemia. They can also reveal the sex of a fetus, which can be important in sex-linked disorders (Lo et al., 1989).

ULTRASOUND

Some parents see their baby for the first time in a *sonogram*. This picture of the uterus, fetus, and placenta (an organ vital to fetal development) is created by *ultrasound*, high-frequency sound waves directed into the mother's abdomen. Ultrasound provides the clearest images yet of a fetus in the womb, with little or no discomfort to the mother. Ultrasound is used to measure fetal growth, to judge gestational age, to detect multiple pregnancies, to evaluate uterine abnormalities, to detect major structural abnormalities in the fetus, and to determine whether a fetus has died, as well as to guide other procedures like amniocentesis. Results from ultrasound may suggest other procedures that may be needed (D'Alton & DeCherney, 1993).

Physicians use ultrasound to guide them in doing a fetal biopsy (a test on a sample of fetal skin) to diagnose certain disorders. But fetal biopsy is experimental, its safety and accuracy still in question (D'Alton & DeCherney, 1993). Moreover, a recent report indicates that ultrasound screening does not reduce fetal and neonatal death (Ewigman et al., 1993). So there seems to be no reason to use it in low-risk pregnancies—especially since some research suggests that repeated and frequent ultrasound may affect fetal growth (Newnham et al., 1993).

UMBILICAL CORD BLOOD SAMPLING

By inserting a needle into tiny blood vessels of the umbilical cord under the guidance of ultrasound, doctors can take samples of a fetus's blood. They can then get a blood count, examine liver function, and assess various other body functions.

This procedure can test for infection, anemia, certain metabolic disorders and immunodeficiencies, and heart failure, and it seems to offer promise for identifying still other conditions. The technique is associated with such problems as pregnancy loss, bleeding from the umbilical cord, early labor, and infection (Chervenak, Isaacson, & Mahoney, 1986; Kolata, 1988). It should be used only when diagnostic information cannot be obtained by safer means (D'Alton & DeCherney, 1993).

PREIMPLANTATION GENETIC DIAGNOSIS

This technique identifies genetic defects in embryos comprising four to eight cells which were conceived by in vitro fertilization (fertilization outside the mother's body). In one study, researchers extracted and examined a single cell for cystic fibrosis (Handyside, Lesko, Tarin, Winston, & Hughes, 1992). Defective embryos were not implanted in the mother's body.

EMBRYOSCOPY

By inserting a tiny viewing scope into a pregnant woman's abdomen, doctors can get a clear look at embryos as young as 6 weeks. The procedure is promising for early diagnosis and treatment of embryonic and fetal abnormalities (Quintero et al., 1993).

These techniques for prenatal diagnosis of birth defects, coupled with the legalization of abortion, have encouraged many couples with troubling medical histories to take a chance on conception. For example, a couple who know that they both carry a recessive gene for a disorder may conceive and then take tests to learn whether the fetus has the condition. They may be reassured that their baby will be normal, or, if the fetus is affected, they may terminate the pregnancy or plan for the special needs of a child with a disability.

---

several thousand human genes. They determine what proteins are made by these genes and detect the presence or absence of proteins associated with particular disorders. Such knowledge can lead to new predictive tests, both before and after birth; to drugs to prevent or treat disease; and to "gene therapy"—technology for repairing abnormal genes. The Human Genome Project, a 15-year, $3 billion research effort under the joint leadership of the National Institutes of Health and the United States Department of Energy, is designed to locate all the human genes and to identify those that cause particular disorders.

To implement the findings from the project, individuals would need to undergo genetic testing to find out whether they carry harmful genes. Critics claim that the social risks of universal genetic testing outweigh its benefits. (See Box 2-3.)

What do you think?   *If you learned through genetic testing that your newborn baby was at risk for a hereditary disorder, would you want to know about it*
1. *If it was a disorder that would show up in early childhood?*
2. *If it would show up in young adulthood?*
3. *If it would show up at age 50 or later?*

THE IMPORTANCE OF ENVIRONMENT

The power of heredity is great—but so is the power of the environment. Recent efforts to acknowledge the role of genetics may have gone too far in attributing too much human outcome to the impact of our genes. Actually, environmental factors seem to be at least as important as genetic ones (Plomin & Rende, 1991).

Heritability describes the statistical estimate of how much of a contribution heredity makes toward individual differences in a specific trait, at a certain point in time. By measuring the incidence rate of the same trait, or the degree of similarity for a given trait, in identical twins as compared with fraternal twins, in adoptive children as compared with their adoptive and biological parents, and in various family members, researchers have concluded that the heritability of traits rarely exceeds 50 percent.* Therefore there is a great deal of room for environmental influence (Plomin, 1990).

heritability   *Statistical estimate of contribution of heredity to individual differences in a specific trait.*

Such influences cover the full range of the environment described in Bronfenbrenner's (1979) ecological approach. We will be discussing many aspects of these systems throughout the book—from the influence of family, which includes social class, income level, parents' personalities, and number of children in the home, out through the larger institutions of society, including day care, school, and governmental policies.

HOW HEREDITY AND ENVIRONMENT INTERACT

"Nature versus Nurture": Hereditary and Environmental Factors

Which has more effect—nature or nurture? Heredity or environment? At one time scientists tried to answer this question by ascribing a certain percentage of a characteristic to the impact of heredity, another percentage to the influence of the environment. But today developmentalists see the relationship between genetic and environmental factors as fundamentally intertwined. As one geneticist put it, "Genes and environment loop out into each other and feed back on each other in a complex way that we have just begun to understand" (Kendler, in Mann, 1994, p. 1687). Current research emphasis is more on how these two influences work together to affect development. Scientists explain some of the variance between people through the concepts of reaction range and canalization.

reaction range   *In genetics, a potential variability, depending on environmental conditions, in the expression of a hereditary trait.*

Reaction Range.   To evaluate any nature-nurture situation, we consider it in terms of a *reaction range.* For anything that is influenced by heredity, there is a range of possible responses that a child can make, depending on the child's environ-

*Studies using these methods will be described later in this chapter.

BOX 2-3 ▪ FOOD FOR THOUGHT

THE PROS AND CONS OF GENETIC TESTING

Widespread genetic testing has many implications. What arguments do people offer about its controversial aspects? The following points emphasize some pros and cons about the procedure. After reading them, you can consider whether we are premature in using genetic testing before it has been further perfected—or whether the benefits outweigh the risks.

ARGUMENTS IN FAVOR OF GENETIC TESTING

1. Knowing a person's genetic profile can lead to early detection and more effective treatment of hereditary disorders. For example, a woman who learns she has a genetic tendency for breast cancer might be advised to undergo mammograms (x-ray photographs of the breast, taken to reveal malignant tumors) at an earlier age and more frequently than would otherwise be recommended. If a cancer is detected in its early stage, her life may be saved.
2. Early detection may lead to prevention or timely intervention. A person who learns of a genetic predisposition to lung cancer may be motivated to stop smoking. A newborn found to have a disease like phenylketonuria (PKU) can be treated early enough to prevent permanent damage.
3. Such information can help in making major decisions, such as whether to have children, what type of occupation to pursue, what climate to live in, and other such lifestyle choices.
4. Society may be able to protect the general welfare by testing people in jobs that bear on the public's safety. For example, if genes were discovered that controlled alcoholism or Alzheimer's disease, airlines and railroads might screen pilots and engineers to see whether they were at risk. Of course, just because people have a gene that might predispose them toward diseases like these does not mean that they would in fact develop them (Orentlicher, 1990).

ARGUMENTS AGAINST GENETIC TESTING

1. Genetic information may be disseminated in a way that violates a person's privacy. Although medical data are supposedly confidential, it is almost impossible to keep such information private. A study at the University of Minnesota found that at least 50 people had access to each patient's medical charts (Gruson, 1992).
2. Parents who learn that a child has an incurable disease may develop a different attitude toward the child, either because they consider the child disabled or because they are afraid to become too attached to a child who may die young (Marshall, 1993).
3. Discrimination on the basis of genetic information is possible. An informal survey found 50 cases in which people had been denied jobs, insurance coverage, or other benefits because of their genes (Gruson, 1992). One man, who had been driving with no accidents and no traffic tickets for 20 years, had his auto insurance policy canceled when his insurance company learned he carried a gene for a rare neurological condition (Henig, 1989). Because of such abuses, a panel of experts has recommended the passage of laws forbidding employers from collecting genetic information, unless it is clear that a worker's performance will be affected, and preventing insurers from considering genetic risk in the issuance or pricing of insurance (Institute of Medicine, IOM, 1993). People found to have genetic risks should be covered under the Americans with Disabilities Act.
4. Current tests are often imprecise and thus unreliable in predicting when, or even whether, a person may develop a particular disease. People deemed at risk of a disease may never develop it (Voelker, 1993).
5. Someone who learns that she or he has the gene for a disease for which there is no cure is bound to suffer great anxiety. What is the point of knowing you have a potentially debilitating condition when you cannot do anything about it? The Institute of Medicine (1993) panel recommends against genetic testing for diseases for which there is no known cure because the test will provide no benefits.
6. Routine genetic testing of newborns, which may show that the presumed father is not the biological father, may harm a child if the family rejects that child (Voelker, 1993). The IOM panel favors voluntary rather than mandatory testing in the belief that parents who choose to have their baby screened will act appropriately on the findings.

ment. Body size, for example, depends on biological processes, which are genetically regulated. Even so, a range of sizes is possible, depending on environmental factors like nutrition. Societies where diets have suddenly improved have seen an entire generation of children grow up to tower over their parents. The better-fed children share their parents' genes but have responded to their healthier world. Once an entire society's diet is adequate over more than one generation, however, children tend to grow to heights similar to those of their parents. Ultimate height is limited by a range of normal human height, so you don't find people only a foot tall—or any who are 10 feet tall!

Genes are not expressed directly as behavior; rather, they may be expressed differently in different environments. How our inherited genes show themselves depends to a considerable extent on our specific environment. For example, genes have a strong effect on weight, but actual body size depends on what a person does. If Vicky has a genetic tendency toward obesity, this will not make her eat a lot, but if she does take in more calories than her body needs, she will be fatter than another girl with a similar genetic tendency who eats less.

Canalization. The impact of genetic programming can be described by the concept of *canalization,* for which we can use the metaphor of canals. After a heavy rainstorm, the rainwater needs to go somewhere; if there are potholes or grooves in a street, the water will go into them rather than flowing evenly down the street. But if canals have been dug along the edges of the street, the ridges and holes in the main part of the street will not matter; the water will go into the canals.

Some human characteristics are so strongly programmed by the genes that they are said to be highly canalized; that is, there is less opportunity for variance in their expression. (They go into genetically "dug" canals.) It takes a more extreme change in environment to alter them. A physical characteristic like eye color is highly canalized; the environment has little or no effect on its expression. Even some kinds of behavior—like sitting up and walking—are highly canalized; unless an environment is extremely deprived, a baby will automatically follow a typical sequence of motor development. But more complex traits having to do with intelligence and personality are not canalized so highly, since they are much more subject to the experiences in a child's life—the kind of family she or he grows up in, the school attended, the people encountered.

Maturation. One reason it is so hard to untangle the relative effects of heredity and environment is that human beings keep changing throughout life. Some changes seem to be caused by the environment; others are influenced more by the genes. For example, crawling, walking, and running develop in that order at certain approximate ages. *Maturation* is the unfolding of a biologically based sequence of physical changes and behaviors as a person develops.

Yet maturation is not unchangeable: Environmental forces affect its timing. This was seen in classic studies in Iranian orphanages where infants received little attention and no exercise. These babies did not sit up or walk until quite late, compared with well-cared-for Iranian children (Dennis, 1960). Yet even under these deprived conditions, maturation did occur, if at a slowed pace.

The balance between nature and nurture seems most complex in the development of intellect and personality. Consider language. Before children can talk, they have to reach a certain level of neurological and muscular maturation. At 6 months of age, Jason could not speak this sentence, no matter how enriched his

canalization *Limitation on some inherited characteristics so that their expression can take, at most, only a few outcomes.*

maturation *Unfolding of a biologically based sequence of physical changes and behaviors.*

home life might be. Yet environment plays a large part in language development. If Jason's parents encourage his first sounds by talking back to him, he is likely to start to speak earlier than if his early vocalizing is ignored. Heredity, then, provides the groundwork for development, but environment affects the pace at which "construction" proceeds and even the specific form of the structure.

Interplay between Heredity and Environment.   Any phenotype is always the result of complex interacting factors. Still, some traits show the impact of heredity more than others. For example, some physical characteristics, like eye color and blood type, are clearly inherited. But more complex traits having to do with health, intelligence, and personality are subject to an interplay of both kinds of forces.

One simple example shows the interaction of heredity and environment: Why are Vicky and her little brother, Bobby, so different? Correlations for cognitive abilities among siblings are only about .40, and for personality they are only about .20 (Plomin, 1989). Usually, in fact, siblings are more different than alike. The explanation lies partly in heredity: Each child in a family inherits different chromosomes from the same parents. Then each child's genetic predisposition is likely to lead him or her to choose a unique set of experiences. Thus Vicky, who was born with artistic talent, *asks* to enroll in a special art program, which then fosters and develops her talent. We see, then, how people actively mold their own environments (Bouchard, 1994).

Also, each child—even in the same family—experiences a unique environment, also referred to as *nonshared environmental effects* (Plomin, 1990). For example, when Vicky was born, her parents were younger, poorer, and living in a cramped city apartment—and very excited by the birth of their first baby. By the time of Bobby's birth, they had moved to a little house in the suburbs, and they were busier and more involved in their careers. They were also more experienced as parents and may have taken Bobby's developmental milestones more for granted. Finally, Vicky was there to be a big sister. All these factors contributed to a different family environment for Bobby. Other events in both children's lives—like illnesses and school experiences—all exert their own influences.

How much is inherited? How much is environmentally influenced? We now know that most characteristics result from the interaction between heredity and environment. Still, the degree of each influence is helpful to know because—among other reasons—it can affect how people act toward children. If, for example, intelligence can be influenced by environment, parents will be inspired to talk to and read to their children and offer them toys that help them learn. On the other hand, if a child's activity level is mostly inherited, they can better accept and work with the child's temperament.

As we have seen, knowing which birth defects are inherited makes genetic counseling possible. Finding that a problem is hereditary does *not* necessarily mean that you cannot do anything about it. For example, children born with the enzyme disorder phenylketonuria (PKU) will be mentally retarded if the defect is not treated. But if they are put on a special diet within the first 3 to 6 weeks of life, they develop normally.

Then too, people's genes influence how they react to the environment. We can see this with regard to cognitive functioning. A child born with a severe level of retardation will be retarded, no matter how favorable the environment is. But if a child is born with milder cognitive limitations, the environment will be more crucial. An enriched environment will help the child to blossom, as was the case with the two young authors with Down syndrome whose parents had offered them a great deal of intellectual stimulation right from birth (Kingsley & Levitz, 1994). Other people born with the same severity of the syndrome, who grew up in families with fewer resources or in institutions, would probably not have achieved the same level of functioning.

What do you think? *Think about your own family. In what ways are you more like your mother? In what ways, like your father? How are you similar and dissimilar to your siblings? Which differences would you ascribe to heredity and which to environment?*

EFFECTS OF HEREDITY AND ENVIRONMENT

Ways to Study the Relative Effects of Heredity and Environment

Researchers use a variety of methods to find out how heredity and environment interact to create differences between people. Some focus more on inherited factors; others focus on environment. The most powerful way to study genetic influences on behavior involves breeding animals for certain traits, like aggressiveness or activity level. Because, for ethical reasons, similar studies cannot be done on human beings, scientists have relied on three other types of research—family, adoption, and twin studies (Plomin, Owen, & McGuffin, 1994; Plomin, 1990).

Family (Kinship) Studies. In family studies, researchers look at resemblances among people who are related to each other. Through this method, we discover the degree to which relatives share certain traits and whether the closeness of the genetic relationship is associated with the degree of similarity. If the closeness of the relationship is associated with degree of similarity in a trait, we can see the influence of heredity. One problem with family studies, however, is that they do not provide a good way to assess possible environmental sources of similarity (Plomin, 1990). With only a family study, for example, we cannot know whether obese children of obese parents inherited the tendency or whether they are obese because their diet is like that of their parents.

Adoption Studies. Adoption studies investigate genetic and environmental influences by looking at the levels of similarity between adopted children and their adoptive parents and siblings and between the children and their biological families. When adopted children are more like their biological parents and siblings on a trait (like obesity), we see the influence of heredity. When they resemble their adoptive families more, we see the influence of environment. Similarly, studies like the Colorado Adoption Project (DeFries, Plomin, & Fulker, 1994) compared resemblance between adoptive siblings and genetically related siblings.

Studies of Twins. This method compares identical twins (who have the same genetic makeup) with fraternal twins (who are no more similar genetically than are any other siblings). When identical twins are more alike on a trait than fraternal twins, we see the effects of heredity.

A number of studies have examined identical twins who had been separated in infancy and reared apart from each other. These studies, which combine twin and adoption strategies, have shown strong resemblances between the twins. Such

Separated at birth, these reunited monozygotic triplets—Bobby, Eddy, and David—show the powerful impact of heredity.

findings support a strong hereditary basis for many physical and psychological characteristics. One problem with this approach is that the home environments of both twins may be very similar, even though their adoptive families are different. For example, both children are likely to grow up in homes at similar socioeconomic levels. Thus the similarity between identical twins reared apart may reflect environmental similarities as well as genetic ones.

Some Characteristics Influenced by Heredity and Environment

Most behavioral dimensions are not a matter of "either-or" but are expressed in a range of possible responses. As we pointed out earlier, most behavioral traits are influenced by a number of genes, each of which exerts a small effect. Also, the environment exerts a great influence. In most cases, physical and psychological characteristics are transmitted multifactorially—through the interaction of genetic and environmental factors. Let's look at some characteristics to see how heredity and environment interact. (See Table 2-5.)

Physical Traits and Conditions.   When Robert Shafran went away to college, students he had never met greeted him like an old friend and called him "Eddy." After seeing a snapshot of Eddy Galland, who had attended the same school the year before, Robert said, "What I saw was a photograph of myself." When a third look-alike turned up, the youths learned that they were identical triplets who had been separated at birth (Battelle, 1981).

The carbon-copy physical appearance of identical twins is well known. They are also more concordant (alike) than fraternal twins in such medical disorders as hypertension, heart disease, rheumatic arthritis, peptic ulcer, and epilepsy (Plomin et al., 1994).

Obesity is strongly influenced by heredity. It is twice as likely that both identical twins will be overweight as that both fraternal twins will be (Stunkard, Harris, Pedersen, & McClearn, 1990). People genetically at risk of obesity must work hard not to get fat. But the environment also affects weight gain. The kind and amount of food eaten in a particular home or in a particular social or ethnic group and the amount of exercise that is encouraged are environmental factors affecting whether someone will be thin or heavy.

Our days on earth seem to be affected to a great degree by our genes. Identical twin men, for example, are more concordant for strokes—17.7 percent, compared with 3.6 percent for male fraternal twins (Brass, Isaacsohn, Merikangas, & Robinette, 1992). In one study, adopted children (born in the 1920s) whose biological parents died before age 50 were twice as likely to have died young as adopted children whose biological parents were alive at 50 (T. Sorensen, Nielsen, Andersen, & Teasdale, 1988). But many health practices can temper predispositions toward particular illnesses and increase longevity.

Intelligence.   Researchers in behavioral genetics have focused more on intelligence than on all other characteristics combined, generally using IQ scores as its measure. What have they found? Heredity seems to exert a major influence on general intelligence, and this becomes increasingly important throughout the life span (Plomin et al., 1994). Since genes do not direct specific behaviors, how do they affect intellectual performance? Apparently, many genes—each with its own small effect—combine to create an overall influence on intelligence. Genes establish a range of possible reactions to a range of possible experiences (Weinberg, 1989).

TABLE 2-5

SOME CONDITIONS AND CHARACTERISTICS SHOWING GENETIC INFLUENCE	
CONDITION/CHARACTERISTIC	**DEGREE OF GENETIC INFLUENCE**
Behavioral and personality dimensions	
General intelligence	Substantial
Verbal reasoning	Substantial
Vocational interest	Substantial
Scholastic achievement	Substantial
Processing speed	Substantial
Spatial reasoning	Substantial
Memory	Substantial
Extroversion	Substantial
Neuroticism	Substantial
Openness	Substantial
Conscientiousness	Substantial
Agreeableness	Substantial
Behavioral and personality disorders	
Reading disability	Substantial
Major affective disorder (depression)	Substantial
Autism	Substantial
Alzheimer's disease	Substantial
Schizophrenia	Substantial
Alcoholism	Modest
Specific language disorder	Some evidence
Panic disorder	Some evidence
Eating disorder	Some evidence
Antisocial personality disorder	Some evidence
Tourette's Syndrome	Some evidence

SOURCE: Based on information in Plomin et al., 1994; Bouchard, 1994.

There is *no* evidence that differences in IQ scores between cultural, ethnic, or racial groups are due to hereditary factors. But many studies point to a strong genetic influence on differences between individuals *within a group*. About 50 percent of the difference in intelligence between persons in a group is believed to be genetically determined, with the remaining variation due to each person's experiences (Weinberg, 1989). Such percentages have clear implications for social policy, since the half of the variance that is environmentally determined is responsive to a number of strategies that help children with low IQ scores do better both academically and socially, as we'll see later. Evidence for the role of heredity in intelligence has emerged from several adoption and twin studies. Adopted children's IQs have been compared with IQs of their adoptive siblings and parents and with either the IQs or the educational levels of their biological mothers (from whom they had been separated since the first week of life). Resemblances to the biological mothers have been consistently higher than to the family members children have lived with (Horn, 1983; Scarr & Weinberg, 1983).

Also, heredity seems to become more important as people grow older. In the adoption studies, young siblings scored similarly, whether related by blood or adoption; but adolescents' scores had zero correlation with those of their adoptive siblings. Furthermore, the adolescents' IQs correlated more highly with their biological mothers' levels of schooling than with their adoptive parents' IQs. The family environment seems more influential for younger children, but adolescents are more apt to find their niches in life on the basis of inborn abilities and interests (Scarr & Weinberg, 1983). They actively select environments that are compatible with their heredity (as Vicky will do, when she chooses to go to art classes in elementary school and then to an arts college). This tendency helps to explain why identical twins reared apart often become very like each other.

Longitudinal twin studies have also found the influence of heredity on intelligence increasing with age. Among 500 pairs of twins, identical twins became more and more alike in IQ from infancy to adolescence, while fraternal twins became less alike. And individual children followed their own distinct patterns of "spurts and lags" in mental development. The home environment had some impact, but genetic factors had more (Plomin, Pedersen, McClearn, Nesselrode, & Bergeman, 1988). But again, we have to remember that genetics accounts only in part for variations in intelligence; changing the environment can have considerable impact on a child's learning and intelligence.

personality *Person's unique way of behaving, feeling, and reacting.*

Personality.   *Personality* is a person's overall pattern of character, behavioral, temperamental, emotional, and mental traits—in other words, the distinguishable, relatively enduring ways in which one person's behavior differs from another's. Something so complicated cannot be ascribed to any one major influence, either hereditary or environmental. But specific aspects of personality do seem to be inherited, at least in part. (See Box 2-4 for a discussion of one such trait, shyness.)

There is modest consensus that personality can be described by five main traits: extroversion, neuroticism, conscientiousness, agreeableness, and openness. Recent analyses of these traits suggest a heritability of about .40 (Bouchard, 1994).

Temperament.   In 1956 two psychiatrists and a pediatrician (A. Thomas & Chess, 1984; A. Thomas, Chess, & Birch, 1968) launched the New York Longitudinal Study (NYLS), following 133 children from infancy into adulthood. They concluded that *temperament*—a person's basic style of approaching and reacting to situations—seems to be inborn.

They looked at how active children were; how regular they were in hunger, sleep, and bowel habits; how readily they accepted new people and situations; how they adapted to changes in routine; how sensitive they were to noise, bright lights, and other sensory stimuli; whether they tended to be cheerful or sad; how intensely they responded; and whether they persisted at tasks or were easily distracted. The children varied enormously in all these characteristics, almost from birth, and the variances tended to continue. But the environment was also very important: Many children changed their behavioral style, apparently reacting to special experiences or parental handling. (See Chapter 7.)

Studies of babies from different ethnic groups suggest that some temperamental traits are inborn. Newborns of different backgrounds have shown a number of differences (Freedman, 1979). In western cultures, for example, when infants' noses are briefly pressed with a cloth, they show a "defensive reaction"; they immediately turn their heads away or swipe at the cloth. Chinese babies, however, do not put up a fight, but simply open their mouths promptly to restore breathing. Findings like this suggest that even the most fundamental-seeming behaviors are subject to genetic and ethnic variability. We need to be very careful therefore about declaring any particular inherited characteristic to be "normal" for all children.

What do you think? *In some cultures children are encouraged to stay close to their parents and not to speak, especially in the presence of strangers. American society, however, values boldness, and American parents are often advised to help shy children become more outgoing. Would it be better if all societies placed more value on all types of personalities? If so, how could this be done?*

Personality Disorders. Certain personality disorders illustrate the intertwining of hereditary and environmental factors. There is evidence for a hereditary influence on alcoholism, depression, infantile autism, and schizophrenia. (The first three conditions, as well as other personality disorders, are discussed elsewhere in this book.) They all tend to run in families and to show greater concordance between identical twins than fraternal twins. But heredity alone does not dictate such disorders. People seem to inherit the tendency for a condition, which can then be triggered by environmental factors.

Schizophrenia is a dramatic example of this interrelationship between nature and nurture. This psychological disorder is marked by a loss of contact with reality and by such symptoms as hallucinations, delusions, and other thought disorders. Many studies suggest that it has a strong genetic component (Plomin & Rende, 1991). But since not all identical twins are concordant for the illness, it cannot be *only* genetic. It is possible that the condition *itself* is not transmitted, but that a predisposition toward it is. If certain environmental stresses occur in the life of someone who is so genetically predisposed, that person may develop schizophrenia. A Swedish study, for example, found that men who had grown up in a city were more likely to develop schizophrenia than were men from rural areas (G. Lewis, David, Andreasson, & Allebeck, 1992). So we see that genes alone do

BOX 2-4 ■ FOOD FOR THOUGHT

SHYNESS

At age 4, Jason went with his parents to an office Christmas party. For the first hour he didn't say a word; for the next hour he clung to his mother's side as he stared wide-eyed at the other children, the strange adults, and the array of toys. By the time he felt comfortable enough to venture away from her, the party was over.

Vicky, also 4, was at the same party. She had barely burst into the room when she ran up to the Christmas tree, grabbed the nearest brightly wrapped package, asked a strange man standing nearby if he could help her open it, and hardly glanced at her parents.

Which of these two do you think will have an easier time in our society?

CAUSES OF SHYNESS

Classical psychoanalytic thought has held for years that such differences between children are created by early experience: Perhaps Jason is wary of the world because he has not learned to trust, while Vicky's experiences have been more positive. Research, however, strongly suggests that shyness and boldness are inborn characteristics, which are related to various physiological functions and which tend to persist throughout life. These traits do not seem related to sex or socioeconomic class (Plomin, 1989).

Jerome Kagan, a professor of psychology at Harvard University, has led a series of longitudinal studies of some 400 children who were followed for over 5 years, starting at just under 2 years of age (Garcia-Coll, Kagan, & Reznick, 1984; Kagan, 1989; Kagan, Reznick, Clarke, Snidman, & Garcia-Coll, 1984; Reznick et al., 1986; Robinson, Kagan, Reznick, & Corley, 1992). Shyness, or what these researchers call "inhibition to the unfamiliar," was strong in about 10 to 15 percent of the children, first showing up at 21 months of age and persisting in most cases at $7\frac{1}{2}$ years. The opposite trait, "boldness," or comfort in strange situations, was also especially strong in about 10 to 15 percent. Most of the children fell between the two extremes.

Both the genetic influence and the stability of the trait were strongest for the children at either extreme, whose personality characteristics were associated with various physiological signs that may give clues to the heritability of the traits. When asked to solve problems or learn new information, the very shy children had higher and less variable heart rates than the middle-range and bolder children, and the pupils of the shy children's eyes dilated more. The shy children seemed to feel more anxious in situations that the other youngsters did not find particularly stressful.

A genetic factor in shyness also showed up in another study. Two-year-olds who had been adopted soon after birth closely resembled their biological mothers in terms of shyness. However, these babies also resembled their adoptive mothers, showing an environmental influence as well (Daniels & Plomin, 1985). The parents of shy babies tended to have less active social lives, exposing neither themselves nor their babies to new social situations. This was true for the adoptive parents, and even more so for biological parents raising their own children.

Thus there is an intertwining of factors. While a *tendency* toward shyness may be inherited, the environment can either accentuate or modify it. Some shy children become more outgoing and spontaneous, apparently in response to parents' efforts to help them become more comfortable with new people and situations. And what the parents do tends to reflect what the society values.

Although some traits, like shyness or a tendency toward fussiness, seem to be hereditary, sensitive handling by parents who understand their children's temperaments can often help children to change the way they meet life's challenges.

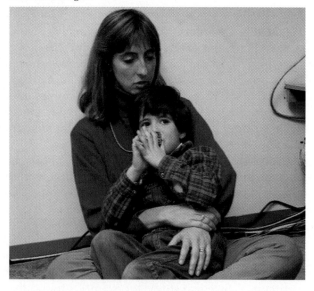

not cause a condition like schizophrenia, but that it is caused by many factors, with the social context of environment playing a critical role.

What do you think?   *If you were to take a position in the debate over the role of heredity and environment, what would you think of the following arguments?*

1. *Some people and groups are genetically inferior to others. Our laws and institutions should take these differences into account.*

2. *The environment shapes so much of our lives and limits or expands so many of our opportunities that people born into impoverished environments should be given extra help so that they will have prospects equal to those of people born into richer environments.*

In this chapter we have focused largely on heredity. But we need to remember how much the environment affects the degree of influence heredity has. As we proceed, we will examine the ways they interact to make us the people we are. The first environment for every human being is the world within the womb, which we discuss next, in Chapter 3.

SUMMARY

1   Parenthood offers a unique opportunity for love and nurturing. Even though the economic and cultural pressures to have children have diminished, most couples do become parents. Nevertheless, compared with those of earlier generations, today's couples tend to have fewer children and to start having them later.

2   Fertilization involves the union of an ovum and a sperm, which form a one-celled zygote. At conception, each normal human being receives 23 chromosomes from the mother and 23 from the father. These align into 23 pairs of chromosomes—22 pairs of autosomes and 1 pair of sex chromosomes. Chromosomes carry the genes that determine inherited characteristics.

3   Although conception usually results in a single birth, multiple births can occur. When two ova are fertilized, fraternal (dizygotic) twins result; these are different in genetic makeup and may be of different sex. When a single fertilized ovum divides in two, identical (monozygotic) twins result. These have the same genetic makeup and therefore are always of the same sex. Larger multiple births result from one of these processes or a combination of the two.

4   The sex of the child depends on whether the father contributes an X or a Y chromosome at the time of fertilization. The mother always contributes an X chromosome. A Y chromosome from the father results in a male. An X chromosome from the father results in a female.

5   Patterns of genetic transmission are dominant inheritance, recessive inheritance, sex-linked inheritance, incomplete dominance, polygenic inheritance, and multifactorial transmission. Various human characteristics, and several diseases and birth defects, are transmitted through these patterns.

6   If an organism carries genes for contradictory traits, the trait expressed will not be random. Instead, one trait will generally be dominant, and that is the one that will be expressed. Observable traits constitute a person's *phenotype,* while the underlying genetic pattern is called the *genotype.*

7   Recessive traits can be expressed only if both parents contribute the same recessive gene at fertilization.

8   Sometimes a trait combines the attributes on both alleles and neither characteristic dominates. This is known as *incomplete dominance.*

9   Some recessive traits may be carried on an X chromosome. Since males have only one X chromosome, two recessive genes are not needed for the trait to be expressed in

them. Females, who carry two X chromosomes, need two recessive genes for a recessive sex-linked trait to be expressed. Thus, sex-linked inheritance is much more common among males.

10 Traits that result from an interaction of a number of genes are transmitted by polygenic inheritance.

11 Multifactorial transmission involves the interaction of genetic and environmental forces.

12 Genetic and chromosomal abnormalities can result in birth defects. The most common chromosomal abnormality is Down syndrome.

13 Through genetic counseling, expectant parents can receive information about the mathematical odds of having a child with certain birth defects. Amniocentesis, chorionic villus sampling, maternal blood tests, ultrasound, umbilical-cord blood sampling, preimplantation genetic diagnosis, and embryoscopy are procedures used to determine whether the fetus is developing normally or is afflicted with certain birth defects.

14 It is difficult to disentangle the relative effects of heredity and environment on development. Today developmentalists consider these factors to interact. Methods for studying their relative effects include family, adoption, and twin studies.

15 Physical and psychological traits are strongly influenced by heredity. The influence of heredity on intelligence seems to increase with age. Some aspects of personality are also influenced by heredity. Temperamental characteristics such as shyness and disorders such as alcoholism, infantile autism, schizophrenia, and depression are all influenced by heredity. However, environmental factors seem to be at least as important as hereditary ones.

KEY TERMS

heredity (65)
environment (65)
nature-versus-nurture controversy (65)
fertilization (67)
zygote (67)
fraternal, or dizygotic, twins (68)
identical, or monozygotic, twins (68)
chromosome (68)
gene (69)
DNA (deoxyribonucleic acid) (69)
allele (72)
homozygous (72)
heterozygous (72)
dominant inheritance (72)
recessive inheritance (72)
genotype (73)
phenotype (73)

sex-linked inheritance (74)
carrier (74)
polygenic inheritance (75)
multifactorial transmission (75)
Down syndrome (81)
genetic counseling (82)
karyotype (83)
amniocentesis (84)
chorionic villus sampling (CVS) (84)
ultrasound (84)
heritability (87)
reaction range (87)
canalization (89)
maturation (89)
personality (94)
temperament (95)

SUGGESTED READINGS

Kingsley, J. & Levitz, M. (1994). *Count us in: Growing up with Down syndrome.* New York: Harcourt Brace & Co. A moving memoir by two young men with Down syndrome who describe growing up with the disability. The book, based on transcribed conversations the two friends had with each other and with others, discusses their attitudes toward friendship, love, marriage, sex, sports, school, and jobs and describes their problems and their successes.

Singer, S. (1985). *Human genetics* (2d ed.). New York: Freeman. A solid account of genetic principles and how they apply to people. Beginning with Mendel's principles, the text considers genes, gene pools, genetic disorders, and counseling.

Stoppard, M. (1993). *Conception, pregnancy, and birth.* New York: Dorling Kindersley. A comprehensive source for information, unusual in focusing on the experiences of both the mother and the newborn. The book includes case studies and in-depth coverage of obstetrical tests used in the 1990s and is an eminently readable work.

Watson, J. (1968). *The double helix: Being a personal account of the discovery of the structure of DNA.* New York: Atheneum. Classic, gossipy account of one of the great discoveries in genetic research. Watson pats himself on the back in an amusing and memorable set of portraits.

CHAPTER 3
PRENATAL DEVELOPMENT

If I could have watched you grow
as a magical mother might,
if I could have seen through my magical transparent
belly,
there would have been such ripening within. . . .

Anne Sexton, 1966

In this chapter, we watch as the one-celled zygote becomes a bright-eyed infant. We see how the embryo and then the fetus grow and how the rest of a person's life can be influenced by the prenatal environment. We also consider how parenthood may be achieved in ways that would have been impossible only a few years ago. After reading this chapter, you should be able to answer questions like the following:

PREVIEW QUESTIONS

- ♦ What happens during the three stages of prenatal development?
- ♦ What capabilities does the fetus have?
- ♦ How do both parents' lifestyles affect the fetus?
- ♦ What kinds of birth defects can be transmitted by mothers and fathers?
- ♦ How can infertility be treated or overcome?
- ♦ How does a new baby change parents' lives?

Jason's life begins long before he gives his first lusty yell after leaving his mother's womb. Fortunately, from the time Julia realized that she was pregnant, she has been making dozens of decisions that have changed her own life. Her pregnancy motivates her to give up smoking; after several earlier tries, this time she succeeds. She foregoes the occasional beer she would ordinarily enjoy. She becomes more aware and critical of her diet. She questions everything she does in terms of how it will affect the baby. Almost every choice she makes now is influenced by the presence of this child, whose arrival will alter her life in ways she cannot yet imagine.

Julia's reaction to her pregnancy is determined by many factors. The womb is the developing child's first environment, and its impact on the child is immense. Its influences range from what the mother herself does and what happens to her, to the father's contribution, to the social and cultural environment that determines the kind of prenatal care she gets, to the wider world, with all its beneficial and harmful elements. All these elements are related in complex ways.

THE EXPERIENCE OF PREGNANCY

The birth of a baby—especially a firstborn—changes the life of everyone in the family. Jason's arrival changes both his parents' personal identities; their emotional outlook; and their relationships with each other, with their own parents, and with the rest of the world. Even before a baby is born, lasting transformations take place. For the expectant mother the physiological changes during pregnancy are unlike any at any other time of her life (Abrams & Viederman, 1988). Then, the psychological effects for both expectant parents are profound.

Emotional attachment to the fetus takes time. Julia and Jess have been yearning to have a child. So at first, as the medical signs begin to confirm Julia's pregnancy, she and Jess are excited, nervous, joyful, and uncertain, all at once. But the baby is still months away, and their first reactions to parenthood arise from their fantasies and anxieties about what it will be like. Yet even before they have a baby to hold, they feel attached to their developing child.

Still they are ambivalent as they realize how much this baby will change their lives. They wonder, "Can we afford this?" "Won't this tie me down?" "Are we ready to be parents?" But because Julia and Jess really want this baby, their positive feelings soon outweigh the negative ones. Julia feels the intimate physical presence of the fetus, of course. And Jess, like some other expectant fathers, experiences a "sympathetic" pregnancy: nausea, backaches, and headaches (Colman & Colman, 1971; Liebenberg, 1969). His symptoms seem to help him be an active partner in the pregnancy.

By the eighth month, Julia and Jess are aware of the fetus's sleep-wake cycles and temperament, feel attached to the fetus (whom they have nicknamed "Thumper"), and imagine what Thumper looks like and what its sex is (Stainton, 1985). Julia sometimes has nightmares that her baby will be born with a birth defect. When she awakens, she realizes that the odds of having a normal, healthy baby are in her favor. By the end of the pregnancy, both parents' emotional attachment to the coming baby appears to be well established.

As Julia and Jess accept their relationship with the child they will have, they try to recognize that their child will be a distinct individual, with his or her own unique personality. They acknowledge their willingness to raise and care for the child. Their awareness of what parenthood entails helps them further their own development (Valentine, 1982).

Julia and Jess begin to resolve their relationships with their own parents as they realize they are about to take on the same roles they once rebelled against. Typically, both prospective parents learn to appreciate parenthood and gain new respect for their own parents. Often, the pregnancy triggers feelings of wanting to be *better* parents than their own parents had been and raises anew issues that had been buried for years. As the new life develops, so do the parents.

Some psychological issues are most prominent before the birth of the first child; others arise in each successive pregnancy. When Vicky's little brother, Bobby, will be born, for example, Ellen and Charles will have even more responsibility; they will again feel anxious about health; and they will have a new worry—how the new baby will affect Vicky.

PRENATAL DEVELOPMENT

If Jason were to be born in China rather than the United States, his birthday would be the supposed date of his conception rather than the date of his birth—and thus would recognize the importance of his 9 months in the womb. Let's see what happens during these months.

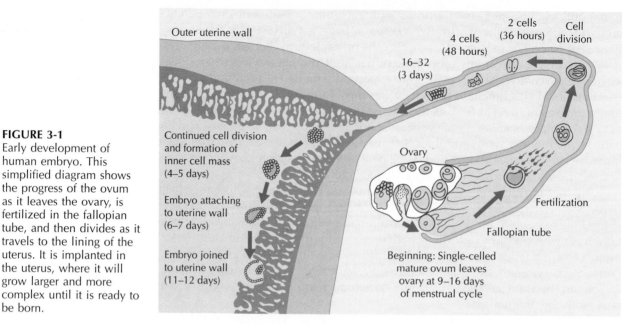

FIGURE 3-1
Early development of human embryo. This simplified diagram shows the progress of the ovum as it leaves the ovary, is fertilized in the fallopian tube, and then divides as it travels to the lining of the uterus. It is implanted in the uterus, where it will grow larger and more complex until it is ready to be born.

Labels in figure:
Outer uterine wall
2 cells (36 hours)
Cell division
4 cells (48 hours)
16–32 (3 days)
Continued cell division and formation of inner cell mass (4–5 days)
Ovary
Embryo attaching to uterine wall (6–7 days)
Fertilization
Embryo joined to uterine wall (11–12 days)
Fallopian tube
Beginning: Single-celled mature ovum leaves ovary at 9–16 days of menstrual cycle

THE THREE STAGES OF PRENATAL DEVELOPMENT

In Nepal one term for pregnancy means "being with two bodies" (Escarce, 1989), a feeling shared by many women as their bodies change with pregnancy.

gestation *Period of time from conception to birth; normally 266 days.*

The average length of pregnancy, or **gestation,** is 266 days. After fertilization and throughout the prenatal (gestational) period, a complicated genetic program influences the development of trillions of specialized cells. The single fertilized cell quickly divides, grows, and divides again. During the three stages of prenatal development—*germinal, embryonic,* and *fetal*—the number of cells rapidly increases, as the new being becomes increasingly complex. (Figure 3-1 shows the early development of the ovum and embryo; a month-by-month description of normal prenatal development is given in Table 3-1).

Germinal Stage (Fertilization to 2 Weeks): The Period of the Zygote

germinal stage *First 2 weeks of development of a conceptus, beginning at fertilization, characterized by rapid cell division and increasing complexity, and ending when the conceptus attaches to the wall of the uterus.*

During the **germinal stage,** the organism divides, becomes more complex, and implants itself in the wall of the uterus. The germinal stage lasts about 10 days to 2 weeks after conception, ending when the embryo attaches itself to the uterus.

Within 36 hours after fertilization, the single-celled zygote enters a period of rapid cell division (*mitosis*). Seventy-two hours after fertilization, it has divided into 32 cells; a day later, it has about 70 cells. This division continues until the original single cell develops into the trillions of specialized cells that make up a person.

While the fertilized ovum is dividing, it is also making its way down the fallopian tube to the uterus, which it reaches in 3 or 4 days. By the time it gets there, its form has changed into a fluid-filled sphere called a *blastocyst,* which then floats freely in the uterus for a day or two. Some cells around the edge of the blastocyst cluster on one side to form the *embryonic disk,* a thickened cell mass from which

TABLE 3-1

	MONTH	DESCRIPTION
	First month	During the first month, growth is more rapid than at any other time during prenatal or postnatal life: The embryo reaches a size 10,000 times greater than the zygote. By the end of the first month, it measures about $\frac{1}{2}$ inch in length. Blood flows through its veins and arteries, which are very small. It has a minuscule heart, beating 65 times a minute. It already has the beginnings of a brain, kidneys, liver, and digestive tract. The umbilical cord, its lifeline to the mother, is working. By looking very closely through a microscope, it is possible to see the swellings on the head that will eventually become eyes, ears, mouth, and nose. Its sex cannot yet be determined.
	Second month	By the end of the second month, the fetus is less than 1 inch long and weighs only $\frac{1}{13}$ ounce. Its head is half its total body length. Facial parts are clearly developed, with tongue and teeth buds. The arms have hands, fingers, and thumbs, and the legs have knees, ankles, and toes. It has a thin covering of skin and can make handprints and footprints. Bone cells appear at about 8 weeks. Brain impulses coordinate the function of the organ system. Sex organs are developing; the heartbeat is steady. The stomach produces digestive juices; the liver, blood cells. The kidneys remove uric acid from the blood. The skin is now sensitive enough to react to tactile stimulation. If an aborted 8-week-old fetus is stroked, it reacts by flexing its trunk, extending its head, and moving back its arms.
	Third month	By the end of the third month, the fetus weighs about 1 ounce and measures about 3 inches in length. It has fingernails, toenails, eyelids (still closed), vocal cords, lips, and a prominent nose. Its head is still large—about one-third its total length—and its forehead is high. Sex can be easily determined. The organ systems are functioning, and so the fetus may now breathe, swallow amniotic fluid into the lungs and expel it, and occasionally urinate. Its ribs and vertebrae have turned to cartilage. The fetus can now make a variety of specialized responses: It can move its legs, feet, thumbs, and head; its mouth can open and close and swallow. If its eyelids are touched, it squints; if its palm is touched, it makes a partial fist; if its lip is touched, it will suck; and if the sole of the foot is stroked, the toes will fan out. These reflexes will be present at birth but will disappear during the first months of life.
	Fourth month	The body is catching up to the head, which is now only one-fourth the total body length, the same proportion it will be at birth. The fetus now measures 8 to 10 inches and weighs about 6 ounces. The umbilical cord is as long as the fetus and will continue to grow with it. The placenta is now fully developed. The mother may be able to feel the fetus kicking, a movement known as *quickening,* which some societies and religious groups consider the beginning of human life. The reflex activities that appeared in the third month are now brisker because of increased muscular development.
	Fifth month	The fetus, now weighing about 12 ounces to 1 pound and measuring about 1 foot, begins to show signs of an individual personality. It has definite sleep-wake patterns, has a favorite position in the uterus (called its *lie*), and becomes more active—kicking, stretching, squirming, and even hiccuping. By putting an ear to the mother's abdomen, it is possible to hear the fetal heartbeat. The sweat and sebaceous glands are functioning. The respiratory system is not yet adequate to sustain life outside the womb; a baby born at this time does not usually survive. Coarse hair has begun to grow for eyebrows and eyelashes, fine hair is on the head, and a woolly hair called *lanugo* covers the body.

TABLE 3-1

	MONTH	DESCRIPTION
	Sixth month	The rate of fetal growth has slowed down a little—by the end of the sixth month, the fetus is about 14 inches long and weighs 1¼ pounds. It has fat pads under the skin; the eyes are complete, opening, closing, and looking in all directions. It can hear, it cries, and it can make a fist with a strong grip. A fetus born during the sixth month still has only a slight chance of survival, because the breathing apparatus has not matured. However, some fetuses of this age do survive outside the womb.
	Seventh month	By the end of the seventh month, the fetus, 16 inches long and weighing 3 to 5 pounds, now has fully developed reflex patterns. It cries, breathes, swallows, and may suck its thumb. The lanugo may disappear at about this time, or it may remain until shortly after birth. Head hair may continue to grow. The chances that a fetus weighing at least 3½ pounds will survive are fairly good, provided it receives intensive medical attention. It will probably need to be kept in an isolette until a weight of 5 pounds is attained.
	Eighth month	The 8-month-old fetus is 18 to 20 inches long and weighs between 5 and 7 pounds. Its living quarters are becoming cramped, and so its movements are curtailed. During this month and the next, a layer of fat is developing over the fetus's entire body, which will enable it to adjust to varying temperatures outside the womb.
	Ninth month	About a week before birth, the fetus stops growing, having reached an average weight of about 7½ pounds and a length of about 20 inches, with boys tending to be a little longer and heavier than girls. Fat pads continue to form, the organ systems are operating more efficiently, the heart rate increases, and more wastes are expelled through the umbilical cord. The reddish color of the skin is fading. At birth, the fetus will have been in the womb for about 266 days, although gestational age is usually estimated at 280 days, since most doctors date the pregnancy from the mother's last menstrual period.

the baby will develop. This mass is already differentiating into two layers. The upper layer, the *ectoderm,* will eventually become the outer layer of skin and the nails, hair, teeth, sensory organs, and nervous system, including the brain and spinal cord. The lower layer, the *endoderm,* will become the digestive system, liver, pancreas, salivary glands, and respiratory system. Then, a middle layer, the *mesoderm,* will develop and differentiate into the inner layer of skin, the muscles, skeleton, and excretory and circulatory systems.

During the germinal stage, other parts of the blastocyst develop into the organs that will nurture and protect the unborn child: the *placenta,* the *umbilical cord,* and the *amniotic sac.* The placenta, an unusual multipurpose organ, is connected to the embryo by the umbilical cord. Through this cord the placenta delivers oxygen and nourishment to the developing baby and removes its body wastes. The placenta also helps combat internal infection and gives the unborn child immunity to various diseases. It produces the hormones that support pregnancy, prepare the mother's breasts for lactation, and eventually stimulate the uterine contractions that will expel the baby from the mother's body. The amniotic sac is a fluid-filled membrane that encases the developing baby, protecting it and giving it room to move.

The *trophoblast,* the outer cell layer of the blastocyst, produces very small threadlike structures that penetrate the lining of the uterine wall and enable the blastocyst to cling there until it is implanted (attached to the uterine lining). Upon implantation, the blastocyst has about 150 cells; when it is fully implanted in the uterus, it is an *embryo.*

embryo *Conceptus between 2 weeks and 8 to 12 weeks after conception.*

What turns that single fertilized egg into an embryo with a specific shape and pattern that characterize it as a particular kind of animal? Only recently was it discovered that an identifiable group of genes do this. These genes produce molecules called *morphogens* which get switched on after fertilization, and, in humans, begin sculpting arms, hands, fingers, vertebrae, ribs, a brain, all the other body parts (Riddle, Johnson, Laufer, & Tabin, 1993; Kraus, Concordet, & Ingham, 1993; Echeland et al., 1993).

Embryonic Stage (2 to 8–12 Weeks)

Development during the Embryonic Stage. During the *embryonic stage,* the organs and major body systems—respiratory, digestive, and nervous—develop. Because growth and development proceed rapidly, this is a critical period when the embryo is most vulnerable to influences of the prenatal environment. A *critical period* is a specific interval during development when an event has its greatest impact. An organ system or structure that is still developing at the time of exposure is most likely to be affected; a structure or organ already developed will be in least danger. Almost all developmental birth defects (cleft palate, incomplete or missing limbs, blindness, deafness) occur during the first *trimester* (3-month period) of pregnancy. Defects can still occur later in pregnancy, but those are likely to be less serious. The most severely defective embryos usually do not survive beyond the critical first trimester and are aborted spontaneously.

embryonic stage *Second stage of pregnancy (2 to 8–12 weeks), characterized by differentiation of body parts and systems and ending when the bone cells begin to appear.*

critical period *Specific time during development when an event has its greatest impact.*

Spontaneous Abortion in the Embryonic Stage. In ancient times, people believed that a woman could be frightened into miscarrying by a clap of thunder or jostled into it if her chariot hit a rut in the street. But today, we realize that the conceptus is well protected against almost all jolts and cannot be shaken loose any more easily than a good unripe apple can be shaken from the tree.

Most miscarriages result from abnormal pregnancies. Since normal prenatal development depends on many precisely controlled events, it is inevitable that sometimes something will go seriously wrong. When this happens, a common result is a natural end to the pregnancy. A *miscarriage,* technically referred to as a *spontaneous abortion,* is the expulsion from the uterus of an embryo or fetus that is not able to survive outside the womb. About one-third (31 percent) of all conceptions end in miscarriage (Wilcox et al., 1988), and three out of four miscarriages occur within the first trimester (J. F. Miller et al., 1980).

spontaneous abortion *Natural expulsion from the uterus of a conceptus that cannot survive outside the womb; also called miscarriage.*

Women are at higher risk of miscarriage if they smoke; drink alcohol or coffee; have miscarried in the past; experience vaginal bleeding in pregnancy; are over 35; or have uterine abnormalities, endocrine problems, or certain infections. Chromosomal abnormalities of the embryo are present in about 50 to 70 percent of all spontaneous abortions (B. S. Apgar & Churgay, 1993; Mishell, 1993).

While the risk to the miscarrying mother is small, an infection, a hemorrhage, or an embolism (obstruction of a blood vessel) can sometimes occur. The risk of such complications is greatest for women over 29, as well as for women who have less access to health care, such as single women and members of minority groups. The risk is also greater for women who miscarry in the second trimester (B. S. Apgar & Churgay, 1993; S. M. Berman, MacKay, Grimes, & Binkin, 1985).

Since a miscarriage can lead to feelings of guilt, depression, anger, and a fear of becoming pregnant again, parents need to acknowledge their grief over the loss, to investigate and treat any medical reasons for it, and, in some cases, to seek counseling to help them deal with what is a very real trauma.

Fetal Stage (8–12 Weeks to Birth)

fetus *Conceptus between 8 to 12 weeks and birth.*

fetal stage *Final stage of pregnancy (from 8–12 weeks to birth), characterized by increased detail of body parts and greatly enlarged body size.*

With the appearance of the first bone cells at about 8 weeks, the embryo begins to become a *fetus;* by 12 weeks, the organism is fully in the *fetal stage.* Right up until birth, "finishing touches" (like fingernails, toenails, and eyelids) develop, and the body changes in form and grows about 20 times in length.

The appearance of the first bone cells at about 8 weeks is considered the beginning of the fetal stage. However, since some organs continue to form beyond 8 weeks, the embryonic period is sometimes designated as the first 12 weeks. During the fetal stage, the fetus grows rapidly, and the organs and body systems become more complex.

PRENATAL ABILITIES AND ACTIVITIES

Fetuses are not passive passengers in their mothers' wombs. They kick, turn, flex their bodies, turn somersaults, squint, swallow, make a fist, hiccup, and suck their thumbs. They respond to sound and vibrations, showing they can hear and feel. Julia is convinced that her fetus is more active when she is lying down than when she is standing. This may stem from the development of the fetus's vestibular system in the middle ear. This system, which controls the sense of balance, begins to function at about 4 months of gestation, probably allowing the fetus to feel changes in the mother's posture.

Even inside the womb, each fetus is a unique human being. Women who bear more than one child often notice differences in the amount of fetal activity from one to another. One mother of a child who later turned out to be hyperactive said, "I knew while Curt was still in the womb that he was going to be a pistol! He bounced around so much inside me that I would automatically put my hand over my abdomen to keep him from popping out!" (M. A. Stewart & Olds, 1973, p. 253). Similarly, many mothers claim that their offspring were as placid before birth as they are afterwards.

Furthermore, fetuses move in different ways. One kicks with his feet or punches with his hands, another squirms slowly, and a third makes sharp, spasmodic movements. Differences in kind or amount of fetal activity seem to predict how active, restless, or resistant to handling a baby will be during the first year (Sontag, 1966). Some of these patterns seem to persist into adulthood, supporting the notion of inborn temperament. Thanks to the use of ultrasound, much has been learned about fetal movement, and scientists are exploring links between activity in the womb and future limb development.

Fetal Therapy

Sometimes, through the methods described in Chapter 2, doctors can detect and then treat correctable conditions. Fetuses can swallow and absorb medicines, nutrients, vitamins, and hormones that are injected into the amniotic fluid. Blood can be transfused through the umbilical cord beginning as early as the eighteenth week of pregnancy, and drugs that might not pass through the placenta can be injected directly through the cord. Surgery has even been performed in the womb, although most current thinking recommends letting the pregnancy come to term and treating the infant soon after birth (Marwick, 1993). However, the availability of powerful therapeutic techniques even in the womb provides another dramatic illustration of the importance of this time of life.

This pregnant woman reading nursery rhymes aloud may be familiar with research indicating that fetal learning seems to take place. Newborns prefer their own mothers' voices to those of other women, and also seem to remember stories they heard while they were still in the womb.

What do you think?   *The debate about induced abortion concerns the conflict between the rights of the mother and the rights of the fetus. Whose rights do you think should take precedence? In what circumstances?*

Fetal Hearing

When Ellen was 7 months pregnant, she went to a fireworks display. At each burst, she felt the fetus within her rock about, and these agitated movements did not stop until the flares and Roman candles did. Stories like this are common; most parents are convinced that a child does hear before birth—and they seem to be right. Over the past 60 years, scientific experiments have shown that fetuses respond to bells and vibrations and can discriminate between different tones (Bernard & Sontag, 1947; Sontag & Richards, 1938; Sontag & Wallace, 1934, 1936).

In one experiment on fetal responses to sound and vibration, researchers turned on a handheld vibrator and put its tip to the mother's abdomen, just over the place where the fetus's head was (as confirmed by ultrasound). Then they measured fetal heart rate and movements, again with ultrasound. After testing 60 fetuses, they found that the first responses to sound and vibration came at 26 weeks of gestation; response increased steadily over the next 6 weeks and plateaued at about 32 weeks (Kisilevsky, Muir, & Low, 1992).

Fetal Learning

Not only can fetuses hear inside the womb; they also seem able to remember and discriminate what they have heard. The fact that newborns prefer their own mothers' voices to those of other women, and female voices to male voices, suggests that babies may develop preferences for the kinds of sounds they heard before birth (DeCasper & Spence, 1986).

Researchers testing this hypothesis asked pregnant women to tape-record three different readings—one from the book *The Cat in the Hat* by Dr. Seuss, one called *The Dog in the Fog* (the last 28 paragraphs of *The Cat in the Hat*, with major nouns changed), and a third story, *The King, the Mice, and the Cheese* (DeCasper & Spence, 1986). During the last 6 weeks of pregnancy, the women recited just one of the readings (the "target" story) an average of 67 times.

On the third day after birth, babies who had heard one of the readings prenatally sucked more (on nipples that activated recordings of these stories) to hear the story they had heard in the womb. This suggested that they recognized their own target story. On the other hand, babies in a control group, who had not heard a reading before birth, responded equally to all three recordings. It seems that babies can learn even before birth.

THE PRENATAL ENVIRONMENT

During her pregnancy, Ellen finds it easier and easier to think of the fetus as a person, especially after she has chosen the baby's name—Victoria. She knows that her baby will be a girl, since, as a first-time mother over 35, she had amniocentesis. (Ellen is happy about having a baby girl, but for a different perspective on sex determination by amniocentesis, see Box 2-1.) From her reading, Ellen learns that a mother's nutrition, drug intake, and perhaps even moods alter the environment of the developing fetus and affect its growth.

At one time the prospective father was thought to have no active role (besides the obvious initial one) with respect to the health of the fetus. But today we know that various environmental factors can affect a man's sperm and the children he conceives, as we'll see later in this chapter. Meanwhile, one way Charles helps to ensure the birth of a healthy child is to stop smoking. While the mother's role has been recognized far longer, we are still discovering many elements that can affect her fetus. A fetus can withstand many shocks and stresses, but providing the best prenatal environment possible gives it the best start in life. Advances in knowledge about prenatal life have given rise to an ethical debate, explored in Box 3–1.

Most of what we know about prenatal hazards we have learned either from animal research or from reports by mothers, after childbirth, on what they had eaten while they were pregnant, what drugs they had taken, how much radiation they had been exposed to, what illnesses they had had, and so forth. Both methods have limitations: It is not always accurate to apply findings from animals to human beings, and women do not always remember what they did during pregnancy. Because of ethical considerations, it is impossible to set up the kind of controlled experiments that might provide more definitive answers. Nevertheless, we know a great deal about prenatal influences.

teratogenic *Descriptive of an environmental factor that produces birth defects.*

Particular factors in the prenatal environment affect different fetuses differently. Some environmental factors that are ***teratogenic,*** or birth-defect-producing, in some cases have little or no effect in others. Research suggests that the timing of an environmental event, its intensity, and its interaction with other factors are all relevant. (See Figure 3-2.) What are some prenatal influences?

MATERNAL FACTORS

Prenatal Nutrition

A woman's diet *before* she conceives can affect her child's future health. Her diet during pregnancy may be even more vital. Pregnant women who gain between 22 and 46 pounds are less likely to miscarry, or to bear stillborn (dead at birth) or

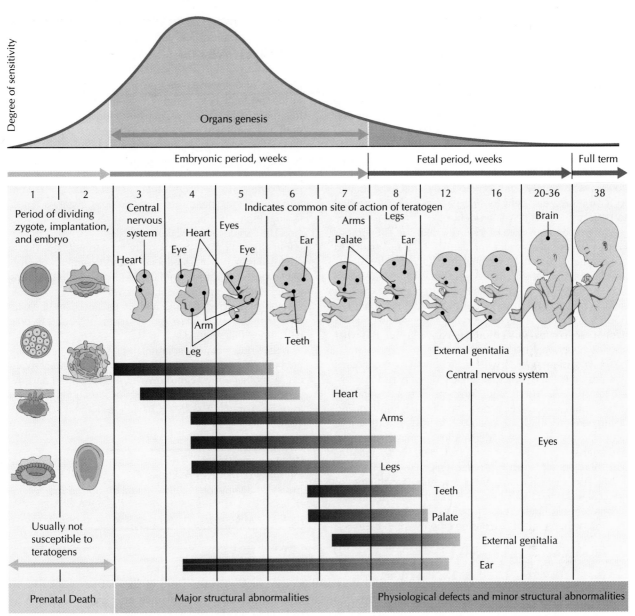

FIGURE 3-2
Critical periods in prenatal development that determine sensitivity to teratogens. The embryo is most vulnerable in the first 8 weeks. Exposure early in the embryonic period may lead to organ defects, whereas later exposure is likely to cause growth retardation or functional problems. (SOURCE: Moore, 1989.)

low-birthweight babies (Adams & Parker, 1990). Gaining too little is riskier than gaining too much (National Center for Health Statistics, 1986). Many women gain less than they should—partly because of societal pressures to look thin. Women at greatest risk of gaining too little are smokers; are underweight or overweight before pregnancy; are under age 20 or over age 35; have only a grade school education; already have three or more children; or are poor, black, or unwed.

Only recently have we learned about the devastating results of a lack of folic acid (a B vitamin) in a pregnant woman's diet. For some time, scientists have known that China has the highest incidence in the world of babies born with the neural-tube defects anencephaly or spina bifida. (See Table 2-2.) But it was not

BOX 3-1 ■ FOOD FOR THOUGHT

WHAT CONSTITUTES FETAL ABUSE?

A young German woman is rendered brain-dead in a car crash in her twelfth week of pregnancy. Although her parents want her to be disconnected from life support, the hospital's ethics committee plans to keep her alive for months, until they can deliver a viable infant (Fisher, 1992).

The birth of a healthy baby boy in Chicago ends a long conflict with county officials who tried to force the mother to have a cesarean delivery that doctors said was needed to protect her fetus ("Woman delivers. . .," 1993).

A woman convicted of forging a check to support her crack habit is jailed for the remainder of her pregnancy to prevent harm to her fetus (Chavkin & Kandall, 1990).

In cases like these, the issue is the conflict between a fetus's right to be born healthy and a pregnant woman's right to privacy and to make her own decisions about her body. It is tempting to legally require a pregnant woman to adopt practices that will ensure her baby's health. But what about her personal freedom?

Can society force a woman to submit to procedures that pose a risk to her, like a surgical delivery or intrauterine transfusions? These procedures are intrusive. Legal coercion could jeopardize the doctor-patient relationship, and such coercion could also open the door to go further into pregnant women's lives—demanding prenatal screening and fetal surgery and restricting their diet, work, and athletic and sexual activity (Kolder, Gallagher, & Parsons, 1987). For these reasons, the overwhelming attitude of medical, legal, and social critics is that the state should intervene only in limited circumstances.

Intervention might be considered only when there is a high risk of serious fetal disease; a high degree of accuracy in the test for a defect; strong evidence that the proposed treatment will be effective; danger that deferring treatment until after birth will cause serious damage; minimal risk to the mother and modest interference with her privacy; and unsuccessful, though persistent, efforts at educating her and obtaining her informed consent. Many procedures that have been ordered by courts in situations not meeting these criteria were thus performed on "dubious legal grounds" (Kolder et al., 1987).

The American Medical Association (1990) opposes criminal sanctions or civil liability for harmful behavior to a fetus. Instead, it urges education and treatment for pregnant women. If failure to follow medical advice can bring forced surgery, confinement, or criminal charges, some women may avoid doctors altogether, depriving their fetuses of prenatal care. If so, more mothers and babies would be harmed than helped.

Says one team of pediatricians, "A mother's love cannot be coerced by jailing pregnant women and errant mothers. A mother's love can, however, be supported and developed through drug abstinence, vocational training, and fostering parenting skills" (Chavkin & Kandall, 1990, p. 225).

What do you think?   *Is society's interest in protecting the rights of the fetus so strong that it justifies coercive measures against pregnant women? Or do the mother's rights always come first? How can the rights of both mother and baby be balanced for the good of both?*

---

until the 1980s that they linked that fact with the time of the babies' conception. Traditionally, Chinese couples wed in January or February and try to conceive as soon as possible—that is, in the barren winter when rural women have few fresh fruits and vegetables, important sources of folic acids, to eat (Tyler, 1994).

After medical detective work established the lack of folic acid as the cause of these defects, China embarked on a mass program to give folic acid supplements to prospective mothers (Tyler, 1994). Women of childbearing age are now urged to include the vitamin in their diets, even before becoming pregnant, to prevent neural-tube defects (American Academy of Pediatrics [AAP] Committee on Genetics, 1993).

Mothers with inadequate diets are more likely to bear low-birthweight infants, babies who are born dead or die soon after birth, or babies whose brains do not develop normally (J. L. Brown, 1987; Read, Habicht, Lechtig, & Klein, 1973; Winick, Brasel, & Rosso, 1972). Giving dietary supplements to malnourished pregnant women results in bigger, healthier, more active, and more visually alert infants (J. L. Brown, 1987; Vuori et al., 1979). In addition, better-nourished mothers tend to breastfeed longer, thus benefiting their babies (Read et al., 1973).

A well-balanced daily diet for pregnant women includes a variety of foods from each of the following categories: grains (bread, cereal, rice, and pasta), fruits and vegetables rich in vitamin C, dark-green vegetables, other fruits and vegetables (including yellow ones rich in vitamin A), protein (meat and meat alternatives), dairy products, and fats and oils. Women need to eat more than usual when pregnant—typically, 300 to 500 more calories a day, including extra protein (Winick, 1981). Teenagers, women who are ill or undernourished or under stress, and women who took birth control pills until shortly before pregnancy need extra nutrients (J. E. Brown, 1983).

Maternal Drug Intake

Practically everything the mother takes in makes its way to the new life in her uterus. Drugs may cross the placenta, just as oxygen, carbon dioxide, and water do. Each year as many as 375,000 infants may be affected by their mothers' drug abuse during pregnancy (Silverman, 1989). The organism is especially vulnerable in its first few months, when development is most rapid, and when drugs will have the strongest effects.

Serious problems have shown up in a mother's—or father's—use of drugs. Some can be treated if the presence of a drug in a newborn baby's body can be detected early. But it has often been difficult to determine exactly which drugs were taken, since doctors have usually had to rely on the parents' own, often-inaccurate testimony.

A test for the presence of drugs in a newborn's system analyzes the baby's *meconium,* the fetal waste matter that is excreted during the first few days after birth. Researchers who tested 3010 newborns from a high-risk urban population found that 44 percent were positive for cocaine, morphine, or cannabinoid, the active ingredient in marijuana, even though only 11 percent of the mothers had admitted to using drugs (Ostrea, Brady, Gause, Raymundo, & Stevens, 1992). It is clear that the technique used to assess the extent of drug abuse influences the result. Since identifying these babies early can make a major difference in their lives, it is important to be as accurate as possible. Let's look now at the effects on children of their mothers' use of various legal and illegal drugs.

Medical Drugs. Drugs known to be harmful include the antibiotics streptomycin and tetracycline; the sulfanomides; excessive amounts of vitamins A, B_6, C, D, and K; certain barbiturates, opiates, and other central nervous system depressants; several hormones, including birth control pills (Bracken, Holford, White, & Kelsey, 1978), progestin, diethylstilbestrol (DES), androgen, and synthetic estrogen; Accutane, a drug often prescribed for severe acne (Lott, Bocian, Pribram, & Leitner, 1984); and even aspirin (Stuart, Gross, Elrad, & Graeber, 1982). The American Academy of Pediatrics (AAP) Committee on Drugs (1994) recommends that *no* medication be prescribed for a pregnant or breastfeeding woman unless it is absolutely essential for her health or her child's.

The effects of taking a drug during pregnancy do not always show up immediately. In the late 1940s and early 1950s, the synthetic hormone diethylstilbestrol (DES) was widely prescribed (ineffectually, as it turned out) to prevent miscarriage. Not until years later, when the daughters of women who had taken DES during pregnancy reached puberty, did about 1 in 1000 develop a rare form of vaginal or cervical cancer (Melnick, Cole, Anderson, & Herbst, 1987). "DES daughters" also have had more trouble bearing their own children, with higher risks of miscarriage or premature delivery (A. Barnes et al., 1980), and "DES sons" seem to show higher rates of infertility and reproductive abnormalities (Stenchever et al., 1981).

What do you think? *Hundreds of adults now alive suffered gross abnormalities of development because their mothers took the tranquilizer thalidomide during pregnancy. The families of many of these people sued the pharmaceutical company that manufactured the drug. Does the company have a moral and a legal obligation to give money to the disabled?*

Nonmedical Drugs. Some other drugs that can affect babies can cause problems for the mother too, and drug abuse is not limited to the young and the poor. One study found similar levels of substance abuse in two groups of women—poor ones who received prenatal care in public clinics and well-off ones who went to private doctors (Chasnoff, Landress, & Barrett, 1990). Let's look at the effects of such abuse.

fetal alcohol syndrome (FAS) *Combination of mental, motor, and developmental abnormalities affecting the offspring of some women who drink heavily during pregnancy.*

Alcohol. Each year in the United States, more than 40,000 babies are born with alcohol-related birth defects. About 1 infant in 750 suffers from *fetal alcohol syndrome (FAS),* a combination of slowed prenatal and postnatal growth, facial and bodily malformations, and disorders of the central nervous system. Central nervous system problems can involve poor sucking response, brain-wave abnormalities, and sleep disturbances in infancy and, throughout childhood, slower information processing, short attention span, restlessness, irritability, hyperac-tivity, learning disabilities, and motor impairments.

Some FAS problems recede after birth; but others—like retardation, learning disabilities, and hyperactivity—tend to persist into adulthood. Unfortunately, enriching these children's environment or education does not seem to enhance their cognitive development (Spohr, Willms, & Steinhausen, 1993; Streissguth et al., 1991). For every child with FAS (about 6 percent of the offspring of alcoholic mothers), as many as 10 others may be born with *fetal alcohol effects,* a less severe condition that can include mental retardation, retardation of intrauterine growth, and minor congenital abnormalities.

Even moderate alcohol intake may harm the fetus. A study of nearly 32,000 pregnancies found that having one or two drinks a day can raise the risk of growth retardation. The risk increased sharply with heavier alcohol intake; less than one drink a day had a minimal effect (Mills, Graubard, Harley, Rhoads, & Berendes, 1984). In another study, infants whose mothers averaged one alcoholic drink a day while pregnant processed information more slowly; the more the mothers drank, the greater the effect (S. W. Jacobson, Jacobson, Sokol, Martier, & Ager, 1993).

The interrelationship among developmental realms—and the bidirectional influences in a child's life—is seen in the way a mother's alcohol use affects her baby's physical, cognitive, and emotional development. A study of 44 white, middle-class mothers and babies found that the babies of mothers who had drunk even moderate amounts of alcohol while pregnant were more irritable at 1 year of age than babies of nondrinking pregnant women. The babies' crying, whining, and tantrums annoyed their mothers, interfering with the mother-baby bond,

One danger of a mother's drinking during her pregnancy is that her child will be born with Fetal Alcohol Syndrome (FAS), as this 4-year-old boy was.

which in turn would most likely disturb the children's emotional development. Also, these babies achieved lower scores on intelligence tests (O'Connor, Sigman, & Kasari, 1993).

Many women have gotten the message that there is no safe level of drinking during pregnancy and that it is best to avoid alcohol from the time they begin *thinking* about becoming pregnant until they stop breastfeeding (AAP Committee on Substance Abuse and Committee on Children with Disabilities, 1993). From 1985 through 1988, an eight-state study of 1712 pregnant women, aged 18 to 45, found that with every subsequent year, fewer women were drinking. However, for those women who did drink—who tended to be less educated, younger, unmarried, and smokers—the number of drinks consumed did not drop (Serdula, Williamson, Kendrick, Anda, & Byers, 1991). The need, then, is to reduce alcohol use among all pregnant women, especially those at high risk. (See Box 3-2.)

Marijuana. Findings about marijuana use by pregnant women are contradictory. Some evidence suggests that heavy use can lead to birth defects; other evidence shows no ill effects. Some of this research was conducted in Jamaica (West Indies), where marijuana use is common. In one study researchers analyzed infants' cries and concluded that a mother's heavy use affects her infant's nervous system (Lester & Dreher, 1989). On the other hand, in another study, 3-day-old infants of mothers who had used marijuana prenatally showed no difference from a control group of nonexposed newborns. But at 1 month, the exposed babies were more alert and sociable and less irritable (Dreher, Nugent, & Hudgins, 1994). The authors of this study suggest that rural Jamaican women who use marijuana are more likely to be better educated, to have a higher income, and to have more adults living in the household and that all of these factors may combine to create a more favorable child-rearing environment. Thus scientists cannot look at a single factor in isolation, but need to explore the cultural context in which it occurs.

A Canadian study found temporary neurological disturbances, like tremors

BOX 3-2 ■ THE EVERYDAY WORLD

ALCOHOL AND PREGNANCY

WHAT EVERY WOMAN SHOULD KNOW

♦ *Drinking alcohol can cause birth defects.*
♦ The most severe form is fetal alcohol syndrome (FAS)—facial and body abnormalities; central nervous system disorders; and mental, motor, and growth retardation.
♦ *You can prevent alcohol-related birth defects.* If you do not drink during your pregnancy, your baby will be free of all alcohol-related birth defects.

WHAT WOMEN CAN DO

♦ *Stop drinking when you first begin to think about becoming pregnant.* You may not know you are pregnant until a month or two after you have conceived. Your fetus is especially vulnerable during the early stages of prenatal development.
♦ *If you have been drinking, stop as soon as you know you are pregnant.* It is probably not too late to prevent harm to your baby if you stop drinking now for the rest of your pregnancy.
♦ *Avoid "party drinking."* Binge drinking—five or more drinks at one time—can harm the developing baby.

♦ *Eat well, do not smoke, and do not take drugs.* Alcohol-related birth defects are more likely to occur if, in addition to drinking, you smoke, use prescription or street drugs, or are poorly nourished.
♦ *If you breastfeed your baby, use alcohol sparingly or not at all.* You can transmit alcohol to your baby through your milk, and large amounts can depress the baby's nervous system.

HOW PREGNANT WOMEN CAN GET HELP

♦ *Ask your health care practitioner.* Your doctor or midwife can answer your questions and give you information about drinking and its effects on you and your baby.
♦ *Get help for a drinking problem.* If you think you may have a drinking problem, you probably do. You owe it to your baby, as well as yourself, to get help. Check the yellow pages of your local telephone directory under "Alcoholism Information and Treatment Centers." Alcoholics Anonymous and some hospital and community programs are free.

---

and startles, as well as higher rates of low birthweight in the infants of marijuana smokers (Fried, Watkinson, & Willan, 1984). A United States study found a link between marijuana use just before and during pregnancy and one kind of leukemia (a childhood cancer), possibly due to pesticide contamination of the cannabis leaves (Robison et al., 1989). The safest course for women of childbearing age is *not* to use marijuana.

Nicotine. Pregnant smokers are at higher risk than nonsmokers of bearing low-birthweight babies and of complications ranging from maternal bleeding during pregnancy to death of the fetus or newborn (Armstrong, McDonald, & Sloan, 1992; McDonald, Armstrong, & Sloan, 1992; Landesman-Dwyer & Emanuel, 1979; Sexton & Hebel, 1984). Women who cut down on smoking during pregnancy tend to have bigger babies than those who continue to smoke at the same rate (Li, Windsor, Perkins, Goldenberg, & Lowe, 1993).

Smoking in pregnancy seems to have some of the same effects on school-age children as does drinking in pregnancy: poor attention span, hyperactivity, learning problems, perceptual-motor and linguistic problems, social maladjustment, poor IQ scores, low grade placement, and minimal brain dysfunction (D. Olds, Henderson, & Tatelbaum, 1994; Landesman-Dwyer & Emanuel, 1979; Naeye & Peters, 1984; Streissguth et al., 1984; Wright et al., 1983).

Mothers who stop smoking during pregnancy but smoke afterwards put their children at risk. Among 2256 4- to 11-year-old children in one study, those whose mothers smoked at least a pack a day *after* pregnancy were twice as likely to be anxious, disobedient, hyperactive, or to show some other behavior problem than were children of nonsmokers. The effect was more pronounced in children whose mothers smoked more than a pack a day (Weitzman, Gortmaker, & Sobol, 1992). It is possible that smoking during pregnancy may alter the child's brain structure or function, with resulting long-term effects on behavior; that passive exposure to cigarette smoke after birth may affect a child's central nervous system; that smoking may alter the mother's behavior, thus affecting her child's; or that mothers who smoke may be less tolerant of their children's behavior and more likely to report it as bothersome.

Opiates. Women addicted to such drugs as morphine, heroin, and codeine are likely to bear premature babies who will be addicted to the same drugs and suffer the effects of addiction until at least age 6. Addicted newborns are restless and irritable and often suffer tremors, convulsions, fever, vomiting, and breathing difficulties. They are twice as likely to die soon after birth as nonaddicted babies (Cobrinick, Hood, & Chused, 1959; Henly & Fitch, 1966; Ostrea & Chavez, 1979).

As older babies, they cry often and are less alert and less responsive (Strauss, Lessen-Firestone, Starr, & Ostrea, 1975). And in early childhood—from ages 3 to 6—they weigh less, are shorter, are less well adjusted, and score lower on perceptual and learning tests (Wilson, McCreary, Kean, & Baxter, 1979). Long-term follow-up studies on these children have found that they tend not to do well in school, are unusually anxious in social situations, and have trouble making friends (Householder, Hatcher, Burns, & Chasnoff, 1982).

Cocaine. Cocaine (including crack, its smokable form) is now reported to be the number 1 illicit drug used by pregnant women in the United States (Schutter & Brinker, 1992). A pregnant woman's use of cocaine is associated with a higher risk of spontaneous abortion, prematurity, low birthweight, smaller head circumference, and neurological problems. These babies are not as alert as other babies and not as responsive, either emotionally or cognitively (Alessandri, Sullivan, Imaizumi, & Lewis, 1993; Chasnoff et al., 1989; Chasnoff, Griffith, Freier, & Murray, 1992; L. Eisen et al., 1991; Zuckerman et al., 1989; Hadeed & Siegel, 1989; Chavez et al., 1989). Later organizational and language skills and secure emotional attachment may all suffer (Azuma & Chasnoff, 1993; Hawley & Disney, 1992). Cocaine use seems to interfere with the flow of blood through the placenta, and it may act on fetal brain chemicals to bring about behavioral change.

The impact of cocaine is far-reaching; it represents both the interconnectedness of development and its bidirectional influences. The mother's psychological reasons for using cocaine—which then affects her physically, cognitively, and emotionally—also affect her baby in all three domains. A baby's initial reaction to the drug is then influenced by the child's early environment. Drug-abusing parents are impaired themselves and often depressed, frequently leading to child abuse or neglect.

How the children behave affects their cognitive and emotional progress. For example, cocaine-exposed newborns do not show the kind of learning called *habituation*, in which they stop responding to a stimulus that is presented repeatedly (discussed in Chapter 6). This may affect their ability to regulate attention (Mayes, Granger, Frank, Schottenfeld, & Bornstein, 1993). For example, a very short attention span will interfere with learning. Similarly, the lethargic or irrita-

Nicotine has a number of harmful effects on a fetus. The strongest finding is that smokers are at risk of bearing low-birthweight babies. But if a woman stops smoking by her fourth month of pregnancy, her baby is likely to be of normal size.

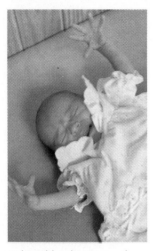

Babies like this 1-month-old baby girl, whose mother used cocaine, begin life with massive problems. Many are preterm and small, many have neurological problems, and many cry for long periods of time, unable to be comforted.

ble behavior of a cocaine-affected infant does not inspire loving feelings. In early childhood, many of these children have trouble loving their parents, making friends, and playing normally. Also, children of addicted mothers often face other environmental risks, like poverty and unstable homes.

But some studies have shown resilience in cocaine-exposed infants, who can often catch up in weight, length, and head circumference by 1 year of age, especially after good prenatal care (Racine, Joyce, & Anderson, 1993; Weathers, Crane, Sauvain, & Blackhurst, 1993). They may also catch up in other ways. It is important to recognize that many of these children can be helped after birth.

Caffeine. Can the caffeine that a pregnant woman swallows in coffee, tea, cola, or chocolate affect her fetus? One study suggests that the amount of caffeine in $1\frac{1}{2}$ to 3 cups of coffee a day may nearly double the risk of miscarriage, and drinking more than 3 cups nearly triples the risk (Infant-Rivard, Fernández, Gauthier, David, & Rivard, 1993). This conflicts with an earlier study that suggested that drinking up to 3 cups of coffee a day during pregnancy does not increase the risk of miscarriage or affect fetal development (Mills et al., 1993). Because such serious questions remain, the U.S. Food and Drug Administration recommends that pregnant women avoid or use sparingly any food, beverages, or drugs that contain caffeine.

Other Maternal Factors

Illness. Some illnesses contracted during pregnancy can have serious effects on the developing fetus, depending partly on *when* the mother gets sick.

When the mother gets rubella (German measles) before the eleventh week of gestation, it is almost certain to cause deafness and heart defects in the baby. But between 13 and 16 weeks of pregnancy, the chances of such effects are only about 1 in 3, and after 16 weeks, they are nearly nil (E. Miller, Cradock-Watson, & Pollock, 1982). Such defects are rare these days, since most children are inoculated against rubella, lowering the odds that a pregnant woman will contract the disease. Furthermore, a nonpregnant woman can find out through a blood test whether she is immune to rubella. If not, she can be immunized.

Diabetes, tuberculosis, and syphilis can also cause problems in fetal development, and both gonorrhea and genital herpes can have harmful effects on the baby at the time of delivery. The incidence of genital herpes simplex virus (HSV) has increased among newborns, who can acquire the disease from the mother or father either at or soon after birth (Sullivan-Bolyai, Hull, Wilson, & Corey, 1983). Newborns with HSV may suffer blindness, other abnormalities, and even death.

A mild parasite-caused infection called *toxoplasmosis* usually produces either no symptoms or symptoms like those of the common cold. But in a pregnant woman, it can cause brain damage, blindness, or even death of the baby. To avoid infection, pregnant women should not eat raw or very rare meat, should not handle cats, and should not dig in a garden where cat feces may be buried. Women who already have a cat should have it checked for the disease, should not feed it raw meat, and should not empty the litter box.

Medical advances have lowered the risks of many illnesses. Tests can now determine whether pregnant women and their fetuses may have been infected by

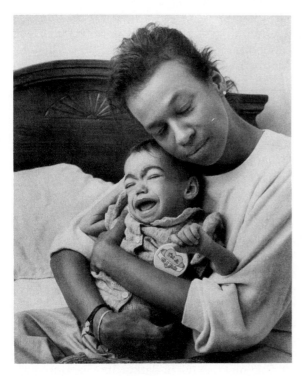

This 26-year-old mother contracted AIDS from her husband, who had gotten it from a former girlfriend, an intraveneous drug user. The father died first of this modern plague, then the 21-month-old baby, and last the mother.

viruses (like those that cause chicken pox and herpes) or by parasites (like the one that causes toxoplasmosis). If so, the women can be treated.

Acquired Immune Deficiency Syndrome (AIDS). *Acquired immune deficiency syndrome (AIDS)* may be contracted by a fetus if the mother has the disease or has in her blood the human immunodeficiency virus (HIV) that causes AIDS. The contents of the mother's blood are shared with the fetus through the placenta, and blood is a carrier of HIV. Women most often contract HIV by intravenous drug use or by sexual intercourse with an infected person, usually a drug user.

Although between 14 and 30 percent of HIV-positive mothers transmit the virus to their newborns, the Working Group on HIV Testing of Pregnant Women and Newborns (1990) does not recommend mandatory screening. Instead, it favors informing all pregnant women and new mothers about AIDS and the tests for it and providing medical care. One test can often detect the infection soon after birth, and the infant can be treated immediately with a drug. Early diagnosis and treatment are important, since children who acquire HIV at about the time of birth are likely to show symptoms before 1 year of age (G. B. Scott et al., 1989).

Incompatibility of Blood Type. Heredity can interact with the prenatal environment to cause incompatibility of blood type between mother and baby, most commonly due to the *Rh factor.* When a fetus's blood contains this protein substance (is Rh-positive) but its mother's blood does not (is Rh-negative), antibodies in the mother's blood may attack the fetus. The result can be miscarriage or stillbirth, jaundice, anemia, heart defects, mental retardation, or death soon after birth. Usually, the first Rh-positive baby of an Rh-negative mother is not affected, but with

Acquired immune deficiency syndrome (AIDS) *Viral disease that undermines effective functioning of the immune system*

Rh factor *Protein substance found in the blood of most people; when it is present in the blood of a fetus but not in the blood of the mother, death of the fetus can result.*

each pregnancy the risk becomes greater. A vaccine can be given to an Rh-negative mother; when administered within 3 days of childbirth or abortion, it will prevent her body from making antibodies that will attack future Rh-positive fetuses. Babies already affected by Rh disease can receive blood transfusions, sometimes even before birth.

Medical X-Rays.   We have known for more than 60 years that radiation can cause gene *mutations*—changes in a gene that produce a new, often harmful characteristic (D. P. Murphy, 1929). Since the greatest damage seems to occur early in pregnancy, radiation exposure should be avoided, especially during the first 3 months (Kleinman, Cooke, Machlin, & Kessel, 1983). Today ultrasound makes medical x-rays less necessary.

Maternal Age.   What is the best age to have a baby? In Chapter 16, we discuss teenage mothers and their babies, whose problems stem more often from social than from medical problems. The concerns for mothers past 30, however, are for the physical well-being of mother and child. In recent years, as more women have delayed childbearing until the mid-thirties or even the forties, researchers have focused on the risks and have come up with encouraging findings. In one group of almost 4000 pregnancies of mostly white, well-educated nonsmokers who received prenatal care, women over 35 had only a slightly higher risk of bearing unusually small babies and were no more likely to deliver prematurely or to have stillbirths than were younger first-time mothers (G. S. Berkowitz, Skovron, Lapinski, & Berkowitz, 1990). However, older mothers were twice as likely to have such complications of pregnancy as diabetes and high blood pressure. Furthermore, as women age, they become less fertile, are more likely to have miscarriages, and are more at risk of having children with birth defects.

Even so, the trend toward later motherhood seems to be a blessing for babies. Although mothers over 35 have a higher risk of birth-related complications, the risk to the baby's health is only slightly higher than for infants of younger women (Berkowitz et al., 1990). On the plus side, babies of older mothers seem to benefit from their mothers' greater ease with parenthood. When 105 new mothers aged 16 to 38 were interviewed and observed with their infants, the older mothers reported more satisfaction with parenting and spent more time at it. They were more affectionate and sensitive to their babies and more effective in encouraging desired behavior (Ragozin, Basham, Crnic, Greenberg, & Robinson, 1982).

Environmental Hazards.   Chemicals, radiation, extremes of heat and humidity, and other hazards of modern life can affect prenatal development. Infants exposed to high levels of lead prenatally scored lower on intelligence tests than those exposed to low or moderate levels (Bellinger, Leviton, Waternaux, Needleman, & Rabinowitz, 1987; Needleman & Gatsonis, 1990). Children exposed prenatally to heavy metals showed higher rates of childhood illness and lower levels of performance on a children's intelligence test (Lewis, Worobey, Ramsay, & McCormack, 1992). Women who worked with chemicals used in manufacturing semiconductor chips had about double the rate of miscarriages as did women workers who did not handle those chemicals (Markoff, 1992).

Nuclear radiation is especially dangerous. It affected Japanese infants after the atomic bomb explosions in Hiroshima and Nagasaki (Yamazaki & Schull, 1990)

Moderate exercise seems to be beneficial for pregnant women and their babies, as long as the women do not work out too strenuously.

and German infants after the spill-out at the nuclear power plant at Chernobyl in the Soviet Union (West Berlin Human Genetics Institute, 1987). In utero exposure to radiation has been linked to greater risk of mental retardation, small head size, chromosomal malformations, Down syndrome, seizures, and poor performance on IQ tests and in school. The critical period seems to be 8 through 15 weeks after fertilization (Yamazaki & Schull, 1990).

Physical Activity. Fortunately, not all things an expectant mother does or is exposed to are harmful to a fetus. Julia can continue jogging and cycling, and Ellen can keep swimming and playing tennis, since moderate exercise does not seem to endanger the fetuses of healthy women (Carpenter et al., 1988). Regular exercise prevents constipation and improves respiration, circulation, muscle tone, and skin elasticity, all of which contribute to a more comfortable pregnancy and an easier, safer delivery. The American College of Obstetrics and Gynecology's (1994) guidelines encourage women in low-risk pregnancies to be guided by their own stamina and abilities.

Among 996 Swiss and Italian mothers, 38 percent reported having taken part in some sporting activity, and almost 62 percent of this group said they had not felt physically overtaxed by either work or sport at any time during pregnancy (Fricker, Hindermann, & Bruppacher, 1989). A study of 45 women in midpregnancy who pedaled exercise bicycles found that only when they were at the point of exhaustion did their fetuses show any decline in heart rate. Even in these cases, this decline was short-lived and occurred only just after the exercise was stopped. All the fetuses showed normal heart response within half an hour after the exercise session. Moreover, all the babies except two who had unrelated complications were fine at birth. The safest course seems to be for pregnant women to exercise moderately—not pushing themselves and not raising their heart rate above 150—and to taper off their workouts rather than stopping abruptly.

PATERNAL FACTORS

The father, too, can transmit environmentally caused defects. Exposure to lead, marijuana and tobacco smoke, large amounts of alcohol and radiation, DES, and certain pesticides may produce abnormal sperm (R. Lester & Van Theil, 1977). Nervous system tumors in children have been associated with such occupations of their fathers as electrical or electronic worker, auto mechanic, miner, printer, paper or pulp mill worker, and aircraft industry worker (M. R. Spitz & Johnson, 1985). One study showed a relationship between a paternal diet low in vitamin C and birth defects and certain types of cancers in his children (Fraga et al., 1991).

A harmful influence is nicotine from a father's smoking. In one study, babies of fathers who smoked were lighter at birth by about 4 ounces per pack of cigarettes smoked per day by the father (or the cigar or pipe equivalent) (D. H. Rubin et al., 1986). Another study found that children of men who smoked were twice as likely as other children to contract cancer in adulthood (Sandler, Everson, Wilcox, & Browder, 1985). In both studies, however, it was difficult to distinguish between prebirth and childhood exposure to smoke.

A man's use of cocaine can also cause birth defects in his children, since cocaine seems to attach itself to his sperm. Cocaine-bearing sperm enters the ovum at conception. This research contradicts the earlier belief that harm results from fetal exposure to drugs only when the baby's organs are developing, from 3 to 12 weeks into the pregnancy. It now appears that fathers must share the responsibility for birth defects caused not only by cocaine, but also by other toxins, like lead and mercury, which might "hitch-hike" onto sperm the same way (Yazigi, Odem, & Polakoski, 1991). One route for the transmission of cocaine from the sperm to the baby may still lie with the mother, however. It is possible that when a cocaine-using woman has sexual intercourse, the man's sperm in her reproductive tract can pick up the drug and carry it to the ovum.

A later paternal age (averaging in the late 30s) is associated with increases in several rare conditions, including Marfan's syndrome (deformities of the head and limbs), dwarfism, and a bone malformation (G. Evans, 1976). Advanced age of the father may also be a factor in about 5 percent of cases of Down syndrome (Antonarakis & Down Syndrome Collaborative Group, 1991). Further, recent research has found that more male cells than female ones undergo mutations (which often have harmful effects), that mutations increase with paternal age, and that therefore older fathers may be a significant source of birth defects in their children (Crow, 1993; 1994).

Fortunately, many environmental influences are under the parents' control. Box 3-3 suggests what prospective parents can do to create a healthy prenatal environment.

A NOTE ON PRENATAL HAZARDS

We need to consider the many ways development can go awry and how best to avoid problems. But we should not forget that normal fetal development is overwhelmingly the rule. Both Ellen and Julia, despite their different lifestyles and different activities, feel good during pregnancy, both physically and emotionally—and both their fetuses, like most, develop normally. Pregnancy is a time of excitement, planning, and thinking. Today's techniques for monitoring fetal devel-

BOX 3-3 ▪ THE EVERYDAY WORLD

CREATING A HEALTHY PRENATAL ENVIRONMENT

Women and men can help ensure the best prenatal environment for their developing child if they follow a certain regimen:

♦ *Begin good medical care early.* Even a low-risk pregnancy can become high-risk if prenatal care is absent or poor. The mother should see a qualified practitioner regularly, beginning with the first hint of pregnancy, and should participate actively in her medical care. Both partners should meet the doctor, ask questions, and report symptoms. For high-risk pregnancies, the mother should see an obstetrician who has experience with her particular condition.

♦ *Eat well.* The mother should eat a well-balanced diet, with whatever vitamin supplements her practitioner recommends.

♦ *Be fit.* Regular moderate exercise is good for both mother and baby. If she hasn't exercised before pregnancy, the mother should take up a moderate activity like walking. She should monitor herself: If she experiences discomfort, bleeding, or other symptoms, she should tell her practitioner.

♦ *Gain weight sensibly.* The mother should gain weight gradually, steadily, and moderately to help prevent a variety of complications, including diabetes, hypertension, varicose veins, hemorrhoids, and a difficult delivery due to an overly large fetus. She should eat well but sensibly, avoiding crash dieting.

♦ *Don't smoke.* Both prospective parents should stop smoking as soon as they decide to conceive.

♦ *Don't drink alcohol.* The mother should stop drinking to reduce the risk of birth defects, particularly of fetal alcohol syndrome, which results from high alcohol intake. The father should drink little or not at all.

♦ *Avoid caffeine.* The mother should avoid or use sparingly any food, beverages, or drugs that contain caffeine.

♦ *Don't take drugs.* Both parents should avoid taking street drugs ever—but especially before and during the pregnancy—and neither should inject drugs intravenously. During pregnancy, the mother needs to be especially careful to avoid all drugs, including aspirin. A doctor who prescribes something for the mother should be told of the pregnancy and queried as to whether the drug is absolutely essential.

♦ *Avoid chemicals as much as possible.* Both parents should make every effort to avoid known harmful chemicals at work or elsewhere.

♦ *Prevent infections or treat them promptly.* Both parents should try to prevent all infections—common colds, flu, urinary tract and vaginal infections, and sexually transmitted diseases—whenever possible. The father can transmit something to the mother, which could have dire effects. If the mother does contract an infection, she should have it treated promptly by a physician who knows she is pregnant.

♦ *Don't try to be Superwoman.* The mother needs to resist the temptation to overachieve and overdo. Getting enough rest during pregnancy is far more important then getting everything done, especially in high-risk pregnancies. The father needs to help the mother get this rest, especially if she has been working full time. If the doctor recommends beginning maternity leave earlier than planned, the mother should take that advice.

opment and our increased knowledge of ways to improve the child's prenatal world make pregnancy much less a cause for concern than it was in earlier days. However, some concerns still remain. These concerns can often be met through comprehensive prenatal care.

PRENATAL CARE

Suppose you are a woman in one of ten western European countries or one in the Middle East, all of which have high standards of maternity care and entitlements to health services and social support.* In any one of these countries you would

*The ten European countries evaluated are Belgium, Denmark, Germany, France, Ireland, Netherlands, Norway, Spain, Switzerland, and Great Britain. The Middle Eastern country is Israel.

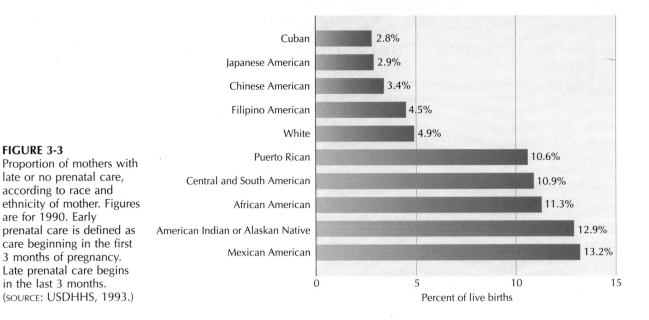

FIGURE 3-3
Proportion of mothers with late or no prenatal care, according to race and ethnicity of mother. Figures are for 1990. Early prenatal care is defined as care beginning in the first 3 months of pregnancy. Late prenatal care begins in the last 3 months. (SOURCE: USDHHS, 1993.)

Chart data:
- Cuban: 2.8%
- Japanese American: 2.9%
- Chinese American: 3.4%
- Filipino American: 4.5%
- White: 4.9%
- Puerto Rican: 10.6%
- Central and South American: 10.9%
- African American: 11.3%
- American Indian or Alaskan Native: 12.9%
- Mexican American: 13.2%

Percent of live births

receive either free or very low cost prenatal and postnatal care, including paid maternity leave from work. This care is offered because early prenatal care reduces rates of infant death, low birthweight, and other birth complications.

You would want to seek prenatal care early because only after your pregnancy was confirmed and officially registered would you begin to get benefits like transportation privileges and preferential hospital booking for delivery. You would probably go first to a general practitioner, who would coordinate your care with a midwife and an obstetrician. The midwife would give you most of your prenatal care and attend the birth—unless your pregnancy was considered high-risk, in which case a doctor would assist you. If you had a complicated pregnancy, your midwife would visit you at home; in some countries you would receive one such visit routinely.

As a pregnant woman in these countries, you would never need to ask how or where you would receive care or who would pay for it. In the United States, you would face a very different situation. You cannot get the benefits of uniform national standards for maternity care, and thus you cannot be assured of consistent, high-quality care. Nor can you count on financial coverage.

In the United States, about 24 percent of pregnant women do not receive care in the first 3 months. Furthermore, those most at risk of bearing low-birthweight babies—teenage, minority, and unmarried women and women with little education—get the least care (S. S. Brown, 1985; Ingram, Makuc, & Kleinman, 1986; Singh, Forrest, & Torres, 1989; USDHHS, 1992). In 1990, about 5 percent of white mothers and about 11 percent of black mothers had no care at all or none until the last 3 months of pregnancy. (See Figure 3-3.) Hispanic women are 3 times as likely as other groups to receive no prenatal care at all (Council on Scientific Affairs of the American Medical Association, 1991).

One way that this bleak picture might change would be if local and federal governments linked prenatal care to comprehensive social and financial benefits. There is need for a wide range of educational, social, and medical services (including outreach workers to identify women in need and help with transportation, baby-sitting, and housing problems). The state of New Jersey has launched a program offering a full range of prenatal health services to all women in the state (J. F. Sullivan, 1989). If more states follow, the future should be healthier for many American babies.

WHEN CONCEPTION IS AN ISSUE

Since human beings seldom abandon their desires simply because they run into obstacles, it is no surprise to find that infertile couples who want children eagerly embrace ways that bypass ordinary biological processes.

INFERTILITY

The most common reason for seeking alternative ways to parenthood is the inability to conceive. Rates of *infertility* (inability to conceive after 12 to 18 months of trying to have a baby) have tripled over the past three decades: About 15 percent of couples overall who want a baby cannot conceive (J. B. Staub & Lipshultz, 1990). This increase seems to be due to several factors—the growing number of couples who delay starting a family until the woman is in her thirties (often not realizing that fertility declines with age), an increase in sexually transmitted infections, and the side effects of such contraceptives as birth control pills and intrauterine devices (Cramer et al., 1985). There is also an association between infertility and cigarette smoking by women: Women who smoke heavily are less fertile than light smokers (Baird & Wilcox, 1985).

infertility *Inability to conceive after 12 to 18 months of trying to have a baby.*

Infertility burdens a marriage emotionally. People—especially women—may have trouble accepting the fact that they cannot do what comes so naturally and easily to others. Spouses may become angry with themselves and each other and may feel empty, worthless, and depressed (Abbey, Andrews, & Halman, 1992). Their sexual relationship suffers as sex becomes a matter of "making babies, not love" (Sabatelli, Meth, & Gavazzi, 1988). Such couples may benefit from professional counseling or support from other infertile couples; RESOLVE, a national nonprofit organization based in Boston, offers such services.

Causes of Infertility

Infertility becomes more of a problem with age. Only about 5 percent of couples are infertile when the women is in her early twenties, but about 15 percent are infertile a decade later, and the proportion rises with advancing age (Menken, Trussell, & Larsen, 1986). Although most research is based on the woman's age, the man's age is also a factor; in early adulthood both partners are equally likely to be infertile (Glass, 1986).

The most common cause of infertility in men is the production of too few sperm. Only one sperm is needed to fertilize the ovum, but a sperm count lower than 60 million to 200 million per ejaculation makes conception unlikely. Another cause is a blocked passageway, making sperm unable to exit; a third cause is impaired ability of sperm to swim well enough to reach the cervix. If the problem is in the woman's body, she may not be producing ova; the ova may be abnormal; the fallopian tubes may be blocked, preventing ova from reaching the uterus;

mucus in the cervix may prevent sperm from penetrating it; or a disease of the uterine lining may prevent implantation of the fertilized ovum.

Sometimes surgery can correct the problem. Sometimes hormones can raise a man's sperm count or increase a woman's ovulation; some fertility drugs cause superovulation, producing two, three, or more babies at a time. In more than 1 out of 10 cases, however, both man and woman seem normal but still are not able to conceive. Some infertile couples choose to remain childless; others adopt a child or turn to new technology.

ALTERNATIVE WAYS TO CONCEIVE

Many couples yearn to have children who carry on their own hereditary legacy— to see in future generations the almond-shaped eyes of one ancestor or the artistic talent of another. Those who can afford the considerable expense can become parents through new technology that enables them to have children who are genetically at least half their own. The four methods discussed below are all controversial for one reason or another, but they can lead to conception.

Artificial Insemination

artificial insemination
Injection of sperm into a woman's cervix.

Artificial insemination involves injection of sperm—often the husband's sperm— directly into the woman's cervix. If a husband seems infertile, a couple may choose *artificial insemination by a donor (AID)*. The donor may be matched with the husband for physical characteristics, and the husband's sperm may be mixed with the donor's so that the possibility exists that the husband is the biological father. Many couples who conceive in this way never tell the children or anyone else about the children's origins. In the United States, some 170,000 women are artificially inseminated each year, resulting in 65,000 births (Office of Technology Assessment, 1988).

In Vitro Fertilization

In 1978 headlines announced the birth of Louise Brown, the first "test-tube baby."[*] After 12 years of trying to conceive, Louise's parents authorized a gynecologist to extract an ovum from Mrs. Brown's ovary, allow it to mature in an incubator, and then fertilize it with Mr. Brown's sperm. The doctor then implanted the embryo in Mrs. Brown's uterus, where it grew.

in vitro fertilization (IVF)
Fertilization that takes place outside the mother's body.

In vitro fertilization (IVF), fertilization that takes place outside the mother's body, is becoming increasingly common for women whose fallopian tubes are blocked or damaged. It can also address male infertility by a new technique that involves injecting a single sperm into an ovum in a dish (Kolata, 1993). Usually, several ova are fertilized and implanted in order to increase the chances of success. Conception and live-birth rates by IVF compare favorably with those for spontaneous conception, but decline with the mother's age (Tan et al., 1992). Although these children tend to be smaller than average, their head circumference is normal and their mental development is in the normal range (Brandes et al., 1992).

[*]This popular term is a misnomer: The fertilization is seldom performed in a test tube. Even the term *in vitro* is wrong; it is Latin for "in glass," while most labs use plastic dishes.

Three-year-old Judith, shown here with her mother, is the center of a legal controversy. Since she was conceived by artificial insemination after her father's death, she was not recognized as his legitimate child. Her case illustrates the many ethical and legal quandaries involved in new ways to conception.

In vitro fertilization is very expensive, costing an average of $72,000 for each successful pregnancy (Neumann, Gharib, & Weinstein, 1994). This cost considers the typical expense of $8,000 for a single attempt and takes into account the fact that most attempts do not produce children. Some insurers cover it; some do not.

Ovum Transfer

Women who cannot produce normal ova may use donor eggs, ova donated by fertile women—the female counterpart of AID. There are two methods of *ovum transfer*. In the first, an ovum is taken from a donor's body and fertilized in the laboratory, and the resulting embryo implanted in another woman's uterus. In the second, a donor egg is fertilized by artificial insemination. A few days later, the donor's uterus is flushed out and the embryo is inserted into the recipient's uterus (Sauer, Paulson, & Lobo, 1990).

ovum transfer
Implantation of a fertilized donor egg from another woman in the recipient mother's uterus.

Surrogate Motherhood

In *surrogate motherhood* a woman is impregnated by the prospective father (usually by artificial insemination). She carries the baby to term and gives the child to the father and his wife. The surrogate undergoes the entire pregnancy, with its risks and emotions. Surrogate motherhood is in legal limbo, partly as a result of the "Baby M" case, in which a surrogate mother changed her mind and wanted to keep the baby (Hanley, 1988a, 1988b; Shipp, 1988). She was not granted custody of the child, but she does have visiting rights. The American Academy of Pediatrics (AAP Committee on Bioethics, 1992) recommends that surrogate parenting be considered a tentative, preconception adoption agreement in which, before birth, the surrogate mother is the sole decision maker. The AAP also recommends a prebirth agreement on the time period during which the surrogate may assert her parental rights.

surrogate motherhood
Pregnancy carried to term by a woman impregnated by the prospective father, usually by artificial insemination. She then gives the infant to the father and his wife; involves mutual agreement before conception.

Technology and Conception: Ethical Issues

In one case, a couple who had arranged for in vitro fertilization and freezing of seven embryos later divorced. One of them then wanted to be able to use the embryos to conceive; the other wanted them destroyed. In another case, a couple conceived an embryo through IVF and hired another woman to carry it to term; she did not want to give up the infant until, in a Solomon-like judgment, the court threatened to send the baby to a foster home. Although the genetic parents agreed to this, the birth mother instead gave them temporary custody. These are just two of the many complicated ethical quandaries that have arisen from new ways of reproduction (Angell, 1990).

To many people, the most objectionable aspect of surrogacy, aside from the possibility of forcing the surrogate to relinquish the baby, is the payment of money. Payment for adoption is forbidden in many states, but surrogate motherhood is not adoption, since the biological father is the legal father. The creation of a "breeder class" of poor and disadvantaged women who carry the babies of the well-to-do strikes many people as wrong.

What do you think?

- *Must people who use these new means of conception be infertile, or should any couple be free to make such arrangements simply for convenience?*
- *Should single people and homosexual couples have access to these methods?*
- *Should the children know about their parentage?*
- *If a test-tube baby is born with a major defect, is the physician liable?*
- *Should chromosome tests be performed on all prospective donors and surrogates?*
- *What is the risk that children fathered or mothered by the same donor or surrogate (genetic half siblings) might someday meet and marry, putting their children at risk of birth defects?*
- *What happens if a couple who have contracted with a surrogate divorce before the birth?*

One thing seems certain: As long as there are people who want children and who are unable to conceive or bear them, human ingenuity and technology will come up with new ways to satisfy their need.

ADOPTION

Adoption, the oldest solution to infertility, is found in all cultures throughout history. It is not only for infertile couples but also for couples who do not want to bear their own children or who already have children and seek to enlarge their families by taking children who need a home.

Since 1970, more Americans—including single and older people, working-class families, and homosexual couples—have become adoptive parents. Among African Americans, adoption is not so closely tied to infertility, but instead to the wish to provide a family for a known child, often a relative, who needs parents (Bachrach, London, & Maza, 1991). In this cultural context, many of these adoptions are informal, with no legal papers, no social workers, no government involvement, just the desire to love and raise a child (L. Richardson, 1993).

Because advances in contraception and legalization of abortion have reduced the number of adoptable healthy white American babies, many adoptable children are from minority groups, beyond infancy, disabled, or of foreign birth. Adoptions are more likely to be arranged through private attorneys and doctors rather than through agencies.

Adoption is well accepted in the United States, but there are still prejudices and mistaken ideas about it. One is the belief that adopted children have problems because they are not raised by their biological parents. Some negative views of adoption were reinforced by past studies that selected samples of adoptees from people seeking mental health services. However, later research found differences between attitudes and characteristics of adopted and nonadopted children that favored the adoptees. Adopted children were more confident, viewed the world more positively, felt more in control of their lives, and saw their adoptive parents as more nurturing than did the nonadopted control-group children (Marquis & Detweiler, 1985).

That is not to say that adopting a child is easier than bearing one. To the contrary, besides the usual issues of parenthood, adoptive parents have extra challenges—acceptance of their infertility (if this is why they adopted), awareness that they are not repeating their own parents' experience, the need to explain the adoption to their children, and discomfort about their children's interest in the biological parents.

Anna, shown here nestled in the arms of her adoptive parents, seems to be a living embodiment of a study that found that adopted children viewed the world more positively than a control group of nonadopted children, felt better able to control their lives, and saw their adoptive parents as more nurturing.

THE TRANSITION TO PARENTHOOD

No matter how children are conceived or whether they are raised by biological or adoptive parents, the birth itself and the few weeks afterward are among the most dramatic periods in life.

Both women and men often feel ambivalent about becoming parents. Along with excitement, most new parents feel some anxiety about the responsibility of caring for a child and about the feeling of permanence that a pregnancy imposes on their marriages. Pregnancy also affects a couple's sexual relationship—sometimes making it even more intimate, sometimes creating barriers.

THE MARITAL RELATIONSHIP

What happens in a marriage with the birth of a first child? It varies considerably. Vicky's and Jason's parents showed two different patterns. Ellen and Charles, Vicky's parents, seem to meld together more as teammates in a new shared project, the care of their new baby. But after Jason's birth, Julia feels overwhelmed by the job of caring for the baby and disturbed by what she sees as Jess's unwillingness to assume his fair share of caregiving. There are hurt feelings and many arguments between them.

One team conducted a longitudinal study in which they followed 128 middle- and working-class couples from the time of their first pregnancy until that child's third birthday. At the beginning of the study, the husbands' ages averaged 29 years and the wives' 27 years. Although some marriages improved, many suffered overall, especially for the wives (Belsky & Rovine, 1990). Many spouses loved each other less, became more ambivalent about their relationship, argued more, and communicated less. This was true no matter what the sex of the child was and whether or not couples had a second child by the time the first was 3 years old. But when the researchers looked, not at the *overall* quality of the marriage, but at such *individual* measures as love, conflict, ambivalence, and effort put into the relationship, at least half of the sample showed either no change on a particular measure or a small positive change.

What distinguishes marriages that deteriorate after parenthood from those that improve? This study found no single determining factor. Rather, a number of different factors, related to both parents and child, seemed influential. In declining marriages, partners were more likely to be younger and less well educated, to earn less money, and to have been married fewer years. One or both partners tended to have low self-esteem, and husbands were likely to be less sensitive (Belsky & Rovine, 1990). Other research has found that the more the division of labor in a marriage changes from egalitarian to traditional, the more marital happiness declines, especially for nontraditional wives (Belsky, Lang, & Huston, 1986).

RELATIONSHIP WITH THE BABY

But what about the relationship with the baby? Is there a way to predict how parents will react? Some researchers have correlated the mother's attitudes during pregnancy with her bonds to the infant she bears and have found relationships.

In one study, 100 pregnant English women were interviewed using the Adult Attachment Interview (AAI), an 18-question, structured interview dealing with the women's attachment during childhood to their own parents or substitute caregivers (Fonagy, Steele, & Steele, 1991). Had they felt rejected? Been upset, ill, or hurt? Suffered loss or abuse? How did they explain their parents' behavior? What was their current relationship with their parents? How influential did they consider their childhood experiences to be on their current behavior and future parenting style?

When their babies were 1 year old, the babies' attachment to their mothers was tested in an experimental situation. In 75 percent of the cases, the researchers were able to use the AAI responses to predict the extent of a baby's attachment to the mother. This may mean that it might be possible to identify and help women at risk of fostering insecure attachments in their children.

Another study found a pregnant woman's level of anxiety related to her baby's security of attachment. Higher levels of maternal anxiety during pregnancy tended to lead to less secure attachment in their 1-year-olds (Del Carmen, Pedersen, Huffman, & Bryan, 1993). However, the babies' behavior at 3 months of age also affected attachment patterns. Babies who fussed and cried a lot gained their mothers' attention, and when the mother was able to soothe her baby, the attachment between them became more secure.

Two surprising findings emerged from the Belsky and Rovine (1990) study: Couples who were most romantic prebaby had more problems postbaby, maybe because of unrealistic expectations. And women who had planned their pregnancies were unhappier, possibly because they had expected life with baby to be better than it turned out to be. [This finding contradicts earlier research that found just the opposite—that when babies are planned and couples are prepared for raising them, marriages are *not* affected for the worse (H. Feldman, 1981).] The mothers who had the hardest time adjusting had babies with irregular temperaments who were harder to take care of. Again, we see how babies influence their environments right from infancy.

Are adoptive parents' experiences different from biological parents? Researchers in Israel looked at 104 couples before they became parents, and then again when their babies—half adopted, half biological offspring—were 4 months old (Levy-Shiff, Goldschmidt, & Har-Even, 1991). The adoptive parents reported more positive expectations and more satisfying parenting experiences than did the others. The adoptive parents, who tended to be older and married longer, may have been more mature and resourceful. Or they may have appreciated parenthood more when it finally came. Or they may have been denying any difficulties, to reassure themselves that they were no different from biological parents.

So we see that many elements go into forming parent-child bonds and that the new baby exerts a strong influence on his or her own life. In Chapter 4 we will take a close look at the first few weeks of this baby's life.

What do you think?   *During pregnancy, prospective parents usually have a number of emotional issues to resolve. Which concerns would be most likely to affect you?*
- *Accepting the idea that your child will be an individual with his or her own interests, which may not be compatible with your own*
- *Resolving your relationship with your own parents*
- *The effect your new baby will have on your marriage*

SUMMARY

1   Prenatal development occurs in three stages. The germinal stage (fertilization to 2 weeks) is characterized by rapid cell division and increased complexity of the organism. The embryonic stage (2 to 8–12 weeks), which begins when the organism is fully implanted in the uterus, is marked by rapid growth and differentiation of major body systems and organs. The fetal stage (8–12 weeks to birth) begins with the appearance of the first bone cells and is characterized by rapid growth and change in body form. The average length of pregnancy, or gestation, is 266 days.

2   About one-third of all conceptions end in spontaneous abortion (miscarriage). Three out of four miscarriages occur in the first trimester of pregnancy. Chromosomal abnormalities are present in about 50 percent of spontaneous abortions.

3   There are individual differences among fetuses in activity level. Fetuses appear to be able to hear and learn.

4   The developing organism can be greatly affected by its prenatal environment. Some environmental factors, called teratogenic factors, produce birth defects.

5   Important prenatal influences include the mother's nutrition, the mother's intake of drugs (including caffeine, nicotine, and alcohol as well as illicit drugs), illness of the mother, incompatibility of blood type between mother and fetus, and factors in the external environment. Paternal factors have also been related to birth defects in offspring. Despite these risk factors, normal fetal development is the rule.

6   Good prenatal and postnatal maternal care is essential for healthy development.

7   An important ethical debate today considers the conflict between a fetus's right to be born healthy and a mother's right to privacy and bodily autonomy.

8   About 15 percent of couples who want to have a baby are infertile (unable to conceive after 12 to 18 months of trying). Artificial insemination, in vitro fertilization, ovum trans-

fer, and surrogate motherhood represent new ways for infertile couples to attain parenthood. Adoption is the oldest solution to infertility and also provides a home for a child who otherwise would not have one.

9 The transition to parenthood affects the marital relationship. A woman's attitude during pregnancy is related to the quality of her relationship with her baby.

KEY TERMS

gestation (104)
germinal stage (104)
embryo (107)
embryonic stage (107)
critical period (107)
spontaneous abortion (107)
fetus (108)
fetal stage (108)

teratogenic (110)
fetal alcohol syndrome (FAS) (114)
Rh factor (119)
infertility (125)
artificial insemination (126)
in vitro fertilization (IVF) (126)
ovum transfer (127)
surrogate motherhood (127)

SUGGESTED READINGS

Brodzinsky, D. M., Schechter, M. D., & Henig, R. M. (1992). *Being adopted: The lifelong search for self.* New York: Doubleday. This book by a psychologist, a psychiatrist, and a medical writer is written from a developmental perspective. It discusses the impact of adoption on the adoptee from infancy through old age.

Dorris, M. (1990). *The broken cord.* New York: HarperCollins. A moving account of the struggles of a Native American child with fetal alcohol syndrome, written by his adoptive father.

Eisenberg, A., Murkoff, H. E., & Hathaway, S. E. (1991). *What to expect when you're expecting* (rev. 2d ed.). New York: Workman. An excellent, comprehensive description of pregnancy, month to month, that incorporates research on care for both mother and baby.

Nilsson, L., Ingelman-Sundberg, A., & Wirsen, C. (1990). *A child is born* (2d ed.). New York: Delacorte. A completely new edition of this classic depiction of fetal development. The material about the parents' experience of pregnancy has been updated but the beautiful photographs of the developing fetus are unchanged.

Reuben, C. (1992). *The healthy baby book.* New York: Tarcher-Perigee. This guide to preventing birth defects includes specific "what to do" guidelines for before, during, and after pregnancy. Examines the effects of diet, medications, infectious diseases, environmental hazards, among others.

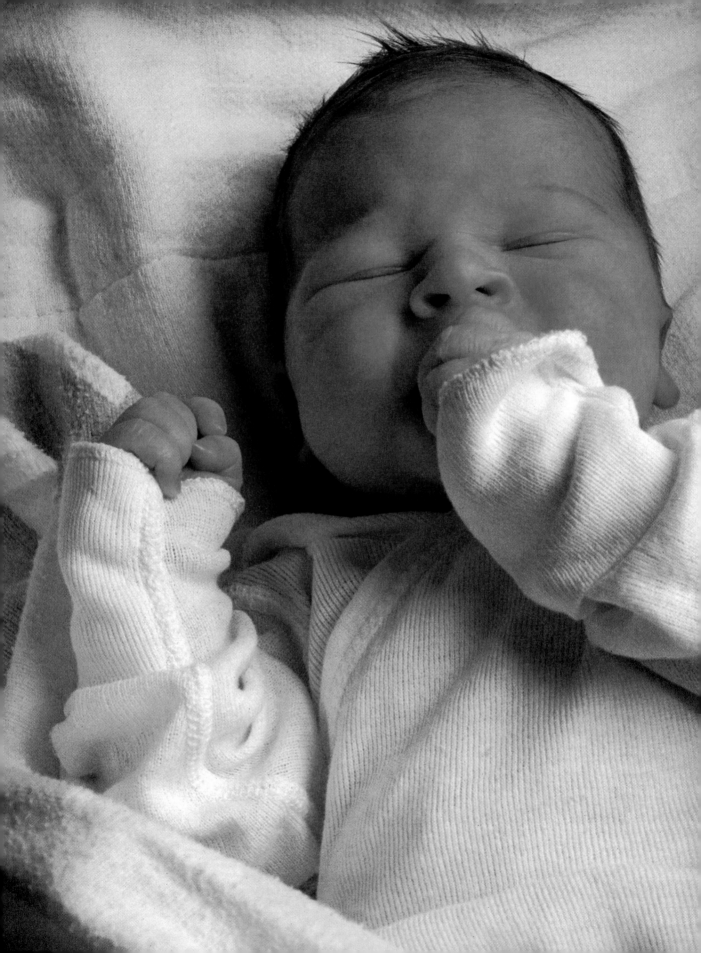

CHAPTER 4
BIRTH AND THE NEWBORN BABY

The experiences of the first three years of life are almost entirely lost to us, and when we attempt to enter into a small child's world, we come as foreigners who have forgotten the landscape and no longer speak the native tongue.

Selma Fraiberg, *The Magic Years,* 1959

Now we explore how babies come into the world—the phases, methods, joys, and complications of birth. We'll look at what newborn babies are like and how to assess their status. We'll describe the body systems that are vital for babies' independent survival after they are no longer attached to the mother through the umbilical cord. We'll also characterize the *states of arousal* of infants (their sleepwake cycles) and the meaning of these states in everyday life. Finally we introduce the neonate's first relationship with another human being, the mother. After reading this chapter, you should be able to answer questions like the following:

PREVIEW QUESTIONS

♦ What happens during the three stages of childbirth, and how do different methods of childbirth affect the baby?

♦ How does the stress of childbirth affect babies?

♦ How do complications at birth affect babies, and what can be done to prevent and treat low birthweight?

♦ What can newborn infants do, and how can we tell whether they are developing normally?

♦ How can adults comfort crying babies?

Ellen woke up feeling new sensations in her uterus, heavy with child. The baby was not due for another 2 weeks, at the end of the normal full-term gestation of 266 days, but she believed that she was feeling birth contractions.

About every 10 or 15 minutes, she felt a mild tightening of her uterus, lasting for 15 to 25 seconds. These contractions were stronger and more regular than similar contractions she had occasionally felt over the past few months. As the intervals between them became shorter, the sensation intensified. They reminded her of the waves she had seen when a storm was building out at sea; they kept swelling, breaking faster and harder.

Some hours later, Vicky's cries announced her arrival in the outside world before her legs had fully emerged from Ellen's body. When the doctor held her up before Ellen and Charles, Vicky was already gazing about the room, looking at the flurry of activity and listening to a buzz of excited voices. The world was pouring into her senses, and, like a new immigrant in an unknown land, Vicky was taking it all in.

THE BIRTH PROCESS

After struggling through a difficult passage, the infant is faced with more than learning the language and customs of her newfound home. A baby has to start to breathe, eat, adapt to the climate, and respond to confusing surroundings. This is a mighty challenge for a being who weighs but a few pounds and whose organs and body systems are still not fully mature. Fortunately, infants are remarkably capable when they come into the world, with body systems and senses already working, however immaturely.

BIRTH AND BIOLOGY: THE PHASES OF CHILDBIRTH

> There is a lot else going on besides the pain in the belly. I felt my nose and teeth going numb, rather as from drinking too much wine. I also saw the colors in the kitchen getting brighter and stronger. I'm not into mystical things, or thinking about auras, but yes, labor is a kind of high if you flow with it, and a room full of loving people does produce energy . . . gives you strength (Rothman, 1992, p. 290).

Childbirth, or labor, takes place in three overlapping phases (see Figure 4-1), plus a fourth phase of recovery. The following description applies to the typical, normal, vaginal delivery. There are variations from this pattern, some of which are described in later sections.

The First Stage of Childbirth

The *first stage,* the longest, typically lasts 12 hours or more for a woman having her first child. There is a great deal of variability, however, and in later births, the first stage tends to be shorter. During this stage, uterine contractions cause the cervix to widen—a process called *dilation*—until it becomes large enough for the baby's head to pass through. At first, the contractions occur about every 8 to 10

FIGURE 4-1
Birth of a baby. (*a*) During the first stage of labor, a series of stronger and stronger contractions dilates the cervix, the opening to the mother's womb. (*b*) During the second stage, the baby's head moves down the birth canal and emerges from the vagina. (*c*) During the brief third stage, the placenta and umbilical cord are expelled from the womb. Then the cord is cut. SOURCE: Adapted from Lagercrantz & Slotkin, 1986.

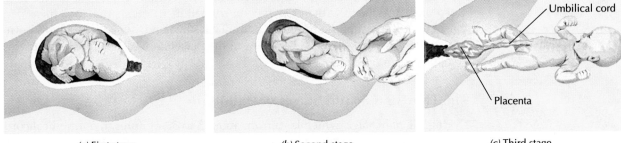

(*a*) First stage   (*b*) Second stage   (*c*) Third stage

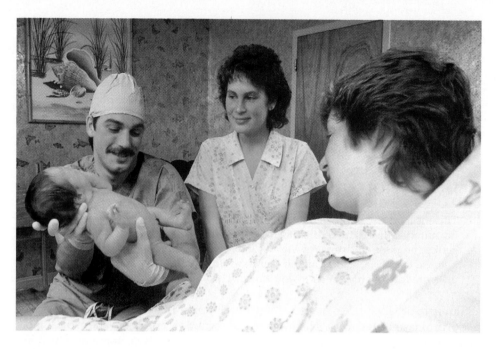

"Labor" is an apt term. Birth is hard work for both mother and baby—but work that yields a rich reward. The work will continue for years as the parents learn to care for their child and the child learns how to make a life in the world.

minutes and last about 30 seconds. Toward the end of labor, they may come every 2 minutes and last 60 to 90 seconds.

Much of the discomfort of labor is caused by the stretching of the lower part of the uterus, especially the cervix. Before the cervix can dilate enough to let the baby pass through, it needs to soften and thin out, through a process called *effacement*. Effacement and early dilation begin during the last weeks of pregnancy. If a woman's cervix dilates quickly during labor, she will feel little or no pain. But if her cervix is rigid and is forcibly dilated by the contractions of her uterus, the contractions will be painful.

The Second Stage of Childbirth

The *second stage* typically lasts about $1\frac{1}{2}$ hours or less. It begins when the baby's head begins to move through the cervix and the vaginal canal. It ends when the baby emerges completely from the mother's body. This is also known as the "pushing stage," since the mother feels the urge to push and can help the birth progress by bearing down hard with her abdominal muscles at each contraction. This helps the baby to leave her body. If this stage lasts longer than 2 hours, a doctor may grasp the baby's head with *forceps* (spoon-shaped instruments that look like salad tongs) to pull it out of the mother's body. This stage ends when the baby is born. It is still attached by the umbilical cord to the placenta, which is inside the mother's body.

The Third and Fourth Stages of Childbirth

During the *third stage,* which lasts from about 5 to 30 minutes, the umbilical cord and the placenta are expelled. The couple of hours after delivery constitute the *fourth stage,* when the mother rests in bed and her recovery from labor and delivery is checked. The birth attendant may massage the uterus to help it contract, will examine the vagina and cervix for any tears or excessive bleeding, and will check the mother's pulse, blood pressure, and breathing rate.

BIRTH AND SOCIETY: HELPING THE MOTHER AND BABY

The basic biology of childbirth, of course, does not change, but the ways that society helps mothers and babies are always shifting. These ways differ greatly from culture to culture and among subcultures in the same society. (See Box 4-1.)

Methods of Childbirth

Charles spent the night in the hospital with Ellen, was in the delivery room during Vicky's birth, and cut the umbilical cord. Both expectant parents had taken a 6-week course given by the hospital; if they had had other children, the "expectant siblings" could have taken a special course and could also have been in the delivery room during the birth. Ellen was happy to use the hospital's special birthing beds, which provided options for a number of different positions; to have her baby in her room with her; and to take a class in, and to get help with, breast-feeding immediately after birth.

Historically, the primary concern in delivering a baby has been to find a method that is comfortable for the mother and safe for both mother and baby. More recently, as safety has been assured in most births in developed countries, health workers have focused on making the experience more pleasant for the mother and the baby and on bringing the father and other family members into the process. Such efforts reflect a growing sensitivity to the emotional needs of all family members.

Medicated Delivery. Biblical scholars still debate whether God's injunction to Eve, "In travail shalt thou bring forth children," implied labor or sorrow. In any case, most societies have evolved ways to speed delivery, make the mother's work easier, and lessen her discomfort. General anesthesia, which renders the woman completely unconscious, is rarely used today. More common is regional (local) anesthesia, which blocks the nerve pathways that would carry the sensation of pain to the brain. Or the mother can receive a relaxing analgesic. All these drugs pass through the placenta to enter the fetal blood supply and tissues.

A number of studies indicate the dangers to the baby of obstetric medication. Children have shown the effects as early as the first day of life, in poorer motor and physiological responses (Murray, Dolby, Nation, & Thomas, 1981), and through the first year, in slower development in sitting, standing, and moving around (Brackbill & Broman, 1979). The babies born in medicated deliveries (Murray et al., 1981) had caught up by 1 month of age, but their mothers felt differently about them. Why?

First, many professionals believe that there is no such thing in human beings as a "maternal instinct." Much of a woman's motherly feeling comes about because of her baby's behavior. An infant who nurses eagerly and acts alert sets up positive feelings in the mother. If the first encounters between mother and baby do not draw a strong reaction from the baby, the mother's early impressions of her baby may remain. Second, it is possible that mothers who choose unmedicated deliveries may feel more positive about parenting and that their attitudes affect how they act with their babies.

BOX 4-1 ■ AROUND THE WORLD

HAVING A BABY IN THE HIMALAYAS

In 1993 and 1994, Sally Olds spent three weeks in Badel, a remote hill village in the small Asian country of Nepal. The following account from her journal describes a visit that she, the friend she traveled with, and their guide made to the village midwife.

Sabut Maya Mathani Rai has been helping childbearing mothers for almost 50 of her 75 years. Buddi, our guide, proudly tells us that she helped his mother at his birth 27 years ago, and then helped her again eleven years ago at the birth of Kiran, the child of his mother's twentieth pregnancy. Only three days ago she attended the birth of a baby girl. She is now training two other women in the village just as her own mother had taught her.

We ask Sabut Maya what she does when she attends a woman about to give birth. "First I feel on the outside of the woman's belly," she says. "I look to see where is the head and the other organs. I help the mother push down when her time comes."

"Do you use forceps or anything like that to help pull the baby out?" Marge asks.

She jerks her head up and sideways in the Nepali gesture that means no. "I don't have any instruments. I just use my hands. If the baby is upside down, I turn it from the outside."

Nepali hill women usually give birth right after—or in the middle of—working in house or fields. The delivery may occur inside or outside of the house, depending on when the woman goes into labor. Women usually give birth kneeling. This position allows the mother to use her strong thigh and abdominal muscles to push the baby out. If the mother has other children, they usually watch, no matter how small they are. But the husbands don't want to watch and the women don't want them there.

Most women are not attended by a midwife; they handle the delivery and dispose of the placenta and umbilical cord themselves. Buddi's mother gave birth on the path as she was walking back from working in the fields, and then asked for her husband's knife to cut the cord.

"If the baby is not coming fast, I use special medicine," the midwife says. "I put grasses on the mother's body and I massage her with oil from a special plant. I don't give the mother any herbs or anything like that to eat or drink, only hot water or tea. Sometimes someone in the family gives her liquor. I don't give her anything to bite down on for pain. She usually doesn't need anything like that. I'm just a helper. I don't have the medicines or the equipment that you have in your country."

Nor does the midwife make any cuts to widen the vagina; although first-time mothers take longer to give birth, they never tear, Sabut Maya tells us. Apparently their ligaments are flexible. Since the women eat the typical low-fat, low-sugar Nepali diet, rich in minerals and grains, they gain little extra weight and have small babies.

In a complicated birth—if, say, the baby isn't emerging or the mother gets sick—the midwife calls the *shaman*, the only kind of intervention available in Badel. Inevitably, some babies die and some mothers die. I think of my own daughter whose baby, after 16 hours of labor, did not move into the vaginal canal, and I shudder, thinking what would have happened if they had not had access to an emergency cesarean delivery. In most cases, however, all goes well, and most deliveries are easy and quick.

How is the newborn cared for? "After the baby is born

However, some research suggests otherwise. Babies born to both medicated and nonmedicated mothers were compared on strength, tactile sensitivity, activity, irritability, and sleep. No evidence appeared of *any* drug effect (Kraemer, Korner, Anders, Jacklin, & Dimiceli, 1985). Poorly designed and misleading research may have kept appropriate drugs from some mothers, making them suffer unnecessary discomfort, while causing guilt in others who did take drugs.

Because the woman is the only person who can gauge her pain and is the most concerned about her child's well-being, she should be the one who decides about obstetric medication. The American Academy of Pediatrics Committee on Drugs (1978) recommends the minimum dose for relief of the mother's pain. Alternative methods of childbirth try to minimize the use of drugs while maximizing the parents' active involvement.

Natural and Prepared Childbirth. In 1914 a British physician, Dr. Grantly Dick-

I wash the baby. I leave this much of the cord on the baby [indicating about half an inch] and I tie it up with very good cotton. Then I wrap a piece of cotton cloth around the baby's tummy. This stays on for a few days until the cord falls off." Sometimes a small piece of the umbilical cord is saved and inserted into a metal bead that will be given to the child to wear on a string around the neck, to ward away evil spirits. A family member flings the placenta high up on a tree near the house to dry out; it eventually is thrown away.

No one but the mother—not even the father—is allowed to hold the baby at first. This may help to protect both mother and baby from infection and disease when they are both most vulnerable. Then, at three days of age for a girl, or seven days for a boy (girls are thought to mature earlier), a purification rite and naming ceremony takes place. The mother washes the clothes she has been wearing and cleans the place in the house where she stayed with her baby. Then, in the presence of both parents' families, who have brought chickens and beer to feast on later, the shaman conducts a rite to exorcise any evil spirits that may have attended the birth.

Marge and I tell how in our culture women lie on their backs, a position unknown in most traditional societies, and how the doctor sometimes breaks the woman's water. We also describe how a doctor sometimes puts on surgical gloves and reaches inside the women to turn a baby in a breech or other position. Looking at Sabut Maya's dirt-blackened hands and fingernails, I emphasize the use of gloves so that she won't take it into her head to try western techniques in an effort to be "modern." But I vastly un-

derestimated her good sense, and I am ashamed of myself when I see her shake her head and hear the translation of her response: "We don't have gloves and we don't have instruments. We don't do any of those things." She repeats, "I'm just a helper." What Sabut Maya really is is a doula (see page 145). It seems ironic that it has taken the western world so long to rediscover some of the wisdom that so-called "primitive" societies have known for centuries.

So yes, in developed countries, women and babies involved in complicated childbirths are better off. But for the great majority of births, it seems that women do better in Badel than they do in the United States. Their bodies are strong, their babies are small, their support system is known and their accomplishment is hailed.

Findings that recently emerged from a study in California bear out these observations in Nepal. In the California group, recently arrived women from Mexico and Southeast Asia had better pregnancy results than native-born American women, despite the newcomers' often extreme poverty. This may be because the immigrant women gained less weight, had healthier diets, used less alcohol and drugs, and had more social support (Rumbaut & Weeks, 1994).

What do you think   *What can we learn from ancient wisdom to help our own childbearing women—without giving up the advanced medical techniques that save lives? And what can we do to bring the best of what we have to save the lives of women around the world, without invalidating those practices that serve them well?*

SOURCE: © Sally Wendkos Olds, 1995

Read, claimed that pain in childbirth was not inevitable but was caused largely by fear. To eliminate fear, he developed the concept of *natural childbirth*. This involves educating women in the physiology of reproduction and delivery and training them in breathing, relaxation, and physical fitness. By midcentury, Dr. Fernand Lamaze was using the psychoprophylactic, or *prepared childbirth*, method of obstetrics. This technique substituted new breathing and muscular responses to the sensations of uterine contractions for the old responses of fear and pain.

The Lamaze method of prepared childbirth has become very popular in the United States. It entails learning about the anatomy and physiology involved in childbirth to reduce fear, training in such techniques as rapid breathing and panting to ease pain, and focusing on sensations other than the birth contractions.

Charles served as Ellen's labor "coach" to help her relax. (Friends or mothers often assume this role.) His voice became a conditioned stimulus, helping Ellen to alternately relax and tense her muscles. His attendance at classes with Ellen,

In classes for expectant parents, mothers learn breathing and muscular exercises to make labor easier, and fathers learn how to assist through labor and delivery.

his help in her exercises, and his participation in the delivery increased Ellen's sense of worth and reduced her fear of loneliness (Wideman & Singer, 1984).

cesarean delivery

Surgical procedure to remove the baby from the uterus.

Cesarean Delivery. *Cesarean delivery* is a surgical procedure to remove the baby from the uterus. Almost one in four babies are delivered in this way in the United States (nearly 1 million a year), an increase from 5.5 percent in 1970 to 23.5 percent in 1991 (Centers for Disease Control and Prevention, 1993; Stafford, 1990).

The operation is commonly performed when labor does not progress as quickly as it should, the baby seems to be in trouble, or the mother is bleeding vaginally. Often a cesarean is needed when the baby is in the breech position (feet first) or in the transverse position (lying crosswise in the uterus), or when the baby's head is too big to pass through the mother's pelvis. Surgical deliveries are more likely when the birth involves a first baby, a large baby, or an older mother. The increase in cesarean rates is partly a reflection of an increase in these situations since 1970 (Parrish, Holt, Easterling, Connell, & LoGerfo, 1994).

Cesarean deliveries have a superior safety record in delivering breech babies (Sachs et al., 1983). But there is little evidence that they improve the overall survival of very low birthweight infants (Malloy, Rhoads, Schramm, & Land, 1989). In a comparison of 21 countries, no association was found between national cesarean rates and birth outcomes (Notzon, 1990).

Disadvantages of cesarean deliveries include a higher risk of maternal infection than in vaginal deliveries, a longer hospital stay and recovery from childbirth, greater expense, and the psychological and physical impacts of surgery (Sachs et al., 1983). Also, the benefits need to be weighed against the risks. One risk is depriving the infant of the experience of labor. (See Box 4-2.)

Critics of current childbirth practices claim that many cesareans are unnecessary, especially in the United States, where cesarean birth rates are among the highest in the world. (See Figure 4-2.) Perhaps in response to such criticism, the rate of increase has slowed since 1980 (Notzon, 1990).

Studies have linked cesarean births with several nonmedical factors. Women with median family incomes of over $30,000 a year have cesarean deliveries at nearly twice the rate as women with median incomes under $11,000 (Gould, Davey, & Stafford, 1989). Research supports the association between cesarean delivery and the physician's opinion that she or he may be sued for malpractice (Localio et al., 1993).

A California study of more than 45,000 births to women who had had a previous cesarean delivery found that future babies were more likely to be delivered vaginally if the women had private medical insurance, and if they went to a nonprofit teaching hospital with a high volume of births rather than a proprietary, nonteaching hospital with fewer births (Stafford, 1990). Two reports warn against the increasingly common practice of vaginal delivery in subsequent births after an initial cesarean delivery. Although most such births go well, there is some risk

FIGURE 4-2

Cesarean delivery rates per 100 hospital deliveries in selected countries, 1985 (or most recent year for which data were available). Asterisks denote incomplete information.
SOURCE: Notzon, 1990, p. 3287.

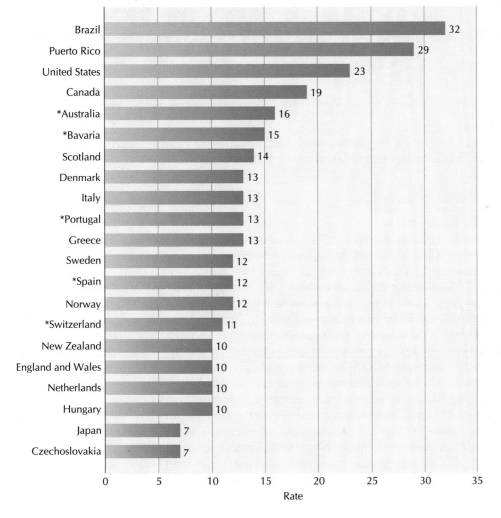

BOX 4-2 ■ FOOD FOR THOUGHT

THE STRESS OF BEING BORN

Life presents all of us with many stresses, starting very early—possibly within the womb and certainly during the struggle of a typical birth. First, the head is squeezed and subjected to pressure as the baby pushes through the narrow birth canal. Then, as contractions of the uterus compress the placenta and umbilical cord, they cause more pressure on the head, plus intermittent oxygen deprivation. Last, the newborn baby is forcibly expelled from the warm shelter of the womb to bright lights, loud noises, and unfamiliar handling.

Yet most babies come through this struggle very well. They are helped by the release of two stress hormones—adrenaline and noradrenaline. These stress hormones are secreted in extra quantities throughout life—in animals as well as human beings—in any dangerous situation, helping the threatened organism prepare for "fight or flight." They are also released early in prenatal life, and at birth their levels soar, to levels higher than in an adult having a heart attack. The first task of these hormones may be to help the fetus make the transition to life outside the womb.

How does this happen? The surge of these hormones at birth clears the lungs of excess liquid and produces a substance that keeps the lungs open and makes breathing possible. The hormones also mobilize fuel to nourish cells and supply blood to the heart and brain. All this activity helps the baby to survive such hardships as lack of food or low levels of oxygen in the first hours of life. Furthermore, by making the baby alert and ready to interact with another person, these hormones may even promote the mother-infant bond.

Babies born by emergency cesarean surgery, after the onset of labor, show levels of the stress hormones that are almost as high as vaginally born infants. But babies born through elective cesarean deliveries *before labor has begun* do not experience this surge of hormones, which seems to be triggered by contractions of the mother's uterus. Many of these babies have trouble breathing, possibly because smaller amounts of stress hormones are released during birth. These findings support concerns about the overuse of elective cesareans, which may be bringing many babies into the world at a disadvantage.

SOURCE: Lagercrantz & Slotkin, 1986.

(1 in 100, according to one study) of rupturing the uterus, with potential injury to the baby (R. O. Jones et al., 1991; J. R. Scott, 1991).

Medical Monitoring

electronic fetal monitoring
Use of machines that track the baby's heartbeat during labor and delivery.

Electronic fetal monitoring is the use of machines that track the baby's heartbeat during labor and delivery. This provides valuable information (especially in detecting a lack of oxygen) in high-risk deliveries, including those of low-birthweight babies and fetuses who seem to be in distress.

But monitoring has drawbacks. It has a high "false-positive" rate—monitors suggesting that babies are in trouble when they are not. For example, the normal release of hormones sometimes causes an irregular heartbeat in the fetus, which is picked up by electronic fetal monitoring (Lagercrantz & Slotkin, 1986). Such false warnings may prompt doctors to deliver by the riskier cesarean method rather than vaginally. Further, research has shown that (1) monitored babies do not do any better, (2) monitoring has not lessened the incidence of cerebral palsy (a disorder of the central nervous system, sometimes occurring as the result of birth trauma), and (3) advances in infants' survival are generally attributed not to monitoring but to better neonatal care (Levano et al., 1986; Lewin, 1988). Also, many women find monitoring uncomfortable since the equipment makes moving around during labor more difficult. Finally, the technology is costly—in terms of the machines themselves and the more expensive cesarean deliveries they often lead to.

Why, then, are monitors used so much? One reason is that they replace the nurses who would otherwise have to check on babies periodically—and we are suffering from a nationwide nursing shortage. Also, in an age when doctors are often sued for not having done everything possible to deliver a healthy baby, the use of a monitor often seems prudent. So although current recommendations are *against* routine fetal monitoring (E. A. Friedman, 1986; Levano et al., 1986), it is likely to persist.

Alternative Settings for Giving Birth

Ellen, giving birth for the first time in her mid-thirties, wanted as much medical and technological support as she could muster. Like 99 percent of women in the United States (Wegman, 1993), she had her baby in a hospital where she was assisted by an *obstetrician,* a physician who specializes in delivering babies.

Julia, on the other hand, felt that a hospital would be too big and impersonal. She joined a small but growing number of women with a good medical history and an uncomplicated pregnancy who give birth at home; in small, homelike birth centers; or in larger maternity centers. Like many of these women, Julia was attended by a certified *midwife,* someone who holds a degree in nursing and has been specially trained to assist at births. The vast majority of American women are still attended by medical doctors (91.4 percent), although the number of midwife-assisted births (4.1 percent) has risen by almost 400 percent over the past twenty years (Wegman, 1989, 1993).

Julia was also attended by a *doula,* a woman who gives both emotional and practical support to a childbearing mother. In a study of 412 women having their first babies, 212 had a doula with them (Kennell, Klaus, McGrath, Robertson, & Hinckley, 1991). The doula-present group had fewer cesarean deliveries, less use of anesthesia, shorter labors, and fewer forceps deliveries. Such positive benefits of the emotional support from a female companion argue for such a person as part of the childbirth support team.

Still, in the United States, childbirth is seen mostly as a medical event that occurs in a hospital under the supervision of a physician. In other countries, like the Netherlands, pregnancy and labor are considered normal events that require medical intervention only when there is a specific reason. About 35 percent of Dutch babies are born at home, and about 43 percent of deliveries are attended by midwives (Treffers, Eskes, Kleiverda, & van Alten, 1990). Most of these births are to women at low risk, and their outcomes compare favorably with hospital births attended by obstetricians.

Low-risk pregnancies and uncomplicated births can work well within any arrangement. But since there may be a sudden emergency during any childbirth, it is vital to have backup plans. A good birth center will have a contract with an ambulance service, an agreement with a local hospital, and on premises emergency equipment for resuscitation and administration of oxygen. Plans for a home birth should include arrangements for emergency transportation to a nearby hospital.

Many hospitals *are* big and impersonal, with rigid rules that seem designed more for the smooth functioning of the institution than for the benefit of patients. In recent years, however, as hospitals have competed more for maternity cases, they have become more responsive to patients' desires. Many have birth centers, where fathers or other birth coaches may remain with the mother during labor

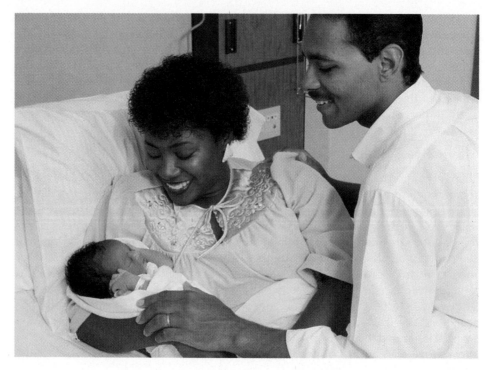

Parents in the delivery room with a newborn usually feel excited, proud, and relieved. A fast, easy delivery is more important than the amount of pain the mother feels in making the memory of birth a happy one.

and delivery, and rooming-in policies that let babies stay in the mother's room for much or all of the day. Maternity centers and birth centers are usually staffed mainly by midwives, with one or more doctors and nurse-assistants. They are designed for low-risk, uncomplicated births and offer prenatal care, birth in a home-like setting, and discharge the same day.

What are the psychological implications of the new ways of giving birth? First, techniques that minimize drugs may give the baby a better start in life. Second, the active participation of both parents reinforces close family attachments. And third, women's insistence on assuming a major role in childbirth has contributed to the growing belief that people should take more responsibility for their own health rather than sit back passively and rely on doctors. In view of what is known about the importance of feeling in control of one's life, the availability of alternative means of childbirth seems like a healthy trend. The crucial element is *choice*.

PARENTS' REACTIONS TO CHILDBIRTH

Exultation, relief, pride, wonder—all are typical reactions to the birth of a child. Also typical, however, are pain and anxiety. What variables in the birth process are most likely to make it a happy or an unhappy memory for the mother? Speed and ease of delivery seem more important than relief of pain. Women whose babies are born after a long labor and by use of forceps are most likely to be dissatisfied with a vaginal birth, and women who have an emergency cesarean delivery tend to be more dissatisfied than those who have their babies by elective cesarean or vaginal delivery.

Not much research has been done into men's experience of childbirth, even though a father's participation has proved especially popular. In 1945, one small hospital in Texas began allowing fathers into the delivery room. By 1983, 99 percent of hospitals surveyed allowed fathers in (May & Perrin, 1985; Wideman & Singer, 1984). Fathers who are present at the birth of a child often see the event as a "peak emotional experience" (May & Perrin, 1985), but attendance at the birth does not necessarily make a man a better father. Fathers typically become emotionally committed to their newborn babies, whether or not they were at the birth (Palkovitz, 1985).

COMPLICATIONS OF CHILDBIRTH

While the great majority of births result in normal, healthy babies, a small minority of babies are born very small, remain in the womb too long, or suffer birth trauma or other complications. Fortunately, the resiliency of the human spirit, combined with medical and psychological progress, enables many children to overcome a poor start in life.

The most effective way to reduce the number of low-birthweight babies is widespread prenatal care, which includes checkups, like the one this woman is having, to follow the fetus's development.

Low Birthweight

In 1992, 7.1 percent of all babies born in the United States were of *low birthweight*—they weighed less than 2500 grams (5½ pounds) at birth. Very low birthweight babies weigh less than 1500 grams (3⅓ pounds); in 1992 they accounted for 1.3 percent of births in the United States, a slight increase over previous years (Wegman, 1994). Low birthweight is associated with more than 60 percent of deaths in the first year of life (MMWR, 1993).

Some low-birthweight babies are born early. Babies born before full-term gestation are called *preterm* (premature) *infants,* and they may or may not be the appropriate size for their gestational age. Others are *small-for-date infants.* They weigh less than 90 percent of all babies of the same gestational age because they experienced delayed fetal growth, probably because of inadequate prenatal nutrition. They may or may not be preterm.

low birthweight
Substandard weight at birth—below 2500 grams (5½ pounds).

preterm infants *Infants born early, that is, prematurely, before the gestation period is complete.*

small-for-date infants
Infants weighing less than 90 percent of all babies of the same gestational age.

Who Is Likely to Have a Low-Birthweight Baby? A number of factors are correlated with low birthweight (S. S. Brown, 1985; see Table 4-1). These include:

- *Demographic factors,* like race, age, education, and marital status
- *Medical factors predating the pregnancy,* like previous abortions, stillbirths, or medical conditions
- *Medical factors associated with the current pregnancy,* like vaginal bleeding or too little weight gain
- *Prenatal behavioral and environmental factors,* like poor nutrition, inadequate prenatal care, smoking, use of alcohol and drugs, and exposure to toxic substances

Many of these factors are interrelated. Teenagers' higher risk probably stems more from poor nutrition and inadequate prenatal care than from age. Socioeconomic status cuts across almost all risk factors. Poor women who smoke are more likely to have low-birthweight babies than affluent women who smoke, probably because factors like poor nutrition and poor prenatal care compound the effects of smoking.

Even before pregnancy, women can cut down their chances of having a low-

TABLE 4-1

PRINCIPAL MATERNAL RISK FACTORS FOR DELIVERING UNDERWEIGHT INFANTS	
FACTORS	**CORRELATIONAL RISKS**
Demographic and socioeconomic conditions	Age (under 17 or over 34) Race (black) Poverty Unmarried Low level of education
Conditions predating current pregnancy	No children or more than four Low weight for height Genital or urinary abnormalities or past surgery Diseases such as diabetes or chronic hypertension Lack of immunity to certain infections, such as rubella Poor obstetric history, including previous low-birthweight infant and multiple miscarriages Genetic factors in the mother (such as low weight at her own birth)
Conditions of current pregnancy	Multiple pregnancy (twins or more) Poor weight gain (less than 14 pounds) Less than 6 months since previous pregnancy Low blood pressure Hypertension or toxemia Certain infections, such as rubella and urinary infections Vaginal bleeding in the first or second trimester Placental problems Anemia or abnormal blood count Fetal abnormalities Incompetent cervix Spontaneous premature rupture of membranes
Lifestyle factors	Smoking Poor nutritional status Abuse of alcohol or other substances Exposure to DES or other toxins, including those in the workplace High altitude
Conditions involving health care	Absent or inadequate prenatal care Premature delivery by cesarean section or induced labor

SOURCE: Adapted from S. S. Brown, 1985.

birthweight baby—by eating well, not smoking or using drugs, drinking little or no alcohol, and getting good medical care. The most effective way to reduce the number of low-birthweight babies is widespread good prenatal care. Low birthweight can often be prevented, to the benefit of society.

Cross-Cultural Aspects of Low Birthweight. Although the United States is more successful than any other country in the world in *saving* low-birthweight babies, the rate of such births in the United States is higher than those in 30 other European, Asian, and Middle East nations. And the low-birthweight rates among black American babies are higher than rates in 73 countries, including a number of African, Asian, and South American nations (UNICEF, 1992).

The high rates for African American women (see Table 4-2) reflect greater poverty and a greater tendency to teenage pregnancy. But the data show that even college-educated black women are more likely than white women to bear low-birthweight babies (S. S. Brown, 1985; Schoendorf, Hogue, Kleinman, & Rowley, 1992). This may be due to poorer medical care, or it may stem from health problems that span generations. There is some evidence that a mother's birthweight and her early childhood environment may predict her children's birthweights. In any case, the high ratio of low-birthweight babies is the major factor in the high mortality rates of black babies. Asian American women are the least likely to bear low-birthweight babies, and Hispanic American mothers' rates for both premature birth and low birthweight seem to be close to the statistics for white births (Wegman, 1990).

Consequences of Low Birthweight. The most pressing fear for very small babies is that they will die in infancy. Because their immune systems are not fully developed, they are more vulnerable to infection. Their reflexes may not be mature enough to perform functions basic to survival, like sucking, and they may need to be fed intravenously (through the veins). Because they have less fat to insulate them and to generate heat, it is harder for them to stay warm. Respiratory distress syndrome (also called *hyaline membrane disease*) is common. Because many low-birthweight babies lack surfactant, an essential lung-coating substance that keeps the air sacs in the lungs from collapsing, they may breathe irregularly, or stop breathing and die. A new treatment giving surfactants to high-risk neonates, 1.3 to 2.85 pounds at birth, increased survival rates (Horbar et al., 1993).

In the past, even when low-birthweight babies survived the dangerous early days, they were left with disabling conditions. Now many survivors do fairly well. In an analysis of 80 studies published since 1979, only about a 6-point difference in IQ showed up between low-birthweight infants and children of normal birthweight—97.7 versus 103.78, both in the average range (Aylward, Pfeiffer, Wright,

TABLE 4-2

COMPARISON OF BLACK AND WHITE INFANTS

Black infants are more likely than white ones to die in the first year from Sudden Infant Death Syndrome, respiratory distress syndrome, infections, injuries, disorders related to short gestation and low birthweight, pneumonia and influenza, and as a result of maternal complications of pregnancy. Rates for deaths due to congenital abnormalities are virtually the same for black and white infants.

	LOW BIRTHWEIGHT (LESS THAN 5 POUNDS, OR 2500 GRAMS), % OF BIRTHS (1992)	VERY LOW BIRTHWEIGHT (LESS THAN 3.3 POUNDS, OR 1500 GRAMS), % OF BIRTHS (1992)	INFANT MORTALITY RATE, PER 1000 (1991)	DECLINE IN INFANT MORTALITY RATE, 1940–1991
Black	13.3	3.0	17.6	83.1%
White	5.8	1.0	7.3	75.9%

SOURCE: Wegman, 1994.

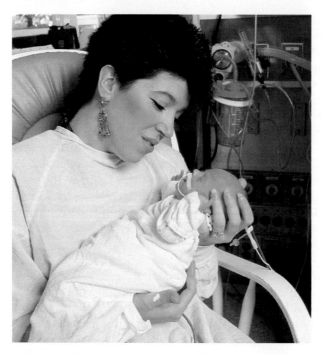

The tiniest babies thrive on human touch. This mother's holding and stroking of her low-birthweight baby girl will help establish a bond between mother and child, and will also help the baby grow and be more alert.

& Verhulst, 1989). However, this difference may not have made an actual difference in the children's lives.

Learning disabilities, which are more common in low-birthweight children, may not be picked up by IQ measures. Of 90 Canadian 5½-year-olds who had weighed less than 3.3 pounds at birth, about half seemed to be at mild to moderate risk of future learning disabilities (Saigal, Szatmari, Rosenbaum, Campbell, & King, 1990). In another study, about one-half of a sample of eighty-eight 7-year-olds who had weighed less than 3.3 pounds at birth needed special education, compared with 15 percent of a normal-weight, full-term control group (Ross, Lippe, & Auld, 1991).

More *extremely* low birthweight babies are surviving today. In a group of 128 infants weighing less than 1.76 pounds (800 grams) born from 1983 to 1985, 36 percent survived, compared with only 20 percent of such babies born from 1977 to 1980 at the same hospital (E. L. Hoffman & Bennett, 1990). However, babies born after only 23 weeks of gestation are at high risk for skull abnormalities and other disorders (Allen, Donohue, & Dusman, 1993).

What do you think? *Given the poor prognosis for babies born between 22 and 25 weeks of gestation, should they be resuscitated aggressively at birth? Or is this a poor use of limited health care resources? How should such decisions be made? Who should make them—parents or health care providers? What criteria are important: gestational age, birthweight, parents' desires and fertility history, findings on ultrasound, or all of these?*

Treatment of Low-Birthweight Babies.   Much of the increase in neonatal survival is due to improved care. Newborn anemia is treated with iron supplements, low blood sugar with intravenous feedings of glucose, and jaundice by medicine or putting the baby under fluorescent lights.

Most important, the low-birthweight baby is placed in an *isolette* (an antiseptic, temperature-controlled crib) and fed through tubes. To prevent the isolation and potential sensory impoverishment of life in an isolette, hospital workers and parents now handle these small babies. Gentle massage seems to foster growth, behavioral organization, weight gain, motor activity, and alertness (T. M. Field, 1986; Schanberg & Field, 1987).

Parents tend to view a low-birthweight baby negatively and to be anxious about the baby's health. Afraid the baby may die, they may be afraid of becoming too attached, so they often feel less comfortable and touch the infant less (Stern & Hildebrandt, 1986). Frequent visits can give parents a more realistic idea of how the baby is doing and help them become more attached. Regularly visited babies seem to recover faster and leave the hospital sooner (Levy-Shiff, Hoffman, Mogilner, Levinger, & Mogilner, 1990; Zeskind & Iacino, 1984).

The Impact of the Social Environment.   Whether low-birthweight children will develop problems later seems to depend on the interaction of several factors. One is the home they grow up in. Research suggests that children in higher socioeconomic circumstances are better able to overcome the early disadvantage of low birthweight (Aylward et al., 1989; McGauhey, Starfield, Alexander, & Ensminget, 1991; Ross, Lippe, & Auld, 1991).

For example, a study of very low birthweight Dutch children shows the impact of social factors on cognitive development. When the home environment was stimulating, even children at high risk (based on birthweight) were able to catch up on their cognitive delay; but in less stimulating homes, children at both high and low risk levels showed cognitive decline. This began to show up at age 2 (Weisglas-Kuperus, Baerts, Smrkovsky, & Sauer, 1993).

Reports from the Infant Health and Development Program (IHDP—1990) support these findings. Almost 1000 low-birthweight children in eight areas of the United States, most from poor, inner-city families, were measured on a number of criteria from birth to age 3. The parents of about half the babies received counseling and information about children's health and development and learned games and activities to play with their children. At 1 year, the babies entered an educational day care program. At 30 months of age children in the experimental group were more persistent, enthusiastic, and competent than a control group of low-birthweight children whose parents had not received counseling (Spiker, Ferguson, & Brooks-Gunn, 1993). At age 3, the experimental-group children were doing better on cognitive and social measures, were much less likely to show mental retardation, and showed fewer behavior problems, compared with the controls (Brooks-Gunn, Klebanov, Liaw, & Spiker, 1993).

Still, there were differences within the experimental group. Those who came from nonstimulating homes where they got little parental attention and care were more likely to be undersized and do poorly on cognitive tests at 3 years than were those from more favorable home environments (Kelleher et al., 1993). Those whose cognitive performance stayed high had mothers who scored high themselves on cognitive testing and who were responsive and stimulating to their children (Liaw & Brooks-Gunn, 1993). Babies who had more than one risk factor (like poorer neonatal health, not receiving the intervention, and having a less educated or less responsive mother) fared the worst. Of all factors, the home environment seemed most influential.

The IHDP studies make clear the need to study child development in an overall context, considering the strong interrelationship among many factors. The studies show how biological and environmental influences interact; they show the complex consequences of such influences in all aspects of development; and they show the impact of the environment, both before and after birth. They also show the resilience possible even among babies with problems at birth. Intervention early in life seems to help prevent downward trends in intelligence test scores over the first 3 years.

Postmaturity

As many as 7 percent of women have not gone into labor 2 weeks after their estimated due date. A baby is considered *postmature* 42 weeks after the start of the mother's last menstrual period. Postmaturity can last as long as 5 weeks. Postmature babies tend to be long and thin. They have kept growing in the womb but have had an insufficient blood supply toward the end of gestation. Possibly because the placenta has aged and become less efficient, it delivers less oxygen. The babies' greater size complicates labor: The mother has to deliver a baby the size of a normal 1-month-old.

Since postmature fetuses are at higher risk of brain damage or even death, doctors faced with a gestation of more than 42 weeks sometimes induce labor with drugs and sometimes perform cesarean deliveries. Each has risks. For example, if the due date has been miscalculated, a baby who is actually premature may be delivered. To help avoid this mistake, doctors monitor the baby's status with ultrasound. This lets them see whether the heart rate speeds up when the fetus moves; if not, the baby may be short of oxygen. Another test involves examining the volume of amniotic fluid; a low level may mean the baby is not getting enough food.

Birth Trauma

birth trauma *Injury sustained at the time of birth.*

anoxia *Oxygen deprivation at birth.*

Passage through the birth canal is a harrowing journey for a small number of babies (2.1 per 1000), who are injured in the process (Wegman, 1994). **Birth trauma** (injury sustained at the time of birth) may be caused by *anoxia* (oxygen deprivation at birth), neonatal diseases or infections, or mechanical injury. Some trauma leaves permanent brain damage, causing mental retardation or behavior problems.

The effects of birth injuries can often be counteracted by a favorable environment. In a longitudinal study of almost 900 children born on the island of Kauai, Hawaii, those whose births had been difficult, whose birthweight had been low, or who had been sick when born were examined at ages 10 and 18 and again in their early thirties. These children's later physical and psychological development was impaired *only* when they grew up in persistently poor environmental circumstances (E. E. Werner, 1985). Unless the early damage was so severe as to require institutionalization, when these children had a stable and enriching environment, they did well. In fact, they had fewer language, perceptual, emotional, and school problems than children who had not experienced unusual stress at birth but who had suffered "environmental trauma" in poor homes where they received little intellectual stimulation or emotional support (E. E. Werner, 1989; E. Werner et al., 1968).

We see, then, that, given a supportive environment, children—even those who suffered significant birth injuries—are remarkably resilient. Even very alarming one-time events can be less important than day-to-day experience.

Stillbirth

A stillbirth is a tragic union of opposites—birth and death. Sometimes fetal death is diagnosed prenatally; in other cases, the baby's death is discovered during labor or delivery. Fortunately, fewer than 1 in 100 infants are stillborn (DeFrain, Montens, Stork, & Stork 1986).

Parents of a stillborn baby should be encouraged to grieve for the baby they have lost. To feel the reality of their loss, they may benefit from seeing and holding the dead infant, obtaining an autopsy report, and having a funeral. Some parents try to "find" the lost child by immediately beginning another pregnancy, but this seems only to complicate their grief rather than help resolve it. First, they need to experience the intensity of their grief. The period up to 6 months to a year after the stillbirth is usually a time of depression, apathy, and self-devaluation. Then, possibly after receiving counseling and emotional support, the parents begin to resume their roles in society. They do not forget their stillborn child, and they may commemorate the anniversary, but they can now focus on life and the living (Kirkley-Best & Kellner, 1982).

THE NEWBORN

WHO IS THE NEWBORN?

The first 4 weeks of life mark the *neonatal period,* a time of transition from intrauterine life—when the fetus is supported entirely by its mother—to an independent existence. This transition generally takes longer for low-birthweight babies, who enter the world with less fully developed body systems.

An average newborn, or **neonate,** is about 20 inches long and weighs about $7\frac{1}{2}$ pounds. At birth, 95 percent of full-term babies weigh between $5\frac{1}{2}$ and 10 pounds and measure between 18 and 22 inches in length (Behrman & Vaughan, 1983). Birth size is related to race, sex, parents' size, and the mother's nutrition and health. Boys tend to be a little longer and heavier than girls, and a firstborn child is likely to weigh less at birth than later-born siblings.

neonate *Infant up to 1 month of age.*

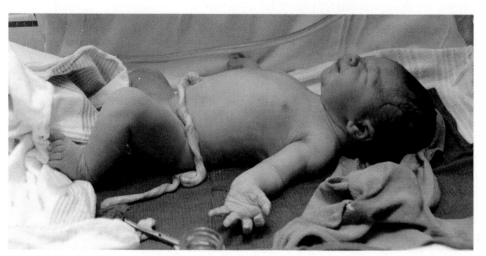

Annie, shown here only moments after her birth, is still attached to her umbilical cord. According to her weight and measurement, she was exactly average—but according to her parents, she is well above average in every other way!

FIGURE 4-3
People are drawn to animals with babyish features: big eyes, bulging foreheads, and retreating chins (as shown in row at left). Such features may be a biological adaptation that encourages survival, since animals with small eyes and long snouts (as shown in row at right) do not elicit the same kind of affection. SOURCE: Lorenz, 1971.

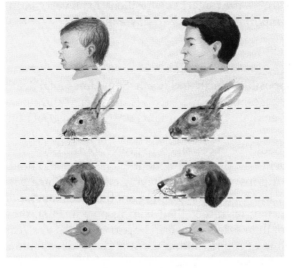

Babies have distinctive features—a large head, big eyes set low, fat cheeks, and a small nose and retreating chin (which make nursing easier). Some ethologists believe that such features, both in babies and in other animals, elicit affection in adults. (See Figure 4-3.)

In their first few days, neonates lose as much as 10 percent of their body weight, primarily because of a loss of fluids. On about the fifth day, babies begin to gain, and usually they are back to birthweight by the tenth to the fourteenth day. Light full-term infants lose less weight than heavy ones, and firstborns lose less than later-borns.

A newborn's head is one-fourth of total body length. It is long and misshapen because of the "molding" that eased its passage through the mother's pelvis. This temporary molding was possible because the infant's skull bones are not yet fused; they will not be completely joined for 18 months. The places on the head where the bones have not yet grown together—the soft spots, or fontanels—are covered by a tough membrane. The fontanels will close within the first month of life. Since the cartilage in a newborn's nose is also malleable, the trip through the birth canal leaves the nose looking squashed for a few days.

Many newborns have a pinkish cast because their skin is so thin that it barely covers the capillaries through which blood flows. Some neonates are very hairy, since all of the *lanugo*, the fuzzy prenatal body hair, has not yet dropped off; it will fall off in a few days. All new babies are covered with *vernix*, an oily protection against infection that dries over a few days' time.

In the Middle Ages, special healing powers were attributed to "witch's milk," a secretion that sometimes issues from the swollen breasts of newborn boys and girls. Like the blood-tinged vaginal discharge of some baby girls, this results from high levels of the hormone estrogen, secreted by the placenta just before birth.

HOW DOES THE NEWBORN FUNCTION?

Babies behave uniquely right from birth. Vicky sticks her tongue out repetitively; Jason makes rhythmic sucking movements. Some infant boys have frequent erections; others never do. Some babies smile often; others, rarely.

New babies differ in their activity levels, too, differences that may hold important clues about later functioning. In one study, children whose movements had been measured during the first days of life were assessed again at 4 and 8 years of age. Their patterns of activity showed continuity of development. The most vigorous newborns continued to be very active as 4- and 8-year-olds, while the least active infants were less active later (Korner et al., 1985). The basic functioning of the body systems, however, is quite similar for most normal babies.

The Newborn's Body Systems

The newborn's need to survive on its own puts a host of new demands on the body systems, all of which typically prove up to the task. Before birth, blood circulation, breathing, ingestion of nutrients, elimination of waste, and temperature regulation were all accomplished through the mother's body. After birth, babies must do all of this themselves. But most newborns do it so well that nobody even remarks on the feat. See Table 4-3 for a comparison of prenatal and postnatal life.

Circulatory System. Before birth, the fetus and mother have independent circulatory systems and separate heartbeats; but the fetus's blood is cleansed through the umbilical cord, which carries "used" blood to the placenta and returns clean blood. After birth, the infant's own system must take over to circulate blood through his or her body. A neonate's heartbeat is fast and irregular, and blood pressure does not stabilize until about the tenth day after birth.

Respiratory System. The umbilical cord also brings oxygen to the fetus and carries back carbon dioxide. A newborn needs much more oxygen and must now get it all alone. Most babies start to breathe as soon as they are exposed to the air. If breathing has not begun within about 5 minutes, the baby may suffer permanent brain injury caused by a lack of oxygen (*anoxia*).

Gastrointestinal System. In the uterus, the fetus also relies on the umbilical cord to bring food from the mother and to carry fetal body wastes away. At birth, new-

TABLE 4-3

A COMPARISON OF PRENATAL AND POSTNATAL LIFE		
CHARACTERISTIC	**PRENATAL LIFE**	**POSTNATAL LIFE**
Environment	Amniotic fluid	Air
Temperature	Relatively constant	Fluctuates with atmosphere
Stimulation	Minimal	All senses stimulated by various stimuli
Nutrition	Dependent on mother's blood	Dependent on external food and functioning of digestive system
Oxygen supply	Passed from maternal bloodstream via placenta	Passed from neonate's lungs to pulmonary blood vessels
Metabolic elimination	Passed into maternal bloodstream via placenta	Discharged by skin, kidneys, lungs, and gastrointestinal tract

SOURCE: Timiras, 1972, p. 174.

borns have a strong sucking reflex to take in milk and their own gastrointestinal secretions to digest it. During the first few days after birth, they secrete *meconium*, a stringy, greenish-black waste matter formed in the fetal intestinal tract. When their bowels and bladder are full, their sphincter muscles open automatically; the baby will not be able to control these muscles for many months.

Three or four days after birth, about half of all babies develop neonatal jaundice: Their skin and eyeballs look yellow. This kind of jaundice is caused by immaturity of the liver and occurs most often in low-birthweight babies; usually it is not serious and has no long-term effects. It is treated by putting the baby under fluorescent lights and by giving medicine. The medicine, which seems to prevent some of the consequences of jaundice, is particularly valuable for babies in poor families or in countries where special lights are not available (Valaes, Petmezaki, Henschke, Drummond, & Kappas, 1994).

Temperature Regulation.   The layers of fat that developed during the last couple of months of fetal life enable healthy full-term infants to keep their body temperature constant after birth, despite changes in air temperature. They also maintain body temperature by increasing their activity when air temperature drops. Because low-birthweight infants have less fat to insulate them and to generate heat, they are placed in temperature-controlled isolettes.

Medical and Behavioral Screening: Is the Baby Healthy?

Vicky and Jason are monitored after birth to see whether they have any problems requiring special care. Doctors and psychologists use such tools as the Apgar and Brazelton scales and screen for certain medical conditions.

Apgar scale   *A method of assessing the baby's health immediately after birth.*

Immediate Medical Assessment: Apgar scale.   At 1 minute after delivery—and then again 5 minutes later—most babies are assessed using the *Apgar scale.* (See Table 4-4.) Its name, after its developer, Dr. Virginia Apgar (1953), helps us remember its five subtests: *a*ppearance (color), *p*ulse (heart rate), *g*rimace (reflex irritability), *a*ctivity (muscle tone), and *r*espiration (breathing).

The infant is rated 0, 1, or 2 on each measure, for a maximum score of 10. Ninety percent of normal infants score 7 or better. A score below 7 means the baby

TABLE 4-4

APGAR SCALE			
SIGN*	0	1	2
Appearance (color)	Blue, pale	Body pink, extremities blue	Entirely pink
Pulse (heart rate)	Absent	Slow (below 100)	Rapid (over 100)
Grimace (reflex irritability)	No response	Grimace	Coughing, sneezing, crying
Activity (muscle tone)	Limp	Weak, inactive	Strong, active
Respiration (breathing)	Absent	Irregular, slow	Good, crying

*Each sign is rated in terms of absence or presence from 0 to 2; highest overall score is 10.
SOURCE: Adapted from V. Apgar, 1953.

needs help to establish breathing. A score below 4 means the baby needs immediate lifesaving treatment. If resuscitation is successful, bringing the baby's score to 4 or over, no long-term damage is likely to result. But scores from 0 to 3 at 10, 15, and 20 minutes after birth may signal the danger of cerebral palsy or other neurological (central nervous system) problems (American Academy of Pediatrics Committee on Fetus and Newborn, 1986).

A low Apgar score does not always mean that a baby is suffocating. An infant's tone and responsiveness may be affected by the amount of sedation or painkilling medication the mother received. Neurological and cardiorespiratory conditions may interfere with one or more vital signs. Premature infants may score low simply because of their physiological immaturity.

Recently there has been some criticism of the Apgar test: that it is not as sensitive as newer measures (one new test measures the oxygen in the newborn's blood) and that it has little predictive value, mostly because of sloppy administration. However, the Apgar test is quick, inexpensive, and easy to administer. Rather than abandon it, hospital workers should be taught to perform it better and to act quickly on the basis of its results.

Screening Newborns for Medical Conditions.   Children who inherit the enzyme disorder phenylketonuria (PKU) will become mentally retarded unless they are fed a special diet beginning in the first 3 to 6 weeks of life. Screening tests that can be administered immediately after birth can often discover such correctable defects.

The extent of neonatal screening is an important social policy issue. Routine screening of all newborns for such rare conditions as PKU (1 case in 14,000 births), hypothyroidism (1 in 4250), and galactosemia (1 in 62,000)—or other, even rarer disorders—is expensive. Yet the cost of testing thousands of newborns to detect one case of a rare disease is often less than the cost of caring for a mentally retarded person for a lifetime. For this reason, all states now require routine screening for PKU and congenital hypothyroidism; states vary on requirements for other screening tests (American Academy of Pediatrics Committee on Genetics, 1992; B. C. Williams & Miller, 1991).

However, there is a risk in doing these tests. They can generate false-positive results—suggesting that a problem exists when it does not. Such cases trigger anxiety, cost, and unnecessary treatment. Also, a healthy newborn mistakenly identified as ill may suffer a disruption of the parent-child relationship, which may affect the child's future psychological development.

What do you think?   *Which of the following guidelines, which have been suggested to minimize faulty screening (Clayton, 1992), seem most important and most feasible?*

■   *Ascertain that the benefits to affected children of early diagnosis are strong enough to outweigh the costs of testing and the costs of false-positive results in unaffected children.*
■   *Regularly evaluate all screening programs.*
■   *Inform parents of planned tests and let them decide whether they want them.*
■   *Give parents any information about genetic disorders that may affect future children.*

Assessing Responses: The Brazelton Scale.   The Brazelton Neonatal Behavioral Assessment Scale measures newborn babies' responses to their environment

(Brazelton, 1973). It assesses *interactive behaviors* like alertness and cuddliness; *motor behaviors* like reflexes, muscle tone, and hand-mouth activity; *control of physiological state,* like a baby's ability to quiet down after being upset; and *response to stress,* the startle reaction. The test takes about 30 minutes, and scores are based on a baby's best performance, rather than on an average. Testers try to get babies to do their best, sometimes repeating an item and sometimes asking the mother to alert her baby.

Infants' States of Arousal

states of arousal
Conditions of alertness in a baby; the sleep-wake cycle.

All babies are born with an internal "clock," which regulates their cycles of eating and sleeping, and perhaps even their moods. These cycles, which govern the various *states of arousal,* seem to be inborn. (See Table 4-5.) Although the different states are common to all neonates, their patterns differ from one baby to another. Vicky sleeps 20 hours a day, while Jason's pattern is at the other extreme—he sleeps only 11 hours. The average amount of sleep is 16 hours a day, but there is great variation (Parmelee, Wenner, & Schulz, 1964).

Although sleep dominates the neonatal period, the cliché "sleeping like a baby" is misleading. As every sleepy parent knows, neonates do *not* sleep for long periods. They wake up every 2 or 3 hours, alternating short stretches of sleep with shorter periods of consciousness. To the relief of parents, this pattern soon changes. At about 3 months, babies grow more wakeful in late afternoon and early evening, and they start to sleep through the night. By 6 months, more than half their sleep occurs at night.

Newborns have about six to eight sleep periods, which alternate between quiet and active sleep. Active sleep appears rhythmically in cycles of about 1 hour and accounts for 50 to 80 percent of a newborn's total sleep time. Active sleep is

TABLE 4-5

STATES OF AROUSAL IN INFANCY				
STATE	EYES	BREATHING	MOVEMENTS	RESPONSIVENESS
Regular sleep	Closed; no eye movement	Regular and slow	None, except for sudden, generalized startles	Cannot be aroused by mild stimuli.
Irregular sleep	Closed; occasional rapid eye movements	Irregular	Muscles twitch, but no major movements	Sounds or light bring smiles or grimaces in sleep.
Drowsiness	Open or closed	Irregular	Somewhat active	May smile, startle, suck, or have erections in response to stimuli.
Alert inactivity	Open	Even	Quiet; may move head, limbs, and trunk while looking around	An interesting environment (with people or things to watch) may initiate or maintain this state.
Waking activity and crying	Open	Irregular	Much activity	External stimuli (hunger, cold, pain, being restrained, or being put down) bring about more activity, perhaps starting with soft whimpering and gentle movements and turning into crying or kicking.

SOURCES: Adapted from information in Prechtl & Beintema, 1964; Wolff, 1969.

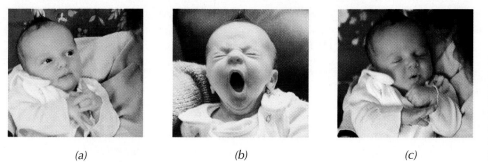

(a)   (b)   (c)

Life in infancy is one state after another, as Richard, according to his own internal "body clock," goes from alert interest to drowsiness, and then into the complete relaxation of sleep.

probably the equivalent of rapid eye movement (REM) sleep, which in adults is associated with dreaming. Over the first 6 months, the amount of this active sleep diminishes and accounts for only 30 percent of sleep time, and the length of the cycle becomes more consistent (Coons & Guilleminault, 1982). The amount of REM sleep continues to decrease steadily throughout life.

As babies become more awake, alert, and active, they develop according to their own unique patterns. These early patterns can have far-reaching effects, showing bidirectional influence. Parents, for example, respond very differently to a placid baby and an excitable one, to one they can quiet easily and one who is inconsolable, to a baby who is awake and alert, and to one who seems uninterested in people or places. The parents' attitudes and behaviors, in turn, influence the baby. Thus, children affect their own lives in basic ways.

Parents spend a great deal of time and energy trying to change their babies' states. Sometimes they try to ease a waking baby back to sleep; at other times, they want to feed an infant too sleepy to nurse. Mostly, they try to quiet a crying baby. While crying is usually more distressing than serious, it is particularly important to quiet low-birthweight babies, because quiet babies maintain their weight better. Steady stimulation is the time-proven way to soothe crying babies—letting them hear a rhythmic sound or suck on a pacifier, rocking them, walking them, or wrapping them snugly. (See Box 4-3.)

THE MOTHER-INFANT BOND

To find out how and when the special intimacy between mothers and their babies forms, some researchers have followed the *ethological approach* (introduced in Chapter 1). This approach considers behavior to be biologically determined and is concerned with what makes it evolve. As we explained, it relies on naturalistic observation, focuses on animals and birds, and emphasizes critical, or sensitive, periods for the development of behavior.

Imprinting

When, as described in Chapter 1, the ethologist Konrad Lorenz (1957) got newborn ducklings to follow him as they would the mother duck and to become attached to him, he demonstrated the behavior known as *imprinting*. The findings of Lorenz and other ethologists—that abnormal development or even death follows if rituals associated with the births of baby animals like ducks, sheep, and goats are prevented or interrupted—have raised questions for human babies.

imprinting *Rapid learning process early in life that establishes a behavior pattern.*

BOX 4-3 ■ THE EVERYDAY WORLD

COMFORTING A CRYING BABY

All babies cry. It is their only way to let us know they are hungry, uncomfortable, lonely, or unhappy. And since few sounds are as distressing as a baby's cry, parents usually rush to feed or pick up a crying infant. As babies quiet down and either fall asleep or gaze about in alert contentment, they may show that their problem has been solved.

At other times, the caregiver cannot figure out what the baby wants. The baby keeps crying. It is worth trying to find ways to help, because babies whose cries bring relief seem to become more self-confident, seeing that they can affect their own lives. By the end of the first year, babies whose cries have brought tender, soothing care cry less and communicate more in other ways, while babies of punitive or ignoring caregivers cry more (Ainsworth & Bell, 1977; Bell & Ainsworth, 1972).

Parents need not fear spoiling their babies by responding to their cries. Infants cannot be spoiled by being picked up and held; the holding itself may be what they are crying for. In Chapter 7 we discuss several kinds of crying and what the crying may mean—including whether it indicates illness.

For healthy babies who just seem unhappy, the following may help (Eiger & Olds, 1987):

♦ Hold the baby, maybe laying the baby on his or her stomach on your chest, to feel your heartbeat and breathing. Or sit with the baby in a comfortable rocking chair.

♦ Put the baby in a carrier next to your chest and walk around.

♦ If you are upset, ask someone else to hold the baby; infants sometimes sense and respond to their caregivers' moods.

♦ Pat or rub the baby's back, in case a bubble of air is causing discomfort.

♦ Wrap the baby snugly in a small blanket; some infants feel more secure when firmly swaddled from neck to toes, with arms held close to the sides.

♦ Make the baby warmer or cooler; put on or take off clothing or change the room temperature.

♦ Give the baby a massage or a warm bath.

♦ Sing or talk to the baby, or provide a continuous or rhythmic sound like music from the radio; a simulated heartbeat; or background noise from a whirring fan, vacuum cleaner, or another appliance.

♦ Take the baby out of the house—for a ride in a stroller or car seat—at any hour of the day or night. In bad weather, some parents walk around in an enclosed mall; the distraction helps them as well as the baby.

♦ If someone other than a parent is taking care of the baby, it sometimes helps if the caregiver puts on a robe or a sweater that the mother or father has recently worn so the baby can sense the familiar smell.

Is There a Critical Period for Forming the Bond between Infants and Their Mothers?

mother-infant bond

Feeling of close, caring connection between mother and newborn.

In 1976 two researchers said that if mother and newborn are separated during the first hours after birth, the *mother-infant bond*—the mother's feeling of close, caring connection with her newborn—may not develop normally (Klaus & Kennell, 1976). They reached this conclusion by comparing mothers and babies who had "extended contact" right after birth with mothers and babies who, following the usual hospital routine, were kept apart for long periods. They reported differences in bonding that persisted over the first few years of life.

This research inspired many hospitals to establish rooming-in policies that let mothers and babies remain together from birth throughout the hospital stay. Although such humane changes are welcome, follow-up research has not confirmed a critical time for bonding (Chess & Thomas, 1982; Lamb, 1982a, 1982b; Rutter, 1979b). While some mothers seemed to achieve closer bonding with their babies after early extended contact, no long-term effects were shown. In 1982 Klaus and Kennell modified their original position, and in 1983 the psychiatrist Stella Chess wrote, "By now the whole 'critical period concept' has been generally discredited in human development theory" (p. 975).

This finding has relieved the worry and guilt sometimes felt by adoptive parents and parents who had to be separated from their infants after birth. Concern with bonding is still a vital issue, however. Some developmentalists urge research on groups at risk of problems in bonding (such as poor, young, or single mothers and fathers) to find out what factors other than early contact affect parent-child bonds (Lamb et al., 1983).

Happily, the human organism is resilient, and many babies have overcome traumatic early experiences. As Chess concluded, "The emotionally traumatized child is not doomed, the parents' early mistakes are not irrevocable, and our preventive and therapeutic intervention can make a difference at all age-periods" (1983, p. 976).

Although, as neonates, Vicky and Jason sleep most of the time and utter no language but a cry, their families find them fascinating company. The gripping reflex of tiny fingers, the wide-eyed gaze, the innocent flat features, and the little well-formed bodies draw loving attention and admiration. By the end of the neonatal period, most babies have charmed an appreciative audience, which has raptly followed their remarkable development in all facets of life—physical, intellectual, and social.

SUMMARY

1   Normal full-term gestation covers 266 days from conception. The birth process occurs in three major stages: (1) dilation of the cervix, (2) descent and emergence of the baby, and (3) expulsion of the placenta and umbilical cord. The fourth stage is a period of recovery for the mother.

2   Whether obstetrical medication causes harm to the baby, and how much, is controversial. Some research suggests that physical effects of medication may persist through at least the first year of life, but critics question the methodology and conclusions of some of these studies.

3   Natural and prepared childbirth can offer both physical and psychological benefits.

4   By 1991, the rate of cesarean deliveries had risen to 23.5 percent in the United States. However, surgical (cesarean) delivery has not improved the survival rate for very low birthweight infants. In addition, the stress involved in the normal birth process seems to help the fetus make the transition to life outside the uterus.

5   Electronic fetal monitoring is the use of machines that monitor fetal heartbeat during labor and delivery.

6   Delivery at home or in birth centers is a feasible alternative for some women with normal low-risk pregnancies.

7   Prolonged labor, use of forceps, and cesarean (rather than vaginal) delivery are most likely to be associated with mothers' dissatisfaction with the birth experience. Most fathers become attached to their newborns, whether or not they attend the birth.

8   Approximately 7 percent of all American babies are of low birthweight, weighing less than 2500 grams ($5\frac{1}{2}$ pounds) at birth. These low-birthweight babies can be either preterm (premature) or small for date or both. Low birthweight is associated with infant mortality and sickness as well as learning disabilities. A supportive postnatal environment can often improve the outcome. A number of demographic factors, medical conditions (both preexisting and connected with the pregnancy), and lifestyle factors are associated with the likelihood of having a low-birthweight baby. The most effective way to reduce the number of low-birthweight babies is to provide widespread prenatal care, as is done in many western European countries.

9   Postmature babies are those born after a gestation of more than 42 weeks. They sometimes suffer from inadequate delivery of oxygen. Postmature fetuses are at a heightened risk of brain damage and death.

10 A small minority of babies suffer birth trauma, or injury sustained at the time of birth. This may result in mental retardation or behavior problems, although a supportive postnatal environment can often result in a more favorable outcome.

11 Stillbirth occurs in less than 1 percent of pregnancies. Grieving for the dead child helps parents deal with their loss.

12 The neonatal period, the first 4 weeks of life, is a time of transition from life inside the womb to life outside it.

13 At birth, the neonate's circulatory, respiratory, gastrointestinal, and temperature-regulation systems become independent of the mother's.

14 At 1 minute and again at 5 minutes after birth, the neonate is assessed medically using the Apgar scale, which measures five factors (appearance, pulse, grimace, activity, and respiration) that indicate how well the newborn is adjusting to extrauterine life. The newborn may also be screened for one or more medical conditions. The Brazelton Neonatal Behavioral Assessment Scale may be used to assess the way a newborn is responding to the environment and to predict future development.

15 Newborns alternate between states of sleep, wakefulness, and activity, with sleep taking up the major (but a diminishing) amount of their time. There is considerable individual difference in patterns, and a baby's patterns are clues to later functioning.

16 Researchers following the ethological approach have tried to determine it there is a critical period for the formation of the mother-infant bond. Their research seems to indicate that there is no such period.

KEY TERMS

cesarean delivery (142)
electronic fetal monitoring (144)
low birthweight (147)
preterm infants (147)
small-for-date infants (147)
birth trauma (152)
anoxia (152)

neonate (153)
Apgar scale (156)
states of arousal (158)
imprinting (159)
mother-infant bond (160)

SUGGESTED READINGS

Boston Women's Health Book Collective. (1992). *The new our bodies, ourselves.* New York: Simon & Schuster. Updated and expanded, this new edition of a book written by women discusses all aspects of women's health, with particularly strong sections on pregnancy, childbirth, and the postnatal period.

Friedman, R., & Gradstein, B. (1992). *Surviving pregnancy loss.* Boston: Little, Brown. This book provides guidance on dealing with a pregnancy loss, be it a miscarriage, stillbirth, or ectopic pregnancy, or a loss associated with a technology-assisted pregnancy. The personal accounts by women who have experienced pregnancy loss firsthand are especially moving.

Griswold, R. L. (1993). *Fatherhood in America: A History.* New York: Basic Books. A fascinating account of the changing roles of fathers over the years, focusing on the connections between masculinity, feminism, and American culture. Drawing on personal letters and diaries, as well as analyses of movies, magazines, and other cultural aspects, the author shows how the role of father as breadwinner has expanded and changed.

Jason, J., & van der Meer, A. (1989). *Parenting your premature baby.* New York: Dell. The senior author of this book, a pediatrician and herself the mother of a premature baby, covers what to expect in neonatal intensive care units, how to meet the baby's special needs, and the long-term outlook for premature infants. The book contains photos of healthy, normal-looking children who were once premature babies.

Kitzinger, S. (1988). *Your baby, your way—Making pregnancy decisions & birth plans.* New York: Pantheon. A book written by a childbirth educator that offers a step-by-step guide for making decisions concerning childbirth.

INFANCY AND TODDLERHOOD

The abilities of infants and toddlers have long been underestimated. Until recently, psychologists did relatively little research on the period from birth to age 3; although it was known to be a time when foundations are laid, the "bricks" seemed perhaps too ordinary to require study.

At 15 months, Jason walks along a sidewalk with his parents and accidentally kicks a can. When the can goes flying, Jason does a double take. Then he begins deliberately kicking the can along the sidewalk, delighted by his discovery of this new way to affect the world. This process of development from the total dependence of the newborn to the self-aware independence of the 3-year-old is the theme of Chapters 5, 6, and 7.

These chapters, like others throughout this book, consider three types of development: physical, cognitive, and personality. In reality, of course, development is never compartmentalized so neatly. Each of its aspects connects to the other aspects and supports their development. Jason's cognitive growth is a natural accompaniment of his physical and emotional growth; Vicky's emotional development is influenced by her mental development. We see children most clearly when we see how these factors combine in one child.

CHAPTER 5
PHYSICAL DEVELOPMENT AND HEALTH IN INFANCY AND TODDLERHOOD

There he lay upon his back
The yearling creature, warm and moist with life
To the bottom of his dimples,—to the ends
Of the lovely tumbled curls about his face.

Elizabeth Barrett Browning, *Aurora Leigh,* 1857

In this chapter, we talk about how babies develop physically—and how adults can foster healthy growth and development. We look at babies' and toddlers' sensory capacities and see that, at first, their perception does not match an adult's perception. Babies are also, of course, less adept at motor skills than adults, and they need to develop coordinated movement, a progression with important implications for all aspects of development. We also discuss two sober topics—infant mortality and sudden infant death syndrome—and one that promises to safeguard children's health—immunizations. After you have studied this chapter, you should be able to answer questions like the following:

PREVIEW QUESTIONS

- ◆ What principles govern physical development? How does the environment affect it?
- ◆ How does early brain growth affect development—and how does the environment affect brain growth?
- ◆ What are the primitive reflexes? What is their significance?
- ◆ How should babies be nourished?
- ◆ How do the senses function in infancy?
- ◆ What milestones in motor development mark the first 3 years?
- ◆ What social policies can enhance children's health and lower rates of infant mortality?

What is going on in Jason's home? Jess and Julia are checking every corner of their apartment—moving breakables to high places, covering electrical outlets, and jamming books so tightly into the shelf that even *they* can hardly pull one out—much less Jason. All this child-proofing is needed because of Jason's newest ability: crawling. This stage in his physical development affects the way he influences his environment and the way he reacts to it, intellectually and emotionally as well as physically.

Jason's physical growth and developing coordination are intertwined with his cognitive and social development throughout infancy and toddlerhood. We begin to examine this early development in this chapter and continue in Chapters 6 and 7 as we explore the first 3 years of life.

Infancy lasts for about the first year and a half; it ends when the child begins walking and stringing words together. Toddlerhood lasts from about 18 to 36 months of age. Toddlers become more and more verbal, independent, and able to move about in their world.

HOW PHYSICAL DEVELOPMENT TAKES PLACE

Vicky, like all normal babies, learns by doing. Her hand knows how to tug, how to lift, how to find her mouth—long before she can understand or say the names of the things she knows. When she does begin to speak, she "speaks" with her body as well as her mouth. "Up," she says and thrusts her dimpled arms up high. By touching a pretzel, by picking up a shoe, by playing with her toes, she learns about the world and about herself.

At first, Vicky does not differentiate herself from the world. With experience, she begins to tell her body apart from other things. She recognizes Charles's face and smiles in pleasure; she sees a strange man and stares at him unsmilingly, knowing he is unfamiliar. She learns that she can drop a toy but that her thumb is always there for sucking. She finds out, when she splashes water all over the bathroom and hurls sand at other children, that she can affect other objects and other people.

It is impossible to understand babies and toddlers without knowing about their physical development. This development depends on *maturation,* the unfolding of patterns of behavior in a biologically determined, age-related sequence. These changes are programmed by the genes. Before children can master new abilities, they must be biologically ready. Thus maturation is important for such motor skills as crawling, walking, carrying, and toilet training and for a host of other physical and cognitive abilities. Only after their muscles and legs are sturdy enough can children explore a room.

maturation *The unfolding of patterns of behavior in a biologically determined, age-related sequence.*

As Vicky becomes more mobile—crawling and then walking—people react differently to her, and she begins to hear warnings like "No, don't go there" and "Don't touch." She also receives loving help as her baby-sitter picks her up after a fall, comforts her, and encourages her to stand on her feet again. Physical changes are an integral part of an infant's and toddler's psychological development.

Normal physical development follows a predetermined sequence, even though the times when individual babies perform specific activities vary widely. It is important to remember that there is no "right" age when a child should reach a certain height or weight or should be performing specific activities. But even though the range of normal development is broad, almost all children progress in a definite order from certain activities to others. Even though Jason is able to sit up at 6 months of age and Vicky cannot do it until 11 months, both can hold up their chins before they can raise their chests, both sit with support before they sit alone, and both stand before they walk. Basically, children learn simple movements before they learn complicated ones.

TWO PRINCIPLES OF PHYSICAL DEVELOPMENT

Before Jason learns how to walk, he can do things with his hands. Before Vicky can use her hands skillfully, she can move her arms with purpose. These aspects of development illustrate two principles of physical development, both in growth and in motor development.

In accordance with the cephalocaudal principle, infants can use their hands adeptly before their legs are very useful, as this baby reaching for a toy demonstrates.

cephalocaudal principle
Principle that development proceeds in a "head-to-tail" direction: The upper body parts develop before the lower parts.

proximodistal principle
Principle that development proceeds in a near-to-far manner: The parts of the body near its center (spinal cord) develop before the extremities.

The *cephalocaudal principle* (from Latin and Greek, meaning "head to tail") dictates that development will proceed from the head to the lower parts of the body. An embryo's head, brain, and eyes develop before the lower parts and are disproportionately large until the other parts catch up. The head of a 2-month-old embryo is half the length of the entire body, and the head of a newborn infant is one-fourth the size of the rest of the body. The brain of a 1-year-old is 70 percent of its full adult weight; the rest of the body is only about 10 to 20 percent of adult weight. Furthermore, infants learn to use the upper parts of their bodies before the lower parts. Babies see objects before they can control their trunk, and they learn to do many things with their hands long before their legs are very useful.

According to the *proximodistal principle* (from Latin, "near to far"), development proceeds from the center of the body to the outer parts. The head and trunk of the embryo develop before the limbs, and the arms and legs before the fingers and toes. Babies first develop the ability to use their upper arms and upper legs (which are closest to the center), then the forearms and forelegs, then hands and feet, and finally, fingers and toes.

Both these principles govern development before and after birth.

PHYSICAL DEVELOPMENT OF THE TWO SEXES

Males are physically more vulnerable than females from conception throughout the life span. Baby boys are, on average, a bit bigger than baby girls. But aside from these two differences, infant boys and infant girls are very similar.

Although some research has found baby boys more active than baby girls (Maccoby & Jacklin, 1974), other studies have found the two sexes equally active during the first 2 years of life (Maccoby, 1980). Gender differences do not show up in sensitivity to touch, and very little difference appears in strength (although boys may be a little stronger). Further, girls and boys are more alike than different in reaching such maturational milestones as sitting up, walking, and teething. Gender differences are somewhat more pronounced in personality and social development. (See Chapter 7.) By the time small children of either sex can run, jump, and play with toys requiring fairly sophisticated coordination, they are very different from the neonates described in Chapter 4.

GROWTH

GROWTH OF THE BODY

Height and Weight

Children grow faster during the first 3 years than they ever will again. At 5 months, the average baby's birthweight has doubled to a weight of about 15 pounds; by 1 year, the birthweight has tripled to about 22 pounds. This rapid rate tapers off during the second year, when about 5 to 6 pounds are gained, so that birthweight is quadrupled by the second birthday. During the third year, the gain is somewhat less, about 4 to 5 pounds.

Height increases by about 10 to 12 inches during the first year (making the typical 1-year-old about 30 inches tall), by about 5 inches during the second year (so that the average 2-year-old is about 3 feet tall), and by about 3 to 4 inches during the third year. (See Figure 5-1.)

This growth may not be smooth and continuous. Rather, it seems to occur in spurts, often after long periods of no growth. In a provocative, small-scale study done on 31 white babies (3 days to 21 months old when first measured), the babies would stay the same size for 2 to 63 days. Then they would spring up as much as a full inch in less than 24 hours (Lampl, Veldhuis, & Johnson, 1992). If this finding is borne out by larger studies on wider populations, its implications will be significant. Instead of worrying when a child's growth seems to have halted, parents and physicians should give the child several months to catch up.

As a young child grows, body shape changes too. The rest of the body catches up with the head, which becomes proportionately smaller until full adult height

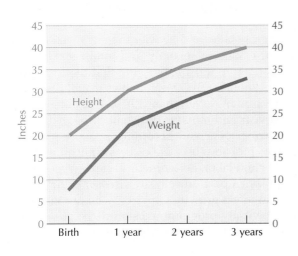

FIGURE 5-1
Growth in height and weight during infancy and toddlerhood. Growth in both height and weight is most rapid during the first few months of life and then tapers off somewhat by the third birthday.

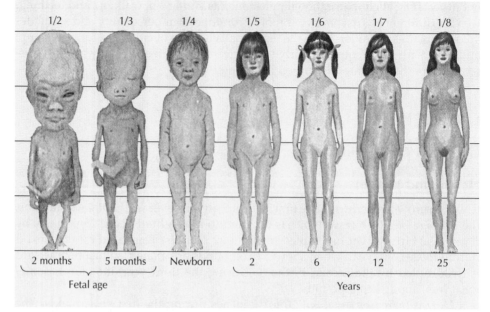

FIGURE 5-2
Changes in the proportions of the human body during growth. The most striking change is that the head becomes smaller in proportion to the rest of the body: The fractions indicate head size as a proportion of total body length at different ages. More subtle is the stability of the trunk proportions (from neck to crotch). Thus the increasing leg proportion is almost exactly the reverse of the decreasing head proportion.

is reached, as shown in Figure 5-2. Most children become leaner in the first 3 years; the 3-year-old is slender, compared with the chubby, potbellied 1-year-old.

Influences on Growth

Some differences show up between racial groups. For example, the bones of African American children harden earlier than those of white children, and the permanent teeth appear sooner. Also, black children mature earlier and tend to be larger than white children (American Academy of Pediatrics, AAP, 1973).

The genes that a child inherits have a great influence on body type—whether she or he will be tall or short, thin or stocky, or somewhere in between (Stunkard, Foch, & Hrubec, 1986; Stunkard, Harris, Pedersen, & McClearn, 1990). However, the environment also exerts a major influence on height and weight, through nutrition, living conditions, and general health. Again we see how hereditary and environmental factors interact.

Well-fed, well-cared-for children grow taller and heavier than less well nourished and nurtured children. They also mature sexually and attain maximum height earlier, and their teeth erupt sooner. In most babies, the first tooth erupts sometime between the ages of 5 and 9 months. By 1 year, babies usually have 6 to 8 teeth; by age $2\frac{1}{2}$, they have 20 (Behrman & Vaughan, 1983). The differences usually begin to show up by the first year and remain consistent throughout life (AAP, 1973). Today, children are growing taller and becoming sexually mature sooner than children of a century ago, probably because of better nutrition, improved sanitation, and the decrease in child labor. Better medical care—especially immunization and antibiotics—also plays a part, since heart disease, kidney disease, and some infectious illnesses can affect growth. Children who are ill for a long time may never achieve their genetically programmed stature, because they may never be able to make up for the growth time lost while they were sick.

GROWTH OF THE BRAIN

What makes newborns respond to the touch of a nipple? What tells them to start the sucking movements that allow them to control their intake of milk? These are functions of the *nervous system*, which consists of the brain, the spinal cord (a bundle of nerves running through the backbone), and a growing network of nerves, which eventually reaches every part of the body. Through this network, sensory messages travel to the brain and motor commands travel back. This complex communication system governs what a person can do both physically and mentally (Casaer, 1993; Kolb, 1989; W. M. Cowan, 1979; and Behrman, 1992).

The brain's normal growth before and after birth is fundamental to future development. The increases in brain weight and volume, both crucial markers of normal growth, are measured before birth by ultrasound and after birth by measuring the circumference of the baby's head. The timetable for brain development is important; measurement provides a valuable way to check for normal progress.

Development of the Nervous System

The greatest growth of cell bodies in the central nervous system occurs between 25 and 40 weeks of gestational age and in the first few months after birth. Different parts of the central nervous system experience growth spurts at different times. The *neurons* (nerve cells) do the vital job of receiving and sending information to other parts of the body. All neurons have a *nucleus* (a center), which contains the cell's genetic information (the programming that determines what each cell does) in deoxyribonucleic acid (*DNA*). Most neurons have *dendrites*—narrow, branching extensions of the cell body—which receive incoming signals from other neurons. The longer and more complex a neuron's dendrites, the more connections can be made.

The neurons are supported and protected by the *glial cells*. One type of glial cell covers parts of the neuron with a coating composed of a fatty tissue called *myelin*. *Myelination,* the process of covering these cells, allows for faster response times to visual, auditory, and other neuronal signals. For example, we know that certain visual pathways are myelinated by 2 to 3 months after birth, when babies smile in response to seeing their caregivers.

Most of the neurons of the *cerebral cortex* are produced by 20 weeks of gestation. (The cerebral cortex is the part of the *cerebrum* involved in higher-level functions, like thinking and problem solving. The cerebrum is the most highly developed part of the brain.) By 40 weeks of gestational age, the neurons of the spinal column, the *brain stem* (the part of the brain responsible for many basic functions), and large parts of the cerebrum are almost fully developed. But not until the first year of life does the *cerebellum* (the part of the brain that coordinates motor activity) have its greatest growth spurt.

Before and after birth, neurons and glial cells migrate to various parts of the brain, where they grow and differentiate to perform various functions. Although the full timetable for differentiation is not known exactly, we do know that some changes in the primary visual cortex occur between 25 and 32 weeks of gestation, whereas cerebellum differentiation comes later and lasts until the end of the second year. In a newborn infant, the subcortical structures are the most fully developed; these regulate such basic biological functions as breathing and digestion. Cells in the cortex are not yet well connected. Connections between cortical cells

FIGURE 5-3

Fetal brain development from 25 days of gestation through birth. As the brain develops, the front part expands greatly to form the cerebrum (the large, convoluted upper mass). Specific areas of the cerebral cortex (the gray outer covering of the brain) are devoted to particular functions, such as sensory and motor activities. But large areas are "uncommitted" and thus are free for higher intellectual activities, such as thinking, remembering, and problem solving. The subcortex (the brain stem and other structures below the cortical layer) handles reflex behavior and other lower-level functions. The newborn's brain contains most of the cells it will eventually have, but it is only about 25 percent of its adult weight. A rapid increase in cortical connections during the first 2 years of life results in a dramatic weight gain (to 80 percent of adult weight) and in the capacity for thought. SOURCE: Restak, 1984.

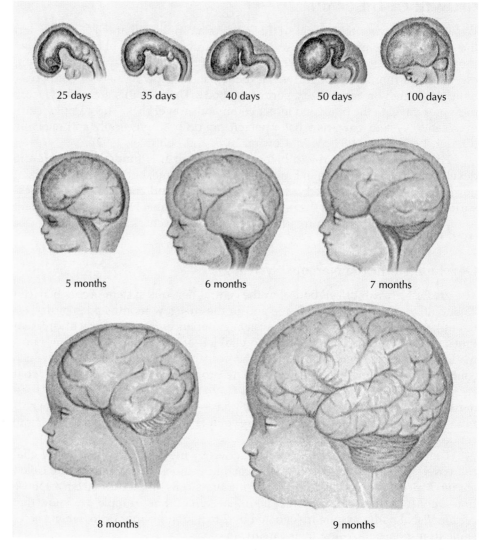

25 days   35 days   40 days   50 days   100 days

5 months   6 months   7 months

8 months   9 months

increase astronomically as the child matures, allowing more flexible, higher-level motor and intellectual functioning.

We can look at the way the brain develops using the analogy of a statue. Instead of starting with grains of sand and gluing them together, a sculptor starts with a block of stone and chisels the unwanted pieces away. This is roughly what happens in the brain. The prenatal brain produces more cells and connections between cells than it needs. Those that do not function will die out after birth. This pruning of excess cells helps to create an efficient nervous system.

In the uterus, an estimated 250,000 brain cells form every minute through cell division (*mitosis*). By birth, most of the 100 billion cells in a mature brain are already formed (W. M. Cowan, 1979; see Figure 5-3).

Both the type and the severity of brain damage are related to the timing of brain growth. That is, when a particular region of the brain is growing, it is most vulnerable to injury. (See Figure 3-2.). Cerebral palsy is most likely to occur from insults occurring up to the middle period of gestation, although a major catastrophe at any age can result in cerebral palsy or mental retardation, or both.

The brain is only 25 percent of its adult weight at birth. It reaches about 70 percent of its eventual weight during the first year and 80 percent by the end of the second year. It continues to grow more slowly until, by age 12, it is almost adult size. Cell death continues until about 16 years of age and then at a much slower pace throughout life. An infant's neurological growth permits development in motor and intellectual activities. Although programmed by the genes, this development is also strongly affected by environmental influences.

How the Environment Influences Brain Development

Until the middle of the twentieth century, scientists believed that the brain grew in an unchangeable, genetically determined pattern. We now know that the brain can be "molded" by experience, especially during early life, when it grows most quickly. The technical term for this is *plasticity*. We can measure plasticity by studying differences in the number of nerve cells, in the connections between them, and in their chemistry.

Early experiences may have lasting effects, for better or worse, on the capacity of the central nervous system to learn and to store information (Greenough, Black, & Wallace, 1987; Wittrock, 1980). Both chronic malnutrition of a fetus and fetal alcohol syndrome, for example, can result in brain damage; and undernourishment in the critical period just after birth can have the same effect.

Permanent physical changes can occur in response to early experience. Some kittens have been fitted with goggles that allow them to see only vertical lines. (See Figure 5-4.) In maturity, these cats will be unable to see horizontal lines and will bump into horizontal boards in front of them. If the goggles let them see only horizontal lines, they will be effectively blind to vertical columns (H. V. Hirsch & Spinelli, 1970). This seems to be due to modifications in the cortical layers early in life as the result of experience—that is, the kinds of lines they are used to seeing. Apparently, most of the neurons (nerve cells) in the visual cortex, the part of the cerebral cortex that controls vision, are programmed to respond to lines only in the direction that the cats have been permitted to see. This does not happen when the same procedure is carried out with adult cats, suggesting that crucial cells in the visual cortex develop early in life.

On the other hand, animal experiments have shown that an early enriched environment can enhance brain growth and functioning. Enrichment can be physical (providing toys) or social (having other animals to interact with). In a series of experiments, rats and other animals were raised in cages enriched with stimulating apparatus like wheels to run on, rocks to climb on, and levers to manipulate. These animals were then compared with littermates raised in standard cages or in isolation. The "enriched" animals had heavier brains with thicker cortical layers, more cells in the visual cortex, greater complexity of cells, more connective cells, and higher levels of neurochemical activity (making it easier to form connections between brain cells) (Rosenzweig, 1984; Rosenzweig & Bennett, 1976). Furthermore, the brain's plasticity seems to continue, to a lesser degree, throughout most of life. Similar differences in brain function showed up when older animals were exposed to differing environments. The changes were like the changes in the brains of younger animals, though smaller in degree.

The implications here for human development—and for social policy—are

FIGURE 5-4
This kitten is wearing training goggles. One lens contains horizontal stripes and the other, vertical stripes. The eye that sees only horizontal stripes will be blind to vertical lines when the animal matures, and the eye that sees only vertical stripes will be blind to horizontal lines.

profound. Since some developmentalists believe that children deprived of stimulation early in life are left with permanently stunted brains, a recent report stresses the need for early intervention in the lives of underprivileged children (Carnegie Corporation, 1994). Such intervention could include intensive educational programs from the first month of life. Data on brain development have already sparked successful efforts to stimulate the physical and mental development of children with Down syndrome, to keep aging people mentally alert, and to help victims of brain damage recover function. These findings also help explain the compensatory value of enrichment, which, as we saw in Chapter 4, helps some infants with birth complications to develop normally.

Reflex Behaviors

reflex behavior
Involuntary reaction to stimulation.

When Vicky blinks at a bright light, she is showing a *reflex behavior,* an automatic, involuntary response to external stimulation. Human beings have many reflexes; some seem to offer protection that extends to survival itself.

The so-called *primitive reflexes,* or newborn reflexes, are present at birth or soon after, and many can be elicited even before birth. (See Table 5-1.) In a normal baby, these primitive reflexes disappear at different times during the first year. For example, the Moro reflex drops out at about 3 months; the rooting reflex, at 9 months; and the Babinski reflex, at 6 to 9 months. Other reflexes are clearly protective—like yawning, coughing, gagging, sneezing, shivering, and blinking. These, of course, do not drop out as children mature.

Although some primitive reflexes are needed for early survival (like rooting to get food), others may be part of our evolutionary legacy (like grasping, by which infant monkeys hold on to the hair of their mothers' bodies). The primitive reflexes are controlled by the subcortex. Their disappearance on schedule is evidence that the cortex is developing normally, causing the shift from reflex to voluntary behavior. This timetable for the development and dropping out of primitive reflexes enables us to evaluate a baby's neurological development by seeing which reflexes are present or absent.

One of the first tests after a baby's birth is for normal reflexes. The primitive reflexes appear and drop out later in preterm infants than in full-term infants. In addition, reflexes vary somewhat according to ethnic group and culture. For example, western newborns typically show the Moro reflex. To elicit this reflex, the baby's body is lifted, and the head supported. The head support is then released, and the head is allowed to drop. Caucasian newborns reflexively extend both arms and legs, cry persistently, and move about in an agitated manner. Navajo babies, however, do not extend their limbs in the same way, rarely cry, and almost immediately stop any agitated motion.

Newborns in Australia, Bali, India, Italy, Kenya, Nigeria, and Sweden also show some kind of unique behavior. It is hard to imagine that these reflexive differences displayed so soon after birth have anything to do with environment or culture. Instead, investigations like this suggest that even those reflexes that seem to be the most fundamental are subject to genetic and ethnic variability. We need to be very careful, therefore, about declaring any particular inherited characteristic to be "normal" for all children.

TABLE 5-1

HUMAN PRIMITIVE REFLEXES

REFLEX	STIMULATION	BABY'S BEHAVIOR
Rooting	Baby's cheek is stroked with finger or nipple.	Head turns; mouth opens; sucking movements begin.
Darwinian (grasping)	Palm of baby's hand is stroked.	Makes strong fist; can be raised to standing position if both fists are closed around a stick.
Swimming	Baby is put into water face down.	Makes well-coordinated swimming movements.
Tonic neck	Baby is laid down on back.	Turns head to one side, assumes "fencer" position, extends arms and legs on preferred side, flexes opposite limbs.
Moro (startle)	Baby is dropped or hears loud noise.	Extends legs, arms, and fingers; arches back; draws back head.
Babinski	Sole of baby's foot is stroked.	Toes fan out; foot twists in.
Walking	Baby is held under arms, with bare feet touching flat surface.	Makes steplike motions that look like well-coordinated walking.
Placing	Backs of baby's feet are drawn against edge of flat surface.	Withdraws foot.

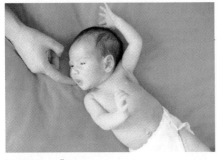

Rooting reflex

Darwinian reflex

Tonic neck reflex

Moro reflex

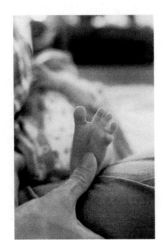

Babinski reflex

Walking reflex

NUTRITION IN INFANCY

Most babies in developed countries* seem to grow normally and to stay healthy under a variety of different feeding regimens. Still, experts do recommend some practices over others. Some ways to tell whether a baby is well nourished are listed in Table 5-2.

Breastfeeding

In the United States, among better-educated, older women from higher-income groups, who have attended childbirth classes, nursing is the preferred way to feed babies (Kurinij, Shiono, & Rhoads, 1988). Today, more than half of new mothers breastfeed, and at least 5 times as many mothers now (as compared with 1971) continue to nurse their babies until at least the fifth or sixth month. After a 6-year decline in breastfeeding rates between 1984 and 1989, the rate rose steadily from 1991 through 1993 (Ross Products Division of Abbott Laboratories, 1994; Eiger & Olds, 1987; Ryan, Rush, Krieger, & Lewandowski, 1991).

Benefits of Breastfeeding. Even though modern infant formulas approximate human milk and many babies thrive on it, breast milk is still almost always the best food for newborns. It has been called the "ultimate health food" because it offers so many benefits (Eiger & Olds, 1987, p. 26). Breast milk is a complete source of nutrients for the first 4 to 6 months, more digestible than cow's milk and less likely to produce allergic reactions. Because the way babies suck at the breast is different from the way they suck on a bottle, their teeth and jaws tend to develop better when they are breastfed (Labbok & Hendershot, 1987). Babies fed exclusively by breast for their first 4 months are less likely to suffer from otitis media, a disorder of the inner ear (Duncan et al., 1993). Breastfed children get varying degrees of protection against diarrhea and respiratory infections like pneumonia

*As opposed to developing countries, where poor sanitary conditions, inadequate medical care, and other problems contribute to health problems for all ages.

TABLE 5-2

HOW TO TELL WHETHER A BABY IS WELL NOURISHED*	
ADEQUATE (GOOD)	**LESS THAN ADEQUATE (POOR)**
General appearance of vitality, well-being, and alertness	Strained expression; dull and listless; apathetic
Bright, clear eyes; smiling, happy expression; no dark circles under eyes	Sad-looking; dark circles under eyes; little smiling; prone to tears
Recovers quickly from fatigue; endurance during activity	Chronic fatigue; tires easily; takes excessive time to bounce back from physical activity; lack of endurance
Full of energy; vigorous	Lack of energy; weakness
Smooth, glossy hair	Dry, brittle, easily "pluckable" hair
Good appetite; curious and eager to try new foods	Poor appetite; unwilling to try new foods; may have many food dislikes
Good posture; stands erect; well-developed muscles	Poor posture; slumping; muscles weak and underdeveloped
Skin is firm and resilient and "feels alive"; subcutaneous fat layers	Skin is dry; has little or no tone; little or no subcutaneous fat
Interested in environment; curious; responsive	Irritable, nervous, slow to react; indifferent, passive, unresponsive; unable to cope with stimuli
Good growth; adequate weight and height for age	Stunted growth; thin and small for age; underweight for height
Attentive; eager to learn and experiment	Shortened attention span; reduced capacity to concentrate

*While it is not easy to evaluate marginal inadequate nutrition, some of the characteristics listed here may be helpful.
SOURCE: Adapted from Alford & Boyle, 1982, p. 56.

Breast milk can be called the "ultimate health food" because it offers so many benefits to babies. Nursing provides mothers, too, with physical and emotional advantages.

and bronchitis (Fallot, Boyd, & Oski, 1980; Forman et al., 1984; Howie et al., 1990; A. L. Wright, Holberg, Martinez, Morgan, & Taussig, 1989).

Breastfeeding is an emotional as well as a physical act. The warm contact with the mother's body fosters bonding, or emotional linkage, between mother and baby, although such bonding also, of course, takes place with bottle-feeding.

The Cultural Context of Breastfeeding. A mother's ethnic, cultural, and socio-economic status affect her decision on how she feeds her baby. Although from 1991 to 1993 breastfeeding rates rose fastest among younger, poorer, and minority women (Ross Products Division of Abbott Laboratories, 1994), nursing is still less popular than bottle-feeding in these populations. Some women do not know the benefits of nursing; others do not want to go against community norms.

It is ironic that many poor women do not breastfeed (MacGowan et al., 1991), since breast milk is more economical than formula. The provincial government of Quebec considers breastfeeding so important for babies' health that it pays low-income women to encourage them to nurse. The expense is outweighed, say these Canadian policy makers, by future health care savings (Farnsworth, 1994).

In the United States, white mothers are more inclined to breastfeed than are African American or Mexican American mothers, even after economic factors are taken into account (Romero-Gwynn & Carias, 1989). Black mothers tend to stop nursing earlier than white mothers, partly because they are more likely to be employed (Fetterly & Graubard, 1984; Kurinij et al., 1988; Rassin et al., 1984). Mothers who work full time generally stop nursing earlier than those who remain at home or work part time (Gielen, Faden, O'Campo, Brown, & Paige, 1991).

Encouraging Breastfeeding. In the southeast Asian country of Laos, women from the highland Hmong tribes always breastfeed their babies, but Hmong immigrants to America thought American children were taller and bigger because they were bottlefed; they saw formula as the American way. One United States–sponsored health program has countered this trend away from breastfeeding with the help of Hmong women who teach health, nutrition, and breastfeeding skills to other Hmong mothers. This social policy helped to increase breastfeeding among its low-income clients from 19 to 48 percent ("In any language. . . .," 1992).

Virtually every woman can breastfeed her baby, with the right kind of information, encouragement, and support. Women are more likely to breastfeed if they begin within the first 10 hours after birth, have a vaginal rather than a cesarean delivery, nurse on "demand" rather than by rigid 3- or 4-hour schedules, and do not return to work soon after the baby's birth (Romero-Gwynn & Carias, 1989). Once back at work, they need nearby child-care centers and employers who understand family needs.

One source of difficulty involves unrealistic expectations. Many mothers expect nursing to be easy and natural; when they encounter problems at the beginning, they switch to the bottle. However, most mothers need to learn to nurse and many babies have to learn to suckle, a process that may take weeks. In traditional societies, other women help the mother and baby in this learning process; support during the early weeks is just as important in the west.

One program of prenatal education and counseling boosted the breastfeeding rate among urban black low-income women; the women were motivated most by learning how their babies' health would benefit (Kistin, Benton, Rao, & Sullivan, 1990). Promoting breastfeeding is an inexpensive public health measure, which seems to be cost-effective, especially among low-income populations (Kramer, 1991).

Occasionally breastfeeding is inadvisable—if a mother has AIDS, which can be transmitted through her milk (Hilts, 1991; Van de Perre et al., 1991), or an infectious illness that she could transmit to her baby through close contact; if the baby is too ill; if the mother must take a medicine or uses an illicit drug that would not be safe for the baby (AAP Committee on Drugs, 1994; Chasnoff, Lewis, & Squires, 1987); or if the mother has had a silicone breast implant (J. J. Levine & Ilowite, 1994). Other women have strong feelings against it or are prevented by work or travel. Julia, for example, has only a 2-week maternity leave. Nursing mothers need to observe the same care as pregnant women in what they eat and drink and which drugs they take.

Bottle-Feeding

Babies fed with properly prepared formula and raised with love also grow up healthy and well adjusted. Most bottle-fed babies receive a formula based on either cow's milk or soy protein. These formulas are manufactured to resemble mother's milk as closely as possible, although they contain supplemental vitamins and minerals that breast milk does not have. For the first 4 to 6 months, breast milk or formula is the only food most babies need. After 4 months or so, infants fed either way need supplemental iron to prevent anemia (Calvo, Galindo, & Aspres, 1992).

Long-term studies comparing breastfed and bottle-fed children found no significant differences in either physical health or psychological adjustment (Fergusson, Horwood, & Shannon, 1986; McClelland, Constantian, Regalado, & Stone, 1978; Schmitt, 1970). The quality of the relationship between parent and child is more important than the feeding method:

A baby raised in a loving home can grow up to be healthy and psychologically secure no matter how he or she receives nourishment. While nursing is usually a beautiful, happy experience for both mother and child, the woman who nurses grudgingly, tight-lipped and stiff-armed, because she feels she *should*, will probably do more harm to her baby by communicating her feelings of resentment and unhappiness than she would if she were a relaxed, loving, bottle-feeding mother (Eiger & Olds, 1987, pp. 33–34).

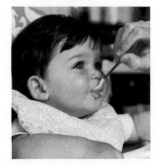

What do you think? *"Every mother should breastfeed her baby." Do you agree or disagree? Give reasons.*

Babies do not need solid foods until they are at least 4 months old—and they do not eat neatly until much later. This kind of feeding is appropriate when a baby can sit with support, has good control of head and neck muscles, and can let the spoon-feeder know when enough is enough.

Cow's Milk, Juice, and Solid Foods

Infants fed plain cow's milk in the early months of life suffer from iron deficiency, and those fed cow's milk in the second half of the first year show a 30 percent increase in intestinal blood loss and a significant loss of iron in the stool (Sadowitz & Oski, 1983). The American Academy of Pediatrics (1989; AAP Committee on Nutrition, 1992b) recommends that babies receive breast milk or iron-fortified formula for the first year.

At 1 year, babies can switch to cow's milk if they are getting a balanced diet of supplementary solid foods that provide one-third of their caloric intake. The milk they drink should be homogenized whole milk fortified with vitamin D—not skim milk or reduced-fat (1 or 2 percent) milk, since they need calories for proper growth. They do not need specially blended follow-up, or "weaning," formulas (AAP, 1989b).

Babies usually love fruit juices. But a study of toddlers aged 14 to 27 months who had failed to grow normally found that large quantities of juice seemed to be interfering with the children's appetites so that they had no room for higher-calorie, more nutritious foods. Also, some got diarrhea (Smith & Lifshitz, 1994). Children 2 or 3 years old should not drink more than 4 to 8 ounces of juice a day, and younger children should have less.

The first time Julia fed pureed green beans to Jason, he spit the spoonful out, spraying green all over her blouse. Many babies reject new foods at first, but as they are repeatedly offered, the babies become familiar with the foods and grow to like them. In one study of 4- to 6-month-old babies, breastfed babies accepted new foods better than bottle-fed babies did. This may be because a mother's milk often takes on the flavor of the foods she eats, accustoming the breastfed infant to varied flavors (S. A. Sullivan & Birch, 1994).

Although the American Academy of Pediatrics recommends waiting to start solid foods until 4 to 6 months of age, many infants begin getting solids—usually cereal or strained fruits—by 2 months of age. This practice often results from aggressive marketing of baby food and parents' belief that solid food will help babies sleep through the night. Nutritionists condemn early feeding of solids as "forced feeding," since babies who cannot sit without support or control their heads and necks cannot effectively communicate when they have had enough (Fomon et al., 1979). Some observers believe that overfeeding of infants will cause lifelong obesity, an issue discussed in Box 5-1.

BOX 5-1 ▪ THE EVERYDAY WORLD

IS OBESITY A PROBLEM IN INFANCY?

Seven babies on Long Island were fed a diet that sounds healthy—skim milk rather than whole milk, no animal fat or sugar, and restricted snacking. But their well-intentioned parents, trying to prevent obesity in their children, were starving them. The babies were not getting enough calories (Pugliese, Weyman-Daum, Moses, & Lifschitz, 1987).

In the United States, obesity is the chief nutritional problem of all age groups. It occurs when people consume more calories than they expend as energy, and the excess calories are stored as fat. This imbalance clearly shows the interplay of physical, psychological, and cultural causes. Although a tendency toward overweight seems to be largely inherited, individual eating habits often follow patterns set in a particular household, which in turn are influenced by standards set by the larger culture (Stunkard et al., 1986; Stunkard et al., 1990).

Those Long Island parents may have underfed their babies because they believed that people who become obese in later life were overfed as infants. This belief rests on research in rats; feeding rat pups too many calories makes them develop too many fat cells, which persist through life

(J. Hirsch, 1972). But research on people has cast doubt on the long-term effects of obesity in infants. One researcher found almost no relationship between measures of obesity before age 6 and the same measures at age 16 (Roche, 1981).

After age 6, however, there was an increasingly strong correlation: Obese children aged 6 or older were more likely to be obese adults. A 40-year follow-up of Swedish children found that whether obese infants became obese adults depended very much on obesity in the family, especially in the mother. If she was obese, her child was likely to remain obese, even if the child ate a recommended diet (Mossberg, 1989). This study again seems to support a genetic basis for obesity.

There is no evidence that obesity hurts babies. For proper growth, young children should not be on any kind of special diet without a clear indication that it is needed (AAP Committee on Nutrition, 1986). The best thing that parents can do to avoid obesity is to adopt a more active lifestyle for the entire family. The parents as well as the children are likely to reap the benefits.

EARLY SENSORY CAPACITIES

"The baby, assailed by eyes, ears, nose, skin, and entrails at once, feels that all is one great blooming, buzzing confusion," wrote the psychologist William James in 1890. We now know this is far from true. Infants are able to make some sense of their perceptions, and they can discriminate in the areas of sight, hearing, smell, taste, and touch.

SIGHT

Vision is the least developed sense at birth. The eyes of newborns are smaller than those of adults, the retinal structures are incomplete, and the optic nerve is underdeveloped. At birth, the eyes of normal babies do not look straight because of the tissue of their eyelids, but this look will disappear soon. They blink at bright lights, and the ability to shift gaze to follow a moving target develops rapidly in the first months. A newborn's eyesight is poor, and peripheral vision is very narrow at birth. It more than doubles between 2 and 10 weeks of age (Tronick, 1972). A neonate's eyes focus best from about 1 foot away—just about the typical distance from the face of a person holding a newborn. This may be an adaptive measure to promote mother-infant bonding.

Vision becomes much more acute during the first year, reaching 20/20 levels by about the sixth month (Aslin, 1987). (This measure of vision means that a person can read letters on a specified line on a standard eye chart from 20 feet away.) The first 3 years seem to represent a critical period for the development of binocular vision (using both eyes to focus on objects, allowing the perception of depth and distance). If children whose two eyes are not aligned properly do not have corrective surgery by age 3, their binocular sight does not develop as well as those whose visual problem is repaired early (Bertenthal & Campos, 1987).

Color perception also develops early. By about 2 months, babies can tell red and green; by about 3 months, they can see blue (Haith, 1986). Four-month-old babies can distinguish among red, green, blue, and yellow; and, like adults, they prefer red and blue (Bornstein, Kessen, & Weiskopf, 1976; Teller & Bornstein, 1987).

Depth Perception

A classic contribution to the study of infants' perceptions, and to the nature-nurture controversy, made use of a *visual cliff* (Walk & Gibson, 1961). Researchers tested the thesis that children are born with no knowledge of space and come to know about height, depth, and distance only through experience. They put babies on a glass tabletop, over a checkerboard pattern. The glass formed a continuous surface, but to an adult's eye, it appeared that one side of the checkerboard pattern was a flat ledge and the other a vertical drop—there was an illusion of depth (a "visual cliff"). Would infants see the illusion and feel in danger?

Young infants do see a *difference* between the "ledge" and the "drop." Six-month-old babies crawl freely on the ledge, but they avoid the drop, even when they see their mothers on the "far side." When even younger infants, aged 2 and 3 months, are placed face down over the visual cliff, their hearts slow down, probably in response to the illusion of depth (Campos, Langer, & Krowitz, 1970).

These findings suggest that depth perception is either innate or learned very early. Newer research suggests that depth perception is closely tied to motor development (see below). However, the ability to *perceive* depth (as shown by a

visual cliff *Apparatus for testing depth perception.*

This baby seems to be weighing the perceived risk of going to mother's enticing arms. Even at this young age, babies can perceive depth and want to avoid falling off the "visual cliff."

slowed heart rate, which indicates interest) does not indicate a *fear* of heights (which would be indicated by a *faster* heart rate). The sense of danger does not develop until later and is related to children's ability to get around by themselves. Apparently, some mix of inborn abilities and learned responses is reflected in the performance on the visual cliff. As usual, when researchers attempt to sort out nature and nurture, they see how closely the two interact.

Visual Preferences

visual preference *An infant's tendency to look longer at certain stimuli than at others, which depends on the ability to differentiate between sights.*

When Jess went shopping for Jason's first toy, he saw a variety of crib toys with bold black-and-white designs. Very young babies like to look at such designs, partly because of the sharp contrasts. The amounts of time babies spend looking at different sights tell us about their *visual preferences,* which depend on the ability to tell one sight from another. The ability to view things selectively is present from birth.

How do researchers study visual preferences in very young babies? To perform his now-classic experiments, R. L. Fantz designed a special apparatus containing a chamber in which an infant can lie and look at a visual stimulus chosen by the experimenter. While the baby is in this chamber, an observer can peek through a tiny hole in the chamber ceiling to see a corneal reflection of the stimulus over the pupil of the baby's eye. As soon as this reflection is seen on one or both of the baby's eyes, the observer starts to time the baby's visual fixation, stopping only when the baby closes or turns away his or her eyes.

Using the Fantz visual preference methodology, researchers have found that babies under 2 days old show definite preferences. Babies prefer curved lines to straight; complex patterns to simple; three-dimensional objects to two-dimensional ones; pictures of faces to pictures of other things; and new sights to familiar ones (Fantz, 1963, 1964, 1965; Fantz, Fagen, & Miranda, 1975; Fantz & Nevis, 1967).

Neonatal "pattern vision"—which is related to visual preferences—is correlated with future cognitive development. Thirty-three newborns thought to be at high risk for developing neurological and intellectual handicaps were tested on their ability to tell one pattern from another. On the basis of their performance, they were designated "normal," "suspect," or "abnormal." Then their reflexes and neuromuscular maturation were examined. At age 3 or 4 years, 19 of them were given an intelligence test. The ratings on the neonatal visual pattern test predicted the children's IQ scores better than did the ratings on the neurological tests (Miranda, Hack, Fantz, Fanaroff, & Klaus, 1977).

What do you think? *Design an apparatus or procedure to study one aspect of vision in infancy (like perception of depth or color). Why would this apparatus or method be an effective way to study the phenomenon?*

HEARING

Hearing begins in the womb and is acute even before birth. Fetuses respond to sounds, and they may learn some sounds in the womb. Immediately after birth, hearing may be impaired because of fluid that fills the inner ears as a result of the birth process. A day or two after birth, when the fluid disappears, hearing

TABLE 5-3

MILESTONES OF HEARING	
AGE (MONTHS)	**CONDITION**
3	Is startled by loud sounds; is soothed by mother's voice; turns in general direction of sound source.
6	Responds to mother's voice; turns head and eyes toward sound but may not find source on first attempt.
10	Looks directly, promptly, and predictably to sound source.
12	Begins to show voluntary control over response to sounds; may or may not pay attention to a sound. Thus, a hearing loss becomes harder to distinguish from lack of concentration.

SOURCE: Bolles, 1982, p. 200.

becomes efficient again. Sounds continue to be important during infancy. In the crib, babies cannot see much, but they can hear a steady flow of sounds. So an infant's world may buzz and sing more than it blooms and smiles. Some milestones of hearing ability are shown in Table 5-3.

Newborns can hear and can even discriminate some sounds from others. At less than 3 days old, Vicky can tell her mother's voice from a stranger's, and Ellen's voice seems to have special importance. In one study of such young infants, a baby was able to turn on a recording of his or her mother reading a story by sucking on a nipple connected to a special apparatus. At certain times, though, the baby's sucking turned on a recording of another woman reading a story. As young as they were, these babies sucked about 24 percent more when it was their mother's voice on the recording (DeCasper & Fifer, 1980). Apparently, since they knew this voice, they were more interested in hearing it. Early recognition of voices may be a mechanism for bonding between parents and child and may be based on recognition of voices heard while the fetus is still in the womb.

A 2-month-old infant born in Chile was adopted by an American couple. Over the next couple of years, when the baby was able to express a preference for a particular radio station, she almost always chose one broadcasting in Spanish. This bears out research findings. In an experiment with sixteen 2-day-old babies whose parents spoke either English or Spanish, the newborns were able to show their preference for hearing one language or the other by the way they sucked. With the infant in a quiet alert state, headphones were placed over both ears, a nipple put in the baby's mouth, and recordings of either a Spanish or an English voice were presented. Most of the babies sucked more vigorously when they heard their parents' native language than when they heard the other language, suggesting that infants as young as 2 days old prefer to activate recordings of their native language for longer periods than a foreign language. The researchers suggest that the babies had become familiar with the language prenatally (Moon, Cooper, & Fifer, 1993).

Also, 3-day-old infants can distinguish between new speech sounds and those they have heard before (L. R. Brody, Zelazo, & Chaika, 1984), and 1-month-old babies can discriminate between sounds as close as "ba" and "pa" (Eimas, Siqueland, Jusczyk, & Vigorito, 1971). Such findings suggest that newborns are biologically prepared for acquiring language.

Infants' early sensitivity to sounds may provide another way to estimate their

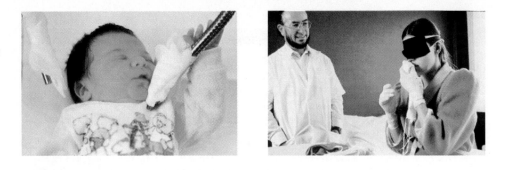

The nose knows. Three-day-old infants, like this one, are more peaceful when they smell pieces of gauze that their mothers had worn than when they smell cloth worn by other women. And blindfolded mothers can identify by smell the shirts their own babies have worn from shirts worn by other babies.

intelligence. Most attempts to predict later IQ scores have proved disappointing. Yet one study found a significant correlation between the ability to discriminate between sounds at 4 months of age and IQ score at 5 years. Thus auditory sensitivity to changes in the environment may be an early indicator of cognitive functioning (O'Connor, Cohen, & Parmelee, 1984). In Chapter 6, we will look further at the relationship between early sensory abilities (specifically, the ability to process sensory information efficiently) and childhood IQ.

SMELL

Newborns can tell distinctive odors apart. They seem to show by their expressions that they like the way vanilla and strawberries smell but do not like the aromas of rotten eggs or fish (Steiner, 1979). They can also tell where odors are coming from. When an ammonium compound is dabbed on one side of a newborn's nose, even a 1-day-old baby will turn his or her nose to the other side (Rieser, Yonas, & Wilkner, 1976).

Smell is a powerful means of communication among human beings, beginning soon after birth. Six-day-old breastfed infants prefer their mother's breast pad over that of another nursing mother, but 2-day-old infants do not, suggesting that babies need a few days' experience to learn how their mothers smell (Macfarlane, 1975).

TASTE

Most people's preference for lemonade over lemons seems to suggest an inborn sweet tooth. Newborns can distinguish among tastes; they prefer sweet tastes to sour or bitter ones. The sweeter the fluid, the harder they suck and the more they drink (Haith, 1986). This preference for sweet tastes is adaptive, since human breast milk is quite sweet. Newborns reject bad-tasting food, probably a survival mechanism.

TOUCH

Touch seems to be the first sense to develop, and for the first several months, it is the most mature sensory system. When you stroke a hungry newborn's cheek near the mouth, the baby will respond by trying to find a nipple. Early signs of this rooting reflex show up in 2-month-old fetuses. By 32 weeks of gestation, all body parts are sensitive to touch, and an infant's sensitivity to touch increases during the first 5 days of life (Haith, 1986).

PAIN SENSITIVITY

In recent years physicians have shied away from giving newborn babies anesthesia during surgery because they believed that neonates cannot feel pain and because of the known side effects of many pain relievers. But even on the first day of life, babies can and do feel pain, and sensitivity to pain increases during the next few days. Preterm and full-term newborns undergoing circumcision and such procedures as heel lancing (to obtain blood samples) cry, have increased heart rates and blood pressure, and sweat during and after the procedures. They also react to pain through body movements, like pulling a leg away from a pinprick, grimacing, and crying (Anand & Hickey, 1987). It seems that the nervous system of a newborn is more highly developed than we used to think.

Although most doctors performing circumcision either do not give infants analgesics or give them some whose effectiveness is questionable (Wellington & Rieder, 1993), the American Academy of Pediatrics recommends the use of pain relievers in most surgery on infants.

Among 415 newborns undergoing heart operations, those who received deep anesthesia that protected them from pain during the surgery and kept them unconscious for a day afterward recovered much better than babies given light anesthesia. The "light anesthesia" babies produced high levels of stress hormones, which may have made them more susceptible to problems (Anand & Hickey, 1992). Topical anesthesia has been proven safe and effective in neonatal circumcision (Benini, Johnston, Faucher, & Aranda, 1993; Weatherstone et al., 1993).

MOTOR DEVELOPMENT OF INFANTS AND TODDLERS

Vicky's activity began long before birth—and has never stopped. In the womb, she moved around, kicked, turned somersaults, and sucked her thumb. In her postnatal life, she lifts her head, looks around, kicks her legs, and flails her arms. These first simple movements, representing a generalized kind of activity, are controlled by the subcortex. By about the fourth month, babies begin to make more deliberate movements.

Increasing control over different body parts reflects the growing role of the cortex, allowing infants to do more specific tasks. As soon as they learn one new skill, they keep practicing it and getting better at it. This becomes tiresome for parents when a child's new skill involves dropping small objects from the high chair—and then crying to get them so she or he can drop them again! But this repetition is an important part of learning, and each newly mastered ability prepares a baby to tackle the next skill in the sequence. The more babies can do, the more they can explore; the more they can explore, the more they can learn—and the more they can do.

Developing motor skills reveal progress in a baby's ability to move deliberately and accurately. Skills proceed from the simple to the complex, and they follow the cephalocaudal and proximodistal principles described earlier. First, for example, Vicky picks up relatively large objects (large for her) with her whole hand; then she graduates to using neat little pincer motions with thumb and forefinger to pick up very small objects (which she usually carries automatically to her mouth). After she gains control over separate movements of her arms, hands, legs, and feet, she will be able to put these movements together to walk. The ability to walk and the precision grip (in which the thumb and index finger meet at

TABLE 5-4

MILESTONES OF MOTOR DEVELOPMENT			
SKILL	25 PERCENT	50 PERCENT	90 PERCENT
Rolling over	2.1 months	3.2 months	5.4 months
Grasping rattle	2.6 months	3.3 months	3.9 months
Sitting without support	5.4 months	5.9 months	6.8 months
Standing while holding on	6.5 months	7.2 months	8.5 months
Grasping with thumb and finger	7.2 months	8.2 months	10.2 months
Standing alone well	10.4 months	11.5 months	13.7 months
Walking well	11.1 months	12.3 months	14.9 months
Building tower of two cubes	13.5 months	13.5 months	20.6 months
Walking up steps	14.1 months	16.6 months	21.6 months
Jumping in place	21.4 months	23.8 months	2.4 years
Copying circle	3.1 years	3.4 years	4.0 years

NOTE: This table shows the approximate ages when 25 percent, 50 percent, and 90 percent of children can perform each skill, according to the Denver Training Manual II.
SOURCE: Adapted from Frankenburg et al., 1992.

the tips to form a circle) are two of the most distinctively human motor capabilities. Neither is present at birth.

MILESTONES OF MOTOR DEVELOPMENT

Babies do not have to be taught basic motor skills like crawling, walking, and grasping. They just need room to move and freedom from interference. As soon as the central nervous system, muscles, and bones are mature enough, babies keep surprising the adults around them with their new abilities.

Motor development is marked by a series of achievements in development. The *Denver Developmental Screening Test* was designed to identify children who are not developing normally, but it can also be used to chart normal progress between the ages of 1 month and 6 years (Frankenburg, Dodds, Fandal, Kazuk, & Cohrs, 1975).

Denver Developmental Screening Test *Screening test given to children (1 month to 6 years old) to identify abnormal development; it assesses gross motor skills, fine motor skills, language development, and personal and social development.*

The test covers such gross motor skills (those using large muscles) as rolling over and catching a ball and such fine motor skills (using small muscles) as grasping a rattle and copying a circle. It also assesses language development (like knowing the definition of words) and personal and social development (like smiling spontaneously and dressing). The newest edition of the test, the Denver II (Frankenburg, Dodds, Archer, Shapiro, & Bresnick, 1992), has revised norms and a number of new items, including an 86 percent increase in language items.

The test provides norms for the ages at which 25 percent, 50 percent, 75 percent, and 90 percent of children pass in each skill. (See Table 5-4 for some milestones.) A child who fails to pass an item at an age when 90 percent of children ordinarily pass is considered developmentally delayed. A child with two or more delays in two or more categories may need special attention.

The Denver norms were standardized on a western population and are not necessarily valid in assessing children from other cultures. For example, one study showed that southeast Asian children did not play pat-a-cake, pick up raisins, and dress themselves at the expected ages (V. Miller, Onotera, & Deinard, 1984). But that did not indicate abnormally slow development. In their culture, children do not play pat-a-cake, raisins look like a medicine they are told to avoid, and they are not expected to dress themselves until a later age than western children.

In the following discussion, when we talk about what the "average" baby can do, we refer to the 50 percent Denver norms. There is, however, no "average" baby. Normality covers a wide range; about half of all babies master these skills before the ages given and about half afterward.

What do you think? *Under what circumstances would you recommend assessing an infant's development?*

Head Control

At birth, most newborns can turn their heads from side to side while lying on their backs. While lying chest down, many can lift their heads enough to turn them. Within the first 2 to 3 months, they lift their heads higher and higher. By 4 months of age, almost all infants can keep their heads erect while being held or supported in a sitting position.

Hand Control

Newborns are born with a grasping reflex. If the palm of an infant's hand is stroked, the baby automatically closes the hand tightly. At about $3\frac{1}{2}$ months, most infants can grasp an object of moderate size, like a rattle, but have trouble holding a small object. Next they begin to grasp objects with one hand and transfer them to the other, and then to hold (but not pick up) small objects. Sometime between 7 and 11 months, their hands become coordinated enough to pick up a tiny object like a pea with pincerlike motion. After that, hand control becomes increasingly precise. At 14 months, the average baby can build a tower of two cubes. About 3 months before the third birthday, the average toddler can copy a circle fairly well.

Heads up! For the first two or three months, babies keep lifting their heads higher and higher—especially when they have an interesting object or person to look at.

Babies are born with a grasping reflex, and their ability to grasp objects grows steadily. Here, Annie finds her aunt's nose to be a convenient hand-hold.

Locomotion

After 3 months, the average infant begins to roll over purposefully, first from front to back and then from back to front. (Before this time, babies sometimes roll over accidentally, and so even the youngest ones should never be left alone on a surface from which they might roll off.)

Babies sit either by raising themselves from a prone (face down) position or by plopping down from a standing position. The average baby can sit without support by 5 to 6 months and can assume a sitting position without help 2 months later.

At about 6 months, most babies begin to get around under their own power, in several primitive ways. They wriggle on their bellies and pull their bodies along with their arms, dragging their feet behind. They hitch or scoot by moving along in a sitting position, pushing forward with their arms and legs. They bear-walk, with hands and feet touching the ground. And they crawl on hands and knees with their trunks raised, parallel to the floor. By 9 or 10 months, babies get around quite well by such means, and so parents have to keep a close eye on them. This kind of locomotion has important psychological implications, as we'll see.

All these developments are milestones along the way to the major motor achievement of infancy: walking. Humans begin to walk later than other species, possibly because babies' heavy heads and short legs make balance difficult (Thelen, cited in Bushnell & Boudreau, 1993). For some months before they can stand without support, babies practice walking while holding onto furniture—sitting down abruptly when they reach table's end, and crawling or lurching from chair to sofa. Soon after they can stand alone well, most infants take their first unaided steps, tumble, go back to crawling, and then try again. The average baby is walking regularly, if shakily, within a few days, and within a few weeks—soon after the first birthday—is walking well and thus achieves the status of toddler.

During the second year, children begin to climb stairs one at a time. (Since they can crawl upstairs before that—and tumble down long before—vigilance and baby gates are needed.) At first they put one foot and then the other on the same step before going on to the next higher one; later they will alternate feet. Going down the stairs comes later. In their second year, toddlers are running and jumping; their parents, trying to keep up with them, are running out of energy. At age 3, most children can balance briefly on one foot, and some begin to hop.

ENVIRONMENTAL INFLUENCES ON MOTOR DEVELOPMENT

Human beings seem to be genetically programmed to sit, stand, and walk. All these skills unfold in a predetermined pattern, and children have to reach a certain level of physiological maturity before they can exercise them. But the environment also plays an important role. Motor development does not seem to be affected by sex or parents' education (Bayley, 1965). It does seem to respond to other factors.

For example, a study of 425 8- to 14-month-old babies found that those who had been born in the winter and spring began to crawl about 3 weeks earlier than those born in summer and fall (Benson, 1993). It is possible that with milder weather and more daylight, the winter and spring babies were more active at critical times of development. This would suggest that experience plays an important part in motor development.

Cross-Cultural Differences

Nko, an African baby, stands and walks much earlier than either Vicky or Jason; Jung, an Asian child, is slower; and Rosa, a Mexican baby, is more advanced in manipulative skills, but slower in getting around. Babies in different societies de-

The major motor achievement of infancy, walking, occurs at different ages. Some babies find it easier to take their first steps when they have something to push. At this age, the pushability of the toy is more important than its service as a doll carriage.

velop along somewhat different patterns. What is normal and typical for children in one culture may not be so in another. This holds true even for such seemingly basic behaviors as reflexes, as we pointed out earlier (Freedman, 1979).

Black African babies tend to be more advanced than white infants in gross motor skills like standing and walking, and Asian infants are apt to show slower development in such skills. Some of these differences may be related to temperament. Asian babies, for example, tend to be more docile. This may explain why they show a calmer response when a cloth is pressed to their noses—and why they are also less likely to explore and move away from their parents (Kaplan & Dove, 1987).

Child-rearing practices and cultural norms seem to play a part. A cross-sectional study of 288 normal full-term babies from the Yucatan peninsula in Mexico found that at 3 months of age, these babies were ahead of American babies in motor skills. By 11 months, however, the Mexican babies were so far behind American babies that an American baby at the typical level of a Mexican baby might be considered neurologically impaired (Solomons, 1978).

The difference again might reflect child-rearing practices. The Mexican babies were slow by American norms, but were not considered delayed under the standards of their own culture. These babies' delayed skills in moving about may be related to several conditions in their lives. As infants, they are swaddled, and so their movement is restricted; later they are restrained by being carried more, by sleeping in hammocks (which become net "cages," compared with the open space of a firm-mattressed crib), and by not being put on the ground to play (because of insects and local beliefs about the dangers of cold floors). On the other hand, Mexican babies may be more advanced in manipulative skills; without toys to play with, they discover and play with their fingers earlier than American babies. The difficulty of coming up with environmental explanations for such differences, however, is highlighted by the fact that Navajo babies—also swaddled for most of the day—begin to walk at about the same age as other American babies (Chisholm, 1983).

Other research also points to environmental influences on gross motor skills. Children of the Ache in eastern Paraguay do not begin to walk until 18 to 20 months of age—about 9 months later than American babies (Kaplan & Dove, 1987). This delay may stem from early child-rearing practices. Ache mothers pull their babies back to their laps when the babies begin to crawl away. Mothers closely supervise their babies because of the hazards of nomadic life—and also because their primary responsibility is child rearing rather than subsistence labor. Children whose parents spend less time with them may become independent sooner because their other caretakers may supervise them less closely. This may apply to American babies now, who, in an era of prevalent day care, seem to be developing more quickly.

Slower-developing children often catch up, given a supportive environment. In their early years Ache children show the slowest motor development reported for any human group, but as 8- to 10-year-olds, they climb tall trees, chop branches, and play in ways that enhance their motor skills. Development, then, may be viewed "as a series of immediate adjustments to current conditions as well as a cumulative process in which succeeding stages build upon earlier ones" (Kaplan & Dove, 1987, p. 197).

Different cultures encourage their children to develop along different lines. Before we adopt or condemn another culture's child-rearing practices, we have to ask, "What's best for *our* children at this time and in this place?"

How Environment Can Slow Development

When children are well nourished, receive good health care, enjoy physical freedom and the opportunity to practice motor skills, their motor development is likely to be normal. An environment that is grossly deficient in any of these areas may retard motor development significantly, as was seen in a classic study of orphans in three institutions in Iran (Dennis, 1960).

In two orphanages, the children were hardly ever handled by the overworked attendants. The younger babies spent almost all their time on their backs in a crib. They drank from propped bottles. They were never put in a sitting position or placed stomach down. They had no toys and were not taken out of bed until they could sit without help (often not until 2 years of age). These children were delayed in their motor development, apparently because the deficient environment kept them from moving around and provided little stimulation. The children in a third orphanage were fed in the arms of attendants, were placed on their stomachs and propped up so that they could sit, and had many toys. Their motor development was normal.

When the children in the first two orphanages did start to get about, they moved around in a sitting position, pushing their bodies forward with their arms and feet, rather than creeping on hands and knees. Since they had never been placed on their stomachs, they had had no opportunity to practice raising their heads or pulling their arms and legs beneath their bodies—the movements needed for crawling. Also, since they had never been propped in a sitting position, they had not practiced raising their hands and shoulders to learn how to sit at the usual age. However, this delay seemed temporary. Older children in one of the two "poor" institutions, whose motor development had also presumably been delayed as infants and toddlers, worked and played normally.

Fortunately, such severe levels of environmental deprivation are rare. But the environment does play a part in motor development, and the more deficient it is, the greater its effect can be.

Can Motor Development Be Speeded Up?

Although some classic short-term experiments showed the importance of maturation for motor development, the Iranian studies described above and some provocative recent experiments point to the role of experience as well.

Classic Research. In one famous experiment, Arnold Gesell (1929) trained one identical twin, but not the other, in stair-climbing, block-building, and hand coordination. As the twins got older, the untrained twin became just as expert as the other one. Gesell concluded that "the powerful influence of maturation on infant behavior patterns is made clear." Children seem to perform certain activities when they are ready.

Toilet training, for example, is often begun long before babies can control the necessary muscles. Before children can control elimination, they have to learn a great deal. At first, elimination is involuntary: When the bladder or bowels are

These twins seem to be mastering stair-climbing at about the same age, confirming results of classic studies in which an identical twin who had not been trained in climbing stairs quickly caught up with the trained twin. Children perform certain activities only when they are ready to.

full, the appropriate muscles open automatically. To control these muscles, children have to learn that there is a proper time and place to allow them to open, they have to become familiar with the feelings that indicate the need to eliminate, and they have to learn to tighten the muscles until they are on the potty—and only then to loosen them. When a child is "successful" at a very early age, it is usually because the *parent* is trained to recognize the child's readiness and can get the child to the potty in time.

In another classic study, Myrtle McGraw (1940) measured the effects of early toilet training. She put one twin on the toilet every hour of every day from 2 months of age, but did not put the other twin on until 23 months. The first twin began to show some control at 20 months; by about 23 months, he had achieved almost perfect success. The other twin quickly caught up. The findings from these older studies suggested that for some abilities—like the control of elimination—experience or training counts for little if the child is not mature enough to benefit from it.

More Recent Research. More recent research indicates that short-term training of infants in certain motor activities *can* influence early development, showing the impact of the environment. One experiment randomly assigned thirty-two 6-week-old baby boys to one of five groups, three experimental and two control. (See Figure 5-5.) The babies in one experimental group were trained by their parents in stepping; those in the second group, in sitting; and those in the third group in stepping *and* sitting. Training lasted 7 weeks and consisted of two 3-minute daily sessions. One control group was not trained in either activity but was tested every week; the other control group was not trained and was tested only at 14 weeks (Zelazo, Zelazo, Cohen, & Zelazo, 1993).

After 14 weeks, all the babies were tested. The infants trained in stepping alone or in stepping and sitting stepped more than those untrained in stepping movements; and the infants trained in sitting alone or in stepping and sitting sat

FIGURE 5-5
Infants trained in sitting and stepping for 7 weeks performed more of those activities than did untrained infants. (*a*) Mean number of steps per minute and standard error for five groups at 14 weeks of age; (*b*) mean duration of sitting per 2 minutes and standard error for five groups at 14 weeks of age. SOURCE: Zelazo, Zelazo, Cohen, & Zelazo, 1993, p. 689.

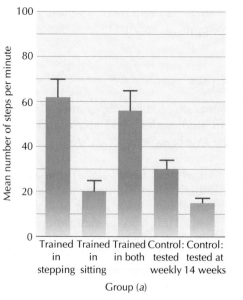

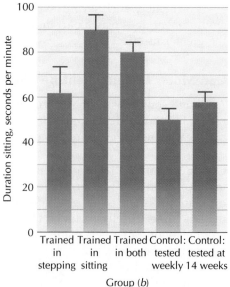

more. So it seems that training in early motor development can accelerate a behavior, but that training effects are very specific to the pattern trained. Training does not seem in generalize to other kinds of motor abilities. These results, say the authors, "rule out a strict view of maturation as biological unfolding . . . relatively unaffected by experience" (Zelazo et al., 1993, p. 690).

This study built on previous ones, which found that training infants in walking—starting at 1 week of age—led to early walking (Zelazo, Zelazo, & Kolb, 1972). Babies who had been trained in stepping walked at an average of 10.12 months, while those in an untrained control group did not begin until an average of 12.35 months. This study suggested that there is a critical period during which the walking response can be transformed from a reflex to a voluntary action. This reflex may have a function in helping infants become more mobile.

In recent years, many parents have put their babies in infant baby walkers, partly because the babies like them and also because parents think the walkers help the babies learn to walk earlier. This latter belief is mistaken, however, according to pediatricians. Furthermore, the walkers are responsible for many childhood injuries. Safety experts recommend not using them at all (C. Collins, 1994).

What do you think? *Do you think that it is wise or dangerous to teach babies skills, like walking, before they are old enough to develop them on their own?*

THE FAR-REACHING EFFECTS OF MOTOR DEVELOPMENT

Have you ever driven for the first time to a place where you had previously gone only as a passenger? As a driver, you probably saw landmarks and were aware of turns you have never noticed as a passenger. After getting there under your own steam, you most likely felt more familiar with the route than you had earlier. Something similar seems to happen to babies after they begin to get around on their own, after always having been carried or wheeled. The emergence of "self-produced locomotion" is a turning point in the second half of the first year of life, influencing all domains of development—physical, cognitive, and emotional.

How Motor Development Influences Perception

Jason did not recognize his mother's face before 4 months of age, not because of any problem in his relationship with Julia, but because his vision was not good enough before then. Similarly, Vicky could not crawl before 8 months of age, not because she was confined but because her muscles and her coordination were not well enough developed before then (Bushnell & Boudreau, 1993). Once either of these physical milestones occurs, it becomes a "setting event" (Bertenthal, Campos, & Barrett, 1984). That is, it increases the likelihood of other new developments for the baby.

Haptic Perception. Not until babies develop enough eye-hand coordination to reach for objects can they begin to develop *haptic perception*. This is the ability to acquire information about objects from handling them as opposed to looking at them. As babies become able to make various hand movements, they can perceive different properties of objects. Up to 3 months of age, as infants clutch objects tightly in their fists, they can perceive temperature, size, and maybe hardness. Between about 4 and 10 months they make repetitive finger and hand movements, scratching, rubbing, waving, banging, squeezing, and poking objects and then passing them from one hand to the other. They now begin to perceive texture and weight. Toward the end of the first year, when they are strong enough to sit without supporting themselves with one hand, they can use both hands in complex ways, which allows them to become aware of shapes. Thus their ability to perceive such characteristics is limited by the level of their motor development (Bushnell & Boudreau, 1993).

Depth Perception. Motor development also influences *depth perception,* the ability to perceive objects and surfaces in three dimensions. We perceive depth by an object's image on the retina of our eyes. *Kinetic cues* depend on the change in this image with movement, of either the person of what she or he is looking at—and we have to know which one is moving. To find out, a baby might hold his or her head still for a moment. Thus a baby needs to have good enough control over the head, to be able to move it and hold it still. This ability is well established by about 3 months. *Binocular cues* (both eyes working together) for depth are present by about 5 months. Some time between 5 and 7 months, babies respond to *static monocular cues,* available in the retinal image of a single eye. These cues include relative size and differences in texture and shading. To judge depth from these cues, babies have to know about actual size and other properties. This information may come from manipulating objects and the resulting haptic perception (Bushnell & Boudreau, 1993).

The Impact of Crawling

Between 7 and 9 months, babies show vast changes. Vicky's behavior shows that she is starting to understand concepts like "near" and "far." She imitates more complex behaviors, and she shows new fears—of strangers, heights, and unfamiliar objects. But she also shows a new sense of security around her parents or other caregivers.

Since changes like these involve so many different psychological functions, affect processes that are so different from each other, and occur over such a short time span, some observers tie them all in with a reorganization of brain function. This neurological development may be set in motion by a basic skill that emerges at this time—a baby's ability to crawl, which makes it possible to get around without depending on anyone else (Bertenthal & Campos, 1987; Bertenthal, Campos, & Barrett, 1984).

How does crawling exert such a powerful influence on babies' lives? Basically, it gives them a new view of the world. When they are carried, they pay little attention to their surroundings. But when they begin to crawl, they become sensitive to where objects are and how big they are in relation to each other. They start to pay attention to what things look like. Crawling babies are able to differentiate similar forms that are unlike in color, size, and location in space (Campos, Bertenthal, & Benson, 1980). Also, babies are more successful in finding a toy that was hidden in a box when they crawl around the box than when they are carried around it (Benson & Uzgiris, 1985).

Moving around on their own also helps babies learn to judge distances and to perceive depth. Depth perception seems to be due less to maturation and age

When babies can get around under their own power, they can take the initiative in going after something they want—like a furry cat's tail. This independent locomotion has important psychological consequences.

than to babies' experience in getting around by themselves. When they start to move around by themselves, they put themselves in danger of falling. To keep them from getting hurt, caregivers usually hover over babies, remove them from dangerous locations, or cry out and jump up when the children are about to get into trouble. Babies are sensitive to these actions and emotions—and they learn to be afraid of places from which they might fall.

The ability to move from one place to another also has social implications. For one, crawling babies seem to be better able to differentiate themselves from the rest of the world. As they move about, they learn to perceive depth and see that the people and objects around them look different depending on how near or far they are. Also, being able to get around means that children are no longer "prisoners" of place. If Vicky wants to be close to her mother and far away from a strange dog, she can move toward the one and away from the other. This step develops mastery over the world, enhancing self-confidence and self-esteem.

These new abilities get babies into new situations, and they learn to look for clues to whether a situation is secure or dangerous. This shows growth in the skill of *social referencing*. Crawling babies look at (*socially reference*) their parents more than babies who have not yet begun to crawl. They seem to pick up emotional signals from their parents' faces or gestures, which, in turn, influence their behavior (Garland, 1982).

We see, then, how motor development can have far-reaching effects in helping babies see their world and themselves in a new way. Parents often feel that their babies and toddlers are never still, but even these active little people do sleep—some more than others. Box 5-2 explores cultural influences on children's early sleep patterns.

BOX 5-2 ■ AROUND THE WORLD

EARLY SLEEP PATTERNS

Until her first birthday, Vicky sleeps in the "family bed" with her parents. At first, Jason sleeps in a cradle next to his parents' bed but is soon moved into a crib in a separate room. There is considerable cultural variation in newborns' sleeping arrangements. In the United States, the commonest practice, reflecting the prevailing recommendations of child-care experts, is having a separate bed, and ideally a separate room, for the infant. White and college-educated mothers are less likely to take their babies into bed with them than are African American mothers and mothers whose education ended with high school (Morelli, Rogoff, Oppenheim, & Goldsmith, 1992).

Some experts, however, find benefits in the shared sleeping pattern. One research team that has been monitoring sleep patterns of mothers and their 3-month-old infants found that those who sleep together tend to wake each other up during the night and that this may prevent the baby from sleeping too long and too deeply and having long breathing pauses that might even be fatal (McKenna & Mosko, 1993).

In many cultures, infants sleep with their mothers for the first few years of life, often in the same bed. In interviews, middle-class American parents and Mayan mothers in rural Guatemala revealed their child-rearing values and goals in their explanations about sleeping arrangements (Morelli et al., 1992).

The American parents, many of whom kept their infants in the same room but not in the same bed for the first 3 to 6 months, said they moved the babies to separate rooms because they wanted to make them self-reliant and independent. The Mayan mothers kept infants and toddlers in their beds until the birth of a new baby, when the older child would sleep with another family member or in a bed in the mother's room. They valued close parent-child relationships and expressed shock at the idea that anyone would put a baby to sleep in a room all alone.

We see, then, how societal values influence parents' behaviors. Throughout this book we will see many ways in which parents' behaviors, often culturally determined, affect their children.

DEATH IN INFANCY

One of the most tragic losses in life is the death of a child. Even though the parents of a baby who died may not have gotten to know their child well, they usually grieve deeply and are often overwhelmed by depression.

INFANT MORTALITY

infant mortality rate
Proportion of babies who die within the first year of life.

Fewer parents know this grief today than in the past, since we have made great strides in protecting the lives of new babies. Today in the United States, the *infant mortality rate*—the proportion of babies who die in the first year of life—is the lowest ever. In 1993, provisional statistics indicate that there were 828.8 deaths in the first year for every 100,000 live births, compared with 26 per 1000 in 1960 (Wegman, 1994).

However, there are some disturbing aspects of this record, which have implications for social policy. First, while infant mortality rates have declined for both black and white babies, black babies are still dying at more than twice the rate for white ones (at rates of 17.6 and 7.3, respectively). This gap is greatest in the neonatal period, suggesting unequal access to modern technology. The infant mortality rate was only slightly higher for Latinos than for non-Hispanic white babies; Puerto Rico had the highest rate, which was still less than that for African American infants (Wegman, 1993, 1994). Second, major regional variations exist, with the lowest rates in New England and the west, and the highest in the District of Columbia and the south (Wegman, 1993). Third, the United States infant mortality rate is higher than those of 21 other countries with populations of 2.5 million or more (Wegman, 1993, 1994; see Figure 5-6).

The term *neonatal mortality* refers to death in the first 4 weeks of life. Almost two-thirds of babies who die in the first year succumb in these first 4 weeks (U.S. Department of Health and Human Services, USDHHS, 1990). Birth defects are the leading cause of infant mortality for white babies. Disorders related to preterm and low birthweight are the leading cause of death for black babies. Other important causes of infant mortality are sudden infant death syndrome (SIDS) (see the next section), respiratory conditions, and the effects of pregnancy complications (Wegman, 1994). The decline in neonatal mortality since the 1960s is due to medical advances in keeping very small babies alive and in treating sick newborns. (See Chapter 4).

Postneonatal mortality is death from the age of 1 month to 1 year. In the United States, the two leading causes are sudden infant death syndrome and birth defects. Other important causes include respiratory disease, infections, parasitic disease, and accidents. Again, while this rate has also been lowered, black babies still die disproportionately more than white babies (6.3 black babies per 1000 live births, compared with 2.8 white babies—Wegman, 1993, 1994).

The *postneonatal* mortality rate improved during the first half of the twentieth century, largely because of better nutrition and sanitation. But the rapid drop

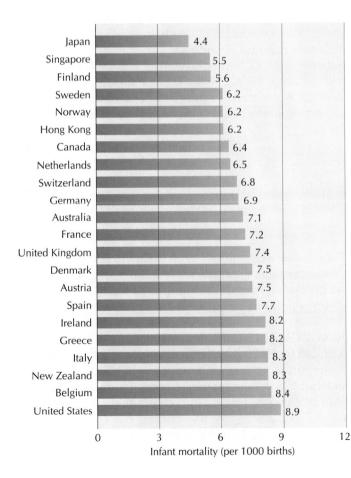

FIGURE 5-6
Infant mortality rate (deaths before 1 year per 1000 live births) is one indicator of a nation's health status. The United States infant mortality rate is higher than those of 21 other countries with populations of 2.5 million or more. This is largely because of the very high mortality rate for minority babies. According to 1991 statistics, the overall U.S. infant mortality rate was 8.9, but the rate for white babies was 7.3 and for black babies, the rate was 17.6. NOTE: Some data are provisional; rates for Spain and Finland are for 1990. SOURCE: Wegman, 1993.

in *neonatal* mortality since 1970 has meant that a larger proportion of infant deaths now occur after the first month. Many of the deaths occur in poor families that have little or no access to medical care. This is especially poignant in the case of Native American babies, who have a low rate of neonatal death. They leave the hospital healthy—but during the first year die at twice the rate of white babies. The causes are often preventable accidents and treatable conditions like pneumonia and gastroenteritis (Honigfeld & Kaplan, 1987).

Our present rates of infant death are chilling. The American Academy of Pediatrics Task Force on Infant Mortality (1986) asks several questions. First, why—in a wealthy country like the United States—is infant mortality not *declining* at a faster rate? Second, why is there such a large disparity in mortality rates between black and white babies? And, third, what effects have governmental budget cuts in health care had on babies? We have the knowledge and the technology to diagnose and treat high-risk pregnancies and help vulnerable infants, but much of this know-how has not benefited poor and minority-group mothers and babies. This situation can be helped if all prospective mothers get good prenatal care and general health care. Besides the tragedy of early death, infant mortality is a sign of children's health problems in general. By analyzing this picture, we can better understand children's health needs.

SUDDEN INFANT DEATH SYNDROME (SIDS)

sudden infant death syndrome (SIDS) *Sudden and unexpected death of any infant under 1 year of age, in which the cause of death remains unexplained after a thorough investigation that includes an autopsy; also known as crib death.*

Sudden infant death syndrome (SIDS) is the sudden and unexpected death of any infant under 1 year of age, in which the cause of death remains unexplained after a thorough investigation that includes an autopsy. About 6000 American babies a year, or about 1.5 out of every 1000 born, die of SIDS. It is the leading cause of deaths in infants from 1 to 12 months old in the United States and in a number of other industrial countries (Kleinman & Kiely, 1990; USDHHS, 1992). It occurs most often between 2 and 4 months of age, very rarely before 3 weeks or after 9 months (Zylke, 1989).

Causes of SIDS

Although we do not have definitive information about what causes SIDS, correlations have been found with a number of risk factors, and research on the condition continues.

Risk Factors for SIDS. Babies who succumb are more likely to be of low birthweight, black, and male. Their mothers are more likely to be young, unmarried, and poor; to have received little or no prenatal care; to have been ill during pregnancy; to smoke or abuse drugs or both; and to have had another baby less than a year before the one who died. The fathers are also more likely to be young (Mitchell et al., 1993; Babson & Clark, 1983; Hunt & Brouillette, 1987; Kleinberg, 1984; D. C. Shannon & Kelly, 1982a, 1982b; USDHHS, 1990). The babies' problems are worsened by living in low socioeconomic circumstances, but SIDS also strikes infants in advantaged families. SIDS deaths are most common in winter. The condition is not contagious, nor is it caused by choking or vomiting.

Current Theories. One theory suggests that SIDS may be caused by a neurological anomaly, with perhaps an abnormality in brain chemistry. Difficulties in the regulation of respiratory control (Hunt & Brouillette, 1987) or in making the transition from sleep to wakefulness have both been suggested by research (Schechtman, Harper, Wilson, & Southall, 1992). Further support for the effects of parental smoking as a cause has come from several studies (Haglund, 1993; Milerad & Sundell, 1993; Schoendorf & Kiely, 1992; Mitchell et al., 1993). Another study suggested that some SIDS-labeled deaths were really accidents (M. Bass, Kravath, & Glass, 1986).

What do you think?   *Can you think of other possible causes of SIDS that researchers should investigate?*

Effects on the Family

In studies of SIDS-bereaved families, all the parents said SIDS was the most severe family crisis they had ever known (DeFrain & Ernst, 1978; DeFrain, Taylor, & Ernst, 1982). One mother said, "This is the most painful time I have ever had to accept. It is hard to be a mother one day and not the next. The first months my arms actually ached to hold her again. I kept thinking I could hear her in bed playing, but it was just the furnace kicking on" (Defrain et al., 1982, p. 19).

Parents also feel guilty and sense criticism, and siblings react with emotional troubles, which may show up as nightmares or school problems. It usually takes about 18 months for a family to regain happiness. A mother said, "So many people tell you when your child dies that things will someday be okay. At that time you seriously doubt that you can ever feel happy and normal again. But it does happen; and it is a blessing and a relief that it does" (DeFrain et al., 1982, p. 69).

Preventing SIDS

A major change in recommendations for the sleep position of newborns has come from studies in Tasmania (an Australian island), the Netherlands, New Zealand, and the United Kingdom. They suggest that SIDS may be related to a baby's sleeping in the prone position (lying on the stomach). The American Academy of Pediatrics, citing declines in SIDS rates where infants are put to sleep on their back or side, recommends this practice for healthy babies (Willinger, Hoffman, & Hartford, 1994). The only babies who should still be put to bed stomach-down are premature infants with respiratory distress, infants with swallowing or upper airway difficulties, or babies with other special problems (Dwyer, Ponsonby, Newman, & Gibbons, 1991; AAP Task Force on Infant Positioning and SIDS, 1992). Once babies can roll over by themselves, some will choose the prone position; this usually poses no problem as long as they are not on soft bedding like pillows, comforters, blankets, or sheepskin.

Besides the supine (back down) or side sleeping position, the 1993 International State of the Art Conference on SIDS recommended several other preventive measures. Ideally, *both* parents and other caregivers should stop smoking completely. At the very least, they should smoke less and not around the baby. To keep the baby's temperature within a healthy range, caregivers should feel the baby's upper chest or nape of the neck, the face, and the forehead; should remove outdoor clothes when taking the baby inside or into a car; and should cover a feverish infant with less clothing and blankets (Köhler & Markestad, 1993).

IMMUNIZATION FOR BETTER HEALTH

By the middle of the twentieth century, immunization seemed to have banished such widespread and often fatal diseases as measles, rubella (German measles), mumps, pertussis (whooping cough), diphtheria, and poliomyelitis, at least in the United States. But between 1980 and 1985, the proportion of American children aged 1 to 4 who were immunized against the major childhood illnesses dropped. A 1994 report found that fewer than half the 2-year-olds in major American cities had gotten all their shots, and those who did get them all had not received them at recommended intervals (Zell, Dietz, Stevenson, Cochi, & Bruce, 1994).

LOWER IMMUNIZATION RATES: IMPLICATIONS FOR SOCIAL POLICY

This failure to protect children is reflected in rising rates of a number of childhood diseases. Between 1985 and 1990, mumps, measles, rubella, and pertussis cases rose, although some declines were reported between 1990 and 1991 (USDHHS, 1993). Now only 11 to 58 percent of 2-year-olds are protected against measles, rubella, polio, mumps, diphtheria, pertussis, and tetanus (Zell et al., 1994).* Immunization rates are especially low among American children from mi-

*As we go to press in 1995, a vaccine to prevent chickenpox has been approved by the federal government and is expected to be recommended for all children over 1 year of age, and for adolescents and adults who have not had the disease.

TABLE 5-5

RECOMMENDED CHILDHOOD IMMUNIZATIONS*						
AGE	DPT†	POLIO	MMR‡	HEPATITIS B§ (HBV)	HAEMOPHILUS (HIB)	TETANUS-DIPHTHERIA
Birth				✔		
1–2 months				✔		
2 months	✔	✔			✔	
4 months	✔	✔			✔	
6 months	✔				✔	
6–18 months				✔		
12–15 months					✔	
15–18 months	✔	✔				
4–6 years	✔	✔				
11–12 years			✔			
14–16 years						✔

*Except where public health authorities require otherwise.
†Diphtheria, tetanus, pertussis (whooping cough).
‡Measles, mumps, rubella.
§The AAP Committee on Infectious Disease (1992) has recommended both universal infant immunization and adolescent immunization against HBV, since selective immunization to high-risk populations failed to control the infection.
SOURCE: Adapted from American Academy of Pediatrics, 1994.

TABLE 5-6

TRENDS IN PREVENTABLE CHILDHOOD DISEASES			
	LOWEST NUMBER OF CASES (YEAR)	NUMBER OF CASES IN 1991*	INCREASE FROM BEST YEAR TO 1991, %
Measles	1,497 (1983)	9,488	533.8
Mumps	2,982 (1985)	4,031	35.2
Pertussis	1,248 (1981)	2,575	106.3
Rubella	225 (1988)	1,372	509.8

*Provisional data reported through December 28, 1991.
SOURCE: Centers for Disease Control.

nority groups and from poverty-stricken families, but the problem cuts across all racial, ethnic, and economic groups (Institute of Medicine, 1994). Table 5-5 shows current recommendations for childhood immunization.

Apparently, we have developed a new disease cycle: "alarm-action" and "relaxation-inaction." The rising disease rate in 1977 provoked renewed alarm and action, leading to a new social policy in which the federal government promoted education and provided money for vaccinations. The disease rate among children then declined, until 1981, when the budget of the Childhood Immunization Initiative program was cut by one-third and the rate began to climb again (Bumpers, 1984; see Table 5-6). Now the U.S. government is again responding to this crisis in health care. In 1994 Congress appropriated more than $800 million to provide free vaccine to the uninsured and those on Medicaid, to offer education, and to make vaccines more available (Leary, 1994b).

According to an expert panel of the Institute of Medicine (1994), more than 90 percent of the nation's children begin their immunizations on schedule—and more than 90 percent are fully inoculated by age 5, when it is required for school attendance. The panel recommended that states mount similar campaigns to inoculate younger children, tracking records by computer; that doctors and clinics set more flexible schedules for giving shots, offer hours on evenings and weekends for working parents, and reach out to educate and remind parents; and that government and private agencies work together.

Another reason for the drop in immunizations is some parents' fears that the vaccines will cause brain damage to their children. This fear arose in response to cases of brain damage that some people attributed to a child's having been injected with pertussis vaccine (to prevent whooping cough), which is usually given along with immunizations for diphtheria and tetanus (DPT vaccine). However, the association between DPT and neurologic illness appears to be very small. In a study of 218,000 children in the United States, only 424 cases (0.2 percent) of such illness were found (Gale et al., 1994). The danger from the diseases that this vaccine prevents is still greater than the danger from the vaccine. In addition, a new vaccine that prevents whooping cough and causes no serious side effects has been successfully tested in Sweden and may soon be commercially available ("New whooping cough vaccine. . ., 1994).

To overcome some barriers to full protection, researchers are currently designing a "supervaccine," one that could provide lifetime immunity with a single dose; would be easy to administer, store, and transport; and would be effective any time after birth (Leary, 1994a).

BOX 5-3   THE EVERYDAY WORLD

PUTTING RESEARCH FINDINGS TO WORK

If you are a parent, or are about to become a parent, or if you care for infants or toddlers, you can put into practice important findings that have emerged from research. The following recommendations are based on theories and findings discussed in Chapters 5, 6, and 7.

♦ *Respond to babies' signals.* This is probably the most important thing a caregiver can do. Meeting an infant's needs—whether for food, cuddling, or comforting—establishes a sense of trust that the world is a friendly place. Answering cries or requests for help gives babies a sense of having some control over their lives, an important awareness for emotional and intellectual development. Adults often worry about spoiling children by meeting their needs quickly, but the children who have the most problems in life are those whose needs go unmet. The idea is "Baby a baby when he's a baby, and you won't have to baby him the rest of his life" (Chapters 6 and 7).

♦ *Provide interesting things for babies to look at and do.* By watching a mobile swaying over a crib and handling simple household objects or brightly colored and vividly patterned toys, babies learn about shapes, sizes, and textures. Playing helps them develop their senses and motor skills. Handling objects helps them distinguish between themselves and things that are not themselves (Chapters 5 and 6).

♦ *Talk to babies and read to them.* By hearing and responding to speech directed especially to them, babies learn how to express themselves. You'll be most effective if you pitch your voice high and speak slowly, use short words and simple sentences, leave off word endings (saying "go" instead of "going," for example), ask questions, repeat words and phrases, and talk about things in the baby's world. You'll probably do most of these things intuitively as you talk in "baby talk," or "motherese" (Chapter 6).

♦ *Give babies the power to make changes.* If you hang a mobile over the crib, make it possible for the baby to make the mobile move. Give toys that the baby can shake to make a noise, or can change in shape, or can make move. Babies need to learn that they have some control over their world and that they can have an effect on the things in it.

♦ *Give babies freedom to explore.* It's better to baby-proof an environment (by taking away things that can be broken or swallowed, by removing sharp objects that can injure, and by jamming books into a bookcase so tightly that a baby can't pull them out) than it is to confine a baby in a playpen. Babies need opportunities to crawl and eventually walk and to exercise their large muscles. They also need to learn about their environment to feel in control of it. And they need the freedom to go off on their own to develop a sense of independence (Chapters 5, 6, and 7).

IMMUNIZATION WORLDWIDE

The contagious diseases of childhood are largely the same the world over. The World Summit for Children brought more than 70 world leaders to the United Nations in September 1990 to announce public health goals for children. Among these goals was the eradication of more than 35 percent of childhood deaths worldwide by immunizing all children (United Nations, 1990).

A comparison of immunization rates in 1985, 1986, and 1987 in the United States and in several European countries* found that American preschoolers are less likely to be protected against polio, tetanus, diphtheria, and measles than are their European counterparts (B. C. Williams, 1990).

Why are immunization rates higher in these other countries? The difference seems to be the way health care is provided. All the European countries examined have publicly subsidized health surveillance, with easy access at little or

*Denmark, France, (West) Germany, the Netherlands, Norway, and England and Wales.

no cost. In the United States, many children are not covered by health insurance and those who are may not have preventive-care coverage.

Immunization is cost-effective. Every dollar spent to immunize against measles, mumps, and rubella saves $13.40 over treating children with these illnesses, and every dollar spent on pertussis immunization saves $11.10 (Harvey, 1990).

What do you think? *If you were to design a campaign to promote universal immunization, which population groups would you target? How would you approach each group? Who should be responsible for assuring immunization for all children—government, parents, or community groups?*

We see how the environment, often in the form of social policy, can exert a great influence on children's health; the environment also has a major impact on cognitive and social-personality development. For research findings offering clues to optimizing children's early environments, see Box 5-3. During the first 3 years children make great advances in these realms, as we'll see in Chapters 6 and 7.

SUMMARY

1   Normal physical growth and motor development depend upon maturation, the unfolding of patterns of behavior in a biologically determined sequence. Two complementary principles are the cephalocaudal principle (development proceeds from the head to the lower body parts) and the proximodistal principle (development proceeds from the center of the body to the outer parts).

2   A child's body grows most rapidly during the first year of life. Growth proceeds at a rapid but diminishing rate for the next 2 years.

3   Growth is influenced by heredity, sex, and race as well as environmental factors such as nutrition and health care.

4   The greatest growth of cell bodies in the central nervous system is between 25 and 40 weeks of gestational age and in the first few months after birth. The newborn baby's brain is 25 percent of its eventual adult weight at birth and reaches 80 percent of its adult weight by the end of the second year. The environment can influence brain development positively or negatively, depending on the experience.

5   "Primitive reflexes" disappear as involuntary (subcortical) control of behavior gives way to cortical control. The timetable for their disappearance reflects whether neurological development is proceeding normally.

6   Breastfeeding offers physiological benefits to the infant and may facilitate the formation of the mother-infant bond. However, the quality of the relationship between parents and infant is more important than the feeding method.

7   At about 4 to 6 months, babies should begin to eat solid foods. Obesity in infancy does not necessarily predict obesity later in life.

8   Sensory capacities, all of which operate to some extent at birth, develop rapidly in the first few months of life. Very young infants show pronounced ability to discriminate among stimuli. Touch seems to be the first sense to develop and is the most mature sensory system for the first several months. Vision is the least well developed sense at birth.

9   Early motor development occurs when an infant is maturationally ready to engage in certain activities.

10   Environmental factors influence the expression of specific motor behaviors. Children raised in isolated, impoverished conditions may show motor retardation, but environmental influences have to be significant to accelerate or retard motor development

markedly. Cross-cultural differences may lead to differences in patterns of motor behavior. However, short-term experiments aimed at speeding up specific types of motor development have generally yielded variable results.

11 Motor development (such as eye-hand coordination and crawling) influences many aspects of physical, cognitive, and emotional development.

12 Although the infant mortality rate in the United States has improved, it is still disturbingly high, especially among African Americans. It is related to poor prenatal care, which often contributes to low birthweight.

13 Sudden infant death syndrome (SIDS) is the leading cause of death in infants between 1 month and 1 year of age, affecting about 6000 infants each year in the United States. The cause of SIDS has not been determined. Decline in SIDS rates is associated with putting the baby to sleep on the back or side rather than on the stomach.

14 Many U.S. children do not receive all their vaccinations on schedule. This is a particular problem for children under age 5.

KEY TERMS

maturation (167)
cephalocaudal principle (168)
proximodistal principle (168)
reflex behavior (174)
visual cliff (181)
visual preference (182)

Denver Developmental Screening Test (186)
infant mortality rate (196)
sudden infant death syndrome (SIDS) (198)

SUGGESTED READINGS

Baumslag, N., & Michels, D. (1995). *Milk, money & madness: The battle for the breast.* Westport, CT: Bergin & Garvey. The authors, a pediatrician and a science writer, cover the history, culture, biology, and politics of breastfeeding. The book has many illustrations.

DeFrain, J., Ernst, L., Jakub, D., & Taylor, J. (1991). *Sudden infant death: Enduring the loss.* Lexington, MA: Heath. This investigation of the experiences and special problems of families who have lost a child to sudden infant death syndrome is compassionate and accepting of the many ways that people deal with tragedy.

Eiger, M. S., & Olds, S. W. (1987). *The complete book of breastfeeding.* New York: Workman. A classic guidebook for nursing mothers that draws on research findings and incorporates many suggestions appropriate for the lifestyles of today's families.

Leach, P. (1990). *Babyhood* (rev. ed.). New York: Knopf. A comprehensive look at the period of infancy, covering everything about a newborn baby. Written for the layperson, the text covers the whole field of study about babies.

CHAPTER 6
COGNITIVE DEVELOPMENT IN INFANCY AND TODDLERHOOD

CHAPTER 6
COGNITIVE DEVELOPMENT IN INFANCY AND TODDLERHOOD

I wish I could travel by the road that crosses baby's mind, and out beyond all bounds;
Where messengers run errands for no cause between the kingdoms of kings of no history;
Where Reason makes kites of her laws and flies them, and
Truth sets Fact free from its fetters.

Rabindranoth Tagore, 1913

In this chapter, we follow babies' progress during the first 3 years. We examine the Piagetian, psychometric, and information-processing approaches to the study of cognition, and we assess babies' intelligence by watching them play. We learn how they learn. We look at the ability to learn and use language. We also look at how babies and toddlers respond to intellectual stimulation, how parents and other caregivers can stimulate them, and how society can help provide stimulation. After you have studied this chapter, you should be able to answer questions like the following:

PREVIEW QUESTIONS

♦ How do the Piagetian, psychometric, and information-processing approaches address and measure infants' cognitive development?
♦ How do infants learn?
♦ How do babies and toddlers learn to speak and understand language?
♦ What are the milestones of language development in the first 3 years?
♦ How do toddlers display competence, how can their parents help them acquire it, and how can society help parents?
♦ How does play advance babies' cognitive and emotional development?

"'Icky! 'Icky!" 18-month-old Vicky shouts as she waves her hand at photos of herself. Her recognition of herself in the photos, her awareness of her name, and her ability to pronounce a close approximation of it are all signs of her cognitive development, giving her more tools for understanding and functioning.

If newborns could speak, we would have realized centuries ago that we were underestimating their intelligence. This underestimation persisted almost to the present because of two major movements toward the end of the nineteenth century. On one hand, psychologists were proposing theories of human development. On the other, doctors were establishing a routine under which babies were born in hospitals, exposed to sedative drugs, and isolated from their mothers. Thus observations of newborns were biased. Furthermore, the first tests to study infants' intelligence were based on tests for adults or animals, none of which were suited to human infants. This has changed over the past few decades, when there has been more research on infants' abilities than during all previous history (Lipsitt, 1982; Rovee-Collier & Lipsitt, 1982).

We now know that the normal, healthy human baby is remarkably competent. Infants are born with all their senses working, with the ability to learn, and with a capacity for acquiring and using language. From birth, humans actively affect their environment as well as react to it.

THREE APPROACHES TO STUDYING COGNITIVE DEVELOPMENT

One-year-old Vicky loves to play games. One day Charles put some Cheerios in his hand, closed it, and put his hand on the tray of Vicky's high chair. With both hands, she pulled his fingers open, saw the Cheerios, and released his fingers to try to get the cereal. His fingers free, Charles again closed them over the Cheerios. After two more tries to get the Cheerios, Vicky held Charles's fingers open with one hand while she picked up the Cheerios with her other. One day, when she was holding a toy in one hand, she opened Charles's fingers with her free hand and then held them open with her chin, flashing a roguish smile as she scooped up the Cheerios.

Vicky is showing the intelligent behavior that babies her age are capable of—behavior involving complex and self-initiated learning. How did her intelligence develop? What accounts for individual differences among children with regard to intelligent behavior? Can we measure a baby's intelligence? Can we predict how smart that baby will be later? These questions are hard to answer because intelligence is hard to define, describe, analyze, and account for fully.

First, what do we mean by intelligence? ***Intelligent behavior*** has two key aspects. First, it is *goal-oriented:* conscious and deliberate rather than accidental. Second, it is *adaptive*—used to solve problems. Intelligence is influenced by both inherited ability and experience, as we saw in Chapter 2. Intelligence is what makes a person able to acquire, remember, and use knowledge; to understand concepts and relationships among objects, ideas, and events; and to apply knowledge and understanding to everyday problems.

Most investigators of intelligence have taken one of three approaches:

- The *Piagetian approach* looks at the quality of cognitive functioning, or *what* people can do. It is concerned with the evolution of mental structures and how children adapt to their environment. It maintains that cognition develops in universal stages.
- The *psychometric approach* tries to measure individual differences in intelligence in terms of quantity, or *how much* intelligence a person has. It uses *intelligence tests;* the higher the test score, the more intelligent a person is assumed to be.
- The *information-processing approach* follows the path information takes from initial perception until it is used. It analyzes the processes underlying intelligent behavior, or *how* people use their intelligence. It also focuses on individual differences.

All three approaches help us understand intelligence. No single approach gives us a full picture, but a combination of them opens several windows to examine what is intelligent, effective behavior. Let us see what each perspective can tell us about the cognitive development of infants and toddlers.

intelligent behavior
Behavior that is goal-oriented—conscious and deliberate rather than accidental—and adaptive: used to identify and solve problems.

Piagetian approach *Study of cognitive development based on describing qualitative changes in thinking that are typical of children at particular stages; named after its founder, Jean Piaget.*

psychometric approach *Study of cognitive development based on attempts to measure the quantity of intelligence.*

information-processing approach *Study of cognitive development based on the mental capacities and processes that support thought.*

PIAGETIAN APPROACH: COGNITIVE STAGES

cognitive development
Growth in mental powers and qualities that permit understanding.

Jean Piaget explored *cognitive development,* the growth in children's thought processes that enables them to acquire and use knowledge. To examine how thought evolves, Piaget watched the development of his own three children. His observations provided the basis for his first stage of cognitive development—the sensorimotor stage—and inspired much research on infant cognition. Many contemporary psychologists, however, believe that, as important as Piaget's contributions were, he underestimated children's abilities. We will discuss the evidence for this criticism after we describe the sensorimotor stage.

Sensorimotor Stage (Birth to About 2 Years)

Jason is in the kitchen with his father. The baby hears the sounds of cabinet doors being opened and closed, hears the whoosh of water from the sink faucet, and watches the activity around him. As Jess cooks dinner, he keeps up a stream of conversation with his son. This everyday scene is a rich source of sensory experiences for Jason, who is in Piaget's first cognitive stage, the *sensorimotor stage.*

sensorimotor stage *In Piaget's theory, the first stage in human cognitive development (birth to about age 2), during which infants acquire knowledge through sensory experience and motor activity.*

This is when infants learn about themselves and their world through their own developing sensory and motor activity. During the first 2 years, said Piaget, babies change from creatures who respond primarily through reflexes and random behavior into goal-oriented toddlers. They will now organize their activities in relation to their environment, coordinate information from their senses, and progress from trial-and-error learning to using rudimentary insights in solving simple problems.

Cognitive Concepts of the Sensorimotor Stage. During the sensorimotor stage, said Piaget, babies develop several cognitive concepts. The most important, he said, is *object permanence,* the realization that an object or person continues to exist even when out of sight. This is the basis for children's awareness that they exist apart from objects and other people. It allows Jason to feel secure in the knowledge that even after his mother has left the room, she continues to exist and will return. It is essential to understanding time, space, and a world full of objects. The development of this concept is what peekaboo is all about. (See Box 6-1.)

object permanence *In Piaget's theory, awareness that a person or thing continues to exist when out of sight.*

Another concept is causality, the recognition that certain events cause other events. In one study, babies saw films that showed physically impossible events, like a ball moving toward a second ball which then moved before the first ball touched it. Infants under 10 months of age showed no surprise, but older babies did. Evidently, the older infants realized that something necessary for movement of the second ball was missing (Michotte, 1962, in Siegler & Richards, 1982).

This rudimentary awareness of causality develops at about 10 months, when many babies begin making experiments. Vicky plays with light switches and delights in making the light go on and off. Her favorite toys are those she can do something with—whirl around, make noises with, or drop. By her actions, she shows that she realizes that she is causing certain events.

But, said Piaget, babies still have limited representational ability—the ability to mentally represent objects and actions in memory. This ability to remember and imagine things and events—largely through symbols like words, numbers, and mental pictures—blossoms, he said, as children are about to enter the next cognitive stage, the preoperational stage (discussed in Chapter 9).

BOX 6-1 ■ AROUND THE WORLD

PLAYING PEEKABOO

In a mud hut in rural South Africa a Bantu mother smiles at her 9-month-old son, covers her eyes with her hands, and asks, "Uphi?" (Where?) After 3 seconds, the mother says, "Here!" and uncovers her eyes to the baby's delight. In a Tokyo apartment a Japanese mother, using different language and covering her eyes with a cloth, plays the same game with her 12-month-old daughter, who shows the same joyous response.

"Peekaboo" is played across diverse cultures using similar routines. In all cultures where the game is played,* the moment when the mother reappears is exhilarating. It is marked by exaggerated gestures and consistent voice tones, high-pitched or low, drawn out or intense.

Why is this game so popular? Psychoanalysts maintain that it helps babies master anxiety when their mother disappears. Cognitive psychologists see it as a way babies play with developing ideas about the existence, disappearance, and reappearance of objects—the concept of object permanence. It may also be a clue to the development of a sense of humor, a social routine that helps babies learn the kinds of rules that will govern language (like taking turns, as in conversation), and preparation for developing attention and learning.

Infants get pleasure from the immediate sensory stimulation of the game, heightened by their fascination with faces and voices, especially the high-pitched tones the adult usually uses. The combination of face and voice signals is compelling. As babies develop the cognitive competency to predict future events, expectations become important and the game takes on new dimensions.

The way the game develops over the first year reflects intertwining changes in the baby's perceptual, cognitive, and motor development. (See table.) By 1 year, children have gone from being relatively passive observers to actively initiating the game and engaging adults in play—thus showing bidirectional influence. Seeing Charles's tee shirt on the floor, Vicky drapes it over her head and toddles over to him. "Where's Vicky?" he asks. She whips the shirt off her face, and as her father exclaims, "Peekaboo!" Vicky laughs.

DEVELOPMENT AS MEASURED BY THE GAME OF PEEKABOO

BABY'S AGE	WHAT ADULT DOES	WHO USUALLY INITIATES	WHAT BABY DOES
3-5 months	Moves own face in and out of infant's view	Adult	Smiles and laughs; begins to develop expectation of what will happen next.
5-8 months	1. Gets baby's attention 2. Covers eyes or face or hides 3. Uncovers or reappears 4. Uses voice cues throughout 5. Smiles and laughs	Adult	Smiles and laughs; shows anticipatory looking and smiling to adult's "alert call" just before her reappearance.
8-15 months	Responds to baby's cues	Baby	Increasingly takes active role in initiating game; if game is discontinued, baby repeats own turn, "talks," looks at or touches adult to resume. In game: 1. Covers eyes or face or hides. 2. Uncovers or reappears. 3. Smiles and laughs.

*The cultures analyzed in this report include those found in Malaysia, Greece, India, Iran, Russia, Brazil, Indonesia, Korea, and South Africa.

SOURCE: Fernald & O'Neill, 1993.

Annie's delight in playing peekaboo rests on the development of object permanence, the knowledge that a familiar face and surroundings are still there even when she cannot see them. Object permanence develops gradually over the first 18 months of life.

Baby sucks thumb   Baby enjoys sucking

(a) Primary circular reaction: Action and response both involve infant's own body (1 to 4 months).

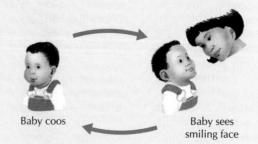

Baby coos   Baby sees smiling face

(b) Secondary circular reaction: Action gets a response from another person or object, leading to baby's repeating original action (4 to 8 months).

Baby steps on rubber duck   Baby squeezes rubber duck   Duck squeaks

(c) Tertiary circular reaction: Action gets one pleasing result, leading baby to perform similar actions to gets similar results (12 to 18 months).

FIGURE 6-1

Primary, secondary, and tertiary circular reactions. According to Piaget, infants learn to reproduce pleasurable events they discover accidentally. In a primary circular reaction (*a*), Vicky happens to suck her thumb, enjoys the feeling, and puts her thumb back in her mouth or keeps it there. The stimulus of the thumb elicits the sucking reflex; the pleasure of sucking then stimulates Vicky to keep on sucking. A secondary circular reaction (*b*) involves something outside Jason's body. He coos; his mother smiles; and because Jason likes to see Julia smiling, Jason coos again.

In a tertiary circular reaction (*c*), Vicky tries different ways to reproduce a response she discovered accidentally. When she steps on a rubber duck, the duck squeaks. Vicky then tries to produce the squeak in another way, this time by squeezing it or sitting on it.

circular reaction *In Piaget's theory, a simple behavior that is repeated often.*

scheme *Organized pattern of behavior.*

Substages of the Sensorimotor Stage.   Looking more closely at the sensorimotor stage, we see the enormous cognitive growth that occurs before age 2. (See Table 6-1). Much of this growth occurs through what Piaget called *circular reactions,* in which an infant learns how to reproduce pleasurable or interesting events originally discovered by chance. Initially, an activity produces a sensation so welcome that the child wants to repeat the activity. The repetition then feeds on itself in a continuous cycle in which cause and effect become almost indistinguishable. (See Figure 6-1.) The six substages of the sensorimotor stage flow from one to another as a baby's *schemes,* or organized patterns of behavior, become more elaborate. Note the progress babies make in developing object permanence.

TABLE 6-1

SIX SUBSTAGES OF PIAGET'S SENSORIMOTOR STAGE OF COGNITIVE DEVELOPMENT	
SUBSTAGE	**DESCRIPTION**
Substage 1 (birth to 1 month): Use of reflexes	Infants exercise their inborn reflexes and gain some control over them. They do not coordinate information from their senses. They do not grasp an object they are looking at. They have not developed object permanence.
Substage 2 (1 to 4 months): Primary circular reactions	Infants repeat pleasurable behaviors that first occur by chance (such as sucking). Activities focus on infant's body rather than the effects of the behavior on the environment. Infants make first acquired adaptations; that is, they suck different objects differently. They begin to coordinate sensory information. They still have not developed object permanence.
Substage 3 (4 to 8 months): Secondary circular reactions	Infants become more interested in the environment and repeat actions that bring interesting results and prolong interesting experiences. Actions are intentional but not initially goal-directed. Infants show partial object permanence. They will search for a partially hidden object.
Substage 4 (8 to 12 months): Coordination of secondary schemes	Behavior is more deliberate and purposeful as infants coordinate previously learned schemes (such as looking at and grasping a rattle) and use previously learned behaviors to attain their goals (such as crawling across the room to get a desired toy). They can anticipate events. Object permanence is developing, although infants will search for an object in its first hiding place, even if they saw it being moved.
Substage 5 (12 to 18 months): Tertiary circular reactions	Infants show curiosity as they purposefully vary their actions to see results. They actively explore their world to determine how an object, event, or situation is novel. They try out new activities and use trial and error in solving problems. Infants will follow a series of object displacements, but since they cannot imagine movement they do not see, they will not search for an object where they have not observed it being hidden.
Substage 6 (18 to 24 months): Mental combinations	Since toddlers have developed a primitive symbol system (such as language) to represent events, they are no longer confined to trial and error to solve problems. Their symbol system allows toddlers to begin to think about events and anticipate their consequences without always resorting to action. Toddlers begin to demonstrate insight. Object permanence is fully developed.

NOTE: Infants show enormous cognitive growth during Piaget's sensorimotor stage, as they learn about the world through their senses and their motor activities. Note their progress in problem solving, object permanence, and the coordination of sensory information.

Substage 1: Use of Reflexes (Birth to 1 Month). As neonates exercise their inborn reflexes, they gain some control over them. They begin to engage in a behavior even when the stimulus that elicits it as an automatic reflex is not present. For example, newborns suck reflexively when their lips are touched. During the first month, they learn to find the nipple even when their lips are not touched, and they suck at times when they are not hungry. Thus infants become energetic initiators of activity, not just passive responders. Their inborn schemes for sucking are modified and extended by experience.

Object permanence is completely lacking; the presence or absence of any object seems random and unpredictable.

Substage 2: Primary Circular Reactions and Acquired Adaptations (1 to 4 Months). Jason lying in his crib sucking his thumb exemplifies a *primary circular reaction,* a simple, repetitive act centered on the baby's own body to reproduce a pleasant sensation first achieved by chance.

One day Jason begins to suck while his thumb happens to be in his mouth. He likes the feeling and tries to recapture it through trial and error. Once he does, he deliberately tries to put his thumb into his mouth, keep it there, and keep sucking. In so doing, he makes his first *acquired adaptation:* He learns to adjust or accommodate his actions by sucking on his thumb differently from the way he sucks on a nipple. The result is a reorganized scheme for sucking.

A baby also starts to coordinate and organize different kinds of sensory information—like vision and hearing. When Vicky hears her father's voice, she turns toward the sound and discovers that it comes from Charles's mouth. Her world is beginning to make sense.

Object permanence is absent. Vicky follows a moving object with her eyes; but when something disappears, she does not look for it. However, she may stare briefly at the spot where the object was last seen, as if passively watching for it.

Substage 3: Secondary Circular Reactions (4 to 8 Months). The third substage coincides with a new interest in manipulating objects. Babies engage in *secondary circular reactions,* intentional actions repeated not merely for their own sake, as in substage 2, but to get results beyond their own body.

For example, Jason now enjoys shaking a rattle to hear its noise. He is learning ways to prolong interesting experiences; for example, he finds that by making a soft sound when a friendly face appears, he can make the face stay longer. However, his behavior is not fully goal-oriented; before he will pursue a goal, he must first discover it accidentally.

Object permanence is developing: Jason looks for an object that he has dropped or that is hidden from him, but only if he can see a part of it. If it is completely hidden, he acts as if it does not exist.

This baby, in the stage of secondary circular reactions, is studying what happens when he pulls the string on his toy. Perhaps he discovered accidentally that the bells rang the first time he pulled the string and is now recreating that interesting experience.

Substage 4: Coordination of Secondary Schemes (8 to 12 Months). By the time they reach the fourth substage, infants have built on the schemes they were born with, adapting and elaborating on them through experience. Babies now begin to separate schemes from the original context in which they were learned and re-combine schemes to deal with new situations. In other words, they generalize from past experience, calling upon responses they have previously mastered to solve new problems.

When an obstacle arises—as when Vicky's father playfully withholds an object she wants—Vicky may grab for the object, push Charles's hand away, or hit his hand. The infant tries out, modifies, and coordinates previous schemes—like grabbing, pushing, and hitting—searching for what works in the new situation.

Object permanence is developing rapidly. Vicky looks for an object if she sees it being hidden. But if she sees it being moved from one hiding place to another, she will look for it in the *first* hiding place.

Substage 5: Tertiary Circular Reactions (12 to 18 Months). In the fifth stage, babies experiment with novel rather than purely repetitive behavior. Once they can walk, their curiosity focuses on new objects, which they inspect to learn about them. They engage in *tertiary circular reactions;* they vary their original actions to see what will happen rather than merely repeat pleasing behavior they have ac-cidentally discovered. Vicky might step on a rubber duck and hear it squeak. Then she might try pressing it; after that, she might sit on the duck.

For the first time, children show originality in problem solving, which they do by trial and error. Instead of merely building on past responses, they try out new behaviors until they find the most effective way to attain a goal. When Vicky wanted to get the Cheerios from Charles, she tried prying and holding his fingers open first with both hands, then with one hand, and finally with her chin.

Object permanence has developed further. Infants look in the last place they have seen something being hidden rather than in the first place, as in substage 4. Still, they cannot imagine movement they do not see. If Charles were to put a toy in his hand, put his hand behind a pillow, leave the toy there, and bring out his closed hand, Vicky would look for her toy in her father's hand. She would not search for it behind the pillow, because she did not *see* him put it there.

Substage 6: Beginning of Thought—Mental Combinations (18 to 24 Months). At about 18 months, said Piaget, children become capable of symbolic thought. That is, they are able to make mental representations (symbols) of events, enabling them to think about actions before taking them and to go beyond action-oriented behavior. Since they now have some understanding of cause and effect, they no longer have to go through trial and error to solve new problems. Rather, mental representations let them try out solutions in their minds and discard the ones they decide will not work. Piaget's daughter, Lucienne, demonstrated this develop-ment of insight when she figured out how to pry a watch chain out of a partially closed match box, opening and closing her mouth to signify her idea of widen-ing the slit in the box (Piaget, 1952).

The ability to manipulate symbols frees children from immediate experience and lets them use language. They can now imitate actions even after whatever or whomever they are copying is no longer in front of them. They are able to pretend, as Vicky does at 20 months when she pretends to drive a car. This simple "pretend" play is the forerunner of the more elaborate dramatic play that occurs at age 3 and older as she becomes better able to remember and imagine. Memory and imagination will improve vastly during early childhood.

Object permanence is fully developed. When children see an object being moved, they look for it in the last hiding place. They will also search for objects they have not seen being hidden. Vicky would now look behind the pillow for the toy, even if she had not seen Charles putting it there.

What do you think?   *You are designing a toy or book for an infant or toddler. Based on Piaget's findings about the sensorimotor stage, what elements would you include in your design?*

Evaluation of Piaget's Concept of a Sensorimotor Stage

Piaget's theories are highly regarded for their innovative contribution to our understanding of cognitive development. Yet while research has supported some of his claims, it has refuted others.

Support for Piaget's Theory.   Object permanence seems to progress in the sequence Piaget described (J. Kramer, Hill, & Cohen, 1975). Also, researchers have developed tests based on Piaget's theories to measure cognitive development in infants. Standardized tests of sensorimotor development, like the Infant Psychological Development Scales (IPDS) (Uzgiris & Hunt, 1975), combine the Piagetian approach with the psychometric (described in the next section).

In one study, 23 babies were tested on the IPDS every 3 months between 1 and 2 years of age, and at 31 months they were given the Stanford-Binet Intelligence Scale, a test of childhood intelligence. A positive correlation appeared between scores on the Stanford-Binet and scores on each of the eight subscales of the IPDS. The age of attaining object permanence was the strongest predictor of later scores on the intelligence tests at 31 months (Wachs, 1975). Thus an infant's sensorimotor abilities seem to be useful predictors of childhood intelligence.

Limitations of the Concept.   Research challenges Piaget's view that infants up to 18 months old cannot think about objects not physically present or about past events. In fact, infants seem able to conceptualize much earlier. Research on memory, discussed later in this chapter, shows that even very young infants have symbolic capabilities and can remember past events. Other studies contradict several aspects of Piaget's theory.

For example, Piaget may have underestimated infants' grasp of *object permanence* because of his testing methods. Babies may fail to search for hidden objects because they are not able to perform a sequence of actions—like moving a cushion to look for something hidden behind it. Infants as young as $3\frac{1}{2}$ months of age, tested by a simpler, more age-appropriate procedure, behaved as if they remembered an object they could not see (Baillargeon & DeVos, 1991). In this experiment, $3\frac{1}{2}$-month-olds watched a short or a tall carrot slide along a track. The track's center was hidden by a screen with a large window. The short carrot did not appear in the window when passing behind the screen. Neither did the tall carrot.

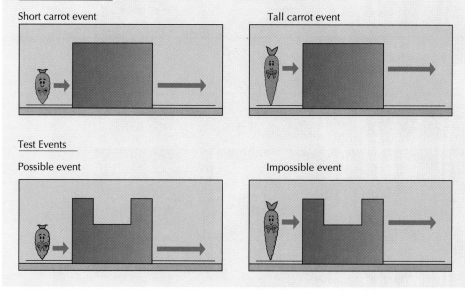

Habituation Events

Short carrot event

Tall carrot event

Test Events

Possible event

Impossible event

FIGURE 6-2
Object permanence in infants. In this experiment, 3½-month-old infants watched a short or a tall carrot slide along a track. The track's center was hidden by a screen with a large window. The short carrot did not appear in the window when passing behind the screen; the tall carrot should have appeared in the window but did not. The babies looked longer at the tall than the short carrot event, suggesting that they were surprised that the tall carrot did not appear. SOURCE: Baillargeon & DeVos, 1991.

The babies looked longer at the tall carrot event, suggesting that they were surprised that the tall carrot did not appear. (See Figure 6-2.)

Research also refutes Piaget's belief that the *senses are unconnected at birth* and are only gradually integrated through experience. We now know that newborns will look at a source of sound, showing a connection between hearing and sight. One-month-olds will look longer at either a bumpy or smooth pacifier, depending on which kind they had sucked, suggesting an integration between vision and touch (Meltzoff & Borton, 1979; see Figure 6-3).

Some controversial findings suggest that *invisible imitation* develops considerably earlier than Piaget described. Invisible imitation uses parts of the body babies cannot see, like the mouth. Piaget maintained that invisible imitation develops after visible imitation—using the hands or feet, for example, which babies can see. But research has found differently.

In one study, babies less than 72 hours old imitated an adult's opening his mouth and sticking out his tongue and copied head movements of adults (Meltzoff & Moore, 1983, 1989). In another, babies with an average age of 36 hours imitated three different emotional expressions—a smile, a pout, and the wide-opened mouth and eyes that usually denote surprise (T. M. Field, Woodson, Greenberg, & Cohen, 1982). Since some other research has contradicted these findings (Abravanel & Sigafoos, 1984; Hayes & Watson, 1981), the age when invisible im-

FIGURE 6-3
Research refutation of Piaget's belief that the senses are unconnected at birth and are only gradually integrated through experience. One-month-old infants sucked on either a bumpy or smooth pacifier, which they could not see. After the pacifier was removed, the babies looked longer at the kind they had sucked, suggesting an integration between vision and touch. SOURCE: Mandler, 1990, p. 238.

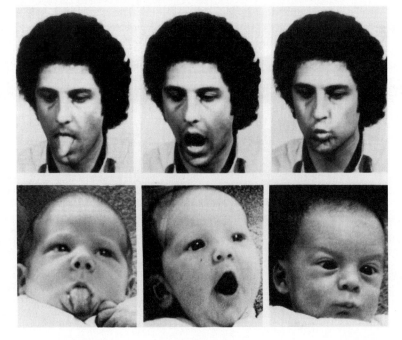

Infants as young as 2 or 3 weeks old, like those shown here, have been recorded as they stuck out their tongues, opened their mouths, and pushed their lips forward after adults did. Some researchers maintain that this shows invisible imitation; others question this conclusion.

itation first takes place remains questionable. However, it does seem to occur earlier than Piaget stated.

Neonatal invisible imitation suggests that human beings are born with a primitive ability to match the acts of other human beings. This may be one aspect of an underlying representational system that lets babies both perceive and produce human acts (Meltzoff & Moore, 1989). Early imitation may be the way infants identify people they see and distinguish "those like me" (people) from things (Meltzoff & Moore, 1992). Early mutual-imitation games, common between parents and infants, may be an important type of early communication that reinforces this aspect of development (Meltzoff & Gopnik, 1993).

Another area of study is *deferred imitation,* the ability to imitate an action a baby saw earlier. This ability shows that a baby has a long-term memory of an event and a mental representation for it, a "picture" in the mind. Piaget said that children do not show deferred imitation until 18 months, but research has demonstrated this in infants of 14 months (Meltzoff, 1985, 1988b) and even 9 months (Meltzoff, 1988a).

In one series of experiments by Andrew Meltzoff, adults pulled apart a two-piece toy or shook a rattle in front of the babies, who could not touch the toys at the time. The babies were returned to the lab 24 hours later (for the 9-month-olds), or 1 week later (for the 14-months-olds). Upon seeing the toys again, more of the babies in the experimental group (who had seen the adults' action) did the same things the adults had done, compared with the babies in the control group, who had also been in the lab the same day and had seen the toys but not the actions. Older babies were more likely to reproduce the actions, perhaps showing a superior ability to receive and encode the information in memory.

Finally, research suggests that an *understanding of number* begins before age 2, when Piaget claimed children first begin to use symbols like words and numbers. Five-month-old babies may be able to add and subtract small numbers of objects (Wynn, 1992), suggesting that the ability to grasp the rudiments of arithmetic may be inborn and that when parents teach their babies numbers, they may only be teaching them the names ("one, two, three") for concepts the babies already know.

Karen Wynn used Mickey Mouse dolls in a series of number experiments. (See Figure 6-4.) For the problem "1 plus 1," she showed 5-month-old babies one doll, then hid the doll behind a screen. The baby saw a hand place another doll behind the screen, and then the screen was pulled away to show two dolls. The length of time that the baby looked at the dolls was calculated.

Sometimes the screen was pulled away to show a false answer; in the "1 plus 1" situation, the babies sometimes saw only one doll or three dolls. In other experiments the researcher started by showing two dolls, then took one away, and the babies saw either one or two dolls. In all the experiments, the babies looked longer at the surprising "wrong" answers than the expected "right" ones. Wynn suggests that the babies had "computed" the right answers in their minds.

Babies seem to be able to think earlier than Piaget claimed. Either they are born with the capacity to form concepts, or they acquire this ability very early in life, without having to go through a long sensorimotor stage.

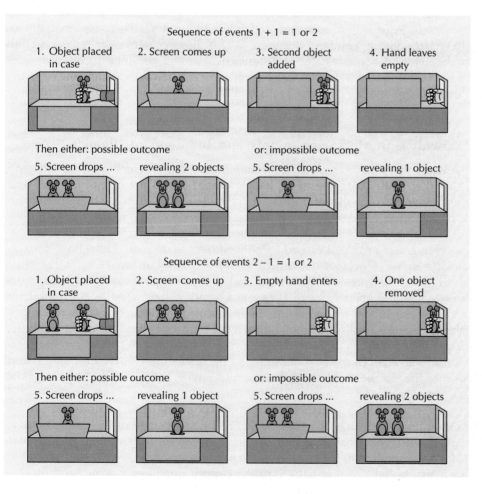

FIGURE 6-4
Can 5-month-old infants count? For the problem "1 plus 1," the researcher showed a baby one doll, then hid it behind a screen. The baby saw a hand place another doll behind the screen; then the screen was pulled away. Sometimes there was a false answer; the babies sometimes saw only one doll or three dolls. In the "2 minus 1" trials the researcher showed two dolls, then took one away, and the babies saw either one or two dolls. The babies consistently looked longer at the surprising "wrong" answers than the expected "right" ones, which suggests that they had "computed" the right answers in their minds. SOURCE: Wynn, 1992.

The French psychologist Alfred Binet (1857–1911) devised a test that exemplifies the psychometric view of intelligence.

PSYCHOMETRIC APPROACH: INTELLIGENCE TESTS

Early in the twentieth century, school administrators in Paris asked psychologist Alfred Binet to devise a test to identify children who could not handle academic work and who should be removed from regular classes and given special training to improve their performance. The test that Binet and his colleague Theodore Simon developed was the forerunner of psychometric tests that try to score intelligence by numbers. One is the Stanford-Binet Intelligence Scale, an American version of the original Binet-Simon tests. (See Chapter 9.) Binet's original purpose was to find out which children were the least educable. Today psychometric testing is also used to discover unusually able youngsters, who may benefit from enriched or accelerated learning. It is most widely used for children over 3, and especially for school-age children.

What Do Intelligence Tests Measure?

The goal of the psychometric approach is to determine and measure quantitatively the factors that make up intelligence. *IQ (intelligence quotient) tests* are supposed to assess *how much* a person has of certain abilities, like comprehension and reasoning. Psychometric tests consist of questions or tasks (usually verbal and performance) that aim to indicate cognitive functioning in these areas. The test scores show how well, relative to other persons, someone can perform the tasks.

Intelligence is hard to define, much less to measure. There undoubtedly are differences among children, but there is also disagreement over how accurately psychometric tests assess those differences. We will continue to discuss issues around intelligence testing in Chapters 9 and 12, when we examine the cognitive development of older children. For now, let's see why it is especially hard to gauge a baby's intelligence.

Difficulties in Measuring Infants' and Toddlers' Intelligence

We know that infants are intelligent from birth—but measuring their intelligence is another matter. For one thing, babies cannot talk. They cannot tell you what they know and how they think. The most obvious way to gauge their intelligence is by assessing what they do, but young infants do not do much. Experimenters try to catch babies' attention and coax them into a particular behavior. But if Vicky does not grasp a rattle, it is hard to tell whether she does not know how, does not feel like doing it, or does not realize what is expected of her.

Infant test scores are unreliable; that is, they tend to vary widely from one time to another. Their value in assessing a baby's *current* abilities is questionable; and they are almost useless for predicting *future* functioning. It is next to impossible to predict adult or even childhood IQ from test scores of normal children before the age of 2. A more useful predictor of childhood IQ is the parents' IQ or educational level (Kopp & Kaler, 1989; Kopp & McCall, 1982). Not until the third year of life do the child's own scores, along with these factors, help to predict later intelligence test scores.

Even for toddlers, predictions from psychometric tests are unreliable. In one longitudinal study, IQs changed markedly, by an average of $28\frac{1}{2}$ points between ages $2\frac{1}{2}$ and 17, and the IQs of one in seven children shifted by more than 40 points (McCall, Appelbaum, & Hogarty, 1973). As children are tested closer to their fifth birthday, the relationship between their current intelligence scores and those in later childhood becomes stronger (Bornstein & Sigman, 1986).

Why do early intelligence scores fail to predict later ones? For one thing, the tests traditionally used for babies measure mostly sensory and motor abilities, while tests for older children are heavily verbal. Thus these different tests seem to measure different and unrelated kinds of intelligence (Bornstein & Sigman, 1986). But even when we look at motor skills alone, children who are good at the large-muscle activities tested at an early age may not be as adept at fine motor, or manipulative, skills, which are considered to be a sign of intelligence a little later on. A 1-year-old who can build towers with blocks may not, by age 7, be able to copy a design made from colored blocks.

Psychologists are better able to predict the future IQ of a disabled infant. Yet some children born with mental and motor handicaps make impressive strides in tested intelligence as they grow older. A supportive environment can help such a child (Kopp & Kaler, 1989; Kopp & McCall, 1982).

In addition, human beings have a "strong self-righting tendency" (Kopp & McCall, 1982). That is, given a favorable environment, infants will follow the developmental patterns for their species unless they have suffered severe damage. Sometime between the ages of 18 and 24 months, this self-righting tendency diminishes as children acquire skills (like verbal abilities) in which there will eventually be great variations in proficiency. As these skills develop, individual differences become more pronounced and lasting.

Nancy Bayley of the University of California at Berkeley developed a test to assess the developmental status of babies from 2 months to 2½ years.

What do you think?   *What do you consider the essence of intelligent behavior in infants and toddlers? How would you measure this?*

Developmental Testing of Infants and Toddlers

Despite the problems in measuring the intelligence of very young children, sometimes there are reasons to test them. If parents are worried that a baby is not doing the same things as other babies the same age, testing may reassure them that

By giving the Bayley Scales to this 33-month-old child, the tester may be able to detect sensory or neurological problems, emotional disturbances, or problems in the child's environment.

TABLE 6-2

SAMPLE TASKS IN THE BAYLEY SCALES OF INFANT DEVELOPMENT	
AGE, MONTHS	**TASKS MOST CHILDREN THIS AGE CAN DO**
5.8	Grasp edge of piece of paper held out by examiner
5.9	Vocalize pleasure and displeasure
6.0	Reach persistently for cube placed just out of reach
6.1	Turn head to watch spoon dropped to floor by child's side
6.3	Say several syllables
11.5	Stop doing something (like putting an object into the mouth) when adult says, "No, no"
11.7	Try to imitate words like *mama, dada,* and *baby*
12.1	Imitate rattling of spoon in cup with stirring motion to make noise
12.6	Put round block into round hole of form board

SOURCE: Kessen, Haith, & Salapatek, 1970.

the child's development is normal. Or tests may alert them to abnormal development and the need to make special arrangements for the child.

Interpretation of developmental test results is based on observations of large numbers of children. After determining what most infants or toddlers can do at particular ages, researchers develop standardized norms, assigning a developmental age to each specific activity. A child's performance is then evaluated in comparison to these norms.

Bayley Scale of Infant Development
Standardized test of infants' mental and motor development.

One widely used developmental test is the *Bayley Scales of Infant Development* (Bayley, 1969; revised Bayley II, 1993). The Bayley II is designed to assess the developmental status of children from 1 to 42 months of age. It is used primarily with children who are at risk or suspected of being at risk for abnormal development (B. Thompson et al., 1994). The Bayley II (see Table 6-2) is organized according to three categories:

1. *Mental scale* measures such abilities as perception, memory, learning, and verbal communication.
2. *Motor scale* measures gross motor (large-muscle) and fine motor (manipulative) skills.
3. *Behavior rating scale* is a 30-item rating, completed by the examiner, of the child's test-taking behaviors.

The separate scores calculated for each scale are useful for assessing a child's current abilities, but not for predicting later intelligence. They are most helpful for early detection of emotional disturbances and sensory, neurological, and environmental deficits.

What do you think? *What are the pros and cons of developmental testing in infancy and toddlerhood?*

Can Infants' and Toddlers' Intelligence Test Scores Be Increased?

Good parenting skills and an enriched day care environment can apparently increase young children's intelligence test scores. In Project CARE, one experimental group of babies from disadvantaged homes received home visits and day care, starting before they were 5 months old (Wasik, Ramey, Bryant, & Sparling, 1990). Trained visitors came to the homes of the babies' parents, helping them to solve problems of child rearing and daily life and encouraging them to play educational games with their children. Meanwhile, the babies' activities at the day care center were designed to stimulate language and to foster their social and cognitive development. Babies in a second experimental group received only the home visits, and a third (control) group got no systematic intervention.

At nine times, between ages 6 months and $4\frac{1}{2}$ years, the 65 children were given cognitive tests. On each occasion after the first (6-month) assessment, the experimental group that received *both* home and day care intervention did better than the other two groups. The children who received only the home visits did no better than the control group. However, since other studies that reported no intervention effects during the preschool years found them later, it is possible that such effects might emerge later for these home-visit-only children too. In any case, these results suggest that the attention babies get, both at home and in day care, affects cognitive development.

What do you think? *What elements would you include in an intervention to enhance cognitive functioning in disadvantaged infants and toddlers? How would you measure success? What ethical issues would you have to consider?*

INFORMATION-PROCESSING APPROACH: PERCEPTIONS AND SYMBOLS

At 2 months, Jason makes sucking motions and waves his arms as Julia comes near him. Anyone can see that he recognizes her and that the sight and sound of her fill him with joy. But how does recognition take place? What is going on in Jason's head? Neither Piaget nor the psychometricians have a good answer.

The information-processing approach is the newest scientific explanation of intelligence. It sees people as manipulators of perceptions and symbols. Its goal is to discover what people do with information from the time they perceive it until they use it. Like the psychometric approach, information-processing theory focuses on individual differences in intelligent behavior. But it concentrates on describing the processes that people go through in acquiring information or solving problems, rather than merely assuming differences in mental functioning from answers given or problems solved.

Information Processing during Infancy as a Predictor of Intelligence

Because of the poor correlation between scores on developmental tests for infants and later IQ tests, many people believed that the cognitive functioning of infants had little in common with that of older children and adults. In other words, they thought there was a discontinuity in cognitive development. Today, discoveries about the ability of young babies to process information that they see or hear challenges this view. When we assess how infants process information rather than how they perform on psychometric tests, we see that mental development seems to be fairly continuous from birth into childhood (McCall & Carriger, 1993; Bornstein & Sigman, 1986; L. A. Thompson, Fagen, & Fulker, 1991).

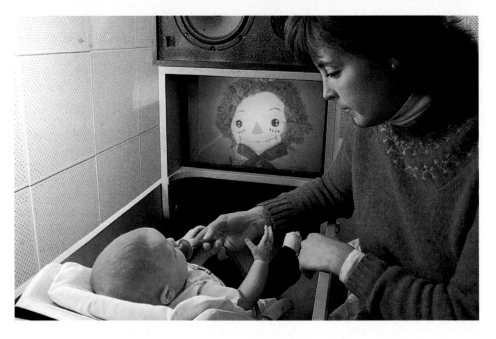

Can this baby tell the difference between Raggedy Ann and Raggedy Andy? Researchers may find out by seeing whether the baby has habituated (gotten used to) one face. If the baby stops sucking on the nipple when a new face appears, this shows that he recognizes the difference.

How *do* infants process information? Many of the answers come from studies that measure habituation.

habituation *Simple type of learning in which familiarity with a stimulus reduces, slows, or even stops a response.*

Habituation. *Habituation* is a type of learning in which repeated exposure to a stimulus (like a sound or a sight) results in a reduced response to that stimulus. Habituation allows us to conserve energy by remaining alert to things and events in the environment only as long as they seem to merit attention because they seem either desirable or threatening.

How Habituation Is Measured. In a typical habituation study, researchers repeatedly present a stimulus (usually a sound or visual pattern) and then monitor such responses as heart rate, sucking, eye movements, and brain activity. A baby who has been sucking typically stops when the stimulus is first presented and does not start again until after it has ended. After the same sound or sight has been presented again and again, it loses its novelty and no longer causes the baby to stop sucking. When this happens, the infant has habituated to it. A new sight or sound, however, will capture the baby's attention and the baby will again stop

dishabituation *Increase in responsiveness after the presentation of a new stimulus; see habituation.*

sucking. This increase in responding to a new stimulus is *dishabituation.*

If infants pay more attention to new stimuli than to familiar ones, they discriminate the new from the old; therefore they must be able to remember the old. To compare new information with information they already have, they must be able to form mental images, or representations, of stimuli. Infants acquire information by forming such images. The efficiency of their information processing depends on the speed with which they form and refer to the images.

Habituation studies have found that newborns can tell sounds they have already heard from those they have not and that neonates less than 1 week old can distinguish between visual patterns (J. S. Werner & Siqueland, 1978). Their discriminatory ability becomes more refined by 5 months of age (Fantz, Fagan, & Miranda, 1975). The greater the difference between patterns, the less time a baby needs to tell them apart (Fagan, 1982; see Figure 6-5).

The Significance of Habituation. Because habituation is a sign of normal development, its presence or absence, as well as the speed with which it occurs, tells us about a baby's development. Since the capacity for habituation increases during the first 10 weeks of life, it reflects maturation (Rovee-Collier, 1987). Habituation studies show how well babies can see and hear, how much they can remember, and what their neurological status is. Babies with low Apgar scores (see Chapter 4) and those with brain damage, distress at the time of birth, or Down syndrome show impaired habituation (Lipsitt, 1986), as do neonates whose mothers took cocaine while pregnant (Eisen et al., 1991). Full-term neonates can habituate to stimuli in all sensory modalities (sight, hearing, touch, taste, and smell), while preterm newborns generally habituate only to some stimuli in some circumstances (Rovee-Collier, 1987).

Poor habituation during the neonatal period often foreshadows slow development; a child who does not habituate at all is likely to have future learning problems (Lipsitt, 1986).

Studying Infants' Information Processing. Mental development is the process of transforming the novel into the familiar, the unknown into the known. Researchers gauge the efficiency of infants' information processing by measuring their variations in attention: how quickly babies habituate to familiar stimuli, how fast their attention is recovered when they are exposed to new stimuli, and how much time they spend looking at the new and the old (McCall & Carriger, 1993; Bornstein, 1985a; Bornstein & Sigman, 1986). Efficient habituation correlates with other signs of advanced mental development—like a preference for complexity, rapid exploration of the environment, sophisticated play, fast problem solving, and the ability to match pictures.

Infants who are efficient at taking in and interpreting what they see, or at remembering what they see or hear, score well later on childhood intelligence tests. In longitudinal studies, habituation and attention-recovery abilities during the first 6 months of life were moderately good predictors of scores on psychometric intelligence tests taken between ages 2 and 8 (Bornstein & Sigman, 1986). Infants' ***visual-recognition memory,*** the ability to remember and recognize something they have seen, seems to be a particularly good predictor of later language ability. It correlates positively with vocabulary test scores during childhood (Fagen & McGrath, 1981).

Another study looked at the relationship between ***visual novelty preference*** at 5 and 7 months and IQ and cognitive performance at 1, 2, and 3 years. At 5 and 7 months, 113 infants were shown sets of abstract patterns and photographs of faces. The babies who preferred looking at new pictures rather than ones they had seen before tended to score higher on the Bayley Scales at 2 years and the Stanford-Binet intelligence test at 3 years. Visual novelty preference (preference for the new pictures) seems to predict general intelligence. Infant visual novelty preference also predicted several specific cognitive abilities at later ages, including language skills and memory ability at 3 years (L. A. Thompson et al., 1991).

Other research has looked at infants' information processing in terms of how well they identify by sight items that they had earlier felt with their hands but had not seen. This ability, known as ***cross-modal transference,*** shows a fairly high level of abstraction; it implies central processing of tactile and visual information. One study compared high-risk, very low birthweight babies with normal full-term babies from the same low-income population. The combination of two scores—the infants' visual recognition memory at 7 months and cross-modal transfer at

FIGURE 6-5
Visual recognition in infancy. The more two pictures or patterns differ, the less time a baby needs to look at them. A 5-month-old baby may need only 4 seconds of study time to tell apart two very different patterns (top pair); but 17 seconds may be needed to recognize faces.
SOURCE: Fagan, 1982.

visual-recognition memory
Recognition of a visual stimulus.

visual novelty preference
Preference for new rather than familiar pictures.

cross-modal transference
Ability to identify by sight items earlier felt but not seen.

1 year—was positively and significantly correlated with the children's IQ scores at 3, 4, and 5 years (S. A. Rose, Feldman, Wallace, & McCarton, 1991).

Early sensitivity to sounds may also predict aspects of later cognitive functioning. A high positive correlation showed up between the ability of 4-month-old infants to discriminate sounds and their IQ scores at age 5 (O'Connor, Cohen, & Parmelee, 1984).

exploratory behavior
Activity prompted by curiosity about the environment.

Exploratory Behavior. When Vicky becomes curious about her world, she squeezes, jabs, rubs, shakes, and bangs objects—activities called *exploratory behavior.* These actions are related to her ability to solve problems and become competent. The degree to which she initiates them provides clues to her early cognitive development (Caruso, 1993).

In a longitudinal study, researchers looked at the antecedents of *exploratory competence* in 13-month-olds. This quality was assessed by studying the way the toddlers played and paid attention to various stimuli (Tamis-LeMonda & Bornstein, 1993). These children's information-processing skills had been tested earlier, and their performance on some information-processing measures at 5 months predicted their exploratory competence at 13 months. For instance, 5-month-olds who looked longer at such sights as a bull's-eye, a female face, and a third pattern were more likely to engage in symbolic play at 13 months. Also, the more the 5-month-olds cooed and made other contented sounds, looked at their mothers or an object, or touched an object, the more exploratory competence they showed at 13 months. So even as early as 5 months, babies show some level of information processing that predicts competence in the second year.

Influences on Information Processing and Cognitive Development

A major influence on cognitive development is how caregivers act toward children. In several experiments, researchers looked at how responsive American and Japanese mothers were to their babies, first when the babies were 2 to 5 months

This mother's responsiveness to her baby's signals may be reflected in the child's later cognitive development. While almost all mothers respond similarly to distressed babies, they vary greatly in the way they interact with their nondistressed children.

old and then again at 1, 1½, 2½, and 4 years of age, when the children were assessed on various cognitive abilities (Bornstein & Tamis-LeMonda, 1989). The mothers were assessed according to their responsiveness to their babies' behavior. When a baby babbled or looked at the mother (nondistress activities) or cried (a sign of distress), what did the mother do? Did she smile at, talk to, pick up, pat, feed, or pay attention to the baby in some way?

Almost all the mothers responded quickly when their babies were upset. However, the extent of *nondistress* responsiveness varied greatly, with no links to the mothers' education or socioeconomic status. Although the mothers' responses to 2-month-old babies were not associated with the children's later development, their responses when the babies were 4 or 5 months old were. As toddlers, the children of the most responsive mothers had more advanced representational abilities; as 4-year-olds they scored higher on the Wechsler Preschool and Primary Scale of Intelligence (WPPSI) and other learning tasks. In other research, mothers' responsiveness to 4-month-old babies was associated with later cognitive achievements (along with the babies' abilities to process information); but the way they acted with their 1-year-olds was not (Bornstein, 1985b). These different findings may point to a sensitive period, when babies are about 4 months old, for a caregiver's impact on intellectual growth.

How does adult responsiveness help children develop intellectually? It might raise their self-esteem and make them feel they have some control over their lives. It might make them feel secure enough to explore and motivate them to persist. Also, it might help them regulate themselves to pay attention and learn.

Other research focused on mothers' responsiveness to preterm infants. The ones whose mothers were most sensitive, responsive, and positively involved with them became adolescents who scored higher on IQ tests and considered themselves more competent than the children of less responsive mothers (Beckwith & Cohen, 1989). Findings like these support other data showing that the environment a child grows up in can do a great deal to offset the negative effects of complications at the time of birth. Although most of these studies have been done with mothers, their findings are probably just as relevant for fathers and other primary caregivers.

What do you think? *What characterizes intelligent behavior in the first three years of life? What are some ways to measure this?*

INFANTS' LEARNING

Do babies *learn* to suck on a nipple? They probably do not; sucking is a reflex they are born with. But sucking quickly becomes a learned behavior when it leads to a comfortably full stomach. Similarly, a baby's first cry is not learned behavior; but babies soon learn to *use* crying to get what they need or want.

Learning is a relatively permanent change in behavior that results from experience. We are born with the *ability* to learn, but learning itself takes place only with experience. Babies learn from what they see, hear, smell, taste, and touch. Learning is a form of adaptation to the environment. Before we examine some ways in which learning takes place, we need to clarify the relationship between learning and maturation.

learning *Relatively permanent change in behavior that results from experience.*

MATURATION AND LEARNING

Even if Vicky was born with the soul of a poet, she will not be able to speak like one until her mouth and vocal cords have developed enough to form verbal sounds and her brain and nervous system are mature enough to assign meanings to sounds and remember them. Certain neurological, sensory, and motor capacities must be developed before learning can occur. Thus *maturation*—the unfolding of patterns of behavior in a biologically determined, age-related sequence— is necessary for learning.

The connection between maturation and learning is seen in the development of crawling. Young babies placed on a "visual cliff" (described in Chapter 5) show they perceive depth, but they do not become *afraid* of the "deep" side until they have begun to get around on their own (Bertenthal & Campos, 1987). Perhaps they have fallen off something—or perhaps when they were on a high place, they heard their caretakers cry out in fear. In any case, they learned from experience that the edge of a "cliff" is something to fear.

A skill that develops through maturation (crawling) contributes to a baby's ability to learn about and interpret the environment. On the other hand, the environment can sometimes influence maturation and, by extension, also influence learning—as in the experiment described in Chapter 5 in which kittens were fitted with training goggles and then, as mature cats, were able to see the lines only in the direction that they had seen through the goggles (H. V. Hirsch & Spinelli, 1970).

TYPES OF LEARNING

Babies learn through habituation, classical conditioning, and operant conditioning—and through combinations of these modes.

Classical Conditioning

In Chapter 1 we saw how Vicky, after her father had taken many pictures of her, eventually blinked *before* the flash on his camera went off. This is an example of *classical conditioning*, in which an organism learns to respond automatically to a stimulus that originally did not provoke the response. In Vicky's case, this stimulus was her father's camera. In classical conditioning, the learner anticipates an event before it happens.

One of the earliest demonstrations of classical conditioning in human beings showed that emotions such as fear can be conditioned (Watson & Rayner, 1920). An 11-month-old baby known as "Little Albert," who loved furry animals, was brought into a laboratory. Just as he was about to grasp a white rat, a loud noise frightened him, and he began to cry. After repeated pairings of the rat with the loud noise, the child whimpered with fear when he saw the rat. The fear also generalized to rabbits, dogs, a Santa Claus mask, and other furry white objects. Under today's ethical standards for research, this experiment would never be permitted because it would be unethical to arouse fear in the name of science. However, the experiment did show that a baby could be conditioned to fear things he had not been afraid of before.

What do you think? *Watson and Rayner's experiments with "Little Albert" remain controversial. Where would you draw the line between society's need to learn and an infant's rights?*

maturation   *Unfolding of patterns of behavior in a biologically determined, age-related sequence.*

classical conditioning
Learning in which a previously neutral stimulus (conditioned stimulus) acquires the power to elicit a response (conditioned response) by association with an unconditioned stimulus that ordinarily elicits a particular response (unconditioned response).

An Indian snake charmer's baby eagerly plays with a snake the father has trained, showing that fear of snakes is a learned response. Children can be conditioned to fear animals that are associated with unpleasant or frightening experiences (as "Little Albert" was in a classic study by John B. Watson and Rosalie Rayner).

At how young an age can a baby be classically conditioned? Babies only 2 hours old have been classically conditioned to turn their heads and suck if their foreheads are stroked at the same time they are given a bottle of sweetened water (Blass et al., 1984, in Rovee-Collier, 1987). Furthermore, newborn infants have learned to suck when they hear a buzzer or a tone; to show the Babkin reflex (turning their heads and opening their mouths) when their arms are moved (instead of the usual stimulus, pressure on the palm of the hand); to dilate and constrict the pupils of their eyes; to blink; and to show a change in heart rate (Rovee-Collier & Lipsitt, 1982).

Operant Conditioning

Jason's smiling to get loving attention from his parents (described in Chapter 1) is an example of *operant conditioning,* in which a baby learns to make a certain response in order to produce a particular effect. Operant conditioning, in which the learner operates on and influences the environment, can be used to learn voluntary behaviors (as opposed to involuntary behaviors like blinking).

operant conditioning
Learning in which a response continues to be made because it has been reinforced.

In one study the nipples sucked by 2-day-old infants were connected to a music source. The babies kept sucking when their sucking turned on the music, but stopped when their sucking turned the music off (Butterfield & Siperstein, 1972). Studies like this, which change what babies do by reinforcing certain behaviors, show that neonates can learn by operant conditioning, *if* the conditioning encourages them to perform some kind of behavior they can already do (like sucking or turning the head), rather than something they would not ordinarily do.

Classical and operant conditioning can occur separately or together to produce increasingly complex behavior. In studies with 1- to 20-week-old infants, the babies received milk if they turned their heads left at the sound of a bell. The babies who did not learn to turn their heads through this operant conditioning were then classically conditioned. When the bell sounded, the left corner of the baby's mouth was touched, and the baby turned his or her head and received the milk. (The touch was the unconditioned stimulus; turning the head the unconditioned response. The bell was the conditioned stimulus; turning the head to the bell became the conditioned response.)

By 4 to 6 weeks, all the babies had learned to turn their heads when hearing the bell. Then the babies learned to differentiate the bell from a buzzer (Papousek, 1959, 1960a, 1960b, 1961). When the bell rang, they were fed on the left; when the buzzer rasped, they were fed on the right. At about 3 months of age, the babies had learned to turn to the side that had brought food. By 4 months, they even learned to reverse their responses (turning to the right at the bell and to the left at the buzzer)—an impressively complex response.

INFANTS' MEMORY AND LEARNING

Very soon after birth, memory is working, and it quickly becomes more efficient. The foundation for memory may be laid even before birth, as we saw in the studies reported in Chapter 3, which suggest that very young infants "remember" a story they had heard while in the womb (DeCasper & Spence, 1986).

Still, it is virtually impossible to remember anything that happened when we were less than 1 year old. We're not sure why. Perhaps, as Freud believed, we repress our early memories; or perhaps we simply replace them with later, more complex ones. But it is clear that infants do have memory: Newborns who heard a certain speech sound one day after birth remembered that sound 24 hours later

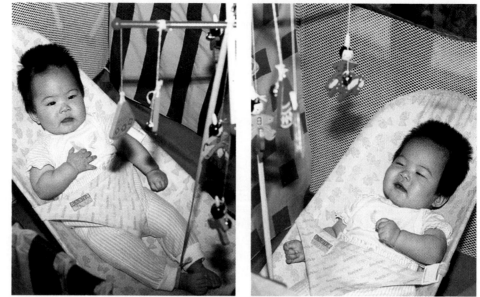

Babies less than 2 months old can remember, after a hiatus of 2 to 4 weeks, that they were able to activate a mobile by kicking their foot; they show this by kicking as soon as they see the mobile. The series of experiments in this research varied the contexts in which the babies learned, and contextual cues helped to establish memory.

(Swain, Zelazo, & Clifton, 1993). In this experiment, 36 infants heard one of two words, either *beagle* or *tinder*. One experimental group heard the same word two days in a row; a second experimental group heard a different word each day; and a control group heard one of the words for the first time on the second day. Both experimental groups habituated to the words on the first day (shown by no longer turning their heads to the sound of the word) and then recovered head turning after a 24-hour delay. The babies presented with the same word over both days seemed to remember it best.

Babies less than 2 months old remember past events, especially if the events gave them pleasure. Researchers studying 6-week-old babies tied a ribbon to each baby's left leg and attached the ribbon to a mobile hung above the crib. The babies quickly learned that kicking would activate the mobile. Then the mobile was taken away. When the mobiles were hung again 2 to 4 weeks later, ribbons were *not* attached to the babies' legs. But when the babies saw the mobiles again, they kicked, especially with their left legs, showing they remembered that kicking activated the mobile (Rovee-Collier & Fagen, 1976, 1981; M. W. Sullivan, 1982).

In another study, babies trained with different mobiles on different days learned to expect a different mobile each time (Fagen, Morrongiello, Rovee-Collier, & Gekoski, 1984). Responding more to a new mobile than to the old one showed their ability to incorporate the idea of change. Findings like these "suggest that infants are 'built' to organize and find structure in what must otherwise appear to be a random and chaotic world" (p. 942).

Part of this structure involves the context—the setting—in which a baby learns. Infants as young as 3 to 6 months recognize differences in settings, and they seem to encode information about the context, along with whatever else they are learning. This finding emerged from other experiments in which babies learned to activate a mobile by kicking.

The babies were trained in a playpen with two sides covered by cloth in one of four patterns: stripes, squares, dots, or triangles. Upon retesting, either 24 hours, 3 weeks, or 6 months later, the babies remembered how to activate the mobile *if* they were retested in a playpen with the same pattern as the one in which they were trained. But if they were retested in a differently patterned playpen, they did not retrieve the original memory and did not remember how to activate the mobile (Rovee-Collier, Schechter, Shyi, & Shields, 1992; Shields & Rovee-Collier, 1992; T. A. Amabile & Rovee-Collier, 1991).

Early memories can last a long time. One study found that $2\frac{1}{2}$-year-olds remembered an experience with a rattle that occurred at the age of $6\frac{1}{2}$ months (Perris, Myers, & Clifton, 1990). The ability that memory provides to organize the world is closely related to the development of intelligence and the ability to learn.

What do you think? *If long-term memory exists for a distinctive—but seemingly unemotional—event like an experiment with a rattle, what important consequences might follow a traumatic experience suffered in infancy?*

Babies also learn from observing and imitating models. (Social learning, described in Chapter 1, is also discussed in Chapter 9.) Children learn many complicated abilities through a mix of different kinds of learning and maturation.

DEVELOPMENT OF LANGUAGE

At $4\frac{1}{2}$ months, Jason chuckles out loud. He also says "ngoo-ooo" and "ngaaah." At 7 months, he makes more sounds, mostly sounding like "da" or "ga." At 11 months, he says "Dada," and at 14 months, he points to everything, asking "What zis?" or saying "Da" for "I want that." At 17 months, he points to the right places when asked "Where is your nose? Tongue? Belly button?" By 21 months, he says, or tries to say, at least 50 words, and he understands many more. He can now tell you exactly what he does or does not want, in his own language. When asked "Do you want to go to bed?" he answers "Eh-eh-eh," accompanied by vigorous arm waving. In other words, "No!" He has also said his first three-word sentence: "Choo-choo bye-bye da-da." (His mother translates, "The train went away and now it's all gone.")

Jason's language ability is a crucial element in his cognitive growth. Once he knows the words for things, he can use symbols to represent objects; he can reflect on people, places, and things in his world; and he can communicate his needs, feelings, and ideas to exert control over his life. (See Table 6-3 for a list of early language milestones.)

Researchers have used a variety of methods to study the development of *language,* the communication system that uses words and grammar. Studies of habituation, based on heart rate or sucking behavior, tell us when babies can distinguish one sound from another. A procedure in which electrodes fastened to a baby's scalp measure the brain responses elicited by sounds, and any difference in these responses, also measures a baby's ability to differentiate between sounds. Researchers audiotape and videotape children and rely on records kept by trained observers during set intervals. We have learned a great deal about babies' ability to communicate—even before they say a single word.

language *Communication system that uses words and grammar.*

STAGES IN DEVELOPMENT OF LANGUAGE

Prespeech

The word *infant* is based on the Latin for "without speech." Before babies say their first "real" words, they make sounds that progress from crying to cooing and babbling, to accidental imitation, and then to deliberate imitation. These sounds are known as *prelinguistic speech.*

prelinguistic speech *Communicative use of sound by infants without using words or grammar.*

TABLE 6-3

LANGUAGE MILESTONES FROM BIRTH TO 3 YEARS	
AGE IN MONTHS	**DEVELOPMENT**
Birth	Can perceive speech, cry, make some response to sound.
$1\frac{1}{2}$ to 3	Coos and laughs.
3	Plays with speech sounds.
5 to 6	Makes consonant sounds, trying to match what she or he hears.
6 to 10	Babbles in strings of consonants and vowels.
9	Uses gestures to communicate and plays gesture games.
9 to 10	Begins to understand words (usually "no" and baby's own name); imitates sounds.
9 to 10	Loses ability to discriminate sounds not in own language.
9 to 12	Uses a few social gestures.
10 to 14	Says first word (usually a label for something); imitates sounds.
10 to 18	Says single words.
13	Understands symbolic function of naming.
13	Uses more elaborate gestures.
14	Uses symbolic gesturing.
16 to 24	Learns many new words, expanding vocabulary rapidly, going from about 50 words to up to 400; uses verbs and adjectives.
18 to 24	Says first sentence (2 words).
20	Uses fewer gestures; names more things.
20 to 22	Has comprehension spurt.
24	Uses many two-word phrases; no longer babbles; wants to talk.
30	Learns new words almost every day; speaks in combinations of three or more words; understands very well; makes many grammatical mistakes.
36	Says up to 1000 words, 80 percent intelligible; makes few mistakes in syntax; grammar is close to informal adult speech.

SOURCES: Bates, O'Connell, & Shore, 1987; Capute, Shapiro, & Palmer, 1987; Lenneberg, 1969.

Crying.   Crying is the newborn's only means of communication. To a stranger, all cries may sound alike, but a baby's parents can often tell the cry for food from the cry of pain. Different pitches, patterns, and intensities signal hunger, sleepiness, or anger.

Cooing.   Between 6 weeks and 3 months, babies start to laugh and coo when happy. Cooing includes making squeals, gurgles, and vowel sounds like "ahhh." A kind of "vocal tennis" begins at about 3 months when they begin to play with speech sounds, matching the sounds they hear from the people around them (Bates et al., 1987).

Babbling.   Babbling—repeating consonant-vowel strings like "ma-ma-ma-ma"—occurs suddenly between 6 and 10 months, and is often mistaken for a baby's first word. Early babbling is not real language, since it does not hold meaning for the baby, but it becomes more wordlike, leading to early speech. Cross-cultural studies—like one that looked at babies growing up in families that spoke French, Chinese, or Arabic—found that babies do not, as was once believed, "try out" all speech sounds in all human languages, but instead, move in the direction of their own language (Boysson-Bardies, Sagart, & Durand, 1984).

   In the babbling stage, one difference shows up between babies. "Word babies" seem to understand words earlier and produce word sounds in their babbling, while "intonation babies" babble in sentencelike patterns and tend not to

BOX 6-2 ■ FOOD FOR THOUGHT

WHAT THE BABBLING OF HEARING-IMPAIRED BABIES TELLS US ABOUT THE DEVELOPMENT OF LANGUAGE

A deaf baby, whose parents are also deaf, makes a series of rhythmic, repetitive motions in front of her torso. Another baby, also the nonhearing child of nonhearing parents, makes similar hand motions around his head and face. These children are babbling. But instead of repeating syllables with their voices ("ma-ma-ma") as hearing babies do, they use gestures. The babies repeat and string together a few motions over and over again. (See Figure 6-6.) The gestures, like the syllables uttered by hearing babblers, do not have any meaning by themselves. The hand-babbling begins before 10 months of age, the same time when hearing infants begin voice-babbling.

Apparently, the deaf babies are copying the sign language they see their parents using, just as hearing babies copy voice utterances. The researchers who described and analyzed the hand motions of two nonhearing babies and two hearing babies found that the nonhearing babies' motions were much more systematic and deliberate than the random clenching fists and fluttering fingers of the hearing babies (Petitto & Marentette, 1991). They then concluded that babies learn sign language (which is structured very much like spoken languages) in the same basic way that other babies learn speech. First, they string together meaningless units; then, as parents reinforce the babies' gestures, the babies attach meaning to them. This suggests that there is an inborn language capacity in the brain that underlies the acquisition of both spoken and signed language. In other words, babbling—whether vocal or manual—is tied to brain maturation rather than to maturation of the vocal cords. This suggests that both nativist and learning-theory explanations for how children learn language are valid.

FIGURE 6-6

Example of manual babbling used by a nonhearing baby who had been exposed to sign language. These four hand shapes represent a sequence, as the baby repeated the series of hand movements over and over again. Each motion is comparable to a syllable in a sequence of vocal babbling. SOURCE: Petitto & Marentette, 1991.

---

break their babbling down into individual words (Dore, 1975). The importance of babbling is shown by its appearance in a different form among deaf babies (Petitto & Marentette, 1991; see Box 6-2). Although these babies may also babble vocally, they do so about 5 months later than hearing babies do (Oller & Eilers, 1988).

Imitating Language Sounds. Language development among babies with normal hearing and speech begins with accidental imitation of sounds they hear. Then they imitate themselves making these sounds. At about 9 to 10 months, they deliberately imitate other sounds, without understanding them. Once they have a repertoire of sounds, they string them together in patterns that sound like language but seem to have no meaning (Eisenson, Auer, & Irwin, 1963; Lenneberg, 1967).

Prelinguistic speech can be rich in emotional expression. Starting at about 2 months, when infants' cooing begins to express contentment, the range of emotional tone increases steadily. Long before children can express ideas in words, parents become attuned to their babies' feelings through the sounds they make (Tonkova-Yompol'skaya, 1973).

Recognizing Language Sounds. Long before babies can utter anything but a cry, they can distinguish between speech sounds. In the first months of life, they can tell apart such similar sounds as "ba" and "pa" (Eimas, Siqueland, Jusczyk, & Vigorito, 1971). This ability seems to be inborn.

Before 6 months of age, babies have learned the basic sounds of their native language, the first step in understanding speech. In one study 6-month-old Swedish and American babies routinely ignored variations in sounds common to their own language, but could distinguish variations in an unfamiliar language (Kuhl, Williams, Lacerda, Stevens, & Lindblom, 1992). Other experiments found that 9-month-old American babies (but not 6-month-olds) listened longer to words with the stress pattern most common in English—strong-weak as in *butter* (but'-ter) rather than weak-strong as in *restore* (re-store'). This preference seems to develop as babies become increasingly familiar with their own language. It seems to be the beginning of the ability to segment continuous speech into words, an ability needed for acquiring a vocabulary (Jusczyk, Cutler, & Redanz, 1993).

By 9 or 10 months, children lose the ability to differentiate sounds that are not part of the language they hear spoken. Japanese infants can easily tell "ra" from "la," but Japanese adults, who speak a language that does not have the "L" sound, have trouble with the same discrimination (Bates, O'Connell, & Shore, 1987). Language perception is, then, shaped by experience (hearing words) earlier than had been thought.

Babies understand many words before they can say them. The first words most babies understand, at about 9 or 10 months, are their own names and the word "no"—the two words a baby is likely to hear most often. They also comprehend words with special meaning for them; 14-month-old Vicky's parents may start spelling words in front of her—if, for example, it is not time yet to give her a b-a-n-a-n-a.

Throughout the prespeech period, caregivers have been communicating with babies in many ways. By 1 year, the baby has some sense of intentional communication, a primitive idea of reference, and a set of signals to communicate with familiar caregivers (Bates et al., 1987). The linguistic stage is now set for speech.

Gestures.   Before babies say their first words, they have developed a repertoire of nonverbal gestures. At 9 months Jason *pointed* to an object, sometimes making a noise ("eh-eh-eh") to show that he wanted it. Between 9 and 12 months, he learned a few *conventional social gestures:* waving bye-bye, nodding his head to mean yes, and shaking his head to signify no. By about 13 months, he used more elaborate *representational gestures* that had a more complex meaning: For example, he would hold up his arms to show that he wanted to be picked up or hold an empty cup to his mouth.

Symbolic gestures go beyond pointing and games like pat-a-cake, to represent specific objects, events, desires, and conditions. (See Table 6-4.) Symbolic gestures emerge just before or at about the same time that babies say their first words. At first, typically at about 14 months, children use symbolic gestures to make requests; at about 15 months to describe attributes (like blowing to mean "hot"); and about 2 weeks later to "name" objects. In one study of thirty-eight 17-month-olds, 87 percent used at least one such gesture, and the average child used four (Acredolo & Goodwyn, 1988). Gestures usually appear before children have a vocabulary of 25 words. They drop out when children learn the word for the idea they were gesturing and can say it instead (Lock, Young, Service, & Chandler, 1990).

More than half the children developed symbolic gestures as a result of routines with their parents. Vicky, for example, bounces her torso to mean "horse,"

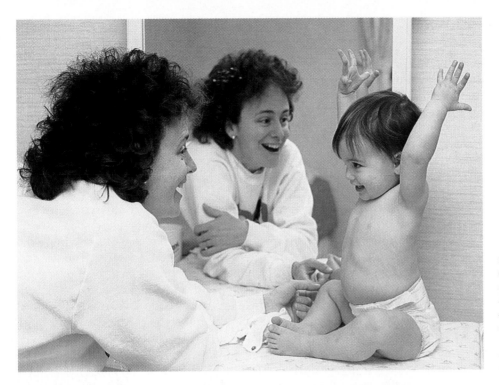

"So big!" Before babies say their first words, they have developed a repertoire of nonverbal gestures. When Mother asks, "How big is Alyssa?" the baby's hands are likely to shoot up. Later gestures will become more elaborate, expressing more complex meanings.

stemming from bouncing on her father's knee. While children make up most of these gestures themselves, their parents' role is important. It takes two to communicate: If others do not interpret and respond to the gestures, children are likely to drop them and try to get attention in ways, like grabbing or making sounds.

Symbolic gestures show that even before children can talk, they understand that objects and concepts have names and that they can use symbols to refer to the things and happenings in their everyday lives.

TABLE 6-4

SYMBOLIC GESTURES SHOWN BY TODDLERS	
CATEGORY	**EXAMPLE**
Making request	"Go out": Child makes knob-turning gesture without touching doorknob. "Nurse": Child pats mother's chest. "Food": Child smacks lips.
Naming attribute	"Hot": Child blows or waves hand. "Many": Child waves hand back and forth. "Big": Child raises arms.
Naming object	"Flower": Child sniffs. "Dog": Child pants. "Airplane": Child holds out arms.
Naming event	"Baseball game": Child claps.
Replying	"I don't know": Child opens palms.

SOURCE: Adapted from Acredolo & Goodwyn, 1988, p. 454.

First Words

linguistic speech *Spoken language; besides words and grammar, it relies on pronunciation, intonation, and rhythm to convey meaning.*

holophrase *Single word that conveys a complete thought; the typical speech form of children aged 12 to 18 months.*

The average baby says his or her first word sometime between 10 and 14 months, initiating *linguistic speech*—spoken language that conveys meaning. Before long, the baby will use many words and will show some understanding of grammar, pronunciation, intonation, and rhythm as well. For now, an infant's total verbal repertoire is likely to be "mama" or "dada." Or it may be a simple syllable that has more than one meaning. As with Jason, "Da" may mean "I want that," "I want to go out," "Where's Daddy?" and so forth. A word like this is called a *holophrase,* because it expresses a complete thought in a single word. Its meaning depends upon the context in which the child utters it.

How Vocabulary Grows.   An average 15-month-old uses 10 different words or names (Nelson, 1973). Vocabulary grows throughout the single-word stage, which typically lasts until the age of about 18 months. Children come to rely more on words, as more occasions inspire them to speak a word or a name. The sounds and rhythms of speech grow more elaborate, and even if a great deal of speech is still babbling—even over the age of 1 year—it *is* quite expressive.

Among the first 50 words spoken by a group of 1- and 2-year-olds, the most common were *names* of things, either in the general sense ("bow-wow" for dog) or the specific ("Unga" for one particular dog). Others were *action* words ("bye-bye"), modifiers ("hot"), words that express *feelings or relationships* (the ever-popular "no"), and a few *grammatical* words ("for") (Nelson, 1973, 1981).

By 13 months most children understand that a word stands for a specific thing or event. They add words slowly to their vocabulary until a "naming explosion" occurs, usually between 16 and 24 months. Within a few weeks, the tod-

Annie and Vera clearly enjoy each other's company as they use their developing linguistic abilities to communicate. Language ability, a crucial element in cognitive growth, also enhances social development.

dler goes from saying about 50 words to saying about 400 (Bates, Bretherton, & Snyder, 1988).

Language development often proceeds in spurts, with some children showing a surge in understanding at about 20 to 22 months. Such a spurt can occur at any point in the second year, although some children never seem to show one. For those who do, a spurt in the number of words spoken usually occurs within two months (Reznick & Goldfield, 1992).

Creating Sentences

At 18 months, Vicky first spoke two words to express a single thought. "Shoe fall," she said to her father, who was pushing her in her stroller. Her father paused, saw the shoe on the sidewalk, and picked it up.

First Sentences.   The range in ages at which children begin combining words are similar for children learning spoken language and for children of deaf parents who learn sign language. Generally, children put words together between 18 and 24 months, about 8 to 12 months after they say their first word. But this is variable. Although prelinguistic speech is fairly closely tied to chronological age, linguistic speech is not. Knowing a child's age tells us little about his or her language development (R. Brown, 1973a, 1973b).

Furthermore, there does not seem to be a direct relationship between different aspects of language development. In one study children who at 20 months of age were early talkers continued to be verbally precocious at age $4\frac{1}{2}$, but were not likely to be early readers (Crain-Thoreson & Dale, 1992).

Vicky's first sentence was typical in that it dealt with everyday events, things, people, or activities (Braine, 1976; M. L. Rice, 1989; Slobin, 1973). This early speech is called "telegraphic" because it includes only essential words, like telegrams. When Jason says, "Jasa fweep," he seems to mean "I want to sweep." Telegraphic speech was once thought to be universal, but we now know that children vary in the extent to which they use it (Braine, 1976), and the form itself varies depending on the language being learned (Slobin, 1983). It still conforms to some degree to the grammar a child hears; Jason does not say "Fweep Jasa" when he wants to push a toy broom around. Interpretation of these early sentences often depends upon their context.

Learning Grammar.   Children's speech becomes increasingly complex. First, tense and case endings, articles, and prepositions are missing ("shoe fall"); and frequently, so are subjects or verbs ("That ball" and "Mommy sock"). Next, the child may string two basic relationships together ("Jason hit" and "Hit ball") to get a more complicated relationship ("Jason hit ball"). The first sentences generally consist of nouns, verbs, and adjectives.

Sometime between 20 and 30 months, children acquire the fundamentals of syntax. They begin to use articles (*a, the*), prepositions (*in, on*), conjunctions (*and, but*), plurals, verb endings, past tense, and forms of the verb *to be* (*am, are, is*). By 3 years of age, speech becomes longer and more complex. Although children often omit parts of speech, they get their meaning across, and they are fluent speakers (R. Brown, 1973a, 1973b). At 2 years, 10 months, Jason, who wanted to help his mother wash dishes, said clearly and grammatically (despite his frustration), "I can't get this glove on my hand." It was a simple sentence, but since he had never heard it before, his saying something completely novel like this illustrates the complex achievement that the command of language represents.

Language continues to develop, of course, and by late childhood, children are quite competent in grammar, although they continue to enlarge their vocabulary and improve their style.

Characteristics of Early Speech

Children's speech is not just an immature version of adult speech. It has a character all its own. This is true whatever language the child is speaking (Slobin, 1971). Early speech has a number of distinct characteristics.

Jason's uncle gave him a toy car, which Jason, at 13 months, called his "koo-ka." Weeks later, when Jason's father came home with a gift and said, "Look, Jason, here's a little car for you," Jason said "koo-ka" and ran and got the one from his uncle. To him, *that* was a little car, and it took some time before he called any other toy cars by the same word. Jason was *underextending a concept* by restricting "little car" to a single object.

underextending a concept *Using a word correctly but in too restricted a way.*

overextending a concept *Using a word incorrectly because of a failure to restrict its meaning appropriately.*

At 14 months, Jason jumped in excitement at the sight of a gray-haired man on the television screen and shouted, "Gampa!" At 15 months, Vicky saw a cow and squealed, "Oof-woof!" Both these toddlers were overgeneralizing, or *overextending a concept.* Jason thought that because his grandfather had gray hair, all gray-haired men could be called "Grandpa." Vicky may have thought that because a dog has four legs and a tail, all animals with these characteristics are "oof-woofs"; or, not knowing the word for cow, she simply may have used the closest word she knew.

As children develop a larger vocabulary, they overextend less and less. Feedback from adults on the appropriateness of what they say is a major way to move beyond this tendency. ("No, honey, that man looks like Grandpa, but he's somebody else's grandpa, not yours." "Sweetie, that is a *cow*.")

Children *simplify*. They use telegraphic speech to say just enough to get their meaning across ("No drink milk!").

Children *overregularize rules,* applying them rigidly, without knowing that some rules have exceptions. But when Jason says "mouses" instead of "mice" or Vicky says "I thinked" rather than "I thought," this represents progress. Both children initially used the correct forms of these irregular words, in simple imitation of what they heard. Once they learn grammatical rules for plurals and past tense (a crucial step in learning language), they apply them universally. The next step involves learning exceptions to rules, which they will do by early school age.

Children *understand grammatical relationships they cannot yet express.* At first, Vicky may understand that a dog is chasing a cat, but she cannot string together enough words to express the complete action. Her sentence comes out as "Puppy chase" rather than "Puppy chase kitty."

THEORIES OF LANGUAGE ACQUISITION

learning theory *Theory that most behavior is learned from experience.*

nativism *Theory that views human beings as having an inborn capacity for language acquisition.*

Although both maturation and environment affect the development of language, different linguists assign major importance to one or the other. B. F. Skinner (1957) was the foremost proponent of *learning theory,* which says that language learning is based on experience, specifically on aspects of the child's environment. Noam Chomsky (1957), on the other hand, upholds the most commonly accepted view, *nativism,* which maintains that there is an inborn capacity for learning language.

Learning Theory

According to learning theory, children learn language in the same way they learn other kinds of behavior—through conditioning and reinforcement. Caregivers reinforce children (usually by smiling, paying attention, and responding) for making sounds that resemble adult speech. So children make more of these sounds, generalizing and abstracting as they go along. At first, children utter sounds at random, and those that sound like adult speech are reinforced. The children repeat the reinforced sounds. Then children imitate the sound they hear adults making and are again reinforced for doing so. Thus children in English-speaking countries learn English rather than another language. Imitation may explain why children outgrow incorrect usages even though parents, who generally correct the *truth* of what children say, usually do not correct how they say it (R. Brown, Cazden, & Bellugi, 1969).

As support for their position, learning theorists note that children reared at home, who presumably hear more adult speech and get more attention and more reinforcement than those who grow up in institutions, babble more (Brodbeck & Irwin, 1946). However, learning theory does not account for children's imaginative ways of saying things they have never heard. Vicky, for example, described the brown smudge left on a napkin she used to wipe chocolate from her lips as her "lip shadow" and a sprained ankle as a "sprangle."

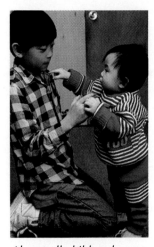

Almost all children learn their native language, mastering the basics in the same age-related sequence without formal teaching. Nativists say that this shows that all human beings are born with the capacity to acquire language. It also helps that proficient speakers, like this toddler's older brother, tend to simplify their speech when talking to babies.

Nativism

In the nativist view, human beings have an inborn capacity for acquiring language: They learn to talk as naturally as they learn to walk. Evidence for this viewpoint comes from several facts:

- Almost all children around the world learn their native language, mastering it in the same age-related sequence without formal teaching.
- Human beings, the only animals to master a spoken language, are the only species whose brain is larger on one side than the other, and who seem to have an inborn mechanism for language localized in the larger hemisphere (the left for most people).
- Newborns respond to language: They move their bodies in the rhythm of the adult speech they hear (Condon & Sander, 1974); they can tell their mother's voice from those of strangers (DeCasper & Fifer, 1980); and in the first months of life, they can differentiate similar sounds (Eimas et al., 1971).

One researcher suggests that neonates can put sounds into categories because all human beings are "born with perceptual mechanisms that are tuned to the properties of speech" (Eimas, 1985, p. 49). Contact with the sounds of a particular language leads children to "tune in" the corresponding preset "channels" and "tune out" unused ones. These perceptual mechanisms, along with the vocal cords and the specialized speech centers of the brain, let a child quickly "join the community of language" (Eimas, 1985, p. 52).

How do babies go from simple sound recognition to create complex utterances that follow the specific rules of their language? Noam Chomsky (1972) proposes that an inborn *language acquisition device (LAD)* programs children's brains to analyze the language they hear and to extract from it the rules of grammar. Using these rules, they can then make up original sentences.

language acquisition device (LAD) *In nativist linguistics, the inborn "mechanism" that enables the human to learn a language.*

The observation that deaf children make up their own sign language when they do not have models to follow is further evidence that internal mechanisms play a role in a young child's growing capacity for linguistic expression (H. Feldman, Goldin-Meadow, & Gleitman, 1979; Hoff-Ginsberg & Shatz, 1982). The case of Simon, a 9-year-old deaf child of deaf parents, is cited as support for this theory. Simon used correct grammar in American Sign Language (ASL), even though he learned incorrect grammar from his parents and a different sign language, with different rules of grammar, at his school (Newport & Singleton, 1992).

Still, the nativist approach does not explain why children differ so much in grammatical skill and fluency, how they come to understand the meanings of words, or why language development depends on having someone to talk with.

Most developmentalists today draw on both nativism and learning theory. They believe that children have an inborn capacity to acquire language, which is then activated and enhanced by experience.

INDIVIDUAL DIFFERENCES IN LANGUAGE DEVELOPMENT

What determines how quickly and how well a baby learns to speak? Again, we see both nature and nurture.

Genetic and Temperamental Factors

A genetic influence is apparent in the moderate positive correlation between parents' intelligence and the rate at which their biological children develop communication skills during the first year of life. This relationship shows up for adopted children and their biological mothers, but not their adoptive parents (Hardy-Brown & Plomin, 1985; Hardy-Brown, Plomin, & DeFries, 1981).

Another influence on language development, which may also be inborn, is a child's temperament. Children who are cooperative, interested in other people, and happy at age 2 are more advanced at ages 2, 3, and 7 in how they express themselves and how they respond to what other people say (Slomkowski, Nelson, Dunn, & Plomin, 1992).

What might account for this relationship between temperament and cognitive factors? First, extroverted children may talk more and have the kind of personality that makes other people want to talk more to them, thus providing more practice in speaking. Then, the "goodness of fit" between a child's temperament and a parent's style may be important. Findings like these emphasize the interaction between different domains in a child's life (like the child's own temperament and the environment created by parents) and also illustrates bidirectional influence (how the child contributes to creating the environment).

Environmental Factors

Many differences in language abilities that surface by the end of the second year reflect differences in environment (Nelson, 1981).

Child-Directed Speech ("Motherese").   You do not have to be a mother to speak "motherese." If you pitch your voice high, simplify your speech by using short words and sentences, speak slowly, ask questions, and repeat your words often

"Motherese"—a simplified form of language used for speaking to babies and toddlers—seems to come naturally, not only to mothers—but also to fathers, grandparents, and slightly older children.

child-directed speech (CDS), or "motherese" *A simplified kind of speech used in talking to babies and toddlers; it includes a high-pitched tone, short words and sentences, slow tempo, repetition, and many questions.*

when you speak to a baby, you are speaking ***child-directed speech (CDS)***, or ***motherese***. Most adults—and even children—do it naturally. Until recently, the idea that CDS enables children to learn language, or at least to pick it up faster, was widely accepted, but recently its value has been questioned. Let's look at the debate.

Infants' preference for simplified speech is already present before 1 month of age; it does not seem to depend on any specific experience (Cooper & Aslin, 1990). However, parents usually do not start speaking CDS until babies show by their expressions, actions, and sounds that they have some understanding of what is being said to them. The influence infants exert appeared in a study that found that women use CDS less when asked to make tapes addressed to unseen children (Snow, 1972). Interaction with an infant encourages the use of CDS.

The Value of Child-Directed Speech. Those who consider CDS important believe that it serves several functions (Snow, 1972). Emotionally, it helps adults and children develop a relationship. Socially, it teaches children how to carry on a conversation—how to introduce a topic, comment and expand on an idea, and take turns talking. Linguistically, it teaches children how to use new words, structure phrases, and put ideas into language. Because CDS is confined to simple, down-to-earth topics, children can use their own knowledge of familiar things to help them work out the meanings of the words they hear (Snow, 1977).

Some researchers have found positive correlations between use of CDS and the rate of 2-year-olds' language growth (Hoff-Ginsberg, 1985, 1986). Social class differences have also been found. Upper-middle-class mothers are more likely to follow their children's conversational cues—by answering questions or pursuing a topic that the child has brought up—whereas working-class mothers more often speak to their children to tell them what to do (Hoff-Ginsberg, 1991). The type of activity that parent and child do together is important. Reading to a child is especially conducive to a supportive style of parent-child conversation, while toy play leads to the highest rates of mothers' commands (Hoff-Ginsberg, 1991).

The value of CDS seems to be supported by research on twins. Twins usually speak later than single-born children; one study suggests why. After observing 6 pairs of twins and 12 singletons at ages 15 and 21 months, researchers found substantial differences in mother-child interactions, mostly due to the practical pressures on harried mothers of twin infants (Tomasello, Mannle, & Kruger, 1986).

Compared with mothers of singletons, mothers of twins speak less frequently to and pay less attention to each child, and have shorter conversations. When they do speak to their babies, more of what they say involves directing a child to do something rather than chattier comments and questions. Twins' mothers imitate more and elaborate less on topics the children bring up. Directive speech is less effective than questioning in encouraging children's fluency (Nelson, 1981). While twins have each other to talk to—and often develop a private language between themselves—their interaction is not as influential as the kind they would have with an adult.

Another researcher found some value of CDS in a study of language functioning in 2½-year-olds, but still concluded that "the differences among mothers that predicted rate of language growth in their children were not differences in the use of motherese per se" (Hoff-Ginsberg, 1985, p. 384). What are these differences? One seems to be an adult's goals in talking to a child—whether, for example, she or he uses scaffolding, that is, prods a child to speak in ways just beyond the range of the child's current competence, which may motivate the child to move up to the next level of language skill (Hoff-Ginsberg, 1986).

Investigators who question the value of CDS contend that children speak sooner and better if they hear and can respond to more complex speech from adults. The children can then select from this speech the parts they are interested in and are able to deal with. In fact, say these researchers, children discover the rules of language faster when they hear complex sentences that use these rules more often and in more ways (Gleitman, Newport, & Gleitman, 1984).

Cross-Cultural Patterns in Child-Directed Speech. Still, CDS persists—and not only in the United States. In talking to her infant or toddler about a dog, an American mother is likely to use the word *doggie;* a Japanese mother says *koino-chan,* the "baby-talk" equivalent of *inu,* the word for dog. The American mother may say, "The doggie goes woof-woof," while the Japanese mother refers to the dog's barking as "wanwan."

A cross-sectional study of 30 American and 30 Japanese mothers and their babies illustrates both universal and culturally mediated responses. Observers who listened to the mothers speaking to their 6-, 12-, and 19-month-old babies at home found a number of similarities, underscoring the use of CDS in various cultures. Both Japanese and American mothers simplify their language, repeat often, and speak differently to children of different ages. Aspects of CDS seem to be universal responses to babies' immaturity (Fernald & Morikawa, 1993).

Cultural differences appeared in the mothers' styles of interaction, reflecting beliefs about child rearing. For example, American mothers label objects much more while playing with their babies ("That's a car. See the car? You like it? It's got nice wheels"), showing their interest in teaching vocabulary. Japanese mothers show their interest in fostering politeness by their use of toys in ritual give-

and-take routines ("Here! It's a vroom vroom. I give it to you. Now give this to me. Yes! Thank you").

Japanese mothers encourage mutual dependence between mother and child, as seen in their more extensive and longer use of CDS, compared with American mothers. American parents' briefer and less extensive use of CDS reflects American values of independence for children. The way adults talk to children teaches them the norms of their culture, along with the rules of their language (Fernald & Morikawa, 1993).

However parents speak, the important thing is their interest in and close interaction with their babies. The more they talk with their children, the sooner the babies can pick up the nuances of speech and can correct wrong assumptions. According to one pair of researchers, "No child has been observed to speak a human language without having had a communicative partner from whom to learn" (Hoff-Ginsberg & Shatz, 1982, p. 22).

Other Environmental Factors.   As babies grow into toddlers, environmental factors other than motherese, or "baby talk," become more important. For one, parents' imitation of babies' sounds affects the pace of language learning (Hardy-Brown & Plomin, 1985; Hardy-Brown, Plomin, & DeFries, 1981). Then too the vocabularies of 14- to 26-month-olds are related to how much their mothers talk to them (Huttenlocher, Haight, Bryk, Seltzer, & Lyons, 1991). A strong relationship has appeared between the frequency of various words in mothers' speech and the order in which children learn these words. Among 2-year-olds in day care centers in Bermuda, those whose caregivers spoke to them often (especially to give or ask for information rather than to control behavior) had better language skills than children who did not have such conversations with adults (McCartney, 1984). Conversely, when children with normal hearing grew up in homes with deaf parents who communicated only through sign language, the children's speech development was slowed (Moskowitz, 1978).

The environment also seems to influence whether children will be *referential*—using their first words primarily to *refer* to objects and events (using nouns and verbs to name and describe things)—or *expressive*—using first words to *express* social routines (using pronouns and repeating formulas, like "stop it") (Nelson, 1981). Referential children learn new words faster than do expressive children (Clark, 1983). The differences between these two kinds of speakers are correlated with parental speaking styles (Lieven, 1978; Olsen-Fulero, 1982). Referential children are more often firstborns from well-educated families, whose parents encourage labeling by asking their children many questions (Nelson, 1973). In contrast, more of the speech of parents of expressive children involves telling them what to do.

Vocabularies get a strong boost when adults seize the right opportunity to teach children new words. If Julia says, "This is a ball," when Jason is already paying attention to the ball, he is more likely to remember the word than if he were playing with something else and she tried to divert his attention to the ball and teach him the word then (Dunham, Dunham, & Curwin, 1993).

To speak and communicate, children need practice and interaction. Hearing speech on television is not enough: Dutch children who watched German television every day did not learn German (Snow et al., 1976). Language is a social act. By talking to babies, adults show how to use new words, structure phrases, and

BOX 6-3 ▪ THE EVERYDAY WORLD

TALKING WITH BABIES AND TODDLERS

"Yes, you like this, don't you? . . . Yes, you do. . . . You love your bath. . . . And your daddy loves you. . . . Now let's wash your tummy. . . . Now. . . ." These remarks may not sound highly intellectual, but they are a vital influence on a baby's development. Talking, reading, and singing to babies help them learn a language; learn that they are valued, special people; and learn how to get along with other people. Here are suggestions for talking with a baby at different stages of language development:

♦ *Babbling stage.* When a baby babbles, repeat the syllables. Make a game of it, and soon the baby will repeat your sound. This kind of game gives a baby the idea that a conversation consists of taking turns, an idea babies seem to grasp at about 7½ or 8 months of age. A round of stimulating chitchat like "dee, dee, dee; dah, dah, dah" helps babies to experience the social aspect of speech.

♦ *First words.* By the time babies speak their first words, at about 1 year, you can help them learn even more by repeating these first words and pronouncing them correctly. If you can't understand what the baby is saying, smile and say something yourself. Babies can understand many more words than they can utter, and they can learn the names for the objects in their world. Julia points to Jason's doll and says, "Please give me Kermit." If Jason doesn't respond, she reaches over, picks up the doll, and says "Kermit." Jason's ability to

understand grows as he learns to discover through language what another person is thinking.

♦ *Multiword speech.* Help a toddler who has begun to string words together to make sentences by expanding on what the child says. If Vicky says "Mommy sock," Ellen replies, "Yes, that is Mommy's sock." Even though expansion may not speed up the acquisition of grammar, it has a strong social use.

♦ *Reading to young children.* Encourage a child's participation in reading-aloud sessions by asking challenging, open-ended questions rather than those calling for a yes or a no response. Start with simple questions ("Where is the ball?") and then pose more challenging ones ("What color is the ball?" "Who is playing with the ball?" "What is happening to the boy in the corner?"). Then expand on the child's answers, correct wrong ones, give alternative possibilities, and bestow praise. By using methods like these rather than just reading aloud, you will help develop both vocabulary and expressive language skills.

Above all, talking and reading with a child should be fun. Not every conversation should be a lesson or a test. The baby should be able to decline to play occasionally, because sometimes a small child just doesn't feel like talking. Most children who begin talking fairly late catch up eventually—and many make up for lost time by later talking nonstop to anyone who will listen!

express speech; and they show children how to carry on a conversation—how to introduce a topic, comment on and add to it, and take turns talking.

However, too much direction from adults—commands, requests, and instructions—is not helpful (Nelson, 1973). Adults help a child most by paraphrasing what a child says, expanding on it, talking about what interests the child, staying quiet long enough to give the child a chance to respond, and using read-aloud sessions to ask questions (M. L. Rice, 1989). (See Box 6-3.)

THE DEVELOPMENT OF EARLY LITERACY

From an early age most children love to be read to, and the way parents read to their young children sets the stage for how children speak, and eventually how they read. In one month-long experiment, researchers trained parents to use special techniques in reading to their children. The study compared two groups of middle-class children aged 21 to 35 months. In the experimental group, the parents adopted new *dialogic* reading routines; the parents in the control group read to their children as frequently as the experimental parents, but were not trained in the new techniques.

The parents in the experimental group asked their children challenging, open-ended questions rather than questions calling for simple yes-no answers. (Instead of asking, "Is the cat asleep?" they would ask, "What is the cat doing?") They expanded on the children's answers to their questions, corrected wrong answers, gave alternative possibilities, and bestowed praise. The parents helped their children become the teller of the story while the adults became active listeners; they prompted, rewarded, and expanded children's efforts to talk (Whitehurst et al., 1988). After 1 month, the children in the experimental group were 8.5 months ahead of the control group in level of speech and 6 months ahead in vocabulary; 9 months later, the experimental group was still 6 months ahead of the controls (Whitehurst et al., 1988). The intervention group received a boost in their *preliteracy skills,* the competencies helpful in learning to read, such as learning what letters look like and sound like.

These techniques hold promise for helping children with below-normal language abilities who are at risk of developing reading problems. Investigators taught the techniques to the day care teachers of 2-year-olds from low-income families (who were not read to frequently) who attended a low-quality day care center in Mexico (Valdez-Menchaca & Whitehurst, 1992). After 6 or 7 weeks of intervention, children in an experimental group (whose teachers used dialogic techniques in reading to them individually) did significantly better on several standardized language tests and spontaneous language than did children in a control group (whose teachers spent time with them individually, doing arts and crafts). Findings like these have important implications for social policy wherever illiteracy is a problem (Valdez-Menchaca & Whitehurst, 1992).

COMPETENCE

WHAT IS COMPETENCE?

In 1965 Burton L. White and his colleagues began the Harvard Preschool Project to test and observe some 400 preschoolers and rate them on their competence in both cognitive and social skills (B. L. White, 1971; B. L. White, Kaban, & Attanucci, 1979). They found significant individual differences among children, which were related to factors in the children's environment.

The most competent children—the researchers called them A's—showed such *social skills* as getting and holding the attention of adults in acceptable ways, using adults as resources, and showing both affection and hostility. They got along well with other children, were proud of their accomplishments, and wanted to act grown-up. Among their *cognitive skills* were using language well, showing a range of intellectual abilities, planning and carrying out complicated activities, and "dual focusing" (paying attention to a task while being aware of what else was going on). Children classified as B's were less accomplished in these skills; and children classified as C's were very deficient. Follow-up studies 2 years later showed stability in the classifications.

One way to help children become competent is to allow them freedom to explore in a safe environment full of interesting things to see and touch. Annie's mother is nearby, ready to answer the 2-year-old's questions about her exciting discovery, tell her what it is, and initiate a conversation about it.

WHAT INFLUENCES COMPETENCE?

To find out how the A and C children became the way they were, the researchers identified A's and C's who had younger siblings, and they looked at the ways the A and C mothers acted with their younger children. (The researchers focused on mothers, feeling that few fathers spent enough time with children of this age to be influential, a conclusion they might not draw today.) Of course, this assumes that these mothers acted the same with the younger siblings as they had with the older ones, an assumption that could not be tested in this study design.

In mothering the younger siblings, significant differences appeared after about 8 months. At this age babies start to understand language, and the way parents talk to them is important. Then, as babies begin to crawl, some parents react with pleasure, some with annoyance. Since babies become attached to the person they spend the most time with, this person's personality is important.

The major differences revolved around three aspects of child rearing—the ability to "design" a child's world, to serve as a "consultant" for a child, and to provide a balance between freedom and restraint. Mothers from all socioeconomic levels fell into both groups: Some welfare mothers raised A children and some middle-class women raised C's.

The A mothers designed a safe physical environment full of interesting things to see and touch (common household objects as often as expensive toys). They tended to be "on call" to their babies, without devoting their entire lives to them. A number had part-time jobs, and those who did stay home generally spent less than 10 percent of their time interacting with their infants. They went about their daily routine but were available when needed to answer a question, label an object, or share in a discovery. These women generally had positive attitudes toward life, enjoyed being with young children, and gave of themselves. They were energetic, patient, tolerant of messiness, and fairly casual about minor risks. They were firm and consistent, setting reasonable limits while showing love and respect. When they wanted to change their babies' behavior, they distracted infants under 1 year of age and used a combination of distraction, physical removal, and firm words with older children.

The C mothers were a diverse group. Some were overwhelmed by life, ran chaotic homes, and were too absorbed in daily struggles to spend much time with their children. Others spent too much time: hovering, being overprotective, pushing their babies to learn, and making them dependent. Some were physically present but rarely made real contact. These mothers provided for their children materially but confined them in cribs or playpens.

The researchers identified several guidelines for raising competent children. (See Box 6-4.) But they did not investigate the children's own contributions to their mothers' child-rearing styles. It is quite possible that the A children had personalities that made their mothers *want* to respond as they did. Perhaps they showed more curiosity, more independence, and more interest in what their mothers said and did than did the C children.

What do you think? *White and his colleagues defined competence in terms of social and cognitive skills. What characteristics would you include in your definition of competence in young children? How would these characteristics vary with the age of the child—and how would you measure them?*

BOX 6-4 ■ THE EVERYDAY WORLD

HELPING CHILDREN BE MORE COMPETENT

The findings from the Harvard Preschool Project and from studies using the HOME (Home Observation for Measurement of the Environment) scales can be useful to caregivers of young children and can be translated into the following guidelines:

1. The best time for enhancing a child's competence is from the age of 6 to 8 months up until about 2 years, but it is never too late.
2. Encourage children to have close social relationships with important people in their lives, especially from the first few months after their first birthday.
3. Make the most of the time you spend with a child.
4. Give children help when they need it rather than pressing it on them too soon, ignoring them, or seeing them as a burden to be dealt with quickly.
5. Stay fairly close to young children but do not hover so much that you discourage them from developing attention-seeking skills.

6. Talk to children about whatever they are interested in at the moment and play with them on their level instead of trying to redirect their attention to something else.
7. Speak with them. They will not pick up language from listening to the radio or television or overhearing conversations. They need interaction with adults.
8. Create an environment that fosters learning—one that includes books, interesting objects, and a place to play.
9. Give them physical freedom to explore. Do not confine them regularly in a playpen, crib, jump seat, or small room.
10. Use punishment sparingly; instead, find opportunities for positive feedback.

SOURCES: Bradley & Caldwell, 1982; Bradley, Caldwell, & Rock, 1988; Bradley et al., 1989; Stevens & Bakeman, 1985; B. L. White, 1971; B. L. White, Kaban, & Attanucci, 1979.

HOME: HOME OBSERVATION FOR MEASUREMENT OF THE ENVIRONMENT

To assess the impact of a child's home surroundings on later cognitive growth, researchers developed a measure called the *Home Observation for Measurement of the Environment (HOME)*. One factor measured by HOME is parental responsiveness, which is seen as an important influence on children's cognitive development. HOME gives credit to the parent of a toddler for caressing or kissing the child during an examiner's visit; to the parent of a preschooler for spontaneously praising the child at least twice during the visit; and to the parent of an older child for answering the child's questions. Examiners evaluate how parent and child talk to each other and give high marks for a parent's friendly, nonpunitive attitude.

The scale also assesses the number of books in the home, the presence of playthings that encourage the development of concepts, and parents' involvement in children's play. High scores on all these factors are fairly reliable in predicting children's IQ; when combined with the parents' level of education, they are even more accurate. A longitudinal study found significant positive correlations between how responsive parents were to their 6-month-old babies (measured using HOME) and how well the children did at age 10 on IQ and achievement tests and teachers' ratings of classroom behaviors (Bradley & Caldwell, 1982; Bradley, Caldwell, & Rock, 1988).

The influence of parents is also seen in a study of 931 African American, Mexican American, and white children. This research showed that in looking at children growing up in inner-city neighborhoods, the day-to-day aspects of the home (like how responsive parents are and whether the child has access to stimulating play materials) are more closely related to cognitive development than are such aspects of the wider environment as socioeconomic status (Bradley et al., 1989). Across all three ethnic groups, a favorable home environment could offset problems in infancy, but when a child's early development status *and* early home environment were both very low, the chances for a good outcome for the child were much less than when only one of these measures was low.

What do you think?   *How would you assess the relationship between a child's cognitive functioning and the home environment? What characteristics would you measure?*

PLAY BETWEEN PARENTS AND THEIR INFANTS AND TODDLERS

Soon after Jason is born, his parents play with him. When he is awake, Jess or Julia is likely to look into his face, talk to him playfully, and touch him lovingly. Within a few weeks, they make him laugh by kissing him on his stomach or bouncing him gently in their arms. As he matures, he initiates some of this play, and throughout his infancy and toddlerhood more and more interactions occur, including the peekaboo games he loves. (See Box 6-1.)

In all these activities, Jason's parents are helping him develop. Play is the work of children, the way they learn the tasks they have to master to function well in life. These tasks include relating to other people, regulating themselves, and learning about expectations. Babies who are developing normally show their mastery of these tasks in how they communicate, how they show their emotions, and how they initiate social exchanges.

Psychologists look at parent-child play to assess the development of infants and toddlers. For 3- to 9-month-olds, researchers set up a sequence of three 2-minute face-to-face episodes: a normal social interaction, a disturbed one, and another normal one (Tronick, 1989; Weinberg, 1989). In the normal episodes, the parent is told to play with the baby as she or he normally does; the disturbed episodes may include the parent's watching the baby while keeping an unresponsive "poker" face or looking depressed and withdrawn.

Babies show a wide range of emotions and communications in these situations. Normally developing babies will generally smile, coo, and make joyful gestures in the first free-play episode; will try to communicate but look either sad or anxious in the disturbed one; and will show mixed positive and negative signals in the third episode. Babies' responses that differ markedly from the norm may signal problems (Beeghley, 1993).

Other studies investigate toddlers' development in these same realms, looking at such behaviors as taking turns, paying attention, and initiating play activities. Such assessments seem to hold promise for testing children with developmental disabilities. Toddlers with Down syndrome, for example, respond much like normal children in some ways (like maturity of play with objects) and differently in others (like taking the initiative in play with others). Autistic children also show characteristic patterns. Such patterns do not always show up in standard psychometric testing, and therefore the kind of test that assesses play patterns can provide valuable information about high-risk children.

Interaction in play and other daily activities is a key to much of childhood development—cognitive, social, and emotional. Children call forth responses from the people around them and they, in turn, react to those responses. In Chapter 7, we will look more closely at these bidirectional influences as we explore early personality and social development.

SUMMARY

1   Intelligence involves both adaptive and goal-oriented behavior. Three major approaches for studying intelligence are the Piagetian, psychometric, and information-processing approaches.

2   The Piagetian approach is concerned with the qualitatively changing nature of cognitive development, or the way people acquire and use knowledge about the world. During the sensorimotor stage, children develop from primarily reflexive infants to toddlers capable of symbolic thought. A major development of the sensorimotor stage is object permanence, the realization that an object or person continues to exist even when out of sight. Much recent research suggests that infants develop sensorimotor behaviors earlier than Piaget's theory holds.

3   The psychometric approach seeks to determine and measure quantitatively the factors that make up intelligence. Psychometric tests for infants emphasize sensory and motor ability. These tests are generally poor predictors of later intelligence.

4   The information-processing approach is concerned with the processes underlying intelligent behavior, that is, how people manipulate symbols and what they do with the information they perceive. Assessment of how efficiently an infant processes information appears to be promising as a predictor of later intelligence.

5   Learning is a relatively permanent change in behavior that occurs as a result of experience. Maturation produces changes in cognitive abilities and enables learning to take place.

6   Very young infants are capable of several types of learning, including habituation (reduced response to a stimulus that has become familiar), classical conditioning (learning a conditioned response to a stimulus that is originally neutral), and operant conditioning (learning a response to produce a particular effect). Complex learning can be achieved through various learning modes, used separately or in combination.

7   Infants show memory ability virtually from birth, and this ability improves rapidly.

8   The development of language is a crucial aspect of cognitive growth.

9   Prelinguistic speech, which precedes the first words, includes crying, cooing, babbling, and imitating. Babies also communicate through the use of gestures. During the second year of life, the typical toddler begins to speak; the second year is also important for growth of language comprehension.

10   Early speech is characterized by simplifying, underextending and overextending concepts, and overregularizing rules.

11   Two major theories of language acquisition are learning theory (which emphasizes the role of reinforcement) and nativism (which maintains that people have an inborn capacity to acquire language).

12   Individual differences in language acquisition are influenced by both genetic and temperamental factors as well as environmental factors. Communication with an adult partner is essential if a child is to learn to speak. It is not clear whether hearing simple, direct, repetitive language (child-directed speech or "motherese") is important to infants' language development.

13   Early literacy is influenced by the way caregivers read to children.

14   Parents' child-rearing styles (especially during the first 2 years) affect children's cognitive, social, and emotional competence. Parents of the most competent children are

skilled at "designing" a child's environment, are available as "consultants" to a child, and use appropriate control.

15 Play between parents and their infants helps infants master such tasks as relating to others, self-regulation, and learning about expectations. Play is also used to assess the development of infants and toddlers.

KEY TERMS

intelligent behavior (209)
Piagetian approach (209)
psychometric approach (209)
information-processing approach (209)
cognitive development (210)
sensorimotor stage (210)
object permanence (210)
circular reaction (212)
scheme (212)
Bayley Scales of Infant Development (222)
habituation (224)
dishabituation (224)
visual-recognition memory (225)
visual novelty preference (225)
cross-modal transference (225)

exploratory behavior (226)
learning (227)
maturation (228)
classical conditioning (228)
operant conditioning (229)
language (231)
prelinguistic speech (231)
linguistic speech (236)
holophrase (236)
underextending a concept (238)
overextending a concept (238)
learning theory (238)
nativism (238)
language acquisition device (LAD) (239)
child-directed speech (CDS) ("motherese") (241)

SUGGESTED READINGS

Pinker, S. (1994). *The language instinct: How the mind creates language.* New York: Morrow. This in-depth work on language development proposes that language is an instinct, wired into our brains from birth. The author, a well-known linguist, answers questions such as how language evolves, how the brain computes it, and how children learn it. He discusses modern linguistic theory in a way that is easily understandable to the average reader.

Wilde, J. A. (1993). *The child's discovery of the mind.* Cambridge, MA: Harvard University Press. According to Piaget, children have little understanding before the age of six. But in the last 20 years, Piaget's methods have been challenged and his conclusions revised. Here is a fascinating survey of the research in this area, studying the implications for children's intellectual and social development.

Youcha, G. (1995). *Minding the children: Child care in America from colonial times to the present.* New York: Scribner. This lively and vivid history of child care sheds light on today's concerns and controversies over the issue.

CHAPTER 7

PERSONALITY AND SOCIAL DEVELOPMENT IN INFANCY AND TODDLERHOOD

But what am I?
An infant crying in the night:
An infant crying for the light:
And with no language but a cry.

Alfred, Lord Tennyson, "In Memoriam," 1850

This chapter is about the shift from the dependence of infancy to the independence of childhood. We'll see the relationship between that shift and the impact parents and children have on each other. We consider Erik Erikson's theories about the formation of basic trust and the development of autonomy in infancy and toddlerhood; we also consider how recent research on the development of self-control and self-regulation expands on his concepts. We look at the emotions babies have and their ways of expressing those emotions. We consider how babies are like one another and how they differ in terms of temperament, gender, and early experiences. We also explore relationships between babies and their parents as well as their other caretakers, their siblings, and other children. Finally, we consider the impact of early day care. As we discuss all these issues, we ask basic questions about the roots of personality:

PREVIEW QUESTIONS

- ◆ What emotions do babies have? How early do they show them?
- ◆ How do infants develop trust? How do toddlers develop autonomy?
- ◆ How do babies themselves, their families, and others in their world contribute to their personality and social and emotional development?
- ◆ What genetic and environmental influences seem to lead to disturbances in development?
- ◆ How do brothers and sisters influence each other?
- ◆ How does early day care affect children's development?

Jason, at age 2, makes it clear that he has finished dinner. From his high chair, he throws down his spoon, plate, food, and bib. He makes something else clear too—he knows he should not be doing this. When Julia speaks sharply to him about raining peas, potatoes, and plastic on the floor, he lowers his eyes and seems to say, "I know I did something you didn't like—but love me anyway."

Jason, in the "terrible twos," is showing an important aspect of early social development. Beyond the tears and the tantrums, the "no's" and the noise, toddlers' emphatic expressions of what they want to do—as opposed to what adults want them to do—signal the shift from infancy to childhood.

EARLY PERSONALITY DEVELOPMENT

Personality is a person's unique and relatively consistent way of feeling, thinking, and behaving. Some aspects of personality seem to be largely inherited; others are more highly influenced by early experience; most reflect the interaction between heredity and environment. First we discuss the awareness that begins in infancy that some aspects of the world and some of the people in it can be trusted, while others cannot. Then we talk about how toddlers learn to regulate their behavior, an essential step toward independence. (Table 7-1 shows highlights of early personality and social development.)

personality *A person's unique and relatively consistent way of feeling, thinking, and behaving.*

THE DEVELOPMENT OF TRUST

Infants come into this world needing care and sustenance. For a far longer period than the young of other mammals, human babies are dependent on other people for food, protection, their very lives. How do they come to trust that their needs will be met? Infants' early experiences are the key.

The first of the eight crises, or critical developmental stages of personality development, identified by Erik H. Erikson (1950) is *basic trust versus basic mistrust.* This stage begins in infancy and continues until about 18 months of age. In these early months, babies develop a sense of how reliable the people and objects in their world are. (Refer to Table 1-3.) They need to develop a balance between trust (which lets them form intimate relationships) and mistrust (which enables them to protect themselves). If trust predominates, as it should, children de-

basic trust versus basic mistrust *In Erikson's theory, the first critical alternative of psychosocial development, in which infants (birth to 18 months) develop a sense of how reliable people in their world are.*

TABLE 7-1

HIGHLIGHTS OF INFANTS' AND TODDLERS' PERSONALITY AND SOCIAL DEVELOPMENT, BIRTH TO 36 MONTHS	
APPROXIMATE AGE IN MONTHS	**CHARACTERISTICS**
0–3	Infants are open to stimulation. They begin to show interest and curiosity, and they smile readily at people.
3–6	Babies can anticipate what is to happen and experience disappointment when it does not. They show this by becoming angry or acting wary. They smile, coo, and laugh often. This is a time of social awakening and early reciprocal exchanges between the baby and the caregiver.
7–9	Babies play "social games" and try to get responses from people. They "talk" to, touch, and cajole other babies to get them to respond. They express more differentiated emotions, showing joy, fear, anger, and surprise.
9–12	Babies are intensely preoccupied with their principal caregiver, may become afraid of strangers, and act subdued in new situations. By 1 year, they communicate emotions more clearly, showing moods, ambivalence, and gradations of feeling.
12–18	Babies explore their environment, using the people they are most attached to as a secure base. As they master the environment, they become more confident and more eager to assert themselves.
18–36	Toddlers sometimes become anxious because they now realize how much they are separating from their caregiver. They work out their awareness of their limitations in fantasy, in play, and by identifying with adults.

SOURCE: Adapted from Sroufe, 1979.

velop the virtue of *hope*—the belief that they can fulfill their needs and obtain their desires (Erikson, 1982). If mistrust predominates, children will view the world as unfriendly and unpredictable and will have trouble forming relationships.

The critical element in fostering trust seems to be sensitive, responsive, consistent caregiving. This can be provided by the mother or someone else. Erikson saw feeding as the setting for establishing the right mix of trust and mistrust, with the mother playing the leading role. But mothers are not the only important influences. A child's own contribution—either as a result of inborn temperament or in response to life circumstances —can influence his or her development.

SELF-REGULATION

Jason is about to poke his finger into an electrical outlet. In his "child-proofed" apartment, the sockets are covered, but here in his grandmother's home, the outlets are not so equipped. When Jason hears his father shout "No!" the 1-year-old pulls his hand back. The next time Jason goes near an outlet, he starts to point his finger, hesitates, and says, "No." He has stopped himself from doing something he remembers he is not supposed to do. This shows the beginning of *self-regulation*—control of one's own behavior to conform to social expectations.

self-regulation *Control of one's own behavior to conform to social expectations.*

The growth of self-regulation links all major domains of development—physical, cognitive, and emotional. The first sign of this drive toward autonomy, or self-determination, comes as the result of physical maturation. "Me do!" is the byword as toddlers use their developing muscles to try to do everything themselves—to walk, to feed and dress themselves, and to expand the boundaries of their world. As toddlers become more mobile, they must learn how to protect themselves and how to get along in society. At 12 to 18 months they are achieving a level of cognitive awareness that lets them absorb information. They are also experiencing the first of what for many people is a lifelong emotional struggle between a desire for approval from the most important people in their lives, their parents—and, at the same time, a need for independence from them.

According to Erikson, toddlers need to develop autonomy. During this stage, parents need to ignore messy faces, bibs, tables, and floors, and let children learn how to master such basic tasks as feeding themselves.

The Development of Autonomy

Jason is continually absorbing information about the behaviors Jess and Julia approve of. As he processes, stores, and acts upon this information, a gradual shift from external to internal control takes place. Erikson referred to this stage as the second crisis: *autonomy versus shame and doubt.*

From about 18 months to 3 years, children make more of their own decisions and use some self-restraint. A major issue during toddlerhood is the development of *self*-regulation and *self*-control versus *outside* regulation and control. Ideally, having come through the first stage with a sense of basic trust in the world and an awakening sense of self, toddlers begin to trust their own judgment and to substitute it for their parents'. Erikson referred to the emergence of this as the *virtue of will.* Because one of a toddler's favorite ways of testing limits is to shout "No!" this new behavior is called *negativism.*

Shame and doubt also have a place in the way toddlers learn to regulate themselves, since unlimited liberty is neither safe nor healthy. Some self-doubt helps them recognize what they are not yet ready to do, and a sense of shame helps them learn to live with others. Toddlers need adults to set limits. Too few or too many limits may make children compulsive about controlling themselves; and fear of losing self-control may fill a child with inhibitions and loss of self-esteem.

Self-control is a child's ability to adjust what she or he does to fit what is socially acceptable. However, when the child wants *very* badly to do something, the rules are easily forgotten; Vicky runs into the street after a ball and Jason takes a forbidden cookie. Not until about age 3 do they develop a significant level of self-regulation, which involves greater flexibility, conscious thought, and the ability to wait for gratification.

Erikson sees toilet training as an important step toward self-control and autonomy. So is language; as children are better able to make their wishes understood, they become more powerful and independent. Meanwhile, caregivers provide a safe harbor—a place from which the child can set out to discover the world and to which the child can keep coming back for support.

The "terrible twos" are a normal manifestation of this need for autonomy. The emergence of a strong, often stubborn will in a 2-year-old is normal. Toddlers *have* to test the new notion that they are individuals, that they have some control over their world, and that they have new, exciting powers. No longer content to let someone else decide what they should do, they are now driven to try out their own ideas and find their own preferences. This often looks like a tendency to say "no" just for the sake of resisting authority, but this "negative" behavior is healthy and normal and should eventually lead to positive results. (See Box 7-1.)

How Children Learn Self-Regulation

At first, babies learn about one situation at a time—to soothe themselves by sucking a thumb or to stay away from an electrical outlet. Their learning is still limited to specific instances, however. (Jason may stay away from the outlet only for a little while and only when Jess is around—and he may keep poking his finger into other perilous places.) By $1\frac{1}{2}$ to 2 years of age, they think and remember well enough to connect what they do with what they have been told to do. At 2, they know (but do not always follow) the rules about what and how to eat and how

BOX 7–1 ■ THE EVERYDAY WORLD

REDUCING NEGATIVISM AND ENCOURAGING SELF-REGULATION

"No! I won't go home! I want to stay and play!" Vicky, at age 3, shouts, running away from Charles as she sees him walking to the sandbox. Getting Vicky to do anything her parents suggest has become harder and harder since she began exhibiting *negativism,* but this is normal behavior for her stage of development.

Caregivers who view children's expressions of self-will as a normal, healthy striving for independence, not as stubbornness, can help them learn to regulate themselves, contribute to their sense of competence, and avoid excessive conflict. Almost all children show negativism to some degree; it usually begins before 2 years of age, tends to peak at about $3\frac{1}{2}$ to 4, and declines by age 6. Many children playfully tease others to show their control—but do not really mean what they say and will eventually comply with requests. The following suggestions can help adults help themselves and children (Haswell, Hock, & Wenar, 1981; Kopp, 1982; Power & Chapieski, 1986):

♦ *Be flexible.* Learn the child's natural rhythms and special likes and dislikes. The most flexible parents tend to have the least resistant children.

♦ *Think of yourself as a safe harbor,* with limits safe enough for a child to explore the world—and come back for support.

♦ *Make the home "child-friendly."* Fill it with unbreakable objects that are safe to explore.

♦ *Avoid physical punishment.* It does not work and may even lead a toddler to do more damage.

♦ *Offer* a choice or even a limited one—to give the child some control. For example, "Would you like to have your bath now or after we read a book?"

♦ *Be consistent* in enforcing necessary requests.

♦ *Don't interrupt an activity unless absolutely necessary.* Try to wait until the child's attention has shifted to something else.

♦ *If you must interrupt, give warning:* "We have to leave the playground soon." This gives the child time to prepare and either finish an activity or think about resuming it another time.

♦ *Suggest alternative activities.* When Ashley is throwing sand in Keiko's face, say, "Oh, look! Nobody's on the swings now. Let's go over and I'll give you a good push!"

♦ *Suggest; don't command.* Accompany requests with smiles or hugs, not criticism, threats, or physical restraint.

♦ *Link requests with pleasurable activities.* "It's time to stop playing, so you can go to the store with me."

♦ *Remind the child of what you expect.* "When we go to this playground, we *never* go outside the gate."

♦ *Wait a few moments before repeating a request* when a child doesn't comply immediately.

♦ *Use "time out"* to end conflicts. In a nonpunitive way, remove either yourself or the child from a tense situation. Very often this results in the resistance diminishing or even disappearing.

♦ *Expect less self-control during times of stress* (like illness, divorce, the birth of a sibling, or a move to a new home).

to dress for sleep or play. By about age 3, they develop greater self-regulation. (Jason now stays away from all electrical outlets and anything that looks like one.)

How does this change take place? A relatively recent line of research has focused on the role of caregivers: what standards of behavior they present to children, when and how they present them, and how children respond (Gralinski & Kopp, 1993). The data from one study support Jess and Julia's early insistence on Jason's learning to stay away from electrical outlets. The earliest and most important standard of behavior in the minds of the 71 white, middle-class mothers studied was keeping their children safe. Then these parents gradually shifted their emphasis. Next came concerns for personal property ("Don't color on the walls") and other people ("No hitting, biting, or pinching"). Then come food-related rules ("Eat only in the kitchen"), self-care ("Use the potty"), learning how to delay ("Wait till Mom gets off the phone"), becoming independent ("You can walk up these steps yourself"), and learning family routines ("Put your toys away") and manners ("Say 'please' ").

These mothers began teaching their children quite early and increased their "do's and don'ts" gradually when the children were between the ages of 13 and 18 months. At 18 months, both the number and kind of teachings increased. Another increase came when the children were 2 years old, and then again at $2\frac{1}{2}$. At about $3\frac{1}{2}$ years, the children were faced with new and more elaborate social rules ("Do not appear naked in front of company, do not pick your nose, and do not go to a neighbor's house too early in the morning"). The parents seemed to intuitively know their children's developmental stages and needs.

The children were most likely to comply with rules regarding their own safety and other people's possessions, which were the first rules to be introduced. They might have listened to these requests more because their parents had emphasized them so strongly, or perhaps because these rules were more firmly entrenched. The older the children got, the more they went along with parental requests. There was a strong association between compliance and cognitive, linguistic, and emotional development.

In support of ecological systems theory, the requests radiated out: from taking care of the child, to concerns relating to people and property close to the child, and finally to social and cultural ideals. But this progression may not apply to all parent-child groups. These white middle-class children were growing up in relatively privileged circumstances. How do parents whose children live in high-risk, violent neighborhoods teach them to be safe? Would the emphasis shift as much or as soon? The authors of this study call for research among other populations, looking for long-term developmental implications of self-regulation and its role in children's lives.

Earlier research looked at how adults *socialize* children—how they teach them the behaviors their culture considers appropriate—and concluded: The most effective caregivers are warm, sensitive, responsive, and authoritative (Maccoby & Martin, 1983). But when a toddler is about to run into the street or touch a hot stove, there is no time for explanations. As one team of researchers concluded, "We do not know how caregivers balance sensitivity to a toddler's burgeoning desire for autonomy with a realization that enforcing safety rules often requires authoritarian behaviors. . . . [I]t would help our understanding of socialization to know how safety rules are enforced, if enforcement differs from other types of rule dictums, and if and how child behavioral characteristics influence parents' safety rules" (Gralinski & Kopp, 1993, p. 582).

socialize *To teach children the behaviors their culture considers appropriate.*

What do you think? *How might the neighborhood, society, and culture in which a person lives affect the rules a young child is taught?*

FACTORS IN PERSONALITY DEVELOPMENT

EMOTIONS: THE BASIS OF PERSONALITY AND SOCIAL DEVELOPMENT

Lying in her crib, Vicky seems perfectly content. But is she? How does she feel? How do her *emotions*—subjective reactions to the environment which are accompanied by physiological responses and which are generally experienced as pleasant or unpleasant—affect the way she thinks and acts?

All normal human beings seem to have the same basic emotions—such sub-

emotions *Subjective feelings such as sadness, joy, and fear, which arise in response to situations and experiences and can be expressed through some kind of altered behavior.*

jective feelings as sadness, joy, and fear—which motivate human behavior. The different emotions are expressed in characteristic ways, are accompanied by certain neurochemical processes in the body, and arise in response to various situations and experiences (Izard & Malatesta, 1987). People differ in how often they feel a particular emotion, in the kinds of events that produce it, and in how they act as a result. Emotional reactions to events and people, which are intimately tied in with cognitive perceptions, form a fundamental element of personality.

Basic expressions of emotion seem to be universal. In one study, 33 Japanese and American babies, aged 5 and 12 months, were videotaped as experimenters gently but firmly restrained the babies' arms for up to 3 minutes. At 5 months, the Japanese babies showed a less intense reaction than the American babies did, but by 12 months the Japanese and American babies showed similar negative expressions, often furrowing their brows, squinting their eyes, and stretching their mouths sideways. In both cultures, older babies became more distressed than younger ones. A basic developmental progression of emotional expression seems to override cultural differences (Camras, Oster, Campos, Miyake, & Bradshaw, 1992).

Studying Babies' Emotions

When you hear a baby cry, you know the child is unhappy. But it is difficult to know whether an infant is crying because of anger, fear, loneliness, or discomfort. It is hard to tell what babies are feeling, or how their feelings first develop.

However, studies conducted by Carroll Izard and his colleagues suggest that in the first few months of life, infants express a wide range of emotions. In one study, the researchers videotaped the facial expressions of 5-, 7-, and 9-month-olds as the babies played games with their mothers, were surprised by a jack-in-the-box, were given shots by a doctor, and were approached by a stranger. When college students and health professionals were asked to identify the babies' emotional expressions just from the tapes, they believed they could recognize joy, sadness, interest, and fear, and, to a lesser degree, anger, surprise, and disgust (Izard, Huebner, Resser, McGinness, & Dougherty, 1980). When observers were trained with *Izard's Facial Expression Scoring Manual,* which is based on patterns of facial movements, they felt even more confident about their identifications (Izard, 1971, 1977). Although we do not know that these babies actually had the feelings they were credited with, they did show a range of expressions that were similar to adults' expressions of these emotions. So it is at least possible that these expressions reflected similar feelings.

How Emotions Develop: The Emerging Sense of Self

Jason cried as soon as he was born and smiled somewhat later, but he did not laugh until he was about 4 months old. Jason was following a normal timetable. This timing seems to spring from a biological "clock" of the brain's maturation, which triggers specific emotions at different ages. (See Table 7-2.) This chronology may have value for survival. Expressions of pain from helpless 2-month-olds may bring the help they need, whereas anger expressed by the same babies in the same situation 7 months later may mobilize them to help themselves—say, to push away an offender (Trotter, 1983).

This emotional timetable can be altered by environmental influences. For example, abused infants show fear earlier than other babies do, very likely having learned the feeling through their experiences (Gaensbauer & Hiatt, 1984).

TABLE 7-2

TIMETABLE OF EMOTIONAL DEVELOPMENT	
EMOTION	**APPROXIMATE AGE OF EMERGENCE**
Interest	
Distress (in response to pain)	Present at birth or
Disgust (in response to unpleasant taste or smell)	soon after
Anger, surprise, joy, fear, sadness, shyness	First 6 months
Empathy, jealousy, embarrassment	18–24 months
Shame, guilt, pride	30–36 months

SOURCES: Adapted from information in Izard & Malatesta, 1987; and M. Lewis, 1987, 1992.

Very soon after birth, babies show signs of interest, distress, and disgust; within the next few months, these primary emotions differentiate into joy, anger, surprise, sadness, shyness, and fear. "Self-conscious" emotions like empathy, jealousy, shame, guilt, embarrassment, and pride come later—some not until the second year or later. In the second year, babies typically develop *self-awareness*—the understanding that they are separate from other people and things. This lets them reflect on their actions and measure them against social standards (Izard & Malatesta, 1987; Kopp, 1982; M. Lewis, 1987).

When does self-awareness emerge? Michael Lewis and his colleagues have found it to be present by the age of 18 months. This is also the age when *self-recognition*—babies' ability to recognize their own images—emerges. To test for self-recognition, researchers counted the number of times children aged 6 to 24 months touched their noses. Then the researchers dabbed rouge on the babies' noses, sat them in front of a mirror, and noted whether they touched their noses more often. The big increase in nose-touching by 18-month-olds suggested that children of this age know their noses are not normally red and that this is, then, the age when babies recognize themselves (M. Lewis & Brooks, 1974).

self-awareness *Ability to recognize one's own actions, intentions, states, and abilities.*

self-recognition *Ability to recognize one's own image.*

What do you think? *What experiences can effect the timing of emotional expressions? How might they do this?*

How Infants Show Their Emotions

It is easy to tell when the newborn Vicky is unhappy. She emits a piercing cry in an ever-rising crescendo; she flails her arms and legs, and she stiffens her body. It is harder to tell when she is happy. During her first month, she quiets at the sound of a human voice or when she is picked up, and she smiles when her hands are moved together to play pat-a-cake. With every passing day, she responds more to people—smiling, cooing, reaching out, and, eventually, going to them.

These early signals hold clues to babies' feelings. They are important steps in development. When babies want or need something, they cry; when they want to reach out to their parents, they often break into an engaging smile or a chortle. When their messages bring a response, their sense of connection with other people grows. Their sense of power is also enhanced as they see that cries bring help and comfort, and smiles and laughter elicit smiles and laughter in return.

Over time, the meaning of emotional signals changes. At first, crying signals physical discomfort. Later, it more often expresses psychological distress. An early

This baby won't be "spoiled" by being picked up; babies whose cries of distress bring relief seem to gain confidence in their power to affect their world, and they end up crying less.

smile comes spontaneously as an expression of internal well-being; later smiles express pleasure in other people (Izard & Malatesta, 1987).

Crying. Crying is the most powerful way—and sometimes the only way—infants can signal that they need something. From the first week of life, infants cry when they feel hunger, cold, or pain and when they are undressed or awakened. Over the next few weeks, they also cry when their feedings are interrupted, when stimulated while in a fussy state, and when left alone in a room.

Babies have four patterns of crying (Wolff, 1969): the basic *hunger cry* (a rhythmic cry, which is not always associated with hunger), the *angry cry* (a variation of the rhythmic cry in which excess air is forced through the vocal cords), the *pain cry* (a sudden onset of loud crying without preliminary moaning, sometimes followed by holding the breath), and the *frustration cry* (two or three drawn-out cries, with no prolonged breath-holding). Babies in distress cry louder, longer, and more irregularly than hungry babies and are more apt to gag and interrupt their crying (Oswald & Peltzman, 1974).

Responding to Crying. Parents often worry they will spoil a child by responding too much to crying. But as we pointed out in Chapter 4, babies whose cries of distress bring relief seem to gain confidence in their power to affect their world. By the end of the first year, babies whose mothers have regularly responded to their crying with tender, soothing care cry less (Ainsworth & Bell, 1977; Bell & Ainsworth, 1972). By 1 year, they are communicating more in other ways—with babbling gestures and facial expressions—than babies of more punitive or ignoring mothers, whose babies cry more. While parents do not need to leap to a baby's side at every whimper, it seems safe to err in the direction of responding more rather than less—and not to worry about spoiling a baby.

Crying as a Diagnostic Tool. Analyzing babies' cries may reveal when infants are sick or at risk of not developing normally. Sound-wave analyses show that many newborns cry at a very high pitch for the first day or two in response to the trauma of birth, but screeching like this that lasts into the first month may reflect central nervous system problems. The cries of newborn preterm and full-term babies have been associated with their scores on developmental tests at 18 months and at 5 years (B. M. Lester, 1987). Abnormal crying patterns have also been linked with a number of medical conditions, including sudden infant death syndrome (B. M. Lester et al., 1989). Thus analysis of crying shows promise in detecting early signs of trouble.

Parents are often very sensitive to differences in babies' crying. When 28 mothers listened to a tape recording of the first 10 seconds of cries by 2-day-old infants who had been snapped on the soles of the feet with a rubber band, the mothers were especially distressed by the more high-pitched cries. When the cries included an up-and-down warbling, the mothers thought the babies sounded sick (Zeskind & Marshall, 1988). Some parents respond to this kind of cry with extra care, but others find it so upsetting that they neglect or abuse the baby. Again, we see the bidirectional nature of parent-child interaction.

Smiling. Vicky's winning smile is one way she makes people fall in love with her. Her smile sets in motion a cycle of trust and affection, as adults smile back, and the infant smiles even more.

Smiling develops in stages. The earliest faint smile appears soon after birth and occurs spontaneously as a result of central nervous system activity. It frequently appears as the infant is falling asleep (Sroufe & Waters, 1976).

In the second week, Vicky often smiles drowsily after feeding, possibly responding to Ellen's sounds. After the second week, she is more likely to smile when she is alert but inactive. At about 1 month, her smiles become more frequent and more social. The first social smiles are brief. Whereas the early reflex smile uses only the lower facial muscles, the social smile also involves the eye muscles. Babies this age smile when their hands are clapped together (Kreutzer & Charlesworth, 1973) and when they hear a familiar voice. During the second month, babies can recognize different people, and they smile more at people they know. At about 3 months, their smiles are broader and longer-lasting.

Some infants smile much more than others, a difference that can have important consequences. A happy, cheerful baby who rewards the parents' caretaking efforts with smiles and gurgles is likely to form a better relationship with them—and with others—than one who smiles less.

Gregory's cheerful disposition, which helps him reward adults' caretaking efforts with smiles and gurgles, is likely to help him form more positive relationships with the people around him (like his father) than if he smiled less.

Laughing.   During his fourth month, Jason starts to laugh out loud at being kissed on his stomach, hearing certain sounds, and seeing his parents do unusual things. Babies' laughter may also be related to fear, since sometimes they show both fear and laughter in reaction to the same thing—like an object looming toward them (Sroufe & Wunsch, 1972).

As Jason grows older, he laughs more often and at more things. At the age of 4 to 6 months, he giggles in response to sound and touch, but by 7 to 9 months, he laughs in more complex situations—as when Jess plays peekaboo with him. The change reflects cognitive development. By laughing at the unexpected, Jason shows he knows what to expect.

Laughter also helps discharge tension. At 2 years of age, an edge of hysteria tinges Jason's laughter at a pop-up dinosaur in a book. Though his initial reaction to the pop-up is to laugh, he quickly sobers and says, "I don't like dat." By using laughter at difficult times, he shows competence. We see, again, a relationship between emotional and cognitive development.

EMOTIONAL COMMUNICATION BETWEEN BABIES AND ADULTS

The Mutual Regulation Model

Jason smiles at Julia; she interprets this as an invitation to play and kisses his stomach, sending him into gales of giggles. But the next day, when she begins to kiss his stomach, he looks at her glassy-eyed and turns his head away. Julia interprets this as "I want to be quiet now." Following this cue, she tucks him into a baby carrier and lets him rest quietly against her body.

This process, called the *mutual regulation model* (E. Z. Tronick & Gianino, 1986), illustrates how infants as young as 3 months take an active part in regulating their emotional states and in influencing their relationships. Babies differ in the amount of stimulation they need or want; too little leaves them uninterested, too much overwhelms them. Overstimulation is a special danger for low-birthweight infants, but it can also affect other babies.

mutual regulation model
Process by which child and caregiver communicate emotional states to each other and respond appropriately.

"Reading" the Messages of Another Person.   Babies and adults send a variety of signals to each other. A healthy interaction occurs when a caregiver "reads" a baby's behaviors accurately and responds appropriately. Adults do not, of course, always understand the babies' messages. When babies do not achieve the results they want, they may become upset at first, but they usually keep on sending signals so they can "repair" the interaction. Normally, interaction moves back and forth between poorly regulated and well-regulated states, and babies learn from these shifts how to send appropriate signals and what to do when their first signals do not bring what they want.

When a baby's goals for connecting with people and objects and for retaining a comfortable emotional balance are met, the baby feels joyful or at least interested, says E. Z. Tronick (1989). But if someone taking care of a baby either ignores an invitation to play or insists on playing after the baby has signaled she or he does not feel like it, the baby will feel angry or sad. Both partners are important and each stimulates the other.

The ability to understand other people's feelings seems to be an inborn ability that helps human beings form attachments to others, live in society, and protect themselves. Even very young infants can normally perceive emotions expressed by other people, and they adjust their own behavior accordingly. At 10 weeks of age, they meet anger with anger (Lelwica & Haviland, 1983). At 3 months, infants faced with a stony-faced, unresponsive mother will make faces, sounds, and gestures to get a reaction (J. F. Cohn & Tronick, 1983; E. Z. Tronick, 1980). Nine-month-olds show more joy, play more, and look longer when their mothers seem happy; they look sad and turn away when their mothers seem sad (Termine & Izard, 1988). This is one more example of the competence very young babies show. They do not just passively receive other people's actions; they do a great deal to act on and change the way people act toward them.

How a Mother's Depression Affects Mutual Regulation. *Depression* is an emotional state characterized by sadness and such other symptoms as difficulties in eating, sleeping, and concentrating. Depressed mothers may ignore or override their baby's emotional signals, often with severe consequences. Such mothers tend to be punitive, to consider their children bothersome and hard to care for, and to feel as if their lives are out of control (T. M. Field et al. 1985; Whiffen & Gotlib, 1989; B. S. Zuckerman & Beardslee, 1987).

Their babies often stop sending emotional signals and try to comfort themselves by behaviors like sucking or rocking. If this defensive reaction becomes habitual, babies will feel that they have no power to draw responses from other people, that their mothers are unreliable, and that the world is untrustworthy.

This cycle may explain why children of depressed mothers react differently from children of nondepressed mothers from an early age, apparently reflecting the change depression causes in a mother's behavior. Children of depressed mothers are at risk of various emotional and cognitive disturbances. As infants, they are more likely to be drowsy, show tension by squirming and arching their backs, cry often, and look sad or angry more often and show interest less often than other babies (Pickens & Field, 1993; T. Field, Morrow, & Adelstein, 1993). They seem less upset when separated from their mothers than do other babies (G. Dawson et al., 1992); they are also less motivated to explore the environment and more apt to prefer less challenging tasks (Redding, Harmon, & Morgan, 1990).

As toddlers they tend to engage in a low level of symbolic play. Among forty-five 2-year-olds whose reactions to such mishaps as a doll breaking and juice

depression *An emotional state characterized by sadness and such other symptoms as difficulties in eating, sleeping, and concentrating.*

spilling were studied, the children of depressed mothers tended to suppress their frustration and tension (P. M. Cole, Barrett, & Zahn-Waxler, 1992). Later they are likely to grow poorly and perform poorly on cognitive measures, have accidents, and have behavior problems that often last into adolescence (T. Field, Morrow, & Adelstein, 1993; T. Field et al., 1985; B. S. Zuckerman & Beardslee, 1987).

Further, babies of depressed mothers may be at risk of becoming depressed themselves. The left frontal region of the human brain seems to be specialized for "approach" emotions like joy, whereas the right frontal region is specialized for "withdrawal" emotions like distress. In one study of the brain activity of 11- to 17-month-old infants, babies of depressed mothers showed less activity in the left frontal region than did other babies. This may suggest they are predisposed to depression later on (G. Dawson, Klinger, Panagiotides, Hill, & Spieker, 1992).

Depressed mothers and their babies can get help from professional or para-professional home visitors. These workers help families get access to community resources, invite mothers to parenting groups or drop-in social hours, and model and reinforce positive interaction with babies (Lyons-Ruth, Connell, & Grunebaum, 1990). Such help can be effective: In one experiment, after an average of about 47 home visits over a 13-month period, 18-month-olds scored higher on the Bayley mental scale and were more likely to be rated as securely attached to their mothers than a control group of nonvisited babies of depressed mothers.

Fortunately, most mothers are not depressed, and most serve as important mediators between their children and the world at large, as in the process known as social referencing.

Social Referencing

If, at a formal dinner table, you have ever glanced to see which fork the person next to you was using, you have used social referencing to "read" other people's nonverbal signals in learning how to act. Through *social referencing,* one person forms an understanding of an ambiguous situation by seeking out another person's perception of it. Babies learn how to do this at a very early age.

social referencing
Understanding an ambiguous situation by seeking out another person's perception of it.

Babies face many situations they neither understand nor know how to respond to. Should they trust a stranger, play with a new toy, or dip their toes in the ocean? They are likely to evaluate ambiguous situations by first looking at their caregivers (Feinman & Lewis, 1983). Sometime after 6 months of age, when babies begin to judge the possible consequences of events and distinguish among and react to various emotional expressions, they learn to "read" other people's emotional and cognitive reactions.

An experiment using the visual cliff (described in Chapter 5) found that when the "drop" looked very shallow or very deep, 1-year-olds did not look toward their mothers; they could judge for themselves whether to cross over. But when they were uncertain about the depth of the "cliff," they paused at the "edge," looked down, and then looked up to their mothers' faces. Meanwhile, the mother posed one of several expressions—fear, anger, interest, happiness, or sadness. The particular emotion influenced the babies' actions. Most of the babies whose mothers showed joy or interest crossed the "drop"; very few whose mothers looked angry or afraid crossed over; and an intermediate number of those whose mothers looked sad did (Sorce, Emde, Campos, & Klinnert, 1985). Apparently, babies socially reference facial expressions most often in puzzling situations, and they use the information they get to determine how to respond.

INDIVIDUAL DIFFERENCES IN PERSONALITY

Even in the womb, fetuses begin to show unique personalities. They already have different activity levels and favorite positions in utero. After birth, individual differences become more apparent. What accounts for these differences? Part of the answer seems to lie in the way babies are treated. As we pointed out, infants of depressed, unresponsive mothers sometimes become sad themselves: They cry, ignore people, or show less motivation to explore. Babies whose parents reject, neglect, or abuse them often show signs of emotional disturbance (Rutter, 1974; L. Yarrow, 1961).

However, infants' emotional responses often follow patterns that persist through the years, suggesting that basic mood is inborn. At 2 months, for example, both Vicky and her cousin, Bart, received shots: Vicky whimpered a little when she got hers, but Bart screamed. At 19 months, Bart yanked a shovel out of Vicky's hand and threw sand in her face; when Bart took Vicky's toys, she usually found something else to play with. Babies as young as 8 weeks of age already show signs of emotional differences that form an important part of the personality (Izard, Hembree, et al., in Trotter, 1987). Such differences in mood constitute one aspect of inborn temperament.

Temperamental Differences

Besides her cheerful disposition, Vicky is an easy baby to take care of because she eats, sleeps, and eliminates at regular times and adapts quickly to new situations. Bart, however, sleeps and eats little and irregularly, laughs and cries loudly, and has to be convinced that new people and new experiences are not threatening before he will have anything to do with them. Jason is mild in his responses, both positive and negative: He does not like most new situations, but if allowed to proceed at his own slow pace, he eventually becomes interested and involved.

Each of these babies is showing aspects of *temperament*—one's characteristic style of approaching and reacting to people and situations. Temperament is the *how* of behavior, rather than the *what* (abilities) or the *why* (motivation). Vicky and Jason may be equally adept at dressing, but Vicky will do it more quickly, be more willing to put on a new shirt, and be less distracted if the cat jumps onto the bed.

Components of Temperament. The New York Longitudinal Study (NYLS), introduced in Chapter 2, followed 133 people from early infancy into adulthood. Researchers interviewed, tested, and observed subjects and interviewed their parents and teachers. Based on their data, they identified nine aspects or components of temperament that showed up soon after birth (A. Thomas, Chess, & Birch, 1968):

1. *Activity level:* how and how much a person moves
2. *Rhythmicity, or regularity:* predictability of biological cycles like hunger, sleep, and elimination
3. *Approach or withdrawal:* how a person initially responds to a new stimulus, like a new toy, food, or person
4. *Adaptability:* how easily an initial response to a new or altered situation is modified in a desired direction
5. *Threshold of responsiveness:* how much stimulation is needed to evoke a response

Stella Chess

Alexander Thomas
This husband-wife team of researchers traced temperamental traits from infancy into young adulthood, and found that many remain stable, while others change considerably, often due to life changes.

temperament   A person's style of approaching other people and situations.

6. *Intensity of reaction:* how energetically a person responds
7. *Quality of mood:* whether a person's behavior is predominantly pleasant, joyful, and friendly or unpleasant, unhappy, and unfriendly
8. *Distractibility:* how easily an irrelevant stimulus can alter or interfere with a person's behavior
9. *Attention span and persistence:* how long a person pursues an activity and continues in the face of obstacles.

Three Patterns of Temperament.   Almost two-thirds of the children studied in the New York Longitudinal Study fitted into one of three categories identified by these researchers. (See Table 7-3.) Forty percent of the children in the NYLS sample were, like Vicky, *easy children,* who are generally happy, rhythmic in their biological functioning, and accepting of new experiences. Ten percent of the children in the sample were, like Bart, *difficult children,* who are more irritable and harder to please, irregular in biological rhythms, and more intense in expressing emotion. *Slow-to-warm-up children,* like Jason, were 15 percent of the sample. They react mildly and adapt slowly to new people and situations (A. Thomas & Chess, 1977).

Many children (like 35 percent of the NYLS sample) do not fit neatly into any of these three groups. A baby may have regular eating and sleeping schedules but be afraid of new people. A child may be extremely easy to relatively easy most of the time—but not always. Another child may warm up slowly to new foods but adapt quickly to new baby-sitters. All these variations are normal (A. Thomas & Chess, 1984).

Influences on Temperament.   The NYLS considered temperamental differences to be inborn and largely hereditary (A. Thomas & Chess, 1977, 1984). Individual differences in basic temperament do not seem to be determined by parents' attitudes (A. Thomas & Chess, 1984) or by gender, birth order, or social class (Persson-Blennow & McNeil, 1981).

But more recent research compared temperamental traits (including activity level, irritability, and soothability) of newborn identical and fraternal twins (a different sample from the NYLS sample) and found a substantial level of environmental influence. The considerable concordance for temperamental traits in *both*

easy child   *Child with a generally happy temperament, regular biological rhythms, and a readiness to accept new experiences.*

difficult child   *Child who has an irritable temperament, irregular biological rhythms, and intense responses to situations.*

slow-to-warm-up child   *Child whose temperament is generally mild and who is hesitant about accepting new experiences.*

TABLE 7-3

THREE TEMPERAMENTAL PATTERNS		
EASY CHILD	**DIFFICULT CHILD**	**SLOW-TO-WARM-UP CHILD**
Has moods of mild to moderate intensity, usually positive	Displays intense and frequently negative moods	Has mildly intense reactions, both positive and negative
Responds well to novelty and change	Responds poorly to novelty and change	Responds slowly to novelty and change
Quickly develops regular sleep and feeding schedules	Sleeps and eats irregularly	Sleeps and eats more regularly than difficult child, less regularly than easy child
Takes to new foods easily	Accepts new foods slowly	
Smiles at strangers	Is suspicious of strangers	Shows mildly negative initial response to new stimuli (like a first encounter with a new person, place, or situation)
Adapts easily to new situations	Adapts slowly to new situations	
Accepts most frustrations with little fuss	Reacts to frustration with tantrums	
Adapts quickly to new routines and rules of new games	Adjusts slowly to new routines	Gradually develops liking for new stimuli after repeated, unpressured exposures
	Cries often and loudly; also laughs loudly	

SOURCE: Adapted from A. Thomas & Chess, 1984.

kinds of twins suggested an environmental as well as a hereditary influence. In the neonatal period, the overwhelming influences of the intrauterine environment and conditions of birth may outweigh genetic influences on temperament, which do not emerge until later in infancy (Riese, 1990).

Unusual events or parents' handling of a child can change temperamental style. One "difficult" girl in the NYLS who was having a hard time as a child suddenly showed musical and dramatic talent at about age 10, leading her parents to see her in a new way and to respond differently to her; by age 22, she was a well-adjusted young woman. Another "difficult" child was doing well with quiet and firm limit-setting by her parents—until she was 13, when her father died and her overwhelmed mother could not cope with the child's needs; this girl developed a severe behavior disorder. An "easy" child got into trouble at age 14 after experimenting with drugs; he gave up drugs a year later when he began following an Indian guru; several years later, he broke with the guru; in his early twenties, he was doing well (A. Thomas & Chess, 1984).

Other evidence of environmental influence comes from a study of babies from three African cultures, which found differences across cultures in temperamental characteristics. The researchers attributed the differences to different child-rearing customs (like a lack of concern with "clock time" in a tribe whose babies have irregular biological rhythms), mothers' attitudes (expecting different behaviors from boys and girls), and ecological settings (DeVries & Sameroff, 1984).

While some cross-cultural variations may result from genetic differences among groups, they also seem to reflect early experiences. The NYLS researchers found the same thing: Children respond to the way their parents treat them. One analysis of NYLS data found that how mothers feel about their roles—whether they are happy or unhappy about either being employed or being at home full-time—seems to affect children's adjustment. Dissatisfied mothers were more likely to be intolerant of, disapprove of, or reject their 3-year-olds' behavior, and the rejected children were likely to become "difficult" (Lerner & Galambos, 1985).

Among 148 firstborn infants, some at 3 months of age had cried a lot and been rated emotionally negative by their mothers, but at 9 months smiled, laughed, and vocalized a lot. This kind of change tended to occur when parents were psychologically healthy and in a good marriage, had high self-esteem, and had harmonious dealings with their babies. Parents of babies who went from generally positive emotional states at 3 months to negative ones 6 months later showed more negative characteristics themselves (Belsky, Fish, & Isabella, 1991).

Effects of Temperament on Adjustment: "Goodness of Fit." About one-third of the NYLS subjects developed behavior problems at some time. Most were mild disturbances that showed up between ages 3 and 5 and had cleared up by adolescence, but some remained or had grown worse by adulthood.

No temperamental type was immune to trouble. Even easy children had problems when their lives held too much stress. One kind of stress is being expected to act in ways contrary to basic temperament. If a very active child is expected to sit still for long periods, if a slow-to-warm-up child is pushed to adjust to many new people and situations, or if a persistent child is constantly taken away from absorbing projects, trouble may result. The key to healthy adjustment is a good fit between children and the demands made upon them.

"Goodness of fit" between parent and child—the degree to which parents feel comfortable with their child—shows how children influence their parents' feelings toward them. Energetic, active parents may become impatient with a slow-moving, docile child, while more easygoing parents might welcome such a personality. One of the most important things parents can do is to accept a child's basic temperament instead of trying to cast him or her into a mold of the parents' design. For example, the parents of a rhythmic baby can use a demand feeding schedule, letting the baby set the pace; the parents of an irregular baby can help by setting a flexible schedule. Parents need to give a slow-to-warm-up child time to adjust to new situations, and they need to ask relatives, friends, and teachers to do the same.

Parents can help their children make the most of the temperament they are born with—by setting firm, consistent limits for an active, intense child; by preparing a nonadaptable child for transitions ("In 5 minutes, it will be time to put away your toys"); and by stimulating an easygoing, docile child.

The notion of inborn temperament relieves parents of some heavy emotional baggage. When they recognize that a child acts in a certain way not out of willfulness, laziness, or stupidity but largely because of inborn temperament, they are less likely to feel guilty, anxious, or hostile or to be rigid or impatient. They can focus on helping the child use his or her temperament as a strength rather than seeing it as an impediment.

What do you think? *Give additional examples of how parents can change "poorness of fit" to "goodness of fit."*

Gender Differences

Are personality differences between girls and boys due to femaleness and maleness? As we saw in Chapter 5, there seem to be few physiological differences between baby boys and baby girls. Researchers have studied infants' activity levels,

Although we can tell from their clothes which of these babies is a girl and which a boy, sex differences in the way baby girls and baby boys react emotionally or play cannot be described clearly until after age 2.

their responses to things they see as opposed to things they hear, their irritability levels, and their interest in exploring their surroundings instead of staying close to a parent. Findings of gender differences have rarely held up when the studies are repeated by the same or other investigators. Sex differences cannot be described clearly until after age 2.

A parent's behavior toward a child is affected by the parent's own sex and by the age and personality of the infant, but there are some consistent findings. Baby boys get more attention in infancy, but the attention baby girls get is designed to make them smile more and be more social (Birns, 1976). Mothers' facial expressions show a wider range of emotion with baby daughters than with sons—which may explain why girls are better than boys at interpreting emotional expression (Malatesta, in Trotter, 1983).

A study using home observations of how parents treated children at 1 year, 18 months, and 5 years of age found the biggest gender-based differences at 18 months. This was seen most often in play, when both mothers and fathers tended to encourage the children to play in gender-typed ways. It was also found with regard to communication: Parents tended to encourage girls to communicate but to discourage boys' efforts. Mothers and fathers were equally likely to gender-type. By age 5, the parents were treating both sexes the same, possibly because the children had already become gender-typed and needed no more influence in this direction (Fagot & Hagan, 1991—see Table 7-4). Gender typing may take hold early: In the second year of life children are learning many new skills, and inexperienced parents, still unsure of their own parenting skills, may unconsciously adopt stereotyped responses.

What do you think? *Why do you think parents treat baby boys and girls differently?*

1. *They want to socialize their child according to cultural norms.*
2. *Unsure of their parenting skills, they unconsciously adopt gender-stereotyped responses.*
3. *There is another explanation.*

Give reasons for your answer.

TABLE 7-4

PARENTS' GENDER-RELATED BEHAVIORS TOWARD CHILDREN AT DIFFERENT AGES	
AGE	**PARENTS' BEHAVIOR**
12 months	Boys received more positive reactions for play with "boys'" toys and for aggressive behavior.
18 months	Girls received more positive responses for attempts to communicate. Boys received more negative reactions to attempts to communicate, more positive reactions for play with "boys'" toys and for aggressive behavior. Mothers gave more instruction than fathers to children trying to communicate, especially to girls. Fathers gave more positive responses to large motor play. Fathers gave fewer positive responses to boys playing with "girls'" toys; mothers did not make this distinction.
5 years	No differences in parent reactions to boys and girls. Fathers gave more positive responses to large motor play.

SOURCE: Adapted from Fagot and Hagan, 1991.

Thus, although gender differences may not be present at birth, environmental shaping of boys' and girls' personalities begins very early in life. As we look more closely at the crucial influence of children's families, we will see other differences among children.

What do you think?   *Do you believe it is appropriate for parents to treat their male and female infants and toddlers differently? Does this encourage appropriate gender identity? Or does it encourage gender stereotypes?*

THE FAMILY AND PERSONALITY DEVELOPMENT

The families children grow up in are probably the largest single influence on their development. Were their births planned and welcomed? How old were their parents? How well do the personalities of parents and child mesh? Are the parents healthy? Are they wealthy or poor? How many people live at home? Influence travels in the other direction too. Children also affect their parents, transforming parents' daily moods, priorities, and future plans—even a marriage itself.

Family life in the 1990s is quite different from a century ago, and family life is likely to change even more in the future. A child growing up today is likely to have only one sibling, a mother who works outside the home, and a father who is more involved in his children's lives than his own father was. The child is likely to receive a considerable amount of daily care from nonrelatives, first in a caregiver's home or a day care center and then at a preschool. Today's children have a 40 to 50 percent chance of spending part of their childhood with only one parent, probably the mother and probably because of divorce (P. C. Glick & Lin, 1986).

Family life for these typical American children is also very different from the life led by children in many other societies. Children's early social experiences vary greatly around the world. Among the Efe people of the African country of Zaire, for example, children don't first form a close relationship with one person, the mother, and then go on to form other ties patterned on that one (Tronick, Morelli, & Ivey, 1992). Instead, from birth, Efe infants are cared for by five or more people in a typical hour and are routinely breastfed by other women as well as their mothers. As 3-year-olds they spend about 70 percent of their time with people other than their mothers.

This social pattern suits the Efe way of life and may result in a distinctive set of social skills for these children. Thus American children, who spend more time alone or with just one or two family members, may learn to amuse themselves earlier than the Efe, but the Efe may learn more social skills at an earlier age. The important thing to remember from studying children in other cultures is that many of the psychological assumptions we take for granted in the west are narrowly culture-based. We need to be able to modify and broaden them to include other cultural practices.

Studying the Child in the Family

The awareness of different social experiences in children's lives has revolutionized the study of socialization—how children learn the behaviors their culture considers appropriate. In the past, almost all research focused on mothers and their children, but now researchers are studying the bonds between children and their fathers, their brothers and sisters, their grandparents, and other caregivers.

Another important research trend is the focus on the entire family. Do Ellen and Charles act differently with Vicky when either one is alone with her from the way they act when all are together? How does Julia and Jess's marital relationship, which is beginning to show strains, affect the relationship each one has with Jason? How does the fact that a child is growing up in a single-parent household affect development? Questions like these have yielded provocative findings. For example, when both parents are present and talking to each other, they tend to pay less attention to the child. In some families, the spouses' closeness to each other may detract from their ability to be close to their children; in others, the parenting experience strengthens the marriage tie (Belsky, 1979). By looking at the family as a unit, we get a fuller picture of the network of relationships among family members. We are particularly interested in how babies form attachments to the people close to them and in the significance of these bonds.

Attachment: A Reciprocal Connection

When Jason's mother is near, he looks at her, smiles at her, talks to her, and crawls after her. When she leaves, he cries; when she comes back, he squeals with joy. When he is frightened or unhappy, he clings to her. Jason has formed his first attachment to another person.

attachment *Active, affectionate, reciprocal relationship between two people; their interaction reinforces and strengthens the bond; the term often refers to an infant's relationship with his or her parents.*

Attachment is an active, affectionate, reciprocal, enduring relationship between two people—known in unscientific circles as *love*. The interaction between the two people continues to strengthen their bond. It may be, as Mary Ainsworth (1979), a pioneering researcher on attachment, has said, "an essential part of the ground plan of the human species for an infant to become attached to a mother figure" (p. 932)—who does not have to be the infant's biological mother but may be any primary caregiver.

Ainsworth (1964) described four overlapping stages of babies' attachment behavior during the first year:*

1. Before about 2 months, infants respond indiscriminately to anyone.
2. At about 8 to 12 weeks, babies cry, smile, and babble more to the mother than to anyone else, but they continue to respond to others.
3. At 6 or 7 months, babies show a sharply defined attachment to the mother, with a waning of friendliness to others.
4. Overlapping with the above, babies develop an attachment to one or more familiar figures like the father or siblings. Fear of strangers may appear between 6 to 8 months.

Studying Attachment. Attachment research illustrates how scientists build on the work of those who have gone before. Ainsworth first studied attachment in the early 1950s as a junior colleague of John Bowlby (1951). Bowlby was convinced of the importance of the mother-baby bond, partly from examining studies of bonding in animals (see discussions of ethology, the study of animal behavior, in Chapters 1 and 4) and partly from seeing disturbed children in a psychoanalytic

*This sequence would not necessarily apply to babies like those of the Efe, who are cared for from birth by a number of different people.

TABLE 7-5

NUMBER OF EPISODE	PERSONS PRESENT	DURATION	BRIEF DESCRIPTION OF ACTION
1	Mother, baby, and observer	30 secs.	Observer introduces mother and baby to experimental room, then leaves.
2	Mother and baby	3 min.	Mother is nonparticipant while baby explores; if necessary, play is stimulated after 2 minutes.
3	Stranger, mother, and baby	3 min.	Stranger enters. First minute: Stranger silent. Second minute: Stranger converses with mother. Third minute: Stranger approaches baby. After 3 minutes mother leaves unobtrusively.
4	Stranger and baby	3 min. or less*	First separation episode. Stranger's behavior is geared to that of baby.
5	Mother and baby	3 min. or more†	First reunion episode. Mother greets and comforts baby, then tries to settle him or her again in play. Mother than leaves, saying "bye-bye."
6	Baby alone	3 min. or less*	Second separation episode.
7	Stranger and baby	3 min. or less*	Continuation of second separation. Stranger enters and gears behavior to that of baby.
8	Mother and baby	3 min.	Second reunion episode. Mother enters, greets baby, then picks him or her up. Meanwhile stranger leaves unobtrusively.

*Episode is curtailed if the baby is unduly distressed.
†Episode is prolonged if more time is required for the baby to become reinvolved in play.
SOURCE: Adapted from Ainsworth, Blehar, Waters, & Wall, 1978, p. 37.

clinic in London. He recognized the baby's role in fostering attachment and warned against separating mother and baby.

Ainsworth was also influenced by studies of attachment in monkeys and studies of the behavior of babies in a strange room. After studying attachment in African babies from Uganda (1967), she tried to replicate her studies in Baltimore. But because of cultural differences between Africa and the United States, she had to change her approach, which had relied on naturalistic observation in babies' homes, and devised the now famous *Strange Situation*. This laboratory technique, designed to reveal behaviors of closeness between an adult and an infant, is now the most common way to study attachment. Typically, the adult is the mother (although other adults have also taken part in studies), the infant is 10 to 24 months old, and the sequence takes less than half an hour. (See Table 7-5.)

In the eight-episode Strange Situation, (1) the mother and the baby enter an unfamiliar room; (2) the mother sits down and the baby is free to explore; (3) an unfamiliar adult enters; (4) the mother goes out, leaving the baby alone with the stranger; (5) the mother comes back and the stranger leaves the room; (6) the mother leaves the baby alone in the room; (7) the stranger comes back instead of the mother; and finally, (8) the stranger goes out as the mother returns. The mother encourages the baby to explore and play again and gives comfort if the baby seems to need it (Ainsworth, Blehar, Waters, & Wall, 1978). Of particular concern is the baby's response when the mother returns (episodes 5 and 8).

Strange Situation *A laboratory technique used to study attachment.*

Patterns of Attachment. When Ainsworth and her colleagues observed 1-year-

secure attachment
Attachment pattern in which an infant separates readily from the primary caregiver and actively seeks out the caregiver when she or he returns.

avoidant attachment
Attachment pattern in which an infant rarely cries when the primary caregiver leaves and avoids contact on his or her return.

ambivalent (resistant) attachment Attachment pattern in which an infant becomes anxious before the primary caregiver leaves but both seeks and resists contact on the caregiver's return.

disorganized-disoriented attachment Attachment pattern in which an infant shows contradictory behaviors.

Securely attached children, as this toddler seems to be, can confidently explore the world away from their parents.

olds in the Strange Situation and also at home, they found three main patterns of attachment: *secure attachment* (the most common category, into which 66 percent of American babies fell) and two forms of anxious, or insecure, attachment—*avoidant attachment* (20 percent of American babies) and *ambivalent, or resistant, attachment* (12 percent). Later, Main and Solomon (1986) identified *disorganized-disoriented attachment*.

Secure Attachment. *Securely attached* babies cry or protest when the mother leaves and greet her happily when she returns. They use her as a secure base: They leave her to go off and explore, returning occasionally for reassurance. They are usually cooperative and relatively free of anger. At 18 months they get around better on their own than anxiously attached toddlers (Cassidy, 1986).

Avoidant Attachment. *Avoidant* babies rarely cry when the mother leaves, and avoid her on her return. They do not reach out in time of need and tend to be angry. They dislike being held, but dislike being put down even more.

Ambivalent, or Resistant, Attachment. *Ambivalent (resistant)* babies become anxious even before the mother leaves and are very upset when she goes out. When she returns, they show their ambivalence by seeking contact with her while at the same time resisting it by kicking or squirming. Resistant babies do little exploration and are hard to comfort.

Disorganized-Disoriented Attachment. Babies with disorganized-disoriented attachment often show inconsistent, contradictory behaviors. They greet the mother brightly when she returns but then turn away, or approach without looking at her. They seem confused and afraid and may represent the least secure pattern (Main & Solomon, 1986).

How Attachment Is Established. Based on a baby's interaction with his or her mother, the baby builds a "working model" of what can be expected from her, says Ainsworth. Different kinds of emotional attachments bring about different cognitive representations and thus different expectations. As long as the mother continues to act in basically the same ways, the model holds up. But if she changes her behavior—not just once or twice but consistently—the baby can revise the model, and the security of attachment may change. Attachment security evolves from trust, which lets the child explore the world from a secure base and then go on to develop the Eriksonian virtues related to autonomy and initiative.

What the Mother Is Like. Several important differences in the quality of mothering seem to be related to babies' patterns of attachment. Mothers of securely attached 1-year-olds are sensitive to their infants throughout the first year of life (Isabella, 1993). They take their cues from their babies about when to feed them and respond to the babies' signals to stop, slow down, or speed up feeding (Ainsworth, 1979). Mothers who have affectionate, attentive, and responsive interactions with their 5-month-olds tend to have positive personalities, higher levels of education, and supportive husbands (Fish, Stifter, & Belsky, 1993).

Mothers whose relationships with their own parents were good (as assessed by the Adult Attachment Interview, described in Chapter 3) tend to have securely attached babies (Fonagy, Steele, & Steele, 1991). A pregnant mother's level of anx-

Both Anna and Diane contribute to the attachment between them by the way they act toward each other. The way the baby molds herself to her mother's body is one of the many activities shown by babies that leads to responses from adults. As early as the eighth week of life, babies direct some behaviors more to their mothers than to anyone else.

iety is also related to her 1-year-old's attachment status: The more anxious she was during pregnancy, the less securely attached her baby is likely to be (Del Carmen, Pedersen, Huffman, & Bryan, 1993).

A mother's emotional state also affects how she acts toward her baby. Babies of highly anxious employed mothers tend to develop avoidant attachments, as measured at 18 months using the Strange Situation. In one study, mothers who reported high levels of anxiety about being separated from their infants at 5 months, tended to be more intrusive when the babies were 10 months old. In a laboratory free-play session, they stimulated the baby too much, took away objects when the baby was still interested, and did not let the baby influence the pace and focus of play. The mother's working itself does not seem to be at the root of such behaviors; rather, it is her feelings about working. Some mothers may be overcontrolling because they feel a need to compensate for their absences. Thus a mother's anxiety about separation and her style of interaction with her baby seem to mediate the relationship between employment and infant attachment (Stifter, Coulehan, & Fish, 1993).

What the Baby Is Like. It's not only the mother who contributes to security of attachment: Infants actively influence their caregivers. Among 114 white middle-class mothers and their infants aged $2\frac{1}{2}$ to 13 months, both mothers and infants contributed in unique ways to the quality of attachment. Mothers of securely attached babies (measured by the Strange Situation) were more sociable, nurturant, and empathic and experienced more positive emotion, but they also openly expressed more anger and sadness around their children. Mothers of insecurely attached babies felt more insecure and helpless and experienced more anger and sadness but were less open in showing these feelings around their children.

Insecurely attached babies cried more, demanded more attention, and showed more sadness and anger. The insecure babies' behavior may have made their moth-

This Zuni Indian baby's comfort in his mother's arms shows trust and reinforces the mother's feelings for her child, which she then displays through her sensitivity to the baby's needs (even when those needs include chewing on jewelry). Again we see how babies actively influence their worlds.

ers feel sad, angry, and helpless; and the mothers' behavior in turn probably affected the babies. A baby's temperament seems to influence attachment, since the researchers identified such infant predictors of attachment security as frustration levels and rates of crying (Izard, Haynes, Chisholm, & Baak, 1991).

Other research found that infant irritability may be related to resistant attachment. Two-day-old babies who showed distress when a pacifier was taken out of their mouths showed insecure attachment at 14 months (Calkins & Fox, 1992). Furthermore, heart rate varied more in insecure children, suggesting that biological factors also play a role in attachment (Izard, Porges, et al., 1991). So we see how important the baby's personality is, partly because of how it affects the mother and partly because of its direct impact on attachment status.

Virtually any activity on a baby's part that leads to a response from an adult can be an attachment behavior: sucking, crying, smiling, clinging, and looking into the caregiver's eyes (Bowlby, 1958; Richards, 1971; Robson, 1967). As early as the eighth week of life, babies direct some of these behaviors more to their mothers than to anyone else. Their overtures are successful when the mothers respond warmly, express delight, and give the babies frequent physical contact along with freedom to explore (Ainsworth, 1969). Evidence that babies gain a sense of the consequence of their own actions—a feeling of power and confidence in their ability to bring about results—comes through in research that finds that babies who fuss and cry a lot, and whose mothers respond by soothing them, tend to be securely attached (Del Carmen et al., 1993).

A current controversy among attachment researchers is over how much influence a baby's own temperament—the tendency to cuddle, cry, or adapt to new situations—exerts on attachment (Vaughn, Waters, et al., 1992). Some research suggests that personality has some impact but is not the primary cause of attachment level. Other research has found similar levels of a baby's attachment to both parents, suggesting that the baby's temperament may in fact play a role (Fox, Kimmerly, & Schafer, 1991).

An infant's early characteristics may be a predictor of whether the baby is likely to become securely or anxiously attached. Many resistant babies have had problems as neonates; others have shown developmental lags that may have made them harder to care for (Egeland & Farber, 1984). Anxious attachment is not inevitable, however, even for infants with other problems. Parents can often compensate for physical or mental impairment in their children, so that the children become securely attached (Van IJzendoorn et al., 1992). Also, very low birthweight does not seem to be associated with impaired attachment (Easterbrooks, 1989; Macey, Harmon, & Easterbrooks, 1987). And a comparison of hearing-impaired toddlers and children with normal hearing found no differences in security of attachment and mother-toddler play between the two groups, suggesting that a good parent-child relationship does not depend on the early development of normal language (Ledeberg & Mobley, 1990). It is the interaction between adult and infant that determines the quality of attachment.

Changes in Attachment. Although attachment patterns normally persist, they can—and often do—change. In one study, almost half of a group of 43 middle-class babies changed attachment pattern between ages 12 and 19 months (R. A. Thompson, Lamb, & Estes, 1982). The fluctuations were associated with changes in the babies' daily lives, including mothers' taking jobs outside the home and changes in child care. The changes were not all in one direction: Some babies became less securely attached, but most who changed became more securely attached, showing the resilience exhibited by so many children.

What accounts for this? Although a mother's caretaking skills are important in forming the initial attachment, her emotional signals—the joy she shows in feeding or bathing her baby—may help the attachment pattern evolve, especially during the second year of life. Some initially resistant infants of young, immature mothers become more secure as their mothers gain experience, skill, and more positive attitudes (Egeland & Farber, 1984). Also, other people can make a difference in a child's life, allowing attachment to, say, a father, a grandmother, or a baby-sitter.

Long-Term Effects of Attachment. Do infants who are securely attached to their mothers grow into children who are very dependent on adults? Research yields an emphatic no. In fact, the more secure a child's attachment is to a nurturing adult, the easier it is for the child to leave that adult. Children who have a secure base do not need to cling to their mothers. Their freedom to explore lets them try new things, attack problems in new ways, and be more comfortable with the unfamiliar. The associations between a baby's level of attachment and characteristics noted years later underscores the continuity of development and the way important experiences carry over into many domains of development.

These effects may persist long after birth. At ages 2 and 3, securely attached children are more likely to know their own names, as well as both their own and their mothers' sex (Pipp, Easterbrooks, & Harmon, 1992). From ages 3 to 5, they are more curious, are more competent, get along better with other children, and are more likely to form close friendships (Youngblade & Belsky, 1992; J. L. Jacobson & Wille, 1986; Waters, Wippman, & Sroufe, 1979; Arend, Gove, & Sroufe, 1979). They are also more likely to be independent in preschool, seeking help from teachers only when they need it (Sroufe, Fox, & Pancake, 1983).

Their advantages continue into middle childhood and adolescence (Sroufe, Carlson, & Shulman, 1993). When 10- and 11-year-olds were observed in summer day camp, those with secure histories were better at making and keeping friends and functioning in a group than children who had been classified as avoidant and resistant. In group tasks they made fewer false starts and finished faster, they were more self-reliant, and they were better coordinated physically.

In a reunion of fourteen 15-year-olds who had gone to camp together, the secure-history adolescents were rated higher on emotional health, self-esteem, ego resiliency, and peer competence. They also scored high ratings in the "capacity to be vulnerable," which measured openness to their feelings.

Children with insecure attachment often have other problems, like inhibitions at age 2, hostility toward other children at age 5, and dependency during the school years (Calkins & Fox, 1992; Lyons-Ruth, Alpern, & Repacholi, 1993; Sroufe, Carlson, Schulman et al., 1993).

The campers, who had been studied from infancy on, showed continuity over time in their personalities and in their ability to adapt to circumstances. This may come from their early expectations about themselves and their relationships, which then lead to certain ways of relating to other people, causing others to act toward them in certain ways. Thus if children think well of themselves and expect to get along with people, they create positive social opportunities that strengthen these beliefs and the gratifying interactions that result from them; the reverse is also true (Sroufe, Carlson, Schulman et al., 1993).

Critique of Attachment Research.   Almost all the research on attachment is based on the Strange Situation. This research has yielded many findings that help us understand attachment, but critics question its conclusions.

The Strange Situation *is* strange; it's also artificial. It sets up a series of eight brief, laboratory-based episodes, asks mothers not to initiate interaction, exposes children to repeated comings and goings of adults, and expects the children to pay attention to them. Since attachment reflects a wider range of behaviors than the Strange Situation taps, a more comprehensive method may be needed to measure it more sensitively, especially to see how mother and infant interact during natural, *non*stressful situations (T. M. Field, 1987).

Furthermore, the Strange Situation may be an especially poor way to study attachment in some situations. Children of mothers who work outside the home, for example, are used to regular separations from them and to the presence of other caregivers and may, therefore, not react the same as children of mothers who are at home (K. A. Clarke-Stewart, 1989; L. W. Hoffman, 1989). It may also be less valid for use in other cultures. Research on Japanese infants, who are less commonly separated from their mothers than are American babies, show high rates of resistant classifications, which may reflect the extreme stressfulness of the Strange Situation for these babies (Miyake, Chen, & Campos, 1985). Further, it does not seem to be valid in assessing the attachment of children with disabilities like Down syndrome (Vaughn, Goldberg, et al., 1994).

Some researchers, therefore, have turned to other measures, like a more objective Q-sorting technique. In this procedure judges sort a set of items into categories, from the most to the least characteristic of a child. The Waters and Deane (1985) Attachment Q-set has raters compare descriptions of a child's actual behavior with descriptions of the "hypothetical most secure child."

Finally, other researchers claim that the correlations between attachment in infancy and later development may stem not from the attachment itself but from the child's own personality characteristics that affect both attachment and later development (Sroufe, Carlson & Schulman, 1993). After reviewing the literature, Michael E. Lamb (1987) concluded that the association between attachment in infancy and development in childhood is weak and inconclusive and that differences among older children may stem from parent-child interaction *after* infancy. Because interaction patterns are often set early and remain consistent over the years, it is hard to tell when they are most influential. We should learn more about attachment as researchers develop and use measures other than the Strange Situation and as they integrate new attachment patterns into research designs.

What do you think?   *Can you think of ways other than the Strange Situation to study attachment? What behaviors would suggest that a baby is securely or insecurely attached? Which of these behaviors would be valid indicators of attachment in other cultures?*

The Mother's Role

Until recently, most developmentalists seemed to agree with Napoleon, who said, "The future good or bad conduct of a child entirely depends upon the mother." Although we now recognize that mothers are not the only important people in babies' lives, they are still central characters in the drama of development.

What Do Babies Need from Their Mothers?   In a famous series of experiments, rhesus monkeys were separated from their mothers 6 to 12 hours after birth and raised in a laboratory. The infant monkeys were put into cages with one of two kinds of surrogate "mothers"—a plain cylindrical wire-mesh form or a form cov-

In a series of classic experiments, Harry Harlow and Margaret Harlow showed that food is not the most important way to a baby's heart. When infant rhesus monkeys could choose whether to go to a wire surrogate "mother" or a warm, soft terry-cloth "mother," they spent more time clinging to the cloth mother, even if they were being fed by bottles connected to the wire mother.

ered with terry cloth. Some monkeys were fed from bottles connected to the wire "mothers"; others were "nursed" by the warm, cuddly cloth ones.

When the monkeys were allowed to spend time with either kind of "mother," they all spent more time clinging to the cloth surrogates—even if they were being fed only by the wire ones. In an unfamiliar room, the babies "raised" by cloth surrogates showed more natural interest in exploring than those "raised" by wire surrogates—even when the appropriate "mothers" were there. Apparently, the monkeys also remembered the cloth surrogates better. After a year's separation, the "cloth-raised" monkeys eagerly ran to embrace the terry-cloth forms, whereas the "wire-raised" monkeys showed no interest in the wire forms (Harlow & Zimmerman, 1959). None of the monkeys in either group grew up normally, however (Harlow & Harlow, 1962), and none were able to mother their own offspring (Suomi & Harlow, 1972).

It is hardly surprising that a dummy mother would not provide the same kind of stimulation and opportunities for development as a live mother. These experiments show that (contrary to the psychoanalytic emphasis on satisfaction of biological needs) feeding is *not* the most important thing mothers do for their babies. "Mothering" includes the comfort of close bodily contact and, in monkeys, the satisfaction of an innate need to cling. Surely, human infants also have needs that must be satisfied, or at least acted upon, if they are to grow up normally. A major task of child development researchers is to find out what those needs are.

One function mothers (and other caregivers) serve is to help children get what they want. Babies as young as 6 months can make things happen: They can induce their mothers to pick up a toy out of their reach and play with them (Mosier & Rogoff, 1994). How do the babies do this? They catch the mother's attention by looking at her, pointing or using other gestures, and eventually using words. In these ways they show they have learned to use their mothers to help them solve problems. Babies contribute actively to the interactions they have with others.

While the mother-child attachment is important, it is not the only attachment babies form. The mother may be the only one who can suckle her infants, but other people—fathers, grandparents, siblings, friends, and caregivers—can also comfort and play with them and give them a sense of security. Fathers are especially important.

The Father's Role

The days of ignoring or minimizing a father's contribution to his children's development seem to be over. In television commercials fathers diaper and bathe their infants. Stores offer strollers with longer, man-sized handles and baby carriers that fit men over 6'4". Psychologists are devoting more research to the father's role in a child's life. The findings from such research underscore the importance of sensitive, responsive fathering. Close ties form between fathers and babies during the first year of life, and fathers exert a strong influence on their children's social, emotional, and cognitive development.

Bonds and Attachments between Fathers and Infants. Many fathers form close bonds with their babies soon after birth. Proud new fathers admire their babies and feel drawn to pick them up. The babies contribute to the bond simply by doing the things all normal babies do: opening their eyes, grasping their fathers' fingers, or moving in their fathers' arms.

Fathers and children often form close bonds during the first year of life. This father, engrossed with his infant daughter, is likely to go on to exert a strong influence on her social, emotional, and cognitive development.

As early as 3 months after birth, it may be possible to predict the security of attachment between father and child. Fathers who show delight in their 3-month-olds, who see themselves as important in their children's development, who are sensitive to the babies' needs, and who hold time with them as a high priority are likely to have infants who are securely attached to them at 1 year (Cox, Owen, Henderson, & Margand, 1992).

Babies develop attachments to both their parents at about the same time, and one study found that the security of attachment to mother and father is quite similar (N. A. Fox, Kimmerly, & Schafer, 1991). But another study found that although babies prefer either the mother or the father to a stranger, they usually prefer their mothers to their fathers, especially when upset (Lamb, 1981). This is probably because mothers typically care for them more often than fathers do.

How Do Fathers Act with Their Infants?   The amount of child care by men in industrialized countries seems to be increasing (Lamb, 1987). Despite a common belief that women are biologically predisposed to care for babies, men seem to be just as sensitive and responsive to infants (Lamb, 1981).

Studies of fathers in Jamaica and in middle-class African American families demonstrate how strongly involved with their infants these fathers are (Roopnarine et al., in press; Hossain & Roopnarine, in press). However, in both groups the mothers are more involved, and the fathers spend more time playing with their babies than feeding or bathing them. Other studies also show that American fathers *play with* their babies more than they *care for* them (Easterbrooks & Goldberg, 1984).

A father's involvement is influenced by many factors. One is the mother's attitude. She often serves as the "gatekeeper" of the father's involvement with the baby, both in her direct actions and in the way she talks about him (Yogman, 1984). Another factor is the mother's employment. Women who work full time stimulate their babies more than women who stay at home full time, and they play with their babies more than the fathers do. They also spend more time tak-

These fathers in "Bootee Camp" in Irvine, California, are learning how to care for their babies and getting support from other new fathers at the same time.

ing care of their babies than do the babies' fathers (Pedersen, Cain, & Zaslow, 1982). Fathers who are their babies' primary caretakers behave more like mothers than like "typical" fathers (T. M. Field, 1978). It will be interesting to see whether father-infant attachment changes in families like these.

Different roles and different societal expectations about what fathers and mothers are supposed to do influence the fathers' styles of interacting with their babies. When Jess tosses the infant Jason up in the air and then wrestles with the toddler Jason, he is typical of American fathers, who tend toward vigorous father-infant play (Yogman et al., 1977; Yogman, 1984). Swedish and German fathers usually do not play with their babies this way (Lamb, Frodi, Frodi, & Hwang, 1982; Parke, Grossman, & Tinsley, 1981). African Aka fathers (Hewlett, 1987) and fathers in New Delhi, India, also tend to play gently with their small children (Roopnarine, Hooper, Ahmeduzzaman, & Pollack, 1993; Roopnarine, Talokder, Jain, Josh, & Srivastav, 1992). Such cross-cultural variation in fathers' play styles casts doubts that rough play is determined by male biology, but suggests it is culturally influenced.

What Is the Significance of the Father-Infant Relationship? The father-infant relationship has cognitive ramifications. A study of 48 working-class Irish fathers found a high level of child care and a strong positive correlation between father care and the babies' scores at age 1 on measures of cognitive development (Nugent, 1991). These fathers talked to their babies, played with them, fed, diapered, soothed, and sang to them. The men most likely to care for their infants were younger, happily married men who had, after their children's birth, modified their work schedules and shared domestic duties with their wives.

In another study, a group of toddlers—two-thirds of whose mothers were employed outside the home—showed the benefits of the father's involvement in caring for and playing with them, especially when his attitude was sensitive and positive. The father's behavior had a particularly strong influence on competence

This baby seems very suspicious of the woman reaching out for her. The baby seems to be showing a classic reaction of stranger anxiety, a common phenomenon (at least in the western world), which involves a wariness of unfamiliar people and places.

in problem solving, and the father's involvement helped to make boys' attachment to their mothers more secure (Easterbrooks & Goldberg, 1984). Furthermore, secure attachments to fathers seem to help children form close friendships at age 5 (Youngblade & Belsky, 1992).

The very fact that a child's two parents have two different personalities—no matter what those personalities are—influences development in unknown ways. We don't know, for example, what effects stem from babies' learning that the same action will bring different reactions from mother and father. One thing seems clear: Anyone who plays a large part in a baby' day-to-day life will exert an important influence.

What do you think?   *"Despite the women's liberation movement and changes in child care, a mother will always be more important to young children than a father." Do you agree or disagree?*

Stranger Anxiety and Separation Anxiety

At 8 months, Vicky suddenly seems like a different baby. She used to be friendly, smiling at strangers and cooing happily whenever someone—anyone—was around. But now, if a new person approaches, she grows quiet and suspiciously eyes the unfamiliar face. It used to be easy to leave Vicky with a new baby-sitter. But now she howls when either parent is out of sight. Vicky is showing two new anxieties—*stranger anxiety,* wariness of a person she does not know, and *separation anxiety,* distress when a familiar caregiver leaves her.

Both separation anxiety and stranger anxiety used to be considered emotional and cognitive milestones of infancy, reflecting recognition of and attachment to the mother. But more recent research suggests that both these phenomena are variable and depend largely on a baby's temperament and life circumstances.

stranger anxiety   *Wariness of strange people and places often shown by infants in the second half of the first year.*

separation anxiety   *Distress shown by an infant when a familiar caregiver leaves.*

Sibling rivalry is not the whole story: Children react in a variety of ways to the arrival of a baby sibling. Some take pride in being the "big ones," who can dress themselves, use the potty, eat with the grown-ups, and even hold the baby.

Although Vicky's reaction is typical, it is not universal, For one thing, there are cross-cultural differences in stranger anxiety. Navajo infants, for example, show less fear of strangers during the first year of life than Anglo infants do. Then there are differences within a culture. Navajo babies who had many opportunities to interact with other people—who belonged to an extended family or lived close to the trading post—were less wary of new people than were other Navajo infants (Chisholm, 1983).

In the United States, babies rarely react negatively to strangers before 6 months of age, commonly do so by 8 or 9 months, and do so more and more throughout the first year (Sroufe, 1977). Even then, however, a baby may react positively to a new person—especially if the person waits for a little while before approaching the baby, then does it gradually, gently, and playfully. This kind of approach lets the infant's natural curiosity and inborn tendency to relate to other people win out. But if a stranger suddenly reaches for a baby, or touches or picks him or her up before the baby has gotten used to the stranger's presence, the baby is more likely to cry.

Research that measured physiological and behavioral responses of 9-month-olds to brief separations from their mothers suggests that infants' stress may be due less to the separation than to the quality of the substitute care. When caregivers were warm and responsive and played with the infants *before* they cried, the babies cried much less than when they were with less responsive caregivers (Gunnar, Larson, Hertsgaard, Harris, & Brodersen, 1992). This effect was most marked with babies whose temperaments disposed them to be quick to anger in situations where they seemed to feel a loss of control.

Stability of substitute care is also important. The pioneering work done by René Spitz (1945, 1946) on institutionalized children emphasized the need for care as close as possible to good mothering. Research has emphasized the need for *continuity* and *consistency* in caregiving, so children can form early emotional bonds to particular people.

One factor affecting a baby's reaction to a stranger is how the caregiver reacts to the new person (Dickstein & Parke, 1988; Klinnert, Emde, Butterfield, & Campos, 1986). For example, when Ellen's mother visited from out of town after not having seen the family for 7 months, Ellen greeted her eagerly. Vicky apparently decided this stranger was a person she could trust, and she soon went willingly into her grandmother's arms.

In one study, the mothers of 10-month-old babies who were approached by an unfamiliar woman spoke to their babies either positively or neutrally about the woman, or spoke to the woman herself positively or neutrally, or remained silent (Feinman & Lewis, 1983). When the mothers spoke positively about the stranger, the babies—especially those with easy temperaments—were friendlier to her than in any of the other situations, and were more likely to lean toward her and offer her a toy. Apparently, the babies socially referenced their mothers in this ambiguous situation and acted accordingly.

Today, neither early and intense fear of strangers nor intense protest when the mother leaves is considered to be a sign of secure attachment. As we saw, researchers now measure attachment more by what happens when the parent returns than by how many tears the baby shed at departure time. Rather, whether a baby cries when a parent leaves or someone new approaches may say more about a baby's temperament than about the security of his or her attachment (R. J. Davidson & Fox, 1989).

DISTURBANCES IN DEVELOPMENT

In most cases, the resiliency of the human spirit prevails: Even in the face of sizable obstacles, personality often develops normally from infancy on. But there are situations and conditions that can disrupt this development. Some, like infantile autism, appear to have a biological basis, while others result from deprivations in a child's early emotional environment.

Autism

A baby lies in his crib, oblivious to other people. Despite his parents' efforts, they cannot get him to cuddle or make eye contact with them. The baby is eventually diagnosed as autistic. *Infantile autism* is a rare and severe developmental disorder marked by an inability to communicate with or respond to other people. It develops in the first $2\frac{1}{2}$ years of life, often as early as the fourth month, and it continues to affect the child through life. Some autistic children never learn to speak but can sing a wide repertory of songs. Boys are 3 to 4 times more likely than girls to be afflicted (Mauk, 1993).

infantile autism *Rare developmental disorder involving the inability to communicate with and respond to other people.*

Some 60 to 75 percent of autistic children are retarded (Mauk, 1993). But they often do well on tasks of manipulative or visual-spatial skill and may perform unusual mental feats, like memorizing entire train schedules. They may scream when their place at the table is changed, insist on always carrying a particular object (like a rubber band), and obsessively repeat a behavior like hand-clapping.

One study examined the responses of three groups of children—normal, mentally retarded, and autistic—to adults' negative emotions. The adults expressed fear (using facial expressions and gestures upon seeing a toy robot), distress (pretending to hurt themselves), and discomfort (pretending to feel sick). The normal children (average age, 20 months) and the retarded ones (average age, 42 months) were very attentive to the adults in all three situations. But the autistic children (average age, about 42 months) seemed to ignore or not notice these adults. This failure to notice emotional signals of the people around them is a typical symptom of autism, and it is a crucial one, since it limits children's social and emotional development and thus contributes to their deficiencies (Sigman, Kasari, Kwon, & Yirmiya, 1992).

Treatment for autistic children includes special education with an emphasis on language, communication, and social interaction. Behavioral methods help children break down tasks into logical steps, and medication may be given to increase their attention span. Most autistic people eventually become able to take care of themselves in day-to-day tasks, but at least 70 percent need a supervised living arrangement as adults (Mauk, 1993).

Although in the past "cold and unresponsive" parents were blamed for causing autism, it is now recognized as a biological disorder of the nervous system (Mauk, 1993). Interference with brain development seems to occur either during early prenatal life or during the first or second year after birth (Courchesne,

Yeung-Courchesne, Press, Hesselink, & Jernigan, 1988). Concordance is considerably higher between identical twins than fraternal twins—96 percent versus 23 percent (Ritvo, Freeman, Mason-Brothers, Mo, & Ritvo, 1985). Autism is probably inherited, there being seemingly minimal impact by the environment.

Environmental Deprivation

When the attachments between infants and their parents are disrupted or impaired because children are separated from their parents or have painful relationships with them, the consequences can be grave. In Chapter 8 we talk about the emotional scars left by parental abuse and neglect. In less severe psychological deprivation, children's basic psychological needs may still go unmet.

In Czechoslovakia, 30-year longitudinal studies have followed children whose births were not wanted, who had alcoholic fathers, who were born to single parents, or whose parents were divorced. Some of the data attest to the resilience of children, but the troubling effects of such conditions also surfaced (Matejcek & Dytrych, 1993).

Despite these children's adverse early environments, *most* developed normally and did not differ from children in a control group who did not fall into any of these categories. This shows that people are not necessarily victims of their environments, that there are individual differences in the ability to cope with less than optimal life conditions, and that many children overcome serious obstacles.

However, there was a greater likelihood of a variety of problems for these children, especially for the unwanted ones. Children born after their mothers had twice requested and been denied abortion were compared with a control group whose births were welcomed. During the first 8 years, the unwanted children were more likely to be overweight, to be treated for acute illness, and to have school problems. Boys were affected more often than girls. As adolescents and young adults, this group was at greater risk for social and emotional problems.

These researchers recommend a number of social policy provisions to monitor and help such children. A Czechoslovakian governmental health service already mandates regular visits to a pediatrician from birth to 5 years, along with periodic evaluations of the family's social functioning. Other proposed measures include providing age-appropriate stimulation and learning opportunities, helping parents form close bonds with their children, and encouraging teachers and leaders of extracurricular activities to give the children experiences of success.

RELATIONSHIPS WITH OTHER CHILDREN

Although parents exert a major influence over children's lives, other children are important too—both in the home and out of it.

SIBLINGS

If you have brothers or sisters, your relationships with them are likely to be the longest-lasting you will ever have. You and your siblings may have fought as children, or you may have been each other's best friends. Either way, these are the people who share your roots, who "knew you when," who accepted or rejected the same parental values, and who probably deal with you more candidly than almost anyone you will ever know. Of course, sometimes the beginning of the sibling relationship—when a new baby is born into a family—takes some adjustment by the older child.

The Arrival of a New Baby

Vicky, aged 3, came into the bedroom where Ellen was nursing Vicky's new baby brother, Bobby. She stared for a few minutes and then pleaded, "Mommy, can't you throw that baby in the garbage?"

Children react in a variety of ways to a new sibling. Some regress to earlier behaviors: They suck their thumbs, wet their pants, ask to suck from breast or bottle, or use baby talk. Others withdraw, refusing to talk or play. Some suggest taking the baby back to the hospital, giving it away, or flushing it down the toilet. Some take pride in being the "big ones," who can dress themselves, use the potty, and help care for the baby. Most behavioral problems of older siblings disappear by the time the younger one reaches 8 months of age (Dunn, 1985).

The birth of a younger sibling often changes the way a mother acts toward her first child. The mother is likely to play less with her first child, to be less sensitive to his or her interests, to give more orders, to have more confrontations, and to initiate fewer conversations and games (Dunn, 1985; Dunn & Kendrick, 1982). However, the extent of these changes often depends on the older child's personality. If that child—say, Vicky—takes the initiative by coming up to her mother to start a conversation or play a game, she is likely to have less of a problem with sibling rivalry than if she withdraws, because she will have found a way to salvage her close relationship with her mother.

There is little research on helping children adjust to a new sibling. Popular advice is to prepare the older children for the birth of a new baby and to make any changes in the child's life (like moving the child to another bedroom or from a crib to a bed, or starting nursery school) well beforehand to minimize feelings of being displaced (Spock & Rothenberg, 1985). Parents should accept a child's anxiety and jealousy as normal, while at the same time protecting the new baby from any harmful expression of those feelings. They can encourage the older child to play and help with the baby and can emphasize how much they value *each* child. Finally, older siblings adjust better if their fathers give extra time and attention to them to make up for the mother's sudden involvement with the infant (Lamb, 1978).

Babies and toddlers become closely attached to their older brothers and sisters, especially when, as with these Chinese children, the older siblings assume a large measure of care for the younger ones.

How Siblings Interact

The interaction between siblings is complex, swathed in layers of contradictory emotions. Babies begin interacting with their older siblings to a significant degree after the first 6 months. One-year-olds spend almost as much time with their siblings as with their mothers and far more time with their siblings than their fathers (Dunn & Kendrick, 1982; Lawson & Ingleby, 1974). In many societies around the world, including our own, older siblings have considerable responsibility for taking care of babies, often when the older ones are only about 4 or 5.

Generally, brothers and sisters get along quite well. One study focused on 34 pairs of same-sex middle-class siblings at home. The younger children averaged 20 months of age; their brothers and sisters were 1 to 4 years older. The older siblings more often initiated both positive and negative behaviors, while the younger

Research suggests that these 1-year-olds in day care are likely to be as, or more, sociable, self-confident, persistent, achieving, and better at solving problems than children cared for at home. The most important element of infant day care is probably the teacher, who exerts a strong influence on the children in her care.

ones imitated more. Older boys were more aggressive; older girls, more likely to share, cooperate, and hug. Sibling interaction was "rich and varied, clearly not based predominantly on rivalry" (Abramovitch, Corter, & Lando, 1979, p. 1003).

Although sibling rivalry is often present, so is genuine affection. Young children usually become quite attached to their older brothers and sisters. Babies become upset when their siblings go away, greet them when they come back, prefer them as playmates, and go to them for security when a stranger enters (Dunn, 1983; R. B. Stewart, 1983).

The parent-child relationship is influential in shaping sibling bonds. The more securely attached babies and young children are to their parents, the better they get along with their siblings. They are less jealous when their mothers play with the other child, and they are less aggressive toward either the mother or the sibling (Teti & Ablard, 1989).

Finally, the environment siblings create for each other affects not only their future relationship but each one's personality development as well (Dunn, 1983). For example, when little girls imitate their big brothers, they may take on some characteristics commonly thought of as masculine. Four-year-olds who have close relationships with their siblings are better able to understand another person's viewpoint than are 4-year-olds who do not have such relationships (Light, 1973).

CHANGES IN SOCIABILITY

Although the family is the center of a baby's social world, infants and—even more so—toddlers show interest in people outside the home, particularly people their own size. Since more babies now spend time in day care settings in close contact with other babies, more researchers are studying how infants and toddlers react to each other.

Interest and Imitation

Babies' interest in other children rises and falls. From the first days in a hospital nursery, infants who have been lying quietly in their cribs start to cry when they hear another baby's cries (Martin & Clark, 1982; Sagi & Hoffman, 1976; Simner, 1971). During the first few months of life, they are interested in other babies and respond to them in about the same way they respond to their mothers: They look, they smile, they coo (T. M. Field, 1978). From age 6 months until about 1 year, they increasingly smile at, touch, and babble to another baby, especially when they are not distracted by the presence of adults or toys (Hay, Pedersen, & Nash, 1982). At about 1 year, however, when the biggest items on their agenda are learning to walk and to manipulate objects, they pay more attention to toys and less to other people (T. M. Field & Roopnarine, 1982).

This stage does not last long, though; children show a growing interest in what other children do. In three experiments, 14- to 18-month-olds watched another toddler play with toys in certain ways—for example, putting beads in a cup and sounding a buzzer. The toddler-observers were then tested to see whether they imitated the activities, showing they remembered them. In the first experiment, the test took place in the laboratory after 5 minutes; in the second experiment, after seeing the other toddler in the laboratory, the toddler-observers were tested at home 2 days later; and in the third experiment, after seeing another child at day care, they were tested at home 2 days later (Hanna & Meltzoff, 1993).

In all three experiments, the toddlers in the experimental groups played with the toys in the way they had seen them played with more than did toddlers in control groups, who were presented with the toys but had not seen another child playing with them. The fact that significant imitation of a peer occurred, even across a change of setting and over 2 days, suggests that even at this early age children learn from each other.

Toddlers also play games like hide-and-seek and follow-the-leader. These games help them connect with other children and pave the way for more complex games involving talking and symbolic play that take over during the preschool years (Eckerman et al., 1989). As children grow older, they enter more and more into the world beyond their own home, and their social skills become increasingly important.

Sociability and Conflict

In the second year, babies understand relationships better. A 10-month-old who holds out a toy to another baby pays no attention to whether the other's back is turned. But a child in the second year of life knows when the offer has the best chance of being accepted and how to respond to another child's overtures (Eckerman, Davis, & Didow, 1989; Eckerman & Stein, 1982). Sociability keeps developing, and even children as young as 2 years old adjust their social behavior to the age of their partners (Brownell, 1990). When 2-year-olds were paired either with other 2-year-olds or with 18-month-old toddlers, the older children made more of an effort to draw the younger ones into a play situation. They may not have needed to make as much of an effort with children their same age, who were more skilled socially. The mixed-age setting seemed to advance the social development of children at both age levels.

Some people, of course, are more sociable than others. As we pointed out in discussing temperament, the readiness to accept new people, the ability to adapt to change, and a baby's usual mood seem to be inherited traits that remain fairly stable over time (A. Thomas et al., 1968). But babies are also influenced by the attitudes of those around them. Sociable infants tend to have sociable mothers (M. Stevenson & Lamb, 1979). Children who spend time with other babies from infancy on become sociable earlier than those who spend all their time at home.

Even conflict has a social purpose. In one observational study, 1- and 2-year-olds, in groups of three children who had not known each other before, were watched while playing with—and sometimes while squabbling over—toys (M. Caplan, Vespo, Pedersen, & Hay, 1991). Overall these children got along well. Just before or just after half of their squabbles, they were sharing, showing, and demonstrating toys to each other. The 2-year-olds got into more conflicts than the 1-year-olds, but they also resolved them more—often by sharing toys when there were not enough for all the children. Conflict at this early age may be important in helping children learn how to negotiate and to solve disputes, a skill they will need throughout life. As children grow older and enter more and more into the world beyond their own home, their social skills become increasingly important. The first step into the wider world for many children is the entrance into out-of-home child care.

THE IMPACT OF EARLY DAY CARE

What happens to the development of children who, from the age of a few weeks, or a few months, are cared for by baby-sitters or day care workers? Does day care—and especially, infant day care—help or harm children? What kinds of care are best, or worst? Few questions in child development arouse as much controversy. The answers are important, since more than half of all American mothers of children under 1 year of age are going out to work, a higher proportion than at any time in the nation's history. About 53 percent of children under 1 year of age and 61 percent of children 4 or under receive care outside the home from someone other than their mother (U.S. Bureau of the Census, 1990).

WHAT IS GOOD DAY CARE?

The questions we ask are important too. What kind of day care are we talking about, care in a center or the more common care in the home of a nonrelative who "takes in" children? What is "high-quality" care? By what criteria do we judge harm and benefit? How can we distinguish the effects of the day care experience from the effects of the parenting the child gets at home? Do more competent, caring parents select better child care? What happens when parents *want* good care but cannot find any that is available and affordable?

Research is trying to find answers to these questions. But many studies are open to criticism, and the findings from them are often ambiguous, inconsistent, or contradictory. Furthermore, although most children are cared for either in their own homes or in someone else's home (see Figure 7-1), much of what we know about the effects of day care comes from studies of high-quality, well-funded university-based centers, which is hardly typical of the care most children receive. We have relatively little information about the effect of the most common kinds

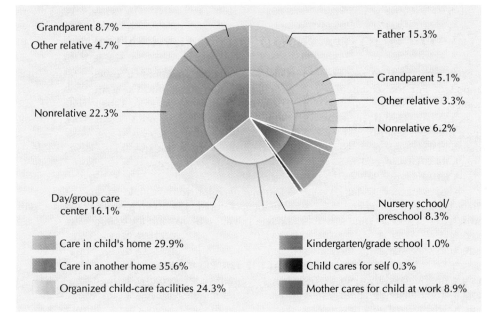

Grandparent 8.7%

Other relative 4.7%

Father 15.3%

Grandparent 5.1%

Other relative 3.3%

Nonrelative 6.2%

Nonrelative 22.3%

Day/group care center 16.1%

Nursery school/ preschool 8.3%

Care in child's home 29.9%

Care in another home 35.6%

Organized child-care facilities 24.3%

Kindergarten/grade school 1.0%

Child cares for self 0.3%

Mother cares for child at work 8.9%

FIGURE 7-1
Primary child-care arrangements used by employed mothers for children under 5. SOURCE: U.S. Bureau of the Census, 1990.

of child care. With these caveats, let's see what research has yielded so far about the impact of day care on children's cognitive, emotional, and social development.

Good day care is like good parenting. Children can thrive physically, intellectually, and emotionally in day care that has small groups, a high adult-to-child ratio, and a stable, competent, highly involved staff. Caregivers should be trained in child development, sensitive to children's needs, authoritative but not too restrictive, stimulating, and affectionate (Belsky, 1984). Children develop best when they have access to educational toys and materials, when they are cared for by adults who teach them and accept them (are neither too controlling nor merely custodial), and when they have a balance between structured activities and freedom to explore on their own (Clarke-Stewart, 1987).

What do you think? *Hired to direct a day care center, you have complete freedom to design it. What would you include? How would you assess the quality of your center?*

By and large, children in good day care programs do at least as well physically, cognitively, and socially as those raised at home. High-quality day care seems to enhance emotional development too, and may even improve relationships with parents. Parents may feel less stress because their child is well cared for while they earn the income they need and because they get some relief from the demands of parenting. For suggestions on choosing good child care, see Box 7-2.

DAY CARE AND COGNITIVE DEVELOPMENT

The most clear-cut conclusions emerge in the cognitive realm for children aged 2 to 4 who attend day care centers. On a number of cognitive measures children in adequate or superior group day care seem to do as well as, or better than, chil-

BOX 7-2 ■ THE EVERYDAY WORLD

HOW TO CHOOSE A GOOD DAY CARE CENTER

What makes a day care center good? A number of factors are important. For one, children get the best care when small numbers of children interact with a few adults. When groups are too large, adding more adults to the staff does not help. It does not seem to matter how many years of formal education the caregivers have had. What does matter is how much they have specialized in a child-related field, like developmental psychology, early childhood education, or special education. Adults with such special training tend to give better care, and children in their care do better on tests of school-readiness skills (Abt Associates, 1978).

A licensed center meets minimum state standards for health, fire, and safety (if it is inspected regularly), but many centers and home care facilities are not licensed or regulated. Furthermore, licensing does not tell anything about the program's quality (American Academy of Pediatrics, AAP, 1986b).

Here are some things to look for in deciding whether to use a particular day care facility (AAP, 1986b; Olds, 1989).

DOES THE CENTER. . .
♦ Provide a safe, clean setting?
♦ Have trained personnel who are warm and responsive to all the children?
♦ Promote good health habits?

♦ Offer a stimulating environment to help children master cognitive and communicative skills?
♦ Encourage children to develop at their own rate?
♦ Nurture self-confidence, curiosity, creativity, and self-discipline?
♦ Stimulate children to ask questions, solve problems, make decisions, and engage in a variety of activities?
♦ Foster social skills, self-esteem, and respect for others?
♦ Help parents improve their child-rearing skills?
♦ Promote cooperation between parents, personnel, public and private schools, and the community?

BE WARY IF THE PROGRAM. . .
♦ Is not licensed or registered with the state.
♦ Refuses to let parents visit unannounced.
♦ Employs staff members who are not educated, trained, or experienced in child-related subjects.
♦ Is overcrowded, unclean, or poorly supervised.
♦ Does not have enough heat, light, or ventilation.
♦ Has no written plans for meals or emergencies.
♦ Has no smoke alarms, fire extinguishers, or first-aid kit.
♦ Does not set aside separate areas for playing, feeding, resting, and diapering.
♦ Has no policy on handling injuries or infections or on managing sick children.
♦ Does not have a medical consultant.

---

dren raised at home by parents or baby-sitters or in day care homes. Where differences appear, day care children tend to score higher on IQ tests, show more advanced eye-hand coordination, play more creatively, know more about the physical world, count and measure better, have better language skills, and are more advanced in knowing such information as their names and addresses.

This cognitive gain is often temporary—a speeding up in acquiring these skills rather than a permanent advantage. Some studies show that the advantages do not hold up once the children leave the center, and by the end of first grade, home-reared children have caught up. Furthermore, the gains seem unrelated to the length of time children are in day care or to the age when they entered (Clarke-Stewart, 1992).

Children from low-income families or stressful homes benefit the most from good day care. The average child in a good program is not much affected for better or for worse, but disadvantaged children in good programs tend not to show the declines in IQ often seen when such children reach school age. Children in day care may be more motivated to learn (AAP, 1986b; Belsky, 1984; Bronfenbrenner, Belsky, & Steinberg, 1977).

The findings about infant day care (care for children under 1 year, or under

3 years, depending on the study) are more complex. Some studies show that children aged 18 months to 5 years score higher on intelligence tests if they attended infant day care (Clarke-Stewart & Fein, 1983). This advantage seems to be temporary. However, at least one study found that children who had been in high-quality infant care were more likely to be assigned to gifted programs in elementary school and, as sixth graders, to get higher math grades (T. Field, 1991).

But another study, which looked at 1181 3- to 4-year-olds, suggests that while children from low-income families and girls from any families do as well or better than home-reared children, boys from high-income families in full-time infant care may be at risk for lower cognitive development. At 3 and 4 years of age, these children were tested on a number of behavioral and cognitive measures, including a picture vocabulary test (Baydar & Brooks-Gunn, 1991). Children whose mothers had gone to work when the babies were 3 to 6 months old did worse on these tests than those whose mothers had gone back either earlier or later. Those whose mothers did not return to work until the second or third year of the children's lives (an economic impossibility for many parents) scored about the same as mother-reared children. The type of care the children got seemed to make a difference: Mother care and grandmother care were better for children from low-income homes; in high-income families, baby-sitter care for girls and mother care for boys were better.

One study comparing care at different levels of quality suggests some reasons for cognitive gains. This research involved 166 children from nine day care centers in Bermuda, where 84 percent of 2-year-olds spend most of the workweek in day care. When caregivers spoke often to children—especially to give or ask for information rather than to control behavior—and encouraged children to start conversations with them, the children did better on tests of language development than did children who did not have such conversations with adults (McCartney, 1984).

A follow-up study found that the children who talked often with their caregivers were also more sociable and considerate (D. Phillips, McCartney, & Scarr, 1987). In fact, the quality and amount of verbal stimulation seemed even more important for social development than the children's family background. Here again, we see the intertwining of different aspects of development and the connection between cognitive influences and personality.

DAY CARE AND SOCIAL DEVELOPMENT

Children who spent much of their first year in day care tend to be as, or more, sociable, self-confident, persistent, achieving, and better at solving problems than children who were at home. Day-care preschoolers also tend to be more comfortable in new situations, more outgoing, less timid and fearful, more helpful and cooperative, and more verbally expressive (Clarke-Stewart, 1989; 1992). One study of children who started day care at an average age of just under 7 months found that between 5 and 8 years of age, they had more friends and were more physically affectionate with them, took part in more extracurricular activities, and were more assertive than children who had been at home (T. Field, 1991).

Day care children also tend to be more disobedient and less polite to adults, bossier and more aggressive with other children, louder, more boisterous, and more demanding in general (Clarke-Stewart, 1989; 1992). But are these "negative" characteristics bad for the children? Or do these traits just pose an inconvenience for adults? Are children who have been in infant day care more advanced in thinking for themselves and less inclined to go along with what others want? Alison Clarke-Stewart suggests that these children may seem more "bratty than children who stay at home because they want their own way and do not have the skills to achieve it smoothly, rather than because they are maladjusted" (1989, p. 269).

The most important element of child care is probably the teacher, who serves as a substitute parent in the world beyond the family. She* enhances cognitive development by the way she talks to and guides the children; she offers a caring, protective presence; and she helps children form trusting relationships with nonrelatives. The teacher exerts a strong influence on how children get along with their peers.

Researchers looked at 4-year-olds who had entered day care at various times in infancy, toddlerhood, and early childhood. They found that children who were securely attached to their first child-care teachers got along better with classmates than did those who had been classified as avoidant or ambivalent with their first teachers. The secure children were more sensitive and empathic, played in more complex ways, and were better liked by other children (Howes, Matheson, & Hamilton, 1994).

A child's relationship with the teacher touches several dimensions of social development, including security, socialization, and dependence. Forty-eight children who had entered full-time child care—either centers or family day care homes—between 2 and 11 months of age were followed for 3 years (Howes, Hamilton, & Matheson, 1994). As 4-year-olds, those who as toddlers had felt secure with their teachers were now more gregarious and less aggressive, and toddlers who had gotten along well with the teacher now got along well with other children. But children who as preschoolers were dependent on their teachers were more socially withdrawn and aggressive. Different aspects of the teacher-child relationship seem to be related to different kinds of social competence and seem to be important at different times of the child's life.

DAY CARE AND EMOTIONAL DEVELOPMENT

A major emotional issue regarding infant child care is its effect on children's attachments to their mothers. Does being cared for by other people for much of a baby's time affect this bond? The effects depend upon many factors, including the mother's satisfaction with her marriage; whether and why she works full time or part time; the child's age, sex, and temperament; and the kind and quality of care the baby gets. Early child care in itself does not seem to pose a risk; the risk lies in poor-quality care and poor family environments (Scarr, Phillips, & McCartney, 1989). The quality of child care tends to be higher outside the United States. (See Box 7-3 for a look at high-quality care in Sweden.)

The first year of life seems the most critical. When babies from stable families receive high-quality care, most studies report positive findings (L. W. Hoffman, 1989). But when infants get unstable or poor-quality day care, they are more likely to avoid their mothers and to have emotional and social problems later on. These effects are worse when there is a poor fit between the mother's and baby's

*Although a few men have chosen careers in early childhood care and education, most day care workers and teachers are women.

BOX 7-3 ▪ AROUND THE WORLD

HOW SWEDEN CARES FOR PARENTS AND CHILDREN

In most societies throughout history other people have helped mothers to care for children. Today the issue of nonparental child care in the United States has taken on a new urgency for several reasons: the great numbers of mothers working outside the home, the rise of group day care as a business venture, and the belief that day care should enhance children's development rather than just offer baby-sitting. Sweden is often held up as a model.

Swedish family policy came about because of rapid industrialization and ensuing labor shortages. To enable women to work and also bear and rear future workers, Sweden developed a system including good pay, generous parental leaves, and high-quality early child care (Lamb & Sternberg, 1992; Hwang & Broberg, 1992).

Every Swedish family receives an allowance from the state for each child, from birth through age 16. Both mothers and fathers can take parental leave, ranging from 2 weeks at 90 percent of regular salary through 18 months, part paid, part unpaid, for one parent at a time. Thus almost all Swedish babies have one parent home for the first year, and children up to 18 months of age are cared for at home by their parents.

In 1989 more than 80 percent of Swedish babies were cared for by parents, and 8 percent were cared for by relatives or private baby-sitters. Only 8 percent under 18 months were in day care operated by local municipalities, but about half of all children over this age received such care. Since the national government sets guidelines for quality, municipal child care is of a very high caliber. Standards are set for the physical facility, staffing and staff training, size of groups, and so forth. Family day care, however, which is common, is almost unregulated; efforts are being made to develop guidelines for "daymothers."

Child care, seen as every family's right, is financed mostly from public funds. Parents pay an average of only 10 to 15 percent of the real cost; the state and the municipality each contribute just under half the remaining costs from revenues received from employers and both business and personal taxes.

Research has shown the positive effects of high-quality infant day care in Sweden (Andersson, 1992). Children aged 8 and 13 who had entered out-of-home care before age 1 (usually during the second half of the first year) were compared with children cared for at home. The day care youngsters generally did better in school and were rated more highly by teachers on such social and emotional variables as school adjustment and social competence. The *type* of care did not affect children's social, emotional, or cognitive development. The most important factor seems to be how well children are cared for in their own homes and what the emotional climate is like there. Parents are still children's most important caregivers.

What do you think? *How appropriate is it to "transplant" a social policy program from a small, affluent, homogeneous country like Sweden to a country like the United States, which is much larger and much more diverse racially and ethnically? Can we—should we—adopt the Swedish philosophy that society as a whole shares responsibility for the care and welfare of its children?*

---

personalities, when the family is under great stress, and when the mother is not responsive to the baby (Gamble & Zigler, 1986; Young & Zigler, 1986).

Some controversial research suggests that extensive substitute care in the first year may affect some children negatively, especially boys. In one study, most (57 percent) of a group of children who had been cared for by someone else for 20 or more hours a week, beginning before age 9 months and through the first year, formed secure attachments to their mothers. But baby boys who received more than 35 hours a week of substitute care tended to be insecurely attached to both parents (Belsky & Rovine, 1988).

However, factors other than substitute care can affect attachment. The most vulnerable boys had been "difficult babies" at 3 months of age and had mothers who were dissatisfied with their marriages, were insensitive to other people, and were strongly career-motivated. Other research has found that working mothers*

---

*All mothers are, of course, "working mothers" since rearing children and caring for a family are valuable—if unpaid—forms of work. Here, however, we define *working mother* as one who works for pay, usually outside the home.

who are warm, accepting, and available when they are home do have securely attached 18-month-old sons (Benn, 1986). We cannot generalize about day care without considering the specifics of the people, the care, and situation.

The timing of the mother's first going out to work is related to quality of attachment. In one study, 18-month-old boys whose mothers started work when the babies were from 6 to 12 months old were more likely to be insecurely attached than those whose mothers went to work when the babies were younger (Benn, 1986). Taken together, studies suggest that women who go back to work should try to do so before the baby is 4 to 6 months old, or after 1 year (Baydar & Brooks-Gunn, 1991; Benn, 1986).

After reviewing studies of parent-infant attachment, Lois W. Hoffman (1989) concluded, however, that if there *is* a relationship between a mother's employment during her baby's first year of life and the baby's attachment security, it is weak. Most studies find that most babies of full-time employed mothers *are* securely attached. Perhaps a mother's working outside the home during the first few months of a baby's life is a form of stress that, when combined with other stresses, can interfere with attachment—but working in itself does not make a difference.

Also, as suggested earlier, the Strange Situation may not be the most appropriate measure of quality of attachment for children of working mothers. At least some babies who seem insecurely attached in the Strange Situation may really be showing independence. Because they are used to their mothers' comings and goings, they are not anxious about them, pay little attention to them, and simply do what works for them on a day-to-day basis—that is, they show an appropriate "avoidant" pattern (Clarke-Stewart, 1989).

Clearly, day care is a complex issue. The importance of its quality has been shown by research findings; the most positive outcomes for children are associated with stable, high-quality care. The age when a child enters care and the child's gender may also matter, although different studies come up with diverse findings. Given that day care seems to have the potential to affect development positively, high-quality care accessible to all families who need and want it seems warranted. It seems to be a cost-effective way to foster healthy development in these early years. In Part Three, we'll see how young children build on the foundation laid during these important first 3 years.

SUMMARY

1   According to Erikson, an infant experiences the first in a series of eight crises that influence personality development. The first crisis is finding the appropriate balance between a sense of basic trust and mistrust about the world. The virtue of this stage is hope. The resolution of this crisis is influenced greatly by events surrounding the feeding situation and by the quality of the mother-infant relationship. Between the ages of $1\frac{1}{2}$ and 3 years, the child faces the second crisis: autonomy versus shame and doubt. The virtue of this stage is will. Erikson emphasizes the importance of parents in helping a child resolve this crisis.

2   There is some controversy over what emotions infants have and when they appear. Emotional expression and self-awareness appear to be tied to maturation of the brain, although experiences also affect the timing of their arrival.

3   Self-awareness and self-recognition emerge at about 18 months.

4   Babies communicate their feelings through crying, smiling, and laughing, and it is

likely that they do so through a variety of facial expressions as well. Crying, smiling, and laughing reveal much about the progress of development.

5 Babies play an active part in regulating emotional states.

6 Children of depressed mothers are at risk for a variety of emotional and cognitive disturbances.

7 Babies demonstrate social referencing, or seeking out another person's reactions to an ambiguous situation.

8 Individual differences in personality result in part from temperament, sex, and family relationships.

9 The New York Longitudinal Study (NYLS) has identified nine fairly stable aspects of temperament—a person's characteristic style of approaching and reacting to people and situations—which appear to be inborn. Most children can be classified as *easy, difficult,* or *slow to warm up.* Temperament can be influenced by environmental factors. A child's temperament has implications for psychological well-being and for parenting practices.

10 Significant physiological and behavioral differences between the sexes typically do not appear until after infancy. However, parents treat their baby sons and daughters differently, which can result in some personality differences.

11 Mother-infant attachment has received considerable theoretical and research attention. Patterns of attachment (secure, avoidant, ambivalent, and disorganized-disoriented), as determined by using the controversial Strange Situation test, may have long-term implications for the child's development. Characteristics of baby and mother both influence security of attachment.

12 Fathers and babies typically become attached early in the baby's life. The nature of infants' and toddlers' experiences with their mothers and fathers appears to differ, and both kinds of experiences are valuable.

13 Stranger anxiety (wariness of strangers) and separation anxiety (distress upon departure of a familiar caregiver) may occur during the second half of a baby's first year. Their occurrence seems to be related to a baby's temperament and life circumstances.

14 Infantile autism is a rare developmental disorder characterized by the inability to communicate with or respond to other people. It appears to be a biological disorder of the nervous system.

15 Environmental deprivation is associated with a variety of developmental problems.

16 Siblings interact with and influence each other both positively and negatively from an early age. Parents' actions and attitudes can help reduce sibling rivalry.

17 Infants and toddlers are social creatures whose interest in each other fluctuates with their developmental priorities. Individual differences in babies' sociability tend to remain stable over time.

18 Good quality day care appears to have generally positive impact on cognitive, social, and emotional development. A major controversy concerns the effect of early and extensive day care on attachment. Unfortunately, much U.S. day care is not of high quality.

KEY TERMS

personality (255)
basic trust versus basic mistrust (255)
self-regulation (256)
autonomy versus shame and doubt (257)
socialize (259)
emotions (259)
self-awareness (261)
self-recognition (261)
mutual regulation model (263)
depression (264)
social referencing (265)
temperament (266)
easy child (267)

difficult child (267)
slow-to-warm-up child (267)
attachment (272)
Strange Situation (273)
secure attachment (274)
avoidant attachment (274)
ambivalent (resistant) attachment (274)
disorganized-disoriented attachment (274)
stranger anxiety (283)
separation anxiety (283)
infantile autism (285)

SUGGESTED READINGS

Brazelton, T. B. (1992). *Touchpoints: Your child's emotional and behavioral development.* Reading, MA: Addison-Wesley. This comprehensive reference book by the pediatrician who developed the Brazelton Neonatal Behavioral Assessment Scale discusses and gives advice to parents relating to issues that come up during the first six years of children's lives. The author defines "touchpoints" as universal spurts of development and periods of regression during childhood.

Kopp, C. (1994). *Baby's steps: The "whys" of your child's behavior in the first two years.* New York: W. H. Freeman. An authority in the field focuses on how development leads children to act the way they do. Special "Snapshot" sections give entertaining real-life examples, and there are suggestions for how you can help your own baby or toddler.

Olds, S. W. (1989). *The working parents' survival guide.* Rocklin, CA: Prima. A comprehensive guide for parents that draws on research about the effects of their employment on their children and offers practical suggestions for their care, both by parents and substitute caregivers.

Stern, D. N. (1990). *Diary of a baby.* New York: Basic Books. A noted developmental psychologist describes what a baby sees, feels, and experiences in the first 22 months of life.

EARLY CHILDHOOD

Change continues in early childhood—ages 3 to 6—but not so rapidly as in infancy and toddlerhood. Even though revolutionary developments no longer appear daily or weekly, they still characterize the three major aspects of development.

During this period Vicky and Jason both become more adept physically, more competent cognitively, and more complex socially. For example, Jason's language ability improves dramatically as he masters the rules of English syntax and the secrets of conversation. He can explain himself to others and can deliberately learn from what they have to say. Vicky increasingly thinks of herself as a member of groups: As part of a family she learns from others in the family how to behave; as a girl she learns how females should act; as a child she learns childhood games and lore from her peers.

In Chapters 8, 9, and 10 we see continued advances in children's development. Physically, the young child takes on more and more adult proportions. Cognitively, she or he begins to use symbols and can sometimes have strikingly adult insights. Emotionally, children begin to identify with others and show a social conscience as well. By the end of this period the adults who love Jason can look at him and say, "He is one of us," with a depth of meaning that was impossible when he first emerged from toddlerhood.

CHAPTER 8
PHYSICAL DEVELOPMENT AND HEALTH IN EARLY CHILDHOOD

"I love you,"
said a great mother.
"I love you for what you are
knowing so well what you are.
And I love you more yet, child,
deeper yet than ever, child,
for what you are going to be,
knowing so well you are going far,
knowing your great works are ahead,
ahead and beyond,
yonder and far over yet."

Carl Sandburg, *The People, Yes,* 1936

By the time children reach early childhood (ages 3 to 6), they have come through the dangers of infancy to enter a healthier time of life. In this chapter we examine physical development and see how it is linked with other domains of development during early childhood.

For example, sleep patterns of young children are influenced by both cultural attitudes and emotional experiences. Motor development affects and is influenced by cognitive and emotional development, as, for example, in children's increasing proficiency in fine motor coordination, which lets them express their thoughts and feeling through art. Children's health and safety are linked to many environmental influences, including their parents' life circumstances, which affect how well they can care for their children. This is especially evident in the tragic results of child abuse and neglect, poverty, and homelessness.

While the most obvious effects of these conditions may be physical, all affect other aspects of a child's development as well. We look at such issues in their ecological context, focusing on the child, the family, the neighborhood, and the larger culture. All exert their influence; all are connected. When you have read this chapter, you should be able to answer such questions as the following:

PREVIEW QUESTIONS

- ◆ How do children grow physically between ages 3 and 6?
- ◆ What are the major motor achievements of early childhood?
- ◆ How does children's artwork show the maturation of their intellect?
- ◆ What are normal sleep needs and common sleep problems in early childhood?
- ◆ How healthy are the years of early childhood?
- ◆ What are the causes of child abuse and neglect? What are the consequences?

It is Vicky's third birthday. In comparison with a year ago, Vicky is very different. She is bigger and is capable of bigger things. In her next 3 years there will be still greater changes. Vicky grows more slowly now than in her first 3 years, but she makes much progress in coordination and muscle development and begins to do many more things.

PHYSICAL GROWTH AND CHANGE

APPEARANCE, HEIGHT, AND WEIGHT

Boys and girls lose their chubby toddler shapes and begin to take on the slender, athletic appearance of childhood. As children's abdominal muscles develop, their potbellies slim down. Their trunks, arms, and legs all grow longer. Children's heads are still relatively large, but (in keeping with the cephalocaudal principle— see Chapter 5) the other parts of their bodies continue catching up as body proportions steadily become more adultlike. ·

The pencil mark on the wall that shows Vicky's height at 3 years is almost 38 inches from the floor. Although a 3-year-old does not grow as quickly as an infant or toddler, Vicky is 4 inches taller than she was a year ago. Boys at age 3 are slightly taller and heavier than girls, with more muscle per pound of body weight. Girls have more fatty tissue. Over the next few years, both Vicky and Jason will continue to grow a steady 2 to 3 inches per year and gain 4 to 6 pounds annually, until they reach the growth spurt of puberty. (See Table 8-1.)

STRUCTURAL AND SYSTEMIC CHANGES

The changes in how children look reflect developments inside their bodies. Muscular and skeletal growth progresses, making children stronger. Cartilage turns to bone at a faster rate than before, and bones become harder, giving the child a firmer shape and protecting the internal organs. These changes, coordinated by the maturing brain and nervous system, promote the development of both gross (large-muscle) and fine (small-muscle) motor skills. The increased capacities of the respiratory and circulatory systems improve physical stamina and, along with the developing immune system, keep children healthier.

NUTRITION

Ellen looks at the tiny amount of food Vicky eats these days and wonders where she is getting all her energy—surely not from those small portions. This change

TABLE 8-1

PHYSICAL GROWTH, AGES 3 TO 6 (50TH PERCENTILE)*				
	HEIGHT, INCHES		WEIGHT, POUNDS	
AGE	BOYS	GIRLS	BOYS	GIRLS
3	38	$37\frac{1}{4}$	$32\frac{1}{4}$	$31\frac{1}{4}$
$3\frac{1}{2}$	$39\frac{1}{4}$	$39\frac{1}{4}$	$34\frac{1}{4}$	34
4	$40\frac{1}{4}$	$40\frac{1}{2}$	$36\frac{1}{2}$	$36\frac{1}{4}$
$4\frac{1}{2}$	42	42	$38\frac{1}{2}$	$38\frac{1}{2}$
5	$43\frac{1}{4}$	43	$41\frac{1}{2}$	41
$5\frac{1}{2}$	45	$44\frac{1}{2}$	$45\frac{1}{2}$	44
6	46	46	48	47

*Fifty percent of children in each category are above this height or weight level; and 50 percent are below it.
SOURCE: Lowrey, 1978.

Although preschoolers eat less in proportion to their size than infants do, they can fulfill their nutritional needs quite easily—and even enjoy the process. Since they eat so little, it's important that their snacks, as well as their regular meals, be nutritious.

in Vicky's appetite is normal. As children's growth rate slows, they need fewer calories per pound of body weight. Preschoolers eat less in proportion to their size than do infants, which often makes parents worry that their children are not eating enough.

Actually, the nutritional demands of early childhood are easily satisfied. A small child's daily protein requirement can be met with two glasses of milk and one serving of meat or an alternative like fish, cheese, or eggs. Vitamin A can come from carrots, spinach, egg yolk, or whole milk (among other foods). Vitamin C is in citrus fruits, tomatoes, and leafy dark-green vegetables (E. R. Williams & Caliendo, 1984). Calcium, essential to build bone mass in childhood, can come from dairy products, broccoli, and salmon. Lactose-intolerant children who have a bad reaction to milk can get necessary nutrients from a variety of other foods. No one food is essential to a child's diet.

Concerns about the cholesterol levels in children's diets have led to recommendations that children over age 2 should receive only about 30 percent of their total calories from fat, less than 10 percent of the total from saturated fat. Meat and dairy foods should remain in the diet to provide protein, iron, and calcium, but milk and other dairy products can now be skim or low-fat, and meats should be lean (AAP Committee on Nutrition, 1992a). Meeting energy and nutrient requirements could be difficult in a low-fat diet for 2- and 3-year-olds, who tend to have small appetites, drink a lot of milk, and resist new foods (Sigman-Grant, Zimmerman, & Kris-Etherton, 1993).

How much do young children eat? Over a 6-day period, 15 children aged 2 to 5 years took in roughly the same number of calories every day, even though they often ate very little at one meal and a great deal at another (Birch, Johnson, Andersen, Peters, & Schulte, 1991). Since small children are able to control their food intake in an orderly way, parents should not urge them to eat more than they want; this might interfere with a child's normal mechanism for balancing energy intake.

However, children whose diets are heavy in sugared cereal, cake, candy, and other low-nutrient foods will not have enough appetite for the food needed for healthy growth. So parents should offer only nutritious foods, including snacks. (See Box 8-1.) Many parents, of course, do this: In a study comparing 2- to 5-year-old children of mothers who work outside the home with children of nonemployed mothers, both ate equally well. But both groups of children had some dietary problems—too little calcium, iron, zinc, and vitamin E, and too much fat (R. K. Johnson, Smiciklas-Wright, Crouter, & Willits, 1992).

What do you think? *Much television advertising aimed at young children fosters poor nutrition by promoting fats and sugars rather than proteins and vitamins. How might parents counteract these pressures?*

gross motor skills
Physical skills involving the large muscles (like jumping or running).

fine motor skills *Abilities involving the small muscles (like buttoning or copying figures).*

MOTOR DEVELOPMENT

MOTOR SKILLS

Children aged 3 to 6 make great strides in motor skills—both *gross motor skills,* physical skills like jumping and running, which involve the large muscles, and *fine motor skills,* abilities like buttoning and copying figures, which involve the

BOX 8-1 ▪ THE EVERYDAY WORLD

ENCOURAGING HEALTHY EATING HABITS

Vicky refuses to eat anything but peanut butter and jelly sandwiches. Jason seems to live on bananas. Mealtimes seem more like art class, as they make snowmen out of mashed potatoes or lakes out of applesauce—and food remains uneaten on the plate.

A diminished appetite in early childhood is normal, however. Adults should not urge children to eat more than they want. If offered nourishing food, young children tend to take in what they need. A child who is energetic, with good muscle tone, bright eyes, glossy hair, and the ability to spring back quickly from fatigue, is unlikely to be inadequately nourished (E. R. Williams & Caliendo, 1984). The following suggestions can make mealtimes pleasanter and children healthier.

♦ Keep a record of what a child eats. The child may in fact be eating enough.

♦ Serve simple, easily identifiable foods. Preschoolers often balk at mixed dishes like casseroles.

♦ Serve finger foods as often as possible.

♦ Introduce only one new food at a time, along with a familiar one the child likes.

♦ Offer small servings, especially of new or disliked foods; give second helpings if wanted.

♦ After a reasonable time, remove the food and do not serve more until the next meal. A healthy child will not suffer from missing a meal, and children need to learn that certain times are appropriate for eating.

♦ Give the child a choice—whether to have rye or whole wheat bread, a peach or an apple, yogurt or milk. No one food is essential; some substitute can provide the same nutrients.

♦ Encourage a child to help prepare food by making sandwiches or mixing and spooning out cookie dough.

♦ Have nutritious snack foods handy and allow the child to select favorites.

♦ Turn childish delights to advantage. Serve food in appealing dishes; dress it up with garnishes or little toys; make a "party" out of a meal.

♦ Don't fight "rituals," in which a child eats foods one at a time, in a certain order.

♦ Make mealtimes pleasant with conversation on interesting topics, keeping talk about eating itself to a minimum.

---

small muscles. With both types of motor skills, they merge abilities they previously had with ones they are now acquiring to produce more complex capabilities. This combination is known as a *system of action*.

Gross Motor Skills

At 3, Jason can walk in a straight line. At 4, he can walk in a circle chalked on a playground. At 5, he manages to run in adult style, hard and fast. Meanwhile, Vicky's throwing ability is developing. At 3, she can throw without losing her balance, although her aim, form, and distance are still weak. At 4, she can play ringtoss when the peg is nearly 5 feet away. And at 5, she begins shifting her weight, stepping forward and getting her weight behind the throw.

These increasingly complex motor behaviors are possible because the sensory and motor areas of the cortex are better developed, permitting better coordination between what children want to do and what they can do. Their bones are stronger, their muscles are more powerful, and their lung power is greater.

Many advances take place in early childhood. (See Table 8-2.) At about $2\frac{1}{2}$ children begin to jump with both feet, a skill they have not been able to master before this time, probably because their leg muscles were not yet strong enough to propel their body weight upward. By $3\frac{1}{2}$ children comfortably alternate feet on a staircase, and by 5 they easily descend the large rungs of a ladder. Hopping is another skill hard to master well until about 4 years of age. Children begin to gal-

TABLE 8-2

3-YEAR-OLDS	4-YEAR-OLDS	5-YEAR-OLDS
Cannot turn or stop suddenly or quickly	Have more effective control of stopping, starting, and turning	Can start, turn, and stop effectively in games
Can jump a distance of 15 to 24 inches	Can jump a distance of 24 to 33 inches	Can make a running jump of 28 to 36 inches
Can ascend a stairway unaided, alternating the feet	Can descend a long stairway alternating feet, if supported	Can descend a long stairway unaided, alternating feet
Can hop, using largely an irregular series of jumps with some variations added	Can hop four to six steps on one foot	Can easily hop a distance of 16 feet

SOURCE: Corbin, 1973.

lop at about 4, do fairly well by 5, and are really skillful by $6\frac{1}{2}$. Skipping is harder, and although some 4-year-olds can skip, it is not until age 6 that most children can do this (Corbin, 1973).

Boys are slightly stronger than girls and have slightly more muscle, even in early childhood (Garai & Scheinfeld, 1968). By $6\frac{1}{2}$ boys typically throw and catch a ball better than girls, probably because parents and coaches tend to spend more time teaching boys these skills, both of which do not evolve as the result of maturation alone, but instead respond to learning and to practice (Corbin, 1973). Girls typically do better than boys at several other tasks involving limb coordination. Five-year-old girls, for example, are better than boys at doing jumping jacks, foot tapping, balancing on one foot, hopping, and catching a ball (Cratty, 1979). Girls tend to excel at small-muscle coordination. These differences may reflect societal attitudes that encourage different types of activities for boys and girls.

The gross motor skills of early childhood are required for sports, dancing, and other activities that begin during middle childhood and may last a lifetime. There seems to be virtually no limit to the number and kind of motor acts children can learn, at least to some degree, by the age of 6. But children vary greatly in adeptness, depending on their genetic endowment and their opportunities to learn and practice motor skills.

Children under age 6 are rarely ready to take part in *any* organized sport. Only 20 percent of 4-year-olds can throw a ball well, and only 30 percent are good at catching (AAP Committee on Sports Medicine and Fitness, 1992). The best way to help children develop physically is to encourage them to be active at an appropriate level for their state of maturity, in unstructured free-play situations. Parents and teachers can help by offering young children the opportunity to climb and jump on safe, well-sized equipment; by providing balls and other toys small enough to be easily grasped and soft enough not to be harmful; and by offering gentle coaching when a child seems to need help.

Fine Motor Skills

Three-year-olds have made significant gains in eye-hand and small-muscle coordination. At 3, Vicky can take a crayon and a big sheet of newsprint and draw a circle. She can pour milk into her cereal bowl, and she can button and unbutton her clothes well enough to dress herself and use the toilet. At 4, Jason can cut along a line with scissors, draw a person, make designs and crude letters, and fold paper into a double triangle. At 5, children can string beads, control a pencil, and copy a square, and they show a preference for using one hand over the other.

HANDEDNESS

In the 1992 United States presidential election all three candidates—Bill Clinton, George Bush, and Ross Perot—were left-handed. Ten percent of the population is left-handed, males more likely than females. What is the significance of left-handedness for development? The preference for using one hand more than the other, which is usually evident by 3 years of age, is called *handedness.* Although the concept seems simple, determination of a person's handedness may be difficult, since not everybody prefers one hand for every task.

handedness *Preference for using a particular hand.*

The propensity for human beings to be right-handed seems to arise from the development of the human brain. Since the left hemisphere of the brain controls the right side of the body and since the left hemisphere is usually dominant, most people favor their right side. In people whose brains are more symmetrical (through heredity or aspects of fetal growth), the right hemisphere tends to dominate, making them left-handed (Coren, 1992; Porac & Coren, 1981).

Advantages and Disadvantages of Left or Right Dominance

Although right-handedness is usually the preferred characteristic (see Box 8-2), both "lefties" and "righties" experience some advantages and some disadvantages. Benjamin Franklin, Michelangelo, Leonardo da Vinci, and Pablo Picasso were all left-handed. All had highly developed spatial imagination, a quality that may be stronger in left-handed people. This may explain the high proportion of

---

BOX 8-2 ■ AROUND THE WORLD

CULTURAL ATTITUDES TOWARD HANDEDNESS

Around the world and over the ages, many cultures have considered right-handedness "better" than left-handedness. In Japan, many parents try to force their children to use the right hand, even going to such extremes as binding the left hand with tape. In many Islamic societies, the left hand is used for private washing after toileting; using the same hand for writing, for eating, or for serving food (among other things) is considered offensive. In the United States, some elderly adults who showed an early preference for the left hand remember being forced to learn how to write with the right hand.

Traces of the idea that left-handedness is abnormal or evil can be found in words like *sinister* (suggesting something evil) from the Latin word meaning "on the left," and *gauche* (meaning "awkward"), the French word for "left." And the favorable connotations of right-handedness live on in *dexterity* and *adroitness* (both meaning "skillfulness")—the first from the Latin and the second from the French word for "right." The word *right* itself has favorable connotations: "correct," "moral," "fitting," and "proper."

No culture has encouraged left-handedness and, though none has completely abolished it, some societies have reduced its incidence. In "extremely permissive" societies, 10.4 percent of the population is left-handed (about the proportion in the United States); in "permissive" societies, the proportion drops to 5.9 percent; and in "harsh, restrictive" societies, it is only 1.8 percent (Hardyck & Petrinovich, 1977).

However, since scientific evidence so far does not provide any reason for favoring "righties," prejudice against the left-handed is on the wane in western industrial countries. Other parts of the world may soon follow on the right (oops, we mean the *correct*) path to equal rights (oops, we mean equal *treatment*) for the left-handed.

---

left-handed architects. Left-handed people may also be more likely to have special intellectual gifts. A study of more than 100,000 twelve- and thirteen-year-olds identified nearly 300 who scored extremely high on the Scholastic Aptitude Test (SAT). Twenty percent of this top-scoring group were left-handed, twice the rate of left-handedness in the general population (Bower, 1985). Furthermore, lefties tend to recover faster from brain damage (Hardyck & Petrinovich, 1977).

However, left-handed people suffer more from allergies, sleep problems, and migraine headaches and are more prone to stuttering, alcoholism, and other substance abuse. They also have higher rates of the reading disability *dyslexia* and the behavior problem *attention deficit disorder* (both discussed in Chapter 12) (Coren & Halpern, 1991; Geschwind & Galaburda, 1985).

A number of factors are associated with handedness. People with histories of birth stress are more likely to be left-handed, and left-handedness is also associated with delayed maturation. An abnormal infusion of hormones prenatally may have caused both the left-handedness and an immune deficiency. Although some scientists think genes determine dominance, twin studies do not support this. Identical twins are no more likely to be similar for handedness than fraternal twins, or than any two people in the population at large (Coren & Halpern, 1991).

On the whole, however, there is no compelling evidence that left-handed people are significantly different from right-handed ones in cognitive or physical abilities. Knowing which hand you hold your pencil in or pitch a ball with tells little about your overall physical or cognitive ability.

ARTISTIC DEVELOPMENT

Left-handed people, like this girl, are likely to be better at spatial tasks and to recover more quickly from brain damage. They also, however, are more likely to be allergic and to have reading and behavior problems. For the most part, neither left- nor right-handedness is clearly superior.

At 4, Jason draws one car or truck after another. When his mother encourages him to draw a person, he does—and then carefully draws wheels instead of feet. Jason's parents encourage his drawing, but they attach little importance to his artistic output. In this respect, they are similar to many earlier professional observers of child development. Now, however, we can see what children's early artwork is saying, thanks largely to the efforts of Rhoda Kellogg. With progress in fine motor development, children are able to reflect their cognitive development in their art. They also express themselves emotionally in their drawings.

Stages of Children's Art Production

Rhoda Kellogg (1970) has examined more than 1 million drawings by children, half under age 6. Since she has found drawings by young children similar in different cultures and countries, she concludes that early drawing reflects maturation of the brain. Let's see how. (See Figure 8-1.)

Two-year-olds *scribble*. Although adults tend to dismiss scribbling as random and meaningless, Kellogg has identified 20 basic scribbles, such as vertical and zigzag lines. In this first stage of drawing, the child is concerned chiefly with the placement of scribbles. Kellogg has identified 17 patterns of placement of scribbles on paper which appear by age 2.

By age 3, the *shape stage* appears. Now a child draws diagrams in six basic shapes—circles, squares or rectangles, triangles, crosses, Xs, and odd forms. Once in this stage, children quickly move on to the *design stage*, where they mix two basic shapes into a complex pattern. These designs are abstract rather than representational. Most adults, including parents and teachers, dismiss the drawings

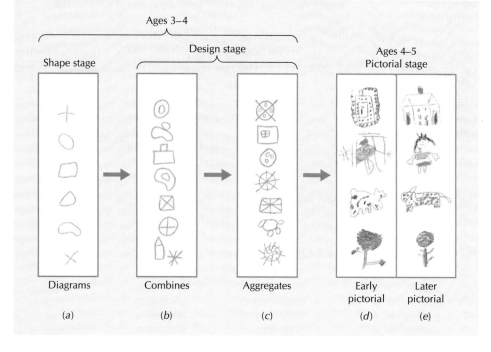

FIGURE 8–1
Artistic development in early childhood. There is a great difference between the very simple shapes shown in (a) and the detailed drawings in (e). The challenge for adults is to encourage children's creativity while acknowledging their growing facility in drawing. SOURCE: Kellog, 1970.

of early childhood because they are not pictures *of* anything. But Kellogg argues: "Adults who coach children to draw real-life objects are not really being helpful; they may even be causing harm" (1970, p. 35).

The *pictorial stage* begins between ages 4 and 5. Early drawings at this stage tend to suggest things from real life; later drawings are better defined. Although most adults tend to see the later drawings as a sign of progress, Kellogg points out that the switch from abstract design to representation marks a fundamental change in the purpose of children's drawing. They move away from a concern with form and design, primary elements in art. Usually after the first years of school, children who once happily drew with crayons abandon all interest in art, often because of the "guidance" of adults who encourage them to portray reality (Kellogg, 1970).

Kellogg quotes artist Pablo Picasso: "Adults should not teach children to draw but should learn from them" (1970, p. 36). In other words, we can sustain children's early creativity by letting them draw what they like without imposing suggestions or standards. They may surprise us. "What the great artist struggles to achieve, the child creates naturally" (1970, p. 39).

What do you think?   *Drawings from children's early pictorial stage show energy and freedom. Those from the later pictorial stage show care and accuracy. Why do you think these changes are happening? What do you think of this switch?*

Art Therapy

Therapists who help children deal with emotional traumas encourage them to draw pictures. A child who draws her feelings does not have to put them into words nor understand them and does not have to worry about saying the wrong thing (Groth-Marnat, 1984).

The colors the child chooses and what the child depicts may help express deep emotions (Garbarino, Dubrow, Kostelny, & Pardo, 1992). "The therapeutic use of play and art can help children reinstate their sense of inner control . . . and self-esteem, and develop . . . trust" (p. 204). Such therapy, which aims to restore a child's emotional health, is often valuable for children who have physical health problems. Fortunately, early childhood is no longer a dangerous time of life from a medical standpoint.

HEALTH

Because of widespread vaccination, many of the major diseases that used to fell young children are now fairly rare. Today accidents are more of a threat.

HEALTH PROBLEMS IN EARLY CHILDHOOD

Although these years are basically healthy, some problems do exist.

Minor Illnesses

Vicky's cheeks are flushed, her normally bright eyes are glazed, and her eyelids are drooping. She looks and acts sick; however, the minor illnesses of childhood may help Vicky build immunity to more serious illness.

Coughs, sniffles, stomachaches, and runny noses are part of childhood. These minor illnesses typically last from 2 to 14 days but are seldom serious enough to need a doctor's attention. Respiratory problems are common during these years—though less common than in infancy—because the lungs are not fully developed. Three- to five-year-olds average seven to eight colds and other respiratory illnesses a year. Later, during middle childhood, children average fewer than six such illnesses (Denny & Clyde, 1983), because of the gradual development of the respiratory system and natural immunity (resistance to disease).

Parmelee (1986) suggests that minor illnesses may have cognitive and emotional as well as physical benefits, since illness helps children learn how to cope with physical distress, and the coping enhances their sense of competence. It also can help them understand someone else's problems.

For example, when Vicky sees her parents, her playmates, her brother, and other people going through similar bouts with illness, she has a better understanding of their feelings. Because she remembers how she felt, she learns *empathy*—the ability to put herself in another person's place and feel what that person is feeling. Also, she can help to comfort and care for another.

Vicky's illness also helps her understanding of language. She may have confused two meanings of the word *bad*—for the way she feels physically when her throat hurts and for her emotional state when she has done something wrong. Thus she may think she is sick (feels "bad") because she hit her brother (was a "bad" girl). Her illness gives Ellen a chance to clarify meanings, and reassure her: "I know you feel bad because you're sick, but you'll soon be well." It also points up the value of avoiding the word *bad* as applied to a child's behavior or to the child as a person.

Major Illnesses

What used to be a very vulnerable time of life is much safer now. Illness-caused deaths in childhood are relatively rare compared with such deaths in adulthood (Starfield, 1991). Children's death rates from all kinds of illness have come down in recent years. Since 1950, deaths from influenza and pneumonia have dropped by 84 percent, although respiratory diseases are still the major cause of death among infants and children worldwide. The 5-year survival rate for cancer (in medical terms, considered a cure) has risen sharply for children under 15 diagnosed between 1977 and 1988, compared with those diagnosed between 1967 and 1973 (American Cancer Society, 1993).

HIV and AIDS in Children.   Children infected with the human immunodeficiency virus (HIV) are at a high risk to develop AIDS (acquired immune deficiency syndrome). In addition, the child's entire family may be stigmatized by the community, and the child may be shunned in the neighborhood or kept out of school, even though there is virtually no risk of infecting classmates. Infected people do not transmit HIV to others, even when they share toys, toothbrushes, eating utensils, toilets, and bathtubs (Rogers et al., 1990).

According to the American Academy of Pediatrics Task Force on Pediatric AIDS (1991), children who carry the HIV virus but do not show any disease symptoms should be treated like well children at home and in school. They do not need to be isolated, either for their own health or for that of other children. But children who show symptoms of HIV infection need special care and special education. These children may develop central nervous system dysfunction that can interfere with their ability to learn and can also cause behavior problems. Under the provisions of the Education for All Handicapped Children Act, these children should be educated in the least restrictive environment—first at school and then, as the disease progresses, at home.

Most children with AIDS show developmental delays and behave like younger, less competent children. The AIDS epidemic claims many victims other than those who die of related illnesses. Among those most grievously affected are children of stricken mothers. By the end of 1995, an estimated 24,600 children and 21,000 adolescents will have lost their mothers (Michaels & Levine, 1992). Most of these orphans will come from low-income African American and Hispanic families.

Who will care for these children? Some will be taken in by relatives, often already overburdened by their own families or by age, as in the case of grandparents called upon to raise second families. Some will go into foster care or adoptive homes. Most will face periods of uncertainty and instability in which their grief at losing their mothers will be aggravated by their fears about the future. This social catastrophe poses great challenges to society.

Accidental Injuries

Between ages 2 and 6, Vicky hurts herself about once every three hours—from falling down, bumping into furniture, and playing with other children. This is typical, based on a study in day care centers (McGrath, Fearon, & Achat, 1994). Most of these "boo-boos" are minor and forgotten after a hug and a kiss.

Since children are naturally venturesome and naive, parents and other adults have to be sure they take precautions to avoid accidents, as this little girl is doing by wearing a life preserver.

Still, accidents are the leading cause of death in childhood, usually because of automobiles. Children in the United States are far more likely to die as the result of injury than are European children (B. C. Williams & Miller, 1991, 1992).

All 50 states and the District of Columbia have laws requiring young children to be restrained in cars, either in specially designed seats or by standard seat belts (AAP, 1990). The restraints are effective: Children who are *not* restrained are 11 times more likely to die in an automobile accident than those who are restrained (Decker, Dewey, Hutcheson, & Schaffner, 1984). But the laws are not always effective. Active young children often rebel against the discomfort of wearing seat belts, and parents frequently give in. An Australian study found that educating preschoolers about the importance of wearing restraints was more effective than threatening parents with police checks and fines (Bowman, Sanson-Fisher, & Webb, 1987). However, young children are more likely to be hit *by* cars than to be injured *in* them (B. C. Williams & Miller, 1992).

Most fatal nonvehicular accidents occur in and around the home: Children drown in bathtubs, pools, and buckets containing liquids (as well as in lakes, rivers, and oceans); are burned in fires and explosions; fall from heights; drink or eat poisonous substances (see Table 8-3); choke on small objects; get caught in mechanical contrivances; fall out of supermarket shopping carts; and suffocate in traps like abandoned refrigerators.

Children in day care suffer fewer injuries than do children cared for at home. Almost half of all day care center injuries occur on playgrounds; one in three are from falls, often resulting in skull injury and brain damage (Thacker, Addiss, Goodman, Holloway, & Spencer, 1992; Sacks et al., 1989). Children can be protected by covering ground surfaces with impact-absorbing materials like wood chips, loose sand, or mats.

Children are naturally venturesome and unaware of danger. It is hard for caretakers to balance between overprotecting children and letting them learn from risk. Laws like those requiring car restraints, "child-proof" caps on medicine bot-

TABLE 8-3

THE FIVE MOST COMMON POISONS INGESTED IN AMERICA, 1983–1992 (ALL AGES)	
TOXIC SUBSTANCE	PERCENTAGE* OF ALL POISONINGS
1 Cleaning products	9.4
2 Analgesics (like aspirin)	9.3
3 Cosmetics	7.5
4 Plants	6.5
5 Cough/cold preparations	5.1

*Percentages based on 12.5 million incidents reported nationally.
SOURCE: Krenzelok, 1994.

tles, and mandatory helmets for bicycle riders have improved child safety. Suggestions for reducing accident risks are given in Table 8-4.

DENTAL HEALTH

By age 3, all a child's primary, or deciduous, teeth are in place. Vicky can now chew whatever she wants. Even though the first "baby teeth" will fall out by age 6, they are important for jaw and permanent tooth development. Furthermore, the habits established now are important for lifelong dental health. The widespread use of fluoride and high levels of dental care have dramatically reduced the incidence of tooth decay in children (Herrmann & Roberts, 1987).

TABLE 8-4

REDUCING ACCIDENT RISKS FOR CHILDREN	
ACTIVITY	PRECAUTIONS
Bicycling	Helmets reduce risk of head injury by 85 percent and brain injury by 88 percent.
Skateboarding and roller blading	Children should wear helmets and protective padding on knees, elbows, and wrists.
Using fireworks	Families should not purchase fireworks for home use.
Lawn mowing	Children under 12 should not operate walk-behind mowers; those under 14 should not operate ride-on mowers; small children should not be close to a moving mower.
Swimming	Swimming pools should not be installed in backyards of homes with children under 5; pools already in place need a fence around all four sides, with gates having high, out-of-reach, self-closing latches.
Playing on a playground	A safe surface under swings, slides, and other equipment can be 10-inch-deep sand, 12-inch-deep wood chips, or rubber outdoor mats; separate areas should be maintained for active play and quiet play, for older and younger children.
Using firearms	Guns should be kept unloaded and locked up, with bullets locked in separate place; children should not have access to keys; adults should talk with children about the risks of gun injury.
Eating	To prevent choking, young children should not eat hard candies, nuts, grapes, and hot dogs (unless sliced lengthwise, then across); food should be cut into small pieces; children should not eat while talking, running, jumping, or lying down.

SOURCE: Adapted from American Academy of Pediatrics, AAP, 1993; AAP & Center to Prevent Handgun Violence, 1994.

Thumb-Sucking

Aside from giving a baby a pacifier to help satisfy sucking needs, parents can usually safely ignore the habit of thumb-sucking in children under 4 years of age. However, the permanent teeth, which begin to appear at about age 6, are developing during early childhood and will be affected if thumb-sucking does not stop before age 6. If children stop sucking their thumbs or fingers by then, their teeth are not likely to be permanently affected (Herrmann & Roberts, 1987).

Prolonged thumb-sucking seems to be more of a habit than the result of emotional disturbance. It responds better to treatment designed to break the habit, like a dental appliance, than to psychological counseling, which has little or no effect. Children over 4 who are still thumb-suckers are sometimes fitted with a dental appliance that corrects any existing malformation of the teeth and also discourages sucking. Success rates with these appliances have been high—about 80 percent (Haryett, Hansen, & Davidson, 1970).

HEALTH IN CONTEXT: ENVIRONMENTAL INFLUENCES

Why do some children have fewer illnesses and injuries than others? Again we see the importance of looking at the ecological context of health. A child's own genetic heritage contributes to some illness: Some children are predisposed toward some medical conditions. But a major role is played by influences in the home, the school, the neighborhood, and the larger society. Environmental factors like nutrition, parental care, frequency of contact with other children, and the presence of noxious substances exert their influence. Besides purely physical factors, family situations involving stress and economic hardship may make some children more vulnerable than others.

Exposure to Illness

Children in larger families are sick more often than those in small families (Loda, 1980). Children in day care centers are two to four times more likely to pick up mild infectious diseases (like colds, flu, and diarrhea) than are children raised at home. They also have a higher risk of contracting more serious gastrointestinal diseases and hepatitis A (Thacker et al., 1992).

Caregivers can cut the rate of illness by more than half by teaching children how to wash their hands after using the toilet; washing their own hands frequently, especially after changing diapers; separating children in diapers from those who are toilet-trained; preparing food away from toilet areas; regularly disinfecting toys and equipment; and discouraging children from sharing food. Safe playground equipment and supervision can help prevent falls and other injuries. In fact, children in *high-quality* day care, where nutrition is well planned and illnesses are detected and treated early, tend to be healthier than those not in day care programs (AAP, 1986c).

Stress

Stressful events in the family—like moves, job changes, divorce, and death—seem to increase the frequency of minor illnesses and home accidents. In one study, children whose families had experienced 12 or more such stressful events were

TABLE 8-5

STRESSFUL EVENTS THAT CAN AFFECT CHILDREN'S HEALTH

Moving to a different house
Parent's changing job, losing job, or starting new job
Serious or prolonged disagreement between parents and their own parents or in-laws
Death of close friend or relative of child or parents
Increased financial problems of parents related to mortgage or business
Serious financial problems of parents
Serious or prolonged argument between parents or with a former spouse
Divorce or legal separation of parents
Reconciliation of parents after divorce or legal separation
Parents' sexual problems
Assault of mother by father
Serious illness or accident suffered by either parent
Serious illness or accident suffered by sibling
Serious illness among other family members
Mother's pregnancy
Court case involving either parent

SOURCE: Adapted from Beautrais, Fergusson, & Shannon, 1982.

more than twice as likely to have to go into the hospital as children from families who had experienced fewer than 4 traumatic events (Beautrais, Fergusson, & Shannon, 1982) (See Table 8-5.). Because entry into day care is stressful for many children (Craft, Montgomery, & Peters, 1992), parents and day care workers can give children tours of the center before they enter and can provide extra nurturance and attention during the first days away from home.

Children are also affected by adults' stress. Anything that reduces a caregiver's ability to cope may result in poor safety and sanitary measures. A distraught adult may forget to put away a kitchen knife or a poisonous cleaning fluid, to fasten a gate, or to make sure a child washes before eating.

Poverty

Poverty is unhealthy—and dangerous. Low income is the *chief* factor associated with poor health (J. L. Brown, 1987), and young children are the largest poverty group in the United States (Strawn, 1992). In the relatively affluent United States, about one in five children is poor, in terms of the official "poverty level" (about $12,000 a year for a family of three). About 40 percent of African American children and 32 percent of Latino children are poor, compared with fewer than 13 percent of white children (Children's Defense Fund, CDF, 1994).

A nationwide study, the results of which were published early in this decade, showed that among 2182 children 17 years old or younger about 10 percent had no medical insurance; 10 percent had no regular source of health care; and 18 percent got their medical care in emergency rooms, community clinics, or hospital outpatient departments (D. L. Wood, Hayward, Corey, Freeman, & Shapiro, 1990). Uninsured, poor, or nonwhite children were less likely to have seen a doctor in the past year, and uninsured children were less likely to have up-to-date immunizations.

Health Implications of Poverty.   Poor children often do not eat properly, grow properly, or get the immunizations and medical care they need. Often living in

BOX 8-3 ▪ FOOD FOR THOUGHT

HOW HOMELESSNESS AFFECTS CHILDREN

More than one-third of homeless people are young children and their single mothers, the fastest-growing segment of the homeless population (Bassuk, 1991). Every night, an estimated 100,000 American children sleep in emergency shelters, welfare hotels, abandoned buildings, cars, or on the street. The effects of such deprivation are devastating, physically and psychologically (Bassuk, 1991; J. L. Bass, Brennan, Mehta, & Kodzis, 1990; Y. Rafferty & Shinn, 1991; Bassuk & Rosenberg, 1990).

Most homeless children are under the age of 5, spending these crucial early years in an unstable and insecure environment. They tend to suffer severe depression and anxiety and to have high rates of developmental delays and learning difficulties, especially in language and motor skills. About half the homeless children in 14 family shelters in Massachusetts needed psychiatric referral (Bassuk & Rubin, 1987).

Homeless children and their parents are cut off from a supportive community, family ties, and institutional resources. The children suffer more health problems than do poor children who have homes. (See Figure 8-2.) They are three times more likely than other children to have missed immunizations, and they experience high rates of diarrhea, hunger, malnourishment, asthma, and elevated levels of lead. They are also at risk of anxiety, depression, and behavior problems like aggression and withdrawal. They have more problems in school, partly because they miss more of it; tend to do poorly on standardized reading and math tests; and are more likely to repeat a grade or be placed in special classes than are children with homes (Bassuk, 1991; Y. Rafferty & Shinn, 1991).

Homeless families need decent, permanent, and affordable housing. They also need safe, clean emergency shelters where they can get nutritious meals and have enough privacy so children can do their homework, get their sleep, and not be exposed to disease. These families also need health and child care, as well as other social services. Homelessness is a multifaceted problem requiring a multifaceted solution.

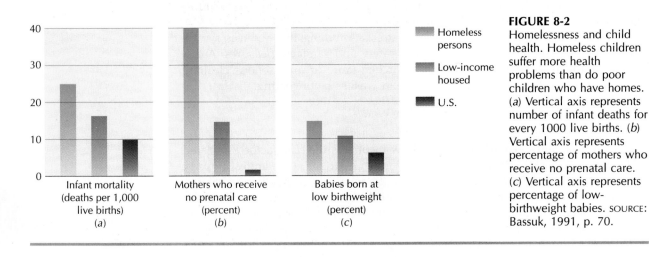

FIGURE 8-2
Homelessness and child health. Homeless children suffer more health problems than do poor children who have homes. (*a*) Vertical axis represents number of infant deaths for every 1000 live births. (*b*) Vertical axis represents percentage of mothers who receive no prenatal care. (*c*) Vertical axis represents percentage of low-birthweight babies. SOURCE: Bassuk, 1991, p. 70.

crowded, unsanitary housing, parents are too busy trying to feed and clothe their children to supervise them adequately. The children are at high risk of injury, partly because their parents do not know how to keep them safe or what to do if they hurt themselves, and partly because they do not have back-up caregivers (Santer & Stocking, 1991).

The problems of poor children begin before birth: Poor mothers often do not eat well or receive adequate prenatal care. Their babies are likely to be of low birthweight, to be stillborn, or to die soon after birth. Poor children are often

Homeless children spend their crucial early years in an unstable, insecure, chaotic environment. This family of five is living temporarily in a hotel. A month after federal officials seized the hotel, tenants complained that, although most drug dealing had stopped, living conditions were as bad as, or worse than, ever.

malnourished, and malnourished children tend to be weak and susceptible to disease. They are likely to suffer lead poisoning, hearing and vision loss, and iron-deficiency anemia, as well as stress-related conditions like asthma, headaches, insomnia, and irritable bowel. They also tend to have behavior problems, psychological disturbances, and learning disabilities (J. L. Brown, 1987; Egbuono & Starfield, 1982; Starfield, 1991). The problems of poor children who do not have homes are the greatest of all. (See Box 8-3.)

Death rates for African American children and teenagers are considerably higher than for white Americans for every cause except suicide, car injuries, and accidental poisoning and falls (B. C. Williams & Miller, 1992). Worldwide, the United States compares unfavorably with 10 European countries on low birthweight, infant survival rates, immunization rates, and children's death rates, especially those due to violence (National Center for Health Statistics, 1986–1990; World Health Organization, 1989). This country also compares unfavorably on childhood deaths from injury. (See Table 8-6.) The reasons for this difference reflect the lack of access to health care.

Social Policy and Poverty.   In the European countries listed in Table 8-6, no child has to go without either preventive health services or medical care if the family cannot afford it. The government provides free health care for everyone without asking whether they are "poor enough" to be eligible. More than 90 percent of European preschoolers receive recommended immunizations.

How can child health standards in the United States be raised? Free or low-cost health care can be made available for children and pregnant and nursing women; systems to track health care can prevent children from slipping between the cracks of different agencies; and more health care workers can be assigned to inner-city and rural areas. The major "safety net" for poor children has been the Aid to Families with Dependent Children (AFDC) program, funded by federal

TABLE 8-6

INJURY DEATHS PER 100,000 AMONG CHILDREN AGE 0–19 (1984–1986) FROM ALL CAUSES	
United States	
Total	30.5
Black	34.4
White and Other	29.8
Switzerland	24.9
West Germany†	23.3
Belgium*	23.2
Norway	22.3
France	21.5
Denmark	18.7
Ireland	17.9
Spain‡	16.9
England and Wales	15.6
Netherlands	13.1

*1983–1984 and 1986.
†The survey was taken before unification.
‡1983–1985.
SOURCE: National Center for Health Statistics, 1984–1988; World Health Organization, 1989.

and state governments. However, with the erosion of AFDC benefits over the past few years, growing numbers of families—including those from the working poor—fail to quality for any benefits (Strawn, 1992). All children need an adequate diet and adequate health care. If they get it, society will benefit.

What do you think? *A federal commitment to the problems of the elderly poor has lowered poverty rates in that population (see Figure 8-3): In 1990 the federal government spent an average of $11,350 per elderly person. In contrast, federal*

FIGURE 8-3
While poverty rates have dropped among the elderly, largely because of a federal commitment to funding for that age group, they have risen over the past two decades for children. The highest rates are for children under 6.
SOURCE: Strawn, 1992.

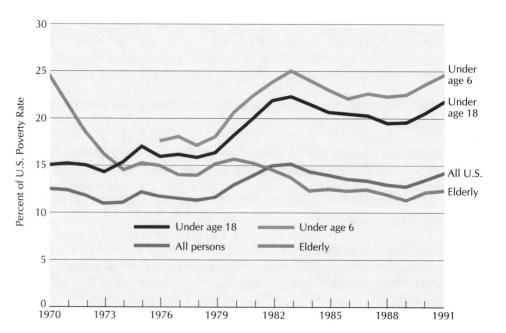

spending per child under age 18 was only $1,020 on average (Strawn, 1992). Who do you think should be responsible for children's well-being when parents cannot take good enough care of them: government, religious and community institutions, or the private sector? Why and how?

Lead Poisoning

To many experts in child health, lead poisoning is the most important environmental problem in the United States today (Bellinger, Stiles, & Needleman, 1992). It affects all economic levels—and its effects may last for years. Lead poisoning can cause seizures, mental retardation, or death (AAP Committee on Environmental Health, 1993). Some 3 million American children under age 6 are estimated to have lead levels high enough to interfere with normal cognitive development. Those at greatest risk are children (especially boys) from minority groups, living in poverty (Pirkle et al., 1994).

Children get lead in the bloodstream by drinking lead-contaminated water, eating contaminated food, putting contaminated fingers in their mouths, or inhaling dust particles in homes or schools with lead-based paint. Even low blood levels of lead can bring down performance on cognitive tests and in schoolwork and can affect both gross and fine motor function (Baghurst et al., 1992; Bellinger et al., 1992; Dietrich, Berger, & Succop, 1993).

Fortunately, moderate lead poisoning can be treated. In one study children aged 1 to 7 years got medicine to bring down their lead levels and were tested three times: once at the beginning of the study; after 7 weeks; and again after 6 months. The final test showed a relationship between lower blood lead levels and improved test scores (Ruff et al., 1993).

The larger goal for society, however, is the prevention of lead poisoning. Effective measures can be taken: A recent decline in blood lead levels in the United States was attributed to the removal of lead from gasoline and soldered food cans (Pirkle et al., 1994).

What do you think? *How can lead poisoning be prevented? Who should assume the responsibility for preventing it—government, building owners, educators, parents, or some combination of these?*

SLEEP PATTERNS AND PROBLEMS

Sleep patterns change throughout life, and early childhood has its own distinct rhythms. (See Figure 8-4.) Young children no longer wake up every 2 to 3 hours, but tend to sleep through the night and take one daytime nap; and they experience more deep sleep than they will later in life (Webb & Bonnet, 1979).

NORMAL SLEEP BEHAVIOR

"Daddy, leave the light on!" Jason calls after his father has tiptoed out of the room in the mistaken belief that Jason has finally fallen asleep. Daddy turns the light back on. Silence reigns for 5 minutes, and then: "I want a drink of water," "What's that noise outside by window?" "I'm cold." Jason is showing a typical change in bedtime behavior.

Taking a favorite blanket, stuffed animal, or other cuddly object to bed is normal. Many children depend on such transitional objects to help them fall asleep, but they eventually outgrow this need.

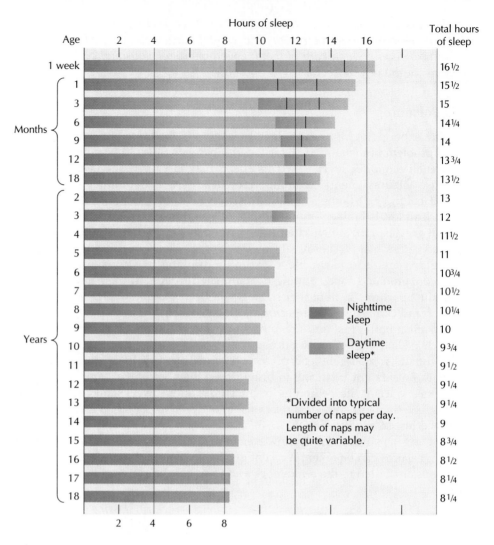

FIGURE 8-4
Typical sleep requirements in childhood. Children go from sleeping about equal amounts day and night to getting all their sleep in one long, extended nighttime period. While the pattern of steadily decreasing hours of sleep holds true generally, individual children may need more or fewer hours than shown here. SOURCE: Ferber, 1985.

transitional objects
Objects used repeatedly by a child as a bedtime companion.

Preschoolers go to sleep differently from infants and toddlers. It is hard for children aged 3 to 6 to let go of a stimulating world full of people and to be by themselves in bed. As a result, they take longer than younger children to fall asleep. While children under 2 will play quietly by themselves or with a sibling before falling asleep, children 3 years old and older are more likely to want a light left on and to sleep with a favorite toy or blanket. Such *transitional objects* help a child make the transition from dependent baby to independent child.

Parents sometimes worry that their child cannot fall asleep without a tattered blanket, a stuffed animal, or some other cuddly object. But there seems to be no basis for worry. In one study, 11-year-olds who at age 4 had slept with cuddly objects were now outgoing, sociable with adults, and likely to be self-confident; they still enjoyed playing by themselves and were not likely to be worriers. At age 16, teenagers who as children had insisted on taking a cuddly object to bed were just as well adjusted as those who had not (Newson, Newson, & Mahalski, 1982).

BOX 8-4 ■ THE EVERYDAY WORLD

HELPING CHILDREN TO SLEEP WELL

Helping a child get a good night's sleep clearly helps the parents too. When a young child has trouble going to sleep or wakes often during the night, the parents can neither relax nor sleep; they get cranky and become irritated with the child, and the entire family feels the strain. Here are some ways to make bedtime pleasant and nighttime refreshing for everyone (American Academy of Pediatrics, AAP, 1992b; L. A. Adams & Rickert, 1989; Graziano & Mooney, 1982):

HELPING CHILDREN GO TO SLEEP

♦ Establish a regular, unrushed bedtime routine—about 20 minutes of quiet activities, like reading a story, singing, or having quiet conversation.
♦ Allow no scary or loud television shows.
♦ Avoid highly stimulating, active play before bedtime.
♦ Keep a small night light on if it makes the child feel more comfortable.
♦ Stay calm but don't yield to requests for "just one more" story, one more drink of water, or one more bathroom trip.
♦ If you're trying to break a child's habit, offer rewards for good bedtime behavior, like stickers on a chart, or simple praise.
♦ Try putting your child to sleep a little later. Sending a

child to bed too early is a common reason for sleep problems.
♦ If a child's fears about the dark or going to sleep have persisted for a long time, look for a program to help the child learn how to relax, how to substitute pleasant thoughts for frightening ones, and how to cope with stressful situations.

HELPING CHILDREN GO BACK TO SLEEP

♦ If a child gets up during the night, take him or her back to bed. Speak calmly, pat the child gently on the back, but be pleasantly firm and consistent.
♦ After a nightmare, reassure a frightened child and occasionally check in on the child. If frightening dreams persist for more than 6 weeks, consult your doctor.
♦ After night terrors, do not wake the child. If the child wakes, don't ask any questions. Just let the child go back to sleep.
♦ Help your child get enough sleep on a regular schedule; overtired or stressed children are more prone to night terrors.
♦ Walk or carry a sleepwalking child back to bed. Childproof your home with gates at the top of stairs and at windows and with bells on the child's bedroom door, so you'll know when she or he is out of bed.

PROBLEMS WITH SLEEP

Sometimes troubles with sleep may indicate a deep-seated emotional problem. Any sleep problem that persists needs to be examined. Walking or talking during sleep, however, are both fairly common and usually harmless, and most sleep problems yield to fairly simple parental measures. (See Box 8-4.)

Bedtime Struggles

Many children—from 20 to 30 percent, according to one study—engage in bedtime struggles lasting more than 1 hour and wake their parents frequently at night. When researchers looked at 96 children between 6 months and 4 years of age, they found five experiences that distinguish children with these problems (Lozoff, Wolf, & Davis, 1985). One is sleeping in the same bed with parents: It is simply more tempting and easier to wake someone in the same bed than in the next room. But the other four conditions signal the presence of family stress. The children's families were more likely to have experienced an accident or illness; or the children were more likely to have mothers who were depressed, were ambivalent toward the child, or had recently changed their schedules to be away for most of the day.

Night Terrors and Nightmares

Night terrors and nightmares both begin to appear in early childhood. About 1 in 4 children aged 3 to 8 suffer from one or the other (Hartmann, 1981). Boys are more likely than girls to experience night terrors, but there is no sex difference for nightmares (Parkes, 1986).

A *night terror* is characterized by abrupt awakening from deep sleep in a state of panic. The child may scream and sit up in bed, breathing quickly and staring. Yet she or he is not really awake, quiets down quickly, and the next morning does not remember anything. These episodes alarm parents more than they do children, and they are rarely a serious problem. They usually go away by themselves, do not signal underlying emotional problems, and may simply be an effect of very deep sleep. If they are severe and long-lasting and occur once a week or more, causing conflict between child and parents, some physicians prescribe a short course of therapy with an antihistamine or antidepressant drug (McDaniel, 1986).

Whereas night terrors usually occur within an hour of falling asleep, *nightmares* come toward morning and are often vividly recalled (Hartmann, 1981). An occasional bad dream is not a cause for alarm, especially in children under 6, who are most likely to have them. But persistent nightmares, especially those that make a child fearful and anxious during waking hours, may be a signal that the child is under too much stress. Repetitive dream themes often point to a specific problem the child cannot solve when awake, which rises to the surface during sleep.

Nighttime Fears

Fear of the dark and fears at bedtime can be treated. A group of children 6 to $13\frac{1}{2}$ years old who had had severe and chronic fears for an average of 5 years attended a 3-week self-control training program with their parents. The children learned how to relax, how to substitute pleasant thoughts for frightening ones, and how to talk to themselves to cope with stressful situations. Of 34 children followed up $2\frac{1}{2}$ to 3 years after treatment, 31 had maintained significant improvement (Graziano & Mooney, 1982). A number of children and parents felt the children's ability to deal with their night fears helped them become more confident in facing problems in general.

Bed-Wetting (Enuresis)

enuresis *Bed-wetting.*

Most children stay dry, day and night, by 3 to 5 years of age. But *enuresis*, repeated urination during the day or night in clothing or in bed, is a common chronic condition. Since the condition is most common at night, it is considered a sleep problem. Diagnosis hinges on at least two occurrences per week for at least 3 months after 5—or its causing significant stress or impairment in important areas of functioning, like school (*Diagnostic and Statistical Manual of Mental Disorders*, DSM-IV, 1994). About 7 percent of 5-year-old boys wet the bed, compared with 3 percent of girls; at age 10, it is 3 percent of boys and 2 percent of girls. Most outgrow the problem without any special help; by age 18, only 1 percent of males and even fewer females have the problem (DSM-IV, 1994). Fewer than 1 percent of bed-wetters have any true physical disorder; heredity and rate of development may be factors.

Enuresis runs in families. About 75 percent of bed-wetters have a close relative who also wet the bed, and identical twins are more similar for enuresis than are fraternal twins (DSM-IV, 1994). Among over 1000 children in New Zealand, family history was the strongest predictor of childhood bed-wetting (Fergusson, Horwood, & Shannon, 1986). Psychosocial factors like social and economic background or stressful life events like divorce had little effect on bed-wetting.

Instead, factors related to biology—in addition to family history—seem crucial. Factors associated with enuresis include small size at birth, small functional bladder capacity (the ability to hold urine without contracting), developmental delays in infancy and toddlerhood, and a deficiency of a particular hormone (Rappaport, 1993; Fergusson et al., 1986).

Children and their parents need to be reassured that the problem is common and not serious and that the child is not to blame and should not be punished. In general, parents need not do anything unless children themselves see the bed-wetting as a problem. The most effective treatments include rewarding children for staying dry; waking children when they begin to urinate by using devices that ring bells or buzzers; giving antidepressant drugs—this as a last resort only, and for no more than 6 months after the last occurrence, and then tapering off (McDaniel, 1986); and teaching children to practice controlling the sphincter muscles and to stretch the bladder (Rappaport, 1993).

Sleep problems are sometimes the first symptom experienced by children abused by adults. These unfortunate youngsters also suffer other grave consequences of maltreatment, especially when those responsible are the most important people in their lives, their parents.

MALTREATMENT OF CHILDREN: ABUSE AND NEGLECT

Some parents cannot or will not meet their children's most basic needs. Unfed, neglected children starve; left without clothing, they freeze; left alone, they perish in fires. Other children are actively abused: kicked, beaten, burned, shaken, thrown against walls and radiators, strangled, suffocated, sexually molested, even buried alive. They are humiliated and terrorized by the people who are supposed to nurture them. Maltreatment takes several forms and any one form of maltreatment is almost always accompanied by one or more of the others (Belsky, 1993):

- *Child abuse* involves physical injury, in a pattern often referred to as the *battered child syndrome* (Kempe, Silverman, Steele, Droegemueller, & Silver, 1962).
- *Sexual abuse* is any kind of sexual contact between a child and an older person.
- *Child neglect* is the failure to provide such necessary care as food, clothing, and supervision.
- Emotional neglect may cause the syndrome known as *nonorganic failure to thrive:* A baby fails to grow and gain weight at home despite adequate nutrition but improves when moved to a hospital and given emotional support.
- *Emotional abuse* involves action or failure to act, causing damage to a child's behavioral, cognitive, emotional, or physical functioning. It may include rejection, terrorization, isolation, exploitation, degradation, ridicule, or corruption.

child abuse *Maltreatment of children causing physical or psychological injury.*

battered child syndrome *Condition showing symptoms of physical abuse.*

sexual abuse *Sexual contact between a child and an older person.*

child neglect *Withholding of such necessary care as food, clothing, and supervision.*

nonorganic failure to thrive *Failure to grow and gain weight despite adequate nutrition, possibly due to emotional neglect.*

emotional abuse *Action or failure to act that damages children's behavioral, cognitive, emotional, or physical functioning.*

stop using words that hurt.

Start using words that help.

Words can hit a child as hard as a fist. And leave scars that last a lifetime. Even when you're upset...stop! Think about what you're saying. For helpful information, write: National Committee for Prevention of Child Abuse, Box 2866E, Chicago, IL 60690.

Physical abuse is not the only maltreatment children can receive. Emotional abuse can include rejection, terrorization, isolation, exploitation, degradation, ridicule, or corruption. Any of these can have grave consequences in both childhood and adulthood.

Mistreatment of children is more widely recognized today. Its incidence is hard to determine because methods for collecting data are flawed and interpretation difficult. But it seems that more than 2.7 million children in the United States are mistreated—resulting in some 2000 deaths annually (National Research Council, NRC, 1993). The rise since 1976, when the first national statistics of abuse were compiled, may represent an actual increase in mistreatment or better reporting, or both. Neglect, the most common form, is probably underreported. Sexual abuse has shown the largest increase. Emotional abuse, the least studied, seems to be present in all forms of child maltreatment.

CAUSES OF ABUSE AND NEGLECT

Why do adults hurt or neglect children? The answer is complex, since the cause of maltreatment involves many factors. We can look at the problem using an ecological perspective, as described by Urie Bronfenbrenner. (See Chapter 1.) This considers factors associated with the child, the abuser, the community, and the larger society.*

The Microsystem: The Abuser or Neglecter and the Child

More than 90 percent of all child abuse occurs at home (Child Welfare League of America, 1986).

The Abuser or Neglecter.   In the past, the mother was usually the abusing parent, probably since she was the person who spent the most time with the child. More recent analyses, however, suggest that men (who may or may not be the child's father) are committing more child abuse. This is true especially for sexual abuse and serious and fatal injuries (Bergman, Larsen, & Mueller, 1986; Browne & Finkelhor, 1986).

In the past, physicians and psychologists focused on the physical aspects of abuse and saw it as an individual disorder or psychological disturbance of the parents. Today we look more closely at how different factors interact to cause abuse. Maltreatment is seen as a symptom of an extreme disturbance of child rearing, which usually appears in the context of other serious family problems like poverty, alcoholism, stress, or antisocial behavior. However, most parents with these problems do not abuse or neglect their children. So such factors do not inevitably predict mistreatment.

While over 90 percent of abusers are not psychotic and do not have criminal personalities, many are lonely, unhappy, anxious, depressed, angry, aggressive, and under great stress. They often have health or substance abuse problems that impair their ability to raise children, and they tend to have low self-esteem and poor impulse control. About one-third of abusing parents were abused themselves as children. Some abusing parents may use their power over their children in a misplaced effort to gain control over their own lives. Neglectful parents, who tend to be impulsive and infantile, often have trouble planning life choices. Adult sexual abusers seem to have a wide range of personality disorders.

Abusers often hate themselves for what they do, yet feel powerless to stop.

*Unless otherwise referenced, this discussion is indebted to Belsky, 1993, and National Research Council, 1993.

Often deprived of good parenting themselves, they do not know how to be good parents to their own children. Often abuse begins when a parent who is already anxious, depressed, or hostile starts out to control a child physically, but then loses control over his or her own behavior and ends up shaking, beating, or otherwise harming the child.

Abusing parents tend to be ignorant of normal child development, expecting children to be toilet-trained, not to cry, or to stay clean and neat at an unrealistically early age. They tend to view as highly stressful behavior what most parents take in stride, and they have more confrontations with their children. Less effective in resolving problems, they recognize and feel bad about their inadequacy and incompetency as parents. They often expect their children to take care of *them* and become enraged when this does not happen.

Abusive parents have trouble reading babies' emotional expressions; thus they may be misinterpreting their babies' needs rather than ignoring them. A parent may try to feed a child who is actually crying in pain and then be frustrated when the baby spits the food back (Kropp & Haynes, 1987).

Neglectful parents, on the other hand, are likely to be apathetic, incompetent, and irresponsible and to ignore their children. Mothers of infants who fail to thrive tend to have been poorly nurtured themselves and to have had stressful relationships with their babies' fathers. These mothers tend to have more complications during pregnancy and childbirth than other mothers, gaining less weight, delivering earlier, and bearing smaller babies. They also have more trouble feeding their infants (Altemeir, O'Connor, Sherrod, & Vietze, 1985). They do not hug or talk to them; are unable to organize a safe, warm home environment; and seem to resent their babies (P. H. Casey, Bradley, & Wortham, 1984).

Abusive parents are more likely to have marital problems than other couples and to fight physically with each other. They have more children and have them closer together, and their households are more disorganized. They experience more stressful events than other families (J. R. Reid et al., 1982). The arrival of a new man in the home—a stepfather or the mother's boyfriend—often triggers abuse by the man. The adults tend to cut themselves off from neighbors, family, and friends, leaving them with no one to turn to in times of stress and no one to see what is happening. Neglectful parents are isolated within the family, tending to be emotionally withdrawn from spouse and children (Wolfe, 1985).

The Child. When parents who think poorly of themselves, had troubled childhoods, and have problems handling negative emotions have children who are particularly needy or demanding, abuse often results. Abused children's greater needs may stem from poor health, "difficult" personalities, or specific disabilities. They are more likely to have been preterm or low-birthweight babies; to be hyperactive, mentally retarded, or physically handicapped; or to show behavioral abnormalities (J. R. Reid et al., 1982). Victims of sexual abuse seem to have a greater-than-average need for affection, which may make them easy prey to child molesters (Tsai & Wagner, 1979).

Of course, most children with these characteristics are not abused. It is the interaction with other factors that results in maltreatment. It is possible that child-related components do not cause the initial abuse but rather serve to keep it up. Then the abuse itself affects children—often making them more aggressive and defiant and perpetuating the cycle.

The Exosystem: Jobs, Neighborhood, and Social Support

The outside world can create a climate for family violence. Unemployment, job dissatisfaction, social isolation, limited social ties, lack of assistance or relief for the primary caregiver, and poverty are all closely correlated with child and spouse abuse. But none of these are determining factors.

What, then, makes one low-income neighborhood a place where children are at high risk for being abused, while another, matched for ethnic population and income levels, is safer? Four inner-city Chicago neighborhoods had differing rates of child maltreatment. In the community called "North," eight children died from maltreatment from 1984 to 1987 (1 death for every 2541 children), about double the rate in "West," where one death occurred among 5571 children (Garbarino & Kostelny, 1993).

What accounted for these differences? Researchers interviewed community leaders in the area with the highest rate of abuse and in the area with the lowest. They found a depressed atmosphere in the high-abuse community. Criminal activity was obvious, physical spaces of community programs were dark and dreary, and people had trouble thinking of anything good to say. Even people who worked in local agencies knew little about community services and resources; had no sense of a social support system, either structured or informal; and showed no positive feelings about their political leaders.

In the low-abuse neighborhood, people readily talked about their community and, while acknowledging its problems, described it as a poor but decent place to live. A picture came through of a neighborhood with robust social support networks, well-known community services, and strong political leadership from the state senator serving the area. The research team concluded that "North" was an environment with "an ecological conspiracy against children" (Garbarino & Kostelny, 1993, p. 213).

The Macrosystem: Cultural Values and Patterns

Two cultural factors that seem to lead to child abuse are violent crime and belief in physical punishment of children.

Compared with other nations, the United States is a violent place. Homicide, wife battering, and rape are all common; resistance to gun control legislation is high. In this country children, who are often considered their parents' property, are the only people whom it is legal to hit. Although the Eighth Amendment to the United States Constitution prohibits cruel and unusual punishment for criminals, the 1977 Supreme Court ruling that school personnel may strike disobedient children is in effect. Thirty states still permit corporal punishment in schools, and minority and handicapped children are paddled more often than their classmates. In countries where violent crime is infrequent and children are rarely spanked—like Japan, China, and Tahiti—child abuse is rare (Celis, 1990).

LONG-TERM EFFECTS OF ABUSE AND NEGLECT

There is no single behavioral or emotional result of childhood abuse or neglect, but either one can produce grave consequences (Emery, 1989). Abused children often show delays in speech, linking emotional and cognitive development (Coster, Gersten, Beeghly, & Cicchetti, 1989). They are also more likely than are

TABLE 8-7

DEVELOPMENTALLY RELATED REACTIONS TO SEXUAL ABUSE	
AGE	**MOST COMMON SYMPTOMS**
Preschoolers	Anxiety
	Nightmares
	Inappropriate sexual behavior
School-age	Fear
	Mental illness
	Aggression
	Nightmares
	School problems
	Hyperactivity
	Regressive behavior
Adolescents	Depression
	Withdrawn, suicidal, or self-injurious behaviors
	Physical complaints
	Illegal acts
	Running away
	Substance abuse
More than one age group	Nightmares
	Depression
	Withdrawn behavior
	Neurotic mental illness
	Aggression
	Regressive behavior

SOURCE: Kendall-Tackett, Williams, & Finkelhor, 1993.

nonabused children to become aggressive themselves, delinquent, or criminal in adulthood (Dodge, Bates, & Pettit, 1990; Widom, 1989). Teenagers who failed to thrive in infancy are likely to have physical, cognitive, and emotional problems, apparently due to emotional neglect (Oates, Peacock, & Forrest, 1985). Teenagers who had been abused as children may react by running away (which may be a healthy move toward self-protection) or by adopting such self-destructive activities as drug use (NRC, 1993).

Sexual abuse carries its own specific consequences, which tend to vary according to a child's developmental status, as shown in Table 8-7. Sexually abused girls are more likely to become preoccupied with sex and to have problems with behavior and school achievement than are nonabused girls (Einbender & Friedrich, 1989). Adults who were sexually abused children are often fearful, anxious, depressed, angry, hostile, or aggressive. They often suffer from low self-esteem, do not trust people, and feel isolated and stigmatized. Not surprisingly, they tend to be sexually maladjusted. They often engage in self-destructive behavior like drug abuse, or antisocial behavior like crime, and they are likely to be raped or sexually assaulted as adults.

The severest trauma occurs in these situations: when a nonabusive parent does not believe the child's account of abuse and does not try to protect the child; when the child is removed from the home; and when the child has suffered more than one type of abuse (Kendall-Tackett, Williams, & Finkelhor, 1993; Browne & Finkelhor, 1986; Bryer, Nelson, Miller, & Krol, 1987; Burgess, Hartman, & Mc-Cormack, 1987). Sexual abuse leads to more symptoms when the abuser is someone close to the child; when the sexual contact has been frequent and over a long period of time; when force has been used; when there has been oral, anal, or vaginal penetration; and when the child has a negative outlook and coping style (Kendall-Tackett et al., 1993).

Emotional maltreatment has been linked to children's lying, stealing, low self-esteem, emotional maladjustment, dependency, underachievement, depression, failure to thrive, aggression, learning disorders, homicide, and suicide, as well as to psychological distress in later life (S. N. Hart & Brassard, 1987).

Why Some Children Do Not Show Scars of Abuse

According to one analysis, two-thirds of abused children grow up to become good parents; only one-third abuse their own children (Kaufman & Zigler, 1987). Many abused and neglected children are resilient, apparently because of protective factors, which range from characteristics of the child to the presence of supportive people, to other life experiences.

High intelligence seems to help: Children who test high on IQ tests tend to maintain good achievement test scores even when experiencing high levels of stress (Garmezy, Masten, & Tellegen, 1984). Also important is the way the child interprets events: Children who see abuse as coming from the parents' weaknesses or frustrations rather than as rejection of them seem to overcome the trauma better. One group of abused children who became well-adjusted adults showed such qualities as high self-esteem and advanced cognitive abilities (Zimrin, 1986).

A supportive person to whom the child can form an attachment helps: Women who had been abused as children but do not abuse their own children are likely to have had someone to whom they could turn for help, to have received therapy, and to have a good marriage or adult love relationship. Also, they are more openly angry about and better able to describe their own experience of abuse. Furthermore, they are more likely to have been abused by one parent and to have had a loving, supportive relationship with the other (Egeland, Jacobvitz, & Sroufe, 1988; Kaufman & Zigler, 1987). A comparable group of abused women who became abusers themselves had experienced more life stress and were more anxious, dependent, immature, and depressed than the nonabusers.

Growing up to become an abuser is far from an inevitable result of being abused as a child. The expectation that the one always causes the other may have led to self-fulfilling prophecies in some cases; in other cases, adults who were abused children feel like "walking time bombs," ready to explode into violence against their own children (Kaufman & Zigler, 1987).

HELPING FAMILIES IN TROUBLE OR AT RISK

One kind of help for families in which abuse is likely to occur is to prevent it. Another kind aims to stop abuse that has already occurred and repair its damage.

Preventing Maltreatment

Since abuse and neglect are much more common among young, poor, and uneducated parents, programs that seek to keep young people in school and prepare them for an occupation before they have children may forestall abuse.

This adult volunteer uses dolls to help young children realize they have control over their bodies and need not let anyone—even friends or family members—touch them. Educational programs for preventing sexual abuse need to walk a fine line between alerting children to danger and frightening them.

Other programs help parents who feel overwhelmed by the demands of parenting. The programs often train young parents thought to be at risk, giving them pointers in encouraging good behavior and discouraging misbehavior, teaching them activities to help children develop language and social skills, and giving expectant and new mothers information about babies' health (Wolfe, Edwards, Manion, & Koverola, 1988). Efforts may also include programs that offer subsidized day care, volunteer homemakers, home visitors, and temporary "respite homes" or "relief parents" to occasionally take children (Belsky, 1993; Wolfe, 1985).

Providing Help for the Abused and Their Families

Intervention can be implemented at the family, community, and cultural levels, and different programs can be undertaken at the same time to work together.

The Microsystem: The Family. Sometimes a child must be separated from abusive parents, but if at all possible, it is better to keep the child in the family and stop the abuse. One effective way to do this is to treat abusers as criminal offenders: People arrested for family violence are less likely to repeat the maltreatment (Bouza, 1990; Sherman & Berk, 1984).

Services for abused children and adults include shelters, education, and therapy. One effective program teaches parents child-management skills while providing therapy to help them deal with stress (G. R. Patterson, Chamberlain, & Reid, 1982). Parents Anonymous and other groups provide free, confidential group services. One evaluation of people attending such groups found physical abuse stopped after 1 month of attendance and verbal abuse decreased after 2 months (Ehresman, 1988).

For helping the victims of sexual abuse, the first step is to recognize the signs.

These include any extreme change of behavior such as loss of appetite; sleep disturbance or nightmares; regression to bed-wetting, thumb-sucking, or frequent crying; torn or stained underclothes; vaginal or rectal bleeding or discharge; vaginal or throat infection; painful, itching, or swollen genitals; unusual interest in or knowledge of sexual matters; and fear or dislike of being left in a certain place or with a certain person (USDHHS, 1984).

Young children need to be told that their bodies belong to them and that they can say no to anyone who might try to touch them or kiss them against their will, even if it is someone they love and trust. They also need to know that they are never to blame for what an adult does and that they can talk to their parents about anything without fear of punishment. And they need to be reassured that most adults want to help and take care of children, not hurt them. Abused children may receive play or art therapy and day care in a therapeutic environment.

The Exosystem: The Community.   In communities at high risk for child abuse, programs that reach beyond the family can be effective. One preschool program helped abused or neglected 3- to 5-year-olds who had become severely withdrawn. A teacher's aide and other preschoolers were trained to suggest or direct play activities and to give or receive objects during play, with the aim of encouraging the maltreated children to play with them. The trained 4-year-old "initiators" helped the withdrawn children become more sociable more effectively than the adults did (Fantuzzo et al., 1988). This kind of program shows the practical impact that child development research can have on the lives of children.

Medical treatment needs to be prompt and sensitive to a child's trauma level. A team approach includes physicians, nurses, social workers, and lawyers—all of whom need to be trained to identify abuse, collect evidence, document personal histories, and refer abusive families for help. Child protection agencies are established to investigate allegations of maltreatment and refer families to sources of help. Yet because of understaffing and underfunding, many cannot do so. One national survey found more than one-third of confirmed cases of maltreatment received no help (McCurdy & Daro, 1993).

When authorities remove children from their homes, the usual alternative is foster care, which has increased markedly during the past decade. This should be a temporary, emergency solution, but although the median stay in foster care is 1.5 years, in some cities the average is 5 years, often with placement in several different homes. Foster care removes a child from immediate danger; but it is often unstable, may also be an abusive situation, and further alienates the child from the family (NRC, 1993).

The Macrosystem: Cultural Values.   Abused children are often caught in a web of such conflicting societal values as protecting children's safety versus preserving families, respecting individual privacy versus maintaining confidentiality. When a child's life is in the balance, which value should take precedence? These are not easy questions to answer, especially since many allegations of abuse are never confirmed. Parents unjustly accused of abuse—as are some parents of babies who succumb to SIDs—suffer grievously and unfairly. Still, the newspapers are full of stories describing the deaths of children whose precarious situations were known to authorities—but who remained in the hands of the parents who had been abusing them and who ultimately struck the fatal blows.

What do you think? *In a case of suspected child abuse, three policies are possible: (1) Ignore it on grounds that parents have to discipline their children, (2) provide the abuser with counseling and provide a second chance, or (3) permanently separate the child from the abuser. How can social policy balance the child's best interest with the rights of the alleged abuser and any third parties like a spouse or other children in the home?*

The plight of abused and neglected children is one for which our society has not yet found effective remedies. Little is known about the effects of different kinds of helping actions, and meanwhile these children often grow up with many problems, at great cost to themselves and to society. Some of their problems spill over into the cognitive realm, discussed in Chapter 9.

SUMMARY

1   Children continue to grow quickly between the ages of 3 and 6, but more slowly than they do during infancy and toddlerhood. Boys are, on average, slightly taller and heavier than girls. The muscular, skeletal, nervous, respiratory, circulatory, and immune systems are maturing.

2   Proper growth and health depend on nutrition. Children between 3 and 6 eat less than before; a balanced diet of essential nutrients is important.

3   Motor development advances rapidly in early childhood. Children make great strides in gross and fine motor skills and eye-hand coordination. There are some sex differences in motor abilities that may reflect skeletal differences or societal expectations or both. Handedness is usually evident by age 3.

4   "Self-taught" art appears to reflect brain development. It progresses from scribbling to the shape stage, design stage, and pictorial stage. Art therapy helps children deal with feelings.

5   Minor illnesses such as colds and other respiratory illnesses are common during early childhood and may have cognitive and emotional benefits.

6   Because of the availability of vaccinations, major contagious illnesses are rare among children in developed countries, although incidences of some are rising.

7   Accidents are the leading cause of death in childhood; most accidents occur in or from automobiles or at home.

8   All the primary teeth have erupted by age 3. Preventive measures such as use of fluoride and early dental care have dramatically reduced the incidence of tooth decay in children. Sucking of fingers or thumb before age 6 is unlikely to cause permanent problems.

9   Factors such as exposure to other children, stress, poverty and hunger, and homelessness increase children's risk of illness or injury. Lead poisoning, a common environmental problem, interferes with cognitive development. It can be prevented and treated.

10   Sleep patterns change during early childhood, as they do throughout life. Young children tend to sleep through the night, take one daytime nap, and sleep more deeply than later in life.

11   It is normal for children to develop bedtime rituals to delay going to sleep. However, prolonged bedtime struggles and persistent nightmares may indicate emotional disturbances that need attention.

12   Night terrors, nightmares, and nighttime fears may appear in early childhood.

13   Enuresis (bed-wetting) is the most common chronic condition seen by pediatricians. It appears to have a genetic basis and is influenced by biological factors.

14 Statistics from the early part of this decade show that more than 2.7 million American children are mistreated, resulting in 2000 deaths annually. Characteristics of the victim and abuser, the family, the community, and the larger culture all contribute to child abuse and neglect. Abuse and neglect can have grave long-term effects; however, some prevention and intervention programs seem to be effective.

KEY TERMS

gross motor skills (306)
fine motor skills (306)
handedness (309)
transitional object (322)
enuresis (324)
child abuse (325)

battered child syndrome (325)
sexual abuse (325)
child neglect (325)
nonorganic failure to thrive (325)
emotional abuse (325)

SUGGESTED READINGS

Beckman, P. J., & Beckman Boyes, G. (1993). *Deciphering the system: A guide for families of young children with disabilities.* Cambridge, MA: Brookline. This comprehensive guide provides basic information about parents' rights under recent legislation affecting young children with disabilities, including the Individuals with Disabilities Education Act. It will take you through the service system, telling you what to expect from the educational assessment process, how to work with multiple service providers, and how to set up due process meetings. You'll also find a resource list and a glossary to help you understand professional jargon.

Golden, M. (1995). *Saving our sons: Raising black children in a turbulent world.* New York: Doubleday. The author gives a moving personal account of her experiences raising her son, first in Nigeria and then in the United States. She also talks to a wide range of people, from psychologists to criminal offenders, searching for answers to questions of race and society.

Leach, P. (1990). *Your baby and child from birth to age 5.* New York: Knopf. A *very* comprehensive book on child care, encompassing physical, cognitive, and emotional development in the first five years of a child's life.

Needleman, H. L., & Landrigan, P. J. (1994). *Raising children toxic free.* New York: Farrar, Straus and Giroux. Two experts, both of whom have testified before Congress on these issues, clarify the confusion surrounding lead, asbestos, pesticides, and other environmental hazards. They explain what the dangers are and what parents can realistically do to protect their children from these dangers.

Webber, J. (1993). *Children's Medications Guide Book.* Englewood Cliffs, NJ: Prentice-Hall. A mother and pharmacist is the author of this guide for parents who want to know more about the medications that are prescribed for their children and about nonprescription medications. Provides information on use, dosage, precautions, and side effects.

CHAPTER 9
COGNITIVE DEVELOPMENT
IN EARLY CHILDHOOD

CHAPTER 9
COGNITIVE DEVELOPMENT IN EARLY CHILDHOOD

337

Children live in a world of imagination and feeling. . . . They invest the most insignificant object with any form they please, and see in it whatever they wish to see.

Adam G. Oehlenschlager

Children's cognitive skills blossom in early childhood. Here we examine some aspects of this development as revealed by recent research as well as by such earlier theorists as Jean Piaget and Lev Semenovich Vygotsky. We see how children's thinking has advanced and in what ways it is still limited. We look at young children's increasing fluency with language and what impact this has on their lives. We examine memory, drawing on the information-processing approach; and we see how psychometric studies measure performance on standardized intelligence tests. We also explore such influences as family, school, and television. After reading this chapter, you'll be able to answer such questions as the following:

PREVIEW QUESTIONS

- ◆ What research shows that young children are more competent than psychologists once believed?
- ◆ How do children develop the ability to use language?
- ◆ How do young children remember? What does research tell us about their cognitive competence?
- ◆ How can we assess intelligence, and what factors influence cognitive achievement in early childhood?
- ◆ How do early educational experiences such as preschool and kindergarten affect children's cognitive development?
- ◆ What impact does television have on young children's cognitive development?

Vicky, at 5½, is full of stories about her friends—Amy and Verselle, waitresses who take her order in a restaurant; Chip and Johnson, who persistently get into trouble when they're not on trips to far-off places; and others, like Kara, who baby-sits a little girl very like a younger Vicky and who eventually marries Chip.

All these friends exist only in Vicky's mind; all are imaginary. As a bright, firstborn, creative girl, Vicky is not unusual—in fact, is normal—in having imaginary companions. About 15 to 30 percent of children between ages 3 and 10 create such "friends" (Manosevitz, Prentice, & Wilson, 1973). But Jason, whose only friends are in the real world, is also bright and imaginative—and also normal.

Girls are more likely to make up companions than are boys (or more likely to acknowledge them). Girls' imaginary playmates are usually human, while boys' are more often animals (Singer & Singer, 1990). Some children of either sex have such companions, and some do not—one more example of individual differences among children, how they may differ greatly and still be normal.

Vicky's imaginary friends reflect an ability that began late in the sensorimotor period but that flourishes during early childhood—the ability to pretend. The increasing complexity of her imaginary companions' activities and relationships shows how the ability to make-believe becomes more elaborate with cognitive growth.

ASPECTS OF COGNITIVE DEVELOPMENT

COGNITIVE CONCEPTS STUDIED BY PIAGET AND SUBSEQUENT RESEARCHERS

Concepts Identified by Piaget: Typical Advances of Early Childhood

Jean Piaget explored thinking in early childhood, which he named the *preoperational stage.* Some of the cognitive concepts he identified become apparent in early childhood, and others begin at the same time but are not fully achieved until middle childhood. (See Table 9-1.) Let's look at them.

TABLE 9-1

COGNITIVE ADVANCES OF EARLY CHILDHOOD*		
ADVANCE	**SIGNIFICANCE**	**EXAMPLE**
Use of symbols	Children can think about something without needing to see it in front of them.	Jason knows the name "Pumpkin" stands for his cat. He can talk or hear about her without having the cat in front of him. Words also stand for objects, people, and events.
Understanding of numbers	Children can count and can deal with quantities.	Vicky has two carrots on her plate. She leaves the table and comes back to find only one. "Who took my carrot?" she demands.
Understanding of identities	The world is more orderly and predictable; children are aware that superficial alterations do not change basic things.	When Jason cannot find his cat, he says, "Maybe Pumpkin put on a bear suit and went to someone else's house to be their pet bear." But when asked, Jason shows that he knows that Pumpkin would, even if she put on a bear suit, still be his cat.

*Although the beginnings of these ways of thought are present in early childhood, their full achievement usually does not take place until middle childhood.

(continued)

TABLE 9-1

ADVANCE	SIGNIFICANCE	EXAMPLE
Understanding of cause and effect	It becomes more evident that the world is orderly; also, children realize that they can cause events to happen.	Vicky knows that if she jumps into a puddle, she will get her sneakers dirty. She can choose to jump anyway; she can do it barefoot; or she can resist the temptation.
Empathy	Relationships with others become possible as children become able to imagine how others might feel.	Jason tells a friend who brought him crayons, "I already have some." Then he quickly adds, "But I wanted more."
Ability to classify	It becomes possible to organize objects, people, and events into meaningful categories.	Vicky lists which of her classmates are "nice" and which are "mean" and says, "The nice ones are my friends."
Theory of mind	It becomes possible to explain and predict other people's actions by imagining their beliefs, feelings, and thoughts.	Jason wants to play ball with some bigger boys. His mother says no so Jason asks his father, but he does not tell Jess that Julia has already said no. He knows that if Jess knew, he would say no, too.

symbolic function *Ability, described by Piaget, to use mental representation, shown in language, symbolic play, and deferred imitation.*

The Symbolic Function: The Use of Symbols to Represent Specific Objects. "I want an ice cream cone!" announces Jason, aged 4, trudging indoors from the hot, dusty backyard. He has not seen anything that triggered this desire—no open freezer door, no television commercial. He no longer needs this kind of sensory cue to think about something. He remembers ice cream (his mental representation includes coldness and taste), and he purposefully seeks it out. This absence of sensory or motor cues characterizes the major development of this stage, the *symbolic function*: the ability to use symbols to represent things.

symbol *In Piaget's terminology, a personal mental representation of a sensory experience.*

Significance of the Symbolic Function. A *symbol* is a mental representation to which a person has attached meaning. It is something that stands for something else. The most common symbol is the word—spoken or written. Knowing the symbols for things helps us to think about them and their qualities, to remember them, and to talk about them—without having them in front of us. Children can now use language to represent absent things and events not taking place at the present time. They now learn not only by sensing and doing but also by thinking symbolically, not only by acting but also by reflecting on their actions.

Indications of the symbolic function. Children show the symbolic function in three major ways: deferred imitation, symbolic play, and language. ***Deferred imitation*** is the repetition (imitation) of an observed action after time has passed. In ***symbolic play,*** children make an object stand for (symbolize) something else. *Language* involves using a common symbol system (words) to communicate.

One evening in the bathtub, Vicky, at age 5, illustrates all of these. She "swims" around, moving her mouth as a fish does. She then orders Ellen to throw her some foam bathtub letters, which Vicky catches in her mouth and "eats." Vicky is showing *deferred imitation:* She saw the pet fish in her kindergarten class and formed and stored a mental symbol (probably a visual image); later—when she could no longer see the fish—see reproduced the behavior by calling up the stored symbol. She shows *symbolic play* by making the foam letters stand for fish food and *language* when she asks Ellen to give her the toys.

Understanding Identities.
The world becomes more orderly and predictable as children develop a basic knowledge of identities—the concept that certain things are the same even though they may change in form, size, or appearance.

Understanding Cause and Effect.
Vicky's persistent "why" questions show she is beginning to link cause and effect. When we listen to children talk, we hear them spontaneously using such words as *because* and *so.* "He's crying because he doesn't want to put his pajamas on—he wants to be naked," said 27-month-old Vicky, watching (and listening to) another child crying loudly as he was being dressed for bed. Even at this early age, children seem to understand some causal relationships.

Researchers asked 3- and 4-year-olds to look at pictures like those on the left in Figure 9-1 and then to choose the picture on the right that would tell what happened (Gelman, Bullock, & Meck, 1980). The children showed an understanding of causality, telling stories like "First you have dry glasses, and then water gets on the glasses, and you end up with wet glasses."

Putting Oneself in Another Person's Place: Empathy.
Although Piaget believed that *empathy*—the ability to put oneself into another's place—comes later in childhood, young children do show it. Ten- to 12-month-old babies cry when they see another child crying; by 13 or 14 months, they pat or hug a crying child; by 18 months, they may hold out a new toy to replace a broken one or give a bandage to someone with a cut finger (M. R. Yarrow, 1978). By early childhood, such empathy shows itself more and more.

Empathy is essential in forming relationships. When Jason, 4, was going home

As Anna pretends to take Grover's blood pressure, she is showing a major cognitive achievement, deferred imitation—the ability to act out an action she observed some time before.

deferred imitation   *Ability to observe an action and imitate it after time.*

symbolic play   *Play in which an object stands for something else.*

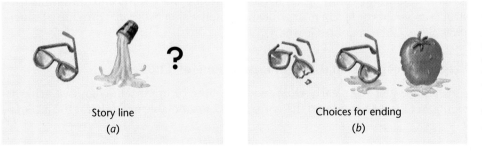

| Story line
(a) | Choices for ending
(b) |

FIGURE 9-1
Examples of sequences to test understanding of causality. A child is asked to look at pictures like those in (*a*) to pick the one in (*b*) that would show what happened, and to tell a story about what happened.

As this little girl plays with blocks, she demonstrates that she can group items into categories by at least one dimension—color. She can probably do it by several dimensions, according to recent research.

with his parents after a visit to his grandmother, he said, "Don't be sad, Grandma. We'll come see you again. And you can come see us." Jason's grandmother had not cried or talked about feeling sad, but he imagined how she must have been feeling. The relationship between the cognitive and the emotional is underscored by the finding that children from families that talk a lot about feelings and causality usually achieve such understanding at an earlier age than children from families that do not talk often about these things (Dunn, Brown, Slomkowski, Tesla, & Youngblade, 1991; Dunn, 1991).

Ability to Classify.   Children develop more proficiency at classifying, or grouping items into logical categories. Beginning in the second year of life, children become more logical in organizing the objects, people, and events in their world. Many 4-year-olds can classify by two criteria, like color, shape, or kind of toy (Denney, 1972). As children use the ability to classify to order many aspects of their lives, they categorize people as "good," "bad," "friend," "nonfriend," and so forth. Thus classification is a cognitive ability with social and emotional implications.

Understanding Numbers.   As we saw in Chapter 6, understanding of some basic number concepts seems to begin in infancy. By early childhood children recognize five counting principles:

1   *The 1-to-1 principle:* When counting, you say only one number word for each item being counted. You pick up one item and say "one" or "two" or whatever number the item represents.
2   *The stable-order principle:* You use number words in a set order—"1-2-3" and so forth, rather than "3-1-2."
3   *The order-irrelevance principle:* It does not matter which item in a group you start counting with. You can pick up the item closest or farthest from you; the total count will be the same.
4   *The cardinality principle:* The last number word used is the total number of items being counted. If there are five items, the last number will be "5."
5   *The abstraction principle:* You can count all sorts of things (Gelman & Gallistel, 1986; Sophian, 1988).

Children now have the words for comparing quantity: They can say one tree is *taller* than another or one cup holds *more* juice than another. As early as 3 or 4 years of age, they know that if they have a certain amount of something (like one cookie) and they get more (another cookie), they have more than they had before. When something is taken away, they know they have less.

This kind of quantitative knowledge seems to be universal, although it develops at different rates in different cultures and in different families, depending on how important counting is in the culture or the family, and how much instruction parents or teachers or educational television programs provide (Resnick, 1989; Saxe, Guberman, & Gearhart, 1987).

Piaget's Preoperational Stage: Limitations of Thought

As we have just seen, early childhood is a time of important cognitive achievements. Yet Piaget considered the years from 2 to 7 notable not only for the achievement of new abilities, but for the absence of others. His label for this second cognitive stage—the *preoperational stage*—emphasizes what it *lacks*. It precedes the stage in which children can think logically.

In the preoperational stage, Piaget said children can think in symbols but cannot yet use logic. He proposed that symbolic thought begins in the final substage of the sensorimotor period when toddlers begin to generate ideas and solve problems through mental representations, which are limited to things that are physically present. Some of Piaget's most important findings concern the lack of logic in children's thinking. Preoperational thinking is rudimentary compared with thinking in middle childhood. Table 9-2 lists some of the limitations in the way preoperational children think, according to Piaget.

Centration.   Preoperational children demonstrate *centration:* They focus on one aspect of a situation and neglect others, often coming to illogical conclusions. This occurs because they cannot *decenter,* or think simultaneously about several aspects of a situation. A classic example is Piaget's famous experiment designed to test the development of *conservation*—the awareness that two things that are equal remain so if their appearance is altered, so long as nothing is added or taken away. He found that children do not fully understand this principle until the stage of concrete operations and that they develop different kinds of conservation at different ages. Figure 9-2 shows how conservation has been tested using different dimensions.

In one type of conservation task, conservation of liquid, Jason is shown two identical glasses, each one short and wide and each one holding the same amount of water. Jason is asked whether the amount of water in the two glasses is equal. Once he agrees, the water in one glass is poured into a third glass, say, a tall, thin one. Jason is now asked whether both contain the same amount of water, or whether one contains more. Then he is asked why he thinks so.

In early childhood—after watching an experimenter pour the water out of one of the short, fat glasses into a tall, thin glass or even after pouring it himself—Jason will say the taller glass (or the wide glass) contains more water. When asked why, he says, "This one is bigger this way," stretching his arms to show the height (or the width). Preoperational children cannot consider height *and* width at the same time. Since they center on one aspect, like height, they cannot solve the problem. Their logic is flawed because their thinking is tied to what they "see"; if one glass *looks* bigger, they think it must *be* bigger. This leads them to confuse appearance with reality.

Confusing Appearance with Reality.   In early childhood, children have trouble distinguishing between what things appear to be and what they really are. Not until about age 5 or 6 will Vicky understand the distinction between appearance and reality. This is important, since the difference between what *is* and what *seems to be* figures in many everyday situations and can have serious implications. For one thing, parents often think children are lying when, in fact, they cannot tell the difference between appearance and reality. It also may account for some of children's fears. For example, if something *looks* scary—like a wooden mask that has hung on the wall since before Vicky was born—she may think it *is* a thing to be frightened of, even though she has seen it for years—and has never seen it cause harm to anyone!

---

preoperational stage   *In Piaget's theory, the second major period of cognitive development (approximately age 2 to age 7), in which children are able to think in symbols but are limited by their inability to use logic.*

centration   *In Piaget's terminology, thinking about one aspect of a situation while neglecting others.*

decenter   *In Piaget's terminology, to think simultaneously about several aspects of a situation.*

conservation   *Piaget's term for awareness that two stimuli which are equal (in length, weight, or amount, for example) remain equal in the face of perceptual alteration, so long as nothing has been added to or taken away from either stimulus.*

TABLE 9-2

LIMITATION	DESCRIPTION	EXAMPLE
Centration: Inability to decenter	Child focuses on one aspect of a situation and neglects others.	Jason cries when Jess gives him a cookie broken in half. Because each half is smaller than the whole cookie, Jason thinks he is getting less.
Irreversibility	Child fails to understand that an operation or action can go both ways.	Jason does not realize that both halves of the cookie can be put next to each other to show the whole cookie.
Focus on states rather than transformations	Child fails to understand the significance of the transformation between states.	In the conservation task, Jason does not understand that transforming the liquid (pouring it from one glass to another) does not change the amount.
Transductive reasoning	Child does not use deductive or inductive reasoning; instead, he jumps from one particular to another and sees cause where none exists.	"I had bad thoughts about my brother. My brother got sick. So I made my brother sick." Or "I was bad so mommy and daddy got divorced."
Egocentrism	Child assumes everyone else thinks as she does.	Vicky takes out her game and tells her mother, "This is *your* treat." She assumes Ellen likes to play the game as much as she does.
Animism	Child attributes life to objects not alive.	Vicky thinks clouds are alive because they move.
Inability to distinguish appearance from reality	Child confuses what is real with outward appearance.	Vicky thinks a sponge made to look like a rock really is a rock because it looks like a rock.

Conservation task	Show child (and have child acknowledge that both items are equal)	Perform transformation	Ask child	Preoperational child usually says
Number	Two equal rows of candies	Space one row farther apart	Are there the same number of candies in each row or does one row have more?	The longer one has more.
Length	Two sticks of the same length	Move one stick.	Are both sticks the same size or is one longer?	The one on the right (or left) is longer.
Liquid	Two glasses holding equal amounts of liquid	Pour liquid from one glass into a taller, narrower glass.	Do both glasses have the same amount or does one have more?	The taller one has more.
Matter (mass)	Two balls of clay of the same size	Roll one ball into a sausage shape.	Do both pieces have the same amount of clay or does one have more?	The sausage has more.
Weight	Two balls of clay of the same weight	Roll one ball into a sausage shape.	Do both weigh the same or does one weigh more?	The sausage weighs more.
Area	Two toy rabbits, two pieces of cardboard (representing grassy fields), with blocks or toys (representing barns on the fields); same number of "barns" on each board	Rearrange the blocks on one piece of board.	Does each rabbit have the same amount of grass to eat or does one have more?	The one with the blocks close together has more to eat.
Volume	Two glasses of water with two equal balls of clay in them	Roll one ball into a sausage shape and put it back in its glass.	Will the water rise the same amount in each glass or will one rise more?	The water in the glass with the sausage will rise more.

FIGURE 9-2
Tests of different kinds of conservation.

John H. Flavell and his colleagues posed a variety of appearance-reality tasks. They used familiar items and simple language to make the tasks as easy as possible. They showed preschoolers a red car, then covered the car with a filter that made the car look black; when the children were asked what color the car really was, they said "black." When the children put on special sunglasses that made milk look green, the children said the milk *was* green, even though they had just seen white milk. When an experimenter put on a Halloween mask in front of the children, the children thought the person was someone different. Children under 6 or 7 made the same mistakes, confusing appearance and reality (Flavell, Green, Wahl, & Flavell, 1987). Nor does training help children learn to distinguish appearance and reality (Flavell, Zhang, Zou, Dong, & Qi, 1983).

The difficulty in distinguishing between appearance and reality seems universal in children until sometime between ages 3 and 6. When they realize that the same object or event can be represented differently by the same person and by different people, they can distinguish appearance from reality.

Irreversibility. Preoperational logic is also limited by *irreversibility:* failure to understand that an operation or action can go two or more ways. In the liquid conservation task, once Jason can imagine restoring the original state of the water by pouring it back into the other glass, he will realize that the amount of water in both glasses is the same.

irreversibility *Failure to understand that an operation or action can go two or more ways.*

Focus on States Rather Than on Transformations. Preoperational children commonly think as if they were watching a filmstrip with a series of static frames. They focus on successive states and cannot understand the transformation from one state to another. In the conservation experiment, they do not grasp the meaning of pouring the water from one glass to the other. That is, they do not understand it is the same amount of water, even though its appearance changes.

Transductive Reasoning. There are two types of logical reasoning: deduction and induction. *Deduction* is based on general observations that lead to a particular result: "Eating a lot of candy can make people sick. I ate a lot of candy today, so I may get sick." *Induction* involves looking at one or more particular situations and drawing general conclusions: "Yesterday, I ate a lot of candy and felt sick. Last week, I ate a lot of candy and felt sick. The same thing happened to Jason. So it looks as if eating a lot of candy can make people sick."

Preoperational children, said Piaget, do not think along either of these lines. Instead, they reason by *transduction:* They look at one particular situation as the basis for another particular situation, without taking the general into account. This kind of reasoning leads children to see a causal relationship where none exists. Vicky thinks, "I had bad thoughts about my brother. My brother got sick. So I made my brother sick." Because the bad thoughts and the brother's sickness occurred around the same time, Vicky assumes illogically that one caused the other. The same kind of reasoning often makes children believe they caused a divorce.

transduction *In Piaget's terminology, a child's method of thinking about two or more experiences without relying on abstract logic.*

Egocentrism. At age 4, Jason was at the beach. Awed by the constant thundering of the waves, he asked his father, "When does it stop?" "It doesn't," Jess replied. "Not even when we're *asleep?*" asked Jason. His thinking was so egocentric, so focused on himself as the center of his universe, that he could not consider anything—not even the mighty ocean—as continuing its motion when he was not there to see it.

Egocentrism is the inability to see things from another's point of view. It is not selfishness, but self-centered understanding; and it is at the heart of the limited thinking of young children. Egocentrism is a form of centration: Young children center so much on their own points of view that they cannot take in another's view at the same time. Three-year-olds are not, of course, as egocentric as newborn babies, who cannot distinguish between the universe and their own bodies; but they still think the universe centers on them. This inability to decenter helps explain why preoperational children have trouble separating reality from what goes on inside their own heads and why they show confusion about what causes what. When Vicky believes her "bad thoughts" have made her brother sick, she is thinking egocentrically. Egocentrism explains why young children talk to themselves or seem to "talk past" other people.

egocentrism *As used by Piaget, a child's inability to consider another person's point of view.*

What do you think? *Since young children are considered egocentric, should caregivers try to get them to understand another person's point of view?*

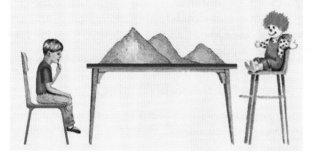

FIGURE 9-3
Piaget's "mountain task," in which a preoperational child cannot describe the "mountain" from the doll's point of view. Piaget concluded that this showed the child's egocentrism.

Studying Egocentrism. Piaget designed the *three-mountain task,* in which a child sits on a chair facing a table that holds three large mounds. The investigator places a doll on a chair on the opposite side of the table, and asks the child to tell or show how the "mountains" would look to the doll. (See Figure 9-3.) Young children usually cannot answer the question correctly; instead, they describe the mountains from their own perspective. Piaget saw this as evidence that they could not imagine a different point of view (Piaget & Inhelder, 1967). However, as we saw in our discussion of empathy, the ability to put oneself into another's place begins to appear at a younger age than Piaget believed.

In fact, another experimenter (Hughes, 1975) posed the same type of problem in a different way. In the "doll and the police officer" task, the child sits in front of a square board, with dividers that separate it into four sections. A toy police officer is put at the edge of the board, and a doll is set into one section. The doll is moved from one section to another, and each time the child is asked, "Can the police officer see the doll?" Then another toy officer is brought into the action, and the child is told to hide the doll from both officers. Among 30 children between ages 3½ and 5, they gave the correct answer or did the right thing 90 percent of the time (Hughes, 1975).

Why were these children able to take another person's point of view (the police officer's) when those doing the mountain task were not? It may be because the "police officer" task calls for thinking in more familiar, less abstract ways. Most children do not look at mountains and do not think about what other people might see when looking at one, but even 3-year-olds know about dolls and police officers and hiding.

Animism. *Animism* is the tendency to attribute life to objects that are not alive. When Piaget asked young children whether the wind and clouds were alive, their answers led him to think they were confused about what is alive and what is not. Piaget attributed this to egocentrism; one child, for example, said the moon is alive "because we are."

animism *Tendency to attribute life to objects that are not alive.*

However, when later researchers questioned 3- and 4-year-olds about differences between a rock, a person, and a doll, the children showed they understood that people are alive and rocks and dolls are not (Gelman, Spelke, & Meck, 1983). They did not attribute thoughts or emotions to rocks, and they cited the fact that dolls cannot move on their own as evidence that dolls are not alive. In another study, even 3-year-olds knew that animals can go uphill by themselves and that statues (even ones that look like animals), wheeled vehicles, and rigid objects cannot. Thus they showed an understanding of which things are capable of independent movement (Massey & Gelman, 1988).

The "animism" Piaget saw in young children may have been due to the fact that the things he asked about (like wind and clouds) show movement—and are very far away. Since children know so little about wind and clouds, they are less certain about them than about familiar things like rocks and dolls.

Can Cognitive Abilities Be Accelerated through Training?

Some programs designed to train cognitive abilities seem to work when a child is on the verge of acquiring the concept being taught. However, certain kinds of training are more effective than others.

In a study of conservation training, 3- and 4-year-olds were shown sets of items, like checkers, candies, and sticks. A child was asked to pick the two rows that had the same number of items or to show which two objects were the same length. Then the objects were moved or changed, and the child was asked whether they were the same. The child was then given one of three verbal rules explaining *why* they were the same:

1 *Identity*, or sameness of materials: "No matter where you put them, they are still the same candies."
2 *Reversibility*, or the possibility of returning the items to their original arrangement: "We just have to put the sticks back together to see they are the same length."
3 *Compensation*, or showing that a change in one dimension was balanced by a change in the other: "Yes, this stick does go farther in this direction, but at the other end, the stick is going farther, and so they balance each other."

The type of training affected how well the children learned conservation. The children who were told the "identity" rule made the most progress. Those who learned reversibility also advanced. But those who were taught compensation benefited little from the training (D. Field, 1981).

The 4-year-olds (who presumably were closer to acquiring conservation on their own) were more apt than the 3-year-olds to learn conservation and retain it up to 5 months later. The 3-year-olds were not able to conserve as many quantities and tended to lose whatever abilities they did gain. This kind of training seems to benefit children when their cognitive structures are well enough developed to handle the principle of conservation. Training gives such children a strategy for integrating the conservation principle into their thought processes.

What do you think?   *Should parents and preschools teach such Piagetian concepts as classification and conservation? Or is it better to let these concepts develop naturally?*

Assessing Piaget's Theory

Piaget's Underestimation of Children's Abilities.   No thinker about cognitive development has been more influential than Piaget. Yet research suggests he underestimated the abilities of preoperational children, just as he did with sensorimotor children. Ironically, Piaget may have *under*estimated young children's cognitive capabilities because he *over*estimated their understanding of and use of language. He assumed that wrong answers revealed faults in thinking, whereas errors may have arisen from the way he phrased the problems. Often children apparently misinterpreted tasks they were asked to do and answered questions that were not the ones the experimenter asked. Also children may not have been able to verbalize what they knew. The research method used influences our conclusion.

Preoperational children do, of course, have more cognitive limitations than children in the next higher stage, that of concrete operations. However, when faced with tasks based on what they are familiar with and explained in language they understand, they show greater competence than they do on traditional Piagetian tasks. A major revision of psychological thinking has come about in response to Piaget's position that children under age 6 have no conception and appreciation of a mental life. Research into what has been called *theory of mind* disputes his point of view and shows that young children are much more cognitively aware than Piaget believed. (See Box 9-1.)

theory of mind
Understanding of mental processes.

Other Criticisms.   As we pointed out in Chapter 1, some researchers question the basic stage nature of Piaget's theory. Because various cognitive abilities seem to develop gradually within a stage period, rather than appear all at once, the stages do not seem as distinct as Piaget defined them (Flavell, 1992). Furthermore, in outlining the typical sequence and age ranges for developing abilities, Piaget failed to consider differences among children, among families, and among cultures.

What do you think?   *Piaget has been criticized for underestimating the thinking of young children. His critics claim that children do better on simplified versions of cognitive tasks (like the egocentrism task described earlier) than on the tasks Piaget set for them. How fair is this criticism? Do the simplified tasks measure the same concepts as the original Piagetian tasks?*

Piaget's Contributions, Theoretical and Practical.   We cannot discount Piaget's great importance in describing cognitive development: His theory is a critical starting point for studying children's thinking. Piaget identified many aspects of childhood thought that had not been considered before. He pinpointed ways in which children's thinking differs from adults' thinking. He inspired much research designed to test his theories. Some of today's most innovative techniques are built on those used by Piaget.

Piaget's descriptions of children's thought helps teachers decide when and how to present various concepts to children. Also, health professionals have become aware that young children may center upon the length of a needle or the size of an x-ray machine and ignore the caregiving aspects of such equipment, that they may not understand the reversibility of mending a broken leg, or that they may not accept logical explanations of why they cannot have a drink before surgery. Parents can better explain concepts like death if they realize that young children do not understand that death is *irreversible*—that a dead person, animal, or flower cannot come to life again.

One of Piaget's most important contributions is his emphasis on the importance of language in the symbolic function. Let's look at the way language abilities develop in early childhood.

BOX 9-1 ■ FOOD FOR THOUGHT

THEORY OF MIND

"Why did Mommy rush me to school this morning?" "Why does Pedro look so sad?" "What made Kenisha get so mad at me?" The ability to make sense of how other people are acting is a major step in cognitive development. How and when do children come to understand what another person is thinking and feeling? All of us constantly try to explain and predict another person's actions by imagining what his or her beliefs, desires, feelings, and emotions are. This process is known in some circles as "folk psychology" or, more currently among psychologists, as "theory of mind."

Piaget was the first scholar to investigate children's understanding of such aspects of their mental life as thoughts and dreams. He interviewed children, asking them such questions as "Where do dreams come from?" or "What do you think with?" Based on the answers, Piaget concluded that before age 6 children cannot tell the difference between thoughts, dreams, and real physical entities and have no conception of a mental life (Piaget, 1929).

However, more recent research indicates that children do discover their minds sometime between the ages of 2 and 5, when their knowledge about mental states and attitudes grows dramatically (Astington, 1993; Bower, 1993).

What accounts for the difference between Piaget's conclusions and those of subsequent researchers? Again, it seems to be a matter of method. Piaget focused on questions and tasks that children either didn't understand or couldn't make sense of, and he expected them to be able to put their understanding into words. Both assumptions

obscured the extent of children's understanding. More-contemporary researchers have tried to use vocabulary and objects that children are familiar with and have observed children in everyday activities. Instead of talking in abstractions, they use concrete examples. In this way they learn that 3-year-olds can tell you the difference between a boy who has a cookie and a boy who is thinking about a cookie; they know which boy can touch, share, and eat that treat (Astington, 1993).

THE POWER OF IMAGINATION

Even though sometime between 18 months and 3 years children learn to distinguish between real and imagined events, 4- to 6-year-olds are not always sure that what they imagine cannot become real (P. L. Harris, Brown, Marriott, Whittall, & Harmer, 1991). In one study, 40 children (age range: 3 years, 4 months to 6 years, 10 months) were shown two cardboard boxes and told, "We're going to play a game of pretend." They were to pretend there was a big, scary monster in one box and a little, friendly puppy in the other. Each box had a small hole in it, and the children were asked whether they wanted to put a finger or a stick in the holes. Most of the children claimed they were just pretending about both the monster and the puppy, but most still preferred to go to the box holding the imaginary puppy, and more used the stick in the monster box and their finger in the puppy box (P. L. Harris et al., 1991).

The results of this and other experiments show that young children understand the distinction between fantasy

LANGUAGE IN EARLY CHILDHOOD

At $3\frac{1}{2}$, Jason talks constantly and has a comment about everything. He creates his own language as he describes how Daddy "hatches" wood (chops with a hatchet), or asks Mommy to "piece" his food (cut it into little pieces), or says he is not ready to go to bed because he is not "yawn-y" yet. By the time he's 5, his language sounds quite adult, as he tells his mother, "Don't be ridiculous!" or proudly points to his toys and says, "See how I organized everything?"

Words, Sentences, and Grammar

"How did the first animal get born?" "Who filled the river with water?" "Do smells come from inside my nose?" Young children ask questions about everything—partly because they are hungry for knowledge and partly because they quickly learn that asking "why" will almost always keep a conversation going.

BOX 9-1 ■ FOOD FOR THOUGHT (CONTINUED)
THEORY OF MIND

and reality, that things they imagine are not real. However, they sometimes respond as if imaginary creatures could actually exist. How can this be? One possibility is that when they imagine a puppy or a monster in a box, they wonder whether those creatures might really be there. So they seem to credit their imagination with the power to overcome what they know of as reality (P. L. Harris et al., 1991).

THE ABILITY TO DECEIVE

Telling a lie can be a sign of cognitive development! For a child to deceive someone, the child has to be able to imagine what the other person might think. In one study, 3-year-olds who knew their mother broke a toy lied to a stranger to protect the mother; but when speaking to the mother, they acknowledged they knew she broke the toy. However, they also lied to the mother, telling her they told the stranger that the mother broke the toy (Ceci & Leichtman, 1992). It seems, then, that children this young change their story to accomplish different aims: one, to protect the mother from being punished and then, with the mother, to preserve the child's self-image as a good and truthful person. They change their story depending on their goal, showing that they can, in fact, decenter and see several possibilities in the same situation.

FALSE BELIEFS

Vicky, 5, is shown a candy box and is asked what is in it. "Candy," she says. But when she opens the box, she is surprised to see it holding crayons, not candy. "What will a child who hasn't opened the box think is in it?" the researcher asks. "Candy!" shouts Vicky, grinning at the joke. Then the researcher repeats the procedure with 3-year-old Bobby. He too answers the first question with "Candy"; but when asked what another child would think was in the box, he says, "Crayons." And then Bobby says that he himself had at first thought crayons would be in the box (Flavell, 1993). Not until children are 4 or 5 years old do they understand that they or other people can hold false beliefs (Moses & Flavell, 1990).

KNOWLEDGE ABOUT THINKING

Although young children do know something about thinking, they do not seem to be aware of stream of consciousness, that the mind is constantly engaged in thought (Flavell, 1993). At 3, for example, Jason understands that someone can be thinking of one thing while looking at or doing something else; that a person whose eyes and ears are covered can still think about objects; that someone who looks pensive is thinking; and that thinking is different from talking (Flavell, Green, & Flavell, 1992). At 4, he does not consider "thinking about" and "knowing" as the same thing (Flavell, 1993). But he still seems to think mental activity starts and stops; he does not view it as continuous.

Preschoolers seem to assume that when the mind has nothing to do, it does nothing. Not until middle childhood do children assume that whenever a person is awake, that person is thinking, no matter what else she or he is doing (Flavell, 1993).

From a very early age, children communicate through social speech. They take into account other people's needs and use words to establish and maintain social contacts. Sometimes a prop like a toy phone can make conversation flow more easily.

Linguistic Advances.   Once children pass age 3, speech becomes increasingly more adult. At 3, they use plurals and past tense and know the difference between *I, you,* and *we.* Between ages 3 and 6, children typically learn several new words a day, but they do not always use the words as adults use them. For example, Jason uses the word *tomorrow* to refer to any time in the future, and *yesterday* for any time in the past (Pease & Gleason, 1985).

Between ages 4 and 5, sentences average four to five words. Children now use prepositions like *over, under, in, on,* and *behind.* Between ages 5 and 6, children speak in longer and more complex sentences. They can define simple words and know some opposites. (Vicky's parents are amused by some definitions offered by their 5-year-old, like the one of a teenager: "a cool woman who listens to music.") Children use more conjunctions, prepositions, and articles. Between 6 and 7 years of age, children speak in compound and complex sentences and use all parts of speech.

Preschool children understand more than 14,000 words, learning an average of nine new words a day (M. L. Rice, 1989). How do they make such meteorlike progress? They use *fast mapping,* a process by which they absorb the meaning of a new word after hearing it only once or twice in conversation. Drawing on the context in which a new word is used, children seem to form a quick partial understanding of it and store it in memory. Linguists still do not know how fast mapping occurs, but it seems likely that children draw upon what they do know— the rules for forming words, other similar words, grammatical contexts, and the subject under discussion.

One day Vicky, upset by her parents' quarreling, exclaimed, "Why are you two being such grumpy old bears?" Vicky was using metaphor, a figure of speech that becomes increasingly common in these years. A *metaphor* is a statement that applies a word or phrase usually designating one thing (like a bear) to another thing (like parents). Vicky's use of metaphor reflects her ability to see similarities among objects and events, signaling cognitive growth going beyond language. The capacity to put things in categories reflects transfer of knowledge from one domain to another and helps in acquiring new knowledge (Vosniadou, 1987).

Linguistic Immaturity.   Young children develop their own syntax, as in 5-year-old Jason's: "I seem to cannot do it." Although they speak fluently, understandably, and fairly grammatically, they still have much to learn about language. For one thing, they rarely use the passive voice ("I was dressed by Grandpa"), conditional sentences ("If I were big, I could drive the bus"), or the auxiliary verb *have* ("I have seen that lady before") (C. S. Chomsky, 1969).

They make errors by failing to note exceptions to rules. At age 3, when Vicky said, "I held my doll," she was merely repeating what she had heard. When she discovered rules (like adding *-ed* for past tense), she tended to *overregularize*—use the rule always—and said "I holded my doll." As we noted in Chapter 6, this mistake is a sign of progress. As Vicky hears people talking and takes part in conversations, she notices that *-ed* is not always used to form the past tense of a verb. Such common errors are a case of taking one step backward to take two steps forward.

At the beginning of early childhood, children can give and follow commands that include more than one step, like "Pick up your toys and put them in the closet." However, they frequently misinterpret complex sentences. If Jason is told, "You may watch TV after you clean up your room," he may process the words

fast mapping   *Process by which a child absorbs the meaning of a new word after hearing it only once or twice in conversation.*

in the order in which he hears them and think he may first watch television and then clean up his room.

Young children are often very literal in interpreting the meanings of words. When Ellen told Vicky her shiny red boots were "sharp," Vicky, 5, said, "They can't be sharp because they don't have nails in them!" Another day Vicky said she had kissed her dentist. When Ellen asked, "Did Dr. Margot kiss you back?" Vicky said no. Rephrasing the question, Ellen asked, "Did Dr. Margot kiss you?" This time Vicky said yes. She had thought her mother was asking whether the dentist had kissed Vicky's back. Such misunderstandings have important implications, since children often receive a very different meaning from the one adults intend to communicate. Adults must be very careful what they say to children— especially in anger.

Pragmatics: The Development of Social Speech

After Jason's third birthday, his pronunciation improves quickly, and everyone finds it easier to understand what he says. He wants people to listen, and if they look away, he sometimes moves to face them. He wants to be understood: If people cannot understand what he says, he tries to explain himself more clearly. The function of his speech is changing as quickly as its form. (See Table 9-3.)

The form and function of speech are linked. As children master words, sentences, and grammar, they become more competent at communicating. This is due to *pragmatics,* the practical use of language. Children learn how to ask for things, how to tell a story or a joke, how to begin and continue a conversation, and how to adjust comments to the listener's perspective (M. L. Rice, 1982). Most speech is *social speech,* speech intended to be understood by someone other than the speaker.

Piaget characterized young children's speech as egocentric (not adapted to the listener), but research suggests that much speech is social from an early age.

pragmatics   *The practical use of language.*

social speech   *Speech intended to be understood by a listener.*

TABLE 9-3

DEVELOPMENT OF SOCIAL SPEECH	
AGE	**CHARACTERISTICS OF SPEECH**

$2\frac{1}{2}$	Beginnings of conversation:
	    Speech is increasingly relevant to others' remarks.
	    Need for clarity is being recognized.

3	Breakthrough in attention to communication:
	    Child seeks ways to clarify and correct misunderstandings.
	    Pronunciation and grammar improve markedly.
	    Speech with children the same age expands dramatically.
	    Use of language as instrument of control increases.

4	Knowledge of fundamentals of conversation:
	    Child shifts speech according to listener's knowledge.
	    Literal definitions are no longer a sure guide to meaning.
	    Collaborative suggestions have become common.
	    Disputes can be resolved with words.

5	Good control of elements of conversation.

SOURCE: Adapted from E. B. Bolles, 1982, p. 93.

When 3- to 5-year-olds were asked to communicate their choice of a toy, they behaved very differently with a person who could see and with one who could not see the toy. They pointed to the toy for a sighted listener but described it to a blindfolded listener (Maratsos, 1973). Also, 4-year-olds use "motherese" (see Chapter 6) when speaking to 2-year-olds (Shatz & Gelman, 1973). Even 2-year-olds use social speech as they point out or show objects to others.

Children's general knowledge affects their ability to communicate. Asked to describe a variety of pictures, $4\frac{1}{2}$-year-olds did very well on simple, familiar subjects like monkeys and people but not on abstract designs (Dickson, 1979).

Private Speech

As Jason, 4, picks up Julia's art book, he says quietly to himself, "Now I can use this—I washed my hands so they're clean and I can hold this book." As he jumps onto his bed, he says—also to himself—"Take off my shoes. . . . Now they're off. Now I can jump."

private speech *Talking aloud to oneself with no intent to communicate with anyone else.*

Private speech—talking aloud to oneself with no intent to communicate with anyone else—is normal and common in childhood, accounting for 20 to 60 percent of what children say. The youngest children playfully repeat rhythmic sounds in a pattern like infants' babbling ("Minga minga minga," Vicky, at 3, sings as she plays); slightly older children "think out loud" in speech related to their actions (as Jason did in the above example); and the oldest children mutter in barely audible tones. (See Table 9-4.)

Psychologists disagree about private speech. The behaviorist John Watson saw it as inappropriate activity that parents should get children to stop. Piaget defined it as egocentric speech reflecting a child's inability to recognize another person's viewpoint. He believed young children talk while they do things because they do not yet know the difference between words and what the words stand for.

Instead of looking on such speech as irrelevant or immature, the Soviet psychologist Vygotsky (1962—see Chapter 1) saw it as a special form of communication with oneself. Like Piaget, he believed private speech helps children integrate language with thought and helps them control their actions. Unlike Piaget, he believed private speech increases during the early school years, as children use it to guide and master their actions, and then fades away as they become able to think silently.

Research supports Vygotsky's interpretation. Among nearly 150 middle-class children aged 4 to 10, private speech rose and fell with age, and the most sociable and popular children used it the most, apparently supporting Vygotsky's view that private speech is stimulated by social experience (Berk, 1986; Kohlberg, Yaeger, & Hjertholm, 1968). The brightest children used it earliest—for them, it peaked at about age 4, compared with age 5 to 7 for children of average intelligence; by age 9, it had practically disappeared for all these children.

The impact of culture is reflected in the pattern of private speech among low-income 5- to 10-year-olds in the mountains of Kentucky. In the Appalachian subculture, communication—especially between men and boys—depends more on gestures than words. "Talk is women's work," men tend to say, admonishing their sons to be quiet. This may explain why private speech persists for a longer time: 25 percent of children (especially boys) still used it at age 10. Children used private speech most when trying to solve difficult problems and when no adults were around (Berk & Garvin, 1984).

TABLE 9-4

TYPES OF PRIVATE SPEECH

TYPE	CHILD'S ACTIVITY	EXAMPLES
Wordplay, repetition	Repeating words and sounds, often in playful, rhythmic recitation	José wanders around the room, repeating in a singsong manner, "Put the mushroom on your head, put the mushroom in your pocket, put the mushroom on your nose."
Solitary fantasy play and speech addressed to nonhuman objects	Talking to objects, playing roles, producing sound effects for objects	Darryl says, "Ka-powee ka-powee," aiming his finger like a gun. Ashley says in a high-pitched voice while playing in the doll corner, "I'll be better after the doctor gives me a shot. Ow!" she remarks as she pokes herself with her finger (a pretend needle).
Emotional release and expression	Expressing emotions or feelings directed inward rather than to a listener	Keiko is given a new box of crayons and says to no one in particular, "Wow! neat!" Rachel is sitting at her desk with an anxious expression on her face, repeating to herself, "My mom's sick, my mom's sick."
Egocentric communication	Communicating with another person, but expressing the information so incompletely or peculiarly that it can't be understood	David and Mark are seated next to one another on the rug. David says to Mark, "It broke," without explaining what or when. Susan says to Ann at the art table, "Where are the paste-ons?" Ann says, "What paste-ons?" Susan shrugs and walks off.
Describing or guiding one's own activity	Narrating one's actions, thinking out loud	Omar sits down at the art table and says to himself, "I want to draw something. Let's see. I need a big piece of paper, I want to draw my cat." Working in her arithmetic workbook, Cathy says to no one in particular, "Six." Then, counting on her fingers she continues, "Seven, eight, nine, ten. It's ten, it's ten. The answer's ten."
Reading aloud, sounding out words	Reading aloud or sounding out words while reading	While reading a book, Tom begins to sound out a difficult word. "Sher-lock Holm-lock," he says slowly and quietly. The he tries again. "Sher-lock Holm-lock, Sherlock Holme," he says, leaving off the final s in his most successful attempt.
Inaudible muttering	Speaking so quietly that the words cannot be understood by an observer	Tony's lips move as he works a math problem.

SOURCE: Adapted from Berk & Garvin, 1984.

Understanding the significance of private speech has practical implications, especially when children go to school (Berk, 1986):

- Talking aloud or muttering should not be considered misbehavior.
- A teacher who hears it should be alert to the possibility that children may be struggling with a problem and may welcome adult help.
- Instead of insisting on quiet, teachers can set aside special areas where children can talk (and learn) without disturbing others.
- Children should be encouraged to play with others to develop the internal thought that will eventually displace the thinking out loud.

Delayed Language Development

Albert Einstein did not start to speak until he was 3 years old, a fact that heartens parents of children whose speech develops late. Language development is delayed in about 3 percent of young children, although the overall intelligence of language-delayed children usually seems to be at least average. About 40 percent of late talkers have such problems as hearing impairment or mental retardation (M. L. Rice, 1989). Some have a history of otitis media (an inflammation of the middle ear) between 12 and 18 months of age; these children improve when the infection, with its related hearing loss, is cleared up (Lonigan, Fischel, Whitehurst, Arnold, & Valdez-Menchaca, 1992).

Causes of Delayed Language Development.   It is unclear why children with no detectable problems speak late. They are not necessarily from homes where they do not get enough linguistic input. Even though some of their parents talk to them more in terms of what the children can say rather than what they can understand (Whitehurst et al., 1988), this may be more the result than the cause of their delay. Also, these children may have a cognitive limitation that makes it hard for them to learn the rules of language (Scarborough, 1990).

Current investigations focus on problems in *fast mapping*—absorbing the meaning of a new word based on having heard it in conversation. Studies suggest that children with delayed language skills need to hear a word more often than other children do before they can understand it. However, given frequent exposure, they can incorporate new words into their vocabulary (M. L. Rice, 1989; M. L. Rice et al., in press).

Implications of Delayed Language Development.   The intertwining of different domains of development is most apparent in language, where delay can have not only cognitive, but also social and emotional consequences. Early language problems, like mispronunciation at age 2, poor vocabulary at age 3, or weakness in naming objects at age 5, are often associated with reading disabilities later on (M. L. Rice, Oetting, Marquis, Bode, & Pae, in press; Scarborough, 1990).

Children who do not speak or understand as well as their peers are often judged negatively by adults. In one study, kindergarten teachers, college students, laypersons, and specialists in speech problems listened to audiotaped samples of preschool children's speech and were asked to rate children and parents on various qualities. All groups of adults rated the children with delayed language skills as less bright, less likable, less socially mature, less likely to succeed in kindergarten, and less likely to be classroom leaders. Furthermore, they saw the children's parents as more limited, of lower educational and socioeconomic levels (M. L. Rice, Hadley, & Alexander, 1993).

Other children too are less likely to want to play with children with a limited command of language (Gertner, Rice, & Hadley, 1993). In one study, the language skill most crucial in determining a preschooler's popularity was comprehension. As long as a child could understand what the other children were saying, it did not matter if the child could not speak clearly. According to the study, speech

The family dinner table is a good setting for encouraging literacy, especially when conversations center on topics like the day's activities and complex issues (like why people do things and how things work). Children learn how to choose the right words and put sentences together to make a coherent account.

delays did impose one obvious social disadvantage: Children having a speech delay were less likely to know other children's names, which may have put them at a disadvantage in making connections and friendships.

Thus verbal deficits can have far-reaching consequences. Children considered less intelligent or less mature by adults may be treated differently by them—and may live down to lower expectations. Children who are not accepted by their peers may have trouble approaching other children—and friendship is important for normal social development. In both cases, self-esteem is bound to suffer. The importance of helping children whose language is delayed is obvious.

What do you think? *Can you think of other reasons why children with delayed language are judged negatively? Should intervention aim to improve their language or their social skills—or other people's attitudes?*

Development of Literacy

Literacy—the ability to read and write—is an essential competency in developed countries for cognitive, social, and even emotional success. Researchers seek to determine the factors that encourage its development and those that retard it.

literacy *The ability to read and write.*

Social interaction—the kind of conversation, especially within the home—seems to be a key factor. Furthermore, the kind of social interaction is important. Children develop literacy skills best when adults provide the right kinds of conversational challenges and at the right time, that is, at the time when children are ready for them. These adults use a broad vocabulary that includes less common words, and family dinner-table conversations tend to center on topics like the day's activities and complex issues (like why people do things and how things work) rather than on food, table manners, or purely personal topics. Such conversations help children learn how to handle the mechanics of language—planning syntax, choosing the right words, and putting sentences together to make a coherent account (Snow, 1993).

Literacy can also be encouraged in nonfamily settings. Since children learn how to define words in school rather than at home, preschool teachers can enhance children's vocabulary, a foundation of literacy (Snow, 1990). Some Head Start teachers have helped children expand their vocabularies by using relatively rare words. The children in these teachers' classes scored higher on vocabulary tests and used many of the new words in play (Dickinson, Cote, & Smith, 1993).

Children also become literate through play, especially dramatic play, the kind most closely linked to literacy (Christie, 1991). This is imaginative play in which children make up situations and act out their parts in them—in other words, transform themselves and their setting by make-believe. Play becomes increasingly social, as episodes involve other people and various objects. Story lines become more complex, evolving into well-coordinated scenarios, and roles and themes become more creative and unusual. All these changes offer children rich opportunities to learn, use, and practice language.

What do you think? *You want to set up a program to encourage literacy development in a group of children at high risk for literacy problems. What elements would you include in your program? How would you judge its success?*

Practical Applications of Research on Language Development

Researchers have discovered ways to help normally developing preschoolers, as well as those with delayed language development (M. L. Rice, 1989). The best way to encourage language development is to provide opportunities for a child to interact with adults and children, to have experiences and talk about them, and to have a rich play life. Adults can help by holding conversations with children about things and events the children show an interest in. During the course of these conversations, the adults should paraphrase and elaborate slightly on what the children say, but they need to avoid doing all the talking. By pausing, they provide openings for children to express themselves and to practice using new words and creating new sentences.

Programs of speech and language therapy can help. These should include careful assessment of both child and family by a trained professional; therapeutic strategies focusing on specific language forms; perhaps a specialized preschool program targeting language skills; and follow-up programs either in or out of school in the elementary school years.

DEVELOPMENT OF MEMORY: THE CHILD AS A PROCESSOR OF INFORMATION

When Vicky was 3, she went on an apple-picking trip. Months later, she talked about going on the bus, visiting a farm, picking apples, bringing them home, and eating them. She had a vivid memory of the event and enjoyed talking about it.

During early childhood children show significant improvements in attention and in the speed and efficiency with which they process information. These advances make possible many cognitive strides—one of the most important of them involves memory. Until recently, what children ordinarily remember was rarely studied. Before the mid-1960s, there was little research on memory in children younger than 5, and until about the 1980s most of that research was done in the artificial setting of the psychological laboratory rather than in the field, the everyday world. Now, with a surge in interest in the development of memory, we have a clearer picture of the "remembering child." When young children are tested by methods that pick up their abilities, they turn out to have better memories than was once believed.

Recognition and Recall

Recognition is the ability to identify something encountered before (like distinguishing in an array of pictures those you have seen before from those that are new). *Recall* is the ability to reproduce knowledge from memory (like describing pictures you have seen after they are no longer present). Preschool children, like all age groups, do better on recognition tasks than on recall, and both abilities improve with age (Myers & Perlmutter, 1978).

recognition *Ability to correctly identify a stimulus as something previously known; compare recall.*

recall *Ability to reproduce material from memory; compare recognition.*

The Importance of General Knowledge. The more familiar children are with items, the better they can recall them. Young children can recall material better when items bear an understandable relation to each other. When 3-year-olds and 4-year-olds were shown pairs of pictures, they did much better recalling related pairs than pairs of unrelated pictures. Then too, the type of relationship affected degree of recall. Children were more likely to recall pictures in which one member of the pair was a part of the other (like a tire and a car) rather than those in which one item was the usual habitat of the other (like a fish and a lake). They were least apt to recall pairs in which the two items belonged to the same category (like a hat and a sock) (S. Staub, 1973).

Mastery Motivation, Study Activities, and Strategies. Newer studies suggest that older children remember better than younger ones and that some children remember better than others because of additional factors—how highly motivated a child is to master skills in general and how the child approaches a specific task.

These conclusions emerged from a study of ninety-three 3-and 4-year-olds (Lange, MacKinnon, & Nida, 1989). During three sessions over a 4-month period, the children were tested on their knowledge of a variety of objects, were assessed on how reflective or impulsive they were, were videotaped to analyze how they did two tasks, and were rated by preschool teachers and parents on such characteristics as "takes initiative in carrying out activities," "uses problem-solving strategies," and "tries to pursue difficult tasks." One task was putting together a picture puzzle. In the other, the children were shown an array of toys, which they were permitted to handle before the toys were taken away and replaced by a set of new toys; the children were asked to label these toys before they, too, were removed. Finally, the children were asked to recall what the toys were. The videotapes showed what the children did with the toys—how much they looked at them, picked them up, and moved them around; how they grouped and named them; and whether they repeated the names of the toys to themselves.

The best predictor of how well the child recalled the names of the toys was "mastery motivation." This refers to a child's tendencies to be independent, self-directed, and generally resourceful (as rated by the child's teacher). The only other factor related to recall ability was the child's activities while studying the toys.

Children who named, grouped, or spent time thinking about or repeating to themselves the names of toys (in other words, used strategies to help them remember) recalled them better than children who did fewer of these activities. These two factors did not seem related to each other—that is, mastery motivation did not seem to encourage children's use of particular study strategies (Lange, et al., 1989).

Childhood Memories

Chances are, your earliest memory is about something that occurred when you were at least 3 years old. Memory in early childhood is rarely deliberate: Young children seldom try to commit facts to memory but, instead, remember events that made a particular impression. Most early memories are short-lived. Jason, at $2\frac{1}{2}$ years, looks at pictures of his birthday party 6 months before and recalls that Vicky broke the toy she gave him that day, but he will probably not remember this incident later in life.

This inability to remember early events later in life is called *infantile amnesia*. Piaget (1969) suggested that young children's memories are not retained because early events are not encoded in long-term memory. However, since children even younger than 2 are able to talk about events that took place more than a month earlier and 4-year-olds remember trips they took at 2 years (Nelson, 1992), this explanation does not seem to be supported. Other theorists maintain that early memories are inaccessible in later years, either because they are not encoded in the same way later memories are, or because, as Freud believed, they are repressed because they are emotionally troublesome.

Implicit and Explicit Memories. A third explanation proposes two ways of encoding memories. Some events may be encoded in a way that can produce behavioral changes but without awareness of memory—a kind of memory known as *implicit memory*. Another system of storing events allows for *explicit memory*—memory we know we have (Newcombe & Fox, 1994). This rationale is based on neural maturation.

Both kinds of memory are supported by studies like one in which 9- and 10-year-olds were shown photos, some of preschool classmates whom they had not seen for 5 years or so and some of children they had never known. The children's *skin conductance* (electrical impulses from the skin) were measured. Positive responses appeared in children seeing pictures of former classmates, often even when they were not consciously aware of recognizing the faces (Newcombe & Fox, 1994). This finding suggests we do have memories of which we are not consciously aware, and buried memories may affect our behavior without our understanding the basis for it, as psychoanalysts maintain.

generic memory *Memory that relies on a script.*

script *General outline of a familiar, repeated event.*

Three Types of Memory. *Generic Memory.* *Generic memory*, which begins at about age 2, relies on a *script* that sketches the general outline of a familiar, repeated event without providing details of the specific time or place when an event happened. A script might involve riding the bus to preschool, the color of the walls in a bedroom, or what Grandmother served for lunch (Nelson, 1993). Generic memory seems to help a child act in the present and predict the future. The memory, serving as a script, outlines routines that fit situations that come up again and again. As a result, the child knows what to expect and how to act.

"Remember when we . . . ?" Young children remember best events that are unique and new, and they may recall many details from a special trip or visit for a year or longer.

Episodic Memory. *Episodic memory* refers to something that happened once at a specific time or place—an apple-picking trip, a ride on a train, or the time a child was knocked down by an ocean wave. Even 2-year-olds show episodic memory, but most memories of such early singular events last for a few weeks or months and then fade away.

episodic memory
Memory of an event that happened once, at a specific time or place.

Autobiographical Memory. *Autobiographical memory* refers to personally meaningful memories that form a person's life history. It contains the specific, personal, long-lasting, and significant events and people in one's life (Nelson, 1993). Autobiographical memory begins for most people in early childhood, rarely before 3 years. It increases slowly between ages 5 and 8; memories from then on are often remembered for 20, 40, or more years (Nelson, 1992). Although autobiographic memory can be considered a type of episodic memory, not everything in episodic memory becomes part of it. Only those memories that acquire a special personal meaning remain and become part of autobiographical memory.

autobiographical memory
Memory of specific events in one's own life.

Autobiographical memory serves a social function, letting a person share something of the self with others. It is valued for its own sake "as a kind of personal and social treasure, a continuing reservoir of knowledge about [the] self and others" (Nelson, 1989, p. 9). It also serves a universal human purpose, since this kind of personal, enduring memory forms the basis for song, story, epic, history, and myth in all cultures (Nelson, 1993).

Influences on Children's Memory

Memory researcher Katherine Nelson (1989) has asked, "What happens during the early childhood years that makes enduring memories possible?" (p. 5). Nelson read diaries kept by mothers about the kinds of things their children re-member, interviewed children, tape-recorded her own daughter's bedtime "self-talk" from 21 months of age until age 3, and drew on other studies of early memories.

Language.   The early childhood event that seems necessary for the retention and retrieval of enduring memories is the development of language skills. Nelson and other linguists believe memory is dependent on language. Not until children can put memories into words can they hold them in their minds (Nelson, 1992). Evidence for this view includes the association between early memories and early language development. Two other factors correlated with early memory—higher social class and being female—are also associated with early language development. Individuals differ: Some people have vivid memories from age 3, while others do not remember much before age 8 (Nelson, 1992).

Social Interaction.   Research seems to support Vygotsky's emphasis on interaction: How adults talk with a child about an event influences how well the child will remember it.

In a field experiment, ten 3-year-olds and their mothers visited a museum (Tessler in Nelson, 1989). Half the mothers talked naturally with their children as they walked through the museum; the other half, as requested, did not open discussions but responded to their children's comments. All conversations were tape-recorded. A week later, researchers interviewed mothers and children separately and asked 30 questions about objects seen the week before.

The children remembered *only* those objects they had talked about with their mothers, and the children in the natural-conversation group remembered better. Mothers' styles of talking also had an effect. Four mothers used a narrative style, reminiscing about shared experiences ("Remember when we went to Vermont and saw Cousin Leroy?"), and six mothers adopted a practical style, using memory for a specific purpose like solving a problem ("Where does this puzzle piece go? You remember, we did that one yesterday"). The children of "narrative" mothers averaged 13 correct answers, compared with fewer than 5 for the "practical" group. Thus, it seems that adults' style of talking about events influences how well children remember them.

Another analysis of how parents talk about the past also identified two styles among 24 white middle-class two-parent families (E. Reese & Fivush, 1993). In an *elaborative* style, parents structure a conversation by moving to a new aspect of an event or adding more information. In a *repetitive* style, they repeat either the general thrust or exact content of their own previous statement or question. A repetitive-style parent might ask, "Do you remember how we went to Florida?" and, receiving no answer, ask, "How did we get there? We went in the ———." An elaborative-style parent, on the other hand, would follow up the first question by saying, "Did we go by car or did we go by train?"

Three-year-olds of elaborative-style parents took part in longer conversations and remembered more details. Both fathers and mothers were more likely to use the elaborative style with girls than with boys, but it is hard to know which comes first. Do girls converse more than boys because parents elaborate more with them, or do parents elaborate more because girls talk more? Whatever the case, adults'

BOX 9-2 ■ FOOD FOR THOUGHT

CHILDREN'S EYEWITNESS TESTIMONY

In 1984 six teachers at a California preschool were arrested on multiple charges of child abuse, charges that eventually included rape, sodomy, fondling, oral copulation, and drugging and photographing children in the nude. Years of legal proceedings followed, based on evidence reported by children who had attended the school. In 1990, 6 years later, after the 58-year-old director and her 26-year-old son had both spent years in jail, almost all the charges were dropped and the jury deadlocked on the others. Both defendants were set free (Ceci & Bruck, 1993a, 1993b).

The key issue was whether the testimony of the children could be believed. Some said such young children could not have imagined the bizarre events they reported, like satanic rituals and animal mutilation. Others claimed the children were responding to suggestions made to them during interviews by parents, therapists, and officials. This and similar cases sparked research to determine how reliable young children's statements are.

A major social policy issue is involved here. Child abuse is a crime that by its very nature must often rely only on the testimony of preschool children, the age group most likely to be abused and most likely to be called as legal witnesses (Doris, 1993). To protect these children, adults must be held responsible. But if a child's testimony is not accurate, an innocent adult may be unfairly punished. Thus we need to know about children's memories about events in their lives.

A series of studies conducted by Stephen J. Ceci and Maggie Bruck demonstrate that children can manufacture memories of events that never occurred. For 11 consecutive weeks, an interviewer told a 4-year-old, "You went to the hospital because your finger got caught in a mousetrap. Did this ever happen to you?" At first the boy said, "No, I've never been to the hospital." In the second interview he said, "Yes, I cried." In the third: "Yes. My mom went to

the hospital with me." By the eleventh interview he said, "My daddy, mommy and my brother [took me] in our van. . . . The hospital gave me . . . a little bandage. . . . The mousetrap was in our house . . . down in the basement. . . . I was playing a game. . . . [My brother] pushed me [into the mousetrap]. I caught my finger in it yesterday. I went to the hospital yesterday" (Ceci, in Goleman, 1993a).

The complexity of drawing upon children's memories emerges from a different study in which 5- to 7-year-old girls were examined by a doctor, some for a curvature of the spine and some genitally (Saywitz, Goodman, Nicholas, & Moan, 1991). Many of the girls responded to false suggestions from an interviewer ("How many times did the doctor kiss you?" or "Didn't the doctor look at your feet first?"). Although most of the children did not make a false report of abuse, most of the girls examined genitally did not report such contact unless specifically asked about it, but a few reported vaginal or anal contact that had not occurred. Other research has shown that children given anatomically correct dolls will insert fingers or sticks into the doll's vagina or anus, reporting that someone did that to them—even when those events had not happened (Ceci & Bruck, 1993a).

Ceci and Bruck (1993a) urge expert witnesses in child abuse cases to keep the following in mind: (1) Preschoolers are more suggestible and therefore potentially less reliable than older children; (2) young children may make mistakes, especially after being asked leading questions, even about events involving their own bodies; (3) children's reports are likely to be more reliable if the children have been interviewed only once, as soon after the event as possible, and if they are interviewed by people who do not have an opinion about what took place, who do not ask leading questions, who ask open-ended rather than yes/no questions, who are patient and nonjudgmental, and who do not reward any responses.

---

conversational styles are influential: Reminiscing and elaborating on information help children remember.

Another adult influence on children's memory can come from suggestions offered to children, a controversial aspect of memory with important social policy implications. (See Box 9-2).

Unusual Activities. Vicky's episodic memory of picking apples if typical: Children as young as 3 years old remember more clearly events that were unique and new. They may recall many details from a trip to the zoo or an unusual museum for up to a year or longer (Fivush, Hudson, & Nelson, 1983). While they also have generic memories for events that recur regularly (like eating lunch or going to the beach), the memories of one common event tend to blur into those of another.

Personal Involvement.   Preschoolers tend to remember activities they actively took part in better than objects they merely saw (D. C. Jones, Swift, & Johnson, 1988). In one study, sixty-five 3- and $4\frac{1}{2}$-year-olds visited a replica of a turn-of-the-century farmhouse, where they took part in five activities, including pretending to sew a blanket on a treadle sewing machine and chopping ice with a pick and hammer. Then they were interviewed—either later the same day, 1 week later, or 8 weeks later—to determine what they remembered.

There were few age differences in the children's memories of what they had *done.* However, the older ones were better at recalling items they had seen and handled. The children remembered best objects they used to *do* something. Once again, we see how the kind of task used to assess children affects conclusions about their development.

Culture.   Furthermore, culture plays a large role. Most research on memory has focused on middle-class American or western European children, who have been talking since about age 2. We know virtually nothing about the relationship between memory and language among children who begin to speak later because of different social and cultural practices (Nelson, 1992).

What do you think?   *What kinds of cultural practices might lead to later development of memory and language?*

As we discuss the measurement of intelligence, we will see how language, memory, and the nature of children's thought all play a part.

DEVELOPMENT OF INTELLIGENCE

Assessing Intelligence by Traditional Psychometric Measures

While her mother watches through a one-way mirror, Vicky, 4, sits in a room with a man she has never seen before. He places a toy automobile, a toy dog, and a shoe on the table in front of her and asks her to name each object. Then he says, "Shut your eyes tight now so you can't see them." He puts a screen between her and the objects and then covers the dog. Removing the screen, he asks Vicky, "Which one did I hide?" Vicky opens her eyes, exclaims "The doggie!" and gets credit for a correct answer.

Since 3-year-olds can communicate with words, sit at a table, and manipulate test objects, they can respond to tasks like this. As we pointed out in Chapter 6, psychologists using the psychometric approach want to determine and measure quantitatively the factors that make up intelligence. They use *intelligence quotient (IQ) tests* to assess how much a person has of certain abilities, like comprehension and reasoning. The tests consist of questions or tasks (usually verbal and performance) that seem to reflect cognitive functioning, and the scores show how well someone can execute the tasks relative to other people. Children's performance in such tests can predict future school performance fairly accurately.

Because children get better at solving tasks as they grow, performance is evaluated on the basis of age. Each child's score is compared with **standardized norms**, standards obtained from the scores of a large, representative sample of children of the same age who took the test while it was being developed.

Test developers devise techniques to try to ensure that tests have high *validity* (that is, the tests measure the abilities they claim to measure) and *reliability* (that is, the test results are reasonably consistent from one time to another). Tests can be meaningful and useful only if they are both valid and reliable.

What Do Scores on Intelligence Tests Mean?   Many people believe that IQ test scores represent a fixed quantity of intelligence people are born with. This is not so. The score is simply an indication of how a person is functioning compared with other people. Intelligence tests are called *aptitude tests,* since they aim to measure a person's *aptitude,* or ability to learn. However, they are validated against measures of *achievement,* like school performance; and such measures are affected by factors beyond intelligence. Although the scores of school-age children and adults tend to be fairly stable, some people show marked changes, perhaps reflecting changes in their life circumstances (Kopp & McCall, 1982).

On the whole, test takers have been doing better on the Stanford-Binet in recent years (Anastasi, 1988), forcing test developers to raise previous norms. This improvement may reflect environmental changes, like exposure to educational television, preschools, better-educated parents, and a wider variety of experiences—as well as changes in the tests themselves.

Because children of 3, 4, or 5 are proficient with language, intelligence tests can now include verbal items. As a result, from this age on tests produce more reliable results than the largely nonverbal tests used in infancy. As children approach age 5, there is a higher correlation between their scores on intelligence tests and the scores they will achieve later (Bornstein & Sigman, 1986; Honzik, Macfarlane, & Allen, 1948).

Children are now easier to test than infants and toddlers, but they still need to be tested individually. Even with individual tests of intelligence like the tests we discuss below, disagreement over how accurately such tests assess differences between children is strong; the controversy becomes even stronger regarding school-age children (discussed in Chapter 12).

Stanford-Binet Intelligence Scale.   The *Stanford-Binet Intelligence Scale,* the first individual childhood intelligence test to be developed, takes 30 to 40 minutes. The child is asked to define words, string beads, build with blocks, identify the missing parts of a picture, trace mazes, and show an understanding of numbers. The child's score is supposed to measure practical judgment in real-life situations, memory, and spatial orientation.

The fourth edition of the Stanford-Binet, revised in 1985, differs in several ways from previous editions. It is less verbal: There is an equal balance of verbal and nonverbal, quantitative, and memory items. It assesses patterns and levels of cognitive development instead of providing the IQ as a single overall measure of intelligence. The updated standardization sample is well balanced geographically over the United States; ethnically, in proportion to ethnic groups' representation in the population; and by gender, representing both sexes equally. Also, the updated norms reflect a socioeconomic balance and allow for children with disabilities. (In Chapter 12 we discuss this test in more detail and explore the controversy over intelligence testing of schoolchildren.)

standardized norms
Standards obtained from the scores of a large, representative sample of children of the same age who took the test while it was being developed.

validity   *Degree to which a test measures the abilities it claims to measure.*

reliability   *Degree to which a test yields reasonably consistent results time after time.*

Stanford-Binet Intelligence Scale   *The first individual childhood intelligence test to be developed; measures practical judgment, memory, and spatial orientation.*

Wechsler Preschool and Primary Scale of Intelligence (WPPSI-R).   The *Wechsler Preschool and Primary Scale of Intelligence (WPPSI-R)**, an hour-long individual test used with children aged 3 to 7, yields separate verbal and performance scores as well as a combined score. Its separate scales are similar to those in the Wechsler Intelligence Scale for Children (WISC), discussed in Chapter 12. The 1989 revision includes new subtests and new picture items. It too has been restandardized on a sample of children representing the population of preschool-age children in the United States. Because children of this age tire quickly and are easily distracted, the test may be given in two separate sessions.

What do you think?   *How meaningful is intelligence testing of young children? Give reasons for your answer.*

Assessing Intelligence by Finding the "Zone of Proximal Development" (ZPD)

A form of testing popular in Russia and now influencing testing in the United States is based on Vygotsky's (1978) theory of cognitive development (described in Chapter 1). He says adults teach most effectively in the *zone of proximal development (ZPD).* Children in this "zone" for a particular tasks can almost perform a task on their own.

To take a child's potential into account, testers using the ZPD approach give children test items up to 2 years above their level of actual development and help them answer the items by asking leading questions and giving examples. The testers then find the child's current ZPD, which tells more about a child's potential than does a traditional test score.

INFLUENCES ON COGNITIVE DEVELOPMENT

When Jason was 6 months old, his parents began reading to him at bedtime—a routine he now cherishes. Seeing his books as a kind of toy, Jason sometimes looked at the pictures by himself. Once Julia put a picture book in his stroller and enjoyed the double takes as passersby saw 18-month-old Jason sucking his thumb and "reading." As we have seen, parents' attitudes and actions affect children's cognitive development. Other influences are the child's own personality, day care, and schooling.

HOW DOES PERSONALITY INFLUENCE COGNITIVE DEVELOPMENT?

Cognitive functioning is closely related to emotional functioning and temperament. An active child who is assertive and curious and takes initiative is likely to do well on IQ tests. Children's social and emotional functioning in preschool appears to influence their performance in the first and second grades.

A group of 323 three-year-olds attending public day care centers in New York City were rated on their social and emotional functioning—how well they got along with teachers and other children and adapted to daily routines. The children were followed up in the first and second grades. When their test scores and

---

*"R" means *revised.*

their teachers' academic ratings of them were compared with their preschool social and emotional ratings, a strong relationship appeared. The findings "suggest that the child who is curious, alert and assertive will learn from [the] environment and . . . the child who is passive, apathetic, and withdrawn will . . . learn less about [it] because of diminished contact; he may even actively avoid contact" (Kohn & Rosman, 1973, p. 450).

HOW DO PARENTS INFLUENCE COGNITIVE DEVELOPMENT?

How well children do on intelligence tests is influenced by such factors as their temperament, the match between their cognitive style and the tasks they are asked to do, their social and emotional maturity, their ease in the testing situation, and their socioeconomic status and ethnic background. (We will examine the last two factors in Chapter 12.) Their parents may be the most important influence.

Providing an Environment for Learning

Do parents who raise children who do well on IQ tests do something special? They seem to. Parents of children with higher IQs tend to be warm, loving, and sensitive. They accept the children's behavior, letting them express themselves and explore. When they want to change a child's behavior, they use reasoning or appeals to feelings rather than rigid rules. They tend to use the *authoritative* style of child rearing (discussed in Chapter 10), which combines respect for the child with firm parental guidance. These parents use sophisticated language and teaching strategies and encourage independence, creativity, and growth by reading to children, teaching them to do things, and playing with them. The children respond with curiosity and creativity and do well in school. Parents who provide challenging, pleasurable learning opportunities for a child lay a foundation for optimum cognitive growth (Clarke-Stewart, 1977).

Parents and the attitudes they project are among many factors that affect children's cognitive development. The reading that this mother does with her children will enrich their knowledge and stimulate their imagination—especially if she makes special efforts to ask them open-ended questions.

Scaffolding: How Parents Teach Children

Sometimes, as Vicky and her mother stroll through the neighborhood, they talk about Vicky's imaginary friends. Ellen asks questions that encourage Vicky to bring these friends into her "pretend" play in a slightly more complex way than Vicky has already shown. Ellen is engaging in *scaffolding*, the kind of teaching favored by Vygotsky, in which adults give temporary support until a child can do a task on his or her own. (See Chapter 1.)

scaffolding *Temporary support given a child to do a task.*

In one study of scaffolding, parents worked with their 3-year-old children on three difficult tasks—copying a model made of blocks; classifying by size, color, and shape; and asking the children to retell a story they had heard. Parents tended to be guided by their children's levels of competence and gave more help when children had more trouble. Furthermore, parents became more sensitive to their children's needs later in the experiment than they had been at first. Sensitivity turned out to be significant: The more finely tuned the parents' help was, the better a child did (Pratt, Kerig, Cowan, & Cowan, 1988).

The Quality of Parenting

The interrelationship among the various domains of development emerges from an observational study showing how physical, emotional, and social aspects of parenting affect a child's cognitive development. Once a month for $2\frac{1}{2}$ years until the target children turned 3, researchers visited the homes of 40 families and observed how parents acted with their children (B. Hart & Risley, 1992). Both parents were present in 32 families; 15 families were African American and 25 were white; 6 were on welfare. The researchers coded three broad clusters of parenting: how much attention a parent gave a child per hour; the nature of parent-child social interaction; and what kinds of things parents said to children—prohibitions, questions, or repetitions and elaborations of the children's statements.

There were considerable differences among these families. For example, although all the parents talked to their children, one parent addressed 200 words to a child in the course of an hour, while another addressed almost 4000 words. Within families, parenting patterns remained stable. No relationship appeared between the children's sex and any parenting measures or IQ scores. Most significant were the correlations between some parenting factors and children's later IQ scores and between specific parenting practices and socioeconomic status (SES). Higher-SES parents spent more time with their children, gave them more attention, talked more to them, and showed more interest in what they had to say. Much more of the talk from lower-SES parents included words like "stop," "quit," and "don't." Children whose parents used a lot of prohibition words tended to score lower on tests.

This study pinpoints some specific differences in parenting that may account for typical differences in IQ test scores and in school performance between children from higher- and lower-income families. It also provides guidance to parents by showing the kinds of practices that can help children do better in school.

Another study found socioeconomic status in itself not a determining factor in intelligence scores, but only one of several social and family risk factors. Assessments of 152 children at ages 4 and 13 revealed no single pattern of risk. Instead, a child's IQ was related to *the total number* of such risk factors as the mother's behavior, mental health, anxiety level, education, and beliefs about children's development; family size and social support; stressful life events; the parent's occupation; and disadvantaged minority status. The more risk factors there were, the lower the child's IQ score (Sameroff, Seifer, Baldwin, & Baldwin, 1993).

THE WIDENING ENVIRONMENT

Parents are far from the only influence on cognitive development. Today more young children than ever spend a large part of the day in day care, preschool, or kindergarten—and another large part in front of the television set.

The difference between preschool and day care (discussed in Chapter 7) lies in their primary purpose. Day care provides a safe place where children can be cared for, usually all day, while their parents are at work or school. Preschool emphasizes educational experiences geared to children's developmental needs, typically in sessions of only 2 hours or so. The distinction has blurred, however: Good day care centers seek to meet children's cognitive, social, and emotional needs, and many preschools offer longer days. Here we discuss the educational components of preschool, which also apply to many day care programs.

PRESCHOOL

Preschools have flourished in the United States since 1919, when the first public nursery schools were established. Many privately run preschools serve mainly well-educated, affluent families, but more and more public schools are moving into preschool education. Preschool enrollment has grown rapidly since 1970 despite a sharp decline in the birthrate.

How Good Preschools Foster Development

At preschool children explore a world outside the home and choose from among activities tailored to their interests and abilities. Through these, children experience successes that build confidence and self-image. Preschool helps children from one- or two-child families (like most families today) learn how to get along with other children.

Some preschools stress social and emotional growth. Others, like those based on the theories of Piaget or of the Italian educator Maria Montessori, have a strong cognitive emphasis. A good preschool provides experiences that let children learn by doing; stimulates their senses through art, music, and tactile materials like clay, water, and wood; and encourages them to observe, talk, create, and solve problems. These activities lay the foundation for advanced cognitive functioning.

This little boy's concentration on the task at hand is typical. Preschool is the place to learn new skills and improve old ones, and to grow in many ways—physically, cognitively, socially, and emotionally.

How Academically Oriented Should Preschool Be?

Over the past couple of decades, pressures have built to offer formal education in preschool. The rising demand for day care, the appreciation of the "head start" gained by disadvantaged children in compensatory programs, the numbers of teachers put out of work by declining school enrollments and shrinking school budgets, and the growing desire among parents to give their children a leg up on the educational ladder have combined to bring the three Rs into preschool. Many educators and psychologists, however, maintain that the only children who benefit from early schooling are those from disadvantaged families—and that a relaxed preschool experience is better for middle-class children (Elkind, 1987).

One study compared children who had attended a heavily academic preschool with others from more traditional (relaxed) preschools. In the early grades the children from the academic preschool did better; but 10 years later, the boys from the traditional preschools did better in reading and math than boys from the academic one. The girls from the academic school did better in reading, but not in math (L. B. Miller & Bizzel, 1983). In another study children who had gone to traditional preschool did as well in kindergarten as those who had attended academic preschools. Children from academic preschools were more anxious taking tests, less creative, and more negative about school than those who went to traditional preschools (Hirsh-Pasek, Hyson, & Rescorla, 1989).

Additional findings came from a longitudinal study that compared low-income youngsters from three different types of preschool programs (Schweinhart, Weikart, & Larner, 1986). One stressed social and emotional development and activities initiated by the child; one was highly structured, emphasizing the teaching of numbers, letters, and words; the third took a middle ground. Children from the academic program narrowly outperformed the others—but had more behavior problems. As adolescents, many had lost interest in school and developed such social and emotional problems as vandalism and delinquency. Too early an academic emphasis may affect children's interest or ability to learn for the long run.

The preschool's most important contribution may well be the children's feeling that school is fun, that learning is satisfying, and that they are competent. The question of what makes a good preschool is answered according to a particular culture's values. (See Box 9-3.)

BOX 9-3 ■ AROUND THE WORLD

PRESCHOOLS IN THREE CULTURES

It is morning in a Japanese preschool. After a half-hour workbook session, lively with talk, laughter, and playful fighting among the children, twenty-eight 4-year-olds sing in unison: "As I sit here with my lunch, I think of mom, I bet it's delicious, I wonder what she's made?" The children speak freely, loudly, even vulgarly to each other for much of the day, but then have periods of formal, teacher-directed group recitations of polite expressions of greeting, thanks, and blessings.

In a Chinese preschool, twenty-six 4-year-olds sing a cheerful song about a train, acting out the words by hooking onto each other's backs and chugging around the room. They then sit down and, for the next 20 minutes, follow their teacher's direction to put together blocks, copying pictures she has handed out. They work in an orderly way, and their errors are corrected as the session proceeds. The teacher has taught the children to recite long pieces and sing complicated songs, emphasizing enunciation, diction, and self-confidence, but she discourages spontaneous talk as possible distraction from work.

The eighteen 4-year-olds at an American preschool begin their day with a show-and-tell session in which children speak individually. They sing a song about monkeys and, for the next 45 minutes, separate into different activities—painting, playing with blocks, completing puzzles, playing in the housekeeping corner, and listening to a story. The teacher moves around the room, talking with the children about their activities, mediating fights, and keeping order. She encourages children to express their own feelings and opinions, helps them learn new words to express concepts, and corrects their speech.

What makes a good preschool? Your answer depends on what you regard as the ideal child, the ideal adult, and the ideal society. The ways schools reflect such values show up in a comparison among preschools in Japan, China, and the United States (Tobin, Wu, & Davidson, 1989). The wide-ranging study involved videotaping preschool activities in all three countries, showing the tapes and discussing them with parents and educators, and asking 750 teachers, administrators, parents, and child development specialists to fill out questionnaires. The classroom activities were consistent with the opinions expressed by each cultural group.

One big difference was in the importance of teaching subject matter. Over half the Americans listed "to give children a good start academically" as one of the top three reasons for a society to have preschools. Only 2 percent of the Japanese gave this answer: They tend to see preschools as havens from the academic pressure and competition that children will face in the years to come. Japanese preschoolers are encouraged to develop more basic skills like concentration and the ability to function in a group. Teachers cultivate perseverance, for example, by refusing to help children dress and undress themselves. The Chinese emphasized academics even more than the Americans, with 67 percent giving this answer. Their emphasis on early learning seems to stem from the Confucian tradition of early, strenuous study; from the Cultural Revolution's discouragement of frivolity and its stress on reading, writing, working with numbers, and clear speaking; and from the desire of parents to compensate for their own disrupted educations. This early stress on academics is controversial, and a less academic preschool curriculum is becoming more popular, especially among developmentalists.

Although preschoolers in all three cultures do many of the same activities, China stresses academic instruction, Japan stresses play, and the United States presents a mixed picture. But in all three countries, parents often pressure preschools to give their children a strong educational start so they will achieve prominent positions in the society. It would be interesting to follow today's children to find out whether those who work harder at ages 3 or 4 or 5 do, in fact, achieve more as adults.

SOURCE: Tobin, Wu, & Davidson, 1989.

What do you think? *What do you consider the primary purpose of preschool and kindergarten: to provide a strong academic foundation for elementary school or to give children an opportunity to learn to function as members of a group, or something else?*

KINDERGARTEN

The typical 5-year-old gets a first taste of "real school" as she or he attends kindergarten, a traditional introduction to formal schooling. Entrance in kindergarten is usually a major family transition; some researchers have explored the link between aspects in the marriage of a child's parents and the child's adaptation to kindergarten (P. A. Cowan, Cowan, Schulz, & Heming, 1994).

Working from an ecological model, these researchers conducted a longitudinal study of 72 couples, beginning in late pregnancy and extending for almost 6 years. When parents had a happy childhood themselves, were happily married in the child's early years, and use an authoritative parenting style, their children do better in kindergarten, both socially and academically. Here is one more example of the way influences can reach out from the past to affect many aspects of a child's life.

How Much Like "Real" School Should Kindergarten Be?

During the 1970s and 1980s, kindergarten—historically a year of transition between the relative freedom of home or preschool and the structure of the primary grades—became more like first grade. The pressures that have made preschools more academically oriented filtered down from kindergarten, where today many children spend less time on freely chosen activities that stretch their muscles and imaginations and more time on worksheets and learning to read (Egertson, 1987).

Many kindergarteners now spend a full day in school, and results of studies on the effects of all-day kindergarten are mixed (Robertson, 1984; Rust, cited in Connecticut Early Childhood Education Council, 1983). Advocates of full-day kindergarten say its longer blocks of uninterrupted time permit unhurried experiences and educational activities, more opportunity for pupil-teacher and parent-teacher contact with a teacher responsible for one rather than two classes, and higher energy levels for teachers and children thanks to a structured morning start and a more relaxed afternoon. Opponents say some 5-year-olds cannot handle a 6-hour day and a long separation from their parents, nor exposure to the danger of overemphasis on academic skills and sedentary activities.

Some educators and psychologists express alarm over "treating kindergarten like a miniature elementary school with a heavy cognitive-academic orientation" (Zigler, 1987, p. 258). They caution against sending children to kindergarten too early, pointing to studies showing the "age effect": The youngest children in a class do less well than the oldest (Sweetland & DeSimone, 1987). One solution is a half-day kindergarten taught by licensed, qualified teachers, followed by a half-day of care given by certified child caregivers (Zigler, 1987). This gives some academic preparation and all-day supervision for those who need it.

We know that many 5-year-olds—and even some younger children—can be taught "2 times 2 equals 4," just as we know that 9-month-old infants can be taught to recognize words printed on flash cards. But unless the motivation comes from *them*, or the learning arises naturally from their experience, their time might be better spent on the true business of early childhood—play.

Predicting Future School Success

A number of measures, including psychometric tests, have been used to predict how well a young child will do in school later on. The best time for screening children with no known disability seems to be toward the end of the kindergarten year. Although there is no single measure or set of measures that accurately predicts a child's academic future, some associations have shown up, especially to identify children at either extreme of academic ability (Tramontana, Hooper, & Selzer, 1988).

Compensatory preschool education, like the Head Start program these children are enrolled in, often yields long-term benefits, with long-lasting gains for children. Some positive effects of Head Start have held up through high school.

IQ is among the best predictors of school achievement; children's ability to understand and to express themselves with language predicts reading competence; and visual-motor and visual-perceptual measures predict reading, math, and general achievement, at least through first grade. The most important behavioral measure is a child's ability to pay attention. These qualities are stressed in programs designed for disadvantaged children.

COMPENSATORY PRESCHOOL PROGRAMS FOR DISADVANTAGED CHILDREN

Children from deprived socioeconomic backgrounds often enter school with a considerable handicap. Since the 1960s, large-scale programs have been developed to help such children compensate for what they have missed and to prepare them for school.

Project Head Start

Project Head Start
Compensatory preschool educational program begun in 1965.

The best-known compensatory preschool program in the United States is *Project Head Start.* It was launched in 1965 in the federal government's war against poverty, focusing on children of low-income families.

The program evolved from a planning committee of 14 experts from the fields of child development, health, and education. One of them, Urie Bronfenbrenner, was just beginning to develop his ecological approach to human development. He maintained that intervention must address the interrelationship among children, their families, and their communities (Zigler & Styfco, 1993).

Head Start's administrators responded to this "whole child" approach as they set goals to improve physical health, enhance mental skills, and foster such aspects of social and emotional development as self-confidence, relationships with others, social responsibility, and a sense of dignity and self-worth for the child and the family. To accomplish these aims, the program provides medical, dental, and mental health care; nutrition (at least one hot meal a day); cognitive enrichment; social services for the child and family; and parent involvement. In 1992, 1370 Head Start centers served more than 621,000 children and their families; more than 11 million had been served since the program began in 1965 (Zigler & Styfco, 1993).

Has Head Start lived up to its name? The program has probably had its strongest impact in physical health and well-being for the target children. Head Start children have shown substantial cognitive and language gains, with the neediest children benefiting the most. One reason why they do as well as they do in school is, being healthier, they are absent less than youngsters from impoverished homes who are not in Head Start. They do better on tests of motor control and physical development (McKey et al., 1985). They also do better on IQ tests, probably because they are motivated and are familiar with the content of test questions and the testing situation (Zigler & Styfco, 1993). Head Start has also had a positive impact on self-esteem, socialization, and social maturity (McKey et al., 1985). Furthermore, it has had a favorable effect on families, through the jobs and job training it offers to low-income parents, the parenting education, and the social support (Zigler & Styfco, 1993).

Long-Term Benefits of Compensatory Preschool Education

Compensatory preschool education often shows long-lasting gains that repay society's initial investment. Although increases in IQ tend to be short-lived without further academic enrichment, some positive effects of preschool programs hold up through high school. Students in 10 early intervention programs assessed by the Consortium for Longitudinal Studies were less likely to be held back and more likely to stay in school and to be in regular (not special) classes than were other needy children (L. B. Miller & Bizzel, 1983).

It has been hard to evaluate Head Start because, being community-based and community-directed, the programs vary around the country. Also, with less funding for social programs in recent years, there have been fewer evaluation efforts. As a result, many findings about Head Start are old (Zigler & Styfco, 1993).

Still, there do seem to be long-term benefits for children enrolled in high-quality preschool programs that incorporate special services like those in Head Start (Haskins, 1989). Students in the Perry preschool program were less likely to need special education for slow learners than were children who had no formal schooling until kindergarten or first grade. They were also much more likely at age 19 to have finished high school, to have enrolled in college or vocational training, and to have jobs. They did better on competence tests and were less likely to have been arrested, and women were less likely to have become pregnant (Berrueta-Clement, Schweinhart, Barnett, Epstein, & Weikart, 1985; Haskins, 1989).

Why have Head Start children not equaled the average middle-class child in performance either in school or on standardized tests (R. C. Collins & Deloria, 1983)? This is apparently because intervention started too late and ended too soon. The solution may involve intervening in the lives of infants and offering programs in the elementary years building upon what has gone before (Zigler & Styfco, 1993). Even though such a commitment will be costly, prevention may well be more effective and less expensive in the long run than remediation or than the need for society to support adults who have failed to become law-abiding, self-sustaining citizens.

It seems, then, that early childhood education can help to compensate for deprivation, and that well-planned programs produce long-term benefits that exceed their original cost (Haskins, 1989). However, we need to keep in mind the developmental needs of young children for play, exploration, and freedom from undue demands—and we need to look closely at particular programs. We also need to look closely at television programs, which occupy more hours of many young children's time than preschool does.

EDUCATIONAL TELEVISION

Parents are often criticized for using television as a baby-sitter, but no parent can be with a child every waking moment. "The real question seems to be whether it is a good or a bad baby-sitter" (Huston & Wright, 1994, p. 80).

Children learn from television. But what are they learning? They learn cognitive concepts like letter and number skills. One study found that the more time 3- to 5-year-olds spent watching *Sesame Street* (as opposed to watching other programs or none), the more their vocabulary skills improved (M. L. Rice, Huston, Truglio, & Wright, 1990). This program was specifically designed to teach such skills as using letters and numbers, solving problems, reasoning, and understanding the physical and social environment. Apparently, it has succeeded.

The program's format is designed to attract children's attention and to get them to participate actively. Children pay more attention to children's and women's voices on television, to cartoons rather than real people, and to accompanying narration, and they respond to shows that acknowledge their interests (Huston & Wright, 1994). After children have heard the words to songs, they enjoy singing along when the music is played without the lyrics. Furthermore, learning often carries over to a wide range of verbal skills not specifically taught.

Television can also spark conversation. From early in the second year of life, children talk to their parents about what they see. They label objects ("kitty"), repeat slogans ("Diet Pepsi, one less calorie"), and ask questions ("Where Ernie go?"). Aside from having interesting and pleasant talks with their young children, parents can build on the children's interest and lead them into the kind of exchanges that, as we have seen, enhance language development (Lemish & Rice, 1986).

When *Sesame Street* first rose to popularity, it showed a great deal of aggression in the form of slapstick sequences and name calling; and it perpetuated gender stereotypes by showing fewer females than males and portraying females as passive. Over the years, however, the show changed markedly, especially with regard to gender-stereotyping. The influence of television on children's attitudes toward gender roles and violence seems considerable, and child development professionals have expressed great concern about the need for adults to help young children reap the educational and other benefits of television, with a minimum of negative influence. (See Box 9-4). Television, then, is one of the major influences in the macrosystem of children's social and personality development, as we shall see in Chapter 10.

BOX 9-4 ▪ THE EVERYDAY WORLD

GUIDING CHILDREN'S TELEVISION VIEWING

Jason watches television several hours every day. By his third birthday, like most American children, he watches 2 to 3 hours a day; by age 5, he watches a little more; and then from ages 5 to 7, he watches less. There are wide individual differences, however. Like many boys, Jason watches more cartoons and action-adventure shows than does Vicky, a typical girl (Huston, Wright, Rice, Kerkman, & St. Petes, 1990). By the time both graduate from high school, they will have spent more time in front of the television set than in the classroom (American Academy of Pediatrics, 1986a).

Television has many far-reaching effects: It influences children's attitudes about hurting or helping other people, about gender roles, about alcohol and other drugs, and about sexuality and relationships. It can send positive messages—or negative ones. Children are active viewers of television, at least most of the time: They choose the programs to watch; as they grow older, they watch more complex shows, and they watch cartoons and comedies rather than information shows especially designed for them. Television-viewing patterns seem to be set quite early in life and are greatly influenced by parents' patterns (Huston et al., 1990).

To help children reap the benefits and avoid the dangers of this electronic teacher, caregivers can follow guidelines suggested by the American Academy of Pediatrics (1986a) and Action for Children's Television (undated):

◆ *Plan a child's viewing in advance.* Approach television the way you would a movie, deciding with your child which show to watch, turning the set on for that program, and turning it off when the program is over.

◆ *Set limits.* Restrict a child's viewing to 1 or 2 hours a day at certain set times, taking into account the child's favorite programs.

◆ *Do not use television as a reward or punishment,* although you may want to reserve viewing time until after the child has carried out responsibilities like homework and chores.

◆ *Watch with a child.* This way, you will know what the child is seeing and you will be able to use television to express your own values and feelings about complex issues and to explain confusing scenes.

◆ *Talk to children* about such topics as love, work, war, family life, sex, drugs, and crime. You can open up conversations about the difference between make-believe and real life, about ways characters could solve problems without violence, and about how violence hurts.

◆ *Set a good example.* Change your own viewing habits if necessary to help children develop good habits.

◆ *Provide alternatives.* Encourage and participate in both indoor and outdoor activities like games, sports, hobbies, reading, and household duties. Use television as a baby-sitter as little as possible.

◆ *Resist commercials.* Help children become smart consumers by teaching them how to recognize a sales pitch and how to tell when a product is presented as an advertisement. Talk about foods that can cause cavities and about toys that may be quickly broken.

◆ *Use new technologies.* If you have a videocassette recorder, tape desirable shows or rent movies or special tapes made for children. If you have cable, ask about devices to lock out inappropriate channels.

◆ *Recognize your power* in channeling the power of television so it will enhance a child's life.

SUMMARY

1 According to Piaget, from approximately 2 to 7 years of age, children are in the preoperational stage of cognitive development. The symbolic function—as shown in deferred imitation, symbolic play, and language—enables children to mentally represent and reflect upon people, objects, and events through the use of symbols.

2 Piaget may have underestimated some of the abilities of "preoperational" children. Experiments using situations familiar to young children suggest that these children are better able to identify and understand causal relationships, are less animistic and egocentric, are more empathic, and have a better grasp of classification and number than Piaget described. Researchers have been able to teach young children conservation when they are already on the verge of grasping it.

3   Preoperational thought has a number of limitations. Children in this stage tend to be egocentric. They show centration; they do not understand reversibility, transformations, and conservation; and they reason transductively. They also do not understand the distinction between appearance and reality.

4   Speech and grammar become fairly sophisticated during early childhood, although some immaturities remain. Speech is of two types: private and social. Private speech is not intended to communicate to a listener but appears to help children gain control over their actions. Social speech is intended to communicate with others. Piaget characterized most preschool speech as egocentric, but recent research shows that children's speech is quite social. Delayed language development may reflect problems in fast mapping.

5   Literacy development is affected by social interaction.

6   Recognition memory is better than recall memory in early childhood, as it is throughout life.

7   Generic memory, which begins at around age 2, relies on a script that provides a general outline of a repeated event. Episodic memory, also displayed by 2-year-olds, refers to a specific one-time event. Autobiographical memory, the personally meaningful memories that form an individual's life history, begins in early childhood.

8   Memory is influenced by general knowledge, mastery motivation, study activities, language, social interaction, unusual activities, personal involvement, and cultural expectations.

9   Psychometric tests of intelligence for young children include the Stanford-Binet Intelligence Scale and the Wechsler Preschool and Primary Scale of Intelligence. Since these tests contain more verbal items than do the tests of infancy, they are better at predicting later intelligence and school performance. New approaches include assessing intelligence by finding the "zone of proximal development" (ZPD).

10   Intelligence test scores and achievement are influenced by the child's personality as well as by parent-child interaction.

11   Preschool programs are of many types. A good preschool fosters children's cognitive, social-emotional, and physical development.

12   Evaluations of compensatory programs like Project Head Start indicate that such programs can have both short-term and long-term benefits. However, it is important not to put too much academic pressure on young children.

13   Kindergarten prepares children for formal schooling. The academic content of kindergarten has increased in recent years.

14   Children who view educational television, most notably *Sesame Street,* show enhanced cognitive skills.

KEY TERMS

symbolic function (340)
symbol (340)
deferred imitation (341)
symbolic play (341)
preoperational stage (343)
centration (343)
decenter (343)
conservation (343)
irreversibility (346)
transduction (346)
egocentrism (346)
animism (347)
theory of mind (349)

fast mapping (352)
pragmatics (353)
social speech (353)
private speech (354)
literacy (357)
recognition (359)
recall (359)
generic memory (360)
script (360)
episodic memory (361)
autobiographical memory (361)
standardized norms (365)
validity (365)

reliability (365)
Stanford-Binet Intelligence Scale (365)
Wechsler Preschool and Primary Scale of
  Intelligence (WPPSI-R) (366)

zone of proximal development (ZPD)
  (366)
scaffolding (367)
Project Head Start (372)

SUGGESTED READINGS

Baron, N. S. (1992) *Growing up with language: How children learn to talk.* Reading, MA: Addison-Wesley. The author, a mother and linguistics professor, unravels the mystery of how children, in just a few short years, crack the code and master language. She explains the processes by which they become coherent readers and speakers, and how parents play a vital role. This work is both highly informative and eminently readable.

Ingersoll, B. D., & Goldstein, S. (1993). *Attention deficit disorder and learning disabilities.* New York: Doubleday. This book helps sorts out the realities and myths of treatments for ADD and learning disabilities. The authors discuss established as well as "alternative" treatments, focusing on the latest evidence from scientific studies.

Oppenheim, J., Brenner, B., & Boegehold, B. D. (1986). *Choosing books for kids.* New York: Ballantine. This book suggests ways to foster a love of reading in children and discusses what is happening developmentally and how this affects what children of different ages will read and respond to. It reviews more than 1500 books, ranging from board books for toddlers to fiction for adolescents.

Tobin, J. J., Wu, D. W. H., & Davidson, D. H. (1991). *Preschool in three cultures: Japan, China, and the United States.* New Haven: Yale University Press. A thought-provoking study of preschools in three countries shows that the Japanese, Chinese, and Americans have very different ideas about how to train children for their future roles in society.

CHAPTER 10
PERSONALITY AND SOCIAL DEVELOPMENT IN EARLY CHILDHOOD

I am fainty,
I am fizzy,
I am floppy.

Paul Thompson (age 6), *My Feelings,* 1966

Our study of personality development in early childhood begins with children's understanding about themselves and how that understanding grows. We'll see how their feelings about themselves and other people affect their personalities. As we discuss what makes up personality, we'll see how one component—identification—influences children's recognition of their own gender. Identification also affects the degree to which they will be altruistic (that is, act out of concern for another person, with no expectation of reward), or aggressive, or fearful. We examine the effect on personality and social development of parents' child-rearing practices and look at how personality affects and is affected by others in a child's social network, like brothers and sisters and playmates. Finally, we explore an activity that brings together social, physical, and cognitive abilities—play. When you have read this chapter, you should be able to answer questions like the following:

PREVIEW QUESTIONS

- ♦ How do children develop a self-concept?
- ♦ What is the progression of children's understanding of emotions?
- ♦ How does the search for identity proceed in early childhood?
- ♦ How do boys and girls identify their sex? How does this identification affect their personalities and standards of behavior?
- ♦ How do parents' child-rearing practices influence young children's personality development?
- ♦ What makes young children act aggressively or altruistically?
- ♦ What accounts for common fears in early childhood? What can be done about them?
- ♦ How do young children get along with their siblings? How do they begin to form friendships?
- ♦ Why do young children play? What kinds of play do they engage in?

Jason, at age 4, asked to describe himself, says:

My name is Jason and I live in an apartment with my mommy and daddy. I have a kitty and her name is Pumpkin. We have a television and I like to watch cartoons. I know all of my A-B-Cs. Listen: A-B-C-D-F-G-J-L-K-O-M-P-Q-X-Z. I can run faster than anyone! I can climb to the top of the jungle gym, I'm not scared! Just happy. You can't be happy *and* scared, no way! I have black hair. I go to preschool. I'm really strong. I can lift this chair, watch me! (Adapted from Harter, 1993, p. 2*)

*Much of this discussion of children's developing understanding of themselves, including their self-concept and their understanding of their emotions, is indebted to Susan Harter (1990, 1993).

IMPORTANT PERSONALITY DEVELOPMENTS IN EARLY CHILDHOOD

SELF-UNDERSTANDING

The way Jason describes himself is characteristic of children his age. He names concrete behaviors, specific physical features, preferences, possessions, and family members. He talks about particular skills (running and climbing) rather than generalizing about his abilities (being athletic). His descriptions spill over into demonstrations, showing how what he thinks is tied to what he does. He defines himself by behaviors and characteristics that other people can see.

Self-definition grows out of both cognitive and emotional elements. Developmentalists today generally view the self as a cognitive construction—a system of descriptive and evaluative representations about the self that guide behavior. This is easy to see in Jason's focus on the observable aspects of himself. Not until middle childhood will he describe himself in terms of higher-order generalizations or trait labels (like *popular, smart,* or *dumb*), which combine a number of specific behaviors that form the basis for the child's conclusion about the self.

A Neo-Piagetian Progression

According to neo-Piagetian thinkers, this shift in self-definition occurs in a continuous progression rather than discrete stages (Fischer, 1980). In this chapter we describe two steps: One occurs in early childhood and one at the border to middle childhood.

■ *Single representations.* At age 4 Jason's statements about himself are isolated from one another. His thinking jumps from particular to particular, in no logical order. He thinks in all-or-none terms: He cannot acknowledge that he might be good in some abilities and not in others, nor can he imagine having two emotions at the same time ("You can't be happy *and* scared").

■ *Representational mappings.* Then, at about ages 5 to 6, Jason can link one aspect of himself to another: "I can run fast, and I can climb high. I'm also strong. I can throw a ball real far, I'm going to be on a team some day!" (Harter, 1993, p. 9). He still focuses on the things he is good at, and his thinking is still all-or-none: "I'm good and therefore I can't be bad" (Harter, 1993, p. 10). In middle childhood, as we shall see in Chapter 13, self-descriptions become more balanced and integrated ("I'm good at some things, bad at others"), as the tendency to think in all-or-none terms declines.*

THE EMERGING SELF-CONCEPT

The *self-concept* is what we believe about who we are, our total picture of our abilities and traits. The beginning of the self-concept is laid down early in life and expands later, especially during middle childhood, as we will see in Chapter 13. For now, let's look at some early roots of the self-concept.

self-concept *What people believe about who they are; sense of self.*

---

*In Chapter 13 we describe *representational systems,* showing children's ability to integrate different features of the self to form higher-order generalizations.

The Early Sense of Self

The sense of self begins in infancy. Jason gradually realizes he is separate from other people and things, and he can reflect on himself and his actions. At about 18 months, he has his first moment of *self-recognition* when he recognizes himself in a mirror.

Next in the development of a sense of self is **self-definition,** when Jason identifies the characteristics he considers important to describe himself. At age 4, Jason thinks of himself mostly in terms of externals. Not until about age 6 or 7 will he begin to define himself in psychological terms. In early childhood Jason develops a concept of who he would like to be—the **ideal self.** But since he is still engaging in all-or-none thinking, he has trouble acknowledging that his **real self**—who he actually is—is different from his ideal self. As a result, he defines himself as a paragon of virtues and abilities.

Children between ages 4 and 7 judge their competence as measured in concrete, observable behaviors. However, they usually have an inflated sense of their abilities, for several reasons. First, they do not yet have the cognitive and social skills to compare themselves accurately with others. Second, adults tend to give positive feedback on newly mastered abilities, especially in comparison with a child's past levels of accomplishment. Third, an unrealistically high self-appraisal may serve a developmental function. When **self-esteem**—the judgment we make about our worth—is high, a child is motivated to achieve (Harter, 1990).*

Measures and Characteristics of Self-Esteem

Although young children can make some judgments about their competence at various activities, they are not yet able to rate the different domains in terms of their importance. They do not seem to be able to put into words a concept of self-worth until middle childhood (Harter, 1990). However, they show by their behavior that they have a sense of self-worth.

Preschool and kindergarten teachers were asked to describe behaviors of children with high or low self-esteem. A different group of teachers was then asked to sort 84 items cited by the first group to find which ones seemed most typical of children at both extremes of self-esteem. The assessments of the second group of teachers matched the descriptions of the first group, and the researchers came up with two basic categories of traits defining children with high and low self-esteem. One category consisted of items representing the child's style of approach to the world; the other category comprised the child's reactions to change, frustration, or stress (Haltiwanger & Harter, 1988). Thus we can paint a portrait of two children:

Tonda has high self-esteem. She trusts her own ideas, is self-confident in approaching challenge and initiating activities, sets goals on her own, is curious, questions and explores, is eager to try new things. She describes herself positively and shows pride in her work and achievements. She is comfortable with transitions, adjusts well to stress, perseveres in the face of frustration, and is able to handle criticism and teasing.

*Support for this last function comes from research suggesting that adults who have an inflated sense of their own abilities and are overly optimistic about what they expect to accomplish are less likely to be depressed than are those with more realistic self-appraisals (Taylor, 1989). Maybe it's too bad many of us "outgrow" this early tendency to overrate ourselves!

self-definition *One aspect of the sense of self; cluster of characteristics considered important in describing oneself.*

ideal self *The self one would like to be.*

real self *The self one actually is.*

self-esteem *The judgment people make about their own worth.*

One source of children's self-esteem comes from their parents. This mother's show of positive interest in her daughter's school work lets her child know that she matters. Feeling loved and respected, she is likely to feel good about herself.

James has low self-esteem. He does not trust his own ideas, lacks the confidence to initiate activities or approach challenge, does not show curiosity or interest in exploring, hangs back and watches rather than participates, withdraws and sits apart from other children, describes himself in negative terms, and does not show pride in his work. When frustrated he gives up easily, and when faced with stress he shows immature behavior.

The differences seem to be in children's levels of confidence, curiosity, willingness to explore, and their ability to adapt to change. These behaviors are similar to those that differentiate securely and insecurely attached infants, as we saw in Chapter 7. Behaviors apparently *not* related to self-esteem include a child's levels of competence and activity, ability to pay attention, motivation to finish tasks, ability to make friends, and need for teacher encouragement.

Initiative versus Guilt

Erik Erikson (1950) too saw initiative, which emerged as one marker of self-worth, as a vital characteristic to emerge during early childhood. He named his third crisis of personality development *initiative versus guilt*. This entails a conflict between the sense of purpose, or initiative, which lets a child plan and begin to carry out activities, and the moral reservations the child may have about such plans.

In early childhood, children are faced with two contradictory pressures. They *can* do—and *want* to do—more and more. At the same time, they are learning that some of the things they want to do (like singing a cute song) meet social approval, while others (like taking apart Mommy's clock) do not. How do they resolve their desire to do with their desire for approval?

This conflict marks a split between two parts of the personality—the part that remains a *child*, full of exuberance and a desire to try new things and test

initiative versus guilt
Third of Erikson's psychosocial crises, in which the child must balance the desire to pursue goals with the moral reservations that prevent carrying them out; successful resolution leads to the virtue of purpose.

new powers, and the part that is becoming an *adult,* constantly examining the propriety of motives and actions. Children who learn how to regulate these opposing drives develop the *virtue of purpose,* the courage to envision and pursue goals, without being inhibited by guilt or fear of punishment (Erikson, 1982). If this crisis is not resolved adequately, said Erikson, a child may turn into an adult who suffers from psychosomatic illness (illness with no apparent physical cause), inhibition, or impotence; who overcompensates by showing off; or who becomes self-righteous and intolerant, concerned more with inhibiting impulses than with enjoying spontaneity.

Caregivers can help children strike a healthy balance between a developing sense of initiative that may lead them to overdo new things and a tendency to become too repressed and guilty. They can give them opportunities to do things on their own while providing guidance and firm limits. They can also act in ways that will enhance children's self-esteem.

Sources of Self-Esteem

When asked, "How do you know your parents love you?" Vicky, 4, reels off: "They play with me, they read me stories before I go to bed, they listen to me, they take me to places I like, they make me peanut butter sandwiches, they don't want me to feel sad." When asked how they know their parents, teachers, and other children like them, young children describe concrete behaviors.

This has significant implications for all adults who work with children. Research suggests that the kind of social support in the activities Vicky described is the major ingredient in a child's self-esteem (Haltiwanger & Harter, 1988). Young children's own sense of their competence or skills does not seem to be correlated with how worthwhile they think they are. Instead, it is the acceptance and caring from parents, teachers, and peers—shown in these people's actual behavior—that makes children feel good about themselves. Later, in middle childhood, youngsters' feelings about their own competence and adequacy do become critical in shaping and maintaining self-worth (Harter, 1990).

What do you think?   *How can caregivers become aware of their important role in helping children develop high self-esteem? What practices should they adopt?*

EMOTIONAL GROWTH

"I hate you!" Vicky, age 5, shouts to her mother. "You're a mean mommy!" Angry because Ellen lost her temper and sent Vicky to her room for pinching her baby brother, Vicky cannot imagine ever loving her mother again. "Aren't you ashamed of yourself for making the baby cry?" her father asks Vicky a little later. Vicky nods, knowing the response he wants, but in truth she feels no shame. What does this tell us about Vicky's level of emotional development?

Understanding of Simultaneous Emotions

Young children cannot grasp the idea that they can experience different emotional reactions at the same time. This understanding develops systematically, along two different dimensions of emotions (Harter & Buddin, 1987). One dimension is the *valence,* whether the feelings are both positive (like happy and glad) or negative (like scared and sad), or whether feelings are of opposite valences, one positive and one negative (like glad and sad). The second dimension comprises the *number of targets* at which the emotions are directed—either one target as the focus of two feelings (Vicky's feeling both anger and love for her mother) or two targets, with one emotion directed toward one target (affection for her father) and a different emotion directed at a different target (jealousy of her baby brother).

Children develop a multidimensional understanding of emotions in an age-related sequence, in five levels, across ages 4 to 12 (Harter & Buddin, 1987):

Level 0: At first children do not understand that two feelings can coexist at the same time. Jason says, "You can't have two feelings at the same time because you only have one mind!" At this stage he cannot even acknowledge feeling two different emotions of the same valence (glad and happy).

Level 1: In this transitional period, children can appreciate the simultaneous appearance of two emotions, but only if they are of the same valence and toward a single target: "If my brother hit me, I would be both mad and sad." They cannot understand feeling two emotions toward two different people or feeling contradictory emotions toward the same person.

Level 2: In this transitional stage, children can bring two feelings of the same valence to two different targets: "I was excited I went to Mexico and glad to see my grandparents." But they cannot understand having simultaneous contradictory feelings: "I couldn't feel happy and scared at the same time, I would have to be two people at once!"

Level 3: Children show a conceptual advance: They can now understand having two contradictory feelings at the same time—but only if they are toward two different targets. Vicky can have a negative feeling ("I was mad at Tony for hitting me") and a positive feeling toward a different aspect of the situation ("but I was happy my father let me hit him back"). Still, she cannot understand the concept that the same target can have both positive and negative aspects.

Level 4: In this final level children can describe having contradictory feelings toward the same target. Jason says, "I'm excited about going to my new school, but I'm a little scared too."

Each of these levels involves gradual developmental change on both cognitive and emotional levels. The child continues to grow in the ability to have more than one kind of opinion and feeling at the same time and to understand a wide range of emotions.

Emergence of Emotions Directed toward the Self

In our story of Vicky's misbehavior toward baby Bobby, her failure to show any shame even though she knew she should not have pinched him is typical of young children. Shame, like pride, is a complex emotion directed toward the self and one that young children rarely understand. Shame combines a sense of sadness or regret for an act that violates a person's own standards, along with anger toward the self for committing that act. Pride combines joy over the mastery of a skill, often along with happiness that the achievement was appreciated by others. Susan Harter (1993), calls such feelings *self-affects*.

The ability to feel these emotions requires a certain level of cognitive advance; it also depends upon the kind of socialization a child has received. Thus we see a linkage among the cognitive, social, and emotional domains of development. In another study (Harter, 1993), 4- to 11-year-olds were told two different stories, one in which a child takes money she or he has been told not to take and another in which a child performs a difficult gymnastic feat. Both stories were presented in two ways, one when no one saw the child and one when the child was observed. This study identified a typical progression in children's ability to understand emotions directed toward the self:

Level 1: At ages 4 to 5, children do not mention that either they or their parents feel either pride or shame, whether the children are observed or not.

Level 2: At ages 5 to 6, children are in transition. They say their parents are ashamed or proud of them, but do not mention feeling these emotions themselves.

Level 3: At ages 6 to 7, children report feeling proud or ashamed—but only if they were observed.

Level 4: At ages 7 to 8, children acknowledge that even if no one sees them, they will feel ashamed or proud of themselves. They seem to have internalized the standards for pride and shame.

Not only does this sequence show the gradual development of feelings about the self, it suggests they depend upon how the parents have conveyed values to the children. The parents have been providing *scaffolding* (described in Chapter 9) until the children internalize the values taught by the parents. One of the ways this teaching occurs is through the child's identification with the parent, an important personality and social development.

IDENTIFICATION OF SELF: GENDER IDENTITY

Vicky, age 5, insists on dressing in a new way, begging to wear leggings with a skirt over them, and boots, indoors and out. When asked why, Vicky replies, "Because Katie dresses like this—and Katie's the king of the girls!"

Vicky's interest in changing her "look" illustrates *identification,* a child's adoption of the characteristics, beliefs, attitudes, values, and behaviors of another person or of a group. As if they were adding bits of clay to create a unique sculpture, children choose various aspects of other people's personalities and behaviors that they want to identify with and add these traits to the ones they already have—those they inherited and those that arose from their early experience. Thus they build their own unique personalities and form their own identities.

One aspect of identification affecting people's attitudes and behavior is *gender identity.* The sex we belong to affects how we look; how we move our bodies; and how we work, play, and dress. It influences what we think about ourselves and what others think of us. All those characteristics—and more—are included when we use the word *gender:* what it means to be male or female. *Sex differences* are the physical differences between males and females; *gender differences* are psychological or behavioral differences.

How do young children achieve *gender identity,* the awareness and identification of themselves as male or female? How do they develop *gender roles,* the behaviors their society expects of males and females, as well as general standards of socially and morally correct behavior? How do other aspects of personality develop? Let's see what insights several theoretical perspectives can give us. (See Table 10-1.)

identification   *Process by which a person acquires the characteristics of another person or a group.*

gender   *What it means psychologically to be male or female.*

sex differences   *Actual biological differences between the sexes.*

gender differences   *Psychological or behavioral differences between the sexes.*

gender identity   *Awareness of one's own sex.*

gender roles   *Behaviors and attitudes a culture deems appropriate for males and females.*

What do you think?   *"Males are innately more aggressive, and females more nurturing. While these traits can be altered to some degree, the basic tendencies will remain." Does research support these statements? Whether true or not, what implications do these widely held beliefs have for personality development?*

TABLE 10-1

FOUR PERSPECTIVES ON GENDER IDENTIFICATION			
THEORY	**MAJOR THEORIST**	**KEY PROCESS**	**BASIC BELIEF**
Psychoanalytic	Sigmund Freud	Emotional	Gender identification occurs when child identifies with same-sex parent.
Social-learning	Jerome Kagan	Learning	Identification is a result of observing and imitating models and being reinforced for gender-appropriate behavior.
Cognitive-developmental	Lawrence Kohlberg	Cognitive	Once child learns she is a girl or he is a boy, child actively sorts information by gender into what girls do and what boys do, and acts accordingly.
Gender-schema	Sandra Bem	Cognitive and learning	Child organizes information about what is considered appropriate for a boy or a girl on the basis of what a particular culture dictates, and behaves accordingly. Child sorts by gender because the culture dictates that gender is an important schema.

Explanations for Gender Identity

The commonly accepted explanations for the development of gender identity are social-learning and cognitive theories. The earliest explanation, though, was psychoanalytic theory. According to the psychoanalytic theory of Sigmund Freud, identification results when a child represses the wish to possess the parent of the other sex and identifies with the parent of the same sex, whom the child sees as the "aggressor." This allows the superego to develop and to lead the child into the latency stage. (See Chapter 1.) This view is no longer accepted by most contemporary psychologists, who tend to favor one of the following theories.

Social-Learning Theory: Observing and Imitating Models. Social-learning theorists explain identification in general, and gender identification in particular, as the consequence of observing and imitating models. Typically, one model is a parent, but children also model themselves after other people, as Vicky did with her classmate Katie. An older brother or sister, a teacher, a peer, or a television personality can also serve as models. Children may adopt characteristics from several different models.

How Identification Occurs. Jerome Kagan (1958, 1971) named four interrelated processes that establish and strengthen identification:

1 Children want to *be* like the model. For example, a boy may look to a famous baseball player, thinking he will be able to do what the athlete can do.

As this little girl reaches for her toes—making the same movements her mother does on a matching exercise mat—she demonstrates identification, one of the most important personality developments of early childhood.

2 Children believe they *are* like the model. A girl believes she looks and acts like her mother—tells jokes like her, walks like her. Other people affirm this identification with comments like "You have your mother's eyes."

3 Children *experience emotions* like those the model is feeling. When Vicky, at 5, saw Ellen cry after her own brother's death, Vicky felt sad and cried too, not for an uncle she barely knew but because her mother's grief made her feel sad.

4 Children *act* like the model. In play and in everyday conversation, they adopt the mannerisms of the model. Preschool teachers and parents are often startled to hear their own words and tone of voice come out of children's mouths.

Through identification, children come to believe they have the same characteristics as a model. When they identify with a nurturant and competent model, children are pleased and proud. When the model is inadequate, they may feel unhappy and insecure.

Effects of Identification. According to social-learning theory, young children generally identify with the parent of the same sex; and when they imitate that parent, they are reinforced. A little boy sees he is physically more like his father than like his mother. He imitates his father (especially when he sees him as nurturant, competent, and powerful) and is rewarded for acting "like a boy." The same process occurs for a girl. According to this approach, children learn morally acceptable behavior in the same way as they do gender identity, by imitation and reinforcement. By the end of early childhood, these lessons are internalized; a child no longer needs praise, punishment, or the model's presence to act in socially appropriate ways.

Evaluating Social-Learning Theory. Although social-learning theory seems to make sense, it has been hard to prove. Children do imitate adults, but not always those of the same sex; often children do not imitate a parent at all. When children are tested for similarity to their parents, they turn out to be no more like them in personality than like other parents chosen at random. Those who do score as similar to their own parents are no more like the same-sex parent than like the other parent (Hetherington, 1965; Mussen & Rutherford, 1963).

An analysis of a large number of studies suggests that parents encourage gender-typed activities in play and chores, and fathers are more likely than mothers to differentiate between boys and girls. However, parents may be simply reinforcing children's own preferences rather than creating them (Lytton & Romney, 1991).

Social learning may underlie children's acquisition of gender identity and behavioral standards. But simple imitation and reinforcement do not seem to explain fully how this occurs.

Cognitive-Developmental Theory: Mental Processes.   Vicky learns she is something called a "girl" because people call her a girl. She figures out which things girls are "supposed" to do and does them. She learns her gender the same way she learns everything else—by thinking about her experience. This is the heart of Lawrence Kohlberg's (1966) cognitive-developmental theory.

Gender Identity and Gender Constancy.   To learn their gender, Kohlberg says, children do not depend on adults as models or dispensers of reinforcements and punishments; instead, they actively classify themselves and others as male or female and then organize their behaviors around their gender.

Gender identity—awareness of being male or female—typically begins at about age 2. By age 3, according to Kohlberg, most children have a firm idea of which sex they belong to. Vicky, at age 3, had a short haircut and indignantly corrected people who thought she was a boy.

Gender constancy, or *gender conservation,* is a child's realization that his or her sex will *always* be the same. Three-year-old Jason, for example, told his mother, "When I grow up, I want to be a mommy just like you so I can play tennis and drive a car." But Vicky, at 4, said she would always be a girl and her friend Jason would always be a boy—even if he played with dolls. Jason had not achieved gender constancy; Vicky had.

According to Kohlberg, gender differences in behavior *follow* the establishment of gender constancy. The reason Vicky prefers dolls to trucks is not the approval she gets for those preferences (as in social-learning theory) but her cognitive awareness that such things fit with her idea of herself as a girl. Once children realize they will *always* be male or female, they adopt "sex-appropriate" behaviors.

gender constancy, or **gender conservation**
Awareness that one will always be male or female.

Gender-Schema Theory: A "Cognitive-Social" Approach.   Sandra Bem developed *gender-schema theory,* a "cognitive-social" approach that contains elements of both cognitive-developmental theory and social-learning theory. It revolves around the concept of a *gender schema* (Bem, 1983, 1985). A schema is a mentally organized pattern of behavior that helps a child sort information. A gender schema is a pattern of behavior organized around gender.

Children socialize themselves in their gender roles, says Bem. First they develop a concept of what it means to be male or female by organizing information around the schema of gender. They organize on this basis because they see that society classifies people more by sex than by anything else: Males and females wear different clothes, play with different toys, use separate bathrooms, and line up

gender-schema theory
Theory that children socialize themselves in their gender roles by developing a concept of what it means to be male or female in a particular culture.

gender schema   *Pattern of behavior organized around gender.*

BOX 10-1 ▪ THE EVERYDAY WORLD

RAISING CHILDREN WITHOUT GENDER-ROLE STEREOTYPES

Parents who want to raise their children to feel good about themselves and to feel empowered by their gender, rather than limited by it, need to "inoculate" children against cultural stereotypes, says the psychologist Sandra Bem (1983, 1985), a pioneer in gender-role research. The following guidelines are based on her recommendations:

♦ *Be models of nonstereotyped behavior.* Share or alternate tasks like bathing the baby and keeping household accounts.
♦ *Encourage children to play with nonstereotyped toys.* Parents can say to a boy playing with a baby doll, "What a good daddy you will be when you grow up!" and to a girl playing with a truck, "What a good driver you will be!"
♦ *Expose children to men and women in nontraditional occupations.* Children who know that Aunt Alice is a plumber and Dad's friend Pete is a nurse are unlikely to think that plumbers have to be male and nurses female.
♦ *Monitor young children's reading and television viewing.* Select nonstereotyped books and programs when possible. When reading classic fairy tales and rhymes, point out how old-fashioned the ideas are ("Isn't it funny that people back then thought that girls needed to be rescued all the time?"). Encourage discussion of stereotyping in television programs and movies.
♦ *Emphasize anatomy and reproduction as the main distinctions between males and females.* Children who know the anatomical differences between males and females are less likely to focus on cultural signals like clothing or hairstyle as sex differentiators.
♦ *Teach them that there is great variation within the sexes.* For example, while some girls do not like to play baseball, others do—and some boys do not.

Once this little boy achieves gender constancy, he knows that he will always be male—that if he has children of his own, he will be a father, not a mother—even if he plays with dolls. By not restricting children's toys to the usual ones for their sex, parents encourage children to stretch their imagination.

♦ *Teach them about cultural diversity*—that people in different cultures and at different historical times hold different beliefs and customs about what is appropriate for males and females.

---

separately in school. Thus Vicky asks, "Is this a toy that girls play with?" and Jason asks, "Do boys wear this kind of Halloween costume?"

Then as children see the culture's gender schema—what boys and girls are "supposed" to be and do—they adapt their own attitudes and behavior. From the full range of human attributes, they display those that fit them, according to their society's gender schema. In the United States, girls learn they should be nurturant, while boys learn they should be strong and aggressive. Children then look at themselves. If they act "gender-appropriate," their self-esteem rises; if not, they feel inadequate. This theory assumes that since the gender schema is learned, it can be modified to bring about the healthy development of both sexes. (See Box 10-1.)

Evaluating the Cognitive Theories.   Research supports a link between gender concepts and cognitive development. Children as young as 2 years old can classify pictures as "boys" or "girls" or "mommies" or "daddies." By age 2½, children can tell which pictures they themselves resemble, and they know whether they will be fathers or mothers when they grow up (S. K. Thompson, 1975).

However, cognitive-developmental theory has its weaknesses. Children often act in "gender-appropriate" ways *before* they achieve gender constancy, contradicting Kohlberg's predictions. In addition, the theory does not explain why—of all the differences among people—children pay so much attention to sex in setting up the classifications by which they make sense of their world.

Gender-schema theory is supported by the fact that very little evidence directly links children's acquisition of gender constancy to their gender-related behavior. Rather, children who do not yet have gender constancy still know a lot about what is "appropriate" for males and females (G. D. Levy & Carter, 1989). So instead of saying gender-role development depends on the single essential cognitive factor of gender constancy, it seems reasonable to look at many different factors. These can include how much children know about gender-role stereotypes and how likely they are to categorize various activities or objects by gender (G. D. Levy & Carter, 1989). Bem's goal of deliberately changing a culture's gender schema is a good idea if that means freeing people from constraining stereotypes. But change in ingrained attitudes about human behavior is slow.

Each of these theories focuses on a different aspect of a child's development. The psychoanalytic perspective emphasizes emotional ties to parents; the social-learning viewpoint stresses what and how children learn in various life contexts; and the cognitive approach notes children's growing ability to take in information about the world and their place in it. None of the theories fully explains why boys and girls turn out differently in some respects while retaining so many characteristics in common, but each contributes to our understanding.

How Gender Affects Development

How much difference does being a girl or a boy make in a child's development?

How Different Are Girls and Boys?   Besides having different sex organs, Vicky and Jason are different in size, strength, appearance, physical and intellectual abilities, and personality. Which of their differences arise because Vicky is a girl and Jason a boy, and which are simply differences between them as two individual human beings?

Physical differences between baby boys and girls are slight—boys are slightly larger and more muscular. Infant boys are also somewhat more vulnerable physically. Other differences are almost nonexistent before age 3, although some research suggests boys are more active. Differences become more pronounced after that; but boys and girls, on average, are "more alike than they are different" (Maccoby, 1980).

In their landmark review of more than 2000 studies, Maccoby and Jacklin (1974) found only a few significant differences between boys and girls. Three cognitive differences—girls' superior verbal ability and boys' better mathematical and spatial abilities—do not show up until after the age of 10 or 11. More recent analyses found these differences to be very small indeed. Gender differences in verbal abilities are so small as to be almost meaningless (Hyde & Linn, 1988). Those in math are complex but also small, and have been getting smaller in recent years. In the general population, neither sex shows better understanding of mathematical concepts, girls excel in computation (adding, subtracting, and so on), and boys do not show superior problem-solving ability until high school (Hyde, Fennema, & Lamon, 1990).

Personality differences too are few. The clearest gender difference here is that males tend to be more aggressive, starting in early childhood. Boys play more boisterously; they roughhouse more and are more apt to try to dominate other children and challenge their parents. Boys argue and fight more often and are more apt to use force or threats of force to get their way, while girls try to defuse conflicts by persuasion rather than confrontation (P. M. Miller, Danaher, & Forbes, 1986). Girls cooperate more with parents and tend to set up rules (like taking turns) to avoid clashes with playmates (Maccoby, 1980). Girls are more likely to be *empathic,* that is, to identify with other people's feelings (N. Eisenberg, Fabes, Schaller, & Miller, 1989; M. L. Hoffman, 1977).

We need to be careful not to overemphasize gender differences. Most that do exist are statistically small and are valid for large groups of boys and girls but not necessarily for individuals. By knowing a child's sex, we cannot predict whether a particular boy or girl will be faster, stronger, smarter, more confident, or more of a leader than another child. Still, despite the rarity of behavioral sex differences, both males and females *believe* they are more different than they actually are (Matlin, 1987). Where does that belief come from, and what are its effects?

Attitudes toward Gender Differences.   When Jason and his friend Shani play house in preschool, Shani, as the "mommy," is likely to "cook" and "take care of the baby" while Jason puts on a hat and "goes to work." When he comes home, sits at the table, and says "I'm hungry," Shani drops what she is doing to wait on him. This scenario would be less surprising if both children's mothers did not work outside the home and if both their fathers did not do a fair amount of housework. These children have absorbed the gender roles of their culture rather than those of their own households.

Gender Roles and Gender-Typing.   *Gender roles* are the behaviors, interests, attitudes, and skills a culture considers appropriate for males and females. By tradition, American women have been expected to devote most of their time to being wives and mothers, while men were supposed to devote most of their time to earning money. Those roles include personality expectations too—for example, that women are compliant and nurturant while men are active and competitive.

Gender-typing is a child's learning of his or her gender role. Children learn these roles early through socialization and become increasingly gender-typed between ages 3 and 6. Brighter children learn them faster. Bright children are the first to notice the physical differences between the sexes and the expectations of their society for each sex—and to try to live up (or down) to those expectations (S. B. Greenberg & Peck, 1974).

Strong gender-typing in early childhood may help children develop their gender identity. Ultimately, of course, people vary in the degree to which they take on gender roles. Perhaps children can become more flexible in their thinking about gender differences only after they know for sure they are male or female and will always remain so.

gender-typing   *Process by which a person learns a gender role.*

Gender Stereotypes. *Gender stereotypes* are exaggerated generalizations about male or female behavior, such as: A female is bound to be passive and dependent, while a male is aggressive and independent. Such stereotyped attitudes are found in children as young as age 3 (Haugh, Hoffman, & Cowan, 1980).

Gender stereotypes can restrict children's views of themselves and their future. They affect people in their simplest, most everyday endeavors as well as in far-reaching life decisions. By viewing certain activities as unmasculine or un-feminine, people may deny their natural inclinations and abilities and force themselves into ill-fitting academic, vocational, or social molds.

Androgyny. The healthiest personality, says Bem (1974, 1976), includes a balance of positive characteristics normally thought of as more appropriate for one sex or the other. A person having such a balance—whom Bem describes as *androgynous*—might be assertive, dominant, and self-reliant (so-called "masculine" traits), as well as compassionate, sympathetic, and understanding ("feminine" traits). Androgynous men and women judge a particular situation on its merits and act on the basis of what seems most effective rather than on what is considered appropriate for their sex.

How Gender Differences Come About

What is the root of gender differences? Is it biological? Or does it lie in the cultural environment, as interpreted to young children through parents, other people, and the media? Research does not yield an either-or answer but instead shows that influences extend from the individual child out to the family, the local institutions, and the culture at large. A discussion of the contexts in which children develop in terms of gender can serve as an example of the ways the different ecological levels in children's lives affect many aspects of their personalities.

Biological Influences. Hormones circulating before or about the time of birth seem to cause sex differences in animals. The male hormone testosterone has been linked to aggressive behavior in mice, guinea pigs, rats, and primates; and the female hormone prolactin can cause motherly behavior in virgin or male animals (Bronson & Desjardins, 1969; D. M. Levy, 1966; R. M. Rose, Gordon, & Bernstein, 1972). Of course, human beings are influenced far more by learning than animals are, so conclusions drawn from animal studies may not apply.

Two small but often-cited studies of people who had unusual prenatal exposure to hormones or were born with sexual abnormalities suggest that both biology and environment play a role. In one (Ehrhardt & Money, 1967), girls whose mothers had taken certain hormones during pregnancy were born with abnormal external sex organs. After surgery, the girls looked normal and had normal female reproductive capability, but they acted "boyish" by playing with trucks and guns and competing with boys in sports. Were these behaviors due to prenatal hormones, parental reinforcement of "tomboy" behavior, or some combination? It is unclear. The other study (Money, Ehrhardt, & Masica, 1968) highlights the role of environment. These subjects were chromosomally male and had testes instead of ovaries but looked female and had been raised as girls. All were "typically female" in behavior and outlook: All considered marriage and raising a family very important and had played mostly with dolls and other "girls'" toys. In this case, biology fails to account for gender-typing.

gender stereotypes
Exaggerated generalizations about male or female behavior.

androgynous *Having some characteristics considered typical of males and other characteristics considered typical of females.*

Anna's enjoyment of her truck shows that she is not restricted in her play by gender stereotypes. Contemporary developmentalists discourage such stereotypes, usually favoring encouraging children to pursue their own interests, even when these interests are unconventional for their sex.

Adam is clearly delighted with his toy, which is modeled after a popular television character. Social-learning theorists say that children's ideas about gender behavior, violence, and other issues are influenced by the models they see on the screen. If so, what impact will the Power Rangers have on Adam?

Hormones may predispose people toward certain behaviors, but then the environment shapes these behaviors. In the studies just cited, samples were very small, making the findings inconclusive. Furthermore, since variations among people of the same sex are larger than the average differences between the sexes, biology fails to explain fully the differences in males' and females' behavior.

Family Influences. Even in today's more "liberated" society, parents—and especially fathers—treat sons and daughters differently, beginning in infancy. An analysis of 172 studies between 1952 and 1987 found that parents pressure boys more to act "like real boys" and avoid acting "like girls" than they pressure girls to avoid "boyish" behavior and act in "feminine" ways (Lytton & Romney, 1991). Boys seem to be gender-socialized more strongly than girls: Girls have much more freedom in the clothes they wear, the games they play, and the people they play with (Miedzian, 1991).

On such measures as the amount of parent-child interaction, encouragement to achieve or to be independent, strictness of discipline, clear communication, and warmth and nurturance, most differences are small and nonsignificant. However, those that did appear were in the expected direction—like accepting aggression more in boys and being warmer with girls.

Fathers are more apt to be social with, more approving of, and more affectionate toward their preschool daughters, but more controlling and directive toward their sons, and more concerned with their sons' cognitive achievements than with their daughters' (Bronstein, 1988). However, adult men and women who get along well at work and in relationships are most apt to have had warm ties to fathers who were competent, strong, secure in their own masculinity and nurturant toward their children (Biller, 1981). The father's absence seems to make little difference in a child's gender development, according to an analysis of 67 studies of single-parent families (M. R. Stevenson & Black, 1988). No differences show up for girls, and those for boys are quite small.

What parents do has long-range implications. Even if parents merely reinforce behavioral tendencies already there, by accentuating them and limiting a child's behavior to what is "appropriate" for one sex or the other, they limit children's views of themselves, their activities, and the fulfillment of their unique personalities.

Media Influences. The typical high school graduate has watched more than 25,000 hours of television (Action for Children's Television, undated) and has absorbed highly gender-stereotyped attitudes from the little screen. Television portrays even more stereotyping than is found in real life: About twice as many males as females appear on television, and males are usually more powerful, dominant, and authoritative (Calvert & Huston, 1987). Men depicted on television shows are also typically more aggressive, more active, and more competent than women (Mamay & Simpson, 1981; D. M. Zuckerman & Zuckerman, 1985).

Children's books represent another source of gender images. After research in the 1970s pointed out extensive stereotyping in children's books, many changes were made. Friendship between boys and girls is more common in story lines now, and girls are braver and more resourceful. Still, there are more male characters, females are more likely to need help and males more likely to give it, and the kinds of help given are different (Beal, 1994). The classics, of course, abound in stereotypes.

Can the media help abolish stereotypes? The answer seems to be "Yes, but . . . ." Some changes have been made in recent years, but while women seen on television are now more likely to be working out of the home and men are sometimes shown caring for children or doing the marketing, a high level of gender-stereotyping still prevails. Social-learning theory says that children who watch a lot of television will imitate the models they see and become more gender-typed. Research bears this out. Young children who watched a series of nontraditional episodes, like one showing a father and son having fun cooking together, had less stereotyped views than children who had not seen the series (J. Johnston & Ettema, 1982). If an effort were made, the media could probably shape children's views in terms of possibilities rather than limitations.

By and large, children come to the television set or the library with preformed attitudes, and they watch, read, and process information selectively. Boys turn on more cartoons and action adventure programs than girls do, and both sexes remember television sequences that confirm the stereotypes they already hold better than they remember nonstereotypical sequences (Calvert & Huston, 1987). However, if a mighty effort is made to present nonstereotyped situations, children's attitudes can change.

Cultural Influences.   The government of Nepal has begun distributing posters urging parents to send their daughters to school. In countries like this, where boys are given more opportunities than girls, personalities are strongly influenced by gender. Even in the United States, however, males and females are treated and valued differently. Do societal forces encourage and accentuate biological differences, or does the culture itself create gender differences? This question is hard to answer. In all societies, some roles are considered appropriate for males, others for females. Gender roles vary, but in most societies men are more aggressive, competitive, and powerful than women. The pattern is hard to change.

Yet in many places attitudes and roles *are* changing. In the United States, women are moving into untraditional occupations and are gaining power in business, in government, and in the family. Egalitarian attitudes are more prevalent, especially among younger, better-educated, and higher-income people (Deaux, 1985). Both men and women are exploring aspects of their personalities that were suppressed by the old gender stereotypes.

What do you think?   *Where would you place yourself on the continuum between the following extremes? Explain.*
- *Family A thinks girls should wear only ruffly dresses and boys should never wash dishes or cry.*
- *Family Z treats sons and daughters exactly alike, without making any references to the children's sex.*

CHILD-REARING PRACTICES

HOW CHILD-REARING PRACTICES AFFECT PERSONALITY DEVELOPMENT

As children become their own persons, their upbringing can be a baffling, complex challenge. How are parents raising their children today? Some parents repeat the child-rearing patterns their own parents followed in bringing them up. Others adopt practices very different from those of their parents.

Parents' Styles and Children's Competence: Baumrind's Research

Why does Stacy hit and bite the nearest person when she cannot finish a jigsaw puzzle? What makes Nils sit with the puzzle for an hour until he solves it? Why does Consuelo walk away from it after a minute's effort? Why are children so different in their responses to the same task? What makes them turn out the way they do? One effort to answer these questions relates different styles of parenting to different levels of children's competence.

Three Kinds of Parenting Styles.   To discover associations between how parents reared their children and how competent the children were, Diana Baumrind studied 103 preschool children from 95 families. Through interviews, testing, and home studies, she identified children who were functioning at various levels and categorized three parental styles. She then described typical behavior patterns of children raised according to each style (Baumrind, 1971; Baumrind & Black, 1967).

Authoritarian parents value control and unquestioning obedience. They try to make children conform to a set standard of conduct and punish them forcefully for acting contrary to that standard. They are more detached and less warm than other parents. Their children tend to be more discontented, withdrawn, and distrustful.

Permissive parents value self-expression and self-regulation. They consider themselves resources, not standard-bearers or models, and make few demands, allowing children to monitor their own activities as much as possible. They explain the reasons underlying the few family rules that do exist, consult with children about policy decisions, and rarely punish. They are noncontrolling, nondemanding, and relatively warm. Their preschool children tend to be immature—the least self-controlled and the least exploratory.

Authoritative parents respect a child's individuality, while stressing social values. They direct children's activities rationally, paying attention to the issues rather than to a child's fear of punishment or loss of love. While they have confidence in their ability to guide children, they respect children's interests, opinions, and personalities. They are loving, consistent, demanding, and respectful of children's independent decisions, but firm in maintaining standards and willing to impose limited punishment. They explain the reasoning behind their stands and encourage verbal give-and-take. Their children apparently feel secure in knowing both that they are loved and what is expected of them. These preschoolers tend to be the most self-reliant, self-controlled, self-assertive, exploratory, and content. (Baumrind's findings seem to support White's [1971] findings about "A" and "C" parenting, discussed in Chapter 6.)

Recent research linked authoritative parenting to learning too. Studies of scaffolding (the temporary help parents give children to do a task) found authoritative parents more sensitive in knowing when to shift their level of help and found their children more successful at various tasks (Pratt, Kerig, Cowan, & Cowan, 1988).

Evaluating Baumrind's Work.   Since this research relied on correlational data, it does not prove that these three styles of child rearing *caused* the way children turn out. Rather, the data established associations between each parenting style and a

authoritarian parents   In Baumrind's terminology, parents whose primary child-rearing values are based on control and obedience.

permissive parents   In Baumrind's terminology, parents whose primary child-rearing values are self-expression and self-regulation.

authoritative parents   In Baumrind's terminology, parents whose primary child-rearing values blend respect for the child's individuality with a desire to instill social values in the child.

"Sam, neither your father nor I consider your response appropriate."

Do Sam's parents seem authoritarian, authoritative, or permissive? Children seem to respond in distinct ways to each of these three styles of parenting. (Drawing by Koren; © 1988 The New Yorker Magazine, Inc.)

particular set of behaviors. Also, it is impossible to know from the data whether the children were, in fact, raised by a particular style. It is possible, for example, that some of the well-adjusted children were raised inconsistently, but by the time of the study, their parents had adopted the authoritative pattern. Further, even if parents *usually* act toward their children in a certain way, they do not respond to *all* situations in that way. Also, Baumrind did not consider innate differences between children, assuming that all differences in social competence are related to what parents do. Finally, she did not consider children's influence on their parents. "Easy" children may induce their parents to be authoritative, while "difficult" ones may make their parents authoritarian.

Why Is Authoritative Child Rearing Special?   Authoritative parenting seems to enhance children's competence, probably because of the parents' reasonable expectations and realistic standards. Children from authoritarian homes are so strictly controlled, by either punishment or guilt, that often they cannot make a conscious choice about a particular behavior because they are too worried about what their parents will do. Children from permissive homes receive so little guidance that they often become uncertain and anxious about whether they are doing the right thing.

In authoritative homes, children know when they are meeting expectations and can decide when it is worth risking parental displeasure or other unpleasant consequences to pursue a goal. These children are expected to perform well, fulfill commitments, and participate actively in family duties as well as family fun.

They know the satisfaction of meeting responsibilities and achieving success. This seems to be reflected in their self-confident, competent behavior.

What makes a parent adopt a particular pattern of child rearing? Some answers have emerged from a study of 42 low-income African American mothers and grandmothers caring for 3- to 6-year-olds (Kelley, Power, & Wimbush, 1992). Although black mothers have been described as largely authoritarian, this study found a wide range of approaches. It is clearly misleading to characterize a cultural group with a single term.

What kinds of influences resulted in different child-rearing attitudes and practices? The influences include how religious the woman was, how old, how educated, and whether she was a single parent. However, cultural background more than any of these factors seemed to determine whether a woman spanked or not. Mothers who were more religious tended to be more sensitive to their children's needs (in Baumrind's terminology, more "authoritative"), as did more mature, more educated, and married mothers. Younger, less educated single mothers, who were less religious, tended to emphasize obedience and respect for elders. This latter approach may be more adaptive for children in an inner-city community, in which respect for authority leads to success in a highly structured school and work situation. What this study teaches us is that "different" does not imply "worse" and that values in the majority culture may not apply to all families.

"Poisonous Pedagogy" and Adult Personality: Research Based on Alice Miller's Concept

Alice Miller, a Swiss psychologist, says that much of the violence and the psychological pain we see today stems from the psychological deprivation experienced by young children. She concluded this from two sources: patients she treated in therapy and study of European child-rearing practices over the past two centuries (A. Miller, 1981, 1983).

Miller (1983) identified a psychologically injurious group of child-rearing practices and attitudes that she called "poisonous pedagogy" (PP). This parenting approach weakens the child's self-confidence and curiosity, ridicules the child's lack of competence, and suppresses the expression of authentic feelings—whether sad, angry, or exuberant. It undermines children's capacity to know, express, and act on their own feelings.

Why do parents do this to children? Miller believes they do it *unconsciously*, in reaction to the emotional damage they themselves suffered as children, and *consciously*, in the belief they are helping their children become more competent and self-sufficient. Only by breaking the generation-to-generation transmission of PP, she says, can adults help children grow up to be psychologically healthy.

To assess PP, Harrington (1993) drew on data from a longitudinal study of 100 mostly middle-class families, begun when most of the children studied were 3 years old. About two-thirds were white, one-fourth were African American, and one-twelfth were Asian. A committee of judges translated Miller's concept into specific child-rearing practices. (See Table 10-2.)

When the children were about 4½ years old, their mothers and fathers separately taught them a battery of four different thinking tasks. Researchers rated the encounters and categorized them by the PP scale. (See Table 10-3.) Years later, researchers correlated the preschool PP ratings with scores on measures of psychological adjustment given when the "children" were 18 and 23 years old. Positive

TABLE 10-2

CHILD-REARING PRACTICES JUDGED MOST AND LEAST DESCRIPTIVE OF "POISONOUS PEDAGOGY" (PP)

MOST CHARACTERISTIC OF PP

- I do not allow my child to get angry with me.
- I believe too much affection and tenderness can harm or weaken a child.
- I sometimes tease and make fun of my child.
- I do not allow my child to question my decisions.
- I think children must learn early not to cry.
- I teach my child to keep control of his/her feelings at all times.
- I believe a child should be seen and not heard.
- I believe scolding and criticism make my child improve.

LEAST CHARACTERISTIC OF PP

- I express affection by hugging, kissing, and holding my child.
- My child and I have warm, intimate times together.
- I respect my child's opinions and encourage him/her to express them.
- I feel a child should be given comfort and understanding when she/he is scared or upset.
- I usually take into account my child's preferences in making plans for the family.
- I believe in praising a child when she/he is good and think it gets better results than punishing him/her when she/he is bad.
- I encourage my child to be curious, to explore and question things.

SOURCE: Adapted from Harrington, 1993.

TABLE 10-3

PARENT-CHILD INTERACTIONS IN PRESCHOOL TEACHING TASK: MOST AND LEAST DESCRIPTIVE OF "POISONOUS PEDAGOGY" (PP)

MOST CHARACTERISTIC OF PP PARENT

- Was critical of child; rejected child's ideas and suggestions
- Tended to control the tasks
- Tended toward overcontrol of own needs and impulses
- Appeared ashamed of child; lacked pride in child
- Pressured child to work at the tasks
- Was impatient with the child
- Tended to reject inadequate solutions

LEAST CHARACTERISTIC OF PP PARENT

- Was supportive and encouraging of child in the situation
- Was responsive to child's needs from moment to moment
- Was warm and supportive
- Praised the child
- Reacted to the child in an ego-enhancing manner
- Encouraged the child
- Surrendered control of the situation to the child
- Encouraged the child to proceed independently
- Valued the child's originality

SOURCE: Harrington, 1993.

TABLE 10-4

PERSONALITY CHARACTERISTICS AT AGES 18–23 YEARS ASSOCIATED WITH MOTHERS' POISONOUS PEDAGOGY (PP) IN THE TEACHING SITUATION AT 4.5 YEARS*

PERSONALITY CHARACTERISTICS OF ADULT CHILD OF PP MOTHER

- Has a brittle ego-defense system; has a small reserve of integration; is disorganized and maladaptive when under stress
- Is vulnerable to real or fancied threat; is generally fearful
- Keeps people at a distance; avoids close interpersonal relationships
- Gives up and withdraws where possible in the face of frustration and adversity
- Is basically anxious
- Is thin-skinned, sensitive to anything that can be construed as criticism or an interpersonal slight
- Is concerned with own adequacy as a person
- Tends to be self-defensive
- Feels cheated and victimized by life; is self-pitying
- Seeks reassurance from others
- Is anxious and tense; shows corresponding bodily symptoms
- Feels a lack of personal meaning in life
- Is basically distrustful of people in general
- Is subtly negativistic; tends to undermine and obstruct or sabotage

CHARACTERISTICS OF ADULT CHILD OF NON-PP MOTHER

- Is turned to for advice and reassurance
- Appears straightforward, forthright, candid
- Responds to humor
- Is personally charming
- Has warmth; has the capacity for close relationships; is compassionate
- Has social poise and presence; appears socially at ease
- Is socially perceptive of a wide range of interpersonal cues
- Tends to arouse liking and acceptance in people
- Is able to see to the heart of important problems
- Emphasizes being with others; is gregarious
- Is cheerful

*Listed characteristics yielded a significant correlation with mothers' observed PP.
SOURCE: Adapted from Harrington, 1993, p. 306.

correlations appeared between parents' use of PP practices and poor psychological health in young adulthood, and vice versa. (See Table 10-4.) Young adults whose mothers had used high levels of PP in the preschool teaching situation were deemed less comfortable with themselves and others, more vulnerable to stress, and less psychologically healthy than young adults whose mothers had shown low levels of preschool PP. The mothers' PP levels seemed more influential than the fathers', probably because the mothers spent more time with their young children than the fathers did.

Love and Maturity

In the long run, the most important aspect of parenting during a child's first 5 years seems to be how parents feel about their children and how they show their feelings. Other findings that seem to support Miller's thesis come from a major study of young adults whose mothers had been interviewed about their child-rearing techniques 20 years earlier (McClelland, Constantian, Regalado, & Stone, 1978; Sears et al., 1957). The way these adults turned out bore little or no relation to specific practices (like whether they had gone to bed early or late). The most important influence—dwarfing all others—was how much their parents, especially their mothers, had loved them, enjoyed them, and shown affection for them.

The most beloved children grew up to be the most tolerant of other people, the most understanding, and the most likely to show active concern for others. The least mature adults had grown up in homes where they were considered a nuisance and an interference in adults' lives. Their parents had been intolerant of noise, mess, and roughhousing and had reacted unkindly to children's aggressiveness, to normal childhood sex play, and to expressions of dependency.

Children of easygoing, loving parents seemed to show less moral behavior as they were growing up than did children of stricter parents. Some misbehavior may be a necessary step in moving away from the wholesale adoption of parents' values and developing one's own value system. The researchers concluded:

> Parents also need faith—faith that loving and believing in their children will promote maturity in the long run, even though some of their offsprings' behavior seems outrageous in the short run as they learn to make their own decisions. There are no shortcuts to perfection. Children have to explore some detours if they are to reach the heights. The best we parents can do to help is to love them, and not stand in the way of their groping attempts to grow up or force them at all times to conform to adult-centered codes of moral behavior. (McClelland et al., 1978, p. 114)

Parents already confused about how best to raise children become even more bewildered when the professionals disagree, as described in Box 10-2.

DISCIPLINE

Parents struggle to make the right decisions in bringing up children. They want to raise human beings who think well of themselves and will fulfill their potential. In this struggle, they have to develop effective methods of *discipline.* Discipline is not a synonym for punishment. The word, from the Latin for "knowledge" or "instruction," is defined accordingly in the dictionary. Parents have different ways of teaching children character, self-control, and moral behavior.

discipline *The process of socialization, of teaching children behavior, character, and self-control.*

Discipline can also be equated with *socialization,* the process by which children acquire habits, skills, values, and motives that will enable them to be productive, law-abiding members of society. Parents discipline, or socialize, their children by teaching them behavior, character, and self-control. Current psychological thinking attributes the success of socialization to children's attachment to responsive parents, to their modeling of parental behaviors, to parents' arranging the environment to elicit desirable behavior (as in hanging hooks low enough on the wall so a young child can hang up her own jacket), and to various forms of parent-child interaction. Such procedures eventually help the child to internalize parental teachings in the form of self-discipline (Maccoby, 1992).

socialization *The process by which children acquire habits, skills, values, and motives that will enable them to become productive, law-abiding members of society.*

Internalization

Internalization is the end result of socialization. It results when children take the values and attitudes of society as their own: They behave in socially acceptable

internalization *End result of socialization, when children take on the values and attitudes of society as their own.*

BOX 10-2 ■ FOOD FOR THOUGHT

IS "GOOD-ENOUGH" PARENTING GOOD ENOUGH?

Sandra Scarr (1992) maintains that being reared in one family rather than another—as long as the family is not violent, abusive, or neglectful—makes little difference in children's personality and cognitive development. Countering this view, Diana Baumrind (1993) points to many differences among "normal" parents and says that different parenting practices can and do influence children's lives. Jacquelyn Faye Jackson (1993) expresses concern that public policymakers who accept Scarr's view will be less likely to support intervention, resulting in poorer developmental outcomes for children who need special help. Let's see how each of these thinkers supports her opinion.

SCARR'S THESIS: "GOOD ENOUGH" PARENTING IS GOOD ENOUGH

Most families provide supportive environments for their children, and "good enough" parents probably have the same effect as "superparents." It does not matter if parents take children to a ball game or to a museum, since children's inherited characteristics will outweigh the differentials in their environments. The athletic child will end up playing ball and the artistic child will create, no matter what their parents do. This perspective depends on an environment varied enough so children can choose the activities and experiences that best fit their own inborn tendencies. It excludes children in "very disadvantaged circumstances and adults with little or no choice about occupations and leisure activities" (Scarr, 1992, p. 9). Among environments that support normal development, however, variations in parenting are not very important in determining children's outcomes. "Parents do not have the power to make their children into whatever they want" (p. 15).

Sandra Scarr

One reason developmentalists have overemphasized the role of parents in influencing the way their children turn out is that parents also provide children's genes, and genetic and environmental influences are correlated. Parents who read well bring books into the house, read to the child, and encourage reading. Parents with reading problems raise children in a less literate environment. When children's reading abilities are correlated with their parents' abilities, the effects of heredity are mixed with the effects of the environment.

Since ordinary parents are good enough, they can take comfort in raising their children in ways that are comfortable for them without feeling guilty when they do not hew closely to current wisdom about good parenting.

BAUMRIND'S VIEW: EXCELLENT PARENTING IS BETTER THAN "GOOD ENOUGH"

All nonabusive nonpoor families are not alike in fostering healthy development, and the self a child will become in one "normal" environment is different from what she or he would become in another.

Diana Baumrind

Scarr fails to specify what kinds of environment are "good enough" or what constitutes "normal development," making it hard to evaluate her thesis. She also fails to explore cross-cultural differences, like mainstream Americans' emphasis on independence and self-reliance, contrasted with Japanese Americans who promote mother-child closeness, or African Americans who have close kinship bonds and multiple caregivers. Most subjects in the research Scarr cites are white and middle-class.

Many American children today—from both poor and well-off families—are growing up at risk of violence, drug abuse, poor reading and math skills, eating disorders, school failure, and sexually transmitted disease. "Thus, the average environment of most young people today is not really good enough just because it is expectable" (Baumrind, 1992, p. 1302).

Biology is not destiny. Parents and others can do a great deal to help children overcome inherited problems, like Down syndrome, for example. Parents affect children's development by using such techniques as scaffolding, induction, elaborated and person-centered communication (all described in Chapter 9), monitoring activities, and modeling desirable behavior. All these practices show a high level of parental involvement and commitment, as opposed to only "good enough."

A danger in accepting Scarr's thesis is its implied encouragement for parental denial of their responsibility for children's healthy development. Parents who ascribe a child's dysfunctional behavior to the child's own personality rather than to anything the parent did or did not do are less likely to try to alter the situation, and the children are less likely to turn out well.

BOX 10-2 ▪ FOOD FOR THOUGHT (CONTINUED)

IS "GOOD-ENOUGH" PARENTING GOOD ENOUGH?

JACKSON'S OPINION: INTERVENTIONS *ARE* EFFECTIVE, EVEN FOR CHILDREN FROM BACKGROUNDS FREE FROM ABUSE AND NEGLECT

Jaquelyn Faye Jackson

Scarr's theory can be harmful to children if it affects social policy by discouraging intervention on the grounds that environmental changes cannot change the course of children's development. In fact, research shows such changes can be beneficial.

In one experiment, intensive intervention efforts were made for healthy infants born to low-income African American women whose IQs were 75 or below. The cognitive development scores of such children are usually normal through the toddler years, indicating that they are not organically retarded. The common drop to retardation levels in preschool and elementary school seems to result from poor living conditions and the nonstimulating environment provided by a low-IQ mother. From before 6 months of age until first grade the study children received intensive day care intervention while their mothers got education and job-training skills. Nine years later, the then-adolescent subjects scored on a par with a control group of children of normal-IQ mothers. Thus Scarr's pessimism about intervention seems unwarranted.

SCARR'S RESPONSE TO CRITICS

Although environments provide a range of opportunities, different people react differently to the same environment. "Both biological and environmental explanations are required to account for human development," Scarr claims (1993, p. 1334). Children in minority ethnic groups and socially disadvantaged children do benefit from interventions that transmit values of the dominant culture; the more they absorb dominant values, the smoother their path in life is likely to be. This does not negate the strong effect of individual inherited characteristics. Biology and culture together shape behavior.

"Genetic does not mean intractable!" (p. 1350). It is valuable to know the importance of heredity and not try to cover up scientific truth for the sake of social action. "All children should have opportunities to become species-normal, culturally appropriate and uniquely themselves. . . . But humanitarian concerns should not drive developmental theory," Scarr says (p. 1350).

---

ways, motivated not by a promise of reward or a fear of punishment, but because they believe certain kinds of behavior are desirable.

Parents socialize children in two ways: *power assertion* and *induction.* Power assertion includes spanking, force (like picking up a child throwing a tantrum and moving him to another room), and threat. Inductive techniques involve setting limits and logical consequences, explaining, reasoning, and getting ideas from the child, rather than punishing, threatening, belittling, or making flat demands.

Parents do not use a single style of socializing children. The most effective parents call upon many different strategies, depending on the age and temperament of the child, the particular teaching the parent wants to impart, and the parent's personality and style. For example, parents tend to use reasoning alone in inducing a child to show concern for others or in teaching table manners; they use power assertion to stop play that gets too rough; and they use both power assertion and reasoning in dealing with lying and stealing. Sometimes parents use power assertion to get a child's attention (as by raising their voice or picking up a child who will not move) and will then use reasoning to make their position clear. Surprisingly, in the United States, physical punishment and withdrawal of love tend to follow damage to property, whereas a child's aggression toward a person does not elicit the same two-pronged reaction (Grusec & Goodnow, 1994).

Internalization involves several steps. First the child has to perceive the message accurately; to achieve this, adults need to be clear about what they say and its importance to them. Then too the child has to see the message as appropriate;

so adults need to be truthful, consistent, and relevant. To motivate the child to accept the message as a guide to behavior, adults can help a child feel autonomous by couching the message in humorous or indirect terms. In sum, adults need to be flexible in discipline, matching it to a child's perception of and reactions to a situation (Grusec & Goodnow, 1994).

Reinforcement and Punishment

Parents sometimes offer rewards to their children to get them to do what they want them to do. They use punishment to get the children to stop doing what they do *not* want them to do. Many parents are less comfortable with rewards—seeing them as bribes—than with punishment. But research shows children learn more by being reinforced for good behavior than by being punished for bad behavior.

behavior modification
Therapeutic approach using principles of learning theory to encourage desired behaviors or to eliminate undesired ones; also called behavior therapy.

Reinforcements. *Behavior modification,* or behavior therapy (a form of operant, or instrumental, learning, described in Chapter 1), is a new name for the old practice of providing positive consequences when children do what parents want them to do or providing negative consequences when they do something the parents disapprove of. *External* reinforcements may be social ones like a smile, a word of praise, a hug, or a special privilege. Or they may take the more tangible form of candy, money, toys, or gold stars. Whatever the reinforcement, the child must see it as rewarding and must get it fairly consistently after showing the desired behavior. Eventually, the behavior should provide its own *internal* reward to the child—such as a sense of pleasure and accomplishment.

"Rewarding" with Punishment. "What are we going to do with that child?" Noel's mother says. "The more we punish him, the more he misbehaves!" No wonder. Noel's parents ignore him most of the time when he behaves well but scold or spank him when he acts up. In effect, they reinforce his behavior by paying attention when he does what they do *not* want him to do.

Most children, of course, prefer affection to disapproval. But children who get little positive attention may like disapproval more than no attention at all, and so they deliberately misbehave. When children deliberately misbehave to get attention, they and their parents can be caught in a destructive cycle: The parents try to halt a behavior with punishment and the children increase the behavior to get more attention. Punishment thus becomes a "reward" that encourages the behavior it is intended to stop.

When Does Punishment Work? Most researchers stress the negative effects of punishment. However, there are times when punishment seems necessary. For example, children have to learn very quickly not to run out into traffic and not to bash each other over the head with heavy toys. Sometimes too, undesirable behavior may be so deep-seated that it is hard to catch a child behaving well so the parent can reinforce the good behavior.

If punishment must be used, the following criteria are important for its effectiveness (Parke, 1977).

- *Timing.* The shorter the time between misbehavior and punishment, the more effective the punishment. When children are punished as they *begin* to engage in a forbidden act such as approaching an object they have been told to stay away from, they will go to it less often than if they are not punished until *after* they have actually touched it.

- *Explanation.* Punishment is more effective when accompanied by an explanation. A short, simple explanation is more effective than a long, involved one.
- *Consistency.* The more consistently a child is punished, the more effective the punishment will be. When the same behavior brings punishment only some of the time, it is likely to continue longer than if punished all the time.
- *The person who punishes.* The better the relationship between the punishing adult and the child, the more effective the punishment.

The Dangers of Punishment.   Although punishment can be effective if used with care, at least in the short run, it can also be harmful. Early and severe physical punishment is especially perilous (B. Weiss, Dodge, Bates, & Pettit, 1992). Aside from the risk of injury to the child, harsh physical and verbal punishment may encourage children to imitate the aggression shown by the punisher. Furthermore, such children may have problems interpreting other people's actions and words, tending to attribute hostile motives where none exist, and to consider aggression an effective response to hypothetical problems. On the other hand, children who are punished often may become passive because they feel helpless to escape punishment. Also, children may become frightened when out-of-control parents yell, scream, chase, and hit them, transmitting the message that parental behavior is no longer predictable (Grusec & Goodnow, 1994). Unwanted long-term effects may include a child's avoidance of a punitive parent, undermining the parent's ability to influence behavior.

SPECIFIC DEVELOPMENTAL ISSUES

ALTRUISM, OR PROSOCIAL BEHAVIOR

One day when Jason, at 4, was picnicking in the park, he saw a shabbily dressed man going through a garbage can. Holding up his sandwich, Jason asked his mother, "Can I give this to him?" This was not the only time Jason showed *altruism,* or *prosocial behavior,* acting out of concern for another person, with no expectation of reward. Prosocial acts often entail cost, self-sacrifice, or risk on the part of the person who makes them.

altruism, or **prosocial behavior**   *Acting out of concern for another person with no expectation of reward; selflessness.*

Origins of Prosocial Behavior

Why do some children reach out to comfort a crying friend or stop to help someone who has fallen while crossing a street? What makes them generous, compassionate, and sensitive to other people's needs? Like the origins of many other human characteristics, factors contributing to caring behavior begin with the child and are affected by the child's social context.

The Child.   The child's genetic legacy may predispose him or her toward empathy, according to findings from a study of twins (Zahn-Waxler, Robinson, & Emde, 1992). Socioeconomic status is *not* a factor, and in most studies, no sex differences turn up either.

Prosocial behavior emerges early. Even before their second birthday, children often help others, share belongings and food, and offer comfort. These behaviors emerge at about the same time children are increasingly able to use symbols and to pretend. What we may be seeing is a child's ability to imagine how another person might feel and to develop a feeling of responsibility for others. This ability enables children to develop a moral sense at a very young age (Zahn-Waxler, Radke-Yarrow, Wagner, & Chapman, 1992).

Altruistic children tend to be advanced in reasoning skills and able to take the role of others (Carlo, Knight, Eisenberg, & Rotenberg, 1991). They are also active and self-confident. Other children respond to them, preferring prosocial preschoolers as playmates (C. H. Hart, DeWolf, Wozniak, & Burts, 1992). How do they become this way? The findings of many studies point to the home. The family is important as a model, as a source of explicit standards, and as a guide to adopting models.

What parents themselves do and say is a major influence on whether children will be likely to help other people, strangers or those in their own families.

The Family.   One way parents encourage altruism is to love and respect a child, since altruistic children generally feel secure in their parents' love and affection. Preschoolers who were securely attached as infants (see attachment discussion in Chapter 7) are more likely than insecurely attached children to respond to other children's distress. They have more friends, and their teachers consider them more socially competent. Children who received empathic, nurturant, responsive care as infants develop those qualities themselves (Kestenbaum, Farber, & Sroufe, 1989; Sroufe, 1983).

Parents of prosocial children typically set an example; they also encourage their children to empathize with others and to reflect on the implications of their actions. When Vicky took candy from a store, her father did not lecture her on honesty or tell her what a bad girl she had been. Instead, he explained how the owner of the store would be harmed because she had not paid for the candy, and he took her back to the store to return it. When incidents like this occur, Vicky's parents ask, for example, "How do you think Mr. Jones feels?" or "How would you feel if you were Maria?" They are using inductive techniques.

Parents of prosocial children usually hold them to high standards. The children know they are expected to be honest and helpful. They have responsibilities in the home and are expected to meet them. Parents also point out other models and steer their children toward stories and television programs—like *Mister Rogers' Neighborhood*—that depict cooperation, sharing, and empathy. Such programs encourage children to be more sympathetic, generous, and helpful (Mussen & Eisenberg-Berg, 1977; NIMH, 1982; D. M. Zuckerman & Zuckerman, 1985).

One study identified 406 non-Jewish Europeans who, during the 1930s and 1940s, had risked their lives to rescue Jews in Nazi-occupied countries, and compared these rescuers with people who had not helped. The rescuers' childhood homes turned out to be different from the others' (Oliner & Oliner, 1988). Rescuers' parents had emphasized ethical principles—compassion and caring for others and a sense of fairness extending to people they did not know. They put less emphasis on obedience, earning money, and the importance of self. Rescuers also reported closer early family relationships, especially with parents who had disciplined them more by inductive techniques like reasoning, explanations, persuasion, advice, and suggestions of how to right a wrong than by spanking. Furthermore, the parents had often behaved altruistically themselves.

A more recent examination also found children's altruism related to parents' use of inductive techniques. Among 106 three- to six-year-olds, the most prosocial children were disciplined by inductive techniques. The strongest correlations held for older preschool daughters of inductive mothers (C. H. Hart et al., 1992). Since mothers are still the primary caregivers of most young children, their behavior seems to make more of an impact than fathers' behavior.

The School.   Teachers who are warm and who themselves show prosocial behavior foster helping and caring behavior in their pupils (Eisenberg, 1992). In many countries outside the United States, moral education is part of the curriculum. In China, teachers tell stories about altruistic heroes and encourage children to imitate them.

In suburban San Francisco's Child Development Project (CDP), teachers have instituted a child-centered approach to encourage prosocial behavior (Battistich, Watson, Solomon, Schaps, & Solomon, 1991). From kindergarten on, children hear about prosocial values, read books, and watch films showing altruistic behavior. They are also encouraged to help other students and to perform community service, as well as classroom chores. After 5 years of the program, children in the CDP schools are more helpful, cooperative, and concerned about other people.

The Culture.   Observers of cooperation and competition and of helpfulness and hostility in various countries have tried to explain why societies differ in these respects. One hypothesis is based on differences in the degree to which children experience love rather than rejection.

Among the Papago Indians of Arizona, parents are warm, supportive, and nurturant, whereas Alorese parents in Java are hostile and neglectful. These and other differences may well account for the cooperative, peaceful Papago personality, compared with the hostile, distrustful, and aggressive behavior of the Alorese (Eisenberg, 1992). The founders of *kibbutzim,* communal groups in Israel, aimed to create a society of less selfish, more generous citizens. A measure of their success is that at every age and stage of development, children reared on a kibbutz tend to think more about obligations to others than do children raised at home (Snarey, Reimer, & Kohlberg, 1985).

What do you think?   *In a society in which "good Samaritans" are sometimes reviled for "butting into other people's business" and sometimes attacked by the very persons they try to help, is it wise to encourage children to offer help to strangers?*

AGGRESSION

Babies do not show truly *aggressive behavior,* hostile actions intended to hurt somebody or to establish dominance. But anyone who is around children past the age of 2½ or 3 has seen enough hitting, punching, kicking, biting, and throwing to recognize the age of *hostile aggression.* Within the next 3 years or so, children normally shift from showing aggression with blows to doing it with words (Maccoby, 1980). Let's see how that happens—and why it sometimes does not happen.

aggressive behavior
Hostile actions intended to hurt somebody or to establish dominance.

The Rise and Decline of Aggression

As Vicky, age 3, was playing in the sandbox, another child came up and snatched her shovel. He was interested only in getting the shovel, not in hurting or dominating Vicky. This is *instrumental aggression,* or aggression used as an instrument to reach a goal. In the early stages of aggression, children often focus single-mindedly on something they want and make threatening gestures against anyone keeping it from them. Between ages $2\frac{1}{2}$ and 5, they commonly struggle over toys and the control of space. Aggression surfaces mostly during social play. Some aggression is normal, and the children who fight the most tend to be the most sociable and competent. The ability to show *some* aggression may be a necessary step in social development.

Between ages 2 and 5, as children become better able to express themselves with words, aggression declines in frequency, initiation, and average length of episodes (Cummings, Iannotti, & Zahn-Waxler, 1989). However, individual differences at age 2 tend to be fairly stable, especially among boys. Boys who hit or grab toys from other children at age 2 are still acting aggressively at age 5.

After age 6 or 7, most children become less aggressive as they become less egocentric and more empathic. They can now put themselves into someone else's place, can understand why the other person may be acting in a certain way, and can develop more positive ways of dealing with that person. They also have more positive social skills—they can communicate better and can cooperate in achieving joint goals.

But not all children learn to control aggression. Some become more and more destructive. Aggression may be a reaction to major problems in a child's life. It may also *cause* major problems, by making other children and adults dislike a child. Even in a normal child, aggression can sometimes get out of hand and become dangerous. Researchers therefore, have studied what stimulates aggression.

Triggers of Aggression

The male hormone testosterone (which boys have more of than girls do) *may* underlie the tendency toward aggressive behavior and explain why males are more likely to be aggressive than females. However, social-learning theorists point to other contributing factors, like ineffective parenting (G. R. Patterson, DeBaryshe, & Ramsey, 1989). Parents of children who later become antisocial often fail to reinforce good behavior and are harsh or inconsistent or both in punishing misbehavior. They are not closely involved in their children's lives in such positive ways as making sure the children do their homework. The children tend to do poorly in school and to be rejected by their peers. Depressed, they then seek out other troubled children, who spur them on to more antisocial behavior.

Triggers of aggression in the early lives of these children include reinforcement for aggressive behavior, frustration, and imitation of aggressive models in real life or on television.

Reinforcement. Children's clearest reward, of course, is getting what they want. But sometimes punishment can reinforce aggressive behavior, since some children would rather get negative attention than none at all. Preschool teachers have decreased the amount of aggression shown by 3- and 4-year-old boys by ignoring aggressive behavior and reinforcing cooperative activities (P. Brown & Elliott, 1965). But it is not always safe to ignore aggression, and permitting it by not interfering with it can even communicate approval.

Frustration and Imitation. Frustration—often resulting from punishment, insults, and fears—does not always lead to aggression, but a frustrated child is more apt to be aggressive than a contented one (Bandura, Ross, & Ross, 1961).

Children often imitate what they see on television, including acts of violence. They may also absorb the value that aggression is appropriate behavior.

Frustration and imitation can work together, as one classic study demonstrated. The social-learning theorist Albert Bandura and his colleagues (1961) divided seventy-two 3- to 6-year-olds into two experimental groups and one control group. One by one, each child in the first experimental group went into a playroom. An adult model (male for half the children, female for the other half) quietly played in a corner with toys. The model for the second experimental group began to assemble Tinker Toys, but after a minute, spent the rest of the 10-minute session punching, throwing, and kicking a 5-foot-tall inflated doll. The children in the control group saw no model.

After the sessions, all the children were mildly frustrated by seeing toys they were not allowed to play with. They then went into another playroom. The children who had seen the aggressive model were much more aggressive than those in the other groups, imitating many of the same things they had seen the model say and do. Both boys and girls were more strongly influenced by an aggressive male model than an aggressive female, apparently because they considered aggression more appropriate for males (in line with the gender schema they had learned). The children who had been with the quiet model were less aggressive than those who had not seen any model. We see, then, how adult models can influence children's behavior in more than one direction.

Effects of Televised Violence.   Even children who do not see aggressive models in real life see hundreds of them on television. Three- to five-year-olds spend an average of 2 hours a day watching television (Institute for Social Research, 1985), and children's programs are 6 times as violent as adults' programs (Signorielli, Gross, & Morgan, 1982). A Canadian study found that from 28 to 40 percent of children aged 3 to 10 watched violent television programs (Bernard-Bonnin, Gilbert, Rousseau, Masson, & Maheux, 1991). Research suggests that children are influenced even more by seeing filmed violence than by seeing real people acting aggressively (Bandura, Ross, & Ross, 1963).

Research since the 1950s shows that children who see televised violence behave more aggressively themselves (National Institute of Mental Health, 1982). This is true across geographic locations and socioeconomic levels, for both boys and girls, and for normal children as well as for those with emotional problems.

This does not mean that viewing television violence *causes* aggression, although the findings strongly suggest it. It is possible that children already prone to violence become more so after seeing it on-screen. Also, they may watch more violent television. Then, some third factor may be involved: Maybe children who watch and react aggressively to televised violence are spanked more than other children. However, evidence from a wide range of research, including experimental and longitudinal studies, supports a causal relationship between watching violence and acting aggressively (Huston et al., 1993; Geen, 1994).

Two theoretical explanations for how this happens depend on children's cognitive processing. One mechanism is the *behavioral script,* which serves as a guide for the child's own behavior (Huesmann, 1986). When Jason sees a character getting angry with someone else and showing anger by shooting, he gets an image of shooting in his mind. He also makes a judgment about the reason for the shooting. Once he has learned that being angry is a good enough reason for becoming violent, he may retrieve this script from memory and use it to guide his own behavior when he gets angry.

The other mechanism is *cognitive priming* (L. Berkowitz, 1984). When Vicky sees televised violence, her mind makes associations consisting of aggressive ideas and emotions. People who are frustrated, attacked, in pain, or stressed usually feel like escaping or fighting. If aggressive associations in Vicky's mind have been primed by seeing violence, she will be more likely to fight than to flee.

Aggressive children watch more television than nonaggressive children, identify more strongly with aggressive characters, and are more likely to believe that aggression seen on television reflects real life (Eron, 1982). Aggressive acts make a more vivid impression than any punishment the "bad guy" receives (Liebert & Poulos in Lickona, 1976). Television encourages aggressive behavior in two ways: Children imitate what they see, and they also absorb the values transmitted and come to see aggression as acceptable behavior.

Children who see both heroes and villains on television getting what they want through violence and lawbreaking may become less sensitive to real-life aggression. They may, for instance, fail to protect the victim of a bully. They are also more likely to break rules and less likely to cooperate to resolve differences.

Watching violence seems to make children more willing to hurt people. One experimental group of 5- to 9-year-olds watched a $3\frac{1}{2}$-minute segment from a popular television series, which includes two fistfights, two shootings, and a knifing. A control group watched $3\frac{1}{2}$ minutes of sports. Afterward, the children were asked to play a "game": They could push a "help" button (to help an unseen child win a game) or a "hurt" button (to make a handle touched by that child so hot it would hurt). (Of course, there was no such child.) The effects were frightening: Children who had watched the violent program were more willing than those who had watched the sports program to hurt the unseen child and to inflict more severe pain (Liebert, 1972).

Some effects of televised violence seem to endure for years. Among 427 young adults whose viewing habits had been studied at age 8, the best predictor of aggressiveness in 19-year-old men and women was the degree of violence in the shows they had watched as children (Eron, 1980, 1982). The American Psychological Association (APA, 1993) has called for a major effort to reduce violence on television. The resolution urges government to require limits on televised violence between 6 A.M. and 10 P.M., warning labels for violent material on videotapes, and a national educational campaign to prevent violence.

Reducing Aggression

Parents can often reduce aggressive tendencies by how they react. The least aggressive children have parents who deal with misbehavior by reasoning with them, making them feel guilty, and withdrawing approval and affection. These techniques are more likely to produce children with strong consciences. Children who are spanked, threatened, or have privileges withdrawn are more likely to be aggressive. (Of course, parents may be more likely to use power assertion techniques with aggressive children.) Parents' tendencies to use inductive methods with girls and power assertion with boys may accentuate girls' inclinations to feel guilty and boys' to be aggressive (Sears, Maccoby, & Levin, 1957).

As we pointed out earlier, punishment—especially spanking—may backfire, because hitting children provides a double incentive for violence. The child not only suffers frustration, pain, and humiliation but also sees aggressive behavior in an adult with whom she or he identifies. Parents who spank provide a "living example of the use of aggression at the very moment they are trying to teach the child not to be aggressive" (Sears et al., 1957, p. 266). Parents need to think about the kind of behavior they want to encourage—and how to do it.

Help can come from programs that teach parents how to reinforce good behavior, discipline consistently and appropriately, and become positively involved in their children's lives (G. R. Patterson et al., 1989). This involvement can include monitoring children's television watching—limiting total time and selecting programs promoting prosocial behavior rather than aggression.

What do you think? *Hostile aggression is widely condemned, but instrumental aggression has many defenders. Is it wise to teach a child never to be aggressive?*

FEARFULNESS

Vicky, at 6, is afraid of seeing a violent movie or television show. Before she turns on the set, she asks, "Is this for kids? Will anybody get hurt?" If she is not sure of a show, she will not watch it. Her concern has even invaded her dreams. One morning, after a particularly scary dream, she said, "Mommy, I had a PG-13 dream and I wanted to have a PG dream." She gets upset when she sees starving children and war on the news and is always full of questions after she happens to see a newscast.

What do you think? *Since young children often find actual news broadcasts scarier than fictional shows, should parents try to prevent their viewing them? Or should parents try to reassure children that the frightening events depicted will not happen to them?*

What Do Children Fear, and Why?

Passing fears are common in these years. Many young children are afraid of animals, especially of dogs. By 6 years of age, children are more likely to be afraid of the dark. Other common fears are of thunderstorms and doctors (DuPont, 1983). Most of these fears evaporate as children grow older and lose their sense of powerlessness.

Why do children become so fearful in early childhood? The reasons may stem from their intense fantasy life coupled with their inability to clearly distinguish "pretend" from reality. Because of their inability to distinguish appearance from reality (discussed in Chapter 9), preschoolers are influenced by how things look. Young children are more likely to be frightened by something that *looks* scary (like the character "The Incredible Hulk") than something capable of doing great harm (like a nuclear explosion); when they get older, they know that the "Hulk" is really a mild-mannered hero on the side of good against evil and are worried by abstract possibilities (Cantor, 1994).

Underlying anxieties, which differ according to a child's own experiences, may cause some fears. A preschooler whose mother is sick in bed may become very upset by a story about a mother's death, even if it is an animal mother. Sometimes children's imaginations get carried away, making them worry about being attacked by a lion or being abandoned. Often their fears come from appraisals of real danger—such as the likelihood of being bitten by a dog—or are triggered by actual events, as when a child who was hit by a car becomes afraid to cross the street. Children who have lived through an earthquake, a kidnapping, or some other frightening event fear it will happen again (Kolbert, 1994). In general, children this age know more and have experienced more than before, and they know there are many things to be afraid of. (See Table 10-5.)

What do you think? *One way in which small children confront fears is to play at such potentially frightening activities as dressing up on Halloween, going on scary rides at amusement parks, and listening to ghost stories. Do you approve or disapprove of such play? Why?*

Preventing and Treating Fears

Parents can help prevent children's fears by instilling a sense of trust and normal caution without being too protective and by overcoming their own unrealistic

TABLE 10-5

CHILDHOOD FEARS	
AGE	**FEARS**
0–6 months	Loss of support, loud noises
7–12 months	Strangers; heights; sudden, unexpected, and looming objects
1 year	Separation from parent, toilet, injury, strangers
2 years	A multitude of stimuli, including loud noises (vacuum cleaners, sirens and alarms, trucks, and thunder), animals, dark rooms, separation from parent, large objects or machines, changes in personal environment, unfamiliar peers
3 years	Masks, dark, animals, separation from parent
4 years	Separation from parent, animals, dark, noises (including noises at night)
5 years	Animals, "bad" people, dark, separation from parent, bodily harm
6 years	Supernatural beings (e.g., ghosts, witches), bodily injury, thunder and lightning, dark, sleeping or staying alone, separation from parent
7–8 years	Supernatural beings, dark, media events (e.g., news reports on the threat of nuclear war or child kidnapping), staying alone, bodily injury
9–12 years	Tests and examinations in school, school performances, bodily injury, physical appearance, thunder and lightning, death, dark
Teens	Social performance, sexuality

SOURCE: Adapted from Morris & Kratochwill, 1983.

fears. They can help a child who is already fearful by reassurance and by encouraging open expression of feelings. They should avoid ridicule ("Don't be such a baby!"), coercion ("Pat the nice doggie—it won't hurt you"), and logical persuasion ("The closest bear is 20 miles away, locked in a zoo!"). Neither should they ignore the fear nor allow the child to continue avoiding the feared object or event. None of these approaches works (DuPont, 1983).

Parents cannot reason away fears caused by cognitive immaturity: A young child cannot understand an explanation like "It can't hurt you—it's not real." Instead, preschoolers are comforted by holding a cuddly toy or having something to eat or drink. Not until elementary school can children relieve fear by telling themselves what they are seeing is not real (Cantor, 1994).

Children can overcome fears by gradually experiencing the situations they are afraid of. In one study involving *systematic desensitization*—the gradual exposure to a feared object—experimenters helped first- through third-graders overcome their fears of snakes by providing gradually closer, more frequent contact. After an average of two 15-minute sessions, 39 out of 45 children held snakes in their laps for 15 seconds, compared with only 5 of 22 children in a control group, who did not have the gradual contact (C. M. Murphy & Bootzin, 1973).

Modeling—observing fearlessness in others—is also useful. Preschool children who feared dogs took part in eight brief sessions in which they saw an unafraid child playing happily with a dog. Later, two-thirds of the fearful children were able to climb into a playpen with the dog (Bandura, Grusec, & Menlove, 1967).

systematic desensitization *Gradual exposure to a feared object for the purpose of overcoming the fear.*

THE WIDENING WORLD: RELATIONSHIPS WITH OTHER CHILDREN

The most important people in a baby's world are caregiving adults. Then in early childhood relationships with peers become important, and almost every characteristic activity and personality issue of this age—from play to gender identity and the degree of aggressive or prosocial behavior—involve a child's relationships with other children, either siblings or friends. Before we see how these relationships develop, let's look at children who grow up without any siblings.

THE ONLY CHILD

Although people often think of only children as spoiled, selfish, lonely, or maladjusted, research does not bear out this negative view. According to an analysis of 115 studies comparing only children of various ages and backgrounds with children who have siblings (Falbo & Polit, 1986), only children do very well. In occupational and educational achievement, intelligence, and character (or personality), "onlies" surpassed children with siblings, especially those with many siblings or older siblings. In these three categories, as well as in adjustment and sociability, only children were like firstborns and people with only one sibling. Research in China suggests that being an only child has implications for future development. (See Box 10-3.)

BROTHERS AND SISTERS

Vicky, 6, has enjoyed playing with her brother Bobby, 2½, since he was an infant. At first, she would arrange her dolls around him as he sat in his infant seat, us-

BOX 10-3 ■ AROUND THE WORLD

A NATION OF ONLY CHILDREN

A group of Chinese kindergartners are learning how to fold paper to make toys. When the toys do not come out right, some of the children try again on their own or watch their classmates and copy what they do. But other children become bored and impatient and ask someone else to do it for them, or else they give up, bursting into tears. In some research (Jiao, Ji, & Jing, 1986), the children in the second category tended to come from one-child families—a fact that worries citizens of the People's Republic of China, which in 1979 established an official policy of limiting families to one child each.

The government is serious about this policy, since China's exploding population means there are not enough classroom places for all its children, not enough jobs for adults, not enough food for everyone. To lower the birthrate, family-planning workers oversee factory workshops and agricultural brigades, and special birth control departments exist in every inhabited area. The policy goes beyond using propaganda campaigns and rewards (housing, money, child care, and school priorities) to induce voluntary compliance. There have been millions of involuntary abortions, sterilizations, and vasectomies, and people who have children without permission are fined and denied job promotions and bonuses. As a result, more only children live in China than in any other country, even though most families formed since 1979 in rural areas (where the policy was not rigidly enforced until a recent harsh crackdown) have two or three children.

Chinese nursery schools, kindergartens, and early elementary grades are filled with children who have no brothers or sisters. This situation marks a great change in Chinese society, in which newlywed couples were traditionally congratulated with the wish, "May you have a hundred sons and a thousand grandsons." No culture in human history has ever been composed entirely of only children. Critics ask whether the Chinese are sowing the seeds of their own destruction.

Some research has suggested that only children are more egocentric, less persistent, less cooperative, and less well liked than children with siblings. They were more likely to refuse to help another child or to help grudgingly, less likely to share their toys or to enjoy playing or working with other children, less modest, less helpful in group activities, and more irresponsible (Jiao et al., 1986).

However, new research comparing Chinese school children with and without siblings contradicts previous findings that only children are spoiled, overindulged "little

Since 1979 the People's Republic of China has limited families to one child each. The implications of this policy for children growing up without siblings, cousins, or aunts and uncles are hotly debated by educators, researchers, and politicians.

emperors" (Falbo & Poston, 1993). A sample of 4000 third- and sixth-graders from both urban and rural districts were assessed on academic achievement, physical growth, and personality. Personality traits considered desirable in China include "good manners, doesn't cry, keeps trying until finishes task, not selfish, modest, likes to do things better than others, has own ideas, confident, likes to help others, respects elders, doesn't start fights, and pays attention to teacher." Such traits were rated by the children themselves and by other children, parents, and teachers.

This research did not point to a risk of abnormal de-

BOX 10-3 ■ AROUND THE WORLD (CONTINUED)

A NATION OF ONLY CHILDREN

velopment for only children. In fact, for academic achievement and physical growth, only children did about the same or better than those with siblings. They did especially well on verbal achievement, and in two of the four provinces studied, only children were taller or heavier than the others.

The few personality differences found varied by sex and by urban or rural residence. Only children living in urban areas, and especially boys, were seen to have less desirable personalities; those from rural areas, especially girls, had more desirable personalities. The data for this project were collected immediately after the disastrous 1989 Tiananmen demonstrations, and the Beijing schools undoubtedly reflected the nation's turmoil. The better showing of girls may mean girls are more easily socialized into Chinese personality norms than are boys. In sum: Birth order and the presence or absence of siblings are not determining factors for children's development; they have to be weighed in context with other influences.

China's population policy also has wider implications. If it succeeds, eventually most Chinese will lack aunts and uncles, nephews and nieces, and cousins, as well as siblings. How this will affect individuals, families, and the social fabric is at present incalculable.

A more sinister question is this: What has happened to the girls? A 1990 census suggests that 5 percent of all infant girls born in China (some half a million infants born alive each year) are unaccounted for. Suspicions abound that parents permitted only one child have been willing to have baby girls killed or to withhold care from them so they can have the chance to bear and raise more highly valued sons. A more benign explanation is that these girls are hidden and raised secretly to evade the one-child policy (Kristof, 1991, 1993). In either case, China's one-child policy has ramifications its developers never thought of.

---

ing him as another doll as she played being "Mommy." Now the two of them gallop around the house together, pretending to be horses; they play kickball and other games; and she sometimes talks him into playing "Daddy." Realizing Bobby cannot yet follow rules, Vicky makes allowances for him, sometimes stopping during play to say to Ellen, "Isn't he cute?"

Sibling rivalry is *not* the main pattern between brothers and sisters early in life. While some rivalry exists, so do affection, interest, companionship—and influence. Observations of young sibling pairs (same-sex and mixed-sex) have shown that siblings separated by as little as 1 year or as much as 4 years interact closely with each other in many ways.

Three sets of observations began when the younger siblings were about $1\frac{1}{2}$ years old and the older ones ranged from 3 to $4\frac{1}{2}$. The studies continued until the younger ones were 5 and the older ones, $6\frac{1}{2}$ to 8 (Abramovitch, Corter, & Lando, 1979; Abramovitch, Corter, Pepler, & Stanhope, 1986; Abramovitch, Pepler, & Corter, 1982). Older siblings initiated more behavior, both friendly (sharing a toy, smiling, hugging, or starting a game) and unfriendly (hitting, fighting over a toy, teasing, or tattling). The younger children tended to imitate the older ones—as in using scissors or blowing cake crumbs out of their mouths.

At the older ages, both siblings were less physical and more verbal, both in showing aggression (through commands, insults, threats, tattling, put-downs, bribes, and teasing) and also in showing care and affection (by compliments and comfort rather than hugs and kisses). The age difference apparently has only one effect: In closely spaced pairs, older siblings initiate more prosocial behavior. Same-sex siblings tend to be a bit closer and to play together more peaceably than boy-girl pairs. Siblings tend to get along better when their mother is not with them: Squabbling is often a bid for parental attention. These researchers found prosocial and play-oriented behaviors to be more common than rivalry and concluded, "It is probably a mistake to think of siblings' relationships, at least during the preschool years, as primarily competitive or negative" (Abramovitch et al., 1986, p. 229).

The ties between brothers and sisters set the stage for later relationships. If these interactions are marked by an easy trust and companionship, children may carry this pattern over to their dealings with playmates, classmates, and, eventually, adulthood friends and lovers. If these early encounters have an aggressive cast, this too may influence later social relations.

FRIENDSHIP AND PEER RELATIONSHIPS

At 3, Vicky already has a best friend, Janie, the little girl who lives next door. They ask for each other as soon as they wake up in the morning, and neither is so happy as when she is in the company of her best friend.

Friendship develops as people develop. Although younger children may play alongside or near each other, it is only at about age 3 or so that they begin to have friends. Through friendships and more casual interactions with other children, young children learn how to get along with others. They learn the importance of *being* a friend as the way to *have* a friend. They learn how to solve problems in relationships, they learn how to put themselves in another person's place, and they see models of other kinds of behavior. They learn values (like moral judgments and gender-role norms), and they practice adult roles.

Young children, like people of all ages, define a friend as "someone you like." How do young children choose friends? They usually become friendly with other children who like to do the same kinds of things, and so friends generally have similar energy and activity levels and are of the same age and sex (Gamer, Thomas, & Kendall, 1975). Vicky plays happily for hours with Janie, but when her classmate, Pedro, comes to her house, he and Vicky have more trouble deciding what to do. They often need suggestions from an adult, and Vicky says, "He doesn't want to do what I want to do."

A study of the conceptions of friendship held by 4- to 7-year-olds supports these observations (Furman & Bierman, 1983). Children were asked to recognize and rate pictured activities that would make children friends. They named the most important features of friendships as doing things together, liking and caring for each other, sharing and helping one another, and to a lesser degree, living nearby or going to the same school. Older children rated affection and support higher than did younger ones and rated physical traits like appearance and size lower.

Behavior Patterns That Affect Choice of Playmates and Friends

Although playing with someone and being friends are not the same, the traits that make young children desirable or undesirable seem quite similar for both purposes. Children who have friends talk more and take turns directing and following. Children who do not have friends tend to fight with those who do or to stand on the sidelines and watch them (Roopnarine & Field, 1984). Children like to play with peers who smile and offer a toy or a hand; they reject overtures from disruptive or aggressive children and ignore those who are shy or withdrawn (Roopnarine & Honig, 1985).

Young children learn the importance of being a friend in order to *have* a friend. One way of being a friend can involve a sighted child's helping a blind playmate to enjoy the feel of the sand and the sound of the surf.

One important task of early childhood is learning how to cope with anger-causing situations. Well-liked preschoolers and kindergartners tend to cope well with anger. They respond in relatively direct, active ways that tend to minimize further conflict and help them to keep relationships going. Boys are more likely to express their angry feelings or resist the actions of the child provoking them, whereas girls are more likely to express their disapproval of the other child. Unpopular children are more likely to hit back or tattle (Fabes & Eisenberg, 1992; S. Asher, Renshaw, Geraci, & Dor, 1979).

However, popularity itself helps. Popular children are less likely to be involved in angry conflicts, because other children are less likely to attack them or try to take their toys. Then too, popular children have a strong coping tool: They can threaten not to play with or not to like the other child (Fabes & Eisenberg, 1992). While there is something of a cycle going on here, it seems children who can regulate their anger—either because of inner resources or what they have learned—can handle social situations better than children who cannot. This translates into popularity.

Family Ties and Popularity with Peers

Although young children's relationships with their brothers and sisters often carry over to relationships with other children, patterns established with siblings are not always repeated with friends. A child who is dominated by an elder sibling can easily step into a dominant role with a playmate. Usually children are more prosocial and playful with playmates than with siblings (Abramovitch et al., 1986).

Young children's relationships with their parents may be more significant. The parents of popular children generally have warm, positive relationships with their children. They teach by reasoning more than by punishment (Kochanska,

1992; Roopnarine & Honig, 1988). They are more likely to be authoritative, and their children have learned to be both assertive and cooperative. Parents of rejected or isolated children have a different profile. The mothers do not have confidence in their parenting, rarely praise their children, and do not encourage independence. The fathers pay little attention to their children, dislike being disturbed by them, and consider child rearing women's work (Peery, Jensen, & Adams, 1984, in Roopnarine & Honig, 1985).

The parents' relationship with each other is a factor. Children whose parents do not get along sometimes respond to this stress by playing with other children in ways that try to avoid conflict. As a result, they don't participate fully, they miss having fun, and they don't learn how to get along with others (Gottman & Katz, 1989).

Furthermore, children seem to pick up social behaviors from their parents. An Australian study found a close link between the social skills of kindergartners and their mothers (Russell & Finnie, 1990). Mothers were asked to help their preschool children join the play of two other children whom the target child did not know. The mothers of popular children were most likely to offer effective, group-oriented suggestions that drew their own child's attention to what the other two were doing; they made positive comments about the playing children and gave ideas about joining the pair. On the other hand, the mothers of children who were either disliked or generally ignored by their classmates showed a lack of sensitivity toward the needs of the pair who were playing. They either disrupted the play by taking charge to make the other children let their own child play, or they gave little or no effective help to their child.

How Adults Can Help Children Make Friends

Having a friend is not only a factor in a child's emotional well-being, it also affects school achievement, showing links between social and cognitive development. One study assessed 125 children three times: upon entering kindergarten, 2 months later, and at the end of the school year (Ladd, 1990). Children who already had friends in class when they entered in August liked school better in October. Those who kept these friendships continued to like school better the following May than children who lost those first friends. Also, kindergartners who made new friends scored higher on three tests of achievement, whereas children rejected by their classmates early in the year began to dislike school, were absent more, and did only half as well on academic tests. School administrators would do well to group entering children with friends and to help children keep up old friendships and form new ones.

Adults can help children make friends. Parents can make play dates for them: Children of parents who arrange their children's social lives have more playmates, see them more often, and initiate more get-togethers themselves (Ladd & Hart, 1992; Ladd & Colter, 1988). Parents who monitor preschoolers' play indirectly—by staying nearby but not getting involved in the play—tend to have socially competent children. Children whose parents get right into the play activity are not so well adjusted in the classroom, but it is not clear which comes first. Parents' early monitoring styles may influence the way their children play with others; or parents of children who are aggressive or do not play well on their own may feel they need to maintain more of a presence (Ladd & Colter, 1988).

By arranging play dates, parents promote children's prosocial behavior, along with sociability. Jason's mother reminds him to be a good host, to see that his visiting friends have a good time. Since children who behave prosocially tend to be more popular, this practice in thinking about the needs and wishes of playmates will have long-lasting consequences. Julia also involves Jason in planning, asking: "Who would be fun for you to play with? What kinds of 'fun' things could you do together?" She encourages Jason to make his own phone invitations. With this kind of responsibility for developing relationships, Jason will be better prepared to initiate and manage his own friendships later on. He is also likely to enjoy school more (Ladd & Hart, 1992).

Other helpful adult activities include making a special effort to find a play group for young children who do not often have the opportunity to be with other youngsters; encouraging "loners" to play with small groups of two or three children; praising signs of empathy and responsiveness; and teaching friendship skills indirectly through puppetry, role-playing, and books about animals and children who learn to make friends (Roopnarine & Honig, 1985).

How children get along with their age-mates affects one of the most important activities of early childhood—play.

CHILDREN'S PLAY

PLAY AS THE "BUSINESS" OF EARLY CHILDHOOD

When Vicky comes to breakfast, she pretends that the bits of cereal floating in her bowl are fish, and she "fishes," spoonful by spoonful. Next, she puts on Ellen's old hat, picks up her discarded briefcase, and is the "mother" going to work. She runs outside to splash in the puddles, comes in for an imaginary telephone conversation, turns a wooden block into a truck and makes the appropriate sound effects, and on and on. Vicky's day is one round of play after another.

An adult might be tempted to dismiss Vicky's activities as insignificant. But that would be a mistake: Play is the "work" of the young. Through play, children grow. They learn how to use their muscles; they coordinate what they see with what they do; and they gain mastery over their bodies. They find out what the world is like and what they are like. They acquire new skills and learn how to use them. They become more proficient with language, they get the opportunity to try out different roles, and they cope with complex and conflicting emotions by reenacting real-life situations.

CONCEPTS OF PLAY

Preschoolers engage in many types of play. They gratify the senses by playing with water, sand, and mud. They master a new skill like riding a tricycle. They pretend to be things or other people. By the end of the preschool years, they delight in formal games with routines and rules. Children progress first from playing alone, to playing alongside other children but not with them, and from there to cooperative play where they interact with others.

Children have different styles of playing, and they play at different things. One kindergartner might be putting on dress-up clothes with a friend while another is absorbed in building a block tower. What can we learn about individual children by seeing how they play? To answer such questions, researchers have approached play from both social and cognitive perspectives.

Considering play as a social activity, researchers evaluate children's social competence on the basis of how they play. Social play reflects the extent to which children interact with other children. Cognitive play shows the level of a child's cognitive development. Both enhance development.

Social and Nonsocial Play

In the 1920s, Mildred B. Parten (1932) observed forty-two 2- to 5-year-olds during free-play periods at nursery school. She identified six types of play, ranging from the most nonsocial to the most social. (See Table 10-6.) She found that as children get older, their play tends to become more social and cooperative.

More recent research suggests a different pattern. In a similar study done 40 years later, forty-four 3- and 4-year-olds played much less sociably than the children in Parten's group (K. E. Barnes, 1971). Why did they? The change might have reflected a changed environment: Because these children watched television, they may have become more passive; because they had more elaborate toys and fewer siblings, they may have played alone more. Another possible explanation may be rooted in socioeconomic class. Preschoolers from lower socioeconomic groups engage in more parallel play, while middle-class children play in more associative and cooperative ways (K. Rubin, Maioni, & Hornung, 1976).

Influence of Day Care. Time in some group-based care tends to be associated

TABLE 10-6

TYPES OF SOCIAL AND NONSOCIAL PLAY IN EARLY CHILDHOOD	
CATEGORY	**DESCRIPTION**
Unoccupied behavior	The child does not seem to be playing, but watches anything of momentary interest.
Onlooker behavior	The child spends most of the time watching other children play. The onlooker talks to them, asking questions or making suggestions, but does not enter into the play. The onlooker is definitely observing particular groups of children rather than anything that happens to be exciting.
Solitary independent play	The child plays alone with toys that are different from those used by nearby children and makes no effort to get close to them.
Parallel play	The child plays independently, but among the other children, playing with toys like those used by the other children, but not necessarily playing with them in the same way. Playing *beside* rather than *with* the others, the parallel player does not try to influence the other children's play.
Associative play	The child plays with other children. They talk about their play, borrow and lend toys, follow one another, and try to control who may play in the group. All the children play similarly if not identically; there is no division of labor and no organization around any goal. Each child acts as she or he wishes and is interested more in being with the other children than in the activity itself.
Cooperative or organized supplementary play	The child plays in a group organized for some goal—to make something, play a formal game, or dramatize a situation. One or two children control who belongs to the group and direct activities. By a division of labor, children take on different roles and supplement each other's efforts.

SOURCE: Adapted from Parten, 1932, pp. 249–251.

with sociable play, according to a study of children from three centers (Schindler, Moely, & Frank, 1987). Children attending centers that emphasized social skills and had mixed age groups and a high adult-child ratio played more sociably the longer they had been in day care. This did not hold true for the children in a small center with same-age grouping, which stressed academic skills. The differences between the children in these centers underscore the need to look at every day care situation individually, rather than making sweeping statements about "the effects of day care."

Is Solitary Play Always Less Mature Than Group Play?   Parten and other observers have suggested that young children who play alone may be at risk of developing social, psychological, and educational problems. However, much nonsocial play consists of constructive or educational activities and furthers cognitive, physical, and social development.

An analysis of children in six kindergartens showed that about one-third of solitary play consisted of goal-directed activities like block building and artwork; about one-fourth was large-muscle play; about 15 percent was educational; and only about 10 percent involved just looking (N. Moore, Evertson, & Brophy, 1974). Thus many types of solitary play seem to reflect independence and maturity, not poor social adjustment.

Another study looked at nonsocial play in relation to the cognitive and social competence of 4-year-olds. It used role-taking and problem-solving tests, teachers' ratings of social competence, and popularity with other children. Some kinds of nonsocial play turned out to be associated with a high level of competence. For example, parallel constructive play (activities like playing with blocks or working on puzzles near another child) is most common among children who are good problem solvers, are popular with other children, and are seen by teachers as socially skilled (K. Rubin, 1982).

Not all nonsocial play is immature. Children need some time alone to concentrate on tasks and problems, and some simply enjoy nonsocial activities more than group activities. We need to look at what children *do* when they play, not just at whether they play alone or with someone else.

Cognitive Play

Children's cognitive development in early childhood lets them progress from simple functional (repetitive) play (like rolling a ball) to constructive play (like building a block tower), imaginative play (like playing doctor), and then formal games with rules (like hopscotch and marbles—Piaget, 1951; Smilansky, 1968). (See Table 10-7.) These more complex forms of play foster further cognitive development.

Types of play seem to be similar in other cultures too. For example, categories similar to those described by Parten and by Smilansky showed up in the play of children in Taiwan (Pan, 1994).

Imaginative Play

Vicky, at 13 months, pushes an imaginary spoon holding imaginary food into the mouth of her very real father. Jason, at 2 years, "talks" to a doll as if it were a real person. Michael, 3, wears a kitchen towel as a cape and runs around as Batman. All these children are engaged in *imaginative play*, which involves imaginary sit-

imaginative play *Play involving imaginary situations; also called fantasy play, dramatic play, or pretend play.*

TABLE 10-7

TYPES OF COGNITIVE PLAY	
TYPE	**DESCRIPTION**
Functional play (sensorimotor play)	Any simple, repetitive muscle movement with or without objects, such as rolling a ball or pulling a pull toy
Constructive play	Manipulation of objects to construct or "create" something
Imaginative play	Substitution of an imaginary situation to satisfy the child's personal wishes and needs; pretending to be someone or something (doctor, nurse, Power Ranger), beginning with fairly simple activities but going on to develop more elaborate plots
Games with rules	Any activity with rules, structure, and a goal (such as winning), like tag, hopscotch, marbles; acceptance of prearranged rules

SOURCE: Adapted from Piaget, 1951; Smilansky, 1968.

uations (also called *fantasy play, dramatic play,* or *pretend play*). At one time, the major professional interest in such play was its supposed function in helping children express their emotional concerns, but interest now focuses more on its role in cognitive and general personality development. As we saw in Chapter 9, such play is linked to literacy development.

Imaginative play emerges during the second year of life when sensorimotor play is on the wane. It increases during the next 3 to 4 years, and then declines as children become more interested in playing games with formal rules. Piaget (1962) maintained that children's ability to pretend rests on their ability to use and remember symbols—to retain mental pictures of things they have seen or heard—and that its emergence marks the beginning of the preoperational stage. Other researchers have found that children who play imaginatively tend to be more joyful—to smile and laugh more—than children who do not (Singer & Singer, 1990).

These boys are engaging in a combination of constructive and imaginative play as they perch behind their imaginary "vehicles." Some children like to play alone more than with others, and recent research suggests that solitary play shows just as much competence as social play.

About 10 to 17 percent of preschoolers' play is imaginative play, and the proportion rises to about 33 percent among kindergartners (K. Rubin et al., 1976; K. Rubin, Watson, & Jambor, 1978). The kind of play, as well as its amount, changes during these years from solitary pretending to sociodramatic play involving other children (Singer & Singer, 1990). So Jason, who at age 3 may climb inside a box by himself and pretend to be a train conductor will, by age 6, want to have passengers on his train with whom he can enact minidramas. Through pretending, children learn how to understand another person's viewpoint, develop skills in solving social problems, and become more creative. Children who play this way tend to cooperate more with other children and to be more popular (Singer & Singer, 1990).

Parents of children who play imaginatively tend to get along well with each other, expose the children to interesting experiences, engage them in conversation, and do not spank (Fein, 1981). They also provide a time and place to play, and they encourage imaginative play, as by providing such simple props as costumes, blocks, paints, and toy people (Singer & Singer, 1990). Children who watch a great deal of television play less imaginatively, possibly because they get into the habit of passively absorbing images rather than generating their own.

HOW GENDER AFFECTS PLAY

At age 4, Vicky much prefers to play with other girls than with boys. She constantly classifies toys, games, and activities as "girls'" things or "boys'" things. When she is not sure about some item, she asks about it. Jason too is more interested in playing with children of his own sex.

This tendency toward sex segregation in free play is common among preschoolers, becomes more so in middle childhood, and seems to be universal across cultures (Maccoby, 1988, 1990). One reason for the split seems to be the different styles of play boys and girls typically adopt. Although there are many exceptions, boys tend to like rough-and-tumble play in fairly large groups, while girls are more inclined to quieter play with one other child (Benenson, 1993). At school age, boys more often play in the streets and other public places; girls are more likely to meet in each other's home or yard.

Another factor, says Eleanor Maccoby (1990), is girls' realization, at an age when children try to influence their playmates more and more frequently, that boys often do not pay attention to girls' requests and suggestions and that boys tend to make their wishes known by direct demands. Even among 33-month-old children, boys tend not to withdraw from a place when a girl asks them to, but they are more likely to do so when a boy tells them to. Maccoby suggests that girls may withdraw from boys when they sense this lack of responsiveness.

Children's play groups are powerful instruments of socialization, in which children learn the skills and approaches they will use, often throughout life. The changes in relationships with playmates and in kinds of play, from imaginative play to games with rules, illustrate another leap in development as children enter middle childhood, the years from about age 6 to age 12, which we examine in Chapters 11, 12, and 13.

SUMMARY

1 Developmentalists generally regard the self as a cognitive construct. According to neo-Piagetians, children in early childhood first display single representations and, later, representational mappings.

2 The self-concept is the total picture of one's abilities and traits. Self-esteem involves a sense of self-worth. An important source of self-esteem is the support that a child receives from parents, teachers, and peers.

3 Erikson maintains that the chief developmental crisis of early childhood is initiative versus guilt. Successful resolution of this conflict results in the virtue of purpose and enables the child to plan and carry out activities. Parents can help children achieve a healthy balance by encouraging them to do things on their own while still providing guidance.

4 Young children gradually develop an understanding of simultaneous emotions.

5 The development of emotions directed toward the self, self-affects, depend upon cognitive development as well as socialization.

6 Identification is the adoption of characteristics, beliefs, values, and behaviors of another person or group. It is a major personality development of early childhood.

7 Three major theories about gender identity, the identification and awareness of oneself as male or female, are social-learning, cognitive-developmental, and gender-schema theories. Social learning theorists explain gender identification as a consequence of observing and imitating models, most typically the parent of the same sex. Cognitive-developmental theory maintains that gender identity is related to cognitive development. Children actively classify themselves as male or female and then organize their behavior around this classification. Gender-schema theory combines aspects of social-learning and cognitive-developmental theories. According to gender-schema theory, children organize patterns of behavior around the gender schema of their culture.

8 Sex differences are physical differences between males and females. Gender differences are psychological differences between the sexes. Gender roles are the behaviors and attitudes a culture deems appropriate for males and females. Gender-typing is the learning of culturally determined gender roles. Gender stereotypes are exaggerated generalizations about male or female behavior.

9 In general, the sexes are more similar than different. Gender differences are few, and their extent and significance are minimal. Explanations for the differences that do exist focus on both biological and environmental origins.

10 Even though gender differences are minor, society holds strong ideas about appropriate behaviors for the sexes, and children learn these expectations at an early age. Because gender-role stereotyping can restrict the development of both sexes, androgynous child rearing, which encourages children to express both "male" and "female" characteristics, is being fostered by many people and institutions.

11 Baumrind has identified three types of child-rearing styles: authoritarian, permissive, and authoritative. Each is related to certain behavior patterns in children. The authoritative style is associated with the most positive developmental outcomes.

12 Miller identified a psychologically injurious group of child-rearing practices that she called "poisonous pedagogy," associated with negative developmental outcomes.

13 Parents' love is the most important influence on the social maturity their children will exhibit as adults.

14 Parents discipline or socialize their children by teaching them behavior, character, and self-control. Internalization is the end result of socialization.

15 Parents influence children's behavior partly through rewards and punishments. Rewards are generally more effective than are punishments. Punishments are more effective when they are immediate, accompanied by explanation, consistent, and car-

ried out by somebody with a good relationship with the child. Physical punishment, in particular, can have a number of damaging effects.

16   Whether children display prosocial or aggressive behavior is influenced by the way their parents treat them, as well as by other factors, including what they learn from the media, the values of their culture, and whether they observe prosocial or aggressive models.

17   During early childhood, children show many fears of both real and imaginary objects and events. Systematic desensitization and modeling help children overcome fears.

18   In the United States children without siblings tend to exhibit positive characteristics in the realms of occupational and educational achievement, intelligence, and personality.

19   As siblings move through early childhood, most of their interactions are positive; rivalry is not the dominant pattern. As they mature, siblings interact less often physically and more often verbally. Older siblings tend to be dominant and are both more aggressive and more prosocial.

20   Children who are aggressive or withdrawn tend to be less popular with playmates than children who act friendly. Parental factors influence the ease with which children make friends.

21   Play is both a social and a cognitive activity. Changes in the type of play children engage in reflect their development. Through play, children exercise their physical abilities, grow cognitively, and learn to interact with other children. Play is influenced by interaction with parents, by day care situation, and by gender.

KEY TERMS

self-concept (381)
self-definition (382)
ideal self (382)
real self (382)
self-esteem (382)
initiative versus guilt (383)
identification (386)
gender (386)
sex differences (386)
gender differences (386)
gender identity (386)
gender roles (386)
gender constancy, or
   gender conservation (389)
gender-schema theory (389)

gender schema (389)
gender-typing (392)
gender stereotypes (393)
androgynous (393)
authoritarian parents (396)
permissive parents (396)
authoritative parents (396)
discipline (401)
socialization (401)
internalization (401)
behavior modification (404)
altruism, or prosocial behavior (405)
aggressive behavior (407)
systematic desensitization (413)
imaginative play (421)

SUGGESTED READINGS

Axline, V. M. (1967).   *Dibs in search of self.* New York: Ballantine. This immensely moving and readable classic is the story of the play therapy that enabled a silent, withdrawn child to become his true, intelligent, and emotionally expressive self.

Elium, J., & Elium, D. (1994).   *Raising a daughter: Parents and the awakening of a healthy woman.* The authors, both counselors, take a developmental approach and a conversational style to address the way cultural forces affect girls' development and how parents can encourage healthy growth.

Elium, J., & Elium, D. (1992).   *Raising a son: Parents and the making of a healthy man.* This earlier book by the same author team speaks to parents who feel frustrated and confused by their sons' behavior and offers knowledge and guidance designed to raise healthy, assertive, and loving men.

Faber, A., & Mazlish, E. (1988). *Siblings without rivalry.* New York: Avon. This book offers dozens of practical guidelines and real-life examples for fostering healthy and cooperative sibling relationships.

Hopson, D., & Powell-Hopson, D. (1990). *Different and wonderful: Raising black children in a race-conscious society.* Englewood Cliffs, NJ: Prentice-Hall. On the basis of their research in this area and their experience as parents, two clinical psychologists advise on such issues as toys, choosing day care and schools, and enhancing self-esteem. This book is not just for black parents; it is a great source for anyone working with children of different races.

Miedzian, M. (1991). *Boys will be boys: Breaking the link between masculinity and violence.* New York: Doubleday. The author, a professor of philosophy with a master's degree in social work, analyzes society's equation of masculinity with violence. She describes creative and effective programs and child-rearing practices that dissuade boys from violent behavior, instill empathy, and foster nurturant fathering.

Miller, A. (1981). *The drama of the gifted child.* New York: Harper & Row. This short book describes and gives many examples of how parents destroy their children's ability to feel and express authentic emotions. A classic in several languages, it is a very readable statement of Miller's philosophy.

Taylor, S. E. (1989). *Positive illusions: Creative self-deception and the healthy mind.* New York: Basic Books. This provocative book by a social psychologist draws on a large body of research demonstrating that the best-adjusted adults are not, as has been traditionally believed, firmly in touch with reality. Instead, the healthy human mind seems to cope with life by replacing negative information with positive, often unrealistically optimistic beliefs.

Turecki, S., with Wernick, S. (1994). *The emotional problems of normal children.* New York: Bantam. A compassionate and practical guide with two basic points: that normal children can have problems, and that parents can help them. Illustrated with vivid vignettes from the author's practice as a child and family psychiatrist, this work shows how parents can use their intimate knowledge of the child to intervene. You'll also find guidelines for deciding when to seek professional help and what to expect if you do.

MIDDLE CHILDHOOD

Middle childhood—from about age 6 to age 12—is often called the *school years,* since school is the central experience during this time. It is in school that Vicky and Jason find friends, games, and ideas, and a complex society. In Chapters 11, 12, and 13 we look at the physical, cognitive, and personality development during these school years and at Vicky's and Jason's increasing socialization.

Chapter 11, on physical development, discusses children's steady growth and improving motor abilities. During these years children acquire many of the physical skills needed to participate in games, sports, and other activities. Chapter 12, on cognitive development, presents the child's new ability to think logically and creatively about the here and now. This is the period when many children first realize which aspects of our complex society most interest them and in which areas they are more competent. Chapter 13, on personality development, discusses a stage that traditionally has been considered calm and idyllic. This stage never was as peaceful as some believed, and many societal elements like divorce and prejudice take their toll. Still, children can emerge from the period with a healthy sense of self-esteem.

CHAPTER 11
PHYSICAL DEVELOPMENT AND HEALTH IN MIDDLE CHILDHOOD

The boy is growing
as fast as he can, elongated
wrists dangling, lean meat
showing between the shirt and the belt.
If there were a rack to stretch himself, he would
strap his slight body to it.
If there were a machine to enter,
skip the next ten years and be
sixteen immediately, this boy would
do it.

> Sharon Olds, "Size and Sheer Will,"
> *The Dead and the Living,* 1983

In middle childhood, as we shall see in our discussions of motor development in this chapter, youngsters seem to be always on the run; they are becoming more proficient at running, as at other motor skills. Their play continues to have strong physical components, even as it becomes increasingly cognitive. Because normal growth depends on proper nutrition and good health, we discuss health and illness, and we look at an increasingly common problem, childhood obesity. As we explore health concerns, we examine children's understanding of health and illness, which links physical, cognitive, and emotional issues. We also consider safety. As children develop, they do more, and their risk of accidents increases; we examine some ways to lower the risk. When you have studied this chapter, you will be able to answer such questions as the following:

PREVIEW QUESTIONS

- ◆ What factors influence height and weight in middle childhood?
- ◆ What motor skills do most children have at this age? How do these skills affect children's lives?
- ◆ What are the causes and implications of childhood obesity? How is it treated?
- ◆ What are the principal health problems in middle childhood?
- ◆ How does the understanding of health and illness develop in middle childhood?
- ◆ What can adults do to make middle childhood healthier and safer for children?

Higher and higher pencil marks on the wall of Jason's room show his growth over the years. His height is a source of pride—and worry—as he measures his new abilities (like reaching the highest shelf in the refrigerator) and as he measures himself against his classmates (and finds too many of them taller then he is). By the time he is 12, he can look Julia squarely in the eye, and she can fit into his blue jeans.

Vicky, too, has been growing slowly and steadily during her first 6 years at school. At first, her pace is about the same as Jason's, but later it becomes slightly faster. At 12, she is taller and heavier than Jason. The facial proportions of both children have also changed. In accordance with the cephalocaudal principle of development (see Chapter 5), during the early years the upper parts of the head grew faster than the lower parts. In middle childhood the lower half of the face catches up, and the forehead is not so high. The facial features become more prominent and more distinctly individual.

Both Vicky and Jason are in robust health, and they take for granted their increasing physical power and coordination. Despite all the colds and sore throats children get, middle childhood is a healthy time of life. Debilitating diseases are rare, but among children living in poverty, without access to preventive and curative medical care, ill health is common.

As we consider growth during middle childhood, we discuss mind *and* body, and both affect health and development.

GROWTH DURING THE SCHOOL YEARS

HEIGHT AND WEIGHT

If we were to walk by a typical elementary school just after the three o'clock bell, we would see a virtual explosion of children of all shapes and sizes. Tall ones, short ones, fat ones, and skinny ones would be bursting out of the school doors into the freedom of the open air.

We would see that 6- to 12-year-olds look very different from children a few years younger. They are taller, and most are fairly wiry, although today more are likely to be overweight than in past decades. Girls retain somewhat more fatty tissue than boys, a characteristic that will persist through adulthood.

During each year of middle childhood, children grow about 1 to 2 inches and gain about 5 to 8 pounds or more. Late in this stage, usually between ages 10 and 12, girls begin their growth spurt; suddenly they are taller and heavier than the boys in their class. (See Table 11-1.)

School-age children are taller and thinner than they were as preschoolers. Girls retain somewhat more fatty tissue than boys, a physical characteristic that will persist through adulthood. Black children tend to be slightly taller than white children.

TABLE 11-1

	HEIGHT, INCHES				WEIGHT, POUNDS			
AGE	WHITE MALES	NONWHITE MALES	WHITE FEMALES	NONWHITE FEMALES	WHITE MALES	NONWHITE MALES	WHITE FEMALES	NONWHITE FEMALES
6	46	47	46	47	48	49	47	46
7	49	49	49	49	53	55	52	51
8	51	52	50	51	61	61	57	58
9	53	53	53	53	66	66	63	65
10	55	55	57	57	73	72	70	78
11	57	58	58	59	81	80	87	90
12	59	60	60	61	91	93	95	99

PHYSICAL GROWTH, AGE 6 TO AGE 12 (50TH PERCENTILE)

*Fifty percent of children in each category are above this height or weight level; and 50 percent are below it.
SOURCE: Adapted from Rauh, Schumsky, & Witt, 1967, pp. 515–530.

Variations in Growth: Norms and Ethnic Considerations

The figures given above are just averages. Individual children vary widely—so widely that "if a child who was of exactly average height at his seventh birthday grew not at all for two years, he would still be just within the normal limits of height attained at age nine" (Tanner, 1973, p. 35).

Children from various ethnic groups grow differently. African American boys and girls tend to be a bit taller and heavier than white children of the same age and sex. There is also a difference between richer and poorer children. Children from more affluent homes tend to be larger and more mature than children from poorer homes. This difference arises from differences in nutrition. Later in this chapter, we will discuss malnutrition, which usually hinders growth. Overweight children mature earliest of all, and heavy girls experience the *menarche*, or the first menstruation, earlier than more slender girls.

Ethnic differences affect children's average size. A study of 8-year-old children in several parts of the world found a range of about 9 inches between the mean heights of the shortest children (mostly from southeast Asia, Oceania, and South America) and the tallest (mostly from northern and central Europe, eastern Australia, and the United States) (Meredith, 1969). Although genetic differences probably account for some of this diversity, so do environmental influences. In hot regions, like those parts of east Africa where the Masai people live, their tall, lean build probably helps to cool the body; conversely, the short, fatter build of the Alaskan Inuit helps these people in arctic climates conserve body heat. In general, the tallest children come from parts of the world "where nutritious food is abundant and where . . . infectious diseases are well controlled or largely eliminated" (Meredith, 1969).

Implicit in this wide range of average sizes is a warning. When judging health or screening for abnormalities, observers often rely on measures of a child's physical growth and development. However, in the face of evidence that children from diverse ethnic groups develop differently, it would be useful to establish separate growth standards for different populations. In the United States especially, where members of many disparate cultures live side by side, judgments about what is normal need to be made cautiously.

Abnormal Growth

Of the many types of growth disorders, one arises from the body's failure to produce enough growth hormone. Human growth hormone is effective in improving short-term growth in height; and a synthetic form of this hormone is now available. Researchers studied children whose own bodies failed to produce enough natural growth hormone and who were given the synthetic hormone. After 4 years of treatment, from an average age of 6.3 years, the children showed increases in height, with no side effects. However, how effective this therapy is in the long run will not be known until the children reach final adult height (Albanese & Stanhope, 1993).

This synthetic hormone is also being used for children who are much shorter than other children their age, but whose bodies *are* producing normal quantities of growth hormone. The synthetic hormone has risks. We have no clear idea what the long-term effects on health are likely to be for a person who is genetically designed to be 5 feet 4 inches tall in adulthood but has been artificially "stretched" to, say, 6 feet. Furthermore, there is no evidence that the drug makes children who are normally short any taller as adults. In fact, it may negate its own growth-inducing effects by bringing on puberty sooner, causing a child to stop growing earlier.

Because there are uncertainties about the safety and long-term effects of synthetic growth hormone, the American Academy of Pediatrics (1983) recommends that it be used *only* for children who are naturally deficient in the hormone. Further, since many of the handicaps associated with being short are due not to short stature itself but to a person's feelings about it, genetically short people may gain more from counseling than from long-term hormone therapy.

What do you think?   *Because height matters so much to so many people, should parents be free to give their children growth hormones, even if they do not have a hormone deficiency?*

NUTRITION AND GROWTH

Both Vicky's and Jason's parents have a hard time keeping the refrigerator stocked these days. Both children are now eating far more than they used to—and, always in a hurry to do something else, are gobbling it down fast. They need the extra calories they are consuming now. In these years, average body weight doubles, and physical play demands great expenditures of energy.

Specific Nutritional Requirements

To support the steady growth and constant exertion of the middle years, children need, on average, 2400 calories every day. Daily food intake should contain about 34 grams of protein, plus high levels of complex carbohydrates, found in such foods as potatoes, pasta, bread, and cereals. Simple carbohydrates, found in

A good breakfast starts the day right. Children's play demands energy, and their body weight will double in these middle-childhood years. To support constant exertion and steady growth, children need high levels of complex carbohydrates, like those in potatoes and grain, and a minimum of refined carbohydrates (sweets).

sweets, should be kept to a minimum. Most people in the United States eat more protein than they need. For example, the government-recommended daily allowances (RDAs) for 7- to 10-year-olds is 28 grams, whereas the average intake for both boys and girls is 71 grams (Bittman, 1993).

Even on hectic school mornings—*especially* on those mornings—breakfast is important. It should supply about one-fourth of a child's nutrients. Eating a healthy and balanced breakfast makes children more alert and productive in the classroom (E. R. Williams & Caliendo, 1984).

For some years, many people believed that sugar makes children hyperactive, interferes with learning, or has other negative effects on behavior or mood. However, although sweets are less desirable in anyone's diet because they generally provide empty calories (that is, nonnutritive calories), some recent research suggests that neither sugar nor the artificial sweetener aspartame affects children's behavior, cognitive functioning, or mood adversely (Wolraich et al., 1994; Kinsbourne, 1994; B. A. Shaywitz et al., 1994). Sugar's "bad press" may have resulted from its reputation as an energy food and from its presence in large amounts at such unstructured, emotional situations as birthday parties, where the real cause of disruptive behavior arises from the situation, not the sweets.

Malnutrition

Millions of children around the world, including many in the United States, do not receive the nutrients they need for healthy development. Some 40 to 60 percent of the world's children suffer from mild to moderate malnutrition, and from 3 to 7 percent are severely malnourished (Lozoff, 1989). Nutritional and environmental factors interact: Undernourished children usually live in poverty and suffer environmental deprivation. Thus we see the harsh effects of disadvantaged social conditions, first on children's physical well-being—and then, because malnutrition interferes with normal development—on their cognitive and social abilities as well.

Effects of Malnutrition.   A child's diet from birth to age 2 is a good predictor of social behavior, including responsiveness, in middle childhood. Why is there such a long-term effect? It may arise from a complex feedback system. Mothers of malnourished infants may respond to them less frequently and less sensitively because the infants do not have the energy to engage their mothers' attention and induce the mother to do things with them. As the babies develop poor social skills and become generally unresponsive, other people become less and less interested in interacting with them (B. M. Lester, 1979).

This process gains momentum if the mother is also malnourished. She, too, lacks the energy and ability to engage the attention of other people and to get them to have much to do with her. Mother and child then become caught in a cycle of passive unsociability (Rosetti-Ferreira, 1978).

Links between nutrition and other aspects of development are also clear. African children in Kenya who suffered mild to moderate undernutrition scored lower than well-nourished children did on a test of verbal abilities and on a matrix test that asked the child to select a pattern to fit in with a set of other patterns (Sigman, Neumann, Jansen, & Bwibo, 1989). Another study of Kenyan children found that better nourished children were happier, more active, and more likely to be leaders; poorly nourished children were more anxious on the school playground (Espinosa, Sigman, Neumann, Bwibo, & McDonald, 1992).

The Kenyan children also showed differential effects of poor nutrition. The children's playground behavior was linked to their taking in enough calories, whereas their cognitive scores were related to the levels of fat and animal protein in their diets. Social activities seemed to depend on quantity of food, whereas cognitive skill development demanded a high-quality diet (Sigman et al., 1989).

What do you think? *Malnutrition early in life has long-term effects on physical, social, and cognitive development. What can various sectors of society—government agencies, community groups, and private organizations—do to prevent malnutrition?*

Effects of Intervention. A longitudinal study in Guatemala found evidence that dietary supplementation can offset poor outcomes. Researchers studied 138 schoolchildren, aged 6 to 8, in three farming villages. At younger ages, these children had all received dietary supplements. Some children received a mix of proteins, essential vitamins, and sources of extra calories; others received sources of extra calories and vitamins, but not proteins. Children who as infants had not received protein supplements tended to be passive, dependent on adults, and more anxious; the children who had received protein supplements were happier and livelier and got along better with other children (Barrett, Radke-Yarrow, & Klein, 1982).

This finding supports the conclusion that poor nutrition leads to less activity. Another intervention program improved cognitive performance. When low-income third- to sixth-graders took part in a Massachusetts school breakfast program, their scores on achievement tests rose (Meyers, Sampson, Weitzman, Rogers, & Kayne, 1989).

Studies like the above show how the different domains of development are related. Another powerful example of the intertwining of physical and social effects can be seen in overnutrition, the excess of calories that leads to obesity.

Obesity

At the age of 8, Vicky looks into every mirror she passes. At the last party she attended, she turned down the birthday cake, saying, "It's too fattening. I need to go on a diet and lose weight." Like most girls her age, Vicky is of normal weight. However, her attitude is typical: Preoccupation with weight is becoming increasingly common among young children, an attitude that too often leads to eating disorders like *anorexia* or *bulimia* (discussed in Chapter 14).

According to one study, children in the United States develop a dislike of obesity between the ages of 6 and 9—largely, it seems, because American society equates thinness with beauty (W. Feldman, Feldman, & Goodman, 1988). However, there are more fat children in the United States than ever before. Because of societal attitudes, these children are likely to suffer psychologically as well as physically.

What Is Obesity, and How Common Is It? In a 6-year study of nearly 2600 mostly white, middle-class children under age 12 who were enrolled in a prepaid health maintenance plan, about 4 percent of the total and $5\frac{1}{2}$ percent of 8- to 11-year-olds were considered obese (Starfield et al., 1984). One way to determine *obesity* is to pinch the skin from the upper arm between two fingers and measure its thick-

obesity *Overweight condition marked by a skin-fold measurement in the 85th percentile (thicker than the skin fold of 85 percent of children of the same age and sex).*

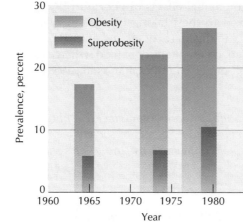

FIGURE 11-1
Estimated trends in obesity and superobesity in children 6 to 11 years old in the United States. The increase in childhood obesity has serious implications for both physical and mental health. SOURCE: Adapted from Gortmaker, Dietz, Sobol, & Wehler, 1987.

ness. A child whose skin fold is in the 85th percentile (thicker than 85 percent of children of the same age and sex) would be considered obese; a child in the 95th percentile would be diagnosed as superobese.

Both obesity and superobesity have increased among school-age children and adolescents. From 1963 to 1980, obesity became 54 percent more common among school-age children and 39 percent more common among adolescents, and superobesity soared by 98 percent and 64 percent, respectively. (Figure 11-1 shows the increase in obesity among schoolchildren.) Among younger children, boys showed the greatest increase; among adolescents, the largest increase was for girls. Rates vary geographically: More obesity occurs in the northeast and midwest than in the west (Gortmaker, Dietz, Sobol, & Wehler, 1987).

What Causes Obesity? Research findings are most often correlational, meaning that we cannot draw cause-and-effect conclusions. However, there seems to be a strong basis for believing that overweight often results from an inherited predisposition, aggravated by behavior involving too little exercise and too much food.

People become overweight when they consume more calories than they expend. The amount of excess calories need not be large: Children who every day eat as little as 50 extra calories (the amount in a single cookie) will put on 5 extra pounds a year (Kolata, 1986). But when two people eat the same amount of calories, why does only one get fat? What makes some people eat more than they need? The following theories offer possible causes for childhood obesity:

■ *Genetic predisposition* is suggested by different lines of research. Investigators have found a genetic mutation that may disrupt the appetite control center in the brain, which tells people they have eaten enough (Zhang et al., 1994). This finding supports data from a study of 540 adopted adults, which found a strong positive correlation between obese people and their biological parents but virtually none with their adoptive parents (Stunkard, Foch, & Hrubec, 1986).

■ *Environment* is also influential, since children tend to eat the same kinds of foods and develop the same kinds of habits as the people around them. Obesity is more common among lower socioeconomic groups, especially among women (Kolata, 1986).

- There is a negative correlation between *activity level* and weight. Are heavier children less active because they are fat, or do they become fat because they are less active? Professional opinion tends toward the second conclusion.
- Evidently, *television* is also a factor. According to two studies—one of nearly 700 six- to eleven-year-olds and one of 6500 adolescents—every hour per day spent watching television results in a 2 percent increase in the prevalence of obesity. Children who watch television a great deal tend to eat more snacks (especially the high-calorie ones seen in commercials) and are less active than other children (Dietz & Gortmaker, 1985).

Treating Childhood Obesity.   A compelling reason for treating childhood obesity is that fat children suffer from the taunts of their peers. They often compensate for their lack of popularity by indulging themselves with treats, making their physical and social problems even worse. An equally important reason for treating overweight children is that, without special attention, they usually become overweight adults. Both their self-esteem and their health are likely to suffer: They will be considered unattractive and will be at risk of high blood pressure, orthopedic problems, and diabetes. However, treatment for children is so recent that we cannot say much about its effectivness.

The basic approach involves a restricted diet, more exercise, and behavior modification. Behavioral therapies, which help children change their eating and exercise habits, have had some effectiveness (L. H. Epstein & Wing, 1987). Because these approaches focus on changing a child's daily routines, they are more productive when they involve parents. Parents can be taught not to use sweets as a reward for good behavior and to stop buying tempting high-calorie foods. Parents can also lose weight themselves, but whether they do or not does not seem to matter to children, as long as the adults support the children's efforts.

Parents need to walk a fine line, however, between helping children and controlling them. One study found that preschoolers whose mothers let them eat

Children, like adults, become overweight when they take in more calories than they expend. The basic approach for preventing or treating obesity involves taking in less food and doing more physical exercise, like this tug of war.

when they are hungry and do not pressure the children to eat everything given to them are more likely to regulate their own calorie intake than are children with more controlling mothers (S. L. Johnson & Birch, 1994).

There is some controversy about exercise, though almost all weight-loss programs include it. "Lifestyle" exercise programs, which include a wide choice of daily activities that can be done from childhood into adulthood, seem to be more effective than aerobic programs based on a limited set of high-intensity, repetitive exercises (L. H. Epstein & Wing, 1987).

There is, however, virtually no controversy among professionals about the use of diet pills for children. Some of these pills can raise blood pressure and cause dizziness, seizures, and even strokes. Yet a study found that nearly 7 percent of American eighth-grade and tenth-grade girls used diet pills or diet candies. Because of the dangers, especially to young people, doctors who specialize in treating obesity have called for making the most popular ingredient of such pills available only by prescription (Burros, 1990).

What do you think? *If obesity "runs in families," either because of heredity or lifestyle, how can parents who have not been able to control their own weight help their children? Will this cause the children too much anxiety? Would it be better to wait until the children themselves want to lose excess weight?*

MOTOR DEVELOPMENT

MOTOR SKILLS IN MIDDLE CHILDHOOD

If we were to follow a group of children on their way home from school, we would see some of them running or skipping and some leaping up onto narrow ledges and walking along, balancing till they jump off, trying to break distance records—but occasionally breaking a bone instead. Some of these youngsters will reach home (or a baby-sitter's house), get a snack, and dash outside again. There they will jump rope, play ball, skate, cycle, sled, throw snowballs, or splash in the swimming hole, depending on the season, the community, and the child. They keep getting stronger, faster, and better coordinated—and they derive great pleasure from testing their bodies and learning new skills.

Many children, however, go inside after school, not to emerge for the rest of the day. Instead of practicing new skills that stretch their bodies, they will stay indoors, often in front of the television set.

During the middle years, children's motor abilities continue to improve with age. (Examples of motor abilities are shown in Table 11-2.)

Gender Differences

Although there is little difference in the skills of young boys and girls, differences become greater as children approach puberty. Boys tend to run faster, jump higher, throw farther, and display more strength than girls (Cratty, 1986). After age 13, the differences between the sexes become even greater; boys' motor abilities improve while girls' stay the same or decline.

Some of the gender difference is due to boys' growing strength, but much of it is culturally caused. Throwing, catching, and dribbling a ball are all skills that

Children's motor abilities improve with age, and as they practice their new skills—alone or with friends, on the playing field or in front of their homes—they improve both physical and mental health.

have to be learned, and boys are routinely taught these skills, while girls generally are not. Since girls' needs for physical activity are getting more attention these days, the discrepancy between the sexes may narrow in years to come. The assessment of girls' abilities is changing. It now seems clear that much of the difference between the boys' and girls' motor abilities has been due to differing expectations, differing levels of coaching, and differing rates of participation. When prepubescent boys and girls take part in similar activities, their abilities are quite similar (E. G. Hall & Lee, 1984).

TABLE 11-2

MOTOR DEVELOPMENT IN MIDDLE CHILDHOOD	
AGE	SELECTED BEHAVIORS
6	Girls are superior in movement accuracy; boys are superior in forceful, less complex acts. Skipping is possible.
	Can throw with proper weight shift and step.
7	One-footed balancing without looking becomes possible.
	Can walk 2-inch-wide balance beams.
	Can hop and jump accurately into small squares.
	Can execute accurate jumping-jack exercise.
8	Have 12-pound pressure on grip strength.
	Number of games participated in by both sexes is greatest at this age.
	Can engage in alternate rhythmic hopping in a 2-2, 2-3, or 3-3 pattern.
	Girls can throw a small ball 40 feet.
9	Boys can run $16\frac{1}{2}$ feet per second.
	Boys can throw a small ball 70 feet.
10	Can judge and intercept pathways of small balls thrown from a distance.
	Girls can run 17 feet per second.
11	Standing broad jump of 5 feet is possible for boys; 6 inches less for girls.
12	Standing high jump of 3 feet is possible.

SOURCE: Adapted from Cratty, 1986.

Such findings support statements by pediatricians that there is no reason to separate prepubertal boys and girls for physical activities. After puberty, however, girls should not be playing heavy-collision sports with boys because their lighter, smaller frames make them too subject to injury (American Academy of Pediatrics Committee on Pediatric Aspects of Physical Fitness, Recreation, and Sports, 1981). Postpubertal girls still need to be physically active, however, for general fitness and for the benefit that weight-bearing exercise offers in the prevention of *osteoporosis*, a thinning of the bones that occurs mostly among elderly women. It is dismaying, therefore, that 75 percent of 15- to 18-year-old girls do not play any sports (Eskenazi, 1988).

PHYSICAL PLAY IN MIDDLE CHILDHOOD

Children's physical play as they move through the middle years leans toward games with rules. Games like hopscotch, leapfrog, hide-and-seek, and tag are universal, enduring across time and around the world (Opie & Opie, 1969). Many children, however, concentrate their play in adult-led activities.

Organized Sports

Nearly 20 million children under age 14 take part in team sports outside of school. However, 75 percent of children who start to play a sport at age 6 or 7 will have quit by age 15 (Rubenstein, 1993). Too often, parents and coaches pressure children to practice long hours, focus on winning rather than playing the game, criticize children's skills, or offer bribes to make them do well (Wolff, 1993). All these tactics discourage rather than encourage participation.

To help children improve their motor skills, organized athletic programs should offer the chance to try a variety of sports, gear coaching to improving skills rather than winning games, and include as many youngsters as possible rather than concentrating on a few star athletes (American Academy of Pediatrics Committee on Sports Medicine and Committee on School Health, 1989). Box 11-1 describes some ways adults can improve children's health and physical fitness.

Rough-and-Tumble Play

Should you come across a couple of children tumbling over each other, you can often tell whether they are fighting or playing only by the expressions on their faces. About 10 percent of schoolchildren's free play on playgrounds consists of *rough-and-tumble play,* vigorous play that involves wrestling, hitting, and chasing. This kind of play is distinct from the kind of vigorous activity that exercises large motor abilities, as in running and climbing. The playful character of rough-and-tumble can be seen in the laughing and screaming that accompany it.

This kind of play reminds us of our evolutionary heritage, since, unlike symbolic play which is distinctly human, rough-and-tumble play was first described in monkeys. It also seems to be universal, since it takes place from early child-

rough-and-tumble play
Vigorous play accompanied by laughing and screaming.

BOX 11-1 ▪ THE EVERYDAY WORLD

IMPROVING CHILDREN'S HEALTH AND FITNESS

American schoolchildren are not as physically fit as they should be—and could be. Their heart and lung fitness is generally inferior to that of a typical middle-aged jogger, and many are overweight.

Why are children in such a rich country in such poor shape? For one thing, only half of all elementary school children take physical education classes as often as twice a week, fewer than half stay active during cold weather, and most are not learning such lifetime fitness skills as running, swimming, bicycling, and walking. For many, their most strenuous exercise involves switching television channels (Dietz & Gortmaker, 1985). Most physical activities, in and out of school, are team and competitive sports and games. These do not promote fitness, will usually be dropped after leaving school, and are usually engaged in by the fittest and most athletic youngsters, not by those who need help the most.

Since adult hypertension has its roots in childhood, the American Academy of Pediatrics Task Force on Blood Pressure Control in Children (1987) recommends measuring blood pressure once a year from age 3 through adolescence. If a child's blood pressure is above the 95th percentile for age and sex after three measurements, treatment should begin. Taking off excess weight, reducing salt intake, and increasing aerobic exercise are usually beneficial; some children are also given drugs to avoid heart damage.

Sometimes just changing everyday behavior brings about considerable improvement. Parents can make exercise a family activity, by regularly hiking or playing ball together, building strength on playground equipment, re-

placing driving with walking whenever possible, using stairs instead of elevators, and limiting television viewing, which has been linked to high cholesterol levels in children (Wong et al., 1992). Excessive television viewing also seems to lower children's metabolic rates, putting them at risk of obesity (Klesges, Shelton, & Klesges, 1993).

More evidence in favor of changing everyday behavior comes from a program of education and behavior modification, involving 24,000 children in Michigan. The children learned how to analyze the foods they ate; how to measure their own blood pressure, heart rate, and body fat; and how to withstand peer and advertising pressure to smoke and to eat junk food. It also encouraged them to take part in physically demanding games. When researchers looked at the effects of the program on 360 second-, fifth-, and seventh-graders, they found heartening results. The children in the program had significantly improved the time in which they could run a mile; they had lowered their cholesterol level, blood pressure, and body fat; and the number of children without any risk factors for developing coronary disease had risen by 55 percent (Fitness Finders, 1984).

This program is in line with recommendations by the American Academy of Pediatrics, which urges schools to provide a sound physical education program with a variety of competitive and recreational sports for all children, emphasizing activities that can be part of a lifetime fitness regimen, such as tennis, bowling, running, swimming, golf, and skating (American Academy of Pediatrics Committee on Sports Medicine and Committee on School Health, 1989).

---

hood through adolescence in such diverse places as India, Mexico, Okinawa, the Kalahari in Africa, the Philippines, Great Britain, and the United States (Humphreys & Smith, 1984).

Anthropologists suggest that this kind of play evolved to provide practice in skills used in fighting and hunting (Symons, 1978). As played today, it serves other purposes, aside from the physical exercise. There is a social function: Children usually choose close friends to tussle with, possibly because they trust their friends not to become aggressive during play. Rough-and-tumble play also helps children assess their own strength as compared with that of other children.

There are individual differences among children's tendencies toward rough-and-tumble play. Boys engage in it more than girls, a difference attributed to hormonal differences that are then reinforced by societal attitudes (Humphreys & Smith, 1984). There are also age differences. In a study of 7-, 9-, and 11-year-olds, the youngest children played this way the most, the oldest the least (Humphreys & Smith, 1987). Cultural differences also appear, with sex differences diminishing or even disappearing in some societies (Blurton Jones & Konner, 1973).

After children outgrow rough-and-tumble play, the kind of activities they move into is associated with their levels of popularity. Among a group of 94 kindergartners and second- and fourth-graders, the popular children moved into games with rules, whereas the unpopular ones became aggressive* (Pellegrini, 1988). It may be that the more socially competent children use rough-and-tumble play as a way to practice prosocial behavior with other popular children, while unpopular children play with children who do not know how to solve social problems, so they cannot learn from one another. These associations provide one more example of how one domain of development interacts with another—in this case, the physical with the social.

HEALTH AND SAFETY

Vicky, aged 10, is home in bed with a cold, her second of the year. She sneezes, snoozes, watches daytime television, and enjoys her break from the school routine. She is lucky; she has had no other illnesses this year, while some of her classmates have had six or seven bouts with colds, flu, or viruses. That number of respiratory infections is common during middle childhood, as germs pass freely among youngsters at school or at play (Behrman, 1992).

Still, middle childhood is a relatively healthy time: The death rate in these years is the lowest in the life span. There are still potential health problems, of course. In addition to obesity, children sometimes suffer from *acute* or *chronic* medical conditions, or both. Many also injure themselves in accidents.

HEALTH CONCERNS

Acute Conditions

What health problems do occur in these years? A longitudinal study of mostly white, middle-class children in a health maintenance plan found varied conditions, from allergies to warts (Starfield et al., 1984). Almost all the youngsters got sick from time to time, but their ailments tended to be brief. During the 6 years

---

*We will look again at the relationship between aggression and unpopularity in Chapter 13.

of the study, almost all the children had *acute medical conditions*—short-term conditions, like upper-respiratory infections, viruses, or eczema. Only one child in nine had persistent conditions, like migraine headaches or nearsightedness. Eighty percent were treated for injuries. Upper-respiratory illnesses, sore throats, strep throats, ear infections, and bed-wetting decreased with age; but acne, headaches, and transitory emotional disturbances increased as youngsters approached puberty (Starfield et al., 1984). As children's physical health changes with age, so does their cognitive understanding of health and illness, as shown in Box 11-2.

acute medical conditions *Medical conditions that persist for a short time.*

Chronic Conditions

Chronic medical conditions are illnesses or impairments expected to last for 3 months or longer, requiring special medical attention and care, long hospitalization, or health services in the home. In middle childhood, most children are free of such conditions that limit their activity, but there has been an increase over the past several years (Starfield, 1991).

Researchers who conducted the 1988 National Health Interview Survey (NHIS) interviewed adults in the households of 17,100 children under 18; no diagnostic tests or medical examinations were conducted. Using a broad definition of chronic illness, one team of researchers analyzed the NHIS data and found that about 31 percent of all children under 18 had a chronic condition (Newacheck, Stoddard, & McManus, 1993). (See Table 11-3.)

chronic medical conditions *Illnesses or impairments that persist for at least 3 months.*

TABLE 11-3

PREVALENCE OF SPECIFIED CHRONIC CONDITIONS AMONG CHILDREN YOUNGER THAN 18 YEARS: UNITED STATES, 1988*				
CONDITION	**CASES/1000**			
	ALL†	**WHITE**	**BLACK**	**HISPANIC**
Respiratory allergies	96.8	114.7	53.6	47.4
Frequent or repeated ear infections	83.4	94.2	53.8	69.7
Asthma	42.5	42.0	51.3	35.1
Eczema and skin allergies	32.9	36.7	21.7	19.2
Speech defects	26.2	24.0	34.5	35.4
Frequent or severe headaches	25.3	28.4	21.1	14.7
Digestive allergies	22.3	27.0	9.9	8.4‡
Frequent diarrhea/bowel trouble	17.1	17.7	12.9	18.5
Deafness and hearing loss	15.3	18.0	6.0‡	15.2
Heart disease	15.2	18.3	7.7‡	10.0
Musculoskeletal impairments	15.2	15.8	10.6	15.2
Blindness and vision impairment	12.7	13.8	8.7‡	13.3‡
Anemia	8.8	8.9	9.2‡	7.5‡
Arthritis	4.6	4.8	5.4‡	2.0‡
Epilepsy and seizures	2.4	1.9	2.4‡	6.2‡
Cerebral palsy	1.8	1.7	0.4‡	3.2‡
Sickle-cell disease	1.2‡	<0.1‡	7.1‡	0.3‡
Diabetes	1.0‡	1.3‡	<0.1‡	0.3‡
Other	19.8	23.6	10.2	9.2‡

*Source: original tabulations of the 1988 National Health Interview Survey.
†Includes white, black, Hispanic, and other races.
‡Indicates prevalence estimate has a relative standard error in excess of 30%.
SOURCE: Newacheck, Stoddard, & McManus, 1993.

BOX 11-2 ■ FOOD FOR THOUGHT

CHILDREN'S UNDERSTANDING OF HEALTH AND ILLNESS

When Vicky was sick, she overhead her doctor refer to *edema* (an accumulation of fluid, which causes swelling) and she thought that her problem was "a demon." Being sick is frightening at any age. For children, who do not understand what is happening, it can be especially distressing and confusing. Children's understanding of health and illness is closely tied to their cognitive development.

At the beginning of middle childhood, children do not always think logically. During this period, children tend to believe that illness is magically produced by human actions, often their own. Magical explanations can last well into childhood. One 12-year-old with leukemia said, "I know that my doctor told me that my illness is caused by too many white cells, but I still wonder if it was caused by something I did" (Brewster, 1982, p. 361). It would be hard for an adult to keep from saying to this child, "There, there, of course it wasn't anything you did."

This reaction may not be helpful. Egocentric explanations for illness can serve as a defense against feelings of helplessness. Children may feel that if something they did made them ill, then they can do something to get better. A researcher warns, "It is never wise to break down defenses until one is sure that more desirable concepts will take their place" (Brewster, 1982, p. 362).

With cognitive development, children's explanations for disease change. They enter a stage in which they explain all diseases—hardly less magically—by germs. "Watch out for germs" say many children this age, who believe germs—and only germs—cause disease. The only "prevention" is a variety of superstitious behaviors to ward off germs. As children approach adolescence, they enter a third stage, where they see that there can be multiple causes of disease, that contact with germs does not automatically lead to illness, and that people can do much to keep healthy.

Over the past few years, as AIDS (acquired immune deficiency syndrome) has spread, attempts have been made to educate the public, including children. To find out how much children understand about this disease, researchers interviewed preschoolers and first-, third-, and fifth-graders (Schvaneveldt, Lindauer, & Young, 1990). The children's knowledge was related to their general perceptions about illness, and accurate understanding was directly related to age. Preschoolers knew practically nothing about AIDS; some did not even remember conversations about it with their parents just the evening before their interviews. Third- and fifth-graders had a fair amount of accurate information about the causes, outcome, and prevention of AIDS, although in both age levels the children held such mistaken beliefs as that AIDS could be contracted from mosquito bites or that it could be prevented by good nutrition. (See Figure 11-2.)

More recent interviews with 361 children in kindergarten through sixth grade supported these conclusions (Schonfeld, Johnson, Perrin, O'Hare, & Cicchetti, 1993). Children's understanding of AIDS follows the same developmental sequence as does their understanding of colds and of cancer. However, they begin to understand the cause of colds earlier than they do of the other two illnesses, probably because they are more familiar with colds. The children's grasp of these concepts was not related to their ethnic, gender, or socioeconomic status.

Although 96 children mentioned drugs as a cause of AIDS, most did not seem to realize that the disease is spread by injection. One second-grader explained how someone gets AIDS: "Well, by doing drugs and something like that . . . By going by a drug dealer who has AIDS. . . . Well, you go by a person who's a drug dealer and you might catch the AIDS from 'em . . . By standing near 'em" (Schonfeld et al., 1993, p. 393).

Effects on Daily Life. Chronic health conditions can affect day-to-day life in a number of ways. Another analysis of the 1988 NHIS data, which focused on six developmental disabilities and their impact on daily life, revealed that 17 percent of children were reported to have had a developmental disability at some time (Boyle, Decouflé, & Yeargin-Allsopp, 1994). Children with one of the six developmental disabilities assessed (cerebral palsy, epilepsy or seizures, blindness, hearing impairment, stuttering, and other speech defects) suffer in their educational functioning as well as in their health. They miss more school, do worse when they are there, and are more likely to repeat a grade than children without these conditions. Of these six conditions, cerebral palsy and epilepsy have the greatest overall impact on a child's life.

BOX 11-2 ▪ FOOD FOR THOUGHT *(continued)*

CHILDREN'S UNDERSTANDING OF HEALTH AND ILLNESS

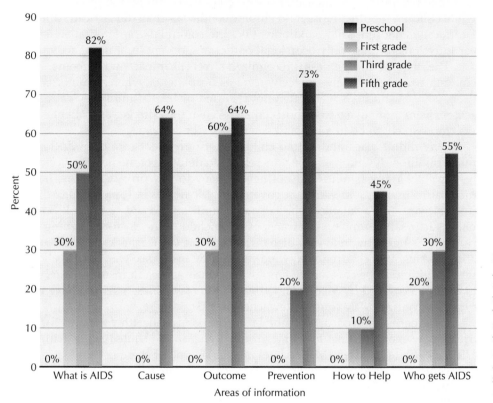

FIGURE 11-2
A study of children's understanding of AIDS found that the older they were, the more they understood. Furthermore, their knowledge was related to their perceptions about illness in general. SOURCE: Schvaneveldt, Lindauer, & Young, 1990.

Research like these studies shows how essential it is to gear teaching about illness to children's levels of understanding. Instruction should focus on how AIDS is *not* transmitted (sharing cups and utensils, coughing, sneezing, through alcohol and cigarettes, hugging or holding hands), as well as how it *is* passed from one person to another (the transfer of bodily fluids, including blood adhering to a needle shared by drug users). The most informative curriculum in the world will fail if it goes over the heads of the pupils for whom it is meant.

Still, children and adolescents with chronic conditions are remarkably resilient (AAP Committee on Children with Disabilities. . . ., 1993). Other research, covering a wide range of ailments, found that most do not exhibit problems in mental health, behavior, or school; and neither the severity nor the type of condition explains who will have psychological difficulties and who will not. The young people who deal best with the stress of chronic illness seem to be those who have the inner resources of intelligence and adaptable temperament; whose parents have high self-esteem, good mental health, and positive beliefs about health care; and whose family is close, flexible, communicative, and has a strong social support network.

Cultural and Ethnic Factors. What effect does the ethnic group a child belongs to have on his or her likelihood of suffering from a chronic condition? When researchers again analyzed 1988 NHIS data, they found differences among various ethnic groups (Newacheck, Stoddard, & McManus, 1993).* Although there was no difference in the prevalence of severe conditions among the groups studied, white children reported more mild chronic conditions than did African American and Latino children. Mild conditions (like the commonly reported allergies and ear infections) impose only occasional bother and do not limit usual activities.

The stage when an illness is recognized affects its impact and outcome: White children were more likely to receive care as outpatients, whereas minority children, whose conditions were often not reported or treated until they were more severe, were more likely to be hospitalized. When they did get outpatient care, it was more likely to be in a hospital emergency department.

Why didn't black and Latino children get outpatient care from doctors for mild conditions? A number of factors related to delivery of medical services seem responsible. Many families did not have money to pay private doctors, had no medical insurance, and were not covered by Medicaid. In some neighborhoods doctors were not available, especially for families who did not speak English. Other factors, like problems in transporting a child to the doctor or getting child care for younger children, may also be responsible (Newacheck et al., 1993). The African American children who were covered by insurance were less likely than white children to be covered by employer-sponsored health insurance and more likely to be covered by Medicaid. Latino children were less likely to have either type of coverage (McManus & Newacheck, 1993).

Differences showed up in another comparison of health measures for children from several distinct Hispanic groups living in the United States with non-Hispanic white children (Mendoza et al., 1991). One of the most dramatic findings concerned differences in the incidence of moderate to severe chronic medical conditions.

Mexican American children, Cuban American children, and non-Hispanic white children had similar rates of chronic illness (ranging from 2.5 to 3.9 percent), but Puerto Rican children living in the mainland United States were much more likely to suffer from such ailments (6.2 percent). It is not clear why these differences exist. The lower rates of chronic illness among Cuban American children might be related to the lower rates of poverty in this group, but Mexican American families, whose rates of chronic illness are also fairly low, tend to have high poverty rates—similar to those of mainland Puerto Rican families. Whatever the reasons, these findings emphasize that Hispanic Americans do not constitute a homogeneous group. It is important to look at each population subgroup individually when deciding how to allocate medical and social services.

Another cultural and ethnic difference that needs to be considered is the belief systems among various groups, an important element in the social context. (See Box 11-3.)

---

*Although people from groups that included Asians, Pacific Islanders, Aleut, Eskimo, Native Americans, and other racial minorities were interviewed, Newacheck and his colleagues reported only on white, African American, and Latino children. These authors point out that, because of the sparseness of information on chronic illness in Asian and Native American children, they could not calculate statistically reliable estimates on the small samples from these and other subgroups.

BOX 11-3 ■ AROUND THE WORLD

HOW CULTURAL ATTITUDES AFFECT HEALTH CARE

One morning Buddi Kumar Rai, a university-educated resident of Badel, a remote hill village in Nepal, carried his 2½-year-old daughter, Kusum, to the shaman, the local "medicine man." Kusum's little face was sober, her usually golden complexion pale, and her almond-shaped eyes droopy from the upper-respiratory infection she had been suffering the past week, complete with fever and a hacking cough.

Two days before, Kusum had been in her father's arms when he had slipped and fallen backwards off a veranda to the ground about 3 feet below, still tightly holding his little daughter. Neither was hurt, but little Kusum had screamed in fright.

Now the shaman told Buddi that Kusum's illness was due to that fright. He prescribed incantations and put a mark, a charcoal smudge the size of a silver dollar, on the child's forehead to drive away the evil spirit that had entered her body when she got her scare.

Two months before this incident, Buddi himself had gone to one of the ten shamans in Badel. "We have no doctors here, no medicine," he said with a shrug. "One time I put on those stupid army boots my uncle gave me, and I walk with my wife to my father-in-law's house in Rakha, maybe two hours. And when I come home, my ankle hurt me so bad I can't walk on that foot. So I call the shaman, and he say my ankle hurts because I crossed the river without praying to the river god. So the shaman chanted over the ankle and told me to go back down to the river and pray, and after a couple of days my foot feels better."

This kind of adherence to ancient beliefs about illness is not unique to remote villages in the Himalayas. It is, in fact, very common in many areas of the industrialized world, where many people cling to beliefs that are at odds with the mainstream scientific and medical philosophy.

To provide better medical care to members of various ethnic and minority groups, public and community policymakers need to understand the cultural beliefs and attitudes that determine what people will do, what decisions they will make, and how they will interact with the broader society. The three key issues relating to illness and disability revolve around *causation, expectations for survival,* and appropriate *social roles* for disabled or chronically ill children and adults.

BELIEFS ABOUT CAUSATION, SURVIVAL, AND SOCIAL ROLES

Many cultures see illness and disability as a form of punishment inflicted upon someone who has either transgressed himself (as did Buddi in failing to pray to the river god), who did something wrong in a previous life, or who is paying for an ancestor's sin. People who believe in such causes will tend to distance themselves from and often be unsympathetic toward the afflicted person. Another belief, common in Latin America and southeast Asia, is that an imbalance of elements in the body causes illness and the patient has to reestablish his or her own equilibrium.

In many societies people believe that a severely disabled child will not survive. Since there is no hope, they do not expend time, effort, or money on the child—which often creates a self-fulfilling prophecy. Such a belief makes it difficult, if not impossible, for parents to plan realistically for the child's future. In some religious households, parents hold out hope for a miracle, which may improve the child's quality of life temporarily but may also discourage such treatments as surgery.

IMPLICATIONS FOR SOCIAL POLICY

Of course, the standard medical systems in the United States are also governed by a cultural belief system. Here, parents are asked to make decisions about their child without consulting members of the extended family. Most American professionals have a high regard for education and recommend as much as possible. Independence and self-sufficiency are valued, and parents are discouraged from "babying" a disabled child. Mothers may be discouraged from breastfeeding a child beyond a certain age, even though that practice is common in their country of origin. People from other cultures may not respond well to American values: Parents may feel a need to consult their own parents, may not consider it important for a daughter to become self-supporting, and may nurse, spoon-feed, and dress normal children at later ages than are common in the United States.

What do you think? *In light of differing cultural beliefs, how can health care workers and policymakers best ensure good care for children of many cultural backgrounds? What practices do they need to consider and evaluate?*

Professionals need to explain clearly, whenever possible in the language of the child's family, what the recommended course of treatment is, the reasoning behind it, and the expected events. Such concern will help to prevent incidents like one that occurred when an Asian mother became hysterical as an American nurse took the mother's baby to get a urine sample. The mother had had three children taken from her in Cambodia. None had returned.

SOURCE: Olds, 1995; Groce & Zola, 1993.

Specific Chronic Conditions

Vision and Hearing Disorders. Most youngsters in middle childhood have keener vision now than they had earlier because their visual apparatus is more developed. Children under 6 years old tend to be farsighted, since their eyes have not matured and are shaped differently from those of adults. By age 6, their vision is more acute, and since both eyes work together better, they can focus better.

Still, some children have vision problems. Almost 13 percent of children under 18 are estimated to be blind or have impaired vision. Visual problems are reported more often for white and Latino children than for African Americans. Deafness and hearing loss affect an estimated 15.3 percent of those under 18, and ethnic differences also appear for reported hearing problems, with 18 percent of white parents reporting them for their children, 6 percent of black parents, and 15.2 percent of Latino parents (Newacheck et al., 1993).

asthma *A chronic respiratory disease characterized by sudden attacks of coughing, wheezing, and difficulty in breathing.*

Asthma. **Asthma,** a chronic respiratory disease that can seriously affect a child's daily life, can in some cases be fatal. It seems to have an allergic basis and is characterized by sudden attacks of coughing, wheezing, and difficulty in breathing. About 4.3 percent of American children under 17 are estimated to be asthmatic, with poor children and African American children most apt to suffer from the illness (Halfon & Newacheck, 1993).

A study in Texas found that Puerto Rican children with asthma were likely to have more severe cases than children in other ethnic groups, possibly because they tended to come from poor families, which have less access to health care. The most common barrier to care reported by families in this study was the inability to pay for medicine (Wood, Hidalgo, Prihoda, & Kromer, 1993).

Poor children with asthma are more likely to receive their care in emergency rooms, hospital-based clinics, and neighborhood health centers than in doctors' offices. The relative inaccessibility of doctor care is associated with the fact that poor children miss more days in school, have to limit their activities more, and spend more days in bed at home and in the hospital than do children from better-off families.

What do you think? *Some observers have suggested ways to help poor children with asthma (Halfon & Newacheck, 1993; Wood et al., 1993). Which of the following possibilities do you think would be most helpful? How could these suggestions be implemented and how should they be funded? What other solutions might work?*

1. *Extended evenings and weekend hours for community health centers*
2. *Education in detecting symptoms and avoiding triggers of attacks (like cigarette smoking and allergy-causing substances in the home)*
3. *Classes in self-management of the disease*

---

stuttering *Involuntary repetition or prolongation of syllables.*

Stuttering. **Stuttering,** involuntary frequent repetition or prolongation of sounds and syllables, is a disorder that interferes with social functioning. As stutterers become frustrated and anxious about ordinary conversation, their self-esteem plummets. The condition runs in families, suggesting a genetic component, and is 3 times more common in boys than in girls. In 98 percent of cases, it begins before age 10; it is more prevalent among young children than older ones. Typically, stuttering starts gradually. About 10 percent of prepubertal children stutter; of these, 80 percent recover, typically before age 16. Sixty percent do so spontaneously, the other 20 percent in response to treatment (*Diagnostic and Statistical Manual of Mental Disorders*, DSM-IV, 1994).

Theories about causes include physical explanations like faulty training in articulation and breathing or problems with brain functioning, including defective feedback about one's own speech; and explanations based on emotional problems, like parental pressures to speak properly and deep-seated conflicts.

Treatment includes psychotherapy and counseling, speech therapy, and drugs. The most effective training methods teach stutterers to unlearn their patterns of motor responses. They learn to speak slowly and deliberately; to breathe slowly and deeply, using abdominal muscles rather than those of the upper chest; and to start up their voices gently, not in the abrupt and almost explosive way in which many stutterers begin to speak. Videotape machines and computers to monitor the voice are among the technological aids for stutterers.

Tics.   *Tics* are repetitive, involuntary muscular movements characterized by suddenness and rapidity. People with tics feel they cannot repress them, although they often manage to suppress the tics for varying lengths of time. Some common tics involve eye-blinking, shoulder-hunching, neck-twisting, head-bobbing, lip-licking, grimacing, grunting, snorting, and uttering guttural or nasal sounds or obscene words. Some tics are transient, lasting less than a year; others last longer. They diminish during sleep and are aggravated by stress (DSM-IV, 1994).

Emotionally caused tics may arise from stresses in the child's past or current relationships and may serve as a release for emotional turmoil. Treatment should include relief of the emotional conflicts underlying these tics. Since not all tics are emotionally caused, however, a child suffering from them should be seen by a physician knowledgeable about neurological disorders, of which tics may be symptoms.

tics   *Involuntary, repetitive muscular movements; also called* stereotyped movement disorder.

Dental Health and Dental Problems

Most of the adult teeth arrive early in middle childhood. The primary teeth begin to fall out at about age 6. They continue to fall out, to be replaced by permanent teeth at a rate of about four teeth per year for the next 5 years. The first molars erupt at about age 6; at about age 13, second molars will come in; and in the early twenties the third molars—the wisdom teeth—appear (Behrman, 1992).

Given the importance of sound teeth for nutrition, general health, and appearance, a major health concern in the United States up until very recently was the high rate of dental problems among children. Now, however, the picture is much brighter. (See Figure 11-3.) A government survey of about 40,000 children aged 5 to 17 found that half of American children have no cavities or other tooth decay (Herrmann & Roberts, 1987). In the 1940s, there was probably 5 times as much tooth decay in children as there is today, and it was rare for a child not to have any cavities at all. Today 82 percent of damaged tooth surfaces have been repaired, compared with only 76 percent in 1980.

This turnaround seems to be due to the widespread use of fluoride in drinking water, toothpaste, and mouthwash; to the use of fluoridated water in food preparation; and to better dental care. Two-thirds of the decay in children's teeth

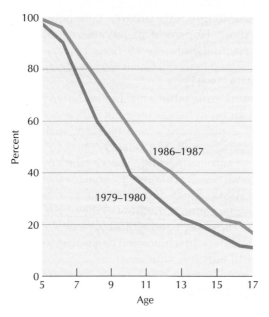

FIGURE 11-3
Percentage of children with no cavities or other decay problems at ages 5 through 17. The improvement in children's dental health seems to have resulted from use of fluoride and from better dental care. SOURCE: Leary, 1988.

is on the rough, chewing surfaces; much of this can be prevented with the use of adhesive sealants, plastic films that harden after being painted onto teeth.

Some children resist dental care because they are afraid of the dentist. Young children are usually cooperative at the dentist's office and with repeated visits they become even more cooperative and less anxious, but in middle childhood

These girls proudly show off a childhood milestone—the normal loss of baby teeth, which will be replaced by permanent ones. American children today have about one-third fewer dental cavities than did children a decade earlier, probably owing to the widespread use of fluoride and to better dental care.

youngsters become more fearful. Is this because children have had more experience with dentists and have learned to fear them? There is little evidence to support this. A more likely cause is children's modeling of their parents' behavior. They see that their parents are nervous about going to the dentist, and the children grow anxious themselves. Fears can be reduced if a child sees another person fearlessly doing something the child is afraid of and also if the child is repeatedly and gradually exposed to the fear-producing stimulus. If parents go to the dentist without showing anxiety, and if they take their children along on their own visits, the children will probably not become fearful (Winer, 1982).

SAFETY CONCERNS: ACCIDENTAL INJURIES

Jason, an extremely agile child, learned how to ride a two-wheel bicycle without training wheels at the age of 3. Now he practices daredevil tricks whenever he can and has fallen often, but he was badly hurt in only one fall, when he fractured his wrist. Although he resisted wearing a helmet at first, with parental insistence he has gotten into the habit of putting his on.

Each year almost 22 million children are injured in the United States, making injury the leading cause of disability and death in children over 1 year of age (Sheps & Evans, 1987).

Which Children Are Most Likely to Be Hurt?

Some children have more accidents than others, either because of physical reasons like poor coordination or because of personality factors, like the tendency to take risks or daydream. Boys, on the average, have more accidents than girls, probably because they take more physical risks (H. Ginsburg & Miller, 1982). Injuries increase from ages 5 to 14, possibly because children become involved in more physical activities (Schor, 1987). (See Figure 11-4.)

A child's family also affects safety. In a longitudinal study of 693 families who sought medical care over a 6-year period, a small number of families accounted for a large number of injuries. After adjustment for family size, 10 percent of the families accounted for almost 25 percent of the injuries (Schor, 1987). Children with siblings have more injuries than only children. Parents of more than

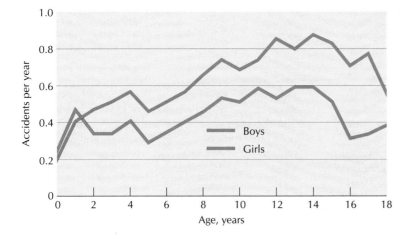

FIGURE 11-4
Average annual rates of injury by age and sex of children. Boys typically have a higher yearly accident rate than girls, except at age 1. Accident rates are especially high for both sexes in late middle childhood and early adolescence. SOURCE: Schor, 1987.

one child may not be as vigilant as parents of one child, or younger children may imitate their older siblings and take more risks, or children in larger families may be more active. Families with high injury rates may be undergoing stress that interferes with the ability to make the home safe or watch over children.

How Are Children Most Likely to Be Hurt?

Most childhood accidents occur in (or are inflicted by) automobiles or occur in the home; but between 10 and 20 percent take place in and around schools. Elementary school children are most likely to be injured from playground falls (Sheps & Evans, 1987). Secondary school students are most often injured in sports. Some of these injuries could be avoided if players were grouped by size, skill, and maturational level rather than by age (AAP Committee on Sports Medicine and Committee on School Health, 1989).

The most common cause of serious injury and death in young schoolchildren is being hit by a moving vehicle. Parents tend to overestimate the safety skills of young children. Many kindergartners and first-graders walk alone to school, often crossing busy streets without traffic lights, although they do not have the skills to do this safely. Many such accidents could be prevented by making parents aware of their children's limitations as pedestrians and by providing school-operated transportation (Dunne, Asher, & Rivara, 1992; Rivara, Bergman, & Drake, 1989).

Each year about 300,000 visits to emergency rooms and 600 deaths of children under 15 are attributed to bicycle accidents. Head injury is the leading cause of disability and death in these accidents (Cushman, Down, MacMillan, & Waclawik, 1991). Children between ages 10 and 14 are more likely to use their bikes for transportation than for play, but accident rates and severity are similar for both types of usage (Agran & Winn, 1993). Even on little-traveled streets close to home, young bicyclists are at risk and need to learn—and adhere to—the rules of the road.

The dangers of riding a bike can be reduced dramatically by using safety-approved helmets (AAP Committee on Accident and Poison Prevention, 1990). Protective headgear is also vital for football, roller skating, roller blading, skateboarding, horseback riding, hockey, speed sledding, and tobogganing. School programs to encourage helmet use can be effective (Weiss, 1992). Parents, teachers, and coaches can help prevent injuries—particularly head injuries—by following the suggestions given in Box 11-4.

One reason for some accidents is children's immaturity, both cognitive (preventing them from being aware of some dangers) and emotional (leading them to take dangerous risks). We discuss cognitive development in middle childhood in Chapter 12 and emotional and social development in Chapter 13.

SUMMARY

1   Physical development is less rapid in middle childhood than in the earlier years. Boys are slightly larger than girls at the beginning of this period, but girls undergo the growth spurt of adolescence at an earlier age and thus tend to be larger than boys at the end of the period. Wide differences in height and weight exist between individuals and between groups.

2   Growth can be stimulated with growth hormones, but these should be used only in cases of natural growth-hormone deficiency.

3   Proper nutrition is essential for normal growth and health. Malnutrition can diminish activity, sociability, and cognitive development. On average, children need 2400 calories a day.

4   Obesity among children is an increasingly common problem. It seems to have both genetic and environmental roots. Behavioral therapies—especially when they involve parents—are the most successful in treating obesity.

5   Because of improved motor development, boys and girls in middle childhood can engage in a wider range of motor activities than can preschoolers. Studies done several decades ago suggest that boys excel in motor skills, but more recent research indicates similar abilities for boys and girls. There is no safety-related reason to separate prepubertal boys and girls for physical activities.

6   About 10 percent of schoolchildren's play is rough-and-tumble play, which appears to be universal and of evolutionary significance.

7   Poor physical fitness among schoolchildren seems to be occurring because children are not physically active enough. With education and behavior modification, children can learn habits to improve their health.

8   Respiratory problems and other common health problems of middle childhood tend to be frequent and of short duration, and medical conditions often recur. Chronic conditions, while relatively rare, appear to be increasing. Children's understanding of illness is related to their cognitive level.

9   Vision improves during middle childhood, although a minority of children have vision problems. Hearing problems and asthma are two additional chronic problems.

10   Stuttering and tics are both fairly common in middle childhood and are more prevalent among boys.

11   Tooth decay rates have declined over the past few decades, mainly because of use of fluoride and improved dental care.

12   Accidental injury is the leading cause of disability and death in children over 1 year of age. Boys, and children from certain families, tend to have more accidents. Most accidents occur in automobiles, at home, or in and around school.

KEY TERMS

obesity (435)
rough-and-tumble play (441)
acute medical conditions (443)
chronic medical conditions (443)

asthma (448)
stuttering (448)
tics (449)

SUGGESTED READINGS

Berger, L., Lithwick, D., and Seven Campers (1992). *I will sing life: Voices from the Hole in the Wall Gang Camp.* Boston: Little, Brown. This spirited and inspiring collection of writings by seven children, ages 7 to 17, who have all attended a camp for children with life-threatening diseases, and the counselors who lead the camp's creative-writing program, offers a window into the minds of children who live with cancer, sickle cell anemia, disability, or AIDS. In moving and witty poetry and prose, they talk about their families, their friends, their beliefs in God, and their feelings about their illnesses.

Krementz, J. (1992). *How it feels to live with a physical disability.* New York: Simon & Schuster. This book introduces 15 children and teenagers with various physical disabilities and allows them to explain in their own words how they meet the particular challenges they face and what their lives are like. Beautifully illustrated with photographs, the book makes physical differentness less intimidating as it becomes clear that these children, despite disability, are essentially regular kids. Although the book is geared for 8- to 10-year-olds, it is suitable for people of all ages.

Wolff, R. (1993). *Good sports: The concerned parent's guide to Little League and other competitive youth sports.* New York: Dell. The author, a father of three, a children's coach, and a sports psychologist, offers advice to parents and coaches about ways to make sports for children safe, fun, and valuable.

CHAPTER 12
COGNITIVE DEVELOPMENT IN MIDDLE CHILDHOOD

CHAPTER 12
COGNITIVE DEVELOPMENT IN MIDDLE CHILDHOOD

Childhood is a world of miracle and wonder: as if creation rose, bathed in light, out of darkness, utterly new and fresh and astonishing. The end of childhood is when things cease to astonish us. When the world seems familiar, when one has got used to existence, one has become an adult.

Eugene Ionesco, *Fragments of a Journal,* 1976

We now examine the cognitive changes that occur in children during the first 6 years of formal schooling, from about ages 6 to 12. We consider the Piagetian, the Vygotskian, the information-processing, and the psychometric perspectives on these changes. Then we look at language—grammar and communication, children's humor, and bilingual education. Since school is so important in children's lives, we take up such school-related issues as the influences on children's academic performance and the experiences of children with special needs. When you have finished reading this chapter, you should be able to answer questions like the following:

PREVIEW QUESTIONS

♦ How is the thinking of schoolchildren different from that of preschoolers?
♦ How is the development of moral reasoning and role-taking ability related to cognitive development?
♦ What advances in memory and language occur during middle childhood?
♦ How is intelligence measured in middle childhood? Why is IQ testing controversial?
♦ What influences affect how children perform in school?
♦ What can schools provide for children with special needs?
♦ How can gifted and talented children's abilities be best nurtured?

Proudly wearing his new backpack, Jason walks to his first-grade classroom. A veteran of preschool and kindergarten, he finds the idea of school exhilarating. He also, however, feels some anxiety around such unspoken questions as "What will my teacher be like? Will the kids like me? Will the work be too hard?"

The first day of "regular" school is a milestone and a sign that a child has entered a distinctly new stage of development. In fact, Jason's anxieties reflect his new ability to realize the challenges he is likely to face. By age 11, Jason will have mastered some of these worries, self-confident in the knowledge that learning is what he does. He will be reading, thinking, talking, and imagining things in ways that were well beyond him only a few years before.

APPROACHES TO COGNITIVE DEVELOPMENT

To discuss cognitive development during these years, we consider four approaches to studying it. The Piagetian approach shows advances in children's thinking and moral judgments in the stage of concrete operations; the Vygotskian

Has this girl developed what Piaget called *conservation*—the realization that even if checkers are rearranged, the number remains the same.

approach stresses the importance of social interaction; the information-processing approach emphasizes the development of attentiveness and of memory; and the psychometric approach has given rise to controversy over intelligence testing.

PIAGETIAN APPROACH: THE STAGE OF CONCRETE OPERATIONS (ABOUT 7 TO 11 YEARS)

At about age 7, children enter a new stage of cognitive development—*concrete operations.* They are less egocentric now and apply logical principles to concrete (actual) situations. They use internal mental operations (thinking) to solve problems set in the here and now. This means that they perform many tasks at a much higher level than they could at the previous (preoperational) stage. For example, children are better at dealing with numbers; understanding the concepts of time and space; distinguishing reality from fantasy; classifying objects, or grouping them in similar categories (see Chapter 9); seriating, or arranging items (like different-size sticks) in order along a particular dimension (like length, from shortest to longest); and understanding conservation.

However, children in this stage are still limited to actual, present situations. They cannot yet think in hypothetical terms, about what *could be* rather than what *is.* The ability to think abstractly does not occur until adolescence, says Piaget.

concrete operations *Piaget's third stage of cognitive development, during which children develop the ability to think logically about the here and now, but not about abstractions.*

Conservation

One of the best-known aspects of Piaget's work is his study of **conservation.** This, as you will recall from Chapter 9, is the ability to recognize that the quantity or amount of something remains the same even if the matter is rearranged, as long as nothing is added or taken away. Piaget and other researchers have tested children's grasp of conservation with regard to such attributes as number, substance, length, area, weight, and volume. (Refer to Figure 9-2.)

conservation *Piaget's term for awareness that two stimuli that are equal (in length, weight, or amount, for example) remain equal in the face of perceptual alteration, so long as nothing has been added to or taken away from either stimulus.*

Testing Conservation.   If we compare the performance of Felipe, who is in the preoperational stage on a conservation task, with Vicky, in the concrete operations stage, we can see how Vicky shows her grasp of logical principles in assessing conservation.

In a typical conservation of substance task, for example, an experimenter shows a child two identical clay balls and asks the child whether the amount of clay in both balls is the same. Once the child agrees that the amount is, indeed, the same, the experimenter or the child changes one of the balls into a different shape—say, a long, thin "sausage." The child is again asked whether the two objects contain the same amount of clay or whether one contains more—and why she or he thinks so. Felipe, the preoperational child, is deceived by appearances: He says that the long, thin roll contains more clay because it *looks* longer. Vicky, the concrete operational child, realizes that appearance does not matter. She understands that a transformation like this changes only how a thing is perceived. She correctly answers that the ball and the "sausage" have the same amount of clay.

When children are asked about the reasoning behind their answers, they reveal their thinking processes and show whether they understand the logical principles underlying the task. Vicky understands the principle of *identity:* She knows the clay is still the same clay, even though it has a different shape. She understands the principle of *reversibility:* She knows that she can reverse the transformation (change the sausage back into a ball) and restore the original shape. Preoperational children do not understand either of these principles. Finally, Vicky can *decenter:* She can focus on more than one relevant dimension (in this case, on both length and width). Felipe, the preoperational child, centers on one dimension (length) while excluding the other and, therefore, does not show conservation ability.

Horizontal Décalage: Development of Different Types of Conservation.   The ability to solve conservation problems varies not only with age but with the particular attribute or dimension involved. Typically, children can solve tasks involving conservation of *substance* (like the one just described) by about age 7 or 8. In tasks involving conservation of *weight*—where they are asked, say, whether the ball and the sausage weigh the same—children typically do not give correct answers until about age 9 or 10. In tasks involving conservation of *volume*—where children must judge whether the sausage and the ball displace an equal amount of liquid when placed in a glass of water—correct answers are rarely given before age 12. In solving these problems, children can apply internal mental operations—they can work out the problems in their heads. They do not have to measure or weigh the objects.

horizontal décalage   *In Piaget's terminology, the development of different types of conservation at different ages; thus, a child can conserve substance before weight, and substance and weight before volume.*

Piaget called the development of different types of conservation at different ages *horizontal décalage.* The phenomenon is fascinating because—since the principle in each task is exactly the same—the time lags show how concrete children's thinking is at this stage. Their reasoning is so closely tied to a particular situation that they cannot readily apply the same basic internal mental operations to different situations.

This gradual mastery of different types of conservation suggests that children do not acquire cognitive abilities all at once, but gradually and continuously. The issue of whether cognitive abilities emerge in discrete stages or gradually has been a major research question. The current thinking, as we pointed out earlier, is that such abilities emerge gradually.

Effects of Experience on Conservation. Piaget stressed the maturational aspects of conservation ability. He believed that children will show the ability to conserve when they are mature enough neurologically. However, cultural factors also affect conservation. For example, black children from higher socioeconomic levels do better on Piagetian tasks than do black children of lower socioeconomic levels (Bardouille-Crema, Black, & Feldhusen, 1986). Children from different countries—like Switzerland, the United States, and Great Britain—typically achieve conservation at different ages.

Schooling seems especially important. Patricia Greenfield (1966) compared African children who lived and went to school in a city with children who lived and went to school in the bush (rural areas) and with children who lived in the bush but had never gone to school. She found wide differences in ability to conserve. Rural children who had gone to school conserved earlier than rural children who had not gone to school. The urban children—who had all gone to school—conserved slightly earlier than the rural children who had gone to school. By age 11 or 12, virtually all the children who had gone to school could conserve liquid quantity, compared with only half the children who had not.

Apparently, something the children were learning in school was helping them understand conservation. This research suggests that maturation alone cannot account for conservation. Both maturation and experience seem to contribute to its development.

By arranging these sticks in order of length, this 6-year-old shows that he understands seriation. This Piagetian task tests the emergence of this cognitive ability, which appears during middle childhood.

Other Important Cognitive Abilities

Two concepts that develop during the school years are *seriation*, the ability to arrange items along a dimension, and *classification*, the ability to sort items into categories.

Seriation. Children show that they understand *seriation* when they can arrange objects in order along one or more relevant dimensions, like weight (lightest to heaviest) or color (lightest to darkest). Piaget (1952) tested this ability by asking children to put sticks in order from shortest to longest.

In the task, Jason is given a handful of sticks of differing lengths and is asked to put them in order from shortest to longest. By age 4 or 5 he can pick out the smallest and the largest sticks. The next harder task comes when he is asked to put 10 sticks in order of size. By age 5 or 6 he can pick out the shortest and the longest and then by trial and error put the rest in order. At 7 or 8 years, however, he can grasp the relationships among the sticks by sight, picking out the shortest, then the next shortest, and so on to the longest.

seriation *Ability to order items along a dimension.*

Transitive Inference. A related ability that develops in middle childhood is *transitive inference*, the ability to recognize a relationship between two objects by knowing the relationship between each of them and a third. Vicky is shown three sticks: a yellow one, a green one, and a blue one. She is shown that the yellow stick is longer than the green one, and the green one is longer than the blue. There is no direct comparison of the yellow and blue sticks, but when she is asked to compare them, she says, "The yellow one is longer than the blue one." She bases her answer on her knowledge of the relationship each of these sticks holds to the green stick (Chapman & Lindenberger, 1988; Piaget & Inhelder, 1967).

transitive inference *Understanding of the relationship between two objects by knowing the relationship of each to a third object.*

Classification. Children's ability to categorize items according to particular attributes, emerges early in childhood. (See Chapter 9.) At first they classify by only one dimension (like color); later they become able to categorize by two dimensions (as color and shape). In middle childhood, children are better able to classify, to organize their world to make it more orderly and understandable.

One classification ability is *class inclusion,* the ability to understand the relationship between a whole and its parts. Preoperational children do not understand this concept. In a typical class inclusion task, Vicky is shown four roses and four carnations. After she identifies them all as flowers, she is asked, "If I make a bouquet of all the roses and you make one of all the flowers, which one is bigger?" At age 5, she said, "The same." She did not understand that the part (the roses) is less than the whole (all the flowers); that is, she lacked the principle of class inclusion. Between ages 7 and 11, children develop this principle and can understand that the larger class of "flowers" includes the subclass of "roses" (Flavell, 1963).

Social Implications of Cognitive Development

If classification skills are immature, a child may be especially vulnerable to gender stereotypes. For example, a child may assume that someone in the category of "doctor" also has to be in the category of "male." The child needs to be able to distinguish the categories of occupation and gender before being able to accept the fact that women can be doctors.

The intertwining of cognitive and social factors is seen in an experiment using cognitive intervention to overcome gender-stereotyping (Bigler & Liben, 1992). Experimenters assigned seventy-five 5- to 10-year-old children to one of three experimental groups and one control group. They trained one experimental group in multiple classification skills, using pictures of men and women engaged in gender-stereotyped occupations. The children had to sort the people by gender, by occupation, and then by combining the two categories. A second experimental group learned multiple classification with neutral items like hats and colors. The third experimental group learned rules for distinguishing gender from the requirements for performing a given job (as "a construction worker must like to build things . . . and must learn to drive big machines"). The control group discussed occupations in general.

After a week of daily 45-minute sessions, the experimental group who classified people by occupation and the experimental group who learned rules about gender and occupation gave less stereotyped responses on measures of gender-stereotyping than did the other two groups. All three experimental groups remembered nonstereotyped information better than did children in the control group. This experiment shows the relationship of cognitive skills like classification to social behaviors like gender-stereotyping. It also supports the value of teaching children gender-neutral criteria for determining who can perform various jobs. Finally, it supports cognitive-developmental theory about gender roles. (See Chapter 10.)

Number and Mathematics

With such developments in logical thought as the greater ability to manipulate symbols, to appreciate concepts like reversibility, and to understand seriation and the idea of part-and-whole, children can now tackle arithmetic.

Advances in Working with Numbers.   Children develop their own informal strategies for adding and subtracting (Resnick, 1989). At first they count on their fingers or other objects. To add 5 and 3, they may create one set of 5 pennies and another set of 3 pennies, and then add both sets to get 8 pennies. However, even after they have counted the 5 pennies, before they can add the extra 3 they have to count all the pennies all over again.

By age 6 or 7 they learn to *count on.* They realize that after they counted the first 5 pennies, they can start counting at 6 rather than 1, to add the 3 more. It may take 2 or 3 more years for them to perform a comparable operation for subtraction, but by age 9 most children can either count up from the smaller number or down from the larger number to get the answer.

Children also become more adept at solving simple story problems like "Pedro went to the store with $5 and spent $2 on candy. How much did he have left?" However, when the unknown is the starting amount ("Pedro went to the store, spent $2 and had $3 left. How much did he start out with?"), the problem is harder. Few children can solve this kind of problem before 8 or 9 years of age (Resnick, 1989).

Intuitive Math.   Research with minimally schooled people in developing countries suggests that the ability to solve addition problems develops nearly universally (Resnick, 1989). In an experiment with Brazilian street vendors aged 9 to 15, a child is presented with a math problem by an experimenter acting as a customer. The customer says, "I'll take two coconuts." Each one costs 40 cruzeiros; she pays with a 500-cruzeiros bill and asks, "What do I get back?" The child counts up from 80: "Eighty, 90, 100, 420," to arrive at the correct answer, 420 cruzeiros.

However, when this same child is given a similar problem in a formal context, as in a classroom ("What is 420 + 80?"), he arrives at the wrong answer of 130. This child incorrectly used a series of steps he learned in school for multiplication problems (Carraher, Schliemann, & Carraher, 1988).

Findings like these show "that neither abstract thought nor conceptual knowledge of mathematics is a privilege of those with many years of Western schooling," but that mathematical concepts are often learned informally (Carraher et al., 1988, pp. 85-86). What implications are there for classroom teaching? Instead of posing abstract problems, it may be more effective to teach math with the use of concrete situations or by using money concepts to help children understand the decimal system.

What do you think?   *Can you describe a situation in which you used intuitive math to solve a math problem?*

Moral Development

Why are we discussing morality in connection with cognitive development? Moral development is, of course, an outgrowth of personality, emotional attitudes, and cultural influences. Psychoanalytic and social-learning theories both draw on these factors to explain moral development. However, one of the most influential conceptions of moral development today is that moral judgment develops along with cognitive growth.

Jean Piaget maintained that young children cannot make sound moral judgments until they achieve a high enough level of cognitive maturity to look at things as another person might see them. Robert Selman extended this view, holding that moral development is linked to "role-taking." We discuss Piaget's and Selman's approaches to moral development here, and we will examine the influential cognitive-developmental theory of Lawrence Kohlberg in Chapter 15.

Piaget: Stages of Constraint and Cooperation. Piaget proposed that moral reasoning develops in two major stages. In the first stage, the *morality of constraint,* the young child thinks rigidly about moral concepts. In this stage children are quite egocentric; they cannot imagine more than one way of looking at a moral issue. They believe that rules cannot be changed, that behavior is right or wrong, and that any offense deserves punishment (unless they themselves are the offenders).

The second stage, the *morality of cooperation,* is characterized by moral flexibility. As children mature, they interact more with other people and come into contact with an increasingly wide range of viewpoints; some of these contradict what they have learned at home. Experience and maturation interact to help them develop their own moral standards. They conclude that there is not one unchangeable absolute of right and wrong. Children can now make more subtle judgments of behavior, considering the intent behind it and using punishment judiciously. They are formulating their own moral codes.

To see how children at different levels of morality thought about behavior, Piaget (1932) would tell them a story about two little boys: "One day Augustus noticed that his father's inkpot was empty and decided to help his father by filling it. While he was opening the bottle, he spilled a lot of ink on the tablecloth. The other boy, Julian, played with his father's inkpot and spilled a little ink on the cloth." Then Piaget would ask, "Which boy was naughtier, and why?"

Children under about age 7 usually consider Augustus naughtier since he made the bigger stain. Older children recognize that Augustus meant well and made the large stain by accident, whereas Julian made a small stain while doing something he should not have been doing. Immature moral judgments center on the degree of offense; more mature judgments consider intent. Table 12-1 shows how the two stages differ on such moral concepts as rules, intention, and punishment.

Selman: Role-Taking Ability. In following the progression from egocentric to moral thinking, Robert Selman (1973) looked at *role-taking ability*—that is, the ability to assume another person's point of view. Since morality involves considering other people's welfare, it is reasonable to suppose that an increased ability to imagine how another person might think and feel should be related to the ability to make moral judgments. In fact, the two are related. Selman divided the development of role-taking into five stages, numbered 0 to 4:

- *Stage 0* (about ages 4 to 6): Children are egocentric, think that their own point of view is the only one possible, and judge accordingly. Suppose that we ask 5-year-old Vicky her opinion about the dilemma in this story: "A little girl has promised her father not to climb trees but then sees a kitten trapped up in a tree. What should the little girl do?" Vicky sees no problem. Since *she* likes kittens, she assumes that everyone else will favor climbing the tree to save the kitten.
- *Stage 1* (about ages 6 to 8): Children realize that other people may interpret a

---

morality of constraint *In Piaget's theory, the first stage of moral reasoning, in which a child thinks rigidly about moral concepts; also called heteronomous morality.*

morality of cooperation *In Piaget's theory, the second stage of moral reasoning, in which a child has moral flexibility; also called autonomous morality.*

role-taking ability *In Selman's terminology, assuming another person's point of view.*

TABLE 12-1

PIAGET'S TWO STAGES OF MORAL DEVELOPMENT		
	STAGE I	**STAGE II**
MORAL CONCEPTS	Morality of constraint.	Morality of cooperation.
POINT OF VIEW	Child views an act as either totally right or totally wrong, and thinks everyone sees it the same way. Children cannot put themselves in place of others.	Children can put themselves in place of others. They are not absolutist in judgments but see that more than one point of view is possible.
INTENTION	Child judges acts in terms of actual physical consequences, not the motivation behind them.	Child judges acts by intentions, not consequences.
RULES	Child obeys rules because they are sacred and unalterable.	Child recognizes that rules are made by people and can be changed by people. Children consider themselves just as capable of changing rules as anyone else.
RESPECT FOR AUTHORITY	Unilateral respect leads to feeling of obligation to conform to adult standards and obey adult rules.	Mutual respect for authority and peers allows children to value their own opinions and abilities and to judge other people realistically.
PUNISHMENT	Child favors severe punishment. Child feels that punishment itself defines the wrongness of an act; an act is bad if it will elicit punishment.	Child favors milder punishment that compensates the victim and helps the culprit recognize why an act is wrong, thus leading to reform.
CONCEPT OF JUSTICE	Child confuses moral law with physical law and believes that any physical accident or misfortune that occurs after a misdeed is a punishment willed by God or some other supernatural force.	Child does not confuse natural misfortune with punishment.

SOURCE: Adapted partly from M. L. Hoffman, 1970; Kohlberg, in M. L. Hoffman & Hoffman, 1964.

situation differently. Vicky, now 7, says, "If the father doesn't know why she climbed the tree, he will be angry. But if he knows why she did it, he will be glad." She realizes the importance of intention—and also that the father's viewpoint may be different from the child's.

■ *Stage 2* (8 to 10 years): Children develop reciprocal awareness. Not only does Vicky, now age 9, know that other people have their own points of view (stage 1), she also realizes that others know that *she* has a particular point of view. Vicky knows that besides telling her father about the kitten, the little girl should also let him know that she did not forget her promise.

■ *Stage 3* (10 to 12 years): Children can imagine a third person's perspective, taking several different points of view into account.

■ *Stage 4* (adolescence or later): People realize that mutual role-taking does not always resolve disputes. Some rival values simply cannot be resolved by communication alone.

Selman's theory illustrates how advances in role-taking ability are related to advances in moral thinking. Such advances are also spurred by social interaction.

VYGOTSKIAN APPROACH: THE IMPACT OF SOCIAL INTERACTION

Lev Vygotsky maintained that social interaction—the exchanges that go on between people, especially within the home—is a key factor in cognitive development.

Social Interactions

According to Vygotsky (1978), all higher planning and organizing functions in cognitive development appear twice: first as the result of interaction with other people, usually adults, and then after the child has internalized what the adults have taught. He expanded these beliefs to the ways children learn, to their performance on intelligence tests, and to their growing skills in thinking, reading, and writing.

Researchers influenced by Vygotsky apply the metaphor of scaffolds, temporary platforms where building workers stand, to this way of teaching (D. Wood, 1980; D. Wood, Bruner, & Ross, 1976). *Scaffolding* is the temporary support that parents, teachers, and others give a child to do a task. There is an inverse relationship between the child's current ability and the amount of support needed. In other words, the more difficulty a child has doing a task, the more direction the caregiver should provide. As the child becomes able to do more, the adult helps less. Once the job is done, the adult takes away the temporary support—or scaffold—which is no longer needed.

scaffolding *Temporary support given a child to do a task.*

Scaffolding in Everyday Life

Adults offer scaffolding in teaching a variety of skills. In one observational study, a group of Mexican women were videotaped teaching 14 young girls how to weave. When working with beginners, the teachers did not instruct by words. Instead, at the more difficult parts of the process, the teachers took over the weaving. The girls watched the women doing this 87 percent of the time, thus learning from observing a model. None of the 14 students experienced failure, because their teachers intervened as soon as they saw the girls having the slightest problem with their cloth (Greenfield, 1984).

Scaffolding seems to come naturally in so many situations that teachers often do not recognize either the method itself or even that they are teaching. One Mexican woman who was interviewed about how girls learn to weave said, "They learn by themselves." Similarly, many western parents, unaware of their roles in teaching toddlers to talk, think that children learn how to talk by themselves rather than through interaction (Chomsky, 1965). Discovering how children learn is at the root of information-processing theory.

INFORMATION PROCESSING IN MIDDLE CHILDHOOD

During middle childhood youngsters mature in a number of cognitive areas. One is the ability to pay attention. This lets them selectively focus on information that is relevant to what they have to do at the moment. They can concentrate longer and screen out irrelevant information. Children who cannot do this have problems in school, where attention and concentration are required.

In middle childhood children can plan their work and devise and use strategies for organizing and counting—abilities that help them learn, remember, and solve problems. Meanwhile, they become increasingly able to take responsibility for doing their own schoolwork.

Instead of focusing on overall changes in children's thought as Piaget did, the information-processing approach explores the separate components of children's mental processes. These researchers look at questions like: How do children create and use strategies? What is involved in selective attention? How does memory work?

Memory is a major issue in information processing. As cognitive development advances, so does memory. The ability to remember improves greatly by middle childhood, as children's memory capacity—the amount of information they can remember—increases, and as they learn to use a variety of memory strategies, or deliberate plans, to help them remember. One ability that develops is *metamemory,* an understanding of how memory processes work.

Memory Capacity

According to the information-processing approach, memory is like a filing system. It involves three basic steps: encoding, storage, and retrieval. After perceiving something, we need to decide where to file it. The first step is to *encode,* or classify it—for example, under "people I know" or "places I have been." Second, we *store* the material so that it stays in memory. Finally, we need to be able to *retrieve* it, or get it out from storage. Forgetting can occur because of a problem with any of the three steps.

Short-term memory increases rapidly in middle childhood. We assess short-term memory by asking children to recall a series of digits in the reverse of the order in which they heard them (to recite "2-8-3-7-5-1" if they have heard "1-5-7-3-8-2"). At ages 5 to 6, children usually remember only two digits; the typical adolescent remembers six.

Young children's poor short-term memory may help to explain why they have difficulty with conservation. They may not be able to remember all the relevant pieces of information necessary to solve the problem (Siegler & Richards, 1982). They may forget that two differently shaped pieces of clay (like a ball and a sausage) were equal initially; so by the time they are asked about the ball and the sausage, they can judge only on present appearance. Their improved short-term memory may be reflected in their ability to solve tasks like this in middle childhood.

Mnemonics: Strategies for Remembering

Jason, at age 6, wants to call his grandmother. "What's Grandma's number?" he asks. As he runs to the telephone, he says the number out loud, again and again. He is using rehearsal, a common technique to improve short-term memory. Jason has discovered that he can take deliberate actions to help him remember.

Devices to aid memory are called *mnemonic strategies.* Mnemonic techniques may be discovered haphazardly; but children can be taught to use them. Some teachers make a special point of teaching the use of mnemonic strategies, pointing out that they will help children remember. Such teaching is especially helpful to children of low to average achievement levels (Moely et al., 1992). Some of the most common mnemonic strategies are rehearsal, organization, elaboration, and external memory aids.

Rehearsal. Some early research suggests that children do not usually use *rehearsal,* or conscious repetition, spontaneously until after first grade (Flavell, Beach, & Chinsky, 1966). When an experimenter pointed to several pictures that children knew they would be asked to recall, first-graders typically sat, waited

rehearsal *Mnemonic strategy to keep an item in short-term memory through conscious repetition.*

Spelling bee winners sometimes use mnemonic strategies like rehearsal (conscious repetition) to fix the correct letters in a word in their minds.

till they were asked for the information, and then tried to recall the pictures in the order in which they had seen them. Second- and fifth-graders, though, moved their lips and muttered almost inaudibly between the time they saw the pictures and the time they were asked to recall them. Not surprisingly, the older children remembered the material better.

When the experimenters asked first-graders to name the pictures out loud when they first saw them (a form of rehearsal), the children remembered the pictures better and also remembered better the order in which they had been presented. In a later experiment, young children were taught to rehearse before they did it spontaneously. They applied rehearsal to the situation in which they were taught, but not to new situations (Keeney, Cannizzo, & Flavell, 1967).

More recent research shows that Jason is not unusual in using rehearsal at the age of 6; children as young as 3 can use it effectively. Although 6-year-olds are more likely to rehearse, 3-year-old rehearsers can remember a grocery list as well as 6-year-olds (Paris & Weissberg-Benchell in Chance & Fischman, 1987).

What do you think?   *Select a mnemonic strategy and design a technique to train children how to use it. How would you assess the success of your teaching?*

organization *Mnemonic strategy of categorizing material in one's mind into related groupings to aid in remembering.*

Organization.   It is much easier to remember material if we mentally categorize it into related groupings, a process known as *organization.* Adults tend to organize automatically. Children younger than 10 or 11 do *not* ordinarily organize automatically, but they can be taught to, or they may acquire the skill by imitating others (Chance & Fischman, 1987). If they see randomly arranged pictures of, say, animals, furniture, vehicles, and clothing, they do not mentally sort the items into categories spontaneously. But if shown how to organize, they recall the pictures as well as older children do. However, the learning is very specific; children do not generalize this learning to other situations.

Elaboration. In the mnemonic strategy called *elaboration,* we link items together in an imagined scene. To remember to buy lemons, ketchup, and napkins, we might imagine a ketchup bottle balanced on a lemon, with a pile of napkins handy to wipe up spilled ketchup. Older children are more likely than younger ones to use elaboration spontaneously, and they remember better when they make up the elaborations themselves. Younger children remember better when someone else makes up the elaboration (Paris & Lindauer, 1976; H. W. Reese, 1977).

elaboration Mnemonic strategy of linking items to be remembered by creating a story about them or a visual image of them.

External Aids. The mnemonic strategies used most commonly by both children and adults involve prompting by something outside the person. You write down a telephone number, make a list, set a timer, or put a library book by the front door. Even kindergartners recognize the value of *external aids,* and as children mature, they use them more (Kreutzer, Leonard, & Flavell, 1975).

Metamemory

At 6 years old, Vicky tells her mother that she has trouble remembering her dreams. Then she has an idea: "Maybe I can put a piece of paper in my brain to take a picture of my dream. This would help me remember."

Vicky is showing her awareness of *metamemory*—knowledge of the processes of memory, an understanding that begins to develop in early childhood. Even 4-year-olds know that if a doll saw two objects, the doll would "remember" the one just seen but would forget the one seen a long time before (Lyon & Flavell, 1993). The understanding that the passage of time affects memory begins early.

metamemory Knowledge of the processes of memory.

From kindergarten through fifth grade, children advance steadily in understanding memory (Kreutzer et al., 1975). Kindergartners and first-graders understand what it means to learn, remember, and forget. They understand that longer study time improves learning and that external aids can help them remember. Perhaps the most sophisticated thing they know about memory, because it combines a knowledge of learning with a knowledge of forgetting, is that relearning something is easier than learning it for the first time.

By third grade, children know that some people remember more than other people and that some things are easier to remember than other things. Because children know more about how memory works, they can now plan better to remember something. They are more likely to think of putting their skates by their schoolbooks if they want to remember to take their skates to school the next day.

PSYCHOMETRIC APPROACH: MEASURING INDIVIDUAL DIFFERENCES IN INTELLIGENCE

Vicky's school gives group intelligence tests every few years, partly to assess the students' abilities and partly to judge how well it is preparing the students. After the fourth grade, when Vicky wants to attend a "magnet" public school that offers special programs, she takes a test individually. Tests like the following help administrators decide whether to admit particular students, whether they would benefit from an enriched program, or whether they need special help.

Wechsler Intelligence Scale for Children (WISC-III) Individual intelligence test for children that includes verbal and performance subtests.

Psychometric Intelligence Tests for Schoolchildren

Schoolchildren are most often tested in groups, but they can also be assessed individually. The most widely used individual test is the *Wechsler Intelligence Scale*

This girl is taking the most widely used test of intelligence for children, the WISC-III, which yields separate scores for verbal and performance abilities.

Kaufman Assessment Battery for Children (K-ABC) *Individual intelligence test for children.*

Otis-Lennon School Ability Test *Group intelligence test for children.*

aptitude tests *Tests that measure children's basic capacity to learn, that is, their general intelligence.*

achievement tests *Tests that assess how much children know in various subject areas.*

for Children (WISC-III). This measures verbal and performance abilities, yielding separate scores for each, as well as a total score. Separating the subtest scores helps pinpoint a child's strengths and also makes it easier to diagnose specific problems. For example, if a child does well on the verbal tests (such as understanding a written passage and knowing vocabulary words) but poorly on the performance tests (such as figuring out mazes and copying a block design), the child may have difficulty with perceptual or motor development. A child who does well on the performance tests and poorly on the verbal tests may have a language problem.

The newest individual test in common use is the *Kaufman Assessment Battery for Children (K-ABC)* (Kaufman & Kaufman, 1983). Developed in the 1980s, it is used in much the same way as is the WISC and is administered to test-takers from $2\frac{1}{2}$ to $12\frac{1}{2}$ years of age. It was designed especially to be used for children from cultural minorities and children with disabilities, who were included in the test's standardization sample. The subtests in the K-ABC's achievement scale measure reading, arithmetic, word knowledge, and general information. Although the subtest items are more like items in a traditional *aptitude test* than like a standard school *achievement test* (see next section), the authors consider the battery a test of what a child has learned rather than of innate abilities.

The K-ABC yields scores on two kinds of information-processing abilities. *Simultaneous processing* requires the integration of a number of stimuli at the same time (like remembering an array of objects seen briefly). *Sequential processing* demands thinking in one step after another (like repeating a series of numbers). This test also uses scaffolding: If a child fails any of the first three items on any subtest, the examiner helps by using different words or gestures or even a different language. Since this test is so new, research has not yet backed up its distinction on the two kinds of processing. However, it seems promising, in view of its acknowledgment of cultural differences and of the importance of information-processing theory.

Another individual test is the Stanford-Binet Intelligence Scale, described in Chapter 9.

A popular group test is the *Otis-Lennon School Ability Test.* Its several levels cover children from kindergarten up to the twelfth grade. Children are usually tested in groups of 10 to 15 and are asked to classify items, to show an understanding of verbal and numerical concepts, to display general information, and to follow directions.

Pros and Cons of Intelligence Testing

The use of psychometric intelligence tests is controversial, with most of the controversy centering on IQ tests. These are called *aptitude tests:* They claim to measure general intelligence, or a child's basic capacity to learn. As we explained in Chapter 9, they are distinct from *achievement tests,* which assess how much a child knows in various subject areas. Achievement tests measure a child's progress and let a school know how effectively it is teaching. There are valid reasons for both promoting and questioning the use of IQ tests for children.

Advantages of IQ Testing. Since IQ tests have been standardized, there is extensive information about their norms, validity, and reliability.* IQ scores are good predictors of achievement in school, especially for highly verbal children, and they

*To refresh your understanding of these terms, return to Chapter 9.

help identify youngsters who are either especially bright or in need of special help. On the other hand, there are serious problems with using intelligence tests, besides those that we have already pointed out regarding tests for infants and handicapped children. The underlying concern is that these tests may be unfair to many children.

Problems with IQ Testing. Robert Sternberg (1985a, 1987), whose triarchic theory of intelligence is discussed in Chapter 15, claims that IQ tests do not assess skills directly, but instead, infer children's ability from how they score. This leads to problems of cultural bias and of underestimating the cognitive abilities of minority-group test-takers. Some critics charge that intelligence tests measure no more than the thinking style of a particular culture—that of white people of European ancestry (Helms, 1992). Others say they do not even do that well, that while the tests do predict academic performance, they underestimate the intelligence of many children who may be bright but for one reason or another do not score high on tests (Gardner, 1983; Sternberg, 1987).

IQ tests miss important aspects of intelligent behavior: "street smarts" (common sense and shrewdness in everyday life), social skills (getting along with other people), creative insight as in music and art, and self-knowledge. Then, because IQ tests are timed, they wrongly equate intelligence with speed. Thus a child who works slowly and deliberately will be penalized.

Another problem with intelligence tests, which aim to measure aptitude rather than what a child has learned, is that the scores turn out to be more closely related to the amount of schooling a child has had than to the child's age (Cahan & Cohen, 1989). It has been impossible to separate "intelligence" and scholastic achievement. Schooling has the greatest impact on verbal abilities, but it also affects performance on number and figure tasks. The fact that people's IQs change over time further challenges the concept of intelligence unaffected by experience.

What do you think?   *How would you define intelligence? How would you test your concept of intelligence? Would you use a traditional IQ test, look at behavior, or use some other measure?*

A child's development itself can enhance performance on intelligence tests. As children mature, learn from experience and schooling, and use their minds, their intelligence scores frequently rise. How motivated a test-taker is and what his or her personality is like can also contribute to a rise—or fall—in intelligence test scores. Furthermore, research suggests that children can be taught how to think more effectively. (See Box 12–1.)

Implications of Intelligence Tests

Cross-Cultural Testing.   As early as 1910, researchers recognized the difficulty of designing intelligence tests for people in diverse cultural groups. Ever since, they have tried to design tests that can measure inborn intelligence without introducing cultural bias, as by designing tests that do not require language. (Testers use gestures, pantomime, and demonstrations for tasks like tracing mazes, finding absurdities in pictures, putting the right shapes in the right holes, and completing pictures.) However, they have not been able to eliminate all cultural content.

For example, cultural variations in the way people view art affect the way a test-taker reacts to a picture. When Jason, an American child, is asked to identify the missing detail in a picture of a face with no mouth, he says, "the mouth." But

BOX 12-1 ▪ THE EVERYDAY WORLD

TEACHING CHILDREN TO THINK

Children *can* be taught to think. Thinking arises at least partly from experience. Therefore, for children to learn how to think—to evaluate a situation, focus on its most important aspects, decide what to do, and do it—they need experience. The following suggestions come from cognitive research (Marzano & Hutchins, 1987; Maxwell, 1987):

♦ Teach thinking skills in the context of everyday activities. This can begin early. As suggested in Chapter 6, asking toddlers open-ended questions (beginning with *what, why,* and *how*) while reading to them encourages them to improve their verbal skills; it also helps them learn to think. The same approach helps older children.

♦ Ask children to "match" information, to compare new data with what they already know. In this way, they learn to identify links among words or concepts (what two items have in common or how they differ). Schoolchildren can categorize a country, for example, as European or African, democratic or totalitarian. This uses the memory strategy of organization, helping them remember the facts.

♦ Demonstrate "critical thinking." Teach children to ask four questions about anything they hear or read: (1) Is it unusual? (2) Is it common knowledge ("The sky is sometimes blue")? (3) If it is not common knowledge, what is the proof? (4) If there is proof, is it reliable? If not, they should learn not to accept the statement.

♦ Show children how to approach a problem: (1) To understand the problem, they need to identify what they know, what they don't know, and what has to be done. (2) They can then design a plan to solve the problem, (3) carry out the plan, and (4) evaluate the plan (decide whether it has worked).

♦ Use "guided imagery" (imagining an event or experience). Sensory images help store information in memory, and the more senses involved, the better. Children studying the Sahara Desert might be asked to "see" it, "touch" the sand, "hear" the wind, and "feel" hot and thirsty. This approach uses the memory strategy of elaboration.

♦ Teach children to go beyond what they have learned. Children studying the American Revolution might be asked, "How do you think the soldiers felt at Valley Forge? What do you suppose they wore? Imagine you were there, and write a letter to your family."

♦ Inspire invention. Ask children to create new information or products, like a gadget to help in some household chore.

♦ Suggest creative projects, like writing a poem or drawing a picture. Encourage children to produce a first version—and then to polish or revise it.

♦ Teach children such helpful procedures as reading a map, performing arithmetical operations, and using a microscope; show some examples of these skills in practice.

♦ Encourage children to set goals within a time frame, and write down the goals to check their progress.

♦ Help them learn how to find the most important points in what they read, see, or hear.

♦ Encourage children to write, since the process of putting thoughts on paper forces the writer to organize those thoughts. Projects that children can enjoy, as well as learn from, include keeping a journal, presenting an argument to parents (for an increase in allowance or a special purchase or privilege), and writing a letter to a business or to a famous person.

Ari, an Asian immigrant child in Israel, said that the *body* was missing. Since the art he was used to would not present a head as a complete picture, he thought the absence of a body was more important than the omission of "a mere detail like the mouth" (Anastasi, 1988, p. 360).

It seems impossible to design a *culture-free* test—a test having *no* culture-linked content. Instead, test developers have tried to produce *culture-fair* tests—tests dealing with experiences common to people in various cultures. However, these tests cannot be truly culture-fair either, because it is almost impossible to screen for culturally determined values and attitudes, which reflect what people in a culture consider to be intelligent behavior. For example, most intelligence tests reflect European traditions rather than African or Asian ones, and designate only one right answer for each test question. Since African American children are often socialized to believe that authority figures reward creative answers rather than obvious ones, they may give unexpected answers, which are then marked wrong (Helms, 1992; Heath, 1989). Cultural differences also affect cognitive processing. For instance, western cultures consider it more intelligent to categorize things by what they *are* (as by putting *bird* and *fish* in the category *animal*); but the Kpelle tribe in Nigeria sorts things by what they *do* (as by grouping *fish* with *swim*) (Sternberg, in Quinby, 1985; Sternberg, 1985a, 1986).

Also, the content of a test—the tasks it poses—calls for skills that the test-developer values; but people from other cultural groups may not value the same abilities. Other cultural attitudes affect the testing situation itself. Does a society value competition or cooperation? A child from a culture that stresses sociability and cooperation will be handicapped taking a test alone. Does a society value speed or deliberation? A child from a society that stresses slow, painstaking work is handicapped in a timed test.

Rapport with the examiner and familiarity with the surroundings are also important. African American and Latino children, disabled children, and children from low socioeconomic levels often earn higher scores when people they know (like their own teachers) give tests in places they know (like their own classrooms) than when they take tests in unfamiliar rooms with unknown examiners (D. Fuchs & Fuchs, 1986; L. S. Fuchs & Fuchs, 1986).

Finally, the test-developer's decision on which answers to accept sometimes seems arbitrary (Miller-Jones, 1989). For example, a 4- to 6-year-old taking the 1973 edition of the Stanford-Binet Intelligence Scale was asked, "What is a house made of?" The answer "A house is made of walls" was marked incorrect; the only "correct" answers gave materials—like wood, bricks, or stone. A critic concluded that "the accepted responses do not incorporate all reasonably intelligent responses to the question" (Miller-Jones, 1989, p. 361).

We might ask why schools should use tests that ignore cultural bias, when, to succeed, the children will have to function in a particular culture. Should tests take a minority culture into account: Should society as a whole make room for that culture? How we answer these questions affects how we apply our knowledge of child development. Two phenomena apparently influenced by culture are the high achievement levels of Asian children (see Box 12-2) and the disparity in intelligence test scores between black and white American children.

What do you think? *Is intelligence related to how well a person perceives and adapts to the culture? Give reasons for your answers.*

Cultural Differences in IQ Test Scores. Although there is considerable overlap in intelligence test scores, with some African Americans scoring higher than most whites, on average black Americans tend to score about 15 points lower on IQ tests than white Americans (L. R. Brody, 1985). Most modern educators say that this difference in scores reflects typical differences in *environment* between the two groups—in education, in cultural traditions, and in other circumstances that affect self-esteem and motivation—as well as in academic performance itself. Let's examine the basis for this belief.

Differences between black and white children's test performance do not appear in infancy. Not until about 2 or 3 years of age do black children lag behind in intelligence test scores (Golden, Birns, & Bridger, 1973). Some research suggests

BOX 12-2 ■ AROUND THE WORLD

HOW CAN ASIAN CHILDREN ACHIEVE SO MUCH?

They seemed to have three strikes against them—southeast Asian boat children. They suffered disruption and trauma as they escaped from their native countries; they lost months or even years, of formal schooling; and they knew no English when they arrived in the United States. Still, Indochinese refugee children quickly began to excel in their new schools (N. Caplan, Choy, & Whitmore, 1992). The academic success of these children mirrors that of many Asian children. How are young Asian Americans able to make such a strong showing by almost every educational measure? Research has yielded a number of answers.

INDIVIDUAL COGNITIVE ABILITY

In a cross-cultural study of American, Japanese, and Chinese children, researchers designed a test to assess children's cognitive abilities on the basis of common experiences (H. W. Stevenson et al., 1985). Test items, given in all three languages, included verbal tasks (repeating lists of words and numbers, following spoken directions, answering questions about stories and everyday facts, and defining words) and nonverbal tasks (learning a code, completing a square, matching shapes, and recalling rhythms). Urban first- and fifth-graders in all three countries also took specially designed reading and math tests.

Asian students do not start out with any overall cognitive superiority. In fact, American first-graders outperform Asians on many tasks, possibly because they are more used to answering adults' questions (Chinese children are expected to "be seen but not heard") and have had more cultural experiences, like going to museums, zoos, and movies (which Asian children do not have until they go to school) (Song & Ginsburg, 1987).

Recent comparisons of Asian and American students found two trends. Although the American students' mathematical abilities declined from first to eleventh grade when compared with the abilities of Asian students, their general information scores became increasingly similar (H. W. Stevenson, Chen, & Lee, 1993). These authors concluded that these differences indict American schools. Since children learn math skills almost entirely in school, high-level teaching makes the difference. On the other hand, general information can be learned outside of school, and American students do acquire it. The superior performance of Asian children seems, then, to be related to cultural and educational differences.

SOCIAL ECOLOGY: FAMILY AND CULTURAL ATTITUDES

In Japan, a child's entrance into school is a greater occasion for celebration than is graduation from high school: First-graders receive such expensive gifts as desks, chairs, and leather backpacks. Japanese and Korean parents spend a great deal of time helping children with schoolwork, and Japanese children who fall behind receive private tutoring or go to *jukus,* private remedial and enrichment schools (McKinney, 1987; Song & Ginsburg, 1987).

Chinese and Japanese mothers—but not Americans—view academic achievement as their children's most important pursuit; and Asian mothers hold higher standards for their children's academic achievement (H. W. Stevenson et al., 1993; H. W. Stevenson, Lee, Chen & Stigler 1990; H. W. Stevenson et al., 1990). American mothers express much more satisfaction with their children's school performance and their schools than do Asian mothers (H. W. Stevenson et al., 1993).

In southeast Asian families, children spend much more time on homework than do American children. Parents help them by setting daily goals and relieving children of household chores. Parents read aloud, set examples of egalitarian role-sharing, and expect equivalent achievements from boys and girls. Older brothers and sisters help younger ones, learning as they teach. Asian students are expected to devote themselves almost entirely to study, whereas

---

that African American babies are precocious on developmental tests (Bayley, 1965; Geber, 1962; Geber & Dean, 1957). The difference that shows up later may reflect the switch from predominantly motor to predominantly verbal tests—and verbal ability is highly influenced by environmental factors. After the first 2 or 3 years of life, the environment seems to make more of a difference.

The influence of the environment also shows up when we compare people from different socioeconomic levels. The same pattern that holds for American white and black test-takers (an average difference of 15 points) also holds for American middle-class and deprived rural and mountain children and for Eng-

BOX 12-2   AROUND THE WORLD *(continued)*

HOW CAN ASIAN CHILDREN ACHIEVE SO MUCH?

American students are more likely to hold after-school jobs, go out on dates, engage in sports, and do chores. Most important perhaps is an overwhelming feeling that learning is valuable, that mastery is satisfying in and of itself, and that effort is more important than ability (H. W. Stevenson et al., 1993; N. Caplan, Choy, & Whitmore, 1992).

In their (often valid) perception of limited chances for success in American life, partly because of language limitations, partly because of unfamiliarity with the culture, and partly because of prejudice from other Americans, many Asian Americans see education as the best route to upward mobility and are, therefore, highly motivated (Sue & Okazaki, 1990).

EDUCATIONAL PRACTICES

Academic and classroom practices differ, too (Song & Ginsburg, 1987; Stigler, Lee, & Stevenson, 1987). Asian teachers spend more time teaching the class as a whole, while American teachers focus more on small groups. Japanese and Chinese teachers spend more than three-fourths of their time with the entire class; American teachers spend less than half. American children spend more time working alone (often at problems they do not understand) or in small groups (with other children who do not understand the work), rather than listening to the teacher teach. Although the American approach offers more individual attention, each child ends up with less total instruction.

Classroom behavior plays a part. American children are out of their seats and engaged in irrelevant activities 5 times more often than are Chinese and Japanese children, who are more obedient. Chinese and Japanese children spend more time on homework, get more help from parents, and like doing homework more than do American children (C. Chen & Stevenson, 1989).

Finally, Asian children spend more time in school each year, more time in classes each day, and more time being taught mathematics—partly because the curriculum is centrally set rather than left up to individual teachers. Although Asian teachers generally do not have as much education as their American counterparts, they are more knowledgeable in their own subjects. To raise American students' proficiency in math and science, it would be necessary not only to provide more hours of education, possibly by lengthening the school day and school year, but also to help American teachers improve their own proficiency.

PSYCHOLOGICAL ADJUSTMENT

The common belief is that high-achieving Asian students suffer psychologically. However, American students report more frequent feelings of stress, academic anxiety, and aggression—with school seen as the most common source of stress, over peers, family, sports, and jobs (H. W. Stevenson et al., 1993). So the poorer academic achievement of American students does not buy them peace of mind.

What happens to students when they leave school? Although 90 percent of Japanese students graduate from high school, compared with 76 percent of American students, only 29 percent go to college, compared with 58 percent in the United States (Simons, 1987). What are these people like as adults? A growing number of Japanese parents, students, and lawyers argue that regimentation stifles individuality; and they are raising legal challenges to many long-established practices (Chira, 1988). Culture shapes attitudes and encourages some kinds of behaviors rather than others. It is apparently culture rather than inborn ability that has helped Asian students achieve so much in school. If cultural standards in either the east or the west change, the relative standing of students will probably change too. The citizens in a culture determine priorities, which are then reflected in their children's lives.

---

lish middle-class and low-income canal-boat and Gypsy children (Pettigrew, 1964). Furthermore, African American children from northern cities score higher than those in the rural south (Baughman, 1971), and middle-class blacks score better than do poor blacks (Loehlin, Lindzey, & Spuhler, 1975).

Researchers have suggested measures to assess ability fairly across racial and ethnic groups. These measures include:

■ Developing ways to tell how much assimilation to majority culture is required by specific test items

- Gauging individual test-takers in terms of whether they hold European, African, or Asian value systems
- Questioning examinees about the meanings of their "wrong" answers
- Using interactive assessment based on Vygotsky's models (see Chapter 9)
- Acknowledging environmental influences—like the tendency of white evaluators to assess white performance more positively than black performance (Kraiger & Ford, 1985)
- Using separate norms for different racial and ethnic groups (Helms, 1992)

One major determinant of intelligence scores that is strongly influenced by the environment is language ability.

DEVELOPMENT OF LANGUAGE IN MIDDLE CHILDHOOD

As a first-grader, Vicky talks her parents' ears off, pronounces her words clearly, and can converse easily about many things. Still, there are many words she does not know and many subtleties of language she does not appreciate. Language abilities continue to grow during middle childhood. Children are now better able to understand and interpret communications—and to make themselves understood.

GRAMMAR: THE STRUCTURE OF LANGUAGE

Imagine that you are home on a winter day. You look out the window at a snow-covered driveway, and you ask your father how you are going to get the family car out of the garage. Your father would probably just tell you where to find the snow shovel—but for the purpose of this discussion, let's assume that he says something like, "Elton promised Madonna to shovel the driveway" or "Elton told Madonna to shovel the driveway." Depending on which answer you receive, you know whether to expect Elton or Madonna to appear, shovel in hand. Many children under 5 or 6 years of age do not understand the difference between these two sentences and think that they *both* mean that Madonna is to do the shoveling (C. S. Chomsky, 1969). Their confusion is understandable, since almost all English verbs that might replace *told* in the second sentence (such as *ordered, wanted,* and *expected*) would put the shovel in Madonna's hand.

Most 6-year-olds have not yet learned how to deal with grammatical constructions in which a word is used the way *promise* is used in the first sentence, even though they know what a promise is and are able to use and understand the word correctly in other sentences. By age 8, most children can interpret the first sentence correctly. They know the concept attached to the word *promise,* and they know how the word can be used.

Even though 6-year-olds use complex grammar and a vocabulary of several thousand words, they still have to master many fine points of language. During the early school years, they rarely use the passive voice (as in "The driveway is being shoveled by Yoko"), verb tenses that include the auxiliary *have* ("Elvis has already shoveled it"), and conditional sentences ("If D.M.C. were home, they would all shovel the driveway").

Up to and possibly after age 9, children develop an increasingly complex understanding of *syntax,* the way words are organized into phrases and sentences

syntax *Way in which words are organized into phrases and sentences.*

TABLE 12-2

ACQUISITION OF COMPLEX SYNTACTIC STRUCTURES

STRUCTURE	DIFFICULT CONCEPT	AGE OF ACQUISITION
John is easy to see.	Who is doing the seeing?	5.6 to 9 years.*
John promised Bill to go.	Who is going?	5.6 to 9 years.*
John asked Bill what to do.	Who is doing it?	Some 10-year-olds still have not learned this.
He knew that John was going to win the race.	Does the "he" refer to John?	5.6 years.

*All children 9 and over know this.
SOURCE: C. S. Chomsky, 1969.

(C. S. Chomsky, 1969). When testing forty 5- to 10-year-old children's understanding of various syntactic structures, Carol S. Chomsky found considerable variation in the ages of children who understood the syntax and of children who did not. (See Table 12-2.)

PRAGMATICS: LANGUAGE AND COMMUNICATION

When the dentist gave 6-year-old Jason a fluoride treatment, she told him not to eat for half an hour. Jason interpreted this to mean that he was not to *swallow* for half an hour. Soon after leaving the examining room, he started to drool and looked very upset, and he was greatly relieved when the dentist, noticing this, told him that he could swallow his saliva.

Even though Jason has arrived at a higher level of linguistic ability, he is still, like many children of his age, having problems with communication. Of course, adults, too, often misinterpret what other people say—resulting in misunderstandings, both cognitive and emotional. Children's failures in interpreting messages often stem from ignorance of *metacommunication,* knowledge of how communication takes place. This knowledge grows throughout middle childhood.

In one experiment to test children's ability to transmit and understand spoken information, kindergartners and second-graders were asked to construct block buildings exactly like those built by another child and to do this on the basis of the first child's audiotaped instructions—without seeing the buildings themselves (Flavell, Speer, Green, & August, 1981). The instructions were often incomplete, ambiguous, or contradictory. The "builders" were then asked if they thought that their buildings looked like the models they were copying and whether they thought the instructions were good or bad.

The older children were more likely to notice when instructions were inadequate and to pause or look puzzled. They were much more likely to know when they did not understand something and to see the implications of unclear communication—that their buildings might not look exactly like the models because they had not received good-enough instructions. The younger children sometimes knew that the instructions were not clear, but they did not seem to realize that this would mean that they might not be able to do the job. Even the older children (8 years old or so) did not show a thorough understanding of communication.

Findings like these have significant implications. Young children often do not

metacommunication
Knowledge of the communication process.

understand what they see, hear, or read, but they may not be aware that they do not understand. Adults need to realize that they cannot take children's understanding for granted. For children's safety, well-being, and academic advancement, we have to be aware whether children do, in fact, know what we want them to know.

CHILDREN'S HUMOR

At 6 years of age, Vicky tells made-up "jokes" like this: "My shoes have been getting untied all day, and most of the night!" She then has a fit of giggles, seeing the incongruity in what she has just said. By age 8, Vicky is telling jokes that combine a safe way to deal with strong emotions (like jealousy) with the growing language ability that lets her enjoy playing with words. So she relates:

"Mom, Bobby is really spoiled!"

"He is *not*."

"Oh, no? You should see what the steamroller did to him!"

Vicky continues to make puns, use wrong words and deliberate mispronunciations, and tell riddles, not only to express her feelings, but also to show her factual knowledge, her mastery of language, and her ability in symbolic, logical, and abstract reasoning. Her appreciation of humor and her ability to create it herself grow as her cognitive abilities develop (McGhee & Chapman, 1980, cited in Masten, 1986).

In one study, children in grades 5 through 8 looked at "Ziggy" cartoons and were asked to rate them on funniness, to explain what made them funny, and to make up captions or titles ("What could the bird be saying to Ziggy that would be funny here?"). The children were also tested for competence.

The most competent children had the best sense of humor—they were most capable of understanding and appreciating humor and creating their own, and these abilities seemed to grow with age. These children were regarded more pos-

In a study, children in grades 5 through 8 were asked to grade "Ziggy" cartoons on funniness, to explain what made them funny, and to make up captions or titles ("What could Ziggy be saying to the cat that would be funny here?"). The most competent children had the best sense of humor. (©1991 by Ziggy & Friends, Inc. All rights reserved. Universal Press Syndicate.)

itively in school. Their teachers considered them more attentive, cooperative, responsive, and productive; and they were popular with their classmates, who saw them as happy, gregarious leaders with good ideas for things to do (Masten, 1986). It seems likely that general cognitive abilities underlie both successful adaptation in the classroom and the development of humor.

DEVELOPMENT OF LITERACY

In the first few grades of school, Vicky, like the other children in her classes, keeps a journal in which she records special experiences. In another notebook she writes and illustrates stories that she shows to her teacher, who helps her edit them. Finally, Vicky reads them to her classmates, who comment and ask questions. In first grade, encouraged to use phonetic spelling to get her thoughts down on paper, she writes "Vicky is pading [petting] da cat." In second grade she learns formal spellings. The new words she uses end up in a personal dictionary. This program enhances her ability to use reading and writing in day-to-day life.

As Vicky's facility with writing grows as a result of the input she receives from her parents, her teachers, and her peers, we see further evidence of the impact of social interaction on the development of literacy. In Chapters 6 and 9 we emphasized the roles of parents and teachers in encouraging literacy. While adults are still important in the school years, now peers also exert a major influence.

In their earlier years children needed to become familiar with the idea of reading. Now they use reading and writing for the same kinds of purposes that adults do. They read for enjoyment, for learning facts and discovering ideas, and to stimulate their own thinking. They write to express ideas, thoughts, and feelings. The social contexts in which they live foster the growth of literacy.

Sociocultural Aspects of Literacy Development

Vygotsky saw the use of symbols to link the mind of the individual with the collective consciousness of culture as a distinctly human behavior. He saw this link occurring through social interaction. In line with this perspective, Anne Haas Dyson (1993) looked into the changes over time in how children use writing to take part in activities valued by their culture. After reading journal entries and stories by 4- to 8-year-old African American children from working-class homes, she concluded that other people's responses give social meaning to a child's use of symbols like words and pictures.

These children initially "wrote" by talking and drawing. They expressed their thoughts and feelings to each other, talked about, and acted out each other's stories. There were individual differences in the way the children created their stories, some concocting action-driven adventures and others focusing on characters. One kindergartner drew a "motorcycle guy" swirling and crashing around a racetrack; another drew a doll and a bird, explaining, "This is the bird that's flying him to the hospital" (Dyson, 1993, p. 31).

The children used their stories to strengthen their relationships with the other children. They put their friends into stories as characters and included words or actions designed to tease or amuse the other children. The stories influenced and were influenced by the children's ongoing social lives.

As children become literate, they strengthen their membership in their culture. They use writing to make social connections, as when third-grader Ayesha

wrote about rap stars seen on television and another child commented on the performers. They also try to gain their peers' attention and respect by the kind of
writing they do, as when they use rhyme, rhythm, and humor. So first-grader
Jameel (inspired by Dr. Seuss) wrote about two friends who sat on each other until Cat was run over by a car and Hat called 911: "Sat on Cat. Sat on Hat. Hat Sat
on CAT. CAT GoN.911 for Cat" (Dyson, 1993, p. 36). Children, then, use language
in particular ways with particular aims, which involve not only the words they
write or speak, but how they themselves relate to the people and the world around
them.

When Friends Write Together: Links between Cognitive and Emotional Domains

In the typical classroom, children work alone and are discouraged from discussing
their work with other children. This is based on the belief that children—especially friends—will distract one another, will turn learning time into playtime,
and will discourage each other from doing their best work. Research based on
Vygotsky's social interaction model suggests that this is not so and that children
progress more when they write with other children, especially friends.

The findings from an experiment comparing 60 fourth-graders, some writing
alone and others in friend or nonfriend pairs, supported the value of collaboration, especially between friends. The children were asked to write pieces that
would become part of a class publication about the rain forest (Daiute, Hartup,
Sholl, & Zajac, 1993). Children working in pairs wrote stories with more solutions
to problems, more explanations and goals, and fewer errors in syntax and word
use than did children working alone. Children working with friends focused more
intently on the work than did the acquaintance pairs, who tended to stray from
the task, joke around, and make less of a joint effort. The friend pairs collaborated
in complex ways, elaborating on each other's ideas, working as a team, and posing alternative ideas.

What makes collaboration between friends so fruitful? Some possible explanations have been offered: Since friends know one another well, they understand
each other's needs, abilities, and likely behaviors; they expect reciprocal commitment from each other; and they are more comfortable and trusting, which may
give them the courage to take intellectual risks (Hartup, in press).

BILINGUALISM AND BILINGUAL EDUCATION

bilingual education
Educational program in which children are taught in more than one language.

bilingualism *Fluency in two languages.*

More than 2.5 million school-age children in the United States come from non-
English-speaking homes (Hakuta & Garcia, 1989). To help these children, many
school districts have implemented programs of *bilingual education.* To encourage *bilingualism,* or fluency in two languages, some schools teach children in their
native language first and then switch to English. Others immerse them in English from the very beginning, using a TESL (Teaching English as a Second Language) approach.

One controversy about bilingual education revolves around which of the two
approaches is more effective. This question is hard to answer, since most research
has focused only on how well children learn English—not how well they do in
school and society in general (Hakuta & Garcia, 1989). One advantage of the first
approach is that, by emphasizing the value of reading and writing their native

language, children become truly bilingual and can also feel proud of their cultural identity.

Another question is whether a child with two languages will fail to become really fluent in either one. This does not seem to be the case. In fact, when the second language has been added with no sacrifice to the first and where bilingualism is admired, children who speak two languages tend to reach higher levels of cognitive achievement (Hakuta, Ferdman, & Diaz, 1987). Knowing one language does not interfere with learning a second; and learning the second does not rob a child of fluency in the first. As one observer commented, having two languages is more like having two children than like having two wives (Fallows, 1986).

Bilingual children can usually switch easily from one language to the other (Zentella, 1981). Changing speech to match the situation, or *code-switching,* seems to come naturally to children. They learn very early, for example, to talk to their parents differently from the way they talk to their friends. One common example of code-switching occurs among some African Americans who speak standard English at school or work and in the outside world, then switch to "black English" when talking with family or friends. Black English, spoken by some black Americans, has a distinctive grammar that seems to derive from African languages. Since it does not conform to standard English, its use in the wider society can be a drawback, whereas its informal use can emphasize cultural bonds.

code-switching *Process of changing one's speech to match the situation.*

Another concern is the cost of bilingualism. For a program to be effective, teachers need to know and be able to teach both languages, and classes need to be small. Many school districts consider bilingual programs a luxury they cannot afford. However, many children who are plunged into English-speaking classrooms without special instruction in English fall behind in their schoolwork and eventually drop out, which, in the end, costs society more than does bilingual education (Cardenas, 1977; Cummins, 1986; McLaughlin, 1985).

Bilingualism is not only an educational issue; it is also a political issue, as in Canada, where Canadian-born children are expected to learn both English and French, although some districts are populated more by one cultural group than the other. In the United States, the issue is more about how best to integrate newcomers. Also, bilingualism has psychological ramifications, since identity is entwined with culture and language, and self-esteem is affected by what happens in school and by proficiency in society.

THE CHILD IN SCHOOL

Jason, in second grade, is in the auditorium listening to the author of a book about the brain. After her talk, the speaker asks the children whether they have any questions. Shyly, Jason asks, "Do headaches come from the brain?" Ten years later, Jason remembers that day with pain. "That woman laughed at me. The way she smiled and her tone of voice made me feel I had asked the dumbest question in the world. I think that's one of the things that happened to me when I was little that made me the way I am today. I *hate* to ask questions in class!"

School assumes a central place in Jason's life. His experience in school affects and is affected by every aspect of his development—cognitive, physical, social, and emotional. Yet child-care professionals and educators often disagree on how school can best enhance children's development, as we can see in the great swings in educational theory over the past several decades.

What happens in school affects and is affected by every aspect of development—cognitive, physical, social, and emotional.

RECENT TRENDS IN EDUCATION

Conflicting views, along with historical events, have brought changes in educational theory and practice during this century. The traditional curriculum, centered on the "three Rs" (reading, 'riting, and 'rithmetic), gave way first to "child-centered" methods that focused on children's interests and then, during the late 1950s, to an emphasis on science and mathematics to overcome the Soviet lead in the space race. Rigorous studies were then replaced during the turbulent 1960s by student-directed learning in "open classrooms," where children engaged in varied activities and teachers served as "facilitators." High school students took more electives and student-initiated courses. Then, in the mid-1970s, a decline in high school students' scores on the Scholastic Aptitude Test (SAT) sent schools back to the "basics."

Today many educators oppose the "back-to-basics" approach. Instead, they recommend teaching in a way that builds on children's natural interests and talents: teaching reading and writing, for example, in the context of a social studies project or teaching math concepts in the study of music. They urge the use of cooperative projects, hands-on experience, using concrete materials to solve problems, and close parent-teacher cooperation. Contemporary educators also emphasize a "fourth R"—reasoning (Rescorla, 1991). Children who are taught thinking skills perform better on intelligence tests and in school.

INFLUENCES ON CHILDREN'S SCHOOLING

Children do not attend school in a social vacuum. Every aspect of the social context of their lives—from their own personalities and characteristics, to their immediate families, to what goes on in their classrooms, and finally to the messages they receive from the larger culture (like "it's not cool to be smart")—plays a role.

Here we focus on factors relating to the child, the parents, the classroom teacher, and the culture, all of which affect children's progress in school.

The Child

Temperament. How does a child's temperament affect the way the child does in school? Does a "teacher's pet" type, who is polite and helpful, make better academic progress? What about a fidgety child who throws tantrums, cannot sit still, and has a short attention span? How important are such characteristics as enthusiasm, interest in the subject, attentiveness, and active participation in class?

To answer these questions, 790 first-graders from a range of ethnic, racial, and economic groups were followed for 4 years (Alexander, Entwisle, & Dauber, 1993). When the researchers compared teachers' ratings of the children, they found that being cooperative and compliant was unrelated to achievement test scores or marks on reading and math. Interest, attention, and active participation were, however, associated with achievement test scores in the first year of the study and with teachers' marks in grades 1, 2, and 4. To progress academically, a child needs to pay attention, to be interested in the subject matter, and to participate actively in school routines.

Temperamentally driven behavior is related to achievement in two ways. First, children who apply themselves to work and cause few problems are likely to get higher marks, which reinforces their behavior and may motivate them toward greater efforts. Second, teachers' marks are subjective and are influenced by whether a child tries hard, pays attention, and participates. These authors believe that children's patterns of classroom behavior are set in first grade and that this time offers a "window of opportunity" for parents and teachers to help a child form good learning habits or to give a child special assistance.

Emotional State. A child's school performance is also related to his or her emotional life. The various aspects of children's personalities are not separate from each other; they interact, with each one influencing the others. One study explored the connection between emotional characteristics and school performance for 143 eight- to eleven-year-olds. Researchers assessed the children on levels of empathy and asked them questions designed to elicit levels of aggression, anxiety, depression, and self-esteem. The children were tested on reading, spelling, and arithmetic and were rated by teachers on aggression and depression (Feshbach & Feshbach, 1987).

The relationship between emotional and cognitive functioning was especially strong for girls. Depression and aggression both seem to interfere with the development of cognitive skills, whereas empathy is associated with good scores in reading and spelling. How are these connections made? Let's look at empathy.

The ability to imagine how another person is feeling is a cognitive skill, which in our society is fostered more in girls than in boys. A child's sensitivity to other people's feelings can help create a more positive social environment in school. It may also help in reading (which often calls for assuming the point of view of a literary character), understanding historical events, and planning that predicts another person's response. Also, cognitive ability can help children understand and profit from their dealings with other people and make them more empathic. On the other hand, problems with schoolwork may make a child depressed or frustrated, leading to aggressiveness.

The Parents

A large body of research shows the importance of an active family role in a number of school-related areas. (See Box 12-3.)

Motivating Children. How do parents motivate their children to do well in school? How do they fail to motivate them? Some try *extrinsic* (external) motivation—giving children money or treats for good grades or punishing them for bad ones. Others encourage children to develop their own *intrinsic* (internal) motivation—praising them for ability and hard work.

Intrinsic motivation seems more effective. In a study of fifth-graders and their parents, the highest achievers had parents who fit Diana Baumrind's description of *authoritative* parents. (See Chapter 10.) They fostered intrinsic motivation by encouraging and praising children and enhancing their autonomy. Their children prefer challenging tasks over easy ones, are curious and interested in learning, and like to solve problems on their own.

On the other hand, *authoritarian* parents, who try too hard—reminding children to do their homework, closely overseeing it, and relying on extrinsic motivation—tend to have low-achieving children. By controlling children too much, they may undermine the children's ability to trust their own opinions about what work to do or to judge their success or failure in school. Parents who fit Baumrind's category of *permissive* parents—who are too uninvolved and do not seem to care how their children do in school—also have low-achieving children (G. S. Ginsburg & Bronstein, 1993).

Since this was a correlational study, we cannot draw firm conclusions about causation. Influence between parents and children tends to be bidirectional: Parents respond to their children's achievement patterns. At their wit's end, the parents of a poor achiever may resort to bribes and threats and feel obliged to sit over him to be sure he does his homework. On the other hand, parents of a child who is already intrinsically motivated may not feel the need to offer rewards or punishments or to take an active role in schoolwork. Some parental involvement, of course, is desirable. Part of the ongoing difficulty of parenting is knowing where to draw the line.

Parental Beliefs. Children are affected not only by what their parents do, but also by what they think. Another distinction between parents of high and low achievers in the study just described was in how much control they thought they had over their own lives. Parents who assumed that outside forces were responsible for their fate had children who were less persistent in doing their work. Such parents may not teach their children that what they do can affect how their lives go (G. S. Ginsburg & Bronstein, 1993).

Many parental beliefs come down via cultural routes. A California survey related parents' beliefs about child rearing, intelligence, and education to children's school performance (Okagaki & Sternberg, 1993). Of the 359 parents studied, some were immigrants from Mexico, Cambodia, Vietnam, and the Philippines; native-born parents were either Mexican American or Anglo-American.

There were significant differences in parental beliefs. Anglo-American parents rated cognitive abilities (like creativity and verbal expression) the most important factors in intelligence, whereas all the other groups held noncognitive elements to be very important. Filipino and Vietnamese parents ranked motivation

BOX 12-3 ■ FOOD FOR THOUGHT

HOW PARENTS INFLUENCE CHILDREN'S SCHOOL ACHIEVEMENT

An 11-year-old student in New York City beams as he shows his mother how to run a computer program in a parent-child class at his school. Other parents explore the possibility of such classes in other schools. The Pepsa program (Parents involved in Education Planning for Students Achievement), unique to this school district, serves a low-income, minority-group population (Wells, 1988a, 1988b). It seems to be the wave of the future as research shows the importance of parents' participation in the academic success of children from all socioeconomic levels.

WHAT PARENTS OF ACHIEVING CHILDREN DO

The following aspects of parental involvement seem important in helping children do well in school (G. S. Ginsburg & Bronstein, 1993; D. L. Stevenson & Baker, 1987; Hess & Holloway, 1984):

♦ *Parents talk to their children.* The parents of achieving children spend time with them, read to them and listen to them read, ask them for information (even when the parents already know the answer), and encourage them to speak correctly and take part in family conversation.

♦ *Parents have high expectations for their children.* These parents encourage their children to master developmental tasks early and do them completely and correctly; they expect children to do well in school and put pressure on them to achieve.

♦ *Parents have warm relationships with their children.* They nurture their children, rarely restrict or punish them, acknowledge their feelings and needs, and help them express negative emotions.

♦ *Parents use the authoritative style of child rearing.* They are firm but reasonable, expecting children to remember—and follow—everyday routines, chores, and schedules. They invite children's input in decision making, state their expectations in a suggestive way rather than a directive one, and provide choices. They tend to be neither permissive nor authoritarian.

♦ *Parents believe in their children.* The parents' conviction that their children can do well boosts the children's self-esteem, motivation, expectations for themselves, and performance.

♦ *Parents foster intrinsic rather than extrinsic motivation.* Instead of offering children money or treats for good grades or depriving them of privileges for bad ones, they praise their children for their ability and their efforts.

♦ *Parents become involved in their children's school.* They take an active role at school, meet with the child's teacher, attend PTA meetings, and take action to address any problems their children have at school.

SUGGESTIONS FOR HELPING CHILDREN READ BETTER

By determining what the parents of achieving children do, researchers have correlated certain adult activities with children's reading achievement (Hess & Holloway, 1984). The following suggestions are based on these research findings:

♦ Show children how reading can enhance their lives by reading yourself and by talking about books and ideas.

♦ Pick up on children's interests by answering their questions about written words in everyday settings (stop signs, signs on stores, signs on restrooms).

♦ Take children to the library and encourage them to select their own books.

♦ Read—and reread—their favorite books to them. Ask them questions that require more than a yes-no answer. Ask them to identify objects in pictures. Refer to the books in conversation.

♦ When they are able, ask them to read to you. (Before children can read, they often memorize stories and enjoy "reading" to you from memory.) Your interest means a great deal.

♦ Buy them books—storybooks, picture dictionaries, alphabet books, and early readers.

♦ Provide writing materials like paper, pencils, and blackboards.

♦ Talk to children about everyday events, things, or people you see on the street, or their favorite television programs. Expand on or clarify what they say.

♦ Play games that involve repetition of language patterns, like filling in words of familiar poems.

♦ Break tasks into manageable pieces, and help children when they run into trouble (like pronouncing a new word).

♦ Encourage children and praise them—always making it fun to learn. Too much pressure leads to tears and learning blocks. Do not try to teach children to read at an early age; this is not correlated with early reading and can push children beyond their abilities.

♦ Above all, believe in the children—and show your confidence. They can do much more when they believe they can do it.

especially highly, emphasizing the importance of working hard to achieve one's goals. Latino parents emphasized social skills, supporting Gardner's (1983) theory of multiple intelligences, which includes interpersonal skills as one important aspect of intelligence. Interestingly, no relationship appeared between parents' beliefs about intelligence and their children's school performance, and there was a negative relationship between beliefs about social skills and performance.

One difference in parents' beliefs about child rearing was reflected in the children's schoolwork. This revolved around conformity to external standards, a value rated low by American-born parents but high by immigrants. Children of parents who valued conformity did not achieve as well in school as did other children, although copying or conforming to what others are doing undoubtedly helps newcomers adapt to their new home.

This study's identification of cultural differences in parental beliefs may help teachers understand and help students develop a way of life that reflects the traditions and values of two cultures. We need to remember, however, that the study was based on western psychological theories, which may not be universally valid. For example, one measure of student self-confidence in the study was a student's maintenance of eye contact while speaking or when spoken to; in some societies children are considered rude if they look directly into adults' eyes. (For a glimpse of school in a different culture, see Box 12-4.)

Parental Involvement in School Activities.   Are children likely to do better in school if their parents come to parent-teacher conferences? Is school success more likely if parents join the PTA? The answer to both questions is yes—especially for younger pupils. One study evaluated the relationship between children's school performance, their mothers' education levels, and their parents' involvement in school activities. The focus on the mother's education rested on the fact that mothers are usually more involved than fathers in school activities (D. L. Stevenson & Baker, 1987).

The mother's education was important in only one sense: More highly educated mothers were more likely to be involved at school, and children of more involved parents performed better. Neither the mother's employment status nor the number of children in the family affected the child's school performance. Since a mother's involvement in school, rather than her education or employment per se, is the crucial variable, it seems likely that if mothers with less education became more involved in school activities, their children would benefit.

The Teacher

Jason loves his second-grade teacher, sometimes calling her "Mommy" by mistake. Ms. Tolliver has become a parent substitute, an imparter of values, and a contributor to Jason's self-esteem. A teacher's influence can even reach into adulthood.

The adult successes of a number of people who had grown up in a poor city neighborhood have been linked to a very special first-grade teacher. As adults, "Miss A's" former pupils showed greater increases in IQ, held better jobs, lived in better housing, and had a neater personal appearance than did other graduates of the school (E. Pederson, Faucher, & Eaton, 1978). What did Miss A do? She showed confidence in children's ability and encouraged them to work hard to justify it. She was affectionate and gave extra time to children who needed it.

BOX 12-4 ■ AROUND THE WORLD

SCHOOL IN A HIMALAYAN VILLAGE

Sally Olds wrote the following description of a school in Badel, an isolated village in Nepal, after her visits to the village in 1993 and 1994.

Those of us who have attended schools and sent our children to schools in the western world in the latter half of the twentieth century have one picture of what a school should be like. The picture is quite different in developing countries. For example, the only light in any of the seven classrooms of the Shree Jalpa Lawor Secondary School in the Nepalese village of Badel comes through a doorway and a single small window. The dim rooms have no furniture except for a few benches and long narrow tables that serve as desks. The school day runs from 10 a.m. till 4 p.m., with an hour's break.

The school's six teachers instruct their 250 students from first through sixth grades in 3 languages—Nepali, English, and Sanskrit—and in mathematics, sociology, history, science, health, and agriculture. In the sixth grade class, the 21 students—15 boys and 6 girls—sitting on those benches rise as we American visitors enter.

At 11, Kiran, the boy in the family we are staying with, is the youngest and smallest child in the class; the oldest are a handsome 17-year-old youth with a deep voice and a bosomy 16-year-old young woman in pigtails. The students show us their school books: They have no story lines, no lively characters, no brightly colored illustrations, nothing to entice a reluctant learner. The children learn mostly by rote.

Kiran's accomplishments look even more impressive than they had before. As young as he is, he is the most proficient speaker of English in his class. Bright-eyed, alert, eager to learn—and to practice what he has learned—he stands out. His motivation may be explained in part by the fact that he comes from a family that encourages education; Kiran's brother is the only university graduate in the village.

In Nepal, teaching is almost entirely a male profession. In this school, however, one quiet sari-clad woman is on the faculty. After learning that she walks two hours each way to get to and from school every day to teach English, we understand why she's not more talkative.

These children are so well behaved most of the time that even during unsupervised hours, they do their work and stay out of trouble. This self-discipline is demonstrated a few days after our visit to the school. One day Kiran trudged home at about 5, exhausted after a school field trip. The children had set out at 6 a.m. and climbed up mountainous terrain for about 3000 feet to an altitude of some 8000 feet. For 11 hours only one teacher was in charge of 100 children—an unheard-of ratio in the United States, where there would be at least one adult for every 10 children.

These children's ability to learn despite lack of the tools and practices considered essential in the developed world may well lie in the reasons they are able to take such a trip. Throughout our days in the village, we don't see children being scolded, spanked or even isolated, either at home or in school. They don't act mean or aggressive, they do what adults ask them to do, and although they horse around with one another, their boisterousness rarely gets out of hand. They are high-spirited and lively, fun to be with, quick to laugh, able to find amusement and delight in the simplest aspects of daily life.

They seem like textbook cases illustrating the results of authoritative parenting and the value of such noncognitive factors as respect for authority, the ability to pay attention, and an interest in learning. Given opportunities for further education and work, they are bound to take advantage of them.

SOURCE: Sally Wendkos Olds, 1995.

Miss A's belief in her pupils undoubtedly had much to do with how well they did. According to the principle of the *self-fulfilling prophecy,* students live up to—or down to—other people's expectations for them. In the "Oak School" experiment, teachers were told at the beginning of the term that some students had shown unusual potential for cognitive growth. Actually, the children identified as potential "bloomers" had been chosen at random. Yet several months later, many of them—especially first- and second-graders—showed unusual gains in IQ. The teachers seemed to like the "bloomers" better. They did not spend more time with them than with the others, nor did they treat them differently in any obvious ways. Subtler influences may have been at work—possibly the teachers' voice, facial expressions, touch, and posture (R. Rosenthal & Jacobson, 1968).

self-fulfilling prophecy
Prediction of behavior, which biases people to act as though the prediction were already true.

Teachers exert a great deal of influence over their pupils. According to the self-fulfilling prophecy, if this teacher believes that this boy is capable of high achievement, he will do better in school than if she has less faith in him.

Although this research has been criticized for methodological shortcomings, other researchers have confirmed the basic principle—that teachers' expectations "can and do function as self-fulfilling prophecies, although not always or automatically" (Brophy & Good, 1974, p. 32). Even first-graders are aware that teachers treat high and low achievers differently. One study found that this awareness did not seem to affect first graders' opinions of themselves very much, but by fifth grade the effect was marked (Weinstein, Marshall, Sharp, & Botkin, 1987).

This principle has important implications for minority-group and poor children. Since many middle-class teachers may be convinced (often subconsciously) that such students have cognitive limitations, they may somehow convey their limited expectations to the children, thus getting from them the little that they expect.

What do you think? *Can you think of an example in your own life of a self-fulfilling prophecy?*

The Culture

The difficulties many minority-group children have in school often stem from social ecology. When their culture values different behavioral styles than the majority culture does, they are handicapped. In the past, these children were considered to be suffering from a cultural *deficit;* today educators refer to cultural *difference,* with its own cognitive and behavioral strengths (Tharp, 1989).

The value of designing educational programs to conform to cultural styles has been demonstrated by the Kamehameha Early Education Program (KEEP), which has had great success in helping primary-grade Hawaiian children improve their cognitive performances. In non-KEEP classes Hawaiian children score very low on standard achievement tests; children in the KEEP classes approach national norms. Inspired by this success, the principles underlying KEEP have also been applied to or suggested for other minority-group students, including Navajo, African American, Eskimo, and Hmongs.

The KEEP principles include the following ways to make the school compatible with children's cultural values:

- *Social organization of the classroom:* In the typical American classroom the teacher speaks to the entire group, with follow-up individual attention. Since Hawaiian culture values collaboration, cooperation, and assisted performance, KEEP classes organize children in small groups of four to five students of mixed sex. With this arrangement, children are continually teaching and learning from each other. For Navajo children, who are trained in self-sufficiency and are separated by sex from about age 8, the most effective groupings include two or three children of the same sex.

- *Adaptation of cultural strengths:* Instead of regarding African American children's physical clowning around with one another as disruptive, teachers can use these tendencies to teach. They can, for example, encourage children to perform in front of the class; then if other students find errors in the performance, they can replace the performers, thus motivating both performers and audience (Williams, 1981).

- *Accommodation for language styles:* Hawaiians show involvement and relationship by overlapping each other's speech, a style often interpreted by teachers as rude interruption. At the other extreme, Navajos speak slowly, with frequent silent pauses; teachers often interrupt, misinterpreting such pauses as signaling the end of a response. When teachers adjust their styles of speaking to their students', children participate more (Tharp, 1989).

- *Sensitivity to rhythms:* Both in speech and in classroom movement, different cultural groups maintain different tempos. When teachers keep the same rhythm the children are familiar with, children participate more in class and learn better. Black children and mothers often interact in a back-and-forth "contest" style; this pattern can be adapted to classroom teaching (Hale, 1982).

- *Adjustment for cognitive styles:* Most western teaching stresses verbal and analytic thought patterns. This approach favors Japanese, Chinese, and white Americans, but not Native Americans, who tend to learn in visual, wholistic ways. At home they often learn by watching what other people do, with little verbal instruction. They are encouraged to listen to an entire story without stopping to discuss parts of it. Teachers can help children in both majority and minority cultures by acknowledging their basic tendencies and encouraging them in aspects of the unfamiliar style (Tharp, 1989).

- *Context of teaching:* Teachers need to put their lessons in the context of the child's experience, previous knowledge, and present skills. KEEP instructors teach reading by encouraging the children to think about their own personal experiences before presenting them with new material. Rules, abstractions, and descriptions need to be related to the children's everyday world so they can better integrate them in a meaningful context.

SCHOOLCHILDREN WITH SPECIAL NEEDS

Just as educators have become more sensitive to teaching children from varied cultural backgrounds, they have also sought to improve education for children of various abilities. We now look at three of the most common educational disabilities, at children with special gifts, and at the way children with both disabilities and special strengths are educated in American schools.

Mentally Retarded, Learning-Disabled, and Hyperactive Children

mental retardation
Below-average cognitive functioning.

Mental Retardation. *Mental retardation* is defined as below-average cognitive functioning, together with a deficiency in adaptive behavior appropriate to current age—and the appearance of such characteristics before age 18 (*Diagnostic and Statistical Manual of Mental Disorders*, DSM-IV, 1994). Low-level cognitive functioning is detected by IQ tests. Adaptive behaviors include such everyday skills as communication and social skills and skills in practical matters like self-care. With a supportive and stimulating early environment and continued guidance and help, many mentally retarded children—including many born with Down syndrome—can expect a reasonably good outcome. Most mentally retarded children can benefit from schooling, at least up to sixth-grade level.

The mentally retarded account for about 1 percent of the population, with about 1.5 males affected for every female. The retarded are generally classified in four categories, based on severity—mildly, moderately, severely, and profoundly retarded. (See Table 12-3.)

In about 30 to 40 percent of cases, the cause of mental retardation is unknown. Known causes include problems in embryonic development, like those caused by a mother's alcohol or drug use (30 percent); mental disorders like autism and environmental influences like lack of nurturance (15 to 20 percent); problems in pregnancy and childbirth, like fetal malnutrition or birth trauma (10 percent); hereditary factors, like Tay Sachs disease (5 percent); and medical conditions acquired in childhood, like trauma or lead poisoning (5 percent) (DSM-IV, 1994).

Learning Disabilities. Nelson Rockefeller, former vice president of the United States, had so much trouble reading that he ad-libbed his speeches instead of us-

TABLE 12-3

LEVELS OF MENTAL RETARDATION	
LEVEL	**DESCRIPTION**
Mildly retarded	About 85 percent of the retarded population. Mildly retarded people can acquire skills up to about the sixth-grade level, hold low-level paid jobs in adulthood, and live in the community. Although they can usually function on their own, they may need guidance and help at times of unusual stress.
Moderately retarded	About 10 percent of the retarded population. Moderately retarded people can learn academic subjects to the second-grade level, can learn occupational and social skills, and in adulthood may work in sheltered workshops or in regular jobs with close supervision. They can do a fair amount for themselves, but usually live in supervised group homes.
Severely retarded	About 3 to 4 percent of the retarded population. Severely retarded people may learn to talk during the school years, can be trained in personal hygiene, and can sometimes learn to recognize such "survival" words as *men, women,* and *stop.* They typically live in group homes or with their families.
Profoundly retarded	About 1 to 2 percent of the retarded population. Profoundly retarded people have minimal sensorimotor functioning, but may respond to some training in getting around, in self-care, and in communicating, especially if they have a one-to-one relationship with a caregiver. They live in group homes, in intermediate-care facilities, with their families, or in institutions.

SOURCE: Diagnostic and Statistical Manual of Mental Disorders, 3d ed., rev., DSM III-R, 1987.

Children with dyslexia have trouble reading and writing, and often doing arithmetic, because they may confuse up and down and left and right. Boys and girls are affected about equally, and dyslexia seems to be at least partly inherited.

ing a script. The inventor Thomas Edison never learned how to spell or write grammatically. World War II hero General George Patton read poorly and got through West Point by memorizing entire lectures (Schulman, 1986). All these people suffered from *dyslexia*—a developmental reading disorder in which reading achievement is at least 2 years below the expected level.

dyslexia *Difficulty in learning to read.*

Dyslexic children—some 3 to 6 percent of the school population—often confuse up and down and left and right; they may read *saw* for *was* and have trouble with arithmetic as well as reading. Dyslexia affects males and females equally, is more common in children from large families and in lower socioeconomic levels, and seems to be at least partly inherited (Council on Scientific Affairs of the American Medical Association, 1989; DeFries, Fulker, & LaBuda, 1987; Shaywitz, Shaywitz, Fletcher, & Escobar, 1990). The reading problem is part of a generalized language impairment ("Dyslexia," 1989). Dyslexic children are late in starting to talk, suffer subtle deficits in both spoken and written language, and have limited memory for verbal materials. If diagnosed before third grade, the child's prognosis is better.

Dyslexia is only one of a number of *learning disabilities (LDs)*—disorders that interfere with a specific aspect of school achievement. Learning disabilities affect an estimated 5 to 10 percent of the population (Interagency Committee on Learning Disabilities, 1987). Since success in school is important for self-esteem, learning disabilities can have devastating effects on the psyche as well as the report card. Although these children often have average or higher general intelligence and apparently normal vision and hearing, they have trouble processing what comes through their senses (Feagans, 1983). As one child said, "I know it in my head, but I can't get it into my hand."

learning disabilities (LDs) *Disorders that interfere with specific aspects of learning and school achievement.*

Mathematical disabilities (MD) may be even more common than reading disabilities; yet they have been relatively neglected (Geary, 1993). Some children have problems because they never learned arithmetic properly, are anxious, or have trouble reading or hearing directions. Others may make mistakes because they use immature arithmetic procedures; this often results from a developmental delay and eventually disappears. A more fundamental problem for some people is remembering arithmetic facts. Math disability, which is often associated with reading disability, may be partly inherited and may be due to a neurological deficit.

Dozens of different disorders affect one or more aspects of learning. Besides reading and math, some children have trouble processing what they hear. Others have poor coordination in either fine motor or gross motor movements, interfering with their ability to write or play games. Still others have speech problems, speaking late and unclearly.

The cause of most such disabilities is unknown. They may be related to behavioral problems; learning-disabled (LD) children tend to be less task-oriented, more easily distracted, and less able to concentrate than other children. There may be a failure of cognitive processing; LD children are less organized as learners and less likely to use memory strategies (Feagans, 1983). Or the cause may be physiological; some children apparently have trouble fast-processing either visual or auditory information (Lehmkuhle et al., 1993; Livingstone et al., 1993; Galaburda et al., 1994). Learning disabilities often run in families; genetic transmission of chromosomal abnormalities may play a role (DeFries et al., 1987; M. D. Levine, 1987). It is also possible that many children classified as LD are youngsters whom schools have failed to teach and control effectively (McGuinness, 1986).

Children at highest risk for learning disabilities are those who were very low birthweight infants, who suffered other birth trauma or malnutrition, who have a "difficult" temperament, or who come from a poor, chaotic family. Those who do best had their problems discovered and responded to early (E. E. Werner, 1993; M. D. Levine, 1987). Among the most successful aids are techniques to help concentration, improve basic skills, and use cognitive strategies. Help from caring, competent adults is important in helping the young people organize life outside school as well as in it, in encouraging progress in both academic and nonacademic areas, and in providing a "second chance" (in school, work, or the military). All this goes toward helping high-risk young people become competent and confident. The children's own characteristics are also vital: Those who best overcome early disabilities have temperamental traits that draw other people toward them, they plan their actions, and they have good self-esteem (Werner, 1993).

Children do not outgrow learning disabilities; some 5 million to 10 million adults suffer from them (Schulman, 1986). Still, if they take appropriate diagnostic tests, learn skills to help them use their strengths to compensate for their weaknesses, and get help for problems like poor self-esteem (often caused by school problems), they can lead satisfying, productive lives. Some go on to college and professional careers; while never cured of their disabilities, they learn how to cope with them.

Hyperactivity and Attention Deficits.   The behavior disorder hyperactivity often accompanies learning disorders. They story is all too familiar: Johnny cannot sit still, cannot finish a simple task, cannot keep a friend, and is always in trouble. His teacher says, "I can't do a thing with him." The doctor says, "Don't worry; he'll grow out of it." The neighbors say, "He's a spoiled brat."

The syndrome that Johnny is probably suffering from, formally known as *attention-deficit hyperactivity disorder (ADHD),* is marked by persistent inattention, impulsivity, low tolerance of frustration, temper tantrums, and a great deal of activity at the wrong time and the wrong place, like the classroom. These traits appear to some degree in all children; but in about 3 to 5 percent of school-

attention-deficit hyperactivity disorder (ADHD) *Syndrome characterized by inattention, impulsivity, and considerable activity at inappropriate times and places.*

age children (4 to 9 times more boys than girls), they are so pervasive that they interfere with the child's functioning in school and daily life. Although some symptoms appear before age 7, ADHD may not be recognized until the child starts school (DSM-IV, 1994).

Hyperactivity is probably caused by a combination of genetic, neurological, biochemical, and environmental factors (Henshaw, 1994; G. Weiss, 1990). One research team found that the brains of adults who had been hyperactive as children metabolized glucose, a sugar, differently from the brains of other adults. Brain differences were especially notable in the areas associated with regulating attention and motor activity (Zametkin et al., 1990). This suggests that the disorder has a neurological aspect. However, there are so many possible causes of hyperactivity that it is difficult to determine the origin of any one case. Environmental factors, including toxins like lead, are also cited (Henshaw, 1994). The syndrome tends to run in families, and may be at least partly inherited (DSM-IV, 1994). Discord in the family seems to sustain and even worsen the symptoms (Henshaw, 1994).

Whatever the cause, parents and teachers can help hyperactive children do better. First, they have to understand and accept the child's basic temperament. Then they can teach the child how to break up work into small, manageable segments; they can incorporate physical activity into the daily classroom schedule; and they can offer alternative ways for the child to demonstrate what she or he has learned, such as individual conferences or tape-recorded reports instead of written reports (M. A. Stewart & Olds, 1973).

ADHD is sometimes treated with drugs, most often stimulants, prescribed to help children focus on the task at hand and reduce problem behaviors like aggression and antisocial behavior. In the short run, the drugs may help, but at the end of a few years, drug-treated children do not do any better on academic achievement tests than do untreated children (McDaniel, 1986). Furthermore, drugs do not help all hyperactive children, and we don't know the long-range effects of giving drugs to what many believe to be basically normal children. It seems best to consider drugs only after trying other approaches and then only in combination with behavior modification programs that teach social skills and control of impulsive behavior (Henshaw, 1994).

One treatment that has received much attention is a diet free of artificial food colorings and flavorings. However, an additive-free diet seems to help only a small number of hyperactive children, and the National Institutes of Health does not recommend it in all cases (Hadley, 1984). Nor does the sugar substitute aspartame affect these children's cognition or behavior (B. A. Shaywitz et al., 1994). Some data suggest that ADHD children may benefit from eating protein-rich breakfasts (Conners, 1988).

The long-range prognosis for ADHD children is mixed. By age 15 only one in four have "recovered"; most continue to show poorer cognitive skills and disruptive behaviors (McGee, Partridge, Williams, & Silva, 1991). Some evidence suggests that about half function normally as adults (Mannuzza, Klein, Bonagura, Konig, & Shenker, 1988). Many have higher rates of job changes, marital disruption, traffic accidents, and brushes with the law (Henker & Whalen, 1989). The long-range problems that occur are most likely to revolve around getting along with other people, drug abuse, and conduct disorders. On the bright side, although hyperactive people generally continue to be restless and impulsive, they also tend to have such positive personality traits as spontaneity, zest, and energy.

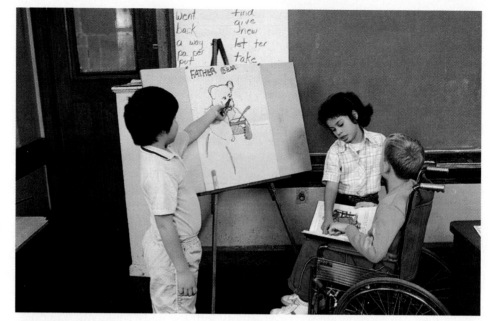

Children with disabilities seem to do best in schools that combine mainstreaming with special classes. This boy in a wheelchair might be in a regular academic class but receive special physical training while his classmates go to gym.

Educating Children with Disabilities.   In 1975, Congress passed the Education for All Handicapped Children Act (Public Law 94-142), which ensures appropriate public education for all children with disabilities. This law requires designing an appropriate program for each child according to his or her needs, involving parents in educational decisions, and allocating funds. Of the children affected by the law, 8 out of 10 are mentally retarded, learning-disabled, or speech-impaired.

The law sets out six principles (Schroeder, Schroeder, & Landesman, 1987). *Zero reject* holds that schools must provide free special education and related services for all children with disabilities between ages 3 or 5 and 18 or 21 years (depending on state laws). *Nondiscriminatory evaluation* requires determining what a child *can* do, not only what she or he cannot do. An *individualized education program* must be written for each child. *Due process* assures fairness of education decisions. *Parental participation* recognizes the importance of parental involvement in their child's education.

The principle of *least restrictive environment* may be the most controversial of the principles on which the law is based. The concept of least restrictive environment calls for **mainstreaming,** integrating disabled with nondisabled youngsters, as much as possible, depending on the disability. Under mainstreaming, children with and without disabilities are in classes with each other for all or part of the day. This approach helps disabled children learn to get along in society and helps nondisabled children know and understand people with disabilities. Critics maintain that children with disabilities are taught better and more humanely in small classes by specially trained teachers.

Mentally retarded children do about the same academically in mainstreamed classes as in special classes (Gruen, Korte, & Baum, 1974). However, they are not accepted socially by their normal classmates; mainstreaming does not diminish the stigma of being retarded (Taylor, Asher, & Williams, 1987).

Mainstreaming requires innovative teaching techniques that meet the needs of all students, and not all teachers can rise to the challenge. Many, however, have

mainstreaming
Integration of disabled and nondisabled children in the same classroom.

effectively taught classes of both disabled and nondisabled students, drawing on teachers' aides, individual tutors, and computers (D. Thomas, 1985). The most effective solution seems to be a combination of mainstreaming and special classes. A mentally retarded child, for example, might be able to take physical education in a regular class, but receive academic instruction in a class with slow learners. Or a child with cerebral palsy might be in a regular academic class but receive special physical training while classmates go to gym.

What do you think? *Does mainstreaming impose too many obstacles for children with disabilities? Would they be better off in special classes or special schools? How does mainstreaming affect the rest of the class?*

Gifted, Creative, and Talented Children

Giftedness. At age 12, Indian-born Balamurati Krishna Ambati is a third-year premedical student at New York University. He mastered calculus at age 4, scored 750 on the math SAT at age 10, and hopes to be a doctor before he turns 18 (Stanley, 1990). His path has not been easy: Although his parents encouraged his achievements from birth, teachers urged him to slow down and peers have not always understood his drive to excel.

Giftedness can be a mixed blessing. Many promising children—more than half, by one report—achieve below their tested potential (National Commission on Excellence in Education, 1983). Why? For one reason, schools do not always meet their needs for cognitive stimulation. About 2.5 million children—some 3 to 5 percent of the school population—are estimated to be gifted, but fewer than 1 million receive special attention (Horowitz & O'Brien, 1986). In considering the gifted, we need to define our terms—and then look at the best way to nurture special abilities.

Sergei, 9, shown here in a Moscow subway station, is a Russian child gifted in many fields. He speaks English fluently, writes murder mysteries, and has a broad knowledge of Soviet and European history. The key to helping such children achieve lies in recognizing and nurturing their natural gifts.

Defining and Identifying Giftedness.

Like intelligence, giftedness is hard to define. The traditional definition, most often used to select children for special programs, is very narrow—an IQ score of 130 or higher (Horowitz & O'Brien, 1986). However, this definition cannot identify creative children (whose unusual answers often lower their test scores), gifted children from minority groups (whose abilities may not be well developed, even though the potential is there), and children with aptitude in a specific area.

giftedness *Possession of one or more of the following traits: superior general intellect, superiority in a single domain (like mathematics or science), artistic talent, leadership ability, or creative thinking.*

A broader definition of *giftedness* includes—but is not limited to—one or more of the following traits: superior general intellect, superiority in a single domain (like mathematics or science), talent in the arts (like painting, writing, or acting), creative thinking (the ability to look at problems in a new way), and/or leadership ability.

Two ways of looking at giftedness stem from new theories of intelligence. According to Robert Sternberg, gifted children process information very efficiently, especially on novel tasks requiring insight (Sternberg, 1985a; J. E. Davidson & Sternberg, 1984). Howard Gardner's (1983) multiple-intelligences theory holds that people can be gifted in one or more of at least seven separate "intelligences," each relatively independent of the others. Some of these "intelligences"— like the musical, the bodily-kinesthetic (moving precisely, as in dance), the interpersonal (understanding others), or the intrapersonal (knowing oneself)—are not tapped by traditional intelligence tests. The others are linguistic (reading and writing), logical-mathematical (using numbers and solving logical problems), and spatial (finding one's way around an environment).

The Lives of Gifted Children.

In the 1920s, Lewis Terman, the professor who brought the Binet intelligence test to the United States, located more than 1500 children with IQs of 135 or higher. He tested them for intelligence, school achievement, character, personality, and interests. They were examined medically, their physical measurements were taken, and their parents and teachers were interviewed. The data that emerged demolished the popular stereotype of the bright child as a puny, pasty-faced bookworm. These gifted children were superior in all areas. They tended to be taller, healthier, better coordinated, better adjusted, and more popular than the average child (Wallach & Kogan, 1965).

Researchers who followed the progress of these subjects into old age found that their cognitive, scholastic, and vocational superiority held up over more than 60 years. They were 10 times more likely than a group not selected on the basis of IQ to have graduated from college and 3 times more likely to have been elected to honorary societies like Phi Beta Kappa. By midlife, they were highly represented in listings like *Who's Who in America*. Almost 90 percent of the men* were in the two highest occupational categories: the professions and higher echelons of business (Terman & Oden, 1959).

These people's lives showed that intelligence tests can spot children with promise and that cognitively gifted children do tend to fulfill that promise. However, there were some methodological problems with Terman's study. For one, the sample was not representative of the United States population at large. All the subjects were Californians, most came from relatively advantaged homes, Jewish children were overrepresented, and African American and Asian children were underrepresented.

*Because of different societal attitudes toward careers for men and women, the sexes were evaluated separately. Both sexes made a good showing.

More recent research has found that cognitively gifted children have fairly mature and sophisticated attitudes about social relationships and are mature in their moral reasoning. However, they do not always behave according to the opinions they express; they may be gifted but they are still children. On the whole, they show average or superior adjustment in their self-concepts, in how they handle their lives, and in how they get along with others (Janos & Robinson, 1985).

Two groups of gifted children, however, tend to have social and emotional problems—those with IQs over 180 and those with high IQs who do not do well in school. The problems of both groups seem to stem in part from unsatisfactory schooling—inflexibility, overemphasis on grades, lack of challenge, and unsupportive teachers (Janos & Robinson, 1985). Many bright children hide their intelligence as they try to fit in with their classmates (R. D. Feldman, 1982). Although the parents of many gifted children are well educated and well off, get along well with each other, and are supportive of their children, the homes of underachieving gifted children tend to be less harmonious (Janos & Robinson, 1985).

What do you think? *Should schools actively seek out the most gifted and creative students and give them special training? If so, what do you think would be the best approach for teaching them?*

Educating Gifted Children. There are two approaches to educating gifted children. *Skipping grades* speeds up children's education, moving them through the curriculum quickly. *Enrichment* broadens and deepens their knowledge by providing extra activities like research projects and special experiences.

Terman's study inspired the movement to enrich gifted children's education and also suggested that skipping grades is not harmful to bright children (C. Rafferty, 1984). Other research, too, found that mathematically gifted children who have skipped a grade did not have social or emotional problems (L. H. Fox & Washington, 1985). Advocates of enrichment believe that putting gifted children with older students is likely to expose them to psychosocial pressures they are not ready for.

As with most issues in child development, individual children have their own unique needs, and the most successful educational programs are tailored to a specific child and a specific situation. All children benefit from being encouraged in their areas of interest and ability.

Creativity

Defining and Identifying Creativity. The unusually bright people studied by Terman did not show signs of unusual creativity: The group did not produce a great musician, an exceptional painter, or a Nobel laureate. Other research, too, has found only modest correlations between creativity and intelligence (Anastasi & Schaefer, 1971; Getzels & Jackson, 1963; McKinnon, 1968).

This is not surprising when you think about the essence of creativity. *Creativity* is the ability to see things in a new light, to see problems that others may fail to recognize, and to come up with new, unusual, and effective solutions. Standardized intelligence tests measure *convergent thinking*—the ability to come up with a single correct answer. Creativity involves *divergent thinking*—the ability to come up with new and unusual answers (Guilford, 1967).

creativity *Ability to see things in a new light, to see problems that others may fail to recognize, and to come up with new, unusual, and effective solutions.*

convergent thinking *Thinking aimed at finding the one "right" answer to a problem.*

divergent thinking *Creative thinking; the ability to discover new, unusual answers.*

What do you think? *What would you include in your definition of creativity? How would you assess it?*

Test-developers have designed ways to test divergent thinking and identify creative children. The Torrance Tests of Creative Thinking, for example, consist of three parts. In "Thinking Creatively with Words," children are asked to think of ways to improve a toy to make it more fun to play with and to list unusual uses for and pose unusual questions about common objects. "Thinking Creatively with Pictures" asks children to draw pictures that start from a colored curved shape, a few lines, or pairs of short parallel lines. "Thinking Creatively with Sound and Words" uses a recording of words (like *crunch* and *pop*) whose sounds suggest their meaning and asks children to write down what the sounds suggest. Another popular test of creativity is illustrated in Figure 12-1.

Current tests of creativity are more useful for research than for educational or vocational counseling. One problem is that scoring depends heavily on speedy responses—and creative people are not always fast workers. Moreover, although the tests are *reliable* (they yield consistent results), there is little or no evidence that they are *valid*—that they identify children who show creativity in life situations (Anastasi, 1988).

Fostering Creativity. Very young children are imaginative in their stories, drawings, and play. Too often, when they enter school, their creativity is stifled as teachers tell them not to color outside the lines, not to make clouds blue and grass red,

QUESTIONS	COMMON ANSWERS	CREATIVE ANSWERS
How many things could these drawings be?		
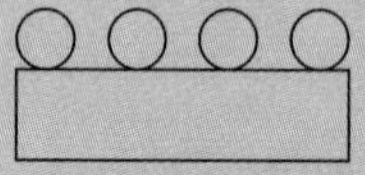	Table with things on top.	Foot and toes.
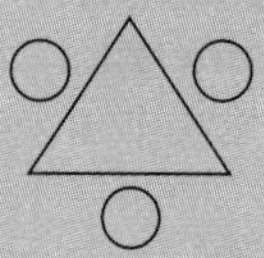	Three people sitting around a table.	Three mice eating a piece of cheese.
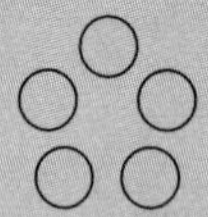	Flower.	Lollipop bursting into pieces.
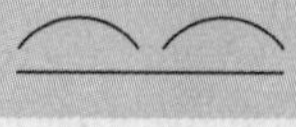	Two igloos.	Two haystacks on a flying carpet.
What do meat and milk have in common?	Both come from animals.	Both are government-inspected.
How many ways could you use a newspaper?	Make paper hats.	Rip it up if you're angry.

FIGURE 12-1
Tests of creativity. It has proven very difficult to develop tests to measure creativity. Part of the reason may be that creative people express their creativity best in situations other than tests. Another reason has to do with the subjectivity of scoring these tests. SOURCE: Adapted from Wallach & Kogan, 1967.

BOX 12-5 ■ THE EVERYDAY WORLD

FOSTERING CREATIVITY

The following suggestions to parents for fostering creativity in children are based on research findings:

♦ *Provide a stimulating environment,* tailored as much as possible to a child's special interests and aptitudes and including lessons or classes and necessary materials. For children who do not show a specific special interest, offer a variety of experiences and materials.

♦ *Focus on a child's strengths* rather than criticizing his or her weaknesses.

♦ *Encourage nonconforming, unpredictable behavior* and help your children avoid or withstand peer pressure. It is easier to do this if you feel secure about your social station, are uninhibited and unconventional yourself, and do not care what other people think.

♦ *Set an example* by pursuing absorbing occupations or cognitive or artistic hobbies.

♦ *Expose children to cultural diversity* and to other creative people; deemphasize traditional gender roles. All this opens up children's thinking and lets them see new possibilities for expressing creativity.

♦ *Respect your children* and show confidence in their ability to do well. Give them both freedom and responsibilities. Give them warm support, but also give them enough space to breathe and think for themselves.

♦ *Do not exert rigid control* over children. The most consistent and best-supported research finding is that parental vigilance, authoritarianism, dominance, and restrictiveness inhibit creativity. Apparently, children who are constantly directed and molded lose the confidence and spontaneity essential for the creative spirit.

SOURCE: T. M. Amabile, 1983; B. Miller & Gerard, 1979.

and to do things the "right" way (Gardner, 1983). Children are more creative when their teachers are open to unconventional questions ("Do rocks grow?"), welcome and praise original ideas, and do not grade everything the children do (Torrance in Chance & Fischman, 1987).

Parents too can encourage their children to be more creative. The families of highly creative children help them in ways described in Box 12-5.

Talent: Recognizing and Encouraging Talented Children.   Studies of internationally known pianists, sculptors, athletes, mathematicians, and neurologists show that artistic success depends on inborn talent, encouragement of that talent, and the artist's own drive to excel (Gardner, 1979; Bloom, 1985).

First, a child's talent has to be recognized. Most of the high achievers in a Chicago study became intensely involved in their field before age 10 to 12. Commonly, a parent or other relative talented in the same area recognized and encouraged the child's talent at an early age.

Second, talent must be nurtured. Often the child's first teacher in the special field emphasized joy and playfulness, making children fall in love with their field. Then, even when the children discovered how demanding the field was, they wanted to master its discipline. Teachers who give rigorous training should take a "longitudinal" approach, getting to know children well, staying with them over several years, and emphasizing long-term goals and individual progress over time.

Talented children receive emotional "highs" from regular participation in such public events as recitals and contests that provide a series of short-term goals and give benchmarks of progress. When they perform well, praise and rewards inspire them to continue to work, and when they do poorly, they want to try to do better the next time.

Finally, the talented child must want to excel. The joys and rewards of the labor must seem like full payment for its rigors. Talented adolescents often devote 15 to 25 hours a week to their activity, and they choose their friends from among others with the same interest.

What do you think? *Talented and gifted children often devote many hours a week to learning the techniques of their field. What do you think are the pros and cons of doing this?*

There is no firm line between being gifted and not being gifted. What we learn about fostering intelligence, creativity, and talent for the small, special population of the gifted and talented can help all children make the most of their potential. The degree to which they do this will affect self-concept and other aspects of their personality, as we shall see in Chapter 13.

SUMMARY

1 From about age 7 to age 11, children are in the Piagetian stage of concrete operations and can use mental operations to solve problems. Children at this stage are less egocentric than before and are more proficient at tasks requiring logical reasoning, such as conservation, seriation, classification, and number abilities, though their reasoning is largely limited to the here and now.

2 According to Piaget, moral development occurs in two stages. The first, morality of constraint, is characterized by moral rigidity. The second, morality of cooperation, is characterized by moral flexibility.

3 Selman's theory links moral development with the ability to take roles.

4 Vygotsky maintained that social interaction is a key factor in cognitive development.

5 Memory improves greatly during middle childhood because children's short-term memory capacity increases rapidly and because children become more adept at using mnemonic strategies such as rehearsal, organization, elaboration, and external aids. Metamemory (the understanding of how memory works) also improves.

6 The intelligence of school-age children is assessed by group tests (such as the Otis-Lennon School Ability Test) and individual tests (such as the WISC-III and the K-ABC). While IQ tests are good predictors of school success, intelligence tests miss other important aspects of intelligent behavior.

7 Developers of intelligence tests have tried to devise "culture-free" tests and "culture-fair" tests, tests that focus on experiences common across cultures. None of these attempts have been completely successful.

8 Differences in performance on intelligence tests between cultural and ethnic groups appear to result from differences in typical environment rather than any inborn differences between groups.

9 Children develop understanding of increasingly complex syntax during middle childhood. Although the ability to communicate improves, even older children may not have a complete awareness of the processes of communication.

10 Children's humor grows as cognitive and linguistic abilities develop.

11 The development of literacy is influenced by social interaction.

12 Many school districts have implemented programs of bilingual education that encourage fluency in two languages.

13 Teachers influence children's success in school and thus their self-esteem. Self-fulfilling prophecies often limit the achievement of poor and minority children. Parents' involvement enhances learning. Children's characteristics like temperament and emotional state also influence school performance.

14 Mental retardation is below-average cognitive functioning, a deficiency in adaptive

behavior appropriate to current age, and the appearance of these characteristics before age 18. Both biological and environmental factors are related to retardation.

15 Learning disabilities are disorders that interfere with specific aspects of school achievement. The causes are unclear. Many learning-disabled children can lead productive lives if they get early individual attention.

16 Under the law in the United States, all children with disabilities are entitled to an appropriate education at public expense. Children must be mainstreamed (placed in regular classes) as much as possible.

17 In Terman's study giftedness was defined as having an IQ score of 135 or higher. This narrow definition misses some gifted children. Although Terman's research found that gifted children tend to be successful as adults, some fail to live up to their potential, possibly because schools do not meet their needs.

18 Creativity involves divergent, rather than convergent thinking. The validity of creativity tests is questionable.

19 The development of gifts, talents, and creativity depends greatly on nurturance. The child's drive is also important. Special school programs stress enrichment or acceleration.

KEY TERMS

concrete operations (459)
conservation (459)
horizontal décalage (460)
seriation (461)
transitive inference (461)
class inclusion (462)
morality of constraint (464)
morality of cooperation (464)
role-taking ability (464)
scaffolding (466)
rehearsal (467)
organization (468)
elaboration (469)
metamemory (469)
Wechsler Intelligence Scale for Children (WISC-III) (469)
Kaufman Assessment Battery for Children (K-ABC) (470)
Otis-Lennon School Ability Test (470)

aptitude tests (470)
achievement tests (470)
syntax (476)
metacommunication (477)
bilingual education (480)
bilingualism (480)
code-switching (481)
self-fulfilling prophecy (487)
mental retardation (490)
dyslexia (491)
learning disabilities (LDs) (491)
attention-deficit hyperactivity disorder (ADHD) (492)
mainstreaming (494)
giftedness (496)
creativity (497)
convergent thinking (497)
divergent thinking (497)

SUGGESTED READINGS

Hallowell, E. M., & Ratey, J. J. (1994). *Driven to distraction: Recognizing and coping with attention deficit disorder from childhood through adulthood.* New York: Pantheon. This book by two psychiatrists, both of whom have the condition themselves, describes the syndrome and offers advice to parents and teachers and to affected adults. It has a comprehensive bibliography.

Healy, J. M. (1990). *Endangered minds: Why our children don't think.* New York: Simon & Schuster. In this thought-provoking book a noted educator examines the reasons children today are less able to concentrate and less able to absorb information than were previous generations. Healy's theory is that forces in today's society (such as the electronic media, unstable family patterns, environmental hazards) are changing the way children think and may even be changing the brain's physical structure.

Kennedy, P., Terdal, L., & Fusetti, L (1993). *The hyperactive child book..* New York: St. Martin's Press. A practical and up-to-date guide on treating, educating, and living with an attention deficit-hyperactivity disorder child. The three authors are a unique team consisting of a clinical psychologist, a pediatrician, and a mother. They provide help in dealing with diagnosis, medications, schools, and the parents' needs.

Kidder, T. (1990). *Among schoolchildren.* New York: Avon. The author spent an entire school year observing a fifth-grade class in Holyoke, Massachusetts, and this is the story of that teacher and her students. It is a remarkable depiction of the demands on a teacher and portrays with compassion the triumphs and failures of her students.

Radford, J. (1990). *Child prodigies and exceptional early achievers.* New York: Free Press/Macmillan. This exploration of the lives of gifted children charts the impact of environmental and genetic influences in their lives. Telling the stories of dozens of early-achieving children, the author, a psychology professor, stresses the importance of stimulating environments and of inspiring mentors and discusses the problems gifted children can encounter.

Sadker, M., & Sadker, D. (1994). *Failing at fairness: How America's schools cheat girls.* New York: Charles Scribner's Sons The authors, both professors of education, argue that both conscious and unconscious sexism of teachers leads to an inferior education for girls. As a result, girls perform worse then boys on standardized tests and suffer declines in self-esteem. The book has social policy implications for educators and child-rearing implications for parents.

Simon, S. B., & Olds, S. W. (1991). *Helping your child find values to live by.* Hadley, MA: Values Press. A self-help manual for parents for establishing moral values and emotional self-awareness in children. The authors explain why values themselves cannot be taught but how parents can teach children a process for arriving at their own values.

Treiber, P. M. (1993). *Keys to dealing with stuttering.* Hauppague, NY: Barron's. The latest research is summarized to help parents understand and manage a child's stuttering, helping the child at home and at school.

CHAPTER 13
PERSONALITY AND SOCIAL DEVELOPMENT IN MIDDLE CHILDHOOD

CHAPTER 13
PERSONALITY AND SOCIAL DEVELOPMENT IN MIDDLE CHILDHOOD

Have you ever felt like nobody?
Just a tiny speck of air.
When everyone's around you,
And you are just not there.

Karen Crawford, age 9

We now trace the rich and varied lives of school-age children as their world expands, and we look at the social and personality growth that accompanies their cognitive growth. We see how youngsters develop a more realistic concept of themselves, and we examine the shift in their relationships as they become more independent of parents and more involved with other people, particularly other children. Through being with peers, they make discoveries about their own attitudes, values, and skills. Still, the family remains a vital influence, and children's lives are profoundly affected by such family issues as parental employment, divorce, and remarriage. Although most children are healthy, some suffer emotional disorders; we look at some of these problems. We also look at resilient children, who emerge from the stresses of childhood healthier and stronger. After you have read this chapter, you should be able to answer such questions as the following:

PREVIEW QUESTIONS

- ◆ How do children develop a self-concept and self-esteem?
- ◆ What is the impact on children of parents' work, divorce, and remarriage?
- ◆ What are sibling relationships like in middle childhood?
- ◆ What is the function of the peer group?
- ◆ How do schoolchildren view friendship? What role does it play in their lives?
- ◆ What are some common childhood emotional disturbances? How are they treated?
- ◆ What enables "resilient" children to withstand stress?

When Vicky was 9½, she went to a 2-week sleep-away Girl Scout camp. It was the first time she had been away from home for so long. The brief notes and cards she sent home during the first week were cheerful and businesslike. Then, 10 days after camp began, she wrote this letter:

Dear Mommy,

I'm very homesick. My counselors expect me to have my sneakers on in one second. And if I don't have them on in 10 seconds, they start yelling at me. If we aren't at a certain place at a certain time, they start yelling—even if we're 2 minutes late! If we go canoeing and we're late for the next period, they blame it all on us! I miss you! I want to come home now! The girls in my cabin are all 10, and they aren't very nice at all. I don't want to stay here any more. I want to be home with you! I miss you and Daddy and everybody else. Please write to me soon.

Love,

Vicky

After shedding a few maternal tears, Ellen reminded herself that parents cannot protect their children from all unhappiness. Nor should they. Children need to learn to overcome the low moments in life, and they have to become independent, fully functioning human beings. (The following summer, Vicky eagerly went to a different community-run camp, one she returned to for two more summers; later she considered these summers high points of her life.)

THE DEVELOPING SELF

The self-concept develops continuously from infancy on. With the cognitive growth during middle childhood, youngsters can develop more realistic concepts of themselves and of what they need to survive and succeed in their culture.

DEVELOPING A SELF-CONCEPT

"Who in the world am I? Ah, *that's* the great puzzle," said Alice in Wonderland, after her size had abruptly changed—again. Solving Alice's "puzzle" entails a lifelong process of getting to know the developing self.

The *self-concept* is our picture of ourself. It is based on our knowledge of what we have been and done; its function is to guide us in deciding what to be and do in the future. The self-concepts built during middle childhood are often strong and lasting. Positive ones (like "I am popular," "I am a good artist," "I am a fast runner") may take shape as children's physical, cognitive, and social abilities let them see themselves as valuable members of society. This is also the time when a negative self-image may arise, to stay with a person long after childhood has been left behind.

As we saw in Chapter 10, young children tend to apply their all-or-nothing thinking to themselves. However, sometime around ages 7 or 8, children develop *representational systems.* This cognitive advance allows them to integrate different features of the self to form higher-order generalizations, as expressed by Vicky, 8: "At school I'm feeling pretty smart in certain subjects, Language Arts and Social Studies. I got As in these subjects on my last report card and was really proud of myself. But I'm feeling really dumb in Arithmetic and Science, particularly when I see how well the other kids are doing" (Harter, 1993, p. 2).

In other words, 8-year-old Vicky can integrate two concepts that she had previously kept in separate mental compartments (smart and dumb). The earlier compartmentalizing of concepts may be a necessary building block for the kind of thinking that allows a child to integrate attributes that seem to contradict each other. This kind of thinking is no longer the black-and-white kind seen in younger children. Vicky's self-descriptions are more balanced now, and she can verbalize her self-concept better. Her cognitive view of herself is crucial for the development of self-esteem, an emotional component of personality.

self-concept *Sense of self that guides one in deciding what to do in the future.*

Self-image has a major impact on personality development. Anna, shown here, is likely to feel good about herself if she considers herself both competent and "good," if she feels a measure of control over her life, and if she feels that the important people in her life love and approve of her.

self-esteem *The judgment people make about their personal worth.*

industry versus inferiority *In Erikson's theory, the fourth crisis that children face; they must learn the skills of their culture or risk developing feelings of inferiority.*

global self-worth *Harter's term for self-esteem.*

SELF-ESTEEM

Middle childhood is an important time for the development of ***self-esteem,*** the sense of self-worth or self-evaluation. As we pointed out earlier, children compare their *real selves* and their *ideal selves* and judge themselves by how well they measure up to the social standards and expectations they have taken into their self-concept.

Children's opinions of themselves have a great impact on their personality development, and especially on their usual mood. Children whose self-esteem is high tend to be cheerful; those with low self-esteem are likely to be depressed (Harter, 1990). A depressed mood can lower energy level, which can affect how well a child does in school and other areas of life, leading to a downward spiral in self-esteem.

There are other differences between children with high and low self-esteem (Harter, 1990). A child with high self-esteem is confident, curious, and independent. She trusts her own ideas, approaches challenges and initiates new activities with confidence. She describes herself positively and is proud of her work. She adjusts easily to change, tolerates frustration, perseveres in pursuing a goal, and can handle criticism and teasing. On the other hand, a child with low self-esteem does not trust her own ideas, lacks confidence, hangs back and watches instead of exploring on her own, withdraws and sits apart from other children, describes herself negatively, and takes no pride in her work. She gives up easily when frustrated and reacts immaturely to stress and inappropriately to accidents.

How do children get a favorable self-image?

Industry and Self-Esteem

According to Erik Erikson, a major determinant of high self-esteem is a child's view of his or her competence. The prime crisis of middle childhood in Erikson's theory is ***industry versus inferiority.*** The issue to be resolved is a child's capacity for productive work. In all cultures children have to learn skills; the specific skills depend on what is valued in a particular society. Arapesh boys in New Guinea, no longer content merely to play, learn to make bows and arrows and to lay traps for rats; Arapesh girls learn to plant, weed, and harvest. Inuit children of Alaska learn to hunt and fish. Children in industrialized countries learn to read, write, count, and use computers.

Efforts at mastery can help children form a positive self-concept. The "virtue" that develops with successful resolution of this crisis is *competence,* a view of the self as able to master skills and complete tasks (Erikson, 1982). As children compare their own abilities with those of their peers, they construct a sense of who they are. If they feel inadequate by comparison, they may retreat to the familiar but less challenging nest of the family, where less may be expected of them. If, on the other hand, they become *too* industrious, says Erikson, they may neglect their relationships with other people and turn into "workaholic" adults.

Sources of Self-Esteem

Another view on how children form an overall favorable opinion of themselves, or a sense of ***global self-worth,*** comes from Susan Harter's (1985; 1990; 1993) research. She suggests that self-esteem comes from two sources: how competent

Middle childhood is a time for learning the skills that one's culture considers important. In rural Haiti children learn how to load a donkey's baskets and lead it to market.

children think they are in important aspects of life and how much social support they receive from other people.

Children as young as 4 years already show by their behavior that they possess a sense of self-worth. But not until middle childhood (about age 8) are youngsters able to express self-judgments in words. This development parallels their growing ability to form cognitive concepts.

Self-Evaluations. Harter (1985) asked children aged 8 and 12 about five domains in life: (1) how well they do in school, (2) how good they are in sports, (3) how accepted they feel by other children, (4) how they behave, and (5) what they look like. The children rated the importance of doing well in each domain relative to their feelings about themselves. Then they rated themselves in each domain. They also answered questions about how much they liked themselves and how happy they were with the way they were. They assessed how they were treated by their parents, teachers, classmates, and close friends. Did these people care about and like the child and treat him or her like a person who mattered and had valuable things to say?

According to this research, the greatest contributor to positive self-worth in middle childhood is how well regarded by important people—parents and classmates, then friends and teachers—a child feels. On their self-evaluation, children rated physical appearance as the most important domain and judged themselves by how good-looking they thought they were. Social acceptance came next. Less critical were competencies in schoolwork, conduct, and athletics. In contrast to the high value that Erikson put on competence in mastering skills, in Harter's studies children's senses of their own competence mattered less than did physical appearance and social acceptance.

According to Harter's research, both self-evaluations in the different domains *and* a sense of support from significant people are important in forming self-worth. One does not compensate for lack of the other. So even if Vicky thinks it's important to be pretty and smart and considers herself both, her self-worth will be undermined if she does not feel valued by her family and other important peo-

BOX 13-1 ▪ FOOD FOR THOUGHT

SELF-ESTEEM AND DISABILITY

Harilyn Rousso, a social worker and psychotherapist, was born with cerebral palsy, raised as a normal child, and sent to regular schools. She offers insights into the impact a physical disability can have on a child's self-esteem.

My mother was quite concerned about the awkwardness of my walk; she feared it would subject me to teasing and rejection. To some extent it did. She made numerous attempts during my childhood to have me go for physical therapy and to practice walking more "normally" at home. I vehemently refused. She could not understand why I would not walk straight.

Now I realize why. My disability, with my different walk and talk and my involuntary movements, having been with me all of my life, was part of me, part of my identity. With these disability features, I felt complete and whole. My mother's attempt to change my walk, strange as it may seem, felt like an assault on myself, an incomplete acceptance of all of me, an attempt to make me over. I fought it because I wanted to be accepted and appreciated as I was.

It is hard to realize that a disability, which seems like a liability, a defect, an eyesore, could be an okay, important part of a child's body and self. It is not that I would choose to be disabled, but rather my disability, like other salient characteristics I was born with, is part of me.

I had learned in childhood to deny my disability because I could not accept society's definition of me as a freak, an inferior person. At some point, disabled children discover that their different bodies are perceived by society as inferior. This is the moment with the most potential for emotional trauma. Like any children subject to prejudice, the consequences depend largely on whether and how these children are helped to understand and deal with the negative societal view of them.

Parents need help in finding ways to explain prejudice to their children and to help their children distinguish physical facts about their disability from societal distortions about these facts.

SOURCE: Rousso, 1984.

---

ple. On the other hand, even if Jason's family and friends shower him with praise and emotional support, if he thinks sports are important but he is not athletic, he will suffer a loss of self-esteem. The presence of a disability also affects self-esteem, as seen in Box 13-1.

Emotional Growth. In middle childhood children can better understand their own emotions, along with other people's emotions. This emotional progression parallels children's cognitive shift: From looking at themselves along a single dimension, they are now able to hold a representation of the self with multiple dimensions. As we saw in Chapter 10, by age 7 or 8 children have internalized complex emotions of shame or pride. The degree to which they feel proud or ashamed of themselves affects what they think of themselves.

The impact these more mature emotions have on self-esteem links the emotional, cognitive, and social domains of development. These emotions require a certain level of cognitive advance; they also depend upon the kind of socialization a child has received.

Parenting Styles. Most parents of children with high self-esteem use what Diana Baumrind termed the *authoritative* approach. These parents combine love and acceptance of their children with strong demands for academic performance and good behavior. Within clearly defined and firmly enforced limits, they show respect for and allow individual expression. They reward more than they punish. The parents themselves tend to have high self-esteem and lead active, rewarding lives (Coopersmith, 1967).

Parents who are both democratic and strict help a child's development in sev-

After their parents, the most important people in many children's lives are their grandparents. A warm and supportive grandfather, who is also handy at fixing a bike, can boost self-esteem—and be fun to be with.

eral ways. By setting clear, consistent rules, they let children know what behavior is expected of them. Knowing what to expect helps children gain internal control; as they function within rule systems, they learn to consider the demands of the outside world. Parents who make demands show that they believe their children can meet them—and that the parents care enough to insist that they do.

There is another way to look at the relationship between parenting and children's self-esteem. Children with high self-esteem may have characteristics that encourage their parents to be loving, firm, and democratic. Children who are self-confident, cooperative, and competent are easy to bring up. Once again we see the bidirectionality of influence between parents and children—how they continually affect each other.

THE CHILD IN THE FAMILY

Vicky and Jason spend more time away from home than they used to. School, friends, games, and movies all draw them away from the house and keep them apart from the family. Yet home and the people who live there are still the most important part of their world.

Relationships with parents, siblings, and extended family members (grandparents, aunts, uncles, and cousins) continue to develop during middle childhood. As proposed in Urie Bronfenbrenner's ecological theory, societal change affects family life, which in turn affects children's development. In recent years such changes include rising rates of divorce, single-parent families, and mothers working outside the home. A review of family research suggests that the negative effects of these factors have been exaggerated—and that the most important factors affecting children's development involve economic well-being, or its lack, and the atmosphere within the home—whether it is warm and loving or is conflict-ridden (Demo, 1991).

Parents who enjoy being with their children, like this mother, are likely to raise children who feel good about themselves—and about their parents.

PARENTS AND CHILDREN

Relationships

School-age children spend relatively little time with their parents; they spend more with their peers. But even though some research suggests that parents spend only about 30 minutes on an average workday interacting with their school-age children, most parents are supportive, loving, and involved with the children (Demo, 1992). Relationships with parents continue to be the most important ones in children's lives.

When 199 mostly middle-class fifth- and sixth-graders answered questionnaires about the important people in their lives, their ratings revealed that different relationships serve different purposes. Ranking ties with their parents the most important, the children looked to them for affection, guidance, lasting and dependable bonds, and affirmation of competence or value as a person. They rated mothers higher than fathers as companions and were generally more satisfied with their relationships with their mothers; girls were closer to mothers than to fathers. After parents, the most important people in children's lives were grandparents, who were seen as warm and supportive offerers of affection and enhancement of worth (Furman & Buhrmester, 1985).

Similar findings showed up among 333 African American, Latino, and white schoolchildren aged 7 to 14. For all ages and all ethnic groups, close family relationships were important. In middle childhood the children's social networks expanded, with extended family becoming more important as providers of social support. This was especially true for black and Latino children; white children received the least extended-family support. As suggested by attachment theory, parents and then extended family members provide a secure environment from which children can expand their social relationships to people outside the family (Levitt, Guacci-Franco, & Levitt, 1993).

Issues

As children's lives change, so do the issues between them and their parents. Parents now worry about a child's school life. They wonder how involved they should be; they wonder what to do about a child who complains about the teacher, misbehaves in school, or pretends to be sick to avoid going.

Another issue is friends. Parents usually want to know where their children are and whom they are with when they are not in school. Some parents tell their children which youngsters they may and may not play with. Disagreements often arise over what household chores children should do, whether they should be paid for doing them, and how much allowance they should get. (Of course, many of these issues do not exist in some societies, where children must work to help the family survive.)

The profound changes in children's lives and in the issues that arise affect the ways parents handle discipline. Yet most parents do not change their *basic* approach to their job as their children mature.

Discipline

Parents have various ways of *discipline*—teaching their children character, self-control, and moral behavior. Most parents use different methods with children of different ages, but retain their dominant style.

Most of the disciplinary techniques Jason's parents use are inductive ones that include reasoning. For example, his father tells him, "You shouldn't hit Jermaine because this will hurt him and make him feel bad." Jason sees from this how his actions can affect others. His mother appeals to his self-esteem ("What happened to the helpful boy who was here yesterday?"), sense of humor ("If you go one more day without a bath, we'll know when you're coming without looking!"), moral values ("A big, strong boy like you shouldn't sit on the train and let an old person stand"), or appreciation ("Aren't you glad that you have a father who cares enough to remind you to wear boots so that you won't catch a cold?"). Above all, Jason's parents let him know he is responsible for what happens to him and has to bear the consequences of his behavior ("No wonder you missed the school bus today—you stayed up too late last night! Now you'll have to walk to school").

This approach to discipline becomes more typical as children gain cognitive awareness. School-age children are less likely to knuckle under to sheer power. They are more likely to defer to parents' wishes when they recognize that their parents are fair, that parental desires contribute to the whole family's well-being, and that parents often "know better" because of their experience. Authoritative parents often defer to children's growing judgment and take strong stands only on important issues.

Yet a parent's underlying philosophy seems to remain fairly consistent over time, especially with regard to control, enjoyment, and emotional investment in a child. In one longitudinal study, parents of boys and girls from varied backgrounds filled out the same questionnaires when their children were 3 years old and again when they were 12 (Roberts, Block, & Block, 1984). The questions related to independence, control, handling aggression and sex, early training, emphasis on health and achievement, expression of feelings, protectiveness, supervision, and punishment. Over the 9-year period, the parents' basic values and

discipline *Teaching intended to help children develop character, self-control, and moral behavior.*

approach to child rearing seemed to remain constant (most emphasized rational guidance and praise), although they did change in some ways appropriate to the children's development.

Control and Coregulation

Control of a child's behavior gradually shifts from parents to child. During the preschool years, a child's gradual acquisition of self-control and self-regulation reduces the need for constant supervision. But not until adolescence or even later are many young people permitted to decide how late to stay out, who their friends should be, and how to spend their money.

Middle childhood is a transitional stage of *coregulation,* in which parent and child share power; "parents continue to exercise general supervisory control, while children begin to exercise moment-to-moment self-regulation" (Maccoby, 1984, p. 191). Coregulation reflects the child's developing self-concept. As children begin to coordinate their own wishes with societal demands, they are more likely to anticipate how other people will react to what they do, or to accept a reminder from parents that others will think better of them if they behave differently.

Coregulation is a cooperative process; it succeeds only if parents and children communicate clearly. If children do not let their parents know where they are, what they are doing, and what their problems are—or if parents become preoccupied with their own activities and do not take an interest in their children's—the parents will not be able to judge when to step in. To make this transitional phase work, parents need to influence their children when the children are with them and to monitor their behavior when they are not—by phone or through a baby-sitter. Most important, children need to learn to monitor their *own* behavior—to adopt acceptable standards, avoid undue risks, and recognize when they need support or guidance from parents (Maccoby, 1984).

HOW PARENTS' WORK AFFECTS CHILDREN

Much of adults' time, effort, and ego goes into their occupations. How does their work affect the family—especially now, when adults' roles are in transition? Let's see some ways parents' work affects children.

Mothers' Work

Most of the research on how women's work affects their children has focused not on the kind of work they do nor its demands on them, but on whether they work at all for pay. Much of the research refers to a time when the working mother was the exception rather than the rule. Today, almost 7 out of 10 married women with children under 18, and 8 out of 10 single mothers, are in the workforce. With more than half of all new mothers going to work soon after giving birth, many children have never known a time when their mothers were *not* working.

How does a mother's employment affect her children? Research has shown a number of beneficial effects and few adverse ones. Its influence is affected by child-related factors like the child's age, sex, temperament, and personality; mother-related factors like whether she works full- or part-time, how she feels about her work, and whether she has a supportive mate; and societal factors like the family's social and economic status and the kind of care the child receives.

coregulation *Transitional stage in the control of behavior in which parents exercise general supervision and children exercise moment-to-moment self-regulation.*

Children whose parents work outside the home become more independent and more self-confident when they know that they are trusted to handle a variety of tasks, like taking a telephone message safely and accurately.

The Mother's Psychological State.   Despite the guilt many working mothers* feel over being away from their children, employed women often feel more competent, more economically secure, and more in charge of their lives. Their self-esteem, sense of personal effectiveness, and overall well-being tend to be higher than that of homemakers, whose work is generally undervalued in our society (Demo, 1992).

The more satisfied a mother is with her life, the more effective she is as a parent. This effect cuts across socioeconomic levels, but may be more significant at lower incomes, especially for single mothers who have had little education. Research indicates lower rates of child abuse from mothers working full-time, compared with at-home or part-time workers (Gelles, 1987). Whether a mother works full- or part-time or is unemployed, if she feels overwhelmed by too many responsibilities, she is more likely to be abusive to her children than if she is comfortable with what she is called upon to do (Demo, 1992).

Interactions in Working-Mother Families.   In working-mother families, the division of labor between parents is less traditional than in one-job families. Even though the typical working mother still does more housework and child care, her husband tends to be more involved than men in homemaker-mother families (Almeida, Maggs, & Galambos, 1993; Demo, 1991). The husband of a working mother can spend more time with his children, since he is less likely to hold a second job. Both parents spend more time with their children on weekends than in families with nonemployed mothers (Demo, 1992).

The father tends to be most involved when the mother works full-time, when they have more than one child, when the children are quite young, and when she earns close to what he does (L. W. Hoffman, 1986). The involved father shows his children a nurturing side—expresses love, tries to help them with their worries and problems, makes them feel better when they are upset, and gives them continuing care and attention (Carlson, 1984). His children see a side of his personality not often visible in men.

Daughters of working women and sons of involved fathers have fewer stereotypes about gender roles than do children in breadwinner-father, homemaker-mother families (Carlson, 1984). This effect depends more on the mother's attitude toward the father's participation in home duties than on how much he actually does (G. K. Baruch & Barnett, 1986).

Children's Reactions to Mothers' Work.   School-age children of employed mothers seem to have two advantages over children of homemaker mothers. They tend to live in more structured homes, with clear-cut rules giving them more household responsibilities, and they are encouraged to be more independent. Encouragement of independence seems to be especially good for girls, helping them to become more competent, to achieve more in school, and to have higher self-esteem (Bronfenbrenner & Crouter, 1982).

Findings for boys are less clear-cut and more varied by social class. Boys in both single- and two-parent lower-income families seem to benefit when their mothers work; these boys achieve more in school. One benefit is the family's higher income. Sons of middle-class working mothers, however, have done less

---

*As in Chapter 7, we use the term *working mother* to describe the mother employed outside the home.

well in school than have sons of homemakers (Heyns & Catsambis, 1986). A newer study may provide the rationale for this effect on boys. It found that 9- to 12-year-old boys whose parents do not monitor them (know where they are, what they are doing, and whom they are with) earn poorer grades than do more closely monitored children (Crouter, MacDermid, McHale, & Perry-Jenkins, 1990). How well parents keep track of their children—especially boys—seems more important than whether the mother works outside the home.

The Ecological Context of the Family.   Among low-income families, women who are better educated and more highly motivated often choose to work to achieve certain goals rather than being on welfare or accepting a meager income from a partner. Because these women have chosen to work, work may affect them positively, benefiting their children. This description fit one group of 189 second-grade children, who seemed to benefit from the employment of their adolescent, single-parent mothers. Children of employed mothers performed better on math, reading, and language tests than did other children. Their achievement may also have resulted from the more favorable environments their mothers' income was able to provide (Vandell & Ramanan, 1992).

Neither the dual-income nor the working-single-parent family follows one single pattern. Probably the most influential factor is the parents' attitudes. One researcher found that "Where the pattern itself produces difficulties, they seem often to stem mainly from the slow pace with which society has adapted to this new family form" (L. W. Hoffman, 1989, p. 290). When good child care is available and affordable, when men assume a large role in the home, and when employers support workers' family roles, families reap the benefits.

What do you think?   *Should a mother whose finances permit, stay home to take care of the children instead of going to work?*

Fathers' Work

Most of the research on how men's work affects their families has focused on the nature of the work itself. Some of the findings regarding men can also apply to women.

When work does not fully satisfy a parent's psychological needs, children may benefit. A man whose work is not exciting may throw himself enthusiastically into family life and, through his children, gain a sense of accomplishment, fun, intellectual stimulation, moral values, and self-esteem. But children may suffer if a man takes out his frustration at having little autonomy at work by being hostile and severe with them, or if a man's work is so fulfilling that he does not invest much of himself in his family. The dominant mood of a man's work may also go home with him—whether it is satisfaction or tension.

Summer vacation poses special problems for working parents: When children are not in school, keeping track of them becomes harder. Mothers who are at home over the summer months become more involved with their children, but in dual-worker families, fathers tend to increase their monitoring when children are out of school and to become more knowledgeable about the children's activities (Crouter & McHale, 1993).

When a man loses his job and becomes irritable and pessimistic, he is likely to nurture his children less and punish them more. The children may react to this treatment with emotional or behavior problems and reduced aspirations (McLoyd, 1989; 1990). Of course, not all unemployed fathers react this way. A man's reactions are tempered by his wife's relationship with him and his children, as well as by the children's personalities and temperaments. Some men find the chance to spend more time with their children a positive aspect of being out of work. In general, though, a father's *not* having a job is considered to have damaging effects on his children, while a mother's *having* one has been thought disruptive for her family (Bronfenbrenner & Crouter, 1982).

Care for School-Age Children of Working Parents

When Jason, 11, comes home from school, he unlocks the door to his apartment, throws down his books, and feeds his cat before sitting down for a snack. Then he calls Julia to check in. Depending on what needs to be done, he may fold laundry, set the table, or start dinner. If he wants to watch television at night, he may do his homework in the afternoon.

Jason is among 2 million *self-care children*—school-age children who regularly care for themselves at home without adult supervision because both parents—or a single custodial parent—work outside the home (C. Cole & Rodman, 1987). Although most self-care takes place after school, some children spend time alone in the morning or evening, too. Most are alone for no more than 2 hours a day (Cain & Hofferth, 1989). Other children go to a structured after-school program, where they do homework under adult supervision, take music or art lessons, or engage in other activities. Others are cared for by a baby-sitter or a relative; and some are cared for by their own parents. Does it matter what kind of after-school care a child gets?

There is no simple answer. Among 150 suburban middle-class children, for example, no differences were found between mother-care and self-care children on a number of dimensions. Both groups did about the same in classroom work, standardized tests, popularity with other children, and parent and teacher ratings (Vandell & Corasaniti, 1988).

In another study, both black and white third-graders from single-parent and two-parent low-income families thrived in after-school programs. These children got higher grades in school, had better work habits, and were better adjusted than children who stayed alone or with their mothers or baby-sitters (Posner & Vandell, undated). However, the type of after-school care is less important than the quality of children's experiences with their families (Vandell & Ramanan, 1991).

The stereotyped picture of the "latchkey child" as a lonely, neglected youngster is giving way to contrary findings. Although there is very little solid information about the impact of self-care on development, research has dispelled one misconception—that most self-care children are from poor, single-parent families in high-risk inner-city settings. Many are from well-educated, middle- to upper-class suburban or rural families (Cain & Hofferth, 1989). In sum, a self-care arrangement can work well if the processes of coregulation and self-regulation have proceeded appropriately. (See Box 13-2.)

Of course, any single influence (like parents' employment) has to be considered in the context of other aspects of a child's world.

BOX 13-2 ▪ THE EVERYDAY WORLD

WHEN SCHOOL-AGE CHILDREN CARE FOR THEMSELVES

How can parents tell when children are ready for self-care? And how can they make the situation as comfortable and safe as possible? The following are some guidelines outlined by professionals:

BEFORE CHILDREN TAKE CARE OF THEMSELVES, THEY SHOULD BE ABLE TO:

♦ Control their bodies well enough to keep from injuring themselves

♦ Keep track of keys and handle doors well enough to avoid locking themselves in or out

♦ Fix a sandwich or other simple snack

♦ Know how to tell time

♦ Safely operate necessary household equipment

♦ Not pose a danger to siblings

♦ Stay alone without being afraid or lonely

♦ Be flexible and resourceful enough to handle the unexpected

♦ Be responsible enough to follow important rules

♦ Understand and remember spoken and written instructions

♦ Read and write well enough to take telephone messages and use a pay phone

♦ Know what to say and do about visitors and callers (not tell strangers that they are alone and not open the door to anyone but family and close friends)

♦ Know how to get help in an emergency (how to call police and firefighters, which friends and neighbors to call, what other resources to call on)

PARENTS AND GUARDIANS CAN HELP IF THEY:

♦ Stay in touch by telephone (as by setting up a regular time for check-in calls, by which they can know where and with whom the child is)

♦ Tell children what to do and how to reach parents or another adult in an emergency

♦ Set up a structure for children's activity in self-care time

♦ Institute safety procedures

♦ Let an answering machine with a man's voice on it answer the phone to give the impression that an adult male is in the home

♦ Agree on a password for the child to use on the phone if she or he is in any kind of trouble

SOURCE: C. Cole & Rodman, 1987; Olds, 1989.

FAMILY ENVIRONMENT

The environment in a child's home has two major components. There is the structure—whether there are two parents, a single parent, or nonrelatives caring for a child, which defines the context in which a child will grow. Then there is the social, economic, and psychological atmosphere in the home (Haurin, 1992).

Researchers who have looked at the effects of both these influences have found that children generally perform better in school and have fewer emotional and behavior problems when they spend their childhood in a home with two parents who have a good relationship with each other. The exact mechanism that causes problems for children growing up in single-parent or stepparent homes is not fully understood, but various possibilities have emerged from the research. How parents act with each other seems to affect children's adjustment more than does marital status (Emery, 1988; Hetherington, 1989).

Atmosphere

In homes with both parents, the way they resolve their differences is associated with children's behavior. In one study, children who at age 5 had angry and distant fathers were at age 8 rated by teachers as self-blaming, distressed, and ashamed. Children who at age 5 had parents who showed contempt for each other by insults, mockery, and disparagement were at age 8 rated as disobedient, likely to break rules, and unable to wait their turn. Whether or not such parents had separated by the time their children were 8 years old, the children still showed mildly antisocial behaviors. Is this because children see models of poor conflict resolution? Or do these parents behave in the same negative ways with the children? Or is some other process at work? In any case, a link exists between parents' behaviors and children's outcomes (Katz & Gottman, 1993).

Whether a couple actually does divorce may be related to how involved a father is with his children. Such involvement is usually deeper when there is at least one son (Katzev, Warner, & Acock, 1994). Fathers are more likely to play with, take out, and do projects with sons than with daughters, possibly because they are more comfortable doing "guy things." An involved father is likely to be more committed to the marriage, and his wife is likely to be more satisfied. Parents who are both involved in child rearing do more, talk more, and tend to have a more intimate relationship than do couples in which the mother does most of the child care (Schwartz, 1994).

Structure

Most children under 18 in the United States live with two parents, but as Figure 13-1 shows, this proportion dropped from 76.6 percent in 1980 to 71.9 percent in 1990. Furthermore, a number of two-parent families are the result of divorce and remarriage.

What difference does the family structure make to children? It seems that involvement with children is at least part of the reason children in two-parent homes show better psychological adjustment. Even if a father is less involved in child rearing than his wife, he is still in the home. According to nationwide data on 17,110 children under 18, children living with single or remarried mothers ("nontraditional" families) were more likely than those living with both biological or adoptive parents ("traditional" families) to have repeated a grade of school, to

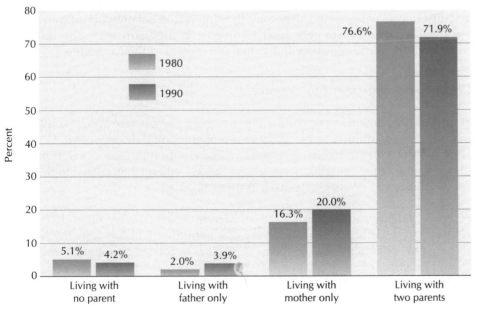

FIGURE 13-1
Living arrangements of children younger than 18, 1980 and 1990. Most children under 18 in the United States live with two parents, but this proportion dropped from 1980 to 1990. A number of these two-parent families are stepfamilies. *Source:* Children's Defense Fund, 1994.

have been expelled, to have been treated for emotional or behavioral problems in the previous year, and to have had more accidental injuries (D. A. Dawson, 1991).

A study of 136 fifth-graders suggests that some differences in psychological adjustment may be related to the fact that traditional parents do more with their children, are more likely to be authoritative, to feel that they have control over their lives, and to avoid severe punishment. In addition to such aspects of parenting, there are other influences, like the financial stress in single-parent homes, the fact that a single parent is often unable to provide as much supervision as two parents can, and the disruptions in families riven by divorce. These too contribute to the differences in child outcomes in the two kinds of families (Bronstein, Clauson, Stoll, & Abrams, 1993). Fortunately, many children adjust well even after their parents' divorce. How well depends on a number of factors.

CHILDREN OF DIVORCE

The central event of Jason's childhood is the collapse of his parents' marriage when he is 7 years old. He knew that they quarreled sometimes, but he always expected them to make up. He sensed the strains between them but tried to pretend they were not there. Now that Jess and Julia have separated, Jason can no longer pretend. He feels confused, angry, and bitterly disappointed. He doubts himself and feels that *he* failed.

More than 1 million children under the age of 18 are involved in divorces each year. About half the children born in the late 1970s and early 1980s (40 percent of white children; 75 percent of black children) will experience their parents' divorce before they turn 16 (Bray & Hetherington, 1993).

No matter how unhappy a marriage has been, its breakup usually comes as a shock to a child. Jason, like other children of divorcing parents, feels afraid of the future, guilty about his own (imaginary) role in causing the divorce, hurt and rejected when Jess moves out, and angry at both parents. Children may become depressed, hostile, disruptive, irritable, lonely, sad, accident-prone, or even suicidal; they may suffer from fatigue, insomnia, skin disorders, loss of appetite, or inability to concentrate; and they may lose interest in schoolwork and in social life. Children of different ages react to divorce in different ways, and different children of the same age show individual differences in their reactions.

Children's Adjustment to Divorce

"Tasks" of Adjustment. The children of divorcing parents face special challenges and burdens in addition to the usual issues of emotional development. In a longitudinal study of 60 divorcing couples whose children ranged in age from 3 to 18 at the time of the separation, six special "tasks" emerged as crucial to the children's adjustment (Wallerstein, 1983; Wallerstein & Kelly, 1980):

1 *Acknowledging the reality of the marital rupture.* Small children often do not understand what happened, and many older children initially deny the separation. Others either are overwhelmed by fears of total abandonment or retreat into fantasies of reconciliation. Most children face the facts by the end of the first year of separation.
2 *Disengaging from parental conflict and distress and resuming customary pursuits.*

At first, children may be so worried that they cannot play, do schoolwork, or take part in other usual activities. They need to put some distance between themselves and their distraught parents and go on with living their own lives. Most children do this by the end of the first 1 to $1\frac{1}{2}$ years after the separation.

3 *Resolving loss.* Absorbing all the losses caused by divorce may be the single most difficult task. Children need to adjust to the loss of the parent they are not living with, the loss of the security of feeling loved and cared for by both parents, the loss of familiar daily routines and family traditions—the loss of a whole way of life. Some children take years to deal with these losses; some never do, carrying a sense of being rejected, unworthy, and unlovable into adulthood.

4 *Resolving anger and self-blame.* Children realize that divorce, unlike death, is voluntary, and they often stay angry for years at the parent (or parents) who could do such a terrible thing to them. They look for the cause of divorce in something they did—or didn't do. When and if they forgive their parents and themselves, they feel more powerful and more in control of their lives.

5 *Accepting the permanence of the divorce.* Some children hold on for years to the fantasy that their parents will be reunited, even after both have remarried. Some accept the permanence of the situation only after they achieve psychological separation from their parents in adolescence or early adulthood.

6 *Achieving realistic hope regarding relationships.* Some children who have adjusted well in other ways come through a divorce feeling afraid to take a chance on intimate relationships themselves, for fear that they will fail as their parents did. They may become cynical, depressed, or simply doubtful of the possibility of finding lasting love.

Many children succeed at all these tasks and come through the divorce with an intact ego. The ability to do this seems to be related partly to a child's own resilience and partly to how parents handle issues entailed in the separation and the challenge of raising children alone.

Influences on Children's Adjustment to Divorce

In general, children of divorce have more social, academic, and behavioral problems than do children from intact homes. This is especially so for boys (Kelly, 1987). However, a number of factors influence how well children will adjust to divorce.

Parenting Styles and Parents' Satisfaction.   Children of divorced authoritative parents usually show fewer behavior problems, do better in school, and have fewer problems getting along with other children than do children of authoritarian or permissive parents (Hetherington, 1986; Guidubaldi & Perry, 1985). These effects are especially significant for boys. Children whose parents are able to control their anger, cooperate in parenting, and not expose the children to quarreling have fewer emotional and social problems (Hetherington, Stanley-Hagan, & Anderson, 1989). When parents argue frequently over child support and custody, their relationship with their children suffers (Donnelly & Finkelhor, 1992).

Children who have emotional or behavioral problems may be responding to the conflict between their parents, both before and after the divorce, rather than to the separation itself (Amato et al. 1993). This may be an indirect result of a mother's distress, which interferes with her ability to be warm and empathic with her children (Kline, Johnston, & Tschann, 1991).

According to studies of families in which the parents had divorced 6 years earlier, custodial mothers who did not remarry had more emotional problems and were less satisfied with their lives than remarried or nondivorced mothers. The unmarried mothers were still in intense, ambivalent, conflicted relationships with their sons, who tended to show behavior problems and spend less time at home with adults. However, the mothers had good relationships with their daughters, who tended to be fairly well adjusted (Hetherington, 1986).

Remarriage of the Mother.   It generally takes 2 to 3 years for children to adjust to a single-parent household. When a mother remarries, they have to adjust again; and sometimes they have to adjust to the breakup of this new marriage (Hetherington et al., 1989). Remarried mothers tend to be happier, better adjusted, and more satisfied with life, and their sons do better with a stepfather. However, their daughters often have more problems than the daughters of divorced women who have not remarried or of nondivorced mothers. Typically, however, these girls eventually adjust (Hetherington, 1986).

Relationship with the Father.   When Jess asked, "What can I do to make this easier for you?" Jason said, "Live close enough so I can ride my bike to your place."

The closer a divorced father lives to his children, the higher his socioeconomic status, and the more recent the separation, the more involved he is likely to be (Amato & Keith, 1991a). Fathers who see their children often, help to make child-rearing decisions, and feel that they have some control over their children's upbringing also tend to make regular child support payments (Braver et al., 1993). These factors have implications for postdivorce counseling and legislation: Perhaps encouraging fathers to take a larger role in their children's lives soon after the separation will set a pattern of intimacy—and child support—that will continue over the years.

This kind of encouragement is vital. Among 16- to 18-year-old boys whose parents had divorced 10 years earlier, the boys' relationships with their fathers were significant for the boys' adjustment. Sons of erratic and rejecting fathers felt hurt, trapped, and humiliated and often reacted with anger against their mothers (Wallerstein, 1987).

Accessibility of Both Parents.   Predictable and frequent contact with the noncustodial parent is important for children. Children who have reliable, frequent contact with the noncustodial parent (typically the father) are usually better adjusted; this is especially true for boys (Kelly, 1987). However, there seems to be no advantage to custody with the same-sex parent (Downey & Powell, 1993).

Joint custody—shared custody by both parents—does not seem to improve a child's situation in an amicable divorce and may worsen it in a bitter divorce (Kline, Tschann, Johnston, & Wallerstein, 1988). Children in shared custody do not have better relationships with their parents than do those in sole custody arrangements (Donnelly & Finkelhor, 1992).

Long-Term Effects of Divorce on Children

The effects of divorce persist beyond childhood. Many children of divorced parents adjust well, but others are still troubled 10 or more years later. In a longitu-

For optimal adjustment, children of divorced parents need reliable, frequent contact with both their parents.

dinal study of thirty-eight 16- to 18-year-olds whose parents had divorced 10 years earlier, three-fourths of the girls and about half of the boys were doing fairly well (Wallerstein, 1987). Most were in school full time, working part time, law-abiding, and living at home (75 percent with their mothers). The girls were getting along well with their mothers and were likely to be dating and involved in sexual relationships. However, the boys were far more likely to be lonely, emotionally constricted, and holding back in relationships with girls. Divorce had left its mark. Burdened by sadness, neediness, and a sense of their own powerlessness, these young people missed their fathers (whom they tended to idealize); were anxious about their own love relationships and chances for successful marriage; and were afraid of being betrayed, hurt, and abandoned (Wallerstein, 1987).

What happens to children of divorce when they become adults? One analysis of 37 studies involving over 81,000 people found some differences between adult children of divorced and nondivorced parents (Amato & Keith, 1991b). The divorce group tended to be slightly more depressed, to have more marital problems, to be in poorer physical health, and to have a lower socioeconomic status. However, the differences were small, stronger in earlier studies (perhaps showing that divorce is less traumatic now than it used to be), weaker among African Americans (where one-parent families are more common), and stronger among people who had sought counseling or therapy. In the general community, the link between parental divorce and negative long-term results for their children was weak.

What do you think? *Do you think that parents who want a divorce should stay married until all their children have grown up? Why or why not?*

ONE-PARENT FAMILIES AND STEPFAMILIES

Single-Parent Families

About 22 percent of American children (more than 10 million) live in homes with only one parent (U.S. Bureau of the Census, 1993). The number of single-parent families in the United States almost tripled between 1960 and 1986, but the rate of increase has slowed.

One-parent families may be created by death or by a mother's never marrying: Nearly a quarter of the nation's unmarried women (23.7 percent) now become mothers, an increase of almost 60 percent since 1982. The increase was especially marked among white women and women who attended college, but an increase also occurred for African American and Hispanic women and women at all educational levels (U.S. Bureau of the Census, 1993). But one-parent families most often result from divorce or separation. Most of the children in these families spend an average of 5 years in a single-parent home, almost always the mother's, before she remarries (Bray & Hetherington, 1993).

The rates for single parenthood are different among different ethnic groups in the United States. Highest rates occur among African Americans (62.6 percent in 1991), followed by Hispanic families (33.1 percent); in white families the rate is about 20 percent (U.S. Bureau of the Census, 1991). Rates also differ in different countries. An Australian report comparing rates in the mid-1980s for eight industrialized countries* found that the United States has the highest percentage

*Australia, France, Japan, Sweden, United Kingdom, United States, Soviet Republic, and West Germany.

of single-parent families (then 28.9 percent), with the lowest rate in Japan (4.1 percent—Burns, 1992).

In 86 percent of single-parent households the mother is the custodial parent, but the number of unmarried father-only families more than doubled between 1980 and 1992. Fathers now head 14 percent of single-parent households (U.S. Bureau of the Census, 1993). Almost 60 percent of custodial fathers are not married; about 40 percent have remarried (Meyer & Garasky, 1993). Custodial fathers typically are older, make more money, and are better educated than are custodial mothers. Married fathers earn the most, followed by single fathers and then single mothers. Still, a substantial number of custodial fathers are poor or nearly poor; 18 percent of father-only families are poor, compared with 43 percent of single-mother families (U.S. Bureau of the Census, 1993). More single fathers than married fathers are black, under 30 years old, and less highly educated (Meyer & Garasky, 1993).

Custodial fathers who do best were actively involved in child care and household tasks before the divorce, sought extra counseling after it, and purposefully worked toward a good relationship with their children. Most are happy with their decision and feel that they are the better choice for custodial parent (Hanson, 1988).

Effects on Children. Jason, like other children growing up in a single-parent household, does not have two adults at home who can share child-rearing responsibilities, take him to activities, serve as gender-role models, and show the interplay of personalities. Also, Julia has more money worries now. Divorce often brings a family's income down to or near the poverty level. Mother-only families suffer from the mother's low earning capacity, the father's failure to pay child support, and meager public benefits. This is associated with negative effects on children's health, well-being, and achievement (McLanahan & Booth, 1989).

The strains of a divorce also affect parenting. For several years after the separation, Julia and Jess—who had both been caring, involved parents—are so preoccupied with personal concerns that they are less attentive and responsive to Jason. The apartment is messy, and his bedtime and bath routines are slipshod (Hetherington, Cox, & Cox, 1975). These effects wear off in time, but Jason continues to feel torn between his two parents, even though they do not show open hostility toward each other. Compared with children of intact families, children in one-parent families report more autonomy and household responsibility; more conflict with siblings and less family cohesion; and less support, control, or punishment from fathers (Amato, 1987).

Effects on Schooling. Although students from one-parent homes tend to have more problems in school (D. A. Dawson, 1991), what looks like a "single-parent" effect is often a "low-income" effect. A study of 18,000 students showed that lower income affected school achievement more strongly than did the number of parents at home. This is an important finding, since one-parent households tend to have lower incomes (Zakariya, 1982). Other factors that influence school achievement are a parent's expectations for the child and the number of books in the home (Milne, Myers, Rosenthal, & Ginsburg, 1986).

Teachers can help children from single-parent homes. When elementary school teachers make systematic efforts to get single parents as well as couples to help children at home, single parents help as much and as effectively as do mar-

This "blended" family consists of a couple and three sets of children: a teenager from the husband's first marriage, two children from the wife's first marriage, and a toddler from the present marriage. Life is more complex in such families, but studies show that most of the children in them adjust and thrive.

ried ones (J. L. Epstein, 1984). Schools can also cooperate in other ways with single parents (most of whom are employed mothers): They can schedule evening, breakfast, or weekend meetings, conferences, and programs; provide late-afternoon transportation after sports or band practice; and send notices and report cards to both parents.

Long-Term Effects of the One-Parent Family.   Do children with only one parent get into more trouble than do those with two parents? Some studies report that they do, and that they may also be at greater risk of marital and parenting problems themselves (Rutter, 1979a). As adults, children from mother-only families are more likely to become poor single parents than are children who live with both parents (McLanahan & Booth, 1989).

Yet the one-parent home is not necessarily pathological, and the two-parent family is not always healthy. In general, children tend to be better adjusted when they have had a good relationship with one parent than when they have grown up in a two-parent home marked by discord and discontent (Rutter, 1983); and an inaccessible, rejecting, or hostile parent can be more damaging than an absent one (Hetherington, 1980).

Stepfamilies

The word *stepparent* conjures up vivid images of wicked and cruel interlopers in the family. Such images often sabotage real-life stepparents' efforts to forge close, warm relationships with their stepchildren. Yet many make the effort, and many succeed. Families made up of "yours, mine, and ours" are common. About 75 percent of divorced men and two-thirds of divorced women remarry; 86 percent of children of remarriages will live with their biological mother and a stepfather (Bray & Hetherington, 1993).

The stepfamily is different from the "natural" family. It has a larger supporting cast, with all the relatives of four adults (the married pair, plus both ex-spouses). It also has special stresses. Children and adults alike may be afraid to trust and love. Children's loyalties to absent or dead parents may interfere with forming ties to the stepparent, especially when the children go back and forth between two households.

The most common stepfamily comprises a mother, her children, and a step-father. One study found that remarried mothers were just as involved with their children as were mothers in intact marriages (Santrock, Sitterle, & Warshak, 1988). Even though many were working, they were nurturant and available to their children. Apparently, the greater satisfaction with life brought by remarriage carries over to a woman's relationships with her children.

Most of the children in this study were doing well and had positive feelings about their stepfathers, who had been in the role an average of 3 years. These men did some caring for and supervising of the children, but deliberately kept some distance from them because of what they saw as the children's needs. Nearly one-fourth of the stepfathers said they had tried to assume a parental role too fast, causing problems. Other research has found that a man has the best chance of gaining acceptance with a stepson if he makes friends with the boy first, supports the mother's parenting, and later moves into an authoritative role (Hetherington, 1986, 1989). This approach does not work so well with a stepdaughter, who is less likely to accept a stepfather as a parent. Boys benefit from having a stepfather; stepdaughters seem to have more behavioral problems than do daughters of non-divorced mothers or divorced mothers who do not remarry (Kelly, 1987).

Many women take their stepchildren to and from school and other activities, provide emotional support and comfort, and discipline them (Santrock et al., 1988). Still, most stepchildren's most enduring ties are with the custodial biological parent. The relationship a child has with that parent helps him or her adjust both to the divorce and the stepfamily.

CULTURAL CONTEXT OF THE FAMILY

A genuine multicultural viewpoint involves looking at far deeper issues than whether people wear saris or kunte cloth, or whether they eat sushi or empanadas. It means delving into values passed on through the generations and expressed in behavior.

Values and Behavior in Different Ethnic Groups

The ethnic group a child belongs to is likely to have its own distinctive socialization goals and adaptive strategies, with consequences for the child's behavior. This was shown in a study of African American, Native American, Asian-Pacific American, and Hispanic families (Harrison, Wilson, Pine, Chan, & Buriel, 1990).

Each ethnic group emphasizes a loyalty to the group and a collective philosophy that stresses group values rather than individual ones. Many adaptive strategies—cultural patterns that promote group survival and well-being—stem from such a perspective. In these minority families, ties are strong among extended family members, who are more likely than are white families to share living quarters and to interact with each other in daily life. These family ties are important in solving problems and coping with stress, especially for recent immigrants and in single-parent families.

By and large, ethnic minority children are encouraged to cooperate, share, and develop an interdependence with others—values that contrast sharply with western ideals of competition, autonomy, individualism, and self-reliance.

In socializing children, parents set their goals in terms of their specific situations within the larger society. Thus social roles in minority families tend to be more flexible than in majority-culture families. Older siblings assume more responsibilities for younger ones, adults more often share breadwinning (from economic need), and alternative family arrangements are more common (because of a perceived, or real, awareness of inadequate support systems in the larger society). The parents of well-motivated, achieving African American children emphasize ethnic pride and self-development, while acknowledging the existence of racial barriers.

Another common adaptive strategy involves becoming comfortable in two cultures. Children learn two languages: the one spoken in the home, which helps to give children a sense of their ethnic identity, and the one spoken in the larger society, which is essential for getting along socially, academically, and eventually at work. These children learn to switch languages and behavior appropriately from one situation to the other. (See the discussion of bilingualism in Chapter 12.)

Anyone planning public policy or working with children from ethnic minorities needs to be aware of how their families differ from the majority culture, and also of how families in one minority culture differ from those in another. By acknowledging and respecting differences among people we can overcome some of the barriers that prevent children from reaching their full potential.

Poverty and Some of Its Effects on Children

Poverty crushes people's spirits, makes them depressed, and interferes with their ability to form and maintain mutually enriching relationships. Impoverished children bear an especially heavy burden from the weight of their parents' distress.

In an ecological analysis, Vonnie McLoyd (1990) focuses on the pervasive effects of the poverty suffered by many black families and traces a typical route from poverty to adults' psychological distress to its effect on child rearing—and finally to its effects on children.

In McLoyd's model, parents who live in poor housing, are worried about their next meal, and feel a lack of control over their lives become anxious, depressed, and irritable. They discipline using the least effort—with physical punishment and authoritarian commands, rather than explaining, reasoning, and negotiating. They may ignore a child's good behavior and pay attention only to misbehavior. Their children in turn have social, emotional, and behavior problems. The children's own characteristics also play a part: Those who have difficult temperaments and are unattractive have even worse problems.

Such results are not inevitable, says McLoyd. When mothers can turn for emotional support, help with child care, and child-rearing information to their own mothers, other relatives, or community representatives, they often respond positively and are able to parent their children more happily and more effectively. The mediating influence of community support holds important implications for community, church, and governmental programs.

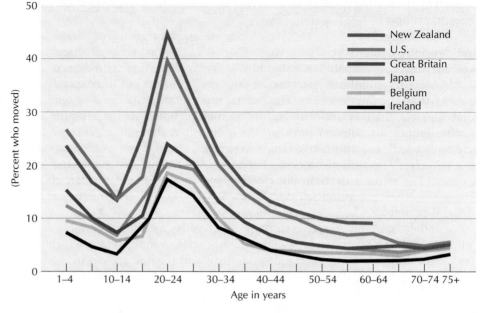

FIGURE 13-2
Percentage of population that changed usual residence in one year for six countries, by age, circa 1981. Children in some countries move much more often than those in others. In the United States such moves seem to be due largely to poverty and to parental separation.
SOURCE: Long, 1992.

When Families Move

Another contextual influence involves frequent moves. Children in some countries move much more often than those in others. (See Figure 13-2.) In the United States such moves seem to be due largely to poverty and to parental separation. Data from the 1988 National Health Interview Survey indicate that children who have moved often are more likely to be poor and in the home of a single parent who is unemployed or a high school dropout (or both) (Long, 1992).

Those who moved three or more times have about twice the risk of emotional, behavior, or school problems as do children who have never moved, even when income and other social factors are taken into account. They are also more at risk for health problems, since they are much less likely to have a regular place to go for medical care. Frequent movers are more likely to be depressed, headstrong, hyperactive, antisocial, and immature; to repeat a school grade, be suspended or expelled; and to receive psychological help. Frequent moving may be a symptom of stress, chaos, and major emotional problems within the family. The moving itself is also disruptive as children feel a loss of control over their lives and leave the friends who become so important in middle childhood (G. A. Simpson & Fowler, 1994; Fowler, Simpson, & Schoendorf, 1993).

Children of Gay and Lesbian Parents

According to a review of the literature on the social and personal development of children of lesbian and gay parents, these children are no more likely to have psychological problems than are those of heterosexual parents (C. J. Patterson, 1992). Nor are they any more likely than children of heterosexual parents to be sexually abused. Their worst problem seems to be teasing from their peers.

Several studies conducted over the past 15 years have focused on such children's sexual identity and gender-role behavior; personal development, including aspects like self-concept, moral judgment, and intelligence; and social relationships. Although research is still sparse and the studies varied in methodology, none indicated any psychological risk for them. Such findings can have social policy implications for legal decisions on custody and visitation disputes, foster care, and adoptions—for anywhere from 6 million to 14 million children in at least 4 million households. These numbers are higher than generally believed, say experts, because so many parents do not openly acknowledge their homosexuality (C. J. Patterson, 1992).

SIBLINGS, PEERS, AND FRIENDS

BROTHERS AND SISTERS

"I fight more with my little brother than I do with my friends," reports Vicky at 8 years of age. "But when I fight with Bobby, we always make up." Vicky recognizes the special nature of her relationship with Bobby. She can see that their tie is deeper and more lasting than a friendship, which may founder on a quarrel or just fade away. She is also aware that her relationship with her brother is ambivalent, marked by special affection as well as intense competition and resentment.

Although American children do less active caretaking of younger siblings than do children in many other countries, scenes like this one are common. The most harmonious sibling relationships tend to be those with older sisters.

How Siblings Help Each Other Develop

Vicky and her brother influence each other *directly* through interaction and *indirectly* through their impact on each other's relationship with their parents. A direct influence is the way siblings help one another develop a self-concept. When Vicky sees that she and Bobby are different despite all their shared bonds, she forms a stronger sense of herself as an individual.

Sibling relations are a laboratory for learning how to resolve conflicts. The ties of blood and physical closeness impel siblings to make up after quarrels, since they know they will see each other every day. They learn that expressing anger does not end a relationship. Younger siblings become quite skillful at sensing other people's needs, negotiating for what they want, and compromising. While firstborns tend to be bossy and more likely to attack, interfere with, ignore, or bribe their siblings, later-borns plead, reason, and cajole. Children are more apt to squabble with same-sex siblings, and two brothers quarrel more than any other combination (Cicirelli, 1976a).

Siblings learn how to deal with dependence in relationships by depending on each other. Although children in America care for younger brothers and sisters less than do children in many other countries, some caretaking does take place. Older children often mind younger ones when parents are at work; they also help younger siblings with homework. This help is most likely to be effective (and accepted) when it comes from a sibling—especially a sister—who is at least 4 years older (Cicirelli, 1976a, 1976b).

Sibling Relationships in Cultural Context

In developing countries, it is common to see a tiny child of 3 rocking a baby. It is also common to see older girls who are kept out of school to care for three or four younger siblings—to keep them out of mischief, toilet-train them, assign chores, and generally supervise. The mother is free to work; the family's survival is at stake. In these settings, sibling care is obligatory.

Sibling caretaking yields many benefits. The younger ones learn skills and knowledge that contribute to their development, and all the siblings form a close bond with each other. This solidarity will carry over into adult life, when they will cooperate, share with, and care for each other. All is not sweetness and light, of course: Siblings fight and compete in developing countries too (Cicirelli, 1994).

In industrialized societies, sibling ties are encouraged but not required. Parents generally try to treat their children equally, which includes not burdening older children with caretaking of younger ones (Weisner, 1993). This view is consistent with the western value of promoting individual development, as opposed to fostering a group ideal.

What do you think?   *Should older siblings have regular formal duties in taking care of younger ones?*

THE PEER GROUP

"Sweep!" Jason bellows as he whisks away a wax-filled bottle cap he and a friend have been flicking in the street game known as "skellzies." This game, played on city streets for some 80 years, is one more in an ancient legacy. Impromptu games of tag, catch, jacks, marbles, and "let's pretend" have historically served the time-honored mandate of childhood: to learn through play. Through play, children are in physical and social contact with others, gain confidence in their ability, and practice using their imagination. Play offers socially acceptable ways to compete, to expend energy, and to act aggressively.

Today we are seeing new social patterns as technology changes the tools and habits of leisure. Television and videocassettes turn many children into "couch potatoes." Computer games demand few social skills. Children engage in more organized sports, which replace children's rules with adult rules and in which adult referees settle disputes so that children do not need to find ways to resolve matters among themselves. Still, as their peers become more and more important, children are spending more time with others their own age than they did in early childhood.

Formation of the Peer Group

Our discussions in earlier chapters told of babies' and toddlers' awareness of one another and of preschoolers' early peer relationships. But it is in middle childhood that the peer group really comes into its own.

Groups form naturally among children who live near each other or go to school together. Children who play together are usually within a year or two of the same age, though an occasional neighborhood play group will form that includes small children along with older ones. Too wide an age range brings problems with differences in size, interests, and ability levels.

Groups are usually all girls or all boys (Hartup, 1984, 1992). Children of the same sex have common interests, girls are generally more mature than boys, and (as we pointed out in Chapter 10), girls and boys develop different styles of playing and talking. As children get older, their groups are usually made up of only one ethnic group, apparently as part of the same drive to be with similar people.

Only among their peers—whether fellow campers or fellow pupils—can children get a sense of how smart, how athletic, or how personable they are.

Although children this age typically have four or five friends with whom they spend most of their "own" time, they usually play with only one or two at a time (Hartup, 1992).

Functions and Influence of the Peer Group

In our highly mobile, age-segregated society, the peer group is a strong influence, for both good and ill.

Positive Effects.   Ninety-one Canadian fifth- and sixth-graders kept week-long diaries of what they did with other children and what they liked and disliked about their friends' behavior. Then another group of 81 children the same age (average age $11\frac{1}{2}$) rated the importance and prevalence of each activity and which behaviors they would most like or dislike in each activity. (See Table 13-1.) As a result of peer activities, children develop skills for sociability and intimacy, enhance relationships, and gain a sense of belonging. They are motivated to achieve and they attain a sense of identity. They also learn (Zarbatany, Hartmann, & Rankin, 1990).

Different peer activities contribute differently to these functions. Noncompetitive activities (like talking) offer opportunities for enhancing relationships, while competitive ones (like sports) help children identify unique aspects of the self. Children need exposure to a variety of activities and may need to be encouraged to take part in those they might not ordinarily seek out (like, say, team sports for girls and child care for boys).

It is with other children, as well as with their parents, that youngsters develop a self-concept and build self-esteem. They form opinions of themselves by seeing themselves as others see them. They have a basis of comparison—a realistic gauge of their own abilities and skills. Only within a large group of their

TABLE 13-1

IMPORTANT AND PREVALENT PEER ACTIVITIES AS RATED BY FIFTH- AND SIXTH-GRADERS		
MOST COMMON ACTIVITIES*		**MOST IMPORTANT ACTIVITIES***
Conversation		Noncontact sports
Hanging out		Watching TV or listening
Walking around at school		to records
Talking on the telephone		Conversation
Traveling to and from school		Talking on the telephone
Watching TV or listening		Physical games
to records		Going to parties
Physical games		Hanging out

MOST LIKED BEHAVIORS		
Invitations to participate	Sharing	Facilitating achievements
Performing admirably	Loyalty	Being nice or friendly
Physically helping	Humor	Absence of unpleasant
Complimenting or encouraging	Instructing	behavior
Giving permission	Helping	

MOST DISLIKED BEHAVIORS		
Physical aggression	Teasing	Annoying or bothersome
Interfering with achievements	Ignoring	behavior
Verbal aggression	Violating rules	Expressing anger
Dishonesty	Criticizing	Unfaithfulness
		Greed or bossiness

*There were some gender differences. Boys liked sports more than girls did and spent more time in contact sports; girls spent more time shopping, talking on the telephone, and talking about hair styles and clothing than boys did.
SOURCE: Zarbatany, Hartmann, & Rankin, 1990.

peers can children get a sense of how smart, how athletic, and how personable they are. Then too, the peer group helps children choose values to live by. Testing their opinions, feelings, and attitudes against those of other children helps them sift through the values they previously accepted unquestioningly from parents and decide which to keep, which to discard. The peer group also offers emotional security. Sometimes another child can provide comfort that an adult cannot. It is reassuring to find out that a friend also harbors "wicked" thoughts that would offend an adult.

Interacting with other children helps children in cognitive ways too. When children work on computer tasks with a partner, for example, they may seem to concentrate less on the task and more on the social interaction, but they enjoy the sessions more and learn more from them than do children working alone (Perlmutter, Behrend, Kuo, & Muller, 1989). Finally, the peer group helps children learn how to get along in society—how to adjust their needs and desires to those of others, when to yield and when to stand firm.

The peer group counterbalances parents' influence, opens new perspectives, helps children form a self-concept and develop social skills, helps them learn, and frees them to make independent judgments.

Negative Effects: Conformity. The peer group may hold out some undesirable values, and some children may not have the strength to resist. Children are most susceptible to pressure to conform during middle childhood.

A classic study on conformity tested the reactions to group pressure of 90 children aged 7 to 13 (Berenda, 1950). The children were shown cards with two lines of clearly different lengths and asked to tell which line was shorter or longer. When the children were alone, they answered correctly; but when they were in a room with eight children who had been told to give wrong answers to 7 of the 12 cards, the target child was torn between describing what she or he actually saw and going along with the group. In the group setting, only 43 percent of the 7- to 10-year-old subjects and 54 percent of the 10- to 13-year-olds gave the right answers. After the test, one 11-year-old girl said:

> I had a funny feeling inside. You know you are right and they are wrong and you agree with them. And you still feel you are right and you say nothing about it. . . . I just gave their answers. If I had the test alone, I wouldn't give the answers I gave. (Berenda, 1950, p. 232)

The effects of conformity can be critical. Peer influence is strongest when issues are unclear. Since we live in a world with many ambiguous issues that call for careful judgment, peer-group influences can have grave consequences. It is usually in the company of peers that children shoplift, begin to use drugs, and act in other antisocial ways. Peer pressure may in some cases change a troublesome child into a delinquent one.

However, children help to shape their own development: Those who already have antisocial leanings are the ones who tend to drift toward other antisocial youngsters and to be further influenced by them. Those without such tendencies are less likely to be in such groups and to be influenced by them (Hartup, 1992).

Some degree of conformity to group standards is a healthy mechanism of adaptation. It is unhealthy only when it becomes destructive or makes people act against their own better judgment.

What do you think? *Since children's peers are so influential, should parents restrict their friendships to children the parents approve of?*

Popularity

We all want other people to like us, and popularity achieves a new importance in middle childhood, when youngsters spend more time with other children and are greatly affected by peer opinions.

Individual Differences in Popularity

The Popular Child. Popular children share a number of characteristics. Typically, they have good cognitive abilities. They are good at solving social problems, helpful to other children, and assertive without being disruptive or aggressive. Their behavior enhances, rather than undermines, other children's goals. They are trustworthy, loyal, and self-disclosing enough to provide emotional support for other children. Their superior social skills make other people enjoy being with them (Newcomb, Bukowski, & Pattee, 1993).

Popular children maintain a strong gender identity within same-sex social groups, rather than showing "undue" interest in being with groups of the other sex. Sroufe, Bennett, Englund, Urban, and Shulman (1993), who studied children in summer camp, maintain the importance of such "gender boundaries" in acquiring peer-group norms and forming a self-concept.

Unpopular children can become better liked if they learn social skills, like carrying on a conversation in which they share information about themselves and show interest in others.

The Unpopular Child. One of childhood's saddest figures is the child who is chosen last for every team, is on the fringes of every group, is not invited to birthday parties, walks home alone after school, and sobs in despair, "Nobody wants to play with me."

Children can be unpopular for many reasons; they can change some of the reasons but not others. Some unpopular youngsters are aggressive, some are hyperactive and inattentive, and some are withdrawn (Newcomb et al., 1993; A. W. Pope, Bierman, & Mumma, 1991; Dodge, Coie, Pettit, & Price, 1990). Others act silly and immature or anxious and uncertain. They are often insensitive to other children's feelings and cannot adapt to new situations (Bierman, Smoot, & Aumiller, 1993).

Unpopular children do not have the social skills that popular ones do. Some expect not to be liked. One experiment involved two groups of unpopular children—third-grade boys and fourth- and fifth-grade girls. Some were told that other children whom they had met once before liked them and looked forward to seeing them again; then they were brought back together with these other children. Children who got this positive "feedback" were liked better by their new acquaintances than were children in a control group who had received no such message. When the children were rated on behavior by independent observers, the girls who got positive messages acted more socially competent (Rabiner & Coie, 1989). Apparently, some unpopular children, expecting not to be liked, do not exert themselves with others.

The process by which a child's early behavior leads to unpopularity can be seen in an observational study of 186 six- and eight-year-old African American boys. The boys were assigned to play groups consisting of six boys who did not know each other. They were then observed during five daily 45-minute sessions. From the beginning of the study, 13 boys who became chronically victimized by the other children were submissive, did not start conversations, did not try to persuade other children to do what they wanted, and played by themselves more than did the other boys. When other children teased or hit them, they showed pain, asked them to stop, gave up toys, or withdrew. The more they submitted, the more the other boys picked on them. Although the victims were not disliked at the beginning of the study, by the end they were not well liked (Schwartz, Dodge, & Coie, 1993). How do children develop the behaviors that will make them popular or unpopular?

Influences on Popularity

Cultural Influences. Chinese children are encouraged to be cautious, to restrain themselves, and to inhibit their urges; quiet and shy youngsters are considered well behaved. In western cultures, however, such children are usually seen as socially immature, fearful, and lacking self-confidence. It is not surprising that shy, sensitive Chinese children are popular with their ethnic peers, but that Canadian and American children with these traits are not well-liked by *their* peers (X. Chen & Rubin, 1992; Bierman et al., 1993). Once again, we see the influence of a child's culture and we are reminded of the need to consider the social context of behavior before deciding on its meaning.

Family Influences. Parent-child relationships are linked to relationships among children, since it is often in the family setting that children acquire the behaviors that affect popularity. Children of parents who punish and threaten are likely to threaten or act mean with other children, and they are less popular than are children of parents who reason and try to help a child understand how another person might feel (C. H. Hart, Ladd, & Burleson, 1990). Unpopular children report the least supportive relationships with their fathers (C. J. Patterson, Kupersmidt, & Griesler, 1990).

Authoritative parenting is associated with better outcomes than authoritarian parenting (Dekovic & Janssens, 1992). Parents of aggressive children are often either coercive or inept in dealing with the children. Their children are so impulsive, mean, and disruptive that other children dislike them. As a result, they tend to seek out friends who are just as antisocial as they are (Hartup, 1989; 1992).

Helping Unpopular Children. Popularity in childhood is not a frivolous issue. Aside from their sadness, sense of rejection, and poor self-esteem, unpopular children are also deprived of a basic developmental experience: the positive interaction with other youngsters that helps them grow. Unpopularity during the preschool years is not necessarily cause for concern, but by middle childhood peer relationships are strong predictors of later adjustment. Children whose elementary school peers like them are more likely to be well-adjusted as adolescents. Those who have trouble getting along with peers are more likely later to have psychological problems, drop out of school, and become delinquent (Newcomb et al., 1993; Morison & Masten, 1991; Kupersmidt & Coie, 1990; Parker & Asher, 1987).

It is not clear whether unpopularity is the *cause* of later disturbances or a *symptom* of problems. Either way, adults can help. Children who are simply *neglected* or overlooked by their classmates or other peers may do better in a different class or a new school, or if they join a new club or go to a new camp. But children who are actively *rejected* by peers—the ones most at risk of developing emotional and behavioral difficulties in later life—need to learn how to make other children like them.

In one experiment, fifth- and sixth-graders were trained in social skills. They learned how to carry on a conversation: how to share information about themselves, how to show interest in others by asking questions, and how to give help, suggestions, invitations, and advice. When they had a chance to practice their new conversational skills in a group project with other children, they became better liked by the others and interacted more with them (Bierman & Furman, 1984).

The experimental group who received the social skills training and took part in the group project showed more general and lasting improvement over a 6-week period (on measures of conversational skills, rates of interaction, peer acceptance, and self-perception) than did a control group who received no training, an experimental group who received the training but did not participate in the peer-group project, and another experimental group who took part in the group project but received no social skills teaching.

Children not only need to learn social skills but also need to be in situations where they can use these skills and where other children can see the changes that have taken place in them. Otherwise, other children may hold on to their former opinions about these youngsters and may not give them a chance to show their new skills. Furthermore, since it seems that children who expect to be liked actually are better liked (Rabiner & Coie, 1989), some kind of positive expectation should be built into programs that are developed to increase children's popularity. However, findings about the impact of family relations on popularity suggest that to be effective, intervention has to look at, and possibly try to change, the quality of parent-child relations rather than focus only on the individual child.

How Can Interracial Peer Groups Be Encouraged?

prejudice *Negative attitudes toward certain groups.*

Peer groups are usually of the same race and of the same or similar socioeconomic status, especially in segregated neighborhoods. Racial segregation in peer groups often results from *prejudice*—negative attitudes toward certain groups, which can corrode the self-esteem of members of these groups. Studies conducted from the 1960s to the mid-1970s found bias against African Americans among both white and black children in northern and southern American cities, from preschool through the early school years (Morland, 1966; J. Williams, Best, & Boswell, 1975).

School integration has brought more acceptance of racial differences, even though children still tend to choose friends of the same race. A study of African American and white third- and sixth-graders who had been in integrated classrooms from kindergarten on found that although the youngsters (particularly the older black children) preferred members of their own race, they rated classmates of the other race quite positively (Singleton & Asher, 1979).

Some schools have worked to reduce prejudice by recruiting and training more minority-group teachers and by emphasizing the cultural contributions of minorities. The most effective programs get children from different racial groups to work together. Like sports teams, interracial learning groups provide a common goal—and result in positive feelings among children (Gaertner, Mann, Murrell, & Dovidio, 1989). The children often go beyond liking each other to becoming true friends.

What do you think? *Should schools actively seek to reduce racial, religious, and ethnic prejudice? What are some ways this could be done?*

Although children usually choose their friends from their own racial group, some manage to overcome barriers of ignorance and prejudice. School programs are often helpful in accomplishing this, especially when they get children from different racial groups to work toward a common goal, as on sports teams or classroom projects.

FRIENDSHIP

Jason and his best friend play ball together and are in the same Scout troop. Vicky and her best friend eat lunch together, play together during recess, talk on the phone after school, and visit each other's home on the weekends. Children look for friends who are similar to them, typically of the same age, sex, and ethnic group and with common interests (Hartup, 1992).

Why Are Friends Important?

Through friendships, children learn to communicate and cooperate. They learn about themselves and others. They obtain partners for physical activities. They grow emotionally, as mutual affection enables children to express intimacy, to bask in a sense of self-worth, and to learn about being in a relationship (Hartup, 1992; Furman, 1982; H. S. Sullivan, 1953).

Children may spend much of their free time in groups, but only as individuals do they form friendships, and even children who are unpopular with a larger group will often make a good friend. Equality of status, of commitment, and of the give-and-take of a reciprocal relationship mark the strongest friendships. These bonds are sturdy enough to withstand the conflicts that inevitably arise between any two friends. Friends often disagree and compete with each other, and learning to resolve conflicts is an important function of friendship (Hartup, 1992).

Girls rely on their best friends more than boys do, and their friendships are affectionate and worth-enhancing. Since these qualities are more characteristic of older children's friendships, school-age girls' closest friendships may be more mature than boys' (Furman & Buhrmester, 1985). Girls tend to have just one or two close friends; boys have more friends, but they tend to be less intimate (Furman, 1982).

Development of Children's Thinking about Friendship

Children's concepts of friendship change vastly during the elementary school years. In middle childhood, a friend is someone a child feels comfortable with, likes to do things with, and can share feelings and secrets with. Friendships help children become more sensitive and loving, more able to give and receive respect. Children cannot be true friends or have true friends until they achieve the cognitive maturity to consider other people's views and needs as well as their own.

On the basis of interviews with more than 250 people between ages 3 and 45, Robert Selman traced changing conceptions of friendship through five overlapping stages. He found that most school-age children are in either stage 2 or stage 3 (Selman & Selman, 1979). Selman's stages and approximate ages are given below:

- *Stage 0: Momentary playmateship (ages 3 to 7).* On this *undifferentiated* level of friendship, children are egocentric and have trouble considering another person's point of view; they tend to think only about what they want from a relationship. Most very young children define their friends in terms of physical closeness ("She lives on my street") and value them for material or physical attributes ("He has the Power Rangers").
- *Stage 1: One-way assistance (ages 4 to 9).* On this *unilateral* level, a "good friend" does what the child wants the friend to do. ("She's not my friend anymore,

These boys' expressions and postures suggest that they feel close to each other. They are probably in Selman's reciprocal, or mutual, stage of friendship. Although some boys develop just one or two close friendships, this is a more common pattern among girls. Boys more commonly have a greater number of less intimate friends.

because she wouldn't go with me when I wanted her to" or "He's my friend because he always says yes when I want to borrow his eraser.")

- *Stage 2: Two-way fair-weather cooperation (ages 6 to 12).* This *reciprocal* level overlaps stage 1. It involves give-and-take but still serves many separate self-interests, rather than the common interests of the two friends. ("We are friends; we do things for each other" or "A friend is someone who plays with you when you don't have anybody else to play with.")
- *Stage 3: Intimate, mutually shared relationships (ages 9 to 15).* On this *mutual* level, children view a friendship as having a life of its own. It is an ongoing, systematic, committed relationship that incorporates more than doing things for each other. Friends become possessive and demand exclusivity. ("It takes a long time to make a close friend, so you really feel bad if you find out that your friend is trying to make other friends too.")
- *Stage 4: Autonomous interdependence (beginning at age 12).* In this *interdependent* stage, children respect friends' needs for both dependency and autonomy. ("A good friendship is a real commitment, a risk you have to take; you have to support and trust and give, but you have to be able to let go too.")

MENTAL HEALTH IN CHILDHOOD

The psychological climate seems to have worsened for American children since the mid-seventies. A survey of 1442 children in 1976 and 2466 in 1989 found that emotional and behavioral problems for 7- to 16-year-olds had increased over those 13 years. The most common problems fell into four categories:

1   Withdrawal or social problems: The child wants to be alone or to play with younger children; the child is secretive, sulky, or lacks energy.
2   Attention or thinking problems: The child has trouble concentrating and doing schoolwork; the child is impulsive.

3 Delinquency or aggression: The child is disobedient, destructive, and antisocial.

4 Anxiety and depression: The child feels sad, fearful, and lonely. (Achenbach & Howell, 1993)

In 1976 about 10 percent of American children were considered to need psychotherapy; in 1989 18 percent were so considered. The rate of decline in mental health held for boys and girls of various ethnic groups and economic levels. When income was taken into account, black and white children had about the same rates of problems; in both years problems were worst for poor children (Achenbach & Howell, 1993). The authors attribute the decline in mental health to no single cause, but to a combination of such societal factors as high levels of violence on the streets and in the media, less monitoring by and less time spent with parents, and discipline problems in the schools (Achenbach, cited in Goleman, 1993).

Still, despite the higher problem ratings, the 1989 scores were not higher than those in several other countries, including France, Australia, Thailand, and Puerto Rico (Achenbach & Howell, 1993). Different cultures seem to produce different problems. A recent study found Embu children of Kenya, whose parents emphasize obedience, more troubled by fears, guilt, and bodily complaints; a comparison group of American children, whose parents tend to value independence, presented problems around arguing, disobedience, and cruelty (Weisz, Sigman, Weiss, & Mosk, 1993).

In a Pittsburgh study boys, black children, and children from poor families were at especially high risk, as were those who had recently experienced a stressful life event, who had repeated a grade in school, or whose parents were having difficulties or had a psychiatric problem (Costello et al., 1988). Some problems seem to be associated with a particular phase of a child's life and will go away on their own, but others need to be treated to prevent trouble in the future. We have already discussed sleep problems, tics, stuttering, and hyperactivity; now we look at some other childhood disturbances.

What do you think?   *Should schools give children "emotional education" to help them deal with psychological issues? Or should this be left to parents?*

EMOTIONAL DISTURBANCES

As many as 20 to 25 percent of school-age children (12 million children) are impaired by emotional problems, but only about one in five troubled children receive help (Achenbach & Howell, 1993).

Acting-Out Behavior

When children fight, lie, steal, and destroy property, they are showing *acting-out behavior*—misbehavior that is an outward expression of emotional turmoil. Almost all children lie occasionally, but when children past the age of 6 or 7 continue telling tall tales, they are often signaling a sense of insecurity. They may be trying to gain attention and esteem or showing hostility toward their parents (Chapman, 1974).

Although occasional minor stealing needs to be dealt with, it is not necessarily a sign of serious trouble. But when children repeatedly steal, they are, again,

acting-out behavior
Misbehavior (for example, lying or stealing) spurred by emotional difficulties.

often showing hostility. Sometimes the stolen items seem to be "symbolic tokens of parental love, power, or authority" (Chapman, 1974, p. 158) of which the child feels deprived. Any chronic antisocial behavior may be a symptom of deep-seated emotional upset.

Separation Anxiety Disorder

Separation anxiety disorder, which may involve school phobia, often begins in childhood. Nicole wakes up on a school morning complaining of nausea, stomachache, or headache. Soon after she has received permission to stay home, the symptom clears up. This goes on day after day, and the longer she is out of school, the harder it will be to get her back. She is timid and inhibited away from home, but willful, stubborn, and demanding with her parents.

Nicole's behavior is typical of children with **school phobia,** a type of **separation anxiety disorder.** This condition involves excessive anxiety for at least 4 weeks concerning separation from home or from people to whom the child is attached. The condition affects some 4 percent of children and young adolescents and may persist through the college years. Children with the disorder often come from close-knit, caring families; they generally develop the anxiety after a life stress like a death of a pet, an illness, or a move to a new school (DSM-IV, 1994).

School phobia seems to have more to do with children's fear of leaving their mothers than a fear of school. Virtually no research has been done on the school situation of these youngsters. If there *is* a problem at school—a sarcastic teacher, a bully in the schoolyard, or overly demanding work—the child's fears may be realistic; the environment may need changing, not the child.

School-phobic children tend to be average or good students, aged 5 to 15; they are equally likely to be boys or girls. Their parents are more likely than other parents to be depressed, suffer from anxiety disorders, and report family dysfunction (G. A. Bernstein & Garfinkel, 1988). The most important element in treatment is an early, gradual return to school. Usually children go back without too much trouble once treatment is begun.

Childhood Depression

"Nobody likes me" is a common complaint in middle childhood, but friendlessness is only one sign of *childhood depression.* Other symptoms are an inability to have fun or concentrate, fatigue, extreme activity or apathy, crying, sleep problems, feelings of worthlessness, weight change, physical complaints, or frequent thoughts about death (DSM-IV, 1994). Any five symptoms for at least 2 weeks may point to depression. If any of these symptoms persist, the child should be given psychological help, not only for immediate relief but also because childhood depression is often the beginning of a problem that persists into adulthood (Kovacs, 1994).

TREATMENT TECHNIQUES

The choice of treatment for a disorder depends on many factors: the nature of the problem, the child's personality, how willing the family is to participate, what it can afford, what is available in the community, and often, the orientation of the professional first consulted.

Everyone feels "blue" at times, but a child's chronic depression can be a danger signal and should be taken seriously, especially when it represents a marked change from the child's usual behavior.

school phobia *Unrealistic fear of going to school; may be a form of separation anxiety disorder.*

separation anxiety disorder *Condition lasting for at least 4 weeks that involves excessive anxiety concerning separation from people to whom a child is attached.*

childhood depression *Affective disorder characterized by inability to have fun or to concentrate, and by an absence of normal emotional reactions.*

Types of Therapy

Psychological treatment can take several forms. In *individual psychotherapy,* a therapist sees a child one on one, to help the child gain insights into his or her personality and relationships and to interpret feelings and behavior. This may be helpful at a time of stress like the death of a parent, even when a child has not shown any signs of disturbance. The therapist may use play materials (like dolls representing family members) to help a child express feelings. The therapist accepts the child's feelings and the child's right to them. Child psychotherapy is usually more effective when combined with counseling for the parents.

Sometimes the parents come with the child, as in *family therapy.* The family therapist sees the whole family together, observes how members act with one another, and points out both the growth-producing and the inhibiting or destructive patterns of family functioning. Sometimes the child whose problem brings the family into therapy is, ironically, the healthiest member, responding to a troubled family situation. Therapy often helps parents to confront their own differences and begin to resolve them. This is often the first step toward solving the children's problems as well.

Behavior therapy, or *behavior modification,* uses principles of learning theory to eliminate undesirable behaviors like temper tantrums or to develop desirable ones like doing homework. A behavior therapist may use operant conditioning to encourage a behavior like putting dirty clothes into the hamper. Every time the child does it, she or he gets a reward like praise, a treat, or a token to be exchanged for toys.

During the 1980s, an increase occurred in the use of *drug therapy* to treat childhood emotional problems (Tuma, 1989). Now antidepressants are commonly prescribed for bed-wetters, stimulants for hyperactive children, and antipsychotics for severe psychological problems.

individual psychotherapy
Treatment technique in which a therapist generally helps a patient gain insight into his or her personality and relationships and helps interpret feelings and behaviors.

family therapy *Treatment technique in which the whole family is treated together and is viewed as the client.*

behavior therapy
Treatment technique using principles of learning theory to alter behavior; also called behavior modification.

drug therapy
Administration of drugs to treat emotional disorders.

Effectiveness of Therapy

Psychological therapy is usually effective (R. J. Casey & Berman, 1985). A review of 75 studies showed that children who received treatment scored better—in com-

Sometimes a child's difficulties bring the entire family into therapy. Family therapy can help all family members examine their interactions and resolve the child's problems, as well as others.

parison with children with similar psychological problems who did not receive treatment—on such measures as self-concept, adjustment, personality, social skills, school achievement, cognitive functioning, and resolution of fears and anxieties.

Treatment for specific problems (like impulsiveness or hyperactivity) brings more improvement than does therapy aimed at more general outcomes like "better social adjustment." No one form of therapy (play or nonplay, individual or group, "child-only" or family) seems superior to another overall, but some kinds are better for some problems (Tuma, 1989). For example, behavior therapy is especially effective for phobias, bed-wetting, and problems with self-control.

Drugs help sometimes, but they should not displace psychotherapy. Drugs are usually most effective when combined with other treatments. Giving pills to change children's behavior is a radical step: Many medicines have side effects, and in some cases the drugs change behavior without getting at the underlying causes. Many therapists turn to drugs only as a last resort.

STRESS AND RESILIENCE

Sources of Stress

Stressful events are part of every childhood. Illness, the birth of a sibling, day-to-day frustration, and parents' temporary absence are common sources of stress. Other nonroutine stresses are also likely to occur in a child's world. Divorce or death of parents, hospitalization, and the day-in, day-out grind of poverty affect many children. Some children survive wars and earthquakes. The increase in the number of homeless families in the United States has brought severe psychological difficulties to children (Bassuk & Rubin, 1987). Violent events like kidnappings and attacks by playground snipers make even relatively protected children realize that their world is not as safe as they had thought and that their parents cannot always guard them. Such realizations affect children in the short and possibly the long run as well (Garmezy, 1983; Pynoos et al., 1987). (See Box 13-3.)

Children's Fears. Most children worry most about things close to their daily lives. A national poll of 758 urban, suburban, and small-town children in the United States, aged 10 to 17, found their biggest worries to be about violent crime against a family member; an adult losing a job; not being able to afford a doctor, shelter, or food; a family member having a drug problem; and a breakup of the family (*CDF Reports,* 1994). According to other research in six countries—Australia, Canada, Egypt, Japan, the Philippines, and the United States—children from many different cultures are remarkably alike in what they are afraid of (Yamamoto, Soliman, Parsons, & Davies, 1987).

When third- through ninth-grade children were asked to rank a list of 20 events in order of how upsetting they would be, the primary fear among children in each country was the same: fear of losing a parent. Next were events that would embarrass them—being kept back in school, wetting their pants in public, or being sent to the principal. For most children, school is a source of insecurity—partly because so many belittling practices (like accusing children of lying or ridiculing them in class) flourish there. Adults can help by respecting children, encouraging them to talk about their worries, and not expecting fears to simply disappear. Most childhood fears are normal, and overcoming them helps children grow, achieve identity, and master their world.

BOX 13-3 ▪ FOOD FOR THOUGHT

CHILDREN WHO LIVE IN CHRONIC DANGER

A 6-year-old from Washington, D.C., asked whether there is anywhere she feels safe, said, "In my basement"; the basement had no windows for bullets to fly through. A 10-year-old told about running away in terror after he saw a man shot in the back on the street. A 6-year-old saw her mother punched in the face by a drug addict. These inner-city children are, unfortunately, typical of many who live surrounded by violence and as a result are fearful, anxious, distressed, and depressed.

Possibly because the subject is so painful or possibly because children may not be reporting all that they see or experience, mothers, who are usually these children's primary caretakers, tend to underestimate the extent of their children's exposure to violence and how it affects them. This may hinder parents' efforts to shield their children from seeing violence or becoming victims of it. The children themselves may take brutal behavior so for granted that they become desensitized to it and may not take necessary precautions to protect themselves.

Children who experience an initial trauma before age 11 are three times more likely than those who undergo trauma as teenagers to develop psychiatric symptoms (J. Davidson & Smith, 1990). (See Table 13-2 for typical reactions at different ages.) Children in an environment with multiple risks—like living in a violent community, in poverty, and receiving inadequate parenting—are most likely to suffer permanent developmental damage (Rutter, 1987).

What happens to children who grow up surrounded by violence? They often have trouble concentrating and re-membering because they don't get enough sleep and are troubled by their fears. They may become anxious and afraid that their mothers will abandon them. Some become aggressive to hide their fears, to protect themselves, or to imitate actions they've seen. Many do not allow themselves to care for other people, since they're afraid of more hurt and loss.

These children need islands of safety in their lives. They need to have caring relationships with adults like teachers or community leaders who can deal with their concerns in the day-to-day context of classroom or group meeting. Play and art activities can help a child express feelings about a traumatic event, reinstate a sense of inner control, develop a feeling of self-worth, and set the stage for a dialogue with an adult whom the child can trust (Garbarino, Dubrow, Kostelny, & Pardo, 1992).

Also, much can be done on the larger societal level. The American Psychological Association's Commission on Violence and Youth recommends community programs built around the interests and needs of young people, including health care, recreation, and vocational training (Youngstrom, 1992). Role models from the community, peer-group discussions, and family intervention should all be offered to deter youths from drugs and violence. The American Academy of Pediatrics makes broad social policy recommendations: regulating and restricting ownership of handguns and ammunition, not romanticizing gun use in television and movies, identifying high-risk adolescents and providing services to them, and developing more community resources (AAP, 1992a).

TABLE 13-2

TYPICAL REACTIONS TO VIOLENCE AT DIFFERENT AGES	
AGE	**REACTION**
Early childhood	Passive reactions and regression (like bed-wetting, clinging, and speaking less); fear of leaving the mother or of sleeping alone; aggressive play; sleep problems
School-age	Aggressiveness, inhibition, somatic complaints (headaches, stomachaches, etc.); learning difficulties (forgetfulness, trouble concentrating); psychological difficulties (anxiety, phobias, withdrawal, denial); grief and loss reactions (hopelessness, despair, depression, inability to play, suicidal thoughts, uncaring behavior, destructiveness); acting tough to hide fears; constricted activities
Adolescence	Some of the same reactions as school-age children, plus acting-out and self-destructive behavior (drug abuse, delinquency, promiscuity, life-threatening reenactments of the trauma); identification with the aggressor (becoming violent, joining a gang)

SOURCE: Garbarino, Dubrow, Kostelny, & Pardo, 1992.

Modern Pressures.   Because families move around more than they used to, children are more likely to change schools and friends and less likely to know many adults well. They know about sex and violence; and when they live in single-parent homes or have to consider parents' work schedules, they often shoulder adult responsibilities.

The child psychologist David Elkind has called today's child the "hurried child" (1981, 1988). Like some other thoughtful observers, he is concerned that the pressures of life today are making children grow up too soon and are making their shortened childhood too stressful. Today's children are pressured to succeed in school, to compete in sports, and to meet parents' emotional needs. Children are exposed to many adult problems on television and in real life before they have mastered the problems of childhood. Yet children are not small adults. They feel and think like children, and they need these years of childhood for healthy development.

Coping with Stress: The Resilient Child

Children's reactions to stressful events differ considerably. Reactions may depend on factors like the event itself (children respond differently to a parent's death and to divorce), the child's age (preschoolers and adolescents react differently), and the child's sex (boys are more vulnerable than girls) (Rutter, 1984). Yet of two children of the same age and sex who are exposed to the same stressful experience, one may crumble while the other remains whole and healthy. Why is this so?

resilient children
Children who bounce back from unfortunate circumstances that would have a highly negative impact on the emotional development of most children.

Resilient children are those who bounce back from circumstances that would blight the emotional development of most children. They are the children of the ghetto who go on to distinguish themselves in the professions. They are the neglected or abused children who go on to form intimate relationships, be good parents, and lead fulfilling lives. In spite of the bad cards they have been dealt, these children are winners. They are creative, resourceful, independent, and enjoyable to be with. What is special about them?

Several studies have identified "protective factors" that seem to contribute to children's resilience (E. E. Werner, 1993; Rosenberg, 1987; Rutter, 1984; Garmezy, 1983; Anthony & Koupernik, 1974). These factors include:

- *The child's personality.* Resilient children tend to be adaptable. They are positive thinkers, friendly, independent, and sensitive to other people. They feel competent and have high self-esteem. Intelligence may be a factor: Good students seem to cope better (Rutter, 1984). These children are often able to deal with their problems by the way they look at the problems—sometimes telling themselves, "It could always be worse."
- *The family.* Resilient children are likely to have good relationships with one or both supportive parents. If they lack this, they are likely to be close to at least one other adult who is interested and caring, and whom they trust. Resilient abused children are likely to have been abused by only one parent rather than both and to have had a loving, supportive relationship with one parent or a foster parent when growing up (Kaufman & Zigler, 1987).
- *Learning experiences.* Resilient children are likely to have had experience solving social problems. They have seen parents, older siblings, or others dealing with frustration and making the best of a bad situation. They have faced chal-

lenges themselves, worked out solutions, and learned that they can exert some control over their lives.

■ *Reduced risk.* Children who have been exposed to only one of a number of factors strongly related to psychiatric disorder (like discord between the parents, low social status, a disturbed mother, a criminal father, and experience in foster care or an institution) are often able to overcome the stress. But when two or more of these factors are present, children's risk of developing an emotional disturbance increases fourfold or more (Rutter in Pines, 1979).

■ *Compensating experiences.* A supportive school environment and successful experiences in sports, in music, or with other children or interested adults can help make up for a dismal home life. In adulthood, a good marriage can compensate for poor relationships earlier in life.

What do you think? *How can adults help children to develop resilience?*

All this research, of course, does not mean that what happens in a child's life does not matter. In general, children with an unfavorable background have more problems in adjustment than do children with a favorable background. What is heartening about these findings is the recognition that childhood experiences do not necessarily determine the outcome of a person's life, that many people do have the strength to rise above the most difficult circumstances, and that we are constantly rewriting the stories of our lives as long as we live. We write important chapters of our life stories during adolescence, as we shall see in Chapters 14, 15, and 16.

SUMMARY

1 Self-concept is the sense of self. It is based on a person's knowledge of what she or he has been and done; it guides future behavior. Self-concept develops greatly in middle childhood. Children develop representational systems allowing them to integrate different features of the self to form higher-order generalizations.

2 Self-esteem, the sense of self-worth or self-evaluation, is important to personality development, especially mood.

3 Erikson's fourth crisis, which occurs during middle childhood, is industry versus inferiority. The "virtue" of this period is competence, a view of the self as able to master and complete tasks.

4 According to Susan Harter, global self-worth comes from two sources: how competent children think they are and how much social support they receive from important people.

5 The peer group assumes particular importance in middle childhood. However, relationships with parents and other family members continue to be the most important relationships in children's lives.

6 Although school-age children require less direct supervision than younger children, it is still important for parents to monitor their activities. Middle childhood involves a transitional stage of coregulation. Disciplinary methods evolve with the child's cognitive development, but there appears to be an underlying consistency in parents' child-rearing attitudes.

7 Children grow up in a variety of family situations besides the traditional nuclear family. These include families in which mothers work outside the home (now a majority of families), families with divorced parents, stepfamilies, one-parent families and families formed by gay or lesbian parents. Ethnic differences also influence family func-

tioning. There are age differences in reaction to family situations. The way parents handle a situation influences how children will adjust to it.

8 Siblings exert a powerful influence on each other, either directly (through their interaction) or indirectly (through their impact on each other's relationship with parents).

9 The peer group influences psychological development. School-age youngsters are most susceptible to pressure to conform, which may encourage antisocial behavior. Most children select peers who are like them in age, sex, and socioeconomic status.

10 Popularity influences self-esteem, and vice versa. Children who think well of themselves are more popular than children with low self-esteem. Children who are not only ignored by their peers but rejected by them are at risk of emotional and behavioral problems. Training in social skills can help such children be accepted by their peers.

11 Racial prejudice among schoolchildren appears to be diminishing as a result of school integration.

12 The basis of friendship changes during middle childhood. Children choose friends they feel comfortable with, and they see friendships as involving give-and-take.

13 Emotional disturbances during childhood are not uncommon. These include acting-out behavior, separation anxiety disorder (including school phobia), and childhood depression. Treatment techniques include individual psychotherapy, family therapy, behavior therapy, and drug therapy.

14 Psychological therapies are generally effective. Drug therapy is effective in certain situations; when used, it should be accompanied by psychotherapy.

15 Normal childhood stresses and fears take many forms and can affect emotional development. As a result of the pressures of modern life, many children are experiencing a shortened and stressful childhood.

16 Some children are more resilient than others; they are better able to withstand stress. Factors related to personality, family, experience, and degree of risk are associated with a child's ability to bounce back from unfortunate circumstances.

KEY TERMS

self-concept (507)
self-esteem (508)
industry versus inferiority (508)
global self-worth (508)
discipline (513)
coregulation (514)
prejudice (536)
acting-out behavior (539)

school phobia (540)
separation anxiety disorder (540)
childhood depression (540)
individual psychotherapy (541)
family therapy (541)
behavior therapy (541)
drug therapy (541)
resilient children (544)

SUGGESTED READINGS

Coles, R. (1990). *The spiritual life of children.* Boston: Houghton Mifflin. The author, a child psychiatrist, interviewed hundreds of children of many faiths about their religious beliefs. In this book he reports their opinions on heaven, hell, God's wishes for humankind, and their doubts.

Comer, J. P., & Poussaint, A. F. (1992). *Raising black children.* New York: Plume. Two leading psychiatrists discuss the special pressures parents face in raising black children, dealing with such issues as drugs, AIDS, and educational pressures. They also offer guidance in helping children cope with the unconscious racism in society. The insights they provide are relevant for *all* parents and children.

Elkind, D. (1988). *The hurried child* (rev. ed.). New York: Addison-Wesley. This book by a well-known psychologist examines how parents can raise healthy children who enjoy childhood, despite social pressures to grow up fast.

Lansky, V. (1989). *Vicky Lansky's divorce book for parents: Helping your children cope with divorce and its aftermath.* New York: New American Library. Based on the author's own experiences as well as those of other families, this practical guide for divorcing parents deals with issues chronologically, from the decision to separate to long-term adjustment.

Marston, S. (1994). *The divorced parent.* New York: Morrow. This book offers success strategies for raising children after the parents' separation or divorce. With a sense of humor and insight into how families work, the author manages to keep in mind the complexity of divorce while offering sound practical suggestions.

Olds, S. W. (1989). *The working parents' survival guide.* Rocklin, CA: Prima Publishing. An in-depth manual for mothers and fathers that draws on up-to-date research to examine the concerns of working parents and their children. It offers practical solutions to a variety of problems, including finding and evaluating good child care, recognizing the appearance of emotional troubles, and helping children adjust to parents' separation.

ADOLESCENCE

Vicky and Jason, both sweltering under ceremonial caps and gowns, are in the auditoriums of their respective high schools. Each one listens to graduation day speeches (remarkably similar from one school to another), sings school songs, and has fleeting thoughts about this turning point in life. From now on, this young man and this young woman will leave behind the world of children and will in many ways enter the world of adults.

The past few years leading to this moment were sometimes stormy, sometimes sublime, always full of changes. In Chapters 14, 15, and 16, we will examine some of those changes.

The physical changes are immense. Jason and Vicky have not only grown taller and heavier, they have also matured, taking on the bodies of adults. Cognitively too, they have blossomed. Both are now better able to think abstractly and hypothetically. Their personalities have matured as well. They have not settled all the issues in their emotional and social lives—they never will settle everything—but they have a clearer sense of their own identities, of who they are and who they wish to become. Vicky and Jason are on the threshold of adulthood.

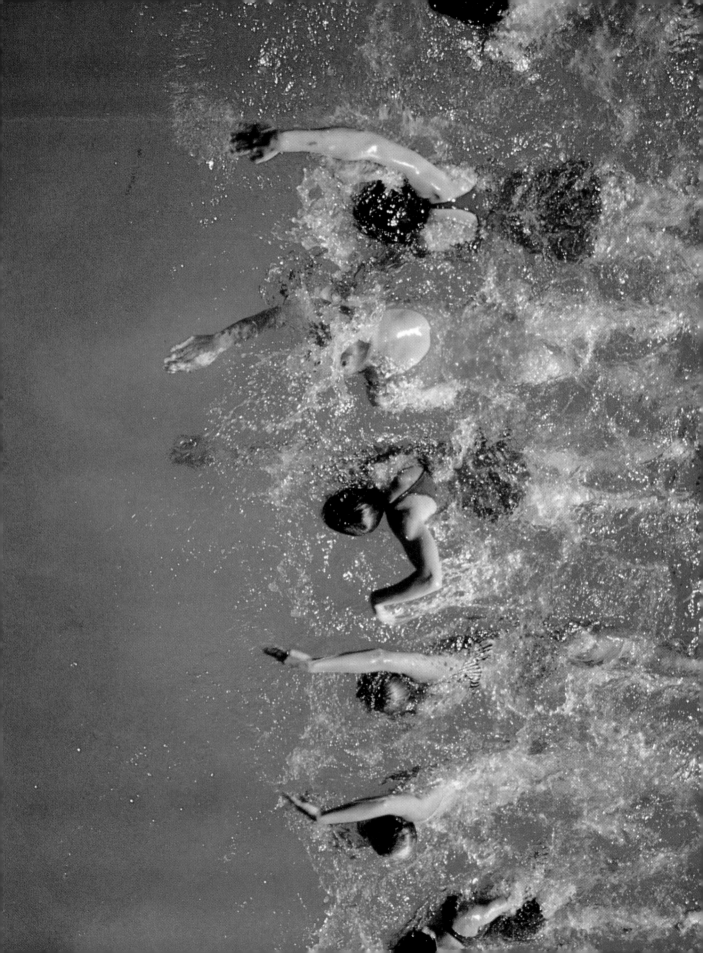

CHAPTER 14
PHYSICAL DEVELOPMENT AND HEALTH IN ADOLESCENCE

Thirteen's anomalous—not that, not this:
Not folded bud, or wave that laps a shore,
Or moth proverbial from the chrysalis.
Is the one age defeats the metaphor.
Is not a town, like childhood, strongly walled
But easily surrounded; is no city.
Nor, quitted once, can it be quite recalled—
Not even with pity.

Phyllis McGinley, "A Certain Age," 1956

In this chapter, we examine the very apparent physical changes of adolescence and how they affect and are affected by psychological changes in these years. First we look at the timing and the psychological impact of the changes. We then discuss some health issues associated with this time of life—nutrition, common eating disorders, drug abuse, and sexually transmitted diseases that adolescents are most at risk for. We also examine two tragic problems affecting growing numbers of adolescents—abuse and neglect, and teenage suicide. Despite problems like these, which affect some adolescents, most young people come through the teenage years in good physical and mental health. When you have finished reading this chapter, you should be able to answers questions like the following:

PREVIEW QUESTIONS

- ◆ What physical changes occur during adolescence?
- ◆ How does early or late sexual maturation affect an adolescent psychologically?
- ◆ What are the most common health problems of adolescence?
- ◆ Which drugs are most abused by adolescents? What are the effects of the drugs they take?
- ◆ Which sexually transmitted diseases are adolescents at risk of contracting?
- ◆ How do abuse and neglect affect adolescents?
- ◆ Why do adolescents commit suicide? How can such deaths be prevented?

Vicky, now 13, cannot pass a mirror without gazing into it, and she never feels the same way twice about what she sees. Every week she seems to have a different body, a perception that both intrigues and perplexes her. "Am I too fat? Why is my nose so big? Will I ever be pretty?" she wonders. Vicky has entered adolescence, and her body is changing as it becomes capable of a new function—sexual reproduction. At a slightly later age, Jason too undergoes great physical changes. But Jason likes the changes he sees. With peach fuzz on his cheeks and a new, deeper voice (nobody mistakes him for his mother on the phone anymore), Jason feels himself leaving childhood behind. By the end of adolescence, Jason has the body of a grown man, and Vicky, the body of a grown woman. Both look very different from the way they did when they entered their teens.

Adolescence is a developmental transition between childhood and adulthood. As with other transitional periods in life (like the beginning of formal schooling), it involves significant changes in one or more domains of development. Early adolescence may be the most extreme transition in the entire life span, entailing changes in every aspect of individual development and every important social context. It provides opportunities for increased growth, but it also carries risks for some young people, who have trouble handling so many changes at once.

adolescence
Developmental transition period between childhood and adulthood.

Many social critics warn that American adolescents today face greater hazards to their physical and mental well-being than did their counterparts of earlier years (Takanishi, 1993). A number of these hazards (like adolescent pregnancy and childbearing, difficult transitions to adult work roles, death by car accidents and homicide) are not typical in other developed countries (Petersen, 1991).

Adolescence is a critical period, a time of increasing divergence between the majority of young people, who are heading for a fulfilling and productive adulthood, and a sizeable minority who will be dealing with major problems. For teenagers who receive help in overcoming the dangers along the way, the future can be bright.

ADOLESCENCE: A DEVELOPMENTAL TRANSITION

Adolescence is generally considered to begin at *puberty*, the process that leads to sexual maturity, when a person is able to reproduce.* Although the physical changes of this time of life are dramatic, they do not burst full-blown at the end of childhood. Puberty is part of a long and complex process that begins even before birth. The biological changes that signal the end of childhood produce rapid growth in height and weight (a rate of growth second only to growth during infancy), changes in body proportions and form, and the attainment of sexual maturity.

puberty *Process that leads to sexual maturity and the ability to reproduce.*

Adolescence is also a social and emotional process. Considered to last almost a decade, it begins at about age 12 and ends in the late teens or early twenties. However, its physical underpinnings have begun long before, and its psychological ramifications continue long after.

MARKERS OF ADOLESCENCE

Early adolescence marks the transition out of childhood, and later adolescence, the transition into adulthood. Neither period is demarcated abruptly. Before the twentieth century, children entered the adult world when they matured physically or when they began a vocational apprenticeship, but today the entry into adulthood is less clear-cut.

One reason is that puberty occurs earlier than it used to, so that now there is a longer lapse of time between puberty and adulthood. Second, our complex society requires a longer period of education, which postpones adulthood. Third,

*Some people use the term *puberty* to mean the end point of sexual maturation and refer to the process as *pubescence,* but our usage conforms to that of most psychologists today.

The Apache Indians of the American southwest celebrate a girl's entrance into puberty with a 4-day ritual that includes special clothing, a symbolic blanket, and singing from sunrise to sunset.

The bar mitzvah, the Jewish ritual that this 13-year-old boy is celebrating, is one of the few formal coming-of-age rites that are still observed in western cultures.

in modern industrial societies there are few definitive markers to establish adulthood, unlike traditional cultures that generally mark its arrival with a "coming-of-age" rite. (See Box 14-1.) The ritual may be held at a certain age, like the bar mitzvah and bat mitzvah observances that still welcome many 13-year-old Jewish boys and girls into adult society. Or it can be tied to a specific event like a girl's first menstruation, which Apache tribes celebrate with a 4-day ritual of sunrise-to-sunset chanting.

What do you think?   *Do you believe that western adolescents today miss something by not having a specific rite of passage from childhood? If so, what kind of observance do you think would be appropriate?*

Vicky thinks she is an adult when she gets her driver's license; Jason, when he collects his first paycheck. Julia says, "I'll know Jason's an adult when he stops calling home collect!"

Young people in America consider themselves adult at different ages, depending on which marker they use. There are *legal* definitions of adulthood: At age 18, people may marry without their parents' permission; at 17, they may enlist in the armed forces; at 18 to 21 (depending on the state), they may enter into binding contracts. Using *sociological* definitions, people call themselves adults when they are self-supporting or have chosen a career, married, or founded a family. There are also *psychological* definitions. Cognitive maturity is often considered to coincide with the capacity for abstract thought. (See Chapter 15.) Emotional maturity may depend on such achievements as discovering one's identity, becoming independent of parents, developing a system of values, and forming

BOX 14-1 ▪ AROUND THE WORLD

FEMALE GENITAL MUTILATION

Many traditional societies have coming-of-age rituals that signal membership in the adult community. These ceremonies often include putting an enduring mark on the body, as by tattooing or scarring the face, removing the foreskin from the penis, or sharpening the teeth. One custom widely practiced in some parts of Africa, the Middle East, and southeastern Asia is surgery on the female genitals, euphemistically called *female circumcision* but termed *female genital mutilation (FGM)* by the World Health Organization. The operation, performed on girls of varying ages from infancy to puberty, may entail *clitoridectomy,* the removal of part or all of the clitoris, or *infibulation,* which involves clitoridectomy plus removal of parts of the labia, the raw edges of which are then sewn together with catgut or held by thorns.

The purposes of these procedures include preserving virginity, reducing the sex drive, maintaining cleanliness, and enhancing beauty. The consequences are often dreadful, including—besides the complete loss of sexual fulfillment—psychological dysfunction and sometimes life-threatening infection from unsterilized instruments and serious loss of blood (Lightfoot-Klein, 1989).

In the countries where these operations are practiced, government officials, physicians, and women's groups have tried to end them, but because most women in the ethnic groups that practice them believe in the procedures and are often the ones who carry them out, they still go on. Furthermore, they are now being carried out in Europe and North America, where many east African refugees have immigrated. Britain, Sweden, and Switzerland have passed laws banning the practice, Canada and France say their laws already prohibit it, and legislation has been introduced in the United States (Farnsworth, 1994; Zimmerman, 1993).

Attitudes are also changing in some areas where the surgery has traditionally been performed. A survey of 150 female third-year high school students in the Sudan found that even though about 96 percent of these girls had had some form of FGM performed on them, more than 70 percent were strongly opposed to the same operation for their sisters and other young girls (Pugh, 1983). These girls' attitudes may have been influenced by the campaign to do away with FGM being led by a growing number of women and health professionals throughout Africa and the world.

What do you think? *Are western objections to female genital mutilation ethnocentric? Should FGM be permitted among those ethnic groups that have traditionally practiced it?*

---

mature relationships of friendship and love. (See Chapter 16.) Some people never leave adolescence, no matter what their chronological age.

What do you think? *How would you define the end of adolescence and entry into adulthood?*

PHYSICAL CHANGES

The biological changes that signal the end of childhood include the adolescent growth spurt; the beginning of menstruation for females; the presence of sperm in the urine of males; the maturation of the primary sex organs (those directly related to reproduction); and development of the secondary sex characteristics (physiological signs of sexual maturity that do not directly involve the reproductive organs).

Puberty

Any eighth- or ninth-grade class photo reveals startling contrasts. Flat-chested little girls stand next to full-bosomed, full-grown young women. Skinny little boys

puberty *Process that leads to sexual maturity and the ability to reproduce.*

TABLE 14-1

USUAL SEQUENCE OF PHYSIOLOGICAL CHANGES IN ADOLESCENCE	
FEMALE CHARACTERISTICS	**AGE OF FIRST APPEARANCE**
Growth of breasts	8–13
Growth of pubic hair	8–14
Body growth	9.5–14.5 (average peak, 12)
Menarche	10–16.5 (average, 12.8)
Underarm hair	About 2 years after appearance of pubic hair
Increased output of oil- and sweat-producing glands (which may lead to acne)	About the same time as appearance of underarm hair
MALE CHARACTERISTICS	**AGE OF FIRST APPEARANCE**
Growth of testes, scrotal sac	10–13.5
Growth of pubic hair	10–15
Body growth	10.5–16 (average peak, 14)
Growth of penis, prostate gland, seminal vesicles	11–14.5 (average, 12.5)
Change in voice	About the same time as growth of penis
First ejaculation of semen	About 1 year after beginning of growth of penis
Facial and underarm hair	About 2 years after appearance of pubic hair
Increased output of oil- and sweat-producing glands (which may lead to acne)	About the same time as appearance of underarm hair

are seen next to broad-shouldered, mustached young men. This variance is normal. There is about a 6- to 7-year range for puberty in both boys and girls.

The Timing of Puberty. Puberty takes about 4 years, beginning about 2 years earlier for girls than for boys. Girls, on average, begin to show pubertal change at 9 or 10 years of age, achieving sexual maturation by 13 or 14. Normal girls, however, may show the first signs as early as age 7 or as late as 14, becoming sexually mature at ages 9 to 16. The average age for boys' entry into puberty is 12, with sexual maturity coming at age 14. But normal boys may begin to show changes from ages 9 to 16, achieving maturity from ages 11 to 18 (Chumlea, 1982). Maturing early or late may have social and psychological consequences.

The physical changes of adolescence unfold in a sequence that is much more consistent than their actual timing, though even this order varies somewhat from one person to another. The usual sequences are shown in Table 14-1. Some people move through puberty very quickly, others more slowly. One girl, for example, may be developing breasts and body hair at about the same rate; but the body hair of another may grow so much faster than her breasts that her adult hair pattern appears a year or so before her breasts develop. The same kinds of variations occur among boys (Tobin-Richards, Boxer, Kavrell, & Petersen, 1984).

How Puberty Begins. Puberty begins when, at some biologically determined time, a young person's pituitary gland sends a message to the sex glands, which then secrete hormones. This precise time is apparently regulated by the interaction of genes, individual health, and environment; it may be related to a critical weight level.

Puberty, then, occurs in response to changes in the body's hormone system, which are triggered by a physiological signal. Its response in a girl is for her ovaries to sharply step up their production of the female hormone estrogen; and in a boy, for his testes to increase the manufacture of androgens, particularly testosterone. Both boys and girls have both types of hormones, but girls have higher levels of estrogen and boys have higher levels of androgens. As early as age 7, the levels of these sex hormones begin to increase, setting in motion the pubertal events. Estrogen stimulates the growth of the female genitals and the development of the breasts; androgens stimulate the growth of the male genitals and body hair.

Hormones are closely associated with emotions, specifically with aggression in boys and with both aggression and depression in girls (Brooks-Gunn, 1988). Some researchers attribute the increased emotionality and moodiness of early adolescence to hormones, but we need to remember that in human beings social influences combine with hormonal ones and may predominate. Even though there is a well-established relationship between the production of the hormone testosterone and sexuality, adolescents begin sexual activity more in accord with what their friends do than with what their glands secrete (Brooks-Gunn & Reiter, 1990).

What do you think? *What do you think are the implications of attaining sexual maturity years before the customary age of marriage, and attaining physical maturity years before attaining physical independence from the family?*

The Relationship between Stress and Puberty. The ways in which physical, cognitive, and personality development influence one another are not always predictable. Some controversial research suggests that conflict between parents and young adolescents may be related more to puberty than to chronological age and that stress may even cause early maturation (Steinberg, 1988). Girls who argue more with their mothers mature faster physically than girls who have calmer relationships. It's possible that a very close mother-daughter tie at a time when a girl is striving for independence might be stressful and that stress might in turn affect the hormonal secretions that govern puberty. Following up these findings, researchers who had followed a group of girls since age 3 found that 16-year-olds who had grown up in a conflict-ridden family or whose fathers had not lived with the family in the girls' childhood tended to begin to menstruate earlier than girls with calmer family settings (Moffitt, Caspi, Belsky, & Silva, 1992).

What might account for this relationship? One possibility is an interaction between heredity and environment. Mothers and daughters resemble each other in age of first menstruation (Garn, 1980). Early maturers tend to marry earlier and have children earlier than their peers. Early marriages are more likely to end in divorce. It is possible that early-maturing mothers tend to have early-maturing daughters, who are more likely to be father-absent because of their mothers' higher probability of divorce (Surbey, 1990).

Evolution may be partly responsible, says psychologist Laurence Steinberg (1987c). Adolescent monkeys and apes commonly leave their parents soon after puberty. Among some species, only the female leaves; among others, both sexes go to found new family groups. This has human parallels. At one time, adolescents routinely left home for apprenticeships in trade; and even now some cultures send young adolescents to live in other households. Today in western countries, sexually mature adolescents may spend 7 or 8 years in their parents' homes. From an evolutionary point of view, it is not surprising that the early years of adolescence bring more conflict than any other time in childhood. The good news is that arguments "rarely undo close emotional bonds or lead adolescents and their parents to reject one another" (Steinberg, 1987c, p. 38).

The conclusions of this research are still being debated. Meanwhile, they demonstrate the interrelationships among various aspects of development.

The Secular Trend

secular trend *Trend noted by observing several generations; in child development, a trend toward earlier attainment of adult height and sexual maturity, which began about a century ago and appears to have ended in the United States.*

On the basis of historical sources, developmentalists have inferred the existence of a *secular trend,* a lowering of the age when puberty begins and young people reach adult height and sexual maturity. A secular trend is a trend that can be seen only by observing several generations. This trend, which includes increases in adult height and weight, began about 100 years ago and has occurred in the United States, western Europe, and Japan, but apparently not in some other countries (Chumlea, 1982).

The most obvious explanation for this secular trend seems to be a higher standard of living. Children who are healthier, better nourished, and better cared for mature earlier and grow bigger. This explanation is supported by evidence: The age of sexual maturity is later in less developed countries than in more industrialized countries. The Bundi girls of New Guinea do not begin to menstruate until a mean age of 18 years, compared with an average age of 12.8 years in the United States (Tanner, 1989).

The secular trend appears to have ended, at least in the United States, probably as a reflection of higher living standards in most segments of our population (Schmeck, 1976). Apparently, the age of sexual maturity has now reached some genetically determined limit and is unlikely to be lowered any further by better nutrition.

The Adolescent Growth Spurt

adolescent growth spurt *Sharp increase in height and weight that precedes sexual maturity.*

During the years from 11 to 13, girls are on the average taller, heavier, and stronger than boys, who achieve their adolescent growth spurt later than girls do. If our society did not have such rigid standards for males being taller than females, this temporary state would be less embarrassing for the boys.

An early sign of maturation is the *adolescent growth spurt*—a sharp increase in height and weight that generally begins in girls between ages $9\frac{1}{2}$ and $14\frac{1}{2}$ (usually at about age 10) and in boys between ages $10\frac{1}{2}$ and 16 (usually at about age 12 or 13). It typically lasts about 2 years. Soon after the growth spurt ends, the young person reaches sexual maturity. Growth in height is virtually complete by age 18 (Behrman, 1992).

Before the growth spurt, boys are typically about 2 percent taller than girls. Between ages 11 to 13, girls are taller, heavier, and stronger. After the spurt, boys are again larger, now by about 8 percent. The growth spurt in males is more intense; its later appearance allows an extra period of growth, since growth before puberty occurs at a faster rate than afterward.

Boys and girls grow differently during adolescence. Jason becomes larger overall; his shoulders will be wider, his legs longer relative to his trunk, and his forearms longer relative to both his upper arms and his height. Vicky's pelvis widens to make childbearing possible; and layers of fat develop under her skin, giving her a more rounded appearance.

In both sexes, the adolescent growth spurt affects practically all skeletal and muscular dimensions. Even the eye grows faster, causing an increase in near-sightedness during this period: About one-fourth of 12- to 17-year-olds are near-sighted (Gans, 1990). The lower jaw usually becomes longer and thicker, both jaw and nose project more, and the incisor teeth of both jaws become more upright.

TABLE 14-2

PRIMARY SEX CHARACTERISTICS: SEX ORGANS	
FEMALE	**MALE**
Ovaries	Testes
Fallopian tubes	Penis
Uterus	Scrotum
Vagina	Seminal vesicles
	Prostate gland

Adolescent boys usually welcome the need to shave, since facial hair is one of the secondary sex characteristics that signal sexual maturation.

These changes are greater in boys than in girls and follow their own time-tables, so that parts of the body may be out of proportion for a while. The result is the familiar teenage awkwardness that accompanies unbalanced, accelerated growth. Balance is restored eventually; but meanwhile, just when they feel the need to charm members of the other sex, adolescents typically have a most un-charming clumsiness. Teenagers generally do not like to be told that this is "just a phase"; but Jason, for one, secretly welcomes the reassurance that his clumsi-ness is a matter of being at an awkward age rather than of having an awkward personality.

Primary Sex Characteristics

The *primary sex characteristics* are the organs necessary for reproduction. In the female, these are the ovaries, uterus, and vagina; in the male, they are the testes, prostate gland, and seminal vesicles. (See Table 14-2.) During puberty, these or-gans enlarge and mature.

primary sex characteristics *Organs directly related to reproduction, which enlarge and mature in early adolescence.*

The principal sign of sexual maturity in girls is menstruation. In boys, the first sign of puberty is the growth of the testes and scrotum, and the principal sign of sexual maturity is the presence of sperm in the urine. A boy is fertile as soon as viable sperm are present. Like menstruation, the timing of the appear-ance of sperm is highly variable. It is difficult to determine when sperm first ap-pear. One longitudinal study found that only 2 percent of 11- to 12-year-old boys have sperm present in the urine, compared with 24 percent of 15-year-old boys (D. W. Richardson & Short, 1978).

A pubescent boy often wakes to find a wet spot or a hardened, dried spot in the bed—a *nocturnal emission,* or an involuntary ejaculation of semen commonly referred to as a *wet dream.* Most adolescent boys have these perfectly normal emis-sions, which may or may not occur in connection with an erotic dream.

Secondary Sex Characteristics

The *secondary sex characteristics* are physiological signs of sexual maturity that do not directly involve the reproductive organs. They include the breasts of fe-males and the broad shoulders of males. Others involve changes in the voice and the texture of skin and growth of pubic, facial, axillary (armpit), and body hair typical of an adult male or female. (See Table 14-3.)

secondary sex characteristics *Physiological signs of sexual maturation (such as breast development and growth of body hair) that do not involve the sex organs.*

The first sign of puberty in girls is usually the budding of the breasts. The nipples enlarge and protrude; the *areolae* (the pigmented areas surrounding the nipples) enlarge; and the breasts assume first a conical and then a rounded shape.

TABLE 14-3

SECONDARY SEX CHARACTERISTICS	
GIRLS	**BOYS**
Breasts	Pubic hair
Pubic hair	Axillary (underarm) hair
Axillary (underarm) hair	Facial hair
Changes in voice	Changes in voice
Changes in skin	Changes in skin
Increased width and depth of pelvis	Broadening of shoulders

The breasts are usually fully developed before menstruation begins. Much to their distress, some adolescent boys experience temporary breast enlargement; this is normal and may last from 12 to 18 months.

Various forms of hair growth also signal maturity. Pubic hair—which is at first straight and silky and eventually becomes coarse, dark, and curly—appears in different patterns in males and females. Axillary hair grows in the armpits. Adolescent boys are usually happy to see hair on the face and chest; but girls are usually dismayed at the appearance of even a slight amount of hair on the face or around the nipples, although this is normal.

The skin of both boys and girls becomes coarser and oilier. The increased activity of the sebaceous glands (which secrete a fatty substance) gives rise to the outbreaks of pimples and blackheads that are the bane of many teenagers' lives. Acne is more common in boys than girls and seems to be related to increased amounts of the male hormone testosterone.

The voices of both boys and girls deepen, partly in response to the growth of the larynx and partly—especially in boys—in response to the production of male hormones.

Menarche

menarche *Girl's first menstruation.*

The most dramatic sign of a girl's sexual maturity is *menarche*—the first menstruation, or monthly shedding of tissue from the lining of the womb. Menarche occurs fairly late in the sequence of female development. (See Table 14-1.) On average, a girl in the United States first menstruates just before her 13th birthday (12.8 years), with a normal range from 10 to 16.5 years. This is about 2 years after her breasts begin to develop and her uterus begins to grow, and after her growth spurt has slowed down.

Although in many cultures menarche is taken as the sign that a girl has become a woman, usually the early menstrual periods do not include ovulation, and many girls are unable to conceive for 12 to 18 months after menarche. Since ovulation and conception do sometimes occur in these early months, however, girls who have begun to menstruate should assume that if they have sexual intercourse, they can become pregnant.

PSYCHOLOGICAL ISSUES RELATED TO PHYSICAL CHANGES

Adolescence is probably the most embarrassing part of the life span. Teenagers are acutely self-conscious and sure that everyone is watching them; meanwhile, their bodies are constantly betraying them. Jason's voice squeaks at times when he wants to seem mature, and his penis becomes obviously erect at the most inopportune moments. Vicky hides her budding breasts under bulky clothing, and every month she worries about getting menstrual blood on her clothes.

But adolescence also offers new opportunities, which young people approach in different ways. It is not surprising that the dramatic physical changes of adolescence have many psychological ramifications. Especially keen are reactions to early or late maturation, to the onset of menstruation, and to changes in physical appearance.

Effects of Early and Late Maturation

One of the great paradoxes of adolescence is the conflict between a young person's yearning to find an individual identity—to assert a unique self—and an overwhelming desire to be exactly like his or her friends. Anything that sets an adolescent apart from the crowd can be unsettling, and youngsters are often disturbed if they mature sexually either much earlier or much later than their friends. Though neither late nor early maturing is necessarily an advantage or a drawback, the timing of maturation can have psychological effects.

Early and Late Maturation in Boys. Some research has found early-maturing boys to be more poised, relaxed, good-natured, popular with peers, and likely to be leaders—and less impulsive than late maturers. Other studies have found them to be more worried about being liked, more cautious, and more bound by rules and routines.

Late maturers have been found to feel more inadequate, rejected, and dominated; to be more dependent, aggressive, and insecure; to rebel more against their parents; and to think less of themselves (Mussen & Jones, 1957; Peskin, 1967, 1973; Siegel, 1982). While some studies have shown that early maturers retain a head start in cognitive performance into late adolescence and adulthood (R. T. Gross & Duke, 1980; Tanner, 1978), many differences seem to disappear by adulthood (M. C. Jones, 1957).

There are pluses and minuses in both situations. Boys like to mature early, and those who do seem to reap benefits in self-esteem (Alsaker, 1992; Clausen, 1975). Being more muscular than late maturers, they are stronger and better in sports and have a more favorable body image. They also have an edge in dating, since they are at the same maturity level as typical girls of their own age (Blyth et al., 1981).

But an early maturer sometimes has trouble living up to expectations that he should act as mature as he looks. He may have too little time to prepare for the changes of adolescence. Late maturers may feel and act more childish; but they may benefit from the longer period of childhood, when they do not have to deal with the demands of adolescence. They may become more flexible as they adapt to the problems of being smaller and more childish-looking than their peers (Livson & Peskin, 1980).

Early and Late Maturation in Girls. Advantages and disadvantages of early and late maturation are less clear-cut for girls. Perhaps this explains why more research has focused on them in recent years. Girls tend *not* to like maturing early; they are generally happier when they mature neither earlier nor later than their peers. Early-maturing girls tend to be less sociable, expressive, and poised; more introverted and shy; and more negative about menarche (M. C. Jones, 1958;

Livson & Peskin, 1980; Ruble & Brooks-Gunn, 1982). Some research suggests that they are apt to have a poor body image and lower self-esteem than later-maturing girls (Alsaker, 1992; Simmons, Blyth, Van Cleave, & Bush, 1979). However, other research has found that maturational status by itself does not affect self-esteem, but that self-esteem depends more on the overall context of the girl's surroundings (Brooks-Gunn, 1988).

One reason why an early-maturing girl may feel less attractive is that her new curviness clashes with cultural standards equating beauty with thinness (Crockett & Petersen, 1987). Earlier maturers may feel dismayed when they do not see the changes as advantageous (Simmons, Blyth, & McKinney, 1983). For example, Vicky's friend Kaia, the star of the school gymnastics team, fears that her developing breasts, menstrual periods, and rounding body may interfere with her agility on the bars. Kaia is a prime candidate for anorexia nervosa (discussed later in this chapter).

These girls may also be reacting to other people's concerns about their sexuality. Parents and teachers sometimes assume that girls with mature bodies *are* sexually active because they look as if they *could* be. Therefore adults may treat an early-maturing girl more strictly and more disapprovingly, and other adolescents may also stereotype and put pressures on her that she is ill-equipped to handle. Also, she may "hang out" with older boys and young men, which might make her vulnerable to their manipulations (Petersen, 1993). This may explain why some research has found that early maturing girls are likely to reach lower levels of educational and occupational achievement in adulthood (Stattin & Magnusson, 1990).

In general, effects of early or late maturation are most likely to be negative when adolescents are very different from their peers either by being much more or much less developed; when they do not see the changes as advantageous; and when several stressful events occur at about the same time, with few or no protective factors (Petersen, 1993; Simmons, Blyth, & McKinney, 1983). But it is hard to generalize about the psychological effects of timing of puberty, because they depend so much on how the adolescent and the people in his or her world interpret the changes.

What do you think? *Did you mature early, late, or "on time"? How did the timing of your maturation affect you psychologically?*

Feelings about Menarche and Menstruation

Menarche is more than a physical event; it is "a concrete symbol of a shift from girl to woman" (Ruble & Brooks-Gunn, 1982, p. 1557). Girls who have begun to menstruate seem more conscious of their femaleness than girls of the same age who have not yet reached menarche. They are more interested in boy-girl relations and in adorning their bodies; when they draw female figures, they show more explicit breasts. They seem more mature in certain personality characteristics (Grief & Ulman, 1982).

In the past, the negative side of menarche—the discomfort and embarrassment that may accompany it—was emphasized. Cultural taboos have reinforced negative attitudes and have often prevented the development of rituals to welcome young girls to womanhood (Grief & Ulman, 1982). Western culture treats menarche not as a rite of passage but as a hygienic crisis, arousing girls' anxieties about staying clean and sweet-smelling rather than instilling pride in their womanliness.

Today, however, most girls take menarche and menstruation in stride. The better prepared a girl is for menarche, the more positive her feelings and the less her distress (Koff, Rierdan, & Sheingold, 1982; Ruble & Brooks-Gunn, 1982). Girls who are uninformed or, worse yet, misinformed, often have unhappy memories of their first menstruation (Rierdan, Koff, & Flaherty, 1986). Those whose menarche comes early are most likely to find it disruptive (Ruble & Brooks-Gunn, 1982), possibly because they are less prepared or because they feel out of step with their friends.

Parents can do much to make menstruation a more positive experience. Vicky's parents helped their daughter see this event as a special sign of maturity. When Ellen saw that Vicky's breasts and pubic hair were beginning to develop, Ellen told her daughter about menstruation—in concrete, personal terms that Vicky could understand. Ellen reassured Vicky that she could engage in all her normal activities, including sports and bathing, during her periods. Then about a year later when Vicky got her first menstrual period, Ellen gave Vicky practical suggestions for coping with discomfort and profuse bleeding. Furthermore, Vicky's father did not pretend to be an ignorant outsider who knew nothing of female biological processes. On the contrary, Charles—unlike many fathers who feel uncomfortable talking about menstruation—encouraged Vicky to ask questions. Both parents maintained an open, matter-of-fact attitude with both Vicky and her brother. Charles even marked his daughter's womanhood by taking Vicky out to a celebratory lunch.

In her diary, Anne Frank wrote down the thoughts about her sexual maturation that were too private for her to talk about with anyone. She expressed the ambivalence about menstruation felt by many young girls—describing it as a nuisance—but also as a "sweet secret."

Feelings about Physical Appearance

Most young teenagers are more concerned about their looks than about any other aspect of themselves, and many do not like what they see in the mirror (Siegel, 1982). Boys want to be tall, broad-shouldered, and athletic; girls want to be pretty, slim but shapely, with nice hair and skin (Tobin-Richards, Boxer, Kavrell, & Petersen, 1984). Anything that makes boys think that they look feminine or girls think that they look masculine makes them miserable. Teenagers of both sexes worry about their weight, their complexion, and their facial features.

Girls tend to be unhappier about their looks than boys of the same age, no doubt because of our culture's greater emphasis on women's physical attributes. When adolescents are asked what they like least about their bodies, often boys say "nothing," while girls complain mostly about their legs and hips (Tobin-Richards et al., 1983).

Most teenagers are more concerned about their physical appearance than about any other aspect of themselves, and they want to mature at about the same time as their friends do.

HEALTH ISSUES IN ADOLESCENCE

These years are healthy ones for most adolescents. Adolescents consult physicians most often for skin and cosmetic problems, coughs and sore throats, and (for girls) prenatal care (Gans, 1990).

HEALTH AND FITNESS

The health problems that do arise in these years are often preventable, stemming as many do from personality, poverty, and lifestyle. While most teenagers do not take health-threatening risks, a sizeable minority of them do. Across ethnic and

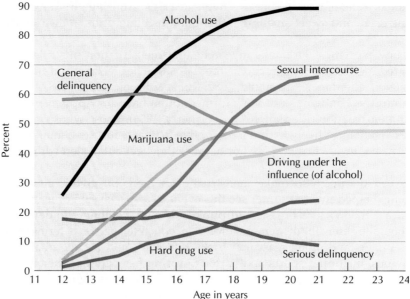

FIGURE 14-1
Age-specific rates for prevalence of some high-risk behaviors, averaged out over 3 years. SOURCE: Adapted from Elliott, 1993.

social class lines, many young adolescents (aged 11 to 14) smoke, drink, use marijuana, and are sexually active. (See Figure 14-1.) Adolescents whose families have been disrupted by parental separation or death are more likely to start these activities early and to engage in them even more over the next few years (Millstein et al., 1992).

Physical Activity—and Inactivity

The combination of youthful energy, well-developed faculties, mature coordination, and strong muscles accounts for the new heights in athletic prowess reached by some adolescents. But sports carry risks, along with glory.

One study of high school sports injuries found that the highest injury rate for either sex is for girls who go out for cross-country running. The next most dangerous sports are, in order, football, wrestling, girls' soccer, and boys' cross-country (about two-thirds the girls' rate) (S. G. Rice, 1993). The high rate of girls' injuries seems to stem partly from such biological factors as puberty and bone density. Prepubescent girls suffer many stress fractures, in part because with their low estrogen levels they have not yet developed maximum bone density. In addition, heavy training often inhibits menstruation, keeping estrogen levels low. Other differences in girls' bodies relative to boys' that may contribute to girls' injuries are wider hips, sharper angles to the thigh bones, and weaker muscles on the inside of the knee.

Not participating in sports or other regular physical exercise, however, may be even more dangerous in the long run. Since a sedentary lifestyle that carries over into adulthood may result in an increase in obesity, diabetes, osteoporosis, and heart disease, recent findings are cause for concern. Only 35 percent of ninth-grade girls and 53 percent of ninth-grade boys participate in 20 minutes of vigorous activity three times a week, and these numbers drop to only 25 and 50 percent, respectively, for high school seniors (Centers for Disease Control & Prevention, 1994).

Some reasons for such low rates of physical activity can be found in social and cultural contexts. In the United States, Illinois is the only state to require physical education in schools (Steinhauer, 1995). Teenage girls—and especially those living in poverty—are the least active. Among the reasons cited for this are lack of access to facilities and lessons, the need to help at home, and lack of encouragement to compete in sports (Updyke, 1994).

Other Health Concerns

Only 6 percent of adolescents suffer from chronic disabilities; in 32 percent of these cases, a mental disorder is responsible (Newacheck, 1989). Other disabilities are caused by chronic respiratory conditions, diseases of the muscle and skeletal system and connective tissue, nervous system disorders, and hearing impairments (Gans, 1990; Newacheck, 1989). (See Figure 14-2.) Dental health is often a problem: 96 percent of high school students have some tooth decay, about 50 percent wear—or should be wearing—braces to correct poor contact between upper and lower jaws, and 23 percent of 15-year-olds have untreated decay in at least one tooth (Gans, 1990).

Health Care

The health status of adolescents is expected to get worse over the next few decades, largely because more young people will be living in poverty. Adolescents from poor families are 3 times as likely to be in fair or poor health and 47 percent more likely to suffer from disabling chronic illnesses than are adolescents from families above the poverty line (Newacheck, 1989). These teenagers need access to medical care; research indicates that they will use it. In one study, teenagers with Medicaid coverage went to doctors at rates similar to teenagers from more affluent families; those without coverage sought less care (Newacheck, 1989).

An estimated 14 percent of young people under age 18 do not receive the medical care they need. Adolescents are less likely than younger children to see a physician regularly (Gans, 1990). Why don't teenagers get medical care? Reasons include lack of money or insurance coverage, medical office hours that conflict with school hours, requirements for parental consent, and a lack of assurance of confidentiality on the part of the health care provider.

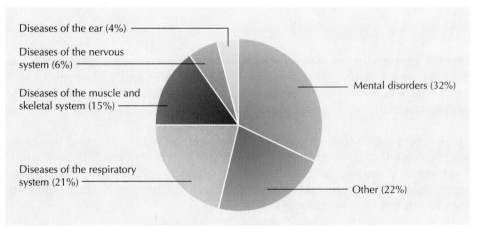

FIGURE 14-2
Causes of mental and physical disability among 10- to 18-year-olds. Six percent of adolescents in this age range have a serious chronic condition that limits their activity. In 32 percent of cases, a mental disorder is responsible. SOURCE: Adapted from Gans, 1990.

We will now discuss such health issues as nutrition and eating disorders, depression, drug abuse, sexually transmitted diseases, physical and sexual abuse, neglect, and suicide. We will examine teenage pregnancy in Chapter 16.

NUTRITION AND EATING DISORDERS

Adolescents' Nutritional Needs

The average teenage girl needs about 2200 calories per day, while the average teenage boy needs about 2800. Protein is important in sustaining growth, and teenagers (like everyone else) should avoid "junk foods" like french fries, soft drinks, ice cream, and snack chips and dips, which are high in cholesterol, fat, and calories and low in nutrients.

The most common mineral deficiencies of adolescents are of calcium, zinc, and iron. Adolescents' need for calcium, which supports bone growth, is best met by drinking enough milk; but people who suffer from lactose intolerance (the inability to digest milk) may obtain calcium from such other foods as salmon and broccoli. Many teenage girls avoid milk for fear of gaining weight, but skim milk actually has a higher calcium content than whole milk. Girls who take calcium supplements to increase their daily intake of this mineral to 110 percent of the U.S. Health Department's recommended daily allowances (RDAs) increase their total body and spinal bone density (Lloyd et al., 1993). This may provide protection in years to come against future bone fractures caused by osteoporosis (thinning of the bones). Protection against osteoporosis is also provided by regular weight-bearing exercise, like walking or running.

Iron-deficiency anemia is common among American adolescents because their diet tends to be iron-poor. Teenagers need a steady source of iron-fortified breads, dried fruits, and leafy green vegetables. Foods with zinc—like meats, eggs, seafood, and whole-grain cereal products—belong in the diet, since even a mild zinc deficiency can delay sexual maturity (E. R. Williams & Caliendo, 1984).

Many adolescents put on weight, and some—especially girls—react by embarking on a lifelong struggle to reduce for the sake of health and beauty. Some are fighting real obesity. But in recent years, two eating problems—*anorexia* and *bulimia*—have become increasingly common. Both reflect our society's standards of female beauty, exalting slenderness above all else, as well as individual pathologies of people who try to meet those standards through bizarre eating patterns.

Obesity

obesity *Overweight condition involving a skin-fold measurement in the 85th percentile.*

Obesity, overweight involving a skin-fold measurement in the 85th percentile, is the most common eating disorder in the United States, affecting 21 percent of adolescents (Center for Health Statistics, 1994). Obese teenagers tend to become obese adults, subject to social, psychological, and physical risks.

Consequences of Overweight. One 60-year longitudinal study found that overweight in adolescence can lead to life-threatening chronic conditions in adulthood—even if the excess weight is lost. The effects are particularly strong for heavy boys, who as adults have death rates nearly double those of men who were more slender as teenagers (Must et al., 1992).

In another study, researchers identified 370 people, aged 16 to 24, who were above the 95th percentile of weight for their age and sex. Seven years later, these people were compared with normal-weight people, some of whom had chronic health conditions. The overweight subjects had suffered many social and economic consequences—possibly as a result of discrimination against heavy people. Compared with nonoverweight subjects in both the healthy and the chronic-condition groups, the women in the overweight group had completed fewer years of school and had lower household incomes and higher rates of poverty; both the overweight women and the overweight men were less likely to be married. These differences held even when original socioeconomic circumstances were taken into account (Gortmaker, Must, Perrin, Sobol, & Dietz, 1993). It seems that being poor makes one more vulnerable to obesity, and being obese makes one more vulnerable to poverty.

Some research has found an association between overweight and poor psychological adjustment (Alsaker, 1992). Other research found social and economic consequences but no effect on self-esteem or other psychological disturbance (Gortmaker et al., 1993).

Causes and Treatment of Overweight.   Obesity results when people consume more calories than they expend. Obese adolescents and adults are widely regarded as having too little "willpower," but this is an oversimplification. Although there are some causes of obesity that people can change—a low rate of physical activity and poor eating habits—other risk factors having nothing to do with willpower seem to make some people susceptible to overweight.

Factors contributing to obesity include genetic regulation of metabolism (obesity often runs in families, as noted in Chapter 2); developmental history (inability to recognize body clues about hunger and when it should be satisfied, or the development of an abnormally large number of fat cells during childhood); emotional stress; and brain damage. No matter what the cause, obese people *can* lose weight. Programs using behavior modification to help adolescents make changes in diet and exercise have had some success in taking off pounds.

Anorexia Nervosa and Bulimia Nervosa

Sometimes a determination *not* to become obese can result in even graver problems than obesity itself, as in the disorders of anorexia nervosa and bulimia nervosa. Both tend to reflect problems in society as well as in families and individuals, since they stem in large part from today's ideal of female beauty—with its unrealistic glorification of slenderness. This cultural influence interacts with family and personal factors to make many adolescent girls and young women obsessed with their weight.

Preoccupations with dieting and weight have become widespread among teenage girls, especially white girls; black girls are less weight- and diet-conscious. Girls who gain weight or diet to lose it tend to be dissatisfied with their self-image and are often depressed. Among 497 urban and suburban high school seniors, two-thirds of the girls were preoccupied with weight and dieting, compared with only 15 percent of the boys (Casper & Offer, 1990). In a different group of 1400 high school students, 63 percent of the girls were trying to lose weight and 28.4 percent of the boys were trying to gain—although most of these adolescents were already of normal weight (Rosen & Gross, 1987). Another study found that more than half of female high school seniors have dieted "seriously." Some never stop (J. D. Brown, Childers, & Waszak, 1988), and some adopt abnormal eating habits.

Anorexia.   Someone suggests to Kaia, 14, that she would perform better in gymnastics if she lost a few pounds. She loses them—and then continues to diet obsessively, refusing to eat. Her body weight becomes less than 85 percent of what is considered normal for her height and age (*Diagnostic and Statistical Manual of Mental Disorders*, DSM-IV, 1994). Meanwhile, Kaia stops menstruating, thick soft hair spreads over her body, and she becomes intensely overactive.

Kaia brags to Vicky that she exists on only three apples a day. She is preoccupied with food—cooking it, talking about it, and urging others to eat—but she eats very little herself. She has a distorted view of herself: She cannot see how shockingly thin she is. She is a good student, described by her parents as a "model" child, and is compulsive about her training schedule. She is also withdrawn, depressed, and obsessed with repetitive, perfectionist behavior (Garner, 1993).

This is a typical scenario for *anorexia nervosa,* or self-starvation, an eating disorder seen mostly in young white women (DSM-IV, 1994). The disorder occurs across socioeconomic levels, may affect both sexes, and is most likely to occur during adolescence, with 17 the average age of onset. The incidence of anorexia has increased in recent years; it is estimated to affect from 0.5 to 1 percent of late adolescent females and an unknown, but growing, percentage of males (DSM-IV, 1994; Garner, 1993).

The course of the disease is highly variable. Some people recover fully after one episode, but others steadily deteriorate or fluctuate between weight gain and relapse. From 2 to 10 percent of people diagnosed with anorexia eventually die, usually of starvation, suicide, or electrolyte imbalance (D. B. Herzog, Keller, & Lavori, 1988; DSM-IV, 1994).

The cause of anorexia is unknown. Many observers consider it a reaction to extreme societal pressure to be slender—a response to a cultural standard of attractiveness that is thinner for women than for men and the thinnest it has been since the 1920s, the time of the last epidemic of similar eating disorders (Silverstein, Perdue, Peterson, et al., 1986; Silverstein, Peterson, & Perdue, 1986). Support for this view comes from the fact that the disorder is especially common among females in sports like figure skating and gymnastics, which have subjective scoring that can be influenced by a competitor's appearance (American College of Sports Medicine, 1992). Other support comes from its prevalence in industrialized societies where food is abundant and attractiveness is equated with thinness, such as the United States, Canada, Europe, Australia, Japan, New Zealand, and South Africa (DSM-IV, 1994).

Others see it as a psychological disturbance related to a fear of growing up, a fear of sexuality, or a malfunctioning family. Such families often seem harmonious on the surface, but the family members are actually overdependent and too involved in each other's lives and have difficulty dealing with conflict (Dove, undated). Some people with anorexia seem to feel that controlling their weight is the only way to control any part of their lives. Depression is often part of the disorder. A Canadian study that followed anorexic patients between 5 and 14 years after treatment found them likely to suffer from depression or anxiety disorders later in life (Toner, Garfinkel, & Garner, 1986).

Still other observers suggest that anorexia may be a physical disorder caused by a deficiency of a crucial chemical in the brain or by a disturbance of the hy-

anorexia nervosa   *Eating disorder, seen mostly in young women, characterized by self-starvation.*

Gymnast Christy Henrich died of multiple organ failure at age 22, after having suffered from anorexia and bulimia as a teenager. These eating disorders are especially common among female figure skaters and gymnasts, and are also on the rise among other adolescents.

pothalamus. Others believe that it may develop because of inadequate coping skills to face new experiences or adverse life events (Garner, 1993). It is probably due to a combination of factors.

Early warning signs include a dieter's lowered weight goals after reaching an initial desired weight, determined secret dieting, excessive exercising, dissatisfaction even after losing weight, and interruption of regular menstruation. As soon as symptoms like these begin to appear, appropriate treatment should be sought.

Bulimia. In *bulimia nervosa,* a person—usually an adolescent girl or a young woman—regularly (at least twice a week, for at least 3 months) goes on huge eating binges within a brief time period (usually up to 2 hours). She or he then tries to nullify the high caloric intake by self-induced vomiting; strict dieting or fasting; vigorous exercise; or using laxatives, enemas, or diuretics to purge the body (DSM-IV, 1994).

bulimia nervosa *Eating disorder in which a person regularly eats huge quantities of food (binges) and then tries to nullify the effects by vomiting, purging, fasting, or excessive exercise.*

People with bulimia are obsessed with their weight and body shape. They do not become abnormally thin, but they become overwhelmed with shame, self-contempt, and depression over their abnormal eating habits. They also suffer extensive tooth decay (caused by repeated vomiting of stomach acid), gastric irritation, skin problems, and loss of hair. There is some overlap between anorexia and bulimia; some victims of anorexia have bulimic episodes, and some people with bulimia lose weight. But the two are separate disorders.

Bulimia affects an estimated 1 to 3 percent of female adolescents and young adults, about 10 times the number of males who have the disorder. The course of the bulimia may be intermittent or chronic, and the long-term outcome is unknown. It is about equally common in countries having high rates of anorexia, as noted above (DSM-IV, 1994).

Bulimia seems to be related to low levels of the brain chemical serotonin, providing a biological basis. Another theory attributes its prevalence in industrialized countries to the same pressures for thinness that create the social climate for anorexia. Then there is a psychoanalytic explanation: that bulimic people use food to appease their hunger for love and attention. The basis for this interpretation rests on reports by some bulimic patients that they felt abused, neglected, and deprived of nurturing from their parents (Humphrey, 1986).

Treatment for Anorexia and Bulimia. Both these eating disorders can be treated, but the relapse rate for anorexia is very high, with up to 25 percent of patients progressing to chronic invalidism and many dying prematurely (Beumont et al., 1993). The immediate goal of treatment for anorexia is to get patients to eat, to gain weight—and to live. They are likely to be admitted to a hospital, where they may be given 24-hour nursing, drugs to encourage eating and inhibit vomiting, and behavior therapy, which rewards eating by granting such privileges as getting out of bed and leaving the room (Beumont, Russell, & Touyz, 1993).

Patients with anorexia seem to need long-term support even after they have stopped starving themselves. Some 27 months after completion of treatment, most of the 63 females in one study had continued to gain weight, had resumed menstruating, and were functioning in school or at work. Still, they continued to have problems with body image. Even though they averaged 8 percent below ideal weight, most thought of themselves as being overweight and as having excessive appetites, and many felt depressed and lonely (Nussbaum, Shenker, Baird, & Saravay, 1985). Since the transition from hospital to home can be difficult, good supervision and counseling are important (Beumont et al., 1993).

Both anorexia and bulimia are also treated by therapies that help patients gain insight into their feelings. Since these patients are at risk of depression and suicide, the discovery that antidepressant drugs can help is heartening (Fluoxetine-Bulimia Collaborative Study Group, Hudson & Pope, 1990; Kaye, Weltzin, Hsu, & Bulik, 1991).

DEPRESSION

Most young people negotiate adolescence without major emotional problems, but some undergo mild to severe bouts of depression. Research among adolescents who have *not* sought psychotherapy suggests that somewhere between 10 and 35 percent of boys and 15 to 40 percent of girls experience depressed moods (Petersen et al., 1993). Before puberty, rates for depression are the same in boys and girls, but at about age 12, the girls start to have higher rates; by age 14, girls' depression rates are twice as high as boys' (Lewinsohn in Goleman, 1990; Rierdan, Koff, & Stubbs, 1988, 1989).

Several factors put adolescent girls at higher risk than boys for depression. One is worry about their appearance, a concern that looms larger for females than males. Girls often feel "ugly"; consider themselves too fat, too short or too tall; or hate their hair or their complexions. In a society in which personality is often judged by appearance, self-image can have long-lasting effects on young people's feelings about themselves. Adults who thought they were attractive during their teenage years have higher self-esteem and are happier than those who did not. Not until the mid-forties do the differences in self-esteem and happiness disappear (Berscheid, Walster, & Bohrnstedt, 1973).

Depression is also associated with the occurrence of several life changes at about the same time. One such change is the move from elementary to secondary school. For either a boy or girl who makes this move at about the same time as puberty, or just after it, there is a higher risk of depression. Since girls enter puberty earlier, they are more likely than boys to experience these two events at about the same time (Petersen, Sarigiani, & Kennedy, 1991). Another risk factor is other stressful family events. Since parents of daughters have a higher divorce rate than do parents of sons, adolescent girls are more likely than boys to experience their parents' divorce (Petersen et al., 1993). Finally, gender-different coping styles may play a role: Men more often distract themselves when they are depressed, whereas women tend to analyze themselves, looking for reasons for depression. These patterns may begin in adolescence, and the male pattern may be more effective in coping with stress (Petersen, Kennedy, & Sullivan, 1991).

Resources for *treating* depressed adolescents are limited. Some possible directions for *preventing* it include programs designed to promote social competence and teach problem-solving skills; targeting of at-risk young people; and carrying out more research on adolescent depression.

USE AND ABUSE OF DRUGS

Much drug taking by adolescents and adults alike seems to be an effort at self-treatment of depression. However, the effort often boomerangs, causing additional problems.

Current Trends in Drug Use

Throughout history, humankind has sought to relieve with drugs the ills that flesh and spirit are heir to. People have relied on drugs to alleviate unhappiness as well as physical ailments and to give their lives a lift. The ancient Greeks drank alcohol; long before the birth of Christ, marijuana was used in China and in India; and cocaine, obtained by chewing coca leaves, was a staple among the sixteenth-century Incas. Many nineteenth-century American women freely drank and gave their babies syrups heavily laced with opium (Brecher, 1972).

Why, then, are we so concerned about drugs today? One reason is the danger of using drugs at a young age. While certain drugs may not be harmful in moderation, adolescents are not known for being moderate. The great majority of adolescents do *not* abuse drugs, but those who do often turn to drugs as short-cut answers to problems, endangering their physical and psychological health and leaving their problems unsolved. Others begin taking drugs mainly out of curiosity or because of peer pressure.

Drug use among adolescents is less prevalent than it was at its peak during the 1960s, and less than it was in the late 1970s and 1980s. The "Monitoring the Future Survey" (National Institute on Drug Abuse, NIDA, 1994) polled about 50,000 eighth-, tenth-, and twelfth-grade students around the United States, a nationally representative sample from over 400 schools. These yearly polls show a decline in use of most drugs from 1979 to 1992; however, a significant increase in drug use occurred between 1992 and 1993 (NIDA, 1993, 1994). These surveys probably underestimate drug use since they do not reach high school dropouts, who are thought to have higher rates.

Young people who use such drugs as alcohol, nicotine, marijuana, LSD, amphetamines, barbiturates, heroin, and cocaine sometimes begin to use them in elementary school. The Monitoring the Future Survey (NIDA, 1994) found that in 1993 67.1 percent of eighth-graders had tried alcohol, 45.3 percent had smoked tobacco, 19.4 percent had tried inhalants (glue, aerosols, and solvents), and 12.6 percent had used marijuana. In the same survey, of 16,300 1993 high school seniors, 31 percent admitted using illicit drugs at least once in the past year, and 42.9 percent said that they had tried an illicit drug at some time (NIDA, 1994).

Twelfth-graders' use of cocaine in the previous 30 days continued the decline begun in 1986; it was down to 1.3 percent in 1993, compared with 1.6 percent in 1988. Lifetime use of crack for seniors was 2.6 percent in 1993. (See Table 14-4.)

The effects of drugs are harmful in adolescence and beyond. In one longitudinal study, more than 1000 high school sophomores and juniors were interviewed again at age 24 or 25. Those who had begun using a certain drug in their teens tended to continue to use it. Users of illicit drugs, including marijuana, were in poorer health than nonusers, had more unstable job and marital histories, and were more likely to have been delinquent. Cigarette smokers tended to be depressed and to have lung problems and breathing problems (Kandel, Davies, Karus, & Yamaguchi, 1986).

Alcohol, marijuana, and tobacco are the three drugs most popular with adolescents.

Alcohol

Many of the same people who worry about the illegal use of marijuana by young people forget that alcohol too is a potent, mind-altering drug, that it is illegal for

TABLE 14-4

LIFETIME PREVALENCE OF DRUG USE BY STUDENTS, 1991, 1992, AND 1993			
DRUG	8TH-GRADERS, PERCENT	10TH-GRADERS, PERCENT	12TH-GRADERS, PERCENT
Marijuana	1991: 10.2 1992: 11.2 1993: 12.6	1991: 23.4 1992: 21.4 1993: 24.4	1991: 36.0 1992: 32.6 1993: 35.3
Cocaine	1991: 2.3 1992: 2.9 1993: 2.9	1991: 4.1 1992: 3.3 1993: 3.6	1991: 7.8 1992: 6.1 1993: 6.1
Crack cocaine	1991: 1.3 1992: 1.6 1993: 1.7	1991: 1.7 1992: 1.5 1993: 1.8	1991: 3.1 1992: 2.6 1993: 2.6
Inhalants	1991: 17.6 1992: 17.4 1993: 19.4	1991: 15.7 1992: 16.6 1993: 17.5	1991: 17.6 1992: 16.6 1993: 17.4
LSD	1991: 2.7 1992: 3.2 1993: 3.5	1991: 5.6 1992: 5.8 1993: 6.2	1991: 8.8 1992: 8.6 1993: 10.3
Alcohol	1991: 70.1 1992: 69.3 1993: 67.1	1991: 83.8 1992: 82.3 1993: 80.8	1991: 88.0 1992: 87.5 1993: 87.0
Cigarettes	1991: 44.0 1992: 45.2 1993: 45.3	1991: 55.1 1992: 53.5 1993: 56.3	1991: 63.1 1992: 61.8 1993: 61.9
All illicit drugs	Figures not available	Figures not available	1981: 65.6 1991: 44.1 1992: 40.7 1993: 42.9

SOURCE: National Institute on Drug Abuse, 1994.

most high school students and many college students, and that it is a much more serious problem nationwide. High school students seem to be drinking less than they used to, college students and young adults, slightly less. Although nearly all high school seniors (87 percent) in the 1993 NIDA survey reported drinking alcoholic beverages in the previous year, the percentage who had had a drink during the previous month was 51 percent, down from the peak rate of 72 percent in 1980. Fewer students reported drinking heavily: 28.9 percent said that they had been drunk during the previous 30 days, compared with 31.6 percent in 1991.

Most teenagers start to drink because it seems a grown-up thing to do, and they continue for the same reasons adults do—to add a pleasant glow to social situations, conform to social expectations, reduce anxiety, and escape from problems. The dangers of driving after drinking are well known: The leading cause of death among 15- to 24-year-olds is alcohol-related vehicle accidents (American Academy of Pediatrics, AAP, Committee on Adolescence, 1987).

There is considerable evidence that alcoholism runs in families, that there is a strong hereditary influence, and that a heightened risk results from the interaction of genetic and environmental factors (McGue, 1993). Identical twins are more similar for alcoholism than are fraternal twins. Sons of alcoholic men are 4 times as likely as sons of nonalcoholic men to develop alcoholism themselves—even when they are adopted at birth and regardless of whether their adoptive parents are alcoholic. Children do not seem to be at unusual risk if their biologi-

To stem the many deaths among young Americans caused by alcohol-related motor vehicle accidents, educational campaigns now stress the importance of naming a "designated driver," one person in a group who agrees not to drink on a specific night.

cal parents are *not* alcoholic even if their adoptive parents are (Schuckit, 1985, 1987). Research has found the same magnitude of heritability for women, who at one time had been thought to become alcoholic largely as a result of social and psychological forces (Kendler, Heath, Neale, Kessler, & Eaves, 1992).

No one is predestined to develop alcoholism. But since genetic factors seem to make some people more vulnerable, children of alcoholic parents should be warned that they may not be able to handle liquor the way their peers do.

Marijuana

Marijuana has been used all over the world for centuries, but only since the 1960s has it become popular among the American middle class. Despite a decline in use since 1979 (37 percent of high school seniors had smoked it during the past 30 days in 1979 compared with 15 percent in 1993, according to the NIDA survey), it is still by far the most widely used illicit drug in this country. In fact, the 1993 rate represents an increase from the 11.9 percent of seniors who had smoked it during the past 30 days in 1992. Eighth- and tenth-graders showed similar increases.

Adolescents start to smoke marijuana for many of the same reasons they begin to drink alcohol. They are curious, they want to do what their friends do, and they want to be adults. Another appeal of marijuana is its value as a symbol of rebellion against parents' values, but this attraction may be slipping, since today's teenagers are much more likely to have parents who smoked (or smoke) marijuana themselves.

Heavy use of marijuana can lead to heart and lung disease, contribute to traffic accidents, and impede memory and learning. It may also lessen motivation, interfere with schoolwork, and cause family problems. Among 49 boys in one study (average age about 16), those who drank alcohol and also smoked marijuana more than twice a week were more likely than those who did not smoke marijuana to have poor eating habits and such health problems as respiratory infections and general fatigue (Farrow, Rees, & Worthington-Roberts, 1987).

Tobacco

Sneaking a cigarette behind the barn was once a humorous staple of adolescent lore. But with new awareness of health hazards, adults' amused indulgence toward young people's use of tobacco has turned to distress. The publication in 1964 of the U.S. Surgeon General's report clearly linked smoking to lung cancer, heart disease, emphysema, and several other illnesses.

Many adolescents got the message. Teenagers express concern about the effects of smoking on health, and smokers feel the disapproval of their peers. Still, in 1993, 29.9 percent of high school seniors smoked regularly, an increase of 2.1 percent over 1992 (NIDA, 1994). Today, more teenage girls than boys smoke, reversing the former male-female ratio. As a result, one type of equality that women have achieved is a death rate from lung cancer almost equal to that of men, although about $2\frac{1}{2}$ times as many men develop the disease (American Cancer Society, 1985).

Smokers usually take their first puff between 10 and 12 years of age; they continue to smoke even though they do not enjoy it at first, and they become physically dependent on nicotine at about age 15. Young people are more likely to smoke if their friends and family do (McAlister, Perry, & Maccoby, 1979; National Institute of Child Health and Human Development, 1978). One reason many adolescent girls do not stop smoking is their fear of putting on weight. Since peer pressure has been effective in inducing people to smoke, its influence in the other direction may be the best preventive mechanism (L. D. Johnston, Bachman, & O'Malley, 1982; McAlister et al., 1979).

SEXUALLY TRANSMITTED DISEASES

While a number of factors influence an adolescent's decision whether to become sexually active (as we will see in Chapter 16), the fear of a sexually transmitted disease is rarely one of them. Yet this age group is suffering a high rate of these diseases.

What Are STDs?

sexually transmitted diseases (STDs) *Diseases spread by sexual contact; also called venereal diseases.*

Sexually transmitted diseases (STDs), also referred to as *venereal diseases,* are diseases spread by sexual contact. Rates of STDs have soared for all ages since the 1960s, with severe effects on adolescents. Of the 12 million cases of STDs each year in the United States, two out of three occur among under-25-year-olds (Donovan, 1993).

The most prevalent STD is chlamydia, which causes infections of the urinary tract, the rectum, and cervix and can lead, in women, to pelvic inflammatory disease (PID), a serious abdominal infection. Other STDs, in order of incidence, are trichomoniasis, gonorrhea, genital (venereal) warts, herpes simplex, hepatitis B, syphilis, and infection by human immunodeficiency virus (HIV), which can cause acquired immune deficiency syndrome (AIDS).

Genital herpes simplex is a chronic, recurring, often painful disease caused by a virus (a different strain of which also causes cold sores on the face). Although no hard figures on its incidence are available, it is highly contagious, with between 200,000 to 500,000 new cases reported every year (Alan Guttmacher Institute, 1993). The condition can be fatal to the newborn infant of a mother who has an outbreak of genital herpes at the time of delivery and to a person with a deficiency of the immune system. It has been associated with increased incidence of cervical cancer. There is no cure, but the antiviral drug acyclovir can prevent active outbreaks.

Human immunodeficiency virus (HIV) attacks the body's immune system, leaving affected persons vulnerable to a variety of diseases, some of which are fatal, like acquired immune deficiency syndrome (AIDS). The HIV virus is transmitted through bodily fluids (mainly blood and semen) and stays in the body for life, even though the person carrying it may not show any signs of illness. Symptoms may not appear until from 6 months to 10 or more years after initial infection. Most victims in the United States are drug abusers who share contaminated hypodermic needles, their sexual partners, homosexual and bisexual men, people who have received transfusions of infected blood or blood products, and infants who have been infected in the womb or during birth. Worldwide, most HIV-infected adults are heterosexual.

The average time from HIV infection to death has been 10 years, with clinical and immunological decline evident much earlier. But about 5 percent of HIV-infected people are characterized as having "non-progressive disease" because they remain healthy and do not show the same declining blood counts as HIV-infected people whose disease progresses. The eventual fate of "non-progressors" is not known, but many seem to be staying healthy 10 or more years after being infected with the virus (Baltimore, 1995).

A 1993 report by the United Nations identifies sexually active teenage girls as the "next leading edge" of the HIV epidemic. In an analysis of information from 31 European, Asian, and African countries, the rate of HIV infection peaked for women at ages 15 to 25, compared with the male peak at ages 25 to 35. Young girls' greater susceptibility to this virus may stem from both physical and cultural causes. Physically, they are less well protected, partly because the membranes in their vaginas are thinner than those of older women, the mucus these membranes produce is thinner, and it contains fewer immunity-producing cells (Futterman et al., 1993).

Many teenagers put themselves at risk for HIV infection. Among 1091 tenth-graders from urban working-class and welfare families and middle-class suburban families, more than two-thirds of sexually active students reported inconsistent or no use of condoms; at least one-third had had two or more partners; and more than 5 percent had had intercourse with a presumably high-risk partner (Walter, Vaughan, & Cohall, 1991).

Fortunately, educating teenagers does have an effect. Among 15- to 19-year-old males, those who received AIDS education and sex education had fewer sexual partners, used condoms more consistently, and had less frequent intercourse (Ku, Sonenstein, & Pleck, 1992). This study counters the widely held notion that educating teenagers about sex makes them *more* sexually active.

AIDS has continued to spread since the early 1980s, when it first exploded as a public health concern. Education has reduced its spread in the homosexual community, blood screening has reduced the risk of contraction by transfusion, and current efforts focus on halting it among drug users. As of now, AIDS is incurable, but in many cases the related infections that kill people can be stopped

BOX 14-2 ▪ THE EVERYDAY WORLD

PROTECTING AGAINST SEXUALLY TRANSMITTED DISEASES

How can people who are sexually active protect themselves against sexually transmitted diseases (STDs)? The following guidelines minimize the possibility of acquiring an STD and maximize the chances of getting good treatment if one is acquired.

♦ Have regular medical checkups. All sexually active persons should request tests specifically aimed at diagnosing STDs.

♦ Know your partner. The more discriminating you are, the less likely you are to be exposed to STDs. Partners with whom you develop a relationship are more likely than partners you do not know well to inform you of any medical problems they have.

♦ Avoid having sexual intercourse with many partners, promiscuous persons, and drug abusers.

♦ Practice "safe sex": Avoid sexual activity involving exchange of bodily fluids. Use a latex condom during intercourse and oral sex. Avoid anal intercourse.

♦ Use a contraceptive foam, cream, or jelly; it will kill many germs and help to prevent certain STDs.

♦ Learn the symptoms of STDs: vaginal or penile discharge; inflammation, itching, or pain in the genital or anal area; burning during urination; pain during intercourse; genital, body, or mouth sores, blisters, bumps, or rashes; pain in the lower abdomen or in the testicles; discharge from or itching of eyes; and fever or swollen glands.

♦ Inspect your partner for any visible symptoms.

♦ If you develop any symptoms yourself, get immediate medical attention.

♦ Just before and just after sexual contact, wash genital and rectal areas with soap and water; males should urinate after washing.

♦ Do not have any sexual contact if you suspect that you or your partner may be infected. Abstinence is the most reliable preventive measure.

♦ Avoid exposing any cut or break in the skin to anyone else's blood (including menstrual blood), body fluids, or secretions.

♦ Practice good hygiene routinely: frequent, thorough hand washing and daily fingernail brushing.

♦ Make sure needles used for ear piercing, tattooing, acupuncture, or any kind of injection are either sterile or disposable. Never share a needle.

♦ If you contract any STD, notify all recent sexual partners immediately so that they can obtain treatment and avoid passing the infection back to you or on to someone else. Inform your doctor or dentist of your condition so that precautions can be taken to prevent transmission. Do not donate blood, plasma, sperm, body organs, or other body tissue. For more information, contact the American Foundation for the Prevention of Venereal Disease (AFPVD), 799 Broadway, Suite 638, New York, NY 10003.

SOURCE: Adapted from American Foundation for the Prevention of Venereal Disease, AFPVD, 1986; Upjohn Company, 1984.

with antibiotics, and HIV-infected people can often live active lives for years if the infection is caught soon enough.

Box 14-2 lists steps that sexually active people can take to protect themselves from STDs. Table 14-5 summarizes the most common STDs and their incidence, causes, most frequent symptoms, treatment, and consequences.

Implications for Adolescents

The reasons for the high rates of sexually transmitted diseases among adolescents are many: increased sexual activity, especially among girls; use of oral contraceptives, which do not protect against STDs, instead of condoms, which often do; the assumption that STDs can be cured easily; adolescents' reluctance to accept that unpleasant things that happen to *other* people can also happen to them; and teenagers' willingness to take risks because they want sex more than they fear disease.

Young girls may be even more susceptible than mature women to STD-caused

TABLE 14-5

THE MOST COMMON SEXUALLY TRANSMITTED DISEASES

DISEASE	NEW CASES ANNUALLY	CAUSE	SYMPTOMS: MALE	SYMPTOMS: FEMALE	TREATMENT	CONSEQUENCES IF UNTREATED
Chlamydia	4 million	Bacterial infection	Pain during urination, discharge from penis.	Vaginal discharge, abdominal discomfort.[†]	Tetracycline or erythromycin.	Can cause pelvic inflammatory disease or eventual sterility.
Tricho-moniasis	3 million	Parasitic infection, sometimes passed on in moist objects like towels and bathing suits	Often absent.	May be absent, or may include vaginal discharge, discomfort during intercourse, odor, painful urination.	Oral antibiotic.	May lead to abnormal growth of cervical cells.
Gonorrhea	1.1 million	Bacterial Infection	Discharge from penis, pain during urination.*	Discomfort when urinating, vaginal discharge, abnormal menses.[†]	Penicillin or other antibiotics.	Can cause pelvic inflammatory disease or eventual sterility; can also cause arthritis, dermatitis, and meningitis.
Genital warts	500,000–1 million	Viral–infection	Painless growths that usually appear on penis, but may also appear on urethra or in rectal area.*	Small, painless growths on genitals and anus; may also occur inside the vagina without external symptoms.*	Removal of warts.	May be associated with cervical cancer. In pregnancy, warts enlarge and may obstruct birth canal.
Herpes	200,000–500,000	Viral infection	Painful blisters anywhere on the genitalia, usually on the penis.*	Painful blisters on the genitalia, sometimes with fever and aching muscles; women with sores on cervix may be unaware of outbreaks.*	No known cure, but controlled with antiviral drug acyclovir.	Possible increased risk of cervical cancer.
Hepatitis B	100,000–200,000 (about 1.5 million carry infection)	Viral infection	Skin and eyes become yellow.	Skin and eyes become yellow.	No specific treatment; no alcohol.	Can cause liver damage, chronic hepatitis.

*May be asymptomatic.
[†]Often asymptomatic

(continued)

TABLE 14-5 (CONTINUED)

DISEASE	NEW CASES ANNUALLY	CAUSE	SYMPTOMS: MALE	SYMPTOMS: FEMALE	TREATMENT	CONSEQUENCES IF UNTREATED
Syphillis	120,000	Bacterial infection	In first stage, reddish-brown sores on the mouth or genitalia or both, which may disappear, though the bacteria remain; in the second, more infectious stage, a widespread skin rash.*	Same as in men.	Penicillin or other antibiotics.	Paralysis, convulsions, brain damage, and sometimes death.
AIDS (acquired immune deficiency syndrome)	45,500	Viral Infection	Extreme fatigue, fever, swollen lymph nodes, weight loss, diarrhea, night sweats, susceptibility to other diseases.*	Same as in men.	No known cure; AZT and other drugs appear to extend life.	Death, usually due to other diseases, such as cancer.

*May be asymptomatic.
†Often asymptomatic
SOURCES: Adapted from Centers for Disease Control, 1986, 1992; Goldsmith, 1989; Morbidity and Mortality Weekly Report, 1987; Alan Guttmacher Institute, 1993; USDHHS, 1993.

infections of the upper genital tract, which can lead to serious, even dangerous, complications. Teenagers are more likely than adults to put off getting medical care (often out of worry that their parents will find out), they are less likely to follow through with treatment, they are often embarrassed to alert their sexual partners when they contract an STD, and STDs are more likely to be misdiagnosed in adolescents (Centers for Disease Control, 1983). Most campaigns aimed at eradicating STDs focus on early diagnosis and treatment. Not until at least equal attention is given to prevention and to the moral obligation to avoid passing on STDs will headway be made in stopping this epidemic.

ABUSE AND NEGLECT DURING ADOLESCENCE

A frail 12-year-old boy arrives at the hospital emergency room with a fractured wrist. After relating an implausible version of the "accident" that caused it, he finally breaks down and tells the physician that his father did it during the most recent of his frequent beatings. A 15-year-old tells the counselor at an abortion clinic that she is pregnant by her own father, who has been forcing her to have sexual relations with him for the past 4 years. No matter how brutal or unloving a home is, most teenagers cannot fight back or run away because they are still dependent on their families.

Adolescents are more likely to be abused—sexually, physically, and emotionally—than any other juvenile age group (National Center on Child Abuse and Neglect, NCCAN, 1988). The rates of abuse and neglect increase overall from age

2 on up through age 17. (See Figure 14-3.) Official figures underestimate the real number of adolescents affected, because they include only cases in which physical injuries occurred because of parental abuse or neglect. Also, cases of neglect or abuse by people other than parents and instances when a child's health or safety was at risk are not counted (Gans, 1990).

While rates of physical and emotional abuse are similar for adolescent boys and girls, teenage girls are 4 times more likely to suffer sexual abuse. At earlier ages, boys are more likely to be abused and neglected than girls. Rates of physical abuse rise by 45 percent from childhood to early adolescence, and emotional abuse soars by 100 percent. Although no consistent racial differences appear in any kind of abuse or neglect, family income has an inverse relationship to reported neglect and abuse. Children and adolescents in families with incomes under $15,000 are more likely to suffer physical, emotional, and sexual abuse than are those in families above that level. Poor children are more than 8 times more likely to suffer serious injury as a result of abuse (NCCAN, 1988).

Physical abuse of teenagers accounts for between 16 and 30 percent of all physical abuse (Blum, 1987). It typically occurs in situations where an adult, enraged by a teenager's disobedience, spanks the youngster or inflicts such facial injuries as bruises, a black eye, or a split lip. (Abused younger children tend to suffer whiplash injuries, fractures, burns, and internal trauma.) Neglect is more common than abuse: 70 percent of all cases of abuse and neglect of adolescents are cases of neglect.

What do you think?   *Why do you think adolescents are at such high risk of abuse and neglect? What can be done to prevent such maltreatment?*

Ideally, treatment of abused and neglected adolescents should take place within the context of the family, school, and community, but this is easier said than done. The federal government is currently mounting a major campaign to teach police officers, teachers, and health professionals how to spot and deal with cases of abuse and neglect.

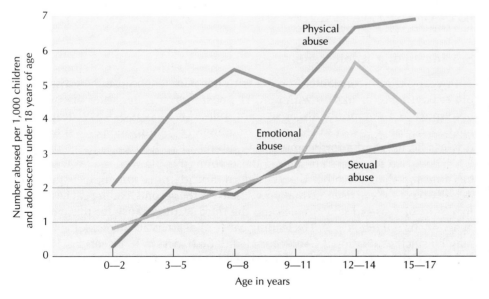

FIGURE 14-3
Differences in physical, sexual, and emotional abuse of children and adolescents. Contrary to many people's beliefs, abuse of children does not stop when the children get older. Emotional abuse peaks in early adolescence (between ages 12 and 14), and rates of both physical and sexual abuse continue to rise through age 17. SOURCE: Adapted from Gans, 1990.

DEATH IN ADOLESCENCE

Death Rates and Causes of Death

Only 27 percent of deaths among 10- to 19-year-olds are from natural causes, showing the general good health and vigor of young people (Gans, 1990). The other 73 percent of adolescent deaths are due to accidents, homicide, and suicide. When adolescents die, violence is usually responsible.

The leading causes of death at this age—accidents, homicide, and suicide—sometimes reflect cultural pressures and sometimes reflect adolescents' lack of experience and immature judgment, which often lead to risk taking and carelessness. In an analysis of risk-taking behaviors, researchers found that adolescents who had dropped out of high school took more risks than those still in school. Students were more likely than those not in school to use safety belts and less likely to ride with a drinking driver, carry a weapon, use drugs, and have sexual intercourse (Centers for Disease Control and Prevention, 1994). For black males aged 15 to 24, homicide is the number one killer—seven times greater than the rate for white males (McGinnis, Richmond, Brandt, Windom, & Mason, 1992).

Teenage boys account for four out of five accidental injuries, and the rate of violent injury for 18- to 19-year-olds is almost $2\frac{1}{2}$ times greater than that for 12- to 15-year-olds (Blum, 1987). The death rate is about 3 times higher for teenage boys than for girls, with boys more likely to die of suicide, homicide, and motor vehicle injuries (Fingerhut & Kleinman, 1989). Death rates for 15- to 19-year-olds are the same for both black and white youths (81 deaths per 100,000), but among 10- to 14-year-olds, African Americans have a death rate 27 percent higher (Fingerhut & Kleinman, 1989). The prime causes of death differ for the races: Automobile accidents are the leading cause for young whites; homicide is the leading cause for young blacks. Among both black and white teenagers, the second leading cause of death is suicide.

What do you think? *How can adolescents be helped to change risky behaviors, like the use of drugs and unsafe sexual activity? How can adults educate and motivate young people? What can society do to make minority-population neighborhoods safer for adolescents?*

Suicide among Adolescents

A 16-year-old girl, constantly at odds with her parents because they disapprove of her boyfriend, breaks up with him. The next morning, her sister discovers her body next to an empty bottle of sleeping pills. An 18-year-old boy, despondent after an accident that resulted in the "totaling" of his car, the revocation of his driver's license, and a forthcoming trial, jumps off an icy bridge to his death.

These two teenagers are among those young people who see no way out of bad times in their life other than ending it. Suicide rates among teenagers—especially boys—have risen, so that now suicide is the second leading cause of death for 15- to 24-year-old white males and the third leading cause for this age group generally (USDHHS, 1992). The leading cause of death is accidents, some of which may be suicides (National Center for Health Statistics, in L. Eisenberg, 1986).

Some child-study professionals believe that suicide rates among teenagers have risen because today's adolescents are under much more stress than their

BOX 14-3 ■ THE EVERYDAY WORLD

PREVENTING SUICIDE

After someone commits suicide, friends and family are usually overwhelmed with grief and guilt. They ask themselves, "Why didn't I know? Why didn't I do something?" Many people intent on killing themselves keep their plans secret, but others send out signals well in advance. An attempt at suicide is sometimes a call for help, and some people die because they are more successful than they intended to be. People who want to help prevent suicide need to learn its warning signs and the kinds of actions that are sometimes effective.

People contemplating suicide often show a marked change of behavior in one or more respects. Some common alarm signals include withdrawal from family or friends; talking about death, the hereafter, or suicide; giving away prized possessions; drug or alcohol abuse; personality changes like increased anger, boredom, and apathy; unusual neglect of appearance; difficulty concentrating at work or in school; staying away from work, school, or other usual activities; complaints of physical problems when nothing is organically wrong; changes in sleeping or eating habits—eating or sleeping much more or much less than usual.

By responding to such changes, it may be possible to get help and avert the loss of a life. A concerned person can act along one or more of the following lines.

♦ Talk to the person about his or her suicidal thoughts. Bringing up the subject will not put ideas into the mind of someone who has not already thought of suicide. It will bring feelings out into the open.

♦ Tell others who are in a position to do something—the person's parents or spouse, other family members, a close friend, a therapist, or a counselor. It is better to break a confidence than to let someone die.

♦ Do as much as possible to relieve the real-life pressures that seem intolerable. This may involve calling a rejecting boyfriend or girlfriend, lending money, or interceding with an employer.

♦ Show the person that she or he has other options besides death, even though none of them may be ideal. One therapist talked nonjudgmentally to a suicidal pregnant teenager. He raised the possibility of a number of alternatives, including abortion, adoption, keeping the baby, telling her parents, telling the baby's father, and committing suicide. After she was able to rank the options in order of preference, suicide no longer headed the list. She and the therapist were now "'haggling' about life" (Shneidman, 1985). This therapist emphasizes the importance of reminding the patient "that life is often the best choice among lousy alternatives and that functioning well may mean choosing the least lousy alternative that is practicably attainable (p. 325).

---

counterparts of earlier days (Elkind, 1984). But many young people who attempt suicide do not want to die. They want only to change their lives, and their suicide attempts are desperate pleas for attention and help. Through impulsiveness or miscalculation, they often die before help can reach them.

Many young people who try to kill themselves have histories of emotional illness; common diagnoses are depression, drug and alcohol abuse, and unstable personality. They tend to be impulsive, to have poor control, and to have low tolerance for frustration and stress (Slap, et al., 1989). They are also likely to think poorly of themselves, to live in a family torn by strife or one they experience as nonsupportive, to have inadequate relationships outside the family, and to feel hopeless (Swedo et al., 1991). Drugs and alcohol play a part in about half of all teenage suicide attempts (National Committee for Citizens in Education, NCCE, 1986).

Suicidal adolescents are often in conflict with their parents and unable to call on them for support when they feel lonely and unloved. Many come from troubled families, and a high proportion have been abused or neglected (Deykin, Alpert, & McNamara, 1985). Although school problems are common, for either academic or behavior reasons, poor performance is not universal. Among a group of high-achieving high school juniors and seniors, 31 percent had considered suicide and 4 percent had tried it (*Who's Who among American High School Students*, in NCCE, 1986). Low achievers may feel their lives are worthless; high achievers may feel under too much pressure to perform.

What can be done to stem the alarming rise in suicide among young people? In the face of individual danger signals, the family and friends of an adolescent who may be contemplating suicide can sometimes help. (See Box 14-3.) However, a more fundamental cause involves the ecological context that young people live in; this needs to be changed at social policy levels.

What Society Can Do to Prevent Suicide

Starting at the most basic level, social policy can emphasize the promotion of physical and mental health. Schools can begin early to help children learn how to solve problems and cope effectively with stress. Programs to enhance self-esteem can be directed toward young children and continued through the school years (Meehan, 1990).

Children, young people, and adults who are at high risk should be identified, so that counseling and guidance can be offered. Someone thinking about suicide may turn first to a crisis center or telephone hot line, which can offer immediate support as well as referral to a mental health professional. Most communities and hospitals now have suicide-prevention hot lines—some operating 24 hours a day—which people can call to talk about their problems; and most college counseling departments provide suicide prevention services. Intervention is especially urgent for people who have already talked about or attempted suicide, since studies show that 10 to 40 percent of people who commit suicide have attempted it before (Meehan, 1990).

Steps can also be taken to reduce access to common methods of suicide. In England and Wales between 1960 and 1975, suicide rates declined, apparently as a result of the elimination of coal gas containing carbon monoxide, which had been a popular method (J. H. Brown, 1979). In the United States and in Australia, the number of suicides from barbiturates declined in proportion to the number of prescriptions written. The number of suicides involving guns has risen in recent years; the ready availability of firearms in the home is associated with a higher risk of suicide (Kellermann et al., 1992). Many suicides are impulsive; if a convenient means is not at hand, the depressed person may not go any further or may at least defer action long enough to get help. Furthermore, a person who leans toward one method may be reluctant to use another (L. Eisenberg, 1980). These findings have important implications for gun control legislation.

Despite the perils of adolescence, most young people emerge from the teenage years with a mature, healthy body and a zest for life. While their bodies have been developing, their intellect has continued to develop too, as we will see in Chapter 15.

SUMMARY

1 Adolescence is a period of transition between childhood and adulthood. It begins with the onset of puberty, a period of rapid physical growth and physiological changes leading to sexual maturity. Puberty ends when a person can reproduce. Puberty takes about 4 years and typically begins earlier in girls.

2   The end of adolescence is not clear-cut in western societies, since no single sign indicates that adulthood has been reached. In some nonwestern cultures, adulthood is regarded as beginning at puberty and is signified by puberty rites in a variety of forms.

3   *Secular trend* refers to a trend that can be observed over several generations. A secular trend toward earlier attainment of adult height and sexual maturity began about 100 years ago, probably because of improvements in living standards; the trend seems to have leveled in the United States.

4   Both sexes undergo an adolescent growth spurt: sharp growth in height and weight and advances in muscular and skeletal development. Soon after the growth spurt ends, the adolescent can reproduce.

5   The primary sex characteristics are the organs directly related to reproduction in the female and the male. These organs enlarge and mature during puberty.

6   The secondary sex characteristics—signs of sexual maturity that do not directly involve the reproductive organs—include the breasts of females and the broad shoulders of males and the body hair, skin, and voice typical of adult men or women.

7   Menarche (first menstruation), the principal sign of sexual maturity in girls, occurs at an average age of 12.8 years in the United States. Timing of menarche varies among cultures and is related to both genetic and environmental factors. In boys, the presence of sperm in the urine is the principal sign of sexual maturity. Adolescent boys may experience nocturnal emissions.

8   The rapid physical changes of adolescence affect self-concept and personality. Early or late maturation also may have an effect, though neither is clearly advantageous or disadvantageous. Girls adjust better to menarche if they are prepared for it.

9   Health problems of adolescents often result from poverty, personality, a risk-taking lifestyle or a sedentary one. For the most part, the adolescent years are relatively healthy.

10 The physical changes of adolescence require a balanced diet. Foods rich in calcium, iron, and zinc are necessary to sustain growth and bring on sexual maturity.

11 Obesity among adolescents is the most common eating disorder; it is associated with social, psychological, and physical factors. It has both genetic and environmental causes. It is most successfully treated by a restricted diet, increased exercise, and behavior modification.

12 Anorexia nervosa is a disorder characterized by self-starvation. A person with bulimia nervosa regularly goes on eating binges and then tries to counter the effect by vomiting, purging, fasting, or excessive exercise. Both of these conditions are more common among females. The causes are unknown. Treatment can include hospitalization, psychotherapy, and sometimes antidepressant drugs.

13 Between 10 and 40 percent of adolescents experience depressed moods, with higher rates for females. Depression is often associated with concern about appearance and the occurrence of several life changes at about the same time.

14 Drug abuse by adolescents is less common today than during the 1960s, 1970s, and 1980s. Still, many young people continue to use legal and illegal drugs. Alcohol abuse is the number 1 drug problem in the United States. Cigarette smoking did not decline among adolescents during the 1980s. More adolescent girls than boys now smoke. Marijuana is the most widely used illicit drug.

15 Sexually transmitted diseases (STDs) are contracted through sexual contact. The most prevalent STD is chlamydia; it is followed by gonorrhea, genital warts, herpes simplex, syphilis, and acquired immune deficiency syndrome (AIDS). Sexually active people can do a great deal to protect themselves against STDs.

16 The extent of abuse and neglect among adolescents has been underestimated. The rates of abuse and neglect increase overall from ages 2 through 17.

17 The three leading causes of death among adolescents are accidents, homicide, and suicide.

KEY TERMS

adolescence (553)
puberty (553)
secular trend (558)
adolescent growth spurt (558)
primary sex characteristics (559)
secondary sex characteristics (559)

menarche (560)
obesity (566)
anorexia nervosa (568)
bulimia nervosa (569)
sexually transmitted diseases (STDs)
  (574)

SUGGESTED READINGS

Byrne, K. (1987). *A parent's guide to anorexia and bulimia.* New York: Holt. In this sensible and reassuring book, the author, herself the mother of a recovering anorexic, discusses how to identify eating disorders, when to seek professional help, and what to expect from these professionals. She also offers suggestions on how to communicate with the eating-disordered member of the family.

Greydanus, D. E. (Ed.). (1991). *Caring for your adolescent: Ages 12-21.* New York: Bantam. This volume, prepared by the American Academy of Pediatrics, covers all aspects of caring for a teenager, including the physical changes of adolescence, nutritional guidelines, weight control, and peer relationships.

Lightfoot-Klein, H. (1989). *Prisoners of ritual: An odyssey into female genital circumcision in Africa.* Binghamton, NY: Haworth Press. An illuminating account of the methods, medical and psychological ramifications, and cultural context of female genital mutilation in the Sudan and other parts of Africa. The author, an educator and family counselor, researched the topic and conducted numerous interviews about it during a 6-year journey in Africa.

McCoy, K., & Wibbelsman, C. (1992). *The new teenage body book.* New York: Putnam. This book, written for teenagers, is clear and thorough in its explanations of what they can expect as their bodies mature. Its presentation of emotional and sexual issues is complete, balanced, and not preachy.

Walker, A., and Parmar, P. (1993). *Warrior marks: Female genital mutilation and the sexual blinding of women.* New York: Harcourt Brace. An account by a novelist and a filmmaker of their research for, and making of, a documentary film about female genital mutilation. The book includes transcripts of interviews with people either involved with or concerned about the practice.

CHAPTER 15
COGNITIVE DEVELOPMENT IN ADOLESCENCE

CHAPTER 15
COGNITIVE DEVELOPMENT IN ADOLESCENCE

I should place [the prime of a man's life] at between fifteen and sixteen. It is then, it always seems to me, that his vitality is at its highest; he has greatest sense of the ludicrous and least sense of dignity. After that time, decay begins to set in.

Evelyn Waugh, aged 16, in a school debate, 1920

To begin our understanding of adolescents' cognitive development, we first examine Jean Piaget's contribution—the concept of formal operations. We also explore areas of cognitive development not covered by Piaget's theory. Then we look at some characteristic aspects of adolescents' thought and at their moral development. Finally, we explore practical aspects of cognitive growth—issues of school and work. After you have studied this chapter, you will be able to answer such questions as the following:

PREVIEW QUESTIONS

- ♦ How does cognitive development in adolescence enable teenagers to consider possibilities about their values and behavior that go beyond their personal experiences?
- ♦ Is adolescents' thought egocentric?
- ♦ How is adolescents' advanced cognitive development related to moral reasoning?
- ♦ How do the three aspects of intelligence in Sternberg's triarchic theory operate in everyday life?
- ♦ How do the transition to secondary school and the high school experience affect adolescents' development?
- ♦ What factors influence high school students' thinking about a career?
- ♦ Why do students drop out of school? What can be done to encourage young people to stay in school?
- ♦ Is part-time work helpful or harmful for most high school students?

Jason, at age 14, is plagued by doubts. He used to have clear opinions about practically everything—opinions that almost always mirrored his parents' thoughts about religion, politics, moral standards, and values. These days, though, the ideas he was once so sure of are no longer compelling. His parents' beliefs do not seem as valid, nor do they answer all his questions. Much seems possible; much is unclear. Where does the truth lie?

The truths he will take for his own emerge from his own cognitive development, which occurs in an overarching social context. Jason was lucky: He was born in a nurturing family with parents who love him and can guide him—even after their divorce—on his way through life. The neighborhood he grew up in was safe, the schools he attends are satisfactory, he receives care when he gets sick, and every expectation is that he will go on for as much education as he wants and is capable of and will secure rewarding employment.

Such supportive environments are denied to many young people. In some environments, the homes, neighborhoods, schools, and other social institutions increase the dangers in their lives and diminish the opportunities. As Joel F. Handler, chair of the Panel on High-Risk Youth, writes in the preface to the report *Losing Generations*,

> High-risk settings do not just happen: they are the result of policies and choices that cumulatively determine whether families will have adequate incomes, whether neighborhoods will be safe or dangerous, whether schools will be capable of teaching, whether health care will be available—in short, whether young people will be helped or hindered while growing up.
>
> (Handler, 1993, pp. vii-viii)

We will now begin to see how the settings in which adolescents live influence how they think, how they reason and act about moral issues, how they do in school, and how they make the transition from school to work. As in other phases of life, there is a dynamic interaction between context and person. Adolescents' individual characteristics affect how they respond to their environments.

ASPECTS OF COGNITIVE DEVELOPMENT

Adolescents not only look different from schoolchildren; they think differently, too. What sets adolescents' thinking on a higher level than children's is the concept of "What if . . .?" Adolescents can think in terms of what *might* be true, rather than just in terms of what they see *is* true. Since they can imagine possibilities, they are capable of hypothetical reasoning. But they often swing between childish and adult thought because they are still limited by forms of egocentric thinking. Cognitive immaturity affects teenagers' everyday life in many ways—including how they think about moral issues.

COGNITION

Cognitive Maturity: Piaget's Stage of Formal Operations

The dominant explanation for the nature of the changes in how teenagers think has been Jean Piaget's. According to Piaget, adolescents enter the highest level of cognitive development. He called this level, which is marked by the capacity for abstract thought, *formal operations.*

formal operations *In Piaget's terminology, the final stage of cognitive development, characterized by the ability to think abstractly.*

The Nature of Formal Operations. Attaining formal operations gives adolescents a new way to manipulate—or operate on—information. In the earlier stage of concrete operations, children could think logically only about the concrete, the here and now. Adolescents are no longer so limited. They can now deal with abstractions, test hypotheses, and see infinite possibilities.

This advance opens many new doors. It enables teenagers to analyze political and philosophical doctrines, and sometimes to construct their own elaborate theories for reforming society. It even allows them to recognize that in some situations there are no definite answers. The ability to think abstractly has emotional ramifications too. Earlier, a child could love a parent or hate a classmate. Now "the adolescent can love freedom or hate exploitation. The adolescent has devel-

What determines how fast the pendulum swings—the length of the string or the weight of the object suspended from it? According to Piaget, an adolescent who has achieved the stage of formal operations can make a hypothesis and figure out a logical way to test it. Research suggests, however, that as many as half of teenagers and more than one-third of adults cannot solve this problem.

oped a new mode of life: the possible and the ideal captivate both mind and feeling" (H. Ginsburg & Opper, 1979, p. 201).

Much of childhood seems to be a struggle to come to grips with the world as it is. Adolescents become aware of the world as it could be.

Seeing New Possibilities. We can glimpse the nature of formal operations in different reactions to a story told by E. A. Peel (1967):

> Only brave pilots are allowed to fly over high mountains. A fighter pilot flying over the Alps collided with an aerial cable-way, and cut a main cable causing some cars to fall to the glacier below. Several people were killed.

A child still at the concrete operational level said, "I think that the pilot was not very good at flying. He would have been better off if he went on fighting." Only one answer came to mind—that the pilot was inept and not doing his real job, fighting.

By contrast, an adolescent who had reached the level of formal operations paid no attention to the designation "fighter pilot" and found a variety of possible explanations for what happened: "He was either not informed of the mountain railway on his route, or he was flying too low; also, his flying compass may have been affected by something before or after takeoff, thus setting him off course and causing the collision with the cable" (Peel, 1967). This response shows the adolescent's new flexibility and complexity of thinking.

The Pendulum Problem. Jason's cognitive development can also be seen through his progress in dealing with a classic Piagetian problem in formal reasoning, the *pendulum problem.* We can trace his development by comparing typical responses from children in the preoperational, the concrete operations, and the formal operations stages.*

Here is the task: Jason is shown a pendulum—an object hanging from a string. He is shown how he can change the length of the string, the weight of the object, the height from which the object is released, and the amount of force he uses to push it. Then he is asked to figure out which factors or combination of factors determines how fast the pendulum swings.

When Jason first saw the pendulum, he was not yet 7 years old and was in the preoperational stage. At this age, he was not able to formulate a plan for attacking the problem. He tried one thing after another in hit-or-miss fashion. First he put a light weight on a long pendulum and pushed it; then he tried swinging a short pendulum with a heavy weight; and then he removed the weight entirely. Not only was his method random, but also he could not understand or report what had actually happened. He thought that the force of his pushes made the pendulum go faster, and although this was not so, he reported it as fact.

The next time Jason was faced with the pendulum, he was 11 years old and in the stage of concrete operations. This time, he did look at some possible solutions, and he even hit on a partially correct answer. But he failed to try out every possible solution systematically. He varied the length of the string and the weight of the object, and he thought that both length and weight affected the speed of the swing. But because he varied both length and weight at the same time, he could not determine which factor was critical, or whether both were.

Not until Jason was confronted with the pendulum again, when he was 15, did he go at the problem systematically. He now realized that any one of the four factors, or some combination of them, might affect the speed of the swing. He designed an experiment to test all the possible hypotheses, varying only one factor at a time while holding the rest constant. In this way, he determined that one factor—the length of the string—determines how fast the pendulum swings (H. Ginsburg & Opper, 1979).

Jason's solution of the pendulum problem showed that he had arrived at the stage of *formal operations,* a cognitive level often attained in early adolescence. Jason can now think in terms of what might be true and not just in terms of what he saw in a concrete situation. Since he could imagine a variety of possible solutions, he was, for the first time, capable of *hypothetical-deductive* reasoning. Once he developed a hypothesis, he could construct a scientific experiment to test the hypothesis. He considered all the possible relationships that might exist and went through them one by one to eliminate the false and arrive at the true. We can see here (as in the story told by Peel) that adolescent thought has a *flexibility* not possible in the concrete operations stage.

This systematic process of reasoning operates for all sorts of problems. People in the formal operations stage are better equipped to integrate what they have learned in the past with their problems of the present and their planning for the future. They are able to apply these thought processes to the problems and issues of day-to-day living and also to the construction of elaborate political and philosophical theories. Of course, people who are capable of formal thought do not always use it.

*This description of age-related differences in the approach to the pendulum problem is adapted from H. Ginsburg & Opper, 1979.

What Brings about Cognitive Maturity?   According to Piaget, both inner and outer changes in the lives of adolescents combine to bring about cognitive maturity. The brain has matured and the social environment is widening, offering more opportunities for experimentation. Interaction between the two kinds of changes is essential. Even if young people's neurological development has advanced enough to allow them to reach the stage of formal reasoning, they may never attain it if they are not encouraged culturally and educationally.

Evidence that peer interaction can help advance cognitive maturity comes from a study in which college students (average age 18.5 years) were faced with a chemistry problem, asked a series of questions, and told to set up their own experiments (Dimant & Bearison, 1991). Students were randomly assigned to work alone or with a partner. Those working in a twosome were told to discuss their answers with each other. Their responses (after being videotaped) were categorized as (1) disagreement, (2) explanation, (3) question, (4) agreement, or (5) extraneous. One dialogue was coded as follows:

Subject A: "What you said can't be. It's no sense." *(disagreement)*

Subject B: "I'm right. I know it." *(disagreement)*

Subject A: "Look here, see *B* [a container in the experiment] didn't work with *D* and *E*, so it can't be *B*." *(explanation)*

Subject B: "Oh, you're right." *(agreement)*

(Dimant & Bearison, 1991, p. 280)

The students who worked in pairs solved more problems than did those who worked alone. However, the nature of the interaction within a pair was important. The more answers a student received from the first three response categories, all of which disturbed that student's reasoning, the greater were the advances in his or her reasoning. The quality and frequency of the interactions brought about cognitive gains.

A 4-year longitudinal study of 165 undergraduates in three disciplines demonstrated that students majoring in the natural sciences, humanities, or social sciences showed improvements in reasoning from their first year of college to their fourth (Lehman & Nisbett, 1990). Although the different courses of study were related to different kinds of reasoning abilities, students in all three fields improved their everyday reasoning. This shows that reasoning skills can be taught and suggests that such teaching can help people change the way they think about uncertainty in everyday life.

Assessing Cognitive Development: Limitations of Piaget's Theory.   What do knowing and thinking mean? How do we define the highest reaches of cognitive development? Using measures like the pendulum problem and conservation of volume implies that cognition can be defined in terms of mathematical and scientific thinking. This narrow view "conveys a view of the individual as living in a timeless world of abstract rules" (Gilligan, 1987, p. 67).

Furthermore, perhaps one-third to one-half of American adults seem never to reach the Piagetian stage of formal operations as measured by the pendulum problem and volume conservation (Papalia, 1972; Kohlberg & Gilligan, 1971). Even by late adolescence or adulthood not everyone seems to be capable of abstract thought.

The Piagetian view does not consider other aspects of intelligence. It does not allow for practical intelligence—the ability to handle "real-world" problems, or the wisdom that helps people cope with an often chaotic world. Nor would it tend to cover such nonscientific subjects as history, languages, writing, and the arts. In fact, as more psychologists have defined cognition in Piaget's terms, more educators have emphasized scientific subjects and taken less interest in the humanities. Piaget's definition of cognitive maturity is significant; but formal reasoning is not the only—and perhaps not even the most important—aspect of mature thinking.

What do you think?   *Would you define the highest level of cognition as (1) formal operational abilities, (2) the ability to solve practical problems, (3) attainment of wisdom, or (4) something else?*

Typical Characteristics of Adolescents' Thought

Jason has trouble these days making up his mind about the simplest things. Vicky makes hers up too quickly—and her impulsiveness sometimes gets her into trouble. Both think that their parents can't do anything right. If adults can look at adolescents' often puzzling, sometimes maddening behavior in the framework described by the psychologist David Elkind (1984), they may be better able to understand the behavior itself and the thought processes underlying it. Based on his clinical work with adolescents and their families, Elkind delineated some typical behaviors and attitudes that stem from their inexperienced ventures into abstract thought.

Finding Fault with Authority Figures.   With their new ability to imagine an ideal world, adolescents realize that the people they once worshiped fall far short of their ideal, and they feel compelled to say so—loudly and often. Parents who do not take this criticism personally, but rather look at it as a growth stage in cognitive and social development, will be able to answer such comments matter-of-factly (and even humorously), acknowledging that nothing—and nobody (not even a teenager!)—is perfect.

Argumentativeness.   Adolescents often use arguing as a way to practice their new abilities to explore the nuances in an issue and to build a case for their viewpoint. If Jason's father encourages and takes part in debates about principles, while carefully avoiding discussing personality, he can help Jason stretch his reasoning ability without getting embroiled in family feuding.

Indecisiveness.   Teenagers have trouble making up their minds even about simple things because they are more aware of how many choices life offers. Should Vicky go to the mall with her girlfriend on a Saturday, or to a movie with her mother, or to the library to look up something for the paper due next week? She may ponder the consequences of each choice for hours, even though her decision will not change her life substantially.

The telephone is often a battleground for parents and teenagers. Even when a parent's point of view is valid, an adolescent's egocentrism often leads to argumentativeness and criticism.

Apparent Hypocrisy. Young adolescents often do not recognize the difference between expressing an ideal and working toward it. Vicky marches against pollution while littering along the way, and Jason aggressively protests for peace. Part of growing up involves realizing that "thinking does not make it so," that values have to be acted upon to bring about change.

Self-Consciousness. Jason, hearing Julia whispering on the phone, "knows" that she is talking about him. Vicky, passing a couple of boys laughing, "knows" that they are ridiculing her. The extreme self-consciousness of young adolescents has a great deal to do with the *imaginary audience,* a conceptualized observer who is as concerned with their thoughts and behavior as they are themselves. Adolescents can put themselves into the mind of someone else—can think about someone else's thinking. But since they have trouble distinguishing what is interesting to them from what is interesting to someone else, they assume that everyone else is thinking about the same thing they are thinking about—themselves.

imaginary audience
Observer who exists only in the mind of an adolescent and is as concerned with the adolescent's thoughts and behaviors as the adolescent is.

The imaginary audience is not restricted to adolescents. As adults, who among us has not agonized over what to wear to an event, thinking that others will actually care what clothes we have on—and then realized that most people were so busy thinking about the impression *they* were making that they hardly noticed our carefully chosen outfit! But because this kind of self-consciousness is especially agonizing in adolescence, it is important to avoid public criticism or ridicule of young teenagers.

personal fable *Conviction that one is special, unique, and not subject to the rules that govern the rest of the world.*

Self-Centeredness. Elkind uses the term *personal fable* for adolescents' belief that they are special, that their experience is unique, and that they are not subject to the rules that govern the rest of the world. According to Elkind, this aspect of teenage egocentrism shows up strongly in early adolescence and underlies much self-destructive behavior by teenagers who think that they are magically protected from harm. A girl thinks that *she* cannot become pregnant; a boy thinks that *he* cannot get killed on the highway; teenagers think that *they* cannot get hooked on drugs. Elkind cites this unconscious assumption of invulnerability ("These things happen only to other people, not to me") to explain much adolescent risk taking.

Although this concept has been widely accepted, recent studies cast doubt on it. Research has found that most people of *any* age are unrealistically optimistic in assessing potential dangers (Taylor, 1989). To find out whether adolescents are more so, researchers compared three groups: 86 mostly white, middle-class teenagers considered at low risk for bad outcomes; the parents of these teenagers; and 95 mostly male, nonwhite teenagers living in homes for adolescents with legal and substance abuse problems. They asked all the subjects to estimate their risks of such events as being in a car accident, having an unwanted pregnancy, becoming alcoholic, being mugged, or becoming sick from air pollution. The subjects were also asked to compare their risks with others' risks. All three groups saw themselves as facing less risk than other people they knew, but these findings were no more pronounced for teenagers than for adults. In fact, for some risks adolescents saw themselves as more vulnerable than their parents saw themselves (Quadrel, Fischoff, & Davis, 1993).

The significance of this research goes beyond its questioning of the "personal fable." If this widely accepted concept is invalid, perhaps other beliefs about adolescent thinking patterns are equally so. This is a ripe area for research to test hypotheses about the characteristics of adolescent thought.

The more adolescents talk about their personal theories and listen to those of other people, the sooner they arrive at a mature level of thinking (Looft, 1971). As adolescents mature in their thought processes, they are better able to think about their own identities, to form adult relationships, and to determine how and where they fit into society. They are also better able to consider moral questions.

MORAL DEVELOPMENT

Neither Vicky nor Jason can have a moral code based on ideals before developing a mind that is capable of imagining ideals. We saw earlier how children's cognitive development enabled them to think through moral issues. Moral reasoning continues to develop as adolescents acquire the capacity to think abstractly and to understand universal moral principles.

Kohlberg's Theory: Levels of Moral Reasoning

According to Lawrence Kohlberg, advanced cognitive development does not *guarantee* advanced moral development, but it must *exist* for moral development to take place.

Kohlberg's Moral Dilemmas. Kohlberg devised a series of moral dilemmas to assess a person's level of moral reasoning. The most famous of these is the following story:

> A woman was near death from cancer. A druggist had discovered a drug that could save her. The druggist was charging $2000 for a small dose of the drug—10 times what it cost him to make. The sick woman's husband, Heinz, borrowed as much as he could, but he could get together only about $1000. He told the druggist that his wife was dy-

ing, and asked him to sell it cheaper or let him pay later. But the druggist said, "No. I discovered the drug and I'm going to make money from it." Heinz, desperate, broke into the man's store to steal the drug for his wife. Should Heinz have done that? Why or why not? (Kohlberg, 1969)

For over 20 years, Kohlberg periodically queried 75 boys who had ranged in age from 10 to 16 years at the start of the study. Kohlberg told them hypothetical stories that posed moral dilemmas of the kind Heinz faced and asked the boys how they would solve them. At the center of each dilemma was a concept of justice.

After telling the stories, Kohlberg and his colleagues asked the boys questions designed to show how they had arrived at their decisions. He was less interested in the answers themselves than in the reasoning that led to them. Two boys who gave opposite answers to a dilemma could both be at the same moral level if their reasoning was based on similar factors.

Kohlberg's Levels and Stages.   From the boys' responses, Kohlberg concluded that the level of moral reasoning is related to a person's cognitive level. The boys' reasoning convinced Kohlberg that people work out moral judgments on their own, rather than merely internalizing the standards of parents, teachers, or peers. Kohlberg identified three levels of moral reasoning, each of which is divided into two stages, as shown in Table 15-1.

preconventional morality *Kohlberg's first level of moral reasoning, in which the emphasis is on external control, obedience to the rules and standards of others, and the desire to avoid punishment.*

morality of conventional role conformity *Second level in Kohlberg's theory of moral reasoning, in which children want to please other people and in which they have internalized the standards of authority figures.*

morality of autonomous moral principles *Third level of Kohlberg's theory of moral reasoning, in which people follow internally held moral principles and decide between conflicting moral standards.*

■ *Level I: **Preconventional morality** (ages 4 to 10 years).* The emphasis in this level is on external control. Children observe the standards of others either to avoid punishment or to obtain rewards.

■ *Level II: **Morality of conventional role conformity** (ages 10 to 13).* Children now want to please other people. They still observe the standards of others, but they have internalized these standards to some extent. Now they want to be considered "good" by people whose opinions are important to them. They are now able to take the roles of authority figures well enough to decide whether an action is good by their standards.

■ *Level III: **Morality of autonomous moral principles** (age 13 or later, if ever).* This is Kohlberg's highest level. For the first time, the person acknowledges the possibility of conflict between two socially accepted standards and tries to decide between them. The control of conduct is now internal, both in standards observed and in reasoning about right and wrong.

At one point, Kohlberg himself questioned his sixth and highest stage (in level III), citing a difficulty in finding people at such a high level of moral development (Muuss, 1988). Still later, however, he proposed a seventh stage that was more religious in orientation (Kohlberg, 1981). Kohlberg's rethinking of his concepts illustrates the dynamic nature of theories, the way they can respond to new research findings or new insights.

Kohlberg's early stages correspond to Piaget's stages of moral development in childhood (described in Chapter 12), but his advanced stages go into adulthood. Kohlberg's stages are also related to Selman's stages (also in Chapter 12): The better a person is at role-taking, the more complicated Heinz's dilemma becomes. When Vicky is at Selman's stage 3 of role-taking development, she says simply that if Heinz were caught, a judge would listen to his explanation, see that

TABLE 15-1

LEVELS	STAGES OF REASONING	TYPICAL ANSWERS TO HEINZ'S DILEMMA
Level 1: Preconventional (ages 4 to 10) Emphasis in this level is on external control. The standards are those of others, and they are observed either to avoid punishment or to reap rewards.	**Stage 1:** *Orientation toward punishment and obedience.* "What will happen to me?" Children obey the rules of others to avoid punishment. They ignore the motives of an act and focus on its physical form (such as the size of a lie) or its consequences (for example, the amount of physical damage).	*Pro:* "He should steal the drug. It isn't really bad to take it. It isn't as if he hadn't asked to pay for it first. The drug he'd take is worth only $200: he's not really taking a $2000 drug." *Con:* "He shouldn't steal the drug. It's a big crime. He didn't get permission; he used force and broke and entered. He did a lot of damage, stealing a very expensive drug and breaking up the store, too."
	Stage 2: *Instrumental purpose and exchange.* "You scratch my back, I'll scratch yours." Children conform to rules out of self-interest and consideration for what others can do for them in return. They look at an act in terms of the human needs it meets and differentiate this value from the act's physical form and consequences.	*Pro:* "It's all right to steal the drug, because his wife needs it and he wants her to live. It isn't that we want to steal, but that's what he has to do to get the drug to save her." *Con:* "He shouldn't steal it. The druggist isn't wrong or bad; he just wants to make a profit. That's what you're in business for—to make money."
Level II: Morality of conventional role conformity (ages 10 to 13) Children now want to please other people. They still observe the standards of others, but they have internalized these standards to some extent. Now they want to be considered "good" by those persons whose opinions are important to them. They are now able to take the roles of authority figures well enough to decide whether an action is good by their standards.	**Stage 3:** *Maintaining mutual relations, approval of others, the golden rule.* "Am I a good boy or girl?" Children want to please and help others, can judge the intentions of others, and develop their own ideas of what a good person is. They evaluate an act according to the motive behind it or the person performing it, and they take circumstances into account.	*Pro:* "He should steal the drug. He is only doing something that is natural for a good husband to do. You can't blame him for doing something out of love for his wife. You'd blame him if he didn't love his wife enough to save her." *Con:* "He shouldn't steal. If his wife dies, he can't be blamed. It isn't because he's heartless or that he doesn't love her enough to do everything that he legally can. The druggist is the selfish or heartless one."
	Stage 4: *Social concern and conscience.* "What if everybody did it?" People are concerned with doing their duty, showing respect for higher authority, and maintaining the social order. They consider an act always wrong, regardless of motive or circumstances, if it violates a rule and harms others.	*Pro:* "You should steal it. If you did nothing, you'd be letting your wife die. It's your responsibility if she dies. You have to take it with the idea of paying the druggist." *Con:* "It is a natural thing for Heinz to want to save his wife, but it's still always wrong to steal. He still knows that he's stealing and taking a valuable drug from the man who made it."
Level III: Morality of autonomous moral principles (age 13, or not until young adulthood, or never) This level marks the attainment of true morality. For the first time, the person acknowledges the possibility of conflict between two socially accepted standards and tries to decide between them. The control of conduct is now internal, both in the standards observed and in the reasoning about right and wrong. Stages 5 and 6 may be alternative methods of the highest level of moral reasoning.	**Stage 5:** *Morality of contract, of individual rights, and of democratically accepted law.* People think in rational terms, valuing the will of the majority and the welfare of society. They generally see these values best supported by adherence to the law. While they recognize that there are times when human need and the law conflict, they believe that it is better for society in the long run if they obey the law.	*Pro:* "This is a situation that forces him to choose between stealing and letting his wife die. In a situation where the choice must be made, it is morally right to steal. He has to act in terms of the principle of preserving and respecting life." *Con:* "Heinz is faced with the decision of whether to consider the other people who need the drug just as badly as his wife. Heinz ought to act not according to his particular feelings toward his wife, but considering the value of all the lives involved."

TABLE 15-1 *(CONTINUED)*

KOHLBERG'S SIX STAGES OF MORAL REASONING

LEVELS	STAGES OF REASONING	TYPICAL ANSWERS TO HEINZ'S DILEMMA
	Stage 6: Morality of universal ethical principles. People do what they as individuals think right, regardless of legal restrictions or the opinions of others. They act in accordance with internalized standards, knowing that they would condemn themselves if they did not.	*Pro:* "The law wasn't set up for these circumstances. Taking the drug in this situation isn't really right, but it's justified." *Con:* "You can't completely blame someone for stealing, but extreme circumstances don't really justify taking the law into your own hands. You can't have people stealing whenever they are desperate. The end may be good, but the ends don't justify the means."

SOURCE: Adapted from Kohlberg, 1969, 1976.

he was right, and let him go. But in Selman's stage 4, Vicky realizes that no matter how good the explanation seems to Heinz, the judge cannot excuse the theft because he must uphold the law.

Adolescent Moral Thinking.   Younger children's thinking about morality generally fits into Kohlberg's first two stages, both at level I, in which they consider morality in terms of obedience to avoid punishment or acting out of self-interest. Some adolescents and adults are also at level I. They think in terms of satisfying their own needs.

Most adolescents, however—like most adults—seem to be at Kohlberg's level II, which contains stages 3 and 4. They have internalized the standards of others, and they conform to social conventions, support the status quo, and think in terms of doing the right thing to please others or to obey the law. As we listen to "law and order" political speeches, we realize how many adults function at stage 4.

Only a small number of people seem to attain level III. At this level, which may be attained in adolescence or adulthood, people can look at two socially accepted standards and choose the one that seems right to them. But even people who have achieved a high level of cognitive development do not always reach a comparably high level of moral development. This is because other factors besides cognition affect moral reasoning. Thus a certain level of cognitive development is *necessary* but not *sufficient* for a comparable level of moral development.

How Do Adolescents at Different Levels React to Kohlberg's Dilemmas?   The different reactions of adolescents to Kohlberg's moral dilemmas illustrate differences in how they think. In Kohlberg's theory, it is the reasoning underlying a person's response to a moral dilemma, not the answer itself, which indicates a person's stage of development. Let us see how young people at all three levels respond to questions about the value of human life (Kohlberg, 1968).

Level I: Preconventional Morality. *Stage 1:* When Tommy,* aged 10, is asked, "Is it better to save the life of one important person or a lot of unimportant people?" he says, "All the people that aren't important because one man just has one house, maybe a lot of furniture, but a whole bunch of people have an awful lot of furniture. . . ."

Tommy seems to be confusing the value of people with the value of their property, and since *many* people have more property than just *one* person, he believes it is better to save their lives.

Stage 2: At age 13, Tommy is asked about "mercy killing": Should a doctor kill a fatally ill woman who requests death because of pain? He answers, "Maybe it would be good to put her out of her pain; she'd be better off that way. But the husband wouldn't want it; it's not like an animal. If a pet dies, you can get along without it—it isn't something you really need. Well, you can get a new wife, but it's not really the same."

Tommy thinks of the woman's value in terms of what she can do for her husband.

Level II: Morality of Conventional Role Conformity. *Stage 3:* At 16, Tommy answers the question about mercy killing by saying, "It might be best for her, but her husband—it's a human life—not like an animal; it just doesn't have the same relationship that a human being does to a family. . . ."

Tommy identifies with the husband's distinctively human empathy and love, but he still does not seem to realize that the woman's life would have value even if her husband did not love her or even if she had no husband.

Stage 4: Richard, aged 16, answers by saying, "I don't know. In one way, it's murder; it's not a right or privilege of man to decide who shall live and who should die. God put life into everybody on earth, and you're taking away something from that person that came directly from God, and you're destroying something that is very sacred; it's in a way part of God, and it's almost destroying a part of God when you kill a person."

Richard sees life as sacred because it was created by God, an authority.

Level III: Morality of Autonomous Moral Principles. *Stage 5:* At 20, Richard says: "There are more and more people in the medical profession who think it is a hardship on everyone, the person, the family, when you know they are going to die. When a person is kept alive by an artificial lung or kidney, it's more like being a vegetable than being a human. If it's her own choice, I think there are certain rights and privileges that go along with being a human being."

Richard now defines the value of life relative to other values: equal and universal human rights, concern for the quality of life, and concern for practical consequences.

Stage 6: At age 24, Richard answers, "A human life takes precedence over any other moral or legal value, whoever it is. A human life has inherent value whether or not it is valued by a particular individual."

Richard now sees the value of human life as absolute, not as derived from or dependent on social or divine authority.

Evaluating Kohlberg's Theory. Subsequent research has confirmed some aspects of Kohlberg's theory but left others in question. In Kohlberg's 20-year-long study

---

*"Tommy" and "Richard" were named in Kohlberg's report.

of American boys (aged 10, 13, and 16 at the first testing), the boys progressed through the stages in sequence and none skipped a stage. Moral judgments correlated positively with the boys' age, education, IQ, and socioeconomic status (Colby, Kohlberg, Gibbs, & Lieberman, 1983).

Cross-Cultural Validity. Cross-cultural studies support this sequence—up to a point. Older subjects from countries other than the United States do tend to score at higher stages than younger subjects, but people from nonwestern cultures rarely score above stage 4 (Edwards, 1977; Nisan & Kohlberg, 1982; Snarey, 1985). It is possible that these cultures do not foster higher development—but it is also likely that Kohlberg's definition of morality as a system of justice is not appropriate for nonwestern societies and that his procedures may not identify higher levels of reasoning in some cultures (Snarey, 1985). Just as culture helps people define intelligent behavior, it also defines moral behavior.

Validity for Females. Critics have also questioned the appropriateness of Kohlberg's definition of morality for American girls and women. Some studies of moral reasoning in adulthood have shown that men tend to score higher than women on Kohlberg's tasks, but other researchers have claimed that this apparent difference is due to the men's higher educational and occupational status rather than gender (Walker, 1984, 1987).

In addition, critics like Carol Gilligan (1982) maintain that women tend to define morality differently from the way men do and base their moral decisions on different factors. Gilligan has conducted her own research on female responses to moral issues. Many women, she says, see morality not in abstract terms of justice and fairness, but in specific terms of selfishness versus responsibility, as an obligation to exercise care and to avoid hurting other people. As we shall see, other researchers too have examined gender differences in moral development.

What do you think? *Which principle seems to be a more basic tenet of moral reasoning: justice or responsibility to other people? Why?*

The Role of Experience. Moral judgments are strongly influenced by education and even by simply telling children the "right" answers to questions involving moral reasoning (Carroll & Rest, 1982; Lickona, 1973). Such findings call into question Kohlberg's belief that children actively work out their moral systems through self-discovery.

Furthermore, the link between a hypothetical answer and actual behavior is not established. Knowing a person's performance on a task of moral judgment does not predict what that person would actually do (Colby & Damon, 1992; Kupfersmid & Wonderly, 1980). This finding is not new: More than 60 years ago, researchers found that children who cheated were just as likely to *say* cheating was wrong as were noncheaters (Hartshorne & May, 1928–1930).

While Kohlberg's stages seem to apply to American males, they are limited in their applicability to women and to people in nonwestern cultures. Questions about assessment methods and about the connection between moral judgments and moral behavior raise serious doubts about some aspects of the theory. Still, Kohlberg has had a major impact. His theory enriched our thinking about how morality develops, emphasizes the association between cognitive maturity and moral maturity, and has stimulated both research and the elaboration of theories about moral development.

What do you think? *Kohlberg's method of assessing moral development by evaluating subjects' reactions to moral dilemmas is widely used. Does this seem like the most appropriate method? Can you suggest an alternative measure?*

The Influence of Social Context on Moral Development

Kohlberg maintains that moral thinking is universal, transcending cultural boundaries. Other research, however, suggests that ecological context exerts a major influence on moral reasoning. (See Box 15-1.) And although both Piaget and Kohlberg considered parents minimally important in helping their children's moral development, recent research has found that, on the contrary, parents can make a major contribution in this area.

Gender Differences in Moral Development. Morality has at least two dimensions: justice with regard to individual rights and care elicited by a sense of responsibility to oneself and others. Kohlberg's theory of moral reasoning focuses on the first dimension, justice, which seems to be a more male-oriented point of view, whereas Carol Gilligan has developed a different way of looking at morality, one that seems to fit in more with the female orientation toward an emphasis on responsibility in relationships.

Some research seems to bear out this dichotomy and to suggest that it shows up in early adolescence (Skoe & Gooden, 1993). Forty-six 11- and 12-year-old girls and boys were interviewed using a new technique, the "Ethic of Care Interview." These interviews incorporate one real-life conflict introduced by the adolescent, along with three hypothetical dilemmas involving family and friends. One, for example, asked what a hypothetical young person should do if "Nicole" or "Jason" accepted a friend's dinner invitation—and then receives an invitation from another friend to see a favorite rock band (from good seats!) on the same evening.

When the students' responses were scored according to five Ethic of Care levels (see Table 15-2), girls scored higher than boys. The girls generated more personal real-life dilemmas (those involving a specific person or group of people whom the subject knew well), whereas boys were more likely to talk about moral conflicts involving people they did not know well, institutions, or issues intrinsic to the self. Girls also tended to be more concerned than boys about maintaining friendships and not hurting other people. The boys were more likely to be concerned about themselves, emphasizing, for example, staying out of trouble.

There seems to be a developmental progression in the ethic of care, with older subjects scoring higher than younger ones (Skoe & Diessner, in press). This may help to explain girls' higher scoring, since girls generally mature earlier than boys. Since research on the ethic-of-care dimension is fairly new, further study is needed to determine whether people do become more responsible as they mature and whether their statements about care are reflected in their actions.

Family Influences on Moral Development. The most effective way to help adolescents move to higher levels of moral reasoning seems to be to give them am-

TABLE 15-2

LEVEL	DESCRIPTION	EXAMPLE
ETHICS OF CARE LEVELS		
1: Survival	Caring for self, with the aim of ensuring one's happiness and avoiding suffering or being hurt.	"Maybe Nicole should tell Janice that she wants to go hear a rock band and maybe she could go to Janice's place some other time."
1.5: Transition from survival to responsibility	A new understanding of the connection between self and others, along with concept of selfishness; although aware of needs of others, care of self is still uppermost.	"Jason should go with his friend who asked him first, because they might not want to ask you ever again if you go with your other friend."
2: Goodness	Caring for others, elaborating the concept of responsibility; "right" is defined by church, parents, society, etc.; conflict arises over issue of hurting.	"Nicole might be able to go to Janice's house for dinner and to the concert with Pam, or she should invite Janice over for the next night. She wouldn't want to hurt either one's feelings."
2.5: Transition from goodness to truth in relationships	Reconsideration of relationship between self and other: Is it "good" to protect others at one's own expense? More flexibility, thoughtfulness, and struggle with dilemmas.	No children scored at this level.
3: Caring for both self and others	Focus on dynamics of relationships through a new understanding of the interconnection between others and self; condemns hurt and exploitation; takes responsibility for choices.	No children scored at this level.

SOURCE: Adapted from Skoe & Gooden, 1993.

ple opportunities to talk about, interpret, and enact moral dilemmas and to expose them to people at a level of moral thinking slightly higher than their own present level. In a study of 63 family triads (mother, father, and child from grades 1, 4, 7, and 10), Walker and Taylor (1991) found that parents could help their children reason at higher levels. These parents were asked to talk with their children about two dilemmas, a hypothetical one and an actual one from the child's own life, which the child described—most commonly, one about friendships, fighting, or honesty.

The children and adolescents who developed the most over a 2-year period had parents who used humor and praise in their discussions, listened to their children, asked for their opinions, and in other ways encouraged them to participate. These parents asked clarifying questions, reworded answers, and checked to be sure the children understood the issues (as in the Socratic style of questioning). They tended to reason with their children at a slightly higher level than the children were currently at, in a style reminiscent of scaffolding, or of Vygotsky's notion of "zone of proximal development."

On the other hand, the children who progressed the least had parents who either lectured about their own opinions or challenged their children's opinions by

BOX 15-1 ■ AROUND THE WORLD

A CHINESE PERSPECTIVE ON MORAL DEVELOPMENT

Kohlberg's story—the dilemma of Heinz, who could not afford a drug for his sick wife—was revised for use in Taiwan so that it described a shopkeeper who would not give a man food for his sick wife. This story would seem unbelievable to Chinese villagers—who in real life would be more likely to hear a shopkeeper say, "You have to let people have things whether they have money or not" (Wolf, 1968, p. 21). In Kohlberg's research, his subjects had to make either-or decisions, based on their individual value systems. But in the Chinese system of morality, people faced with such dilemmas would discuss them openly, would be guided by community standards, and would try to find a solution that pleased as many parties as possible (Dien, 1982).

From the Chinese perspective, human beings are seen as being born with normal tendencies. Their moral development rests on intuitive and spontaneous feelings supported by society, rather than on the kind of analytical thinking, individual choice, and personal responsibility inherent in Kohlberg's theory. Kohlberg's philosophy is oriented toward abstract principles of justice; the Chinese ethos leans toward conciliation and harmony.

The Chinese system also differs from real-life morality in western cultures. In the west, good people may expect to be harshly punished if they are driven by circumstances to break a law. The Chinese are unaccustomed to universally applied laws; they prefer to abide by the decisions of a wise judge.

How, then, can Kohlberg's theory, which is rooted in western values and reflects western ideals, measure moral development in an eastern society that has developed along very different lines? Some critics say that it cannot, and that an alternative view of moral development is required. Such a view would measure morality by the ability to make a judgment based on norms of reciprocity, rules of exchange, available resources, and complex relationships (Dien, 1982).

This viewpoint echoes the forceful protests made by Carol Gilligan (1982, 1987)—who has studied moral development in American women—that Kohlberg's stages esteem male-oriented values of justice and fairness rather than female-oriented moral imperatives of compassion and responsibility for the welfare of others.

These issues are important because of their implications for the education of our high school students. Adolescence is a time of great idealism, a time of searching for answers to important questions, a time when people are receptive to moral education. If our schools and our leaders stress the value of justice and rights, as stressed by Kohlberg, rather than an alternative value of care and responsibility, we may be raising a new generation of citizens who see morality as a black-and-white issue and who see attempts to resolve conflicts in a caring way as "utopian, outdated, impractical," or even as part of "the outworn philosophy of hippies" (Gilligan, 1987, p. 75).

In the interest of national and global harmony, perhaps we need to rethink our concept of morality.

---

questioning and contradicting them, making the children feel defensive. Moral development arises from both cognitive and emotional bases, and parents can help their children in both domains.

Progress to postconventional moral thinking seems to depend on appreciating the relative nature of moral standards. Adolescents begin to understand that every society evolves its own definition of right and wrong and that the values of one culture may seem shocking to another. (Refer to Box 2-1 about selective abortion of female fetuses and to Box 14-1 about female genital mutilation.) Many young people question their views about morality when they enter the wider world of high school or college and encounter people whose values, culture, and ethnic background are different from their own. Some are inspired by the examples of others. (See Box 15-2.)

STERNBERG'S TRIARCHIC THEORY OF INTELLIGENCE

As adolescents' thinking matures, it is useful to look at it in terms of the kinds of thought that become more important and more sophisticated in adult life. Let's look at an example involving three college students.

BOX 15-2 ▪ FOOD FOR THOUGHT

THE ANTECEDENTS OF MORAL LEADERSHIP

What makes a single mother of four young children with no money and only a tenth-grade education dedicate her life to religious missionary work on behalf of her equally poor neighbors? What leads a pediatrician to devote much of his practice to the care of poor children instead of to patients whose parents could provide him with a lucrative income?

In the mid-1980s, two psychologists, Anne Colby and William Damon, sought answers to questions like these. They identified 23 "moral exemplars," people who showed unusual moral excellence in their day-to-day lives, interviewed them in depth, and studied the routes by which they had become the people they were (Colby & Damon, 1992). In this text we emphasize the interaction of cognitive and emotional factors in contributing to the way people think about morality and to how they act about it. In the report of Colby and Damon's research, these aspect of development are closely intertwined.

MORAL EXEMPLARS: WHO THEY ARE

To find their subjects, Colby and Damon worked with a panel of 22 "expert nominators," people who in their professional lives regularly think about moral ideas, such as philosophers, historians, and religious thinkers. Then the researchers drew up a final set of five criteria: a sustained commitment to principles that show respect for humanity; acting consistently with one's ideals; willingness to risk self-interest; inspiring others to moral action; and a sense of humility and lack of concern for one's own ego.

The 23 people chosen as moral exemplars ranged widely in age, education, occupation, and ethnicity. There were 10 men and 13 women, aged 35 to 86, of white, African American, and Latino backgrounds. Education levels varied from eighth grade up through M.D.s, Ph.D.s, and law degrees; occupations included religious callings, business, teaching, and social leadership. Areas of concern involved poverty, civil rights, education, ethics, the environment, peace, and religious freedom.

The research yielded a number of surprises, not least of which was this group's showing on Kohlberg's measure of moral judgment. Each exemplar was posed the Heinz dilemma and a follow-up dilemma asking how the man should be punished if he does steal the drug. Only half scored at the highest level, morality of autonomous moral principles; the others scored at level II, of conventional role conformity. The major difference between the two groups was education: Those with college and advanced degrees were much more likely to score at the higher level, and no one who had not gone to college scored above level II.

Clearly, it is not necessary to score at Kohlberg's highest stages to live an exemplary moral life.

LIFE INFLUENCES AND PERSONAL CHARACTERISTICS

These moral exemplars did not develop in isolation, but responded to social influences. Some influences, like those from parents and other inspiring models, were important from childhood on. Other influences, significant in later years, helped people evaluate their own capacities, form moral goals, and develop strategies to achieve their goals.

Overall, the processes responsible for reliability and stability in moral commitments were *gradual,* taking many years to build up. They were also *collaborative:* Leaders took advice from their supporters and people noted for independent judgment drew heavily on feedback from those close to them. They thrived and grew in close action and communication both with people who shared their goals and with those who had different perspectives.

Along with their enduring moral commitments, certain personality characteristics also seemed to remain with them throughout adulthood: an enjoyment of life, the ability to make the best of a bad situation, solidarity with others, a sense of absorption in work, a sense of humor, not taking themselves too seriously, and humility. They also tended to be optimistic in their belief that change was indeed possible, a trait that helped them battle what often seemed like overwhelming odds and to persist in the face of defeat.

While their decisions in the service of moral action often meant risk and hardship, these people did not see themselves as courageous. Nor did they agonize over their decisions. They saw what had to be done, and since their personal and moral goals coincided, they went ahead and did it. Colby and Damon liken this attitude to the one felt by most people who see nothing extraordinary about a simple moral action like not stealing when you have an opportunity to do so—as, say, from a blind newsdealer. These moral exemplars took the same basic attitude toward moral actions that would be daunting for most people, not calculating personal consequences to themselves or their families, not feeling they were sacrificing themselves—just going ahead and doing what they believed needed to be done.

In the end, of course, there is no clear blueprint for creating a "moral exemplar." Just as it is not possible to write directions to produce a genius in any other field, there is no well-marked route for producing a moral giant. What studying the lives of such people can bring to our lives, however, is the awareness that the seeds of greatness are within us from an early age and can flower within seemingly ordinary people, given the right circumstances.

Three Students

Alix, Barbara, and Courtney applied to graduate programs at Yale University. Alix had earned almost straight A's in college, scored high on the Graduate Record Examination (GRE), and had excellent recommendations. Barbara's grades were only fair, and her GRE scores were low by Yale's high standards, but her letters of recommendation enthusiastically praised her exceptional research and creative ideas. Courtney's grades, GRE scores, and recommendations were good but not among the best.

Alix and Courtney were admitted to the graduate program. Barbara was not admitted to the program, but psychology professor Robert Sternberg hired her as a research associate, and she took graduate classes on the side. Alix did very well for the first year or so, but less well after that. Barbara confounded the admissions committee by doing work as outstanding as her letters of recommendation had predicted. Courtney's performance in graduate school was only fair, but she had the easiest time getting a good job afterward (Trotter, 1986).

Three Aspects of Intelligence

According to Sternberg's *triarchic theory of intelligence* (1985b, 1987), these women represent three different aspects of intelligence. Everyone has each element to a greater or lesser extent, and each is particularly useful in specific kinds of situations:

1. *Componential element—how efficiently people process and analyze information.* The *componential element* is the *critical* aspect of intelligence. It tells people how to approach problems, how to go about solving them, and how to monitor and evaluate the results. Alix was strong in this area; she was good at taking intelligence tests and finding holes in arguments.
2. *Experimental element—how people approach novel and familiar tasks.* The *experimental element* is the *insightful* aspect of intelligence. It allows people to compare new information with what they already know and to come up with new ways of putting facts together—in other words, to think in original ways (as Einstein did when he developed his theory of relativity). Automatic performance of familiar operations (like recognizing words) facilitates insight, because it leaves the mind free to tackle unfamiliar tasks (like decoding new words). Barbara was strong in this area.
3. *Contextual element—how people deal with their environment.* The *contextual element* is the *practical* "real-world" aspect of intelligence. It becomes increasingly valuable in adult life—as in selecting a place to live or a field of work. It involves the ability to size up a situation and decide what to do: adapt to it, change it, or find a new, more comfortable setting. Courtney was strong in this area.

triarchic theory of intelligence *Sternberg's theory describing three types of intelligence: componential (analytic ability), experiential (insight and creativity), and contextual (practical knowledge).*

How These Three Aspects of Intelligence Operate in Everyday Life

Alix's componential ability helped her to sail through tests in undergraduate school. But in graduate school, where more original thinking is expected, it was Barbara's superior experiential intelligence—her fresh insights and innovative ideas—that shone. Courtney was strongest in practical, contextual intelligence—

"street smarts." She knew her way around. She chose "hot" research topics, submitted papers to the "right" journals, and knew where and how to apply for jobs.

Psychometric tests measure componential (critical) intelligence rather than experiential (insightful) or contextual (practical) intelligence. Since experiential and contextual intelligence are very important in adult life, psychometric tests are less appropriate and useful in gauging adults' intelligence than in measuring children's.

An important component of contextual, or practical, intelligence is *tacit knowledge*—"inside information" or "savvy," which is not formally taught or openly expressed, like knowing how to win a promotion or cut through red tape. (In our example, Courtney was strong in tacit knowledge.) Getting ahead in a career, for instance, often depends on tacit knowledge. This includes *self-management* (understanding motivation and knowing how to organize time and energy), *management of tasks* (knowing how to write a grant proposal), and *management of others* (knowing when to reward subordinates). Job performance typically shows only a weak correlation with IQ and employment tests; but one study in which hypothetical work-related scenarios were presented to experts and novices in psychology and business management found a significant relationship between job performance and these three kinds of tacit knowledge (Wagner & Sternberg, 1986).

The Triarchic Abilities Test

Problem 1

John's family moved to Iowa from Arizona during his junior year in high school. He enrolled as a new student in the local high school two months ago but still has not made friends and feels bored and lonely. One of his favorite activities is writing stories. What is likely to be the most effective solution to this problem?

(a) Volunteer to work on the school newspaper staff.

(b) Spend more time at home writing columns for the school newsletter.

(c) Try to convince his parents to move back to Arizona.

(d) Invite a friend from Arizona to visit during Christmas break.

Problem 2

Any retail business that ignores its regular clientele in order to concentrate on new *jids* may discover that sales do not increase. The new interest generated may not be enough to compensate for the loss in sales caused by dissatisfied patrons who begin to shop elsewhere.

Jid most likely means:

(a) Product

(b) Customer

(c) Advertisement

(d) Investment

Both these problems are from a test that Sternberg developed on the basis of his triarchic theory. This group test is designed for test-takers from kindergarten through adulthood. The first problem tests practical intelligence, calling for everyday inferences. The second one tests componential intelligence, the kind most often tested on standard intelligence tests, which include things like learning the meanings of words from context. Other parts of the test include such tasks as coping with novelty in using words, numbers, and figures; doing practical math problems; and planning routes by looking at maps.

"The testing of intelligence," says Sternberg (in press, p. 51), "can be as diverse and multifaceted as is intelligence itself." The triarchic approach emphasizes teaching different kinds of intelligence in conjunction with testing for various aspects, in order to enhance cognitive skills. To encourage the practical application of his theory and research, Sternberg (1986) has developed such a program for use with high school students. These aspects of intelligence are among the many kinds of knowledge that adolescents need to learn. Some do learn a great deal at schools that consider young people's needs and encourage their development.

What do you think?   *Which of Sternberg's three kinds of intelligence are you strongest in? Did your education include a focus on any of these aspects? How might such teaching be integrated into a junior high or high school curriculum?*

SECONDARY SCHOOL

School is one of the most crucial elements in a young person's social environment. Historically in the United States, education has been the ticket to economic and social advancement leading to successful adult life. However, for many students today—especially those from low-income families and neighborhoods—school no longer performs this vital function. Approaching development in the context of where and how young adolescents live and how their social institutions affect them helps us to understand some of the issues that arise in early adolescence. One is the move out of elementary school.

THE TRANSITION TO JUNIOR HIGH OR HIGH SCHOOL

Patterns of Transition

At the end of sixth grade, Jason went through an important American rite of passage. He graduated from the small (500-student) elementary school he had gone to since kindergarten and entered a junior high school with 3 times as many students. Instead of staying with one teacher and the same children for the entire school day, he is now in a less personal setting in which teachers, classrooms, and classmates change constantly throughout the day. In 3 more years, he will move again, this time to an even larger high school.

Vicky is following a different, less typical pattern. Since her elementary school runs from kindergarten to eighth grade, she will stay in a familiar setting with familiar people for a longer time, and then have only one transition to make, when, after completing the eighth grade, she enters high school.

Which pattern is better? What benefits and drawbacks are associated with each? Research has found a number of stresses associated with Jason's more typical sequence. One 5-year longitudinal study followed 594 white students in the

Milwaukee public schools from sixth through tenth grade, comparing students in the 6-3-3 pattern with those in the 8-4 pattern (Blyth, Simmons, & Carlton-Ford, 1983). Researchers looked at students' self-esteem, social adjustment (based on extracurricular activity), academic progress (by grade-point average and performance on achievement tests), and perception of the "anonymity" of their schools (how much they felt other people knew them).

Students who went to junior high school to enter seventh grade had more problems than those who did not leave elementary school until after eighth grade. Girls were especially vulnerable.

Effects of the Transition

Both boys and girls in the 6-3-3 pattern had a decrease in grade-point averages, took less part in extracurricular activities, and saw their schools as more anonymous. Furthermore, the girls' self-esteem dropped, an effect that persisted into tenth grade (Blyth et al., 1983).

Gender-Related Correlates.   Why do girls have more problems? One clue emerges from research that has found that the more life changes are taking place in a student's life, the more likely both GPA and extracurricular participation are to decrease for both sexes and the more likely girls' self-esteem is to drop (Simmons, Burgeson, Carlton-Ford, & Blyth, 1987).

Girls usually enter puberty sooner than boys and begin to date earlier, making it more likely that they will experience "life-change overload" (Petersen, 1993). Furthermore, there is more emphasis on girls' looks and popularity at this age, and they may miss the security of being with old friends. Other research too has shown that girls react more negatively than boys to stress in adolescence, unlike childhood, when males are more vulnerable.

School-Related Correlates.   Some negative consequences may result from a mismatch between the needs of adolescents and the characteristics of the new school. Typically, junior high school students have fewer opportunities to make decisions than do elementary school students; they have less personal, less positive relationships with their teachers; they are more likely to be grouped by ability, a practice that increases competitiveness and concerns about evaluation; and their classwork often requires lower-level cognitive skills than did their work in earlier grades. Furthermore, since junior high teachers tend to judge students by a higher standard, this often results in lowered grades; and since grades are a powerful predictor of self-confidence, a drop in grades can lead to a drop in self-esteem (Eccles et al., 1993).

Home-Related Correlates.   Another factor that can affect adjustment to the new school status is a change in parents' work or marital status. One study found that when parents had either been demoted or laid off at about the same time that their children were moving into junior high school, these young adolescents had a hard time adjusting to their new school status. They had more trouble getting along with other students and were more disruptive in school than were youngsters from stable families or families in which a parent had just been rehired or promoted. They had even more problems than did children whose parents had been laid off permanently during the two years of this study (Flanagan & Eccles, 1993).

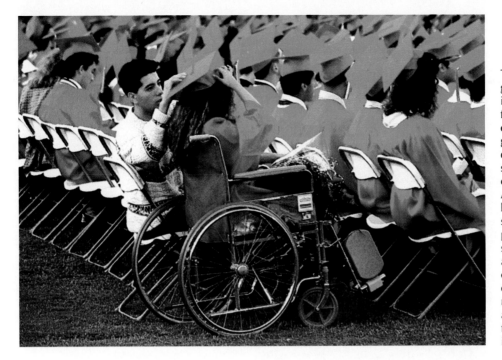

These high school graduates are taking an important step toward their future careers. Dropping out of school does not guarantee poverty, but dropouts do have to scramble harder to start a career. Today, more Americans than ever before graduate from high school, an increase over previous generations that stems from many causes—a general widening of educational opportunities, encouragement of minority-group students, and financial aid programs for students from low-income families.

Total comfort and complete stability, of course, are not only impossible to achieve at any age but also undesirable. Throughout life, we grow and develop as we learn to cope with challenges. We do this best, however, if we can deal with one change at a time. Although this is not always possible, educators and families can focus on designing environments that will help young adolescents meet the needs and desires special to this developmental stage. This may involve opportunities for decision making, participation in rule making, continued close relationships with adults both within and outside the family, and a level of independence appropriate for their age and level of development.

What do you think?   *By what specific ways can parents and teachers help students with the transition to junior high or high school?*

HIGH SCHOOL TODAY

High school is the central organizing experience in both Vicky's and Jason's lives. It offers them opportunities to learn new information, master new skills, and sharpen old ones; to examine career choices; to participate in sports; and to get together with friends. It widens their intellectual and social horizons as it combines encounters with peers and with a variety of adults. Adolescents in less advantaged circumstances, however, are less likely to experience high school as an opportunity but as one more hindrance on the road to adulthood.

The social, vocational, and athletic functions of high school are important, but its primary focus continues to be academic. During the 1970s, scores on standardized tests fell, most dramatically in vocabulary and reading. One analysis attributed the decline to "a decreased academic emphasis on the educational

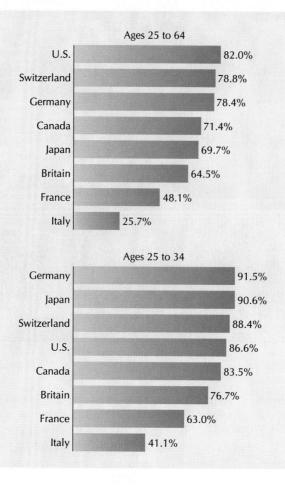

Ages 25 to 64

Country	Percentage
U.S.	82.0%
Switzerland	78.8%
Germany	78.4%
Canada	71.4%
Japan	69.7%
Britain	64.5%
France	48.1%
Italy	25.7%

Ages 25 to 34

Country	Percentage
Germany	91.5%
Japan	90.6%
Switzerland	88.4%
U.S.	86.6%
Canada	83.5%
Britain	76.7%
France	63.0%
Italy	41.1%

FIGURE 15-1
High school graduation rates as a percentage of population. Although the United States boasts a higher rate of high school graduation for adults aged 25 to 64 than seven other industrialized countries, American rates have lagged behind for younger adults. The high rates among minority groups explain the drop in part, and some observers recommend more minority-group and more male teachers in the nation's schools. SOURCE: U.S. Department of Education, 1992.

process" (Rock, Ekstrom, Goertz, Hilton, & Pollack, 1985). However, another reason is the broader base of students who now go to high school. The National Commission on Excellence in Education (1983) found that the average high school or college *graduate* today is not as well educated as the average graduate of previous generations, when fewer people finished high school or college. However, the average *citizen* today is better educated than the average citizen of the past.

Today, more than three-fourths of Americans who are 25 years old and older (76.5 percent) have graduated from high school; some finished at the usual age, and others earned their diplomas later (U.S. Bureau of the Census, 1988). This increase stems from many causes—a general widening of educational opportunities, financial aid programs for students from low-income families, and the policy of some schools to graduate students even though they have not learned basic skills. Still, the United States lags behind many other countries in graduation rates of younger adults (U.S. Department of Education, 1992). (See Figure 15-1.)

One reason for the high dropout rate in the United States stems from the disparity in the quality of schools for advantaged children and those attended by minority-group children living in poverty (National Research Council, NRC, 1993b).

What Makes a High School Good?

A good high school is marked by an active, energetic principal; an orderly, unoppressive atmosphere; teachers who take part in making decisions; a principal and teachers with high expectations for students; an emphasis on academics (as opposed to athletics and other extracurricular activities); and frequent monitoring of students' performance (Linney & Seidman, 1989).

Schools for students from low-income families often fall short of these qualities. It is ironic that the children who need the most help generally attend schools with the fewest material resources. Not only are the physical plants of schools in poor urban or rural areas often dreary, dilapidated, and dispiriting places to be; these schools also have less money to spend on a high teacher-pupil ratio, tutoring, counseling, health care, and English-language instruction for foreign-born students. Despite the efforts of many dedicated educators, such schools often fail to help students from disadvantaged backgrounds build the skills they need for successful adult lives (NRC, 1993a).

Furthermore, some traditional educational practices contribute to the high rate of failure for low-achieving students. One is the practice of *tracking*, or grouping students by abilities. Tracking accentuates the differences between students even more, relegates low-track students to basic skills rather than higher-order learning, gives them less stimulation from their classmates, and often provides poorer teaching. Students placed in low tracks rarely move up, and their awareness of their low academic status often makes them lose interest in even trying to do better (NRC, 1993). Mixed-ability classes stimulate these students better and have both social and psychological benefits for them, while not holding back more competent students (Oakes, Gamoran, & Page, 1992; Rutter, 1983).

Retaining students in grade seems to have negative effects similar to those of tracking (NRC, 1993). Thus school systems often make the problems of low-income students from poor neighborhoods even worse. Parents can sometimes overcome the inadequacy of a school, but when they are poor and overburdened, they may not be able to help their children do better academically.

HOME INFLUENCES ON ACHIEVEMENT IN HIGH SCHOOL

Parents' Interest

Vicky and Jason both come from families that value education and value children. Both sets of parents are involved with their children and their schooling, even though all four parents work outside the home and often have trouble finding time to do everything. These parents keep track of their children's whereabouts (even now that, as adolescents, Vicky and Jason are more independent—and even now that Jess and Julia no longer live together) and of how they are doing in school (even now that Vicky and Jason rarely seek help or advice with schoolwork).

Parents like these try to attend as many parent-teacher meetings as possible, and they make time to talk to their children almost every day—at the dinner table when schedules allow, or at some other time if the parents' work or the children's sports workouts or music lessons mean that the family cannot be together at dinner. (Jason usually speaks to his father by phone on the days when they do not see each other.) Overall, the relationship between the generations is caring and

TABLE 15-3

SURVEY ITEM	SELF-REPORTED GRADES			
	MOSTLY A's	MOSTLY B's	MOSTLY C's	MOSTLY D's
Mother keeps close track of how well child does in school.	92%	89%	84%	80%
Father keeps close track of how well child does in school.	85%	79%	69%	64%
Parents almost always know child's whereabouts.	88%	81%	72%	61%
Child talks with mother or father almost every day.	75%	67%	59%	45%
Parents attend PTA meetings at least once in a while.	25%	22%	20%	15%
Child lives in household with both parents.	80%	71%	64%	60%

NOTE: This table, based on a survey of more than 30,000 high school seniors, shows the percentage of students with various grade averages who gave positive answers to each survey item. In each instance, the higher the grades were, the more likely the parents were to be involved with the child.
SOURCE: National Center for Education Statistics, 1985.

interested, despite occasional conflicts. These parents resolve disagreements in the same authoritative way they always have.

This kind of attention from parents seems to pay off in good grades, according to a survey of more than 30,000 high school seniors in more than 1000 schools (National Center for Education Statistics, NCES, 1985). As Table 15-3 shows, the students with the highest grades have the most involved parents. The father's importance is especially noteworthy. Fathers vary more than mothers in the degree to which they stay on top of children's schoolwork; the more involved a father is, the better his children fare. His importance is also seen in the fact that children who live with both parents earn better grades.

These findings do not prove that parents' interest improves students' grades. The cause-and-effect relationship may, in fact, work the other way: Young people who do well in school may stir parents' interest, encouraging their involvement. It is more likely, however, that parents stimulate their children to do well by showing interest and concern and that the students' achievements then stimulate their parents, so that the effect reinforces itself. Also, parents of teenage students who do well are interested in more than their children's homework and grades. They take the children seriously both in and out of school, and the children reward that interest.

Relationships with Parents

Adolescents who get along well with their parents and whose parents are reasonably well adjusted tend to get higher grades and behave better in school (Forehand, Long, Brody, & Fauber, 1986). Researchers looked at grade-point averages and teachers' behavior ratings of 46 boys and girls whose age averaged $13\frac{1}{2}$, assessed parents' marital conflict and depression, and asked both parents and children to recall disagreements about such issues as cleaning the children's bedrooms, homework, television, and drugs.

Teenagers who had the most parental conflict had the most behavior problems in school. Children of depressed mothers also tended to have problems, but a father's depression did not have the same effect. However, conflict with the father had more impact than did conflict with the mother. Frequent disagreements with mothers did not affect school performance, but students who got along poorly with their fathers had lower grades than did those who got along well. Surprisingly, the parents' marital relationships did not affect their children's grades or behavior.

Why should conflict with the father be especially upsetting? Perhaps teenagers and mothers clash so often over routine matters that young people do not take it seriously, but conflicts with fathers may be over more important issues or simply have more impact because they are less frequent. Or mothers may be better able than fathers to maintain intimacy with children even when they are angry with them. Causation may run in the other direction too: When students do poorly in school, fathers may become more involved, and as they try to oversee students' work or behavior, more conflicts may erupt. In either case, both these studies make clear the need for the father's involvement in the lives of adolescent children, which has been ignored in much research.

Parenting Styles

Studies of about 6400 California high school students compared their achievement on the basis of their parents' fitting into one of Baumrind's child-rearing styles:

Authoritative parents tell adolescents to look at both sides of issues, admit that children sometimes know more than parents, talk about politics, and welcome teenagers' participation in family decisions. Students receive praise and freedom if they get good grades; poor grades bring encouragement to try harder, offers of help, and loss of freedom. *Authoritarian parents* tell adolescents not to argue with or question adults and tell them they will "know better when they are grown up." Good grades bring admonitions to do even better, and poor grades upset parents,

Parenting styles can influence how adolescents do in school. Children of authoritative parents—who admit that teenagers sometimes know more than their elders, who talk about politics, and who welcome teenagers' participation in family decisions—tend to do better.

who punish by reducing allowances or "grounding." *Permissive parents* do not care about grades, make no rules about watching television, do not attend school programs, and neither help with nor check their children's homework. (Permissive parents may be neglectful and uncaring, or caring and concerned but convinced that children should be responsible for their own lives.)

Children of authoritative parents tend to do better in school than do children of parents in the other two groups (Steinberg & Darling, 1994; Steinberg, Lamborn, Dornbusch, & Darling, 1992; Dornbusch, Ritter, Leiderman, Roberts, & Fraleigh, 1987). Students who get low grades are more likely to have authoritarian or permissive parents or parents who waffle between styles. Inconsistency is associated with the lowest grades, possibly because children who do not know what to expect from their parents become anxious and less able to concentrate on their work.

Ethnic differences showed up among the students, supporting the basis of the ecological approach to development in context. The above relationships hold up for white teenagers. But Asian American students, whose parents tend to be authoritarian, still do well, possibly because of the influence of peers, who also value academic achievement. However, Hispanic and African American students—even those of authoritative parents—do not do as well in school, apparently because there is little support from their peers for academic achievement (Steinberg, Dornbusch, & Brown, 1992). As one girl said, "My friends come over, see me reading, and call me a nerd." Parents cannot always overcome influences in the larger environment. If young people feel that shining in school will make them less popular with their peers or will not result in life success, they will not be motivated to succeed there.

This work suggests another influence of context. The lower school achievement of children of single parents, who tend to be more permissive, may be due to the style of parenting, not the single-parent status itself.

Socioeconomic Status

Family income may be the most powerful factor contributing to the setting in which an adolescent lives (National Research Council, NRC, 1993). This environment in turn affects a young person's education, since housing, neighborhoods, schools, health care facilities, social experiences, and opportunities for higher education are all linked to both income and setting. Income may also have a big impact on the family atmosphere itself, which influences school achievement.

Do parents value education? Do they read to their young children and take them to the library? Do they talk to their children? What goals do parents have for their children, and how do they help them reach those goals? Do parents show interest in schoolwork and expect children to go to college? Is the family stable?

Whether a family is rich or poor, the answers to questions like these are important. However, the family's social and economic background has a strong relationship to achievement, partly in its influence on *how* parents rear their children. It is not the parents' occupation, income, or education that makes the difference, but the indirect effect that their socioeconomic status has on their style of parenting (K. R. White, 1982). Furthermore, in poor neighborhoods there are more single-parent families, whose adolescents are more likely to engage in high-risk behaviors (NRC, 1993). Schools in these neighborhoods tend to be less able to meet the needs of their students.

BOX 15-3 ▪ THE EVERYDAY WORLD

SHOULD TEENAGERS HOLD PART-TIME JOBS?

When Vicky announced that she had taken an after-school and weekend job as a waitress, her parents applauded her initiative and industry. They thought it would help her learn how to handle money responsibly and develop good work habits. But Vicky's high school counselor was less enthusiastic. Let's see why.

A higher proportion of teenage students are working today than at any other time in the past few decades. This trend conforms to the American belief in the moral benefits derived from working. But some research makes us wonder whether part-time work has real value for high school students. For those students who have to work to help support their families, the question is moot. But for those who work to earn pocket money, the issue is more complex than it appears.

ARGUMENTS IN FAVOR OF PART-TIME WORK FOR ADOLESCENTS

1 Paid work teaches young people to handle money responsibly.
2 It helps them develop good work habits, like promptness, reliability, and efficient time management (National Commission on Youth, 1980).
3 A good part-time job (one that helps a teenager to master new skills, assume responsibility, and work with people of different ages and backgrounds) helps students learn about a particular field, thus guiding them in choosing a career (National Commission on Youth, 1980).
4 It helps them learn workplace skills, like how to find a job, and how to get along with a variety of people—employers, coworkers, and sometimes the public.
5 By showing adolescents how demanding and difficult the world of work is and how unprepared they are for it, part-time jobs—especially menial ones—sometimes help to motivate young people to continue their education.
6 Some undesirable tendencies of working adolescents may be caused not by working itself but by why some teenagers take jobs. Some may want to work because they are uninterested in school, are alienated from their families, and want money to buy drugs and liquor. Their jobs may actually keep them out of trouble by providing legal ways for them to earn money.

ARGUMENTS AGAINST PART-TIME WORK FOR ADOLESCENTS

1 Teenagers who work are no more independent in making financial decisions than are their classmates who do not hold jobs (Greenberger & Steinberg, 1986).
2 Most students who work part time during high school are in low-level, repetitive jobs where they do not learn skills that will be useful later in life (Hamilton & Crouter, 1980).
3 Working teenagers are not likely to earn any more money as adults than are those who did not hold jobs during high school (Greenberger & Steinberg, 1986).
4 Work seems to undermine performance in school, especially for teenagers who work more than 15 or 20 hours per week. Grades, involvement in school, and attendance decline. Working more than 15 hours a week is related to dropping out of school (NCES, 1987). Since education is so important as preparation for careers and for life, working at an early age may interfere with it.
5 Working has hidden costs. Some teenagers spend their earnings on alcohol or drugs, develop cynical attitudes toward work, and cheat or steal from their employers. Teenagers who work tend to spend less time with their families and to feel less close to them. They have little contact with adults on the job, and they are usually in gender-stereotyped jobs (Steinberg, Fegley, & Dornbusch, 1993; Greenberger & Steinberg, 1986). Those who work long hours are less likely to eat breakfast, exercise, get enough sleep, or have enough leisure time (Bachman & Schulenberg, 1993).
6 The workplace is dangerous for many adolescents. In 1992 more than 64,000 teenagers sought treatment in hospital emergency rooms for injuries on the job (National Institute of Occupational Safety and Health, 1994).

What do you think? *Should teenagers work part time? Give reasons for your position.*

To make extra money, students from many social and economic levels often seek part-time work after school and on weekends. But this step is not necessarily the most productive use of their energy and time, as indicated in Box 15-3.

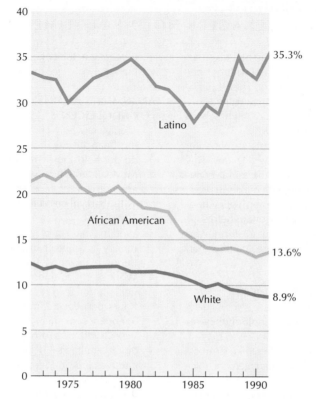

FIGURE 15-2
High school dropout rates. Although rates have declined for white and African American students, they have remained high for Latino students, who often leave school to help support their families. SOURCE: U.S. Department of Education, 1992.

DROPPING OUT OF SCHOOL

Linda, a Native American tribal leader, in her senior year of high school, told her school counselor, "My tribe needs me. I have to leave school." For Linda, there was no question that family and tribe took precedence over academic pursuits. For other students, other reasons lead them to leave school before receiving a diploma. Whatever the reason, leaving school early reduces the opportunities that the future will hold for a young person. Dropping out of high school does not guarantee poverty, but dropouts do have to scramble harder to start a career—if they ever have one. Many employers require a high school diploma, and many jobs require skills based on a solid education.

Who Drops Out?

In 1991, 8.9 percent of white people aged 16 to 24 in the United States were not in school and had never received a high school degree. For African Americans, the percentage was 13.6 percent. Both these percentages represented an increase in school graduation rates over the previous 19 years. However, the dropout rates for Hispanic Americans—35.3 percent in 1991—was roughly the same as it had been in 1972 (U.S. Department of Education, 1991). (See Figure 15-2.) Among the possible reasons for the high Latino dropout rates are language difficulties, financial pressures, and a culture that puts family first. Almost one-half of dropouts leave in the eleventh grade, almost one-third in the senior year, and about one-fourth in the tenth grade. Boys are more likely than girls to drop out ("Students Learning," 1990).

Asian American students have the lowest dropout rate, followed by (in increasing order) white, African American, Hispanic, and Native American students. When socioeconomic status is held constant, however, the large difference among white, African American, and Latino young people narrows or even vanishes. In fact, at equal socioeconomic levels, black students' attainment is higher than white students' (NCES, 1987). Socioeconomic status seems to be a critical factor in determining which students will stay in school long enough to graduate.

Students who are most likely to drop out of school share a number of family characteristics. Those whose parents are poorly educated and in low-level jobs and those who are in large, single-parent families are 3 to 5 times more likely to drop out than are students in more privileged circumstances (NCES, 1987). Even in more affluent families, teenagers from single-parent and remarried families are more likely to drop out of school than are those living with both parents, according to a study of more than 13,000 high school sophomores (Zimiles & Lee, 1991). A gender effect showed up in this study: An adolescent living with a parent of the same sex is less likely to drop out when the custodial parent has not remarried and is more likely to do so in a stepfamily situation. This may be related to the strong attachment that often develops between a child and a same-sex single parent, a relationship that may be disrupted when the parent remarries.

Dropping out in high school can sometimes be predicted as early as the seventh grade. In a longitudinal study, 475 seventh-graders were followed for 5 years. Dropout rates were higher for students who, when first seen, showed aggressive behavior *and* did poorly in school (Cairns, Cairns, & Neckerman, 1989). More than 80 percent of the boys and 47 percent of the girls who showed this behavioral combination in seventh grade dropped out before finishing eleventh grade. Being unpopular with peers in seventh grade did *not* predict dropping out, probably because young people tend to have friends who are like themselves (that is, at similar risk for dropping out or graduating).

Other factors associated with dropping out include having repeated a grade in elementary school, working more than 15 hours a week while in high school, being married, having a child, being alienated from family and community, and such signs of antisocial behavior as suspension, probation, or trouble with the law (NCES, 1987; Williams, 1987).

Why Do They Drop Out?

For students like Linda, cultural values conflict with academic ones. This is also the case for some students who succumb to peer pressure as they see other young people in their social group leaving school. The reasons dropouts give for their decision do not tell the whole story. When asked 2 years later why they had dropped out, one group of males pointed mostly to poor grades, having to support the family, and not liking school; a few said they had been expelled or suspended. Females attributed dropping out mainly to marriage or plans to marry, feeling that "school is not for me," poor grades, or pregnancy; a small number mentioned a job (NCES, 1983).

It is hard to know the exact reasons for dropping out. More than half the girls said they had left because of pregnancy or marriage. However, they may have become pregnant or gotten married precisely because they were not doing well or were not interested in school or were responding to gender or cultural bias in school. If the girls' reasons *were* true, why were they? The boys' explanations tell just as little about their underlying reasons. Some researchers attribute dropping out to lack of motivation and self-esteem, little encouragement of education by parents, cultural bias and low expectations by teachers, inappropriate skill training for non-college-bound youth, and disciplinary problems at home and at school (Hamilton, 1990; Rule, 1981).

What Happens to Dropouts?

Dropouts have trouble getting jobs; the work they do get is in low-level, poor-paying occupations, and they are more likely to lose their jobs. In one study, 27 percent of male high school dropouts and 31 percent of female high school dropouts were looking for work; 32 percent of the women were not looking for work because they were full-time homemakers. Of those who were working, only about 14 percent of the young men and 3 percent of the young women had jobs that required technical skills. Typical jobs were waiting on tables, manual labor, factory work, clerking in stores, baby-sitting, clerical work, and farmwork. More than half the dropouts soon regretted leaving school, and a small percent took part in educational programs (NCES, 1987).

How Can Dropping Out Be Prevented?

Society suffers when young people do not finish school. Dropouts are more likely to end up on welfare, to be unemployed, and to become involved with drugs, crime, and delinquency. In addition, the loss of taxable income burdens the public treasury (NCES, 1987). Both public and private organizations have developed a variety of programs aimed at encouraging young people to stay in school.

One particularly successful federally funded program, Upward Bound, was established in 1964; by 1988, 80 percent of its graduates had gone on to 4-year colleges. Students from low-income families whose parents and siblings did not go to college are selected for the program on the basis of school records, teacher recommendations, a personal interview, and an assessment of applicants' and parents' commitment to the program. It stresses high expectations, has a rigorous curriculum, and offers tutoring and peer counseling. It also offers counseling on drug abuse, self-esteem, study skills, preparing for the Scholastic Aptitude Tests (SATs), applying to college, and career planning (Wells, 1988a). The success of programs like Upward Bound shows that it is possible to prevent dropping out.

What do you think?   *What kind of commitments can government, educators, and parents make to help young people stay in school?*

DEVELOPING A CAREER

"Is there life after high school? Where will all this education lead? What kind of work will I do after school? Do I need still more education?" These are the questions adolescents ask.

STAGES IN VOCATIONAL PLANNING

When she was 6, Vicky was going to be an astronaut. At 12, Vicky laughed at that idea. Math and science were not her best subjects, and she knew she could never make it into the space program. At 15 she did some volunteer work at a hospital and began thinking about psychiatry as a career. Now, as a high school senior, she has decided against the financial and time commitments demanded by medical school and instead is applying to colleges with a 5-year program leading to a master's degree in psychiatric social work.

Jason's aspirations are less sharply focused. At 6 he wanted to be a baseball player. At 12 baseball still sounded good, but so did becoming a dancer—even though he rarely confided this ambition to his schoolmates. As the time to apply to college draws closer, he bounces from one interest to another—baseball, choreography, law, geology, and psychology—and hates to have to drop any of them.

Vicky's development follows three classic stages in career planning: the fantasy period, the tentative period, and the realistic period (Ginzberg et al., 1951). During the *fantasy* period of her elementary school years, Vicky's choices were active and exciting rather than realistic, and her decisions were based on emotions rather than on practical considerations. In the *tentative* period, at about puberty, she began to make a more realistic effort to match her interests with her abilities and values. By the end of high school, she is in the *realistic* period and plans for the right education to meet her career goals.

Jason has not yet reached the realistic period. He is not alone. In one study, more than 6000 high school seniors in Texas were asked to name their top three career choices and to report on their educational plans. They were also asked about their preferred vocational styles: working alone versus working with others; working inside versus outdoors; and working with people, things, or ideas. At a time in their lives when they had to make crucial choices about education and work, these students knew little about occupations. Not surprisingly, they tended to know more about their first career choice and increasingly less about the next two. But even of those who felt that they had a good understanding of their first career choice, only about half planned to get the appropriate amount of education. Some thought they needed much more education for their chosen careers than they actually did, and others were not planning on getting enough training. Furthermore, most students did not seem to be making good matches between their career choices and their interests (Grotevant & Durrett, 1980).

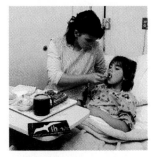

Volunteer work is one way to preview the rewards and frustrations of a particular career. If this teenage "candy-striper" finds hospital work rewarding, she may pursue a career as a doctor or a nurse.

INFLUENCES ON VOCATIONAL PLANNING

How do young people choose their career goals? Many factors enter in, including individual ability and personality, education, socioeconomic and ethnic background, societal values, the advice of school counselors, and life experiences. Important influences on career planning are societal institutions; parents' ambitions for, and encouragement of, their children; and gender.

Societal Aids in the Transition from School to Work

About half of the high school graduates in the United States do not go on to college; of those who do, fewer than half earn 4-year degrees. Still, although some 75 percent of students will not finish college, most vocational counseling at the high school level is oriented toward college-bound youth (NRC, 1993a). Many young people, ignorant about the job market and how they can fit into it, flounder badly. Many do not learn the skills they will need to get a good position. Some take jobs beneath their abilities; some do not find work at all. Again, low income is a determining factor: For people under age 20, being raised in a low-income family is the strongest predictor of joblessness (NRC, 1993a).

Most other industrialized countries offer some kind of structured help to non-college-bound students, but the United States relies almost entirely on market forces to help these youths find work. For many, the marketplace does not work. In a few communities, demonstration programs have been set up to help in the school-to-work transition. The most successful ones offer a coordinated set of services—including remedial teaching of basic skills, counseling, peer group support, mentoring, apprenticeship, and job placement services—over an extended period (NRC, 1993a).

The failure to be vocationally prepared is one of the prime reasons why so many youths from poor families turn to crime as a way to make a living. Young men who have problems with education and employment have a high probability of being arrested and imprisoned or of becoming a victim of crime themselves (NRC, 1993). (Adolescent criminal activity will be discussed in Chapter 16.)

As a result of the lack of formal programs to help young people make the transition from school to work, much of this preparation falls on the shoulders of parents.

How Do Parents Affect Vocational Plans?

Parents' encouragement and financial support are important influences on aspiration and achievement. In general, parental encouragement predicts high ambition better than social class does. When 2622 sixth-, eighth-, tenth-, and twelfth-grade students, black and white and from all social strata, were asked to describe their own expectations for their education and their fathers' and mothers' expectations for them, more than half the students agreed with the perceived goals of each parent (T. E. Smith, 1981). If parents do not encourage their children to pursue higher education and are not willing to help them through college, it is harder for the younger people, even though some students do work their way through school, take out loans, or win scholarships.

How Does Gender Affect Vocational Plans?

A woman who entered engineering school at Ohio State University in 1945 was one of six females in her class. Some 35 years later, women made up about 30 percent of the entering class (R. D. Feldman, 1982). Similar increases have been seen in the number of women studying law, medicine, and other traditionally male occupations—even though they are still vastly underrepresented (Reis, 1991). Women who pursue nontraditional careers are likely to be the eldest child in the family and to have well-educated parents (Matlin, 1987).

Even though there is much more flexibility in career goals today, gender—and gender-stereotyping—often influence choice of career. For example, although there is little or no difference between boys and girls in mathematical or verbal ability and although girls' grades are on average better than boys', many girls are not encouraged to continue in gifted programs, take advanced science and math courses, or pursue demanding careers (Reis, 1991; Read, 1991; Hyde & Linn, 1988; Maccoby & Jacklin, 1974). Many parents, teachers, and career counselors still steer young people into gender-typed careers (Matlin, 1987).

However, the small apparent differences in males' and females' abilities have no real educational or vocational implications. There is no basis for guiding males and females to different careers. Even if differences do exist, there is much over-

Is this career counselor influenced by the student's sex in advising him about possible career choices? Even though there is little or no difference between boys and girls in mathematical or verbal ability, many career counselors still steer young people into gender-typed careers.

lap: Some girls are better at math and science than are some boys, and some boys are better writers and speakers than are some girls. Young people should be encouraged to pursue careers that fit their own interests and abilities, regardless of gender.

What do you think?   *Imagine you are a high school counselor. What kind of program would you put in place to help students make career plans?*

The adolescent's search for identity is closely tied to vocational ambitions. The question "Who shall I be?" is very close to "What shall I do?" The choice of a career is crucial: People who feel they are doing something worth doing and doing it well feel good about themselves. On the contrary, those who feel that their work does not matter to others, or that they are not very good at it, can feel emotionally insecure. A prime issue in adolescence, which we discuss in Chapter 16, is the continuing effort to define the self, to mold an identity, and to emerge with self-knowledge and self-esteem.

SUMMARY

1   Many adolescents attain Piaget's stage of formal operations, which is characterized by the ability to think abstractly. People in the stage of formal operations can engage in hypothetical-deductive reasoning, as demonstrated by performance on the pendulum task. People in the formal operations stage can think in terms of possibilities, deal flexibly with problems, and test hypotheses. Since experience plays an important part in attaining this stage, not all people become capable of formal operations.

2   A number of "egocentric" behaviors characteristic of adolescence include finding fault with authority figures, argumentativeness, self-consciousness, self-centeredness, indecisiveness, and apparent hypocrisy.

3   According to Kohlberg, moral reasoning invokes the development of a sense of jus-

tice and values on three major levels: preconventional, conventional role conformity, and autonomous moral principles. Most adolescents are at Kohlberg's level II. Their moral judgments conform to social conventions, they support the status quo, and they think in terms of doing the "right" thing to please others or to obey the law. Some adolescents, however, are at the preconventional level; others are at the level of autonomous moral principles.

4 Cultural, gender, and family factors play a part in the attainment of the more advanced levels of moral judgment. The validity of Kohlberg's system has been questioned for use in some cultures and for females.

5 Sternberg's triarchic theory includes three aspects of intelligence: componential (the critical aspect), experiential (the insightful aspect), and contextual (the practical aspect). His triarchic abilities test is based on this theory.

6 High school is the central organizing experience—cognitively and otherwise—in the lives of most adolescents. Efforts are being made to improve the quality of education in American high schools. School and teacher characteristics are important influences. The pattern of transition to junior high school or high school influences adjustment.

7 Home atmosphere, parents' involvement, family relationships, and parenting style appear to make more of a difference than does a family's socioeconomic status in students' achievement in high school.

8 Although most adolescents in the United States graduate from high school, the dropout rate is particularly high among Native American, Latino, and African American students. Programs such as Upward Bound aim to encourage young people to stay in school.

9 Vocational choice is influenced by several factors, including societal support, gender, and parents' attitude.

10 More teenagers today work part time after school than they did in the past few decades. Work seems to have little benefit for a teenager's educational, social, or occupational development. Its negative effect on schoolwork is greatest when the teenager works more than 15 or 20 hours a weak.

KEY TERMS

formal operations (589)
imaginary audience (594)
personal fable (594)
preconventional morality (596)
morality of conventional role conformity (596)

morality of autonomous moral principles (596)
triarchic theory of intelligence (605)

SUGGESTED READINGS

Csikszentmihalyi et al. (1993)

Elkind, D. (1984). *All grown up and no place to go.* Reading, MA: Addison-Wesley. A thought-provoking book about the difficulties of being a teenager and raising teenagers today. Elkind argues that teenagers are unprepared for the adult challenges they are asked to face, and so they exhibit many problem behaviors. He specifically relates formal operational thinking abilities to behaviors such as self-centeredness, self-consciousness, and argumentativeness.

Freedman, S. G. (1990). *Small victories: The real world of a teacher, her students, and their high school.* New York: Harper & Row. This account of a year in the life of a New York City teacher shows what an imaginative, dedicated person can bring to the lives of immigrant students and others who live and go to high school in a rundown inner-city neighborhood. The book also includes portraits of other faculty members and students. It leaves the reader with the sense that good teaching is a vocation, not a job.

Greenberger, E., & Steinberg, L. (1986). *When teenagers work.* New York: Basic Books. An absorbing and controversial analysis of research on the impact that working has on teenagers. The authors conclude that working during the teens entails a number of hidden costs that affect development negatively.

CHAPTER 16
PERSONALITY AND SOCIAL DEVELOPMENT IN ADOLESCENCE

This face in the mirror
stares at me
demanding Who are you? What will you become?
And taunting, You don't even know.
Chastened, I cringe and agree
and then
because I'm still young,
I stick out my tongue.

Eve Merriam, "Conversation with Myself," 1964

In this chapter, we talk about changes adolescents face in social and personality development. We consider the search for identity—a search for, or an attempt to create, personal stability and certainty amid many changes and questions. The big question "Who am I?" comprises a mosaic of subquestions, like "What do I really believe?" "What kinds of relationships do I have?" and "Who am I, sexually?" After examining research and theories about adolescents' identity, we discuss three aspects of identity: relationships with parents and siblings, relationships with peers, and sexual identity. We explore two problems of adolescence—pregnancy and juvenile delinquency—and then describe what adolescents typically are like today. After you have read this chapter, you will be able to answer questions such as the following:

PREVIEW QUESTIONS

- ◆ Is "storm and stress" an inevitable part of adolescence?
- ◆ Do adolescent boys and girls seek identity in similar ways?
- ◆ How do teenagers' relationships with parents and peers help them achieve their own identity?
- ◆ What are the prevailing sexual practices and attitudes among adolescents today?
- ◆ What are some causes and consequences of teenage pregnancy and of delinquency?
- ◆ What are adolescents like today?

"The trouble is," said 16-year-old Vicky to her mother after an argument, "that I don't know who I am. You know who you are. You're Ellen Smith Miller. You're a teacher. You're a wife. You're a mother. But who am I? You expect me to be just like you, to think just the way you do, and to do whatever you would do if you were me. But you're *not* me. I don't know who *is* me. I wish I could be myself with you, but I always feel under all this pressure not to talk about the things I think or do that I know you wouldn't approve of.

"Then when I do decide to open up to you, it never is a good time. I guess it's my fault. I don't pick the right times—whenever I want to talk, you're always busy with something else and don't have enough time to listen to me. But if we can't talk to each other, we'll never understand each other." Vicky thinks but doesn't say, "And I'll never find out who I really am."

Vicky expresses what is probably the most crucial task of adolescence—the search for identity, the quest to find out "who I really am." Teenagers need to develop their own values and to be sure that they are not just parroting the ideas of their parents. They have to find out what they can do and to be proud of their accomplishments. They want to develop close relationships with both boys and girls their own age and to be liked and loved and respected for who they are and what they stand for. This means they have to find out what they stand for.

Adolescents search for identity in many ways. Vicky's high school years have been troubled by a recurring disquiet over all the changes she faces. She knows she is no longer a child—but feels she is not yet an adult. As she looks at her mother, who seems to fit all her roles so easily—teacher, mother, wife, friend—Vicky cannot imagine herself filling any of these roles comfortably and well. She is not sure she even wants to. Her biggest problem these days is that she does not know what she wants.

Jason's adolescence is quieter and less troubling to his parents and stepfather. Yes, one night he came home reeking of cheap wine, and, yes, he sometimes offends his mother and her husband with coarse language and annoys his father with loud music. By and large, though, Jason's parents (like Vicky's) share a pride in their child, and a trust that he will do the right thing. He accepts their confidence in him, and—within responsible limits—he does what he pleases. This works out well, since what he wants to do often fits in with what his parents want him to do—achieve in school, socialize with friends they like, and work with the school drama club (usually behind the scenes; he is still shy). Still, like most adolescents he has doubts, anxieties, questions about the future. Like many teenagers whose parents have separated, he still feels pangs of sadness that they are no longer together. Furthermore, he worries that he will not be able to find and keep a girlfriend, that the same kinds of differences that drove his parents apart will arise in his relationships.

THE SEARCH FOR IDENTITY

The search for identity is a lifelong voyage, launched early in childhood and propelled farther in adolescence. As Erik Erikson (1950) emphasizes, this effort to make sense of the self and the world is not "a kind of maturational malaise." It is, instead, a healthy, vital process that contributes to the ego strength of the adult. We have already looked at some of the issues that contribute to an adolescent's sense of self, such as moral reasoning, achievement in school and other pursuits, and thinking about future careers. Now we explore some of the other aspects of this quest which spur personal growth and development.

IDENTITY VERSUS IDENTITY CONFUSION

The chief task of adolescence, says Erikson (1968), is to resolve the conflict of *identity versus identity confusion*—to become a unique adult with a meaningful role in life. To form an identity, the ego organizes a person's abilities, needs, and desires and helps to adapt them to the demands of society.

identity versus identity confusion In Erikson's theory, the fifth crisis of psychosocial development, in which an adolescent must determine his or her own sense of self (identity), including the role she or he will play in society.

This flutist's musical talent and interest can, according to Erikson, help her resolve the adolescent conflict of identity versus identity confusion. If she does not plan a career in music, she will need to decide on an alternate career, thus fulfilling a major task in the search for identity.

In adolescence the search for "who I am" becomes especially insistent, as the young person's sense of identity begins where the process of identification ends. Identification begins with modeling the self on other people, but identity formation involves becoming oneself, as the adolescent synthesizes earlier identifications into a new psychological structure, a unique identity greater than the sum of its parts (Kroger, 1993).

Based on his own life (see Chapter 1) and on his research with adolescents in various societies, Erikson concluded that one of the most crucial aspects in the search for identity is deciding on a career. In the stage of middle childhood, that of *industry versus inferiority,* children acquired the skills needed for success in the culture. Now as adolescents, they need to find ways to use these skills. Rapid physical growth and new genital maturity alert young people to their impending adulthood, and they begin to wonder about their roles in adult society. When young people have trouble settling on an occupational identity, they are at risk for disturbances, like early pregnancy or crime.

Erikson sees the prime danger of this stage as identity (or role) confusion, which can express itself in a young person's taking an excessively long time to reach adulthood (after age 30). (He himself did not resolve his own identity crisis until his mid-twenties.) A certain amount of identity confusion is normal, however. It accounts for both the chaotic nature of much adolescent behavior and teenagers' painful self-consciousness about their appearance.

Cliquishness and intolerance of differences—both hallmarks of the adolescent social scene—are defenses against identity confusion, says Erikson. Adolescents may also show confusion by regressing into childishness to avoid resolving conflicts or by committing themselves impulsively to poorly thought-out courses of action. During the *psychosocial moratorium*—the "time out" period that adolescence provides—many people search for commitments to which they can be faithful. Vicky commits herself to working for racial harmony in her community, Jason becomes a vegetarian, Michelle studies the violin. Very often these youthful commitments, which are both ideological and personal, will shape a person's life for years to come. The extent to which young people can be true to commitments influences their ability to resolve their identity crisis.

From this identity crisis arises the *virtue of fidelity*—sustained loyalty, faith, or a sense of belonging to a loved one or to friends and companions. Fidelity also involves identifying with a set of values, an ideology, a religion, a political movement, a creative pursuit, or an ethnic group (Erikson, 1982). Self-identification emerges when young people *choose* values and people to be loyal to, rather than accepting their parents' choices.

What do you think? *Can you think of values that you hold which are different from those of your parents? How did you come to develop these values?*

Fidelity represents an extensively developed sense of trust. In infancy, it was important to trust others, especially parents; now it is important to be trustworthy oneself. In addition, adolescents now transfer their trust from their parents to other people who can help guide them through life. These may be mentors or loved ones. Love is part of the avenue toward identity, says Erikson. By becoming intimate and sharing thoughts and feelings with another person, the adolescent offers up his or her own tentative identity, sees it reflected in the loved one, and is better able to clarify the self.

Adolescent intimacies differ from mature intimacy, which will involve commitment, sacrifice, and compromise. According to Erikson, mature intimacy cannot occur until after a person has achieved a stable identity. But this sequence describes males' development. Erikson's theory considers women's development as a deviation from a male norm. He said that women achieve identity and intimacy at the same time: An adolescent girl puts her identity aside as she prepares to define herself through the man she will marry. This male orientation has brought criticisms of Erikson's theory. We will now look at a line of research that has explored differences between males' and females' identity development.

RESEARCH ON IDENTITY

Vicky and Jason, and many of their friends, are about to graduate from high school. Vicky's friend Vanessa knows exactly what she is going to do with her life. Vanessa's mother, union leader at a plastics factory, has arranged for Vanessa to enter an apprenticeship program at the factory. Vanessa has never considered doing anything else.

Jason still has no idea of what he wants to do, but he is not worried. Thanks to a scholarship offered by the mayor's office, he expects to go to college, take courses that sound interesting, and make up his mind when he is ready.

Vicky has looked at her interests and her talents and is planning to become a social worker. She has narrowed down her college choices and has applied to three schools—one she is fairly sure of getting into, one "safe" school which she is positive will admit her, and one selective "reach" school, which may not. She knows that her college experiences will either confirm her interest in social work or lead her in another direction. She is open to both possibilities.

Jason's closest friend Jared is agonizing over his future. Should he attend a community college—or join the army? He cannot decide what to do now, or what he wants to do in the long run.

TABLE 16-1

CRITERIA FOR IDENTITY STATUSES		
	POSITION ON OCCUPATION AND IDEOLOGY	
IDENTITY STATUS	CRISIS (PERIOD OF CONSIDERING ALTERNATIVES)	COMMITMENT (ADHERENCE TO A PATH OF ACTION)
Identity achievement	Present	Present
Foreclosure	Absent	Present
Identity diffusion	Present or absent	Absent
Moratorium	In crisis	Present but vague

SOURCE: Adapted from Marcia, 1980.

All four of these high school seniors are wrestling with identity formation. What accounts for the differences in the way they are going about it—and in the eventual results?

Identity Statuses: Crisis and Commitment

According to the psychologist James E. Marcia, these students are in four different statuses of ego development. Marcia expanded and clarified Erikson's theory by designating several identity statuses and correlating them with other aspects of personality.

Marcia defines identity as "an internal, self-constructed, dynamic organization of drives, abilities, beliefs, and individual history" (1980, p. 159). He identified four statuses, differing according to the presence or absence of *crisis* and *commitment,* the two elements that Erikson maintained were crucial to forming identity. (See Table 16-1.) Marcia defines *crisis* as a period of conscious decision making, and *commitment* as a personal investment in an occupation or a system of beliefs (ideology). To evaluate identity status, he developed a 30-minute semistructured interview. (See Table 16-2.)

Marcia related these identity statuses to such personality characteristics as anxiety, self-esteem, moral reasoning, and patterns of behavior. These categories are not permanent; they change as people continue to develop (Marcia, 1979). People commonly move from foreclosure, to moratorium, to achievement (Kroger & Haslett, 1991, in Kroger, 1993). Building on Marcia's theory, other researchers identified a number of family and personality variables related to identity status. (See Table 16-3.)

Based on their answers, Marcia classified people into one of four categories:

1 *Foreclosure* (*commitment with no crisis*). Vanessa is in this category. She has made commitments but, instead of questioning them and exploring other possible choices (going through the crisis period), has accepted other people's plans for her life. Her strong point is a rigid strength: She is happy and self-assured, sometimes even smug and self-satisfied. She has close family ties, be-

crisis *Period of conscious decision making related to identity formation.*

commitment *Personal investment in an occupation or a system of beliefs.*

foreclosure *Identity status described by Marcia in which a person who has not spent time considering alternatives (that is, has not been in crisis) is committed to other people's plans for his or her life.*

TABLE 16-2

IDENTITY-STATUS INTERVIEW	
SAMPLE QUESTIONS	**TYPICAL ANSWERS FOR THE FOUR STATUSES**
About occupational commitment: "How willing do you think you'd be to give up going into _____ if something better came along?"	*Identity achievement.* "Well, I might, but I doubt it. I can't see what 'something better' would be for me." *Foreclosure.* "Not very willing. It's what I've always wanted to do. The folks are happy with it and so am I." *Identity confusion.* "Oh, sure. If something better came along, I'd change just like that." *Moratorium.* "I guess that if I knew for sure, I could answer that better. It would have to be something in the general area—something related. . . . "
About ideological commitment: "Have you ever had any doubts about your religious beliefs?"	*Identity achievement.* "Yes, I even started wondering whether there is a God. I've pretty much resolved that now, though. The way it seems to me is. . . . " *Foreclosure.* "No, not really; our family is pretty much in agreement on these things." *Identity confusion.* "Oh, I don't know. I guess so. Everyone goes through some sort of stage like that. But it really doesn't bother me much. I figure that one religion is about as good as another!" *Moratorium.* "Yes, I guess I'm going through that now. I just don't see how there can be a God and still so much evil in the world or. . . . "

SOURCE: Adapted from Marcia, 1966.

TABLE 16-3

FAMILY AND PERSONALITY FACTORS ASSOCIATED WITH ADOLESCENTS IN FOUR IDENTITY STATUSES*				
FACTOR	**IDENTITY ACHIEVEMENT**	**MORATORIUM**	**FORECLOSURE**	**IDENTITY CONFUSION**
FAMILY	Parents encourage autonomy and connection with teachers; differences are explored within a context of mutuality.	Adolescents are often involved in an ambivalent struggle with parental authority.	Parents are overly involved with their children; families avoid expressing differences; parents use denial and repression to avoid dealing with unwelcome thoughts and events.	Parents are laissez-faire in child-rearing attitudes; are rejecting or not available to children.
PERSONALITY	High levels of ego development, moral reasoning, internal locus of control, self-certainty, self-esteem, performance under stress, and intimacy.	Most anxious and fearful of success; high levels of ego development, moral reasoning, and self-esteem.	Highest levels of authoritarianism and stereotypical thinking, obedience to authority, external locus of control, dependent relationships, low levels of anxiety.	Mixed results, with low levels of ego development, moral reasoning, cognitive complexity, and self-certainty; poor cooperative abilities with others

*These associations have emerged from a number of separate studies. Since they have all been correlational, rather than longitudinal, it is impossible to say that any factor caused placement in any identity status.
SOURCE: Kroger, 1993.

lieves in law and order, likes to follow a powerful leader (like her mother), and becomes dogmatic when her opinions are questioned.

2 *Moratorium* (*crisis, no commitment*). Jared, still in crisis, is struggling with a decision, seems to be heading for a commitment, and will probably achieve identity. He is lively, talkative—and in conflict. He is close to his mother—and competitive and anxious. He is also wrestling with issues of intimacy: He wants to have a girlfriend but has not yet developed a close relationship.

3 *Identity achievement* (*crisis leading to commitment*). Vicky is in this category. She has devoted much thought to major issues in her life (the crisis period), she has made choices, and she now expresses strong commitment to those choices. As an identity achiever, she has *flexible strength:* She is thoughtful but not so introspective that she is paralyzed. She has a sense of humor, functions well under stress, is capable of intimate relationships, and holds to her standards while being open to new ideas.

4 *Identity confusion* (*no commitment, crisis uncertain*). In a carefree way, Jason has considered options, but so far has avoided commitment. Some others in this category are aimless drifters without goals. They tend to be superficial or unhappy, and they are often lonely because they have not made commitments to people.

What do you think? *Describe a time in your life when you fit into one or more of Marcia's categories. Give particulars.*

Gender Differences in Identity Formation

Sigmund Freud's statement "Biology is destiny" implies that the different patterns of development seen in males and females in almost all cultures are an inevitable result of their anatomical differences. Today, psychologists generally believe that "socialization is destiny"—that most differences between males and females arise from societal attitudes and practices, although some research suggests differing rates of maturation between the sexes. (See Box 16-1.) Whatever the reasons, the sexes differ in the struggle to define identity. Only in recent years have researchers explored the female quest for identity.

Research on Female Identity Formation. After studying girls and women, Carol Gilligan concluded that the female definition of self is less concerned with achieving a separate identity than with relationships with others. Girls and women judge themselves on their responsibilities and their ability to care for others as well as themselves. Even highly achieving women attain identity more through cooperation than through competition (Gilligan, 1982, 1987; L. M. Brown & Gilligan, 1990).

James E. Marcia (1979) modified his original interviews to explore issues of female identity. He added questions about attitudes toward premarital intercourse, views on women's role, and concerns related to lifestyle. His findings were surprising: Men in moratorium (those who were in crisis but had not yet made commitments) most closely resembled men who had achieved identity. But the women who most closely resembled the men in the identity achievement category were in foreclosure: They had made a commitment but had not undergone a personal crisis.

Why should this be? Marcia says that society pressures women to carry on

---

moratorium *Identity status described by Marcia in which a person is currently considering alternatives (in crisis) and seems headed for commitment.*

identity achievement *Identity status described by Marcia, which is characterized by commitment to choices made following a crisis period, a period spent in thinking about alternatives.*

identity confusion *Identity status described by Marcia, which is characterized by absence of commitment and which may not follow a period of considering alternatives.*

The psychologist Carol Gilligan has studied females' identity formation in adolescence and adulthood and concluded that girls and women achieve identity differently from boys and men. The female route is less through competition and more through cooperation.

BOX 16-1 ■ FOOD FOR THOUGHT

GENDER DIFFERENCES IN PERSONALITY DEVELOPMENT

According to popular wisdom, Vicky and Jason are bound to develop differently: She as a girl will mature earlier and be more empathic, and he as a boy is more aggressive. But in 80 years of research about development, this belief has rarely been investigated scientifically. Now a statistical analysis of 65 studies of personality growth, involving about 9000 subjects, *has* found gender differences (L. D. Cohn, 1991). Adolescent girls apparently do mature earlier in some ways. The difference is small in general and most notable in junior high and high school; it declines markedly among college-age adults and disappears entirely among older men and women. This lessening of gender differences may be the result of maturation.

The analysis used research conducted on the Washington University Sentence Completion Test, which consists of 36 sentence stems that respondents have to complete. Examples are "At times she (he) worried about . . .," and "A woman (man) should always . . . ."

Overall, gender differences in personality development showed females to be more advanced. Such differences arose by late childhood, increased at about age 13, and were fairly large throughout adolescence. When boys were still egocentric, girls had moved toward social conformity; when boys began to be conformists, girls were becoming more self-aware. It's ironic that boys are often granted earlier dating privileges, independence, and freedom from adult supervision when it's the girls who are more mature.

Gender differences in personality development seem to stem from differences in boys' and girls' social experiences, like the differences in their play. The looser structure of girls' games, which are less rule-bound than those played by boys, may foster the development of moral reasoning. The small groups in which girls play provide more opportunities for conversation and for mimicking adult relationships than do the large groups common in boys' play. Furthermore, children may attach their own meanings to social roles: The competitiveness encouraged in boys may reinforce a tendency toward impulsiveness that all children have, but which is discouraged in girls.

Later in life, both men and women base their moral reasoning on issues related to both justice (as in Lawrence Kohlberg's theory) and care (as in Carol Gilligan's), supporting the belief that "a single path toward maturity exists for both sexes" (L. D. Cohn, 1991, p. 263).

---

social values from one generation to the next, and therefore stability of identity is extremely important for them. He suggests that for women, foreclosure of identity is just as adaptive as a struggle to achieve identity. (However, with the many changes that have taken place over the past few decades in women's roles, identity foreclosure may no longer be adaptive for them.)

Erikson's and Marcia's belief that identity and intimacy develop together for women is supported by research indicating that intimacy matters more to girls than to boys, even in grade school friendships (Blyth & Foster-Clarke, 1987).

Research on Female Self-Esteem. An analysis of interviews with 99 girls in several age groups showed that girls' confidence in themselves and in their perceptions of the world stays fairly high until age 11 or 12. Until then they tend to be perceptive about relationship issues and assertive about their feelings. But when they hit adolescence, they accept stereotyped notions of how they should be and repress their true feelings for the sake of being "nice" (L. M. Brown & Gilligan, 1990).

As they recognize that they are burying parts of themselves, which means they can no longer have authentic relationships, their confidence falters. Only those who continue to be honest with themselves and others by acknowledging their true feelings and expressing them appropriately are able to stay in healthy relationship with themselves, with others, and with the society they are entering, says Gilligan. These girls' self-esteem remains high, they see themselves as competent, and they are more likely to go on to nontraditional careers.

Identity development is especially complicated for young people from minority-group backgrounds. Adults can help young people form a positive sense of themselves, celebrating their cultural heritage and physical appearance.

A survey sponsored by the American Association of University Women (AAUW) of 3000 children in grades 4 through 10 (2400 girls and 600 boys) yielded similar results (Daley, 1991). Although boys' self-esteem dropped, too, by high school age they were still ahead of the girls, and the drop was less steep.

What do you think? *Why do you think self-esteem drops when boys and girls are adolescent? How can adults help teenagers raise self-esteem?*

The AAUW survey also found culture a factor in self-esteem. Many more black girls were still confident in high school compared with white and Latina girls; white girls lost their self-assurance earliest of all three groups. African American girls may feel more self-confident because they often see strong women around them. They seem less dependent on school achievement for their self-esteem, drawing their sense of themselves more from family and community. Ethnicity is a prominent issue in the development of self-esteem.

Ethnic Factors in Identity Formation

Identity development is especially complicated for young people from minority-group backgrounds. Some research using Marcia's (1966) identity-status measures shows a larger proportion of minority-group adolescents than white adolescents scoring in "foreclosure" (Spencer & Markstrom-Adams, 1990). This may be adaptive. For example, Hispanic adolescents in predominantly Hispanic communities may pick up messages that they will find social recognition, strength, and a robust sense of ethnic identity by following the norms of their culture.

What happens when a young person confronts conflicting values between the larger society and the ethnic community, as, say, when a Native American is expected to participate in a tribal ceremony being held on a day when she or he is supposed to be in school? Or when young people internalize (take other people's standards as their own) popular prejudice against their racial or ethnic group? Or when parents uncomfortable with such issues do not discuss them with their children? All these situations can cause identity confusion.

One review of the literature concludes that skin color, language differences, physical features, and stereotyped social standing are extremely important in molding self-concept and that adults can help young people form a positive sense of themselves (Spencer & Markstrom-Adams, 1990). Some steps to foster healthy identity formation among minority-group children include encouraging them to stay in school, caring for their physical and mental health, encouraging social support systems like kin networks and religious centers, and stressing their cultural heritage (Spencer & Markstrom-Adams, 1990).

ACHIEVING SEXUAL IDENTITY

How do adolescents achieve sexual identity? And how do they deal with their parents concerning this exciting yet stressful new aspect of their lives?

A profound change in an adolescent's life is the movement from close friendships only with people of the same sex to friendships and romantic attachments with members of the other sex—or for homosexual people, same-sex romantic feelings. Seeing oneself as a sexual being, coming to terms with one's sexual stirrings, and developing an intimate romantic relationship—all these are critical aspects of achieving sexual identity.

Adolescents' self-images and relationships with peers and parents are bound up with sexuality. Sexual activity—casual kissing, necking and petting, and genital contact—fulfills a number of adolescents' needs, only one of which is physical pleasure. Teenagers become sexually active for many reasons: to enhance intimacy, to seek new experience, to prove their maturity, to keep up with their peers, to find relief from pressures, and to investigate the mysteries of love.

Studying Adolescents' Sexuality

It is difficult to do research on sexuality. Virtually every study about sex—from Kinsey's surveys in the 1940s to those being done now—has been criticized for inaccuracy on the basis that people who answer questions about sex tend to be sexually active and liberal in their attitude toward sex and are not a representative sample of the population. Also, there is no way to corroborate what people say: Some may lie to conceal their sexual activities while others may exaggerate. The problems multiply when surveying young people. For one, parental consent is often needed for the participation of minors, and parents who grant permission may not be typical. Still, even if we cannot generalize findings to the population as a whole, within the groups that take part in surveys we can see trends over time, which reveal changes in sexual mores.

Sexual Attitudes and Behavior

Masturbation. *Masturbation,* or sexual self-stimulation, is the first sexual experience for most people. It is an almost universal practice, yet there has been little research on it.

masturbation *Sexual self-stimulation.*

The research we do have shows an increase since the early 1960s in the number of adolescents who say they masturbate (Dreyer, 1982). In the early 1970s, 50 percent of boys and 30 percent of girls under age 15 said they masturbated; in the late 1970s, 70 percent of boys and 45 percent of girls under 15 admitted to it. Apparently, a significant change did take place, even though we do not know whether boys and girls actually did masturbate more or whether they were simply more willing to say they did.

Still, teenagers continue to regard masturbation as shameful; fewer than one-third questioned by Coles and Stokes (1985) said they felt no guilt about it. This suggests that attitudes toward masturbation have changed more radically among sex educators than among teenagers. Educators today stress that masturbation is normal and healthy, that it cannot cause physical harm, that it helps people learn how to give and receive sexual pleasure, and that it provides a way to gratify sexual desire without entering into a relationship for which a person is not emotionally ready.

sexual orientation *Focus of sexuality, either heterosexual or homosexual.*

Sexual Orientation. It is in adolescence that a person's *sexual orientation* is usually expressed: whether that person will consistently be sexually, romantically, and affectionately interested in members of the other sex *(heterosexual)* or in persons of the same sex *(homosexual).*

heterosexual *Sexually, romantically, and affectionately interested in members of the other sex.*

In one study of 38,000 students in grades 7 through 12, 88.2 percent described themselves as predominantly heterosexual, 1.1 percent as predominantly homo-

homosexual *Sexually, romantically, and affectionately interested in members of the same sex.*

sexual or bisexual (being interested in members of both sexes), and 10.7 percent were unsure of their sexual orientation (Remafedi, Resnick, Blum, & Harris, 1992). The older students were more certain about their sexual orientation than the younger ones: 25.9 percent of 12-year-olds were unsure of their sexual orientation, compared with only 5 percent of 18-year-olds. Those who were "unsure" were more likely to report having homosexual fantasies and attractions and were less likely to have had heterosexual experiences (Remafedi et al., 1992).

What Determines Sexual Orientation?   Why do people become heterosexual or homosexual? Much of the research on this question has been spurred by efforts to explain homosexuality. The oldest theory is that homosexuality represents a kind of mental illness. But several decades of objective scientific research have found no association between homosexuality and emotional or social problems (APA, undated). These findings (along with political lobbying and changes in public attitudes) eventually led the American Psychiatric Association to stop classifying homosexuality as a "mental disorder." The most recent edition of the *Diagnostic and Statistical Manual of Mental Disorders* contains no references at all to homosexuality (DSM-IV, 1994).

Other theories consider biological factors, a family with a dominating mother and a weak father (thought by some to cause male homosexuality), and chance learning (developing a preference for one's own sex after having been seduced by a homosexual). No scientific support has been found for family constellation or chance learning as a cause, but there is some evidence for a biological origin. One report linked male homosexuality to a small region of one chromosome (Hamer et al., 1993), and the same researchers are now looking at the chromosomes of female homosexuals.

According to one theory, sexual orientation is determined by a complex prenatal process involving both hormonal and neurological factors (Ellis & Ames, 1987). If the levels of sex hormones in a fetus of either sex are in the typical female range between the second and fifth months of gestation, the person will be attracted to males after puberty. If the hormone levels are in the male range, the person will be attracted to females. Another finding—of differences in an area of the brain that governs sexual behavior—also points to a possible biological origin for homosexuality (LeVay, 1991). If there is such a predisposition toward either heterosexuality or homosexuality, social and environmental influences would have to be very strong to overcome the original biological programming.

The prevailing view today is that there are a number of reasons why a person becomes heterosexual or homosexual, that for most people sexual orientation is shaped at an early age, that it is not a conscious choice, and that interaction among biological, social, and psychological factors is crucial (American Psychological Association, APA, undated).

Homosexuality.   Many young people have one or more homosexual experiences as they are growing up, usually before age 15. But isolated experiences, or even homosexual attractions or fantasies, do not determine eventual sexual orientation; few go on to make this a regular pattern. Only about 3 percent of adolescent boys and 2 percent of girls have ongoing homosexual relationships, even though about 15 percent of boys and 10 percent of girls have had a homosexual contact during adolescence (Chilman, 1980). The incidence of homosexuality seems to be similar in a number of cultures (Hyde, 1986).

Over the past 50 years attitudes toward sexuality have changed, to include the approval of premarital sex in a loving relationship and a decline in the double standard by which males are freer sexually than females. Most teenagers are not promiscuous; if they are sexually active, it is usually within a monogamous relationship.

Although many people have sought treatment to change their own sexual orientation or that of a child, there is no good evidence that such therapy works (APA, 1990). Furthermore, many mental health providers question the ethics of trying to alter a trait that is not a disorder and that is important to a person's identity (APA, undated).

Attitudes, Behavior, and the "Sexual Evolution."   The early 1920s through the late 1970s witnessed a sexual *evolution* (rather than a *revolution*), both in what people do sexually and in how they feel about their sexual behavior. There has been a steady trend toward acceptance of more sexual activity in more situations. One change has been the approval of premarital sex in a loving relationship. Another is a decline in the *double standard*—the code that gives males more sexual freedom than females. The sexual evolution may have reached a plateau or may even be reversing itself; but meanwhile, like the rest of the population, today's teenagers are more sexually active and liberal than the generation before them. This is especially true of girls.

In 1965, at a large southern university, 33 percent of the male students and 70 percent of the females believed that premarital sexual intercourse was immoral. By 1985, there was a much closer correspondence between the sexes, with only 15.9 percent of the males and 17.1 percent of the females thinking this (I. Robinson, Ziss, Ganza, Katz, & Robinson, 1991). Rates for premarital sexual activity also rose, especially for women. (See Table 16-4.) By age 18 more than half of women and almost three-fourths of men have had intercourse (Alan Guttmacher Institute, AGI, 1994).

The double standard is not dead, though. In a telephone survey of 500 high school students, more boys said that sex was a pleasurable experience and that they felt good about their sexual experiences so far, and more girls said that they were in love with their last sexual partner and that they should have waited until they were older before having sex (Lewin, 1994). College students consider a

TABLE 16-4

PREMARITAL SEXUAL INTERCOURSE AMONG COLLEGE STUDENTS		
	MALES, PERCENT	FEMALES, PERCENT
1965	65.1	28.7
1970	65.0	37.3
1975	73.9	57.1
1980	77.4	63.5
1985	79.3	63.0

SOURCE: I. Robinson, Ziss, Ganza, Katz, & Robinson, 1991.

woman with many sexual partners more immoral than such a man, and college men still hold more liberal attitudes than college women (I. Robinson et al., 1991).

A study of 1880 fifteen- to nineteen-year-old males drew a profile of the average sexually active boy. During the previous year he had had relationships with two girls at different times, each one lasting a few months; and for long periods of time—as much as six months—he had had no sexual partner (Sonenstein, Pleck, & Ku, 1991). A girl is likely to have her first sexual relations with a steady boyfriend; a boy is likely to have his with someone he knows casually (Dreyer, 1982; Zelnik, Kantner, & Ford, 1981; Zelnik & Shah, 1983).

There is often a discrepancy between what people of any age *say* about sex and what they *do*. Most teenagers apparently become sexually active earlier than they say they *should*. In one poll (Louis Harris & Associates, 1986), teenagers gave a median age of 18 as the "right age" to start having intercourse, even though most of the 17-year-olds and nearly half of the 16-year-olds were no longer virgins. (See Table 16-5.) In another study, focused on 3500 junior high and high school students, 83 percent of nonvirgins gave a "best age for first intercourse" higher than the age at which they had experienced it themselves, and 88 percent of young mothers gave an older "best age for first birth" than their own ages at first birth (Zabin, Hirsch, Smith, & Hardy, 1984). Many adolescents, then, hold "values and attitudes consistent with responsible sexual conduct, but not all of them are able to translate these attitudes into personal behavior" (Zabin et al., 1984, p. 181).

Most very young teenagers are still virgins—84 percent of 13-year-olds, 77 percent of 14-year-olds, and 70 percent of the 15-year-olds. Those who begin having sexual relations early are often coerced into it by an older man (AGI, 1994). Teenage girls (and, to a lesser extent, boys) often feel under pressure to engage in activities they do not feel ready for. Social pressure was the chief reason given by

TABLE 16-5

INCIDENCE OF SEXUAL INTERCOURSE, 1988		
	MALES, PERCENT	FEMALES, PERCENT
By age 15	33	25
By age 19	86	80

SOURCES: London, Masher, Pratt, & Williams, 1989; Pratt, 1990; Sonenstein, Pleck, & Ku, 1989; as reported in B. C. Miller & Moore, 1990.

TABLE 16-6

FACTORS ASSOCIATED WITH TIMING OF FIRST INTERCOURSE		
	FACTORS ASSOCIATED WITH EARLY AGE	FACTORS ASSOCIATED WITH LATER AGE
Timing of puberty	Early	Late
Personality style	Risk-taking, impulsive	Traditional values, religious orientation
Substance use	Use of drugs, alcohol, tobacco	Nonuse
Education	Fewer years of schooling	More years of schooling; valuing academic achievement
Family structure	Single-parent family	Two-parent family
Socioeconomic status	Disadvantaged	Advantaged
Race	African American	White, Latino

SOURCES: B. C. Miller & Moore, 1990; Sonnenstein, Pleck, & Ku, 1991.

73 percent of the girls and 50 percent of the boys in the Harris poll when asked why many teenagers do not wait for sex until they are older. One-fourth of the teenagers reported that they had felt pressured to go further sexually than they wanted to. Both boys and girls also mentioned curiosity as a reason for early sex; more boys than girls cited sexual feelings and desires. Only 6 percent of the boys and 11 percent of the girls gave love as a reason. Various social and psychological factors also exert influence. (See Table 16-6.)

A major reason for concern about early sexual activity is the risk of pregnancy (discussed later in this chapter) and of STDs (see Chapter 14). Teenagers who can go to their parents or other adults with questions about sex have a better chance of avoiding some of the common problems associated with burgeoning sexual activity—and a better chance of achieving a mature sexual identity.

Communicating with Parents about Sex

Many parent-teen conflicts are about sex. Vicky's parents dislike her boyfriend, do not want her with him when no adults are home, and do not want her to stay out late with him. They may be protective of their daughter partly because they are uncomfortable with their own sexuality and thus are unsure of how to handle Vicky's.

Parents' values *are* more liberal now than they used to be. Today's parents are more likely to help a pregnant daughter than to punish her or cast her out. Today's parents may worry about whether their daughter's boyfriend should share her bedroom when she brings him home from college for a weekend, but parents of 30 years ago would not have admitted knowing that a daughter was sexually active—and she would not have told them.

An extensive survey of teenagers' views on and experience with sex found that parents' guidance is overwhelmingly positive. Only 3 percent of the teenagers recalled their parents' telling them that sex was not normal and healthy. Yet communication about sex is a problem in many families. Parents often think they have said more than their children have heard. One 15-year-old mother said, "[My mother said] she'd told me to come to her when it was time for me to have sex and she'd get me some birth control, but she must have said it *very* softly" (Coles & Stokes, 1985, p. 37).

Almost one-third (31 percent) of American teenagers and 28 percent of sexually active teenagers have never talked to their parents about sex. Close to half (42 percent) are nervous or afraid to bring it up. Almost two-thirds (64 percent) have never discussed birth control at home (Louis Harris & Associates, 1986). Teenagers who *have* talked to their parents about sex in general and birth control in particular are more likely to use it consistently that those who have not.

But adolescents' ambivalence makes it hard for their parents to talk to them about sex. Although teenagers say they would like to be frank with their parents about sexual behavior, they resent being questioned and tend to consider their sexual activities nobody else's business. Still, when parents ignore obvious signs of sexual activity, young people sometimes become puzzled and angry. Said one 16-year-old girl, looking to the future, "I'm not going to pretend that I don't know what's happening. If my daughter comes in at five in the morning, her skirt backwards and wearing some guy's sweater, I'm not going to ask her, 'Did you have a nice time at the movies?' . . . I don't plan to fail!" (R. C. Sorensen, 1973, p. 61).

SOCIAL ASPECTS OF PERSONALITY DEVELOPMENT IN ADOLESCENCE

One aspect of the search for identity is the need to become independent of parents. Sometimes the identity search is through the peer group. So let's look at adolescent's relationships with parents and peers.

adolescent rebellion
Pattern of tumult that may involve conflict with family, alienation from adult society, and hostility toward adults' values.

In the United States and other western cultures the teenage years have often been seen as a time of **adolescent rebellion,** involving conflict within the family, alienation from adult society, and hostility toward adults' values. Yet studies of adolescents find that fewer than 1 out of 5 fit this pattern of tumult (Offer, Ostrov, & Howard, 1989).

Age does become a powerful bonding agent in adolescence—more powerful than race, religion, community, or sex. American teenagers spend much of their free time with people their own age, with whom they feel comfortable and can identify. They have their best times with their friends, with whom they feel free, open, involved, excited, and motivated. These are the people they most want to be with. Young people are caught up in "generational chauvinism": They tend to believe that most other adolescents share their personal values and that most older people do not (Csikszentmihalyi & Larson, 1984; R. C. Sorensen, 1973).

Nevertheless, adolescents' rejection of parental values is often partial, temporary, or superficial. Teenagers' values tend to remain closer to their parents' values than many people realize. "Adolescent rebellion" often amounts to little more than a series of minor skirmishes.

RELATIONSHIPS WITH PARENTS

The stereotype—that parents and teenagers do not like each other and do not get along with each other—may have been born in the first formal theory of adolescence, that of psychologist G. Stanley Hall. Hall (1904/1916) believed that young people's efforts to adjust to their changing bodies and to the imminent demands of adulthood usher in a period of "storm and stress," which inevitably leads to conflict between the generations. Sigmund Freud (1935/1953) and his daughter, Anna Freud (1946), also thought that parent-child friction was inevitable, growing out of adolescents' need to free themselves from dependency on their parents. But the anthropologist Margaret Mead (1928, 1935), who studied adolescence in other cultures, concluded that when a culture provides a serene and gradual transition from childhood to adulthood, adolescent rebellion is not typical. Peaceful transitions are most likely to occur in cultures where social change is minimal.

But even in dynamic societies, recent research indicates that rebellion need not be a symptom of adolescence. Despite some conflicts, most American adolescents feel close to and positive about their parents, have similar values on major issues, and value their parents' approval (Hill, 1987; Offer, Ostrov, & Howard, 1989). Teenagers who are very rebellious may well need special help.

An Ambivalent Relationship

Young people feel a constant tension between their need to break away from their parents and their dependency on them. Parents have mixed feelings themselves.

"This song is dedicated to our parents, and is in the form of a plea for more adequate supervision."

The title of this song could well be "Ambivalence." Rock music and outrageous outfits may be symbols of a teenager's need to break away from parents and dependency on them. But, like these young musicians, most adolescents do not want to break away too far or too fast. (Drawing by Koren; ©1991 The New Yorker Magazine, Inc.)

Torn between wanting their children to be independent and wanting to keep them dependent, parents find it hard to let go. As a result, parents give teenage children "double messages," saying one thing but communicating the opposite by their actions. Conflict is more likely to surface between adolescents and their mothers rather than their fathers (Steinberg, 1981, 1987a). This may be because mothers have been more closely involved with their children and find it harder to give up their involvement.

Still, the emotions attending this transition do not necessarily lead to a break with either parental or societal values. A number of studies of American teenagers have found little turmoil or chaos (Brooks-Gunn, 1988; Offer et al., 1989). Although teenagers report slightly more negative moods than younger children, they do not talk about wide swings in emotional states, often considered inevitable in adolescence (Larson & Lampman-Petraitis, 1989). Research is fairly consistent in reporting significant conflict in only 15 to 25 percent of families; and these families often had problems *before* the children approached adolescence (W. A. Collins, 1990; Hill, 1987; Offer et al., 1989).

In his classic studies of midwestern boys, Daniel Offer (1969) found a high level of bickering over unimportant issues between 12- and 14-year-olds and their parents, but he found little "turmoil" or "chaos." In a follow-up study of these same boys 8 years later, Offer and Offer (1974) found that most were happy, had a realistic self-image, and were reasonably well-adjusted. Less than one-fifth had experienced a tumultuous adolescence.

Conflict with Parents

Conflict between adolescents and parents is neatly described by the subtitle of one report: "All Families Some of the Time and Some Families Most of the Time" (Montemayor, 1983). This survey of 50 years of literature on relations between adolescents and their parents concludes that the usual conflict is normal and healthy and has taken very similar form over the years.

Parents and teenagers rarely clash over economic, religious, social, and political values. Most arguments are about day-to-day matters like schoolwork, chores, friends, dating, curfews, and personal appearance (Montemayor, 1983; Smetana, Yau, Restrepo, & Braeges, 1991). Later in adolescence, conflict is more likely to revolve around more serious issues, like sexual activity and alcohol use (Carlton-Ford & Collins, 1988). The nature of the conflict is similar in married and divorced families (Smetana et al., 1991).

Discord generally increases during early adolescence, stabilizes in middle adolescence, and then decreases after the young person is about 18 years old. The increased conflict in early adolescence may be related more to puberty than to chronological age, as we noted in Chapter 14. The calmer climate in late adolescence may reflect an eventual adjustment of both parents and teenagers to the momentous changes of early adolescence—or simply the tendency of 18-year-olds to move away from home.

What do you think?   *When teenagers complain that their parents "don't understand" them, do you think they mean that their parents do not know how they feel or that their parents do not sympathize with them? Explain your answer.*

What Adolescents Need from Their Parents

Many arguments between teenagers and their parents are about "how much" and "how soon." How much freedom does Vicky have to schedule her own activities? How soon can Jason take the family car? These are matters of judgment that demand flexible thinking from parents.

Parents have to walk a fine line between granting their adolescents enough independence and protecting them from immature lapses in judgment. If separation or emotional independence from the family comes too early, it can spell trouble for a teenager. This trouble can take the form of alienation, susceptibility to negative peer influences, and such physically or socially unhealthy behavior as drug abuse or premature sexual activity (Steinberg, 1987a; Steinberg & Silverberg, 1986). Still, parents need to let their children take *some* risks. Positive exploration—trying a new activity, making new friends, learning a difficult skill, taking on a new challenge, or resisting peer pressure—poses challenges that lead to growth (Damon, 1984).

The kind of parenting that seems to provide the right balance is, still, authoritative parenting. This offers warmth and acceptance; assertiveness with regard to rules, norms, and values; willingness to listen, explain, and negotiate; and granting of psychological autonomy, encouraging children to form their own opinions (Lamborn, Mounts, Steinberg, & Dornbusch, 1991). Authoritative parents, according to one study, "exert control over the child's behavior, but not over the child's sense of self" (Steinberg & Darling, 1994). Warmth seems to foster the development of self-esteem and social skills, behavioral control helps young people to control their impulses, and granting psychological autonomy helps teenagers become responsible and competent (Steinberg, 1990).

One reason this approach works so well with teenagers is that it takes their cognitive growth into account. By explaining their reasons, parents acknowledge that adolescents can evaluate situations intelligently. This kind of approach also leads to higher school performance (Steinberg & Darling, 1994). The stronger the parents' interest in their teenagers' lives, the more likely the teenagers are to get high marks.

For adolescents as well as younger children, authoritative parenting seems to foster the development of self-esteem and social skills, promote the ability to control impulses, and help in becoming responsible and competent.

How Adolescents Are Affected by Their Parents' Life Situation

Parents' Employment. Most research about how parents' work affects adolescents refers to a mother's employment. In one study, 7 out of 10 teenagers said that their mothers' working had either positive effects or no effects on them (General Mills, Inc., 1981). Teenagers may like the independence they feel when their mothers are out of the house and therefore less likely to direct the adolescents' activities.

Adolescent children of working mothers tend to be better adjusted socially than other teenagers, feel better about themselves, have more of a sense of belonging, and get along better with their families and friends (Gold & Andres, 1978). On the negative side, teenage children of working mothers tend to spend less time on homework and reading and more time watching television (Milne, Myers, Rosenthal, & Ginsburg, 1986). With less supervision, they may be more subject to peer pressure leading to behavior problems.

In the 1950s, the 1960s, and the 1970s, when most mothers who could afford to stay home did so, some research pointed to certain differences between children of employed and at-home mothers. For example, adolescent sons of working women held less stereotyped views of the female role. The daughters of employed women had higher and less gender-stereotyped career aspirations, were more outgoing, scored higher on several academic measures, and seemed better adjusted on social and personality measures (L. W. Hoffman, 1979). More recent analysis, however, suggests that a mother's work status is just one of many factors that shape attitudes toward women's roles (Galambos, Petersen, & Lenerz, 1988).

Maternal employment in itself does not seem to affect teenagers much either way. Whatever effect it has is filtered through other factors, like the warmth in a relationship or a mother's satisfaction with her roles as mother and worker. Teenage sons of working mothers are likely to have more flexible attitudes toward gender roles when they have warm relationships with their mothers, and teenage daughters show unstereotyped gender-role attitudes when their mothers are happy with their own roles (Galambos et al., 1988).

When Adolescents Care for Themselves.   Because his mother is working, Jason, like many other adolescents, is responsible for himself for at least part of the day. Lack of supervision does not in itself leave preteens and young teenagers especially vulnerable to peer pressure. The differences that do show up depend on the nature of self-care, parents' involvement with the self-care, and parenting styles.

Laurence Steinberg (1986) gave questionnaires to 865 ten- to fifteen-year-olds in Madison, Wisconsin. They were asked what they would do in various hypothetical situations involving antisocial behavior (like stealing, vandalism, or cheating on a test) if a "best friend" suggested one course when they really thought something else was right. Students who stayed home alone after school (where they could be in telephone contact with their parents, could follow an agreed-upon schedule of homework and chores, and were in a familiar environment that reminded them of family values) were no more influenced by their friends than were those who were at home with adults or older siblings. But the further removed youngsters were from even the possibility of adult supervision, the more influenced they were by peers. Thus, teenagers who spent time unsupervised at a friend's house were more influenced than those who stayed home alone, and the ones who just "hung out" with a group were most influenced. Yet even in this last group, students whose parents knew where they were turned out to be only slightly more vulnerable to peer pressure. Apparently, these teenagers had internalized parental standards.

Although this study emphasizes the differences among "self-care" adolescents, we need more research before we can draw general conclusions. For one thing, since most of the subjects were suburban, the findings might not apply to young people in the country or in big cities, especially inner-city neighborhoods. For another, it is not clear whether adult supervision lessens susceptibility to peer pressure or whether adolescents who are more peer-oriented resist parental supervision. Finally, these subjects were responding to hypothetical situations; their responses may have been very different from their behavior in real life. Another study of young people from the same schools, however, did find that responses to hypothetical situations correlated with youngsters' reports of actual misconduct (B. B. Brown, Clasen, & Eicher, 1986). So this approach may be able to predict actual behavior.

Adolescents with Single Parents.   Jason's smooth adolescence is not typical in one regard. Adolescents who do not live with their biological fathers run a greater risk of giving in to peer pressure and getting into trouble, and this risk is not alleviated by the mother's remarriage. A nationwide study of 6710 twelve- to seventeen-year-olds found that, across socioeconomic levels, teenagers living with only their mothers were more likely to be truant, run away from home, smoke, have discipline problems in school, or get into trouble with the police (Dornbusch et al., 1985). But the presence of another adult in the home—like a grandparent or a friend of the mother, but *not* a stepfather—lowers the risk almost to the level found in two-parent families, especially for boys. This suggests that some of the problems in single-parent homes may be due to the many pressures on the mother and that nontraditional family groupings can help relieve this pressure and help keep adolescents out of trouble.

In another study, Steinberg (1987b) analyzed the answers of the 865 Wisconsin adolescents whom he had studied and came to a similar conclusion. Adolescents living with both natural parents were less likely to be influenced to commit antisocial acts by their friends than were those in either single-parent homes or stepfamilies. Only among the oldest children was the presence of a stepfather even slightly helpful in lowering susceptibility to peer pressure.

Since single and remarried mothers are less likely to be authoritative parents (Dornbusch, Ritter, Leiderman, Roberts, & Fraleigh, 1987), their children's problems may stem from parenting style rather than from the father's absence.

SIBLING RELATIONSHIPS

Vicky, who used to enjoy playing and looking after her younger brother, is spending much less time with Bobby these days. She is typical of most adolescents, whose relationships with their siblings, as well as their parents, change during these years.

In a study of 363 students in grades 3, 6, 9, and 12, Buhrmester and Furman (1990) found that as children grow older, their relationships with their siblings become progressively more equal and more distant. Adolescent siblings still show intimacy, affection, and admiration for their brothers and sisters. But they spend less time with them (Raffaelli & Larson, 1987), and their relationships are less intense. Older siblings exercise less power over younger ones, fight with them less, are not as likely to look to them for companionship, and are not as close to them. As teenagers work at separating from their families, they spend more time with close friends and with people they are romantically involved with. They have less time and less need for the emotional gratification they used to get from the sibling bond.

These changes in relationships seem to be fairly complete by the time the younger sibling is about 12 years old. By this time, children no longer need the same amount of supervision—supervision that has often been given by older brothers and sisters. At the same time the younger siblings are becoming more competent and independent, the relative difference between older and younger siblings is shrinking. (A 6-year-old is vastly more competent than a 3-year-old, but an 18-year-old and a 15-year-old are more equal.) The change in the relationship between younger and older siblings parallels—and may well come before—the same kind of change between adolescents and their parents, with regard to greater equality, more independence, and less authority exerted by the older over the younger.

The changes that occur in sibling relationships differ, depending on a child's place in the family. The older sister or brother has inherited a position of authority and responsibility that she or he never had in relation to either parents or peers. Then, as the younger sibling grows up, the older one has to give up some of the power and status that has been held for years. Maybe this is why so many older siblings look on their younger brothers and sisters as pesky annoyances. On the other hand, the younger ones still look up to their older siblings and try to be more "grown up" by identifying with them.

Spacing has an effect, too. Siblings who are farther apart in years tend to be more affectionate toward each other and to get along better than do those who are close in age. The more frequent quarrels and greater antagonism between closely spaced brothers and sisters probably arise from a greater rivalry between siblings whose capabilities are close enough so that they compare themselves with each other—or are constantly compared by other people. Gender is another factor: Same-sex siblings are usually closer than a brother and sister.

Although these effects of birth order, spacing, and gender have held up across several studies, they are less important in the quality of sibling relationships than are such factors as the temperament of each child, how the parents act toward them, and how old the children are (Stocker, Dunn, & Plomin, 1989). Between ages 9 and 15, the amount of time that young people spend with both their parents and siblings declines dramatically (Larson & Richards, 1991). Although adolescents are alone for many of the hours that they used to be with their families, they also spend more time with friends.

FIGURE 16-1
The people adolescents spend their time with. This graph shows the percentage of self-reports by 2734 high school students for each category of people. Here and in Figure 16-2, 1 percentage point is equivalent to about 1 hour per week spent with the given people or in the given activity.
SOURCE: Adapted from Csikszentmihalyi & Larson, 1984, p. 71.

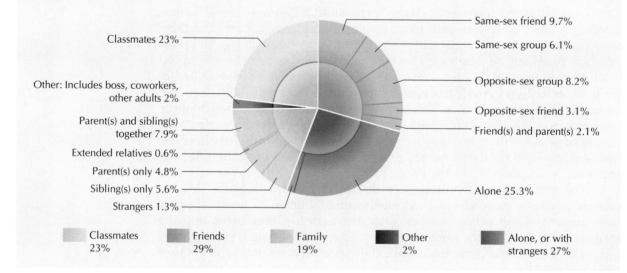

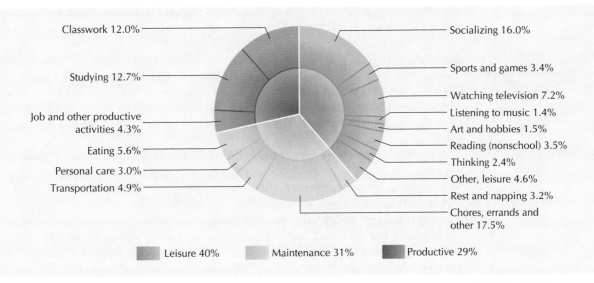

Classwork 12.0%

Studying 12.7%

Job and other productive activities 4.3%

Eating 5.6%

Personal care 3.0%

Transportation 4.9%

Socializing 16.0%

Sports and games 3.4%

Watching television 7.2%

Listening to music 1.4%

Art and hobbies 1.5%

Reading (nonschool) 3.5%

Thinking 2.4%

Other, leisure 4.6%

Rest and napping 3.2%

Chores, errands and other 17.5%

Leisure 40%   Maintenance 31%   Productive 29%

FIGURE 16-2
The things adolescents spend their time doing. SOURCE: Adapted from Csikszentmihalyi & Larson, 1984, p. 63.

RELATIONSHIPS WITH PEERS

Both Vicky and Jason find support in the complex transition of adolescence from their growing involvement with their peers. Adolescents going through rapid physical changes take comfort from being with others going through like changes. As Vicky questions the value of adult standards and the need for parental guidance, she finds it reassuring to turn for advice to friends who can understand and sympathize because they are in the same position themselves. As Jason "tries on" new values, he can test his ideas with his peers with less fear of being ridiculed or "shot down" than he might have with parents or other adults. The peer group is a source of affection, sympathy, and understanding; a place for experimentation; and a supportive setting for achieving autonomy and independence from parents. It is also a place to form intimate relationships with others, providing the basis for adult intimacy (Gecas & Seff, 1990; Coleman, 1980; Newman, 1982). No wonder adolescents like to spend time with their peers!

How Adolescents Spend Their Time—and with Whom

What do teenagers do on a typical day? With whom do they do it? Where do they do it? And how do they feel about what they are doing? To answer these questions, for 1 week 75 high school students in a Chicago suburb carried beepers that rang at random once in every 2 waking hours. Each student was asked to report what she or he was doing at the time the beeper sounded—and where and with whom. From the 4489 self-reports, Csikszentmihalyi & Larson (1984) described what it is like to be a modern teenager.

The results (see Figures 16-1 and 16-2) showed the importance of peers. These adolescents spent more than half their waking hours with friends and classmates and only 5 percent of their time with one or both parents. They were happiest when with friends. Being with the family ranked second; next came being alone; and last, being with classmates. Teenagers have more fun with friends—joking, gossiping, and hanging out—than at home, where activities tend to be more serious and more humdrum.

Friendships in Adolescence

"What *do* you talk about for so long?" Ellen asks, laughing. Vicky has been on the phone for an hour talking with Vanessa, the friend she had left only 45 minutes before picking up the phone. The intensity of friendships is greater in adolescence than at any other time in the life span (Berndt & Perry, 1990).

There is some continuity from middle childhood into adolescence. Both age groups see mutual help, mutual interaction, and mutual liking to be at the core of friendship. At both ages, friendships seem to last about the same lengths of time and to have about the same levels of conflict.

There are also differences. In early adolescence, friends are more intimate and supportive than they had been earlier, they regard loyalty as more critical to a friendship, and they compete less and share more with their friends than do younger children (Berndt & Perry, 1990). The appearance of these features marks a transition to adultlike relationships.

Such changes are due partly to cognitive development. Adolescents are now better able to express their thoughts and feelings and share them with friends. They can also consider another person's point of view better, and so it is easier for them to understand their friends' thoughts and feelings.

Gender affects friendships too. Boys and men tend to count more people as friends than girls and women do, but male friendships are rarely as close as female ones. Emotional support and sharing of confidences are particularly vital to female friendships throughout life (Blyth & Foster-Clark, 1987; Bukowski & Kramer, 1986).

Friendships are likely to be closer and more intense in adolescence than at any other time in the life span. When young people begin to separate from their parents, they look to their close friends for intimacy. This is especially true for girls, who confide more in their friends and count more on their emotional support than boys do.

Adolescents who have close friends are high in self-esteem, consider themselves competent, and do well in school. Those whose friendships are highly conflicted score lower on all these measures (Berndt & Perry, 1990). Adolescents tend to pick friends who are already like them; then too, friends influence each other to become even more alike (Berndt, 1982; Berndt & Perry, 1990). Friends tend to have similar status within the larger peer group (Berndt & Perry, 1990). Similarity is more important to friendship in adolescence than later in life, probably because as teenagers struggle to differentiate themselves from their parents, they need support from people like themselves (L. Weiss & Lowenthal, 1975). This need also shows in the way adolescents imitate each other's behavior and are influenced by peer pressure. As a result, adolescents sometimes find themselves in a tug-of-war between parents and peers.

Adolescents spend more than half their waking hours with other teenagers and only about 5 percent of their time with a parent. Before young people become truly independent, they go from being dependent on parents to being dependent on peers.

Peer Pressure versus Parents' Influence

If the other girls in her group wear tight black leggings and Doc Martens boots, Vicky will not come to school in a plaid skirt and loafers. If her crowd gathers at a fast-food restaurant at night, Vicky will not—at least by choice—spend her evenings in the library. Her friends influence not only her clothes and hairdo but also her social activities, sexual behavior, and use or nonuse of drugs. Members of the adolescent peer group are constantly influencing and being influenced by each other. Even the most outspoken "nonconformists" usually follow the customs of their chosen group.

Still, "peer power" is not everything. Most teenagers have positive ties with their parents (Hill, 1987) and maintain two reference groups—parents and peers. Peers tend to have more to say about everyday social issues; parents have more influence about deeper concerns: what to do about a moral dilemma, what job to take, and what education to pursue (Brittain, 1963; Emmerick, 1978). As adolescents become surer of themselves, they become more autonomous; they are more likely to make up their own minds and to stick with their decisions in the face of disagreement from either parents or peers (Newman, 1982).

Parents' Influence over Adolescents' Choice of Friends

Although parents often feel they have lost any leverage they ever had over their teenage children's choice of friends, they still exert considerable indirect influence. One study of 3781 high school students found significant relationships between parents' behaviors and students' peer groups (B. B. Brown, Mounts, Lamborn, & Steinberg, 1993). The researchers found that such parental practices as monitoring students' behavior and schoolwork, encouraging achievement, and joint decision making were associated with such adolescent behaviors as academic achievement, drug use, and self-reliance. In turn, these behaviors were related to membership in such common adolescent peer groups as "populars jocks, brains, normals, druggies, and outcasts" (p. 471).

It seems that parents help to shape prosocial or antisocial behavior, which then predisposes their children to gravitate toward particular crowds. Thus teenagers whose parents emphasize achievement do better in school. And the teenagers whose behavior is monitored by their parents tend to join the "brains" crowd, whereas the ones who are not monitored and do not take part in joint decision making are more likely to join the "popular" crowd, which is more likely to become involved in drug use.

SOME PROBLEMS OF ADOLESCENCE

Although most people weather adolescence well, some have serious problems. A great deal of research over the years has focused on individual characteristics of troubled adolescents and their families. However, thanks to a recent sensitivity to the context in which young people live, more attention is being paid to the influence of the environment and to reducing young people's exposure to high-risk settings (National Research Council, NRC, 1993a).

One reason teenagers get into trouble is their lack of skills or knowledge; they may not know how to use a condom, when to stop drinking, or when a friend is leading them into dangerous activities. They also face more new, nonroutine situations than adults generally do. Then too, their missteps may be more public since they are often committed in the presence of other people and since the consequences are often dealt with by adults in charge of them, like parents and teachers (Quadrel, Fischoff, & Davis, 1993).

Two all-too-common problems that can affect the rest of a young person's life are an unplanned pregnancy and criminal activity. Neither is "normal" or "typical"; both signal an adolescent in trouble. The danger in assuming that turmoil is a normal, necessary part of these years is that parents, teachers, community leaders, and makers of social policy may fail to recognize when a young person needs help.

TEENAGE PREGNANCY

Over the past two decades, adolescents have become more successful in preventing pregnancy, making the teenage pregnancy rate in the United States fall 19 percent between 1972 and 1990, from 254 pregnancies per 1000 *sexually active* girls aged 15 to 19 to 208 per 1000 (AGI, 1994). Still, the U.S. rate is one of the highest in the world, accounting for 1.1 million teenage pregnancies in 1990 (Children's Defense Fund, CDF, 1993). This high number occurred despite gains in contraception use during this time because a higher proportion of teenagers were having sexual intercourse (AGI, 1994). However, the great majority of unintended pregnancies, abortions, and out-of-wedlock births that occur each year are to adult women. Teenagers account for only about one-fourth of all unplanned pregnancies (AGI, 1994).

About half of pregnant teenagers have their babies and plan to raise them themselves, slightly over a third have abortions, and the rest miscarry. Very few place their children for adoption (AGI, 1994). More than 80 percent of adolescent mothers come from low-income, minority, and disadvantaged groups; girls from more advantaged families tend to have abortions (AGI, 1994; G. Adams, Adams-Taylor, & Pittman, 1989).

Understanding Teenage Pregnancy

International Differences in Adolescent Pregnancy Rates. Why do so many American teenagers become pregnant? In the Netherlands the pregnancy rate for *all* girls aged 15 to 19 is 14 per 1000. In the United States it is 96 per 1000. The abortion rate for the same group in the Netherlands is about 8 per 1000; in the United States it is over 60 per 1000. Are Dutch girls less sexually active than girls in this country? No. The two countries have similar rates of early sexual intercourse. Swedish girls are more advanced sexually than American girls, but Sweden's pregnancy rate is also well below that of the United States: 35 pregnancies per 1000 fifteen- to nineteen-year-olds, with about 27 abortions per 1000.

Some Americans attribute our higher pregnancy rates compared with European teenagers to our unusually large poor population, whose pregnancy rates tend to be higher than those of middle-class adolescents. It is true that the industrialized nations of Europe have no comparable level of urban impoverishment. However, the rates of pregnancy and abortion among white American teenagers are still far above the rates in European countries. Our rate is also double Canada's.

Many also believe that federal welfare programs like Aid to Families with Dependent Children encourage early and frequent pregnancy. But other industrial countries are even more generous in their support of poor mothers, and yet their teenage pregnancy rates are much lower. Unemployment among American teenagers is also popularly cited as a reason for the high pregnancy rate; but unemployment among teenagers is a serious problem in the other countries too.

Some differences between the United States and these other countries may explain our higher adolescent pregnancy rate. One is the confidentiality of service to teenagers. In Sweden it is forbidden to inform parents if teenagers request privacy. Another difference is cost. Contraceptives are provided free to adolescents in Britain, France, Sweden, and, in many cases, the Netherlands.

Europe's industrialized countries also provide extensive sex education. Sweden's compulsory curriculum includes sex education at all grade levels. Dutch schools have no special sex education programs, but the mass media and private groups provide extensive information about contraceptive techniques. Nearly all Dutch teenagers are well informed about birth control.

The primary policy goals behind the various countries' decisions to encourage the use of contraceptives include a wish to prevent teenage girls from becoming pregnant and an eagerness to keep the abortion rate among teenagers from rising. This second concern has proved important in persuading conservative groups to support the policy. The programs that support the successes of European countries have all been proposed and debated in the United States. They generally fail to be implemented because of a concern that they might seem to endorse sexual activity among teenagers. The irony is that, as a result, our teenage pregnancy rate is one of the highest in the world (E. F. Jones et al., 1985).

Most sexually active young people avoid unintended pregnancy. Did this 14-year-old prospective mother and her 18-year-old husband use a birth control method that failed? Or are they among the one-third of adolescents who use no birth control? If so, why?

Why Teenage Girls Do Not Use Contraception.   Most sexually active young people avoid unintended pregnancy. Two-thirds of adolescents use some method of birth control—usually the male condom—the first time they have sex, and between 72 percent and 84 percent of teenage girls use birth control on a regular basis (AGI, 1994). But only 13 percent of one group of adolescent girls used birth control pills correctly all the time, and only 4 in 10 took a pill every day (Oakley, Sereika, & Bogue, 1991).

Teenagers who do not use birth control often say that they did not expect to have intercourse and therefore did not prepare for it. But when asked why their *peers* do not use contraceptives, many tell a different story. Nearly 40 percent say that young people either prefer not to use birth control, do not think about it, do not care, enjoy sex more without it, or want to get pregnant. Other often-mentioned reasons are lack of knowledge about or access to birth control, embarrassment about seeking contraception, or fear that parents will find out they are having sex (Louis Harris & Associates, 1986). Many girls, misinformed, believe that they cannot get pregnant—that pregnancy cannot occur during the first instance of intercourse, or while using certain positions, or at certain times in the menstrual cycle (Quadrel, Fischoff, & Davis, 1993).

Guilt feelings often underlie the explanation that sexual activity was unexpected. Believing that sexual intercourse is wrong, some girls preserve their self-respect by considering themselves swept away by love and unable to help themselves. Unpremeditated sex is acceptable; carefully planned sex is only for "bad" girls. The guiltier a girl feels about premarital sex, the less likely she is to use effective contraception (Herold & Goodwin, 1981). A girl who feels guilty is embarrassed to go to a birth control clinic and have an internal physical examination. She is less likely to read about birth control than one who does not feel guilty, and she is more likely to think that oral contraceptives are hard to get.

Some girls are persuaded to conceive by boyfriends who see the ability to father a child as a proof of manhood. Then too, some—especially those from abusive or neglectful backgrounds—feel that having a baby of their own will give them someone to love and someone who will love them. However, caring for a baby is demanding, and young mothers, barely more than children themselves, often encounter many more problems than they had anticipated.

Who Is Likely to Get Pregnant?   In any discussion of adolescent pregnancy and childbearing, the ecological context of a girl's life has to assume a major place. Social factors affect both premarital sexual activity and the use of birth control.

Poverty is a major underlying cause of teenage childbearing (AGI, 1994). African American and Latina girls, girls who live with a single parent, girls from impoverished families, and girls whose parents are relatively uneducated tend to use no birth control, or to use less effective methods than "the pill" or the diaphragm. On the other hand, girls who make high grades, have career aspirations, or are involved in sports or other activities *are* likely to use birth control effectively (AGI, 1994; B. C. Miller & Moore, 1990; Ford, Zelnick, & Kantner, 1979; Louis Harris & Associates, 1986).

Age, sexual knowledge, and experience are all major factors. The younger a girl is at first intercourse, the longer she is likely to wait before seeking help with contraception—and the more likely she is to become pregnant (Tanfer & Horn, 1985). The less she knows about sex, the less likely she is to protect herself (Louis Harris & Associates, 1986). And the newer she is to sexual activity, the more vulnerable she is. Half of first premarital pregnancies occur in the first 6 months of sexual activity, and one out of five occur in the first month (Zabin, Kantner, & Zelnik, 1979).

Historically, teenagers seldom sought advice about birth control until they had been sexually active for a year or more. But in recent years the proportion of American women using contraceptives at first intercourse has risen, from 47 percent in the years 1975 to 1979, to 65 percent in 1983 to 1988. This change may be partly the result of AIDS education, since the increase was largely due to an increased use of condoms. Ethnic differences appeared in one study of 8450 women, aged 15 to 44: 68 percent of Jewish women, 54 percent of other white women, 45 percent of African American women, and 32 percent of Latina women used contraception at first intercourse (Mosher & McNally, 1991).

What is the father's profile? Often he is considerably older than the mother. Most fathers of babies born to teenage mothers are no longer teenagers themselves, and the younger the girl, the greater the age difference tends to be. Nearly one-third of the fathers of babies born to 15-year-old girls are 21 or older (AGI, 1994). Boys are less likely to use contraceptives than girls are; but two out of five girls who used birth control during recent intercourse relied on their partners' male methods—condoms or withdrawal (G. Adams et al., 1989). With the increased use of condoms, this may be changing.

The image of the irresponsible young man who abandons his pregnant girlfriend belies the amount of support supplied by many young fathers. Some of this support is mandated by law, since many states require fathers to pay child support for the first 18 years of a child's life. Enforcement often involves deducting set amounts from a man's pay. However, despite these laws (which are spottily enforced) and even though paternity can be clearly established through biological testing, many men do not assume responsibility for the children they have fathered, leaving the mother with all the financial and emotional burdens of child-rearing.

Among the consequences of teenage parenthood are medical complications for mother and baby and social problems for adolescents who must assume the responsibilities of parenthood before they are mature enough to handle them.

Consequences of Teenage Pregnancy

The Mother.　Teenage girls are more prone to such complications of pregnancy as anemia, prolonged labor, and toxemia. They are twice as likely as older mothers to bear low-birthweight babies and children with neurological defects and three times more likely to have babies who die in the first year (McKenry, Walters, & Johnson, 1979).

The health problems of teenage mothers and their children often result from social causes rather than medical ones. Many of the mothers are poor, do not eat properly, and get inadequate prenatal care or none at all (S. S. Brown, 1985). These problems of poverty antedate their pregnancies (AGI, 1994). In two large-scale studies—one in the United States and one in Denmark—teenagers' pregnancies turned out better than those of women in any other age group, leading to the conclusion that "if early, regular, and high quality medical care is made available to pregnant teenagers, the likelihood is that pregnancies and deliveries in this age group will not entail any higher medical risk than those of women in their twenties" (Mednick, Baker, & Sutton-Smith, 1979, p. 17).

Even with the best care, however, and the best of physical outcomes, teenage mothers still have problems. They are less likely to finish high school than their age-mates who do not have babies, and many who do finish do so at a later age. In one study, 5 years after giving birth, only half of urban black adolescent mothers had graduated from high school; however, 10 years later, two-thirds had graduated (Furstenberg, Brooks-Gunn, & Morgan, 1987).

Teenage mothers are likely to have money troubles; many receive public assistance, at least for a while. Furthermore, they are at high risk of repeat pregnancies. The risk is highest for those who drop out of school, remain sexually active, and do not use reliable means of birth control. These women "may have resigned themselves to few options other than repeated childbearing" (McAnarney & Hendee, 1989, p. 76). About one-fourth of women in their twenties and thirties who became mothers in adolescence are poor as adults, but for most of them, it was their initial impoverished circumstances that continued to affect their adult lives rather than their early motherhood. About 16 percent would have been poor even without having had a baby (AGI, 1994). Still, early childbearing does restrict future opportunities for both the mothers and their children.

The Children.   Children of teenage parents are at higher risk than other children of entering the state's foster care system, and years may pass before a foster child's final status is settled (AGI, 1981). Children of such young parents are also more likely to have low IQ scores and do poorly in school, and this likelihood increases over the years (Baldwin & Cain, 1980). As preschoolers, these children are often overactive, willful, and aggressive. In elementary school, they tend to be inattentive and easily distracted, and they give up easily. In high school, they are often low achievers (Brooks-Gunn & Furstenberg, 1986). However, a 20-year study that followed more than 400 teenage mothers in Baltimore found that two-thirds of their daughters did not become teenage mothers themselves, and most graduated from high school (Furstenberg, Levine, & Brooks-Gunn, 1990).

What do you think?   *Which of the following choices do you think is usually best for a teenage girl who discovers that she is pregnant: marry the father and raise the child, stay single and raise the child, give the baby to adoptive parents, or have an abortion?*

Preventing Teenage Pregnancy

Programs designed to prevent early pregnancy have two aims: encouraging young teenagers to delay intercourse and improving contraceptive use among adolescents who are already sexually active. Some such programs have been quite successful. The most effective ones combine sexuality education, skills for deciding about having intercourse and communicating with partners, and access to birth control counseling and contraceptives (AGI, 1994; I. C. Stewart, 1994). Since adolescents who have high aspirations for the future are less likely to become pregnant, one of the best preventives is to motivate young people in other areas of their lives and to raise their self-esteem. Programs that focus on this approach rather than on the mechanics of contraception have achieved some success (Carrera, 1986).

Since teenagers who are knowledgeable about sex are more likely to use birth control, parents and schools can help lower the high level of teenage pregnancy by offering education about sex and parenthood—both the facts and the feelings (Conger, 1988). Although many people fear that if teenagers know about sex, they will want to put this knowledge into practice, community- and school-based sex education does not result in more sexual activity by adolescents (M. Eisen & Zellman, 1987). Since the media are a powerful influence on adolescents' behavior, radio and television should present sexual situations responsibly and permit advertising of contraceptives. Box 16-2 offers other suggestions about how to prevent teenage pregnancy.

Helping Pregnant Teenagers and Teenage Parents

An unmarried pregnant teenager is especially vulnerable to emotional upheaval. However she handles her pregnancy, she has conflicting feelings. Just when she needs the most emotional support, she often gets the least: Her boyfriend may be

BOX 16-2 ▪ THE EVERYDAY WORLD

HOW CAN TEENAGE PREGNANCY BE PREVENTED?

Pregnancy in adolescence can be devastating to mother, father, and baby. The following guidelines for preventing early pregnancy are based on findings from research studies and recommendations by those who work with adolescents.

♦ Parents should talk about sex with children from an early age, instilling healthy, positive attitudes and being "askable," so that their children will feel free to go to them with questions. Children whose parents discuss sex with them are likely to delay sexual activity until an appropriate time (Jaslow, 1982).

♦ Schools, churches, and the media should offer realistic sex education. This should include information about risks and consequences of teenage pregnancy, different kinds of birth control methods, and places where teenagers can get medical and contraceptive help (Alan Guttmacher Institute, AGI, 1994).

♦ Counseling programs that include peers should be instituted to encourage sexually active teenage girls to use contraceptives. Teenagers are more responsive to girls close to their own age than they are to adult counselors (Jay, DuRant, Soffit, Linder, & Litt, 1984).

♦ Community programs encouraging teenagers to delay sexual activity should be instituted. Such programs can help young people stand up against peer pressure urging them to be more sexually active than they want to be, can teach them how to say no gracefully, and can offer guidance in problem solving (J. Gross, 1994).

♦ Adolescents' use of birth control services should be kept confidential. Young teenagers cite this as the single most important consideration in choosing a birth control clinic (Zabin & Clark, 1983). Many young people say they would not go to a clinic that insisted on notifying their parents or obtaining consent from parents (Jaslow, 1982).

♦ Specific messages that need to be communicated to young people include the following (S. Gordon & Everly, 1985):

   * If someone says to you, "If you really love me, you'll have sex with me," it is always a line.
   * Sex is never a test of love.
   * It is not romantic to have sex without using a means of birth control—it is stupid.
   * It is perfectly normal not to have sex.
   * Machismo is hurting and exploiting people to make a boy feel more secure.
   * More than 85 percent of boys who impregnate teenage girls will eventually abandon them.
   * Girls who feel they do not amount to anything unless some guy loves them will not amount to much even after they are loved—if they get that far.
   * The most important components of a relationship are love, respect, caring, humor, and honest communication that does not violate private thoughts and experiences.

---

frightened by the responsibility and turn away, her family may be angry, and she may be isolated from her school friends. An interested, sympathetic, and knowledgeable counselor may be of great help. The young mother and her baby also benefit from family support: The prognosis for low-birthweight infants of teenage mothers is better when they and their young mothers live with the mother's mother (S. K. Pope et al., 1993).

Pregnant girls need to learn both job and parenting skills (Buie, 1987). In one school program, 80 low-income teenage mothers learned parenting skills, either from a biweekly visit to their homes (by a graduate student and a teenage aide) or through paid job training as teachers' aides in the nursery of a medical school. The infants of both experimental (parent-training) groups developed better than babies in a control (untrained) group. They weighed more, had more advanced motor skills, and interacted better with their mothers. The mothers who worked as teachers' aides and their children showed the most gains: More mothers returned to work or school, fewer became pregnant again, and their babies made the most progress (T. M. Field, Widmayer, Greenberg, & Stoller, 1982).

The mother bears the major impact of teenage parenthood, but the young father's life is often affected as well. A boy who feels emotionally committed to the girl he has impregnated also has decisions to make. He may pay for an abortion. Or he may marry the girl, a move that will affect his educational and career plans. The father also needs someone to talk to, the help him sort out his own feelings so that he and the mother can make the best decision for themselves and their child.

What do you think? *Since adolescent pregnancy is such a problem, should teenage girls still be urged to follow a stricter standard of behavior than teenage boys? Or should teenage boys be encouraged to be more responsible sexually?*

ADOLESCENT CRIMINAL ACTIVITY

status offender *Juvenile charged with committing an act that is considered criminal only because the offender is a minor (for example, truancy, running away from home, or engaging in sexual intercourse).*

Two kinds of young people get into trouble with the law. One is the ***status offender***—a young person who has been truant, has run away from home, has been sexually active, has not abided by parents' rules, or has done something else ordinarily not considered criminal—except when done by a minor.

The other kind is the young person who has done something considered a crime no matter who commits it—like robbery, rape, or murder. Offenders under age 16 or 18 (depending on the state) are usually treated differently from adult criminals. Court proceedings are likely to be secret, the offender is more likely to be tried and sentenced by a judge rather than a jury, and punishment is usually more lenient. However, for some particularly violent crimes, minors may be tried as adults.

Teenagers—especially boys—are responsible for more than their share of crimes. The rate among girls has increased a little recently, but still girls' crime rates are similar to those of boys only for status offenses like running away from home, incorrigibility, and engaging in sexual intercourse. Teenagers are also more likely to be the victims of crime. While those aged 12 to 17 account for less than 10 percent of the American population, they make up 23 percent of the victims of assault, rape, and robbery (Office of Juvenile Justice and Delinquency Prevention, 1994).

Personal Characteristics of Delinquents

What makes one child get into trouble when another who lives on the same street or even in the same household remains law-abiding? Children who get into trouble early in life are more likely to get into deeper trouble later. Stealing, lying, truancy, and poor achievement in school are all predictors of delinquency (Loeber & Dishion, 1983). Also, delinquents have a slightly lower average IQ than is found in the general population, especially in verbal skills (Quay, 1987).

One study of 55 delinquents who had been patients at a psychiatric hospital suggests that delinquency is a class phenomenon, as well as a result of emotional turmoil that affects young people from all levels of society. The way a young person is treated after committing an antisocial act is often related to which segment of society she or he comes from. Delinquents from affluent families are taken to psychiatrists; delinquents from poor families are booked by the police (Loeber & Dishion, 1983; Offer, Ostrov, & Marohn, 1972). The wealthy adolescent gets help; the poor one gets a police record.

In some cases, delinquency has been related to backgrounds of physical and sexual abuse and to neurological and psychiatric problems (D. O. Lewis et al., 1988). Youths with problems like these may need medical treatment along with psychological help.

The Delinquent's Family

Several family characteristics are associated with juvenile delinquency. In a study of 18,226 boys and girls under 18 in long-term state-operated correction institutes, more than half reported that a family member had also been imprisoned at least once, and nearly three out of four had not grown up with both parents (U.S. Department of Justice, 1988). These figures apply only to young people who were arrested and convicted and thus may reflect who gets caught up in the criminal justice system rather than who actually commits delinquent acts. Some young offenders' families have the resources to keep them out of jail.

Antisocial behavior in adolescents is closely related to parents' inability to keep track of what their children do and with whom they do it. Also, parents of delinquent children are less likely to punish rule-breaking with anything more severe than a lecture or a threat (G. R. Patterson & Stouthamer-Loeber, 1984). The impact of ineffective parenting begins early in childhood. As we pointed out in Chapter 10, parents of delinquents often failed to reinforce good behavior and were harsh or inconsistent or both in punishing misbehavior when their children were younger. Through the years they have not been closely involved in their children's lives in positive ways (G. R. Patterson, DeBaryshe, & Ramsey, 1989).

The Delinquent's Neighborhood

The youth who sees that the only rich people in his neighborhood are the drug dealers is vulnerable to seduction into a life of crime. Because of economic and residential stratification, crime—especially violent crime—is concentrated in low-income urban neighborhoods, whose residents are more likely to be murdered, raped, assaulted, robbed, and to have their cars stolen than are middle-class people. The high rates of poverty in neighborhoods with predominantly minority populations, when combined with the effects of prejudice and discrimination, make these communities at high risk for crime (NRC, 1993a).

The Influence of the Peer Group

Parents worry—with good reason—about a child's "falling in with the wrong crowd." Peers exert a strong influence; young people who take drugs, drop out of school, and commit delinquent acts usually do all of these in the company of their friends. But children don't "fall in" with a group; they seek out their friends or, when rejected by some peers, accept the overtures of others. Of all the groups in a school or neighborhood, what makes one youngster go with the "wrong" one?

Recent research suggests that the process starts out in childhood and has its roots in troubled parent-child interactions (G. R. Patterson, Reid, & Dishion, in press). Children get certain payoffs for antisocial behavior, possibly getting attention or their own way by acting up, or avoiding punishment by lying or cheating on school tests. The children's antisocial behavior then interferes with school-

The increase among girls of drug use and running away from home seems to lead to the kinds of activities that support them, like shoplifting. The strongest predictor of delinquency is a family's failure to supervise and discipline children; the poorest predictor is socioeconomic status.

work and with their ability to get along with their well-behaved classmates. As a result, these children—unpopular and nonachieving—seek out other antisocial children. These children keep influencing each other and often learn new kinds of misconduct from one another.

Since school failure is often related to antisocial behavior, and since contact with antisocial peers at age 10 is related to antisocial behavior at age 12, the common educational practice of *tracking* may be making the problem worse. Grouping children together in the same classroom because of similar academic skills keeps the nonachieving children together. Since these are often the antisocial children, the long-term friendships that grow up in the classroom may solidify problem behaviors and discourage children from improving either schoolwork or behavior (Dishion, Patterson, Stoolmiller, & Skinner, 1991).

Dealing with Delinquency

How can we help young people lead productive, law-abiding lives? How can we protect society? So far, the answers are unclear. Can we turn young offenders away from a life of crime by sentences that consider their youth, bolstered by social solutions like probation and counseling? Or would we have less crime if we treated young offenders as we treat adults, basing sentences on the seriousness of the crime rather than the age of the offender?

One study suggests that how young offenders are treated is less important in most cases than just letting them grow up. Except for a small group of "hardcore" offenders, it is almost impossible to predict which young people will commit crimes as adults. In a longitudinal analysis of police and court records, plus interviews with more than 6000 adults in Racine, Wisconsin, more than 90 percent of the men and 65 to 70 percent of the women had engaged in some adolescent misbehavior, although many had not been caught. But only 5 to 8 percent had been booked for felonies as adults. Why did most of these people become law-abiding? Fewer than 8 percent said that they were afraid of getting caught. Most said they had realized that what seemed like fun in their early years was no longer appropriate (L. W. Shannon, 1982).

Most adolescents outgrow their "wild oats" as maturity brings valuable reappraisals of attitudes and behavior. But society must continue to explore ways to help those who cannot climb out of the morass of delinquency and alienation on their own. The most effective programs for adolescent delinquents lie outside the juvenile justice or prison system and incorporate teaching of social and vocational skills (NRC, 1993a).

Most promising, however, is an approach that prevents delinquency before it occurs. Recently, researchers analyzing the long-term effects of some early childhood intervention programs found a bonus. Adolescents who had taken part in these programs as children were less likely to get into trouble with the law (Zigler, Taussig, & Black, 1993). These programs seemed to serve a preventive function because they embraced an ecological view of child development, treating children through their broad environment rather than through any single aspect of their lives. The programs that focused on preparing children for school showed a "snowball effect": The children's teachers had a more positive attitude toward better-prepared kindergartners, the children liked school better, and they achieved more in later grades. This in turn led to higher self-esteem and aspirations for the future, both of which tend to deter antisocial behavior (Berrueta-Clement, Schweinhart, Barnett, Epstein, & Weikart, 1987).

Some programs offered adults the kinds of practical and social support that helped them become better parents. They learned how to discipline and motivate their children, and to build relationships with the children's teachers, all of which may have helped the children's school performance (Seitz, 1990). Since academic failure is related to delinquency, it makes sense that bettering a child's chances for school success will lower his or her chances of social failure.

What do you think?   *What should a judge do with a first-time juvenile offender who has committed a felony: let the offender off with a warning, investigate the offender's family background before deciding, investigate the offender's socioeconomic status before deciding, sentence the offender to a term in a penal institution, or take some other action? Give reasons for your answer.*

ADOLESCENCE: AN EXCITING TIME OF LIFE

Fortunately, the great majority of adolescents neither become pregnant nor get into trouble with the law. With all its turbulence, normal adolescence is an exciting time, when all things seem possible. Teenagers are on the threshold of love, or life's work, and of participation in adult society. They are getting to know the most interesting people in the world: themselves.

ACKNOWLEDGING THE MAJORITY

According to an analysis of findings from three cohorts of adolescents, most of them manage very well during these years (Offer et al., 1989). The data for this analysis came from three separate studies—in the 1960s, the 1970s, and the 1980s. The three cohorts were more alike than different. The findings were that most

With all its turbulence, normal adolescence is an exciting time of life. Teenagers are on the threshold of love, of life's work, and of participation in adult society. They are getting to know the most interesting people in the world: themselves. Most of them manage very well during these years.

adolescents enjoy life, are happy with themselves most of the time, do not feel inferior to others, and do not have major problems with body image, physical development, or sexuality. They are usually relaxed and confident in new or challenging situations, and they take pleasure in doing good work.

Most of the young people in all three groups did not show any evidence of either a "generation gap" or a "natural rebellion" against their parents. Instead, most got along well with their parents and did not see any major problems with them. Life may not always run smoothly at home, but most teenagers seem to like and be proud of their families (Offer et al., 1989).

Teenagers in the 1960s seemed to be the best off, those in the 1970s the worst. What made the difference? One possibility is a "baby-boom, baby-bust" theory (Easterlin, 1980). This hypothesis suggests that the higher the ratio of adolescents in the population, the more problems they have. In "boom" periods, adolescents have to compete more fiercely for jobs and college admission. Such pressures may help to explain differences in self-image between generations. The adolescents studied in the 1960s were at the end of a "baby bust" generation; those in the 1970s were in the middle of a "baby boom"; and those in the 1980s were again in a "baby bust," offering some support for this theory.

HELPING THE MINORITY

Although high-risk groups like high school dropouts were not studied in the above research, the "boom-bust" theory might help to explain greater problems within disadvantaged populations, which tend to have higher proportions of young people than does the population at large.

As we have seen, the settings in which children and adolescents live have a big impact on their lives. We need to learn how to help the many young people whose environments are not optimal. One way to begin is to conduct research on approaches that can lower the risk. We need to learn, for example,

- How the various aspects of a young person's environment (like home, school, neighborhood, and community) interact to affect development
- What the major risk and protective factors are
- How ethnic, racial, or religious discrimination affects development
- How families manage or are overwhelmed by adversity
- What kinds of supports help families and how to deliver them
- What processes can sustain interest in school and motivation to achieve there
- What constitutes a healthy, functioning neighborhood and how dysfunctional communities can be turned around
- How an effective health care system can be implemented and how adolescents can be brought into it
- What kinds of programs can help young people, especially those who do not go to college, make the transition from school to work
- What kinds of alternatives can be developed to change the course of adolescents who have become involved in crime.

Research also needs to be done on individual characteristics of adolescents. We need to know what makes some young people able to overcome social and economic obstacles to achieve productive, fulfilling lives and how we can apply that knowledge to help others.

Most important, we need to have an open mind about development. Instead of looking at people through the filter of a preconceived theory, it is essential to look at the facts. If people believe that adolescence is normally a time of stress and disturbance, the approximately 20 percent of the teenage population with very real problems may not get the help they need. The adults around these young people may stand back, waiting for them to "grow out" of adolescence and of their problems. Instead, adolescents who show by their behavior that they are disturbed can—and should—be helped now. With support, more of them can recognize and build on their strengths as they are about to enter adult life.

The normal developmental changes in the early years of life are obvious and dramatic signs of growth. The infant lying in the crib becomes an active, exploring toddler. The young child enters and embraces the worlds of school and society. The adolescent, with a new body and new awareness, prepares to step into adulthood. But growth and development do not screech to a stop with adolescence. People change in many ways throughout early, middle, and late adulthood. Some capacities emerge relatively late in life, and human beings continue to shape their own development, as they have been doing since birth. What occurs in a child's world is significant, but it is not the whole story. We each continue to write our own story of human development for as long as we live.

SUMMARY

1 Erik Erikson's fifth psychosocial crisis is the conflict between identity and identity confusion. Finding an occupational identity is a key task of this stage. The "virtue" that should arise from this identity crisis is fidelity.

2 Research by James Marcia, based on Erikson's theory, examined the presence or absence of crisis and commitment in a person's identity formation. On the basis of these factors, Marcia identified four categories of identity formation: identity achievement (crisis leading to commitment), foreclosure (commitment with no crisis), confusion (no commitment, crisis uncertain), and moratorium (crisis, no commitment).

3 Marcia, Gilligan, and other researchers have found differences in the ways males and females define themselves. Intimate relationships appear to be more important for women; achieving a separate identity, for men. Ethnic differences in self-esteem have also been noted.

4 Adolescent sexuality strongly influences developing identity. Masturbation and occasional early homosexual experiences are common. Sexual orientation is most likely the result of an interaction of biological, social, and psychological factors.

5 Sexual attitudes and behaviors are more liberal than in the past. There is more acceptance of premarital sexual activity, and there has been a decline in the double standard for males and females. Because of social pressure, many adolescents become sexually active earlier than they feel they should. More than one-half of women and almost three-fourths of men have had intercourse by the age of 18.

6 Although many parents are more accepting of teenage sexual behavior than in the past, many adolescents have difficulty discussing sexual matters with their parents.

7 Although the relationships between adolescents and parents are not always smooth, there is little evidence that full rebellion characterizes most of these relationships. Parents and their teenage children often hold similar values. Most arguments are about everyday matters.

8 Adolescents need some independence, but too-early separation or emotional independence from the family (or other significant adults) can cause alienation, susceptibility to negative peer influence, and physically or socially unhealthy behaviors. Authoritative parenting seems to be the most beneficial.

9 Relationships with siblings tend to become more equal and somewhat more distant during adolescence.

10 Adolescents spend most of their time with peers. Friendships become more intimate, and romantic relationships develop.

11 Pregnancy is a major problem among adolescents. The adolescent pregnancy rate in the United States is one of the highest in the world. Many teenagers have abortions. Ninety percent of those who have their babies keep them. Teenage pregnancy often has negative consequences for mothers, fathers, children, and society.

12 Comprehensive sex education programs and more communication between parents and their adolescents can encourage teenagers to delay sexual activity and to use contraceptives.

13 Juvenile delinquents fall into two categories. Status offenders commit acts that are not considered criminal for adults. The second kind of juvenile delinquent has committed an act that is considered a crime no matter what the age of the offender.

14 Young people under 18 commit a high share of crimes, particularly crimes against property. The strongest predictor of delinquency is the family's level of supervision and disciplining of children.

15 Even with all the difficulties of establishing a personal, sexual, social, and vocational identity, adolescence—the threshold of adulthood—is typically interesting, exciting, and positive.

KEY TERMS

SUGGESTED READINGS

Apter, T. (1990). *Altered loves: Mothers and daughters during adolescence.* New York: St. Martin's. This is an insightful study of changes in the mother-daughter relationship during adolescence. It is based on the author's interviews with mothers and daughters in England and the United States and on recent psychological studies of family interaction.

Csikszentmihalyi, M., & Larson, R. (1984). *Being adolescent: Conflict and growth in the teenage years.* New York: Basic Books. These authors equipped 75 teenagers with beepers and asked them to report what they were doing and how they were feeling each time they were signaled. This project provided a wealth of information about who teenagers spend time with and how they feel about their lives.

Hardy, J. B., & Zabin, L. S. (1991). *Adolescent pregnancy in an urban environment: Issues, programs, and evaluations.* Washington, DC: Urban Institute Press; and Baltimore, MD: Urban & Schwarzenberg. The authors, with ten contributors, analyze the urban context for teenage pregnancy, discuss services available to young parents and their babies, and describe programs designed to prevent early pregnancies, including birth control and health education.

Pipher, M. (1994). *Reviving Ophelia: Saving the selves of adolescent girls.* This wise and sensitive book by a Nebraska clinical psychologist sounds the alarm about an increased severity in the problems of young girls, which include eating disorders, self-mutilation, drugs and alcohol, unwise sexual behavior, and suicide attempts. The author lays many of these problems at the door of societal pressures, some of which are new to this generation.

Steinberg, L., & Levine, A. (1990). *You and your adolescent: A parent's guide for ages 10–20.* This book is truly comprehensive: It covers, among other topics, puberty, drugs, emotions, sex, cognitive development, school, work, dating, summer activities, friends, independence, and the transition to adulthood. Without being overwhelming, it seems to address almost every issue that might concern the parent of an adolescent.

Wolf, A. E. (1991). *Get out of my life: But first could you drive me and Cheryl to the mall? A parent's guide to the new teenager.* Written by a clinical psychologist who has worked with children and adolescents, this book empathizes with both parents and teens as the author uses humor and anecdotes to describe psychological rules that dictate teenage behavior and to suggest some ways to defuse conflict.

BIBLIOGRAPHY

Abbey, A., Andrews, F. M., & Halman, J. (1992). Infertility and subjective well-being: The mediating roles of self-esteem, internal control, and interpersonal conflict. *Journal of Marriage and the Family, 54,* 405–417.

Abramovitch, R., Corter, C., & Lando, B. (1979). Sibling interaction in the home. *Child Development, 50,* 997–1003.

Abramovitch, R., Corter, C., Pepler, D. J., & Stanhope, L. (1986). Sibling and peer interaction: A final follow-up and a comparison. *Child Development, 57,* 217–229.

Abramovitch, R., Pepler, D., & Corter, C. (1982). Patterns of sibling interaction among preschool-age children. In M. B. Lamb (Ed.), *Sibling relationships: Their nature and significance across the lifespan.* Hillsdale, NJ: Erlbaum.

Abrams, B., & Viederman, M. (1988, Spring). Pregnancy and childbirth: Normal and abnormal reactions. *Outlook* [Newsletter of the Department of Psychiatry, New York Hospital–Cornell Medical Center], p. 7.

Abravanel, E., & Sigafoos, A. D. (1984). Exploring the presence of imitation during early infancy. *Child Development, 55,* 381–392.

Abroms, K. I., & Bennett, J. W. (1981). Changing etiological perspectives in Down's syndrome: Implications for early intervention. *Journal of the Division for Early Childhood, 2,* 109–112.

Abt Associates. (1978). *Children at the Center: Vol. 1. Summary findings and policy implications of the National Day Care Study.* Washington, DC: U.S. Department of Health, Education and Welfare.

Achenbach, T. M., & Howell, C. T. (1993). Are American children's problems getting worse? A 13-year comparison. *Journal of the American Academy of Child and Adolescent Psychiatry, 32,* 1145–1154.

Acredolo, L., & Goodwyn, S. (1988). Symbolic gesturing in normal infants. *Child Development, 59,* 450–466.

Action for Children's Television. (undated). *Treat TV with T.L.C.* One-page flyer. Newtonville, MA: Author.

Adams, G., Adams-Taylor, S., & Pittman, K. (1989). Adolescent pregnancy and parenthood: A review of the problem, solutions, and resources. *Family Relations, 38,* 223–229.

Adams, L. A., & Rickert, V. I. (1989). Reducing bedtime tantrums: Comparison between positive routines and graduated extinction. *Pediatrics, 84,* 756–761.

Adams, L. A., & Rickert, V. I. (1989). Reducing bedtime tantrums: Comparison between positive routines and graduated extinction. *Pediatrics, 84,* 756–761.

Agran, P. F., & Winn, D. G. (1993). The bicycle: A developmental toy versus a vehicle. *Pediatrics, 91,* 752–755.

Ainsworth, M. A., & Bowlby, J. (1991) An ethological approach to personality development. *American Psychologist, 46,* 333–341.

Ainsworth, M. D. (1964). Patterns of attachment behavior shown by the infant in interaction with his mother. *Merrill-Palmer Quarterly, 10,* 51–58.

Ainsworth, M. D. S. (1967). *Infancy in Uganda: Infant care and the growth of love.* Baltimore: Johns Hopkins University Press.

Ainsworth, M. D. S. (1969). Object relations, dependency, and attachment: A theoretical review of the infant-mother relationship. *Child Development, 40,* 969–1025.

Ainsworth, M. D. S. (1979). Infant-mother attachment. *American Psychologist, 34,* 932–937.

Ainsworth, M. D. S., & Bell, S. (1977). Infant crying and maternal responsiveness: A rejoinder to Gewirtz and Boyd. *Child Development, 48,* 1208–1216.

Ainsworth, M. D. S., Blehar, M. C., Waters, E., & Wall, S. (1978). *Patterns of attachment: A psychological study of the strange situation.* Hillsdale, NJ: Erlbaum.

Alan Guttmacher Institute. (AGI) (1981). *Teenage pregnancy: The problem that hasn't gone away.* New York: Viking.

Alen Guttmacher Institute (AGI). (1994). *Sex & America's teenagers.* New York: Author.

Albanese, A., & Stanhope, R. (1993). Growth and metabolic data following growth hormone treatment of children with intrauterine growth retardation. *Hormone Research, 39*, 8–12.

Alessandri, S. M., Sullivan, M. W., Imaizumi, S., & Lewis, M. (1993). Learning and emotional responsivity in cocaine-exposed infants. *Developmental Psychology, 29*, 989–997.

Alexander, K. L., Entwisle, D. R., & Dauber, S. L. (1993). First grade classroom behavior: Its short- and long-term consequences for school performance. *Child Development, 64*, 801–814.

Allen, M. C., Donohue, P. K., & Dusman, A. E. (1993). The limit of viability—Neonatal outcome of infants born at 22 to 25 weeks' gestation. *New England Journal of Medicine, 329*, 1597–1601.

Allore, R., O'Hanlon, D., Price, R., Neilson, K., Willard, H. F., Cox, D. R., Marks, A., & Dun, R. J. (1988). Gene encoding the B subunit of S100 protein is on chromosome 21: Implications for Down syndrome. *Science, 239*, 1311–1313.

Almeida, D. M., Maggs, J. L., & Galambos, N. L. (1993). Wives' employment hours and spousal participation in family work. *Journal of Family Psychology, 7*, 233–244.

Almy, M., Chittenden, E., & Miller, P. (1966). *Young children's thinking: Some aspects of Piaget's theory.* New York: Teachers College Press.

Alsaker, F. D. (1992). Pubertal timing, overweight, and psychological adjustment. *Journal of Early Adolescence, 12*, 396–419.

Altemeir, W. A., O'Connor, S. M., Sherrod, K. B., & Vietze, P. M. (1985). Prospective study of antecedents for nonorganic failure to thrive. *Journal of Pediatrics, 106*, 360–365.

Amabile, T. A., & Rovee-Collier, C. (1991). Contextual variation and memory retrieval at six months. *Child Development, 62*, 1155–1166.

Amabile, T. M. (1983). *The social psychology of creativity.* New York: Springer-Verlag.

Amato, P. R. (1987). Family processes in one-parent, stepparent, and intact families: The child's point of view. *Journal of Marriage and the Family, 49*, 327–337.

Amato, P. R., & Keith, B. (1991a). Parental divorce and adult well-being: A meta-analysis. *Journal of Marriage and the Family, 53*, 43–58.

Amato, P. R., & Keith, B. (1991b). Parental divorce and the well-being of children: A meta-analysis. *Psychological Bulletin, 110*, 26–46.

Amato, P. R., Kurdek, L. A., Demo, D. H., & Allen, K. R. (1993). Children's adjustment to divorce: Theories, hypotheses, and empirical support. *Journal of Marriage and the Family, 55*, 23–54.

American Academy of Pediatrics (AAP). (1973). The ten-state nutrition survey: A pediatric perspective. *Pediatrics, 51*, 1095–1099.

American Academy of Pediatrics (AAP). (1983). Growth hormone treatment of children with short stature. *Pediatrics, 72*, 891–894.

American Academy of Pediatrics (AAP). (1986a). *How to be your child's TV guide: Guidelines for constructive viewing.* Elk Grove Village, IL: Author.

American Academy of Pediatrics (AAP). (1986b). *Positive approaches to day care dilemmas: How to make it work.* Elk Grove Village, IL: Author.

American Academy of Pediatrics (AAP). (1989). Follow-up or weaning formulas. *Pediatrics, 83*, 1067.

American Academy of Pediatrics (AAP). (1992a, January 15). *AAP proposes handgun ban, other measures to curb firearm deaths, injuries.* News release. Elk Grove Village, IL: Author.

American Academy of Pediatrics (AAP). (1992b, Spring). Bedtime doesn't have to be a struggle. *Healthy Kids*, pp. 4–10.

American Academy of Pediatrics (AAP). (1994). *Recommendations for dates of childhood immunizations.* Position paper. Author.

American Academy of Pediatrics (AAP) and Center to Prevent Handgun Violence. (1994). *Keep your family safe from firearm injury.* Washington, DC: Center to Prevent Handgun Violence.

American Academy of Pediatrics (AAP) Committee on Accident and Poison Prevention. (1990). Bicycle helmets. *Pediatrics, 85*, 229–230.

American Academy of Pediatrics (AAP) Committee on Adolescence. (1987). Alcohol use and abuse: A pediatric concern. *Pediatrics, 79*, 450–453.

American Academy of Pediatrics (AAP) Committee on Bioethics. (1992, July). Ethical issues in surrogate motherhood. *AAP News*, pp. 14–15.

American Academy of Pediatrics (AAP) Committee on Drugs. (1978). Effects of medication during labor and delivery on infant outcome. *Pediatrics, 62*, 402–403.

American Academy of Pediatrics (AAP) Committee on Drugs. (1994). The transfer of drugs and other chemicals into human milk. *Pediatrics, 93*, 137–150.

American Academy of Pediatrics (AAP) Committee on Fetus and Newborn. (1986). Use and abuse of the Apgar score. *Pediatrics, 78*, 1148–1149.

American Academy of Pediatrics (AAP) Committee on Genetics. (1992). Issues in newborn screening. *Pediatrics, 89*, 345–349.

American Academy of Pediatrics (AAP) Committee on Genetics. (1993). Folic acid for the prevention of neural tube defects. *Pediatrics, 92*, 493–494.

American Academy of Pediatrics (AAP) Committee on Infectious Diseases. (1992). Universal hepatitis B immunization. *Pediatrics, 89*, 795–800.

American Academy of Pediatrics (AAP) Committee on Nutrition. (1986). Prudent life-style for children: Dietary fat and cholesterol. *Pediatrics, 78*, 521–525.

American Academy of Pediatrics (AAP) Committee on Nutrition. (1992a). Statement on cholesterol. *Pediatrics, 90*, 469–473.

American Academy of Pediatrics (AAP) Committee on Nutrition. (1992b). The use of whole cow's milk in infancy. *Pediatrics, 89*, 1105–1109.

American Academy of Pediatrics (AAP) Committee on Pediatric Aspects of Physical Fitness, Recreation, and Sports. (1981). Competitive athletics for children of elementary school age. *Pediatrics, 67*, 927–928.

American Academy of Pediatrics (AAP) Committee on Sports Medicine and Committee on School Health. (1989). Organized athletics for preadolescent children. *Pediatrics, 84*, 583–584.

American Academy of Pediatrics (AAP) Committee on Sports Medicine and Fitness. (1992). Fitness, activity, and sports participation in the preschool child. *Pediatrics, 90*, 1002–1004.

American Academy of Pediatrics (AAP) Committee on Substance Abuse and Committee on Children with Disabilities. (1993). Fetal alcohol syndrome and fetal alcohol effects. *Pediatrics, 91*, 1004–1006.

American Academy of Pediatrics (AAP) Task Force on Blood Pressure Control in Children. (1987). Report of the second task force on blood pressure control in children. *Pediatrics, 79*, 1–25.

American Academy of Pediatrics (AAP) Task Force on Infant Mortality. (1986). Statement on infant mortality. *Pediatrics, 78*, 1155–1160.

American Academy of Pediatrics (AAP) Task Force on Infant Positioning and SIDS. (1992). Positioning and SIDS. *Pediatrics, 89*, 1120–1126.

American Academy of Pediatrics (AAP) Task Force on Pediatric AIDS. (1991). Education of children with human immunodeficiency virus infection. *Pediatrics, 88*, 645–648.

American Association of Pediatrics (AAP) Committee on Children with Disabilities and Committee on Psychosocial Aspects of Child and Family Health. (1993). Psychosocial risks of chronic health conditions in childhood and adolescence. *Pediatrics, 92,* 876–877.

American Association of Pediatrics (AAP) Committee on Environmental Health. (1993). Lead poisoning: From screening to primary prevention. *Pediatrics, 92,* 176–183.

American Cancer Society. (1985). *1985 cancer facts and figures.* Pamphlet. Washington, DC: Author.

American Cancer Society. (1993). Cancer statistics, 1993. *Cancer Journal for Clinicians, 43,* 7–26.

American College of Obstetrics and Gynecology. (1994). *Exercise during pregnancy and the postpartum pregnancy* (Technical Bulletin No. 189). Washington, DC: Author.

American Foundation for the Prevention of Venereal Disease, Inc. (1986). *Sexually transmitted disease [venereal disease]: Prevention for everyone* (13th rev. ed.). New York: Author.

American Psychological Association (APA). (1993). *Violence and youth: Psychology's response: Vol. 1. Summary report of the American Psychological Association Commission on Violence and Youth.* Washington, DC: Author.

American Psychological Association (APA). (undated). *Answers to your questions about sexual orientation and homosexuality* [brochure]. Washington, DC: Author.

Anand, K. J. S., & Hickey, P. R. (1987). Pain and its effect in the human neonate and fetus. *New England Journal of Medicine, 317,* 1321–1329.

Anand, K. J. S., & Hickey, P. R. (1992). Halothane-morphine compared with high-dose sufentanil for anesthesia and post-operative analgesia in neonatal cardiac surgery. *New England Journal of Medicine, 326,* 1–9.

Anastasi, A. (1988). *Psychological testing* (6th ed.). New York: Macmillan.

Anastasi, A., & Schaefer, C. E. (1971). Note on concepts of creativity and intelligence. *Journal of Creative Behavior, 3,* 113–116.

Andersson, B. E. (1992). Effects of daycare on cognitive and socioemotional competence of thirteen-year-old Swedish children. *Child Development, 63,* 20–36.

Angell, M. (1990). New ways to get pregnant. *New England Journal of Medicine, 323,* 1200–1202.

Anthony, E. J., & Koupernik, C. (Eds.). (1974). *The child in his family: Children at psychiatric risk* (Vol. 3). New York: Wiley.

Antonarakis, S. E., & Down Syndrome Collaborative Group. (1991). Parental origin of the extra chromosome in trisomy 21 as indicated by analysis of DNA polymorphisms. *New England Journal of Medicine, 324,* 872–876.

Apgar, B. S., & Churgay, C. A. (1993). Spontaneous abortion. *Primary Care, 20,* 621–627.

Apgar, V. (1953). A proposal for a new model of evaluation of the newborn infant. *Current Researches in Anesthesia and Analgesia, 32,* 260–267.

Arend, R., Gove, R., & Sroufe, L. A. (1979). Continuity of individual adaptation from infancy to kindergarten: A predictive study of ego-resiliency and curiosity in preschoolers. *Child Development, 50,* 950–959.

Ariès, P. (1962). *Centuries of childhood.* New York: Vintage.

Armstrong, B. G., McDonald, A. D., & Sloan, M. (1992). Cigarette, alcohol, and coffee consumption and spontaneous abortion. *American Journal of Public Health, 81,* 85.

Asher, J. (1987, April). Born to be shy? *Psychology Today,* pp. 56–64.

Asher, S., Renshaw, P., Geraci, K., & Dor, A. (1979, March). *Peer acceptance and social skill training: The selection of program content.* Paper presented at the meeting of the Society for Research in Child Development, San Francisco.

Aslin, R. N. (1987). Visual and auditory development in infancy. In J. D. Osofsky (Ed.), *Handbook of infant development* (2d ed.) New York: Wiley.

Astington, J. W. (1993). *The child's discovery of the mind.* Cambridge, MA: Harvard University Press.

Aylward, G. P., Pfeiffer, S. I., Wright, A., & Verhulst, S. J. (1989). Outcome studies of low birth weight infants published in the last decade: A metaanalysis. *Journal of Pediatrics, 115,* 515–520.

Azuma, S. D., & Chasnoff, I. J. (1993). Outcome of children prenatally exposed to cocaine and other drugs: A path analysis of three-year data. *Pediatrics, 92,* 396–402.

Babson, S. G., & Clarke, N. G. (1983). Relationship between infant death and maternal age. *Journal of Pediatrics, 103,* 391–393.

Bachman, J. G., & Schulenberg, J. (1993). How part-time work intensity relates to drug use, problem behavior, time use, and satisfaction among high school seniors: Are these consequences or merely correlates? *Developmental Psychology, 29,* 220–235.

Bachrach, C. A., London, K. A., & Maza, P. L. (1991). On the path to adoption: Adoption seeking in the United States, 1988. *Journal of Marriage and the Family, 53,* 705–718.

Baghurst, P. A., et al. (1992). Environmental exposure to lead and children's intelligence at the age of seven years. *New England Journal of Medicine, 327,* 1279–1284.

Baillargeon, R., & DeVos, J. (1991). Object permanence in young infants: Further evidence. *Child Development, 62,* 1227–1246.

Baird, D. D., & Wilcox, A. J. (1985). Cigarette smoking associated with delayed contraception. *Journal of the American Medical Association, 253,* 2979–2983.

Baldwin, W., & Cain, V. S. (1980). The children of teenage parents. *Family Planning Perspectives, 12,* 34.

Baltes, P. B., Reese, H. W., & Lipsitt, L. (1980). Life-span developmental psychology. *Annual Review of Psychology, 31,* 65–110.

Baltimore, D. (1995). Lessons from people with nonprogressive HIV infection. *New England Journal of Medicine, 332,* 259–260.

Bandura, A. (1960). *Relationship of family patterns to child behavior disorders* (Progress report, USPHS, Project No. M-1734). Stanford, CA: Stanford University.

Bandura, A., Grusec, J. E., & Menlove, F. L. (1967). Vicarious extinction of avoidance behavior. *Journal of Personality and Social Psychology, 5,* 16–23.

Bandura, A., & Huston, A. (1961). Identification as a process of incidental learning. *Journal of Abnormal and Social Psychology, 63,* 311–318.

Bandura, A., Ross, D., & Ross, S. A. (1961). Transmission of aggression through imitation of aggressive models. *Journal of Abnormal and Social Psychology, 63,* 575–582.

Bandura, A., Ross, D., & Ross, S. A. (1963). Imitation of film-mediated aggressive models. *Journal of Abnormal and Social Psychology, 66,* 3–11.

Bardouille-Crema, A., Black, K. N., & Feldhusen, J. (1986). Performance on Piagetian tasks of black children of differing socioeconomic levels. *Developmental Psychology, 22,* 841–844.

Barnes, A., Colton, T., Gunderson, J., Noller, K., Tilley, B., Strama, T., Townsend, D., Hatab, P., & O'Brien, P. (1980). Fertility and outcome of pregnancy in women exposed in utero to diethylstilbestrol. *New England Journal of Medicine, 302,* 609–613.

Barnes, K. E. (1971). Preschool play norms: A replication. *Developmental Psychology, 5,* 99–103.

Barrett, D. E., Radke-Yarrow, M., & Klein, R. E. (1982). Chronic malnutrition and child behavior: Effects of early caloric supplementation on social and emotional functioning at school age. *Developmental Psychology, 18,* 541–556.

Baruch, G. K., & Barnett, R. C. (1986). Father's participation in family work and children's sex role attitudes. *Child Development, 57,* 1210–1223.

Bass, J. L., Brennan, P., Mehta, K. A., & Kodzis, S. (1990). Pediatric problems in a suburban shelter for homeless families. *Pediatrics, 85,* 33–38.

Bass, M., Kravath, R. E., & Glass, L. (1986). Death-scene investigation in sudden infant death. *New England Journal of Medicine, 315,* 100–105.

Bassuk, E. L. (1991). Homeless families. *Scientific American, 265,* 66–74.

Bassuk, E. L., & Rosenberg, L. (1990). Psychosocial characteristics of homeless children and children with homes. *Pediatrics, 85,* 257–261.

Bassuk, E. L., & Rubin, L. (1987). Homeless children: A neglected population. *American Journal of Orthopsychiatry, 57,* 279–286.

Bates, E., Bretherton, I., & Snyder, L. (1988). *From first words to grammar: Individual differences and dissociable mechanisms.* New York: Cambridge University Press.

Bates, E., O'Connell, B., & Shore, C. (1987). Language and communication in infancy. In J. D. Osofsky (Ed.), *Handbook of infant development* (2d ed.). New York: Wiley.

Battelle, P. (1981, February). The triplets who found each other. *Good Housekeeping,* pp. 74–83.

Batistich, V., Watson, M., Solomon, D., Schaps, E., & Solomon, J. (1991). The Child Development Project: A comprehensive program for the development of prosocial character. In W. M. Kurtines & J. L. Gewirtz (Eds.), *Handbook of moral behavior and development: Vol. 3. Application* (pp. 1–34). Hillsdale, NJ: Erlbaum.

Baughman, E. E. (1971). *Black Americans.* New York: Academic.

Baumrind, D. (1971). Harmonious parents and their preschool children. *Developmental Psychology, 41,* 92–102.

Baumrind, D. (1993). The average expectable environment is not good enough: A response to Scarr. *Child Development, 64,* 1099–1117.

Baumrind, D., & Black, A. E. (1967). Socialization practices associated with dimensions of competence in preschool boys and girls. *Child Development, 38,* 291–327.

Baydar, N., & Brooks-Gunn, J. (1991). Effects of maternal employment and child-care arrangements on preschoolers' cognitive and behavioral outcomes: Evidence from the children of the National Longitudinal Survey of Youth. *Developmental Psychology, 27,* 932–945.

Baydar, N., Brooks-Gunn, J., & Furstenberg, F. F. (1993). Early warning signs of functional illiteracy: Predictors in

childhood and adolescence. *Child Development, 64,* 815–829.

Bayley, N. (1965). Research in child development: A longitudinal perspective. *Merrill-Palmer Quarterly of Behavior and Development, 11,* 184–190.

Bayley, N. (1969). *Bayley scales of infant development.* New York: Psychological Corporation.

Bayley, N. (1993). *Bayley scales of infant development: II.* New York: Psychological Corporation.

Beal, C. R. (1994). *Boys and girls: The development of gender roles.* New York: McGraw-Hill.

Beautrais, A. L., Fergusson, D. M., & Shannon, F. T. (1982). Life events and childhood morbidity: A prospective study. *Pediatrics, 70,* 935–940.

Beckwith, L., & Cohen, S. E. (1989). Maternal responsiveness with preterm infants and later competency. In M. H. Bornstein (Ed.), *Maternal responsiveness: Characteristics and consequences* (New Directions for Child Development, No. 43). San Francisco: Jossey-Bass.

Beeghly, M. (1993). Parent-infant play as a window on infant competence: An organizational approach to assessment. In K. MacDonald (Ed.), *Parent-child play: Descriptions and implications.* Albany, NY: State University of New York Press.

Behrman, R. E. (1985). Preventing low birth weight: A pediatric perspective. *Journal of Pediatrics, 107,* 842–854.

Behrman, R. E. (1992). *Nelson textbook of pediatrics* (13th ed.). Philadelphia: Saunders.

Behrman, R. E., & Vaughan, V. C. (Eds.). (1983). *Nelson textbook of pediatrics* (12th ed.). Philadelphia: Saunders.

Bell, S., & Ainsworth, M. D. S. (1972). Infant crying and maternal responsiveness. *Child Development, 43,* 1171–1190.

Bellinger, D. C., Stiles, K. M., & Needleman, H. L. (1992). Low-level lead exposure, intelligence, and academic achievement: A long-term follow-up study. *Pediatrics, 90,* 855–861.

Bellinger, D., Leviton, A., Waternaux, C., Needleman, H., & Rabinowitz, M. (1987). Longitudinal analysis of prenatal and postnatal lead exposure and early cognitive development. *New England Journal of Medicine, 316,* 1037–1043.

Belsky, J. (1979). Mother-father-infant interaction: A naturalistic observational study. *Developmental Psychology, 15,* 601–607.

Belsky, J. (1984). Two waves of day care research: Developmental effects and conditions of quality. In R. Ainslie (Ed.), *The child and the day care setting.* New York: Praeger.

Belsky, J. (1993). Etiology of child maltreatment: A developmental-ecological analysis. *Psychological Bulletin, 114,* 413–434.

Belsky, J., Fish, M., & Isabella, R. (1991). Continuity and discontinuity in infant negative and positive emotionality: Family antecedents and attachment consequences. *Developmental Psychology, 27,* 421–431.

Belsky, J., Lang, M., & Huston, T. L. (1986). Sex typing and division of labor as determinants of marital change across the transition to parenthood. *Journal of Personality and Social Psychology, 50,* 517–522.

Belsky, J., & Rovine, M. (1990). Patterns of marital change across the transition to parenthood: Pregnancy to three years postpartum. *Journal of Marriage and the Family, 52,* 5–19.

Belsky, J., & Rovine, M. J. (1988). Nonmaternal care in the first year of life and the security of infant-parent attachment. *Child Development, 59,* 157–167.

Beltramini, A. U., & Hertzig, M. E. (1983). Sleep and bedtime behavior in preschool-aged children. *Pediatrics, 71,* 153–158.

Bem, S. L. (1974). The measurement of psychological androgyny. *Journal of Consulting and Clinical Psychology, 42,* 155–162.

Bem, S. L. (1976). Probing the promise of androgyny. In A. G. Kaplan & J. P. Bean (Eds.), *Beyond sex-role stereotypes: Readings toward a psychology of androgyny.* Boston: Little, Brown.

Bem, S. L. (1983). Gender schema theory and its implications for child development: Raising gender-aschematic children in a gender-schematic society. *Signs, 8,* 598–616.

Bem, S. L. (1985). Androgyny and gender schema theory: A conceptual and empirical integration. In T. B. Sonderegger (Ed.), *Nebraska Symposium on Motivation, 1984. Psychology and gender.* Lincoln: University of Nebraska Press.

Benenson, J. F. (1993). Greater preference among females than males for dyadic interaction in early childhood. *Child Development, 64,* 544–555.

Benini, F., Johnston, C. C., Faucher, D., & Aranda, J. V. (1993). Topical anesthesia during circumcision in newborn infants. *Journal of the American Medical Association, 270,* 850–853.

Benn, R. K. (1986). Factors promoting secure attachment relationships between employed mothers and their sons. *Child Development, 57,* 1224–1231.

Benson, J. B. (1993). Season of birth and onset of locomotion: Theoretical and methodological implications. *Infant Behavior and Development, 16,* 69–81.

Benson, J. B., & Uzgiris, I. C. (1985). Effect of self-inflicted locomotion on infant search activity. *Developmental Psychology, 21*, 923–931.

Berenda, R. W. (1950). *The influence of the group on the judgments of children.* New York: King's Crown.

Bergman, A. B., Larsen, R.M., & Mueller, B. A. (1986). Changing spectrum of serious child abuse. *Pediatrics, 77*, 113–116.

Berk, L. E. (1986, May). Private speech: Learning out loud. *Psychology Today*, pp. 34–42.

Berk, L. E., & Garvin, R. A. (1984). Development of private speech among low-income Appalachian children. *Developmental Psychology, 20*, 271–286.

Berkowitz, G. S., Skovron, M. L., Lapinski, R. H., & Berkowitz, R. L. (1990). Delayed childbearing and the outcome of pregnancy. *New England Journal of Medicine, 322*, 659–664.

Berkowitz, L. (1984). Some effects of thoughts on anti- and prosocial influences of media events: A cognitive-neoassociation analysis. *Psychological Bulletin, 95*, 410–427.

Berman, P. W. (1987). Children caring for babies: Age and sex differences in response to infant signals and to the social context. In N. Eisenberg (Ed.), *Contemporary topics in developmental psychology.* New York: Wiley-Interscience.

Berman, P. W., & Goodman, V. (1984). Age and sex differences in children's responses to babies: Effects of adult caretaking requests and instructions. *Child Development, 55*, 1071–1077.

Berman, S. M., MacKay, H. T., Grimes, D. A., & Binkin, N. J. (1985). Deaths from spontaneous abortion in the United States. *Journal of the American Medical Association, 253*, 3119–3123.

Bernard, J., & Sontag, L. W. (1947). Fetal reactivity to sound. *Journal of Genetic Psychology, 70*, 205–210.

Bernard-Bonnin, A-C., Gilbert, S., Rousseau, E., Masson, P., & Maheux, B. (1991). Television and the 3- to 10-year-old child. *Pediatrics, 88*, 48–54.

Berndt, T. J. (1982). The features and effects of friendship in early adolescence. *Child Development, 53*, 1447–1460.

Berndt, T. J., & Perry, T. B. (1990). Distinctive features and effects of early adolescent friendships. In R. Montemayor, G. R. Adams, & T. P. Gullotta (Eds.), *From childhood to adolescence: A transitional period?* Newbury Park, CA: Sage.

Bernstein, G. A., & Garfinkel, B. D. (1988). Pedigrees, functioning, and psychopathology in families of school phobic children. *American Journal of Psychiatry, 145*, 70–74.

Berrueta-Clement, J. R., Schweinhart, L. J., Barnett, W. S., Epstein, A. S., & Weikart, D. P. (1985). *Changed lives: The effects of the Perry Preschool Program on youths through age 19.* Ypsilanti, MI: High/Scope.

Berscheid, E., Walster, E., & Bohrnstedt, G. (1973, June). The happy American body: A survey report. *Psychology Today*, pp. 119–131.

Bertenthal, B. I., & Campos, J. J. (1987). New directions in the study of early experience. *Child Development, 58*, 560–567.

Bertenthal, B. I., Campos, J. J., & Barrett, K. C. (1984). Self-produced locomotion: An organizer of emotional, cognitive, and social development in infancy. In R. N. Emde & R. J. Harmon (Eds.), *Continuities and discontinuities in development.* New York: Plenum.

Beaumont, P. J., Russell, J. D., & Touyz, S. W. (1993, June 26). Treatment of anorexia nervosa. *Lancet*, pp. 1635–1640.

Bierman, K. L., & Furman, W. (1984). The effects of social skills training and peer involvement on the social adjustment of preadolescents. *Child Development, 55*, 151–162.

Bierman, K. L., Smoot, D. L., & Aumiller, K. (1993). Characteristics of aggressive-rejected, aggressive (nonrejected), and rejected (nonaggressive) boys. *Child Development, 64*, 139–151.

Bigler, R. S., & Liben, L. S. (1992). Cognitive mechanisms in children's gender stereotyping: Theoretical and educational implications of a cognitive-based intervention. *Child Development, 63*, 1351–1363.

Biller, H. B. (1981). The father and sex role development. In M. E. Lamb (Ed.), *The role of the father in child development.* New York: Wiley.

Birch, L. L., Johnson, S. L., Andresen, G., Peters, J. C., & Schulte, M. C. (1991). The variability of young children's energy intake. *New England Journal of Medicine, 324*, 232–235.

Birns, B. (1976). The emergence and socialization of sex differences in the earliest years. *Merrill-Palmer Quarterly, 22*, 229–254.

Bittman, M. (1993, October 27). Eating well: Need more protein? Probably not. *New York Times*, p. C11.

Blauvelt, H. (1955). Dynamics of the mother-newborn relationship in goats. In B. Schaffner (Ed.), *Group processes.* New York: Macy Foundation.

Bloom, B. S. (1985). *Developing talent in young people.* New York: Ballantine.

Blum, R. (1987). Contemporary threats to adolescent health in the United States. *Journal of the American Medical Association, 257*, 3390–3395.

Blurton Jones, N. G., & Konner, M. J. (1973). Sex differences in behavior of London and Bushman children. In R. P. Michael & J. H. Crook (Eds.), *Comparative ecology and behavior of primates.* London: Academic.

Blyth, D. A., & Foster-Clark, F. S. (1987). Gender differences in perceived intimacy with different members of adolescents' social networks. *Sex Roles, 17*, 689–718.

Blyth, D. A., et al. (1981). The effects of physical development on self-image and satisfaction with body-image for early adolescent males. In R. G. Simmons (Ed.), *Research on community and mental health* (Vol. 2). Greenwich, CT: JAI.

Blyth, D. A., Simmons, R. G., & Carlton-Ford, S. (1983). The adjustment of early adolescents to school transitions. *Journal of Early Adolescence, 3*(1–2), 105–120.

Bolles, E. B. (1982). *So much to say.* New York: St. Martin's.

Bornstein, M. H. (1985a). Habituation of attention as a measure of visual information processing in human infants. In G. Gottlieb & N. A. Krasnegor (Eds.), *Development of audition and vision in the first year of postnatal life: A methodological overview.* Norwood, NJ: Ablex.

Bornstein, M.H. (1985b). How infant and mother jointly contribute to developing cognitive competence in the child. *Proceedings of the National Academy of Science, 82*, 7470–7473.

Bornstein, M., Kessen, W., & Weiskopf, S. (1976). The categories of hue in infancy. *Science, 191*, 201–202.

Bornstein, M. H., & Sigman, M. D. (1986). Continuity in mental development from infancy. *Child Development, 57*, 251–274.

Bornstein, M. H., & Tamis-LeMonda, C. S. (1989). Maternal responsiveness and cognitive development in children. In M. H. Bornstein (Ed.), *Maternal responsiveness: Characteristics and consequences* (New Directions for Child Development, No. 43). San Francisco: Jossey-Bass.

Bornstein, M. H., Tal, J., & Tamis-LeMonda, C. S. (1991). Parenting in cross-cultural perspective: The United States, France, and Japan. In M. H. Bornstein (Ed.), *Cultural approaches to parenting.* Hillsdale, NJ: Erlbaum.

Bouchard, T. J. (1994). Genes, environment, and personality. *Science, 264*, 1700–1701.

Bouza, A. V. (1990). *The police mystique: An insider's look at cops, crime, and the criminal justice system.* New York: Plenum.

Bower, B. (1985). The left hand of math and verbal talent. *Science News, 127, 263.*

Bower, B. (1993). A child's theory of mind. *Science News, 144,* 40–42.

Bowlby, J. (1951). *Maternal care and mental health.* Geneva: World Health Organization.

Bowlby, J. (1958). The nature of the child's tie to his mother. *International Journal of Psychoanalysis, 39,* 1–23.

Bowman, J. A., Sanson-Fisher, R. W., & Webb, G. R. (1987). Interventions in preschools to increase the use of safety restraints by preschool children. *Pediatrics, 79,* 103–109.

Boyle, C. A., Decouflé, P., & Yeargin-Allsopp, M. (1994). Prevalence and health impact of developmental disabilities in U.S. children. *Pediatrics, 93,* 399–403.

Boysson-Bardies, B., Sagart, L., & Durand, C. (1984). Discernible differences in the babbling of infants according to target language. *Journal of Child Language, 11,* 1–15.

Brackbill, Y., & Broman, S. H. (1979). *Obstetrical medication and development in the first year of life.* Unpublished manuscript.

Bracken, M., Holford, T., White, C., & Kelsey, J. (1978). Role of oral contraception in congenital malformations of offspring. *International Journal of Epidemiology, 7,* 309–317.

Bradley, R. H. (1989). Home measurement of maternal responsiveness. In M. H. Bornstein (Ed.), *Maternal responsiveness: Characteristics and consequences.* (New Directions for Child Development, No. 43). San Francisco: Jossey-Bass.

Bradley, R., & Caldwell, B. (1982). The consistency of the home environment and its relation to child development. *International Journal of Behavioral Development, 5,* 445–465.

Bradley, R., Caldwell, B., & Rock, S. (1988). Home environment and school performance: A ten-year follow-up and examination of three models of environmental action. *Child Development, 59,* 852–867.

Bradley, R. H., Caldwell, B. M., Rock, S. L., Ramey, C. T., et al. (1989). Home environment and cognitive development in the first 3 years of life: A collaborative study involving six sites and three ethnic groups in North America. *Developmental Psychology, 25,* 217–235.

Braine, M. (1976). Children's first word combinations. *Monographs of the Society for Research in Child Development, 41* (1, Serial No. 164).

Brandes, J. M., Scher, A., Itzkovits, J., Thaler, I., Sarid, M., & Gershoni-

Baruch, R. (1992). Growth and development of children conceived by in vitro fertilization. *Pediatrics, 90,* 424–429.

Brass, L. M., Isaacsohn, J. L., Merikangas, K. R., & Robinette, C. D. (1992). A study of twins and stroke. *Stroke, 23,* 221–223.

Braver, S. L., Wolchik, S. A., Sandler, I. N., Sheets, V. L., Fogas, B., & Bay, R. C. (1993). A longitudinal study of noncustodial parents: Parents without children. *Journal of Family Psychology, 7,* 9–23.

Bray, J. H., & Hetherington, E. M. (1993). Families in transition: Introduction and overview. *Journal of Family Psychology, 7,* 3–8.

Brazelton, T. B. (1973). Neonatal behavioral assessment scale. Philadelphia: Lippincott.

Brecher, E., & the Editors of *Consumer Reports.* (1972). *Licit and illicit drugs.* Mount Vernon, NY: Consumers Union.

Brewster, A. B. (1982). Chronically ill hospitalized children's concepts of their illness. *Pediatrics, 69,* 355–362.

Brittain, C. (1963). Adolescent choices and parent-peer cross-pressures. *American Sociological Review, 28,* 385–391.

Brodbeck, A. J., & Irwin, O. C. (1946). The speech behavior of infants without families. *Child Development, 17,* 145–156.

Brody, L. R., Zelazo, P. R., & Chaika, H. (1984). Habituation-dishabituation to speech in the neonate. *Developmental Psychology, 20,* 114–119.

Brody, N. (1985). The validity of tests of intelligence. In B. B. Wolman (Ed.), *Handbook of intelligence* (pp. 353–389). New York: Wiley.

Bronfenbrenner, U. (1979). *The ecology of human development.* Cambridge, MA: Harvard University Press.

Bronfenbrenner, U. (1986). Ecology of the family as a context for human development: Research perspectives. *Developmental Psychology, 22,* 723–742.

Bronfenbrenner, U. (1994). Ecological models of human development. In T. Husen & T. N. Postlethwaite (Eds.), *International encyclopedia of education* (2d ed., Vol. 3). Oxford, UK: Pergamon Press/Elsevier Science.

Bronfenbrenner, U., Belsky, J., & Steinberg, L. (1977). *Daycare in context: An ecological perspective on research and public policy* (Review prepared for Office of the Assistant Secretary for Planning and Evaluation, U.S. Department of Health, Education, and Welfare).

Bronfenbrenner, U., & Crouter, A. (1982). Work and family through time and space. In S. B. Kamerman & C. D. Hayes (Eds.), *Families that work: Children in a changing world.* Washington, DC: National Academy.

Bronson, F. H., & Desjardins, C. (1969). Aggressive behavior and seminal vesicle function in mice: Differential sensitivity to androgen given neonatally. *Endocrinology, 85,* 871–975.

Bronstein, P. (1988). Father-child interaction: Implications for gender role socialization. In P. Bronstein & C. P. Cowan (Eds.), *Fatherhood today: Men's changing role in the family.* New York: Wiley.

Bronstein, P., Clauson, J., Stoll, M. F., & Abrams, C. L. (1993). Parenting behavior and children's social, psychological, and academic adjustment in diverse family structures. *Family Relations, 42,* 268–276.

Brooke, J. (1988, April 26). Technology aids vaccination effort. *New York Times,* p. C3.

Brooks-Gunn, J. (1988). Pubertal processes and the early adolescent transition. In W. Damon (Ed.), *Child development today and tomorrow.* San Francisco: Jossey-Bass.

Brooks-Gunn, J., & Furstenberg, F. F. (1986). The children of adolescent mothers: Physical, academic, and psychological outcomes. *Developmental Review, 6,* 224–251.

Brooks-Gunn, J., Klebanov, P. K., Liaw, F., & Spiker, D. (1993). Enhancing the development of low-birthweight, premature infants: Changes in cognition and behavior over the first three years. *Child Development, 64,* 736–753.

Brooks-Gunn, J., & Reiter, E. O. (1990). The role of pubertal processes. In S. S. Feldman & G. R. Elliott (Eds.), *At the threshold: The developing adolescent.* Cambridge, MA: Harvard University Press.

Brophy, J. E., & Good, T. L. (1974). *Teacher-student relationships.* New York: Holt.

Brown, B. B., Clasen, D. R., & Eicher, S. A. (1986). Perceptions of peer pressure, peer conformity dispositions, and self-reported behavior among adolescents. *Developmental Psychology, 22,* 521–530.

Brown, B. B., Mounts, N., Lamborn, S. D., & Steinberg, L. (1993). Parenting practices and peer group affiliation in adolescence. *Child Development, 64,* 467–482.

Brown, J. E. (1983). *Nutrition for your pregnancy.* Minneapolis: University of Minnesota Press.

Brown, J. H. (1979). Suicide in Britain: More attempts, fewer deaths, lessons for public policy. *Archives of General Psychiatry, 36,* 1119–1124.

Brown, J. L. (1987). Hunger in the U.S. *Scientific American, 256*(2), 37–41.

Brown, L. M., & Gilligan, C. (1990, April). *The psychology of women and the development of girls.* Paper presented at the Laurel-Harvard Conference on the

Psychology of Women and the Education of Girls, Cleveland.

Brown, L. M., & Gilligan, C. (1992). *Meeting at the crossroads: Women's psychology and girls' development.* Cambridge, MA: Harvard University Press.

Brown, P., & Elliott, H. (1965). Control of aggression in a nursery school class. *Journal of Experimental Child Psychology, 2,* 103–107.

Brown, R. (1973a). Development of the first language in the human species. *American Psychologist, 28,* 97–106.

Brown, R. (1973b). *A first language: The early stages.* Cambridge, MA: Harvard University Press.

Brown, R., Cazden, C. B., & Bellugi, U. (1969). The child's grammar from I to III. In J. P. Hill (Ed.), *Minnesota Symposia on Child Psychology* (Vol. 2). Minneapolis: University of Minnesota Press.

Brown, S. S. (1985). Can low birth weight be prevented? *Family Planning Perspectives, 17,* 112–118.

Browne, A., & Finkelhor, D. (1986). Impact of child sexual abuse: A review of the research. *Psychological Bulletin, 99,* 66–77.

Brownell, C. A. (1990). Peer social skills in toddlers: Competencies and constraints illustrated by same-age and mixed-age interaction. *Child Development, 61,* 838–848.

Bryer, J. B., Nelson, B. A., Miller, J. B., & Krol, P. A. (1987). Childhood sexual and physical abuse as factors in adult psychiatric illnesses. *American Journal of Psychiatry, 144,* 1426–1430.

Buhrmester, D., & Furman, W. (1990). Perceptions of sibling relationships during middle childhood and adolescence. *Child Development, 61,* 138–139.

Buie, J. (1987, April 8). Pregnant teenagers: New view of old solution. *Education Week,* p. 32.

Bukowski, W. M., & Kramer, T. L. (1986). Judgments of the features of friendship among early adolescent boys and girls. *Journal of Early Adolescence, 6,* 331–338.

Bumpers, D. (1984). Securing the blessings of liberty for posterity: Preventive health care for children. *American Psychologist, 39,* 896–900.

Burgess, A. W., Hartman, C. R., & McCormack, A. (1987). Abused to abuser: Antecedents of socially deviant behaviors. *American Journal of Psychiatry, 144,* 1431–1436.

Burke, B. M. (1992). Genetic counselor attitudes towards fetal sex identification and selective abortion. *Social Science and Medicine, 34,* 1263–1269.

Burns, A. (1992). Mother-headed families: An international perspective and the case of Australia. *Social Policy Report of the Society for Research in Child Development, VI,* Spring, 1992.

Burns, J. F. (1994, August 27). India fights abortion of female fetuses. *New York Times,* p. A5.

Burros, M. (1990, October 3). Children are focus of diet-pill issue. *New York Times,* pp. C1, C4.

Bushnell, E. W., & Boudreau, J. P. (1993). Motor development and the mind: The potential role of motor abilities as a determinant of aspects of perceptual development. *Child Development, 64,* 1005–1021.

Butterfield, E., & Siperstein, G. (1972). Influence of contingent auditory stimulation upon non-nutritional suckle. In J. Bosma (Ed.), *Oral sensation and perception: The mouth of the infant.* Springfield, IL: Thomas.

Cahan, S., & Cohen, M. (1989). Age versus schooling effects on intelligence development. *Child Development, 60,* 1239–1249.

Cain, V. S., & Hofferth, S. L. (1989). Parental choice of self-care for school-age children. *Journal of Marriage and the Family, 51,* 65–77.

Cairns, R. B., Cairns, B. D., & Neckerman, H. J. (1989). Early school dropout: Configurations and determinants. *Child Development, 60,* 1437–1452.

Calkins, S. D., & Fox, N. A. (1992). The relations among infant temperament, security of attachment, and behavioral inhibition at twenty-four months. *Child Development, 63,* 1456–1472.

Calvert, S. L., & Huston, A. C. (1987). Television and children's gender schemata. In L. S. Liben & M. S. Signorella (Eds.), *Children's gender schemata.* San Francisco: Jossey-Bass.

Calvo, E. B., Galindo, A. C., & Aspres, N. B. (1992). Iron status in exclusively breast-fed infants. *Pediatrics, 90,* 375–379.

Campos, J., Bertenthal, B., & Benson, N. (1980, April). *Self-produced locomotion and the extraction of form invariance.* Paper presented at the meeting of the International Conference on Infant Studies, New Haven, CT.

Campos, J. J., Langer, A., & Krowitz, A. (1970). Cardiac responses on the visual cliff in prelocomotor human infants. *Science, 170,* 196–197.

Camras, L. A., Oster, H., Campos, J. J., Miyake, K., & Bradshaw, D. (1992). Japanese and American infants' responses to arm restraint. *Developmental Psychology, 28,* 578–583.

Cantor, J. (1994). Confronting children's fright responses to mass media. In D. Zillman, J. Bryant, & A. C. Huston (Eds.), *Media, children, and the family: Social scientific, psychoanalytic, and clinical perspectives.* Hillsdale, NJ: Erlbaum.

Caplan, M., Vespo, J., Pedersen, J., & Hay, D. F. (1991). Conflict and its resolution in small groups of one- and two-year-olds. *Child Development, 62,* 1513–1524.

Caplan, N., Choy, M. H., & Whitmore, J. K. (1992, February). Indochinese refugee families and academic achievement. *Scientific American,* 36–42.

Capute, A. J., Shapiro, B. K., & Palmer, F. B. (1987). Marking the milestones of language development. *Contemporary Pediatrics, 4,* 24.

Cardenas, J. A. (1977). Response I. In N. Epstein (Ed.), *Language, ethnicity and the schools.* Washington, DC: Institute for Educational Leadership.

Carlo, G., Knight, G. P., Eisenberg, N., & Rotenberg, K. J. (1991). Cognitive processes and prosocial behaviors among children: The role of affective attributions and reconciliations. *Developmental Psychology, 27,* 456–461.

Carlson, B. E. (1984). The father's contribution to child care: Effects on children's perceptions of parental roles. *American Journal of Orthopsychiatry, 54,* 123–136.

Carlton-Ford, S., & Collins, W. A. (1988, August). *Family conflict: Dimensions, differential reporting, and developmental differences.* Paper presented at the annual meeting of the American Sociological Association, Chicago.

Carnegie Corporation Task Force on Meeting the Needs of Young Children. (1994). *Starting points: Meeting the needs of our youngest children.* New York: Carnegie Corporation of New York.

Carpenter, M. W., Sady, S. P., Hoegsberg, B., Sady, M. A., Haydon, B., Cullinane, E. M., Coustan, D. R., & Thompson, P. D. (1988). Fetal heart rate response to maternal exertion. *Journal of the American Medical Association, 259,* 3006–3009.

Carraher, T. N., Schliemann, A. D., & Carraher, D. W. (1988). Mathematical concepts in everyday life. In G. B. Saxe & M. Gearhart (Eds.), Children's mathematics. *New Directions in Child Development, 41,* 71–87.

Carrera, M. A. (1986, April 11). *Future directions in teen pregnancy prevention.* Talk presented to the annual meeting of the Society for the Scientific Study of Sex, Eastern Region.

Carroll, J. L., & Rest, J. R. (1982). Moral development. In B. Wolman (Ed.), *Handbook of developmental psychology.* Englewood Cliffs, NJ: Prentice-Hall.

Carter, D., & Welch, D. (1981). Parenting styles and children's behavior. *Family Relations, 30,* 191–195.

Caruso, D. (1993). Dimensions of quality in infants' exploratory competence at one year. *Infant Behavior and Development, 16,* 423–439.

Case, R. (1985). *Intellectual development: Birth to adulthood.* Orlando, FL: Academic.

Case, R. (1992). Neo-Piagetian theories of child development. In R. Sternberg & C. Berg (Eds.), *Intellectual development.* New York: Cambridge University Press.

Casey, P. H., Bradley, R., & Wortham, B. (1984). Social and nonsocial home environment of infants with nonorganic failure-to-thrive. *Pediatrics, 73,* 348–353.

Casey, R. J., & Berman, J. S. (1985). The outcome of psychotherapy with children. *Psychological Bulletin, 98,* 388–400.

Casper, R. C., & Offer, D. (1990). Weight and dieting concerns in adolescents, fashion or symptom? *Pediatrics, 86,* 384–390.

Cassidy, J. (1986). The ability to negotiate the environment: An aspect of infant competence as related to quality of attachment. *Child Development, 57,* 331–337.

CDF Reports (1994, January). Living in fear. Vol. 15, No. 2.

Ceci, S. J., & Bruck, M. (1993a). Child witnesses: Translating research into policy. *Social Policy Report of the Society for Research in Child Development, VII,* 3.

Ceci, S. J., & Bruck, M. (1993b). Suggestibility of the child witness: A historical review and synthesis. *Psychological Bulletin, 113,* 403–439.

Ceci, S. J., & Leichtman, M. D. (1992). "I know that you know that I know that you broke the toy": A brief report of recursive awareness among 3-year-olds. In S. J. Ceci, M. D. Leichtman, & M. E. Putnick (Eds.), *Cognitive and social factors in early deception* (pp. 1–9). Hillsdale, NJ: Erlbaum.

Celis, W. (1990). More states are laying school paddle to rest. *New York Times,* pp. A1, B12.

Centers for Disease Control. (1983). *CDC Surveillance Summaries* (Vol. 32). Atlanta: Author.

Centers for Disease Control and Prevention (CDC). (1993). Rates of cesarean delivery—United States, 1991. *Morbidity and Mortality Weekly Report, 42,* 285–289.

Centers for Disease Control and Prevention (CDC). (1994). Health risk behaviors among adolescents who do and do not attend school—United States, 1992. *Journal of the American Medical Association, 271,* 1068–1070.

Cesaer, P. (1993). Old and new facts about perinatal brain development. *Journal of Child Psychology and Psychiatry, 34,* 101–109.

Chance, P., & Fischman, J. (1987, May). The magic of childhood. *Psychology Today,* pp. 48–58.

Chapman, A. H. (1974). *Management of emotional problems of children and adolescents* (2d ed.). Philadelphia: Lippincott.

Chapman, M., & Lindenberger, U. (1988). Functions, operations, and decalage in the development of transitivity. *Developmental Psychology, 24,* 542–551.

Chasnoff, I. J., Griffith, D. R., Freier, C., & Murray, J. (1992). Cocaine/polydrug use in pregnancy: Two-year follow-up. *Pediatrics, 89,* 284–289.

Chasnoff, I. J., Griffith, D. R., MacGregor, S., Dirkes, K., & Burns, K. A. (1989). Temporal patterns of cocaine use in pregnancy: Perinatal outcomes. *Journal of the American Medical Association, 261,* 1741–1744.

Chasnoff, I. J., Landress, H., & Barrett, M. (1990). The prevalence of illicit-drug or alcohol use during pregnancy and discrepancies in mandatory reporting in Pinellas County, Florida. *New England Journal of Medicine, 332,* 1202–1206.

Chasnoff, I. J., Lewis, D. E., & Squires, L. (1987). Cocaine intoxification in a breast-fed infant. *Pediatrics, 80,* 836–838.

Chavez, G. F., Mulinare, J., & Cordero, J. F. (1989). Maternal cocaine use during early pregnancy as a risk factor for congenital urogenital anomalies. *Journal of the American Medical Association, 262,* 795–798.

Chavkin, W., & Kandall, S. R. (1990). Between a "rock" and a hardplace: Perinatal drug abuse. *Pediatrics, 85,* 223–225.

Chen, C., & Stevenson, H. W. (1989). Homework: A cross-cultural examination. *Child Development, 60,* 551–561.

Chen, X., & Rubin, K. H. (1992). Correlates of peer acceptance in a Chinese sample of six-year-olds. *International Journal of Behavioral Development, 15,* 259–273.

Chervenak, F. A., Isaacson, G., & Mahoney, M. J. (1986). Advances in the diagnosis of fetal defects. *New England Journal of Medicine, 315,* 305–307.

Chess, S. (1983). Mothers are always the problem—or are they? Old wine in new bottles. *Pediatrics, 71,* 974–976.

Chess, S., & Thomas, A. (1982). Infant bonding: Mystique and reality. *American Journal of Orthopsychiatry, 52,* 213–222.

Child Welfare League of America. (1986). *Born to run: The status of child abuse in America.* Washington, DC: Author.

Children's Defense Fund (1993). Birth to teens. *CDF Reports,* 0276-6531.

Children's Defense Fund. (1994). *The state of America's children yearbook 1994.* Washington, DC: Author.

Chilman, C. S. (1980). *Adolescent sexuality in a changing American society: Social and psychological perspectives* (NIH Publication No. 80-1426). Bethesda, MD: U. S. Department of Health, Education and Welfare, Public Health Service, National Institute of Health.

Chira, S. (1988, July 27). In Japan, the land of the rod, an appeal to spare the child. *New York Times,* pp. A1, A10.

Chisholm, J. S. (1983). *Navajo infancy: An ethnological study of child development.* New York: Aldine.

Chomsky, C. S. (1969). *The acquisition of syntax in children from five to ten.* Cambridge, MA: MIT Press.

Chomsky, N. (1957). *Syntactic structures.* The Hague: Mouton.

Chomsky, N. (1965). *Aspects of a theory of syntax.* Cambridge, MA: MIT Press.

Chomsky, N. (1972). *Language and mind* (2d ed.). New York: Harcourt Brace Jonanovich.

Christie, J. F. (1991). *Psychological research on play: Connections with early literacy development.* Albany, NY: State University of New York Press.

Chumlea, W. C. (1982). Physical growth in adolescence. In B. B. Wolman (Ed.), *Handbook of developmental psychology.* Englewood Cliffs, NJ: Prentice-Hall.

Cicirelli, V. G. (1976a). Family structure and interaction: Sibling effects on socialization. In M. F. McMillan & S. Henao (Eds.), *Child psychiatry: Treatment and research.* New York: Brunner/Mazel.

Cicirelli, V. G. (1976b). Siblings teaching siblings. In V. L. Allen (Ed.), *Children as teachers: Theory and research on tutoring.* New York: Academic.

Cicirelli, V. G. (1994). Sibling relationships in cross-cultural perspective. *Journal of Marriage and the Family, 56,* 7–20.

Clark, E. V. (1983). Meanings and concepts. In P. H. Mussen (Ed.), *Handbook of child psychology.* New York: Wiley.

Clarke-Stewart, A. (1977). *Child care in the family: A review of research and some propositions for policy.* New York: Academic.

Clarke-Stewart, A. (1992). Consequences of child care for children's development. In A. Booth (Ed.), *Child care in the 1990s: Trends and consequences.* Hillsdale, NJ: Erlbaum.

Clarke-Stewart, K. A. (1987). Predicting child development from day care forms and features: The Chicago study. In D. A. Phillips (Ed.), *Quality in child care: What does the research tell us? Re-*

search monographs of the National Association for the Education of Young Children. Washington, DC: National Association for the Education of Young Children.

Clarke-Stewart, K. A. (1989). Infant day care: Maligned or malignant. *American Psychologist, 44*, 266–273.

Clausen, J. A. (1975). The social meaning of differential physical and sexual maturation. In S. E. Dragastin & G. H. Elder, Jr. (Eds.), *Adolesence in the life cycle.* New York: Halsted.

Clausen, J. A. (1993). *American lives.* New York: Free Press.

Clayton, E. W. (1992). Issues in state newborn screening programs. *Pediatrics, 90*, 641–646.

Cobrinick, P., Hood, R., & Chused, E. (1959). Effects of maternal narcotic addiction on the newborn infant. *Pediatrics, 24*, 288–290.

Cohn, J. F., & Tronick, E. Z. (1983). Three-month-old infants' reaction to simulated maternal depression. *Child Development, 54*, 185–193.

Cohn, L. D. (1991). Sex differences in the course of personality development: A meta-analysis. *Psychological Bulletin, 109*, 252–266.

Colby, A., & Damon, W. (1993). Gaining insight into the lives of moral leaders. *Chronicle of Higher Education, 39*, 84–84.

Colby, A., Kohlberg, L., Gibbs, J., & Lieberman, M. (1983). A longitudinal study of moral development. *Monographs of the Society for Research in Child Development, 48*(1–2, Serial No. 200).

Cole, C., & Rodman, H. (1987). When school-age children care for themselves: Issues for family life educators and parents. *Family Relations, 36*, 92–96.

Cole, P. M., Barrett, K. C., & Zahn-Waxler, C. (1992). Emotion displays in two-year-olds during mishaps. *Child Development, 63*, 314–324.

Coleman, J. (1980). Friendship and the peer group in adolescence. In J. Adelson (Ed.), *Handbook of adolescent development.* New York: Wiley.

Coles, R., & Stokes, G. (1985). *Sex and the American teenager.* New York: Harper & Row.

Collins, C. (1994, November 10). Baby walkers: The question of safety. *New York Times*, p. C2.

Collins, R. C., & Deloria, D. (1983). Head Start research: A new chapter. *Children Today, 12*(4), 15–19.

Collins, W. A. (1990). Parent-child relationships in the transition to adolescence: Continuity and change in interaction, affect, and cognition. In R. Montemayor, G. R. Adams, & T. P. Gullotta (Eds.), *From childhood to adolescence: A transitional period?* Newbury Park, CA: Sage.

Colman, A., & Colman, L. (1971). *Pregnancy: The psychological experience.* New York: Herder & Herder.

Condon, W., & Sander, L. (1974). Synchrony demonstrated between movements of the neonate and adult speech. *Child Development, 45*, 456–462.

Conger, J. J. (1988). Hostages to fortune: Youth, values, and the public interest. *American Psychologist, 43*, 291–300.

Connecticut Early Childhood Education Council (CECEC). (1983). *Report on full-day kindergarten.* Author.

Conners, C. K. (1988). Does diet affect behavior and learning in hyperactive children? *Harvard Medical School Mental Health Letter, 5*(5), 7–8.

Coons, S., & Guilleminault, C. (1982). Development of sleep-wake patterns and non–rapid eye movement sleep stages during the first six months of life in normal infants. *Pediatrics, 69*, 793–798.

Cooper, R. P., & Aslin, R. N. (1990). Preference for infant-directed speech in the first month after birth. *Child Development, 61*, 1584–1595.

Coopersmith, S. (1967). *The antecedents of self-esteem.* San Francisco: Freeman.

Corbin, C. (1973). *A textbook of motor development.* Dubuque, IA: Brown.

Coren, S. (1992). *The left-hander syndrome: The causes and consequences of left-handedness.* New York: Free Press.

Coren, S., & Halpern, D. F. (1991). Left-handedness: A marker for decreased survival fitness. *Psychological Bulletin, 109*(1), 90–106.

Costello, A. J., Edelbrock, C., Burns, B. J., Dulcan, M. K., Brent, D., & Janiszewsku, S. (1988). Psychiatric disorders in pediatric primary care. *Archives of General Psychiatry, 45*, 1107–1116.

Coster, W. J., Gersten, M. S., Beeghly, M., & Cicchetti, D. (1989). Communicative functioning in maltreated toddlers. *Developmental Psychology, 25*, 1020–1029.

Council of Scientific Affairs of the American Medical Association. (1989). Dyslexia. *Journal of the American Medical Association, 261*, 2236–2239.

Council on Scientific Affairs of the American Medical Association. (1991). Hispanic health in the United States. *Journal of the American Medical Association, 265*, 248–252.

Courchesne, E., Yeung-Courchesne, R., Press, G. A., Hesselink, J. R., & Jernigan, T. L. (1988). Hypoplasia of cerebellar vermae lobules VI and VII in autism. *New England Journal of Medicine, 318*, 1349–1354.

Cowan, P. A., Cowan, C. P., Schulz, M. S., & Heming, G. (1994). Prebirth to preschool family factors in children's adaptation to kindergarten. In R. D. Parke & S. G. Kellam (Eds.), *Exploring family relationships with other social contexts. Family research consortium: Advances in family research* (pp. 75–114). Hillsdale, NJ: Erlbaum.

Cowan, W. M. (1979). The development of the brain. *Scientific American, 241*, 113–133.

Cox, M. J., Owen, M. T., Henderson, V. K., & Margand, N. A. (1992). Prediction of infant-father and infant-mother attachment. *Developmental Psychology, 28*, 474–483.

Craft, M. J., Montgomery, L. A., & Peters, J. (1992, October 2). *Comparative study of responses in preschool children to the birth of an ill sibling.* Nursing seminar series presentation, University of Iowa College of Nursing, Iowa City.

Crain-Thoreson, C., & Dale, P. S. (1992). Do early talkers become early readers? Linguistic precocity, preschool language, and emergent literacy. *Developmental Psychology, 28*, 421–429.

Cramer, D. W., Schiff, I., Schoenbaum, S. C., Gibson, M., Belisle, S., Albrecht, B., Stillman, R. J., Berger, M. M., Wilson, E., Stadel, B. V., & Seibel, H. (1985). Tubal infertility and the intrauterine device. *New England Journal of Medicine, 313*, 941–947.

Cratty, B. (1979). *Perceptual and motor development in infants and children* (2d ed.). Englewood Cliffs, NJ: Prentice-Hall.

Cratty, B. J. (1986). *Perceptual and motor development in infants and children* (3d ed.). Englewood Cliffs, NJ: Prentice-Hall.

Crnic, K. A., & Greenberg, M. T. (1990). Minor parenting stresses with young children. *Child Development, 61*, 1628–1637.

Crockett, L. J., & Petersen, A. C. (1987). Pubertal status and psychosocial development: Findings from the Early Adolescent Study. In R. M. Lerner & T. T. Foch (Eds.), *Biological-psychosocial interactions in early adolescence: A lifespan perspective.* Hillsdale, NJ: Erlbaum.

Crouter, A. C., MacDermid, S. M., McHale, S. M., & Perry-Jenkins, M. (1990). Parental monitoring and perception of children's school performance and conduct in dual- and single-earner families. *Developmental Psychology, 26*, 649–657.

Crouter, A. C., & McHale, S. M. (1993). Temporal rhythms in family life: Seasonal variation in the relation between parental work and family processes. *Developmental Psychology, 29*, 198–205.

Crow, J. F. (1993). How much do we know about spontaneous human mutation rates? *Environmental and Molecular Mutagenesis, 21,* 122–129.

Crow, J. F. (1994). Spontaneous mutation as a risk factor. *Experimental and Clinical Immunogenetics.*

Csikszentmihalyi, M., & Larson, R. (1984). *Being adolescent: Conflict and growth in the teenage years.* New York: Basic Books.

Cummings, E. M., Iannotti, R. J., & Zahn-Waxler, C. (1989). Aggression between peers in early childhood: Individual continuity and developmental change. *Child Development, 60,* 887–895.

Cummins, J. (1986). Empowering minority students: A framework for intervention. *Harvard Educational Review, 56,* 18–36.

Curtiss, S. (1977). *Genie.* New York: Academic.

Cushman, R., Down, J., MacMillan, N., & Waclawik, H (1991). Helmet promotion in the emergency room following bicycle injury: A randomized trial. *Pediatrics, 88,* 43–47.

Czeizel, A. E., & Dudas, I. (1992). Prevention of the first occurrence of neural-tube defects by periconceptual vitamin supplementation. *New England Journal of Medicine, 327,* 1832–1835.

D'Alton, M. E., & DeCherney, A. H. (1993). Prenatal diagnosis. *New England Journal of Medicine, 32,* 114–120.

Daiute, C., Hartup, W. W., Sholl, W., & Zajac, R. (1993, March 26). *Peer collaboration and written language development: A study of friends and acquaintances.* Paper presented at the meeting of the Society for Research in Child Development, New Orleans.

Daley, S. (1991, January 9). Little girls lose their self-esteem on way to adolescence, study finds. *New York Times,* p. B6.

Daling, J. R., Weiss, N. S., Metch, B. J., Chow, W. H., Siderstrom, R. M., Moore, D. E., Spadone, L. R., & Stadel, B. V. (1984). Primal tubal infertility in relation to the use of an intrauterine device. *New England Journal of Medicine, 312,* 937–941.

Damon, W. (1984). Peer education: The untapped potential. *Journal of Applied Developmental Psychology, 5,* 331–343.

Daniels, D., & Plomin, R. (1985). Origins of individual differences in infant shyness. *Developmental Psychology, 21,* 118–121.

Davidson, J., & Smith, R. (1990). Traumatic experiences in psychiatric outpatients. *Journal of Traumatic Stress, 3,* 459–475.

Davidson, J. E., & Sternberg, R. J. (1984). The role of insight in intellectual gift-edness. *Gifted Child Quarterly, 28*(2), 58–64.

Davidson, R. J., & Fox, N. A. (1989). Frontal brain asymmetry predicts infants' response to maternal separation. *Journal of Abnormal Psychology, 98*(2), 127–131.

Dawson, D. A. (1991). Family structure and children's health and well-being: Data from the 1988 National Health Interview Survey on child health. *Journal of Marriage and the Family, 53,* 573–584.

Dawson, G., Klinger, L. G., Panagiotides, H., Hill, D., & Spieker, S. (1992). Frontal lobe activity and affective behavior of infants of mothers with depressive symptoms. *Child Development, 63,* 725–737.

Deaux, K. (1985). Sex and gender. *Annual Review of Psychology, 36,* 49–81.

DeCasper, A., & Fifer, W. (1980). Newborns prefer their mother's voices. *Science, 208,* 1174–1176.

DeCasper, A. J., & Spence, M. J. (1986). Prenatal maternal speech influences newborns' perception of speech sounds. *Infant Behavior and Development, 9,* 133–150.

Decker, M. D., Dewey, M. J., Hutcheson, R. H., & Schaffner, W. (1984). The use and efficacy of child restraint devices. *Journal of the American Medical Association, 252,* 2571–2575.

DeFrain, J., & Ernst, L. (1978). The psychological effects of sudden infant death syndrome on surviving family members. *Journal of Family Practice, 6,* 985–989.

DeFrain, J., Montens, L., Stork, J., & Stork, W. (1986). *Stillborn: The invisible death.* New York: Free Press.

DeFrain, J., Taylor, J., & Ernst, L. (1982). *Coping with sudden infant death.* New York: Free Press.

DeFries, J. C., Fulker, D. W., & LaBuda, M. C. (1987). Evidence for a genetic etiology in reading disability of twins. *Nature, 329,* 537–539.

DeFries, P. J., Plomin, R., & Fulker, D. W. (1994). *Nature and nurture during middle childhood.* Cambridge, UK: Blackwell.

Dekovic, M., & Janssens, J. M. A. M. (1992). Parents' child-rearing style and child's sociometric status. *Developmental Psychology, 28,* 925–932.

Del Carmen, R. D., Pedersen, F. A., Huffman, L. C., & Bryan, Y. E. (1993). Dyadic distress management predicts subsequent security of attachment. *Infant Behavior and Development, 16,* 131–147.

Demo, D. H. (1991). A sociological perspective on parent-adolescent disagreements. *New Directions for Child Development, 51,* 111–118.

Demo, D. H. (1992). Parent-child relations: Assessing recent changes. *Journal of Marriage and the Family, 54,* 104–117.

Denney, N. W. (1972). Free classification in preschool children. *Child Development, 43,* 1161–1170.

Dennis, W. (1960). Causes of retardation among institutional children: Iran. *Journal of Genetic Psychology, 96,* 47–59.

Denny, F. W., & Clyde, W. A. (1983). Acute respiratory tract infections: An overview. In W. A. Clyde & F. W. Denny (Eds.), Workshop on acute respiratory diseases among children of the world. *Pediatric Research, 17,* 1026–1029.

deRegt, R. H., Minkoff, H. L., Feldman, J., & Schwartz, R. H. (1986). Relation of private or clinic care to the cesarean birth rate. *New England Journal of Medicine, 315,* 619–624.

DeVries, M. W., & Sameroff, A. J. (1984). Culture and temperament: Influence on infant temperament in three East African societies. *American Journal of Orthopsychiatry, 54,* 83–96.

Deykin, E. Y., Alpert, J. J., & McNamara, J. J. (1985). A pilot study of the effect of exposure to child abuse or neglect on adolescent suicide behavior. *American Journal of Psychiatry, 142,* 1299–1303.

Diagnostic and statistical manual of mental disorders (3d ed., rev.) (DSM III-R). (1987). Washington, DC: American Psychiatric Association.

Diagnostic and statistical manual of mental disorders (4th ed.) (DSM-IV). (1994). Washington, DC: American Psychiatric Association.

Dickinson, D. K., Cote, L., & Smith, M. W. (1993). Learning vocabulary in preschool: Social and discourse contexts affecting vocabulary growth. In C. Daiute (Ed.), The development of literacy through social interaction. *New Directions in Child Development, 61,* 67–78.

Dickson, W. P. (1979). Referential communication performance from age 4 to 8: Effects of referent type, context, and target position. *Developmental Psychology, 15,* 470–471.

Dickstein, S., & Parke, R. D. (1988). Social referencing in infancy: A glance at fathers and marriage. *Child Development, 59,* 506–511.

Dien, D. S. F. (1982). A Chinese perspective on Kohlberg's theory of moral development. *Developmental Review, 2,* 331–341.

Dietrich, K. N., Berger, O. G., & Succop, P. A. (1993). Lead exposure and the motor developmental status of urban six-year-old children in the Cincinnati Prospective Study. *Pediatrics, 91,* 301–307.

Dietz, W. H., & Gortmaker, S. L. (1985). Do we fatten our children at the television set? Obesity and television viewing in children and adolescents. *Pediatrics, 75*, 807–812.

Dimant, R. J., & Bearison, D. J. (1991). Development of formal reasoning during successive peer interactions. *Developmental Psychology, 27*, 277–284.

Dion, K. K., Berscheid, E., & Walster, E. (1972). What is beautiful is good. *Journal of Personality and Social Psychology, 24*, 285–290.

Dishion, T. J., Patterson, G. R., Stoolmiller, M., & Skinner, M. L. (1991). Family, school, and behavioral antecedents to early adolescent involvement with antisocial peers. *Developmental Psychology, 27*, 172–180.

Dodge, K. A., Bates, J. E., & Pettit, G. S. (1990). Mechanisms in the cycle of violence. *Science, 250*, 1678–1683.

Dodge, K. A., Coie, J. D., Pettit, G. S., & Price, J. M. (1990). Peer status and aggression in boys' groups: Developmental and contextual analysis. *Child Development, 61*, 1289–1309.

Donnelly, D., & Finkelhor, D. (1992). Does equality in custody arrangement improve the parent-child relationship? *Journal of Marriage and the Family, 54*, 837–845.

Donovan, P. (1993). Project offers counseling and condoms to Philadelphia students. *Family Planning Perspectives, 25*, 180.

Donovan, P. (1993). *Testing positive: Sexually transmitted disease and the public response.* New York: Alan Guttmacher Institute.

Dore, J. (1975). Holophrases, speech arts, and language universals. *Journal of Child Language, 2*, 21–40.

Doris, J. (1993). Paper presented at the Child Witness Conference. Family Life Development Center, Cornell University, New York.

Dornbusch, S. M., Carlsmith, J. M., Bushwall, S. J., Ritter, P. L., Leiderman, H., Hastorf, A. H., & Gross, R. T. (1985). Single parents, extended households, and the control of adolescents. *Child Development, 56*, 326–341.

Dornbusch, S. M., Ritter, P. L., Leiderman, P. H., Roberts, D. F., & Fraleigh, M. J. (1987). The relation of parenting style to adolescent school performance. *Child Development, 58*, 1244–1257.

Dove, J. (undated). *Facts about anorexia nervosa.* Bethesda, MD: National Institutes of Health, Office of Research Reporting, National Institute of Child Health and Human Development.

Downey, D. B., & Powell, B. (1993). Do children in single-parent households fare better living with same-sex parents? *Journal of Marriage and the Family, 55*, 55–71.

Dreher, M. C., Nugent, K., & Hudgins, R. (1994). Prenatal marijuana exposure and neonatal outcomes in Jamaica: An ethnographic study. *Pediatrics, 93*, 254–260.

Dreyer, P. H. (1982). Sexuality during adolescence. In B. B. Wolman (Ed.), *Handbook of developmental psychology.* Englewood Cliffs, NJ: Prentice Hall.

Duncan, B., Ey, J., Holberg, C. J., Wright, A. L., Martinez, F. D., & Taussig, L. M. (1993). Exclusive breast-feeding for at least four months protects against otitis media. *Pediatrics, 91*, 867–872.

Dungy, C. I., Christensen-Szalanski, J., Losch, M., & Russell, D. (1992). Effect of discharge samples on duration of breast-feeding. *Pediatrics, 90*, 233–236.

Dunham, P. J., Dunham, F., & Curwin, A. (1993). Joint-attentional states and lexical acquisition at 18 months. *Developmental Psychology, 29*, 827–831.

Dunn, J. (1983). Sibling relationships in early childhood. *Child Development, 54*, 787–811.

Dunn, J. (1985). *Sisters and brothers.* Cambridge, MA: Harvard University Press.

Dunn, J. (1991). Young children's understanding of other people: Evidence from observations within the family. In D. Frye & C. Moore (Eds.), *Children's theories of mind: Mental states and social understanding.* Hillsdale, NJ: Erlbaum.

Dunn, J., Brown, J., Slomkowski, C., Tesla, C., & Youngblade, L. (1991). Young children's understanding of other people's feelings and beliefs: Individual differences and antecedents. *Child Development, 62*, 1352–1366.

Dunn, J., & Kendrick, C. (1982). *Siblings: Love, envy and understanding.* Cambridge, MA: Harvard University Press.

Dunne, R. G., Asher, K. N., & Rivara, F. P. (1992). Behavior and parental expectations of child pedestrians. *Pediatrics, 89*, 486–490.

DuPont, R. L. (1983). Phobias in children. *Journal of Pediatrics, 102*, 999–1002.

Dwyer, T., Ponsonby, A. B., Newman, N. M., & Gibbons, L. E. (1991). Prospective cohort study of prone sleeping position and sudden infant death syndrome. *Lancet, 337*, 1244–1247.

Dyson, A. H. (1993). A sociocultural perspective on symbolic development in primary grade classrooms. In C. Daiute (Ed.), The development of literacy through social interaction. *New Directions in Child Development, 61*, 25–39.

Dyslexia (1989, September 23). *Lancet,* pp. 719–720.

Easterbrooks, M. A. (1989). Quality of attachment to mother and to father: Effects of perinatal risk status. *Child Development, 60*, 825–830.

Easterbrooks, M. A., & Goldberg, W. A. (1984). Toddler development in the family: Impact of father involvement and parenting characteristics. *Child Development, 55*, 740–752.

Easterlin, R. A. (1980). *Birth and fortune.* New York: Basic Books.

Eccles, J. S., Wigfield, A., Midgley, C., Reuman, D, et al. (1993). Negative effects of traditional middle schools on students' motivation. *Elementary School Journal, 93*, 553–574.

Echeland, Y., Epstein, D. J., St-Jacques, B., Shen, L., Mohler, J., McMahon, J. A., & McMahon, A. P. (1993). Sonic hedgehog, a member of a family of putative signality molecules, is implicated in the regulation of CNS polarity. *Cell, 75*, 1417–1430.

Eckerman, C. O., Davis, C. C., & Didow, S. M. (1989). Toddlers' emerging ways of achieving social coordination with a peer. *Child Development, 60*, 440–453.

Eckerman, C. O., & Stein, M. R. (1982). The toddler's emerging interactive skills. In K. H. Rubin & H. S. Ross (Eds.), *Peer relationships and social skills in childhood.* New York: Springer-Verlag.

Edwards, C. P. (1977). The comparative study of the development of moral judgment and reasoning. In R. Monroe, R. Monroe, & B. B. Whiting (Eds.), *Handbook of cross-cultural human development.* New York: Garland

Egbuono, L., & Starfield, B. (1982). Child health and social status. *Pediatrics, 69*, 550–557.

Egeland, B., & Farber, E. A. (1984). Infant-mother attachment: Factors related to its development and changes over time. *Child Development, 55*, 753–771.

Egeland, B., Jacobvitz, D., & Sroufe, L. A. (1988). Breaking the cycle of abuse. *Child Development, 59*, 1080–1088.

Egertson, H. A. (1987, May 20). Recapturing kindergarten for 5-year-olds. *Education Week,* pp. 19, 28.

Ehresman, L. W. (1988, Fall). Two decades of effective child abuse prevention and treatment: Beating the odds. *Missing and abused.*

Ehrhardt, A. A., & Money, J. (1967). Progestin induced hermaphroditism: I.Q. and psychosocial identity. *Journal of Sexual Research, 3*, 83–100.

Eiger, M. S., & Olds, S. W. (1987). *The complete book of breastfeeding.* New York: Bantam.

Eimas, P. D. (1985). The perception of speech in early infancy. *Scientific American, 252*(1), 46–52.

Eimas, P., Siqueland, E., Jusczyk, P., & Vigorito, J. (1971). Speech perception in infants. *Science, 171*, 303–306.

Einbender, A. J., & Friedrich, W. N. (1989). Psychological functioning and behavior of sexually abused girls. *Journal of Consulting and Clinical Psychology, 57,* 155–157.

Eisen, L. N., Field, T. M., Bandstra, E. S., Roberts, J. P., Morrow, C., Larson, S. K., & Steele, B. M. (1991). Perinatal cocaine effects on neonatal stress behavior and performance on the Brazelton scale. *Pediatrics, 88,* 477–480.

Eisen, M., & Zellman, G. L. (1987). Changes in incidence of sexual intercourse of unmarried teenagers following a community-based sex education program. *Journal of Sex Research, 23,* 527–544.

Eisenberg, L. (1980). Adolescent suicide: On taking arms against a sea of troubles. *Pediatrics, 66,* 315–320.

Eisenberg, L. (1986). Does bad news about suicide beget bad news? *New England Journal of Medicine, 315,* 705–706.

Eisenberg, N. (1992). *The caring child.* Cambridge, MA: Harvard University Press.

Eisenberg, N., Fabes, R. A., Schaller, M., & Miller, P. A. (1989). Sympathy and personal distress: Development, gender differences, and interrelations of indexes. In N. Eisenberg (Ed.), *Empathy and related emotional responses* (New Directions for Child Development, No. 44). San Francisco: Jossey-Bass.

Eisenson, J., Auer, J. J., & Irwin, J. V. (1963). *The psychology of communication.* New York: Appleton-Century Crofts.

Elder, G. H., Jr. (1974). *Children of the Great Depression: Social change in the life experience.* Chicago: University of Chicago Press.

Eliopoulos, C., Klein, J., Phan, M. K., Knie, B., Greenwald, M., Chitayat, D., & Koren, G. (1994). Hair concentrations of nicotine and cotinine in women and their newborn infants. *Journal of the American Medical Association, 271,* 621–623.

Elkind, D. (1981). *The hurried child.* Reading, MA: Addison-Wesley.

Elkind, D. (1984). *All grown up and no place to go.* Reading, MA: Addison-Wesley.

Elkind, D. (1987, May). Superkids and super problems. *Psychology Today,* pp. 60–61.

Elkind, D. (1988). *Miseducation.* New York: Knopf.

Elliot, D. S. (1993). Health enhancing and health compromising lifestyles. In S. G. Millstein, A. C. Petersen, & E. O. Nightingale (Eds.), *Promoting the health of adolescents: New directions for the twenty-first century.* New York: Oxford University Press.

Ellis, L., & Ames, M. A. (1987). Neurohormonal functioning and sexual orientation: A theory of homosexuality-heterosexuality. *Psychological Bulletin, 101,* 233–258.

Emde, R. N. (1992). Individual meaning and increasing complexity: Contributions of Sigmund Freud and Rene Spitz to developmental psychology. *Developmental Psychology, 28,* 347–359.

Emery, R. E. (1988). *Marriage, divorce, and children's adjustment.* Newbury Park, CA: Sage.

Emery, R. E. (1989). Family violence. *American Psychologist, 44,* 321–328.

Emmerick, H. (1978). The influence of parents and peers on choices made by adolescents. *Journal of Youth and Adolescence, 7,* 175–180.

Epstein, J. L. (1984, May). Single parents get involved in children's learning [Summary]. *CSOS Report.* Baltimore, MD: Johns Hopkins University Center for Social Organization of Schools (CSOS).

Epstein, L. H., & Wing, R. R. (1987). Behavioral treatment of childhood obesity. *Psychological Bulletin, 101,* 331–342.

Erikson, E. H. (1950). *Childhood and society.* New York: Norton.

Erikson, E. H. (1964). *Insight and responsibility.* New York: Norton.

Erikson, E. H. (1968). *Identity: Youth and crisis.* New York: Norton.

Erikson, E. H. (1973). The wider identity. In K. Erikson (Ed.), *In search of common ground: Conversations with Erik H. Erikson and Huey P. Newton.* New York: Norton.

Erikson, E. H. (1982). *The life cycle completed.* New York: Norton.

Eron, L. D. (1980). Prescription for reduction of aggression. *American Psychologist, 35,* 244–252.

Eron, L. D. (1982). Parent-child interaction, television violence, and aggression in children. *American Psychologist, 37,* 197–211.

Escarce, M. E. W. (1989). A cross-cultural study of Nepalese neonatal behavior. In J. K. Nugent, B. M. Lester, & T. B. Brazelton (Eds.), *The cultural context of infancy: Vol. 1. Biology, culture, and infant development* (pp. 65–86). Norwood, NJ: Ablex.

Eskenazi, G. (1988, June 8). Girls' participation in sports improves. *New York Times,* pp. A29, A33.

Espinosa, M. P., Sigman, M. D., Neumann, C. G., Bwibo, N. O., & McDonald, M. A. (1992). Playground behavior of school-age children in relation to nutrition, schooling, and family characteristics. *Developmental Psychology, 28,* 1188–1195.

Evans, G. (1976, July). The older the sperm . . . *Ms.,* pp. 48–49.

Evans, M. I., Drugan, A., Bottoms, S. F., Platt, L. D., Rodeck, C. A., Hansmann, M., & Fletcher, J. C. (1991). Attitudes on the ethics of abortion, sex selection, and selective pregnancy termination among health care professionals, ethicists, and clergy likely to encounter such situations. *American Journal of Obstetrics and Gynecology, 164,* 1092–1099.

Evans, R. I. (1967). *Dialogue with Erik Erikson.* New York: Harper & Row.

Ewigman, B. G., Crane, J. P., Frigoletto, F. D., LeFevre, M. L., Bain, R. P., McNellis, D., & the RADIUS Study Group. (1993). Effect of prenatal ultrasound screening on perinatal outcome. *New England Journal of Medicine, 329,* 821–827.

Fabes, R. A., & Eisenberg, N. (1992). Young children's coping with interpersonal anger. *Child Development, 63,* 116–128.

Fagan, J. F. (1982). Infant memory. In T. M. Field, A. Huston, H. Quay, L. Troll, & G. Finley (Eds.), *Review of human development.* New York: Wiley.

Fagen, J. W., & McGrath, S. K. (1981). Infant recognition memory and later intelligence. *Intelligence, 5,* 121–130.

Fagen, J. W., Morrongiello, B. A., Rovee-Collier, C., & Gekoski, M. J. (1984). Expectancies and memory retrieval in the three-month-old infants. *Child Development, 55,* 936–943.

Fagot, B. I., & Hagan, R. (1991). Observations of parent reaction to sex-stereotyped behaviors: Age and sex effects. *Child Development, 62,* 617–628.

Falbo, T., & Polit, D. F. (1986). Quantitative review of the only child literature: Research evidence and theory development. *Psychological Bulletin, 100,* 176–189.

Falbo, T., & Poston, D. L. (1993). The academic, personality, and physical outcomes of only children in China. *Child Development, 64,* 18–35.

Fallot, M. E., Boyd, J. L., & Oski, F. A. (1980). Breast-feeding reduces incidence of hospital admissions for infection in infants. *Pediatrics, 65,* 1121–1124.

Fallows, J. (1986, November 24). Viva bilingualism. *The New Republic,* pp. 18–19.

Fantuzzo, J. W., Jurecic, L., Stoval, A., Hightower, A. D., Goiins, C., & Schachtel, D. (1988). Effects of adult and peer social initiations on the social behavior of withdrawn, maltreated preschool children. *Journal of Consulting and Clinical Psychology, 56,* 34–39.

Fantz, R. L. (1963). Pattern vision in newborn infants. *Science, 140,* 296–297.

Fantz, R. L. (1964). Visual experience in infants: Decreased attention to familiar patterns relative to novel ones. *Science, 146,* 668–670.

Fantz, R. L. (1965). Visual perception from birth as shown by pattern selectivity. In H. E. Whipple (Ed.), New issues in infant development. *Annals of the New York Academy of Science, 118,* 793–814.

Fantz, R. L., Fagen, J., & Miranda, S. B. (1975). *Early visual selectivity.* In L. Cohen & P. Salapetek (Eds.), *Infant perception: From sensation to cognition: Vol. 1. Basic visual processes* (pp. 249–341). New York: Academic.

Fantz, R. L., & Nevis, S. (1967). Pattern preferences and perceptual-cognitive development in early infancy. *Merrill-Palmer Quarterly, 13,* 77–108.

Farnsworth, C. H. (1994, April 5). Quebec bets on subsidized milk, mother's kind. *New York Times,* p. A4.

Farrow, J. A., Rees, J. M., & Worthington-Roberts, B. S. (1987). Health, developmental, and nutritional status of adolescent alcohol and marijuana abusers. *Pediatrics, 79,* 218–223.

Feagans, L. (1983). A current view of learning disabilities. *Journal of Pediatrics, 102,* 487–493.

Fein, G. (1981). Pretend play in childhood: An integrative review. *Child Development, 52,* 1095–1118.

Feinman, S., & Lewis, M. (1983). Social referencing at ten months: A second-order effect on infants' responses. *Child Development, 54,* 878–887.

Feldman, H. (1981). A comparison of intentional parents and intentionally childless couples. *Journal of Marriage and the Family, 43,* 593–600.

Feldman, H., Goldin-Meadow, S., & Gleitman, L. (1979). Beyond Herodotus: The creation of language by linguistically deprived deaf children. In A. Lock (Ed.), *Action, gesture, and symbol: The emergence of language.* New York: Academic.

Feldman, R. D. (1982). *Whatever happened to the quiz kids: Perils and profits of growing up gifted.* Chicago: Chicago Review Press.

Feldman, W., Feldman, E., & Goodman, J. T. (1988). Culture versus biology: Children's attitudes toward thinness and fatness. *Pediatrics, 81,* 190–194.

Ferber, R. (1985). *Solve your child's sleep problems.* New York: Simon & Schuster.

Fergusson, D. M., Horwood, L. J., & Shannon, F. T. (1986). Factors related to the age of attainment of nocturnal bladder control: An 8-year longitudinal study. *Pediatrics, 78,* 884–890.

Fernald, A., & Morikawa, H. (1993). Common themes and cultural variations in Japanese and American mothers' speech to infants. *Child Development, 64,* 637–656.

Fernald, A., & O'Neill, D. K. (1993). Peekaboo across cultures: How mothers and infants play with voices, faces, and expectations. In K. MacDonald (Ed.), *Parent-child play* (pp. 259–285). Albany: State University of New York Press.

Feshbach, N. D., & Feshback, S. (1987). Affective processes and academic achievement. *Child Development, 58,* 1335–1347.

Fetterly, K., & Graubard, M. S. (1984, March 23). Racial and educational factors associated with breast-feeding—United States, 1969 and 1980. *Morbidity and Mortality Weekly Report,* pp. 153–154.

Field, D. (1981). Can preschool children really learn to conserve? *Child Development, 52,* 326–334.

Field, T. (1991). Quality infant day-care and grade school behavior and performance. *Child Development, 62,* 863–870.

Field, T., Morrow, C., & Adlestein, D. (1993). Depressed mothers' perceptions of infant behavior. *Infant Behavior and Development, 16,* 99–108.

Field, T., Sandberg, D., Garcia, R., Vega-Lahr, N., Goldstein, S., & Guy, L. (1985). Pregnancy problems, postpartum depression, and early mother-infant interactions. *Developmental Psychology, 21,* 1152–1156.

Field, T. M. (1978). Interaction behaviors of primary versus secondary caretaker fathers. *Developmental Psychology, 14,* 183–184.

Field, T. M. (1986). Interventions for premature infants. *Journal of Pediatrics, 109,* 183–190.

Field, T. M. (1987). Interaction and attachment in normal and atypical infants. *Journal of Consulting and Clinical Psychology, 55,* 853–859.

Field, T. M., & Roopnarine, J. L. (1982). Infant-peer interaction. In T. M. Field, A. Huston, H. C. Quay, L. Troll, & G. Finley (Eds.), *Review of human development.* New York: Wiley.

Field, T. M., Widmayer, S., Greenberg, R., & Stoller, S. (1982). Effects of parent training on teenage mothers and their infants. *Pediatrics, 69,* 703–707.

Field, T. M., Woodson, R., Greenberg, R., & Cohen, D. (1982). Discrimination and imitation of facial expressions by neonates. *Science, 218,* 179–181.

Finegan, J. A. K., Quarrington, B. J., Hughes, H. E., Mervyn, J. M., Hood, J. E., Zacher, J. E., & Boyden, M. (1990). Child outcome following mid-

trimestr amniocentesis: Development, behaviour, and physical status at age 4 years. *British Journal of Obstetrics and Gynaecology, 97,* 32.

Fingerhut, L. A., & Kleinman, J. C. (1989). *Trends and current status in childhood mortality, United States, 1900–85.* Vital and Health Statistics, Series 3, No. 26(DHHS Publication No. PHS 89-1410). Hyattsville, MD: National Center for Health Statistics.

Fischer, K. (1980). A theory of cognitive development: The control and construction of hierarchies of skills. *Psychological Review, 87,* 477–531.

Fish, M., Stifter, C. A., & Belsky, J. (1993). Early patterns of mother-infant dyadic interaction: Infant, mother, and family demographic antecedents. *Infant Behavior and Development, 16,* 1–18.

Fisher, M. (1992, November 30). Dead mother, living fetus: Rights prevail, but whose? *International Herald Tribune,* p. 2.

Fitness Finders. (1984). *Feelin' good.* Spring Arbor, MI: Author.

Fivush, R., Hudson, J., & Nelson K. (1983). Children's long term memory for a novel event: An exploratory study. *Merrill-Palmer Quarterly, 30,* 303–316.

Flanagan, C. A., & Eccles, J. S. (1993). Changes in parents' work status and adolescents' adjustment at school. *Child Development, 64,* 246–257.

Flavell, J. (1963). *The developmental psychology of Jean Piaget.* New York: Van Nostrand.

Flavell, J. H. (1986). The development of children's knowledge about the appearance-reality distinction. *American Psychologist, 41,* 418–425.

Flavell, J. H. (1992). Cognitive development: Past, present, and future. *Developmental Psychology, 28,* 998–1005.

Flavell, J. H. (1993). Young children's understanding of thinking and consciousness. *Current Directions in Psychological Science, 2,* 40–43.

Flavell, J. H., Beach, D., & Chinsky, J. (1966). Spontaneous verbal rehearsal in a memory task as a function of age. *Child Development, 37,* 283–299.

Flavell, J. H., Green, F. L., & Flavell, E.R. (1992). *Young children's knowledge about thinking.* Unpublished manuscript, Stanford University.

Flavell, J. H., Green, F. L., & Flavell, E.R. (1995). Young children's knowledge about thinking. *Monographs of the Society for Research in Child Development, 60,* (Serial No. 243).

Flavell, J. H., Green, F. L., Wahl, K. E., & Flavell, E. R. (1987). The effects of question clarification and memory aids on young children's performance on appearance-reality tasks. *Cognitive Development, 2,* 127–144.

Flavell, J. H., Speer, J. R., Green, F. L., & August, D. L. (1981). The development of comprehension monitoring and knowledge about communication. *Monographs of the Society for Research in Child Development, 46*(5, Serial No. 192).

Flavell, J. H., Zhang, X.-D., Zou, H., Dong, Q., & Qi, S. (1983). A comparison between development of the appearance-reality distinction in the People's Republic of China and the United States. *Cognitive Development, 15,* 459–466.

Fluoxetine-Bulimia Collaborative Study Group. (1992). Fluoxetine in the treatment of bulimia nervosa: A multicenter placebo-controlled, double-blind trial. *The Archives of General Psychiatry, 49,* 139–147.

Fomon, S. J., Filer, L. J., Anderson, T. A., & Ziegler, E. E. (1979). Recommendations for feeding normal infants. *Pediatrics, 63,* 52–59.

Fonagy, P., Steele, H., & Steele, M. (1991). Maternal representations of attachment during pregnancy predict the organization of infant-mother attachment at one year of age. *Child Development, 62,* 891–905.

Ford, J., Zelnik, M., & Kantner, J. (1979, November). *Differences in contraceptive use and socioeconomic groups of teenagers in the United States.* Paper presented at the meeting of the American Public Health Association, New York.

Forehand, R., Long, N., Brody, G. H., & Fauber, R. (1986). Home predictors of young adolescents' school behavior and academic performance. *Child Development, 57,* 1528–1533.

Forman, M. R., Graubard, B. I., Hoffman, H. J., Beren, R., Harley, E. E., & Bennett, P. (1984). The Pima infant feeding study: Breast feeding and gastroenteritis in the first year of life. *American Journal of Epidemiology, 119,* 335–349.

Fowler, M. G., Simpson, G. A., & Schoendorf, K. C. (1993). Families on the move and children's health care. *Pediatrics, 91,* 934–940.

Fox, L. H., & Washington, J. (1985). Programs for the gifted and talented: Past, present, and future. In F. D. Horowitz & M. O'Brien (Eds.), *The gifted and talented: Developmental perspectives.* Washington, DC: American Psychological Association.

Fox, N. A., Kimmerly, N. L., & Schafer, W. D. (1991). Attachment to mother/attachment to father: A meta-analysis. *Child Development, 62,* 210–225.

Fraga, C. G, Motchnik, P. A., Shigenaga, M. K., Helbock, H. J., Jacob, R. A., &

Ames, B. N. (1991). Ascorbic acid protects against endogenous oxidative DNA damage in human sperm. *Proceedings of the National Academy of Sciences of the United States of America, 88,* 11003–11006.

Frankenburg, W. K., Dodds, J., Archer, P., Shapiro, H., & Bresnick, B. (1992). The Denver II: A major revision and restandardization of the Denver Developmental Screening Test. *Pediatrics, 89,* 91–97.

Frankenburg, W. K., Dodds, J. B., Fandal, A. W., Kazuk, E., & Cohrs, M. (1975). *Denver Developmental Screening Test: Reference manual.* Denver: University of Colorado Medical Center.

Freedman, D. G. (1979, January). Ethnic differences in babies. *Human Nature,* pp. 15–20.

Frenkiel, N. (1993, November 11). Family planning: Baby boy or girl? *New York Times,* pp. C1, C6.

Freud, A. (1946). *The ego and the mechanisms of defense.* New York: International Universities Press.

Freud, S. (1953). *A general introduction to psychoanalysis* (J. Riviere, Trans.). New York: Permabooks. (Original work published 1935).

Fricker, H. S., Hindermann, R., & Bruppacher, R. (1989). In J. K. Nugent, B. M. Lester, & T. B. Brazelton (Eds.), *The cultural context of infancy: Vol. 1. Biology, culture, and infant development.* Norwood, NJ: Ablex.

Fried, P. A., Watkinson, B., & Willan, A. (1984). Marijuana use during pregnancy and decreased length of gestation. *American Journal of Obstetrics and Gynecology, 150,* 23–27.

Friedman, E. A. (1986). How much fetal monitoring and cesarean section is enough? *New England Journal of Medicine, 315,* 641–643.

Friedrich, L. K., & Stein, A. H. (1973). Aggressive and prosocial television programs and the natural behavior of preschool children. *Monographs of the Society for Research in Child Development, 38* (Whole No. 4).

Fromkin, V., Krashen, S., Curtiss, S., Rigler, D., & Rigler, M. (1974). The development of language in Genie: Acquisition beyond the "critical period." *Brain and Language, 15*(9), 28–34.

Fuchs, D., & Fuchs, L. S. (1986). Test procedure bias: A meta-analysis of examiner familiarity effects. *Review of Educational Research, 56,* 243–262.

Fuchs, L. S., & Fuchs, D. (1986). Effects of systematic formative evaluation of student achievement: A metaanalysis. *Exceptional Children, 53,* 199–205.

Furman, W. (1982). Children's friendships. In T. M. Field, A. Huston, H. C.

Quay, L. Troll, G. E. Finley (Eds.), *Review of human development.* New York: Wiley.

Furman, W., & Bierman, K. L. (1983). Developmental changes in young children's conceptions of friendship. *Child Development, 54,* 549–556.

Furman, W., & Buhrmester, D. (1985). Children's perceptions of the personal relationships in their social networks. *Developmental Psychology, 21,* 1016–1024.

Furstenberg, F. F., Brooks-Gunn, J., & Morgan, S. P. (1987). Adolescent mothers and their children in later life. *Family Planning Perspectives, 19,* 142–152.

Furstenberg, F. F., Levins, J. A., & Brooks-Gunn, J. (1990). The children of teenage mothers: Patterns of early childbearing in two generations. *Family Planning Perspectives, 22,* 54–61.

Futterman, D., Hein, K., Reuben, N., Dell, R., & Shaffer, N. (1993). Human immunodeficiency virus–infected adolescents: The first 50 patients in a New York City program. *Pediatrics, 91,* 730–735.

Gaensbauer, T., & Hiatt, S. (1984). The psychobiology of affective development. Hillsdale, NJ: Erlbaum.

Gaertner, S. L., Mann, J., Murrell, A., & Dovidio, J. F. (1989). Reducing intergroup bias: The benefits of recategorization. *Journal of Personality and Social Psychology, 57,* 239–249.

Galambos, N. L., Petersen, A. C., & Lenerz, K. (1988). Maternal employment and sex typing in early adolescence: Contemporaneous and longitudinal relations. In A. D. Gottfried & A. W. Gottfried (Eds.), *Maternal employment and children's development: Longitudinal research.* New York: Plenum.

Gale, J. L., Thapa, P. B., Wassilak, S. G., Bobo, J. K., Mendelman, P. M., & Foy, H. M. (1994). Risk of serious acute neurological illness after immunization with diptheria-tetanus-pertussis vaccine: A population-based case-control study. *Journal of the American Medical Association, 271,* 37–41.

Gamble, T. J., & Zigler, E. (1986). Effects of infant day care: Another look at the evidence. *American Journal of Orthopsychiatry, 56,* 26–42.

Gamer, E., Thomas, J., & Kendall, D. (1975). Determinants of friendship across the life span. In F. Rebelsky (Ed.), *Life: The continuous process.* New York: Knopf.

Gans, J. E. (1990). *America's adolescents: How healthy are they?* Chicago: American Medical Association.

Garai, J. E., & Scheinfeld, A. (1968). Sex differences in mental and behavioral traits. *Genetic Psychology Monographs, 77,* 169–299.

Garbarino, J., Dubrow, N., Kostelny, K., & Pardo, C. (1992). *Children in danger: Coping with the consequences of community violence.* San Francisco: Jossey-Bass.

Garbarino, J., & Kostelny, K. (1993). Neighborhood and community influences on parenting. In T. Luster & L. Okagaki (Eds.), *Parenting: An ecological perspective* (pp. 203–226). Hillsdale, NJ: Erlbaum.

Garcia-Coll, C., Kagan, J., & Reznick, J. S. (1984). Behavioral inhibition in young children. *Child Development, 55,* 1005–1019.

Gardner, H. (1979, March 29). Exploring the mystery of creativity. *New York Times,* pp. C1, C17.

Gardner, H. (1983). *Frames of mind: The theory of multiple intelligences.* New York: Basic Books.

Garland, J. B. (1982, March). *Social referencing and self-produced locomotion.* Paper presented at the meeting of the International Conference on International Studies, Austin, TX.

Garmezy, N. (1983). Stressors of childhood. In N. Garmezy & M. Rutter (Eds.), *Stress, coping and development in children.* New York: McGraw-Hill.

Garmezy, N., Masten, A., & Tellegen, A. (1984). The study of stress and competence in children. A building block for developmental psychopathology. *Child Development, 55,* 97–111.

Garn, S. M. (1980). Continuities and change in maturational timing. In O. G. Brim, Jr. & J. Kagan (Eds.), *Constancy and change in human development.* Cambridge, MA: Harvard University Press.

Garner, D. M. (1993, June 26). Pathogenesis of anorexia nervosa. *Lancet,* pp. 1631–1635.

Geary, D. C. (1993). Mathematical disabilities: Cognitive, neuropsychological, and genetic components. *Psychological Bulletin, 114,* 345–362.

Geber, M. (1962). Longitudinal study and psychomotor development among Baganda children. *Proceedings of the Fourteenth International Congress of Applied Psychology, 3,* 50–60.

Geber, M., & Dean, R. F. A. (1957). The state of development of newborn African children. *Lancet,* pp. 1216–1219.

Gecas, V., & Seff, M. A. (1990). Families and adolescents: A review of the 1980s. *Journal of Marriage and the Family, 52,* 941–958.

Geen, R. G. (1994). Television and aggression: Recent developments in research and theory. In D. Zillman, J. Bryant, & A. C. Huston (Eds.), *Media, children, and the family: Social scientific, psychoanalytic, and clinical perspectives.* Hillsdale, NJ: Erlbaum.

Gelles, R. J. (1987). The family and its role in the abuse of children. *Psychiatric Annals, 17,* 229–232.

Gelman, R., Bullock, M., & Meck, E. (1980). Preschoolers' understanding of simple object transformations. *Child Development, 51,* 691–699.

Gelman, R., & Gallistel, C. R. (1986). *The child's understanding of number.* Cambridge, MA: Harvard University Press.

Gelman, R., Spelke, A., & Meck, E. (in press). Work on animism in children.

General Mills, Inc. (1981). *The General Mills American family report 1980–81: Families at work: Strengths and strains.* Minneapolis, MN: Author.

Gertner, B. L., Rice, M. L., & Hadley, P. A. (1993). *The influence of communicative competence on peer preferences in a preschool classroom.* Manuscript submitted for publication.

Geschwind, N., & Galaburda, A. M. (1985). Cerebral lateralization. Biological mechanisms, associations and pathology: I. A hypothesis and a program for research. *Archives of Neurology, 42,* 428–459.

Gesell, A. (1929). Maturation and infant behavior patterns. *Psychological Review, 36,* 307–319.

Getzels, J. W., & Jackson, P. W. (1963). The highly intelligent and the highly creative adolescent: A summary of some research findings. In C. W. Taylor & F. Baron (Eds.), *Scientific creativity: Its recognition and development.* New York: Wiley.

Gielen, A. C., Faden, R. R., O'Campo, P., Brown, C. H., & Paige, D. M. (1991). Maternal employment during the early postpartum period: Effects on initiation and continuation of breastfeeding. *Pediatrics, 87,* 298–305.

Gilligan, C. (1982). *In a different voice: Psychological theory and women's development.* Cambridge, MA: Harvard University Press.

Gilligan, C. (1987). Adolescent development reconsidered. In C. E. Irwin (Ed.), *Adolescent social behavior and health.* San Francisco: Jossey-Bass.

Ginsburg, G. S., & Bronstein, P. (1993). Family factors related to children's intrinsic/extrinsic motivational orientation and academic performance. *Child Development, 64,* 1461–1474.

Ginsburg, H., & Miller, S. M. (1982). Sex differences in children's risk-taking behavior. *Child Development, 53,* 426–428.

Ginsburg, H., & Opper, S. (1979). *Piaget's theory of intellectual development* (2d ed.). Englewood Cliffs, NJ: Prentice-Hall.

Ginzberg, E., et al. (1951). *Occupational choice: An approach to a general theory.* New York: Columbia University Press.

Glass, R. B. (1986). Infertility. In S. S. C. Yen & R. B. Jaffe (Eds.), *Reproductive endocrinology: Physiology, pathophysiology, and clinical management* (2d ed.). Philadelphia: Saunders.

Gleitman, L. R., Newport, E. L., & Gleitman, H. (1984). The current status of the motherese hypothesis. *Journal of Child Language, 11,* 43–79.

Glick, J. (1975). Cognitive development in cross-cultural perspective. In F. Horowitz (Ed.), *Review of child development research* (Vol. 4, pp. 595–654). Chicago: University of Chicago Press.

Glick, P. C., & Lin, S.-L. (1986). Recent changes in divorce and remarriage. *Journal of Marriage and the Family, 48,* 737–747.

Golbus, M., Loughman, W., Epstein, C., Halbasch, G., Stephens, J., & Hall, B. (1979). Prenatal genetic diagnosis in 3000 amniocenteses. *New England Journal of Medicine, 300,* 157–163.

Gold, D., & Andres, D. (1978). Developmental comparison between adolescent children with employed and nonemployed mothers. *Merrill-Palmer Quarterly, 24,* 243–254.

Golden, M., Birns, B., & Bridger, W. (1973, March). *Review and overview: Social class and cognitive development.* Paper presented at the meeting of the Society for Research in Child Development, Philadelphia.

Goldsmith, M. F. (1989). "Silent epidemic" or "social disease" makes STD experts raise their voices. *Journal of the American Medical Association, 261,* 3509–3510.

Goldstein, H., & Tanner, J. (1980, March 15). Ecological considerations in the creation and the use of child growth standards. *Lancet,* pp. 582–585.

Goleman, D. (1990), May 10). Why girls are prone to depression. *New York Times,* p. B15.

Goleman, D. (1993a, June 11). Studies reveal suggestibility of very young as witnesses. *New York Times,* pp. A1, A23.

Goleman, D. (1993b, December 8). New study portrays the young as more and more troubled. *New York Times,* p. C16.

Gordon, D., & Young, R. (1976). School phobia: A discussion of etiology, treatment, and evaluation. *Psychological Bulletin, 39,* 783–804.

Gordon, S., & Everly, K. (1985). Increasing self-esteem in vulnerable students: A tool for reducing pregnancy among teenagers. In *Impact '85.* Syracuse, NY: Ed-U Press.

Gortmaker, S. L., Dietz, W. H., Sobol, A. M., & Welher, C. A. (1987). Increasing pediatric obesity in the United States. *American Journal of the Diseases of Childhood, 141,* 535–540.

Gortmaker, S. L., Must, A., Perrin, J. M., Sobol, A. M., & Dietz, W. H. (1993). Social and economic consequences of overweight in adolescence and young adulthood. *New England Journal of Medicine, 329,* 1008–1012.

Gottman, J. M., & Katz, L. F. (1989). Effects of marital discord on young children's peer interaction and health. *Developmental Psychology, 25*(3), 373–381.

Gould, J. B., Davey, B., & Stafford, R. S. (1989). Socioeconomic differences in rates of cesarean section. *New England Journal of Medicine, 321,* 233–239.

Gralinski, J. H., & Kopp, C. B. (1993). Everyday rules for behavior: Mothers' requests to young children. *Developmental Psychology, 29,* 573–584.

Graziano, A. M., & Mooney, K. C. (1982). Behavioral treatment of "nightfears" in children: Maintenance and improvement at $2\frac{1}{2}$ to 3-year follow-up. *Journal of Counseling and Clinical Psychology, 50,* 598–599.

Greenberger, E., & Steinberg, L. (1986). *When teenagers work.* New York: Basic Books.

Greenfield, P. (1966). On culture and conservation. In J. S. Bruner, R. R. Olver, & P. Greenfield (Eds.), *Studies in cognitive growth.* New York: Wiley.

Greenfield, P. M. (1984). A theory of the teacher in the learning activities of everyday life. In B. Rogoff & J. Lave (Eds.), *Everyday cognition: Its development in social context.* Cambridge, MA: Harvard University Press.

Greenough, W. T., Black, J. E., & Wallace, C. S. (1987). Experience and brain development. *Child Development, 58,* 539–559.

Grief, E. B., & Ulman, K. J. (1982). The psychological impact of menarche on early adolescent females: A review of the literature. *Child Development, 53,* 1413–1430.

Groce, N. E., & Zola, I. K. (1993). Multiculturalism, chronic illness, and disability. *Pediatrics, 91,* 1048–1055.

Gross, J. (1994, April 5). Blending care and law enforcement, hospitals try to stem in child abuse. *New York Times,* p. A18.

Gross, R. T., & Duke, P. (1980). The effect of early versus late physical maturation on adolescent behavior. In I. Litt (Ed.), Symposium on adolescent medicine [Special issue]. *Pediatric Clinics of North America, 27,* 71–78.

Grotevant, H., & Durrett, M. (1980) Occupational knowledge and career development in adolescence. *Journal of Vocational Behavior, 17,* 171–182.

Groth-Marnat, G. (1984). *Handbook of psychological assessment.* New York: Van Nostrand Reinhold.

Gruen, G., Korte, J., & Baum, J. (1974). Group measure of locus of control. *Developmental Psychology, 10,* 683–686.

Grusec, J. E., & Goodnow, J. J. (1994). Impact of parental discipline methods on the child's internalization of values: A reconceptualization of current points of view. *Developmental Psychology, 30,* 4–19.

Gruson, L. (1992, April 22). Gains in deciphering genes set off effort to guard data against abuses. *New York Times,* p. C12.

Gualtieri, T., & Hicks, R. E. (1985). An immunoreactive theory of selective male affliction. *Behavioral and Brain Sciences, 8,* 427–441.

Guidubaldi, J., & Perry, J. D. (1985). Divorce and mental health sequelae for children: A two year follow-up of a nationwide sample. *Journal of the American Academy of Child Psychiatry, 24,* 531–537.

Guilford, J. P. (1967). *The nature of human intelligence.* New York: McGraw-Hill.

Guisinger, S., & Blatt, S. J. (1994). Individuality and relatedness: Evolution of a fundamental dialectic. *American Psychologist, 49,* 104–111.

Gunnar, M. R., Larson, M. C., Hertsgaard, L., Harris, M. L., & Brodersen, L. (1992). The stressfulness of separation among nine-month-old infants: Effects of social context variables and infant temperament. *Child Development, 63,* 290–303.

Haddow, J. E., Palomaki, G. E., Knight, G. J., Williams, J., Polkkiner, A., Canick, J. A., Saller, D. N., & Bowers, G. B. (1992). Prenatal screening for Down's syndrome with use of material serum markers. *New England Journal of Medicine, 327,* 588–593.

Hadeed, A. J., & Siegel, S. R. (1989). Maternal cocaine use during pregnancy: Effect on the newborn infant. *Pediatrics, 84,* 205–210.

Hadley, J. (1984, July-August). Facts about childhood hyperactivity. *Children Today,* pp. 8–13.

Haglund, B. (1993). Cigarette smoking and sudden infant death syndrome: Some salient points in the debate. *Acta Paediatrica, 389*(Suppl.), 37–39.

Haith, M. M. (1986). Sensory and perceptual processes in early infancy. *Journal of Pediatrics, 109,* 158–171.

Hakuta, K., Ferdman, B. M., & Diaz, R. M. (1987). Bilingualism and cognitive development: Three perspectives. In S. Rosenberg (Ed.), *Advances in applied psycholinguistics: Vol. 2. Reading, writing, and language learning* (pp. 284–319). New York: Cambridge University Press.

Hakuta, K., & Garcia, E. E. (1989). Bilingualism and education. *American Psychologist, 44,* 374–379.

Hale, J. (1982). *Black children: Their roots, culture, and learning styles.* Provo, UT: Brigham Young University Press.

Halfon, N., & Newacheck, P. W. (1993). Childhood asthma and poverty: Differential impacts and utilization of health services. *Pediatrics, 91,* 56–61.

Hall, E. G., & Lee, A. M. (1984). Sex differences in motor performance of young children: Fact or fiction? *Sex Roles, 10,* 217–230.

Hall, G. S. (1916). *Adolescence.* New York: Appleton. (Original work published 1904).

Halsey, C. L., Collin, M. F., & Anderson, C. L. (1993). Extremely low birth weight children and their peers: A comparison of preschool performance. *Pediatrics, 91,* 807–811.

Haltiwanger, J., & Harter, S. (1988). *A behavioral measure of young children's presented self-esteem.* Unpublished manuscript, University of Denver.

Hamer, D. H., Hu, S., Magnuson, V. L., Hu, N., & Pattatucci, A. M. L. (1993). A linkage between DNA markers on the x chromosome and male sexual orientation. *Science, 261,* 321–327.

Hamilton, S. (1990). *Apprenticeship for adulthood.* New York: Free Press.

Hamilton, S., & Crouter, A. (1980). Work and growth: A review of research on the impact of work experience on adolescent development. *Journal of Youth and Adolescence, 9,* 323–338.

Handler, J. F. (1993). In National Research Council (Ed.), *Losing generations: Adolescents in high-risk settings* (pp. vii–ix).

Handyside, A. H., Lesko, J. G., Tarín, J. J., Winston, R. M. L., & Hughes, M. R. (1992). Birth of a normal girl after in vitro fertilization and preimplantation diagnostic testing for cystic fibrosis. *New England Journal of Medicine, 327,* 905–909.

Hanley, R. (1988a, February 4). Surrogate deals for mothers held illegal in Jersey. *New York Times,* pp. A1, B6.

Hanley, R. (1988b, February 4). Legislators are hesitant on regulating surrogacy. *New York Times,* p. B7.

Hanna, E., & Meltzoff, A. N. (1993). Peer imitation by toddlers in laboratory, home, and day care contexts: Implications for social learning and memory. *Developmental Psychology, 29,* 701–710.

Hanson, S. M. H. (1988). Divorced fathers with custody. In P. Bronstein & C. P. Cowan (Eds.), *Fatherhood today: Men's changing role in the family.* New York: Wiley.

Hardy-Brown, K., & Plomin, R. (1985). Infant communicative development: Evidence from adoptive and biological families for genetic and environmental influences on rate differences. *Developmental Psychology, 21,* 378–385.

Hardy-Brown, K., Plomin, R., & DeFries, J. C. (1981). Genetic and environmental influences on rate of communicative development in the first year of life. *Developmental Psychology, 17,* 704–717.

Hardyck, C., & Petrinovich, L. F. (1977). Left-handedness. *Psychological Bulletin, 84,* 385–404.

Harlow, H. F., & Harlow, M. K. (1962). The effect of rearing conditions on behavior. *Bulletin of the Menninger Clinic, 26,* 213–224.

Harlow, H. F., & Zimmerman, R. R. (1959). Affectional responses in the infant monkey. *Science, 130,* 421–432.

Harrington, D. M. (1993). Child-rearing antecedents of suboptimal personality development: Exploring aspects of Alice Miller's concept of the poisonous pedagogy. In D. C. Funder, R. D. Parke, C. Tomlinson-Keasey, & K. Widaman (Eds.), *Studying lives through time: Personality and development* (pp. 289–313). Washington, DC: American Psychological Association.

Harris, L., & Associates. (1986). *American teens speak: Sex, myths, TV, and birth control. The Planned Parenthood poll.* New York: Planned Parenthood Federation of America.

Harris, P. L., Brown, E., Marriott, C., Whittall, S., & Harmer, S. (1991). Monsters, ghosts, and witches: Testing the limits of the fantasy-reality distinction in young children. In G. E. Butterworth, P. L. Harris, A. M. Leslie, & H. M. Wellman (Eds.), *Perspective on the child's theory of mind.* Oxford, UK: Oxford University Press.

Harrison, A. O., Wilson, M. N., Pine, C. J., Chan, S. Q., & Buriel, R. (1990). Family ecologies of ethnic minority children. *Child Development, 61,* 347–362.

Hart, B., & Risley, T. R. (1992). American parenting of language-learning children: Persisting differences in family-child interactions observed in natural home environments. *Developmental Psychology, 28,* 1096–1105.

Hart, C. H., DeWolf, M., Wozniak, P., & Burts, D. C. (1992). Maternal and paternal disciplinary styles: Relations with preschoolers' playground behavioral orientation and peer status. *Child Development, 63,* 879–892.

Hart, C. H., Ladd, G. W., & Burleson, B. R. (1990). Children's expectations of the outcome of social strategies: Relations with sociometric status and maternal disciplinary style. *Child Development, 61,* 127–137.

Hart, S. N., & Brassard, M. R. (1987). A major threat to children's mental health: Psychological maltreatment. *American Psychologist, 42,* 160–165.

Harter, S. (1985). Competence as a dimension of self-worth. In R. Leahy (Ed.), *The development of the self.* New York: Academic.

Harter, S. (1990). Causes, correlates, and the functional role of global self-worth: A life-span perspective. In J. Kolligan & R. Sternberg (Eds.), *Competence considered: Perceptions of competence and incompetence across the life-span* (pp. 67–97). New Haven, CT: Yale University Press.

Harter, S. (1993). Developmental changes in self-understanding across the 5 to 7 shift. In A. Sameroff & M. Haith (Eds.), *Reason and responsibility: The passage through childhood.* Chicago: University of Chicago Press.

Harter, S., & Buddin, B. J. (1987). Children's understanding of the simultaneity of two emotions: A five-stage developmental acquisition sequence. *Developmental Psychology, 23,* 388–389.

Hartmann, E. (1981, April). The strangest sleep disorder. *Psychology Today,* pp. 14–18.

Hartshorne, H., & May, M. A. (1928–1930). *Studies in the nature of character* (Vols. 1–3). New York: Macmillan.

Hartup, W. W. (1984). The peer context in middle childhood. In W. A. Collins (Ed.), *Development during middle childhood.* Washington, DC: National Academy.

Hartup, W. W. (1989). Social relationship and their developmental significance. *American Psychologist, 44,* 120–126.

Hartup, W. W. (1992). Peer relations in early and middle childhood. In V. B. Van Hasselt & M. Hersen (Eds.), *Handbook of social development: A lifespan perspective* (pp. 257–281). New York: Plenum.

Hartup, W. (in press). Cooperation, close relationships, and cognitive development. In W. M. Bukowski, A. F. Newcomb, & W. W. Hartup (Eds.), *The company they keep: Friendships and their developmental significance* (pp. 12–47). New York: Cambridge University Press.

Harvey, B. (1990). Toward a national child health policy. *Journal of the American Medical Association, 264,* 252–253.

Haryett, R. D., Hansen, R. C., & Davidson, P. O. (1970). Chronic thumbsucking: A second report on treatment and its physiological effects. *American Journal of Orthodontics, 57,* 164.

Haskins, R. (1989). Beyond metaphor: The efficacy of early childhood education. *American Psychologist, 44,* 274–282.

Haswell, K., Hock, E., & Wenar, C. (1981). Oppositional behavior of preschool children: Theory and intervention. *Family Relations, 30,* 440–446.

Haugh, S., Hoffman, C., & Cowan, G. (1980). The eye of the very young beholder: Sex typing of infants by young children. *Child Development, 51,* 598–600.

Haurin, R. J. (1992). Patterns of childhood resilience and the relationship to young adult outcomes. *Journal of Marriage and the Family, 54,* 846–860.

Hawley, T. L., & Disney, E.R. (1992). Crack's children: The consequences of maternal cocaine abuse. *Social Policy Report of the Society for Research in Child Development, VI(4),* 1–23.

Hay, D. F., Pedersen, J., & Nash, A. (1982). Dyadic interaction in the first year of life. In K. H. Rubin & H. S. Ross (Eds.), *Peer relationships and social skills in children.* New York: Springer.

Hayes, A., & Batshaw, M. L. (1993). Down syndrome. *Pediatric Clinics of North America, 40,* 523–535.

Hayes, L. A., & Watson, J. S. (1981). Neonatal imitation: Fact or artifact? *Developmental Psychology, 17,* 655–660.

Heath, S. B. (1989). Oral and literate tradition among black Americans living in poverty. *American Psychologist, 44,* 367–373.

Helms, J. E. (1992). Why is there no study of cultural equivalence in standardized cognitive ability testing? *American Psychologist, 47,* 1083–1101.

Henig, R. M. (1989, December 24). High-tech fortunetelling. *New York Times Magazine,* pp. 20–22.

Henker, B., & Whalen, C. K. (1989). Hyperactivity and attention deficits. *American Psychologist, 44,* 216–223.

Henly, W. L., & Fitch, B. R. (1966). Newborn narcotic withdrawal associated with regional enteritis in pregnancy. *New York Journal of Medicine, 66,* 2565–2567.

Herold, E. S., & Goodwin, M. S. (1981). Premarital sexual guilt and contraceptive attitudes and behavior. *Family Relations, 30,* 247–253.

Herrmann, H. J., & Roberts, M. W. (1987). Preventive dental care: The role of the pediatrician. *Pediatrics, 80,* 107–110.

Herzog, D. B., Keller, M. B., & Lavori, P. W. (1988). Outcome in anorexia nervosa and bulimia. *Journal of Nervous and Mental Disorders, 176,* 131–143.

Hess, R. D., & Holloway, S. D. (1984). Family and schools as educational institutions. In R. D. Parke (Ed.), *Review of Child Development Research 7: The family.* Chicago: University of Chicago Press.

Hetherington, E. M. (1965). A developmental study of the effects of sex of the dominant parent on sex role preference, identification and imitation in children. *Journal of Personality and Social Psychology, 2,* 188–194.

Hetherington, E. M. (1980). Children and divorce. In R. Henderson (Ed.), *Parent-child interaction: Theory, research and prospects.* New York: Academic.

Hetherington, E. M. (1986). Family relations six years after divorce. In *Remarriage and parenting today: Research and theory.* New York: Guilford.

Hetherington, E. M. (1989). Coping with family transitions: Winners, losers, and survivors. *Child Development, 60,* 1–14.

Hetherington, E. M., Cox, M., & Cox, R. (1975). *Beyond father absence: Conceptualizing of effects of divorce.* Paper presented at the meeting of the Society for Research in Child Development, Denver.

Hetherington, E. M., Stanley-Hagan, M., & Anderson, E. (1989). Marital transitions: A child's perspective. *American Psychologist, 44,* 303–312.

Hewlett, B. S. (1987). Intimate fathers: Pattenrs of paternal holding among Aka pygmies. In M. E. Lamb (Ed.), *The father's role: Cross-cultural perspectives.* Hillsdale, NJ: Erlbaum.

Heyns, B., & Catsambis, S. (1986). Mother's employment and children's achievement: A critique. *Sociology of Education, 59,* 140–151.

Hill, J. P. (1987). Research on adolescents and their families: Past and prospect. In C. E. Irwin (Ed.), *Adolescent social behavior and health.* San Francisco: Jossey-Bass.

Hilts, P. J. (1991, August 29). Study shows passing AIDS in breast milk is easier than thought. *New York Times,* p. B13.

Hirsch, H. V., & Spinelli, D. N. (1970). Visual experience modifies distribution of horizontally and vertically oriented receptive fields in cats. *Science, 168,* 869–871.

Hirsch, J. (1972). Can we modify the number of adipose cells? *Postgraduate Medicine, 51*(5), 83–86.

Hirsh-Pasek, K., Hyson, M. C., & Rescorla, L. (1989, August). *Academic environments in early childhood: Challenge and pressure.* Paper presented at the annual meeting of the American Psychological Association, New Orleans.

Hoff-Ginsberg, E. (1985). Some contributions of mothers' speech to their children's syntactic growth. *Journal of Child Language, 12,* 367–385.

Hoff-Ginsberg, E. (1986). Function and structure in maternal speech: Their relation to the child's development of syntax. *Developmental Psychology, 22,* 155–163.

Hoff-Ginsberg, E. (1991). Mother-child conversation in different social classes and communicative settings. *Child Development, 62,* 782–796.

Hoff-Ginsberg, E., & Shatz, M. (1982). Linguistic input and the child's acquisition of language. *Psychological Bulletin, 92,* 3–26.

Hoffman, E. L., & Bennett, F. C. (1990). Birth weight less than 800 grams: Changing outcomes and influences of gender and gestation number. *Pediatrics, 86,* 27–34.

Hoffman, L. W. (1979). Maternal employment. *American Psychologist, 34,* 859–865.

Hoffman, L. W. (1986). Work, family, and the child. In M. S. Pallak & R. O. Perloff (Eds.), *Psychology and work: Productivity, change, and employment.* Washington, DC: American Psychological Association.

Hoffman, L. W. (1989). Effects of maternal employment in the two-parent family: A review of the recent research. *American Psychologist, 44,* 283–292.

Hoffman, M. (1970). Moral development. In P. H. Mussen (Ed.), *Carmichael's manual of child psychology.* New York: Wiley.

Hoffman, M., & Hoffman, L. W. (Eds.). (1964). *Review of child development research.* New York: Russell Sage Foundation.

Hoffman, M. L. (1977). Sex differences in empathy and related behaviors. *Psychological Bulletin, 84,* 712–722.

Honigfeld, L. S., & Kaplan, D. W. (1987). Native-American post-neonatal mortality. *Pediatrics, 80,* 575–578.

Honzik, M. P., Macfarlane, J. W., & Allen, L. (1948). The stability of mental test performance between two and 18 years. *Journal of Experimental Education, 17,* 309–323.

Horbar, J. D., Wright, E. C., Onstad, L., & the Members of the National Institute of Child Health and Human Development Neonatal Research Network. (1993). Decreasing mortality associated with the introduction of surfactant therapy: An observational study of neonates weighing 601 to 1300 grams at birth. *Pediatrics, 92,* 191–196.

Horn, J. (1983). The Texas Adoption Project: Adopted children and their intellectual resemblance to biological and adoptive parents. *Child Development, 54,* 268–275.

Horowitz, F. D. (1992). John B. Watson's legacy: Learning and environment. *Developmental Psychology, 28,* 360–367.

Horowitz, F. D., & O'Brien, M. (1986). Gifted and talented children: State of knowledge and directions for research. *American Psychologist, 41,* 1147–1152.

Hossain, Z., & Roopnarine, J. L. (in press). African-American fathers' involvement with infants: Relationship to their functioning style, support, education, and income. *Infant Behavior and Development.*

Householder, J., Hatcher, R., Burns, W., & Chasnoff, I. (1982). Infants born to narcotic-addicted mother. *Psychological Bulletin, 92,* 453–468.

Howes, C., Hamilton, C. E., & Matheson, C. C. (1994). Children's relationships with peers: Differential associations with aspects of the teacher-child relationship. *Child Development, 65,* 253–263.

Howes, C., Matheson, C. C., & Hamilton, C. E. (1994). Maternal, teacher, and child care history correlates of children's relationships with peers. *Child Development, 65,* 264–273.

Howie, P. W., Forsyth, J. S., Ogston, S. A., Clark, A., & Florey, C. D. (1990). Protective effect of breast feeding against infection. *British Journal of Medicine, 300,* 11–16.

Hudson, J. I., & Pope, H. G. (1990). Affective spectrum disorder: Does antidepressant response identify a family of disorders with a common pathophysiology? *American Journal of Psychiatry, 147*(5), 552–564.

Huesmann, L. R. (1986). Psychological processes promoting the relation between exposure to media violence and aggressive behavior by the viewer. *Journal of Social Issues, 42,* 125–139.

Hughes, M. (1975). *Egocentrism in preschool children.* Unpublished doctoral dissertation, Edinburgh University, Edinburgh, UK.

Humphrey, L. L. (1986). Structural analysis of parent-child relationships in eating disorders. *Journal of Abnormal Psychology, 95*(4), 395–402.

Humphreys, A. P., & Smith, P. K. (1984). Rough-and-tumble in preschool and playground. In P. K. Smith (Ed.), *Play in animals and humans.* Oxford, UK: Blackwell.

Humphreys, A. P., & Smith, P. K. (1987). Rough and tumble, friendship, and dominance in schoolchildren: Evidence for continuity and change with age. *Child Development, 58,* 201–212.

Hunt, C. E., & Brouillette, R. T. (1987). Sudden infant death syndrome: 1987 perspective. *Journal of Pediatrics, 110,* 669–678.

Huston, A. C., & Wright, J. C. (1994). Educating children with television: The forms of the medium. In D. Zillman, J. Bryant, & A. C. Huston (Eds.), *Media, children, and the family: Social scientific, psychoanalytic, and clinical perspectives.* Hillsdale, NJ: Erlbaum.

Huston, A. C., Wright, J. C., Rice, M. L., Kerkman, D., & St. Petes, M. (1990). Development of television viewing patterns in early childhood: A longitudinal investigation. *Developmental Psychology, 26,* 409–420.

Huston, A., et al. (1993). *Big world, small screen: The role of television in American society.* Lincoln: University of Nebraska Press.

Huttenlocher, J., Haight, W., Bryk, A., Seltzer, M., & Lyons, T. (1991). Early vocabulary growth: Relation to language input and gender. *Developmental Psychology, 27,* 236–248.

Hwang, C-P., & Broberg, A. G. (1992). The historical and social context of child care in Sweden. In M. D. Lamb, K. J. Sternberg, C-P. Hwang, & A. G. Broberg (Eds.), *Child care in context.* Hillsdale, NJ: Erlbaum.

Hyde, J. S. (1986). *Understanding human sexuality* (3d ed.). New York: McGraw-Hill.

Hyde, J. S., Fennema, E., & Lamon, S. J. (1990). Gender differences in mathematics performance: A meta-analysis. *Psychological Bulletin, 107,* 139–155.

Hyde, J., & Linn, M. C. (1988). Gender differences in verbal abilities: A meta-analysis. *Psychological Bulletin, 104,* 53–69.

In any language breastfeeding is best for baby. (1992, December). *Food and Nutrition,* pp. 12–13.

Infant Health and Development Program. (1990). Enhancing the outcomes of low-birth-weight, premature infants. *Joural of the American Medical Association, 263,* 3035–3042.

Infante-Rivard, C., Fernández, A., Gauthier, R., David, M., & Rivard, G.-E. (1993). Fetal loss associated with caffeine intake before and during pregnancy. *Journal of the American Medical Association, 270,* 2940–2943.

Ingram, D. D., Makuc, D., & Kleinman, J. C. (1986). National and state trends in use of prenatal care, 1970–1983. *American Journal of Public Health, 76(4),* 415–423.

Institute for Social Research. (1985). How children use time. In *Time, goods and well-being.* Ann Arbor: University of Michigan.

Institute of Medicine, National Academy of Sciences (IOM). (1993, November). *Assessing genetic risks: Implications for health and social policy.* Washington, DC: National Academy of Sciences.

Interagency Committee on Learning Disabilities. (1987). *Learning disabilities: A report to the U.S. Congress.*

Isabella, R. A. (1993). Origins of attachment: Maternal interactive behavior across the first year. *Child Development, 64,* 605–621.

Izard, C. E. (1971). *The face of emotions.* New York: Appleton-Century Crofts.

Izard, C. E. (1977). *Human emotions.* New York: Plenum.

Izard, C. E., Haynes, O. M., Chisholm, G., & Baak, K. (1991). Emotional determinants of infant-mother attachment. *Child Development, 62,* 906–917.

Izard, C. E., Huebner, R. R., Resser, D., McGinness, G. C., & Dougherty, L. M. (1980). The young infant's ability to produce discrete emotional expressions. *Developmental Psychology, 16,* 132–140.

Izard, C. E., & Malatesta, C. Z. (1987). Perspectives on emotional development I: Differential emotions theory of early emotional development. In J. D. Osofsky (Ed.), *Handbook of infant development* (2d ed.) New York: Wiley.

Izard, C. E., Porges, S. W., Simons, R. F., Haynes, O. M., & Cohen, B. (1991). Infant cardiac activity: Developmental changes and relations with attachment. *Developmental Psychology, 27,* 432–439.

Jack or Jill? (1993). *Lancet, 341,* 727–728.

Jacklin, C. N. (1989). Female and male: Issues of gender. *American Psychologist, 44,* 127–133.

Jackson, J. F. (1993). Human behavioral genetics, Scarr's theory, and her views on interventions: A critical review and commentary on their implications for African American children. *Child Development, 64,* 1318–1332.

Jacobson, J.L., & Wille, D. E. (1986). The influence of attachment pattern on developmental changes in peer interaction from the toddler to the preschool period. *Child Development, 57,* 338–347.

Jacobson, J. L., Jacobson, S. W., Padgett, R. J., Brumitt, G. A., & Billings, R. L. (1992). Effects of prenatal exposure on cognitive processing and efficiency and sustained attention. *Developmental Psychology, 28,* 297–306.

Jacobson, S. W., Jacobson, J. L., & Frye, K. F. (1991). Incidence and correlates of breast-feeding in socioeconomically disadvantaged women. *Pediatrics, 88,* 728–736.

Jacobson, S. W., Jacobson, J. L., Sokol, R. J., Martier, S. S., & Ager, J. W. (1993). Prenatal alcohol exposure and infant information processing ability. *Child Development, 64,* 1706–1721.

Janos, P. M., & Robinson, N. M. (1985). Psychosocial development in intellectually gifted children. In F. D. Horowitz & M. O'Brien (Eds.), *The gifted and talented: Developmental perspectives.* Washington, DC: American Psychological Association.

Jaslow, C. K. (1982). Teenage pregnancy (ERIC/CAPS Fact Sheet). Ann Arbor, MI: Counseling and Personnel Services Clearinghouse.

Jason, J. M. (1989). Infectious disease–related deaths of low birth weight infants, United States, 1968 to 1982. *Pediatrics, 84,* 296–303.

Jay, M. S., DuRant, R. H., Shoffitt, T., Linder, C. W., & Litt, I. F. (1984). Effect of peer counselors on adolescent compliance in use of oral contraceptives. *Pediatrics, 73,* 126–131.

Jiao, S., Ji, G., & Jing, Q. (1986). Comparative study of behavioral qualities of only children and sibling children. *Child Development, 57,* 357–361.

Johnson, R. K., Smiciklas-Wright, H., Crouter, C., & Willits, F. K. (1992). Maternal employment and the quality of young children's diets: Empirical evidence based on the 1987–1988 nationwide food consumption inquiry. *Pediatrics, 90,* 245–249.

Johnson, S. L., & Birch, L. L. (1994). Parents' and children's adiposity and eating styles. *Pediatrics, 94,* 653–661.

Johnston, J., & Ettema, J. S. (1982). *Positive images: Breaking stereotypes with children's television.* Newbury Park, CA: Sage.

Johnston, L. D., Bachman, J. G., & O'Malley, P. M. (1982). *Student drug use, attitudes, and beliefs: National trends 1975–1982.* Rockville, MD: National Institute on Drug Abuse.

Jones, D. C., Swift, D. J., & Johnson, M. A. (1988). Nondeliberate memory for a novel event among preschoolers. *Developmental Psychology, 24,* 641–645.

Jones, E. F., Forrest, J. D., Goldman, N., Henshaw, S. K., Lincoln, R., Rosoff, J. I., Westoff, C. F., Wulf, W., & Wulf, D. (1985). Teenage pregnancy in developed countries: Determinants and policy implications. *Family Planning Perspectives, 17,* 53–63.

Jones, M. C. (1957). The late careers of boys who were early- or late-maturing. *Child Development, 28,* 115–128.

Jones, M. C. (1958). The study of socialization patterns at the high school level. *Journal of Genetic Psychology, 93,* 87–111.

Jones, R. O., Nagashima, A. W., Hartnett-Goodman, M. M., & Goodlin, R. C. (1991). Rupture of low transverse cesarean scars during trial of labor. *Obstetrics and Gynecology, 77,* 815–817.

Jusczyk, P. W., Cutler, A., & Redanz, N. J. (1993). Infants' preference for the predominant stress patterns of English words. *Child Development, 64,* 675–687.

Justice, E. M. (1985). Categorization as a preferred memory strategy: Developmental changes during elementary school. *Developmental Psychology, 21,* 1105–1110.

Kaback, M., Lim-Steele, J., Dabholkar, D., Brown, D., Levy, N., Zeiger, K., for the International TSD Data Collection Network (1993). Tay-Sachs disease—Carrier screening, prenatal diagnosis, and the molecular era. *Journal of the American Medical Association, 270,* 2307–2315.

Kagan, J. (1958). The concept of identification. *Psychological Review, 65,* 296–305.

Kagan, J. (1971). *Personality development.* New York: Harcourt Brace Jovanovich.

Kagan, J. (1984). *The nature of the child.* New York: Basic Books.

Kagan, J. (1989). *Unstable ideas: Temperament, cognition, and self.* Cambridge, MA: Harvard University Press.

Kagan, J., Reznick, J. S., Clarke, C., Snidman, N., & Garcia-Coll, C. (1984). Behavioral inhibition to the unfamiliar. *Child Development, 55,* 2212–2225.

Kamin, L. J. (1974). *The science and politics of IQ.* Potomac, MD: Erlbaum.

Kamin, L. J. (1981). Commentary. In S. Scarr (Ed.), *Race, social class, and individual differences in I.Q.* Hillsdale, NJ: Erlbaum.

Kandel, D. B., Davies, M., Karus, D., & Yamaguchi, K. (1986). The consequences in young adulthood of adolescent drug involvement. *Archives of General Psychiatry, 43,* 746–754.

Kaplan, H., & Dove, H. (1987). Infant development among the Ache of eastern Paraguay. *Developmental Psychology, 23,* 190–198.

Katz, L. F., & Gottman, J.M. (1993). Patterns of marital conflict predict children's internalizing and externalizing behaviors. *Developmental Psychology, 29,* 940–950.

Katzev, A. R., Warner, R. L., & Acock, A. C. (1994). Girl or boy? Relationship of child gender to marital instability. *Journal of Marriage and the Family, 56,* 89–100.

Kaufman, A. S., & Kaufman, N. L. (1983). *Kaufman assessment battery for children: Administration and scoring manual.* Circle Pines, MN: American Guidance Service.

Kaufman, J., & Zigler, E. (1987). Do abused children become abusive parents? *American Journal of Orthopsychiatry, 57,* 186–192.

Kaye, W. H., Weltzin, T. E., Hsu, L. K., & Bulik, C. M. (1991). An open trial of fluoxetine in patients with anorexia nervosa. *The Journal of Clinical Psychiatry, 52,* 464–471.

Keeney, T. J., Cannizzo, S. R., & Flavell, J. H. (1967). Spontaneous and induced verbal rehearsal in a recall task. *Child Development, 38,* 953–966.

Kelleher, K. J., Casey, P. H., Bradley, R. H., Pope, S. K., Whiteside, L., Barrett, K. W., Swanson, M. E., & Kirby, R. S. (1993). Risk factors and outcomes for failure to thrive in low birth weight preterm infants. *Pediatrics, 91,* 941–948.

Kellermann, A. L., Rivara, F. P., Somes, G., Reay, D. T., Francisco, J., Banton, J. G., Prodzinski, J., Flinger, C., & Hackman, B. B. (1992). Suicide in the home in relation to gun ownership. *New England Journal of Medicine, 327,* 467–472.

Kelley, J. L., Power, T. G., & Wimbush, D. D. (1992). Determinants of disciplinary practices in low-income black mothers. *Child Development, 63,* 573–582.

Kellogg, R. (1970). Understanding children's art. In P. Cramer (Ed.), *Readings in developmental psychology today.* Delmar, CA: CRM.

Kelly, J. B. (1987, August). *Longer-term adjustment in children of divorce: Converging findings and implications for practice.* Paper presented at the annual meeting of the American Psychological Association, New York.

Kempe, C. H., Silverman, F. N., Steele, B. N., Droegemueller, W., & Silver, H. K. (1962). The battered child syndrome. *Journal of the American Medical Association, 181,* 17–24.

Kendall-Tackett, K. A., Williams, L. M., Finkelhor, D. (1993). Impact of sexual abuse on children: A review and synthesis of recent empirical studies. *Psychological Bulletin, 113,* 164–180.

Kendler, K. S., Heath, A. C., Neale, M. C., Kessler, R. C., & Eaves, L. J. (1992). A population-based twin study of alcoholism in women. *Journal of the American Medical Association, 268*(14), 1877–1882.

Kennell, J., Klaus, M., McGrath, S., Robertson, S., & Hinckley, C. (1991). Continuous emotional support during labor in a US hosital. *Journal of the American Medical Association, 265,* 2197–2201.

Kessen, W., Haith, M., & Salapatek, P. (1970). Infancy. In P. H. Mussen (Ed.), *Carmichael's manual of the child psychology* (Vol. 1, 3d ed.). New York: Wiley.

Kimbrough, R. D., LeVois, M., & Webb, D. R. (1994). Management of children with slightly elevated blood lead levels. *Pediatrics, 93,* 188–191.

Kingsley, J., & Levitz, M. (1994). *Count us in.* New York: Harcourt Brace.

Kinsbourne, M. (1994). Sugar and the hyperactive child. *New England Journal of Medicine, 330,* 355–356.

Kirkley-Best, E., & Kellner, K. R. (1982). The forgotten grief: A review of the psychology of stillbirth. *American Journal of Orthopsychiatry, 52,* 420–429.

Kisilevsky, B. S., Muir, D. W., & Low, J. A. (1992). Maturation of human fetal reponses to vibroacoustic stimulation. *Child Development, 63,* 1497–1508.

Kistin, N., Benton, D., Rao, S., & Sullivan, M. (1990). Breast-feeding rates among black urban low-income women: Effects of prenatal education. *Pediatrics, 86*(5), 741–746.

Kitzmiller, J. L., Gavin, L. A., Gin, G. D., Jovanovic-Peterson, L., Main, E. K., & Zigrang, W. D. (1991). Preconception care of diabetes: Glycemic control prevents congenital abnormalities. *Journal of the American Medical Association, 265,* 731–736.

Klaus, M. H., & Kennell, J. H. (1976). *Maternal-infant bonding.* St. Louis: Mosby.

Klaus, M. H., & Kennell, J. H. (1982). *Parent-infant bonding* (2d ed.). St. Louis: Mosby.

Kleinberg, F. (1984). Sudden infant death syndrome. *Mayo Clinic Proceedings, 59,* 352–357.

Kleinman, J. C., Cooke, M., Machlin, S., & Kessel, S. S. (1983). *Variations in use of obstetric technology* (DHHS Publication No. PHS 84-1232). Washington, DC: U.S. Government Printing Office.

Kleinman, J. C., & Kiely, J. L. (1990). Postneonatal mortality in the United States: An international perspective. *Pediatrics, 86,* 1091–1097.

Klerman, G. L., & Weissman, M. M. (1989). Increasing rates of depression. *Journal of the American Medical Association, 261,* 2229–2235.

Klesges, R. C., Shelton, M. L., & Klesges, L. M. (1993). Effects of television on metabolic rate: Potential implications for childhood obesity. *Pediatrics, 91*(2), 281–295.

Kline, M., Johnston, J. R., & Tschann, J. M. (1991). The long shadow of marital conflict: A model of children's postdivorce adjustment. *Journal of Marriage and the Family, 53,* 297–309.

Kline, M., Tschann, J., Johnston, J., & Wallerstein, J. (1988, March). *Child outcome in joint and sole custody families.* Paper presented at the annual meeting of the American Orthopsychiatry Association, San Francisco.

Klinnert, M. D., Emde, R. N., Butterfield, P., & Campos, J. J. (1986). Social referencing: The infant's use of emotional signals from a friendly adult with mother present. *Developmental Psychology, 22,* 427–432.

Kochanska, G. (1992). Children's interpersonal influence with mothers and peers. *Developmental Psychology, 28*(3), 491–499.

Koff, E., Rierdan, J., & Sheingold, K. (1982). Memories of menarche: Age, preparation, and prior knowledge as determinants of initial menstrual experience. *Journal of Youth and Adolescence, 11,* 1–9.

Kohlberg, L. (1966). A cognitive-developmental analysis of children's sex-role concepts and attitudes. In E. E. Maccoby (Ed.), *The development of sex differences.* Stanford, CA: Stanford University Press.

Kohlberg, L. (1968, April). The child as a moral philosopher. *Psychology Today,* pp. 25–30.

Kohlberg, L. (1969). Stage and sequence: The cognitive-developmental approach to socialization. In D. A. Goslin (Ed.), *Handbook of socialization theory and research.* Chicago: Rand McNally.

Kohlberg, L. (1981). *Essays on moral development.* San Francisco: Harper & Row.

Kohlberg, L., & Gilligan, C. (1971, Fall). The adolescent as a philosopher: The discovery of the self in a postconventional world. *Daedalus,* pp. 1051–1086.

Kohlberg, L., Yaeger, J., & Hjertholm, E. (1968). Private speech: Four studies and a review of theories. *Child Development, 39,* 691–736.

Kohler, L., & Markestad, T. (1993). Consensus statement on prevention programs for SIDS. *Acta Paediatrica, 38* (Suppl.), 126–127.

Kohn, M., & Rosman, B. L. (1973). Relationship of preschool social-emotional functioning to later intellectual achievement. *Developmental Psychology, 6,* 445–452.

Kolata, G. (1986). Obese children: A growing problem. *Science, 232,* 20–21.

Kolata, G. (1988, March 29). Fetuses treated through umbilical cords. *New York Times,* p. C3.

Kolata, G. (1993, July 6). Miniature scope gives the earliest pictures of a developing embryo. *New York Times,* p. C3.

Kolb, B. (1989). Brain development, plasticity, and behavior. *American Psychologist, 44,* 1203–1212.

Kolbert, E. (1994, January 11). Canadians curbing TV violence. *New York Times,* pp. C15, C19.

Kolder, V. E., Gallagher, J., & Parsons, M. T. (1987). Court-ordered obstetrical interventions. *New England Journal of Medicine, 316,* 1192–1196.

Kopp, C. B. (1982). Antecedents of self-regulation: A developmental perspective. *Developmental Psychology, 18,* 199–214.

Kopp, C. B., & Kaler, S. R. (1989). Risk in infancy: Origins and implications. *American Psychologist, 44,* 224–230.

Kopp, C. B., & McCall, R. B. (1982). Predicting later mental performance for normal, at-risk, and handicapped in-

fants. In P. B. Baltes & O. G. Brim (Eds.), *Lifespan development and behavior* (Vol. 4). New York: Academic.

Korner, A. F., Zeanah, C. H., Linden, J., Berkowitz, R. I., Kraemer, H. C., & Agras, W. S. (1985). The relationship between neonatal and later activity and temperament. *Child Development, 56,* 38–42.

Kraemer, H. C., Korner, A., Anders, T., Jacklin, C. N., & Dimiceli, S. (1985). Obstetric drugs and infant behavior: A re-evaluation. *Journal of Pediatric Psychology, 10,* 345–353.

Kraiger, K., & Ford, K. (1985). A meta-analysis of ratee race effects in performance ratings. *Journal of Applied Psychology, 70,* 56–65.

Kramer, J., Hill, K., & Cohen, L. (1975). Infants' development of object permanence: A refined methodology and new evidence for Piaget's hypothesized ordinality. *Child Development, 46,* 149–155.

Kramer, M. S. (1991). Poverty, WIC, and promotion of breastfeeding. *Pediatrics, 87,* 399–400.

Krauss, R., & Glucksberg, S. (1977). Social and nonsocial speech. *Scientific American, 263*(2), 100–105.

Krauss, S., Concordet, J. P., & Ingham, P. W. (1993). A functionally conserved homolog of the Drosophila segment polarity gene hh is expressed in tissues with polarizing activity in zebrafish embryos. *Cell, 75,* 1431–1444.

Krenzelok, E. (1994). *An overview of 10 years of poisoning data.* (AAPCC TESS, 1983–1992). Presentation to 16th International Congress, European Association of Poison Centers and Clinical Toxicologists, Vienna, Austria.

Kreutzer, M., & Charlesworth, W. R. (1973). Infant recognition of emotions. Paper presented at the meeting of the Society for Research in Child Development, Philadelphia.

Kreutzer, M., Leonard, C., & Flavell, J. (1975). An interview study of children's knowledge about memory. *Monographs of the Society for Research in Child Development, 40* (1, Serial No. 159).

Kristof, N. D. (1991, June 17). A mystery from China's census: Where have young girls gone? *New York Times,* pp. A1, A8.

Kristof, N. D. (1993, July 21). Peasants of China discover new way to weed out girls. *New York Times,* pp. A1, A6.

Kroger, J. (1993). Ego identity: An overview. In J. Kroger (Ed.), *Discussions on ego identity.* Hillsdale, NJ: Erlbaum.

Kropp, J. P., & Haynes, O. M. (1987). Abusive and nonabusive mothers'

ability to identify general and specific emotion signals of infants. *Child Development, 58,* 187–190.

Kruper, J. C., & Uzgiris, I. (1987). Fathers' and mothers' speech to young infants. *Journal of Psycholinguistic Research, 16,* 597–614.

Ku, L. C., Sonenstein, F. L., & Pleck, J. H. (1992). The association of AIDS education and sex education with sexual behavior and condom use among teenage men. *Family Planning Perspectives, 24,* 100–106.

Kuczmarski, B. (1994). *Health objectives for the nation: Prevalence of overweight among adolescents, 1988–1991.* Hyattsville, MD: National Center for Health Statistics.

Kuhl, P. K., Williams, K. A., Lacerda, F., Stevens, K. N., & Lindblom, B. (1992). Linguistic experience alters phonetic perception in infants by 6 months of age. *Science, 255,* 606–608.

Kupersmidt, J. B., & Coie, J. D. (1990). Preadolescent peer status, aggression, and school adjustment as predictors of externalizing problems in adolescence. *Child Development, 61,* 1350–1362.

Kupfersmid, J., & Wonderly, D. (1980). Moral maturity and behavior: Failure to find a link. *Journal of Youth and Adolescence, 9,* 249–261.

Kurinij, N., Shiono, P. H., & Rhoads, G. G. (1988). Breastfeeding incidence and duration in black and white women. *Pediatrics, 81,* 365–371.

Labbok, M. H., & Hendershot, G. E. (1987). Does breastfeeding protect against malocclusion? An analysis of the 1981 child health supplement to the National Health Interview Survey. *American Journal of Preventive Medicine, 3,* 4.

Ladd, G. W. (1990). Having friends, keeping friends, making friends, and being liked by peers in the classroom: Predictors of children's early school adjustment. *Child Development, 61,* 1081–1100.

Ladd, G. W., & Colter, B. S. (1988). Parents' management of preschooler's peer relations: Is it related to children's social competence? *Developmental Psychology, 24,* 109–117.

Ladd, G. W., & Hart, C. H. (1992). Creating informal play opportunities: Are parents' and preschoolers' initiations related to children's competence with peers? *Developmental psychology, 28,* 1179–1187.

Ladson, S., Johnson, C. F., & Doty, R. E. (1987). Do physicians recognize sexual abuse? *American Journal of Diseases of Children, 141,* 411–415.

Lagercrantz, H., & Slotkin, T. A. (1986). The "stress" of being born. *Scientific American, 254*(4), 100–107.

Lamb, M. E. (1978). Influence of the child on marital quality and family interaction during the prenatal, perinatal, and infancy periods. In R. Lerner & G. Spanier (Eds.), *Child influences on marital and family interaction: A life-span perspective*. New York: Academic.

Lamb, M. E. (1981). The development of father-infant relationships. In M. E. Lamb (Ed.), *The role of the father in child development* (2d ed.). New York: Wiley.

Lamb, M. E. (1982a). The bonding phenomenon: Misinterpretations and their implications. *Journal of Pediatrics, 101,* 555–557.

Lamb, M. E. (1982b). Early contact and maternal-infant bonding: One decade later. *Pediatrics, 70,* 763–768.

Lamb, M. E. (1987). Predictive implications of individual differences in attachment. *Journal of Consulting and Clinical Psychology, 55,* 817–824.

Lamb, M. E., Campos, J. J., Hwang, C. P., Leiderman, P. H., Sagi, A., & Svejda, M. (1983). Maternal-infant bonding: A joint rebuttal. *Pediatrics, 72,* 574–575.

Lamb, M. E., Frodi, A. M., Frodi, M., & Hwang, C. P. (1982). Characteristics of maternal and paternal behavior in traditional and non-traditional Swedish families. *International Journal of Behavior Development, 5,* 131–151.

Lamb, M. E., & Sternberg, K. J. (1992). Sociocultural perspectives on nonparental child care. In M. D. Lamb, K. J. Sternberg, C.-P. Hwang, & A. G. Broberg (Eds.), *Child care in context.* Hillsdale, NJ: Erlbaum.

Lamborn, S. D., Mounts, N. S., Steinberg, L., & Dornbusch, S. M. (1991). Patterns of competence and adjustment among adolescents from authoritative, authoritarian, indulgent, and neglectful families. *Child Development, 62,* 1049–1065.

Lampl, M., Veldhuis, J. D., & Johnson, M. (1992). Saltation and stasis: A model of human growth. *Science, 258,* 801–803.

Landesman-Dwyer, S., & Emanuel, I. (1979). Smoking during pregnancy. *Teratology, 19,* 119–126.

Lange, G., MacKinnon, C. E., & Nida, R. E. (1989). Knowledge, strategy, and motivational contributions to preschool children's object recall. *Developmental Psychology, 25,* 772–779.

Larson, R., & Lampman-Petraitis, C. (1989). Daily emotional states as reported by children and adolescents. *Child Development, 60,* 1250–1260.

Larson, R., & Richards, M. H. (1991). Daily companionship in late childhood and early adolescence: Changing developmental contexts. *Child Development, 62,* 284–300.

Lawson, A., & Ingleby, J. D. (1974). Daily routines of preschool children: Effects of age, birth order, sex and social class, and developmental correlates. *Psychological Medicine, 4,* 339–415.

Leary, W. E. (1988, June 22). Survey finds sharp drop in tooth decay. *New York Times,* p. A1.

Leary, W. E. (1994a, March 29). Researchers closing in on a single-dose vaccine for children. *New York Times,* p. C3.

Leary, W. E. (1994b, April 24). Barriers to immunization peril children, expert says. *New York Times,* p. A26.

Ledeberg, A. R., & Mobley, C. E. (1990). The effect of hearing impairment on the quality of attachment and mother-toddler interaction. *Child Development, 61,* 1596–1604.

Lehman, D. R., & Nisbett, R. E. (1990). A longitudinal study of the effects of undergraduate training on reasoning. *Developmental Psychology, 26,* 952–960.

Lehmkuhle, S., Garzia, R. P., Turner, L., Hash, T., & Baro, J. A. (1993). A defective visual pathway in children with reading disability. *New England Journal of Medicine, 328,* 989–996.

Lelwica, M., & Haviland, J. (1983). *Ten-week-old infants' reactions to mothers' emotional expressions.* Paper presented at the biennial meeting of the Society for Research in Child Development, Detroit.

Lemish, D., & Rice, M. L. (1986). Television as a talking picture book: A prop for language acquisition. *Journal of Child Language, 13,* 251–274.

Lenneberg, E. H. (1967). *Biological functions of language.* New York: Wiley.

Lerner, J. V., & Galambos, N. L. (1985). Maternal role satisfaction, mother-child interaction, and child temperament: A process model. *Child Development, 21,* 1157–1164.

Lester, B. M. (1979). A synergistic process approach to the study of prenatal malnutrition. *International Journal of Behavioral Development, 2,* 377–394.

Lester, B. M. (1987). Developmental outcome prediction from acoustic cry analysis in term and preterm infants. *Pediatrics, 80,* 529–534.

Lester, B. M., Anderson, L. T., Boukydis, C. F. Z., Garcia-Coll, C. T., Vohr, B., & Peucker, M. (1989). Early detection of infants at risk for late handicap through acoustic cry analysis. *Research in Infancy, 25*(6), 99–118.

Lester, B. M., & Dreher, M. (1989). Effects of marijuana use during pregnancy on newborn cry. *Child Development, 60,* 765–771.

Lester, R., & Van Theil, D. H. (1977). Gonadal function in chronic alcoholic men. *Advances in Experimental Medicine and Biology, 85A,* 339–414.

Levano, K. J., Cunningham, F. G., Nelson, S., Roark, M., Williams, M. L., Guzick, D., Dowling, S., Rosenfeld, C. R., & Buckley, A. (1986). A prospective comparison of selective and universal electronic fetal monitoring in 34,995 pregnancies. *New England Journal of Medicine, 315,* 615–619.

LeVay, S. (1991). A difference in hypothalamic structure between heterosexual and homosexual men. *Science, 253,* 1034–1037.

Levine, J. J., & Ilowite, N. T. (1994). Sclerodermalike esophagel disease in children breast-fed by mothers with silicone breast implants. *Journal of the American Medical Association, 271,* 213–216.

Levine, M. D. (1987). *Developmental variation and learning disorders.* Cambridge, MA: Educators Publishing.

Levitt, M. J., Guacci-Franco, N., & Levitt, J. L. (1993). Convoys of social support in childhood and early adolescence: Structure and function. *Developmental Psychology, 29,* 811–818.

Levy, D. M. (1966). *Maternal overprotection.* New York: Norton.

Levy, G. D., & Carter, D. B. (1989). Gender schema, gender constancy, and gender-role knowledge: The roles of cognitive factors in preschoolers' gender-role stereotype attributions. *Developmental Psychology, 25,* 444–449.

Levy-Shiff, R., Goldschmidt, I., & Har-Even, D. (1991). Transition to parenthood in adoptive families. *Developmental Psychology, 27,* 131–140.

Levy-Shiff, R., Hoffman, M. A., Mogilner, S., Levinger, S., & Mogilner, M. B. (1990). Fathers' hospital visits to their preterm infants as a predictor of father-infant relationship and infant development. *Pediatrics, 86,* 289–293.

Lewin, G. (1994, May 18). Boys are more comfortable with sex than girls are, survey finds. *New York Times,* p. A20.

Lewin, T. (1988, March 22). Despite criticism, fetal monitors are likely to remain in wide use. *New York Times,* p. 24.

Lewis, D. O., Pincus, J. H., et al. (1988). Neuropsychiatric, psychoeducational and family characteristics of 14 juveniles condemned to death in the United States. *American Journal of Psychiatry, 145,* 584–589.

Lewis, G., David, A., Andreasson, S., & Allebeck, P. (1992). Schizophrenia and city life. *Lancet, 340,* 137–140.

Lewis, M. (1987). Social development in infancy and early childhood. In J. D. Osofsky (Ed.), *Handbook of infant development* (2d ed.). New York: Wiley.

Lewis, M. (1992). Shame, the exposed self. *Zero to Three, XII*(4), 6–10.

Lewis, M., & Brooks, J. (1974). Self, other, and fear: Infants' reaction to people. In H. Lewis & L. Rosenblum (Eds.), *The origins of fear: The origins of behavior* (Vol. 2). New York: Wiley.

Lewis, M., Worobey, J., Ramsay, D. S., & McCormack, M. K. (1992). Prenatal exposure to heavy metals: Effect on childhood cognitive skills and health status. *Pediatrics, 89,* 1010–1015.

Li, C. Q., Windsor, R. A., Perkins, L., Goldenberg, R. L., & Lowe, J. B. (1993). The impact on infant birth weight and gestational age of cotinine-validated smoking reduction during pregnancy. *Journal of the American Medical Association, 269,* 1519–1524.

Liaw, F., & Brooks-Gunn, J. (1993). Patterns of low-birth-weight children's cognitive development. *Developmental Psychology, 29,* 1024–1035.

Lickona, T. (1973). *An experimental test of Piaget's theory of moral development.* Paper presented at the meeting of the Society for Research in Child Development, Philadelphia.

Lickona, T. (Ed.). (1976). *Moral development and behavior.* New York: Holt.

Liebenberg, B. (1969). Expectant fathers. *Child and Family, 8,* 265–278.

Liebert, R. M. (1972). Television and social learning: Some relationships between viewing violence and behaving aggressively. In J. P. Murray, E. A. Rubinstein, & G. A. Comstock (Eds.), *Television and social behavior* (Vol. 2). Washington, DC: U.S. Government Printing Office.

Lieven, E. M. (1978). Conversations between mothers and young children. In N. Waterson & C. Snow (Eds.), *The development of communication: Social and pragmatic factors in language acquisition.* New York: Wiley.

Light, R. J. (1973). Abused and neglected children in America: A study of alternative policies. *Harvard Educational Review, 43,* 556–598.

Lightfoot-Klein, H. (1989). *Prisoners of ritual.* Binghamton, NY: Haworth.

Linney, J. A., & Seidman, E. (1989). The future of schooling. *American Psychologist, 44,* 336–340.

Lipsitt, L. (1982). Infant learning. In T. M. Field, A. Huston, H. Quay, L. Troll, & G. Finley (Eds.), *Review of human development.* New York: Wiley.

Lipsitt, L. P. (1986). Learning in infancy: Cognitive development in babies. *Journal of Pediatrics, 109,* 172–182.

Livson, N., & Peskin, H. (1980). Perspectives on adolescence from longitudinal research. In J. Adelson (Ed.), *Handbook of adolescent psychology.* New York: Wiley.

Lloyd, T., Andon, M. B., Rollings, N., Martel, J. K., Landis, J. R., Demers, L.

M., Eggli, D. F., Kieselhorst, K., & Kulin, H. E. (1993). Calcium supplementation and bone mineral density in adolescent girls. *Journal of the American Medical Association, 270,* 841–844.

Lo, Y.-M. D., Patel, P., Wainscoat, J. S., Sampietro, M., Gillmer, M. D. G., & Fleming, K. A. (1989, December 9). Prenatal sex determination by DNA amplification from maternal peripheral blood. *Lancet,* pp. 1363–1365.

Localio, A. R., Lawthers, A. G., Bengston, J. M., Hebert, L. E., Weaver, S. L., Brennan, T. A., & Landis, J. R. (1993). Relationship between malpractice claims and cesarean delivery. *Journal of the American Medical Association, 269,* 366–373.

Lock, A., Young, A., Service, V., & Chandler, P. (1990). Some observations on the origin of the pointing gesture. In V. Volterra & C. J. Erting (Eds.), *From gesture to language in hearing and deaf children.* New York: Springer.

Locke, R. (1979, January 7). Preschool aggression linked to TV viewing. *Wisconsin State Journal,* p. 2.

Loda, F. A. (1980). Day care. *Pediatrics in Review, 1*(1), 277–281.

Loeber, R., & Dishion, T. (1983). Early predictors of male delinquency: A review. *Psychological Bulletin, 94,* 68–99.

Loehlin, J., Lindzey, G., & Spuhler, J. (1975). *Race differences in intelligence.* San Francisco: Freeman.

Long, L. (1992). International perspectives on the residential mobility of America's children. *Journal of Marriage and the Family, 54,* 861–869.

Lonigan, C. J., Fischel, J. E., Whitehurst, G. J., Arnold, D. S., & Valdez-Menchaca, M. C. (1992). The role of otitis media in the development of expressive language disorder. *Developmental Psychology, 28,* 430–440.

Looft, W. R. (1971). *Toward a history of life-span developmental psychology.* Unpublished manuscript, University of Wisconsin, Madison.

Lorenz, K. (1957). Comparative study of behavior. In C. H. Schiller (Ed.), *Instinctive behavior.* New York: International Universities Press.

Lorenz, K. (1971). *Studies in animal and human behavior* (Vol. 2). Cambridge, MA: Harvard University Press.

Lott, I. T., Bocian, M., Pribram, H. W., & Leitner, M. (1984). Fetal hydrocephalus and ear anomalies associated with maternal use of isotretinoin. *Journal of Pediatrics, 105,* 597–600.

Louis Harris & Associates. *See* Harris, L., & Associates.

Lowrey, G. H. (1978). *Growth and development of children* (7th ed.). Chicago: Year Book Medical.

Lozoff, B. (1989). Nutrition and behavior. *American Psychologist, 44,* 231–236.

Lozoff, B., Wolf, A. W., & Davis, N. S. (1985). Sleep problems seen in pediatric practice. *Pediatrics, 75,* 477–483.

Lyon, T. D., & Flavell, J. H. (1993). Young children's understanding of forgetting over time. *Child Development, 64,* 789–800.

Lyons-Ruth, K., Alpern, L., & Repacholi, B. (1993). Disorganized infant attachment classification and maternal psychosocial problems as predictors of hostile-aggressive behavior in the preschool classroom. *Child Development, 64,* 572–585.

Lyons-Ruth, K., Connell, D. B., & Grunebaum, H. U. (1990). Infants at social risk: Services as mediators of infant development and security of attachment. *Child Development, 61,* 85–98.

Lytton, H., & Romney, D. M. (1991). Parents' differential socialization of boys and girls: A meta-analysis. *Psychological Bulletin, 109,* 267–296.

Maccoby, E. (1980). *Social development.* New York: Harcourt Brace Jovanovich.

Maccoby, E. E. (1984). Middle childhood in the context of the family. In W. A. Collins (Ed.), *Development during middle childhood.* Washington, DC: National Academy.

Maccoby, E. E. (1988). Gender as a social category. *Developmental Psychology, 24,* 755–765.

Maccoby, E. E. (1990). Gender and relationships: A developmental account. *American Psychologist, 45,* 513–520.

Maccoby, E. E. (1992). The role of parents in the socialization of children: An historical overview. *Developmental Psychology, 28,* 1006–1017.

Maccoby, E. E., & Martin, J. A. (1983). Socialization in the context of the family: Parent-child interaction. In P. H. Mussen (Series Ed.), & E. M. Hetherington (Vol. Ed.), *Handbook of child psychology: Vol. 4. Socialization, personality, and social development* (pp. 1–101). New York: Wiley.

Maccoby, E., & Jacklin, C. (1974). *The psychology of sex differences.* Stanford, CA: Stanford University Press.

Macey, T. J., Harmon, R. J., & Easterbrooks, M. A. (1987). Impact of premature birth on the development of the infant in the family. *Journal of Consuling and Clinical Psychology, 55,* 846–852.

Macfarlane, A. (1975). Olfaction in the development of social preferences in the human neonate. In *Parent-infant interaction* (CIBA Foundation Symposium, 33). Amsterdam: Elsevier.

MacGowan, R. J., MacGowan, C. A., Serdula, M. K., Lane, J. M., Joesoef, R.

M., & Cook, F. H. (1991). Breast-feeding among women attending women, infants, and children clinics in Georgia, 1987. *Pediatrics, 87*, 361–366.

Main, M., & Solomon, J. (1986). Discovery of an insecure disorganized/disoriented attachment pattern: Procedures, findings, and implications for the classification of behavior. In M. Yogman & T. B. Brazelton (Eds.), *Affective development in infancy*. Norwood, NJ: Ablex.

Malloy, M. H., Rhoads, G. G., Schramm, W., & Land, G. (1989). Increasing cesarean section rates in very low-birth weight infants: Effect on outcome. *Journal of the American Medical Association, 262*, 1475–1478.

Mamay, P. D., & Simpson, P. L. (1981). Three female roles in television commercials. *Sex Roles, 7*, 1223–1232.

Mandler, J. M. (1990). A new perspective on cognitive development in infancy. *American Scientist, 78*, 236–243.

Mannuzza, S., Klein, R. G., Bonagura, N., Konig, P. H., & Shenker, R. (1988). Hyperactive boys almost grown up: II. Status of subjects without a mental disorder. *Archives of General Psychiatry, 45*, 13–18.

Manosevitz, M., Prentice, N. M., & Wilson, F. (1973). Individual and family correlates of imaginary companions in preschool children. *Developmental Psychology, 8*, 72–79.

Maratsos, M. (1973). Nonegocentric communication abilities in preschool children. *Child Development, 44*, 697–700.

March of Dimes Birth Defects Foundation. (1983). *Genetic counseling*. White Plains, NY: Author.

Marcia, J. E. (1966). Development and validation of ego identity status. *Journal of Personality and Social Psychology, 3*, 551–558.

Marcia, J. E. (1979, June). *Identity status in late adolescence: Description and some clinical implications*. Address given at a symposium on identity development, Rijksuniversitat Groningen, Netherlands.

Marcia, J. E. (1980). Identity in adolescence. In J. Adelson (Ed.), *Handbook of adolescent psychology*. New York: Wiley.

Markoff, J. (1992, October 12). Miscarriages tied to chip factories. *New York Times*, pp. A1, D2.

Marquis, K. S., & Detweiler, R. A. (1985). Does adopted mean different? An attributional analysis. *Journal of Personality and Social Psychology, 48*, 1054–1066.

Marshall, E. (1993). A tough line on genetic screening. *Science, 262*, 984–985.

Martin, G. B., & Clark, R. D. (1982). Distress crying in neonates: Species and peer specificity. *Developmental Psychology, 18*, 3–9.

Martinez, G. A., & Kreiger, F. W. (1985). The 1984 milk-feeding patterns in the United States. *Pediatrics, 76*, 1004–1008.

Marwick, C. (1993). Coming to terms with indicators for fetal surgery. *Journal of the American Medical Association, 270*, 2025–2029.

Marzano, R. J., & Hutchins, C. L. (1987). *Thinking skills: A conceptual framework*. (ERIC Document Reproduction Service No. ED 266436).

Massey, C. M., & Gelman, R. (1988). Preschoolers' ability to decide whether a photographed unfamiliar object can move itself. *Developmental Psychology, 24*, 307–317.

Masten, A. S. (1986). Humor and competence in school-aged children. *Child Development, 57*, 461–473.

Matejcek, Z., & Dytrych, A. (1993). Specific learning disabilities and the concept of psychological sub-deprivation: The Czechoslovak experience. *Learning Disabilities Research and Practice, 8*, 44–51.

Matlin, M. W. (1987). *The psychology of women*. New York: Holt, Rinehart, & Winston.

Mauk, J. E. (1993). Autism and pervasive developmental disorders. *Pediatric Clinics of North America, 40*, 567–578.

Maxwell, L. (1987). *Eight pointers on teaching children to think*. Washington, DC: Office of Educational Research and Improvement, U.S. Department of Education.

May, K. A., & Perrin, S. P. (1985). Prelude: Pregnancy and birth. In S. M. H. Hanson & F. W. Bozett (Eds.), *Dimensions of fatherhood*. Beverly Hills, CA: Sage.

Mayes, L. C., Granger, R. H., Frank, M. A., Schottenfeld, R., & Bornstein, M. H. (1993). Neurobehavioral profiles of neonates exposed to cocaine prenatally. *Pediatrics, 91*, 778–783.

McAlister, A. L., Perry, C., & Maccoby, N. (1979). Adolescent smoking: Onset and prevention. *Pediatrics, 63*, 650–658.

McAnarney, E. R., & Hendee, W. R. (1989). Adolescent pregnancy and its consequences. *Journal of the American Medical Association, 262*, 74–77.

McCall, R. B., Appelbaum, M. I., & Hogarty, P. S. (1973). Developmental changes in mental performance. *Monographs of the Society for Research in Child Development, 38*(Serial No. 150).

McCall, R. B., & Carriger, M. S. (1993). A meta-analysis of infant habituation and recognition memory performance as predictors of later IQ. *Child Development, 64*, 57–79.

McCartney, K. (1984). Effect of quality of day care environment on children's language development. *Developmental Psychology, 20*, 244–260.

McClelland, D., Constantian, C., Regalado, D., & Stone, C. (1978, January). Making it to maturity. *Psychology Today*, pp. 42–53, 114.

McCurdy, K., & Daro, D. (1993, April). *Current trends in child abuse reporting and fatalities: The results of the 1992 annual fifty state survey* (Working paper No. 808). Chicago: National Committee for Prevention of Child Abuse.

McDaniel, K. D. (1986). Pharmacological treatment of psychiatric and neurodevelopmental disorders in children and adolescents (Part 1, Part 2, Part 3). *Clinical Pediatrics, 25*, 65–71, 198–224.

McDonald, A. D., Armstrong, B. G., & Sloan, M. (1992). Cigarette, alcohol, and coffee consumption and prematurity. *American Journal of Public Health, 82*, 87.

McGauhey, P. J., Starfield, B., Alexander, C., & Ensminget, M. E. (1991). Social environment and vulnerability of low birth weight children: A social-epidemiological perspective. *Pediatrics, 88*, 943–953.

McGee, R., Partridge, F., Williams, S., & Silva, P. A. (1991). A twelve-year follow-up of preschool hyperactive children. *Journal of the American Academy of Child and Adolescent Psychiatry, 30*, 224–232.

McGinnis, J. M., Richmond, J. B., Brandt, E. N., Windom, R. E., & Mason, J. O. (1992). Health progress in the United States: Results of the 1990 objectives for the nation. *Journal of the American Medical Association, 268*(18), 2545–2552.

McGraw, M. B. (1940). Neural maturation as exemplified in achievement of bladder control. *Journal of Pediatrics, 16*, 580–589.

McGue, M. (1993). From proteins to cognitions: The behavioral genetics of alcoholism. In R. P. Plomin & G. E. McClearn (Eds.), *Nature, nurture, and psychology*. Washington, DC: American Psychological Association.

McGue, M., Bacon, S., & Lykken, D. T. (1993). Personality stability and change in early adulthood: A behavioral genetic analysis. *Development Psychology, 21*, 96–109.

McGue, M., Bouchard, T. J., Iacono, W. G., & Lykken, D. T. (1993). Behavioral genetics of cognitive ability: A lifespan perspective. In R. P. Plomin & G. E. McClearn (Eds.), *Nature, nurture, and psychology*. Washington, DC: American Psychological Association.

McGuinness, D. (1986, February 5). Facing the "learning disabilities" crisis. *Education Week*, pp. 22, 28.

McKenna, J. J., & Mosko, S. (1993). Evolution and infant sleep: An experimental study of infant-parent co-sleeping and its implications for SIDS. *Acta Paediatrica*, 389(Suppl), 31–36.

McKenry, P. C., Walters, L. H., & Johnson, C. (1979). Adolescent pregnancy: A review of the literature. *Family Coordinator*, 23(1), 17–28.

McKey, R. H., Condelli, L., Ganson, H., Barrett, B. J., McConkey, C., & Plantz, M. C. (1985). *The impact of Head Start on children, families, and communities.* Washington, DC: CSR, Inc.

McKinley, D. (1964). *Social class and family life.* New York: Free Press.

McKinney, K. (1987). *A look at Japanese education today* (Research in Brief, IS 87-107 RIB). Washington, DC: U.S. Department of Education, Office of Educational Research and Improvement.

McKinnon, D. W. (1968). Selecting students with creative potential. In P. Heist (Ed.), *The creative college student: An unmet challenge.* San Francisco: Jossey-Bass.

McLanahan, S., & Booth, K. (1989). Mother-only families: Problems, prospects, and politics. *Journal of Marriage and the Family, 51,* 557–580.

McLaughlin, B. (1985). *Second language acquisition in childhood: Vol. 2. School-age children* (2nd ed.). Hillsdale, NJ: Erlbaum.

McLoyd, V. (1989). Socialization and development in a changing economy: The effects of paternal job and income loss on children. *American Psychologist, 44,* 293–302.

McLoyd, V. C. (1990). The impact of economic hardship on black families and children: Psychological distress, parenting, and socioemotional development. *Child Development, 61,* 311–346.

McManus, M. A., & Newacheck, P. (1993). Health insurance differentials among minority children with chronic conditions and the role of federal agencies and private foundations in improving financial access. *Pediatrics, 91,* 1040–1047.

Mead, M. (1928). *Coming of age in Samoa.* New York: Morrow.

Mead, M. (1935). *Sex and temperament in three primitive societies.* New York: Morrow.

Mednick, B. R., Baker, R. L., & Sutton-Smith, B. (1979). *Teenage pregnancy and perinatal mortality* (Contract No. 1-117-82807). Unpublished manuscript.

Meehan, P. J. (1990). Prevention: The endpoint of suicidology. *Mayo Clinic Proceedings, 65,* 115–118.

Melnick, S., Cole, P., Anderson, D., & Herbst, A. (1987). Rates and risks of diethylstilbestrol-related clear-cell ade-nocarcinoma of the vagina and cervix. *New England Journal of Medicine, 316,* 514–516.

Meltzoff, A. N. (1985). Immediate and deferred imitation in fourteen- and twenty-four-month-old infants. *Child Development, 56,* 62–72.

Meltzoff, A. N. (1988a). Infant imitation after a 1-week delay: Long-term memory for novel acts and multiple stimuli. *Developmental Psychology, 24,* 470–476.

Meltzoff, A. N. (1988b). Infant imitation and memory: Nine-month-olds in immediate and deferred tests. *Child Development, 59,* 217–225.

Meltzoff, A., & Gopnik, A. (1993). The role of imitation in understanding persons and developing a theory of mind. In S. Baron-Cohen, H. Tager-Flusberg, & D. J. Cohen (Eds.), *Understanding others' minds: Perspectives from autism.* Oxford, UK: Oxford University Press.

Meltzoff, A. N., & Borton, R. W. (1979). Intermodal matching by human neonates. *Nature, 282,* 403–404.

Meltzoff, A. N., & Moore, M. K. (1983). Newborn infants imitate adult facial gestures. *Child Development, 54,* 702–709.

Meltzoff, A. N., & Moore, M. K. (1989). Imitation in newborn infants: Exploring the range of gestures imitated and the underlying mechanisms. *Developmental Psychology, 25,* 954–962.

Meltzoff, A. N., & Moore, M. K. (1992). Early imitation within a functional framework: The importance of person identity, movement, and development. *Infant Behavior and Development, 15,* 479–505.

Mendoza, F. S., Ventura, S. J., Valdez, R. B., Castillo, R. O., Saldivar, L. E., Baisden, K., & Martorell, R. (1991). Selected measures of health status for Mexican-American, mainland Puerto Rican, and Cuban-American children. *Journal of the American Medical Association, 265,* 227–232.

Menken, J., Trussell, J., & Larsen, U. (1986). Age and infertilty. *Science, 233,* 1389–1394.

Meredith, H. V. (1969). Body size of contemporary groups of eight-year-old children studied in different parts of the world. *Monographs of the Society for Research in Child Development, 34*(1).

Meyer, D. R., & Garasky, S. (1993). Custodial fathers: Myths, realities, and child support policy. *Journal of Marriage and the Family, 55,* 73–89.

Meyers, A. F., Sampson, A. E., Weitzman, M., Rogers, B. L., & Kayne, H. (1989). School breakfast program and school performance. *American Journal of Diseases of Children, 143,* 1234–1239.

Michaels, D., & Levine, C. (1992). Estimates of the number of motherless youth orphaned by AIDS in the United States. *Journal of the American Medical Association, 268,* 3456–3461.

Miedzian, M. (1991). *Boys will be boys: Breaking the link between masculinity and violence.* New York: Doubleday.

Milerad, J., & Sundell, H. (1993). Nicotine exposure and the risk of SIDS. *Acta Paediatrica* 389(Suppl.), 70–72.

Miller, A. (1981). *The drama of the gifted child.* New York: Harper & Row.

Miller, A. (1988). *For your own good: Hidden cruelty in child-rearing and the roots of violence* (2d ed.). New York: Farrar, Straus & Giroux.

Miller, B., & Gerard, D. (1979). Family influences on the development of creativity in children: An integrative review. *Family Coordinator, 28*(3), 295–312.

Miller, B. C., & Moore, K. A. (1990). Adolescent sexual behavior, pregnancy, and parenting: Research through the 1980s. *Journal of Marriage and the Family, 52,* 1025–1044.

Miller, C. A. (1987). A review of maternity care programs in western Europe. *Family Planning Perspectives, 19,* 207–211.

Miller, E., Cradock-Watson, J. E., & Pollock, T. M. (1982, October 9). Consequences of confirmed maternal rubella at successive stages of pregnancy. *Lancet,* pp. 781–784.

Miller, J. B. (1991). The development of women's sense of self. In J. V. Jordan, A. G. Kaplan, J. B. Miller, I. P. Stiver, & J. L. Surrey (Eds.), *Women's growth in connection: Writings from the Stone Center.* New York: Guilford.

Miller, J. F., Williamson, E., Glue, J., Gordon, Y. B., Grudzinskas, J. G., & Sykes, A. (1980, September 13). Fetal loss after implantation: A prospective study. *Lancet,* pp. 554–556.

Miller, L. B., & Bizzel, R. P. (1983). Long-term effects of four preschool programs: Sixth, seventh, and eighth grades. *Child Development, 54,* 727–741.

Miller, P. H. (1983). *Theories of developmental psychology.* San Francisco: Freeman.

Miller, P. H. (1993). *Theories of personality development* (3d ed.). New York: Freeman.

Miller, P. M., Danaher, D. L., & Forbes, D. (1986). Sex-related strategies in coping with interpersonal conflict and children aged five and seven. *Developmental Psychology, 22,* 543–548.

Miller, V., Onotera, R. T., & Deinard, A. S. (1984). Denver Developmental Screening Test: Cultural variations in southeast Asian children. *Journal of Pediatrics, 104,* 481–482.

Miller-Jones, D. (1989). Culture and testing. *American Psychologist, 44,* 360–366.

Mills, J. L., Graubard, B. I., Harley, E. E., Rhoads, G. G., & Berendes, H. W. (1984). Maternal alcohol consumption and birth weight: How much drinking is safe during pregnancy? *Journal of the American Medical Association, 252,* 1875–1879.

Mills, J. L., Holmes, L. B., Aarons, J. H., Simpson, J. L., Brown, Z. A., Jovanovic-Peterson, L. G., Conley, M. R., Graubard, B. I., Knopp, R. H., & Metzger, B. E. (1993). Moderate caffeine use and the risk of spontaneous abortion and intrauterine growth retardation. *Journal of the American Medical Association, 269,* 593–597.

Millstein, S. G. (1989). Adolescent health: Challenges for behavioral scientists. *American Psychologist, 44,* 837–842.

Millstein, S. G., Irwin, C. E., Adler, N. E., Cohn, L. D., Kegeles, S. M., & Dolcini, M. M. (1992). Health-risk behaviors and health concerns among young adolescents. *Pediatrics, 89,* 422–428.

Milne, A. M., Myers, D. E., Rosenthal, A. S., & Ginsburg, A. (1986). Single parents, working mothers, and the educational achievement of school children. *Sociology of Education, 59,* 125–139.

Milunsky, A. (1992). *Heredity and your family's health.* Baltimore, MD: Johns Hopkins University Press.

Miranda, S., Hack, M., Fantz, R., Fanaroff, A., & Klaus, M. (1977). Neonatal pattern vision: Predictor of future mental performance? *Journal of Pediatrics, 91,* 642–647.

Mishell, D. R. (1993). Recurrent abortion. *Journal of Reproductive Medicine, 38,* 250–259.

Mitchell, E. A., Ford, R. P. K., Stewart, A. W., Taylor, B. J., Bescroft, D. M. O., Thompson, J. M. P., Scragg, R., Hassall, I. B., Barry, D. M. J., Allen, E. M., & Roberts, A. P. (1993). Smoking and the sudden infant death syndrome. *Pediatrics, 91,* 893–896.

Miyake, K., Chen, S., & Campos, J. (1985). Infants' temperament, mothers' mode of interaction and attachment in Japan: An interim report. In I. Bretherton & E. Waters (Eds.), Growing points of attachment theory and research. *Monographs of the Society for Research in Child Development, 50*(1–2, Serial No. 109), 276–297.

Moely, B. E., Hart, S. S., Leal, L., Santulli, K. A., Rao, N., Johnson, T., & Hamilton, L. B. (1992). The teacher's role in facilitating memory and study strategy development in the elementary school classroom. *Child Development, 63,* 653–672.

Moffitt, T. E., Caspi, A., Belsky, J., & Silva, P. A. (1992). Childhood experience and the onset of menarche: A test of a sociobiological model. *Child Development, 63,* 47–58.

Money, J., Ehrhardt, A., & Masica, D. N. (1968). Fetal feminization induced by androgen insensitivity in the testicular feminizing syndrome: Effect on marriage and maternalism. *Johns Hopkins Medical Journal, 123,* 105–114.

Montemayor, R. (1983). Parents and adolescents in conflict: All families some of the time and some families most of the time. *Journal of Early Adolescence, 3,* 83–103.

Moon, C., Cooper, R. P., & Fifer, W. P. (1993). Two-day-olds prefer their native language. *Infant Behavior and Development, 16,* 495–500.

Moore, A. U. (1960). *Studies on the formation of the mother-neonate bond in sheep and goats.* Paper presented at the meeting of the American Psychological Association.

Moore, K. L. (1993). *Before We Are Born: Basic Embryology and Birth Defects,* 4th edition. Philadelphia: Saunders.

Moore, N., Evertson, C., & Brophy, J. (1974). Solitary play: Some functional reconsiderations. *Developmental Psychology, 10,* 830–834.

Morbidity and Mortality Weekly Report (MMWR). (1987, August 14). Update: Acquired immunodeficiency syndrome—United States.

Morbidity and Mortality Weekly Report (MMWR). (1990). Low birthweight—United States, 1975–1987. *39,* 148–151.

Morbidity and Mortality Weekly Report (MMWR). (1993, March 12). Infant mortality—United States, 1990. *42,* 161–165.

Morelli, G. A., Rogoff, B., Oppenheim, D., & Goldsmith, D. (1992). Cultural variation in infants' sleeping arrangements: Questions of independence. *Developmental Psychology, 28,* 604–613.

Morison, P., & Masten, A. S. (1991). Peer reputation in middle childhood as a predictor of adaptation in adolescence: A seven-year follow-up. *Child Development, 62,* 991–1007.

Morland, J. (1966). A comparison of race awareness in northern and southern children. *American Journal of Orthopsychiatry, 36,* 22–31.

Moses, L. J., & Flavell, J. H. (1990). Inferring false belief from actions and reactions. *Child Development, 61,* 929–945.

Mosher, W. D., & McNally, J. W. (1991). Contraceptive use at first premarital intercourse: United States, 1965–1988. *Family Planning Perspectives, 23*(3), 108–116.

Mosier, C. E., & Rogoff, B. (1994). Infants' instrumental use of their mothers to achieve their goals. *Child Development, 65,* 70–79.

Moskowitz, B. A. (1978). The acquisition of language. *Scientific American, 239*(5), 92–108.

Mossberg, H.-O. (1989, August 26). 40-year follow-up of overweight children. *Lancet,* pp. 491–493.

MRC Vitamin Study Research Group. (1991). Prevention of neural tube defects: Results of the Medical Research Council vitamin study, *Lancet, 338,* 131–137.

Muret-Wagstaff, S., & Moore, S. G. (1989). In J. K. Nugent, B. M. Lester, & T. B. Brazelton (Eds.), *The cultural context of infancy: Vol. 1. Biology, culture, and infant development.* Norwood, NJ: Ablex.

Murphy, C. M., & Bootzin, R. R. (1973). Active and passive participation in the contact desensitization of snake fear in children. *Behavior Therapy, 4,* 203–211.

Murphy, D. P. (1929). The outcome of 625 pregnancies in women subjected to pelvic radium roentgen irradiation. *American Journal of Obstetrics and Gynecology, 18,* 179–187.

Murray, A. D., Dolby, R. M., Nation, R. L., & Thomas, D. B. (1981). Effects of epidural anesthesia on newborns and their mothers. *Child Development, 52,* 71–82.

Mussen, P. H., & Eisenberg-Berg, N. (1977). *Roots of caring, sharing and helping: The development of prosocial behavior in children.* San Francisco: Freeman.

Mussen, P. H., & Jones, M. C. (1957). Self-conceptions, motivations, and interpersonal attitudes of late- and early-maturing boys. *Child Development, 28,* 243–256.

Mussen, P. H., & Rutherford, E. (1963). Parent-child relations and parental personality in relation to young children's sex role preferences. *Child Development, 34,* 589–607.

Must, A., Jacques, P. F., Dallal, G. E., Bajema, C. J., & Dietz, W. H. (1992). Long-term morbidity and mortality of overweight adolescents. *New England Journal of Medicine, 327,* 1350–1355.

Muuss, R. E. H. (1988). *Theories of adolescence* (5th ed.). New York: Random House.

Myers, N., & Perlmutter, M. (1978). Memory in the years from 2 to 5. In P. Ornstein (Ed.), *Memory development in children.* Hillsdale, NJ: Erlbaum.

Naeye, R. L., & Peters, E. C. (1984). Mental development of children whose mothers smoked during pregnancy. *Obstetrics and Gynecology, 64,* 601.

National Center for Education Statistics (NCES). (1983). High school dropouts: Descriptive information from high school and beyond. *NCES Bulletin.* Washington, DC: U.S. Department of Education.

National Center for Education Statistics (NCES). (1985). *The relationship of parental involvement to high school grades* (Publication No. NCES-85-205b). Washington, DC: U.S. Government Printing Office.

National Center for Education Statistics (NCES). (1987). *Who drops out of high school? From high school and beyond.* Washington, DC: Office of Educational Research and Improvement, U. S. Department of Education.

National Center for Health Statistics. (1986). *Maternal weight gain and the outcome of pregnancy, United States, 1980. Vital statistics* (DHHS Publication No. 86-1922). Washington, DC: U.S. Government Printing Office.

National Center for Health Statistics. (1990). *Health United States 1989 and prevention profile* (DHHS Publication No. 90-1232). Washington, DC: U.S. Government Printing Office.

National Center for Health Statistics. (1993). *Health United States 1992 and prevention profile.* Washington, DC: U.S. Government Printing Office.

National Center on Child Abuse and Neglect. (1988). *Study findings. Study of national incidence and prevalence of child abuse and neglect: 1988* (Contract No. 105-85-1702). Washington, DC: U.S. Department of Health and Human Services.

National Commission on Excellence in Education. (1983, April). *A nation at risk: The imperative for educational reform* (Stock No. 065-000-00177-2). Washington, DC: U.S. Government Printing Office.

National Commission on Youth. (1980). *The transition to adulthood: A bridge too long.* New York: Westview.

National Committee for Citizens in Education (NCCE). (1986, Winter Holiday). Don't be afraid to start a suicide prevention program in your school. *Network for Public Schools,* pp. 1, 4.

National Down Syndrome Society. (1993, Fall). *Update,* p. 3.

National Institute of Child Health and Human Development. (1978). Smoking in children and adolescents. *Pediatric Annals, 7,* 130–131.

National Institute of Mental Health (NIMH). (1982). *Television and behavior: Ten years of scientific progress and implications for the eighties: Vol. 1. Summary report* (DHHS Publication No. ADM 82-1195). Washington, DC: U.S. Government Printing Office.

National Institute on Drug Abuse (NIDA). (1994). *Monitoring the future.* Washington, DC: National Institutes of Health.

National Research Council. (1993a). *Losing generations: Adolescents in high-risk settings.* Washington, DC: National Academy Press.

National Research Council. (1993b). *Understanding child abuse and neglect.* Washington, DC: National Academy Press.

Neal, A. G., Grout, H. T., & Wicks, J. W. (1989). Attitudes about having children: A study of 600 couples in the early years of marriage. *Journal of Marriage and the Family, 51,* 313–328.

Needleman, H. L., & Gatsonis, C. A. (1990). Low-level lead exposure and the IQ of children: A meta-analysis of modern studies. *Journal of the American Medical Association, 263,* 673–678.

Nelson, K. (1973). Structure and strategy in learning to talk. *Monographs of the Society for Research in Child Development, 38*(1–2).

Nelson, K. (1981). Individual differences in language development: Implications for development and language. *Developmental Psychology, 17,* 170–187.

Nelson, K. (1989). Remembering: A functional developmental perspective. In P. R. Solomon, G. R. Goethels, C. M. Kelly, & B. R. Stephens (Eds.), *Memory: An interdisciplinary approach.* New York: Springer-Verlag.

Nelson, K. (1992). Emergence of autobiographical memory at age 4. *Human Development, 35,* 172–177.

Nelson, K. (1993). The psychological and social origins of autobiographical memory. *Psychological Science, 47,* 7–14.

Neumann, P. J., Gharib, S. D., & Weinstein, M. D. (1994). The cost of a successful delivery with in vitro fertilization. *New England Journal of Medicine, 331,* 239–243.

New whooping cough vaccine is said to eliminate side effects. (1994, November 25). *New York Times,* p. A20.

Newacheck, P. W. (1989). Improving access to health services for adolescents from economically disadvantaged families. *Pediatrics, 84,* 1056–1063.

Newacheck, P. W., Stoddard, J. J., & McManus, M. (1993). Ethnocultural variations in the prevalence and impact of childhood chronic conditions. *Pediatrics, 91,* 1031–1047.

Newcomb, A. F., Bukowski, W. M., & Pattee, L. (1993). Children's peer relations: A meta-analytic review of popular, rejected, neglected, controversial, and average sociometric status. *Psychological Bulletin, 113,* 99–128.

Newcombe, N., & Fox, N. A. (1994). Infantile amnesia: Through a glass darkly. *Child Development, 65,* 31–40.

Newman, P. R. (1982). The peer group. In B. Wolman (Ed.), *Handbook of developmental psychology.* Englewood Cliffs, NJ: Prentice-Hall.

Newnham, J. P., Evans, S. F., Michael, C. A., Stanley, F. J., & Landau, L. I. (1993). Effects of frequent ultrasound during pregnancy: A randomised controlled trial, *Lancet, 342,* 887–891.

Newport, E. L., & Singleton, J. L. (1992, June) Paper presented at the meeting of the American Psychological Society, San Diego.

Newson, J., Newson, E., & Mahalski, P. A. (1982). Persistent infant comfort habits and their sequelae at 11 and 16 years. *Journal of Child Psychology and Psychiatry, 23,* 421–436.

Nisan, M., & Kohlberg, L. (1982). Universality and variation in moral judgment: A longitudinal and cross-sectional study in Turkey. *Child Development, 53,* 865–876.

Nordlicht, S. (1979). Effects of stress on the police officer and family. *New York State Journal of Medicine, 79,* 400–401.

Notzon, F. C. (1990). International differences in the use of obstetric interventions. *Journal of the American Medical Association, 263,* 3286–3291.

Nugent, J. K. (1991). Cultural and psychological influences on the father's role in infant development. *Journal of Marriage and the Family, 53,* 475–485.

Nussbaum, M., Shenker, I. R., Baird, D., & Saravay, S. (1985). Follow-up investigation in patients with anorexia nervosa. *Journal of Pediatrics, 106,* 835–840.

Oakes, J., Gamoran, A., & Page, R. N. (1992). Curriculum differentiation: Opportunities, outcomes, and meanings. In P. W. Jackson (Ed.), *Handbook of research on curriculum* (pp. 570–608). New York: Macmillan.

Oakley, D., Sereika, S., & Bogue, E. (1991). Oral contraceptive pill use after an initial visit to a family planning clinic. *Family Planning Perspectives, 23,* 150–154.

Oates, R. K., Peacock, A., & Forrest, D. (1985). Long-term effects of nonorganic failure to thrive. *Pediatrics, 75,* 36–40.

O'Bryant, S. L. & Corder-Boltz, C. R. (1978). The effects of television on children's stereotyping of women's work roles. *Journal of Vocational Behavior, 12,* 233–244.

O'Connor, M. J., Cohen, S., & Parmelee, A. H. (1984). Infant auditory discrimination in preterm and full-term infants as a predictor of 5-year intelligence. *Developmental Psychology, 20,* 159–165.

O'Connor, M. J., Sigman, M., & Brill, N. (1987). Disorganization of attachment in relation to maternal alcohol consumption. *Journal of Consulting and Clinical Psychology, 55,* 831–836.

O'Connor, M. J., Sigman, M., & Kasari, C. (1993). Interactional model for the association among maternal alcohol use, mother-infant interaction, and infant cognitive development. *Infant Behavior and Development, 16,* 177–192.

Offer, D. (1969). *The psychological world of the teenager: A study of normal adolescent boys.* New York: Basic Books.

Offer, D., & Offer, J. B. (1974). Normal adolescent males: The high school and college years. *Journal of the American College Health Association, 22,* 209–215.

Offer, D., Ostrov, E., & Howard, K. I. (1989). Adolescence: What is normal? *American Journal of Diseases of Children, 143,* 731–736.

Offer, D., Ostrov, E., & Marohn, R. C. (1972). *The psychological world of the juvenile delinquent.* New York: Basic Books.

Office of Juvenile Justice and Delinquency Prevention. (1994). *National crime victimization survey.* Washington, DC: U.S. Bureau of Justice.

Office of Technology Assessment (1988). *Artificial insemination practice in the United States: Summary of a 1987 survey.* Washington, DC: U.S. Government Printing Office.

Okagaki, L., & Sternberg, R. J. (1993). Parental beliefs and children's school performance. *Child Development, 64,* 36–56.

Olds, D. L., Henderson, C. R., & Tatelbaum, R. (1994a). Intellectual impairment in children of women who smoke cigarettes during pregnancy. *Pediatrics, 93,* 221–227.

Olds, D. L., Henderson, C. R., & Tatelbaum, R. (1994b). Prevention of intellectual impairment in children of women who smoke cigarettes during pregnancy. *Pediatrics, 93,* 228–233.

Olds, S. W. (1980, January). Miscarriage: Why me? *Self,* pp. 82–83.

Olds, S. W. (1985). *That eternal garden: Seasons of our sexuality.* New York: Times Books.

Olds, S. W. (1989). *The working parents' survival guide.* Rocklin, CA: Prima.

Olds, S. W. (in press). *That is our way.*

Oliner, S. P., & Oliner, P. M. (1988). *The altruistic personality: Rescuers of Jews in Nazi Europe.* New York: Free Press.

Oller, D. K., & Eilers, R. (1988). The role of audition in infant babbling. *Child Development, 59,* 441–449.

Olsen-Fulero, L. (1982). Style and stability in mother conversational behavior: A study of individual differences. *Journal of Child Language, 9,* 543–564.

Olsen-Fulero, L. (1982). The role of audition in infant babbling. *Child Development, 59,* 441–449.

Opie, I., & Opie, P. (1969). *Children's games in street and playground.* London: Oxford University Press.

Orentlicher, D. (1990). Genetic screening by employers. *Journal of the American Medical Association, 263,* 1005–1008.

Ostrea, E. M., Brady, M., Gause, S., Raymundo, A. L., & Stevens, M. (1992). Drug screening of newborns by meconium analysis: A large-scale, prospective, epidemiologic study. *Pediatrics, 89,* 107–113.

Ostrea, E. M., & Chavez, C. J. (1979). Perinatal problems (excluding neonatal withdrawal) in maternal drug addiction: A study of 830 cases. *Journal of Pediatrics, 94,* 292–295.

Oswald, P. F., & Peltzman, P. (1974). The cry of the human infant. *Scientific American, 230*(3), 84–90.

Palkovitz, R. (1985). Fathers' birth attendance, early contact, and extended contact with their newborns: A critical review. *Child Development, 56,* 392–406.

Pan, W. H.-L. (1994). Children's play in Taiwan, In J. L. Roopnarine, J. E. Johnson, & F. H. Hooper (Eds.), *Children's play in diverse cultures.* Albany: State University of New York Press.

Papalia, D. (1972). The status of several conservation abilities across the lifespan. *Human Development, 15,* 229–243.

Papousek, H. (1959). A method of studying conditioned food reflexes in young children up to age six months. *Pavlovian Journal of Higher Nervous Activity, 9,* 136–140.

Papousek, H. (1960a). Conditioned motor alimentary reflexes in infants: 1. Experimental conditioned sucking reflex. *Ceskoslovenska Pediatrie, 15,* 861–872.

Papousek, H. (1960b). Conditioned motor alimentary reflexes in infants: 2. A new experimental method of investigation. *Ceskoslovenska Pediatrie, 15,* 981–988.

Papousek, H. (1961). Conditioned head rotation reflexes in infants in the first months of life. *Acta Paediatrica, 50,* 565–576.

Paris, S. G., & Lindauer, B. K. (1976). The role of inference in children's comprehension and memory for sentences. *Cognitive Psychology, 8,* 217–227.

Parke, R. (1977). Some effects of punishment on children's behavior—Revisited. In P. Cantor (Ed.), *Understanding a child's world.* New York: McGraw-Hill.

Parke, R. D., Grossman, K., & Tinsley, B. R. (1981). Father-mother-infant interaction in the newborn period: A German-American comparison. In T. M. Field, A. M. Sostek, P. Viete, & P. H. Leideman (Eds.), *Culture and early interaction.* Hillsdale, NJ: Erlbaum.

Parker, J. G., & Asher, S. R. (1987). Peer relations and later personal adjustment: Are low-accepted children at risk? *Psychological Bulletin, 102,* 357–389.

Parkes, J. D. (1986, September 1). The parasomnias. *Lancet,* pp. 1021–1025.

Parmelee, A. H. (1986). Children's illnesses: Their beneficial effects on behavioral development. *Child Development, 57,* 1–10.

Parmelee, A. H., Wenner, W. H., & Schulz, H. R. (1964). Infant sleep patterns: From birth to 16 weeks of age. *Journal of Pediatrics, 65,* 576.

Parmentier, M., Libert, F., Schurmans, S., Schiffmann, S., Lefort, A., Eggerickx, D., Mollereau, C., Gerard, C., Perret, J., et al. (1992). Expression of members of the putative olfactory receptor gene family in mammalian germ cells. *Nature, 355,* 453–455.

Parrish, K. M., Holt, V. L., Easterling, T. R., Connell, F. A. & LeGerfo, J. P. (1994). Effect of changes in maternal age, parity, and birth weight distribution on primary cesarean delivery rates. *Journal of the American Medical Association, 271,* 443–447.

Parten, M. (1932). Social play among preschool children. *Journal of Abnormal and Social Psychology, 27,* 243–269.

Patterson, C. J. (1992). Children of lesbian and gay parents. *Child Development, 63,* 1025–1042.

Patterson, C. J., Kupersmidt, J. B., & Griesler, P. C. (1990). Children's perceptions of self and of relationships with others as a function of sociometric status. *Child Development, 61,* 1335–1349.

Patterson, G. R., Chamberlain, P., & Reid, J. B. (1982). A comparative evaluation of a parent-training program. *Behavior Therapy, 13,* 638–650.

Patterson, G. R., DeBaryshe, B. D., & Ramsey, E. (1989). A developmental perspective on antisocial behavior. *American Psychologist, 44,* 329–335.

Patterson, G. R., Reid, J. B., & Dishion, T. J. (in press). *Antisocial boys.* Eugene, OR: Castalia.

Patterson, G. R., & Stouthamer-Loeber, M. (1984). The correlation of family management practices and delinquency. *Child Development, 55,* 1299–1307.

Pease, D., & Gleason, J. B. (1985). Gaining meaning: Semantic development. In J. B. Gleason (Ed.), *The development of language.* Columbus, OH: Merrill.

Pebley, A. R. (1981). Changing attitudes toward the timing of first birth. *Family Planning Perspectives, 13,* 171–175.

Pedersen, F. A., Cain, R., & Zaslow, M. (1982). Variation in infant experience associated with alternative family roles. In L. Laosa & I. Sigel (Eds.), *The family as a learning environment.* New York: Plenum.

Pederson, E., Faucher, T. A., & Eaton, W. W. (1978). A new perspective of the effects of first-grade teachers on children's subsequent adult status. *Harvard Educational Review, 48,* 1–31.

Peel, E. A. (1967). The psychological basis of education (2d ed.). Edinburgh, UK: Oliver & Boyd.

Pellegrini, A. D. (1988). Elementary-school children's rough-and-tumble play and social competence. *Developmental Psychology, 24,* 802–806.

Perlmutter, M., Behrend, S. D., Kuo, F., & Muller, A. (1989). Social influences on children's problem solving. *Developmental Psychology, 25,* 744–754.

Perris, E. E., Myers, N. A., & Clifton, R. K. (1990). Long-term memory for a single infancy experience. *Child Development, 61,* 1796–1807.

Persson-Blennow, I., & McNeil, T. F. (1981). Temperament characteristics of children in relation to gender, birth order, and social class. *American Journal of Orthopsychiatry, 51,* 710–714.

Peskin, H. (1967). Pubertal onset and ego functioning. *Journal of Abnormal Psychology, 72,* 1–15.

Peskin, H. (1973). Influence of the developmental schedule of puberty on learning and ego functioning. *Journal of Youth and Adolescence, 2,* 273–290.

Petersen, A. C. (1991, April). *American adolescence: How it affects girls.* Paper presented at the Gisela Konopka Lecture, University of Minnesota, Minneapolis.

Petersen, A. C. (1993). Creating adolescents: The role of context and process in developmental trajectories. *Journal of Research on Adolescence, 3,* 1–18.

Petersen, A. C., Compas, B. E., Brooks-Gunn, J., Stemmler, M., Ey, S., & Grant, K. E. (1993). Depression in adolescence. *American Psychologist, 48,* 155–168.

Petersen, A. C., Sarigiani, P. A., & Kennedy, R. E. (1991). Adolescent depression: Why more girls? *Journal of Youth and Adolescence, 20,* 247–271.

Petitto, L. A., & Marentette, P. F. (1991). Babbling in the manual mode: Evidence for the ontogeny of language. *Science, 231,* 1493–1495.

Pettigrew, T. F. (1964). Negro American intelligence. In T. F. Pettigrew (Ed.), *Profile of the Negro American* (pp. 100–135). Princeton, NJ: Van Nostrand.

Phillips, D. P., & Carstensen, L. L. (1986). Clustering of teenage suicides after television news stories about suicide. *New England Journal of Medicine, 315*(11), 685–689.

Phillips, D. P., & Paight, B. A. (1987). The impact of televised movies about suicide. *New England Journal of Medicine, 317,* 809–811.

Phillips, D., McCartney, K., & Scarr, S. (1987). Child-care quality and chil-

dren's social development. *Developmental Psychology, 23,* 537–543.

Piaget, J. (1929). *The child's conception of the world.* New York: Harcourt Brace.

Piaget, J. (1932). *The moral judgment of the child.* New York: Harcourt Brace.

Piaget, J. (1951). *Play, dreams, and imitation* (C. Gattegno & F. M. Hodgson, Trans.). New York: Norton.

Piaget, J. (1952). *The origins of intelligence in children.* New York: International Universities Press.

Piaget, J. (1969). *The child's conception of time* (A. J. Pomerans, trans.). London: Routeledge & Kegan Paul.

Piaget, J., (1962). Comments on Vygotsky's critical remarks concerning *The language and thought of the child* and *Judgment and reasoning in the child.* In L. S. Vygotsky, *Thought and language.* Cambridge, MA: MIT Press.

Piaget, J., & Inhelder, B. (1967). *The child's conception of space.* New York: Norton.

Pickens, J., & Field, T. (1993). Facial expressivity in infants of depressed mothers. *Developmental Psychology, 29,* 986–988.

Pines, M. (1979, August). Superkids. *Psychology Today,* pp. 53–63.

Pipp, S., Easterbrooks, M. A. & Harmon, R. J. (1992). The relation between attachment and knowledge of self and mother in one- to three-year-old infants. *Child Development, 63,* 738–750.

Pirkle, J. L., Brody, D. J., Gunter, E. W., Kramer, R. A., Raschal, D. C., Flegal, K. M., & Matte, T. D. (1994). The decline in blood lead levels in the United States. *Journal of the American Medical Association, 272,* 284–291.

Plomin, R. (1989). Environment and genes: Determinants of behavior. *American Psychologist, 44,* 105–111.

Plomin, R. (1990). The role of inheritance in behavior. *Science, 248,* 183–188.

Plomin, R., Owen, M. J., & McGuffin, P. (1994). The genetic bases of behavior. *Science, 264,* 1733–1739.

Plomin, R., Pedersen, N. L., McClearn, G. E., Nesselroade, J. R., & Bergeman, C. S. (1988). EAS temperaments during the last half of the life span: Twins reared apart and twins reared together. *Psychology and Aging, 3,* 43–50.

Plomin, R., & Rende, R. (1991). Human behavioral genetics, *Annual Review of Psychology, 42.*

Pollock, L. A. (1983). *Forgotten children.* Cambridge, UK: Cambridge University Press.

Pope, A. W., Bierman, K. L., & Mumma, G. H. (1991). Aggression, hyperactivity, and inattention-immaturity: Behavior dimensions associated with peer rejection in elementary school

boys. *Developmental Psychology, 27,* 663–671.

Pope, S. K., Whiteside, L., Brooks-Gunn, J., Kelleher, K. J., Rickert, V. I., Bradley, R. H., & Casey, P. H. (1993). Low-birth-weight infants born to adolescent mothers: Effects of coresidency with grandmother on child development. *Journal of the American Medical Association, 269,* 1396–1400.

Porac, C., & Coren, S. (1981). *Lateral preferences and human behavior.* New York: Springer-Verlag.

Posner, J. K., & Vandell, D. L. (undated). *Low-income children's after school care: Are there beneficial effects of after school programs?* Unpublished manuscript, University of Wisconsin–Madison.

Power, T. G., & Chapieski, M. L. (1986). Child-rearing and impulse control in toddlers: A naturalistic investigation. *Developmental Psychology, 22,* 271–275.

Pratt, M. W., Kerig, P., Cowan, P. A., & Cowan, C. P. (1988). Mothers and fathers teaching 3-year-olds: Authoritative parenting and adult scaffolding of young children's learning. *Developmental Psychology, 24,* 832–839.

Prechtl, H. F. R., & Beintema, D. J. (1964). The neurological examination of the full-term newborn infant. *Clinics in Developmental Medicine* (No. 12). London: Heinemann.

Pugh, D. (1983, November 11). Bringing an end to multilation. *New Statesman,* pp. 8–9.

Pugliese, M. T., Weyman-Daum, M., Moses, N., & Lifschitz, F. (1987). Parental health beliefs as a cause of nonorganic failure to thrive. *Pediatrics, 80,* 175–182.

Pynoos, R. S., Frederick, C., Nader, K., Arroyo, W., Steinberg, A., Eth, S., Nunez, F., & Fairbanks, L. (1987). Life threat and post-traumatic stress in school-age children. *Archives of General Psychiatry, 44,* 1057–1063.

Quadrel, M. J., Fischoff, B., & Davis, W. (1993). Adolescent (in)vulnerability. *American Psychologist, 48,* 102–116.

Quay, H. (1987). Intelligence. In H. C. Quay (Ed.), *Handbook of juvenile delinquency.* New York: Wiley.

Quinby, N. (1985, October). On testing and teaching intelligence: A conversation with Robert Sternberg. *Educational Leadership,* pp. 50–53.

Quintero, R. A., Abuhamad, A., Hobbins, J. C., & Mahoney, M. J. (1993). Transabdominal thin-gauge embryofetoscopy: A technique for early prenatal diagnosis and its use in the diagnosis of a case of Meckel-Gruber syndrome. *American Journal of Obstetrics and Gynecology, 168,* 1552–1557.

Rabiner, D., & Coie, J. (1989). Effect of expectancy induction on rejected peers' acceptance by unfamiliar peers. *Developmental Psychology, 25,* 450–457.

Racine, A., Joyce, T., & Anderson, R. (1993). The association between prenatal care and birth weight among women exposed to cocaine in New York City. *Journal of the American Medical Association, 270,* 1581–1586.

Raffaelli, M., & Larson, R. W. (1987). *Sibling interactions in late childhood and early adolescence.* Paper presented at the biennial meeting of the Society for Research in Child Development, Baltimore.

Rafferty, C. (1984, April 23). Study of gifted from childhood to old age. *New York Times,* p. B5.

Rafferty, Y., & Shinn, M. (1991). Impact of homelessness on children. *American Psychologist, 46,* 1170–1179.

Ragozin, A. S., Basham, R. B., Crnic, K. A., Greenberg, M. T., & Robinson, N. M. (1982). Effects of maternal age on parenting role. *Developmental Psychology, 18,* 627–634.

Rappaport, L. (1993). The treatment of nocturnal enuresis—Where are we know? *Pediatrics, 92,* 465–466.

Raskin, P. A., & Israel, A. C. (1981). Sex-role imitation in children: Effects of sex of child, sex of model, and sex-role appropriateness of modelled behavior. *Sex Roles, 1,* 1067–1076.

Rassin, D. K., Richardson, J., Baranowski, T., Nader, P. R., Guenther, N., Bee, D. E., & Brown, J. P. (1984). Incidence of breast-feeding in a low socioeconomic group of mothers in the United States; Ethnic patterns. *Pediatrics, 73,* 132–137.

Rauh, J. L., Schumsky, D. A., & Witt, M. T. (1967). Heights, weights, and obesity in urban school children. *Child Development, 38,* 515–530.

Ravitch, D. (1983, October). The education pendulum. *Psychology Today,* pp. 62–71.

Read, C. R. (1991). Gender distribution in programs for the gifted. *Roeper Review, 13,* 188–193.

Read, M. S., Habicht, J.-P., Lechtig, A., & Klein, R. E. (1973, May). *Maternal malnutrition, birth weight, and child development.* Paper presented at the International Symposium on Nutrition, Growth and Development, Valencia, Spain.

Redding, R. E., Harmon, R. J., & Morgan, G. A. (1990). Maternal depression and infants' mastery behaviors. *Infant Behavior and Development, 113,* 391–396.

Reese, E., & Fivush, R. (1993). Parental styles of talking about the past. *Developmental Psychology, 29,* 596–606.

Reese, H. W. (1977). Imagery and associative memory. In R. V. Kali & J. W. Hagen (Eds.), *Perspectives on the development of memory and cognition.* Hillsdale, NJ: Erlbaum.

Reid, J. R., Patterson, G. R., & Loeber, R. (1982). The abused child: Victim, instigator, or innocent bystander? In D. J. Berstein (Ed.), *Response structure and organization.* Lincoln: University of Nebraska Press.

Reis, S. M. (1991). The need for clarification in research designed to examine gender differences in achievement and accomplishment. *Roeper Review, 13,* 193–198.

Reissland, N. (1988). Neonatal imitation in the first hour of life: Observations in rural Nepal. *Developmental Psychology, 24,* 464–469.

Remafedi, G., Resnick, M., Blum, R., & Harris, L. (1992). Demography of sexual orientation in adolescents. *Pediatrics, 89,* 714–721.

Rescorla, L. (1991). Early academics: Introduction to the debate. In L. Rescorla, M. C. Hyson, & K. Hirsh-Pasek (1991), Academic instruction in early childhood: Challenge or pressure? *New Directions in Child Development, 53,* 5–11.

Resnick, L. B. (1989). Developing mathematical knowledge. *American Psychologist, 44,* 162–169.

Restak, R. (1984). *The brain.* New York: Bantam.

Reznick, J. S., & Goldfield, B. A. (1992). Rapid change in lexical development in comprehension and production. *Developmental Psychology, 28,* 406–413.

Reznick, J. S., Kagan, J., Snidman, N., Gersten, M., Baak, K., & Rosenberg, A. (1986). Inhibited and uninhibited children: A follow-up study. *Child Development, 57,* 660–680.

Rice, M. L. (1982). Child language: What children know and how. In T. M. Field, A. Huston, H. C. Quay, L. Troll, & G. E. Finley (Eds.), *Review of human development research.* New York: Wiley.

Rice, M. L. (1989). Children's language acquisition. *American Psychologist, 44,* 149–156.

Rice, M. L., Hadley, P. A., & Alexander, A. L. (1993). Social biases toward children with speech and language impairments: A correlative causal model of language limitations. *Applied Psycholinguistics, 14,* 445–471.

Rice, M. L., Huston, A. C., Truglio, R., & Wright, J. (1990). Words from "Sesame Street": Learning vocabularly while viewing. *Developmental Psychology, 26,* 421–428.

Rice, M. L., Oetting, J. B., Marquis, J., Bode, J., & Pae, S. (in press). Frequency of input effects on word comprehension of children with specific language impairment. *Journal of Speech and Hearing Research.*

Rice, S. G. (1993). [Injury rates among high school athletes, 1979–1992]. Unpublished raw data.

Richards, M. P. M. (1971). Social interaction in the first week of human life. *Psychiatria, Neurologia, Neurochirugia, 74,* 35–42.

Richardson, D. W., & Short, R. V. (1978). Time of onset of sperm production in boys. *Journal of Biosocial Science, 5,* 15–25.

Richardson, L. (1993, November 25). Adoptions that lack papers, not purpose. *New York Times,* pp. C1, C6.

Riddle, R. D., Johnson, R. L., Laufer, E., & Tabin, C. (1993). Sonic hedgehog mediates the polarizing activity of the ZPA. *Cell, 75,* 1401–1416.

Rierdan, J., Koff, E., & Flaherty, J. (1986). Conceptions and misconceptions of menstruation. *Women and Health, 10,* 33–45.

Rierdan, J., Koff, E., & Stubbs, M. L. (1988). Gender, depression, and body image in early adolescents. *Journal of Early Adolescence, 8,* 109–117.

Rierdan, J., Koff, E., & Stubbs, M. L. (1989). A longitudinal analysis of body image as a predictor of the onset and persistence of adolescent girls' depression. *Journal of Early Adolescents, 9,* 454–466.

Riese, M. L. (1990). Neonatal temperament in monozygotic and dizygotic twin pairs. *Child Development, 61,* 1230–1237.

Rieser, J., Yonas, A., & Wilkner, K. (1976). Radial localization of odors by human newborns. *Child Development, 47,* 856–859.

Rindfuss, R. R., Morgan, S. P., & Swicegood, G. (1988). *First births in America,* Berekeley: University of California Press.

Rindfuss, R. R., & St. John, C. (1983). Social determinants of age at first birth. *Journal of Marriage and the Family, 45,* 553–565.

Ritvo, E. R., Freeman, B. J., Mason-Brothers, A., Mo, A., & Ritvo, A. M. (1985). Concordance for the syndrome of autism in 40 pairs of afflicted twins. *American Journal of Psychiatry, 142,* 74–77.

Rivara, F. P., Bergman, A., B., & Drake, C. (1989). Parental attitudes and practices toward children as pedestrians. *Pediatrics, 84,* 1017–1021.

Roberts, G. C., Block, J. H., & Block, J. (1984). Continuity and change in parents' child-rearing practices. *Child Development, 55,* 586–597.

Robertson, L. F. (1984, November). Why we went back to half-days. *Principal,* pp. 22–24.

Robinson, I., Ziss, K., Ganza, B., Katz, S., & Robinson, E. (1991). Twenty years of the sexual revolution, 1965–1985: An update. *Journal of Marriage and the Family, 53,* 216–220.

Robinson, J. L., Kagan, J., Reznick, J. S., & Corley, R. (1992). The heritability of inhibited and uninhibited behavior: A twin study. *Developmental Psychology, 28,* 1030–1037.

Robison, L. L., Buckley, J. D., Daigle, A. E., Wells, R., Benjamin, D., Arthur, D. C., & Hammond, G. D. (1989). Maternal drug use and risk of childhood nonlymphoblastic leukemia among offspring. *Cancer, 63,* 1904–1911.

Robson, K. S. (1967). The role of eye-to-eye contact in maternal-infant attachment. *Journal of Child Psychology and Psychiatry, 8,* 13–25.

Roche, A. F. (1981). The adipocyte-number hypothesis. *Child Development, 52,* 31–43.

Rock, D. A., Ekstrom, R. B., Goertz, M. E., Hilton, T. L., & Pollack, J. (1985). *Factors associated with decline of test scores of high school seniors, 1972 to 1980.* Washington, DC: U.S. Department of Education, Center for Statistics.

Rodman, H., & Cole, C. (1987). Latchkey children: A review of policy and resources. *Family Relations, 36,* 101–105.

Rogers, M. F., White, C. R., Sanders, R., Schable, C., Ksell, T. E., Wasserman, R. L., Ballanti, J. A., Peters, S. M., & Wray, B. B. (1990). Lack of transmission of human immunodeficiency virus from infected children to their household contacts. *Pediatrics, 85,* 210–214.

Rogoff, B., & Morelli, G. (1989). Perspectives on children's development from cultural psychology. *American Psychologist, 44,* 343–348.

Romero-Gwynn, E., & Carias, L. (1989). Breast-feeding intentions and practice among Hispanic mothers in southern California. *Pediatrics, 84,* 626–631.

Roopnarine, J. L., Brown, J., Snell-White, P., Riegraft, N. B., Crossley, D., Hossain, Z., & Webb, W. (in press). Father involvement in children and household work in common-law dual-earner and single-earner Jamaican families. *Journal of Applied Developmental Psychology.*

Roopnarine, J., & Field, T. (1984). Play interaction of friends and acquaintances in nursery school. In T. Field, J. Roopnarine, & M. Segal (Eds.), *Friendships in normal and handicapped children.* Norwood, NJ: Ablex.

Roopnarine, J., & Honig, A. S. (1985, September). The unpopular child. *Young Children,* pp. 59–64.

Roopnarine, J. L., Hooper, F. H., Ahmeduzzaman, M., & Pollack, B. (1993).

Gentle play partners: Mother-child and father-child play in New Delhi, India. In K. MacDonald (Ed.), *Parent-child play* (pp. 287–304). Albany: State University of New York Press.

Roopnarine, J. L., Talokder, E., Jain, D., Josh, P. & Srivastav, P. (1992). Personal well-being, kinship ties, and mother-infant and father-infant interactions on single wage and dual-wage families in New Delhi, India. *Journal of Marriage and the Family, 54,* 293–301.

Rose, R. M., Gordon, T. P., & Bernstein, I. S. (1972). Plasma testosterone levels in the male rhesus: Influences of sexual and social stimuli. *Science, 178,* 643–645.

Rose, S. A., Feldman, J. F., Wallace, I. F., & McCarton, C. (1991). Information processing at 1 year: Relation to birth status and developmental outcome during the first 5 years. *Developmental Psychology, 27,* 723–737.

Rosen, J. G., & Gross, J. (1987). Prevalence of weight reducing and weight gaining in adolescent girls and boys. *Health Psychology, 6,* 131–147.

Rosenberg, M. S. (1987). New directions for research on the psychological maltreatment on children. *American Psychologist 42,* 166–171.

Rosenthal, M. K. (1982). Vocal dialogues in the neonatal period. *Developmental Psychology, 18,* 17–21.

Rosenthal, R., & Jacobson, L. (1968). *Pygmalion in the classroom.* New York: Holt.

Rosenzweig, M. R. (1984). Experience, memory, and the brain. *American Psychologist, 39,* 365–376.

Rosenzweig, M. R., & Bennett, E. L. (Eds.). (1976). *Neural mechanisms of learning and memory.* Cambridge, MA: MIT Press.

Rosetti-Ferreira, M. C. (1978). Malnutrition and mother-infnat asynchrony: Slow mental development. *International Journal of Behavioral Development, 1,* 207–219.

Ross, G., Lippe, E. G., & Auld, P. A. M. (1991). Educational status and school-related abilities of very low birth weight premature children. *Pediatrics, 88,* 1125–1134.

Ross Products Division of Abbott Laboratories. (1994). *Ross mothers' survey.* Columbus, OH: Author.

Rothman, B. K. (1992). *In labor: Women and power in the birthplace* (2nd ed.). New York: Norton.

Rousso, H. (1984, December). Fostering healthy self-esteem. *The Exceptional Parent,* pp. 9–14.

Rovee-Collier, C. (1987). Learning and memory in infancy. In J. D. Osofsky (Ed.), *Handbook of infant development* (2d ed.). New York: Wiley.

Rovee-Collier, C., & Fagen, J. W. (1976). Extended conditioning and 24-hour retention in infants. *Journal of Experimental Child Psychology, 21,* 1.

Rovee-Collier, C., & Fagen, J. W. (1981). The retrieval of memory in early infancy. In L. P. Lipsitt (Ed.), *Advances in infancy research* (Vol. 1). Norwood, NJ: Ablex.

Rovee-Collier, C., & Lipsitt, L. (1982). Learning, adaptation, and memory in the newborn. In P. Stratton (Ed.), *Psychobiology of the human newborn.* New York: Wiley.

Rovee-Collier, C., Schechter, A., Shyi, G., & Shields, P. (1992). Perceptual identification of contextual attributes and infant memory retrieval. *Developmental Psychology, 28,* 307–318.

Rubenstein, C. (1993, November 18). Child's play, or nightmare on the field? *New York Times,* pp. C1, C10.

Rubin, D. H., Krasilnikoff, P. A., Leventhal, J. M., Weile, B., & Berget, A. (1986, August 23). Effects of passive smoking on birthweight. *Lancet,* pp. 415–417.

Rubin, D. H., Leventhal, J. M., Krasilnikoff, P. A., Kuo, H. S., Jekel, J. F., Weile, B., Levee, A., Kurzon, M., & Berget, A. (1990). Relationship between infant feeding and infectious illness: A prospective study of infants during the first year of life. *Pediatrics, 85,* 464–471.

Rubin, K. (1982). Nonsocial play in preschoolers: Necessary evil? *Child Development, 53,* 651–657.

Rubin, K., Maioni, T. L., & Hornung, M. (1976). Free play behaviors in middle-class and lower-class preschoolers: Parten and Piaget revisited. *Child Development, 47,* 414–419.

Rubin, W., Watson, K., & Jambor, T. (1978). Free-play behaviors in preschool and kindergarten children. *Child Development, 49,* 534–536.

Ruble, D. N., & Brooks-Gunn, J. (1982). The experience of menarche. *Child Development, 53,* 1557–1566.

Ruff, H. A., Bijur, P. E., Markowitz, M., Ma, Y.-C., & Rosen, J. F. (1993). Declining blood lead levels and cognitive changes in moderately lead-poisoned children. *Journal of the American Medical Association, 269,* 1641–1646.

Rule, S. (1981, June 11). The battle to stem school dropouts. *New York Times,* pp. A1, B10.

Russell, A., & Finnie, V. (1990). Preschool children's social status and maternal instructions to assist group entry. *Developmental Psychology, 26,* 603–611.

Rutter, M. (1974). *The qualities of mothering: Maternal deprivation reassessed.* New York: Aronson.

Rutter, M. (1979a). Maternal deprivation, 1972–1978: New findings, new concepts, new approaches. *Child Development, 50,* 283–305.

Rutter, M. (1979b). Separation experiences: A new look at an old topic. *Pediatrics, 95,* 147–154.

Rutter, M. (1983). Stress, coping, and development: Some issues and some questions. In N. Garmezy & M. Rutter (Eds.), *Stress, coping, and development in children.* New York: McGraw-Hill.

Rutter, M. (1984, March). Resilient children. *Psychology Today,* pp. 57–65.

Rutter, M. (1987). Continuities and discontinuities from infancy. In J. Osofsky (Ed.), *Handbook of infant development.* New York: Wiley.

Ryan, A. S., Rush, D., Krieger, F. W., & Lewandowski, G. E. (1991). Recent decline in breast-feeding in the United States, 1984 through 1989. *Pediatrics, 88,* 719–727.

Ryerson, A. J. (1961). Medical advice on child rearing, 1550–1900. *Harvard Educational Review, 31,* 302–323.

Rymer, R. (1993). *Genie: An abused child's flight from silence.* New York: HarperCollins.

Sabatelli, R. M., Meth, R. L., & Gavazzi, S. M. (1988). Factors mediating the adjustment to involuntary childlessness. *Family Relations, 37,* 338–343.

Sachs, B. P., McCarthy, B. J., Rubin, G., Burton, A., Terry, J., & Tyler, C. W. (1983). Cesarean section. *Journal of the American Medical Association, 250,* 2157–2159.

Sacks, J. J., Smith, M. D., Kaplan, K. M., Lambert, D. A., Sattin, W., & Sikes, K. (1989). The epidemiology of injuries in Atlanta day-care centers. *Journal of the American Medical Association, 262,* 1641–1645.

Sadowitz, P. D., & Oski, F. A. (1983). Iron status and infant feeding practices in an urban ambulatory center. *Pediatrics, 72,* 33–36.

Sagi, A., & Hoffman, M. (1976). Empathic distress in newborns. *Developmental Psychology, 12,* 175–176.

Saigal, S., Szatmari, P., Rosenbaum, P., Campbell, D., & King, S. (1990). Intellectual and functional status at school entry of children who weighed 1000 grams or less at birth: A regional perspective of births in the 1980s. *Journal of Pediatrics, 116,* 409–416.

Salive, M. E., Guralnik, J. M., & Glynn, R. J. (1993). Left-handedness and mortality. *American Journal of Public Health, 83,* 265–267.

Sameroff, A. J., Seifer, R., Baldwin, A., & Baldwin, C. (1993). Stability of intelligence from preschool to adolescence: The influence of social and family risk factors. *Child Development, 64,* 80–97.

Sandler, D. P., Everson, R. B., Wilcox, A. J., & Browder, J. P. (1985). Cancer risk in adulthood from early life exposure to parents' smoking. *American Journal of Public Health, 75,* 487–492.

Santer, L. J., & Stocking, C. B. (1991). Safety practices and living conditions of low-income urban families. *Pediatrics, 88,* 111–118.

Santrock, J. W., Sitterle, K. A., & Warshak, R. A. (1988). Parent-child relationships in stepfather families. In P. Bronstein & C. P. Cowan (Eds.), *Fatherhood today: Men's changing role in the family.* New York: Wiley.

Sauer, M. V., Paulson, R. J., & Lobo, R. A. (1990). A preliminary report on oocyte donation extending reproductive potential to women over 40. *New England Journal of Medicine, 323,* 1157–1160.

Sauer, M. V., Paulson, R. J., & Lobo, R. A. (1993). Pregnancy after age 50: Application of oocyte donation to women after natural menopause. *Lancet, 341,* 321–323.

Saxe, G. B., Guberman, S. R., & Gearhart, M. (1987). Social processes in early number development. *Monographs of the Society for Research in Child Development, 52,* 216.

Saywitz, K. J., Goodman, G. S., Nicholas, E., & Moan, S. F. (1991). Children's memories of a physical examination involving genital touch: Implications for reports of child sexual abuse. *Journal of Consulting and Clinical Psychology, 59,* 682–691.

Scarborough, H. S. (1990). Very early language deficits in dyslexic children. *Child Development, 61,* 1728–1743.

Scarr, S. (1992). Developmental theories for the 1990s: Development and individual differences. *Child Development, 63,* 1–19.

Scarr, S. (1993). Biological and cultural diversity: The legacy of Darwin for development. *Child Development, 64,* 1333–1353.

Scarr, S., Phillips, D., & McCartney, K. (1989). Working mothers and their families. *American Psychologist, 44,* 1402–1409.

Scarr, S., & Weinberg, R. (1983). The Minnesota Adoption Study: Genetic differences and malleability. *Child Development, 54,* 260–267.

Schanberg, S. M., & Field, T. M. (1987). Sensory deprivation stress and supplemental stimulation in the rat pup and preterm human neonate. *Child Development, 58,* 1431–1447.

Schechtman, V. L., Harper, R. M., Wilson, A. J., & Southall, D. P. (1992). Sleep state organization in normal infants and victims of the sudden infant death syndrome. *Pediatrics, 89,* 865–870.

Schindler, P. J., Moely, B. E., & Frank, A. L. (1987). Time in day care and social participation in young children. *Developmental Psychology, 23,* 255–261.

Schiro, A. (1988, August 25). Parents agree to detente in the clothes war. *New York Times,* pp. C1, C6.

Schmeck, H. M., Jr. (1976, June 10). Trend in growth of children lags. *New York Times,* p. 13.

Schmitt, M. H. (1970). Superiority of breast-feeding: Fact or fancy? *American Journal of Nursing,* 1488–1493.

Schoen, E. J. (1990). The status of circumcision of newborns. *New England Journal of Medicine, 322,* 1308–1312.

Schoendorf, K. C., Hogue, C. J. R., Kleinman, J. C., & Rowley, D. (1992). Mortality among infants of black as compared with white college-educated parents. *New England Journal of Medicine, 326,* 1522–1526.

Schoendorf, K. C., & Kiely, J. L. (1992). Relationship of sudden infant death syndrome to maternal smoking. *Pediatrics, 90,* 905–908.

Schonfeld, D. J., Johnson, S. R., Perrin, E. C., O'Hare, L. L., & Cicchetti, D. V. (1993). Understanding of acquired immunodeficiency syndrome by elementary school children—A developmental survey. *Pediatrics, 92,* 389–395.

Schor, E. L. (1987). Unintentional injuries: Patterns within families. *American Journal of the Diseases of Children, 141,* 1280.

Schroeder, S. R., Schroeder, C. S., & Landesman, S. (1987). Psychological services in educational settings to persons with mental retardation. *American Psychologist, 42,* 805–808.

Schuckit, M. A. (1985). Genetics and the risk for alcoholism. *Journal of the American Medical Association, 254,* 2614–2617.

Schuckit, M. A. (1987). Biological vulnerability to alcoholism. *Journal of Consulting and Clinical Psychology, 55,* 301–309.

Schulman, S. (1986, February). Facing the invisible handicap. *Psychology Today,* pp. 58–64.

Schutter, S., & Brinker, R. (1992). Conjuring a new category of disability from prenatal cocaine exposure: Are the infants unique biological or caretaking casualties? *Topics in Early Childhood Special Education, 11,* 84–111.

Schvaneveldt, J. D., Lindauer, S. L. K., & Young, M. H. (1990). Children's understanding of AIDS: A developmental viewpoint. *Family Relations, 39,* 330–335.

Schwartz, D., Dodge, K. A., & Coie, J. D. (1993). The emergence of chronic peer victimization in boys' play groups. *Child Development, 64,* 1755–1772.

Schweinhart, L. J., Weikart, D. P., & Larner, M. B. (1986). A report on the High/Scope preschool curriculum comparison study: Consequences of three preschool curriculum models through age 15. *Early Childhood Research Quarterly, 1,* 15–45.

Scott, G. B., Hutto, C., Makuch, R. W., Mastrucci, M. T., O'Connor, T., Mitchell, C. D., Trapido, E. J., & Parks, W. P. (1989). Survival in children with perinatal acquired immunodeficiency virus type 1 infection. *New England Journal of Medicine, 321,* 1791–1796.

Scott, J. P. (1958). *Animal behavior.* Chicago: University of Chicago Press.

Scott, J. R. (1991). Mandatory trial of labor after cesarean delivery: An alternative viewpoint. *Obstetrics and Gynecology, 77,* 811–814.

Sears, R. R., Maccoby, E. E., & Levin, H. (1957). *Patterns of child rearing.* New York: Harper & Row.

Seitz, V. (1990). Intervention programs for impoverished children: A comparison of educational and family support models. *Annals of Child Development, 7,* 73–103.

Selman, R. L. (1973, March). *A structural analysis of the ability to take another's social perspective: Stages in the development of role-taking ability.* Paper presented at the meeting of the Society for Research in Child Development, Philadelphia.

Selman, R. L., & Selman, A. P. (1979, April). Children's ideas about friendship: A new theory. *Psychology Today,* pp. 71–80.

Serdula, M., Williamson, D. F., Kendrick, J. S., Anda, R. F., & Byers, T. (1991). Trends in alcohol consumption by pregnant women: 1985 through 1988. *Journal of the American Medical Association, 265,* 876–879.

Sexton, M., & Hebel, R. (1984). A clinical trial of change in maternal smoking and its effect on birth weight. *Journal of the American Medical Association, 251,* 911–915.

Shannon, D. C., & Kelly, D. H. (1982a). SIDS and near-SIDS (Part 1). *New England Journal of Medicine, 306,* 959–965.

Shannon, D. C., & Kelly, D. H. (1982b). SIDS and near-SIDS (Part 2). *New England Journal of Medicine, 306,* 1022–1028.

Shannon, L. W. (1982). *Assessing the relationship of adult criminal careers to juvenile careers.* Iowa City: University of Iowa, Iowa Urban Community Research Center.

Shatz, M., & Gelman, R. (1973). The development of communication skills: Modifications in the speech of young children as a function of listener. *Monographs of the Society for Research in Child Development, 38*(5, Serial No. 152).

Shaywitz, B. A., Sullivan, C. M., Anderson, G. M., Gillespie, S. M., Sullivan, B., & Shaywitz, S. E. (1994). Aspartame, behavior, and cognitive function in children with attention deficit disorder. *Pediatrics, 93,* 70–75.

Shaywitz, S. E., Shaywitz, B. A., Fletcher, J. M., & Escobar, M. D. (1990). Prevalence of reading disability in boys and girls. *Journal of the American Medical Association, 246,* 998–1002.

Sheps, S., & Evans, G. D. (1987). Epidemiology of school injuries: A 2-year experience in a municipal health department. *Pediatrics, 79,* 69–75.

Sherman, L. W., & Berk, R. A. (1984, April). The Minneapolis domestic violence experiment. *Police Foundation Reports,* pp. 1–8.

Shields, P. J., & Rovee-Collier, C. (1992). Long-term memory for context-specific category information at six months. *Child Development, 63,* 245–259.

Shipp, E. R. (1988, February 4). Decision could hinder surrogacy across nation. *New York Times,* p. B6.

Shneidman, E. (1985). The definition of suicide. New York: Wiley.

Siegel, O. (1982). Personality development in adolescence. In B. B. Wolman (Ed.), *Handbook of developmental psychology.* Englewood Cliffs, NJ: Prentice-Hall.

Siegler, R. S., & Richards, D. (1982). The development of intelligence. In R. Sternberg (Ed.), *Handbook of human intelligence.* London: Cambridge University Press.

Sigman, M. D., Kasari, C., Kwon, J-H., & Yirmiya, N. (1992). Responses to the negative emotions of others by autistic, mentally retarded, and normal children. *Child Development, 63,* 796–807.

Sigman, M., Neumann, C., Jansen, A. A. J., & Bwibo, N. (1989). Cognitive abilities of Kenyan children in relation to nutrition, family characteristics, and education. *Child Development, 60,* 1463–1474.

Sigman-Grant, M., Zimmerman, S., & Kris-Etherton, P. M. (1993). Dietary approaches for reducing fat intake of preschool-age children. *Pediatrics, 91,* 955–960.

Signorielli, N., Gross, L., & Morgan, M. (1982). Violence in television programs: Ten years later. In D. Pearl, L. Bouthilet, & J. Lazar (Eds.), *Television and behavior: Ten years of scientific progress and implications for the eighties: Technical reviews* (Vol. 2). Washington, DC: National Institute of Mental Health.

Silverman, S. (1989). Scope, specifics of maternal drug use, effects on fetus are beginning to emerge from studies. *Journal of the American Medical Association, 261,* 1688–1689.

Silverstein, B., Perdue, L., Peterson, B., et al. (1986). The role of the mass media in promoting a thin standard of bodily attractiveness for women. *Sex Roles, 14,* 519–532.

Silverstein, B., Peterson, B., & Perdue, L. (1986). Some correlates of the thin standard of bodily attractiveness for women. *International Journal of Eating Disorders, 5*(5).

Simmons, R.G., Blyth, D. A., & McKinney, K. L. (1983). The social and psychological effects of puberty on white females. In J. Brooks-Gunn & A. C. Petersen (Eds.), *Girls at puberty: Biological and psychological perspectives.* New York: Plenum.

Simmons, R. G., Blyth, D. A., Van Cleave, E. F., & Bush, D. M. (1979). Entry into early adolescence: The impact of school structure, puberty, and early dating on self-esteem. *American Sociological Review, 44,* 948–967.

Simmons, R. G., Burgeson, R., Carlton-Ford, S., & Blyth, D. A. (1987). The impact of cumulative change in early adolescence. *Child Development, 58,* 1220–1234.

Simner, M. L. (1971). Newborn's response to the cry of another infant. *Developmental Psychology, 5,* 135–150.

Simons, C. (1987, March). They get by with a lot of help from their *kyoiku* mamas. *Smithsonian,* pp. 44–52.

Simpson, G. A., & Fowler, M. G. (1994). Geographic mobility and children's emotional/behavioral adjustment and school functioning. *Pediatrics, 93,* 303–309.

Simpson, J. L., & Elias, S. (1993). Isolating fetal cells from maternal blood: Advances in prenatal diagnosis through molecular technology. *Journal of the American Medical Association, 270,* 2357–2361.

Singer, D. G., & Singer, J. L. (1990). *The house of make-believe: Play and the developing imagination.* Cambridge, MA: Harvard University Press.

Singh, S., Forrest, J. D., & Torres, A. (1989). *Prenatal care in the United States: A state and county inventory.* New York: Alan Guttmacher Institute.

Singleton, L., & Asher, S. (1979). Racial integration and children's peer preferences: An investigation of developmental and cohort differences. *Child Development, 50,* 936–941.

Skinner, B. F. (1938). *The behavior of organisms: An experimental approach.* New York: Appleton-Century.

Skinner, B. F. (1957). *Verbal behavior.* New York: Appleton-Century-Crofts.

Skoe, E. E., & Diessner, R. E. (1994). Ethic of care, justice, identity, and gender: An extension and replication. *Merrill-Palmer Quarterly, 40,* 272–289.

Skoe, E. E., & Gooden, A. (1993). Ethic of care and real-life moral dilemma content in male and female early adolescents. *Journal of Early Adolescence, 13,* 154–167.

Slap, G. B., Vorters, D. F., Chaudhuri, S., & Centor, R. M. (1989). Risk factors for attempted suicide during adolescence. *Pediatrics, 84,* 762–772.

Slobin, D. I. (1971). Universals of grammatical development in children. In W. Levelt & G. B. Flores d'Arcais (Eds.), *Advances in psycholinguistic research.* Amsterdam: New Holland.

Slobin, D. (1973). Cognitive prerequisites for the acquisition of grammar. In C. Ferguson & D. Slobin (Eds.), *Studies of child language development.* New York: Holt, Rinehart, & Winston.

Slobin, D. (1983). Universal and particular in the acquisition of language. In E. Wanner & L. Gleitman (Eds.), *Language acquisition: The state of the art.* Cambridge, UK: Cambridge University Press.

Slomkowski, C. L., Nelson, K., Dunn, J., & Plomin, R. (1992). Temperament and language: Relations from toddlerhood to middle childhood. *Developmental Psychology, 28,* 1090–1095.

Smetana, J. G., Yau, J., Restrepo, A., & Braeges, J. L. (1991). Adolescent-parent conflict in married and divorced families. *Developmental Psychology, 27,* 1000–1010.

Smilansky, S. (1968). *The effects of sociodramatic play on disadvantaged preschool children.* New York: Wiley.

Smith, M. M., & Lifshitz, F. (1994). Excess fruit juice consumption as a contributing factor in nonorganic failure to thrive. *Pediatrics, 93,* 438–443.

Smith, T. E. (1981). Adolescent agreement with perceived maternal and paternal educational goals. *Journal of Marriage and the Family, 43,* 85–93.

Snarey, J. R. (1985). Cross-cultural universality of social-moral development: A critical review of Kohlbergian research. *Psychological Bulletin, 97,* 202–232.

Snarey, J. R., Reimer, J., & Kohlberg, L. (1985). Development of social-moral reasoning among kibbutz adolescents: A longitudinal cross-cultural study. *Developmental Psychology, 21,* 3–17.

Snow, C. E. (1972). Mother's speech to children learning language. *Child Development, 43,* 549–565.

Snow, C. E. (1977). Mother's speech research: From input to interaction. In C. E. Snow & C. A. Ferguson (Eds.), *Talking to children: Language and acquisition.* London: Cambridge University Press.

Snow, C. E. (1990). The development of definitional skill. *Journal of Child Language, 17,* 697–710.

Snow, C. E. (1993). Families as social contexts for literacy development. In C. Daiute (Ed.), The development of literacy through social interaction. *New Directions in Child Development, 61,* 11–24.

Snow, C. E., Arlman-Rupp, A., Hassing, Y., Jobse, J., Joosten, J., & Verster, J. (1976). Mothers' speech in three social classes. *Journal of Psycholinguistic Research, 5,* 1–20.

Solomons, H. (1978). The malleability of infant motor development. *Clinical Pediatrics, 17,* 836–839.

Sonenstein, F. L., Pleck, J. H., & Ku, L. C. (1991). Levels of sexual activity among adolescent males in the United States. *Family Planning Perspectives, 23,* 162–167.

Song, M., & Ginsburg, H. P. (1987). The development of informal and formal mathematical thinking in Korean and U.S. children. *Child Development, 58,* 1286–1296.

Sontag, L. W. (1966). Implications of fetal behavior and environment for adult personality. *Annals of the New York Academy of Science, 134,* 782–786.

Sontag, L. W., & Richards, T. W. (1938). Studies in fetal behavior: Fetal heart rate as a behavioral indicator. *Child Development Monographs, 3*(Whole No. 4).

Sontag, L. W., & Wallace, R. I. (1934). Preliminary report of the Fels fund: A study of fetal activity. *American Journal of Diseases of Children, 48,* 1050–1057.

Sontag, L. W., & Wallace, R. I. (1936). Changes in the heart rate of the human fetal heart in response to vibratory stimuli. *American Journal of Diseases of Children, 51,* 583–589.

Sophian, C. (1988). Early developments in children's understanding of number: Inferences about numerosity and one-to-one correspondence. *Child Development, 59,* 1397–1414.

Sorce, J. F., Emde, R. N., Campos, J., & Klinnert, M. D. (1985). Maternal emotional signaling: Its effect on the visual cliff behavior of 1-year-olds. *Developmental Psychology, 21,* 195–200.

Sorensen, R. C. (1973). *Adolescent sexuality in contemporary America.* Tarrytown, NY: World.

Sorensen, T., Nielsen, G., Andersen, P., & Teasdale, T. (1988). Genetic and environmental influences on premature death in adult adoptees. *New England Journal of Medicine, 318,* 727–732.

Spencer, M. B. (1990). Development of minority children: An introduction. *Child Development, 61,* 267–269.

Spencer, M. B., & Markstrom-Adams, C. (1990). Identity processes among racial and ethnic minority children. *Child Development, 61,* 290–310.

Spiker, D., Ferguson, J., & Brooks-Gunn, J. (1993). Enhancing maternal interactive behavior and child social competence in low birth weight, premature infants. *Child Development, 64,* 754–768.

Spitz, M. R., & Johnson, C. C. (1985). Neuroblastoma and paternal occupation: A case-control analysis. *American Journal of Epidemiology, 121,* 924–929.

Spitz, R. A. (1945). Hospitalism: An inquiry into the genesis of psychiatric conditioning in early childhood. In D. Fenschel et al. (Eds.), *Psychoanalytic studies of the child* (Vol. 1, pp. 53–74). New York: International Universities Press.

Spitz, R. A. (1946). Hospitalism: A follow-up report. In D. Fenschel et al. (Eds.), *Psychoanalytic studies of the child* (Vol. 1, pp. 113–117). New York: International Universities Press.

Spock, B., & Rothenberg, M. B. (1985). *Baby and child care.* New York: Pocket Books.

Spohr, H-L., Willms, J., & Steinhausen, H-C. (1993). Prenatal alcohol exposure and long-term developmental consequences. *Lancet, 341,* 907–910.

Sroufe, L. A. (1977). Wariness of strangers and the study of infant development. *Child Development, 48,* 731–746.

Sroufe, L. A. (1979). Socioemotional development. In J. Osofsky (Ed.), *Handbook of infant development.* New York: Wiley.

Sroufe, L. A. (1983). Individual patterns of adaptation from infancy to preschool. In M. Perlmutter (Ed.), *Proceedings of Minnesota symposium on child psychology.* Hillsdale, NJ: Erlbaum.

Sroufe, L. A., Bennett, C., Englund, M., Urban, J., & Shulman, S. (1993). The significance of gender boundaries in preadolescence: Contemporary correlates and antecedents of boundary violation and maintenance. *Child Development, 64,* 455–466.

Sroufe, L. A., Carlson, E., & Schulman, S. (1993). Individuals in relationships: Development from infancy through adolescence. In D. C. Funder, R. D. Parke, C. Tomlinson-Kesey, & K. Widaman (Eds.), *Studying lives through time: Personality and development* (pp. 315–342). Washington, DC: American Psychological Association.

Sroufe, L. A., Fox, N. E., & Pancake, V. R. (1983). Attachment and dependency in a developmental perspective. *Child Development, 54,* 1615–1627.

Sroufe, L. A., & Waters, E. (1976). The ontogenesis of smiling and laughter: A perspective on the organization of development in infancy. *Psychological Review, 83,* 173–189.

Sroufe, L. A., & Wunsch, J. (1972). The development of laughter in the first year of life. *Child Development, 43,* 1326–1344.

Stafford, R. S. (1990). Alternative strategies for controlling rising cesarean section rates. *Journal of the American Medical Association, 263,* 683–687.

Stainton, M. C. (1985). The fetus: A growing member of the family. *Family Relations, 34,* 321–326.

Stanley, A. (1990, May 7). Prodigy, 12, fights skeptics, hoping to be a doctor at 17. *New York Times,* pp. A1, B2.

Starfield, B. (1978). Enuresis: Focus on a challenging problem in primary care. *Pediatrics, 62,* 1036–1037.

Starfield, B. (1991). Childhood morbidity: Comparisons, clusters, and trends. *Pediatrics, 88,* 519–526.

Starfield, B., Katz, H., Livingston, G., Benson, P., Hankin, J., Horn, S., & Steinwachs, D. (1984). Morbidity in childhood—A longitudinal view. *New England Journal of Medicine, 310,* 824–829.

Stattin, H., & Magnusson, D. (1990). *Pubertal maturation in female development.* Hillsdale, NJ: Erlbaum.

Staub, J. B., & Lipschultz, L.I. (1990). Treatments for infertile men. *Medical Aspects of Human Sexuality, 24,* 40–45.

Staub, S. (1973). *The effect of three types of relationships on young children's memory for pictorial stimulus pairs.* Unpublished doctoral dissertation, Harvard University Graduate School of Education, Cambridge, MA.

Steinberg, L. (1981). Transformations in family relations at puberty. *Developmental Psychology, 17,* 833–840.

Steinberg, L. (1986). Latchkey children and susceptibility to peer pressure: An ecological analysis. *Developmental Psychology, 22,* 433–439.

Steinberg, L. (1987a). Impact of puberty on family relations: Effects of pubertal status and pubertal timing. *Developmental Psychology, 23,* 451–460.

Steinberg, L. (1987b). Single parents, stepparents, and the susceptibility of adolescents to antisocial peer pressure. *Child Development, 58,* 269–275.

Steinberg, L. (1987c, September). Bound to bicker. *Psychology Today,* pp. 36–39.

Steinberg, L. (1988). Reciprocal relation between parent-child distance and pubertal maturation. *Developmental Psychology, 24,* 122–128.

Steinberg, L. (1990). Autonomy, conflict, and harmony in the family relationship. In S. Feldman & G. Elliott (Eds.), *At the threshold: The developing adolescent.* Cambridge, MA: Harvard University Press.

Steinberg, L., & Darling, N. (1994). The broader context of social influence in adolescence. In R. Silbereisen & E. Todt (Eds.), *Adolescence in context.* New York: Springer.

Steinberg, L., Dornbusch, S. M., & Brown, B. B. (1992). Ethnic differences in adolescent achievement: An ecological perspective. *American Psychologist, 47,* 723–729.

Steinberg, L., Fegley, S., & Dornbusch, S. M. (1993). Negative impact of part-time work on adolescent adjustment: Evidence from a longitudinal study. *Developmental Psychology, 29,* 171–180.

Steinberg, L., Lamborn, S. D., Dornbusch, S. M., & Darling, N. (1992). Impact of parenting practices on adolescent achievement: Parenting, school involvement, and encouragement to succeed. *Child Development, 47,* 723–729.

Steinberg, L., & Silverberg, S. B. (1986). The vicissitudes of autonomy in early adolescence. *Child Development, 57,* 841–851.

Steiner, J. E. (1979). Human facial expressions in response to taste and smell stimulation. *Advances in Child Development and Behavior, 13,* 257.

Steinhauer, J. (1995, January 4). Girls don't want to have gym. *New York Times,* pp. C1, C6.

Stenchever, M. A., Williamson, R. A., Leonard, J., Karp, L. E., Ley, B., Shy, K., & Smith, D. (1981). Possible relationship between in utero diethylstilbestrol exposure and male fertility. *American Journal of Obstetrics and Gynecology, 140,* 186–193.

Stern, M., & Hildebrandt, K. A. (1986). Prematuring stereotyping: Effects on mother-infant interaction. *Child Development, 57,* 308–315.

Sternberg, R. J. (1984, September). How can we teach intelligence? *Educational Leadership,* pp. 38–50.

Sternberg, R. J. (1985a). *Beyond IQ: A triarchic theory of human intelligence.* New York: Cambridge University Press.

Sternberg, R. J. (1985b, November). Teaching critical thinking, Part I: Are we making critical mistakes? *Phi Delta Kappan,* pp. 194–198.

Sternberg, R. J. (1986). *Intelligence applied: Understanding and increasing your intellectual skills.* San Diego: Harcourt Brace.

Sternberg, R. J. (1987, September 23). The uses and misuses of intelligence testing: Misunderstanding meaning, users over-rely on scores. *Education Week,* pp. 22, 28.

Sternberg, R. J. (in press). Metaphors of mind underlying the testing of intelligence. In P. W. Reynolds & J. C. Roden (Eds.), *Advances in Psychological Assessment* (Vol. 8).

Stevens, J. H., & Bakeman, R. (1985). A factor analytic study of the HOME scale for infants. *Developmental Psychology, 21,* 1196–1203.

Stevenson, D. L., & Baker, D. P. (1987). The family-school relation and the child's school performance. *Child Development, 58,* 1348–1357.

Stevenson, H. W., Chen, C., & Lee, S.-Y. (1993). Mathematics achievement of Chinese, Japanese, and American children: Ten years later. *Science, 258,* 53–58.

Stevenson, H. W., Lee, S., Chen, C., & Lummis, M. (1990). Mathematics achievement of children in China and the United States. *Child Development, 61,* 1053–1066.

Stevenson, H. W., Lee, S., Chen, C., Stigler, J. W., et al. (1990). Contexts of achievement: A study of American, Chinese, and Japanese children. *Monographs of the Society for Research in Child Development, 55*(1–2, Serial No. 221).

Stevenson, H. W., Stigler, J. W., Lee, S., Lucker, G. W., Kitamura, S., & Hsu, C. (1985). Cognitive performance and academic achievement of Japanese, Chinese, and American children. *Child Development, 56,* 718–734.

Stevenson, M. R., & Black, K. N. (1988). Paternal absence and sex-role development: A meta-analysis. *Child Development, 59,* 793–814.

Stevenson, M., & Lamb, M. (1979). Effects of infant sociability and the caretaking environment on infant cognitive performance. *Child Development, 50,* 340–349.

Stewart, I. C. (1994, January 29). Two-part message [Letter to the editor]. *New York Times,* p. A18.

Stewart, M. A., & Olds, S. W. (1973). *Raising a hyperactive child.* New York: Harper & Row.

Stewart, R. B. (1983). Sibling attachment relationships: Child-infant interactions in the strange situation. *Developmental Psychology, 19,* 192–199.

Stifter, C. A., Coulehan, C. M., & Fish, M. (1993). Linking employment to attachment: The mediating effects of maternal separation anxiety and interactive behavior. *Child Development, 64,* 1451–1460.

Stigler, J. W., Lee, S., & Stevenson, H. W. (1987). Mathematics classrooms in Japan, Taiwan, and the United States. *Child Development, 58,* 1272–1285.

Stocker, C., Dunn, J., & Plomin, R. (1989). Sibling relationships: Links with child temperament, maternal behavior, and family structure. *Child Development, 60,* 715–727.

Strauss, M., Lessen-Firestone, J., Starr, R., & Ostrea, E. (1975). Behavior of narcotics-addicted newborns. *Child Development, 46,* 887–893.

Strawn, J. (1992). The states and the poor: Child poverty rises as the safety net shrinks. *Social Policy Report of the Society for Research in Child Development, VI*(3).

Streissguth, A. P., Aase, J. M., Clarren, S. K., Randels, S. P., LaDue, R. A., & Smith, D. F. (1991). Fetal alcohol syndrome in adolescents and adults. *Journal of the American Medical Association, 265,* 1961–1967.

Streissguth, A. P., Martin, D. C., Barr, H. M., Sandman, B. M., Kirchner, G. L., & Darby, B. L. (1984). Intrauterin alcohol and nicotine exposure: Attention and reaction time in 4-year-old children. *Developmental Psychology, 20,* 533–541.

Stuart, M. J., Gross, S., J., Elrad, H., & Graeber, J. E. (1982). Effects of acetyl-salicylic-acid ingestion on maternal and neonatal hemostasis. *New England Journal of Medicine, 307,* 909–912.

Students' learning and graduation rates slip. (1990, May 3). *New York Times,* p. B12.

Stunkard, A. J., Foch, T. T., & Hrubec, Z. (1986). A twin study of human obesity. *Journal of the American Medical Association, 256,* 51–54.

Stunkard, A., Harris, J. R., Pedersen, N. L., & McClearn, G. E. (1990). The body-mass index of twins who have been reared apart. *New England Journal of Medicine, 322,* 1483–1487.

Sue, S., & Okazaki, S. (1990). Asian-American educational achievements: A phenomenon in search of an explanation. *American Psychologist, 45,* 913–920.

Sullivan, H. S. (1953). *The interpersonal theory of psychiatry.* New York: Norton.

Sullivan, J. F. (1989, December 5). Prenatal care offered to all in New Jersey. *New York Times,* pp. B1, B8.

Sullivan, M. W. (1982). Reactivation: Priming forgotten memories in infants. *Child Development, 53,* 516.

Sullivan, S. A., & Birch, L. L. (1994). Infant dietary experience and acceptance of solid foods. *Pediatrics, 93,* 271–277.

Sullivan-Bolyai, J., Hull, H. F., Wilson, C., & Corey, L. (1983). Neonatal herpes simplex virus infection in King County, Washington. *Journal of the American Medical Association, 250,* 3059–3062.

Suomi, S., & Harlow, H. (1972). Social rehabilitation of isolate-reared monkeys. *Developmental Psychology, 6,* 487–496.

Surbey, M. K. (1990). Family composition, stress, and human menarche. In T. E. Ziegler & F. B. Bercovitch (Eds.), *Socioendocrinology of primate reproduction.* New York: Wiley-Liss.

Swain, I. U., Zelazo, P. R., & Clifton, R. K. (1993). Newborn infants' memory for speech sounds retained over 24 hours. *Developmental Psychology, 29,* 312–323.

Swedo, S., Rettew, D. C., Kuppenheimer, M., Lum, D., Dolan, S., & Goldberger, E. (1991). Can adolescent suicide attempter by distinguished from at-risk adolescents? *Pediatrics, 88,* 620–629.

Sweetland, J. D., & DeSimone, P. A. (1987). Age of entry, sex, and academic achievement in elementary school children. *Psychology in the Schools, 24,* 406–412.

Symons, D. (1978). *Play and aggression: A study of rhesus monkeys.* New York: Columbia University Press.

Tabor, A., Philip, J., Madsen, M., Bang, J., Obel, E., & Norgaard-Petersen, B. (1986, June 7). Randomised controlled trial of genetic amniocentesis in 4606 low-risk women. *Lancet,* pp. 1287–1292.

Takanishi, R. (1993). The opportunitis of adolescence—Research, interventions, and policy. *American Psychologist, 48,* 85–87.

Tamis-LeMonda, C. S., & Bornstein, M. H. (1993). Antecedents of exploratory competence at one year. *Infant Behavior and Development, 16,* 423–439.

Tan, S. L., Royston, P., Campbell, S., Jacobs, H. S., Betts, J., Mason, B., & Edwards, R. G. (1992). Cumulative conception and live birth after in-vitro fertilisation. *Lancet, 339,* 1090–1094.

Tanfer, K., & Horn, M. C. (1985). Contraceptive use, pregnancy and fertility patterns among single American women in their 20's. *Family Planning Perspectives, 17,* 10–19.

Tanner, J. M. (1973). Growing up. *Scientific American, 229*(3), 35–43.

Tanner, J. M. (1978). *Fetus into man: Physical growth from conception to maturity.* Cambridge, MA: Harvard University Press.

Tanner, J. M. (1989). *Fetus into man: Physical growth from conception to maturity.* (2d ed.). Cambridge: Harvard University Press.

Task Force on Pediatric AIDS of the American Psychological Association. (1989). Pediatric AIDS and human immunodeficiency virus infection. *American Psychologist, 44,* 258–264.

Taylor, A. R., Asher, S. R., & Williams, G. A. (1987). The social adaptation of mainstreamed mildly retarded children. *Child Development, 58,* 1321–1334.

Taylor, S. E. (1989). *Positive illusions: Creative self-deception and the healthy mind.* New York: Basic Books.

Teller, D. Y., & Bornstein, M. H. (1987). Infant color vision and color perception. In P. Salapatek & L. B. Cohen (Edsl), *Handbook of infant perception: Vol. 1. From sensation to perception* (pp. 185–236). Orlando, FL: Academic.

Terman, L. M., & Oden, M. H. (1959). *Genetic studies of genius: Vol. 5. The gifted group at mid-life.* Stanford, CA: Stanford University Press.

Termine, N. T., & Izard, C. E. (1988). Infants' responses to their mothers' expressions of joy and sadness. *Developmental Psychology, 24,* 223–229.

Teti, D. M., & Ablard, K. E. (1989). Security of attachment and infant-sibling relationships: A laboratory study. *Child Development, 60,* 1519–1528.

Thacker, S. B., Addiss, D. G., Goodman, R. A., Holloway, B. R., & Spencer, H. C. (1992). Infectious diseases and injuries in child day care. Opportunities for healthier children. *Journal of the American Medical Association, 268,* 1720–1726.

Tharp, R. G. (1989). Psychocultural variables and constants: Effects on teaching and learning in schools. *American Psychologist, 44,* 349–359.

Thomas, A., & Chess, S. (1977). *Temperament and development.* New York: Brunner/Mazel.

Thomas, A., & Chess, S. (1984). Genesis and evolution of behavioral disorders: From infancy to early adult life. *American Journal of Psychiatry, 141,* 1–9.

Thomas, A., Chess, S., & Birch, H. G. (1968). *Temperament and behavior disorders in children.* New York: New York University Press.

Thomas, D. (1985). The dynamics of teacher opposition to integration. *Remedial Education, 20*(2), 53–58.

Thompson, B., Wasserman, J. D., Gyurke, J. S., Matula, K., Mitchell, J. H., & Carr, B. (1994, January). *The validity of mental and motor scores from the new Bayley Scales of Infant Development–II: A second-order factor analysis.* Paper presented at the annual meeting of the Southwest Educational Research Association, San Antonio, TX.

Thompson, L. A., Fagen, J. F., & Fulker, D. W. (1991). Longitudinal prediction of specific cognitive abilities from infant novelty preference. *Child Development, 62,* 530–538.

Thompson, R. A., Lamb, M. E., & Estes, D. (1982). Stability of infant-mother attachment and its relationship to changing life circumstances in an unselected middle-class sample. *Child Development, 53,* 144–148.

Thompson, S. K. (1975). Gender labels and early sex-role development. *Child Development, 46,* 339–347.

Timiras, P. S. (1972). *Developmental physiology and aging.* New York: Macmillan.

Tobin, J. J., Wu, D. Y. H., & Davidson, D. H. (1989). *Preschools in three cultures: Japan, China, and the United States.* New Haven, CT: Yale University Press.

Tobin-Richards, M. H., Boxer, A. M., Kavrell, S. A. Mc., & Petersen, A. C.

(1984). Puberty and its psychological and social significance. In R. M. Lerner & N. L. Galambos (Eds.), *Experiencing adolescence: A sourcebook for parents, teachers, and teens.* New York: Garland.

Tobin-Richards, M. H., Boxer, A. M., & Petersen, A. C. (1983). The psychological significance of pubertal change: Sex differences in perceptions of self during early adolescence. In J. Brooks-Gunn & A. C. Petersen (Eds.), *Girls at puberty: Biological, social, and psychological perspectives.* New York: Plenum.

Tomasello, M., Mannle, S., & Kruger, A. C. (1986). Linguistic environment of 1- and 2-year-old twins. *Developmental Psychology, 22,* 169–176.

Toner, B. B., Garfinkel, P. E., & Garner, D. M. (1986). Long-term follow-up of anorexia nervosa. *Psychosomatic Medicine, 48,* 520–529.

Tonkova-Yompol'skaya, R. V. (1973). Development of speech intonation in infants during the first two years of life. In C. A. Fergusin & D. Slobin (Eds.), *Studies of child language development.* New York: Holt.

Tramontana, M. G., Hopper, S. R., & Selzer, S. C. (1988). Research on the preschool prediction of later academic achievement: A review. *Developmental Review, 8,* 89–146.

Treffers, P. E., Eskes, M., Kleiverda, G., & van Alten, D. (1990). Home births and minimal medical interventions. *Journal of the American Medical Association, 264,* 2207–2208.

Tronick, E. Z. (1972). Stimulus control and the growth of the infant's visual field. *Perception and Psychophysics, 11,* 373–375.

Tronick, E. Z. (1980). On the primacy of social skills. In D. B. Sawin, L. O. Walker, & J. H. Penticuff (Eds.), *The exceptional infant: Psychosocial risk in infant environment transactions.* New York: Brunner/Mazel.

Tronick, E. Z. (1989). Emotions and emotional communication in infants. *American Psychologist, 44,* 112–119.

Tronick, E. Z., & Gianino, A. F. (1986). The transmission of maternal depression to the infant. In E. Z. Tronick & T. Field (Eds.), *Maternal depression and infant disturbance.* San Francisco: Jossey-Bass.

Tronick, E. Z., Morelli, G. A., & Ivey, P. K. (1992). The Efe forager infant and toddler's pattern of social relationships: Multiple and simultaneous. *Developmental Psychology, 28,* 568–577.

Trotter, R. J. (1983, August). Baby face. *Psychology Today,* pp. 14–20.

Trotter, R. J. (1986). Profile: Robert J. Sternberg: Three heads are better than one. *Psychology Today, 20,* 56–62.

Trotter, R. J. (1987, May). You've come a long way, baby. *Psychology Today,* pp. 34–45.

Tsai, M., & Wagner, N. (1979). Incest and molestation: Problems of childhood sexuality. *Resident and Staff Physician,* 129–136.

Tuma, J. M. (1989). Mental health services for children: The state of the art. *American Psychologist, 44,* 188–199.

Tyler, P. E. (1994, January 11). Chinese start a vitamin program to eliminate a birth defect. *New York Times,* p. C3.

UNICEF. (1992). *State of the world's children.* New York: Oxford University Press.

United Nations. (1990). *Declaration of the world summit for children.* New York: Author.

Upjohn Company. (1984). *Writer's guide to sex and health.* Kalamazoo, MI: Author.

U.S. Bureau of the Census. (1988). *Fertility of American women: June 1987* (Current Population Reports, Series P-20, No. 427). Washington, DC: U.S. Government Printing Office.

U.S. Bureau of the Census. (1988). *Households, families, marital status and living arrangements: March, 1988* (Advance report, Series P. 20, No. 432). Washington, DC: U.S. Government Printing Office.

U.S. Bureau of the Census. (1990). *Who's minding the kids: Child care arrangements: 1986–1987* (Current Population Reports, Series, P-70, No. 20). Washington, DC: US Government Printing Office.

U.S. Bureau of the Census. (1991). *Household and family characteristics, March 1991* (Publication No. AP-20-458). Washington, DC: U.S. Government Printing Office.

U.S. Bureau of the Census. (1993). Statistics on characteristics of single-parent households.

U.S. Department of Education. (1991). *Digest of education statistics* (Publication No. NCES 91-697). Washington, DC: U.S. Government Printing Office.

U.S. Department of Education. (1992). *Dropout rates in the U.S., 1991* (Publication No. NCES 92-129). Washington, DC: U.S. Government Printing Office.

U.S. Department of Health and Human Services (USDHHS). (1981). Statistics on the incidence of depression.

U.S. Department of Health and Human Services (USDHHS). (1982). *Prevention '82* (DHHS Publication No. PHS 82-50157). Washington, DC: U.S. Government Printing Office.

U.S. Department of Health and Human Services (USDHHS). (1984). *Child abuse prevention: Tips to parents.* Washington, DC: Office of Human Development Services, Administration for Children, Youth, and Families, National Center on Child Abuse and Neglect.

U.S. Department of Health and Human Services (USDHHS). (1990). *Health United States 1989* (DHHS Publication no. PHS 90-1232). Washington, DC: U.S. Government Printing Office.

U.S. Department of Health and Human Services (USDHHS). (1992). *Health United States 1991, and prevention profile* (DHHS Publication No. PHS 92–1232). Washington, DC: U. S. Government Printing Office.

U.S. Department of Health and Human Services (USDHHS). (1993, August). *Health: U. S. 1992* (DHHS Publication No. 93-1232). Washington, DC: U.S. Government Printing Office.

U.S. Department of Justice (1988). Statistics.

Uzgiris, I. C., & Hunt, J. (1975). *Assessment in infancy.* Urbana: University of Illinois Press.

Vaillant, G. E., & Vaillant, C. O. (1990). Natural history of male psychological health, XII: A 45-year study of predictors of successful aging. *American Journal of Psychiatry, 147,* 31–37.

Valaes, T., Petmezaki, S., Henschke, C., Drummond, G. S., & Kappas, A. (1994). Contrl of jaundice in preterm newborns by an inhibitor of bilirubin production: Studies with tin-mesoporphyrin. *Pediatrics, 93,* 1–11.

Valdez-Menchaca, M. C., & Whitehurst, G. J. (1992). Accelerating language development through picture book reading: A systematic extension to Mexican day care. *Developmental Psychology, 28,* 1106–1114.

Valentine, D. P. (1982). The experience of pregnancy: A developmental process. *Family Relations, 31,* 243–248.

Valenzuela, M. (1990). Attachment in chronically underweight young children. *Child Development, 61,* 1984–1996.

Van de Perre, P., Simonon, A., Msellati, P., Hitimana, D.-G., Vaira, D., Bazubagira, A., Van Goethem, C., Stevens, A.-M., Karita, E., Sondag-Thull, D., Dabis, F., & Lepage, P. (1991). Postnatal transmission of human immuno-deficiency virus type 1 from mother to infant. *New England Journal of Medicine, 325,* 593–598.

Van IJzendoorn, M. H., Goldberg, S., Kroonenberg, P. M., & Frenkel, O. J. (1992). The relative effects of maternal and child problems on the quality of attachment: A meta-analysis of attachment in clinical samples. *Child Development, 63,* 840–858.

Van Noord-Zaadstra, B. M., Looman, C. W. N., Alsbach, H., Habbema, J. D. F., teVelde, E. R., & Karbaat, J. (1991). Delaying childbearing: Effect of age on fecundity and outcome of pregnancy. *British Medical Journal, 302,* 1361.

Van Riper, M., Ryff, C., & Pridham, K. (1992). Parental and family well-being in families of children with Down syndrome: A complete study. *Research in Nursing and Health, 15,* 227–235.

Vandell, D. L., & Corasaniti, M. A. (1988). The relation between third graders' after-school care and social, academic, and emotional functioning. *Child Development, 59,* 868–875.

Vandell, D. L., & Ramanan, J. (1991). Children of the National Longitudinal Survey of Youth: Choices in after-school care and child development. *Developmental Psychology, 27,* 637–643.

Vandell, D. L., & Ramanan, J. (1992). Effects of early and recent maternal employment on children from low-income families. *Child Development, 63,* 938–949.

Vaughn, B. E., Goldberg, S., Atkinson, L., Marcovitch, S., MacGregor, D., & Seifer, R. (1994). Quality of toddler-mother attachment in children with Down syndrome: Limits to interpretation of Strange Situation behavior. *Child Development, 65,* 95–108.

Vaughn, B. E., Stevenson-Hinde, J., Waters, E., Kotsaftis, A., et al. (1992). Attachment security and temperament in infancy and early childhood: Some conceptual clarifications. *Developmental Psychology, 28,* 463–473.

Veroff, J., Douvan, E., & Kulka, R. (1981). *The inner American.* New York: Basic Books.

Visher, E., & Visher, J. (1983). Stepparenting: Blending families. In H. I. McCubbin & C. R. Figley (Eds.), *Stress and the family: Vol. 1. Coping with normative transitions.* New York: Brunner/Mazel.

Voelker, R. (1993). The genetic revolution: Despite perfection of elegant techniques, ethical answers still elusive. *Journal of the American Medical Association, 270,* 2273–2277.

Vosniadou, S. (1987). Children and metaphors. *Child Development, 58,* 870–885.

Vuori, L., Christiansen, N., Clement, J., Mora, J., Wagner, M., & Herrera, M. (1979). Nutritional supplementation and the outcome of pregnancy: 2. Visual habituation at 15 days. *Journal of Clinical Nutrition, 32,* 463–469.

Vygotsky, L. S. (1956). *Selected psychological investigations.* Moscow: Izdstel'sto Akademii Pedagogicheskikh Nauk SSSR.

Vygotsky, L. S. (1962). *Thought and language.* Cambridge, MA: MIT Press.

Vygotsky, L. S. (1978). *Mind in society: The development of higher psychological processes.* Cambridge, MA: Harvard University Press.

Wachs, T. (1975). Relation of infants' performance on Piaget's scales between 12 and 24 months and their Stanford Binet performance at 31 months. *Child Development, 46,* 929–935.

Wagner, R. K., & Sternberg, R. J. (1986). Tacit knowledge and intelligence in the everyday world. In R. J. Sternberg & R. K. Wagner (Eds.), *Practical intelligence: Nature and origins of competence in the everyday world.* Cambridge, UK: Cambridge University Press.

Walk, R. D., & Gibson, E. J. (1961). A comparative and anytical study of visual depth perception. *Psychology Monographs, 75* (15).

Walker, L. (1984). Sex differences in the development of moral reasoning: A critical review. *Child Development, 55,* 677–691.

Walker, L. (1987, August). *A longitudinal study of moral stages.* Paper presented at the annual meeting of the American Psychological Association, New York.

Walker, L. J., & Taylor, J. H. (1991). Family interactions and the development of moral reasoning. *Child Development, 62,* 264–283.

Wallach, M. A., & Kogan, N. (1965). *Modes of thinking in young children: A study of the creativity-intelligence distinction.* New York: Holt.

Wallerstein, J. S. (1983). Children of divorce: The psychological tasks of the child. *American Journal of Orthopsychiatry, 53,* 230–243.

Wallerstein, J. S. (1987). Children of divorce: Report of a ten-year follow-up of early latency-age children. *American Journal of Orthopsychiatry, 57,* 199–211.

Wallerstein, J. S., & Kelly, J. B. (1980). *Surviving the break-up: How children actually cope with divorce.* New York: Basic Books.

Walter, H. J., Vaughan, R. D., & Cohall, A. T. (1991). Psychosocial influences on acquired immunodeficiency syndrome risk-behaviors among high school students. *Pediatrics, 88,* 846–852.

Warren, K. S. (1988, March 19). Protecting the world's children: An agenda for the 1990s. *Lancet,* p. 659.

Wasik, B. H., Ramey, C. T., Bryant, D. M., & Sparling, J. J. (1990). A longitudinal study of two early intervention strategies: Project CARE. *Child Development, 61,* 1682–1696.

Waters, E., & Deane, K. E. (1985). Defining and assessing individual differences in attachment relationships: Q-methodology and the organization of behavior in infancy and early childhood. *Monographs of the Society for Research in Child Development, 50,* 41–65.

Waters, E., Wippman, J., & Sroufe, L. A. (1979). Attachment, positive affects, and competence in the peer group: Two studies in construct validation. *Child Development, 50,* 821–829.

Watson, J. B. (1958). *Behaviorism (rev. ed.).* New York: Norton.

Watson, J. B., & Rayner, R. (1920). Conditioned emotional reactions. *Journal of Experimental Psychology, 3,* 1–14.

Weathers, W. T., Crane, M. M., Sauvain, K. J., & Blackhurst, D. W. (1993). Cocaine use in women from defined population: Prevalence at delivery and effects on growth in infants. *Pediatrics, 91,* 350–354.

Weatherstone, K. B., Rasmussen, L. B., Erenberg, A., Jackson, E. M., Claflin, K. S., & Leff, R. D. (1993). Safety and efficacy of a topical anesthesia during circumcision in newborn infants. *Journal of the American Medical Association, 270,* 850–853.

Webb, W. B., & Bonnet, M. (1979). Sleep and dreams. In M. E. Meyer (Ed.), *Foundations of contemporary psychology.* New York: Oxford University Press.

Wegman, M. E. (1989). Annual summary of vital statistics—1988. *Pediatrics, 84,* 943–956.

Wegman, M. E. (1990). Annual summary of vital statistics—1989. *Pediatrics, 86,* 835–847.

Wegman, M. E. (1993). Annual summary of vital statistics—1992. *Pediatrics, 92,* 743–754.

Wegman, M. E. (1994). Annual summary of vital statistics—1993. *Pediatrics, 94,* 792–803.

Weinberg, R. A. (1989). Intelligence and IQ: Landmark issues and great debates. *American Psychologist, 44,* 98–104.

Weinstein, R. S., Marshall, H. H., Sharp, L., & Botkin, M. (1987). Pygmalion and the student: Age and classroom differences in children's awareness of teacher expectation. *Child Development, 58,* 1079–1093.

Weisglas-Kuperus, N., Baerts, W., Smrkovsky, M., & Sauer, P. J. E. (1993). Effects of biological and social factors on the cognitive development of very low birth weight children. *Pediatrics, 92,* 658–665.

Weisman, S. R. (1988, July 20). No more guarantees of a son's birth. *New York Times,* pp. A1, A9.

Weisner, T. S. (1993). Ethnographic and ecocultural perspectives on sibling relationships. In Z. Stoneman & P. W. Berman (Eds.), *The effects of mental retardation, disability, and illness on sibling relationships* (pp. 51–83). Baltimore, MD: Paul H. Brooks.

Weiss, B., Dodge, K. A., Bates, J. E., & Pettit, G. S. (1992). Some consequences of early harsh discipline: Child aggression and a maladaptive social information processing style. *Child Development, 63,* 1321–1335.

Weiss, B. D. (1992). Trends in bicycle helmet use by children: 1985 to 1990. *Pediatrics, 89,* 78–80.

Weiss, G. (1990). Hyperactivity in childhood. *New England Journal of Medicine, 323,* 1413–1415.

Weiss, L., & Lowenthal, M. (1975). Life-course perspectives on friendship. In M. Lowenthal, M. Thurner, & D. Chiriboga (Eds.), *Four stages of life.* San Francisco: Jossey-Bass.

Weissman, M. M., Gammon, D., John, K., Merikangas, K. R., Warner, V., Prusoff, B. A., & Sholomskas, D. (1987). Children of depressed parents: Increased psychopathology and early onset of major depression. *Archives of General Psychiatry, 44,* 847–853.

Weisz, J. R., Sigman, M., Weiss, B., & Mosk, J. (1993). Parent reports of behavioral and emotional problems among children in Kenya, Thailand, and the United States. *Child Development, 64,* 98–109.

Weitzman, M., Gortmaker, S., & Sobol, A. (1992). Maternal smoking and behavior problems of children. *Pediatrics, 90,* 342–349.

Wellington, N., & Rieder, M. J. (1993). Attitudes and practices regarding analgesia for newborn circumcision. *Pediatrics, 92,* 541–543.

Wellman, H., & Lempers, J. (1977). The naturalistic communicative abilities of two-year-olds. *Child Development, 48,* 1052–1057.

Wells, A. S. (1988a, September 7). For those at risk of dropping out, an enduring program that works. *New York Times,* p. B9.

Wells, A. S. (1988b, January 3). The parents' place: Right in the school. *New York Times Education Supplement,* p. 63.

Werler, M. M., Shapiro, S., & Mitchell, A. A. (1993). Periconceptional folic acid exposure and risk of occurrent neural tube defects. *Journal of the American Medical Association, 269,* 1257–1261.

Werner, E. E. (1985). Stress and protective factors in children's lives. In A. R. Nichol (Ed.), *Longitudinal studies in child psychology and psychiatry.* New York: Wiley.

Werner, E. E. (1989). Children of the garden island. *Scientific American, 260*(4), 106–111.

Werner, E. E. (1993). Risk and resilience in individuals with learning disabilities: Lessons learned from the Kauai

longitudinal study. *Learning Disabilities Research and Practice, 8,* 28–34.

Werner, E., Bierman, L., French, F. E., Simonian, K., Connor, A., Smith, R., & Campbell, M. (1968). Reproductive and environmental casualties: A report on the 10-year follow-up of the children of the Kauai pregnancy study. *Pediatrics, 42,* 112–127.

Werner, J. S., & Siqueland, E. R. (1978). Visual recognition memory in the preterm infant. *Infant Behavior and Development, 1,* 79–94.

West Berlin Human Genetics Institute. (1987). Study on effects of nuclear radiation at Chernobyl on fetal development.

Whiffen, V. E., & Gotlib, I. H. (1989). Infants of postpartum depressed mothers: Temperament and cognitive status. *Journal of Abnormal Psychology, 98,* 274–279.

White, B. L. (1971, October). *Fundamental early environmental influences on the development of competence.* Paper presented at Third Western Symposium on Learning, Western Washington State College, Bellingham, WA.

White, B. L., Kaban, B., & Attanucci, J. (1979). *The origins of human competence.* Lexington, MA: Heath.

White, K. R. (1982). The relation between socio-economic status and academic achievement. *Psychological Bulletin, 91,* 461–481.

Whitehurst, G. J., Falco, F. L., Lonigan, C. J., Fischel, J. E., DeBaryshe, B. D., Veldez-Menchaca, M. D., & Caulfield, M. (1988). Accelerating language development through picture book reading. *Developmental Psychology, 24,* 552–559.

Wideman, M. V., & Singer, J. F. (1984). The role of psychological mechanisms in preparation for childbirth. *American Psychologist, 34,* 1357–1371.

Widom, C. S. (1989). The cycle of violence. *Science, 244,* 160–166.

Wilcox, A. J., Weinberg, C. R., O'Connor, J. F., Baird, D. D., Schlatterer, J. P., Canfield, R. E., Armstrong, E. G., & Nisula, B. C. (1988). Incidence of early loss in pregnancy. *New England Journal of Medicine, 319,* 189–194.

Williams, B. C. (1990). Immunization coverage among preschool children: The United States and selected European countries. *Pediatrics, 86*(Suppl.), 1052–1056.

Williams, B. C., & Miller, C. A. (1991). *Preventive health care for young children: Findings from a 10-country study and directions for United States policy.* Arlington, VA: National Center for Clinical Infant Programs.

Williams, B. C., & Miller, C. A. (1992). Preventive health care for young children: Findings from a 10-country study and directions for United States policy. *Pediatrics, 89* (Suppl.).

Williams, E. R., & Caliendo, M. A. (1984). *Nutrition: Principles, issues, and applications.* New York: McGraw-Hill.

Williams, J., Best, D., & Boswell, D. (1975). The measurement of children's racial attitudes in the early school years. *Child Development, 46,* 494–500.

Williams, M. D. (1981). Observations in Pittsburgh ghetto schools. *Anthropology and Education Quarterly, 12,* 211–220.

Williams, S. B. (1987). A comparative study of black dropouts and black high school graduates in an urban public school system. *Education and Urban Society, 19,* 311–319.

Willinger, M., Hoffman, H. T., & Hartford, R. B. (1994). Infant sleep position and risk for sudden infant death syndrome: Report of meeting held January 13 and 14, 1994. *Pediatrics, 93,* 814–819.

Wilson, G., McCreary, R., Kean, J., & Baxter, J. (1979). The development of preschool children of heroin-addicted mothers: A controlled study. *Pediatrics, 63,* 135–141.

Winer, G. A. (1982). A review and analysis of children's fearful behavior in dental settings. *Child Development, 53,* 1111–1133.

Winick, M. (1981, January). Food and the fetus. *Natural History,* pp. 16–81.

Winick, M., Brasel, J., & Rosso, P. (1972). Nutrition and cell growth. In M. Winick (Ed.), *Nutrition and development.* New York: Wiley.

Wittrock, M. C. (1980). Learning and the brain. In M. C. Wittrock (Ed.), *The brain and psychology.* New York: Academic.

Wolf, M. (1968). *The house of Lim.* Englewood Cliffs, NJ: Prentice-Hall.

Wolfe, D. A. (1985). Child-abusive parents: An empirical review and analysis. *Psychological Bulletin, 97,* 462–482.

Wolfe, D. A., Edwards, B., Manion, I., & Koverola, C. (1988). Early intervention for parents at risk of child abuse and neglect: A preliminary investigation. *Journal of Consulting and Clinical Psychology, 56,* 40–47.

Wolff, P. H. (1966). The causes, controls, and organizations of behavior in the newborn. *Psychological Issues, 5*(1, Whole No. 17), 1–105.

Wolff, P. H. (1969). The natural history of crying and other vocalizations in early infancy. In B. M. Foss (Ed.), *Determinants of infant behavior* (Vol. 4). London: Methuen.

Wolff, R. (1993). *Good sports: The concerned parent's guide to Little League and other competitive youth sports.* New York: Dell.

Wolraich, M. L., Lindgren, S. D., Stumbo, P. J., Steglink, L. D., Appelbaum, M. I., & Kiritsky, M. C. (1994). Effects of diets high in sucrose or aspartame on the behavior and cognitive performance of children. *New England Journal of Medicine, 330,* 301–307.

Woman delivers a baby boy after refusing a caesarean. (1993, December 30). *New York Times,* p. A12.

Wong, N. D., Nei, T. K., Qaqundah, P. Y., Davidson, D. M., Bassin, S. L., & Gold, K. V. (1992). Television viewing and pediatric hypercholesterolemia. *Pediatrics, 90,* 75–79.

Wood, D. (1980). Teaching the young child: Some relationships between social interaction, language, and thought. In D. Olson (Ed.), *The social foundations of language and thought.* New York: Norton.

Wood, D., Bruner, J., & Ross, G. (1976). The role of tutoring in problem solving. *Journal of Child Psychiatry and Psychology, 17,* 89–100.

Wood, D. L., Hayward, R. A., Corey, C. R., Freeman, H. E., & Shapiro, M. F. (1990). Access to medical care for children and adolescents in the United States. *Pediatrics, 86,* 666–673.

Wood, P. R., Hidalgo, H. R., Prihoda, T. J., & Kromer, M. E. (1993). Hispanic children with asthma. *Pediatrics, 91,* 62–69.

Working Group on HIV Testing of Pregnant Women and Newborns. (1990). HIV infection, pregnant women, and newborns: A policy proposal for information and testing. *Journal of the American Medical Association, 264,* 2416–2420.

Wright, A. L., Holberg, C. J., Martinez, F. D., Morgan, W. J., & Taussig, L. M. (1989). Breast-feeding and lower respiratory tract illness in the first year of life. *British Medical Journal, 299,* 946–949.

Wright, J. T., Waterson, E. J., Barrison, I. G., Toplis, P. J., Lewis, I. G., Gordon, M. G., MacRae, K. D., Morris, N. F., & Murray Lyon, I. M. (1983, March 26). Alcohol consumption, pregnancy, and low birthweight. *Lancet,* pp. 663–665.

Wynn, K. (1992). Evidence against empiricist accounts of the origins of numerical knowledge. *Mind and Language, 7,* 315–332.

Yamamoto, K., Soliman, A., Parsons, J., & Davies, O. L. (1987). Voices in unison: Stressful events in the lives of children in six countries. *Journal of Child Psychology and Psychiatry, 28,* 855–864.

Yamazaki, J. N., & Schull, W. J. (1990). Perinatal loss and neurological abnormalities among children of the atomic bomb. *Journal of the American Medical Association, 264,* 605–609.

Yarrow, L. (1961). Maternal deprivation: Toward an empirical and conceptual reevaluation. *Psychological Bulletin, 58,* 459–490.

Yarrow, M. R. (1978, October 31). *Altruism in children.* Paper presented at program, Advances in Child Development Research, New York Academy of Sciences, New York.

Yazigi, R. A., Odem, R. R. & Polakoski, K. L. (1991). Demonstration of specific binding of cocaine to human spermatoza. *Journal of the American Medical Association, 266,* 1956–1959.

Yogman, M. J. (1984). Competence and performance of fathers and infants. In A. MacFarlane (Ed.), *Progress in child health.* London: Churchill Livingston.

Yogman, M. J., Dixon, S., Tronick, E., Als, H., & Brazelton, T. B. (1977, March). *The goals and structure of face-to-face interaction between infants and their fathers.* Paper presented at the meeting of the Society for Research in Child Development, New Orleans.

Young, K. T., & Zigler, E. (1986). Infant and toddler day care: Regulations and policy implications. *American Journal of Orthopsychiatry, 56,* 43–55.

Youngblade, L. M., & Belsky, J. (1992). Parent-child antecedents of 5-year-olds' close friendships: A longitudinal analysis. *Developmental Psychology, 28,* 700–713.

Youngstrom, N. (1992). Inner-city youth tell of life in "a war zone." *APA Monitor,* 36–37.

Yudkin, M. (1984, April). When kids think the unthinkable. *Psychology Today,* pp. 18–25.

Zabin, L. S., & Clark, S. D. (1983). Institutional factors affecting teenagers' choice and reasons for delay in attending a family planning clinic. *Family Planning Perspectives, 15,* 25–29.

Zabin, L. S., Hirsch, M. B., Smith, E. A., & Hardy, J. B. (1984). Adolescent sexual attitudes and behavior: Are they consistent? *Family Planning Perspectives, 16,* 181.

Zabin, L. S., Kantner, J. F., & Zelnik, M. (1979). The risk of adolescent pregnancy in the first months of intercourse. *Family Planning Perspectives, 11,* 215–222.

Zahn-Waxler, C., Radke-Yarrow, M., Wagner, E., & Chapman, M. (1992). Development of concern for others. *Developmental Psychology, 28,* 126–136.

Zahn-Waxler, C., Robinson, J. L., & Emde, R. N. (1992). The development of empathy in twins. *Developmental Psychology, 28,* 1038–1047.

Zakariya, S. B. (1982, September). Another look at the children of divorce: Summary report of the study of school needs of one-parent children. *Principal,* pp. 34–37.

Zametkin, A. J., Nordahl, T. E., Gross, M., King, A. C., Semple, W. E., Rumsey, J., Hamburger, S., Cohen, R. M., et al. (1990). Cerebral glucose metabolism in adults with hyperactivity of childhood onset. *New England Journal of Medicine, 323,* 1361–1366.

Zarbatany, L., Hartmann, d. P., & Rankin, D. B. (1990). The psychological functions of preadolescent peer activities. *Child Development, 61,* 1067–1080.

Zelazo, N. A., Zelazo, P. R., Cohen, K. M., & Zelazo, P. D. (1993). Specificity of practice effects on elementary neuromotor patterns. *Developmental Psychology, 29,* 686–691.

Zelazo, P. R., Zelazo, N. A., & Kolb, S. (1972). "Walking" in the newborn. *Science, 176,* 314–315.

Zell, E. R., Dietz, V., Stevenson, J., Cochi, S., & Bruce, R. H. (1994). Low vaccination levels of U. S. preschool and school-age children. *Journal of the American Medical Association, 271,* 833–839.

Zelnik, M., Kantner, J. F., & Ford, K. (1981). *Sex and pregnancy in adolescnece.* Beverly Hills, CA: Sage.

Zelnik, M., & Shah, F. K. (1983). First intercourse among young Americans. *Family Planning Perspectives, 15,* 64–72.

Zentella, A. C. (1981). Language variety among Puerto Ricans. In C. A. Ferguson & S. B. Heath (Eds.), *Language in the USA* (pp. 218–238). New York: Cambridge University Press.

Zeskind, P. S., & Iacino, R. (1984). Effects of maternal visitation to preterm infants in the neonatal intensive care unit. *Child Development, 55,* 1887–1893.

Zeskind, P. S., & Marshall, T. R. (1988). The relation between variations in pitch and maternal perceptions of infant crying. *Child Development, 59,* 193–196.

Zhang, Y., Proenca, R., Maffei, M., Barone, M., Leopold, L., & Friedman, J. M. (1994). Positional cloning of the mouse obese gene and its human homologue. *Nature, 372,* 425–432.

Zigler, E. F. (1987). Formal schooling for four-year-olds? *North American Psychologist, 42,* 254–260.

Zigler, E., & Styfco, S. J. (1993). Using research and theory to justify and inform Head Start expansion. *Social Policy Report of the Society for Research in Child Development, VII*(2).

Zigler, E., Taussig, C., & Black, K. (1992). Early childhood intervention: A promising preventative for juvenile delinquency. *American Psychologist, 47,* 997–1006.

Zimiles, H., & Lee, V. E. (1991). Adolescent family structure and educational progress. *Developmental Psychology, 27,* 314–320.

Zimmerman, D. (1993). Genital mutilation of women now is a challenge in the U.S. *Probe: David Zimmerman's newsletter on science, media, public policy, and health, 2,* 1, 4–5.

Zimrin, H. (1986). A profile of survival. *Child Abuse and Neglect, 10,* 339–349.

Zuckerman, B. S., & Beardslee, W. R. (1987). Maternal depression: A concern for pediatricians. *Pediatrics, 79,* 110–117.

Zuckerman, B., Frank, D., Hingson, R., Amaro, H., Levenson, S. M., Kayne, H., Parker, S., Vinci, R., Aboagye, K., Fried, L., Cabral, H., Timperi, R., & Bauchner, H. (1989). Effects of maternal marijuana and cocaine use on fetal growth. *New England Journal of Medicine, 320,* 762–768.

Zuckerman, D. M., & Zuckerman, B. S. (1985). Television's impact on children. *Pediatrics, 75,* 233–240.

Zylke, J. W. (1989). Sudden infant death syndrome: Resurgent research offers hope. *Journal of the American Medical Association, 262,* 1565–1566.

ACKNOWLEDGMENTS

The authors wish to thank the copyright owners for permission to reprint the following copyrighted material.

INTRODUCTION

Opening quotation: Hartford, J. (1971). "Life Prayer." In *Work Movies* by John Hartford. Copyright © 1971 by Ensign Music Corporation. Reprinted by permission.

CHAPTER 2

Opening quotation: Leonard, W. E. (1923). *Two Lives* by William Ellery Leonard. © 1923 by B. W. Huebsch, Inc. © 1951 Charlotte Charlton Leonard, Viking-Penguin. Reprinted by permission of the author's heirs.

Page 71: Weisman, S. R. (1988). No more guarantees of a son's birth. *The New York Times*, pp. A1, A9. Copyright © 1988 by The New York Times Co. Reprinted by permission.

Figure 2.6: Babu, A., and Hirschhorn, K. (1992). *A Guide to Human Chromosome Defects*. Birth Defects: Original Article Series, 28(2). Reprinted by permission of the March of Dimes Birth Defects Foundation, White Plains, New York.

Figure 2.7: Fuchs, F. (1980). "Genetic Amniocentesis." *Scientific American*, 242(6), 47–53. Copyright © 1980 by Scientific American, Inc. All rights reserved. Reprinted by permission.

Table 2.2: Tisdale, S. (1988). "The gene screen: Looking in on baby." *Health* (formerly *In Health* and *Hippocrates*), 2(3), 68–69. Researched by Valerie Fahey. Excerpted from *Hippocrates* © 1988. Reprinted by permission.

Table 2.5: Adapted in part from Bouchard, T. J. (1994). "Genes, environment, and personality." *Science, 264*, 1700–1701. Copyright 1994 by the American Association for the Advancement of Science. Adapted in part from Plomin, R., Owen, M. J., and McGuffin, P. (1994). "The genetic bases of behavior." *Science, 264*, 1733–1739. Copyright 1994 by the American Association for the Advancement of Science.

CHAPTER 3

Opening quotation: Sexton, A. (1966). "Little Girl, My String Bean, My Lovely Woman." In Anne Sexton, *Live or Die*. Copyright © 1966 by Anne Sexton. Reprinted by permission of Houghton Mifflin Company. All rights reserved.

Figure 3.2: Moore, K. L. (1989). *Before We are Born: Basic Embryology and Birth Defects*, 4th edition, 1993. Reprinted by permission of W. B. Saunders Co.

CHAPTER 4

Opening quotation: Fraiberg, S. (1959). *The Magic Years*. Copyright © 1959 Selma H. Fraiberg; copyright renewed 1987. Reprinted by permission of Charles Scribner's Sons, an imprint of Macmillan Publishing Company.

Box 4.1: Olds, S. W. (1995). Having a baby in the Himalayas. Copyright 1995 by Sally Wendkos Olds. Reprinted by permission.

Figure 4.1: Lagercrantz, H., and Slotkin, T. A. (1986). The 'stress' of being born. *Scientific American*, 254(4). Copyright © 1986 by Scientific American, Inc. All rights reserved. Adapted by permission.

Figure 4.2: Notzon, F. C. (1990). International difference in the use of obstetric interventions. *Journal of the American Medical Association, 263*(24), 3286–3291. Copyright 1990 by the American Medical Association. Reprinted by permission.

Table 4.2: Wegman, M. E. (1994). Annual summary of vital statistics–1992. *Pediatrics, 92*, 743. Copyright 1993. Reproduced by permission of *Pediatrics*.

Table 4.4: Apgar, V. (1953). A proposal for a new method of evaluation of the new born infant. *Current Researches in Anesthesia and Analgesia, 32*, 260–267. Adapted by permission of the International Anesthesia Research Society.

Table 4.5: Adapted in part from Prechtl, H. F. R., and Beintema, D. J. (1964). *The neurological examination of the full-term newborn infant: Clinics in development medicine* (No. 12). London: Butterworth Heinemann. Adapted in part from Wolff, P. H. (1966). "The causes, controls, and organizations of behavior in the neonate." *Psychological Issues*, Monograph 17, 5(1), 1–105. Copyright 1966 by International Universities Press, Inc. Adapted by permission.

CHAPTER 5

Figure 5.3: Restak, R. (1984). Fetal Brain Development. *The Brain*, Fig. 3.1. Copyright © 1984 by Educational Broadcasting Corporation and Richard M. Restak, M.D. Used by permission of Bantam Books, a division of Bantam Doubleday Dell Publishing Group, Inc.

Figure 5.5: Zelazo, N. A., Zelazo, P. R., Cohen, K. M., and Zelazo, P. D. (1993). Specificity of practice effects on elementary neuromotor patterns. *Developmental Psychology, 29,* 686–691. Copyright © 1993 by the American Psychological Association. Reprinted with permission of the American Psychological Association and P. R. Zelazo.

Figure 5.6: Wegman, M. E. (1993). Annual summary of vital statistics–1992. *Pediatrics, 92,* 743–754. Copyright 1992. Reprinted by permission of *Pediatrics.*

Table 5.2: Alford, B., and Boyle, M. (1982). *Nutrition During the Lifecycle,* 56. Englewood Cliffs: Prentice-Hall, Inc. Adapted by permission of the authors.

Table 5.3: Bolles, E. B. (1982). *So Much to Say,* 200. Copyright © 1982 by Edmund Blair Bolles. Reprinted by permission of St. Martin's Press, Inc.

Table 5.4: Frankenberg, W. K., Dodds, J., Archer, P., Shapiro, H., and Bresnick, B. (1992). The Denver II: A major revision and restandardization of the Denver Developmental Screening Test. *Pediatrics, 89,* 91–97. The Denver II Screening Manual is published by Denver Developmental Materials, Inc., Denver, CO. Adapted by permission.

Table 5.5: American Academy of Pediatrics (1994). *Recommended Childhood Immunizations.* Adapted by permission of American Academy of Pediatrics, Elk Grove Village, IL.

CHAPTER 6

Box 6.1 and Table in Box: Fernald, A., and O'Neill, D. K. (1993). Peekaboo across cultures: How mothers and infants play with voices, faces, and expectations. In K. MacDonald (Ed.), *Parent-child play,* 259–285. Albany, NY: State University of New York Press. Reprinted by permission.

Figure 6.2: Baillargeon, R., and DeVos, J. (1991). Object permanence in young infants. *Child Development, 62,* 1227–1246. © The Society for Research in Child Development, Inc. Reprinted by permission.

Figure 6.3: Mandler, J. M. (1990). A new perspective on cognitive development in infancy. *American Scientist, 78,* 236–243. Reprinted by permission of Sigma Xi, the Scientific Research Society.

Figure 6.4: Wynn, K. (1992). Evidence against empiricist accounts of the origin of numerical knowledge. *Mind and Language, 7,* 315–332. Reprinted by permission of Basil Blackwell Ltd.

Figure 6.5: Fagan, J. F. (1982). Infant memory. In T. M. Field, A. Huston, H. Quay, L. Troll, & G. Finley (eds.), *Review of human development.* New York: John Wiley & Sons.

Figure 6.6: Petitto, L. A., and Marentette, P. F. (1991). Babbling in the manual mode: Evidence for the ontogeny of language. *Science, 251,* 1493–1495. Copyright 1991 by the American Association for the Advancement of Science. Reprinted by permission.

Table 6.2: Kessen, W., Haith, M., Salapatek, P. (1970). Infancy. In P. H. Mussen (ed.), *Carmichael's manual of the child psychology, I,* 3rd edition. New York: John Wiley & Sons.

Table 6.3: Capute, A. J., Shapiro, B. K., and Palmer, F. B. (1987). Language milestones from birth to 3 years. *Contemporary Pediatrics,* April 24. Copyright by *Contemporary Pediatrics.* Reprinted by permission.

Table 6.4: Acredolo, L., and Goodwyn, S. (1988). Symbolic gesturing in normal infants. *Child Development, 59,* 450–466. © The Society for Research in Child Development, Inc. Adapted by permission.

CHAPTER 7

Page 259: Gralinski, J. H., and Kopp, C. B. (1993). Everyday rules for behavior: Mothers' requests to young children. *Developmental Psychology, 29,* 573–584. Reprinted by permission.

Table 7.1: Sroufe, L. A. (1979). Socioemotional development. In J. Osofsky (Ed.), *Handbook of Infant Development.* Copyright © 1979 by John Wiley & Sons. Adapted by permission.

Table 7.3: Thomas, A., and Chess, S. (1984). Genesis and evolution of behavioral disorders: From infancy to early adult life. *American Journal of Psychiatry, 141*(1), 1–9. Adapted by permission.

Table 7.4: Fagot, B. I., and Hagan, R. (1991). Observations of parent reaction to sex-stereotyped behaviors: Age and sex effects. *Child Development, 62,* 617–628. © The Society for Research in Child Development, Inc. Adapted by permission.

CHAPTER 8

Opening quotation: Sandburg, C. (1936). *The People, Yes.* Copyright 1936 by Harcourt Brace Jovanovich, Inc. Renewed 1964 by Carl Sandburg. Reprinted by permission of the publisher.

Page 312: Garbarino, J., Dubrow, N., Kostelny, K., and Pardo, C. (1992). *Children in danger: Coping with the consequences of community violence.* Copyright 1992 by Jossey-Bass Inc., Publishers, San Francisco. Reprinted by permission.

Figure 8.1: Kellogg, R. (1970). Understanding children's art. In P. Cramer (ed.), *Readings in developmental psychology today.* Delmar, CA: CRM. Reprinted by permission of Mayfield Publishing Company.

Figure 8.2: Bassuk, E. L. (1991). Homeless families. *Scientific American, 265,* 66–74.

Figure 8.3: Strawn, J. (1992). The states and the poor: Child poverty rises as the safety net shrinks. *Social Policy Report of the Society for Research in Child Development, VI*(3). Copyright by The Society for Research in Child Development. Reprinted by permission.

Table 8.1: Lowrey, G. H. (1978). *Growth and Development of Children,* 7th edition. Copyright © 1978 by Year Book Medical Publishers, Inc., Chicago. Reprinted by permission.

Table 8.4: Adapted in part from American Academy of Pediatrics, Commitee on Accident and Poison Prevention (1990). Bicycle helmets. *Pediatrics, 85,* 229-230. Adapted in part from American Academy of Pediatrics and Center to Prevent Handgun Violence (1994). *Keep your family safe from firearm injury.* Washington, DC: Center to Prevent Handgun Violence. Adapted by permission.

Table 8.5: Beautrais, A. L., Fergusson, D. M., and Shannon, F. T. (1982). Life events and childhood morbidity: A prospective study. *Pediatrics, 70*(6), 935–940. Copyright 1982. Adapted by permission of *Pediatrics.*

Table 8.7: Kendall-Tackett, K. A., Williams, L. M., and Finkelhor, D. (1993). Impact of sexual abuse on children: A review and synthesis of recent empirical studies. *Psychological Bulletin, 113,* 164–180. Copyright © 1993 by the American Psychological Association. Reprinted by permission of the American Psychological Association and the authors.

CHAPTER 9

Table 9.3: Bolles, E. B. (1982). *So Much to Say.* Copyright © 1982 by Edmund

Blair Bolles. New York: St. Martin's Press, Inc. Adapted by permission of Dominick Abel Agency.

Table 9.4: Berk, L., and Garvin, R. (1984). Development of private speech among low income Appalachian children. *Developmental Psychology, 202*(2), 271–284. Copyright 1984 by the American Psychological Association. Adapted by permission.

CHAPTER 10

Opening quotation: Thompson, P. (1992). "My feelings." In Richard Lewis (comp.), *Miracles: Poems by Children of the English-Speaking World.* © 1992, The Touchstone Center, New York. Reprinted by permission.

Page 401: McClelland, D., Constantian, C., Regalado, D., and Stone, C. (1978). Making it to maturity. *Psychology Today, 12*(1), 42–53, 114.

Tables 10.2, 10.3, 10.4: Harrington, D. M. (1993). Child-rearing antecedents of suboptimal personality development: Exploring aspects of Alice Miller's concept of the poisonous pedagogy. In D. C. Funder, R. D. Parke, C. Tomlinson-Keasey, and K. Widaman (eds.), *Studying lives through time: Personality and development,* 289–313. Copyright © 1993 by the American Psychological Association. Adapted by permission of the American Psychological Association and the author.

CHAPTER 11

Opening quotation: Olds, S. (1983). "Size and Sheer Will." In Sharon Olds, *The Dead and the Living.* Copyright © 1983 by Sharon Olds. Reprinted by permission of Alfred A. Knopf, Inc.

Figure 11.1: Gortmaker, S. L., Dietz, W. H., Sobel, A. M., and Wehler, C. A. (1987). Increasing pediatric obesity in the U.S. *American Journal of Diseases of Children, 141,* 535–540. Copyright 1987, American Medical Assocation. Adapted by permission.

Figure 11.2: Schvaneveldt, J. D., Lindauer, S. L. K., and Young, M. H. (1990). Children's understanding of AIDS: A developmental viewpoint. *Family Relations, 39,* 330–335. Copyright 1990 by the National Council on Family Relations, 3989 Central Ave. N.E., Suite 550, Minneapolis, MN 55421. Reprinted by permission.

Figure 11.3: Leary, W. E. (1988, June 22). Survey finds sharp drop in tooth decay. *New York Times,* p. A1. Copyright © 1988 The New York Times Company. Reprinted by permission.

Figure 11.4: Schor, E. L. (1987). Unintentional injuries: Patterns within families. *American Journal of the Diseases of Children, 141,* 1280. Copyright 1987, American Medical Association. Reprinted by permission.

Table 11.1: Rauh, J. L., Schumsky, D. A., and Witt, M. T. (1967). Heights, weights and obesity in urban school children. *Child Development, 38,* 515–530. © 1967 by The Society for Research in Child Development, Inc. Adapted by permission.

Table 11.2: Cratty, B. J. (1986). *Perceptual and motor development,* 3d edition. Adapted by permission of Prentice-Hall, Inc.

Table 11.3: Newacheck, P. W., Stoddard, J. J., and McManus, M. (1993). Ethnocultural variations in the prevalence and impact of childhood chronic conditions. *Pediatrics, 91,* 1031–1047. Reproduced by permission of *Pediatrics.*

CHAPTER 12

Page 463: Resnick, L. B. (1989). Developing mathematical knowledge. *American Psychologist, 44,* 162–169. Reprinted by permission of the American Psychological Association.

Box 12.4: Olds, S. W. (1995). Description of a school in a Himalayan village. Copyright by Sally Wendkos Olds 1995. Reprinted by permission.

Figure 12.1: Wallach, M. A., and Kogan, N. (1967). Creativity and intelligence in children's thinking. *Transaction, 41*(1), 38–43. Copyright © 1967 by Transaction Publishers. Adapted by permission.

Table 12.3: American Psychiatric Association (1987). *Diagnostic and Statistical Manual of Mental Disorders,* third edition, revised. Reprinted by permission of the American Psychiatric Association.

CHAPTER 13

Box 13.1: Rousso, H. (1984). Fostering Healthy Self-Esteem: Part I. *Exceptional Parent,* December 1984, 9–14. Reprinted with the express consent and approval of *Exceptional Parent,* a monthly magazine for parents and families of children with disabilities and special health care needs. Subscription cost is $24 per year for 12 issues; call 1-800-247-8080. Offices at 120 State Street, Hackensack, NJ 07601.

Figure 13.1: Children's Defense Fund (1994, January). Living in fear. *CDF Reports, 15*(2). Reprinted by permission of Children's Defense Fund, Washington, DC.

Figure 13.2: Long, L. (1992). International perspectives on the residential mobility of America's children. *Journal of Marriage and the Family, 54,* 861–869. Copyright 1992 by the National Council on Family Relations, 3989 Central Ave. N.E., Suite 550, Minneapolis, MN 55421. Reprinted by permission of the National Council on Family Relations and the author.

Table 13.1: Zarbatany, L., Hartmann, D. P., and Rankin, D. B. (1990). The psychological functions of preadolescent peer activities. *Child Development, 61,* 1067–1080. © The Society for Research in Child Development, Inc. Reprinted by permission.

Table 13.2: Garbarino, J., Dubrow, N., Kostelny, K., and Pardo, C. (1992). *Children in danger: Coping with the consequences of community violence.* Copyright 1992 by Jossey-Bass, Inc., Publishers, San Francisco. Reprinted by permission.

CHAPTER 14

Opening quotation: McGinley, P. (1956). "A certain age; Portrait of girl with comic book." In Phyllis McGinley, *Times Three.* Originally appeared in *The New Yorker.* Copyright 1952 by Phyllis McGinley. Used by permission of Viking Penguin, a division of Penguin Books USA Inc.

Figure 14.1: Elliott, D. S. (1993). Health enhancing and health compromising lifestyles. In S. G. Millstein, A. C. Petersen, and E. O. Nightingale (Eds.), *Promoting the health of adolescents: New directions for the twenty-first century.* New York: Oxford University Press. Reprinted by permission.

Figure 14.2 and 14.3: Gans, J. E. (1990). *America's adolescents: How healthy are they?* Adapted by permission of the American Medical Association, Chicago.

CHAPTER 15

Page 589: Handler, J. F. (1993). Preface. In National Research Council (ed.), *Losing generations: Adolescents in high-risk settings,* vii–ix. Reprinted by permission.

Pages 595-596: Kohlberg, L. (1969). Stage and sequence: The cognitive-developmental approach to socialization. In D. A. Goslin (ed.), *Handbook of socialization theory and research.* Chicago: Rand McNally. Reprinted by permission of D. A. Goslin.

Pages 606, 607: Sternberg, R. J. (in press). Metaphors of mind underlying the testing of intelligence. In P. W. Reynolds and J. C. Rodens (eds.), *Advances in Psychological Assessment,* vol. 8. Reprinted by permission of the author.

Table 15.1: Adapted in part from Kohlberg, L. (1969). Stage and sequence: The cognitive-developmental approach to socialization. In D. A. Goslin (ed.), *Handbook of socialization theory and research.* Chicago: Rand McNally. Reprinted by permission of D. A. Goslin. Adapted in part from Kohlberg, L. (1976). Moral Stage and Moralization. In T. Lickona (ed.), *Moral Development and Behavior.* New York: Holt, Rinehart and Winston. Reprinted by permission of Thomas Lickona.

Table 15.2: Skoe, E. E., and Gooden, A. (1993). Ethic of care and real-life moral dilemma content in male and female early adolescents. *Journal of Early Adolescence, 13,* 154-167. Copyright © 1993 by Sage Publications. Reprinted by permission of Sage Publications, Inc.

CHAPTER 16

Opening quotation: Merriam, E. (1964, 1973). "A conversation with myself." In Eve Merriam, *A Sky Full of Poems.* Copyright © 1964, 1970, 1973, 1986 by Eve Merriam. Reprinted by permission of Marian Reiner.

Page 630: Marcia, J. E. (1980). Identity in adolescence. In J. Adelson (ed.), *Handbook of adolescent psychology.* Copyright © 1980 by John Wiley & Sons, Inc. Reprinted by permission of John Wiley & Sons, Inc.

Box 16.2: Gordon, S., and Everly, K. (1985). Excerpted from: Increasing self-esteem in vulnerable students: A tool for reducing pregnancy among teenagers. *Impact '85.* Syracuse, NY: Ed-U Press.

Figure 16.1 and 16.2: Csikszentmihalyi, M., and Larson, R. (1984). *Being adolescent: Conflict and growth in the teenage years,* 71 and 63. New York: Basic Books. Adapted by permission of Basic Books, a division of HarperCollins Publishing Company.

Table 16.1: Marcia, J. E. (1980). Identity in adolescence. In J. Adelson (ed.), *Handbook of adolescent psychology.* Copyright © 1980 by John Wiley & Sons, Inc. Reprinted by permission of John Wiley & Sons, Inc.

Table 16.2: Marcia, J. E. (1966). Development and validation of ego identity status. *Journal of Personality and Social Psychology, 3*(5), 551–558. Copyright 1966 by the American Psychological Association. Adapted by permission by the American Psychological Association and author.

Table 16.3: Kroger, J. (1993). Ego identity: An overview. In J. Kroger (Ed.), *Discussions on ego identity.* Hillsdale, NJ: Lawrence Erlbaum Publishers.

Table 16.4: Robinson, I., Ziss, K., Ganza, B., Katz, S., and Robinson, E. (1991). Twenty years of sexual revolution, 1965–1985: An update. *Journal of Marriage and the Family, 53,* 216–220. Copyright 1991 by the National Council on Family Relations, 3989 Central Ave. NE, Suite 550, Minneapolis, MN 55421. Reprinted by permission.

Table 16.6: Adapted in part from Miller, B. C., and Moore, K. A. (1990). Adolescent sexual behavior, pregnancy, and parenting: Research through the 1980s. *Journal of Marriage and the Family, 52*(4), 1025–1044. Copyright 1990 by the National Council on Family Relations, 3989 Central Ave. NE, Suite 550, Minneapolis, MN 55421. Adapted by permission. Adapted in part from Sonnenstein, F. L., Pleck, J. H., and Ku, L. C. (1991). Levels of sexual activity among adolescent males in the United States. *Family Planning Perspectives, 23*(4), 162–167. Adapted by permission of The Alan Guttmacher Institute.

PHOTO CREDITS

Introduction

Introduction opening photo: Shirley Zeiberg; p. 4: Philip N. Hollembeak; p. 7: Deborah Davis/PhotoEdit.

Chapter 1

Chapter 1 opening photo: Julie O'Neil/The Picture Cube; p. 13: Erika Stone; p. 16: Jean Michel Turpin/Gamma Liaison; p. 21: Georges de la Tour: *The Newborn.* Musée des Beaux-Arts de Rennes; p. 22: Keith Myers/The New York Times; p. 24: Bettmann Archive; p. 29, above: Bettmann Newsphotos; p. 29, below: Wellesley College News Office; p. 33: Joe McNally; p. 35: Tom McCarthy/PhotoEdit; p. 37: Yves De Braine/Black Star; p. 38: Courtesy of Dr. Inhelder; p. 40: Thomas McAvoy/LIFE Magazine © Time Warner Inc.; p. 46: Ulrike Welsch/Photo Researchers; p. 50: James Wilson/Woodfin Camp & Associates; p. 55: Roe DiBona.

Chapter 2

Chapter 2 opening photo: Tony Freeman/PhotoEdit; p. 65: Margaret Roche; p. 74: Jalandoni/Monkmeyer; p. 82: Laura Dwight/Peter Arnold, Inc.; p. 92: New York Newsday; p. 96: Rick Friedman/Black Star.

Chapter 3

Chapter 3 opening photo: Taeke Henstra/Photo Researchers; p. 105 (top to bottom): Petit Format/Nestle/Science Source Photo Researchers; Petit Format/Nestle/Science Source/Photo Researchers; Lennart Nilsson, *A Child Is Born.* English translation © 1966, 1977 by Dell Publishing Co. Inc.; J. S. Allen/Daily Telegraph/International Stock Photo; James Stevenson/Photo

Researchers; p. 106 (top to bottom): Lennart Nilsson, *Being Born*; Petit Format/Nestle/Science Source/Photo Researchers; Petit Format/Nestle Science Source/Photo Researchers; Ronn Maratea/ International Stock Photo; p. 109: David Schaefer/Monkmeyer; p. 115: George Steinmetz; p. 117: American Cancer Society; p. 118: Steve Leonard/Black Star; p. 119: Fred R. Conrad/The New York Times; p. 121: L. Rorke/The Image Works; p. 127: Alex Brandon/NYT Pictures; p. 128: Erika Stone.

Chapter 4

Chapter 4 opening photo: Kindra Clineff/The Picture Cube; p. 138: Jim Pickerell/The Image Works; p. 142: Lawrence Migdale/Photo Researchers; p. 146: Ronn Maratea/International Stock Photo; p. 147: Mark M. Walker/The Picture Cube; p. 150: Hank Morgan/Science Source/ Photo Researchers; p. 153: Philip N. Hollembeak; p. 159: Michael R. Elia.

Chapter 5

Chapter 5 opening photo: Nita Winter; p. 168: Laima Druskis/Stock, Boston; p. 175 (clockwise from top left): Kathryn Abbe; Lew Merrim/Monkmeyer; Elizabeth Crews; Elizabeth Crews; Elizabeth Crews; p. 177: Nancy Durrell McKenna/Photo Researchers; p. 179: Lew Merrim/ Monkmeyer; p. 181: Innervisions; p. 184: J. Guichard/Sygma; p. 187: Philip N. Hollembeak; p. 188: Mark Olds; p. 189: Margaret Miller/Photo Researchers; pp. 192, 195: Elizabeth Crews.

Chapter 6

Chapter 6 opening photo: Renate Hiller/Monkmeyer; p. 212: Nancy Olds; p. 214: Joel Gordon; p. 218: Andrew Meltzoff; p. 220: Culver Pictures; p. 221, above: Bancroft Library, University of California, Berkeley; p. 221, below: Laura Dwight; p. 224: James Kilkelly/DOT; p. 226: Elizabeth Crews/The Image Works; p. 228: Mary Ellen Mark; p. 230: Courtesy of Carolyn Rovee-Collier; p. 235: Shirley Zeiberg; p. 236: Cynthia Hinsey; p. 239: Sybil Shackman/Monkmeyer; p. 241: Tony Freeman/PhotoEdit; p. 245: Nancy Olds.

Chapter 7

Chapter 7 opening photo: Alex Low/International Stock Photo; p. 256: George Goodwin/Monkmeyer; p. 262: Linda Benedict-Jones/The Picture Cube; p. 263: Jane Vaicunas; p. 266: Gabriel A.

Cooney; p. 269: Shirley Zeiberg; p. 274: Jean-Claude Lejeune/Stock, Boston; p. 275: Jonathan Finlay; p. 276: Joel Gordon; p. 279: Harlow Primate Laboratory/University of Wisconsin; p. 281: Joel Gordon; p. 282: Spencer Grant/Monkmeyer; p. 283: Shirley Zeiberg; p. 284: Myrleen Fergson Cate/PhotoEdit; p. 287: Eastcott/The Image Works; p. 288: Elizabeth Crews/The Image Works.

Chapter 8

Chapter 8 opening photo: Bob Daemmrich/Stock, Boston; p. 306: David Woo/Stock, Boston; p. 310: Laura Dwight; p. 314: S. Sweezy/Stock, Boston; p. 319: AP/Wide World Photos; p. 321: B. Irwin/Taurus; p. 326: National Committee for the Prevention of Child Abuse; p. 331: Janet Fries/Time Magazine.

Chapter 9

Chapter 9 opening photo: Erika Stone; pp. 341, 342, 351: Erika Stone; p. 357: Jeff Dunn/The Picture Cube; p. 361: Sybil Shackman/Monkmeyer; p. 367: Junebug Clark/Photo Researchers; p. 369: Miro Vintoniv/Stock, Boston; p. 372: Laura Dwight/Peter Arnold, Inc.

Chapter 10

Chapter 10 opening photo: Sybil Shackman/Monkmeyer; p. 383: Erika Stone; p. 388: Lawrence Migdale/Stock, Boston; p. 390: Jim Pickerell/Stock, Boston; p. 393: Erika Stone; p. 394: Safra Nimrod; p. 402, left: Rhoda Baer; right: Jane Scherr; p. 403: Jane Scherr; p. 406: Peter Vandermark/Stock, Boston; p. 409: Bob Daemmrich/Stock, Boston; p. 414: Owen Franken/Stock, Boston; p. 417: Nita Winter; p. 422: Shirley Zeiberg.

Chapter 11

Chapter 11 opening photo: Robert Finken/The Picture Cube; p. 431: Lawrence Migdale/Stock, Boston; p. 433: Lawrence Migdale/Photo Researchers; p. 437: Bob Daemmrich/Stock, Boston; p. 439, above left: George Ancona/International Stock Photo; right: Joseph Nettis/Photo Researchers; below left: Renate Hiller/Monkmeyer; p. 450: Mary Kate Denny/PhotoEdit.

Chapter 12

Chapter 12 opening photo: Erika Stone; pp. 459, 461: Laura Dwight; p. 468: Charles Gupton/The Stock Market;

p. 470: Lew Merrim/Monkmeyer; p. 482: Tony Freeman/PhotoEdit; p. 488: Michael Newman/PhotoEdit; p. 491: Richard S. Orton; p. 494: Andrew Brilliant/The Picture Cube; p. 495: Raphael Gaillarde/Gamma-Liaison.

Chapter 13

Chapter 13 opening photo: Richard Hutchings/Photo Researchers; p. 508: Erika Stone; p. 509: Owen Franken/Stock, Boston; p. 511: Shirley Zeiberg; p. 512: Bernager/Explorer/ Photo Researchers; p. 514: Frank Siteman/Stock, Boston; pp. 522, 525: Erika Stone; p. 529: Janice Fullman/Picture Cube; p. 531, left: Roger V. Dollarhide/Monkmeyer; right: Bob Daemmrich/Stock, Boston; p. 534: Myrleen Ferguson Cate/PhotoEdit; p. 536: Mindy E. Klarman/Photo Researchers; p. 538: Ken Lax/Photo Researchers; p. 540: Gabe Palmer Mugshots/The Stock Market; p. 541: David Young-Wolff/PhotoEdit.

Chapter 14

Chapter 14 opening photo: Jack Fields/Photo Researchers; p. 554, left: Blair Seitz/Photo Researchers; right: Bill Gillette/Stock, Boston; p. 558: Dagmar Fabricius/Stock, Boston; p. 559: Richard Hutchings/Photo Researchers; p. 563, above: Culver Pictures; below: Shirley Zeiberg; p. 568: Kelley Chin/The Kansas City Star/AP Wide World Photo; p. 573: Louis Fernandez/Black Star.

Chapter 15

Chapter 15 opening photo: Will & Deni McIntyre/Photo Researchers; p. 590: Mimi Forsyth/Monkmeyer; p. 594: Jeffry W. Myers/Stock, Boston; p. 609: Spencer Grant/Photo Researchers; p. 613: Blair Seitz/Photo Researchers; p. 619: Billy E. Barnes/Stock, Boston; p. 621: Richard Pasley/Stock, Boston.

Chapter 16

Chapter 16 opening photo: Bob Daemmrich/Stock, Boston; p. 628: Erika Stone; p. 633: Harvard University News Office; p. 634: Bob Daemmrich/The Image Works; p. 637: Nancy Sheehan/The Picture Cube; p. 643: David Young-Wolff/PhotoEdit; p. 648: Nancy Sheehan/The Picture Cube; p. 649: Rick Kopstein/Monkmeyer; p. 651: Bob Daemmrich/Stock, Boston; p. 653: Courtesy of the Children's Defense Fund; p. 658: Mike Kagan/Monkmeyer; p. 660: Myrleen Ferguson/PhotoEdit.

INDEX

Eiger, M. S., 160, 176, 179
Eilers, R., 233
Eimas, P., 183, 234, 239
Einbender, A. J., 329
Eisen, L. N., 117, 225
Eisen, M., 654
Eisenberg, L., 580, 582
Eisenberg, N., 392, 406, 407, 417
Eisenberg-Berg, N., 406
Eisenson, J., 233
Ekstrom, R. B., 610
Elder, G. H., Jr., 19–20
Elias, S., 86
Elkind, D., 21, 369, 544, 581, 593–595
Elliott, D. S., 564
Elliott, H., 408
Ellis, L., 636
Elrad, H., 113
Emanuel, I., 116
Emde, R. N., 30, 265, 284, 405
Emery, R. E., 328, 518
Emmerick, H., 649
Ensminget, M. E., 151
Entwisle, D. R., 483
Epstein, A. S., 373
Epstein, J. L., 525
Epstein, L. H., 437, 438
Erikson, E. H., 25, 27, 28–29, 255–259,
   383–384, 508, 509, 627–629, 632–633
Ernst, L., 199
Eron, L. D., 410
Escobar, M. D., 491
Eskenazi, G., 440
Eskes, M., 145
Espinosa, M. P., 434
Estes, D., 277
Ettema, J. S., 395
Evans, G., 122
Evans, G. D., 451, 452
Evans, M. I., 71
Evans, R. I., 29
Everly, K., 655
Everson, R. B., 122
Evertson, C., 421
Ewigman, B. G., 86

Fabes, R. A., 392, 417
Faden, R. R., 177
Fagen, J., 182, 224
Fagen, J. F., 223, 224
Fagen, J. W., 225, 230
Fagot, B. I., 270
Falbo, T., 413, 414
Fallot, M. E., 177
Fallows, J., 481
Fanaroff, A., 182
Fandal, A. W., 186
Fantuzzo, J. W., 332
Fantz, R. L., 182, 224
Farber, E. A., 277
Farnsworth, C. H., 177, 555
Farrow, J. A., 574
Fauber, R., 612
Faucher, D., 185
Faucher, T. A., 486
Feagans, L., 491, 492
Fegley, S., 615
Fein, G., 423
Feinman, S., 265, 284
Feldhusen, J., 461
Feldman, E., 435
Feldman, H., 130, 240
Feldman, J. F., 226
Feldman, R. D., 497, 620
Feldman, W., 435

Fennema, E., 392
Ferber, R., 322
Ferdman, B. M., 481
Ferguson, J., 151
Fergusson, D. M., 178, 317, 325
Fernald, A., 211, 242–243
Fernández, A., 118
Feshbach, N. D., 483
Feshbach, S., 483
Fetterly, K., 177
Field, D., 348
Field, T., 416
Field, T. M., 151, 217, 264, 265, 278, 282, 289,
   293, 655
Fifer, W., 183, 239
Finegan, J. A. K., 85
Fingerhut, L. A., 580
Finkelhor, D., 326, 329, 521, 522
Finnie, V., 418
Fischel, J. E., 356
Fischer, K., 381
Fischhoff, B., 595, 650, 652
Fischman, J., 468, 499
Fish, M., 268, 274, 275
Fisher, M., 112
Fitch, B. R., 117
Fitness Finders, 441
Fivush, R., 362, 364
Flaherty, J., 563
Flanagan, C. A., 608
Flavell, E. R., 52, 345, 351
Flavell, J. H., 52, 345, 349, 462, 467–469, 477
Fletcher, J. M., 491
Fluoxetine-Bulimia Collaborative Study
   Group, 570
Foch, T. T., 170, 436
Fomon, S. J., 179
Fonagy, P., 130, 274
Forbes, D., 392
Ford, J., 652
Ford, K., 476, 638
Forehand, R., 612
Forman, M. R., 177
Forrest, D., 329
Forrest, J. D., 124
Foster-Clark, F. S., 633, 648
Fowler, M. G., 528
Fox, L. H., 497
Fox, N. A., 276, 278, 281, 284, 360
Fox, N. E., 277
Fraga, C. G., 122
Fraleigh, M. J., 614, 645
Frank, A. L., 421
Frank, M. A., 117
Frankenburg, W. K., 186
Freedman, D. G., 95, 190
Freeman, B. J., 286
Freeman, H. E., 317
Freier, C., 117
Frenkiel, N., 70
Freud, A., 641
Freud, S., 24–28, 29, 387, 632, 641
Fricker, H. S., 121
Fried, P. A., 116
Friedman, E. A., 145
Friedrich, L. K., 48, 50
Friedrich, W. N., 329
Frodi, A. M., 282
Frodi, M., 282
Fromkin, V., 43
Fuchs, D., 473
Fuchs, L. S., 473
Fulker, D., 91
Fulker, D. W., 223, 491
Furman, W., 416, 512, 535, 537, 645

Furstenberg, F. F., 653, 654
Futterman, D., 575

Gaensbauer, T., 260
Gaertner, S. L., 536
Galaburda, A. M., 310
Galambos, N. L., 268, 515, 644
Gale, J. L., 201
Galindo, A. C., 178
Gallagher, J., 112
Gallistel, C. R., 342
Gamble, T. J., 295
Gamer, E., 416
Gamoran, A., 611
Gans, J. E., 558, 563, 565, 579, 580
Ganza, B., 637, 638
Garai, J. E., 308
Garasky, S., 524
Garbarino, J., 312, 328, 543
Garcia, E. E., 480
Garcia-Coll, C., 96
Gardner, H., 471, 486, 496, 499
Garfinkel, B. D., 540
Garfinkel, P. E., 568
Garland, J. B., 195
Garmezy, N., 330, 542, 544
Garn, S. M., 557
Garner, D. M., 568, 569
Garvin, R. A., 354, 355
Gatsonis, C. A., 120
Gause, S., 113
Gauthier, R., 118
Gavazzi, S. M., 125
Gearhart, M., 342
Geary, D. C., 491
Geber, M., 474
Gecas, V., 646
Geen, R. G., 410
Gekoski, M. J., 230
Gelles, R. J., 515
Gelman, R., 341, 342, 347, 354
General Mills, Inc., 643
Geraci, K., 417
Gerard, D., 499
Gersten, M. S., 328
Gertner, B. L., 356
Geschwind, N., 310
Gesell, A., 191
Getzels, J. W., 497
Gianino, A. F., 263
Gibbons, L. E., 199
Gibbs, J., 600
Gibson, E. J., 181
Gielen, A. C., 177
Gilbert, S., 409
Gilligan, C., 47, 592, 600, 601, 603, 632, 633
Ginsburg, A., 524, 643
Ginsburg, G. S., 484, 485
Ginsburg, H., 448, 590, 591, 591n.
Ginsburg, H. P., 474, 475
Ginzberg, E., 619
Glass, L., 199
Glass, R. B., 125
Gleason, J. B., 352
Gleitman, H., 242
Gleitman, L., 240, 242
Glick, J., 20
Glick, P. C., 271
Goertz, M. E., 610
Golbus, M., 85
Goldberg, S., 278
Goldberg, W. A., 281, 283
Golden, M., 473
Goldenberg, R. L., 116
Goldfield, B. A., 237

Young, A., 234
Young, K. T., 295
Young, M. H., 444, 445
Youngblade, L. M., 277, 283, 342
Youngstrom, N., 543

Zabin, L. S., 638, 652, 655
Zahn-Waxler, C., 265, 405, 406, 408
Zajac, R., 480
Zakariya, S. B., 524
Zametkin, A. J., 493
Zarbatany, L., 531, 532

Zaslow, M., 282
Zelazo, N. A., 192, 193
Zelazo, P. R., 183, 192, 193, 229–230
Zell, E. R., 200
Zellman, G. L., 654
Zelnik, M., 638, 652
Zentella, A. C., 481
Zeskind, P. S., 151, 262
Zhang, X.-D., 345
Zhang, Y., 436
Zigler, E., 295, 330, 371–373, 544, 659
Zimiles, H., 617

Zimmerman, D., 555
Zimmerman, R. R., 280
Zimmerman, S., 306
Zimrin, H., 330
Ziss, K., 637, 638
Zola, I. K., 447
Zou, H. 345
Zuckerman, B., 117
Zuckerman, B. S., 264, 265, 394, 406
Zuckerman, D. M., 394, 406
Zylke, J. W., 198

SUBJECT INDEX

Note: **Bold** page numbers indicate glossary terms.

Ability grouping, 611, 658
Abortion, 71, 129, 650–651, 656
  sex discrimination and, 71, 415
  spontaneous, 86, 107–108, 113–114, 117
Abused children, 325–333
  adolescents as, 578–579
  delinquency and, 657
  eyewitness testimony of, 363
  fetuses as, 112
  help for, 330–333
  sexual abuse and, **325**, 327, 329–330, 331–332, 578–579, 657
Accidents:
  during adolescence, 580
  automobile, 314, 452, 572
  bicycle, 452–453
  during early childhood, 313–315, 319, 320
  of infants and toddlers, 193
  during middle childhood, 451–453
Accommodation (Piaget), **38**
Achievement tests, 365, **470**
Acquired adaptation (Piaget), 214
Acquired immune deficiency syndrome (AIDS), 119, 178, 313, 444–445, 574, 575–576, 578, 652
Acting-out behavior, **539**, 539–540
Acute medical conditions, 442–443, **443**
Adaptation:
  acquired, 214
  Piaget on, **38**
Addictive drugs (see Drugs)
Adolescence, 17, 23, **553**
  cognitive development during:
    career development, 618–621
    egocentrism and, 594–595
    high school and, 607–618
    moral development in, 595–603
    Piagetian approach to, 589–593
    planful competence, 5, 53
  personality and social development during:
    antisocial behavior and, 644, 645, 649–650, 656–659
    depression in, 568, 570, 580–582
    gender identity in, 629, 632–634
    identity and, 627–640
    juvenile delinquency and, 656–659
    parent-child relationships and, 639–645
    peer relationships and, 646–650
    pregnancy and, 617, 650–656
    sexual identity and, 634–640
    sibling relationships and, 645–646

Adolescence (*Cont.*):
  theoretical perspectives on, 26, 27, 627–634
  physical development during:
    abuse and neglect in, 578–579
    death and, 572, 580–582
    drug use and abuse, 570–574
      eating disorders, 566–570
    nutritional needs, 566–570
    psychological impact of, 560–563, 567–570
    puberty in, 440, 553–563, 641–643
    sexually transmitted diseases (STDs) and, 574–578
Adolescent growth spurt, **558**, 558–559
Adolescent rebellion, **640**, 640–645, 657
Adoption, 128–129
  bonding in, 160–161
  transition to parenthood in, 129–131
Adoption studies, 91, 93
  intelligence and, 94
  temperament and, 96
Advertising, 375
Affection, of parents for children, 400–401
Affective disorders, 540
African Americans:
  adoption by, 128
  breastfeeding by, 177
  code-switching by, 481
  conservation and, 461
  infant mortality rate, 196–197
  intelligence test scores of, 473–475
  low-birthweight babies of, 149
Age:
  average, 7
  of father, and birth defects, 122
  of first sexual intercourse, 636, 638–639
  linguistic speech and, 236–237
  of mother, at birth of child, 66, 81–82, 120
  pendulum problem and, 590–591
  prosocial behavior and, 405–406
  of puberty, 555–556, 561–562
  (*See also* Stage theories of development)
Age effect, 371
Aggressive behavior, **407**
  in child abuse, 325–333
  cognitive skills and, 483
  in early childhood, 392, 393, 407–411, 415–416
  in sibling relations, 415–416
  (*See also* Violence)
Aid to Families with Dependent Children (AFDC), 319–320, 651
AIDS (acquired immune deficiency syndrome), 119, 178, 313, 444–445, 574, 575–576, 578, 652

Ainsworth, Mary, 41, 273–274
Alcohol, 122, 123
  adolescent use of, 571–573
  fetal alcohol syndrome (FAS) and, 114–115, 116
  use during pregnancy, 114–115, 116
Alcoholism, 310
Alleles, **72**
  heterozygous, 72–73
  homozygous, 72–73
  multiple, 75
Alpha$_1$ antitrypsin deficiency, 76
Altruism (prosocial behavior), **405**, 405–407, 418–419
Ambati, Balamurati Krishna, 495
Ambivalent (resistant) attachment, **274**
American Association of University Women (AAUW), 634
American Indians (*see* Native Americans)
American Psychiatric Association, 636
Amniocentesis, 70, 71, **84**, 85, 110
Amniotic sac, 106–107
Anal stage (Freud), 26, 27
Androgens, 393, 557
Androgynous characteristics, **393**
Anemia, 178, 179, 566
Anencephaly, 77, 85, 111–112
Animal studies, 3
  of attachment, 272–273, 279–280
  on environment and brain development, 173–174
Animism, 344, **347**, 347–348
Anorexia nervosa, 567–570, **568**
Anoxia, **152**, 155
Antisocial behavior:
  during adolescence, 644, 645, 649–650, 656–659
  juvenile delinquency, 656–659
  during middle childhood, 533, 535, 539–540
Anxiety disorders, 540
Apgar scale, **156**, 156–157, 225
Appearance:
  adolescent focus on, 560–563, 567–570
  in early childhood, 305
  reality versus, in early childhood, 343–346
Applied research, 4–5
Aptitude tests, 365, **470**
Argumentativeness, 593
Art therapy, 311–312
Artificial insemination (AI), 70, **126**
Artistic development, in early childhood, 310–312
Asian Americans:
  achievement of students, 474–475
  low-birthweight babies of, 149